ANNOTATED TEACHER'S EDITION

HOLT
Psychology

Sexual Principles in Practice

SPENCER A. RATHUS

HOLT, RINEHART AND WINSTON

A Harcourt Education Company

Austin • Orlando • Chicago • New York • Toronto • London • San Diego

The Author

Dr. Spencer A. Rathus is currently a professor at New York University. Dr. Rathus entered clinical practice and teaching after earning his Ph.D. in 1972. His research interests lie in the areas of abnormal behavior, methods of therapy, human growth and development, and psychological assessment. Since his publication of *Adjustment and Growth: The Challenges of Life* in 1980, Rathus has poured his energies into his textbooks. His college textbooks include an introductory psychology textbook (*Psychology in the New Millennium*), a child development textbook (*Voyages: Childhood and Adolescence*), and an abnormal psychology textbook.

Teacher Consultant

Jim Matiya
Carl Sandburg High School
Orland Park, IL

Academic and Teacher Reviewers

Lydia Fitzgerald
Faribault High Scool
Faribault, MN

Dale Kinney
Ralston Senior High School
Ralston, NE

Dr. Aida Hurtado
University of California,
Santa Cruz
Social Psychology

Dr. Michela Gallagher
University of North Carolina,
Chapel Hill
Experimental/Biological and
Cognitive Psychology

Dr. Keith D. White
University of Florida
Biological Psychology

Dr. David Cohen
University of Texas, Austin
Clinical Psychology

Dr. Terry Davidson
Purdue University
Behavioral Neuroscience

Dr. Jeremiah Faries
Northwestern University
Cognitive Psychology

Dr. Arthur Staats
University of Hawaii
Cognitive Psychology,
Intelligence

Dr. Julie Hubbard
University of Delaware
Child Clinical Psychology

Dr. Anne C. Fletcher
University of North Carolina at
Greensboro
Developmental Psychology,
Adolescence

Dr. Thomas Bradbury
University of California,
Los Angeles
Developmental Psychology

Dr. Daniel N. McIntosh
University of Denver
Social Psychology

Calvin P. Garbin, Ph.D.
University of Nebraska
Quantitative and Research
Methods

Dr. Nancy Russo
Arizona State University
Social Psychology, Gender

Dr. Kevin Williams
State University of New York,
Albany
Behavioral Psychology

Dr. Timothy Anderson
Vanderbilt University
Abnormal Psychology

Dr. Bertram Malle
University of Oregon
Social Psychology

TO THE TEACHER

Dear colleague,

Teaching psychology at the high school level is a challenging, yet rewarding job. We are faced with students who come into the classroom with varying levels of abilities and talents. These students are interested in who they are, what motivates them, what people think, and a myriad of other questions about themselves and other people. They look to the teacher as a facilitator, who guides, directs, and offers guidance about the psychology of human behavior. This psychology text begins your student's exploration into the science of human behavior.

Holt Psychology: Principles in Practice offers the most extensive research and current scholarship of any high school text on the market today. Dr. Spencer Rathus and the team who developed this textbook and teacher's resources package have worked very hard to see that you have a text that uses the most current scientific information with teacher's resources designed to help the student learn.

Holt Psychology: Principles in Practice—including the Pupil's and Teacher's Editions and the Teacher's Resources package—is the most comprehensive set of materials in high school psychology. Enclosed you will find the latest information on teaching high school psychology. The Pupil's Edition also includes the APA's *Ethical Principles for Psychologists and Code of Conduct*.

Maintaining the students' interest in the educational process is one of the primary goals of this psychology program. Dr. Rathus has used vignettes about high school students in a new and refreshing way that grabs your students' attention and keeps them interested. Cultural diversity and awareness also play an important role in each of the chapters.

Teaching psychology at the high school level is a labor of love. I hope you take advantage of the materials being offered by Holt, Rinehart and Winston. They have been carefully developed with you and your students in mind. Psychology is a fascinating subject for both the teacher and the student. *Holt Psychology: Principles in Practice* will help you and your students explore the exciting psychology of human behavior.

Jim Matiya,
Carl Sandburg High School

TABLE OF CONTENTS

M1

It's All About RELEVANCE

CNNfyi.com™ is a site designed to give students in grades 6–12 access to people, places, and environments around the globe while offering "real-world" articles, career and college resources, and online activities.

A DAY IN THE LIFE

opens each chapter and relates the information discussed in that chapter to the everyday events in the lives of a group of fictional high school students. Throughout the chapter, there are occasional references back to the feature to demonstrate the application of the concept.

The first step to success in the social studies classroom is capturing and sustaining the interest of your students. *HOLT PSYCHOLOGY* is designed to be open and friendly to all students, so that they develop an enthusiasm for learning.

Technology that

go.hrw.com FOR STUDENTS

Your students can access interactive activities, homework help, up-to-date maps, and more when they visit **go.hrw.com** and type in the keywords they find in their text.

CHAPTER HOME PAGE

The **Chapter Home Pages** contain pre-screened enrichment links that extend content, teaching resources, and interactive activities that combine guided research with specific product-based projects. The **Home Page** also directs students to **Homework Practice Online, Holt Researcher, Holt Grapher,** and more!

ONLINE TEMPLATES

Your students can use these interactive templates to create newspapers, travel brochures, postcards, journals, creative works, and more. The instructional design of this tool allows students to do something with the content they have learned.

HOMEWORK PRACTICE

This helpful tool allows students to practice and review content by chapter anywhere there is a computer.

HRW ONLINE ATLAS

This helpful online tool contains over 300 well-rendered and clearly labeled country and state maps. The clean design and easy-to-use navigational tools make accessing information simple. These maps are continually updated so you can rest assured that you and your students have the latest and most accurate geographical content available. Maps are available in English and Spanish.

STATE HANDBOOKS

Visit **go.hrw.com** and find fun facts, state maps, flags, and statistics. There are also links to state-specific resources and products that are especially made for teachers and students.

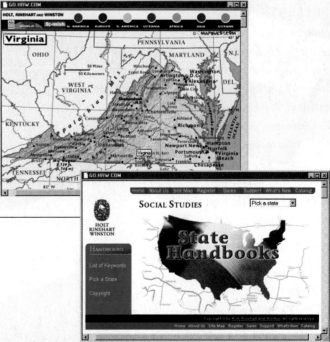

Delivers Content

CNNfyi.com

At **CNNfyi.com**, students will love exploring news stories written by experienced journalists as well as student bureau reporters complete with links to homework help and lesson plans.

Named *"Best Online Current Events Program"* by techlearning.com!

CNN PRESENTS VIDEO LIBRARY

The **CNN PRESENTS** video collection tackles the issue of making content relevant to students head on. Real-world news stories enable students to see the connections between classroom curriculum and today's issues and events around the nation and the world.

CNN PRESENTS...

- **Psychology**
- **America: Yesterday and Today, Beginnings to 1914**
- **America: Yesterday and Today, 1850 to the Present**
- **America: Yesterday and Today, Modern Times**
- **Geography: Yesterday and Today**
- **World Cultures: Yesterday and Today**
- **American Government and Civics**
- **Economics**
- **September 11, 2001: Part 1**
- **September 11, 2001: Part 2**
- **Sociology**

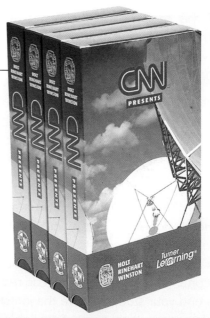

Holt is proud to team up with CNN/TURNER LEARNING to provide you and your students with exceptional current and historical news videos and online resources that add depth and relevance to your daily instruction. This information collection takes your classroom to the far corners of the globe without students ever leaving their desks!

Unique Teacher's

go.hrw.com FOR TEACHERS

Throughout the *Annotated Teacher's Edition*, you'll find **Internet Connect** boxes that take you to specific chapter activities, links, current events, and more that correlate directly to the section you are teaching. Through **go.hrw.com** you'll find a wealth of teaching resources at your fingertips for fun, interactive lessons.

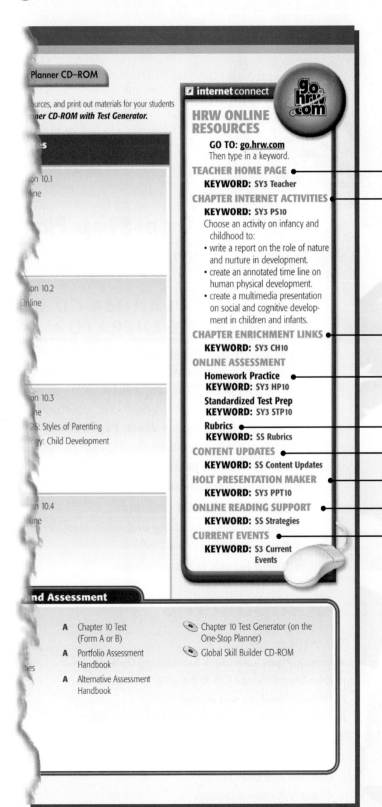

Planner CD-ROM

...urces, and print out materials for your students
...ner CD-ROM with Test Generator.

...es

...on 10.1
...ine

...on 10.2
Online

...on 10.3
...e
...6: Styles of Parenting
...gy: Child Development

...n 10.4
...line

internet connect

HRW ONLINE RESOURCES

GO TO: go.hrw.com
Then type in a keyword.

TEACHER HOME PAGE
KEYWORD: SY3 Teacher

CHAPTER INTERNET ACTIVITIES
KEYWORD: SY3 PS10
Choose an activity on infancy and childhood to:
• write a report on the role of nature and nurture in development.
• create an annotated time line on human physical development.
• create a multimedia presentation on social and cognitive development in children and infants.

CHAPTER ENRICHMENT LINKS
KEYWORD: SY3 CH10

ONLINE ASSESSMENT
Homework Practice
KEYWORD: SY3 HP10
Standardized Test Prep
KEYWORD: SY3 STP10
Rubrics
KEYWORD: SS Rubrics

CONTENT UPDATES
KEYWORD: SS Content Updates

HOLT PRESENTATION MAKER
KEYWORD: SY3 PPT10

ONLINE READING SUPPORT
KEYWORD: SS Strategies

CURRENT EVENTS
KEYWORD: S3 Current Events

DIRECT LAUNCH TO CHAPTER ACTIVITIES

GUIDED ONLINE ACTIVITIES

LINKS FOR EVERY SECTION

INTERACTIVE PRACTICE AND REVIEW

RUBRICS FOR SUBJECTIVE GRADING

UP-TO-DATE INFORMATION

PRESENTATION SUPPORT

PRACTICE FOR READING SUCCESS

WEB RESOURCES FOR CURRENT ISSUES

...nd Assessment

A Chapter 10 Test (Form A or B)
A Portfolio Assessment Handbook
A Alternative Assessment Handbook

Chapter 10 Test Generator (on the One-Stop Planner)
Global Skill Builder CD-ROM

...ties

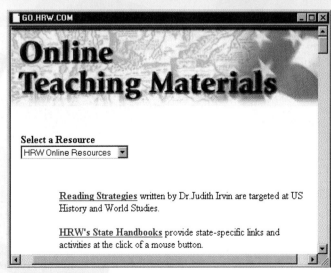

GO.HRW.COM

Online Teaching Materials

Select a Resource
HRW Online Resources

Reading Strategies written by Dr. Judith Irvin are targeted at US History and World Studies.

HRW's State Handbooks provide state-specific links and activities at the click of a mouse button.

Management System

Everything you need is on one disc!

One-Stop Planner® with Test Generator

ONE-STOP PLANNER CD-ROM WITH TEST GENERATOR

Holt brings you the most user-friendly management system in the industry with the **One-Stop Planner CD-ROM with Test Generator.** Plan and manage your lessons from this single disc containing all the teaching resources for **Holt Psychology,** valuable planning and assessment tools, and more.

- **Editable lesson plans**
- **Classroom Presentations**
- **ExamView® Pro test generator**
- **Previews of all teaching and video resources**
- **Easy printing feature**
- **Direct launch to go.hrw.com**

Holt Psychology Program Components

Reading Support
- **Graphic Organizer Activities**
- **Reading Strategies for the Social Studies Classroom**
- **Mastering Critical Thinking Skills**

Research and Activities
- **Creating a Psychology Fair**
- **Essays and Research Themes for Advanced Placement Students**
- **Readings and Case Studies in Psychology**
- **Research Projects and Activities for Teaching Psychology**
- **Study Skills and Writing Guide**

Classroom Resources
- **Lesson Plans with Block Scheduling Options**
- **One-Stop Planner CD-ROM with Test Generator**
- **Porfolio Projects and Activities**
- **Teaching Transparencies with Teacher's Notes**

Review and Assessment
- **Alternative Assessment Handbook**
- **Chapter and Unit Tests**
- **Chapter Review Activities**

MEETING INDIVIDUAL NEEDS

Holt Psychology: Principles in Practice recognizes that most classrooms include students from a variety of backgrounds and with a variety of learning styles. Many of the activities in both the Pupil's Edition and the Annotated Teacher's Edition are suited to students with varying needs. In addition, activities in the chapter interleafs, located at the beginning of each chapter of the Annotated Teacher's Edition, focus explicitly on meeting the individual needs of the following categories of students:

LEARNERS HAVING DIFFICULTY

To assist students who need repetition, have short attention spans, lack self-esteem, and/or learn at a slower rate than other classmates, *Holt Psychology: Principles in Practice* activities provide the opportunity for review and reteaching of basic information in the chapter. Some activities also focus students on their own interests and experiences to motivate them and to encourage them to make connections. Specific methods include the use of audio and visual materials, teacher demonstrations, interactive activities, extended explanations, and summarizing and outlining exercises.

AUDITORY LEARNERS

Strategies targeting students who respond particularly well to auditory stimuli include lectures (both by teachers and guest speakers), audiotapes (either listened to or created by students), class discussion, role-playing, debating, reading aloud, and oral presentation.

VISUAL LEARNERS

For students who are oriented toward visual learning, *Holt Psychology: Principles in Practice* strategies suggest the examination, analysis, and interpretation of materials such as photographs, graphs, and charts. Activities that make use of chalkboards, bulletin boards, and maps also are recommended. Students might be asked to create graphic organizers, posters, maps, or other visual displays.

TACTILE/KINESTHETIC LEARNERS

Tactile/kinesthetic learners benefit from interactive activities and activities that utilize movement and action. Simulations, field trips, role-playing, conducting interviews, using newspaper and magazine articles, constructing models, and creating maps, posters, time lines, and illustrations are all effective strategies used in *Holt Psychology: Principles in Practice*.

GIFTED LEARNERS

Activities requiring research beyond the textbook help meet the needs of gifted learners. Often such activities focus on real-world issues and problem solving through the use of investigation, debate, panel discussions, and other forums for the exchange of ideas. As almost every student is gifted in one way or another, teachers are encouraged to use these types of activities with as many students as possible.

LIMITED ENGLISH PROFICIENCY (LEP)

Instructional strategies in *Holt Psychology: Principles in Practice* are designed to limit stress and anxiety for students who face difficulty in communicating in the classroom or in understanding instructions. Students who do not speak English as their first language may display conversational ability in English and understand a major part of a lesson. However, such students may not yet be able to express themselves in writing or orally well enough to indicate their level of understanding. LEP students also are students whose first language is English but who display insufficient language skills.

It is important to remember that all students for whom English is a second language do not fall within the same ability range, and that many of these students might otherwise be considered gifted or might have attained high academic skills if instructed in their native language.

Because of these diverse characteristics, LEP students benefit from a variety of instructional techniques. These includes oral introduction to assignments and modeling by the teacher, vocabulary activities that emphasize context, opportunities to engage in role-playing and reader's theater, working in small groups or with partners, and responding to visuals. You might consider the following guidelines for effective interaction with LEP students:

SIMPLIFY CONTENT

▶ Speak slowly.

▶ Pronounce words clearly.

▶ Use a controlled vocabulary.

▶ Minimize use of idioms.

CONTEXT AIDS

▶ Use gestures.

▶ Use animated facial expressions.

▶ Act out meaning of words or concepts.

▶ Use varied visual materials.

CHECKING UNDERSTANDING

▶ Make frequent checks for comprehension.

▶ Repeat important concepts.

▶ Expand meaning whenever possible.

▶ Use varied questions and techniques.

Last, remember that LEP students may be new immigrants to the United States—possibly from war-torn countries that are in economic and political turmoil. Students' difficulties in adapting to a new culture could prevent them from taking part in class discussions. Avoid questioning them about life in their former countries unless they are willing to share their experiences. When developing cooperative projects, try to use LEP students' knowledge, experiences, and cultural traditions in ways that will promote their self-esteem.

PORTFOLIO ASSESSMENT

Holt Psychology: Principles in Practice includes a variety of creative Building Your Portfolio projects that help students, teachers, and parents assess the learning and performance progress of an individual student. These projects offer teachers and students more than the traditional instructional pattern of lecture, reading, discussion, and test. Rather than relying simply on rote learning, the portfolio projects call on the creativity and enthusiasm of students to help them apply what they have learned in the text.

A student's portfolio—a collection a student's work in a folder, envelope, box, or other container—serves as a tangible record of his or her progress and performance over a period of time. The portfolio activities are found at the end of each chapter in the Pupil's Edition. The variety of portfolio projects and materials provide a multidimensional view of a student's mastery of skills, understanding of information, and ability to apply those skills and knowledge.

Flexibility and creativity help make Portfolio Assessment an important part of the *Holt Psychology: Principles in Practice* program. Activities throughout both the Pupil's Edition and the Annotated Teacher's Edition provide students with the opportunity to create a wide range of materials for their portfolios. Students should feel free to include any materials in their portfolios that they consider representative of their progress and understanding as they study the field of psychology.

AUTHENTIC ASSESSMENT
The portfolio activities include real-world projects. The projects are designed to be authentic in both content and structure. Students might be asked, for example, to identify a psychological disorder based on a fictional case study or to execute and explain a naturalistic-observation experiment. These activities might require students to accomplish such tasks as conducting polls, creating organizational charts, and developing flowcharts and time lines.

At the heart of authentic assessment lies the concept that students' most important learning takes place when students create the learning themselves. Rather than asking students to simply memorize information that may be forgotten at the end of the course, the portfolio projects involve students as the main participants in the learning process. The activities help students acquire skills they will need to know and use in their lives again and again—for their careers, for their work with volunteer organizations, and for informed and active citizenship.

As they work on the projects, students will sharpen their research skills, learning what types of information to look for and where to find the information they need. Students will also learn how to present information in a variety of forms, including writing; visual displays such as charts, graphs, and illustrations; and oral presentations. Students' organizational skills also will improve as they complete their research and present their findings.

As students complete their projects, they will truly have the sense that they have created something of their own rather than having copied it. The projects do not have "right" and "wrong" answers: Students must come to their own conclusions.

ALTERNATIVE ASSESSMENT
The portfolio projects provide a particularly valuable opportunity for students who are less comfortable with traditional assessment, such as in-class exams. Often, such tests are not reliable indicators of progress for students who have difficulty expressing themselves in traditional formats. The portfolio projects allow students to work with a degree of flexibility in terms of content and structure.

The Task Sheet, Assessment forms, and Building Your Portfolio Checklists in the *Portfolio Projects and Assessment* booklet support the portfolio projects. These worksheets help students and teachers assess the step-by-step progress of students as they work through their projects, and provide checklists that students should follow as they work on their portfolio activities.

The worksheets also assist students in planning their time by helping them pace their work over the entire unit, chapter by chapter, rather than lumping it together at the end of the unit. The worksheets help students in other ways as well, such as by guiding them to sources of needed information and by teaching them how to manage large projects that require progress on various activities.

Also in the Teacher's Resources, teachers will find *Alternative Assessment Forms* that can be used to evaluate a student's progress on various kinds of assignments, such as writing projects, oral or theater presentations, and group projects.

COOPERATIVE LEARNING
The portfolio projects provide an excellent opportunity for cooperative learning. Although students may work alone on a project, they might also accomplish the projects in a variety of ways. At the teacher's discretion, students might work cooperatively rather than individually on projects. Each project is divided into several specific steps, allowing group members to take individual responsibility for one of the steps. Conversely, members might all work on each step together, dividing the tasks of research, writing, illustrating, and oral presentation; or each step could be completed by a different group in the class.

RUBRICS

RUBRIC
RESEARCH

DIRECTIONS: This form is designed to help you evaluate student's research activities. Read the statements below. Then indicate the number from the following scale that reflects your assessment of the student's work.

1=Weak   **2**=Moderately Weak   **3**=Average   **4**=Moderately Strong   **5**=Strong

1. Develops a research plan, conducts an organized search, and makes good use of research time.   1   2   3   4   5

2. Makes good use of indices, electronic finding aids, card catalogs, periodical guides, and so on.   1   2   3   4   5

3. Utilizes the textbook and other in-class resources when appropriate.   1   2   3   4   5

4. Develops a research strand, using one resource to find others by looking at its bibliography and and footnotes.   1   2   3   4   5

5. Creates multiple research paths by searching for information on his or her topic under related topics.   1   2   3   4   5

6. Seeks out more than one source of information on a topic for use in the work product.   1   2   3   4   5

7. Uses primary sources when appropriate.   1   2   3   4   5

8. Evaluates sources for the quality of their information.   1   2   3   4   5

9. Takes gooid research notes, identifying directly-copied material, and recording the source.   1   2   3   4   5

10. Puts research findings into his or her own words.   1   2   3   4   5

ADDITIONAL COMMENTS:

_____

_____

TOTAL POINTS/GRADE: _____

RUBRIC
WRITING ASSIGNMENTS

DIRECTIONS: This form is designed to help you evaluate writing assignments. Read the statements below. Then indicate the number from the following scale that reflects your assessment of the student's work.

1=Weak **2**=Moderately Weak **3**=Average **4**=Moderately Strong **5**=Strong

1.	Each paragraph in the assignment starts with a topic sentence.	1	2	3	4	5
2.	The organization of the writing assignment is clear and easy to follow.	1	2	3	4	5
3.	The assignment is concise and well written.	1	2	3	4	5
4.	The assignment employs the appropriate information or facts.	1	2	3	4	5
5.	The content demonstrates an understanding of the topic and related concepts.	1	2	3	4	5
6.	The assignment is neatly typed or handwritten.	1	2	3	4	5
7.	The spelling, punctuation, and grammar on the writing assignment is accurate.	1	2	3	4	5
8.	If appropriate, the assignment appears to have been well researched.	1	2	3	4	5
9.	The content fulfills all the requirements of the assignment.	1	2	3	4	5
10.	Overall, the work represents the writer's full potential.	1	2	3	4	5

ADDITIONAL COMMENTS:

_____

_____

TOTAL POINTS/GRADE: _____

RUBRIC
DEBATES

DIRECTIONS: This form is designed to help you evaluate student debates. Read the statements below. Then indicate the number from the following scale that reflects your assessment of the group's work.

1=Weak   **2**=Moderately Weak   **3**=Average   **4**=Moderately Strong   **5**=Strong

1. Participants' statements are accurate and well researched.	1	2	3	4	5
2. Participants' contributions demonstrate understanding of the topic and related concepts.	1	2	3	4	5
3. Participants deliver ideas in a clear and concise manner, without too much reliance on notes.	1	2	3	4	5
4. Participants speak loudly and clearly enough to be heard by the audience.	1	2	3	4	5
5. Participants maintain eye contact with each other and with the audience.	1	2	3	4	5
6. Each participant's statements are relevant to the topic and appropriate for his or her side of the debate.	1	2	3	4	5
7. The debate follows the appropriate format and time limits.	1	2	3	4	5
8. Rebuttal statements are appropriate and show that participants listened to and understood the opposing arguments.	1	2	3	4	5
9. The debate fulfills the requirements of the assignment.	1	2	3	4	5
10. Overall, the debate represents the full potential of the participants.	1	2	3	4	5

ADDITIONAL COMMENTS:

_____

_____

TOTAL POINTS/GRADE: _____

RUBRIC
DRAWING CONCLUSIONS

DIRECTIONS: This form is designed to help you evaluate student's skill in drawing conclusions. Read the statements below. Then indicate the number from the following scale that reflects your assessment of the student's mastery of this skill.

1=Weak   **2**=Moderately Weak   **3**=Average   **4**=Moderately Strong   **5**=Strong

1. The student gathers and considers appropriate information and evidence. 1 2 3 4 5

2. The student identifies main points in the information that are relevant to the topic or issue at hand. 1 2 3 4 5

3. The student thoughtfully analyzes and evaluates alternative information, explanations, and points of view. 1 2 3 4 5

4. The student fair-mindedly follows where evidence and explanations lead. 1 2 3 4 5

5. The student draws conclusions that are solidly based on reasoned evidence. 1 2 3 4 5

6. The conclusion employs the appropriate information or facts. 1 2 3 4 5

7. The conclusion shows an understanding of the appropriate concepts or topics. 1 2 3 4 5

8. The conclusion fulfills the requirements of the assignment. 1 2 3 4 5

9. The conclusion is presented in a clear, concise, and appropriate manner. 1 2 3 4 5

10. Overall, the conclusion demonstrates the student's full potential in applying this skill. 1 2 3 4 5

ADDITIONAL COMMENTS:

_____

_____

TOTAL POINTS/GRADE: _____

RUBRIC
PRESENTATIONS

DIRECTIONS: This form is designed to help you evaluate student presentations. Read the statements below. Then indicate the number from the following scale that reflects your assessment of the student's or group's work.

1=Weak   **2**=Moderately Weak   **3**=Average   **4**=Moderately Strong   **5**=Strong

1. The topic of the presentation meets the requirements of the assignment.   1   2   3   4   5

2. The presentation appears to be well researched.   1   2   3   4   5

3. The content of the presentation is appropriate and accurate.   1   2   3   4   5

4. The presentation indicates an understanding of the topic.   1   2   3   4   5

5. The presentation indicates an ability to synthesize information and understand cause-and-effect relationships.   1   2   3   4   5

6. The presentation includes the required number of elements.   1   2   3   4   5

7. Any artwork in the presentation is appropriate and neatly executed.   1   2   3   4   5

8. The presentation is neat and inviting.   1   2   3   4   5

9. If a group project, each group member appears to have participated in the development of the presentation.   1   2   3   4   5

10. Overall, the presentation represents the individual's or group's full potential.   1   2   3   4   5

ADDITIONAL COMMENTS:

_____

_____

TOTAL POINTS/GRADE: _____

RUBRIC
LISTENING

DIRECTIONS: This form is designed to help you evaluate student's skill in listening. Read the statements below. Then indicate the number from the following scale that reflects your assessment of the student's mastery of this skill.

1=Weak   **2**=Moderately Weak   **3**=Average   **4**=Moderately Strong   **5**=Strong

1. Determines exactly what he or she needs to know.   1   2   3   4   5

2. Pays careful attention to relevant verbal information.   1   2   3   4   5

3. Asks effective questions to clarify verbal information.   1   2   3   4   5

4. Encourage others to present information and opinions.   1   2   3   4   5

5. Is able to identify and summarize the speaker's main points.   1   2   3   4   5

ADDITIONAL COMMENTS:

_____

_____

TOTAL POINTS/GRADE: _____

RUBRIC
CREATING A RÉSUMÉ

DIRECTIONS: This form is designed to help you evaluate student-created résumés. Read the statements below. Then indicate the number from the following scale that reflects your assessment of the student's work.

1=Weak   **2**=Moderately Weak   **3**=Average   **4**=Moderately Strong   **5**=Strong

1. The résumé contains the name and age of the individual who is being profiled.	1	2	3	4	5
2. The résumé is well written.	1	2	3	4	5
3. The résumé covers the individual's contributions and life experiences to the period under study.	1	2	3	4	5
4. The résumé focuses on contributions and experiences that are relevant to the topic or current unit of study.	1	2	3	4	5
5. The information contained in the résumé is accurate.	1	2	3	4	5
6. The content of the résumé shows a clear understanding of the individual's relationship to the topic or unit of study.	1	2	3	4	5
7. The résumé is neatly typed or handwritten.	1	2	3	4	5
8. The spelling, punctuation, and grammar in the résumé is accurate.	1	2	3	4	5
9. The résumé fully meets the requirements of the assignment.	1	2	3	4	5
10. The work represents the full potential of the writer.	1	2	3	4	5

ADDITIONAL COMMENTS:

_____

_____

TOTAL POINTS/GRADE: _____

RUBRIC
CAUSE AND EFFECT

DIRECTIONS: This form is designed to help you evaluate student's skill in determining cause-and-effect relationships. Read the statements below. Then indicate the number from the following scale that reflects your assessment of the student's mastery of this skill.

1=Weak   **2**=Moderately Weak   **3**=Average   **4**=Moderately Strong   **5**=Strong

1. The student can differentiate between a cause and an effect.   1   2   3   4   5

2. The student can identify key words and phrases that indicate cause-and-effect relationships.   1   2   3   4   5

3. The student can recognize cause-and-effect relationships separated by other information.   1   2   3   4   5

4. The student recognizes and can identify multiple effects from a single cause.   1   2   3   4   5

5. The student recognizes and can identify multiple causes of a single effect.   1   2   3   4   5

6. The student presents the cause-and-effect relationship in an appropriate manner.   1   2   3   4   5

7. The relationship identified employs the appropriate information or facts.   1   2   3   4   5

8. The cause-and-effect relationship drawn shows understanding of the appropriate concepts or topics.   1   2   3   4   5

9. The relationship identified fulfills the requirements of the assignment.   1   2   3   4   5

10. Overall, the relationship drawn demonstrates the student's full potential in applying this skill.   1   2   3   4   5

ADDITIONAL COMMENTS:

_____

_____

TOTAL POINTS/GRADE: _____

RUBRIC
CHARTS

DIRECTIONS: This form is designed to help you evaluate student-created charts. Read the statements below. Then indicate the number from the following scale that reflects your assessment of the student's work.

1=Weak **2**=Moderately Weak **3**=Average **4**=Moderately Strong **5**=Strong

1. The chart has an appropriate title and headings.	1	2	3	4	5
2. The chart is clearly organized.	1	2	3	4	5
3. Chart lines, boxes, and text are neat and legible.	1	2	3	4	5
4. The chart's content is accurate.	1	2	3	4	5
5. Chart information is divided into relevant parts for presentation.	1	2	3	4	5
6. The spelling, grammar, and punctuation on the chart is accurate.	1	2	3	4	5
7. The chart presents the information in a way that is easy to follow.	1	2	3	4	5
8. Chart content and organization show an understanding of the topic and related concepts.	1	2	3	4	5
9. The chart fulfills all the requirements of the assignment.	1	2	3	4	5
10. Overall, the final result represents the student's full potential.	1	2	3	4	5

ADDITIONAL COMMENTS:

_____

_____

TOTAL POINTS/GRADE: _____

RUBRIC
COMPARING AND CONTRASTING

DIRECTIONS: This form is designed to help you evaluate student's skill in comparing and contrasting. Read the statements below. Then indicate the number from the following scale that reflects your assessment of the student's mastery of this skill.

1=Weak   **2**=Moderately Weak   **3**=Average   **4**=Moderately Strong   **5**=Strong

1. The student attempts comparisons from appropriately parallel categories of items.   1   2   3   4   5

2. The student chooses only a very few specific items to be compared.   1   2   3   4   5

3. The student determines what characteristics the selected items have in common.   1   2   3   4   5

4. The student decides on which of these common areas he or she wishes to concentrate.   1   2   3   4   5

5. The student identifies similarities and differences in the selected common areas.   1   2   3   4   5

6. The comparison employs the appropriate information or facts.   1   2   3   4   5

7. The comparison shows an understanding of the appropriate concepts or topics.   1   2   3   4   5

8. The comparison fulfills the requirements of the assignment.   1   2   3   4   5

9. The comparison is presented in a clear, concise, and appropriate manner.   1   2   3   4   5

10. Overall, the comparison demonstrates the student's full potential in applying this skill.   1   2   3   4   5

ADDITIONAL COMMENTS:

_____

_____

TOTAL POINTS/GRADE: _____

RUBRIC
GROUP ACTIVITY

DIRECTIONS: This form is designed to help you evaluate student work in cooperative learning groups. Read the statements below. Then indicate the number from the following scale that reflects your assessment of the student's work.

1=Weak   **2**=Moderately Weak   **3**=Average   **4**=Moderately Strong   **5**=Strong

1. Each member of the group had a clear understanding of the group's task.	1	2	3	4	5
2. Each member of the group had a clear understanding of his or her expected contribution to the group's task.	1	2	3	4	5
3. Group members listened willingly to one another.	1	2	3	4	5
4. Members of the group showed strong leadership qualities.	1	2	3	4	5
5. Group members encouraged others to express opinions or contribute information.	1	2	3	4	5
6. Group members presented their information or ideas in a clear and logical manner.	1	2	3	4	5
7. Each member of the group fulfilled his or her responsibilities in the completion of the group's task.	1	2	3	4	5
8. The group fulfilled all the requirements of its assigned task.	1	2	3	4	5
9. Overall, the group worked well together.	1	2	3	4	5
10. The group performed to its full potential.	1	2	3	4	5

ADDITIONAL COMMENTS:

_____

_____

TOTAL POINTS/GRADE: _____

RUBRIC
CLASSIFICATORY WRITING

DIRECTIONS: This form is designed to help you evaluate classificatory writing assignments. Read the statements below. Then indicate the number from the following scale that reflects your assessment of the student's work.

1=Weak   **2**=Moderately Weak   **3**=Average   **4**=Moderately Strong   **5**=Strong

1.	Introduces and states the subject in an interesting manner.	1	2	3	4	5
2.	Divides the subject into relevant parts for presentation and evaluation.	1	2	3	4	5
3.	Precisely defines all of the terms applicable to the subject.	1	2	3	4	5
4.	Compares and contrasts the subject to something else, or compares and contrasts parts of the subject to each other.	1	2	3	4	5
5.	Includes sensory and factual details to help the audience picture the subject.	1	2	3	4	5
6.	Presents the subject in a highly organized fashion that is easy for the audience to follow.	1	2	3	4	5
7.	Takes into account the point of view of the audience being addressed.	1	2	3	4	5
8.	The spelling, punctuation, and grammar on the writing assignment is accurate.	1	2	3	4	5
9.	The writing assignment is neatly typed or handwritten.	1	2	3	4	5
10.	If appropriate, evaluates and assesses the subject or the parts of the subject.	1	2	3	4	5

ADDITIONAL COMMENTS:

_____

_____

TOTAL POINTS/GRADE: _____

RUBRIC
DISCUSSIONS

DIRECTIONS: This form is designed to help you evaluate student panel discussions and discussion groups. It may also be used for whole-class discussions. Read the statements below. Then indicate the number from the following scale that reflects your assessment of the discussion group's work.

1=Weak   **2**=Moderately Weak   **3**=Average   **4**=Moderately Strong   **5**=Strong

1. Each member of the group had a clear understanding of the group's task.	1	2	3	4	5
2. Group members presented their ideas and information in a clear and logical manner.	1	2	3	4	5
3. Group members willingly listened to one another.	1	2	3	4	5
4. Each member of the group contributed to the discussion.	1	2	3	4	5
5. Group members encouraged and respected the contributions of other members.	1	2	3	4	5
6. The group kept the discussion focused on the topic or task.	1	2	3	4	5
7. Group members spoke loudly and clearly enough to be heard by all listeners.	1	2	3	4	5
8. Contributions of group members demonstrated understanding of the topic being discussed.	1	2	3	4	5
9. The discussions met all the requirements of the assignment.	1	2	3	4	5
10. Overall, the discussion represented the full potential of the participants.	1	2	3	4	5

ADDITIONAL COMMENTS:

_____

_____

TOTAL POINTS/GRADE: _____

HOLT
PSYCHOLOGY: Principles In Practice

CONTENTS

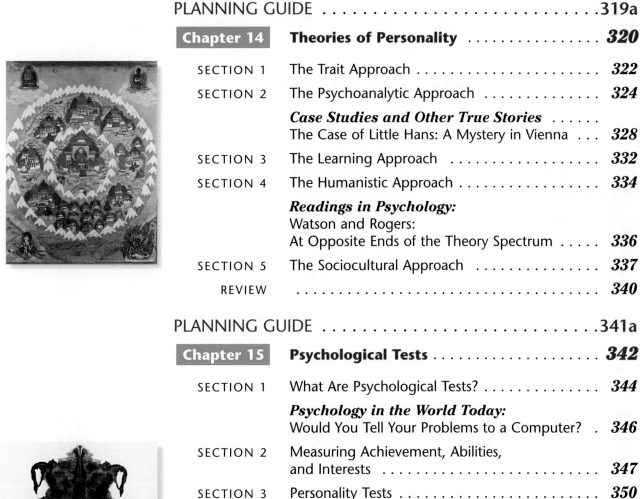

X   *Contents*

Psychology and Your World

Case Studies

ANALYZING PRIMARY SOURCES " "

Technology Activities

internet connect

Skill-Building Activities

SKILLS HANDBOOK

BUILDING SOCIAL STUDIES SKILLS

PSYCHOLOGY IN ACTION UNIT SIMULATIONS

CHARTS AND GRAPHS

Multifactorial Model of Schizophrenia

Genetic Factors

Complications during pregnancy and birth

Stress

SCHIZOPHRENIA

Viral infections

Family environment

How to Use Your Textbook

Use the chapter opener to get an overview of what you will learn.

A Day in the Life appears at the beginning of each chapter. This feature illustrates psychological concepts by following the experiences of teens in everyday life.

Key Terms lists important concepts you will encounter as you read the chapter. The terms will be defined in context.

Chapter 18 — PSYCHOLOGICAL DISORDERS

Read to Discover

1. What is the basis for classifying psychological disorders?
2. What are anxiety disorders?
3. What are the four dissociative disorders?
4. How do the two most common somatoform disorders differ?
5. How do psychologists attempt to explain mood disorders?
6. What are the subtypes of schizophrenia?
7. How do personality disorders differ from other psychological disorders?

A DAY IN THE LIFE

May 16

Janet was at home studying in her bedroom when the phone rang. "Hello?" she answered.

"Hey, Janet, it's me—Dan. Can you talk for a minute?"

Janet and Dan had been friends for years, and she could always tell when he sounded sad. "Of course I can. What's up?" Janet answered, trying to sound positive.

"It's Michelle again," Dan said.

About a year ago, Dan's older sister, Michelle, had been diagnosed with a serious psychological disorder called schizophrenia. Michelle was 23 years old and lived with her husband, Jeff, in a small house in the country. Accepting the fact that Michelle had a psychological disorder had been difficult for Dan. At first, he didn't talk about it with anyone outside his family. Then, after a while, he began confiding in Janet.

"It's so hard sometimes," Dan said sadly. "I really thought she was going to be okay after the doctors finally diagnosed and started treating her last year."

"Did something happen?" Janet asked, genuinely concerned.

"Well, I hadn't seen her in weeks

because Jeff was the only person she would talk to. I finally saw her tonight, and I could tell that something was happening again. She always seems so distracted. It's like she's listening to something only she can hear."

"Has she been taking the medicine that the doctor prescribed?" Janet asked.

"I don't know for sure," Dan answered. "I asked her about it tonight, but she got really defensive. She kept saying that I was trying to confuse her, and then she insisted that Jeff take her home."

"I'm sorry, Dan. I wish there were something I could do," Janet responded sympathetically.

"Thanks," Dan said. "It really helps to be able to talk to someone. At least I'm handling it a lot better than my parents are. My mom thinks that somehow it's her fault—like it is hereditary or Michelle caught it as a baby."

"Do the doctors have any idea how she did get it?" Janet asked.

"Not really," Dan said. "They have a bunch of different theories, but I don't think they know for sure. I'm just hoping that somehow they'll figure out exactly what's wrong so they'll be able to really help her."

"Me, too," Janet replied softly.

Dan's sister, Michelle, has schizophrenia, a serious psychological disorder that causes her to hear things that others cannot hear and, in general, often to lose touch with reality. Most psychological disorders are less serious than schizophrenia, but they still may cause great distress for affected individuals and their families and friends. This chapter describes several types of psychological disorders, including schizophrenia. The treatment of psychological disorders is the focus of Chapter 19.

Key Terms

psychological disorders
culture-bound syndromes
anxiety
phobia
simple phobia
social phobia
panic attack
agoraphobia
obsessions
compulsions
post-traumatic stress disorder
dissociation
depersonalization
somatization
depression
bipolar disorder
mania
schizophrenia
catatonic stupor

WHY PSYCHOLOGY MATTERS

Psychologists help people deal with psychological disorders. Use CNNfyi.com or other current events sources to learn more about how psychologists and other professionals help people cope with disorders.

408 CHAPTER 18

PSYCHOLOGICAL DISORDERS 409

Read to Discover questions begin each chapter of *Holt Psychology: Principles in Practice*. These questions serve as your guide as you read the chapter. Keep them in mind as you explore the chapter content.

Why Psychology Matters is an exciting way for you to make connections between what you are reading in your psychology book and the world around you. In each chapter you will be invited to explore a topic that is relevant to our lives today by using CNNfyi.com connections.

Use these built-in tools to read for understanding.

Truth or Fiction? questions, which are woven throughout the chapters, provide an engaging way to explore many interesting facets of psychology.

Charts, graphs and other visuals illustrate the concepts discussed in the chapter.

Questions help ensure that you understand the information in the visual.

Use these tools to pull together all of the information you have learned.

SECTION 3 REVIEW

go.hrw.com
Homework Practice Online

Keyword: SY3 HP18

1. Explain how dissociative fugue differs from dissociative amnesia.

2. **Critical Thinking** *Evaluating* In some cultures, people are encouraged to go into trancelike states. Should this type of dissociation be considered a sign of a psychological disorder? Why or why not?

Homework Practice Online lets you log on to the HRW Go site to complete an interactive self-check of the material covered in the section.

Critical Thinking helps you explore the section objectives and gain a strong understanding of the section content.

Thinking Critically questions ask you to use the information you have learned in the chapter to extend your knowledge.

Building Social Studies Skills is a way for you to build your skills at analyzing information and gain practice in answering standardized-test questions.

Writing About Psychology activities let you practice your writing skills to explore in more detail topics you have studied in the chapter.

Graphic Organizers will help you pull together and organize important information for your writing assignments.

Psychology Projects is an exciting and creative way to demonstrate your understanding of psychology.

xx

Use these online tools to review and complete online activities.

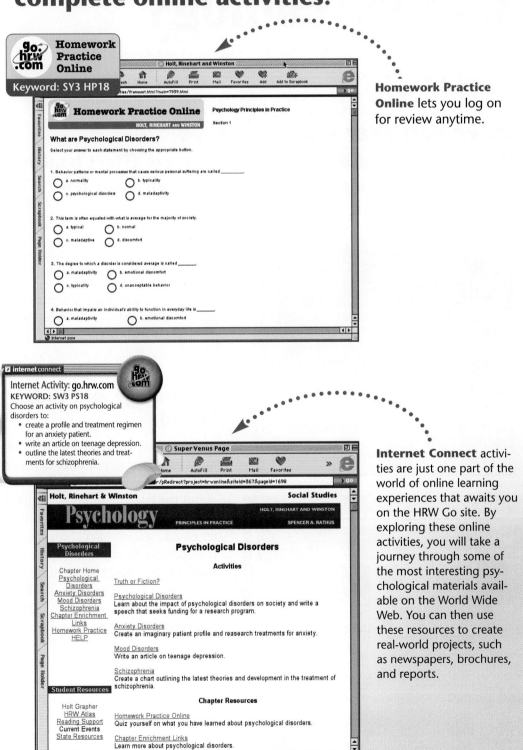

Homework Practice Online lets you log on for review anytime.

Internet Connect activities are just one part of the world of online learning experiences that awaits you on the HRW Go site. By exploring these online activities, you will take a journey through some of the most interesting psychological materials available on the World Wide Web. You can then use these resources to create real-world projects, such as newspapers, brochures, and reports.

Why Psychology Matters

Have you ever wondered. . .

Why do people dream? How does stress affect health? Why are some memories so vivid? Maybe you are curious about the ways people learn.

Blind children share with sighted
CNN Student Bureau's Jana Jacobs reports on a program in Atlanta that brings sighted and blind children together (August 7)

E very day, psychologists study a fascinating topic—people. Why do they do this? To learn why people act and think the way they do.

Psychology and Your World

All you need to do is watch or read the news to see the importance of psychology. You have probably seen news stories about the latest findings of studies carried out by psychologists. Many of these studies could have an effect on your life or the lives of your family and friends. The Why Psychology Matters feature of *Holt Psychology: Principles in Practice* invites you to use the vast resources of **CNNfyi**.com or other current events sources to examine the importance of psychology. Through this feature you will be able to draw connections between what you are studying in your psychology book and the events occurring in the world today.

Learning About People

When you think of the word *psychology*, what comes to mind? Perhaps you picture a person on a couch, talking to a counselor. Maybe you think of a scientist in a laboratory or library carrying out research. These things are important, but the study of psychology includes much more. Psychology involves asking questions and solving problems. It focuses on people and how they perceive the world, how they think, and why they behave the way they do.

Psychologists are interested in how we see ourselves.

The study of psychology helps us understand ourselves. It also helps us understand how we relate to family, friends, and the world around us. This useful information can help you in many aspects of your life.

Psychology and You

Psychologists continue to try to unravel the mysteries of human thought and behavior. With such a complex focus of study, psychology is a dynamic, ever-changing field. *Holt Psychology: Principles in Practice* presents in a clear fashion the most fascinating, up-to-date information on research in the field of psychology. By learning about psychology, you will gain fresh insights into your understanding of yourself and others.

Skills Handbook

CRITICAL THINKING
AND THE STUDY OF PSYCHOLOGY

*T*he study of psychology involves more than simply memorizing a series of names and terms. You will need to develop a variety of critical thinking skills to fully grasp the range of concepts and methods used in the study of psychology. Critical thinking is the reasoned judgment of information and ideas. People who think critically study information to determine its accuracy. They evaluate arguments and analyze conclusions before accepting their validity. Critical thinkers are able to recognize and define problems and develop strategies for resolving them.

The development of critical thinking skills is essential to understanding how psychology applies to you and your world. For example, critical thinking skills enable you to evaluate statistical information you hear in news stories.

Helping you develop critical thinking skills is an important part of Holt Psychology: Principles in Practice. *Using the following critical thinking skills will help you better understand the concepts involved in psychology.*

■ **Analyzing Information** is the process of breaking something down into its parts and examining the relationships among them. An *analysis* of something's parts enables you to better understand the whole. For example, to analyze the relationship between biology and behavior, you might study the nervous system, the brain, and the role of heredity in shaping personality.

■ **Sequencing** is the process of placing events in correct chronological order to better understand the relationships among these events. You can sequence events in two basic ways: according to *absolute* or *relative* chronology. Absolute chronology means that you pay close attention to the actual dates events took place. Placing events on a time line would be an example of absolute chronology. Relative chronology refers to the way events relate to one another. To put events in relative order, you need to know which one happened first, which came next, and so forth.

■ **Categorizing** is the process by which you group things together by the characteristics they have in common. By putting things or events into categories, it is easier to make comparisons and see differences among them.

■ **Comparing and Contrasting** involves examining events, situations, or points of view for their similarities and differences. *Comparing* focuses on both the similarities and the differences. *Contrasting* focuses only on the differences. For example, by comparing gender roles in different cultures you might note that although women have traditionally been primarily responsible for raising children, men and women increasingly share that responsibility. By contrasting, on the other hand, you might note that in many cultures women are still primarily responsible for raising children.

■ **Summarizing** is the process of taking a large amount of information and boiling it down into a short and clear statement. Summarizing is particularly useful when you need to give a brief account of a longer story or event. For example, it might be more useful to summarize the history of psychology than to take time away from your study of current research in the field.

■ Drawing Inferences and Conclusions is forming possible explanations for an event, a situation, or a problem. When you make an *inference,* you take the information you know to be true and come up with an educated guess about what else you think is true about that situation. A *conclusion* is a prediction about the outcome of a situation based on what you already know.

■ Evaluating is assessing the significance or overall importance of something. When evaluating conclusions you should base your judgment on standards that others will understand and are likely to think important.

■ Supporting a Point of View involves identifying an issue, deciding what you think about the issue, and persuasively expressing your position on it. Your stand should be based on specific information. In taking a stand, state your position clearly and give reasons to support it.

■ Making Generalizations and Predictions is the process of interpreting information to form more general statements and guess about what will happen next. A *generalization* is a broad statement that holds true for many types of behaviors or situations. Making generalizations can help you see the "big picture" of events. It is very important, however, that you avoid including situations that do not fit the statement. When this occurs, you run the risk of creating a stereotype, or overgeneralization. A *prediction* is an educated guess about an outcome. When you read about psychology, you should always be asking yourself questions like, "What will happen next? If this person does this, what will that mean for . . .?", and so on. These types of questions help you draw on information you already know to see patterns in psychology.

■ Identifying Bias is the process of identifying a writer's strong feelings. Many people have strong opinions that appear in their writings. Remember that just because you hear something in a source, be it a research study, statistics given in a news story, or a television program, you do not have to agree with what is said. When looking for bias, examine the sources of information the author uses. How reliable are those sources? Consider why the writer supported one view over another. Be sure to distinguish between provable facts and someone's opinions.

■ Finding the Main Idea The ability to identify and understand the main idea is crucial to understanding any complex subject. This is particularly true of the study of psychology because the significant theories and methods may sometimes get lost among numerous detailed examples.

Psychology: Principles in Practice is designed to help you focus on the main ideas in psychology. The Read to Discover questions, along with the "Truth or Fiction?" statements that introduce each chapter are intended to guide your reading. The Section Review questions that close each section are intended to help you gauge whether or not you have grasped the main ideas of the section. You will still need to focus your reading, however. Applying these basic guidelines will help you identify the main ideas in whatever subject you read.

How to Find the Main Idea

1. **Read introductory material.** Read the title and the introduction, if there is one. They often indicate the main ideas to be covered.

2. **Have questions in mind.** As you read, formulate questions about the subject that you think may be answered by the material. Having such questions in mind will help you focus your reading.

3. **Note the outline of ideas.** Pay attention to any headings or subheadings. They will provide a basic outline of the major ideas. You may also want to write down this outline and use it to guide your reading.

4. **Distinguish supporting details.** As you read, distinguish sentences providing supporting details from the general statements they support. A series of examples may lead to a conclusion that restates or reinforces a main idea.

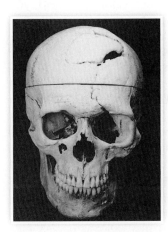

Cause: Phineas Gage experiences severe physical trauma to the underside of the frontal lobes of his cerebral cortex.

Effect: Gage's personality changes. He becomes ill-mannered, foul-mouthed, and undependable.

Cause: A person experiences a very depressing situation.

Effect/Cause: The depressing situation may reduce the activity of noradrenaline in the brain.

Effect: The chemical changes in the brain may worsen the depression.

■ **Identifying Cause and Effect** Identifying and understanding cause-and-effect relationships is one essential concept in the study of psychology. It is necessary to investigate not only what caused a certain behavior or feeling to occur, but also what emotions, thoughts, and behaviors may happen as a result. To help determine the answers, psychologists ask such questions as: What is the individual's or group's background? Is this an isolated incident or does the behavior indicate a pattern? What external events may contribute to this type of feeling or pattern of behavior? Could biological processes be involved in producing this type of behavior?

CLUE WORDS AND PHRASES

CAUSE	EFFECT
as a result of	aftermath
because	as a consequence
brought about	depended on
inspired	gave rise to
led to	originated from
produced	outcome
provoked	outgrowth
spurred	proceeded from
the reason	resulting in

How to Identify Cause and Effect

1. **Look for clues.** Certain words and phrases are immediate clues to the existence of a cause-and-effect relationship. Examples of such clue words and phrases are listed here.

2. **Identify the relationship.** Read carefully to identify how concepts are related. Writers do not always clearly state the link between cause and effect.

3. **Check for complex connections.** Beyond the immediate cause-and-effect relationship, check for other, more complex connections. Note, for instance, whether (1) there were additional causes of a given effect, (2) a cause had multiple effects, and (3) these effects themselves caused further events.

Applying Your Skill

Review the example in the diagram above, taken from the case study on page 65. The diagram demonstrates an important cause-and-effect relationship. Also keep in mind that in some instances an effect may also become a cause.

Practicing Your Skill

From your knowledge of psychology, choose a sequence of feelings, thoughts, and behaviors that may share a cause-and-effect relationship. Draw a simple cause-and-effect chart that could be used as part of a visual presentation. Be sure that the chart shows the relationship between these feelings, thoughts, and behaviors. Then write a paragraph that explains the connections.

■ Problem solving is the process of finding an effective solution to a problem. Listed below are guidelines for the problem-solving process.

1. Identify the problem. Identify just what the problem or difficulty is that you are facing. Sometimes you face a difficult situation made up of several different problems. Each problem may require a different solution.

2. Gather information. Conduct research on any important issues related to the problem. Try to find the answers to questions like the following: What caused this problem? Who or what does it affect? When did it start?

3. List and consider options. Look at the problem and the answers to the questions you asked in Step 2. List and then think about all the possible ways in which the problem could be solved. These are your options—possible solutions to the problem.

4. Consider advantages and disadvantages. Consider the advantages and disadvantages of all the options that you have listed. Make sure that you consider the possible long-term effects of each possible solution. You should also determine what steps you will need to take to achieve each possible solution. Some suggestions may sound good at first but may turn out to be impractical or hard to achieve.

5. Choose and implement a solution. Select the best solution from your list and take the steps to achieve it.

6. Evaluate the effectiveness of the solution. When you have completed the steps needed to put your plan into action, evaluate its effectiveness. Is the problem solved? Were the results worth the effort required? Has the solution created any other problems that now need to be addressed?

Practicing Your Skill

The feature on page 412 discusses the challenges mental-health professionals face in dealing with criminal defendants who may or may not have a psychological disorder severe enough to justify avoiding punishment for the crime. Imagine that you are a psychologist who has been asked by a court to evaluate whether a person is legally sane and can thus be put on trial for a crime. Use the problem-solving guidelines above to help you decide how best to approach the issue.

■ Decision Making Psychologists face many difficult decisions in their practices and during research. With the use of decision-making skills you will be better able to make a decision on important issues. The following activities will help you develop and practice these skills. Decision making involves choosing between two or more options. Listed below are guidelines that will help you with making decisions.

1. Identify a situation that requires a decision. Think about your current situation. What issue are you faced with that requires you to take some sort of action?

2. Gather information. Think about the issue. Examine the causes of the issue or problem and consider how it affects you and others.

3. Identify options. Consider the actions that you could take to address the issue. List these options so that you can compare them.

4. Predict Consequences. Predict the consequences of taking the actions listed for each of your options. Compare these possible consequences. Some options might be easier or seem more satisfying. But do they produce the results that you want?

S5 *Critical Thinking*

5. **Take action to implement a decision.** Choose a course of action from your available options and put it into effect.

Practicing Your Skill

Chapter 19 describes different methods of therapy. Imagine that you are a psychologist who has been asked to help a person develop a more positive outlook and higher self-esteem. Use the decision-making guidelines above to help you decide which method would best help the person.

■ **Conflict Resolution** Every year, psychologists help many people learn how to resolve conflicts. The following guidelines can be useful in resolving conflicts.

1. **Consider Persuasion.** Try to persuade the person you have a conflict with to come around to your point of view. You might want to come up with persuasive arguments for your position, then rank each reason in order of persuasiveness. Finally, present the most persuasive reasons to the other person in an effort to sway his or her point of view.

2. **Compromise.** Realize that sometimes compromise is necessary to resolve a conflict. Consider giving up something to reach an agreement. Decide what you would be willing to give up to resolve the disagreement. Then encourage the person you are having a disagreement with to meet and discuss what he or she would be willing to give up to reach an agreement.

3. **Debate the Issue.** Suggest to the person you are having a disagreement with that you and he or she hold a debate. Gather information about the advantages and disadvantages of your position. Then consider preparing flash cards outlining your best arguments. Finally, recommend that you and the other person debate your disagreement.

4. **Consider Negotiation.** Begin negotiations about the conflict. Suggest to the person you

have a disagreement with that you and he or she meet to discuss your positions and what they would be willing to agree upon. Perhaps by working together to resolve the conflict, you will arrive at a solution that neither of you had considered before.

Practicing Your Skill

Chapter 14 discusses theories of personality. Imagine that you are a psychologist, and that a colleague of yours strongly disagrees with you about which theory of personality best explains a particular client's behavior. Use the conflict resolution guidelines above to help you and your colleague resolve your disagreement about the best way to help the client.

Kohlberg's Stages of Moral Development

Stage	Moral Reasoning Goal	What Is Right?
p r e c o n v e n t i o n a l l e v e l		
1	Avoiding punishment	Doing what is necessary to avoid punishment
2	Satisfying needs	Doing what is necessary to satisfy one's needs
c o n v e n t i o n a l l e v e l		
3	Winning approval	Seeking and maintaining the approval of others using conventional standards of right and wrong
4	Law and order	Moral judgments based on maintaining social order High regard for authority
p o s t c o n v e n t i o n a l l e v e l		
5	Social order	Obedience to accepted laws Judgments based on personal values
6	Universal ethics	Morality of individual conscience, not necessarily in agreement with others

According to Lawrence Kohlberg, people's moral development follows a specific sequence. Not every person reaches the highest stage.

■ Using Primary and Secondary Sources

There are many sources of firsthand psychological information, including self-reports, recorded interviews, diaries, letters, photographs, laboratory data, and other documented research results. These are examples of *primary sources*. Primary sources are considered valuable tools for studying psychology because they offer a close-up view of clinical experiences and research results.

Secondary sources are descriptions or interpretations of events written after the events have occurred by persons who did not participate in the actual events. Textbooks, such as *Holt Psychology: Principles in Practice*, biographies, encyclopedias, and other reference works are secondary sources.

How to Study Primary and Secondary Sources

1. **Study the material carefully.** Consider the nature of the material. Is it anecdotal (telling a story) or scientific? Is the material upon which the conclusion was made based on firsthand information or on the accounts of others? Note the main ideas and supporting details. They are often important clues about the source of the material.

2. **Consider the audience.** Ask yourself: For whom was this information meant originally? For example, case history that was written for and published in a professional journal would probably differ in style and perhaps also in content from a case history relayed orally by a professor during a class lecture.

3. **Check for bias.** Watch for words or phrases that signal the author's one-sided view of a person, event, or concept.

4. **When possible, compare sources.** Study more than one source on a topic, if available. Comparing sources gives you a more complete, balanced account of a subject.

Practicing Your Skill

1. What distinguishes secondary sources from primary sources?

2. Why is it important to consider the origin of a source?

■ Building Vocabulary

As you read *Holt Psychology: Principles in Practice* you will encounter new and unfamiliar words. With regular effort, however, you can master these new terms and turn the study of psychology into an opportunity to enlarge and improve your vocabulary. The steps listed below will help you accomplish this.

How to Build Vocabulary

1. **Identify unusual words.** As you read the chapters, list any words that you cannot immediately define or pronounce.

2. **Study context clues.** Study the sentence and paragraph in which you find the new term. The setting in which the word appears, or the *context*, may give you clues to the word's meaning by providing examples or definitions of more familiar words that have the same meanings.

3. **Use the dictionary.** Use a dictionary to learn the definitions of words on your list.

4. **Review new vocabulary.** Be on the lookout for ways to use the new words in homework assignments, classroom discussions, or in ordinary conversation.

Practicing Your Skill

1. Define *context*. How can a word's context provide clues to its meaning?

2. As you read the rest of this Skill's Handbook, list any unfamiliar words that you encounter. Write down what you think that word means, then check your guesses against a dictionary's definition or this book's Glossary.

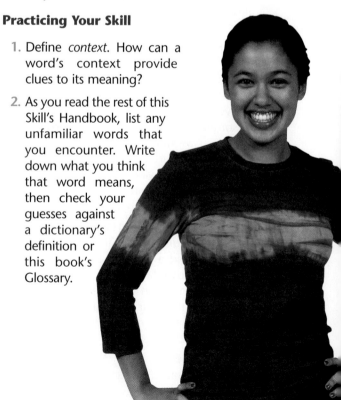

■ Creating an Outline

An outline is a tool for organizing information. It is a logical summary that presents the main points of what you plan to communicate. Creating an outline is an important part of writing a paper. An outline enables you to highlight the main ideas you intend to express in your paper and list the supporting details you want to cover. The writing process itself becomes much easier when the outline on which an essay is based is thorough and well organized.

How to Create an Outline

1. **Order your material.** Decide what information you want to emphasize. Then order or classify your research material with that focus in mind. Determine what information belongs in the introduction, what should be in the body of your paper, and what to reserve for the conclusion.

2. **Identify main ideas.** After organizing your material, identify the main ideas you plan to highlight in each section. These topics will be the main headings of your outline.

3. **List supporting details.** Determine the important details or facts that support each main idea. Rank and list them as subheadings, using additional levels of subheadings as necessary. Subheadings must come in pairs, at the least. That is, no *A*s without *B*s, no *1*s without *2*s, and so forth.

4. **Put your outline to use.** Structure your paper according to your outline. Each main heading, for instance, might form the basis of a paragraph's topic sentence. Subheadings would then make up the content of the paragraph.

Practicing Your Skill

Read Section 1 in Chapter 3. Create an outline to organize the complex biological concepts described in the section. Then use the outline to write a brief essay about the nervous system.

■ Conducting Library Research

To complete research papers or special projects related to the field of psychology, you may need

Using PQ4R

I. What is classical conditioning?
  A. Who is Ivan Pavlov?
  B. What do US, UR, CR, and CS mean?
  C. How is adaptation to the environment related to conditioning?
    1. What is a taste aversion?
    2. What is extinction?
    3. What is spontaneous recovery?
    4. How do generalization and discrimination relate to classical conditioning?
  D. What are some applications of classical conditioning?
    1. What are flooding and systematic desensitization?
    2. What is counterconditioning?
    3. How does the bell-and-pad method for bed-wetting work?

to use resources other than this textbook. Conducting thorough research generally requires using the resources available in a library.

Finding Information

To locate a particular book in a library, you need to know how libraries organize their materials. Books of fiction are alphabetized according to the last name of the author. To classify nonfiction and reference books, libraries use the Dewey decimal system and the Library of Congress system. Both systems assign each book a *call number* that tells you its classification.

To find the book's call number, look in the library's card catalog or online catalog. These sources list books by author, by title, and by subject. Finding a particular book is simple if you know the author's name or the book's title. If you do not have this information, however, or if you just want to find some books about a general subject, you can look up that subject heading.

Using Resources

In a library's reference section, you will find encyclopedias, indexes to magazines and newspapers, specialized dictionaries, atlases, and abstracts. Early in your research, encyclopedias will often be an effective resource. Encyclopedias include articles explaining basic psychological concepts and methods, historical information, and biographical sketches of important figures in the field of psychology.

Libraries also house specialized dictionaries of psychological terms and concepts. These dictionaries define and describe the more important terms, people, and theories.

Periodical indexes can also be extremely useful. They are especially helpful if you are looking for relevant, up-to-date articles containing facts and statistics about a particular subject. *The Readers' Guide to Periodical Literature,* which lists articles published in magazines, can be extremely useful. Additionally, the *New York Times Index* catalogs all news stories published in the the *New York Times,* the U.S. daily newspaper with perhaps the most extensive coverage of current events and issues.

Practicing Your Skill

1. What kinds of references contain information about terms used in psychology?

2. Where would you look to find recent coverage of a controversial new theory?

■ Writing About Psychology

Holt Psychology: Principles in Practice provides you with numerous writing opportunities using psychology-related terminology correctly. Chapter reviews contain exercises that give you the chance to focus your writing on a particular aspect of psychology.

How to Write with a Purpose

Always keep your basic purpose for writing in mind. This purpose may be to analyze, to evaluate, to synthesize, to inform, to persuade, or to hypothesize. Every purpose for writing suggests its own form, tone, and content. The point of view you adopt will shape what you write, as will your intended audience.

Each writing opportunity provided in this textbook will have specific directions about what and how to write. Regardless of your subject matter, you should follow certain basic steps in the writing process. The following guidelines can help you improve your writing.

How to Write a Paper

1. **Identify your purpose in writing.** Read the directions carefully to identify the purpose for your writing. Keep that purpose in mind as you plan and write your paper.

2. **Consider your audience.** When writing for a specific audience, choose the tone and style that will best communicate your message.

3. **Create an outline.** Plan before you begin writing. Organize themes, main ideas, and supporting details into an outline.

4. **Collect information.** Conduct research, if necessary. Your writing will be more effective if you have many details at hand.

5. **Write a first draft.** Remember to use your outline as a guide when you attempt the first draft. Each paragraph should express a single main idea, or a set of related ideas, with details for support. Be careful to clearly demonstrate the relationships between ideas, and to use proper transitions—sentences that build connections between paragraphs. Be sure to use standard grammar, spelling, sentence structure, and punctuation.

6. **Review and edit.** Revise your draft as needed to make your points clearly. Improve your sentences by varying their length and structure, by omitting clichés and substituting more precise language, and by adding appropriate adjectives and adverbs. Then check for correct spelling, punctuation, and grammar.

7. **Write your final version.** Prepare a neat, clean final version. Appearance is important; while it may not boost the quality of the writing, it can affect the way your effort is perceived.

Practicing Your Skill

1. What factor, more than any other, should affect how and what you write? Why?

2. Why is it important to consider the audience for whom you are writing?

3. What steps should you take to edit a first draft? Why is this important?

■ Using the Internet

The Internet is a vast, world-wide collection of linked computers that convey and receive data. Millions of information sources are found on the Internet, in no order and with no one person or organization in control of the content. Government agencies, universities, libraries, non-profit and for-profit organizations, businesses, and individuals put the information "out there" for anyone's use—often for free. In the United States alone, more than 174 million people use the Internet. Millions of students in the United States and around the world have learned to use the Internet as a rich source of information. By learning the fundamentals of on-line research, you will obtain access to this enormously helpful source.

Data on almost every conceivable subject is available to anyone who has access to a computer, an Internet provider, a telephone jack and cable access or a modem. A *modem* is an internal or external device connected to your computer that enables your computer to transmit and receive information electronically via telephone lines.

The World Wide Web

Several attempts have been made to organize the vast amounts of information available on the Internet. One such effort is the World Wide Web. The Web was designed to make all online information part of one matrix of interconnected documents and services. Almost every resource available on the Internet can be accessed via the World Wide Web.

Information on the Web is organized according to category and is stored in a particular, unique location. The location is known as an address, or *URL*—short for Universal Resource Locator—on the Internet. Software programs called *Web browsers* enable a computer to locate addresses and to search subject categories anywhere on the Internet, including the World Wide Web.

Web Pages

Web URLs share certain basic characteristics because most Web documents are created using the same computer language, HyperText Markup Language, or HTML. A Web URL always begins with the four letters *http,* which simply states that the address was created in HTML. Your Web browser can go directly to any URL that you type into its locator box.

All Internet addresses indicate the domain, or the nature of the information's source. These sources are indicated by suffixes on the address. The suffixes include the following: *gov* for government agencies; *com* for a business or commercial enterprises; *org* for nonprofit organizations; and *edu* for educational institutions.

Your browser is like a taxi that does not recognize landmarks, but finds its way only by specific addresses. If you know the address you need, getting there is a snap. Just be sure to type the address exactly as you have seen it, including strange-looking symbols, spaces, and upper- and lower-case letters. This is critical because if you give it an incorrect address— even a "dot" out of place—you will receive a message on your screen that the Web site cannot be retrieved.

Once you have typed in the correct address, your browser will take you to a Web homepage, the opening page of a Web document. Think of it as a table of contents. Web pages contain underlined or highlighted words and images called hyperlinks. Clicking on a hyperlink will take you to a related or "linked" Web page, either within this site or in another location on the Internet. Hyperlinks function in a nonlinear fashion. By clicking on hyperlinks, you can "surf the Net," traveling to a seemingly unlimited number of Web sites.

Navigating the Web

You can navigate your way around the Web in three ways:

- by clicking on the hyperlinks that interest you, and exploring the Web.

- by using search tools, primarily keyword searches, that identify your subject category.

- by commanding the browser to go directly to a specific Internet resource that may be in another collection of organized data.

It is important to write down any potential sources of information in a log. This will enable you to easily find the URL again and command your browser to take you there.

The best way to familiarize yourself with the Internet is to spend some time exploring the Web—clicking on hyperlinks, and finding your way back. If your time on the Internet is limited, however, and you need to conduct research on a specific topic, you will need to focus your search.

The Internet offers many sources for research. Many of the world's libraries and archives can be searched from any computer with online access. Be aware that search tools are constantly changing. Get to know the strengths and weaknesses of your search tool choice. Some large Web sites—such as American Online, CNN, MSN, Netscape, and Yahoo!—offer links to a broad range of information. Sites such as CNNfyi.com allow you to access a wealth of current information. These sites are also useful when transferring information from written to visual form.

A broad search of the Web will give you a sense of just how many documents are related to your subject, but it will not tell you whether these documents will be useful or relevant to your particular research project. Rather than scanning an overwhelming amount of data, you can limit your initial search by these two methods:

- Lists of lists, or menus. Use a keyword search (or the URL, if you have it) to go directly to an on-line reference library, such as the Library of Congress, which lists Web sites by subject and gives their URLs.

- Clearinghouse lists. These are roughly equivalent to on-line encyclopedias merged with directories.

A Trial Run

Let's say you want to research a paper on the following topic: "The Effect of Weather on People's Moods." A hunch told you that the rainy day was putting you and your friends in bad moods. The following steps provide an example of how you might successfully navigate the Web and complete your research.

1. **Decide on your topic:** moods and weather.

2. **Determine your research needs.** Gather no more and no less information than is necessary to complete your project.

3. **Create a list of possible keywords,** for example, climate, rain, depression, happiness, and even rainy-weather cities, such as Seattle and London.

You may find a promising Web site containing hyperlinks that lead you to a Web page in the "health" category. Here you may find a description of "seasonal affective disorder." This sounds like your topic, only it is more about seasons (winter) than rain. Still, it's too close to ignore. So you can go "surfing."

Clicking on one hyperlink may not reveal anything relevant. Another hyperlink on the next "page," however, may tell you about light therapy treatment, and refer you to a hospital research program using light therapy in London.

At this point, you may need to stop and evaluate your approach. Ask yourself: Am I now on a fascinating but completely irrelevant side alley? If you answer yes, which, at some point in time, will happen, you will need to reassess your topic.

Ask yourself whether your topic has changed, and if so, do you want to get it back on your original track or follow this somewhat different and, it seems, more focused direction? Often, the process of researching reveals that a selected topic was too vague at the start.

Sometimes, however, you do not have the option of altering or narrowing your topic, either because it was assigned or because you committed yourself to it. What can you do? Don't get frustrated, there are still several options.

- Try other approaches. University psychology departments, research facilities, and professional psychological associations worldwide usually have Web sites.

- Try using another Web browser. All software packages are not identical. Some are more powerful than others and will retrieve more data, or more specific data.

Above all, be patient with yourself. You are developing a new and complex skill. It takes practice,

experience, and faith in your own intuition to develop truly efficient on-line research skills that will help you as you study about psychology.

Becoming a Strategic Reader

by Dr. Judith Irvin

Everywhere you look, print is all around us. In fact, you would have a hard time stopping yourself from reading. In a normal day, you might read cereal boxes, movie posters, notes from friends, t-shirts, instructions for video games, song lyrics, catalogs, billboards, information on the Internet, magazines, the newspaper, and much, much more. Each form of print is read differently depending on your purpose for reading. You read a menu differently from poetry, and a motorcycle magazine is read differently than a letter from a friend. Good readers switch easily from one type of text to another. In fact, they probably do not even think about it, they just do it.

When you read, it is helpful to use a strategy to remember the most important ideas. You can use a strategy before you read to help connect information you already know to the new information you will encounter. Before you read, you can also predict what a text will be about by using a previewing strategy. During the reading you can use a strategy to help you focus on main ideas, and after reading you can use a strategy to help you organize what you learned so that you can remember it later. Holt Psychology: Principles In Practice *was designed to help you more easily understand the ideas you read. Important reading strategies employed in* Holt Psychology: Principles In Practice *include:*

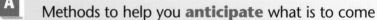

A   Methods to help you **anticipate** what is to come

B   Tools to help you **preview and predict** what the text will be about

C   Ways to help you **use and analyze visual information**

D   Ideas to help you **organize the information** you have learned

A. Anticipate Information

How can I use information I already know to help me understand what a new chapter will be about?

Anticipating what a new chapter will be about helps you connect the upcoming information to what you already know. By drawing on your background knowledge, you can build a bridge to the new material.

1 Each chapter of *Holt Psychology: Principles In Practice* asks you to explore the chapter before you start reading by forming opinions based on your current knowledge.

TRUTH OR fiction ?

Read the following statements about psychology. Do you think they are true or false? You will learn whether each statement is true or false as you read the chapter.
- Psychologists never guess about the answers to the questions they ask.
- You have to do a study more than once to be sure its results are valid.

A Before Reading Agree/Disagree	B After Reading Agree/Disagree
Psychologists never guess about the answers to the questions they ask.	
You have to do a study more than once to be sure its results are valid.	

2 ... **4**

3 Read the text and discuss with classmates.

5 You can also refine your knowledge by reviewing the **Truth or Fiction Revisited** boxes.

Anticipating Information

step 1 Identify the major concepts of the chapter. In *Holt Psychology: Principles in Practice*, these are presented in the **Truth or Fiction** feature at the beginning of each chapter.

▼

step 2 Agree or disagree with each of the statements.

▼

step 3 Read the text and discuss your responses with your classmates.

▼

step 4 After reading the material that deals with the **Truth or Fiction** statement, revisit the statements and respond to them again based on what you have learned.

▼

step 5 Go back and check your knowlege by reviewing the **Truth or Fiction Revisited** boxes.

TRUTH OR fiction ▪ REVISITED ▪

It is not true that psychologists never guess about the answers to the questions they ask. After psychologists ask a research question, they form a hypothesis, or an educated guess, about the answer.

B. Previewing and Predicting

How can I figure out what the text is about before I even start reading a section?

Previewing and **predicting** are good methods to help you understand the text. If you take the time to preview and predict before you read, the text will make more sense to you during your reading.

1 Usually, your teacher will set the purpose for reading. After reading some new information, you may be asked to write a summary, take a test, or complete some other type of activity.

Previewing and Predicting

step 1 Identify your purpose for reading. Ask yourself what you will do with this information once you have finished reading.

▼

step 2 Ask yourself what is the main idea of the text and what are the key vocabulary words you need to know.

▼

step 3 Use signal words to help identify the structure of the text.

▼

step 4 Connect the information to what you already know.

"After reading about self-esteem, you will work with a partner to create a poster and . . ."

2 As you preview the text, use *graphic signals* such as headings, subheadings, and boldface type to help you determine what is important in the text. Each chapter of *Holt Psychology: Principles in Practice* opens by giving you important clues to help you preview the material.

Looking at the chapter's title, main heading, and subheadings can give you an idea of what is to come.

Read to Discover questions give you clues as to the chapter's main ideas.

18 Chapter PSYCHOLOGICAL DISORDERS

Read to Discover

1 Explain the basis for classifying psychological disorders.

2 Distinguish among the anxiety disorders, and outline the theories that explain them.

3 Define *dissociation*, and describe the dissociative disorders.

3 Other tools that can help you in previewing are **signal words**. These words prepare you to think in a certain way. For example, when you see words such as *similar to, same as,* or *different from,* you know that the text will probably compare and contrast two or more ideas. Signal words indicate how the ideas in the text relate to each other. Look at the list below for some of the most common signal words grouped by the type of text structures they include.

SIGNAL
w o r d s

Cause and Effect	Compare and Contrast	Description	Problem and Solution	Sequence or Chronological Order
because	different from	for instance	the question is	not long after
since	same as	for example	a solution	next
consequently	similar to	such as	one answer is	then
this led to...so	as opposed to	to illustrate		initially
if...then	instead of	in addition		before
nevertheless	although	most importantly		after
accordingly	however	another		finally
because of	compared with	furthermore		preceding
as a result of	as well as	first,		following
in order to	either...or	second ...		on (date)
may be due to	but			over the years
for this reason	on the other hand			today
not only...but	unless			when

4 Learning something new requires that you connect it in some way with something you already know. This means you have to think before you read and while you read. You may want to use a chart like this one to remind yourself of the information already familiar to you and to come up with questions you want answered in your reading. The chart will also help you organize your ideas after you have finished reading.

What I know	*What I want to know*	*What I learned*

C. Use and Analyze Visual Information

How can all the pictures, graphs, and cartoons help me be a stronger reader?

Using **visual information** can help you understand and remember the information presented in *Holt Psychology: Principles in Practice.* Good readers make a picture in their mind when they read. The pictures, charts, graphs, time lines, and diagrams that occur throughout *Holt Psychology: Principles in Practice* are placed strategically to increase your understanding.

Analyzing Visual Information

step 1 As you preview the text, ask yourself how the visual information relates to the text.

▼

step 2 Generate questions based on the visual information.

▼

step 3 After reading the text, go back and review the visual information again.

▼

step 4 Connect the information to what you already know.

1 You might ask yourself questions like these:

Why did the writer include this image with the text? What details about this image are mentioned in the text?

2 After you have read the text, see if you can answer your own questions.

What are the people in this picture doing?

Why are they sitting in a circle?

What does this picture tell me about psychology?

3 After reading, take another look at the visual information.

4 Try to make connections to what you already know.

D. Organize Information

Once I learn new information, how do I keep it all straight so that I will remember it?

To help you remember what you have read, you need to find a way of **organizing information**. Two good ways of doing this are by using graphic organizers and concept maps. **Graphic organizers** help you understand important relationships—such as cause-and-effect, compare/contrast, sequence of events, and problem/solution—within the text. **Concept maps** provide a useful tool to help you focus on the text's main ideas and organize supporting details.

Identifying Relationships

Using graphic organizers will help you recall important ideas from the section and give you a study tool you can use to prepare for a quiz or test or to help with a writing assignment. Some of the most common types of graphic organizers are shown below.

Cause and Effect

Psychological events cause people to react in a certain way. Cause-and-effect patterns show the relationship between results and the ideas or events that made the results occur. You may want to represent cause-and-effect relationships as one cause leading to multiple effects,

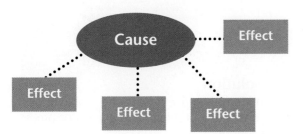

or as a chain of cause-and-effect relationships.

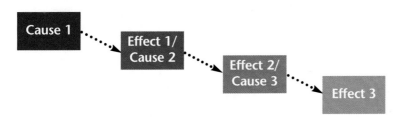

Constructing Graphic Organizers

step 1 Preview the text, looking for signal words and the main idea.

▼

step 2 Form a hypothesis as to which type of graphic organizer would work best to display the information presented.

▼

step 3 Work individually or with your classmates to create a visual representation of what you read.

❱ Comparing and Contrasting

Graphic Organizers are often useful when you are comparing or contrasting information. Compare-and-contrast diagrams point out similarities and differences between two concepts or ideas.

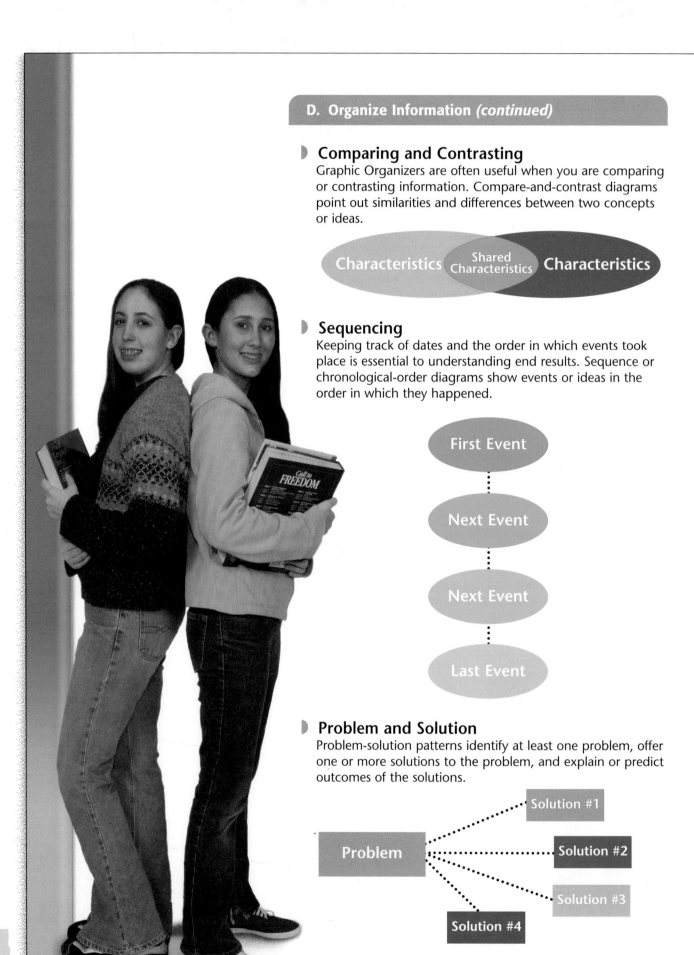

Characteristics   Shared Characteristics   Characteristics

❱ Sequencing

Keeping track of dates and the order in which events took place is essential to understanding end results. Sequence or chronological-order diagrams show events or ideas in the order in which they happened.

First Event

Next Event

Next Event

Last Event

❱ Problem and Solution

Problem-solution patterns identify at least one problem, offer one or more solutions to the problem, and explain or predict outcomes of the solutions.

Solution #1

Problem

Solution #2

Solution #3

Solution #4

Identifying Main Ideas and Supporting Details

One special type of graphic organizer is the concept map. A concept map, sometimes called a semantic map, allows you to zero in on the most important points of the text. The map is made up of lines, boxes, circles, and/or arrows. It can be as simple or as complex as you need it to be to accurately represent the text.

Here are a few examples of concept maps you might use.

Constructing Concept Maps

step 1 Preview the text, looking at what type of structure might be appropriate to display on a concept map.

▼

step 2 Taking note of the headings, bold-faced type, and text structure, sketch a concept map you think could best illustrate the text.

▼

step 3 Using boxes, lines, arrows, circles, or any shapes you like, display the ideas of the text in the concept map.

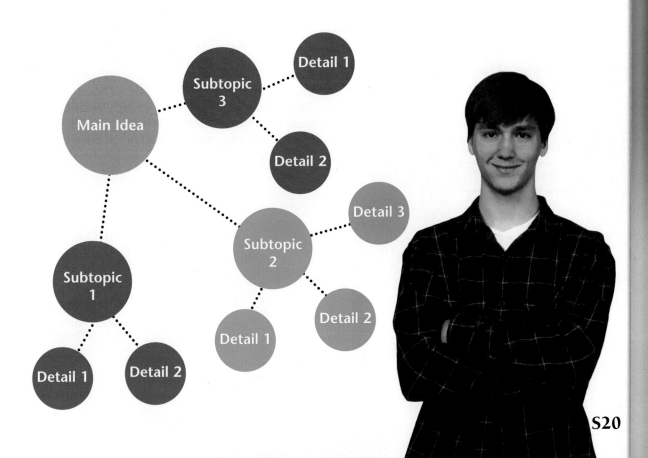

Standardized Test-Taking Strategies

A number of times throughout your school career, you may be asked to take standardized tests. These tests are designed to demonstrate the content and skills you have learned. It is important to keep in mind that in most cases the best way to prepare for these tests is to pay close attention in class and take every opportunity to improve your general social studies, reading, writing, and mathematical skills.

Tips for Taking the Test

1. Be sure that you are well rested.
2. Be on time, and be sure that you have the necessary materials.
3. Listen to the teacher's instructions.
4. Read directions and questions carefully.
5. DON'T STRESS! Just remember what you have learned in class, and you should do well.

Practice the strategies at go.hrw.com

STANDARDIZED
TEST PREP
ONLINE
keyword:
SY3 STP TOC

Tackling Social Studies

The social studies portions of many standardized tests are designed to test your knowledge of the content and skills that you have been studying in one or more of your social studies classes. Specific objectives for the test vary, but some of the most common include the following:

1. Demonstrate an understanding of issues and events in history.
2. Demonstrate an understanding of geographic influences on historical issues and events.
3. Demonstrate an understanding of economic and social influences on historical issues and events.
4. Demonstrate an understanding of political influences on historical issues and events.
5. Use critical thinking skills to analyze social studies information.

Standardized tests usually contain multiple-choice and, sometimes, open-ended questions. The multiple-choice items will often be based on maps, tables, charts, graphs, pictures, cartoons, and/or reading passages and documents.

Tips for Answering Multiple-Choice Questions

1. If there is a written or visual piece accompanying the multiple-choice question, pay careful attention to the title, author, and date.

2. Then read through or glance over the content of the written or visual piece accompanying the question to familiarize yourself with it.

3. Next, read the multiple-choice question first for its general intent. Then reread it carefully, looking for words that give clues or can limit possible answers to the question. For example, words such as *most* or *best* tell you that there may be several correct answers to a question, but you should look for the most appropriate answer.

4. Read through the answer choices. Always read all of the possible answer choices even if the first one seems like the correct answer. There may be a better choice farther down in the list.

5. Reread the accompanying information (if any is included) carefully to determine the answer to the question. Again, note the title, author, and date of primary-source selections. The answer will rarely be stated exactly as it appears in the primary source, so you will need to use your critical thinking skills to read between the lines.

6. Think of what you already know about the time in history or person involved and use that to help limit the answer choices.

7. Finally, reread the question and selected answer to be sure that you made the best choice and that you marked it correctly on the answer sheet.

Strategies for Success

There are a variety of strategies you can prepare ahead of time to help you feel more confident about answering questions on social studies standardized tests. Here are a few suggestions:

1. Adopt an acronym—a word formed from the first letters of other words—that you will use for analyzing a document or visual piece that accompanies a question.

Helpful Acronyms

For a document, use SOAPS, which stands for

S Subject

O Overview

A Audience

P Purpose

S Speaker/author

For a picture, cartoon, map, or other visual piece of information, use OPTIC, which stands for

O Occasion (or time)

P Parts (labels or details of the visual)

T Title

I Interrelations (how the different parts of the visual work together)

C Conclusion (what the visual means)

---

2. Form visual images of maps and try to draw them from memory. Standardized tests will most likely include maps showing many features, such as states, countries, continents, and oceans. Those maps may also show patterns in settlement and the size and distribution of cities. For example, in studying the United States, be able to see in your mind's eye such things as where the states and major cities are located. Know major physical features, such as the Mississippi River, the Appalachian and Rocky Mountains, the Great Plains, and the various regions of the United States, and be able to place them on a map. Such features may help you understand patterns in the distribution of population and the size of settlements.

3. When you have finished studying a geographic region or period in history, try to think of who or what might be important enough for a standardized test. You may want to keep your ideas in a notebook to refer to when it is almost time for the test.

4. Standardized tests will likely test your understanding of the political, economic, and social processes that shape a region's history, culture, and geography. Questions may also ask you to understand the impact of geographic factors on major events. For example, some may ask about the effects of migration and immigration on various societies and population change. In addition, questions may test your understanding of the ways humans interact with their environment.

5. For the skills area of the tests, practice putting major events and personalities in order in your mind. Sequencing people and events by dates can become a game you play with a friend who also has to take the test. Always ask yourself "why" this event is important.

6. Follow the tips under "Ready for Reading" below when you encounter a reading passage in social studies, but remember that what you have learned about history can help you in answering reading-comprehension questions.

Ready for Reading

The main goal of the reading sections of most standardized tests is to determine your understanding of different aspects of a piece of writing. Basically, if you can grasp the main idea and the writer's purpose and then pay attention to the details and vocabulary so that you are able to draw inferences and conclusions, you will do well on the test.

Tips for Answering Multiple-Choice Questions

1. Read the passage as if you were not taking a test.
2. Look at the big picture. Ask yourself questions like, "What is the title?", "What do the illustrations or pictures tell me?", and "What is the writer's purpose?"
3. Read the questions. This will help you know what information to look for.
4. Reread the passage, underlining information related to the questions.

5. Go back to the questions and try to answer each one in your mind before looking at the answers.
6. Read all the answer choices and eliminate the ones that are obviously incorrect.

Types of Multiple-Choice Questions

1. **Main Idea** This is the most important point of the passage. After reading the passage, locate and underline the main idea.

2. **Significant Details** You will often be asked to recall details from the passage. Read the question and underline the details as you read, but remember that the correct answers do not always match the wording of the passage precisely.

3. **Vocabulary** You will often need to define a word within the context of the passage. Read the answer choices and plug them into the sentence to see what fits best.

4. **Conclusion and Inference** There are often important ideas in the passage that the writer does not state directly. Sometimes you must consider multiple parts of the passage to answer the question. If answers refer to only one or two sentences or details in the passage, they are probably incorrect.

Tips for Answering Short-Answer Questions

1. Read the passage in its entirety, paying close attention to the main events and characters. Jot down information you think is important.
2. If you cannot answer a question, skip it and come back later.
3. Words such as *compare, contrast, interpret, discuss,* and *summarize* appear often in short-answer questions. Be sure you have a complete understanding of each of these words.
4. To help support your answer, return to the passage and skim the parts you underlined.

5. Organize your thoughts on a separate sheet of paper. Write a general statement with which to begin. This will be your topic statement.
6. When writing your answer, be precise but brief. Be sure to refer to details in the passage in your answer.

Targeting Writing

On many standardized tests, you will occasionally be asked to write an essay. In order to write a concise essay, you must learn to organize your thoughts before you begin writing the actual composition. This keeps you from straying too far from the essay's topic.

Tips for Answering Composition Questions

1. Read the question carefully.
2. Decide what kind of essay you are being asked to write. Essays usually fall into one of the following types: persuasive, classificatory, compare/contrast, or "how to." To determine the type of essay, ask yourself questions like, "Am I trying to persuade my audience?", "Am I comparing or contrasting ideas?", or "Am I trying to show the reader how to do something?"
3. Pay attention to keywords, such as *compare, contrast, describe, advantages, disadvantages, classify,* or *speculate.* They will give you clues as to the structure that your essay should follow.
4. Organize your thoughts on a separate sheet of paper. You will want to come up with a general topic sentence that expresses your main idea. Make sure this sentence addresses the question. You should then create an outline or some type of graphic organizer to help you organize the points that support your topic sentence.
5. Write your composition using complete sentences. Also, be sure to use correct grammar, spelling, punctuation, and sentence structure.
6. Be sure to proofread your essay once you have finished writing.

Gearing Up for Math

On most standardized tests you will be asked to solve a variety of mathematical problems that draw on the skills and information you have learned in class. If math problems sometimes give you difficulty, have a look at the tips below to help you work through the problems.

Tips for Solving Math Problems

1. Decide what is the goal of the question. Read or study the problem carefully and determine what information must be found.
2. Locate the factual information. Decide what information represents key facts—the ones you must have to solve the problem. You may also find facts you do not need to reach your solution. In some cases, you may determine that more information is needed to solve the problem. If so, ask yourself, "What assumptions can I make about this problem?" or "Do I need a formula to help solve this problem?"
3. Decide what strategies you might use to solve the problem, how you might use them, and what form your solution will be in. For example, will you need to create a graph or chart? Will you need to solve an equation? Will your answer be in words or numbers? By knowing what type of solution you should reach, you may be able to eliminate some of the choices.
4. Apply your strategy to solve the problem and compare your answer to the choices.
5. If the answer is still not clear, read the problem again. If you had to make calculations to reach your answer, use estimation to see if your answer makes sense.

Statistics

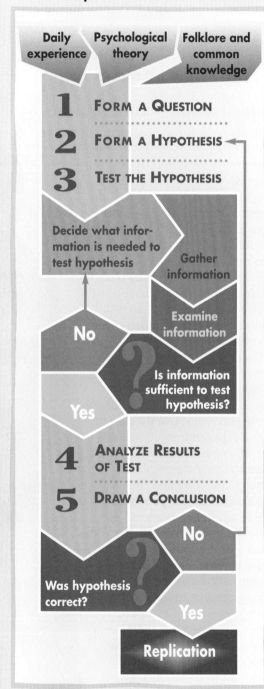

The Steps of Scientific Research

Daily experience · **Psychological theory** · **Folklore and common knowledge**

1 FORM A QUESTION

2 FORM A HYPOTHESIS

3 TEST THE HYPOTHESIS

Decide what information is needed to test hypothesis

Gather information

Examine information

No

? Is information sufficient to test hypothesis?

Yes

4 ANALYZE RESULTS OF TEST

5 DRAW A CONCLUSION

No

? Was hypothesis correct?

Yes

Replication

A flowchart is used to illustrate a sequence of events or the steps in a process. This flowchart demonstrates the steps a researcher generally follows.

Reading Charts and Graphs

Charts and graphs are used to organize and present information visually. They categorize and display data in a variety of ways, depending on the type of chart or graph being used and the subject matter of the data.

Using Charts

There are several type of charts. This textbook uses the following types of charts to illustrate various concepts: flowcharts, Venn diagrams, organization charts, and tables.

A *flowchart* illustrates a sequence of events or the steps in a process. "The Steps of Scientific Research," shown to the left, is an example of a flowchart. Cause-and-effect relationships are also frequently depicted in flowcharts.

Venn diagrams use circles to represent simple relationships among sets. Overlapping regions in the Venn diagram represent the intersection of information. The Venn diagram shown on page S26, for example, demonstrates that Seoul is located within South Korea and South Korea is in Asia. Therefore, it follows that Seoul is located in Asia.

An organization chart, such as the one on page S26 titled "Divisions of the Nervous System," displays the structure of a particular organization or concept. It illustrates the ranking or function of the organization's internal parts and the relationship between those parts.

A *table* is generally a multi-column chart that presents data in categories that are easy to understand and compare. This textbook frequently uses tables to organize data and concepts. For an example, see page 430.

Using Graphs

There are also several types of graphs used in this textbook. Each has certain advantages in displaying data for a particular emphasis.

A *line graph,* for example, plots changes in quantities over time. It consists of a horizontal and a vertical axis. One axis generally lists numbers or percentages, while the other axis usually marks off periods of time. A line is created by plotting data on the grid formed by the intersecting axes and then connecting the dots. "Average Growth Rates for Boys and Girls from Childhood Through Adolescence" is an example of a line graph.

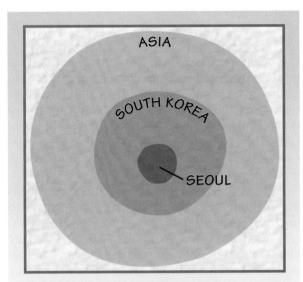

Venn diagrams represent the intersection of information. For example, Seoul is in South Korea, which is in Asia. Therefore, Seoul is in Asia.

A *bar graph* can also be used to display changes in quantities over time. More often, however, bar graphs are used to compare quantities within the same category, and to summarize the differences succinctly. For example, the bar graph on page S27, "Distribution of Pain Receptors" compares the num-

ber of pain receptors and sensitivity to pain and pressure in different parts of the human body.

A *pie graph*, or *circle graph*, displays proportions at a glance by showing sections of a whole, like slices of a pie, with the whole equaling 100 percent. "United States Population by Group" is an example of a pie graph.

How to Read Charts and Graphs
1. **Read the title.** Read the title to identify the focus of the chart or graph, remembering what each kind is designed to emphasize.
2. **Study the parts.** To identify the type of information presented, read the headings, subheadings, and labels that define each axis, bar, or section of the graph. Study the categories used and the specific data given for each category in a chart.
3. **Analyze the details.** Note increases or decreases in quantities. When reading dates, note intervals of time. When viewing a flowchart, follow directional arrows or lines. When reading graphs, look for trends, relationships, and changes in the data.
4. **Put the data to use.** Formulate generalizations or draw conclusions based on the data presented.

Divisions of the Nervous System

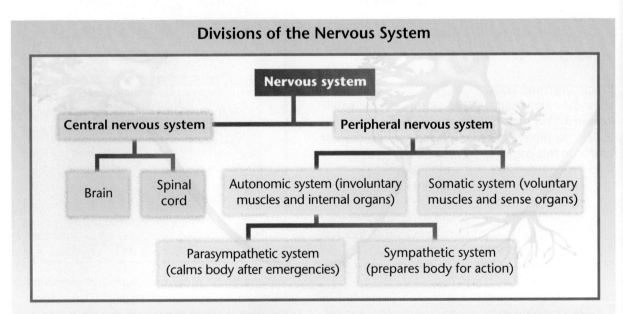

In an organization chart, the structure of a particular concept or organization is illustrated graphically. This organization chart, for example, shows the divisions of the human nervous system, the parts of those divisions, and the relationship between each of those parts.

Average Growth Rate for Boys and Girls from Childhood Through Adolescence

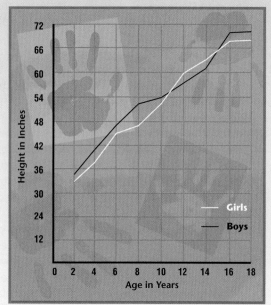

Line graphs are effective tools for illustrating the changes of a particular quantity over time. For example, this line graph demonstrates the change in height of boys and girls throughout the years of adolescence.

Source: Tanner, J.M. (1978). *Fetus into man: Physical growth from conception to maturity*. Cambridge, MA: Harvard University Press. (p. 118)

Practicing Your Skills

Use the flowchart, "The Steps of Scientific Research," on page S25 to answer questions 1 and 2. Then complete questions 3 and 4 using the bar graph on this page.

1. Write a detailed description of the steps illustrated in the chart, but do not use numbers or refer to the chart.
2. Decide whether the information is more easily understood in chart form or in a prose description. Give reasons for your opinion.
3. Which part of the body has the most pain receptors? The fewest?
4. Assuming that the information presented in this graph is valid, do you believe that individuals differ in their sensitivities to pain? How could you account for someone claiming to have a "high pain threshold"?

Analyzing Observations

Conducting a research study is actually only a small part of the research process. Imagine that you decide to conduct a survey about the amount of television teenagers watch daily. After you conducted interviews and received dozens of completed questionnaires you would probably feel overwelmed by the amount of data you had collected. What is the next step?

When faced with this situation, psychologists use mathematical procedures, called *statistics*, to organize, analyze, and interpret the data. Psychologists then use the statistical analyses to construct charts and graphs. In short, statistics help psychologists make sense of their research findings.

Distribution of Pain Receptors

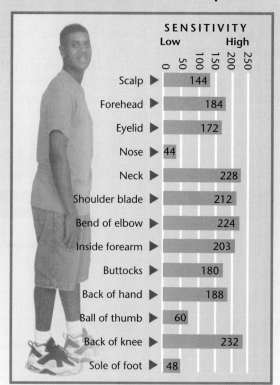

Bar graphs are a common method of comparing quantities within the same category. This bar graph compares the levels of sensitivity to pain in the various parts of the human body.

Source: Strughold, H. (1924). On the density and thresholds in the areas of pain on the epidermis in the various regions of the body. 7 Biol, 80, 367-380 (in German)

United States Population by Group

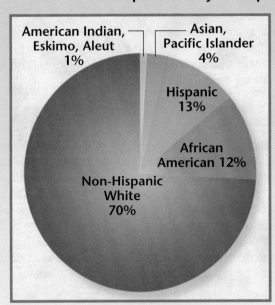

American Indian, Eskimo, Aleut 1%

Asian, Pacific Islander 4%

Hispanic 13%

African American 12%

Non-Hispanic White 70%

Pie graphs are effective tools for illustrating the proportional divisions of a central concept. This pie graph, for example, demonstrates the proportions of the various ethnic groups as a percentage of the U.S. population as a whole. Hypothetically, if the U.S. population was one million, how many African Americans would you expect there to be?

Source: Statistical Abstract of the United States 1995. Figures have been rounded.

Understanding Frequency Distributions

One of the most common forms of statistical analysis researchers use to organize their data is the *frequency distribution*. A frequency distribution is a way of arranging data to determine how often a certain piece of data—such as a score, salary, or age—occurs. In setting up a frequency distribution, researchers arrange the data from highest to lowest, and enter a mark when a piece of data occurs. The sum of each group's marks determines the frequency.

If there are too many different pieces of data to list individually, as is sometimes true for class scores, a researcher may substitute specific numerical spans, called *class intervals*, for individual scores. Again, the data are arranged from highest to lowest. A frequency distribution would allow a teacher to see at a glance how well a group of students did on a test, for instance, but it does not provide any information about individual performance.

Understanding Bell Curves

One of the most useful statistical concepts for psychologists is the *bell curve*, or *normal curve*. The bell curve is an ideal, a hypothetical standard against which actual categories of people or things (such as scores) can be measured and compared.

Usually, bell curves are used to categorize characteristics of people in large groups. The closer the group comes to the center of the curve, where the most "normal" traits congregate, the more validity the study appears to have.

For example, the bell curve, "Distribution of IQ Scores," shown on page S29, illustrates a hypothetical standard against which actual IQ scores can be compared. This curve is a model of an ideal. It shows what would happen if the largest number of scores fell exactly in the middle of a range of scores. A comparison of the actual scores against this bell curve tells psychologists how representative the IQ test really is.

A bell curve is a normal frequency distribution. This means that after counting the occurrence, or *frequency*, of specific data (scores for instance), researchers can create an arrangement, or *distribution*, that is concentrated on or near the curve's center, which represents the norm. The fewest entries of data should appear at the far ends of the distribution—away form the highly concentrated norm.

It follows then, that when the graphed results of an experiment come close to matching a bell curve, the results are assumed to be highly representative of that experiment. If most scores or data cluster towards the ends of the curve, however, the experiment or test is assumed to be unrepresentative of the group.

Bell curves and frequency distributions seem very complicated. However, they are simply ways to condense information and put it in a visual form. Within moments of glancing at a real plotted curve and the bell curve beside it, researchers can judge approximately how far from the norm their experimental group was, and how closely their results conform to what is "perfectly" normal.

Practicing Your Skills

1. Define *Frequency distribution*, and identify a situation in which you have applied this concept.
2. Look at the bell curve on page S29. What percentage of students would be expected to score between 90 and 110? Between 70 and 130?
3. What problems can you identify with basing assumptions on a bell curve?

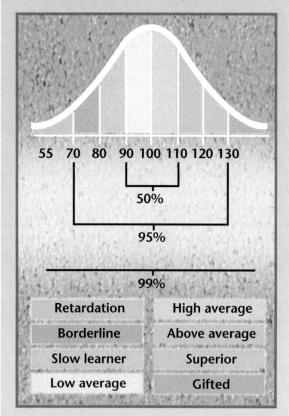

Distribution of IQ Scores

55 70 80 90 100 110 120 130

50%

95%

99%

Retardation	High average
Borderline	Above average
Slow learner	Superior
Low average	Gifted

Bell curves, or normal curves, represent a hypothetical standard against which actual categories of people or things can be measured and compared. This bell curve illustrates a hypothetical standard against which actual IQ scores could be compared. If the actual scores closely represent this standard, the IQ test is considered to be valid.

Mean, Median, and Mode: Measures of Central Tendency

Three other measures are used to compare data that fall within the central points of a distribution: the *mode*, the *mean*, and the *median*.

Mode

Simply, the *mode* is the piece of data (or the score) that occurs most often in a given set of numbers. To find the mode, examine any frequency distribution and choose the number that appears most often. The mode is of limited use to researchers because "occurring most often" in a distribution may mean,

for instance, that this number occurred only twice among fifty different test scores.

Mean

The *mean* is an average. The mean is found by adding all the scores or data together and then dividing that sum by the number of scores. The formula for finding the mean is:

$$\text{mean} = \frac{\text{sum of the scores}}{\text{number of scores}}$$

A significant disadvantage of using the mean is that any extreme score, whether high or low, distorts a researcher's results. For instance, if five waiters earn $300, $350, $325, $390, and $600 per week respectively, the mean—or average—weekly salary for this group would be $393. Yet three of the five waiters earn less than the average amount. In this circumstance, using the mean would not necessarily be representative of the waiters' wages.

Median

The *median* is the score or piece of data that falls precisely in the middle of all the scores when they are arranged in descending order. Exactly half of the students score above the median, and exactly half score below it. In the previous example of waiters' salaries, the median would be $350, because two waiters earned more and two earned less than $350.

The median, unlike the mean, is usually an actual number or score. To find the median of an even number of scores, you would find the median of the two numbers that fall in the middle, and then take the mean of those two central numbers in the distribution.

One major advantage of the median is that extreme scores, high or low, will not affect it. For example, examine the following two distributions:

Group X: 4, 10, 16, 18, 22
Group Y: 4, 10, 16, 18, 97

The median for each group is 15, because that number falls precisely in the middle of all the scores. However, the mean for Group X is 14 (4 + 10 + 16 + 18 + 22 = 70; 70 ÷ 5 = 14), while the mean for Group Y is 29 (4 + 10 + 16 + 18 + 97 = 145; 145 ÷ 5 = 29). The mean changes dramatically simply by introducing one extreme score. The median, however, remains the same.

The kind of central point that researchers choose to use in any given situation depends on what they are trying to find out. The median is not the best choice in all instances. Actually, in a bell curve—the idealized norm—the mode, the mean, and the median are identical.

Variability

Knowing what the mode, the mean, and the median are tells a researcher a great deal but not everything about the data. Researchers also need to know how much *variability* there is among the scores in a group of numbers. That is, researchers must discover how far apart the numbers or scores are in relation to the mean. For this purpose, psychologists use two measures: the range and the standard deviation.

Range

The *range* is the mathematical difference between the highest and lowest scores in a frequency distribution. If the highest grade in a class is 100 and the lowest is 60, the range is 40 (100 – 60 = 40).

Two groups of numbers may have the same mean but different ranges. For example, consider the batting averages of two baseball teams:

Team A: 210 250 285 300 340
Team B: 270 270 275 285 285

The mean for each team is 277. However, the range for Team A is 130 points, whereas the range for Team B is 15 points. This would tell a researcher that Team B is more alike in its batting abilities than is Team A.

The range tells psychologists how similar the subjects in each group are to one another in terms of what is being measured. This information could not be obtained from the mode, the mean, or the median alone, since each is just one number and not a comparison.

The disadvantage of the range, though, is that it takes only the lowest and highest scores of a frequency distribution into account. The middle numbers may be substantially different in two groups that have the same range. For example, here are two distributions:

Group A: 5, 8, 12, 14, 15
Group B: 5, 6, 7, 8, 15

Each group has the same range of 10. But the scores in Group A differ greatly from the scores in Group B.

For this reason, psychologists often use the standard deviation.

Standard Deviation

Psychologists sometimes want to know how much any particular score is likely to vary from the mean, or how spread out the scores are around the mean. To derive these measures, researchers calculate the standard deviation. The closer the standard deviation is to zero, the more reliable that data tends to be.

Let's say that the standard deviation of Team A's batting average is about 44.2, and the standard deviation of Team B's batting average is 6.8. From this information we know that the typical score of Team A will fall within 44.2 points of the mean, and the typical score of Team B will be within 6.8 points of the mean. This tells us that the quality of batting is more consistent on Team B than on Team A.

Two bell curves can have the same mode, mean, and median, but different standard deviations. If you were plotting two bell curves on a line graph, and one curve had a much larger standard deviation than the other, the curve with the larger standard deviation would show a more pronounced bell shape on the graph.

Correlation

Correlation is a measure of the relationship between two variables. A *variable* is any behavior or condition that can change in quantity or quality. Examples of variables that people frequently encounter are age, hair color, weight, and height.

Correlation and causation are two types of relationships between variables that have great importance for psychologists.

When two variables are related, they are said to have a *correlation*. Changes in variables often occur together. Sometimes, an increase or decrease in one is accompanied by a corresponding increase or decrease in the other. For example, a decrease in someone's caloric intake is accompanied by a decrease in that person's weight. Such variables are said to be *positively correlated.*

Sometimes, when one variable increases, the other decreases, or vice-versa. These variables are said to be *negatively correlated.* Examples of positive and negative correlations are illustrated in the chart on page S31.

Correlation coefficient

The *correlation coefficient* describes the degree of relationship between variables. The concept of correlation allows researchers to predict the value of one variable if they know the value of the other and the way that the variables are correlated. A perfect correlation would have a coefficient of +1.00; a perfect negative correlation has a coefficient of –1.00. A correlation coefficient of zero indicates that there is no correlation between two variables.

Perfect positive correlations (+ 1.00 coefficient), when graphed, form a straight line that leans to the right; a perfect negative correlation (–1.00 coefficient), shown on a line graph, would form a straight line to the left. In reality, few correlations are perfect. While one variable may increase or decrease in relation to the other, both variables probably will not change to the same degree.

The following is an example of a strong negative correlation with predictive potential: The more hours Tracy spends commuting to work, the less she enjoys driving. We can predict that if Tracy shortens her commute, her enjoyment of driving will increase.

Causation

Although correlation is an important concept in statistics, it does not explain everything about relationships between variables. For one thing, correlation does not speak to the concept of causation. No correlation, of any degree, in itself proves that one variable causes another.

It is difficult to determine whether one variable actually causes another. Researchers determine causal relationships scientifically rather than relying on the intuitive sense of causality that may be implied in a correlation. They compare the differences between an experimental group—the group that displays the condition that is being studied—and a control group, in which this condition is not present. The *independent variable* is the variable being manipulated by the researcher.

If Group A is exposed to a virus and gets sick, and Group B is exposed to the same virus but has been vaccinated and does not become ill, there appears to be a causal relationship at work. It seems that the vaccine protected Group B from the virus, and therefore from illness. But researchers probably would want to examine how the vaccine actually worked—if it did. It may have been coincidental that Group B remained well.

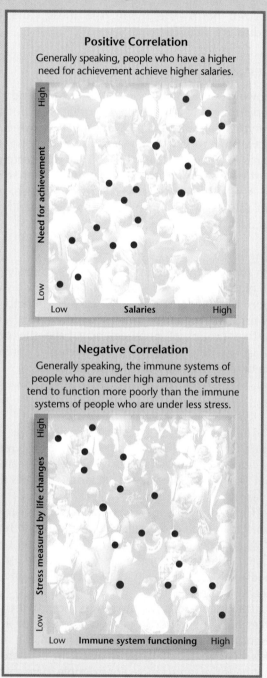

Positive and Negative Correlations

Positive Correlation

Generally speaking, people who have a higher need for achievement achieve higher salaries.

Need for achievement (High / Low) vs. *Salaries* (Low / High)

Negative Correlation

Generally speaking, the immune systems of people who are under high amounts of stress tend to function more poorly than the immune systems of people who are under less stress.

Stress measured by life changes (High / Low) vs. *Immune system functioning* (Low / High)

Correlations represent the relationship between two variables. When two variables show a positive correlation, one rises as the other rises. If the two variables are negatively correlated, one of the variables rises as the other falls.

UNIT 1

Overview

In Unit 1, students will be introduced to the scientific study of psychology. Students will learn what psychology is and how psychologists go about adding to the discipline's existing body of knowledge.

CHAPTER 1 • *What Is Psychology?* presents the goals of psychology, the kinds of work that psychologists do, a brief history of psychology, and contemporary perspectives in the field of psychology.

CHAPTER 2 • *Psychological Methods* describes the steps involved in the scientific method and the various methods psychologists use to conduct research.

UNIT 1

INTRODUCTION TO PSYCHOLOGY

CHAPTERS

1 **What Is Psychology?**

2 **Psychological Methods**

▶ Internet Activity

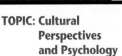

internet connect

TOPIC: Cultural Perspectives and Psychology
GO TO: go.hrw.com
KEYWORD: SY3 UNIT 1

Have students access the Internet through the HRW Go site to research the ways in which cultural perspectives relate to the physical, political, and social environment of a culture group. Organize students into five groups. Assign each group a theory—structuralism, functionalism, behaviorism, gestalt psychology, or psychoanalysis—and have the groups prepare illustrated visual aids to explain how the theories were influenced by the culture, history, and physical environment of the leading proponents of each theory.

▶ Using Visuals

Have students examine the photograph on this page and develop a list of questions about the people in the photograph. Tell students that Unit 1 will help explain why this photograph would be of interest to psychologists, and how psychologists would go about answering the questions posed by the students.

1

What is Psychology?

CHAPTER RESOURCE MANAGER

	Objectives	Pacing Guide	Reproducible and Review Resources
SECTION 1: **Why Study Psychology?** (pp. 4–6)	Identify the goals of psychology, and explain how psychology is a science.	**Regular** 1 day **Block Scheduling** .5 day *Block Scheduling Handbook with Team Teaching Strategies, Chapter 1*	**PS** Reading and Case Studies 1 **RS** Essay and Research Themes for Advanced Placement Students 1 **REV** Section 1 Review, p. 6
SECTION 2: **What Psychologists Do** (pp. 8–11)	Describe the work done by psychologists according to their areas of specialization.	**Regular** 1 day **Block Scheduling** .5 day *Block Scheduling Handbook with Team Teaching Strategies, Chapter 1*	**SM** Mastering Critical Thinking Skills 1 **REV** Section 2 Review, p. 11
SECTION 3: **A History of Psychology** (pp. 12–17)	Explain the historical background of the study of psychology.	**Regular** 1 day **Block Scheduling** .5 day *Block Scheduling Handbook with Team Teaching Strategies, Chapter 1*	**E** Research Projects and Activities for Teaching Psychology **REV** Section 3 Review, p. 17
SECTION 4: **Contemporary Perspectives** (pp. 18–21)	Describe the seven main contemporary perspectives in psychology.	**Regular** 1 day **Block Scheduling** .5 day *Block Scheduling Handbook with Team Teaching Strategies, Chapter 1*	**REV** Section 4 Review, p. 21

Chapter Resource Key

PS	Primary Sources	**A**	Assessment	Video
RS	Reading Support	**REV**	Review	Internet
E	Enrichment		Transparencies	Holt Presentation Maker Using Microsoft® PowerPoint®
SM	Skills Mastery		CD-ROM	

 One-Stop Planner CD–ROM

See the *One-Stop Planner* for a complete list of additional resources for students and teachers.

One-Stop Planner CD–ROM

It's easy to plan lessons, select resources, and print out materials for your students when you use the *One-Stop Planner CD-ROM with Test Generator.*

Technology Resources

One-Stop Planner, Lesson 1.1
Homework Practice Online
HRW Go site

One-Stop Planner, Lesson 1.2
Homework Practice Online
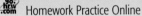 Presents Psychology: Psychologists and Family Counseling
HRW Go site

One-Stop Planner, Lesson 1.3
Homework Practice Online
HRW Go site

One-Stop Planner, Lesson 1.4
Homework Practice Online
Teaching Transparencies 1: Contemporary Psychological Perspectives

Chapter Review and Assessment

HRW Go site

REV Chapter 1 Review, pp. 22–23

REV Chapter Review Activities with Answer Key

A Chapter 1 Test (Form A or B)

A Portfolio Assessment Handbook

A Alternative Assessment Handbook

Chapter 1 Test Generator (on the One-Stop Planner)

Global Skill Builder CD-ROM

☑ internet connect

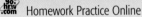

HRW ONLINE RESOURCES

GO TO: **go.hrw.com**
Then type in a keyword.

TEACHER HOME PAGE
KEYWORD: **SY3 Teacher**

CHAPTER INTERNET ACTIVITIES
KEYWORD: **SY3 PS1**
Choose an activity to have students:
• create a pamphlet on contemporary perspectives in psychology.
• write about a day in the life of a psychologist.
• write a biographical sketch of famous psychologists.

CHAPTER ENRICHMENT LINKS
KEYWORD: **SY3 PS1**

ONLINE ASSESSMENT
Homework Practice
KEYWORD: **SY3 HP1**
Standardized Test Prep
KEYWORD: **SY3 STP1**
Rubrics
KEYWORD: **SS Rubrics**

CONTENT UPDATES
KEYWORD: **SS Content Updates**

HOLT PRESENTATION MAKER
KEYWORD: **SY3 PPT1**

ONLINE READING SUPPORT
KEYWORD: **SS Strategies**

CURRENT EVENTS
KEYWORD: **S3 Current Events**

Additional Resources

PRINT RESOURCES FOR TEACHERS
Baxter, P. M. (1993). *Psychology: A guide to reference and information sources.* Englewood, CO: Libraries Unlimited.

Reber, A. S. (1995). *The Penguin dictionary of psychology.* New York: Penguin Books.

Robinson, D. N. (1995). *An intellectual history of psychology.* Madison: University of Wisconsin Press.

PRINT RESOURCES FOR STUDENTS
Reed, J., & Baxter, P. (1992). *Library use: A handbook for psychology.* Washington, DC: American Psychological Association.

Stratton, P., & Hayes, N. (1999). *A student's dictionary of psychology.* New York: Routledge, Chapman & Hall.

Woods, P. J., & Wilkinson, C. S. (Eds.). (1987). *Is psychology the major for you?* Washington, DC: American Psychological Association.

MULTIMEDIA RESOURCES
The way of science (VHS). Films for the Humanities & Sciences, P.O. Box 2053, Princeton, NJ 08543-2053.

Psychology: Core concepts (CD-ROM). Films for the Humanities & Sciences, P.O. Box 2053, Princeton, NJ 08543-2053.

WHAT IS PSYCHOLOGY?

Introducing Chapter 1

Students often have many misconceptions about psychology, the nature of psychology as a science, and the place of psychology among the social sciences. Before you ask students to read Chapter 1, have them write a short essay answering the following four questions: (1) What is psychology? (2) What types of work do psychologists do? (3) What types of things do psychologists study? (4) Why is the study of psychology important? After students have completed the assignment, ask volunteers to read their essays aloud to the class. Follow up this activity by correctly defining psychology and its subject matter and by stating several reasons why psychology is an important social science. Tell students that reading Chapter 1 will help them answer the preceding four questions.

Sections

1 *Why Study Psychology?*

2 *What Psychologists Do*

3 *A History of Psychology*

4 *Contemporary Perspectives*

Chapter 1

WHAT IS PSYCHOLOGY?

Read to Discover

1 What are the goals of psychology, and how is psychology a science?

2 What do psychologists do, and what are their areas of specialization?

3 How has the study of psychology developed over time?

4 What are the seven main contemporary perspectives in psychology?

Each chapter begins with a vignette, called "A Day in the Life," that relates the information discussed in the chapter to the everyday events in the lives of a group of fictional high school students. The text of the chapter occasionally refers back to the vignette to demonstrate the application of the concept being discussed. An icon marked "A Day in the Life" is placed next to these references.

Copy the following graphic organizer onto the chalkboard, omitting the italicized text. Fill in the circles as you discuss each of psychology's goals with the class.

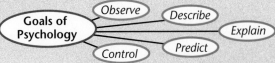

A DAY IN THE LIFE

September 20

The alarm shook Linda out of a dream. Shafts of light pierced the window blinds in her room. She shut off the alarm, rose, and raised the blinds. A world of color splashed in. As she stifled a morning sneeze, Linda recalled that yesterday in psychology class her teacher had challenged the students to touch their noses with their eyes closed. Linda had succeeded, but Todd had jokingly poked himself in the eye. She remembered the incident and laughed. Her laughter

stopped when she remembered that she was going to have a math test today. Then she relaxed. "No sweat; I'm really good at math," she thought. And after school, she had plans to meet some friends. "I wonder if Marc will be there," she pondered. (Linda thought Marc was very attractive.) She reflected sadly that Nick would not be there. Nick had a drug problem, and his parents had convinced him to go to a treatment center for help. Linda sighed to herself, then turned away from the window and went to the kitchen for breakfast. She was hungry.

• • •

Sleeping and waking, our perceptions of the worlds within and around us, memory, emotion, attractions between people—these are some of the topics of interest to psychologists. The kinds of questions that psychologists might ask about Linda's thoughts and behavior on this morning include the following:

- How did the alarm wake Linda? What happened inside her brain that woke her?
- Linda raised the blinds, and her morning became alive with color. How are we able to sense the world outside? Why do most of us see colors while some of us cannot?
- Linda was able to touch her nose with her eyes closed. What body senses enable us to know where our body parts are, and what we are doing when our eyes are closed?
- Linda is good at math. Why do students do well in some high school subjects such as math but struggle in others? How are factors such as motivation and intelligence involved?
- Linda was looking forward to meeting her friends. Why do most of us seek friendship? How is our behavior influenced by other people?
- Linda thought Marc was attractive. What is attraction? What is love? Why do we find some people attractive and others less so?
- Nick was involved with drugs. How do drugs affect people psychologically? In what ways are drugs harmful?
- Linda was hungry for breakfast. What makes us hungry? Why are some people overweight and others dangerously thin?

Psychologists are so intrigued by these types of questions that they make the attempt to answer them their life's work.

Key Terms

- psychology
- behavior
- cognitive activities
- psychological constructs
- theory
- principle
- basic research
- introspection
- associationism
- structuralism
- functionalism
- behaviorism
- Gestalt psychology
- psychoanalysis
- psychodynamic thinking
- biological perspective
- evolutionary perspective
- cognitive perspective
- humanistic perspective
- psychoanalytic perspective
- learning perspective
- social-learning theory
- sociocultural perspective
- ethnic group

▶ WHY PSYCHOLOGY MATTERS

Psychologists have made the study of human behavior the focus of their careers. Use **CNNfyi.com** or other current events sources to learn more about psychology and what psychologists do.

CNNfyi.com

Using Key Terms

Have students prepare a matching test using the key terms and their definitions, which are found in the Glossary or in Chapter 1. Tell students to write the answers to the test on the back of the sheet of paper. Then have students exchange their papers and complete the tests. Finally, direct students to keep their matching tests for later use.

Using Visuals

Have students examine the photograph on page 2 and describe what they see. Then ask students to brainstorm a list of questions that psychologists might have about the scene depicted in the photograph and about the person shown in the scene. Write these questions on the chalkboard. Then read "A Day in the Life" aloud to the class. Have students add to the list of questions on the chalkboard. Finally, have students read the questions on page 3 and discuss how these questions compare to the questions listed on the chalkboard.

► Identify the goals of psychology, and explain how psychology is a science.

This objective is assessed in the Section Review on page 6 and in the Chapter 1 Review.

Opening Section 1

Motivator

Conduct a brainstorming session in which students identify the benefits they hope to gain from learning about psychology. Examples might include developing a greater understanding of themselves and others, or learning more about psychology as a possible future career. When no new ideas are forthcoming, tell students that Section 1 will introduce them to the ways in which psychologists interpret the world and help explain why learning to interpret the world as psychologists do will benefit them now and in the future.

Using Truth or Fiction

Each chapter opens with several "Truth or Fiction" statements that relate to the concepts discussed in the chapter. Ask students whether they think each statement is true or false. Answers to each item as well as explanations are provided at appropriate points within the text under the heading "Truth or Fiction Revisited."

Class Discussion

Have students discuss which commonplace human activities indicate the same kind of curiosity about human behavior and mental processes that prompts some people to study psychology. *(Students may mention reading human interest stories in newspapers, watching or listening to talk shows, filling out quizzes in magazines, and so on.)* Ask students how they think the formal study of human behavior and mental processes differs from casual or personal interest in them.

TRUTH OR fiction ?

Read the following statements about psychology. Do you think they are true or false? You will learn whether each statement is true or false as you read the chapter.

- Psychologists have very little interest in studying people's emotions.
- A book on psychology, with content similar to that found in this textbook, was written by Aristotle more than 2,000 years ago.
- In the Middle Ages, some innocent people were allowed to drown as a way of proving that they were not possessed by demons.
- Some psychologists view our strategies for solving problems as mental programs operated by our very own personal computers—our brains.
- Sigmund Freud's theories continue to influence psychology today.

SECTION 1

Why Study Psychology?

What do you hope to learn from the study of psychology? Perhaps you hope to gain a better understanding of why people act as they do or, more specifically, why *you* act as you do. Or perhaps you want to learn more about your thoughts and feelings; in doing so, you might discover more-effective ways to handle, or help others handle, the stresses of daily life. Whether your reason is general or specific, the study of psychology will give you new ways to look at and interpret the world and the people who inhabit it.

Behavior and Mental Processes

Psychology is the scientific study of behavior and mental processes. **Behavior** is any action that other people can observe or measure. For example, Linda awakened, rose from her bed, raised the blinds, and laughed. All of these activities are behaviors. All are observable by other people.

Behavior also includes activities such as walking and talking, pressing a switch, turning left or right, sleeping, eating, and drinking. Behavior even

includes automatic body functions such as heart rate, blood pressure, digestion, and brain activity. Behavior can be measured by simple observation or by laboratory instruments. For example, brain activity can be measured by scientific instruments such as the electroencephalograph (EEG).

Linda also engaged in mental processes, or **cognitive activities**. These activities include dreams, perceptions, thoughts, and memories. For example, Linda was dreaming when her alarm rang. Brain waves that indicate dreaming can be measured, but dreaming itself is a private mental process—dreams are known only to the dreamer. Linda also perceived a world of color. Activity of the cells in a person's eyes can be measured as they respond to color, but only Linda could see her own mental image of the world. Linda laughed as she remembered the nose-touching psychology lesson. Memories, too, are private mental processes.

Psychologists are also interested in studying people's emotions, or feelings. Emotions can affect both behavior and mental processes. For example, Linda experienced a moment of anxiety when she remembered her math test, and she felt happiness at the thought of seeing Marc. Perhaps Linda's heart raced a bit when she thought about the test or about Marc. Her heart activity was an example of behavior, but her thoughts about the math test and about Marc were private mental processes. We would be unable to observe or measure Linda's thoughts directly. But if she told us about them, we would be observing a behavior—Linda *telling* us about her thoughts. Researchers often use **psychological constructs** to learn more about human behavior. These constructs are used to talk about something we cannot see, touch, or measure directly.

TRUTH OR fiction ■ REVISITED ■

It is not true that psychologists have very little interest in studying people's emotions. Psychologists know that emotions are important because they can influence both behavior and mental processes.

The Goals of Psychology

In general, scientists seek to observe, describe, explain, predict, and control the events they study. Psychologists have the same goals. They observe and describe behavior and mental processes to

Teaching Section 1

Demonstration

Tell students to prepare for a pop quiz on Chapter 1. Before students get too upset, tell them that this is not really a quiz but rather a test of how they react to unexpected situations. Then have them discuss what they experienced when they heard about the quiz. Next, have them distinguish between those thoughts and emotions that helped them deal with the situation and those that hindered their ability to do so. Finally, have students suggest steps they can take to overcome anxiety when faced with unexpected situations. Ask them how this exercise demonstrates the goals of psychology.

Cooperative Learning

Organize the class into five groups. Direct each group to interview teachers in your school who teach one of the following social sciences: history, anthropology, economics, political science, or sociology. In their interviews, the groups should seek answers to the following questions: What is the focus of this discipline? What are the goals of this discipline? What kinds of research topics might be of interest to people in this discipline? Ask volunteers from each group to report their findings to the class. Then have the class compare and contrast psychology with the other social sciences.

better understand them. A better understanding of behavior enables psychologists to explain, predict, and control behavior.

An example of how psychologists apply the goals of psychology can be seen in the case of Buffalo Bills placekicker Scott Norwood. Norwood had toiled for many years perfecting his techniques and preparing for the day when he might play in a Super Bowl. For several hours a day, he practiced and improved his form on the field. He kicked field goals from various distances and in all extremes of weather. Then he got his chance—the Bills and the New York Giants met in Super Bowl XXV. But when Norwood had the opportunity to win the game with a field goal, he missed, handing the victory to the Giants in the final seconds of the game. Norwood had lost his composure, which left him unable to perform under pressure.

Losing one's "cool" and failing to perform effectively in a crucial situation—such as during an important game or while taking a major test—can be very hard on a person. It can hurt an individual's self-esteem and self-confidence.

Sports psychologists help athletes such as Scott Norwood handle performance problems by applying the goals of psychology. First, they observe and describe the behavior. By measuring athletes' heart rates and other body processes, psychologists know that problems may occur when athletes are highly excited. Interviews with athletes reveal that they often feel anxious during big games. They may become distracted by the cheers or jeers of the crowd and lose their concentration. They cannot focus on the jobs they are supposed to be doing.

Psychologists then explain the behavior in terms of the feelings of anxiety and the distractions that hinder the athletes' performance. The relationship between anxiety and performance is somewhat complex. A little anxiety is often a good thing. It motivates us to practice for a game or to study for a test. It makes us alert and ready. On the other hand, too much anxiety is harmful. It may make us shaky and distract us from the task at hand.

Psychologists next predict that athletes will do best when anxiety is moderate and will falter when anxiety becomes too intense. Finally, they help athletes change, and thus control, their behavior and mental processes by teaching them ways of keeping their anxiety at a tolerable level. Psychologists also teach athletes how to filter out the sounds of the fans so they can focus on their task—helping the team win the game.

Some athletes use positive visualization to help them perform successfully in high-pressure situations such as close games.

One method that sports psychologists recommend to help athletes perform more effectively under pressure is called positive visualization. In this method, athletes imagine themselves going through the motions in a critical game situation. For example, a basketball player might imagine taking a free throw in overtime during a close game. She concentrates on blocking the noise of the crowd from her mind and focuses on the rim. She sees herself raising the ball with one hand as she guides it with the other. She then imagines releasing the ball and watching it glide through the net.

The goal of "controlling" behavior and mental processes is often misunderstood. Some people mistakenly think that psychologists seek ways to make people behave as the psychologists want them to—like puppets on strings. This is not so. Psychologists know that people should be free to make their own decisions. Psychologists know much about the factors that influence human behavior, and they use this knowledge to help people accomplish their own goals.

Psychology as a Science

Psychology is a social science, but it has foundations in the natural sciences. The social sciences, which also include history, anthropology, economics, political science, and sociology, deal with the structure of human society and the nature and interactions of the individuals who make up society. These individuals and their behavior and mental processes are the focus of psychology.

Cross-Curricular Link: Language Arts

Tell students that the word *psychology* comes from the Greek word *psyche,* meaning "mind" or "soul," and the Latin word *logia,* meaning "study of." Have students brainstorm as many words as possible that contain the word root *-psych-.* Write these words on the chalkboard. Then have students use the word root to determine the meanings of the words.

Class Discussion

Emphasize the fact that psychologists must not approach the goal of controlling behavior by seeking ways to make people behave as the psychologists want them to. Have students discuss why some people hold this misconception about the role of psychologists.

Readings and Case Studies

Closing Section 1

Analyzing Information

After discussing psychological research and theories, have students analyze why the ability to predict behavior and mental processes is such an important test of a psychological theory. Then have students analyze the relationship between theory and research.

Reviewing Section 1

Have students complete the Section Review questions on page 6.

Extension

Have students ask five family members, friends, and relatives the following question: "What do you think are the main goals of psychology?" Tell students to make note of the responses. In class, have a volunteer tally the results of the poll. Use the results as the basis of a class discussion. Which responses appeared most often? Which appeared least often? Do the responses indicate any misconceptions about the goals of psychology? If so, why might the general public hold such misconceptions about psychology?

The natural sciences, which include biology, chemistry, and physics, are concerned with the nature of the physical world. Some areas that psychologists study, such as the functioning of the brain, are closely related to the natural sciences, particularly biology. Like natural scientists, psychologists seek to answer questions by following the steps involved in scientific research. These steps include conducting surveys and experiments, collecting and analyzing data, and drawing conclusions.

Research As a science, psychology tests ideas through various research methods. Two widely used methods are surveys and experimentation. A survey is a method of collecting data that usually involves asking questions of people in a particular group.

Although most psychologists are interested mainly in human behavior, some choose to focus on animal behavior, such as that of sea snails, pigeons, rats, and gorillas. Some psychologists believe that research findings with certain animals can be applied to human beings. Others argue that humans are so distinct that we can only learn about them by studying people. The truth probably lies somewhere in between. For example, by studying the nerve cells of squid, psychologists have been able to learn about the workings of human nerve

cells. However, only by studying people can psychologists learn about uniquely human qualities such as morality, values, and love.

Psychologists rely on research to learn whether certain methods will work before they use them with clients. When the research is conducted with people, psychologists make every effort to protect the research participants. You will read more about research methods in Chapter 2.

Psychological Theories Psychologists organize their research about behavior and mental processes into theories. A **theory** is a statement that attempts to explain why things are the way they are and happen the way they do. Psychological theories discuss principles that govern behavior and mental processes. A **principle** is a rule or law, such as the principle that you will probably get better grades if you study more. Psychological theories may include statements about behavior (such as sleeping or aggression), mental processes (such as memories and mental images), and biological processes (such as the effect of chemicals in the brain).

A useful psychological theory allows psychologists to predict behavior and mental processes. For example, if a theory about fatigue is useful, psychologists can apply it to predict when people will or will not sleep. If a theory does not accurately predict behavior or mental processes, psychologists consider revising or replacing the theory.

In psychology, as in other sciences, many theories have been found inadequate for accurately explaining or predicting the things with which they are concerned. As a result, these theories have been discarded or revised. For example, many psychologists once believed that stomach contractions were the cause of hunger. But then it was observed that many people feel hungry even when they do not have stomach contractions. As a result, psychologists now believe that stomach contractions are only one of many factors affecting appetite.

Psychologists often conduct surveys to learn about people's behavior and mental processes.

SECTION 1 REVIEW

1. What defining characteristics of psychology differentiate it from other related social sciences?

2. Define *theory* and *principle*.

3. **Critical Thinking** *Summarizing* What is psychology, and what are the five goals of psychology?

CASE STUDIES
AND OTHER TRUE STORIES

Remind students that one of the major arguments against the claims of astrology is that people who believe in it cannot scientifically prove its existence. Have students analyze why the failure of individuals to offer convincing evidence about astrology's benefits would make psychologists skeptical about its existence. Then have students explain why skepticism is a necessary component of scientific research.

Organize students into those who believe strongly that astrology is useful and those who think its claims are fraudulent or exaggerated. Students who are undecided on this issue should serve as the audience. Tell the students who will be arguing for or against the existence of astrology as a valid science to meet separately and collect material to support their points of view. Then stage a debate. The audience has the important role of keeping track of the various anecdotes and explanations and then evaluating their relevance and accuracy.

CASE STUDIES
AND OTHER TRUE STORIES

Thinking Critically About Astrology

This chapter explores the scientific approaches and methods of psychologists. Psychologists are critical thinkers, which means that they are skeptical. They insist on seeing the evidence before they will accept people's claims and arguments about what is truth and what is fiction. As scientists, psychologists know that beliefs about the behavior of cosmic rays, chemical compounds, cells, or people must be supported by evidence. Persuasive arguments and reference to authority figures are *not* scientific evidence.

False sciences do not rely on verifiable evidence. Even so, false science is widespread. Think of the claims made by tabloid newspapers—each week, they announce 10 new sightings of Elvis Presley and 10 new encounters with extraterrestrials.

By examining one false science—astrology—we can learn why false science cannot be relied upon. Astrology is based on the idea that the positions of the stars, Moon, and planets affect human personality and destiny. One can also supposedly foretell the future by studying the positions of these bodies. Astrologers prepare forecasts called horoscopes, which are based on people's birth dates and indicate what is safe for them to do. Read the following description of personality. Would it be on target if you read it in your horoscope?

You have the inner potential for change. You have unused potential that you have not yet turned to your advantage. There are parts of your personality known to you alone. You have the ability to handle conflicting demands. You also have a strong potential for improvement.

This horoscope would actually apply to many different kinds of people. The tendency to believe such a general personality report is called the Barnum effect, after circus promoter P. T. Barnum, who once declared that a good circus had to "have something for everyone." General personality

Thinking critically is an important skill.

reports "have something for everyone," which allows palm readers and fortune-tellers to sound as if they are right on target.

Supporters of astrology might offer the following arguments:

■ Astrology has been practiced for many centuries and is part of human tradition.

■ Astrology seems to provide a path to meaning in life and, for a fortunate few, a road to riches.

■ People in high positions have followed the advice of astrologers.

■ If one heavenly body, the Moon, is powerful enough to sway the tides of the seas, why should the pulls of the stars and planets not affect people's destinies?

■ Astrology is a special art and not a science. Therefore, we should not subject astrology to scientific testing.

Think critically about the claims of astrologers. For example, does the fact that astrology has a lengthy tradition mean that it is true? Are the tides similar to human personality and destiny?

Astrological predictions routinely fail. But does it matter? Will believers in astrology be persuaded by facts? Probably not. Even in our age of scientific enlightenment, millions of people will continue to consult their horoscopes. Psychology, however, is grounded in facts. Psychological findings are of value because they are routinely subjected to careful scrutiny.

> ### WHY PSYCHOLOGY MATTERS
>
> Psychologists, like all scientists, must think critically while they work. Use CNNfyi.com or other current events sources to learn more about how psychologists think critically. Write a one-page report of what you have learned.
>
> CNNfyi.com

Cultural Dimensions

Psychology is of interest to people in many different parts of the world. In Japan, for example, where there are many psychological associations, psychologists are involved in international research, and television programs on psychology are popular. Psychology in India can be traced back to ancient literature that explored consciousness, personality types, and conflict resolution. The scientific study of psychology was established at various Indian universities in the early 1900s. Chinese psychological inquiry dates back to Confucius in about 500 B.C. The early Chinese discussed such issues as nature versus nurture and the mind-body conflict, both of which are still studied today. The first programs in psychology in Africa were established in the 1960s. Research and publication programs have been established, and university graduates are employed as clinical, educational, and industrial psychologists.

2
Section Objective

▶ Describe the work done by psychologists according to their areas of specialization.

This objective is assessed in the Section Review on page 11 and in the Chapter 1 Review.

Opening Section 2

Motivator

Before students read Section 2, ask them to discuss movies they have seen or books they have read that have professional psychologists as characters. What kinds of work did these psychologists do? In which areas of psychology did they specialize? How realistic were their characterizations? Then tell students that the field of psychology has many areas of specialization and that the psychologists who specialize in these areas do many different kinds of work. Tell students that they will learn more about what psychologists do by reading Section 2.

☑ internet connect

go. hrw. com

TOPIC: A Day in the Life of a Psychologist

GO TO: go.hrw.com
KEYWORD: SY3 PS1

Have students access the Internet through the HRW Go site to research the major fields, subfields, and career opportunities that comprise psychology. Then ask students to write a short story that portrays a typical day for a psychologist working in one of the fields or subfields mentioned in the text. Remind students to make their stories as realistic as possible and to refer directly to facts found in their research.

SECTION 2
What Psychologists Do

All psychologists share a keen interest in behavior and believe in the value of scientific research. They also share the belief that theories about behavior and mental processes should be supported by scientific evidence. They accept something as true only if the evidence shows it is so.

Some psychologists are interested mainly in research. They investigate the factors that give rise to behaviors and that explain certain mental processes. They form theories about why people and animals do the things they do. Then they test their theories by predicting when specific behaviors will occur.

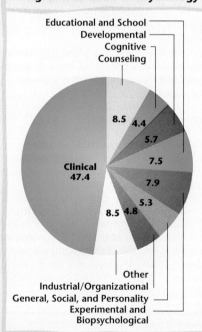

Students Enrolled in Doctoral Programs in Fields of Psychology

- Educational and School
- Developmental
- Cognitive
- Counseling

Clinical 47.4

8.5 4.4
5.7
7.5
7.9
5.3
8.5 4.8

Other
Industrial/Organizational
General, Social, and Personality
Experimental and
Biopsychological

FIGURE 1.1 *Nearly half (47%) of the doctoral students who enroll in doctoral programs in psychology enroll in clinical programs. The next most popular field is counseling psychology. The figure combines students enrolled in public and private institutions.*

Source: Kyle, T. M. & Williams, S. (2000 May); 1998–1999 APA Survey of Graduate Department of Psychology, Tables 13A &13B

Other psychologists consult. That is, they apply psychological knowledge in the form of therapy to help people change their behavior so that they can better meet their own goals. Still other psychologists teach, sharing their knowledge of psychology in classrooms and workshops.

Clinical Psychologists

Clinical psychologists make up the largest group of psychologists. Clinical psychologists are the people most of us think of when we hear the term "psychologist."

Clinical psychologists help people with psychological problems, such as anxiety or depression, or severe psychological disorders, such as schizophrenia. Clinical psychologists help their clients overcome problems and adjust to the demands of their lives. They also help people who have problems with relationships, drug abuse, or weight control. Most likely, a clinical psychologist was helping Linda's friend Nick overcome his drug problem.

A DAY IN THE LIFE

Clinical psychologists are trained to evaluate psychological problems through the use of interviews and psychological tests. Then these psychologists help clients understand and resolve their problems by changing ineffective or harmful behavior. (See Chapter 19.)

Clinical psychologists work in hospitals, in prisons, in college and university clinics, and in private practices. Some clinical psychologists divide their time among clinical practice, teaching, and research.

Clinical psychologists should not be confused with psychiatrists. A psychiatrist is a medical doctor who specializes in the treatment of psychological problems and who can prescribe medication for clients. Psychologists also specialize in the treatment of psychological problems, but because they are not medical doctors, they may not prescribe medication for their clients.

Counseling Psychologists

Like clinical psychologists, counseling psychologists use interviews and tests to identify their clients' problems. Counseling psychologists typically treat people who have adjustment problems rather than serious psychological disorders. For example, a counseling psychologist's clients may have difficulty making decisions about their

8

Teaching Section 2

Meeting Individual Needs: Limited English Proficiency

Students with limited English proficiency may have difficulty distinguishing among the professional specialties. Help them analyze each title's relation to a particular area of expertise. For example, the word *school* in *school psychologist* suggests someone who works with students in a particular school, while an *educational psychologist* deals more with educational methods. Have students use the dictionary to find the meanings of the descriptive parts of the titles.

Drawing Conclusions

Organize the class into small groups, and assign each group one of the professional specialties discussed in the section. Tell the groups to create a series of riddles, using their assigned professional specialties as the answers. For example: "I study the development of self-esteem in children. Who am I?" *(a developmental psychologist)* Have the groups, one at a time, read their riddles to the class, and have the class solve the riddles by identifying each group's professional specialty.

careers, or they may find it hard to make friends. They may be experiencing conflicts with family members, teachers, employers, or colleagues. Counseling psychologists help their clients clarify their goals, overcome their adjustment problems, and meet challenges. Counseling psychologists are often employed in businesses and in college and university counseling and testing centers.

School Psychologists

Your school district may employ one or more school psychologists. School psychologists identify and help students who have problems that interfere with learning. Typical problems that school psychologists deal with include peer group and family problems, psychological problems, and learning disorders, which are problems in learning to read, write, or do math.

School psychologists identify students with problems by talking with teachers, parents, and the students themselves. School psychologists may also administer tests, such as intelligence tests and achievement tests. These tests, which are usually 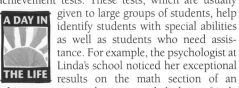 given to large groups of students, help identify students with special abilities as well as students who need assistance. For example, the psychologist at Linda's school noticed her exceptional results on the math section of an achievement test and recommended placing Linda in an advanced math class.

School psychologists also observe students in the classroom to see how they interact with their teachers and peers. After gathering the information they need, school psychologists advise teachers, school officials, and parents about how to help certain students reach their potential or overcome their learning difficulties.

In addition, school psychologists make recommendations regarding the placement of students in special classes and programs. In some school districts, student placement is the major responsibility of the school psychologist.

Educational Psychologists

Like school psychologists, educational psychologists are concerned with helping students learn. But they generally focus on course planning and instructional methods for an entire school system rather than on designing a program of study for an individual student.

School psychologists may administer various types of tests to find out about students' abilities. Educational psychologists may help construct such tests.

Educational psychologists are concerned with theoretical issues that relate to measurement of abilities, learning, and child and adolescent development. Their research interests include the ways in which learning is affected by the following:

- psychological factors, such as motivation, emotions, creativity, and intelligence
- cultural factors, such as beliefs
- economic factors, such as the level of income earned by a person's family
- instructional methods used in the classroom

Some educational psychologists help prepare standardized tests, such as the Scholastic Aptitude Test (SAT). They study various tests to determine the type of test that can most effectively predict success in college. They may also examine individual test items to determine whether these items make a useful contribution to the test as a whole.

Developmental Psychologists

Developmental psychologists study the changes that occur throughout a person's life span. These changes can be of the following types:

- physical (including changes in height and weight, adolescent growth, sexual maturity, and the physical aspects of aging)
- emotional (for example, development of self-concept and self-esteem)

Cross-Curricular Link: Government

In the 1960s, psychologists had a significant impact on governmental policy in the United States. Educational psychologists amassed evidence that revealed that many underprivileged children were not ready either cognitively or socially to begin school in kindergarten. As a result, these children were falling further behind in school with each passing year. In response to this evidence, the federal government created a program called Head Start to give underprivileged children extra enrichment early in their educational careers.

Guided Practice

Lead the class in creating a chart of the various specializations in psychology discussed in the section. Have the students include in the chart the individual areas of specialization, the focus of each specialization, the types of work done by specialists in the area, and whether the specializations are research oriented or client oriented. Also have students suggest topics that might be of particular interest to psychologists in the various research-oriented specialties. Students may wish to make a copy of the master chart for later review.

Independent Practice

Have students use what they learned in the Guided Practice activity to write a job advertisement for a psychologist in one of the areas of specialization discussed in the section. Tell students to specify in their advertisements what the nature of the job will be but not to specify which type of specialist is being sought. Have the students post their advertisements around the classroom, and have the class try to determine which type of psychologist could best fulfill the duties of the job.

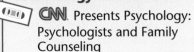

Technology Resources

CNN. Presents Psychology: Psychologists and Family Counseling

What's New in Psychology?

Many new areas of specialization in psychology have emerged in recent years. Some of these are theoretical in nature. Mathematical psychology, for example, uses calculus to develop models of complex behavioral phenomena. Some new areas combine a traditional specialty in psychology with a specialty in another science. Psychopharmacology, for instance, unites physiological psychology and pharmacology in an attempt to understand the processes by which drugs affect behavior. Clinical neuropsychology, another emerging area, focuses on the biological bases of abnormal behavior.

- cognitive (such as changes from childhood to adulthood in mental images of the world outside or how children learn right from wrong)
- social (such as formation of bonds between parents and children, relationships with peers, or intimate relationships between adults)

Developmental psychologists also attempt to sort out the relative influences of heredity and the environment on development. (See Chapters 3 and 10.)

Some developmental psychologists are especially interested in the challenges of adolescence. For example, how do adolescents handle the competing, and often contradictory, messages of peers (who pressure them to act in one way) and parents (who want them to act in another way)? How can psychologists help parents and school officials encourage adolescents to avoid activities that may be harmful to their physical and psychological well-being? What are the causes of depression and suicide among teens? How can people help prevent these painful situations from occurring?

Personality Psychologists

Personality psychologists identify characteristics, or traits. Shyness and friendliness are examples of traits. Personality psychologists look for the many different traits people have, and they study the development of these traits. Personality psychologists share with clinical psychologists an interest in the origins of psychological problems and disorders. These psychologists are also concerned with issues such as anxiety, aggression, and gender roles. Gender roles are the behavior patterns expected of women and men in a given culture.

Social Psychologists

Social psychologists are concerned with people's behavior in social situations. For example, they would be interested in studying the reasons for Linda's attraction to Marc. Whereas personality psychologists tend to look within people for explanations of behavior, social psychologists generally focus on external influences. Social psychologists study the following issues:

- the ways in which women and men typically behave in a given setting
- the physical and psychological factors that attract people to one another

- the reasons people tend to conform to group standards and expectations
- how people's behavior changes when they are members of a group
- the reasons for and the effects of prejudice and discrimination within various groups and from one group to another
- the situations in which people act aggressively and those in which they help others

Experimental Psychologists

Psychologists in all specialties may conduct experimental research. However, experimental psychologists conduct research into basic processes such as the functions of the nervous system. Other basic processes include sensation and perception, learning and memory, and thinking and motivation.

Experimental psychologists would be interested in exploring the biological reasons why Linda's alarm clock woke her. They would want to know what triggered her memory of the psychology class's nose-touching demonstration. In addition, experimental psychologists would be interested in the biological and psychological factors that contributed to Linda's feeling of hunger.

Some experimental psychologists focus on the relationships between biological changes (such as the release of hormones into the bloodstream) and psychological events (such as feelings of anxiety or depression). These experimental psychologists are called biological psychologists.

Experimental psychologists are more likely than other psychologists to engage in basic research. **Basic research** is research that has no immediate application and is done for its own sake. The findings of experimental psychologists are often put into practice by other psychological specialists. For example, basic research into motivation has helped clinical and counseling psychologists develop ways of helping people control their eating habits. Basic research into learning and memory has helped educational psychologists enhance learning conditions in schools.

Other Specialists

You have already read about sports psychologists and how they can help athletes. There are several other specialties in psychology.

Closing Section 2

Industrial and Organizational Psychologists

Industrial psychologists focus on people and work. Organizational psychologists study the behavior of people in organizations, such as business firms. Industrial psychology and organizational psychology are closely related. Psychologists in these fields are often trained in both areas.

Industrial and organizational psychologists are employed by business firms to improve working conditions and increase worker output. They may assist in hiring, training, and promoting employees. They may also devise psychological tests for job applicants and conduct research into the factors that contribute to job satisfaction. In addition, some industrial and organizational psychologists have counseling skills and help employees who have problems on the job.

Environmental Psychologists

Does crowding in cities make people irritable? Does smog have an effect on people's ability to learn? Environmental psychologists ask these types of questions. They focus on the ways in which people influence and are influenced by their physical environment. Environmental psychologists are concerned with the ways in which buildings and cities serve or fail to serve human needs. They investigate the psychological effects of extremes in temperature, noise, and air pollution.

Consumer Psychologists

Consumer psychologists study the behavior of shoppers to explain and predict their behavior. They also assist others in applying the findings of such studies. For example, they work with advertisers to create effective newspaper ads and television commercials. They advise store managers about window displays and shelf arrangement to attract customers. Have you ever noticed that in many supermarkets, milk is shelved far away from the store entrance? That is because milk is an item that many people buy frequently. Its placement at the rear of the store ensures that shoppers will pass—and hopefully buy—other items on the way to the milk shelf.

Forensic Psychologists

When an attorney wants an expert witness to testify whether a person accused of a crime is or is not competent to stand trial, the attorney might call on a forensic psychologist. These psychologists work within the criminal justice system. In addition to testifying about the psychological competence of defendants, they may explain how certain kinds of psychological prob-

*A worker clears rubble from the site of a collapsed building. **What types of psychologists might be interested in studying the effects of such work?***

lems give rise to criminal behavior. Police departments employ psychologists to do the following jobs:

- assist in the selection of police officers
- help police officers cope with job stress
- train police officers in the handling of dangerous situations such as suicide threats, hostage crises, and family violence

Health Psychologists

Health psychologists examine the ways in which behavior and mental processes are related to physical health. They study the effects of stress on health problems such as headaches and heart disease. Health psychologists try to explain why some people follow their doctor's advice and other people do not. Health psychologists also help people adopt healthful behaviors such as exercising.

SECTION 2 REVIEW

Homework Practice Online
Keyword: SY3 HP1

1. In what way are psychiatrists and psychologists different?

2. List three subspecialties of psychology and describe the work of each.

3. **Critical Thinking** *Analyzing Information* If you decided to become a psychologist, which subspecialty of psychology would you prefer and why?

3
Section Objective

▶ Explain the historical background of the study of psychology.

This objective is assessed in the Section Review on page 17 and in the Chapter 1 Review.

Motivator

Call on volunteers to identify the aspects of human behavior and mental processes they would most like to learn about. Encourage students to put their ideas in the form of questions. *(Examples might include "Why don't people's actions always match their words?" and "How do children learn right from wrong?")* Write their questions on the chalkboard. Then tell students that questions about human behavior have intrigued people throughout the ages. Have students read Section 3 to learn more about the history of psychology and psychology's emergence as a science.

Cultural Dimensions

In ancient Greece, long before the time of Plato, and in many other ancient cultures, people believed that thoughts and dreams—as well as madness—were sent by the gods. Peoples of ancient Mesopotamia believed that their gods sent them messages telling them when to plant crops and against whom to make war. The ancient Hebrews believed that God rewarded them with good visions and punished them with evil spirits. Beginning around the sixth century B.C., scholars in India, China, and Greece all began to attribute human thoughts and emotions to an internal source: the mind.

Class Discussion

Ask students to consider whether Socrates' directive to "know thyself" is useful advice. What role does introspection play in helping people learn about themselves? How can learning to know yourself help you understand the world and the people who inhabit it?

SECTION 3
A History of Psychology

People have always been interested in the behaviors of other people. Thus psychology is as old as human history. Interest in the actions, motives, and thoughts of human beings can be traced as far back as the philosophers and scientists of ancient times.

Roots from Ancient Greece

More than 2,000 years ago, Plato (428–348 or 347 B.C.), a student of Socrates in ancient Greece, recorded his teacher's advice: "Know thyself." This phrase has remained a motto of psychological study ever since. Socrates suggested that we can learn

Socrates encouraged people to examine their thoughts and feelings—to know themselves.

much about ourselves by carefully examining our thoughts and feelings. Psychologists call this method of learning **introspection**, which means "looking within."

One of Plato's students, Greek philosopher Aristotle (384–322 B.C.), raised many questions about human behavior that are still discussed. Aristotle outlined the laws of **associationism**, which are still at the heart of learning theory more than 2,000 years later. He showed how experiences often remind us of similar experiences in the past, how the face of a loved one makes us feel secure, and how thought leads to ideas as we dream and as we daydream. One of Aristotle's works is called *Peri Psyches*, which means "about the mind." Aristotle's approach was scientific. He argued that human behavior, like the movements of the stars and the seas, is subject to certain rules and laws. He believed one such universal law was that people are motivated to seek pleasure and to avoid pain—a view still found in some modern psychological theories. *Peri Psyches* also explores topics such as sensation and perception, thought, intelligence, needs and motives, feelings and emotions, and memory.

TRUTH OR fiction ■ REVISITED ■ *It is true that a book with content similar to that found in this textbook was written by Aristotle more than 2,000 years ago. The name of that book is Peri Psyches.*

The ancient Greeks also theorized about various psychological problems, such as confusion and bizarre behavior. Throughout human history, many people have attributed such disorders to supernatural forces. The ancient Greeks generally believed that the gods punished people for wrongdoing by causing them confusion and madness. However, the Greek physician Hippocrates (c. 460–c. 377 B.C.) was an exception. He suggested that such problems are caused by abnormalities in the brain. But this idea that biological factors can affect our thoughts, feelings, and behavior influenced thinking about psychology for more than 2,000 years.

The Middle Ages

During the Middle Ages, most Europeans believed that problems such as agitation and confusion were signs of possession by demons. A popular belief of the

Summarizing Ideas

Ask students to create a two-column chart titled "Early Perspectives in Psychology." Tell them to label one column *Wilhelm Wundt* and the other *William James*. Have students complete their charts by comparing and contrasting the schools of thought introduced by these early psychologists. Then have students write a paragraph explaining why the school of thought developed by Wundt came to be called structuralism and why the school of thought developed by James came to be known as functionalism.

Role-Playing

Select two groups of volunteers to participate in a panel discussion. Tell one group to imagine that they are structuralists trained by Wilhelm Wundt. Tell the other group to imagine that they are functionalists trained by William James. Have the two groups explain their psychological schools of thought to the class. Then have each group try to convince the other group that its school of thought is better able to explain human behavior and mental processes. Ask the class to evaluate the contributions made by both schools to the development of psychology as a science.

time was that possession was punishment for sins or the result of deals made with the devil.

Certain "tests" were used to determine whether a person was possessed. One of the most infamous tests, the water-float test, was based on the principle that pure metals sink to the bottom during the smelting process whereas impure metals float to the surface. Individuals who were suspected of being possessed were thrown into deep water. Suspects who managed to keep their heads above water were assumed to be impure and in league with the devil. They were then executed for associating with the devil. Those who sank to the bottom, on the other hand, were judged to be pure. Unfortunately, some of those enjoyed no better fate—they drowned.

TRUTH
OR
fiction
■ REVISITED ■

It is true that in the Middle Ages some innocent people were allowed to drown as a way of proving that they were not possessed by the devil. The method was based on a water-float test used for judging the purity of metals.

The Birth of Modern Science

People of the 1500s, 1600s, and 1700s witnessed great scientific and intellectual advances. In the 1500s, for example, Polish astronomer Nicolaus Copernicus challenged the view that the sun revolved around Earth, suggesting instead that Earth revolves around the sun. In the 1600s English scientist Sir Isaac Newton formulated the laws of gravity and motion. English Philosopher John Locke, building on principles of associationism, theorized that knowledge is not inborn but is learned from experience. In the late 1700s French scientist Antoine Lavoisier founded the science of chemistry and explained how animals and plants use oxygen in respiration.

The scientific approach also led to the birth of modern psychology in the 1800s. Psychologists argued that ideas about human behavior and mental processes should be supported by evidence. In the late 1800s psychological laboratories were established in Europe and the United States. In these laboratories, psychologists studied behavior and mental processes using methods similar to those Lavoisier had used to study chemistry. Most historians of psychology point to the year 1879 as the beginning of psychology as a modern laboratory science. In that year, German psychologist Wilhelm Wundt established his laboratory in Leipzig.

Wilhelm Wundt and Structuralism

Wilhelm Wundt (1832–1920) and his students founded a field of experimental psychology that came to be known as **structuralism**. Structuralists were concerned with discovering the basic elements of consciousness. Wundt broke down the content of consciousness into two categories: objective sensations and subjective feelings. Objective sensations, such as sight and taste, were assumed to accurately reflect the outside world. Subjective feelings were thought to include emotional responses and mental images.

Wilhelm Wundt

Structuralists believed that the human mind functioned by combining these basic elements of experience. For example, a person can experience an apple objectively by observing its shape, color, texture, and taste. The person can also experience the apple subjectively by remembering how good it feels to bite into one. Using the method of introspection, Wundt and his students carefully examined and reported their experiences.

William James and Functionalism

A decade after Wundt established his laboratory, introspection convinced Harvard University professor William James (1842–1910) that conscious experience cannot be broken down as structuralists believed. James maintained that experience is a continuous "stream of consciousness." He focused on the relationships between experience and behavior and described

William James

his views in *The Principles of Psychology*. Many consider this book, published in 1890, to be the first modern psychology textbook.

James was one of the founders of the school of **functionalism**. Functionalists were concerned with how mental processes help organisms adapt to their environment. They stressed the application of their findings to everyday situations.

⧉ internet connect

TOPIC: Historical Psychologists
GO TO: go.hrw.com
KEYWORD: SY3 PS1
Have students access the Internet through the HRW Go site to research notable psychologists and their contributions to psychology. Then ask the students to create a biography in which they outline the achievements, theories, and importance to psychology of the person they chose. Remind students to use standard spelling, grammar, punctuation, and sentence structure.

Evaluating Ideas

To help students understand the concept of observable behavior, direct them to observe your behavior for a period of five minutes. Tell them to write down everything you do within that period of time. Caution them to remain as objective as possible and to make no inferences about what is going on in your mind. At the end of the time period, ask volunteers to read their lists aloud. Have students discuss any limitations involved in explaining behavior only on the basis of observable behavior.

For Further Research

Have interested students research the history of the American Psychological Association (APA). Students should find out when and where the APA was established, why it was established, and who its founding members were. Students should also note significant milestones for the APA. Have students present their findings to the class in the form of oral reports. Reports should be accompanied by graphics that illustrate the growth of the APA's membership and the increase in the number of divisions within the APA.

Calvin and Hobbes — by Bill Watterson

CALVIN AND HOBBES copyright 1995 Watterson. Reprinted with permission of Universal Press Syndicate. All rights reserved.

Functionalism differed from structuralism in several ways. Whereas structuralism relied only on introspection, the methods of functionalism included behavioral observation in the laboratory as well as introspection. The structuralists tended to ask, What are the elements (structures) of psychological processes? The functionalists, on the other hand, tended to ask, What are the purposes (functions) of behavior and mental processes? What do certain behaviors and mental processes accomplish for the person (or animal)?

Functionalists proposed that adaptive behavior patterns are learned and maintained because they are successful. For example, some students study diligently because they have learned that studying leads to good grades. Less-adaptive behavior patterns are dropped or are discontinued. For example, if you ask someone for a date repeatedly and are refused each time, eventually you will probably stop asking the person out.

Adaptive (successful) actions are repeated and eventually become habits. The formation of habits is seen in such acts as turning doorknobs or riding a bicycle. At first, these acts require our full attention. But through repetition—and success—they become automatic. The multiple tasks involved in learning to type on a keyboard or to write in longhand also become routine through successful repetition. We then perform them without much attention. Habit allows us to take the mechanics of typing or writing for granted and to concentrate instead on *what* we are typing or writing.

John B. Watson and Behaviorism

Picture a hungry rat in a maze. It moves along until it reaches a place where it must turn left or right. If the rat is consistently rewarded with food for turning right at that place, it will learn to turn right when it arrives there the next time—at least, when it is hungry. But what does the rat *think* when it is learning to turn right at that place in the maze?

Does it seem absurd to try to place yourself in the mind of a rat? It did to John B. Watson (1878–1958), when he was asked by examiners to consider this question as a requirement for his doctoral degree in psychology.

He was asked this question because functionalism was the dominant school of psychology at the time. Functionalists were concerned with the stream of consciousness as well as with behavior. Although Watson agreed with the functionalist

John B. Watson

focus on the importance of learning, he believed that it was unscientific to study a construct like consciousness—particularly the consciousness of animals. He saw consciousness as a private event that is known only to the individual. He asserted that if psychology was to be a natural science, like physics or chemistry, it must be limited to observable, measurable events—that is, to behavior. As the founder of the school of **behaviorism**, Watson defined psychology as the scientific study of observable behavior.

B. F. Skinner and Reinforcement

Harvard University psychologist B. F. Skinner (1904–1990) added to the behaviorist tradition by introducing the concept of reinforcement. Skinner

Spark a discussion on the Exploring Diversity feature by asking students to respond to the following statement: "Many people think that what is, is what should be." Have students relate this statement to the long-term dominance of white males in the field of psychology. Then have students analyze why the inclusion of women and people of various ethnic backgrounds in the field of psychology has provided a much greater understanding of human behavior and mental processes.

For Further Research

Have students research the 1954 U.S. Supreme Court case that cited Clark's work on the effects of discrimination—*Brown* v. *Board of Education of Topeka*. Students should determine who brought the case to the Court and why, the basis of the argument made to the Court, and the Court's rationale for its decision. Ask students to summarize their findings in a written report. Then have them explain the significance of the 1954 ruling and analyze why an end to legal discrimination may not eliminate discrimination in society.

EXPLORING

DIVERSITY

Bringing Diversity into Psychology

I n the past, psychology—like many other academic fields—was dominated by white men. Not only were the psychologists themselves mostly white men, but most of their research used white male participants and tended to explore issues that were relevant primarily to white men. However, in recent decades that has changed. Today many psychologists are women and members of traditionally underrepresented ethnic groups. In fact, white men now obtain fewer than half of the doctoral degrees in psychology.

Not only are psychologists as a group more diverse now than they used to be—so is their research. A great deal of current psychological research deals with questions of gender, culture, prejudice, and stereotypes. The work of African American psychologist Kenneth Bancroft Clark exemplifies such research.

Clark was born in the Panama Canal Zone in 1914, the son of West Indian parents. Miriam Clark, his mother, brought her children to the United States for their education. They settled in the Harlem section of New York City.

Although most African American children at the time were advised to attend vocational high schools, where they could learn specific job skills, Kenneth Clark attended an academic high school. He went on to Howard University in Washington, D.C., where he majored in psychology and married Mamie Phipps. The Clarks then attended Columbia University, where they both earned Ph.D. degrees in psychology.

In 1946 the Clarks founded the Northside Center for Child Development. Kenneth and Mamie Clark's clinical work led to several studies showing the negative effect of segregation on the self-esteem of African American children. In one

Kenneth B. Clark

well-known study (Clark & Clark, 1947), African American children were asked to choose between white and black dolls after being given instructions such as "Give me the pretty doll" or "Give me the doll that looks bad." The Clarks reported that most children preferred the white dolls over the black ones and concluded that the children were demonstrating their feelings that society as a whole preferred white people.

In the early 1950s Kenneth Clark began working with the National Association for the Advancement of Colored People (NAACP) to end school segregation. In 1954, when the Supreme Court overturned the "separate but equal" doctrine, it cited Clark's work on the effects of discrimination on the personality development of both African American and white children. In his book *Prejudice and Your Child,* published in 1955, Clark described the effects of segregation on white children as well as on African American children.

Clark's later work examined the quality of education and the problems of juvenile delinquency and crime. He was among the first experts to recommend preschool classes, after-school programs, and community participation.

Think About It

Analyzing Information Kenneth Clark is only one of the many people who have contributed to psychology's diversity. Select one of the following psychologists and prepare an oral report on his or her life and work: J. Henry Alston, Mary Whiton Calkins, Lillian Comas-Diaz, Beverly Greene, Gilbert Haven Jones, Christine Ladd Franklin, Jorge Sanchez, Stanley Sue, Margaret Floy Washburn.

B. F. Skinner

showed that when an animal is reinforced, or rewarded, for performing an action, it is more likely to perform that action again in the future. He demonstrated that laboratory animals, such as rats and pigeons, are capable of learning complex behavior patterns if they are reinforced in the right ways. Behaviorists have taught animals to push buttons, turn in circles, climb ladders, push toys across the floor, and even shoot baskets by rewarding the animals for performing the desired behavior.

According to Skinner, people learn in the same way animals do. Like animals, people learn to behave in certain ways because they have been reinforced for doing so.

The Gestalt School

Look at the two drawings in Figure 1.2 and answer the questions posed in the caption. These drawings demonstrate the idea that the perception of something is affected by the context in which it occurs. For example, in Drawing A, the circles in the centers of the two sets are the same size. However, we may think they are different sizes because of the differing contexts in which they appear. That is, one circle is surrounded by larger circles and the other is surrounded by smaller circles.

In Drawing B, the second symbols in the two rows are identical. The symbol in the top row may look like the letter B because it is with the letters A, C, and D. However, when the identical symbol is with the numbers 12, 14, and 15, it may look more like the number 13. Even though the two symbols are identical, the context in which each one appears influences what we perceive it to be.

German psychologists Max Wertheimer, Kurt Koffka, and Wolfgang Köhler were fascinated by the ways in which context influences people's interpretation of information. In the 1920s they founded the school of **Gestalt psychology**. The psychology of *Gestalt*, which means "shape" or "form" in German, is based on the idea that perceptions are more than the sums of their parts. Rather, they are wholes that give shape, or meaning, to the parts. As such, Gestalt psychology rejects the structuralist idea that experience can be broken down into individual parts or elements.

Gestalt psychologists also reject the behaviorist notion that psychologists should concentrate only on observable behavior. In addition, Gestalt psychologists believe that learning is active and purposeful. They disagree with the behaviorist view that learning is mechanical.

These circus lions probably learned how to do their tricks by being reinforced, or rewarded, for each behavior that contributed to the overall effect the trainers were trying to achieve.

Closing Section 3

Demonstration

To demonstrate Gestalt theory, locate a black-and-white drawing of a familiar animal. Make several photocopies of the image, and on each successive photocopy use correction fluid to blank out an increasing amount of detail. Be sure, however, to leave *some* detail remaining to indicate each part of the animal's body. Then test the drawings on different groups of students. How much detail can you eliminate and still retain a meaningful image? Have students explain how this demonstrates that perceptions are more than the sums of their parts.

Comparing Information

Ask students to create a chart listing the name of each school of thought covered in the section, each school's major theorist, and each school's main principles.

Reviewing Section 3

Have students complete the Section Review questions on page 17.

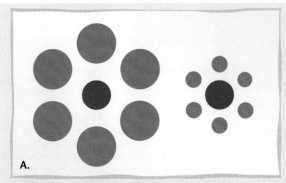

A.

B.

FIGURE 1.2 *Look at Drawing A. Are the circles in the centers of the two sets of circles the same size? In Drawing B, what is the second symbol in each line? We perceive images in terms of the contexts in which they occur, so two images that are identical may appear to be different if their surroundings are different.*

Köhler and the other founders of Gestalt psychology demonstrated that much learning, particularly problem solving, is accomplished by insight, not by mechanical repetition. Insight is the reorganization of perceptions that enables an individual to solve a problem. In other words, insight is the sudden appearance of the Gestalt, or form, that enables the individual to see the solution.

Sigmund Freud and the School of Psychoanalysis

Sigmund Freud

Sigmund Freud (1856–1939), a Viennese physician, was perhaps the most famous of the early psychologists. The school of thought that he founded, called **psychoanalysis**, emphasizes the importance of unconscious motives and internal conflicts in determining human behavior.

Freud's theory, more than the others, has become a part of popular culture. You may be familiar with several Freudian concepts. For example, have you ever tried to interpret a slip of the tongue, or have you ever tried to figure out the meaning of a dream you had? The ideas that people are driven by hidden impulses and that verbal slips and dreams represent unconscious wishes largely reflect Freud's influence on popular culture.

Structuralists, functionalists, behaviorists, and Gestalt psychologists all conducted their research in the laboratory. However, Freud gained his understanding of human behavior through consultations with patients. Freud was astounded at how little insight these patients had into their own ideas and feelings. He came to believe that unconscious processes, particularly sexual and aggressive urges, are more important than conscious experience in governing people's behavior and feelings.

Freud's theory which is sometimes called **psychodynamic thinking**, assumed that most of what exists in an individual's mind is unconscious and consists of conflicting impulses, urges, and wishes. According to Freud's theories, human behavior is aimed at satisfying these desires, even though some of them seem socially inappropriate or even unacceptable. But at the same time, people want to see themselves as good and decent human beings. Thus, they often are consciously unaware of the real motivations for their behavior. Freud attempted to help people gain insight into their unconscious conflicts and find socially acceptable ways of expressing their wishes and meeting their needs.

SECTION 3 REVIEW

1. Describe the main differences between structuralism and functionalism.
2. How did the field of psychology develop?
3. **Critical Thinking** *Drawing Inferences and Conclusions* Identify one example of the influence that Sigmund Freud's psychoanalytic theory has had on popular culture.

Caption Question: Answers

Drawing A: Yes, the circles are the same size. Drawing B: Although both symbols are alike, the symbol in the top line is a B and the symbol in the bottom line is a 13.

Section 3 Review: Answers

1. Structuralism breaks down conscious experience into objective sensations and subjective feelings; the mind functions by combining these two basic elements. Functionalism proposes that adaptive behavior patterns are learned and maintained because they are successful.

2. Students should note that psychology began in ancient Greece and revived during the scientific advances of the 1500s, 1600s, and 1700s. Students should note the contributions of modern psychologists such as William James, B. F. Skinner, and Sigmund Freud.

3. Students may cite examples that indicate that common slips of the tongue are often called Freudian slips.

Section Objective

▶ Describe the seven main contemporary perspectives in psychology.

This objective is assessed in the Section Review on page 21 and in the Chapter 1 Review.

Opening Section 4

Motivator

Have students retrieve the matching tests they created in the Using Key Terms activity on page 3. Ask volunteers to read aloud the definitions of the seven contemporary psychological perspectives discussed in Section 4. Then ask students to copy the names of the seven perspectives on a separate sheet of paper. Tell them to use the definitions to speculate on the nature and research interests of each perspective. Then have students write a short description of each perspective on the basis of their speculations. Tell students to keep these descriptions for later use.

For Your Information

Tell students that a theoretical perspective is a general set of assumptions about the nature of phenomena. In the case of psychology, each of the seven perspectives presented in this section has a different set of assumptions about the nature of human behavior and mental processes. Some students may be confused by the variety of perspectives in psychology and ask why psychologists cannot seem to agree on anything. Remind students that human behavior is complex and that having a variety of perspectives gives us a much richer and fuller view of behavior than could one perspective alone.

Class Discussion

Tell students that virtual reality is a new technology that simulates the sights, sounds, and feel of real or imaginary events. Ask students who have had experience with virtual reality games at amusement arcades to describe the experience for the class. Then have the class speculate on how biologically oriented psychologists might use virtual reality to learn more about human behavior.

SECTION 4

Contemporary Perspectives

Today few psychologists describe themselves as structuralists or functionalists. Few would consider themselves Gestalt psychologists although the school of Gestalt psychology has inspired current research in perception and problem solving. The numbers of traditional behaviorists and psychoanalysts also have been declining. Many current psychologists in the behaviorist tradition have modified the theories of Watson and Skinner. Similarly, many contemporary psychoanalysts do not use the methods Freud did.

Nevertheless, the historical traditions of psychology find expression in contemporary perspectives on psychology. The most important of these are the biological, evolutionary, cognitive, humanistic, psychoanalytic, learning, and sociocultural perspectives. Each perspective emphasizes different topics of investigation and has different approaches.

The Biological Perspective

The **biological perspective** emphasizes the influence of biology on our behavior. This perspective has roots in associationism. Psychologists assume that our mental processes—our thoughts, fantasies, and dreams—are made possible by the nervous system. They point particularly to its key component, the brain. Biologically oriented psychologists look for the connections between events in the brain, such as the activity of brain cells, and behavior and mental processes. They use several techniques, such as CAT scans and PET scans, to show which parts of the brain are involved in various mental processes. (See Chapter 3.) Biological psychology has shown that certain parts of the brain are highly active when we listen to music, other parts are active when we solve math problems, and still other parts are involved with certain psychological disorders. Biological psychologists have also learned that certain chemicals in the brain are connected with the storage of information—that is, the formation of memories.

Moreover, biological psychologists are interested in the influences of hormones and genes. Hormones are chemicals that glands release into the bloodstream to set in motion various body functions, such as growth or digestion. Genes are the basic units of heredity. Biological psychologists study the influences of genes on personality traits, psychological health, and various behavior patterns.

The Evolutionary Perspective

The **evolutionary perspective** focuses on the evolution of behavior and mental processes. British scientist Charles Darwin theorized that in the struggle for survival, the most-adaptive organisms have a greater chance of surviving to maturity, when they can reproduce. For example, people who are naturally resistant to certain diseases are more likely to transmit their genes to future generations. Evolutionary psychologists suggest that many kinds of behavior patterns, such as aggressive behavior, also have a hereditary basis. These psychologists believe that inherited tendencies influence people to act in certain ways.

The Cognitive Perspective

The **cognitive perspective** emphasizes the role that thoughts play in determining behavior. Cognitive psychologists study mental processes to understand human nature. They investigate the ways in which people perceive information and make mental images of the world, solve problems, and dream and daydream. Cognitive psychologists, in short, study what we refer to as the mind.

The cognitive tradition has roots in Socrates' maxim "Know thyself" and in his method of introspection for learning about the self. Cognitive psychology also has roots in structuralism, functionalism, and Gestalt psychology. Each of these schools of thought has addressed issues that are of interest to cognitive psychologists.

Another aspect of the cognitive perspective involves information processing. Many cognitive psychologists have been influenced by computer science. Computers process information to solve problems. Information is first fed into the computer. The information is then placed in the working memory while it is being worked on. After being processed, the information is stored more or less permanently on the computer's hard drive, a compact disk, or a floppy disk.

Many psychologists speak of people as having working memories and storage facilities (or long-term memories). If information has been placed in computer storage or in a person's long-term memory, it must first be retrieved before it can be worked on again. To retrieve information from computer

Teaching Section 4

Guided Practice

To help students understand the differences among the contemporary perspectives in psychology, choose one chapter topic from the table of contents in this textbook (adolescence, for example) and have students explain how that topic would interest biologically oriented psychologists. *(A biological psychologist would be likely to examine the hormonal and chemical changes that occur in adolescence rather than, for example, the social pressures on adolescents.)*

Independent Practice

Tell students to build on the Guided Practice activity by explaining what psychologists who follow the other perspectives might find of interest about the same topic. *(Cognitive psychologists might consider the ways in which adolescents process information; humanistic psychologists might study ways in which adolescents can reach their full potential; psychoanalysts might focus on the unconscious desires and conflicts of adolescents, and so on.)*

---

storage, people must know the name for the data file and the process for retrieving data files. Similarly, cognitive psychologists believe people need certain cues to retrieve information from their long-term memories. Otherwise, it is lost to them.

Cognitive psychologists sometimes refer to our strategies for solving problems as our "mental programs" or "software." In this computer metaphor, our brains are the "hardware" that runs our mental programs. In other words, our brains are our own *very* personal computers.

TRUTH OR fiction ■ REVISITED ■

It is true that some psychologists view our strategies for solving problems as mental programs operated by our own very personal computers—our brains. These psychologists are called cognitive psychologists, and they study how we process information.

Cognitive psychologists believe that people's behavior is influenced by their values, their perceptions, and their choices. For example, an individual who interprets a casual remark as an insult may react with hostility. But the same remark directed at another person might be perceived very differently by that person and thus may meet with a different reaction.

The Humanistic Perspective

The **humanistic perspective** stresses the human capacity for self-fulfillment and the importance of consciousness, self-awareness, and the capacity to make choices. Consciousness is seen as the force that shapes human personality.

Humanistic psychology considers people's personal experiences to be the most important aspect of psychology. Humanistic psychologists believe that self-awareness, experience, and choice permit us to "invent ourselves." In other words, they enable us to fashion our growth and our ways of relating to the world as we go through life. Unlike the behaviorists, who assume that behavior is caused largely by the stimuli that act upon us, humanistic psychologists believe that we are free to choose our own behavior.

The humanistic perspective views people as basically good and desiring to be helpful to others. Humanistic psychologists help people explore their feelings, manage their negative impulses, and realize their potential.

Some cognitive psychologists are interested in the ways in which children view the world.

Critics of the humanistic perspective, particularly behaviorists, insist that psychology should be scientific and address only observable events. They argue that people's inner experiences are unsuited to scientific observation and measurement. However, humanistic psychologists insist that inner experience is vital to the understanding of human nature.

The Psychoanalytic Perspective

The **psychoanalytic perspective** stresses the influence of unconscious forces on human behavior. In the 1940s and 1950s, psychoanalytic theory dominated the practice of psychotherapy and greatly influenced psychology and the arts. Although psychoanalytic thought no longer dominates psychology, its influence continues to be felt. Psychologists who follow Sigmund Freud's approach today focus less on the roles of unconscious sexual and aggressive impulses and more on conscious choice and self-direction.

TRUTH OR fiction ■ REVISITED ■

It is true that Sigmund Freud's theories continue to influence psychology today. However, psychoanalytic theory no longer dominates the field, and contemporary psychologists who follow Freud's approach focus on different factors than Freud did.

Using Visuals

Call students' attention to the photograph on this page. Ask them what information they can infer about the mental and emotional states of the children in the picture. How are the children behaving differently than adults would in the same situation? What are some of the questions a cognitive psychologist might raise about the situation depicted?

For Your Information

Two psychologists, Carl Rogers and Abraham Maslow, developed the humanistic perspective in reaction to both Freudian and behaviorist psychology. These humanists believed that human beings do not act only in response to either unconscious impulses or external stimuli; rather, people have the potential for directing their own growth. Rogers focused on the individual's drive to enhance the self and actualize (or reach) inner potential, while Maslow became known for his explanation of the hierarchy of human needs, including physiological needs related to survival and the need for self-actualization.

Drawing Conclusions

Have the class work together to expand the chart on psychological perspectives shown on page 20. Ask students to brainstorm a list of specific questions about human behavior and mental processes. (You may wish to remind students of the questions they developed in the Section 3 Motivator activity on page 12.) Have a volunteer write these questions on the chalkboard. Then have students determine which psychological perspective best answers each question. Students should then group the questions by perspective and create a fourth column for the chart.

Cooperative Learning

Organize the class into seven groups, and assign each group one of the seven psychological perspectives discussed in the section. Tell the groups to use discarded magazines to locate pictures that illustrate the subject matter and key assumptions of their assigned perspective. Have the members of each group combine their pictures to make a bulletin board display. Have representatives from each group present and discuss their displays. Post the displays in the classroom.

Contemporary Psychological Perspectives

Perspective	Subject Matter	Key Assumption
Biological	Nervous system, glands and hormones, genetic factors	Biological processes influence behavior and mental processes.
Evolutionary	Physical traits, social behavior	Adaptive organisms survive and transmit their genes to future generations.
Cognitive	Interpretation of mental images, thinking, language	Perceptions and thoughts influence behavior.
Humanistic	Self-concept	People make free and conscious choices based on their unique experiences.
Psychoanalytic	Unconscious processes, early childhood experiences	Unconscious motives influence behavior.
Learning	Environmental influences, learning, observational learning	Personal experience and reinforcement guide individual development.
Sociocultural	Ethnicity, gender, culture, socioeconomic status	Sociocultural, biological, and psychological factors create individual differences.

FIGURE 1.3 *Contemporary psychologists differ in their approaches to psychological thought. These seven broad perspectives are the most common ways that psychologists view behavior today.*

Freud believed that aggressive impulses are common reactions to the frustrations of daily life and that we seek to vent these impulses on other people. Because we fear rejection or retaliation, we put most aggressive impulses out of our minds. But by holding aggression in, we set the stage for future explosions. Pent-up aggressive impulses demand outlets. Partial outlets can be provided by physical activity—for example, sports—but we may also direct hostile impulses toward strangers. (That guy who intentionally bumped into you in the hallway, according to Freud, might be venting unconscious anger toward his parents.)

The Learning Perspective

The **learning perspective** emphasizes the effects of experience on behavior. In the views of many psychologists, learning is the essential factor in observing, describing, explaining, predicting, and controlling behavior. However, the term *learning* has different meanings to different psychologists. For example, traditional behaviorists and social-learning theorists have different attitudes toward the role of consciousness in learning.

John B. Watson and other behaviorists found no role for consciousness. They believed that people act and react because of their learning histories and the influence of their situations, not because of conscious choice. Behaviorists are not concerned with what an organism *knows*. They are concerned with what the organism *does*. Behaviorists emphasize the importance of environmental influences and focus on the learning of habits through repetition and reinforcement.

In contrast, **social-learning theory** suggests that people can change their environments or create new ones. Furthermore, social-learning theory holds that people can learn intentionally by observing others. Social-learning theorists believe that conscious observational learning provides people with a storehouse of responses to life's situations. However, people's expectations and values influence whether they *choose* to do what they have learned how to do.

Psychologists who take the learning perspective believe that behavior is learned either from direct experience or by observing other people. For example, people will behave a certain way when they expect to be rewarded for that behavior. Social-

Closing Section 4

Role-Playing

Tell seven volunteers to imagine that they are representatives of the newly formed (fictitious) Psychological Perspectives Association (PPA). Assign each volunteer one of the perspectives discussed in Section 4. Inform the class that these representatives are here today to hold a press conference about their new organization and the perspectives around which the organization was formed. Then have the journalists (the rest of the class) pose questions to the representatives about their respective perspectives and their reasons for forming this organization.

Follow Up

Tell students to retrieve the descriptions of the psychological perspectives they wrote for the Motivator activity on page 18. Have students review and revise their descriptions as needed. Then have them summarize, in outline form, the basic facts about each perspective.

Reviewing Section 4

Have students complete the Section Review questions on page 21.

---

learning theorists have a cognitive leaning. Like cognitive theorists, social-learning theorists believe that people act in a particular way only when they recognize that the circumstances call for that behavior. For example, we act with hostility when we have been provoked, or we act with friendliness when we have been treated well.

The Sociocultural Perspective

The **sociocultural perspective** studies the influences of ethnicity, gender, culture, and socioeconomic status on behavior and mental processes. By taking these factors into account, psychologists can better understand how people act and think. The science of psychology is enriched by awareness of these factors and by taking them into account when conducting research (Denmark, 1998).

One kind of diversity involves ethnicity. Members of an **ethnic group** are united by their cultural heritage, race, language, or common history. The sociocultural perspective helps people appreciate the cultural heritages and historical issues of various ethnic groups. The following items are among the psychological issues related to ethnicity:

- inclusion of people from various ethnic minority groups in psychological research studies
- bilingualism
- ethnic differences in intelligence test scores
- ethnic differences in vulnerability to health problems ranging from obesity to high blood pressure and certain forms of cancer
- prejudice

Sociocultural theorists also study gender, which is the state of being male or being female. Gender is not simply a matter of anatomy. It involves a complex web of cultural expectations and social roles that affect people's self-concepts and aspirations as well as their behavior. One reason for the importance of gender studies is that such studies address issues concerning similarities and differences between males and females.

In the past, much of the scientific research on gender roles and gender differences assumed that male behavior represents the norm (Ader &

One topic explored by followers of the sociocultural perspective is how people of different ethnicities and genders interact with each other.

Johnson, 1994). Such assumptions have changed in recent years. Women, who have entered higher education in great numbers, had traditionally been channeled into domestic pursuits. In the United States, women have attended college only since 1833, when Oberlin College opened its doors to women. Yet today more than half of American college students are women. Two thirds of the doctoral degrees in psychology are awarded to women (Kohout & Williams, 1999).

Following the pattern of American society in general, the field of psychology is becoming more diverse. African Americans make up 6 percent to 7 percent of the first-year students in doctoral departments in psychology, and Hispanics make up 5 percent (APA Research Office, 2000). However, these percentages are far below these groups' representation in the general population.

SECTION 4 REVIEW

go.hrw.com **Homework Practice Online**
Keyword: SY3 HP1

1. How do cognitive psychologists compare people's mental processes to the working of computers?
2. How would a psychoanalyst explain aggression?
3. List the seven leading contemporary perspectives in psychology.
4. **Critical Thinking** *Evaluating* How does knowledge of cultural differences enrich the study of psychology?

name and the rules for retrieving data files, people need certain cues to retrieve information stored in their long-term memory.

2. A psychoanalyst would say that aggression is a common reaction to the frustrations of daily life and that people seek to vent their aggression on other people.

3. biological, evolutionary, cognitive, humanistic, psychoanalytic, learning, sociocultural

4. Knowledge of cultural differences enriches the study of psychology because such knowledge makes possible a much broader understanding of the forces that shape human behavior and mental processes.

Chapter Review: Answers

Writing a Summary

See the section subtitles for the main topics in the chapter.

Identifying People and Ideas

1. the scientific study of behavior and mental processes
2. mental processes
3. a statement that attempts to explain why things are the way they are and happen the way they do
4. Greek philosopher who developed associationism
5. psychology concerned with the resolution of the mind into structural elements

21

Technology

► Chapter 1 Test Generator (on the One-Stop Planner)
► HRW Go site

Reinforcement, Review, and Assessment

► Chapter 1 Review, pp. 22–23
► Chapter Review Activities with Answer Key
► Alternative Assessment Handbook
► Portfolio Assessment Handbook
► Chapter 1 Test (Form A or B)

PSYCHOLOGY PROJECTS

Linking to Community

Have students research what types of psychologists work in their community. Have them consider all the different kinds of psychologists and the possible locations where they might work (for example, clinical psychologists might work in private practice or in local clinics; industrial

---

6. the study of how mental processes help organisms adapt to their environment

7. behaviorist who introduced the concept of reinforcement

8. a school of thought that emphasizes unconscious motives and internal conflicts in determining human behavior

9. the perspective that stresses the human capacity for self-fulfillment and the importance of consciousness, self-awareness, and the capacity to make choices

10. theory that people can change their environments or create new ones

Understanding Main Ideas

1. A theory is a statement that attempts to explain why things are the way they are and happen the way they do, while a principle is a rule or law.

2. clinical psychologists—treat a variety of psychological problems, including serious psychological disorders; counseling psychologists—also treat people, but generally those who have adjustment problems

3. Hippocrates held the view that psychological problems are caused by abnormalities in the brain rather than by supernatural forces.

4. biological, evolutionary, cognitive, humanistic, psychoanalytic, learning, sociocultural

Thinking Critically

1. Many psychologists today use pychodynamic thinking, although they focus less on the roles of unconscious impulses and more on conscious choice and self-direction than Freud.

22

Chapter 1 REVIEW

Writing a Summary

Using standard grammar, spelling, sentence structure, and punctuation, summarize the information in this chapter. Consider:

• the goals of psychology and psychologists' areas of specialization
• the history of psychology and the seven main contemporary perspectives in psychology

Identifying People and Ideas

Identify the following terms or people and use them in appropriate sentences.

1. psychology
2. cognitive activities
3. theory
4. Aristotle
5. structuralism
6. functionalism
7. B. F. Skinner
8. psychoanalysis
9. humanistic perspective
10. social-learning theory

Understanding Main Ideas

SECTION 1 (pp. 4–6)
1. How do the concepts of theory and principle differ?

SECTION 2 (pp. 8–11)
2. Describe what clinical and counseling psychologists do.

SECTION 3 (pp. 12–17)
3. What view held by the ancient Greek physician Hippocrates was ahead of its time?

SECTION 4 (pp. 18–21)
4. What are the seven main contemporary perspectives in psychology?

Thinking Critically

1. Analyzing Information Trace the impact of psychodynamic thinking on current thinking in psychology.

---

2. Making Generalizations and Predictions Sports psychology is an example of a relatively new area of psychological specialization. What do you think might be important areas for psychology in the years ahead? Explain your choices.

3. Analyzing Information Trace the impact of associationism on current thinking in psychology.

4. Evaluating Describe a commonly held belief about gender differences that sociocultural psychologists might want to research. How might they go about proving or disproving this belief?

5. Drawing Inferences and Conclusions Describe the relationship between earlier and later theories related to a given psychological construct.

Writing About Psychology

1. Summarizing Find three newspaper or magazine articles that discuss the work done by different psychologists. Write a summary of the articles, describing what type of psychologist is featured in each article.

2. Analyzing Information A tip line is a telephone service people can call to hear a recording of helpful information. Write a three-minute script for a tip line on the services different psychologists provide. Consider the kinds of concerns people might want to discuss with each type of psychologist. Use the graphic organizer below to help you write your script.

People's Concerns

psychologists might work in factories or other types of businesses; local institutions associated with the criminal justice system might use the services of forensic psychologists, and so on). Have students contact a number of these psychologists and invite them to describe their work to the class on a Psychology Career Day.

Building Social Studies Skills

Interpreting Graphs

Study the bar graph below. Then use the information in the graph to help you answer the questions that follow.

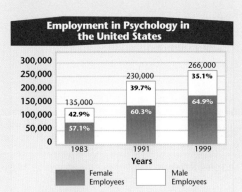

Employment in Psychology in the United States

	1983	1991	1999
Total	135,000	230,000	266,000
Female Employees	57.1%	60.3%	64.9%
Male Employees	42.9%	39.7%	35.1%

Years

☐ Female Employees   ☐ Male Employees

Source: U.S. Census Bureau

1. How many more psychologists were employed in 1999 than in 1983?
   a. 131,000
   b. 135,000
   c. 266,000
   d. 401,000

2. What conclusions can you draw about the field of psychology in the United States from the years 1983 to 1991?

Analyzing Primary Sources

Read the following excerpt, in which Stephen Poland describes his work as a school psychologist. Then answer the questions that follow.

"Another benefit you have as a school psychologist is the opportunity to work in a multitude of settings with learners of all ages and backgrounds. . . . School settings allow you to intervene with children who would never come through the doors of a mental health clinic because their families lack the financial resources, motivation, or the knowledge to access these services. Most schools are 'zero reject' service centers that are mandated [required] to serve whoever comes in the door. The impact of your intervention is magnified in a school because you can work with children and their teachers, other school staff, and their parents."

3. Which of the following statements best describes Poland's point of view?
   a. Teachers and other school staff interfere with the work of school psychologists.
   b. School psychologists are able to work with people who might otherwise not receive professional assistance.
   c. Because schools do not reject students, school psychologists have a very difficult job.
   d. Many parents do not want their child to meet with the school psychologist.

4. According to this excerpt, why do school psychologists assist a variety of people and problems?

PSYCHOLOGY PROJECTS

Cooperative Learning

Using Your Observation Skills As a class, agree to watch the same program on television. The next day, organize small groups of students to discuss the program's characters. What behaviors did you observe? How did you find out about the characters' thoughts (cognitive activities) and feelings (emotions)? Choose one person in your group to record the group's ideas on the role of observation in understanding differences among people. Share your group's ideas with the class.

▶ internet connect

Internet Activity: go.hrw.com
KEYWORD: SY3 PS1
Choose an activity on psychology:
- write a profile about a historical psychologist.
- create a pamphlet that discusses the ways in which contemporary perspectives have changed traditional theories and practice in psychology.
- write a short story illustrating a typical day in the life of a psychologist.

go.hrw.com

Psychological Methods

CHAPTER RESOURCE MANAGER

	Objectives	Pacing Guide		Reproducible and Review Resources
SECTION 1: **Conducting Research** (pp. 26–29)	List and explain the steps scientists follow in conducting scientific research.	**Regular** 1 day	**Block Scheduling** .5 day	**SM** Mastering Critical Thinking Skills **REV** Section 1 Review, p. 29
		Block Scheduling Handbook with Team Teaching Strategies, Chapter 2		
SECTION 2: **Surveys, Samples, and Populations** (pp. 29–34)	Explain the survey method and the importance of proper sampling techniques.	**Regular** 1 day	**Block Scheduling** .5 day	**REV** Section 2 Review, p. 34
		Block Scheduling Handbook with Team Teaching Strategies, Chapter 2		
SECTION 3: **Methods of Observation** (pp. 34–40)	Compare and contrast various methods of observation, and discuss the use of correlation in analyzing results.	**Regular** .5 day	**Block Scheduling** .5 day	**PS** Reading and Case Studies 2 **RS** Essay and Research Themes for Advanced Placement Students 1 **REV** Section 3 Review, p. 40
		Block Scheduling Handbook with Team Teaching Strategies, Chapter 2		
SECTION 4: **The Experimental Method** (pp. 40–44)	Describe the purpose and elements of an experiment.	**Regular** .5 day	**Block Scheduling** .5 day	**E** Research Projects and Activities for Teaching Psychology **REV** Section 4 Review, p. 44
		Block Scheduling Handbook with Team Teaching Strategies, Chapter 2		
SECTION 5: **Ethical Issues** (pp. 44–47)	Evaluate the ethical issues involved in psychological research.	**Regular** 1 day	**Block Scheduling** .5 day	**REV** Section 5 Review, p. 47
		Block Scheduling Handbook with Team Teaching Strategies, Chapter 2		

Chapter Resource Key

PS Primary Sources
RS Reading Support
E Enrichment
SM Skills Mastery

A Assessment
REV Review
 Transparencies
 CD-ROM

 Video
 Internet
 Holt Presentation Maker Using Microsoft® PowerPoint®

 One-Stop Planner CD-ROM

See the *One-Stop Planner* for a complete list of additional resources for students and teachers.

 **One-Stop** Planner CD–ROM

It's easy to plan lessons, select resources, and print out materials for your students when you use the **One-Stop Planner CD-ROM with Test Generator.**

Technology Resources

 One-Stop Planner, Lesson 2.1
 Homework Practice Online
Teaching Transparencies 2: The Steps of Scientific Research
 HRW Go site

 One-Stop Planner, Lesson 2.2
 Homework Practice Online
 CNN Presents Psychology: Twin Studies

 One-Stop Planner, Lesson 2.3
 Homework Practice Online
 Teaching Transparencies 3: Positive and Negative Correlations
Teaching Transparencies 4: Correlation Versus Cause and Effect

 One-Stop Planner, Lesson 2.4
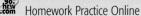 Homework Practice Online
HRW Go site

 One-Stop Planner, Lesson 2.5
Homework Practice Online
HRW Go site

Chapter Review and Assessment

 HRW Go site
REV Chapter 2 Review, pp. 48–49
REV Chapter Review Activities with Answer Key

A Chapter 2 Test (Form A or B)
A Portfolio Assessment Handbook
A Alternative Assessment Handbook

 Global Skill Builder CD-ROM
 Chapter 2 Test Generator (on the One-Stop Planner)

⧉ internet connect

HRW ONLINE RESOURCES

GO TO: go.hrw.com
Then type in a keyword.

TEACHER HOME PAGE
KEYWORD: SY3 Teacher

CHAPTER INTERNET ACTIVITIES
KEYWORD: SY3 PS2
Choose an activity to have students:
• design a hypothetical research program.
• create a model illustrating cause and effect and correlation.
• apply APA standards for ethical decision making to historic experiments.

CHAPTER ENRICHMENT LINKS
KEYWORD: SY3 CH2

ONLINE ASSESSMENT
Homework Practice
KEYWORD: SY3 HP2
Standardized Test Prep
KEYWORD: SY3 STP2
Rubrics
KEYWORD: SS Rubrics

CONTENT UPDATES
KEYWORD: SS Content Updates

HOLT PRESENTATION MAKER
KEYWORD: SY3 PPT2

ONLINE READING SUPPORT
KEYWORD: SS Strategies

CURRENT EVENTS
KEYWORD: S3 Current Events

Additional Resources

PRINT RESOURCES FOR TEACHERS
Hock, R. (Ed.). (1992). *Forty studies that changed psychology: Explorations into the history of psychological research.* Englewood Cliffs, NJ: Prentice-Hall.

Martin, D. W. (1991). *Doing psychology experiments.* Pacific Grove, CA: Brooks/Cole.

Pyke, S., & Agnew, N. (1993). *The science game.* Englewood Cliffs, NJ: Prentice-Hall.

PRINT RESOURCES FOR STUDENTS
Kincher, J. (1995). *Psychology for kids: 40 fun experiments that can help you learn about yourself.* Minneapolis: Free Spirit Publishing.

Kincher, J. (1995). *Psychology for kids II: 40 fun experiments that can help you learn about others.* Minneapolis: Free Spirit Publishing.

Stanovich, K. E. (1992). *How to think straight about psychology.* (3rd ed.). New York: HarperCollins.

MULTIMEDIA RESOURCES
Methodology—The psychologist and the experiment (VHS). McGraw-Hill Films, 674 Via De La Valle, Del Mar, CA 92014.

Understanding research (VHS). Intellimation, P.O. Box 1922, Santa Barbara, CA 93116-1922.

PSYCHOLOGICAL METHODS

Ask students to brainstorm a list of instances in their daily lives when they must follow an established set of procedures to accomplish a task, solve a problem, or answer a question. Have a volunteer note students' responses on the chalkboard. *(Students may say they follow recipes to bake cakes, play games according to established rules, or use established formulas to solve math problems.)* Tell students that psychologists also follow established procedures when they conduct their research. These established procedures, or psychological methods, must be followed to ensure that psychological research is conducted in a scientific manner. Then tell students that psychological methods are the focus of Chapter 2.

Sections

1 **Conducting Research**

2 **Surveys, Samples, and Populations**

3 **Methods of Observation**

4 **The Experimental Method**

5 **Ethical Issues**

Each of the five questions identified on page 24 corresponds to one of these sections.

Chapter 2 PSYCHOLOGICAL METHODS

Read to Discover

1 What steps do scientists follow in conducting scientific research?

2 Why are proper sampling techniques important?

3 What are the various methods of observation, and how is correlation used in analyzing results?

4 What are the purposes and elements of experiments?

5 How are ethical issues involved in psychological research?

24

Each chapter begins with a vignette, called "A Day in the Life," that relates the information discussed in the chapter to the everyday events in the lives of a group of fictional high school students. The text of the chapter occasionally refers back to the vignette to demonstrate the application of the concept being discussed. An icon marked "A Day in the Life" is placed next to these references.

Copy the following graphic organizer onto the chalkboard, omitting the italicized text. Fill in the circles as you discuss with the class how research questions are formed.

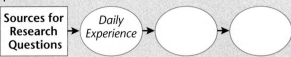

Sources for Research Questions → *Daily Experience* → ◯ → ◯

A DAY IN THE LIFE

September 27

Dan and Marc were at Todd's, and Dan noticed a new fish tank in Todd's room. "Hey, Todd, when did you get this?"

"Last week," explained Todd. "I finally made enough money at the restaurant to be able to buy a fish tank and some fish. I've wanted fish since I was little."

"Cool! What do you have to do to take care of them?" Marc asked.

"You know, feed them, monitor the water temperature, generally watch over the fish and make sure they're doing okay. Like last week, I noticed that they seemed to be acting a little sluggish. They were eating less than usual, so I figured it was because they didn't like the food I was feeding them. I switched to a different kind of fish food."

"Did it help?"

"It seemed to, although it took a couple of days."

"What kind of fish are in here?" Dan asked.

"Some tetras and a Siamese fighting fish. I wanted to get more than one of the fighting fish, but the salesperson at the pet store said that probably wasn't a good idea."

"Why? What would they do to each other?" Dan wanted to know.

"I'm not sure. Attack each other, I think," Todd speculated.

"Too bad the fish can't tell us!" Dan joked.

Marc was quiet as he watched the fish swim around. "Do you have a mirror?" he asked suddenly.

Todd got a small hand mirror, wondering what Marc was up to. Then Marc held up the mirror so the fighting fish could see its reflection. The fish fanned out its fins menacingly, puffed up its cheeks, and started to dart toward its reflection. Marc moved the mirror away.

"I bet that was its attack reaction! It didn't realize that the other fish was only a reflection of itself," Todd exclaimed excitedly. "It thought it was a rival fish, and it prepared itself to fight!"

"I guess fighting fish really do fight each other," concluded Dan.

"Or maybe Todd just has a weird fish," teased Marc.

. . .

Todd, Marc, and Dan were having fun. They did not realize that they were actually conducting scientific research. By creating the right conditions, Todd and his friends were able to observe the fish and how it reacted to changes in the environment. Similarly, psychologists sometimes bring animals or people into laboratory environments where they can observe them under carefully controlled conditions. At other times, psychologists study the behavior of organisms in the field—that is, where the organisms live naturally. In addition, psychologists sometimes get information by conducting experiments, much as the boys did with the fighting fish. There are many different approaches to research. This chapter explores several of them.

Key Terms

- construct
- hypothesis
- replicated
- survey
- target population
- sample
- random sample
- stratified sample
- bias
- volunteer bias
- case study
- longitudinal method
- cross-sectional method
- naturalistic observation
- laboratory observation
- correlation
- positive correlation
- negative correlation
- experiment
- variables
- independent variable
- dependent variable
- experimental group
- control group
- controlled experiment
- placebo
- single-blind study
- double-blind study
- standard deviation
- ethics
- informed consent

▶ WHY PSYCHOLOGY MATTERS

Psychologists use a variety of research methods to learn about human behavior. Use **CNNfyi.com** or other current events sources to learn more about how psychologists study human behavior.

CNNfyi.com

Using Key Terms

Ask students to prepare a crossword puzzle using at least 20 of the key terms and their definitions. Definitions can be found in Chapter 2 or in the Glossary at the back of the textbook. Then have students exchange papers and complete the crossword puzzles. Students may wish to keep their puzzles for later review.

Class Discussion

Ask volunteers to read aloud the "A Day in the Life" vignette on page 25. Have students speculate on how this vignette relates to psychological research methods. Then have students discuss instances in their own lives when they have used informal experiments to test an idea.

Section Objective

▶ List and explain the steps scientists follow in conducting scientific research.

This objective is assessed in the Section Review on page 29 and in the Chapter 2 Review.

Opening Section 1

Motivator

Have students provide examples of experiments they have conducted in a natural science course such as biology, physics, or chemistry. Ask them to describe the steps involved in conducting the experiments. Guide them, if necessary, to describe the five steps of the scientific method. Write these steps on the chalkboard. Tell students that social scientists as well as natural scientists use the scientific method when conducting research. Then have students read Section 1 to learn how psychologists use the scientific method to guide their research.

Using Truth or Fiction

Each chapter opens with several "Truth or Fiction" statements that relate to the concepts discussed in the chapter. Ask students whether they think each statement is true or false. Answers to each item as well as explanations are provided at appropriate points within the text under the heading "Truth or Fiction Revisited."

Cross-Curricular Link: Language Arts

Point out that the way a research question is framed influences the way it is understood and ultimately answered. Have students frame basic research questions and then exchange them with classmates. How many verbal ambiguities can students find in the questions? Challenge them to clarify the questions by using more precise vocabulary and clearer sentence structure.

Class Discussion

Have students recite some proverbs and discuss whether there is evidence to support them. Then have students brainstorm contradictory pairs of sayings. ("Absence makes the heart grow fonder." "Out of sight, out of mind.") What do such contradictory sayings suggest about folk wisdom in general?

26

TRUTH OR fiction?

Read the following statements about psychology. Do you think they are true or false? You will learn whether each statement is true or false as you read the chapter.

- Psychologists never guess about the answers to the questions they ask.
- You have to do a study more than once to be sure its results are valid.
- Asking the students in your psychology class for their opinions on a topic is a good way to figure out how people in the larger community feel about that topic.
- Some psychological studies take years or even decades to complete.
- Taking a pill that does not contain any medicine might have the same effects as taking one that does.
- Psychologists sometimes have to deceive participants in a study.

SECTION 1

Conducting Research

Psychology, like chemistry and biology, is an experimental science. In an experimental science, assumptions (such as about the behavior of chemical compounds, cells, or people) must be supported by evidence. It is not enough to argue that something is true just because someone says it is. Psychologists and other scientists make it their business to be skeptical of claims that lack actual scientific evidence.

Psychologists use a variety of research methods to study behavior and mental processes. These methods differ in a number of ways, but psychologists tend to follow the same general procedure when conducting their research. This procedure consists of five steps: forming a research question, forming a hypothesis, testing the hypothesis, analyzing the results, and drawing conclusions.

Forming a Research Question

Psychologists begin a study by forming a research question. Many research questions arise from daily experience. For example, Todd, Marc, and Dan were wondering about the aggressiveness of Siamese fighting fish. But aggressiveness, like anxiety, is a

psychological **construct**. It can be assumed that it is present, but it cannot be seen or measured directly. Therefore, research questions are best directed toward behavior. This is why Todd, Marc, and Dan asked: What do fighting fish do to each other when they are placed together?

Other research questions arise out of psychological theory. According to social-learning theorists, for example, people learn by observing others. Thus, these theorists might ask, what effects (if any) does watching television violence have on viewers?

Research questions also arise from folklore and common knowledge. For example, questions might arise from such well-known—and often-repeated—statements as "Two heads are better than one," "Opposites attract," and "Beauty is in the eye of the beholder." Psychologists ask, is it true that pairs or groups of people solve problems more effectively than people working alone? Are people with opposite personality traits really attracted to each other? Is beauty a matter of individual preference, or are there common standards for beauty?

Forming a Hypothesis

After psychologists ask a research question, they form a hypothesis about the answer. A **hypothesis** is an educated guess. The accuracy of a hypothesis can be tested by research.

Psychologists may word a hypothesis in the form of an if-then statement. If-then reasoning is an example of social scientific reasoning. Todd engaged in if-then reasoning. *If* Siamese fighting fish are aggressive, he reasoned, *then* they will attack one another. Todd did not realize that he was engaging in social scientific reasoning, but he was. Todd was also making an educated guess. His guess was based on the fact that the fish were called "fighting fish." It was also based on the pet shop salesperson's advice not to put more than one fighting fish in the same tank. Because it is only an educated guess, a hypothesis must be tested.

TRUTH OR fiction
■ REVISITED ■

It is not true that psychologists never guess about the answers to the questions they ask. After psychologists ask a research question, they form a hypothesis, or educated guess, about the answer. Once they have formed their hypotheses, they test them.

Teaching Section 1

Cooperative Learning

Organize the class into small groups. Tell the members of each group to reread the "A Day in the Life" vignette on page 25. Have the students sketch scenes based on the vignette that follow the progression of the story and that illustrate the five steps of scientific research. Each group should then mount the sketches on cardboard to create a film-industry type of storyboard. Have representatives from each group present their storyboards to the class and explain how the storyboards illustrate the steps involved in scientific research.

Meeting Individual Needs: Learners Having Difficulty

To help students master the steps of scientific research, have them trace with their fingers the five steps shown on the flowchart on page 27. Tell students to alternately trace the steps and then state the steps aloud without looking at the chart until they have memorized the entire sequence.

Testing the Hypothesis

Because psychology is a science, psychological knowledge rests on carefully examined human experience. No matter how good a hypothesis sounds and no matter how many people believe it, a hypothesis cannot be considered to be correct until it has been scientifically tested and proved to be right. Psychologists do not rely on people's opinions. Instead, they examine the evidence and draw their own conclusions.

Psychologists answer research questions or test hypotheses through a variety of methods. To test the hypothesis that two fighting fish would attack each other, the best method would probably be to put two real fish in the same tank. But Todd did not have another fighting fish, so this was not possible. Marc suggested using a mirror to create the illusion of another fighting fish. He hoped that Todd's fish would react to its reflection in the same way it would react to a real fish. In that way he, Todd, and Dan would be able to find out whether it is true that fighting fish do attack each other. Thus, holding a mirror in front of the fish was the method Marc chose to test the boys' hypothesis.

Analyzing the Results

After psychologists have tested their hypotheses, they analyze their results. In other words, they ask what their findings mean. After Todd, Marc, and Dan saw the fighting fish fan out its fins and puff up its cheeks apparently in reaction to seeing the image of another fish, they had to figure out how to interpret that reaction. Todd interpreted the fish's actions as going into attack position.

In most psychological studies, psychologists collect a great deal more information, or data, than Marc, Dan, and Todd did with the fish. For example, psychologists would test their hypothesis on more than one fish. They might spend weeks, months, or even years gathering data. The more information collected, the more complex a task it is to analyze it. Often, psychologists look for patterns and relationships in the data. They must decide which data support their hypothesis and which data do not.

Drawing Conclusions

Once psychologists have analyzed their research observations, they draw conclusions about their

The Steps of Scientific Research

Daily experience | Psychological theory | Folklore and common knowledge

1 FORM A QUESTION

2 FORM A HYPOTHESIS

3 TEST THE HYPOTHESIS

Decide what information is needed to test hypothesis

Gather information

Examine information

No

? Is information sufficient to test hypothesis?

Yes

4 ANALYZE RESULTS OF TEST

5 DRAW A CONCLUSION

No

? Was hypothesis correct?

Yes

Replication

FIGURE 2.1 *For research to be valid, proper scientific procedures must be used. These are the steps that researchers generally follow.*

For Your Information

When psychologists have completed a research study, they usually report their findings in psychological journals. In this way, psychologists not only disseminate information but also give other professionals the opportunity to critique their work. Sometimes a reader will spot flawed research methods or faulty conclusions in a research report and then challenge the findings of the study in a future issue of the journal. A critical review process is essential to the scientific method.

Journal Activity

Tell students to write about examples of faulty reasoning, whether in the history of science, in common superstition, or from their own experience. Their essays should identify both the evidence and the reasoning process that led to the incorrect conclusion.

Teaching Transparencies with Teacher's Notes

TRANSPARENCY 2: The Steps of Scientific Research

Closing Section 1

Follow Up

Ask students to make a chart based on the storyboards created for the Cooperative Learning activity on page 27. Have them list the steps of scientific research, describe the elements that illustrate each step, and analyze the boys' actions in terms of scientific research.

Reviewing Section 1

Have students complete the Section Review questions on page 29.

Extension

Remind students that when researchers replicate an experiment, they sometimes use participants who have characteristics that differ from the characteristics of the participants in the original study. Have students locate a study of human behavior in a special-interest psychology magazine or a general-interest periodical. Tell students to identify the characteristics of the participants. Then have students write a brief essay explaining how using participants who have different characteristics might affect the results.

Despite the claims of fortune-tellers, little if any scientific evidence supports the existence of precognition or other forms of ESP. Studies that seem to support ESP usually cannot be replicated.

questions and their hypotheses. These conclusions are useful in the development and validation of theories in psychology. When their observations do not support their hypotheses, they often must change the theories or beliefs from which the hypotheses were derived. Therefore, psychologists need to keep open minds. They must be willing to adjust or modify their hypotheses if their findings make it necessary to do so.

In the fish example, once the boys had seen how the fighting fish reacted to the image of another fish and had interpreted that reaction as an attack reaction, they concluded that, yes, fighting fish do fight each other. They were satisfied that Todd's hypothesis was correct. If the fighting fish had not had such a reaction, Todd, Marc, and Dan would not have been able to conclude that the hypothesis was correct. They would not necessarily have been able to prove that the hypothesis was *incorrect*, however. Maybe the fighting fish realized that it was only looking at a reflection and not at a real fish. Thus, the boys would have had to do more research.

Replication

Even when a study carefully follows proper procedures, its findings might just represent a random occurrence. As Marc put it, maybe Todd just had a weird fish; maybe other fighting fish would react differently. For the findings of a study to be confirmed, the study must be **replicated**. That is, the study must be repeated—and it must produce the same results as before.

When scientists replicate a study but obtain different results than were obtained the first time, the findings of the first study are questioned. This is one reason that most psychologists do not believe that extrasensory perception (ESP) is a valid scientific phenomenon, even though some isolated studies have supported the existence of ESP. These studies have not yielded the same results when replicated.

TRUTH OR fiction ▪ REVISITED ▪

It is true that you have to do a study more than once to be sure its results are valid. The repeating of an experiment is called replication. If a study does not produce the same results more than once, the results may not have been accurate.

Sometimes scientists repeat a study under slightly different circumstances than those in the original study. In the fish example, to confirm the hypothesis that fighting fish attack each other, it would probably be best to replicate the experiment by using two or more real fish rather than one fish and its reflection.

Sometimes researchers repeat a study using a different set of participants. Todd, Marc, and Dan could have tried the same experiment with a few other fighting fish. If these fish acted differently than Todd's did, this would indicate that Todd's fish was somehow unusual. The boys might even try the experiment with different *types* of fighting fish to see if all the fish have the same reaction. They might also try the experiment with both male and female fighting fish. In many animal species, males have different behavior patterns than females. Thus, it is important to study both males and females if the goal is to make generalizations about all members of the species.

In a study in which people are the participants, researchers might want to replicate the study using participants who differ not only in gender but also in such characteristics as age, ethnicity, social and economic background, level of education, and geographic setting. For example, if a study was done for the first time only with teenagers, the researchers might include participants from other age groups the next time. That way, the researchers could be sure that the findings were consistent among a variety of age groups.

Section Objective

▶ Explain the survey method and the importance of proper sampling techniques.

This objective is assessed in the Section Review on page 34 and in the Chapter 2 Review.

Motivator

Bring to class samples from magazines and newspapers that refer to the behaviors and opinions of large numbers of people. Try to present a mix of news articles, feature articles, and advertisements that report widespread trends on everything from voting patterns to consumer preferences in clothing. Have students examine these materials and speculate on how the writers might have obtained their information and what factors would influence how valid and reliable the writers' claims are.

New Questions

Whether the findings of a research study support or contradict the hypothesis of that study, they are likely to lead to new research questions. Once Todd, Marc, and Dan had performed their fish experiment, they might have asked any number of other questions. For example, *why* do fighting fish attack each other? Does it have to do with mating, with turf, or with something else entirely? Is it a reaction they have instinctively from birth, or do they learn it as they mature? Are there any circumstances under which fighting fish do *not* attack each other? Do any other animals have similar attack reactions? Do people ever act like that?

Even if Todd's fish had totally ignored its reflection, that too would have raised new questions. Would it also ignore a real fish? And if so, why is it called a fighting fish? Under what circumstances does it fight?

Once new questions have been asked, the process begins all over again. The researchers must propose a new hypothesis about the answer to the new question. And once again, the hypothesis must be tested.

The rest of this chapter explores the different types of research methods that psychologists use to test hypotheses. These methods include the survey method, various observational methods, and the experimental method. Each of these methods has advantages and disadvantages, and some methods are better suited to certain kinds of research studies than are other methods. It would be convenient if there were one perfect method that could be used in all circumstances. But human beings are complex, and the human experience has many dimensions. Thus, several different research methods are needed to study it.

SECTION 1 REVIEW

Homework Practice Online
Keyword: SY3 HP2

1. List and describe the five steps that scientists follow when conducting research.

2. Why is replication of a research study important?

3. **Critical Thinking** *Analyzing Information* Locate a newspaper or magazine article that discusses the findings of a recent research study. Summarize the study, and then list two new questions that might be asked based on the findings of the study.

SECTION **2**

Surveys, Samples, and Populations

When Todd, Marc, and Dan wanted to know what fighting fish would do to each other, it would have been convenient (as Dan pointed out) if they could have just asked the fish. But, of course, fish cannot talk. People, on the other hand, *can* talk. Thus, when psychologists want to find out about people's attitudes and behaviors, one possible way to gather information is to ask people directly.

The Survey Method

Gathering information by asking people directly is usually accomplished by means of a survey. In a **survey**, people are asked to respond to a series of questions about a particular subject.

Psychologists D. L. DuBois and B. J. Hirsch (1990), for example, used the survey method to examine mixed-race friendships among high school students. (See Figure 2.2.) The survey asked high school students to identify the races of their friends. More than 80 percent of white and African American students reported having a friend of the other race in school. However, far fewer students

Friendship Patterns Among High School Students

Students	White	African American
Have a friend of another race in school	87%	82%
Have a friend of another race outside of school	23%	42%

FIGURE 2.2 *Research indicates that although many students have friends of a different race, fewer students see those friends outside of school.*

Source: "School and Neighborhood Friendship Patterns of Blacks and Whites in Adolescence" by D. L. DuBois and B. J. Hirsch, 1990, *Child Development*, 61, pp. 524–536.

---

1. The five steps are forming a research question (posing a question based on experience, psychological theory, or common knowledge); forming a hypothesis (making an educated guess about the answer); testing the hypothesis (examining the evidence through any of a variety of means); analyzing the results (looking for patterns or relationships in the evidence); and drawing conclusions (determining whether the findings support the hypothesis and adjusting it if they do not).

2. If a replicated study does not result in the same findings as the original study, the original results may not have been accurate.

3. Students should be able to summarize the methods and findings of the study and then formulate two new research questions based on the findings.

Teaching Section 2

Guided Practice

Remind students that survey findings may not necessarily be completely accurate and that respondents in surveys are not always honest. Have students summarize the reasons given in the textbook to account for this fact. Then have students speculate on additional reasons why respondents in a survey might answer incorrectly or dishonestly. *(Possibilities might be that the respondents did not understand the questions, the respondents could not remember the correct answers, and the respondents enjoyed deliberately confusing the researcher.)*

Independent Practice

Have students locate and bring to class examples of surveys found in magazines, mailings, stores and offices, and government buildings. Distribute these materials among the students. Tell them to evaluate the survey questions and determine the attitudes or behaviors the survey is attempting to assess and the likely success of the questions in eliciting desired information. Have volunteers discuss their conclusions with the class.

Using Visuals

Point out that the comic strip on page 30 makes fun of the use of surveys by market researchers trying to learn about consumer preferences. Manufacturers apply this information when making decisions about developing, advertising, and selling new products. Ask students what the comic strip suggests about such surveys. *(They may elicit false information.)* Then have students brainstorm reasons why a magazine survey might not produce reliable results. *(Students may say that some of the people completing the survey might not take it seriously.)*

Class Discussion

Point out that one problem with survey results is that a person's beliefs often conflict with that person's behavior. When asked how much television he or she watches per week, an individual might answer, "Under 10 hours," honestly believing this to be true when in fact a study of the person's behavior would show a different reality. Have students discuss other behaviors that might differ from beliefs in similar ways.

Calvin and Hobbes — by Bill Watterson

reported seeing these friends outside of school. DuBois and Hirsch concluded that the reason may be that even though many of the respondents attended integrated schools, the neighborhoods they lived in may have been segregated.

Psychologists conduct surveys by asking people to fill out written questionnaires or by interviewing people orally. By distributing questionnaires or by conducting interviews over the telephone or in person,

Researchers who conduct studies in densely populated areas have a large pool of possible participants from which to draw.

researchers can rapidly survey thousands of people. Computers often aid in the analysis of the information collected.

The findings of interviews and questionnaires are not necessarily completely accurate. People may not be honest, for whatever reasons, about their attitudes or behavior. Some people may fear that their responses will not be kept confidential. Thus, they answer only what they are willing to reveal to the world at large. Other respondents may try to please the interviewers by saying what they think the interviewers want to hear.

The significant risk of obtaining inaccurate data through interviews and questionnaires became clear from the results of a 1960s survey about toothbrushing habits. If people had brushed their teeth as often as they claimed, and used the amount of toothpaste they said they used, three times as much toothpaste would have been sold in the United States as was actually sold at that time (Barringer, 1993). The survey respondents might not have wanted the interviewers to know that they did not brush their teeth as often as their dentists advised.

Populations and Samples

When researchers conduct any type of study, they must consider what group or groups of people they wish to examine and how respondents will be selected. This is particularly true with surveys.

Imagine that your town or city is about to hold a referendum on whether to institute a 10:00 P.M. curfew for people under the age of 18. How might you most accurately predict the outcome of the referendum? You might conduct a poll by asking people how they are planning to vote. But whom would you select to be in the poll?

30

Suppose you only polled the students in your psychology class. Do you think you would be able to make an accurate prediction? Probably not. Many of the people in your psychology class are probably under the age of 18 and thus might be particularly likely to oppose the curfew because they believe it would restrict their freedom. However, these students are too young to vote. The voters in the actual referendum would all be at least 18. Since the curfew would not restrict them, they might be more inclined to vote for it. Thus, a poll of your psychology class would probably not be very useful for predicting the outcome of this particular referendum.

To accurately predict an outcome, it is necessary to study a group that represents the target population. A **target population** is the whole group you want to study or describe. In the curfew example, the target population consists of all possible voters on the referendum. It does not consist of nonvoters. The question is not whom the referendum will affect if passed, but whether the referendum will be passed or not. Thus, only voters are relevant to the survey.

It would be costly and difficult—if not impossible—to interview or question every member of a target population (in this case, all voters in the area). Instead, researchers study a **sample**, which is only part of the target population.

Selecting Samples

Psychologists and other scientists select samples scientifically to ensure that the samples accurately represent the populations they are supposed to represent. In other words, a sample should be as similar as possible to the target population. Otherwise, researchers will be unable to use the sample to make accurate predictions about the population from which the sample is drawn.

A high school class does not represent all the people in the town or city where a school is located, particularly in terms of opinions on an issue that pertains to age (such as a curfew for people under 18). Thus, the answers of people in a high school class might be biased (and, of course, most high school students are not old enough to vote). In this case, they would probably be biased against the curfew. On the other hand, researchers probably could predict the outcome of the referendum by interviewing as a sample a large number of people who represent all voters in the town or city.

One way that scientists obtain a sample that they hope represents the target population is by using a random sample. In a **random sample**, individuals are selected by chance from the target population. Each member of the population has an equal chance of being chosen. If the random sample is big enough, chances are that it will accurately represent the whole population.

Researchers can also use a stratified sample. In a **stratified sample**, subgroups in the population are represented proportionally in the sample. For instance, about 12 percent of the American population is African American. A stratified sample of the American population would thus be about 12 percent African American. (See Figure 2.3.)

A large random sample is likely to be accurately stratified even if researchers take no special steps to ensure that it is. A random sample of 1,000 to 1,500 people will usually represent the general American population reasonably well. A sample of 5 million motorcycle owners, however, would not. A large sample size by itself does not necessarily guarantee that a sample represents a target population, particularly if the sample is not a random sample. Motorcycle owners probably do not represent all people in the United States.

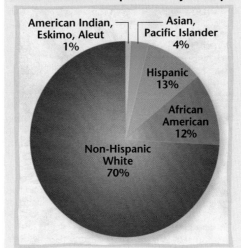

United States Population by Group

American Indian, Eskimo, Aleut — 1%
Asian, Pacific Islander — 4%
Hispanic — 13%
African American — 12%
Non-Hispanic White — 70%

FIGURE 2.3 *In a stratified sample of the U.S. population, various groups should be represented in the same proportions as they are present in the whole population.* **Based on this chart, in a stratified sample consisting of 100 people, how many African Americans would you expect to find in the sample?**

Source: U.S. Census. Figures have been rounded.

EXPLORING

DIVERSITY

Have students speculate on how the increased diversity among sample groups might affect the future of psychological research. How might this add to the body of knowledge concerning human behavior? Then have students analyze how generalizing findings from one specific group of people to all groups might have potential dangers. *(In the health field, for example, symptoms of heart disease in men may not be generalizable to women.)*

For Further Research

Ask students to find reports of psychological studies or surveys in periodicals and books. Have the students summarize the research studies for the class, including information about the demographic characteristics of the participants. Have the class discuss the diversity or lack thereof of the participants and how including a more diverse sample might have affected the findings. Have students also note whether the authors of the studies imposed any limitations on their conclusions because of a lack of diversity.

Think About It: Answer

Students may suggest increasing the number of mothers participating in studies by providing them with child care or increasing the diversity of participants by recruiting in nontraditional environments.

Journal Activity

Tell students to imagine that they have been invited by the American Psychological Association to present a speech to the APA members titled "The Importance of Using Diverse Samples in Psychological Research." Have students write a draft of the speech they would give.

EXPLORING

DIVERSITY

Representing Human Diversity in Research

Most psychologists today appreciate the need to allow for the wide diversity of members of society in their research. This has not always been the case. For example, throughout the history of psychology, men have been included as research participants more often than women. A key reason for this stems from the pool of available research subjects. Many research participants have traditionally been drawn from the armed services and universities. The majority of people in the armed services are male. And only in recent years has the number of women in colleges and universities grown equal to (and exceeded) that of men.

Many research studies draw their participants from college campuses, which have grown increasingly diverse in recent years.

The relatively small research pools led psychologists to mistakenly generalize their findings beyond men. Researchers tended to conclude that what was true for white men was true for all of society. When this sort of overgeneralization occurred, important distinctions between groups tended to be ignored.

Health, for example, has been an area where cultural, ethnic, and gender differences have not always been taken into account. Some surprising results have been obtained as studies have broadened their scope beyond white men. For example, researchers have discovered significant differences between how men and women are affected by heart disease. Although women receive less treatment for heart disease than men, they are at greater risk of dying from the condition. Researchers are studying whether this increased risk exists because of differences in the types of treatment women receive from health-care providers.

Ethnic differences in research results have also arisen as the pool of study participants has broadened. Researchers have learned that African Americans of both genders are more likely to suffer from heart disease than members of the white population. This higher risk arises, in part, from correspondingly higher rates of hypertension and diabetes in the African American population.

Domestic violence is another area of study that has benefited from studies with more diversified groups of participants. Much research has been performed on the prevalence of violence against women. But more recent research has revealed that men, too, are victims of domestic violence. Psychologists have also studied the repercussions that domestic violence has beyond the victim of the physical assault. Children in particular suffer emotionally in a household where violence occurs.

Recent research has also focused on issues significant to members of the older population. Studies have shed light on a variety of topics of concern to the elderly, such as the way older people cope with the changes in their health and in social relationships.

The American Psychological Association (1994b) recommends that the write-up of a study's results include a clear description of the research sample in terms of ethnicity, gender, and any other potentially relevant characteristics. For example, if a sample uses only male participants, the report should include this information. When such descriptions are included, the reader is less likely to assume that a study's findings apply equally to all groups.

THINK ABOUT IT

Analyzing Information What might be some ways to increase the number of participants from traditionally underrepresented groups in psychological studies?

Closing Section 2

Role-Playing

Challenge students to role-play the part of a researcher who is overgeneralizing on the basis of limited observations. Encourage students to ask some of their classmates real questions or to observe actual behaviors and then overgeneralize their findings. For example, a student might ask five female friends if they play sports and report that since each one does, the majority of female high school students play sports. Then have the rest of the class identify the flaws in reasoning that led to each incorrect generalization.

Applying Ideas

Have students work in groups to write a sample survey about lunchroom preferences, administer the survey, and report the results. Tell the groups to evaluate the weaknesses of their surveys in their final analyses, paying special attention to possible volunteer bias.

Reviewing Section 2

Have students complete the Section Review questions on page 34.

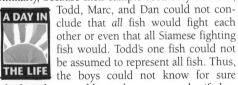

It is not true that asking the students in your psychology class for their opinions on a topic is a good way to figure out how people in the larger community feel about that topic. To find out how community members feel about a topic, you would need to select a sample that represents the community. Your psychology class probably does not.

Generalizing Results

Sometimes, for one reason or another, researchers do not use a sample that represents an entire population. In some cases, the researchers want to know about only one group within the population and thus have no reason to study other groups. In other cases, it may be impractical or impossible to obtain a random or stratified sample.

In such cases, researchers are cautious about generalizing their findings to groups other than those from which their samples were drawn. Similarly, because their sample used only one fish, Todd, Marc, and Dan could not conclude that *all* fish would fight each other or even that all Siamese fighting fish would. Todd's one fish could not be assumed to represent all fish. Thus, the boys could not know for sure whether they would get the same results if they used other types of fish.

The same is true with people. Researchers cannot learn about the preferences of all people by studying only one group of people, such as men. In a study about car preferences, for example, psychologists would avoid generalizing from a sample that was made up only of men because men's preferences for cars might not be the same as women's. In other words, if researchers found that men prefer certain types of cars, the researchers could not conclude that women prefer those same types of cars if the study did not include women.

The gender of the individuals in the sample is not the only characteristic that researchers must take into account. For instance, researchers cannot learn about the attitudes of Americans in general if they limit their observations to people who live in one part of the country (for example, the Midwest) or to people from one socioeconomic background (for example, wealthy people).

Men and women might tend to prefer different types of cars, so a study of people's car preferences would need to have both male and female participants.

Volunteer Bias

Researchers often have little control over who responds to surveys or participates in research studies. Although the researchers may choose to whom they give a questionnaire, they usually cannot force people to complete the questionnaire. Another factor that psychologists must take into account is **bias**, or a predisposition to a certain point of view. People who volunteer to participate in studies often bring with them a **volunteer bias**—that is, they often have a different outlook from people who do not volunteer for research studies.

For one thing, volunteers are usually more willing than other people to disclose personal information. Volunteers may also be more interested in research than people who do not volunteer. Furthermore, they may have more spare time to participate in research studies than other people. Depending on what the study is about, any or all of these factors—as well as others—could skew the results. That is, these factors could slant the results in a particular direction.

Have you ever filled out and returned a questionnaire printed in a magazine? Popular magazines such as *Glamour, Seventeen*, and *Psychology Today* often survey readers' attitudes about various topics

Some studies, such as surveys administered by the Gallup Organization or the National Opinion Research Center, use nationwide samples of several thousand respondents. Other studies, such as those that focus on the brain-wave patterns of people with schizophrenia, may sample only a handful of people. This difference occurs because the type of study being conducted influences the size of the sample needed. To obtain a cross section of American attitudes, it is necessary to survey many diverse individuals. To study a brain pattern associated with a disorder, only individuals with that disorder are needed.

Technology Resources

CNN. Presents Psychology: Twin Studies

Section Objective

▶ Compare and contrast various methods of observation, and discuss the use of correlation in analyzing results.

This objective is assessed in the Section Review on page 40 and in the Chapter 2 Review.

Opening Section 3

Motivator

Organize the class into groups. Tell the groups that you are giving them each a separate task to perform. Then give each group a slip of paper that reads: "Your task is to quietly observe the other groups and record any behaviors that you see." Allow the groups to observe each other for five minutes. Then have a member from each group read aloud the group's instructions and the recorded behaviors. Tell students that everyone observes behavior and makes generalizations. To draw scientific conclusions, however, psychologists follow carefully structured methods of observation.

Journal Activity

Have students write a paragraph explaining why the observations made by the groups during the Motivator activity on page 34 were unscientific.

The Survey Method

Research Method	Description	Advantages	Disadvantages
Survey Method	People respond to a series of questions about a particular subject.	It enables the researcher to gather information about large numbers of people.	People may not be entirely honest in answering questions. Survey samples are not always representative of the target population.

FIGURE 2.4 *One way to learn about people's behaviors and attitudes is simply to ask them. Psychologists often do just that by conducting surveys. Surveys, however, have some disadvantages.*

and behaviors in certain circumstances. Such a questionnaire might, for instance, ask readers how they like to spend their leisure time. Do they prefer to go to the movies, visit with friends, read magazines, or listen to music?

Thousands of readers complete these types of questionnaires and send them in. However, do the respondents represent the general population of the United States? Probably not. In a magazine survey, a disproportionate number of responses to the question posed above would probably be "read magazines." After all, the questionnaire itself comes from a magazine. People who do not like to read magazines probably would not fill out the questionnaire. They would not have seen it in the first place. Such magazine surveys are affected by volunteer bias. For example, readers who have enough time to fill out the questionnaire may tend to have different leisure preferences than people who are too busy to fill out the questionnaire. This volunteer bias might affect the findings.

SECTION 2 REVIEW

Homework Practice Online

Keyword: SY3 HP2

1. What are two different ways by which surveys are conducted?

2. Explain the importance of random and stratified sampling.

3. **Critical Thinking** *Contrasting* Give an example of a survey that might produce different results depending on whether participants volunteered or were selected randomly. How might the results differ, and what would account for the difference?

Methods of Observation

Almost everyone, at one time or another, observes other people. We observe people as they talk, eat, work, play, and interact with others and with us. Based on our observations of other people (and also of ourselves), we tend to make generalizations about human behavior and human nature.

Our observations and generalizations usually serve us fairly well in our daily lives. But no matter how many experiences we have had, most of our personal observations are fleeting and haphazard. We sift through experience for things that interest us, but we often ignore the obvious because it does not fit our ideas about how things ought to be. Thus, we cannot draw scientific conclusions based only on our own unstructured observations.

Even the most respected psychologists may use their personal observations as a starting point for their research and as the basis for their hypotheses. Once they have begun their investigations, however, psychologists use more careful methods of observation. The survey method, discussed above, is one such method of observation. Other methods of observation include the testing, case-study, longitudinal, cross-sectional, naturalistic-observation, and laboratory-observation methods.

The Testing Method

Psychologists sometimes use psychological tests to learn about human behavior. There are several

Teaching Section 3

Meeting Individual Needs: Gifted Learners

Suggest that gifted students conduct further research into the case of Genie. Tell the students to analyze the ways in which various scientists studied and evaluated Genie's case and the information about human development and language development gleaned from Genie's particular case. Ask the students to summarize their findings and share them with the class. Have the class use the findings to evaluate the case-study method as a method of scientific observation.

Demonstration

To demonstrate that people's recollections of events may have gaps and inaccuracies, invite four or five students to improvise a skit along the lines of this chapter's "A Day in the Life" vignette. (You might bring in some simple props and costumes for them to use.) Immediately afterward, and without the class's knowledge, take careful notes on exactly what transpired. One week later, ask students to write a reconstruction of the skit. Then compare the students' reconstructions to your notes. Discuss the various gaps and inaccuracies you uncovered.

types of psychological tests. Intelligence tests measure general learning ability. Aptitude tests measure specific abilities and special talents, such as musical ability and mechanical skills. Still other tests measure vocational interests.

Personality tests are another type of psychological test psychologists use. Personality tests measure people's character traits and temperament. For example, personality tests might be used to assess whether people are socially outgoing or aggressive. Personality tests might also be used to diagnose psychological problems such as anxiety and depression. (See Chapter 15.)

The Case-Study Method

Another research method psychologists use is the case-study method. A **case study** is an in-depth investigation of an individual or a small group. To learn about the people who are being studied, researchers may observe or speak with them, interview others who know them, and find out more about their backgrounds and personal histories. Psychologists use what they learn in a case study to generalize broader principles that apply to the larger population.

Sigmund Freud developed psychoanalytic theory largely on the basis of case studies. Freud carefully studied the people who sought his help. He interviewed some of them for many years, developing as complete a record of their childhoods as he could. He also looked for the factors that seemed to contribute to their current problems.

Some case studies focus on rare circumstances or events. One such case study involved a girl named Genie. When she was only 20 months old, her father locked her in a small room. She was kept there until she was rescued at the age of 13 (Rymer, 1993). Her social contacts were limited to her mother, who fed her, and her father, who often beat her. No one spoke to her. And in all those years, she herself did not say a word.

After her rescue, Genie's language development followed the normal sequence of language development. (See Chapter 8.) Genie never learned to use language as well as most people, however. This case study suggests that there is a special period in early childhood when it is easiest for people to learn language.

Although case studies sometimes offer great insights, psychologists are cautious about generalizing from case studies. This is particularly true of case studies that cannot be replicated, such as

Some aptitude tests measure the test taker's physical or perceptual abilities.

Genie's. Because of the rarity and cruelty of Genie's experience, scientists would never repeat this study. Thus they cannot know for sure, on the basis of Genie's experience alone, whether the theory about a special language-learning period in childhood is correct. Perhaps other unknown factors were responsible for Genie's apparent inability to achieve full language competence.

Furthermore, case studies lend themselves to some of the same pitfalls that surveys do, particularly when the case studies are based on interviews with people about their past experiences. Most people's recollections are filled with gaps and inaccuracies. Some of these inaccuracies occur because people tend not to remember the details of events. Some people even intentionally distort their pasts to impress the researcher. And sometimes without meaning to, researchers subtly encourage people to answer in certain ways to fulfill the researchers' expectations. For example, some psychoanalysts have been criticized for encouraging people to interpret their behavior according to Freud's psychoanalytic theory (Bandura, 1986).

Class Discussion

Have students compare the advantages of using a standardized test to study an individual with the advantages of using a case study. *(A possible answer might be that a standardized test is simpler and probably less expensive to administer; it has a clear focus and an existing means for interpreting results. A case study, on the other hand, is a more open-ended, more flexible, and more in-depth method.)*

For Your Information

Another unusual case that provided information about "normal" psychology was the case of a man known as H.M. As the result of surgery, H.M. had a lesion in the part of his brain known as the hippocampus, which is involved in memory processing. H.M. could receive new information and hold it in his memory for a short while, but he could not add any new memories to his long-term memory storage. H.M.'s unusual symptoms supported the scientific theory that short-term memory and long-term memory are two separate stages in memory processing.

Guided Practice

Write *Longitudinal Method* and *Cross-Sectional Method* on the chalkboard. Under each method, write *Strengths* and *Weaknesses*. Have students suggest entries for each column, and write these entries on the chalkboard. Then have students brainstorm a list of research questions that could be answered using either of these methods. Guide students to understand that the longitudinal method and the cross-sectional method are ideally suited to research questions that focus on human development over the life span.

Independent Practice

Tell students to choose one of the research questions suggested in the Guided Practice activity and design a simple psychological study to answer that question. Make sure students form a research hypothesis to guide their study, and tell them to specify both a longitudinal and a cross-sectional method for obtaining data. Challenge students to develop research designs that minimize the weaknesses of both methods. Have volunteers present their research designs to the class for discussion.

For Your Information

In the 1950s, American Telephone & Telegraph (AT&T) was hiring thousands of college graduates every year. The company hired a psychologist named Douglas W. Bray to predict which new employees would make effective managers. Bray designed a longitudinal study to identify potential managers. Eight years later, and again 20 years later, Bray examined the actual job performances of the people he had assessed. Sure enough, a significant number of those who had scored high had been promoted to top management positions.

Bray, D. W. (1982). The assessment center and the study of lives. *American Psychologist, 37.* 180–189.

Longitudinal and Cross-Sectional Methods

Just as Freud studied some of his patients over a matter of years, so too do some psychological studies observe participants over a long period of time. Some research topics, such as those concerned with development throughout the life span, deal with how people or other organisms change over time.

To study such topics, psychologists often use the **longitudinal method**. In this method, researchers select a group of participants and then observe those participants over a period of time, often years or even decades. By using this method, psychologists can observe the ways in which individuals change over time.

Usually the observations are conducted at intervals, perhaps once a year. For example, if psychologists wanted to find out more about how people learn language, they might select a group of six-month-olds who are not yet using language. Then once a month, the researchers might observe the children to find out how their language skills are changing over time. By the time the children are three or four years old, they are no longer learning language at such a rapid pace. The psychologists might then observe them only once or twice a year.

TRUTH OR fiction ■ R E V I S I T E D ■ *It is true that some psychological studies take years or even decades to complete. These studies may be longitudinal studies, which examine the ways in which individuals change by observing them over a long period of time.*

Needless to say, longitudinal studies are extremely time-consuming. Imagine how much patience you would need knowing that even if you started a study right now, you would not get conclusive results for another 5, 10, or 15 years. Moreover, longitudinal studies tend to be expensive, and they are risky. There is often no guarantee that participants will remain available over the long time period that they are to be studied.

To avoid some of the problems with longitudinal studies, psychologists may use the cross-sectional method to find out about changes over time. In the **cross-sectional method**, instead of following a set of individuals over a number of years, researchers select a sample that includes people of different ages. The researchers then compare the behavior of the participants in the different age groups. For example, in a language-learning study, psychologists might select 12-month-olds, 14-month-olds, and 16-month-olds. They would then observe the language skills of members of each age group and compare the groups with one another in order to make generalizations about how children learn language over time.

Information gained in cross-sectional studies is less reliable than information from longitudinal studies. When psychologists study one individual over a period of time, as in a longitudinal study, they know that any changes they observe in that individual are due to her or his experiences or development. But when they compare groups of people of different ages at the same time, as in a cross-sectional study, psychologists cannot be certain what factors are responsible for differences among the participants. Perhaps the differences are due to developmental changes, but perhaps the participants were simply different from the beginning.

The Naturalistic-Observation Method

One way that psychologists sometimes find out about children's language skills is to observe children as they use language naturally, such as while they interact with other children and adults in play groups. This is called **naturalistic observation**, or field study. People often use naturalistic observation in their daily lives without even knowing it. That is, they observe other people or animals in the "field"—in their natural habitats. In the case of people, field settings include homes, schools, office buildings, restaurants—any place where people spend time.

 A DAY IN THE LIFE If Todd had wanted to use naturalistic observation to observe fish, he would have had to go to a river, a lake, or an ocean—someplace where fish exist naturally. But without realizing it, Todd used naturalistic observation all the time to watch people. In his job at the restaurant, Todd could not avoid noticing the different ways that customers ate their food. Some people gobbled down their meals quickly, almost without pausing. Others ate delicately, carefully chewing each bite. He wondered what accounted for these differences in people's eating habits.

Psychologists also wonder about such questions. They have, like Todd, used naturalistic observation to study how people eat. They have watched people in restaurants to learn, for example, whether slender people and heavy people eat their food differently. Such field research has shown that heavy people tend to eat somewhat more rapidly than slender people. Heavy people also chew less often and leave less food on their plates.

This type of study has led to suggestions about how heavy people might diet more effectively. For example, they might eat more slowly and take less food to begin with so that when they clean their plates, they have eaten less. (See Chapter 13.)

This researcher is using naturalistic observation to study a meerkat, a small mammal native to Africa.

In naturalistic observation, psychologists try not to interfere with the organisms they are observing. In the restaurant example, psychologists would not ask the diners questions or encourage them to eat a particular food. They would simply observe the people eating.

The Laboratory-Observation Method

Some matters simply cannot be studied in a naturalistic setting. For example, Todd could not realistically have observed his tropical fish in their natural habitat.

Sometimes it is more useful for a psychologist to observe behavior in a laboratory rather than in the field. This method is called **laboratory observation**. Laboratories are not necessarily sterile rooms tended by people in white coats; a laboratory is any place that provides the opportunity for observation or experimentation. As such, many laboratories are quite informal.

In fact, Todd's fish tank was a type of laboratory, a small artificial lake. To make the environment suitable for the fish, Todd had to do many things, such as monitor the temperature and acid content of the water. Once he had set up his laboratory, he was able to observe the behavior of the fish. He watched the fish dart under the protecting leaves. He saw how they created and defended their turf.

He observed their mating behavior and watched them breed. Sometimes their behavior amazed him—such as when they immediately swam to the surface of the water when he turned on the light. In just a few days after Todd had brought the fish home, they had learned that they would be fed when the light went on.

Like Todd, psychologists often study animals by using the laboratory-observation method. B. F. Skinner created special enclosed environments, which became known as Skinner boxes, to study the behavior of animals such as rats. In one of these miniature laboratories, a food pellet drops into the box when the rat in the box presses a lever. Rats learn quickly to press the levers, especially when they are hungry. Other psychologists have built mazes to see how effectively rats learn routes through the mazes. (See Chapter 6.) Both the Skinner box and the maze are examples of laboratories.

Psychologists sometimes use a laboratory to control the environment of a study. For example, if they wanted to see whether the amount of light in a room affects how much people eat, they would need to be able to control the lighting in the room where people were eating. Similarly, Todd's fish tank was a place where he could observe the behavior of the fish while he controlled what happened in the environment. He could, for instance, observe how the fish responded if he changed the temperature of the water or the type of food he fed them.

Synthesizing Information

Review with students the seven main theoretical perspectives in psychology presented in Chapter 1 and the six methods of observation charted on page 38. Then write the following headings on the chalkboard: *Biological/Case Study; Cognitive/Cross-Sectional; Humanistic/Naturalistic Observation; Psychoanalytic/Longitudinal; Learning/Laboratory; Sociocultural/Testing*. Ask students to give examples of research topics that might be appropriate for each combination. Have students provide a rationale for their choices.

Formulating Hypotheses

Organize the class into groups. Have the members of each group formulate a hypothesis about some aspect of human behavior that is of interest to all group members. Ask group members to decide which of the methods shown on page 38 could best be used to test the hypothesis, and have them develop a written rationale for their choice. Have the groups present their hypotheses and rationales to the class one at a time. Ask the class to critique each group's method in terms of its advantages and disadvantages and to suggest other methods that might be more efficient.

Class Discussion

Remind students that longitudinal studies are expensive and time-consuming and that the participants may not be available for the duration of the study. Ask students to consider why, despite these drawbacks, some psychologists continue to use the longitudinal method to collect their data. Also ask students to discuss how they would respond to a request to participate in a longitudinal study, knowing that the researchers would track them over a period of years. If they were psychologists, how would they go about persuading respondents to participate in a long-term study?

Journal Activity

Most students are subject to some kind of intelligence, personality, or other testing at some time. Have students write about their personal experiences with such tests. How did the process of being tested make them feel? Were they told how the tests were constructed and for what purposes the results would be used?

Six Methods of Observation

Research Method	Description	Advantages	Disadvantages
Testing Method	Several types of tests measure various elements of human behavior such as abilities, interests, and personality.	Convenient method for researchers to gain insight to certain aspects of an individual's abilities or behavior.	Does not always provide a complete representation of an individual's true abilities or personality.
Case-Study Method	Researchers conduct in-depth investigations of individuals or small groups.	Provides insight into specific cases.	May focus on isolated circumstances or events that cannot be replicated. People interviewed in case studies may distort their past experiences. Researchers may unintentionally encourage people to answer questions a certain way.
Longitudinal Method	A group of participants are observed at intervals over an extended period of time.	Enables researchers to see how individuals change over time.	Time-consuming and expensive. Participants may not be available for the duration of the study.
Cross-Sectional Method	Researchers compare the differences and similarities among people in different age groups at a given time.	Less time-consuming than the longitudinal method for studying changes over time.	Differences between the members of the sample cannot necessarily be attributed to age or development.
Naturalistic-Observation Method	Researchers observe the behavior of people or animals in their natural habitats.	Enables researchers to witness the behavior of people or animals in settings that are not artificial.	Researchers have no control over the setting or the events that occur.
Laboratory-Observation Method	Participants are observed in a laboratory setting.	Enables researchers to precisely control certain aspects of the study.	Laboratories cannot duplicate real-life environments.

FIGURE 2.5 *Psychologists employ several types of observation methods to conduct research.*

Meeting Individual Needs: Learners with Limited English Proficiency

To help students with limited English proficiency understand the terms *positive correlation* and *negative correlation*, have them think of a date between a boy and a girl. If the two people have a positive relationship, they "go together" to the movies. But if the two people develop a negative relationship, they "go in opposite directions" rather than continue the date. Explain that correlations apply to many kinds of relationships.

Applying Information

As a way of helping students consolidate their comprehension, have them create short quizzes covering the main terms and concepts in this section. Then have students exchange their quizzes with classmates and complete the quizzes.

Reviewing Section 3

Have students complete the Section Review questions on page 40.

Analyzing Observations

Once psychologists have made their observations, they must analyze and interpret them. One method they use is **correlation**, which is a measure of how closely one thing is related to another. The stronger the correlation between two things, the more closely those two things are related. For example, there is a strong correlation between height and ability to reach items that are located on the top shelf of a cabinet. The taller the person, the greater that person's ability to reach the top shelf.

In psychology, researchers often look for correlations between various characteristics or traits. For instance, are people with a stronger felt need than others for achievement more likely to advance in their jobs? What is the relationship between stress and health? Between grades earned by students and extracurricular involvement?

Positive and Negative Correlation   To determine whether there is a correlation between achievement and occupational success, a researcher might compare need for achievement as measured by a personality test with the salaries of the test takers. There is, in fact, a correlation between the need for achievement and salaries, and it is a **positive correlation**. (See Figure 2.6.) That is, as one goes up, so does the other. Generally speaking, people who feel a greater need to achieve earn more money (Ginsburg & Bronstein, 1993; Gottfried et al., 1994).

There are, of course, some exceptions. Some people are highly motivated to achieve, but they do not have high-paying jobs. Others are average in their need for achievement but earn very high incomes. Therefore, factors other than a need for achievement also contribute to high salaries. One such factor is the type of job one has; people in some kinds of jobs earn more than people in other kinds of jobs. In addition, for people to succeed, they also have to know how to interact with others, how to manage people, and how to manage multiple tasks at one time (Collier, 1994; Sternberg et al., 1995). Thus, there is a positive correlation between success and a variety of factors.

In contrast, there is a **negative correlation** between stress and health. As one goes up, the other goes down. (See Figure 2.6.) As the amount of stress on people increases, their immune systems become less capable of fighting off illness—thus, the greater the stress, the poorer the health. This is why students under stress are more likely than other students to get colds (Cohen et al., 1993).

Positive and Negative Correlations

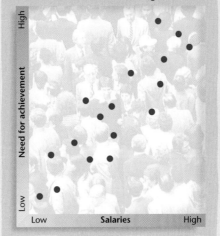

Positive Correlation

Generally speaking, people who have a higher need for achievement achieve higher salaries.

Negative Correlation

Generally speaking, the immune systems of people who are under high amounts of stress tend to function more poorly than the immune systems of people who are under less stress.

FIGURE 2.6   *Each dot represents an observation of one person. When two factors show a positive correlation, one rises as the other rises. When two factors show a negative correlation, one of the factors rises as the other one falls.*

For Your Information

British scientist Francis Galton (1822–1911) and his followers were responsible for developing the statistical methods used to determine correlations. Galton used these methods to test the degree to which individuals resembled their relatives. Other scientists soon applied these methods to their own fields.

Teaching Transparencies with Teacher's Notes

TRANSPARENCY 3: Positive and Negative Correlations

Readings and Case Studies

Essay and Research Themes for A. P. Students

Theme 1

39

4
Section Objective

▶ Describe the purpose and elements of an experiment.

This objective is assessed in the Section Review on page 44 and in the Chapter 2 Review.

Opening Section 4

Motivator

Have students brainstorm a list of questions they might have about human life and development, health, and relationships. Then ask them to discuss how their lives would be different if there were no reliable way to seek answers to these questions—no way to distinguish between false and true hypotheses, between cause and effect, between fact and superstition. Explain that in this section they will learn about the method by which scientists throughout the world seek answers to questions of cause and effect—the experiment.

Correlation Versus Cause and Effect

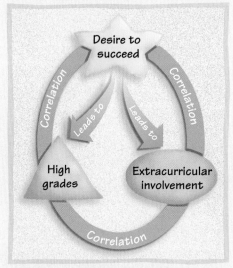

FIGURE 2.7 *Although a correlation may exist between high grades and extracurricular involvement, this does not mean that one causes the other.*

Limits of Correlation Correlation describes relationships. It does not, however, reveal cause and effect. Just because two things are related does not necessarily mean that one causes the other.

For example, suppose you were conducting a study in your school and discovered a positive correlation between students' grades and their level of involvement in extracurricular activities. In other words, suppose you found that students who earn high grades in their classes also participate heavily in extracurricular activities. Does this mean that earning high grades *causes* students to become involved in extracurricular activities or that involvement in extracurricular activities *causes* students to earn high grades? Not necessarily. It might be that there are other factors—such as a general desire to succeed—that encourage or cause *both* high grades and extracurricular involvement. (See Figure 2.7.) Thus, we cannot conclude on the basis of the correlation alone that one causes the other.

Recall that Todd noticed a correlation between the amount of food his fish were eating and the way they were behaving—they were eating less and were acting sluggish. Todd assumed that the fish were sluggish because they were not eating enough. In other words, he assumed that one factor (decreased amount of food eaten) was causing the other (sluggish behavior). On the basis of this assumption, Todd changed the type of food he was feeding the fish.

But Todd's assumption may have been mistaken. Perhaps, the fish were sick and their illness was causing both the odd behavior and the lack of appetite. There could have been a hidden factor at work that was acting on both of the other factors to create a correlation between them. As you will see, experiments allow us to draw conclusions about cause and effect.

SECTION 3 REVIEW

1. What is a case study? Name one drawback of the case-study method.

2. What is the difference between the naturalistic-observation method and the laboratory-observation method?

3. **Critical Thinking** *Analyzing Information* Suppose you want to find out if there is a correlation between age and preferred volume level for listening to music for people between the ages of 15 and 55. Which observational methods might you use to study this?

SECTION 4
The Experimental Method

The method researchers use to answer questions about cause and effect is the experiment. In an **experiment**, participants receive what is called a treatment, such as a change in room temperature or a new drug. Researchers then carefully observe the participants to determine how the treatment influences their behavior (if at all).

When Todd switched fish foods to see if the new food would make the fish eat more and stop acting sluggish, he was conducting an experiment. Changing the food was the treatment. Similarly, when Marc used a mirror to see how the fighting fish would react, that too was an experiment. Holding up the mirror was the treatment.

As with other research methods, the experimental method has some limitations. For example, the

Guided Practice

Bring to class an account of a psychological study in a specialized magazine such as *Psychology Today* or a general-interest magazine such as *Redbook* or *Time*. Summarize the main points of the study for students, and walk them through an analysis of the study. Have students identify the research question, the hypothesis, the independent and dependent variables, the experimental and control groups, the findings of the study, and the conclusions.

Independent Practice

Have students work independently to locate magazine accounts of psychological experiments and subject the experiments to the same analysis described in the Guided Practice activity. Have students summarize their findings in brief, written reports. Ask them to include in their reports any criticisms they have of the study's methodology or conclusions. Have volunteers present their reports and criticisms to the class for discussion.

conditions created in an experiment may not accurately reflect conditions in real life. Almost by their very nature, experiments must simplify things somewhat in order to yield useful information about cause and effect. Nevertheless, experiments do yield useful information much of the time, and for that reason, psychologists frequently turn to the experimental method in their research.

Independent and Dependent Variables

Experiments contain **variables**, which are factors that can vary, or change. In an experiment, the **independent variable** is the factor that researchers manipulate so that they can determine its effect. Suppose researchers are testing the hypothesis that warm temperatures cause aggression in humans. In that experiment, temperature is the independent variable because that is what researchers are manipulating to observe its effect.

In the same experiment, level of aggression is the dependent variable. As you might guess from its name, a **dependent variable** depends on something—the independent variable. The researchers want to find out whether level of aggression depends on temperature.

In Todd's experiment with the fish food, the type of food he was using was the independent variable. The extent to which the fish acted sluggish and the amount they ate were dependent variables.

Experimental and Control Groups

Ideal experiments use experimental and control groups. Members of an **experimental group** receive the treatment. Members of a **control group** do not. Every effort is made to ensure that all other conditions are held constant for both the experimental group and the control group. This method makes it possible for researchers to conclude that the experiments results are caused by the treatment, not by something else.

Researchers randomly assign participants to one group or the other. For example, in an experiment about students' grades and extracurricular involvement, some students would be randomly assigned to participate in extracurricular activities. These students would make up the experimental group. Others would be randomly assigned *not* to participate in extracurricular activities. These students would be the control group. Once researchers ensured that all other factors—such as educational background—were the same for the two groups,

they could then compare the groups to see whether involvement in extracurricular activities makes a difference in the grades participants earn.

When an experiment uses control groups as well as experimental groups, it is called a **controlled experiment**. When Todd switched foods to see if a different food would change the behavior of the fish, he was *not* conducting a controlled experiment. Because the fish acted less sluggish after he switched their food, he assumed that the new food was responsible. But what if another factor caused the change in their behavior? Perhaps they had been sick and had recovered naturally. Or perhaps the temperature of the water had changed without Todd's realizing it.

To know for sure whether the food was responsible for the changed behavior of the fish, Todd would have to do a controlled experiment. First, he would have to randomly organize the fish into two groups. He would give the experimental group the new food. The control group would receive the usual food. If he separated the groups with a piece of glass in the tank, he could keep all other factors —such as water temperature and acidity—the same for both groups of fish. (See Figure 2.8 on page 42.) If after a period of time the fish that received the new food were no longer acting sluggish, but the fish that received the old food still were, he could conclude that the new fish food had made the difference. But if all of the fish continued to act sluggish, or if they all started to become more active again, something other than the new food was the cause.

Another example of a study in which it is useful to have a control group concerns a key question for psychologists: Does psychotherapy work? In other words, do people who undergo therapy feel better, or feel better faster, than people who do not?

Millions of people seek help from psychologists. Many patients believe their therapists have helped them. For example, a former patient might say, "I was in terrible shape before therapy, but I feel much better now." Yet we do not know what would have happened if this person had not sought help. Many people feel better about their problems as time goes on, with or without therapy. In other words, an individual's involvement in therapy is not part of a controlled experiment. There is no control group— an identical person who has *not* gone to a therapist. Of course, we could never find such a person because no two people are exactly the same.

However, researchers can make up for this by conducting an experiment on the effects of therapy

Classifying Information

To help students understand the difference between independent and dependent variables and between experimental and control groups, have them brainstorm several hypotheses they would like to test, such as "Students who receive tutoring will improve their grades." Choose one hypothesis and create a graphic organizer on the chalkboard showing the independent and dependent variables and the experimental and control groups. Have volunteers create graphic organizers for the other hypotheses.

For Further Research

Have students conduct further research into the placebo effect. Some students may wish to research hypotheses about how and why placebos function as they do. Other students may wish to identify references to placebos in specific experiments. Still others may wish to analyze accounts of folk medicine and "miracle cures." Organize students in groups, according to the focus of their research, and tell them to work together to prepare both a written report and an oral presentation. Groups may also wish to prepare visual materials to accompany their presentations.

For Your Information

Placebos can affect the perception of pain, altering brain chemistry and producing endorphins—chemicals that reduce pain much in the same way that morphine does. Scientists know, however, that a drug called naloxone inhibits the effect of morphine. In 1979, researchers wanted to find out if naloxone would also inhibit the pain-reducing effect of placebos. The researchers gave one group of participants a placebo and told them it was a painkiller. Their pain was reduced. Another group of subjects was told they would receive a painkiller, but they were given a placebo plus naloxone. Their pain did not lessen.

Levine, J. D., et al. (1979). Naloxone dose dependability produces analgesia and hyperalgesia in postoperative pain. *Nature, 278.* 740–741.

Journal Activity

Ask students if they can remember as children being given a "placebo" to reduce pain or anxiety (for example, a "lucky" stone to reduce the fear of going to sleep or a kiss to make pain go away). Have them describe in their journals how well these placebos worked.

FIGURE 2.8 *In an experiment to test the hypothesis that a different food changes the behavior of fish, the fish might be divided at random into two groups. The groups are separated by a piece of glass. Except for the type of food received, all other factors, such as water temperature, are kept the same for both groups.*

using a large number of people. In such an experiment, some people would be randomly assigned to an experimental group and would receive therapy. Others with the same problems as those in the first group would be assigned to a control group and would not receive therapy. Even though the people in the experimental group would not be identical to the people in the control group, individual differences would probably average out as long as the groups were large enough. Thus, researchers could determine whether people who receive therapy fare better than those who do not. It would be a controlled experiment.

The Placebo Effect

The question of whether psychotherapy works is further complicated by the fact that people who seek psychotherapy usually expect it to work. Imagine that a person who has a problem is about to see a therapist about it. Chances are, the person is expecting that the visit will be helpful. Otherwise, why would he or she be going?

In research studies and in our daily lives, our expectations affect what happens to us. Feeling better simply because we expect to feel better—and for no other reason—is an example of the placebo (pluh-SEE-boh) effect. A **placebo** is a substance or treatment that has no effect apart from a person's belief in it. For example, one type of placebo is a tablet that appears to contain a real drug but actually has no medicinal value. Someone who has a headache and takes the tablet to feel better might start to feel better even though the tablet does not contain any medicine—as long as the person *thinks* it contains medicine.

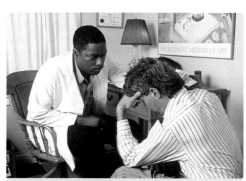

People undergoing therapy might find it helpful not only because of the therapy itself but also because of the expectation that it will help.

TRUTH OR fiction ∎ REVISITED ∎

It is true that taking a pill that does not contain any medicine might have the same effects as taking one that does. This is due to the placebo effect. People expect to feel better after receiving what they believe to be medication.

Single-Blind Studies

Expectations can create bias toward certain points of view. If a person expects that a drug may have certain effects, he or she will be biased toward paying close attention to any sensations that are similar to those effects.

How, then, can researchers deal with the effects of expectations? How can they learn whether the participants' preconceptions about a new drug are biasing their perceptions of its effects?

One way that researchers can avoid the influence of expectations is by keeping participants unaware of, or blind to, the treatment they are receiving. In a **single-blind study**, participants do not know whether they are in the experimental group or the control group.

Figure 2.9 shows experimental conditions in which some people are given a real drug and others are given a placebo. In this example, half of those given the real drug are deceived. They are told they are taking the placebo. Half of those given the placebo also are deceived. They are told they are

taking the drug. The rest of the participants are told the truth about what they are taking.

What does it mean if the people taking the new drug improve faster, regardless of what they have been told, but people who take the placebo do not? It means the drug is effective. What does it mean if all the people who are told they are taking the drug get better faster, regardless of whether they are taking the drug or the placebo? It means that they improve because of their expectations—because of a belief that they are taking a helpful drug—and not because of the drug itself. Thus, the drug in and of itself has few if any benefits.

Double-Blind Studies

Participants may not be the only people involved in an experiment who have expectations. Researchers themselves may also have expectations, such as a belief about the effectiveness of a particular treatment. It is therefore useful if the researchers are also unaware of who has had the treatment and who has had the placebo. A study in which both participants and experimenters are unaware of who receives the treatment is called a **double-blind study**.

Double-blind studies are required by the Food and Drug Administration before new drugs can be put on the market (Carroll et al., 1994). People in these studies are assigned at random to take the real drug or the placebo. Neither the participants nor the people who measure the results know who is taking what. Thus, the people who measure the effects can remain unbiased. After the final measurements are

A Single-Blind Study

FIGURE 2.9 *In a single-blind drug study participants are divided into four groups. People in one group receive the drug and are told that they are receiving the drug. Members of the second group receive the drug and are told that they are receiving a placebo. The third group receives a placebo but is told that it is receiving the drug. People in the fourth group receive a placebo and are told that they are receiving a placebo.*

Section Objective

▶ Evaluate the ethical issues involved in psychological research.

This objective is assessed in the Section Review on page 47 and in the Chapter 2 Review.

Opening Section 5

Motivator

Have students use what they have learned thus far in the chapter to brainstorm hypothetical psychological studies that might involve unfair or damaging treatment to the participants. Write students' responses on the chalkboard. For each study listed, have students determine how irresponsible methodology could be avoided. Then have students discuss whether harming the participants in a research study could ever be justified. Explain that these and related issues are the focus of Section 5.

Section 4 Review: Answers

1. The independent variable is the factor that researchers manipulate to study its effect; the dependent variable is the factor that changes, depending on what happens to the independent variable. In Todd's experiment with fish food, the type of food he was using was the independent variable, and the extent to which the fish acted sluggish was the dependent variable.

2. A controlled experiment is one that uses a control group as well as an experimental group. Members of an experimental group receive the designated treatment; members of the control group do not.

3. Double-blind studies remove researchers' biases, as well as the biases of participants.

---

made, an impartial panel (made up of people who *do* know who had the real drug and who did not) determines, on the basis of the measurements of the unbiased observers, whether the effects of the drug differed from those of the placebo.

Central Tendency and Dispersion

Researchers organize data to generalize about the information. Teachers do this every time they analyze test scores. A common technique is to measure or determine central tendency. When the teacher adds all scores and divides the sum by the number of students who took the test, he or she finds the mean, or average score. The mean is most often used as the central tendency. Other methods of arriving at the central tendency include finding the median and the mode. If scores are organized from the lowest to the highest, or the highest to the lowest, the median score is the middle score. Half of the grades are below this score and half are above. The mode is the most frequent score.

To understand the distribution or dispersion of data, researchers must document the range of scores, or how variable the scores are. The two most frequently used measures of variability are range and **standard deviation**. To find the range, the lowest score in the data is subtracted from the highest. This is a simple technique and gives a crude measure of variability. Standard deviation is a measure of distance of every score to the mean. The larger the standard deviation the more spread out the scores are. If five students got 7 out of 10 questions correct on a test, two students got 10 correct, and one got 5 correct, the mode is 7, the median is 7, and the mean is 7.5. To compute the standard deviation, subtract the mean from each score. 10 minus 7.5 equals 2.5. This is a positive deviation because the score is above the mean. Seven minus 7.5 is negative .2, and 5 minus 7.5 is negative 2.5. Test scores that have a large range have a relatively higher standard deviation while test scores bunched together, as in this case, have a relatively small standard deviation.

SECTION 4 REVIEW

go.hrw.com **Homework Practice Online**
Keyword: SY3 HP2

1. Define *independent variable* and *dependent variable*. Give an example of each.

2. What is a controlled experiment? What is the difference between an experimental group and a control group?

3. **Critical Thinking** *Evaluating* Why might a double-blind study yield more reliable results than a single-blind study?

Ethical Issues

Ethics are standards for proper and responsible behavior. Psychologists follow ethical standards to promote the dignity of the individual, foster human welfare, and maintain scientific integrity. An important aspect of psychologists' work is to lessen human suffering. Along these lines, ethical standards prevent scientists from undertaking research or treatments that will be harmful to human participants. Specific ethical guidelines have been established by the American Psychological Association (APA). Psychologists are required to be familiar with these guidelines. The APA is a scientific and professional organization of psychologists.

Research with People

Ethical standards limit the type of research that psychologists may conduct. Imagine trying to study whether early separation of children from their mothers impairs the children's social development. Scientifically, such a study might collect important psychological data. But it would be unethical to purposefully separate infants from their mothers to study the effects of such a separation. Such a separation would violate the ethical principle that study participants must not be harmed. Thus, psychologists would not seriously consider running an experiment that involves intentional separation.

One alternative research approach to such a study might be to observe the development of children who have already been separated from their mothers since an early age. However, it could be difficult to draw specific conclusions from this type of research. The same factors that led to the separation—such as the death of the parents—may have influenced a child's development as much as (or perhaps more than) the separation itself. Even if there was a positive correlation between separation from the mother and the child's impaired social development, psychologists could not prove cause and effect—that one was caused by the other.

What are the ethical standards researchers adhere to? The APA guidelines provide a number of provisions that detail what is needed to make a study ethical (APA, 1994a). These guidelines include two important principles: confidentiality and informed consent.

CASE STUDIES
AND OTHER TRUE STORIES

Ask volunteers to write and present a skit about the Hawthorne study. Have some of the students play the workers and some play the researchers. After the skit has been presented, select other volunteers to serve as a review panel. Have the Hawthorne researchers present their study and its results to the panelists. Ask the panelists to critique the study and explain how both the study and the conclusions are flawed. Have the class provide additional examples of flaws in the experiment.

Drawing Conclusions

Ask students to consider why being observed may make some people work harder. Have them provide examples from their own lives—whether in school, at home, or while engaged in some sort of sport or hobby—when they performed better than usual because they were receiving extra attention. Then have students brainstorm instances when attention might have a negative effect or no effect at all. What might account for the difference in performance reactions to the extra attention?

CASE STUDIES
AND OTHER TRUE STORIES
The Hawthorne Plant Study: A Flawed Experiment

In 1927, researchers began a study in the Hawthorne plant of the Western Electric Company in Cicero, Illinois. They had been called in by the factory's managers to find out what conditions in the factory might be changed to boost productivity. The researchers designed a study in which productivity was the dependent variable and length of rest periods, workdays, and workweeks were the independent variables.

The researchers selected five women as participants in the study. The women were to work as a team in a room where they could be observed. The researchers introduced rest pauses of varying lengths throughout the workday. They observed the women to see how their productivity was affected. The researchers then began to shorten the workday and, later, the workweek. Again, they observed the changes in productivity.

At first, the researchers observed that as they increased rest periods and shortened the workday and workweek, the women's overall output increased. It appeared that, with more rest, workers returned to their jobs refreshed and therefore were able to produce more. To check their findings, the researchers slowly returned to the original schedule—with shorter rest periods, a longer workday, and a longer workweek.

To the surprise of the researchers, the women's output remained higher than it had been at the beginning of the study. How could that be? The research team concluded that the increase in output was caused not by the independent variables (length of rest pauses, workday, and workweek) but by another variable—the women's awareness that they were being observed. They felt special because of the unusual attention they were receiving; thus, they worked harder.

This phenomenon came to be known as the "Hawthorne effect." It was a valuable finding, and led to the theory that one effective way to increase worker productivity was simply to pay more attention to the workers. However, its value notwith-

standing, the finding was accidental and a result of a flawed study design.

To test the variables they wanted to test, the researchers could have conducted a blind study. In such a study, at least some of the participants would not have known they were being observed. Alternatively, the researchers could have established a control group—a group of participants who knew they were being observed but did not receive any of the treatments that the members of the experimental group received.

The design of the Hawthorne study had some other flaws as well. For one thing, the experimental group was exceedingly small. A sample size of five is really not large enough to be able to generalize conclusions about the larger population. Furthermore, the sample did not remain constant over the course of the whole experiment. Two of the women in the group were replaced in the middle of the study because they talked too much, their productivity was low, and they were considered a negative influence on the others. Their removal may have biased the results in favor of increased productivity.

Moreover, the researchers may have misinterpreted the results of the study. The conclusion that productivity remained high even after the women returned to the original schedule was not completely correct. Total output stayed about the same, but it was achieved in more hours. In other words, hourly productivity actually *dropped.* In addition, the researchers never considered that the longer one does a job, the more skilled one becomes. That in itself may increase productivity.

Because of these flaws, the existence of the Hawthorne effect has been called into question (Jones, 1992). The Hawthorne effect remains only a hypothesis.

> ### WHY PSYCHOLOGY MATTERS
>
> Psychologists study the conditions in which people work. Use CNNfyi.com or other current events sources to learn more about how psychologists study the workplace environment. Write a newspaper article of what you have learned.
>
> CNNfyi.com

internet connect

go hrw .com

TOPIC: Research and Ethics
GO TO: go.hrw.com
KEYWORD: SY3 PS2

Have students access the Internet through the HRW Go site to research Philip Zimbardo's prison experiment and Stanley Milgram's research on obedience to authority. Then have students apply the standards of the American Psychological Association for ethical decision making regarding the collection, storage, and use of psychological data to the experiments. Ask students to write a report in which they critique the experiments by applying contemporary standards regarding experimentation.

Teaching Section 5

Follow Up

Review with students the information on informed consent presented in the section. Then ask students to recall the experiments they designed for the Synthesizing Information activity on page 43. Have each student prepare an informed consent form that he or she could use with prospective participants of the experiment. Ask volunteers to present their informed consent forms to the class for discussion, and have the class critique the appropriateness of the forms in relation to the proposed experiments.

Taking a Stand

Organize students into two groups—those who think it is justifiable to use deception in psychological research and those who think such deception is never justifiable. Tell the members of each group to work together to compile arguments and hypothetical examples. Then have spokespersons from the two groups debate the use of deception in psychological research.

Class Discussion

Have the class discuss the issue of confidentiality between a psychologist and his or her participants or clients. Have students first analyze the basis of the rule of confidentiality and then debate its application to hypothetical cases.

Cross-Curricular Link: Law

Tell students that *confidential communication* is the legal term used to describe the private conversations between psychologists and clients or participants. Point out that private conversations between lawyers and clients also are protected. Lawyers who reveal confidential information told to them by their clients may even lose their right to practice law.

For Your Information

Today most universities, hospitals, and research foundations have ethics review committees that examine all proposed experiments to determine whether they may cause harm in any way.

Participants in psychological studies sign consent forms to indicate that they understand the research.

Confidentiality Psychologists treat the records of research participants and clients as confidential. In other words, the records are private. This is because psychologists respect people's right to privacy. In addition, people are more likely to disclose true information and feelings when they know that what they say will remain confidential (Blanck et al., 1992).

In certain very rare circumstances, such as when a client reveals plans to harm someone, a psychologist may disregard confidentiality in order to protect the well-being of the client or of other people. Such situations, however, are definitely the exception rather than the rule. Even when they do arise, psychologists must think long and hard about whether breaking confidentiality is the appropriate thing to do.

Informed Consent The APA has distinct restrictions against research studies that could pose a serious threat to the physical or psychological health of participants or that might have long-term, irreversible effects on them. However, the APA acknowledges that some worthwhile studies may cause participants to experience some discomfort or other short-term negative effects.

To help avoid situations in which people volunteer to participate in research without knowing that such effects are possible, the APA generally requires that the participants provide informed consent. **Informed consent** means that people agree, or consent, to participate in a research study only after they have been given a general overview of the research and have been given the choice of whether or not to participate. The provision of information and the opportunity to choose give people some degree of control and make participation less stressful (Dill et al., 1982).

Deception On the other hand, some psychological experiments cannot be run without deceiving people. For instance, new drug experiments and other blind studies cannot be conducted without keeping participants unaware of the treatment they are receiving or of the nature of the study. In order for the study to be valid, some participants must be deceived. In drug experiments, many participants might be told they are taking a real drug when they are actually taking a placebo, or vice versa.

Psychologists have debated the ethics of deceiving participants in research (Fisher & Fyrberg, 1994). According to the APA's statement of ethical principles, psychologists may use deception only under specified conditions:

- when they believe that the benefits of the research outweigh its potential harm
- when they believe that the individuals would have been willing to participate if they had understood the benefits of the research
- when participants receive an explanation of the study after it has occurred

Explaining what happened in the study once it is over helps avoid misunderstandings about the research. Explanations also reduce participants' anxieties and let the participants maintain their dignity (Blanck et al., 1992).

TRUTH OR fiction
■ REVISITED ■

It is true that psychologists sometimes have to deceive participants in a study. Deception may be needed to prevent participants from purposefully or accidentally distorting the outcome of the research. But there are strict rules about deception in research.

Cooperative Learning

The subject of animal experimentation is an important and controversial one. Organize students into the following groups to research and report back to the class on various aspects of animal research: Cosmetics, New Drugs, New Surgical Procedures, Brain Experiments, Learning and Behavior. Encourage students to research both the beliefs of animal rights activists and the perspectives of the scientific community. Also have students determine what legal changes have occurred in this field in the past 10 years.

Applying Information

Have students draw up a comprehensive list of all the ethical principles discussed in this section. Then have them provide one example to illustrate each principle.

Reviewing Section 5

Have students complete the Section Review questions on page 47.

Research with Animals

A DAY IN THE LIFE

Needless to say, the experiments Todd, Marc, and Dan conducted were done with animals—Todd's fish. Most studies that use animals (such as those in which researchers have rats run through mazes to find out how they learn) do not harm the animals at all. Even the boys' fish experiments did not harm the fish. Marc's idea of using a mirror to find out about the fighting fish was a much more ethical method than using another real fighting fish. Marc was able to move the mirror, but if he had used another real fish, the two fish might have fought to the death.

Sometimes, however, psychologists and other scientists conduct research that may be harmful to animals. Such research studies often use animals because they cannot be carried out with people for ethical reasons. Experiments on the effects of early separation of children from their mothers are an example. These experiments could not be done with people, but they have been done with monkeys and other animals (e.g., Harlow, 1959). Such research has helped psychologists investigate the formation of bonds of attachment between parents and children. (See Chapter 10.)

There are other examples of psychological studies that rely on animals in order to avoid harming humans. Psychologists and biologists who study the brain sometimes destroy parts of the brains of laboratory animals to learn how those parts influence the animals' behavior. This and other types of research on animals have benefited humans. Advances in the treatment of mental disorders, neuromuscular disorders, strokes, visual and memory defects, headaches, and high blood pressure, among others, can be traced to animal research.

Psychologists use animals only when there is no alternative and when they believe that the potential benefits outweigh the harm. Only a small percentage of all psychological studies involve animals. Some researchers argue that many advances in medicine and psychology could not have taken place without harming animals (Fowler, 1992; Pardes et al., 1991). Yet many people believe that it is no more ethical to harm animals than it is to harm humans. Although the APA has rules of ethics for how animals used in research should be treated, controversy continues to surround the use of animals in scientific research.

In many studies that use animals, researchers are careful to treat the animals kindly.

Ethics in Using Data

Another area in which psychologists follow strict rules about ethics is in how they produce, store, and present their data. When researchers conduct a study, they need to be as objective as possible in planning their study, in collecting their data, and in analyzing their data. Without this objectivity, the researchers may bias their study, perhaps unintentionally, in favor of their hypothesis.

Even more importantly, when information collected by researchers contradicts their hypothesis, they must be willing to discard their hypothesis in light of the evidence. It might be tempting to toss out all the evidence that contradicts the hypothesis and present to others only the evidence that supports the hypothesis. But this would be misleading and thus unethical. It might also become an obstacle to others' attempts to study psychology.

SECTION 5 REVIEW

go.hrw.com **Homework Practice Online**
Keyword: SY3 HP2

1. Explain the purpose of ethical standards in the profession of psychology.
2. Why are confidentiality and informed consent important to psychological research?
3. **Critical Thinking** *Supporting a Point of View* Do you believe that it is ethical or unethical to deceive people about the purposes of research studies? Explain your answer.

Section 5 Review: Answers

1. Ethical standards protect study participants from harm and maintain the scientific integrity of the study.

2. Knowing that confidentiality is being observed will ensure more openness from the participants. Informed consent gives participants a degree of control and makes participation less stressful.

3. Answers should show that students have weighed the possible harm to participants against the benefits of the research.

Chapter Review: Answers

Writing a Summary

See the section subtitles for the main topics in the chapter.

Identifying People and Ideas

1. an educated guess
2. a group that is to be studied or described

Technology

▶ Chapter 2 Test Generator (on the One-Stop Planner)

▶ HRW Go site

Reinforcement, Review, and Assessment

▶ Chapter 2 Review, pp. 48–49

▶ Chapter Review and Activities with Answer Key

▶ Alternative Assessment Handbook

▶ Portfolio Assessment Handbook

▶ Chapter 2 Test (Form A or B)

Linking to Community If there are any academic, industrial, or other research psychologists in the community, invite them to come to the classroom and discuss studies in which they have been involved. If this is not possible, you might wish to invite researchers from other branches of science

---

Chapter 2 REVIEW

3. a predisposition to a certain point of view

4. an in-depth investigation of an individual or a small group

5. a measure of how closely one thing is related to another

6. factors that can vary

7. members of a studied group who do not receive a treatment administered during an experiment

8. a study in which the participants do not know whether they are in the experimental group or the control group.

9. a study in which neither the researchers nor the participants know whether the latter are in the experimental group or control group.

10. consent given by a research participant who has been given a general overview of the research

Understanding Main Ideas

1. Social scientists form a research question, form a hypothesis, test the hypothesis, analyze results, and draw conclusions.

2. One advantage is that a lot of information can be gathered quickly. One disadvantage is that people may not be honest in their answers.

3. In a positive correlation, one factor rises as the other factor rises. In a negative correlation, one factor rises as the other falls.

4. an average, the middle score, the most frequent score, the lowest score in data subtracted from the highest score, the measure of distance of every score to the mean

Writing a Summary

Using standard grammar, spelling, sentence structure, and punctuation, summarize the information in this chapter. Consider:

• the steps of scientific research and various research methods

• the purpose of experiments and ethical considerations in carrying out experiments

Identifying People and Ideas

Identify the following terms or people and use them in appropriate sentences.

1. hypothesis   **6.** variables
2. target population   **7.** control group
3. bias   **8.** single-blind study
4. case study   **9.** double-blind study
5. correlation   **10.** informed consent

Understanding Main Ideas

SECTION 1 (pp. 26–29)

1. Identify and describe the basic methods of social scientific reasoning.

SECTION 2 (pp. 29–34)

2. What are some of the advantages and disadvantages of the survey method?

SECTION 3 (pp. 34–40)

3. Explain the difference between positive correlation and negative correlation.

SECTION 4 (pp. 40–44)

4. Define *mean, median, mode, range,* and *standard deviation*.

SECTION 5 (pp. 44–47)

5. What purposes do ethical standards serve in psychological research?

Thinking Critically

1. Making Generalizations and Predictions Surveys are often used to help predict future events, such as election outcomes. How might these surveys affect the outcome of the events?

2. Drawing Inferences and Conclusions If correlations do not explain cause and effect, why are they useful?

3. Summarizing What are some potential sources for error in conducting research?

4. Evaluating Under what circumstances might a psychologist break the promise of confidentiality?

Writing About Psychology

1. Summarizing Go to the library and locate a psychological study that includes measures of central tendency and dispersion. Check the research by computing the mean, median, mode, range, and standard deviation. Write a report summarizing your findings.

2. Supporting a Point of View Write an essay in which you defend or argue against the use of animal subjects in psychological research. Do some background reading so that you can support your position with facts. Read your essay to the class as part of a class discussion about the ethics of research with animals. Use the graphic organizer below to help you write your report.

Reasons to Support Animal Research	Reasons to Oppose Animal Research

to discuss their experiences in applying the scientific method. A third possibility might be to invite clinical or school psychologists to discuss with the class studies in which the results affect today's teenagers.

Cooperative Learning

Tell students that they will write a pamphlet titled "The Student's Guide to Ethical Research." Organize the class into five groups, and assign each group one of the following sections: Introduction, Confidentiality, Informed Consent, Objectivity, and Experimentation with Animals. Have each group present their sections to the class. Ask the class to make suggestions. Have the class bind the sections into a completed pamphlet. Distribute copies to the class.

Building Social Studies Skills

Interpreting Graphs

Study the bar graph below. Then use the information in the graph to help you answer the questions that follow.

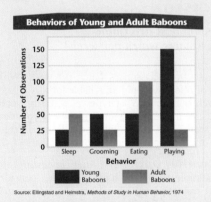

Behaviors of Young and Adult Baboons

Number of Observations (0, 25, 50, 75, 100, 125, 150)
Behavior: Sleep, Grooming, Eating, Playing

Young Baboons / Adult Baboons

Source: Ellingstad and Heimstra, *Methods of Study in Human Behavior,* 1974

1. Which behaviors did young baboons exhibit more frequently than adult baboons?
   a. sleeping and eating
   b. grooming and playing
   c. playing and sleeping
   d. grooming and eating

2. Can you tell which method of observation researchers used to create this chart? If so, which method was used? If not, what methods may have been used?

Analyzing Primary Sources

Read the following excerpt, which is taken from the Ethics Code of the American Psychological Association. Then answer the questions that follow.

"Psychologists seek to contribute to the welfare of those with whom they interact professionally. In their professional actions, psychologists weigh the welfare and rights of their patients or clients, students, supervisees, human research participants, and other affected persons, and the welfare of animal subjects of research. When conflicts occur among psychologists' obligations and concerns, they attempt to resolve these conflicts and to perform their roles in a responsible fashion that avoids or minimizes harm. Psychologists are sensitive to real or ascribed [attributed] differences in power between themselves and others, and they do not exploit or mislead other people during or after professional relationships."

3. Which of the following statements best reflects the ethical values found in the excerpt above?
   a. Psychologists must never do any harm.
   b. Psychologists may mislead patients, but only under extraordinary circumstances.
   c. When not at work, psychologists may behave however they please.
   d. In the event of a conflict, psychologists must work to minimize any harm that may result.

4. According to the excerpt, why must psychologists consider the welfare and rights of their patients?

PSYCHOLOGY PROJECTS

Cooperative Learning

Using Surveys Working in small groups, design a survey of the students in your school. You might find out about their views on a particular issue or their buying habits. Decide on a format and give everyone in the group a role in preparing the questionnaires or in conducting the interviews. Write a summary of the project applying the APA's ethical standards for the collection, storage, and use of the data.

internet connect

Internet Activity: go.hrw.com
KEYWORD: SY3 PS2

Choose an activity on psychological methods to:

- design a hypothetical research program.
- create a 3-D model illustrating cause and effect and correlation.
- apply the APA standards for ethical decision making to historic experiments.

go.hrw.com

5. Ethical standards protect the dignity of research subjects and help maintain scientific integrity.

Thinking Critically

1. People who read or hear about survey results might change their opinions to be on the winning side.

2. Correlations show relationships between factors, which can then be analyzed to yield specific information.

3. Potential sources for error include selecting a nonrepresentative sample, getting dishonest answers, and allowing expectations to bias results.

4. A psychologist should break confidentiality only to protect the well-being of the client or other people.

Writing About Psychology

1. Students' reports should reflect an understanding of central tendency and dispersion.

2. Students should write an essay for or against animal research, backing up opinions with facts.

Building Social Studies Skills

1. b
2. No, because researchers may have used either the naturalistic-observation or the laboratory-observation method.
3. d
4. They must consider a patient's welfare and rights because improving patients' welfare is a goal of psychology.

UNIT 1 REVIEW

▶ TEACH

Organize students into groups to practice their decision-making skills. Ask each group to consider the decision to major in psychology in college or another fictional decision of your choosing. Have the groups follow the four-step process outlined in the Psychology in

▶ PSYCHOLOGY IN ACTION

Ask students to create graphic organizers that illustrate areas of their lives in which they could apply the decision-making skills outlined in the simulation. Have volunteers present their graphic organizers to the class.

Action Simulation to reach a decision. Each member should participate in the process. After Step 3, group members should take a vote on which decision to choose. Have one or more group members present their decision-making process to the class.

▶ EXTEND

Have students review the decision in the Psychology in Action Simulation. Then ask students to imagine that the student group has

chosen the survey method to learn how much television their classmates watch per week. Groups now face the decision of how to conduct their surveys. For example, should the students pose their survey questions in person, by telephone, by mail, or by e-mail? Have groups conduct research and incorporate the decision-making skills outlined in the simulation. Finally, have one or two groups present their decision-making process to the class for evaluation.

UNIT 1

PSYCHOLOGY IN ACTION

YOU MAKE THE DECISION . . .

*What type of research method would best determine
how many hours of television your classmates watch per week?*

Complete the following activity in small cooperative groups. Your group wants to learn how much television your classmates watch per week. But first you need to prepare a presentation in which you explain what type of research method would be the best way to learn about your classmates' viewing habits. Your group has formed the hypothesis that, on average, your classmates watch between 10 and 15 hours per week.

1. Gather Information. Use your textbook and other resources to find information that might help you decide what type of research method would be best to help you learn how much

television your classmates watch per week. What types of research would be reliable for this type of research question? What types of research would be feasible in the time frame you have to complete your work? You may want to divide up different parts of the research among group members.

2. Identify Options. After reviewing the information that you have gathered, consider which research methods you might recommend. Your final decision may be easier to reach if you consider as many options as possible. Be sure to record your options for the preparation of your presentation.

3. Predict Consequences. Now take each option you and the members of your group came up with and consider how each type of research might lend itself to what you need to find out. Ask yourself questions such as,

- Will our group be able to actually observe our classmates as they watch television?
- Will my classmates respond accurately to questions about how much television they watch?

Once you have predicted the consequences, record them as notes for your presentation.

4. Take Action to Implement Your Decision. After you have considered your options, you should create your presentation. Be sure that you are very clear regarding your decision about what research method to use. You will need to support your decision by including information you gathered and by explaining why you rejected other options. You may want to create cluster diagrams or charts to support your decision. When you are ready, decide who in your group will make which part of the presentation. Then make your presentation to the class. Good luck!

UNIT 2

Overview

In Unit 2, students will learn about the connection between the body and the mind, including how biology affects people's behavior and mental processes and how people experience the world around them.

UNIT 2
BODY AND MIND

CHAPTERS

3 *Biology and Behavior*

4 *Sensation and Perception*

5 *Consciousness*

▶ *Internet Activity*

internet connect

TOPIC: Analogies of the Body and Mind
GO TO: go.hrw.com
KEYWORD: SY3 UNIT 2

Have students access the Internet to research biology and behavior, sensation and perception, or consciousness. Then have students create 5 analogies that employ information from the Web sites. Students' analogies should be written in the style of the SAT test and should include an answer key that explains which answer is correct as well as why the other answers are incorrect. Then ask students to quiz their classmates or share their analogies with the class.

▶ *Using Visuals*

Have students look at the photograph on page 51. Ask them to describe what they see. Explain that this unit focuses on how people's bodies, minds, heredity, and experiences affect the way people look at the world. Tell students that because no two people are exactly alike, no two people would look at the photograph and see exactly the same thing.

Biology and Behavior

CHAPTER RESOURCE MANAGER

	Objectives	Pacing Guide	Reproducible and Review Resources
SECTION 1: **The Nervous System** (pp. 54–59)	Explain how messages are transmitted by neurons, and describe the functions of the nervous system.	**Regular** **Block Scheduling** 1 day .5 day *Block Scheduling Handbook with Team Teaching Strategies, Chapter 3*	**E** Research Projects and Activities for Teaching Psychology **SM** Study Skills and Writing Guide, Part 1 **REV** Section 1 Review, p. 59
SECTION 2: **The Brain:** **Our Control Center** (pp. 59–67)	Identify the major structures of the brain, and explain the functions of each structure.	**Regular** **Block Scheduling** 1 day .5 day *Block Scheduling Handbook with Team Teaching Strategies, Chapter 3*	**PS** Readings and Case Studies, 3 **E** Creating a Psychology Fair, Handout 2 **REV** Section 2 Review, p. 67
SECTION 3: **The Endocrine System** (pp. 67–69)	Identify the hormones secreted by the major glands of the endocrine system and the role each one plays.	**Regular** **Block Scheduling** 1 day .5 day *Block Scheduling Handbook with Team Teaching Strategies, Chapter 3*	**SM** Mastering Critical Thinking Skills 3 **REV** Section 3 Review, p. 69
SECTION 4: **Heredity: Our Genetic Background** (pp. 69–72)	Explain the role of chromosomes and genes in heredity and evaluate the methods used by psychologists to study the role of heredity in determining traits.	**Regular** **Block Scheduling** 1 day .5 day *Block Scheduling Handbook with Team Teaching Strategies, Chapter 3*	**RS** Essay and Research Themes for Advanced Placement Students, Theme 2 **REV** Section 4 Review, p. 72

Chapter Resource Key

PS Primary Sources   **A** Assessment   Video

RS Reading Support   **REV** Review   Internet

E   Enrichment   Transparencies   Holt Presentation Maker Using Microsoft® PowerPoint®

SM Skills Mastery   CD-ROM

 One-Stop Planner CD–ROM

See the *One-Stop Planner* for a complete list of additional resources for students and teachers.

One-Stop Planner CD–ROM

It's easy to plan lessons, select resources, and print out materials for your students when you use the **One-Stop Planner CD-ROM with Test Generator.**

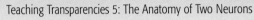
Technology Resources

 One-Stop Planner, Lesson 3.1
Teaching Transparencies 5: The Anatomy of Two Neurons
Teaching Transparencies 6: The Synapse
Teaching Transparencies 7: The Central Nervous System
Homework Practice Online

 One-Stop Planner, Lesson 3.2
Teaching Transparencies 8: Parts of the Human Brain
Teaching Transparencies 9: Sensory and Motor Areas of the Brain
Homework Practice Online
CNN. Presents Psychology: Britain's Brain Bank
HRW Go Site

 One-Stop Planner, Lesson 3.3
Teaching Transparencies 10: The Endocrine System
Homework Practice Online
HRW Go Site

 One-Stop Planner, Lesson 3.4
Homework Practice Online
HRW Go Site

Chapter Review and Assessment

HRW Go site
REV Chapter 3 Review, pp. 74–75
REV Chapter Review Activities with Answer Key

A Chapter 3 Test (Form A or B)
A Portfolio Assessment Handbook
A Alternative Assessment Handbook

Chapter 3 Test Generator (on the One-Stop Planner)
Global Skill Builder CD-ROM

---

internet connect

HRW ONLINE RESOURCES

GO TO: go.hrw.com
Then type in a keyword.

TEACHER HOME PAGE
KEYWORD: SY3 Teacher

CHAPTER INTERNET ACTIVITIES
KEYWORD: SY3 PS3
Choose an activity to have students:
• create a symbol reflecting the functions of the parts of the brain.
• make a chart on the endocrine system.
• write a report on the influence of heredity and environment on psychological traits.

CHAPTER ENRICHMENT LINKS
KEYWORD: SY3 CH3

ONLINE ASSESSMENT
Homework Practice
KEYWORD: SY3 HP3
Standardized Test Prep
KEYWORD: SY3 STP3
Rubrics
KEYWORD: SS Rubrics

CONTENT UPDATES
KEYWORD: SS Content Updates

HOLT PRESENTATION MAKER
KEYWORD: SY3 PPT3

ONLINE READING SUPPORT
KEYWORD: SS Strategies

CURRENT EVENTS
KEYWORD: S3 Current Events

Additional Resources

PRINT RESOURCES FOR TEACHERS
Bloom, F., & Lazerson, A. (1995). *Brain, mind, and behavior* (2nd ed.). New York: W. H. Freeman.

Coren, S. (1991). *The left-handed syndrome: the causes and consequences of left-handedness.* New York: Free Press.

Springer, S. P., & Deutsch, G. (1995). *Left brain, right brain* (4th ed.). New York: W. H. Freeman.

PRINT RESOURCES FOR STUDENTS
Diamond, M., et al. (1985). *The human brain coloring book.* New York: HarperCollins.

Sacks, O. (1998). *The man who mistook his wife for a hat.* New York: Simon & Schuster.

MULTIMEDIA RESOURCES
The brain (VHS). Films for the Humanities & Sciences, P.O. Box 2053, Princeton, NJ 08543-2053.

The man who mistook his wife for a hat (VHS). Films for the Humanities & Sciences, P.O. Box 2053, Princeton, NJ 08543-2053.

3-D Body adventure (CD-ROM). Knowledge Adventure Incorporated. 1-800-542-4240.

BIOLOGY AND BEHAVIOR

Introducing Chapter 3

Ask students how closely they think psychology and biology are related. Have students compare these two fields of scientific study by answering the following questions:

▶ What do biology and psychology have in common?

▶ How do biology and psychology differ?

▶ Do biologists and psychologists use the same medical terms? Why or why not?

Students should save their responses and review them after studying Chapter 3.

Sections

Each of the four questions identified on page 52 corresponds to one of these sections.

Chapter 3 — BIOLOGY AND BEHAVIOR

Read to Discover

1 How are messages transmitted by neurons, and what are the functions of the peripheral nervous system?

2 What are the major structures of the brain, and what is the function of each structure?

3 How do hormones secreted by the major glands of the endocrine system affect the body?

4 What is the role of chromosomes and genes in heredity, and how do psychologists study the role of heredity in determining traits?

52

Using "A Day in the Life"

Each chapter begins with a vignette, called "A Day in the Life," that relates the information discussed in the chapter to the everyday events in the lives of a group of fictional high school students. The text of the chapter occasionally refers back to the vignette to demonstrate the application of the concept being discussed. An icon marked "A Day in the Life" is placed next to these references.

Copy the following graphic organizer onto the chalkboard, omitting the italicized text. Fill in the circles as you provide an overview of the chapter material to the class.

```
  Nervous                                   Endocrine
  System                                     System
            Major Areas of
            Study for Biological
            Psychologists
  Environment                                Heredity
```

A DAY IN THE LIFE

October 11

Marc was rushing through the halls to reach class on time. As he ran, thoughts of Linda floated through his mind. He was in some classes with her, and he was beginning to think that she was very attractive. Distracted by these images of Linda, Marc rounded a corner and bumped into Todd, who stepped down hard on Marc's big toe. Marc grabbed his sneakered foot in his hands, then started to rub his toe, which throbbed with pain. In addition, he felt his heart begin to race. Todd cringed and said, "Oh, sorry. I didn't even see you." Still holding his foot, Marc grunted, "Hey, don't worry. It's no big deal."

• • •

No big deal? At first glance, this incident between Marc and Todd seems very simple, but much more actually occurred than meets the eye. The way in which Marc's body responded to having his foot stepped on is of great interest to psychologists. This may seem surprising—after all, what does biology have to do with psychology? In fact, biological functioning has much to do with psychology.

The ways in which our bodies and minds work in relation to each other are quite remarkable. Biological psychologists (sometimes called biopsychologists) study the ways in which our behavior and psychological processes are linked to biological structures and processes. For example, sensation, perception, memory, and thinking are all psychological processes that have at least a partly biological basis. (You will read about these topics in greater depth in later chapters.)

A major area of study for biological psychologists concerns the workings of the nervous system. The nervous system, which includes the brain, is involved in psychological processes such as thought and emotion, movement and sensation, and much more. Based on our knowledge of the nervous system, we can explain how messages were sent from Marc's toe to his brain and back to his foot, causing him to grab his foot and begin to massage his injured toe.

In addition to the nervous system, biological psychologists study the endocrine system. This system is responsible for the secretion of hormones. Hormones serve a wide variety of functions, such as influencing emotions. Marc's emotional response to having his foot stepped on was due in part to the endocrine system.

Biological psychologists are also interested in heredity and how it affects us both physically and psychologically. Heredity influences not only how we look but also how we act. Biological psychologists study the interactions between our heredity and the environments in which we live.

Key Terms

- central nervous system
- peripheral nervous system
- neurons
- cell body
- dendrites
- axon
- myelin
- axon terminals
- synapse
- neurotransmitters
- spinal cord
- somatic nervous system
- autonomic nervous system
- medulla
- pons
- cerebellum
- reticular activating system
- thalamus
- hypothalamus
- limbic system
- cerebrum
- cerebral cortex
- corpus callosum
- association areas
- endocrine system
- hormones
- heredity
- genes
- chromosomes

WHY PSYCHOLOGY MATTERS

Psychologists study the nervous system to learn about human behavior. Use **CNNfyi**.com or other current events sources to learn more about the relationship between biology and behavior.

CNNfyi.com

Using Key Terms

Explain to students that many biological terms—including most of the key terms in this chapter—are derived from words of Greek or Latin origin. Have students make a list of the key terms and look up their definitions in a dictionary that includes derivations. Demonstrate how to break the words down to their roots and prefixes. Also show students how to use the list of abbreviations in the dictionary to determine a word's origin. Demonstrate by using the following example: *Synapse* (Gk *syn*, meaning "with"; Gk *haptein*, meaning "to fasten").

Section Objective

7

▶ Explain how messages are transmitted by neurons and describe the functions of the peripheral nervous system.

This objective is assessed in the Section Review on page 59 and in the Chapter 3 Review.

Opening Section 1

Motivator

Set up a row of dominoes to illustrate neural transmission. Invite a volunteer to tap the first domino, sending the whole line falling. Explain to students that the process involved in the transmission of messages between neurons is similar to the chain reaction of a row of falling dominoes. Tell students that the neurons, like the dominoes, transmit messages in only one direction and that neurons always transmit messages at the same strength—just as the dominoes do not gain speed as they fall down.

Using Truth or Fiction

Each chapter opens with several "Truth or Fiction" statements that relate to the concepts discussed in the chapter. Ask students whether they think each statement is true or false. Answers to each item as well as explanations are provided at appropriate points within the text under the heading "Truth or Fiction Revisited."

Cross-Curricular Link: Biology

Tell students that all vertebrates have nervous systems similar to the human nervous system. Then explain that most species of invertebrates that have more than one cell also have some sort of a nervous system. Have each student research and compare the nervous systems of two different organisms—one vertebrate and one invertebrate. Have them present their findings, with visuals, in an oral report to the class.

Teaching Transparencies with Teacher's Notes

TRANSPARENCY 5:
The Anatomy of Two Neurons

54

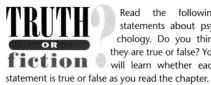

Read the following statements about psychology. Do you think they are true or false? You will learn whether each statement is true or false as you read the chapter.

- Individual cells in the human body can be several feet long.
- Anxiety can give you indigestion.
- A person with brain damage may be able to report that he or she has seen a face but may not be able to identify that it was the face of a close friend.
- Some people are "left-brained" and others are "right-brained."
- The father's genetic contribution—not the mother's—determines the sex of the offspring.

SECTION 7
The Nervous System

The human nervous system is involved in thinking, dreaming, feeling, moving, and much more. It is working when we are active or still, awake or asleep. The nervous system regulates our internal functions. It is also involved in how we react to the external world. Even learning and memory are made possible by the nervous system. When we learn a new behavior or acquire new information, the nervous system registers that experience and changes to accommodate its storage.

The nervous system has two main parts: the central nervous system and the peripheral nervous system. The **central nervous system** consists of the brain and the spinal cord. The **peripheral nervous system** is made up of nerve cells that send messages between the central nervous system and all the parts of the body. In order to understand how the central and the peripheral nervous systems work, we must first understand how nerve cells communicate with one another and how their messages travel through the body.

Neurons

Nerve cells, called **neurons**, run through our entire bodies and communicate with each other. Neurons send and receive messages from other structures in the body, such as muscles and glands. These messages can affect events ranging from the sensation of a pinprick to the first steps of a child, from the writing of a poem to the memory of a past event. Each of us has more than 100 billion neurons, most of which are found in the brain.

Components of a Neuron Neurons are somewhat like trees in structure. Parts of neurons resemble the branches, trunk, and roots of a tree.

The Anatomy of Two Neurons

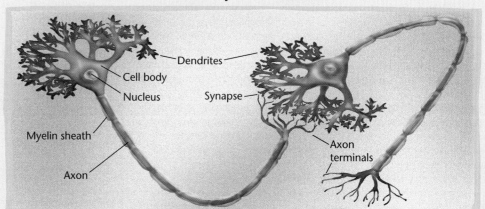

FIGURE 3.1 "Messages" enter neurons through the dendrites. These messages are transmitted along the trunklike axon to other neurons, glands, and muscles. On many neurons, the myelin sheath protects the axon.

54

Teaching Section 1

Guided Practice

Have students stand close together and hold hands to create a "chain." Tell students to imagine that they are sensory neurons and that the last person in the chain is the brain. Devise a code system by which a certain number of hand squeezes represent a certain sensation, such as cold or pain. Explain that by squeezing the hand of the person next to them, the students are simulating the transmission of neural impulses. Have the first "sensory neuron" pass a sensation to the next neuron using the hand-squeeze code, then to the next neuron, and so on to the end of the chain.

Independent Practice

Have students divide into small groups and consider what would have happened to the impulse in the Guided Practice once it was received by the brain. Students should answer the following questions: What factors determined where the original message was sent? *(the location of the neuron in the body and the event that produced the message)* Once the message was received, what type of neurons then carried the message back to the place in the body that first experienced the impulse? *(motor neurons)*

And, as in forests, many nerve cells lie alongside one another like a thicket of trees. Unlike trees, however, neurons can also lie end to end. Their "roots" are intertwined with the "branches" of neurons that lie below. (See Figure 3.1.)

Every neuron consists of a cell body, dendrites, and an axon. The **cell body** produces energy that fuels the activity of the cell. Branching out from the cell body are thin fibers called **dendrites**. The dendrites receive information from other neurons and pass the message through the cell body.

While the dendrites carry information *to* the cell body, the **axon** carries messages *away*. A neuron has many dendrites but usually only one axon. Axons vary greatly in length. Some are just a tiny fraction of an inch, while others stretch to several feet. Because of the length of their axons, some neurons in your legs are several feet long.

TRUTH OR fiction ▪ REVISITED ▪

It is true that individual cells in the body can be several feet long. These cells are nerve cells, or neurons, that are long because they have long axons. Some neurons in the leg stretch from the lower spine to the toes.

Many axons are covered with **myelin**, a white fatty substance that insulates and protects the axon. This myelin sheath, or casing, also helps to speed up the transmission of the message. At the end of the axon, smaller fibers branch out. These fibers are called **axon terminals**.

The Communication Process Messages are sent from the axon terminals of one neuron to the dendrites of other neurons. In order for a message to be sent from one neuron to another neuron, it must cross the **synapse**. The synapse is a junction between the axon terminals of one neuron and the dendrites of another neuron. Messages travel in only one direction. Thus, messages are received by the dendrites and travel through the cell body and the axon to the axon terminals. From there, they cross synapses to the dendrites of other neurons. (See Figure 3.2.) New synapses can develop between neurons that were not previously connected, as when we learn something new.

The information that is sent and the place to which it goes depend on a number of factors. These factors include the locations of the neuron in the

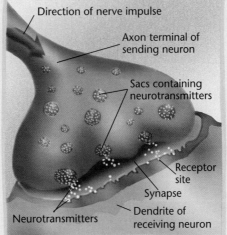

The Synapse

Direction of nerve impulse

Axon terminal of sending neuron

Sacs containing neurotransmitters

Receptor site

Synapse

Neurotransmitters

Dendrite of receiving neuron

FIGURE 3.2 *There is no physical connection between neurons. A neuron relays its message across a junction called a synapse by releasing chemicals called neurotransmitters. They are received by the next neuron.*

A DAY IN THE LIFE

body and the events that produced the message. For example, the pain in Marc's toe was transmitted to his brain through sensory neurons. Sensory neurons are nerve cells that carry information received by the senses *to* the central nervous system. Motor neurons, on the other hand, are nerve cells that carry information *from* the central nervous system to the muscles and the glands and influence their functioning. Motor neurons took the message to Marc's foot so that he pulled up on it and began to rub it. Other motor neurons stimulated Marc's glands, making his heart beat faster. Still other neurons in his brain enabled him to think over the matter and to decide that Todd should be forgiven.

Occasionally, something happens to disrupt the message-sending process. For example, a hard blow to the head from a car accident or a sports injury can cause a concussion—an injury in which the soft tissue of the brain hits against the skull. Sometimes, the person is affected for only a few seconds. Other times, the person may experience effects for a much longer time. In 1993, Dallas Cowboys quarterback Troy Aikman suffered a concussion during a game in the National Football League playoffs. He

Meeting Individual Needs:
Gifted Learners

Have students research the role of the neurotransmitter acetylcholine (ACh) in Alzheimer's disease. Students should prepare a written report in which they define Alzheimer's disease and describe it in biochemical terms. Reports should also answer the following questions: Why is ACh needed for healthy brain functioning? What happens to ACh that may cause Alzheimer's disease? What may reduce ACh in brain cells? How are ACh levels increased?

Evaluating Information

Explain that people who have too much or too little of the neurotransmitters norepinephrine and/or serotonin often suffer from depression. Doctors may prescribe antidepressant drugs to regulate these neurotransmitters in their patients' bodies. Although sales of these drugs total in the billions of dollars, their total effect is often modest and their side effects can be quite harmful. Have students discuss the possibility of treating depression through psychological therapy as an alternative to drug therapy. (Tell students they will learn more about treating depression in Chapter 19.)

Using Visuals

Explain that Troy Aikman's memory loss was a form of retrograde amnesia, a condition in which one cannot remember anything that happened during the time immediately before losing consciousness from a severe head blow. However, memories of other past events remain intact. Tell students they will learn more about amnesia in Chapter 7.

Class Discussion

Tell the class that endorphins are neurotransmitters that naturally reduce pain and boost mood. Explain that flooding the brain with painkillers, antidepressants, or other drugs may cause the brain to stop producing endorphins. Thus, when such a drug is discontinued, a person may experience a period of discomfort—ranging from mild to agonizing—until the brain resumes production of endorphins. Ask students to discuss this and any other possible ramifications of taking antidepressants or painkillers. Do students believe that the benefits outweigh the potential harm?

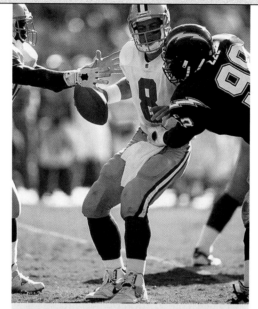

Troy Aikman's concussion in the 1993 football playoffs interfered with his memory of the event.

remembers being at the game, but he cannot remember what happened during the game. Such experiences show that memory is in large part a biological process. (See Chapter 7.)

Neurotransmitters: Chemical Messengers

Neurons send messages across synapses through the release of **neurotransmitters**. Neurotransmitters are chemicals that are stored in sacs in the axon terminals. A neuron fires, or sends its message, by releasing neurotransmitters—much like droplets of water shooting out of a spray bottle. Neurons can fire hundreds of times every second.

There are several types of neurotransmitters. Each has its own structure and fits into a receptor site on the next neuron, similar to the way in which a key fits into a lock. The message is converted into an electrical impulse that travels the length of the neuron. The message is then transmitted to the next neuron by neurotransmitters. The process continues until the message arrives at its destination. This whole process takes only a fraction of a second.

Neurotransmitters are involved in everything people do. Whenever a person waves a hand, yawns, or thinks about a friend, neurotransmitters are involved. Some diseases and psychological dis-

orders may also be caused by the presence of too much or too little of various neurotransmitters.

Researchers have identified dozens of neurotransmitters and their functions. For example, acetylcholine is a common neurotransmitter that is

A DAY IN THE LIFE

involved in the control of muscles. It is used by the motor neurons of the spinal cord and stimulates skeletal muscles. The release of acetylcholine was what led Marc to grab his foot. When the amount of acetylcholine available to the brain decreases, the formation of memories is impaired.

Dopamine is another neurotransmitter. It is involved primarily in motor behavior. A deficiency in dopamine levels plays a role in Parkinson's disease, which is characterized by tremors and uncoordinated, rigid movements. An excess of dopamine may contribute to the psychological disorder schizophrenia. (See Chapter 18.) Other neurotransmitters include noradrenaline, which is primarily involved in preparing the body for action, and serotonin, which is involved in emotional arousal and sleep.

Although we are often unaware of the processes in our bodies, we can be sure that our bodies are hard at work whether we are running or sitting still.

Long-distance runners experience a "runner's high," which may be connected with the release of endorphins. Endorphins are neurotransmitters similar in function to the drug morphine. They have a tranquilizing and painkilling effect on the body.

Synthesizing Information

Have students prepare a narrative of a neural impulse as it travels through the body. The narrative should explain the impulse's voyage through the nervous system, beginning with its arrival at the first sensory neuron's dendrites, then its journey to that neuron's cell body, then to the axon, and so on. The voyage should continue throughout the neural-transmission process, including the point at which the impulse arrives at the central nervous system via sensory neurons and is then transmitted to a motor neuron, where it begins its journey back to the muscles or glands.

Demonstration

Demonstrate the knee-jerk reflex test on a student volunteer. Have the volunteer sit in a chair and cross one leg over the other. Using a rubber reflex hammer, gently strike the soft area just under the kneecap of the volunteer's crossed leg. Have students review the information on the central nervous system to discuss the reflex and describe what happened and why.

At any given moment, millions of neurons are shooting neurotransmitters across synapses and sending complicated messages to various parts of the body. These messages are carried via the spinal cord and the peripheral nervous system.

The Central Nervous System

Figure 3.3 shows the central nervous system, which consists of the neurons of the spinal cord and the brain. (The brain is discussed in Section 2.) The **spinal cord** extends from the brain down the back. It is a column of nerves about as thick as a thumb, and it is protected by the bones of the spine. It transmits messages between the brain and the muscles and the glands throughout the body.

The spinal cord is also involved in spinal reflexes. A spinal reflex is a simple, automatic response to something. For example, if a person touches a hot stove, a message goes immediately from his or her hand to the spinal cord. A message to remove the hand is then sent back to motor neurons in the hand. The removal of the hand is a spinal reflex. (The person may also register pain in his or her brain. But the pain is not what causes the reflex. In fact, the pain may not even be felt until after the hand has been removed.)

Many of our simple actions are reflexive. Have you ever wondered why you blink when you get a speck of dust in your eye? Or why some people sneeze when they sniff pepper? Physicians sometimes test people's reflexes to learn whether their nervous systems are functioning properly. When a doctor taps just below the knee to see if you kick, the purpose is to check your knee-jerk reflex to make sure your neurons are responding the way they are supposed to.

The Peripheral Nervous System

The peripheral nervous system lies outside the central nervous system and is responsible for transmitting messages between the central nervous system and all parts of the body. The two main divisions of the peripheral nervous system are the somatic nervous system and the autonomic nervous system. (See Figure 3.4 on page 58.)

The Somatic Nervous System The **somatic nervous system** transmits sensory messages to the central nervous system. It is activated by touch, pain, changes in temperature, and changes in body position. The somatic nervous system enables us to

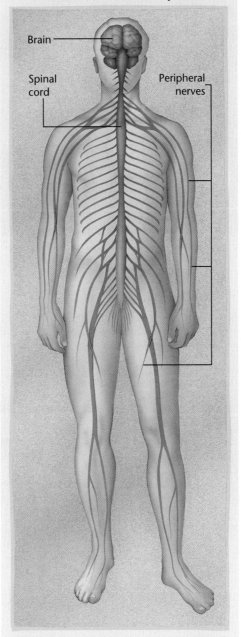

The Central Nervous System

Brain

Spinal cord

Peripheral nerves

FIGURE 3.3 *Your spinal cord is protected by a column of bones called vertebrae. Similarly, your brain is protected by the skull.*

Cultural Dimensions

South American Indians often hunt with arrows tipped with curare, a poison extracted from plants. When an arrow tipped with curare pierces the skin, the poison prevents ACh from lodging within receptor sites in neurons. The lack of ACh prevents muscle contractions, thereby resulting in paralysis. The victim is unable to contract the muscles used in breathing and dies from suffocation.

Using Visuals

Have students look at Figure 3.3. Tell them that the brain is the most complex part of the nervous system. Explain that the spinal cord is a mass of nerve tissue organized into segments that carry sensory and motor information to and from the brain.

Teaching Transparencies with Teacher's Notes

TRANSPARENCY 7: The Central Nervous System

57

Closing Section 1

Organizing Information

Have students construct a diagram of the nervous system listing the various divisions of the nervous system and the types of actions that each of the divisions controls. *(for example, autonomic nervous system: heartbeat, breathing, and blood pressure)*

Reviewing Section 1

Have students complete the Section Review questions on page 59.

Extension

Have interested students complete a brief research paper about paraplegia and quadriplegia. Explain to students that paraplegia, or paralysis of the legs, usually results from damage to the spinal cord below the neck and that quadriplegia, or paralysis of the arms and legs, usually results from damage in the neck region. Students should research the conditions and injuries that cause these forms of paralysis as well as identify which specific areas of the nervous system are affected.

When a doctor hits the knee joint, sensory neurons carry the message from the muscles to the spinal cord. This excites motor neurons, which causes leg muscles to contract, making the leg move.

experience the sensations of hot and cold and to feel pain and pressure. For example, we can feel the softness of a cat's fur, warmth if the cat is sitting on our lap, and pain if the cat scratches us. The somatic system also alerts us that parts of the body have moved or changed position. It sends messages to the muscles and the glands and helps us maintain posture and balance.

The Autonomic Nervous System   The word *autonomic* means "occurring involuntarily," or automatically. The **autonomic nervous system** regulates the body's vital functions, such as heartbeat, breathing, digestion, and blood pressure. We generally do not have to think about these activities—they occur automatically and are essential for keeping us alive.

Psychologists are interested in the autonomic nervous system because of its involvement in the experience of emotion. The response of the autonomic nervous system is particularly important when a person experiences something stressful in the environment.

The autonomic nervous system has two divisions: the sympathetic and the parasympathetic nervous systems. (See Figure 3.4.) These systems generally have opposing functions. The sympathetic system is activated when a person is going into action, perhaps because of some stressful event. It prepares the body either to confront the situation or to run away. This is sometimes called the "fight-or-flight" response. For example, when a person is suddenly attacked by a large angry dog, the sympathetic nervous system is aroused.

The sympathetic nervous system prepares the body by suppressing digestion, increasing the heart

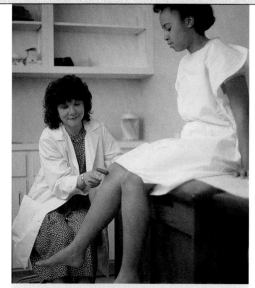

Divisions of the Nervous System

Nervous system

Central nervous system — Peripheral nervous system

Brain | Spinal cord

Autonomic system (involuntary muscles and internal organs) | Somatic system (voluntary muscles and sense organs)

Parasympathetic system (calms body after emergencies) | Sympathetic system (prepares body for action)

FIGURE 3.4   *This chart shows the major divisions of the nervous system. The central nervous system consists of the brain and the spinal cord. The peripheral nervous system transmits messages from the central nervous system to all parts of the body.*

Section Objective

► Identify the major structures of the brain, and explain the functions of each structure.

This objective is assessed in the Section Review on page 67 and in the Chapter 3 Review.

Motivator

Bring to class four or five photographs or other illustrations of the brain structure of several animals, such as various fish, amphibians, reptiles, birds, and/or mammals. Explain to students that the more intellectually advanced an animal is, the larger its cerebral cortex is. Tell students which types of animal brains you have pictures of, and ask students to match each brain to the appropriate animal. Then give students the answers and discuss their responses. Explain to students that they will learn more about the functions of the cerebral cortex in this section.

and respiration rates, and elevating the blood pressure. Do you ever feel queasy when you are in a stressful situation—such as when your teacher springs a surprise quiz on you? This is because your sympathetic nervous system has kicked into action and has suppressed your digestive processes. And when Todd stepped on Marc's toe, Marc felt his heart start to race—another result of the activation of the sympathetic nervous system.

It is true that anxiety can give you indigestion. Anxiety may cause indigestion by inducing activity of the sympathetic nervous system, which suppresses digestion.

In contrast to the sympathetic system, the parasympathetic nervous system restores the body's reserves of energy after an action has occurred. Heart rate and blood pressure are normalized, breathing is slowed, and digestion returns to normal. If you are having trouble remembering which system is which, perhaps it will help to keep in mind that "sympathetic" and "stress" both start with the letter *s,* while "parasympathetic" and "peace" both begin with *p.* The sympathetic system reacts to stress; the parasympathetic system restores peace.

SECTION 1 REVIEW

 Homework Practice Online Keyword: SY3 HP3

1. How do messages travel from one neuron to another?
2. Identify the systems that make up the peripheral nervous system.
3. **Critical Thinking** *Summarizing* In what way do the parasympathetic and the sympathetic nervous systems work together?

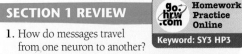

The Brain: Our Control Center

Every person is unique in part because of the capacities for learning and thought made possible by the human brain. In ancient times, hundreds of years before scientists had learned much about how the brain functions, people did not attribute human psychological processes such as thinking to the working of the brain. People thought that what was inside a person's body was not very different from what was inside an animal's body. Therefore, they reasoned, the abilities that make people different from animals—such as creative thought, art, and analytical abilities—could not be explained in biological terms. Instead, it was widely believed that the body was inhabited by souls or demons.

The ancient Egyptians believed that a little person dwelled within the skull and regulated behavior. Greek philosopher Aristotle thought that the soul resided in the heart. B. F. Skinner (1987) noted that the English language still reflects the belief in the heart as the seat of will, thought, hunger, and joy. We use expressions such as "deep in one's heart," "to know something by heart," and "to have a change of heart."

Today, however, we recognize that the mind, or consciousness, dwells within the brain (Goldman-Rakic, 1995; Sperry, 1993). We know that when thoughts of Linda ran through Marc's mind, something was happening in his brain. We now have greater understanding of the brain and the links between biological processes and psychological phenomena.

Parts of the Brain

The human brain is composed of many parts that work together to organize our movements, create our thoughts, form our emotions, and produce our behaviors. Scientists have identified the localized functions of different parts of the brain. The brain is divided into three sections: the hindbrain, the midbrain, and the forebrain. (See Figure 3.5 on page 60.) The hindbrain is the lower portion of the brain and is involved in many vital functions such as heart rate, respiration, and balance. The midbrain includes areas that are involved in vision and hearing. The forebrain, the front area of the brain, is involved in complex functions such as thought and emotion.

The Hindbrain   The medulla, the pons, and the cerebellum are important structures of the hindbrain. The **medulla** is involved in vital functions such as heart rate, blood pressure, and breathing. The **pons** is located in front of the medulla and is involved in regulating body movement, attention, sleep, and alertness.

Applying Information

Have students read the information on the reticular activating system. Ask them what it is, what its function is, and how it is related to arousal and sleep. Then have students discuss the types of noises that wake them during the night. Have students discuss how they usually respond to particular noises. Then ask students to compare their responses. Why do certain noises wake some of the students while other students are unaffected by those same noises? *(The reticular activating system becomes selective and may learn to screen out common disturbances.)*

Demonstration

Locate an anatomical model of the brain. (One may be available in the science department at school.) Use the model in class to identify the various structures and parts of the brain. Have students refer to Figures 3.5 and 3.6 for comparison. Point out that the cerebrum accounts for approximately 85 percent of the brain's weight and is surrounded by the cerebral cortex.

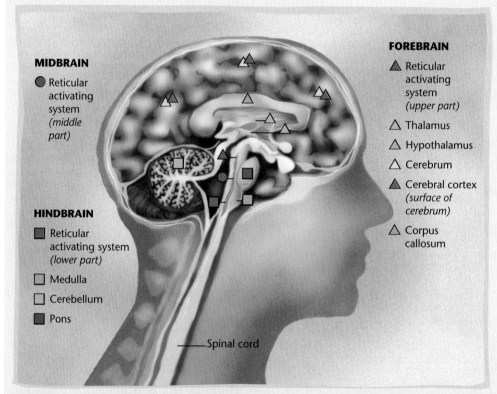

Parts of the Human Brain

MIDBRAIN
● Reticular activating system (middle part)

HINDBRAIN
■ Reticular activating system (lower part)
□ Medulla
□ Cerebellum
■ Pons

FOREBRAIN
▲ Reticular activating system (upper part)
△ Thalamus
△ Hypothalamus
△ Cerebrum
▲ Cerebral cortex (surface of cerebrum)
△ Corpus callosum

— Spinal cord

FIGURE 3.5 *The average human adult brain weighs about three pounds and has more than 10 billion cells, many of which are neurons. Although the brain makes up about 2 to 3 percent of a person's body weight, it requires about 20 percent of the blood's oxygen supply.*

Cerebellum is the Latin word for "little brain." The **cerebellum** looks like the larger part of the brain (the cerebrum), under which it rests, but it is much smaller. It is involved in balance and coordination. A person whose cerebellum is injured may have trouble with coordination. The person may walk unsteadily and even occasionally fall down.

The Midbrain   The midbrain is located between the hindbrain and the forebrain. Areas within the midbrain are involved in vision and hearing. Eye movement, for example, is controlled by an area in the midbrain. In addition, the midbrain contains part of the **reticular activating system**. The reticular activating system begins in the hindbrain and rises through the midbrain into the lower part of the forebrain. This system is important for attention, sleep, and arousal. Stimulation of the reticular activating system makes us alert. It affects arousal by increasing heart rate and blood pressure, and it increases brain activity. Some drugs, such as alcohol, reduce the activity of the reticular activating system, thus affecting alertness and reaction time.

Sudden, loud noises stimulate the reticular activating system and can awaken a sleeping person. However, the reticular activating system can screen out some noises. A person who lives in the city may not be awakened by the sounds of traffic roaring by. This same person may, however, awaken to sounds that are more out of the ordinary, such as a bird singing, even if these sounds are fairly soft.

The Forebrain   Four key areas of the forebrain are the thalamus, the hypothalamus, the limbic system, and the cerebrum. Certain parts of the forebrain are very well developed in human beings. The forebrain is the part of the brain that makes it possible for humans to engage in complex thinking processes.

Thalamus is a Latin word meaning "inner chamber." The **thalamus** is a critical structure of the brain because it serves as a relay station for sensory stimulation. Most of the messages coming from the sense organs go through the thalamus on the way to the higher levels of the brain (those areas responsible for mental processes such as thinking and

reasoning). The thalamus transmits sensory information, such as the pain from Marc's big toe, to the areas of the brain that interpret and respond to the information. The thalamus also relays sensory input from the eyes and the ears to the appropriate parts of the brain for interpretation of the input.

Hypo- is a Greek prefix meaning "under." Thus, the **hypothalamus** lies below the thalamus. The hypothalamus is tiny, but it is extremely important because it is involved in many aspects of behavior and physiological functions. It is vital to the regulation of body temperature, the storage of nutrients, and various aspects of motivation and emotion. It is also involved in hunger, thirst, sexual behavior, caring for offspring, and aggression. Disturbances within the hypothalamus can lead to unusual drinking and eating behaviors.

Among lower animals, stimulation of parts of the hypothalamus triggers behaviors such as fighting, mating, or nest building. Although the hypothalamus is also important to people, our behavior is less mechanical and tends to be influenced by cognitive functions such as thought, choice, and value systems.

The **limbic system** forms a fringe along the inner edge of the cerebrum. It is involved in learning and memory, emotion, hunger, sex, and aggression. If a particular part of the limbic system is damaged, people can recall old memories but do not create new memories. For example, a person with damage to that area may have vivid childhood memories of playing with his or her sister but may not be able to remember that this same sister visited earlier that day. Researchers have also found that destruction of another specific area of the limbic system can lead animals to show passive behavior. Destruction of a different area of the limbic system causes some animals to behave aggressively, even when there seems little reason to do so.

The **cerebrum** (Latin for "brain") is the crowning glory of the brain. Only in human beings does the cerebrum make up such a large part of the brain. The cerebrum accounts for about 70 percent of the weight of the brain. The surface of the cerebrum is wrinkled with ridges and valleys. This surface is the **cerebral cortex**. The cerebral cortex is the outer layer of the brain, just as bark is the outer layer of a tree. (*Cortex* is the Latin word for "bark of a tree.")

The cerebral cortex is the part of the brain that we tend to think of when we talk about the brain. It is the part that makes us uniquely human—the part that thinks. In addition to thinking, the cerebral cortex also deals with memory, language, emotions, complex motor functions, perception, and much more.

The Cerebral Cortex: What Makes Us Unique

The cerebral cortex is composed of two sides—a left side and a right side. Each side is called a hemisphere. (The Greek *hemi-* means "half." Thus, each half of the brain is half a sphere, just as each half of planet Earth is a hemisphere.) To visualize the cerebral cortex, think of a walnut. The shell of the walnut is like the skull. Just as the walnut has two sides that are connected, so does the brain. In the brain, the structure that connects the two hemispheres is called the **corpus callosum**.

Interestingly, information received by one side of the body is transmitted to the *opposite* hemisphere of the brain. For example, if you touch something with your left hand, that information is sent to the right side of your brain. Conversely, if you touch something with your right hand, the left hemisphere of your brain receives the information. The corpus callosum aids in getting information from one side of the brain to the other.

Each hemisphere of the cerebral cortex is divided into four parts, or lobes. The frontal lobe lies behind the forehead, and the parietal lobe lies to the top and rear of the head. The temporal lobe lies to the side, just below the ears. The occipital lobe is at the back of the head. (See Figure 3.6 on page 62.)

Some sensations, such as visual sensations, are received primarily in one lobe. However, each lobe does not necessarily act independently from the others. Some functions require the interplay of several lobes. The involvement of the cerebral cortex in the senses and motor behavior is a good illustration of this interaction.

Guided Practice

Bring to class an illustration or photograph of the brain of an animal other than a human. Explain to students that the size of a specific area of the brain may indicate how important that area's function is for that particular animal. For example, dogs have a larger and better developed area in the brain for smell than people have. Ask students to list other animals whose brain functions may differ significantly from those of humans. Then have students identify the area of the brain that may be different.

Independent Practice

Have students prepare a list of the primary functions of each of the four lobes of the brain. Then have students compare the four lists and brainstorm ways in which each of the four lobes must work together. *(For example, when you watch a theatrical play you use the visual areas in the occipital lobe to see the play and the auditory area in the temporal lobe to hear the play. Your parietal lobe interprets the sights, sounds, and emotions, and the motor cortex in the frontal lobe stimulates motor neurons to clap your hands when the play is over.)*

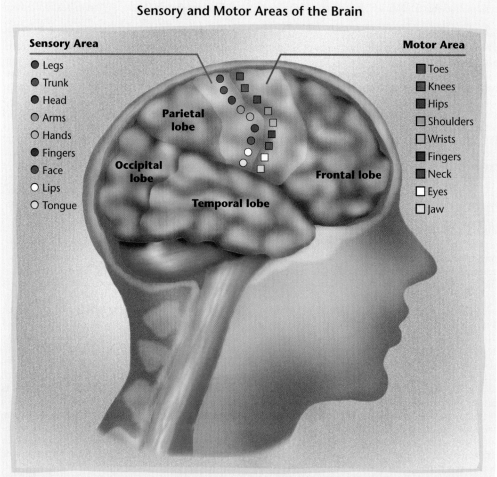

FIGURE 3.6 *Certain areas of the cerebral cortex control specific sensory and motor functions.*

Senses and Motor Behavior The occipital lobe contains the primary visual area of the cerebral cortex. When light strikes the eyes, neurons in the occipital lobe fire, enabling us to see. We also "see" flashes of light if neurons in the occipital lobe are stimulated by electricity.

Damage to different parts of the occipital lobe can create unusual conditions. People with damage to one area may be able to recognize an object, but they may be unable to differentiate it from another object that is similar. For example, if shown a key, they may know that what they see is a key, but they may not be able to tell it apart from another key that looks different. People with damage to another area

may be able to report that they have seen a face, but they may not be able to identify that it is the face of a close friend.

It is true that a person with brain damage may be able to report that he or she has seen a face but may not be able to identify that it was the face of a close friend. Damage to a particular area in the occipital lobe of the cerebral cortex can create this condition.

Applying Information

Have students think of objects that are designed for people who are right-handed. Possibilities include desks, notebooks, and scissors. Then have them discuss how and why left-handed people are often expected to learn how to use these objects.

Evaluating Information

Tell students to review the information on the two key language areas of the brain: Broca's area and Wernicke's area. Then have students answer the following questions: Why does the human brain have such highly developed areas for language? Do other animals' brains have a similar level of development for language? Why or why not? What other areas of the brain are involved in the use of language? *(The centers for vision and hearing enable us to understand written and spoken language; the motor cortex and the cerebellum enable us to move our lips and tongues to speak.)*

The hearing, or auditory, area of the cortex lies in the temporal lobe. Sounds are relayed from the ears to the thalamus to the auditory area. When this occurs, we hear sounds. If a specific area of the temporal cortex is damaged, a person may not be able to recognize very common sounds.

Messages received from the skin senses (see Chapter 4) are projected to the sensory cortex in the parietal lobe. These sensations include warmth, cold, touch, and pain. Different neurons fire, depending on whether you have scratched your nose, touched a hot stove, or been stung by a bee. When Todd stepped on Marc's toe, the pain message was relayed from the toe to the parietal lobe of Marc's brain.

The motor cortex in the frontal lobe, was involved when Marc grabbed his foot and started rubbing it. Neurons in the motor cortex fire when we move certain parts of our body.

Association Areas   Much of the cerebral cortex is composed of areas that involve sensory and motor functions. Other areas, called **association areas**, shape information into something meaningful. For example, certain neurons in the visual area of the occipital lobe fire when we see vertical lines. Others fire in response to horizontal lines. Although one group of cells may respond to vertical lines and another group of cells to horizontal lines, association areas put it all together. As a result, we see a box or an automobile or a road map instead of a confusing display of verticals and horizontals.

The association areas in the frontal lobes, near the forehead, could be called the brain's executive center. It appears to be where we solve problems and make plans and decisions (Chafee & Goldman-Rakic, 2000; Duncan et al., 2000; Levy & Goldman-Rakic, 1999).

Executive functions also require memory, like the memory in your computer. Association areas also provide the core of your working memory (Chafee & Goldman-Rakic, 2000; Levy & Goldman-Rakic, 1999). They are connected with sensory areas in the brain and can tap whatever sensory information is needed or desired. The frontal region of the brain thus retrieves visual, auditory, and other kinds of memories and manipulates them—similar to the way in which a computer retrieves information from files in storage and manipulates it in working memory. Other association areas make possible the complex psychological functions of language.

Language Abilities   Although the left and the right hemispheres of the brain have many of the same functions, they differ in a number of ways. For example, for nearly all right-handed people, language functions are based in the left hemisphere. Language functions are also based in the left hemisphere of about two out of three left-handed people.

Within the hemisphere containing the language functions, two key language areas are Broca's area and Wernicke's area. Damage to either area is likely to cause an aphasia, a difficulty with specific aspects of understanding or producing language.

Wernicke's area, which is located in the temporal lobe, pieces together sounds and sights. People with damage to this area may find it difficult to understand speech, and their speech often is meaningless. For example, when asked to describe a picture of two boys stealing cookies behind a woman's back, one person responded: "Mother is away her working her work to get her better, but when she's looking the two boys looking the other part. She's working another time" (Geschwind, 1979).

Broca's area is located in the frontal lobe near the section of the motor cortex that controls the areas of the face used for speaking. When Broca's area is damaged, people speak slowly and laboriously, using simple sentences.

Left Versus Right Hemispheres   The same hemisphere that contains most language functions is usually more involved in logic, problem solving, and mathematical computation than is the other hemisphere (Borod, 1992; Hellige, 1990). The nonlanguage hemisphere is relatively more concerned with the imagination, art, feelings, and spatial relations. People often speak of certain abilities as belonging to the right brain or to the left brain. Thus, people who are very logical are said to be "left-brained," while people who are particularly creative are called "right-brained." This idea, however, has become exaggerated. Although some differences do exist, the hemispheres do not act independently of each other (Hellige, 1990).

It is not true that some people are "left-brained" and others are "right-brained." Both hemispheres of the brain are involved in most human activities and abilities.

What's New in Psychology?

Studies suggest that people who are deaf use the left hemisphere of the brain to read sign language (Corina et al., 1992). Therefore, if a deaf person has a stroke—in which the blood supply to part of the brain is cut off—in the left hemisphere, he or she will have as much difficulty communicating in sign language as a hearing person would have using spoken language. The brain interprets both sign language and spoken language in the same way.

internet connect

TOPIC: Parts of the Brain
GO TO: go.hrw.com
KEYWORD: SY3 PS3

Have students access the Internet through the HRW Go site to research parts of the brain and how the different parts function to organize and control physical and mental processes. Then ask students to create a symbol or drawing for each part of the brain. The symbol should reflect the function of the part and its role in controlling physical or mental processes.

Demonstration

Have two students sit next to each other on the same chair. Then say that each person can use only one side of his or her body—one should use the left side and the other, the right side. Ask the students to perform a few simple tasks, such as tying a shoe. On the first attempt, have the students complete the tasks by themselves, using only one half of their bodies. Then have both students cooperate to complete the task. Explain that, like the students, each hemisphere of the brain can function by itself, but the brain functions more effectively if the two hemispheres work together.

Evaluating Information

Have students reread the section in the text on split-brain operations. Then ask them to write a brief essay in which they answer the following questions: What have scientists learned from these operations? What, if anything, can you infer from the results of split-brain operations? What information regarding the functioning of the hemispheres calls for more research?

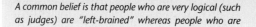

A common belief is that people who are very logical (such as judges) are "left-brained" whereas people who are more creative (such as artists) are "right-brained." This belief, however, has little scientific validity.

Much of what psychologists have learned about left- and right-hemisphere functioning comes from people who have had split-brain operations. In a split-brain operation, the corpus callosum, which connects the two hemispheres, is cut. This procedure, although performed only rarely, is sometimes used to help people with serious neural disorders such as severe cases of epilepsy. People with epilepsy experience seizures, which are bursts of abnormal neuron firings that generally occur in one hemisphere and then spread to the other. Cutting the corpus callosum can reduce the severity of the seizures by preventing them from spreading. After the surgery, patients usually function quite effectively despite their hemispheres' inability to communicate with each other.

However, the surgery does have some subtle effects on functioning. For example, people may be able to describe verbally the objects they hold in their right hand but not what they hold in their left hand (Gazzaniga, 1992). This is because if an object is held in the right hand, the information is sent to the left hemisphere, which (in most people) contains language abilities. However, if the same object is held in the left hand, this information is projected to the right hemisphere, which has very little language ability. It is important to remember that for people with intact corpus callosums, the hemispheres usually work together. Thus, most people can describe objects held in either hand.

Methods of Studying the Brain

Much of our earlier understanding of the brain came from studies of people with head injuries. Today, researchers increase their knowledge of the brain and its functions by using a variety of techniques to study damaged and intact brains.

Accidents   One way that researchers have been able to see how the brain is related to psychological functions is through the study of accidents and brain damage. Brain damage from head injuries can result in loss of vision and hearing, confusion, or loss of memory. In some cases, the loss of large portions of the brain may result in relatively little loss of function. Yet the loss of vital, smaller parts can result in language problems, memory loss, or death. In other words, which particular area is damaged may have a greater effect than the amount of the damage.

Electrical Stimulation of the Brain   Electrical stimulation of the brain has shown that specific areas are associated with specific types of sensations (such as seeing light or feeling a tap on the arm) or motor activities (such as walking). In a classic experiment, José Delgado (1969) used electrical stimulation of the brain to show how an animal could be made to change behavioral patterns. The researchers implanted an electrode into a bull's

For Further Research

Tell students that José Delgado is one of many scientists who have studied the brain. Have each student choose one of the following scientists to research: Gustav Fritsch, Eduard Hitzig, or Wilder Penfield. Each student should prepare a short oral report in which he or she explains the scientist's experiment and the significance of the results.

Ask students what might have happened to Phineas Gage if the rod had injured the motor area of his cerebral cortex or the sensory area of his cerebral cortex. Ask students the following question: Are there parts of the brain that, if injured, would result in a person's death? If so, what are they?

CASE STUDIES
AND OTHER TRUE STORIES

Is Phineas Gage Still the Same Man?

The ability of the brain to withstand some accidents is nothing less than remarkable. In some instances, people have not only survived severe injuries to the brain, but they have continued to live fairly normal lives. Sometimes, though, the victim is not quite the same as before the accident. Consider the case of Phineas Gage.

Young Mr. Gage was a promising railroad worker. His character was outstanding and he was well liked. But all that changed one day in 1848. While he was tamping down the blasting powder for a dynamite charge, Gage accidentally set the powder off. An inch-thick metal rod shot upward through his brain and out the top of his head.

The rod landed many yards away. Gage fell back in a heap, but he was not dead. His coworkers watched in shock as he stood up a few moments later and spoke. They drove him by oxcart to a local doctor, John Harlow. As the doctor marveled at the hole through Gage's head, Gage asked when the doctor thought he'd be able to return to work.

Everyone, including the doctor, was surprised that Phineas Gage even survived the accident. Two months later, the physical effects of Gage's wounds had healed. He walked about, spoke normally enough, and was aware of his surroundings. However, Gage had changed. He no longer was a dependable worker. He had also become foul-mouthed and ill-mannered. It had become clear that the accident had had some serious psychological consequences.

Gage died 13 years later during an epileptic seizure. Dr. Harlow persuaded Gage's family to donate his skull to the Warren Medical Museum at Harvard University. Generations of biologists and

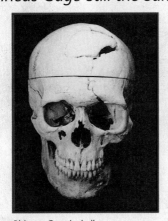

Phineas Gage's skull

psychologists have studied the skull and wondered how Gage's changes in personality might have been caused by damage to his brain.

According to biologists Hanna and Antonio Damasio (1992), the way in which the rod had entered the brain had spared the parts of the frontal lobes that were involved in language and motor behavior. Thus, Gage was able to speak normally and move about easily. However, the rod had severely damaged a part of the underside of the frontal lobes, causing the disturbance in personality. The Damasios note that people who suffer damage to the same part of the brain today experience similar changes in personality. These individuals are often unable to censor their thoughts before speaking. As a result, they may blurt out thoughts that they would have kept to themselves before their brains were injured.

Other researchers also have found changes in patients' personalities after brain injuries. In general, damage to right frontal areas can produce impulsive and rule-breaking behaviors, such as interrupting conversations (Kolb & Taylor, 1981). People with frontal-lobe injuries are also less likely to make spontaneous facial expressions. The combination of excessive talking and lack of facial expressions may make these individuals seem like different people than they were before.

WHY PSYCHOLOGY MATTERS

Many people have suffered injuries that affect their personalities. Use **CNN fyi.com** or other current events sources to learn more about how psychologists help people who have suffered brain injuries. Write a two-paragraph profile about a person who has suffered such an injury.

CNN fyi.com

For Your Information

A local newspaper expressed astonishment at Gage's survival. "The most singular circumstance connected with this melancholy [sad] affair is, that he was alive at two o'clock this afternoon, and in full possession of his reason, and free from pain." Gage later donated the tamping bar to the medical school at Harvard University.

Closing Section 2

Drawing Conclusions

Have students make a chart of the methods used to study the brain. At the top of each column, they should write the name of the method. Then, below each method, have them fill in the following information: how the method is used, what type of information it provides, and conclusions that can be drawn from the results of studies using the method.

Synthesizing Information

Have students use what they have learned in this section to write a narrative "guided tour" of the brain. Students should provide a detailed description—including the function and location—of the major parts of the brain.

Reviewing Section 2

Have students complete the Section Review questions on page 67.

brain. When the brain was stimulated, the bull dramatically stopped his charge and circled to the right.

In another classic study, James Olds and Peter Milner (Olds, 1969) used rats who had electrodes implanted in their brains to learn about the functions of the hypothalamus. When the rats pressed a lever, the electrodes stimulated the portion of the hypothalamus where they were implanted. As it turned out, the rats found this stimulation pleasurable—so pleasurable that the rats would press the lever up to 100 times a minute just to receive the stimulation. In some cases, hungry rats chose electrical stimulation over food. The part of the hypothalamus where the electrodes were implanted thus became known as a "pleasure center."

Electrical stimulation of the brain is not always reliable as a research tool. Stimulation in the same place can produce different effects at different times. On one occasion, a rat may eat when a portion of the brain is stimulated, but on another occasion it may drink. The areas that produce pleasant and unpleasant sensations in people may also vary from person to person and from day to day.

The Electroencephalogram The electroencephalogram (EEG) is a device that records the electrical activity of the brain. Electrodes attached to the scalp with tape or paste detect small amounts of electrical activity called brain waves. Researchers have learned that certain brain wave patterns are associated with feelings of relaxation and with sleep. (See Chapter 5.) Researchers and physicians can use electroencephalogram readings to help diagnose some kinds of psychological disorders and to help locate tumors.

Scans In recent years, scientists have designed new techniques for examining the brain. These techniques use computers to generate images of the brain from various sources of information (Goleman, 1995; Posner & Raichle, 1994). Images of the brain can provide information about brain damage and other abnormalities. Imaging techniques can also be used for early diagnoses of cancers and other problems. In addition, physicians can use imaging to aid them during difficult and intricate surgeries.

In computerized axial tomography (CAT) scans, a moving ring passes X-ray beams around and through the head. The density of the brain tissue determines how much radiation is absorbed. Computers measure the amounts of radiation and piece together a three-dimensional view of the brain that can be displayed on a video monitor.

In magnetic resonance imaging (MRI), a person lies in a very powerful magnetic field. Radio waves then cause parts of the brain to give off extra energy. This energy is measured from multiple angles and is translated by computer into a visual image of the brain's anatomy. MRI is more powerful than a CAT scan and can show details more clearly. For example, MRI is more effective at revealing small injuries and abnormalities in hard-to-see areas.

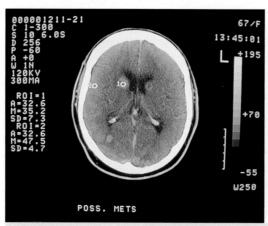

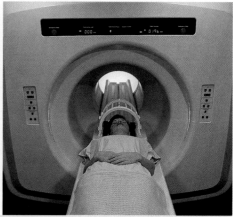

The photograph at left shows an image obtained by a CAT scan. By producing a three-dimensional view of the brain, a CAT scan can reveal hidden brain damage. The photograph on the right shows a person entering MRI apparatus. For people who fear enclosed spaces, the time spent lying in the MRI field can be uncomfortable.

Section Objective

▶ Explain how hormones secreted by the major glands of the endocrine system affect the body.

This objective is assessed in the Section Review on page 69 and in the Chapter 3 Review.

Opening Section 3

Motivator

At the same time, bring two cups of water to the boiling point—one in a microwave oven and another in a pot on the stove. Then pour the water into separate mugs. Have students compare the two cups after two minutes and again after five minutes. Which cup of water reached the boiling point first? Which one stayed hot longer? Explain that like the water in the microwave oven, messages relayed by the nervous system are fast and short-lived. Like the water on the stove, messages relayed by the endocrine system are slower but usually are longer lasting.

Positron emission tomography (PET) scans differ from CAT scans and MRIs because they show the activity of the brain rather than a snapshot of the brain at a given time. Scientists can see the brain actually at work. The person is injected with radioactive sugar. As the sugar reaches the brain, more of it is used where brain activity is greater. A computer image is generated based on the activity. The PET scan has been used by researchers to see which parts of the brain are most active when we are listening to music, working out a math problem, using language, or playing chess (Goldman-Rakic, 1995; Raichle, 1994). The PET scan reveals which parts of the brain are activated while the event is actually taking place. So, if you raise your hand, the computer will show activity in one area. If you suddenly start to sing a song, another area will light up. Research with PET scan suggests that we carry out much of our problem solving in the frontal lobes (Duncan et al., 2000).

Using these research techniques, psychologists have learned that the mind is a product of the brain. Today it is generally agreed that for every mental event there are accompanying, underlying biological events. Imaging techniques have allowed us to explore more deeply how the nervous system, particularly the brain, functions while we are thinking, feeling, and moving. The study of brain abnormalities has also revealed that when parts of the brain have undergone damage, other areas of the brain can sometimes take over the functions of the damaged areas.

A PET scan shows brain activity as it occurs.

SECTION 2 REVIEW

Homework Practice Online
Keyword: SY3 HP3

1. Why is the cerebral cortex important?

2. Describe two differences between the left hemisphere and the right hemisphere of the cerebral cortex.

3. List three different imaging techniques used to study the brain.

4. **Critical Thinking** *Evaluating* Why do you think it benefits people to have brains that are flexible? What would happen if brains were not flexible?

SECTION 3

The Endocrine System

The **endocrine system** consists of glands that secrete substances, called **hormones**, into the bloodstream. The word *hormone* is derived from the Greek *horman,* meaning "to stimulate" or "to excite." Hormones stimulate growth and many kinds of reactions, such as changes in activity levels and moods. Because hormones affect behavior and emotional reactions, psychologists who study the biology of behavior are also interested in the endocrine system.

Like neurotransmitters, hormones have specific receptor sites. Although the various hormones circulate throughout the body, they act only on hormone receptors in certain places. Hormones are produced by several different glands. These glands include the pituitary gland, the thyroid gland, the adrenal glands, and the testes and the ovaries. (See Figure 3.7 on page 68.)

The Pituitary Gland

The pituitary gland lies just below the hypothalamus. It is about the size of a pea, but it is so important that it has been referred to as the "master gland." The pituitary gland, which is stimulated by the hypothalamus, is responsible for the secretion of many different hormones that affect various aspects of behavior.

Growth hormone, for example, regulates the growth of muscles, bones, and glands. Children whose growth patterns seem abnormally slow often catch up to others the same age when doctors give them growth hormone.

Some hormones affect females in relation to pregnancy and mothering. Prolactin stimulates production of milk in nursing women. Oxytocin is responsible for stimulating labor in pregnant women. Sometimes when a pregnant woman is overdue, an obstetrician may induce labor by injecting the woman with oxytocin.

Section 2 Review: Answers

1. The cerebral cortex is the part of the brain that controls the way we think as well as our memory, language, emotions, perceptions, and complex motor functions.

2. The left hemisphere is usually more involved in language and logic, while the right hemisphere plays more of a role in emotions, creativity, and spatial relations.

3. Answers should include the CAT scan, the MRI, and the PET scan.

4. Because the brain is flexible, if one part is injured, another part may be able to assume the function of the damaged part. If the brain were not flexible, then abilities controlled by the damaged area would be completely and forever lost.

Teaching Section 3

Role-Playing

Ask for student volunteers to participate in a role-playing activity. Tell students that each volunteer will be playing one of the following roles: the pituitary gland, the thyroid gland, or the adrenal gland. Then have each volunteer choose people from the class to serve as "hormones." Have each gland and its hormones present facts to the class about the way the gland and the hormones interact. Ask students to discuss whether the role-playing exercise accurately conveyed the information about the endocrine system.

Closing Section 3

Classifying Information

Have students make a table of the glands of the endocrine system in which they identify the hormones secreted by each of the glands as well as the function of each of the hormones.

Reviewing Section 3

Have students complete the Section Review questions on page 69.

The Endocrine System

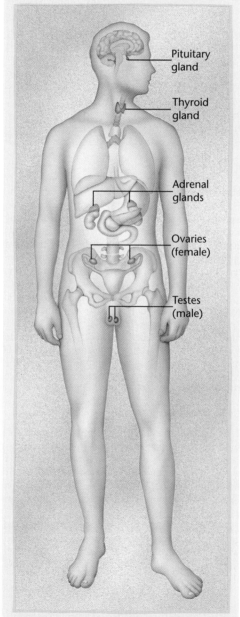

- Pituitary gland
- Thyroid gland
- Adrenal glands
- Ovaries (female)
- Testes (male)

FIGURE 3.7 *The glands of the endocrine system secrete hormones that stimulate various body functions.* **Why do you think psychologists are interested in the endocrine system?**

Oxytocin and prolactin have been shown in some lower mammals to be connected to maternal behaviors such as caring for young (Insel, T. R., 2000). The role of these hormones, if any, in human maternal behaviors remains unclear, however.

The Thyroid Gland

The thyroid gland produces thyroxin. Thyroxin affects the body's metabolism—its rate of converting food to energy. The production of too little thyroxin can lead to a condition called hypothyroidism. People with hypothyroidism often are overweight. For children, too little thyroxin can cause a condition called cretinism, which is characterized by stunted growth and mental retardation.

People who produce too much thyroxin may develop hyperthyroidism. Hyperthyroidism is characterized by excitability, inability to sleep, and weight loss.

The Adrenal Glands

The adrenal glands are located above the kidneys. The Latin prefix *ad-* means "toward" or "at," and *renal* derives from the Latin *renes,* meaning "kidneys."

The outer layer, or cortex, of the adrenal glands secretes cortical steroids. Cortical steroids increase resistance to stress and promote muscle development. They also cause the liver to release stored sugar, making energy available for emergencies.

The adrenal glands also produce adrenaline and noradrenaline. When a person faces a stressful situation, the sympathetic nervous system causes the adrenal glands to release a mixture of adrenaline and noradrenaline. These hormones help arouse the body, enabling the person to cope with the stressful situation. When Todd stepped on Marc's toe, for example, Marc's adrenal glands produced the adrenaline-noradrenaline mixture to help Marc deal with the situation.

Adrenaline also plays a role in the emotions people experience. It can intensify emotions such as fear and anxiety. Another function of noradrenaline is to raise blood pressure. In the nervous system, it also acts as a neurotransmitter.

The Testes and the Ovaries

Other glands are the testes (in males) and the ovaries (in females). These glands produce the hormones testosterone, estrogen, and progesterone.

Section Objective

► Explain the role of chromosomes and genes in heredity and evaluate the methods used by psychologists to study the role of heredity in determining traits.

This objective is assessed in the Section Review on page 72 and in the Chapter 3 Review.

Opening Section 4

Motivator

Have students make a chart with three columns. In the first column, they should list 10 of their physical and emotional traits. In the second column, have them place check marks next to those traits they believe are a result of heredity. In the third column, have them place check marks next to those traits they believe are a result of environment. Have students keep their charts to use again later in this section.

Adrenaline and noradrenaline help people deal with emergencies, such as when parents must rush a child to the hospital.

Testosterone   Testosterone is a male sex hormone, although females have small amounts of this hormone as well. Testosterone is produced by the testes in males. Small amounts of it are also secreted by the ovaries in females. Testosterone plays an important role in development.

In the prenatal period, testosterone influences development of the sex organs. About eight weeks after fertilization, if testosterone is secreted, it stimulates development of male sex organs. If testosterone is not secreted, female sex organs develop.

In adolescence, testosterone aids the growth of muscle and bone as well as the development of primary and secondary sex characteristics. Primary sex characteristics are directly involved in reproduction. Secondary sex characteristics, such as beard growth, distinguish males and females but are not directly involved in reproduction.

Testosterone is a kind of steroid. A small number of athletes use steroids to enhance their athletic ability. Steroids affect muscle mass, heighten resistance to stress, and increase the body's energy supply. Steroids also stimulate the sex drive and raise self-esteem. Because our society is highly competitive, some people are tempted to use steroids, but their use has serious medical and ethical implications. Links have been reported between steroid use and sleep disturbances, liver damage, heart disease, and other medical problems. Ethically, most people believe that the use of steroids is unnatural and unfair to athletes who do not use them.

Estrogen and Progesterone   Estrogen and progesterone are female sex hormones, although low levels are found in males. The ovaries in females produce estrogen and progesterone. Estrogen is also produced in smaller amounts by the testes in males.

Estrogen fosters the development of primary and secondary sex characteristics, such as breast enlargement. Progesterone has multiple functions. It stimulates growth of the female reproductive organs and helps prepare the body for pregnancy. Together, estrogen and progesterone regulate the menstrual cycle and vary greatly during that cycle. Changes in levels of estrogen have been linked to premenstrual syndrome (PMS) in some women. PMS is a collection of symptoms (such as irritability, depression, and fatigue) that some women experience before menstruating.

Estrogen has psychological effects as well as biological effects. Higher levels of estrogen seem to be connected with optimal cognitive functioning and feelings of well-being among women (Ross et al., 2000; Yaffe et al., 2000). Women are also more interested in sexual activity when estrogen levels are high—particularly during ovulation, when they are fertile.

SECTION 3 REVIEW

Homework Practice Online
Keyword: SY3 HP3

1. Explain the effects of the endocrine system on development.

2. **Critical Thinking**   *Analyzing Information* How does the endocrine system affect behavior?

SECTION 4

Heredity: Our Genetic Background

Heredity is the transmission of characteristics from parents to offspring. Psychologists are interested in studying heredity, along with the brain and hormones, as a means of understanding why people behave as they do. Heredity plays a key role in the development of traits both in people and in animals. The traits we inherit help shape our behavior.

Heredity is vital in the transmission of physical traits such as height, hair texture, and eye color. Heredity is also related, to some extent, to some psychological traits (Lykken et al., 1992; Plomin &

Section 3 Review: Answers

1. Answers should note that hormones secreted by the endocrine system stimulate growth.

2. Answers should note that the adrenal glands affect how people deal with stress. Testosterone, estrogen, and progesterone affect people's moods and behavior.

internet connect

TOPIC: The Endocrine System
GO TO: go.hrw.com
KEYWORD: SY3 PS3

Have students access the Internet through the HRW Go site to research the endocrine system and its effects on emotion and behavior. Then ask students to create a chart that outlines the glands in the endocrine system, the hormones produced by each, the function of the hormone, and how they act to stimulate bodily functions.

Teaching Section 4

Taking a Stand

Explain to the students that medical doctors can perform genetic tests on men and women who are planning to have children. These tests, referred to as genetic screening, are meant to identify whether the expectant parent is likely to produce an offspring who is genetically predisposed to—expected to be affected by—certain genetic characteristics or birth defects such as Down syndrome or cystic fibrosis. Have students hold a debate about whether genetic screening should be mandatory for all couples.

For Further Research

Have students research the ways in which genetic disorders are transmitted from parents to offspring. They should cover dominant inheritance, recessive inheritance, sex-linked inheritance, and multifactorial inheritance. Also ask students to find out how couples planning to have children can undergo genetic screening to evaluate the genetic makeup of both members of the couple and how that makeup will affect their offspring. Students should present their findings in a one-page report.

Using Visuals

Tell students that each chromosome consists of more than 1,000 genes. The sequence in the "rungs" of the ladder is the genetic code that will cause the organism to develop specific traits.

For Your Information

Down syndrome is considered a chromosomal abnormality, a genetic disorder that results from an excess or deficiency of genetic material. Explain that two other common types of genetic disorders are disorders resulting from a single mutated gene (which is one defective unit of genetic material) and multifactorial disorders (which are caused by the interaction of one or more abnormal genes with environmental factors). Multifactorial disorders are thought to result from a fetus's genetic predisposition to react adversely to specific environmental factors.

DNA: The Genetic Code

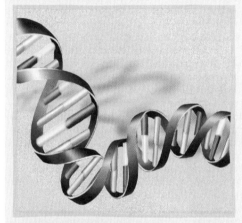

FIGURE 3.8 *The threadlike molecules of DNA that make up chromosomes contain the codes for the development of particular traits.*

Rende, 1991). Researchers have found that some psychological traits such as shyness, leadership ability, aggressiveness, and even an interest in arts and crafts are influenced by heredity. It is important, though, to keep in mind that the environment also plays a role in shaping these traits. Heredity has been shown to be one factor involved in many psychological disorders, including anxiety and depression, schizophrenia, bipolar disorder, and alcoholism (Carey & DiLalla, 1994; Clark et al., 1994; Sher & Trull, 1994). (See Chapter 18.)

Despite their disability, children with Down syndrome enjoy many of the same activities that other children do.

Genes and Chromosomes

Genes are the basic building blocks of heredity. Traits are determined by pairs of genes, with one gene in each pair inherited from each parent. Some traits, such as blood type, are controlled by a single pair of genes. Complex psychological traits, such as intelligence, involve combinations of genes, as well as environmental factors.

Genes are found in threadlike structures called **chromosomes**, which are composed of deoxyribonucleic acid (DNA). DNA takes the form of a double helix. (See Figure 3.8.) Most normal human cells contain 46 chromosomes that are organized into 23 pairs. In each of the 23 pairs, one chromosome comes from the father and the other chromosome comes from the mother. Each chromosome contains instructions for the development of particular traits in the individual.

Researchers have learned that 22 of the 23 pairs of chromosomes are similar in males and females. The 23rd pair, the sex chromosomes, determines whether we are female or male. In males, the 23rd pair consists of an X chromosome (so called because of its X shape) and a Y chromosome (because of its Y shape). Females have two X chromosomes, so they always pass an X chromosome on to their offspring. The chromosome that comes from the father, therefore, determines the sex of the offspring. If the father contributes an X chromosome, then the offspring is female. If the father contributes a Y chromosome, then the offspring is male.

TRUTH OR fiction

■ REVISITED ■

It is true that the father's genetic contribution—not the mother's—determines the sex of the offspring. The mother always contributes an X chromosome. Thus, it is the X or the Y chromosome from the father that determines the sex of the child.

When a child is born without 46 chromosomes in each cell, physical and behavioral disorders may result. One of the most common disabilities of this type occurs when there is an extra, or third, chromosome on the 21st pair. When this happens, a baby will be born with Down syndrome. People with Down syndrome usually have some level of mental retardation and may have heart and respiratory problems.

Analyzing Information

Tell students that some couples pay a considerable amount of money to have X chromosomes and Y chromosomes separated in an attempt to conceive a child that is specifically male or female. This issue raises concerns that, in the future, people will be able to and will want to control the genetic makeup of babies before they are conceived. Ask students to discuss the pros and cons of couples being able to choose specific traits for their children. Ask students the following question: If you had a choice, would you want to choose your child's physical and emotional traits? Why or why not?

Cooperative Learning

Organize students into pairs. Have each student in the pair choose one side of the nature-nurture controversy. Ask each student to write a paragraph describing how a person's viewpoint on this issue might affect his or her attitude about an individual's ability to change or modify behavior. Each pair of students should then present their findings in class in the form of an oral debate.

DILBERT reprinted by permission of United Feature Syndicate, Inc.

The Nature-Nurture Debate

Throughout history, philosophers and scientists have debated the role of biology in determining who we are, as people. This discussion is often called the "nature-nurture debate." *Nature* refers to what people inherit—the biological groundwork that prepares a person to develop in certain ways. *Nurture* refers to environmental factors—what a person is exposed to in life. Nurture includes a variety of factors such as family, education, culture, living conditions, everyday individual experiences, and other factors that make up people's environment.

People who support the "nature" side of the debate argue that people's traits and personality are primarily determined by their biological makeup. The argument is that our inherited characteristics determine the kind of people we are. Supporters of the "nurture" side, argue that the environment we live in and our everyday experiences—not our biological inheritance—determine how we behave and think.

Both of these views are extreme. Today most psychologists agree that the influences of both nature and nurture determine our psychological traits. Biology influences us to act in certain ways, but our environment—along with personal factors such as values and decision making—can modify these plans. It is the interaction of heredity and environment that determines who we are. A person who has the genetic potential to write a brilliant novel will never write that novel if he or she is never taught to read or write. An athlete who has the genetic potential to win a gold medal in figure skating will never win the medal if he or she has never been to a skating rink (or a solidly frozen pond).

Although most psychologists agree that genes and the environment interact, the extent of the role that heredity plays is still a controversial topic. Some

psychologists believe that many of our traits, including intelligence, are determined largely by genetics. Others have criticized this view and are concerned about its implications. The heredity view can be interpreted to suggest that we cannot control our destiny because it is determined by our biology. Taken to the extreme, the heredity view might suggest, for example, that we should not try to change something about ourselves with which we are not satisfied. However, most psychologists are careful to note that heredity is not destiny. They emphasize that the environment does play a role in determining how a person develops.

Kinship Studies

The most common way to sort out the roles that heredity and environment play in determining a trait is to do kinship studies. Kinship refers to the degree to which people are related, based on the genes they have in common. Identical twins share 100 percent of their genes. A parent and his or her child share 50 percent of their genes, as do full brothers and sisters, on average. Aunts and uncles related by blood share an average of 25 percent of their genes with nieces and nephews, and first cousins share an average of 12.5 percent.

Psychologists use this information to determine how much a trait is influenced by genetics and how much by environment. They study certain traits or behavioral patterns in individuals and then compare them to those of relatives. If genes are involved in a certain trait, then people who are more closely related, and who share more genes, should be more likely to exhibit the same trait than people who have less overlap in genes or who are not related. Two common types of kinship studies are twin studies and adoptee studies.

Closing Section 4

Evaluating Information

Have students consider whether their personalities are similar to their parents'. Then tell students that studies have shown that the personalities of parents are often unrelated to the personalities of their children. Ask students to suggest reasons to account for the similarities and differences between them and their parents. Then ask how many of the reasons are primarily genetic and how many are primarily environmental. Discuss whether the students favor genetic or environmental reasons.

Follow Up

Have students find the charts they constructed in the Motivator activity. Ask them to review the charts and change any check marks they feel are incorrect based on what they have learned in Section 4. Then have them briefly describe the roles of heredity and environment in determining each of the 10 traits they listed.

Reviewing Section 4

Have students complete the Section Review questions on page 72.

Section 4 Review: Answers

1. Genes are the building blocks of heredity. They provide the instructions for the development of specific traits. Genes are contained in the chromosomes, the threadlike structures composed of DNA that are in every cell of the body.

2. The role of heredity is studied through various types of kinship research. Answers should include descriptions of twin studies, adoption studies, and studies of twins reared apart.

3. Answers might include family influences, cultural values, everyday individual experiences, and traumatic events.

Identical twins share the same genetic makeup.

Twin Studies   The study of identical and fraternal twins is a useful way to learn about the relative influences of nature and nurture. Because identical twins share the same genetic makeup, differences between identical twins must be the result of the environment. For example, if one of the identical twins loves jazz, but the other twin prefers rock, that difference must be due to the twins' different experiences in the environment—not their heredity.

In contrast, fraternal twins, like other brothers and sisters, share an average of 50 percent of their genes. Thus, differences between fraternal twins might stem from heredity or the environment. The premise behind twin studies is that if identical twins are more similar on a certain trait than are fraternal twins, then that trait is influenced by genetics.

Researchers have found that identical twins resemble one another more strongly than fraternal twins in certain traits, including shyness and activity levels, irritability, sociability, even happiness (McCourt et al., 1999; McCrae & Costa, 2000; Lykken & Tellegen, 1996). Thus, these traits appear to be influenced by heredity.

Identical twins are also more likely than fraternal twins to share psychological disorders such as autism, substance dependence, and schizophrenia (DiLalla & Carey, 1996). In one study on autism, a disorder characterized by limited social and communication abilities, both twins were likely to be autistic in 96 percent of the identical twin pairs. In contrast, both twins were likely to be autistic in only 24 percent of the fraternal twin pairs (Ritvo et al., 1985). This evidence strongly suggests a role for heredity in autism.

Adoptee Studies   One problem with twin studies is that identical twins tend to be treated similarly and are exposed to similar environments (Coon et al., 1990; Segal, 1993). Because they share the same environment as well as the same heredity, it is sometimes difficult to determine whether their similarities are due to nature or nurture.

One way to try to eliminate the effects of common backgrounds is to study children who have been adopted. Children who have been separated from their parents at an early age and then raised elsewhere provide special opportunities for sorting out the effects of nature and nurture. Psychologists look for the relative similarities between children and their adoptive and biological families. If the children act more like their biological families—with whom they share genes—than their adoptive families—with whom they share the environment—then their behavior may be largely influenced by heredity.

Twins Reared Apart   One of the most useful types of kinship studies examines twins who have been reared apart. Twins reared apart are less likely than twins reared together to share common experiences. Thus, similarities are probably due to genetic factors. In a major study that began in 1979, Thomas Bouchard and his colleagues (1990) examined twins who were reared apart. They found that many psychological and personality traits—including intelligence, traditionalism (following rules), risk avoidance, aggression, and leadership—are influenced by heredity.

Twins reared apart even share many of the same mannerisms, such as how they sit or stand. In one study, one pair of twins each wore seven rings, two bracelets on one wrist, and a bracelet and watch on the other wrist (Holden, 1980). Most researchers, however, acknowledge that the environment also has an important effect on the development of traits and mannerisms.

SECTION 4 REVIEW

1. Define *gene* and *chromosome*.

2. Describe two methods used to study the role of heredity in determining traits.

3. **Critical Thinking**   *Finding the Main Idea*
   Why are psychologists interested in heredity?

72

Extension

Have students do research to support or refute the following statement related to the nature-nurture debate: Parenting is the number-one influence on a child's success or failure and happiness or unhappiness in life. Students should present their conclusions in a one-page report with evidence to support their conclusions.

Have students design a survey to determine whether siblings share similar social attitudes. Then have each student survey three sets of siblings—each respondent should answer the questions privately. When students have completed their surveys, ask them whether the siblings they surveyed had social attitudes that were similar to or different from one another. How could one determine whether those attitudes resulted from genetic influences or were a result of the siblings' upbringing?

READINGS IN

PSYCHOLOGY

DOES HEREDITY DETERMINE OUR PERSONALITIES?

In 1979 Thomas Bouchard and several colleagues began conducting the Minnesota Study of Twins Reared Apart (Bouchard et al., 1990). The purpose of the study was to discover the extent to which heredity and environment were each involved in determining various psychological and personality traits. More than 100 pairs of identical and fraternal twins who were separated in infancy and reared apart participated in the study. The researchers examined similarities and differences in numerous traits such as intelligence, leadership abilities, and reaction to stress. They also studied social attitudes such as religious beliefs and the tendency to follow tradition.

In the report, Bouchard emphasized the importance of studying twins reared apart:

Monozygotic [identical] and dizygotic [fraternal] twins who were separated early in life and reared apart are a fascinating experiment of nature. They also provide the simplest and most powerful method for disentangling the influence of environmental and genetic factors on human characteristics.

Bouchard and his colleagues drew several conclusions from their research:

The study of these reared-apart twins led to two general and seemingly remarkable conclusions concerning the sources of the psychological differences—behavioral variation—between people: (i) genetic factors exert a pronounced and pervasive influence on behavioral variability, and (ii) the effect of being reared in the same home is negligible for many psychological traits. . . . For almost every behavioral trait so far investigated, from reaction time to religiosity, an important fraction of the variation among people turns out to be associated with genetic variation.

In other words, the results of the study suggested that heredity plays a greater role than environment in determining personality traits and behavior. Bouchard and his colleagues also noted, however, that the strong influence of heredity on psychological traits does not necessarily mean that environmental factors in general—and parenting in particular—play no role whatsoever. Commenting on the role parents play in determining personality traits in their children, the researchers stated:

Psychologists have been surprised by the evidence that being reared by the same parents in the same physical environment does not, on average, make siblings more alike as adults than they would have been if reared separately in adoptive homes. It is obvious that parents can produce shared effects if they grossly deprive or mistreat all their children. It seems reasonable that charismatic, dedicated parents, determined to make all their children share certain personal qualities, interests, or values, may sometimes succeed. Our findings, and those of others, do not imply that parenting is without lasting effects. The remarkable similarity in [identical twins reared apart] in social attitudes (for example, traditionalism and religiosity) does not show that parents cannot influence those traits, but simply that this does not tend to happen in most families.

The study, which lasted more than a decade, indicated that identical twins reared apart are as similar as identical twins reared together, and that identical twins are more similar than fraternal twins. Based on these results, Bouchard and many other psychologists believe that personality, intelligence, and social attitudes are largely determined by heredity, rather than environment.

Think About It

Drawing Inferences and Conclusions One of the findings of the Bouchard study was that children raised in the same family do not necessarily have similar social attitudes or personalities. Why might differences occur?

Primary Source Note

Description of change: excerpted, bracketed

Rationale: excerpted to focus on main idea; bracketed to clarify meaning

Think About It: Answers

In addition to genetic differences, children raised in the same family are treated differently within the family and have different experiences in their lives outside the family.

Chapter 3 Review: Answers

Writing a Summary

See the section subtitles for the main topics in the chapter.

Identifying People and Ideas

1. the brain and spinal cord
2. nerve cells that run through the body and communicate with one another
3. a white fatty substance that insulates and protects the axon
4. a junction between the axon terminals of one neuron and the dendrites of another neuron
5. the system that regulates the body's vital functions
6. the system that regulates attention, sleep, and arousal
7. glands that secrete hormones into the bloodstream

Technology

► Chapter 3 Test Generator (on the One-Stop Planner)

► HRW Go site

Reinforcement, Review, and Assessment

► Chapter 3 Review, pp. 74–75

► Chapter Review Activities with Answer Key

► Alternative Assessment Handbook

► Portfolio Assessment Handbook

► Chapter 3 Test (Form A or B)

PSYCHOLOGY PROJECTS

Linking to Community Have a neurologist visit the class and discuss the ways in which physicians in your community use the techniques described in the text to study the brain. Ask the neurologist to discuss the following questions:

---

8. the transmission of characteristics from parents to offspring

9. the basic building blocks of heredity

10. threadlike structures that contain genes

Understanding Main Ideas

1. The nervous system is responsible for carrying messages to and from all parts of the body.

2. Students may describe the reflexive action of a hand touching a hot stove. Dendrites of sensory neurons detect the heat and carry the message along their axons to other dendrites until the message reaches the spinal cord. A message to remove the hand is then sent back to motor neurons in the hand.

3. The cerebellum and cerebrum might be called the "little brain" and "big brain," respectively. The cerebellum is located in the hindbrain and controls balance and coordination. The cerebrum is located in the forebrain and is responsible for complex motor and mental functions.

4. occipital (vision), temporal (auditory), parietal (skin senses), and frontal (motor)

5. Structures in the nervous system stimulate the endocrine system to produce hormones. For example, the hypothalamus stimulates the pituitary gland to produce the growth hormone.

6. The "nature-nurture debate" concerns whether behavior is determined more by heredity or by environment.

Thinking Critically

1. The message does not reach its destination, which may result in

Chapter 3 REVIEW

Writing a Summary

Using standard grammar, spelling, sentence structure, and punctuation, summarize the information in this chapter. Consider:

• the anatomy and functions of given brain areas and the nervous system

• the effects of the endocrine system on development and behavior, and the role of chromosomes and genes in heredity

Identifying People and Ideas

Identify the following terms or people and use them in appropriate sentences.

1. central nervous system
2. neurons
3. myelin
4. synapse
5. autonomic nervous system
6. reticular activating system
7. endocrine system
8. heredity
9. genes
10. chromosomes

Understanding Main Ideas

SECTION 1 (pp. 54–59)

1. Why is the nervous system referred to as a communication system?

2. Give an example of spinal reflex, and explain how the nervous system functions in this reflexive action.

SECTION 2 (pp. 59–67)

3. Which brain structures might be called "little brain" and "big brain"? Why? Besides their size, how are these structures different?

4. List the four lobes of the cerebral cortex and one function of each.

SECTION 3 (pp. 67–69)

5. How are the nervous system and the endocrine system related?

SECTION 4 (pp. 69–72)

6. What is meant by the "nature-nurture debate"?

Thinking Critically

1. Analyzing Information Messages travel in only one direction from neuron to neuron. What happens if the message-sending process is disrupted?

2. Contrasting How do the functions of the sympathetic and parasympathetic systems differ?

3. Making Generalizations and Predictions Imagine that you have to give an oral report in class. Describe how you might feel and act before and after the report. How does your knowledge of the nervous system help you understand your reactions?

4. Identifying a Point of View Why do you think some observers think it would be dangerous to adhere to an extreme heredity view of psychological traits?

5. Drawing Inferences and Conclusions Which type of kinship study probably yields the most reliable results? Why? What might be some drawbacks of this type of study?

Writing About Psychology

1. Analyzing Information Write a two-page paper describing the localized functions of the major brain areas.

2. Summarizing The role of parenting is an important issue for those who support the nurture side of the nature-nurture debate. Locate books or journals in the library that deal with parenting. Prepare a one-page summary of the arguments of each side of this debate. Use the graphic organizer below to help you write your summary.

Nature	Nurture

- What can be learned from EEGs, CAT scans, MRIs, and PET scans?
- What can physicians do to help people who have problems commonly diagnosed by these tests?
- How were these problems diagnosed before these techniques were available?

After the neurologist has finished his or her presentation, give students the opportunity to ask additional questions.

Cooperative Learning Organize students into groups of four. Tell students that the role of parenting is a major concern of those who support the nurture side of the nature-nurture debate. Have students locate books in the library that deal with parenting. Each student in a group should choose a different book.

Have students debate the influence of parenting on children's behavior. Then have the groups summarize the significance of parenting on personality.

Building Social Studies Skills

Interpreting Graphs

Study the bar graph below. Then use the information in the graph to help you answer the questions that follow.

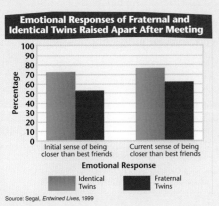

Emotional Responses of Fraternal and Identical Twins Raised Apart After Meeting

Percentage (y-axis: 0, 10, 20, 30, 40, 50, 60, 70, 80, 90, 100)

Emotional Response (x-axis): Initial sense of being closer than best friends | Current sense of being closer than best friends

Legend: Identical Twins | Fraternal Twins

Source: Segal, *Entwined Lives*, 1999

1. Which of the following statements can be concluded from the information on the chart?
   a. Identical twins feel a greater sense of bonding than do fraternal twins.
   b. There are no differences between identical and fraternal twins.
   c. Twins feel closer than siblings who are not twins.
   d. Identical twins have a less strong sense of bonding than do fraternal twins.
2. What additional information would make this chart more useful?

Analyzing Primary Sources

Read the following Aesop's fable, which raises an important issue in the study of psychology. Then answer the questions that follow.

❝The gods were once disputing whether it was possible for a living being to change its nature. Jupiter said "yes," but Venus said "no." So to try the question, Jupiter turned a cat into a maiden and gave her to a young man for a wife. The wedding was duly performed and the young couple sat down to the wedding feast. "See," said Jupiter to Venus, "how becomingly she behaves. Who could tell that yesterday she was but a cat? Surely her nature is changed."

"Wait a minute," replied Venus, and let loose a mouse in the room. No sooner did the bride see this than she jumped up from her seat and tried to pounce upon the mouse. "Ah, you see," said Venus, "nature will out.❞

3. Which of the following statements best describes the meaning of the fable?
   a. Heredity plays a more important role than environment in determining personality traits.
   b. Environment plays a more important role than heredity in determining personality traits.
   c. Heredity and environment are of equal importance in determining personality traits.
   d. Heredity plays no role in shaping personality traits.
4. In the fable, what method of observation do Jupiter and Venus use to resolve the nature-nurture debate?

momentary or permanent inability to remember the incident.

2. The sympathetic nervous system heightens certain bodily functions and suppresses others. The parasympathetic nervous system returns the body to its normal state.

3. Your stomach may feel queasy, you breathe rapidly, and your heart pounds. Afterward, breathing and heart rate return to normal.

4. People might think they are destined to behave or think in a certain way and thus they avoid trying something that might improve their situation or outlook.

5. Studies of identical twins who grew up in different environments are most effective. Researchers can ascribe similar traits to heredity, not upbringing. The drawback is researchers cannot ignore the influence of environment on the developement of traits.

Writing About Psychology:

1. Students should describe the different brain areas and should specify each area's localized functions.

2. Students should describe the positions of both sides of the "nature-nurture debate."

Building Social Studies Skills

1. a

2. Students' answers will vary, but suggestions might include the length of time between the initial meeting and current feelings, and the responses of nontwin siblings raised apart who are meeting for the first time.

3. a

4. They use the case-study method.

PSYCHOLOGY PROJECTS

Cooperative Learning

Reading About Psychology With two or three of your classmates, look for magazine and newspaper articles that deal with biology and behavior. For example, you might find an article describing research that indicates schizophrenia is caused by a chemical imbalance in a person's body, or you might see an article describing a surgical procedure that relieves the tremors of Parkinson's disease. Present a summary of the article to the class. Then place the article in a class file on biology and behavior.

internet connect

Internet Activity: go.hrw.com
KEYWORD: SY3 PS3

Choose a topic on biology and behavior to:
- create a symbol reflecting the functions of the parts of the brain.
- make a chart of the human endocrine system.
- write a report on the influence that heredity and environment have on psychological traits.

Sensation and Perception

CHAPTER RESOURCE MANAGER

	Objectives	Pacing Guide		Reproducible and Review Resources
SECTION 1: Sensation and Perception: The Basics (pp. 78–80)	Distinguish between sensation and perception, and explain how they contribute to an understanding of our environment.	**Regular** 1 day *Block Scheduling Handbook with Team Teaching Strategies, Chapter 4*	**Block Scheduling** .5 day	**SM** Mastering Critical Thinking Skills 4 **REV** Section 1 Review, p. 80
SECTION 2: Vision (pp. 80–85)	Explain how the eye works to enable vision.	**Regular** 1 day *Block Scheduling Handbook with Team Teaching Strategies, Chapter 4*	**Block Scheduling** .5 day	**E** Research Projects and Activities for Teaching Psychology **SM** Study Skills and Writing Guide, Part 2 **REV** Section 2 Review, p. 85
SECTION 3: Hearing (pp. 85–88)	Describe how the ear perceives sound.	**Regular** 1 day *Block Scheduling Handbook with Team Teaching Strategies, Chapter 4*	**Block Scheduling** .5 day	**E** Creating a Psychology Fair, Handout 2 **REV** Section 3 Review, p. 88
SECTION 4: Other Senses (pp. 88–92)	Identify the chemical, skin, and body senses.	**Regular** 1 day *Block Scheduling Handbook with Team Teaching Strategies, Chapter 4*	**Block Scheduling** .5 day	**RS** Essay and Research Themes for Advanced Placement Students, Theme 3 **REV** Section 4 Review, p. 92
SECTION 5: Perception (pp. 93–99)	Summarize the laws of sensory perception.	**Regular** 1 day *Block Scheduling Handbook with Team Teaching Strategies, Chapter 4*	**Block Scheduling** .5 day	**PS** Readings and Case Studies, 4 **REV** Section 5 Review, p. 99

Chapter Resource Key

PS	Primary Sources	**A**	Assessment		Video	
RS	Reading Support	**REV**	Review		Internet	
E	Enrichment		Transparencies		Holt Presentation Maker Using Microsoft® PowerPoint®	
SM	Skills Mastery		CD-ROM			

One-Stop Planner CD–ROM

See the *One-Stop Planner* for a complete list of additional resources for students and teachers.

One-Stop Planner CD–ROM

It's easy to plan lessons, select resources, and print out materials for your students when you use the **One-Stop Planner CD-ROM with Test Generator.**

Technology Resources

 One-Stop Planner, Lesson 4.1
 Homework Practice Online
 CNN Presents Psychology: Synesthesia

 One-Stop Planner, Lesson 4.2
 Homework Practice Online
 Teaching Transparencies 11: The Electromagnetic Spectrum
 Teaching Transparencies 12: The Human Eye
HRW Go Site

 One-Stop Planner, Lesson 4.3
Homework Practice Online
 Teaching Transparencies 13: The Human Ear
HRW Go Site

 One-Stop Planner, Lesson 4.4
 Homework Practice Online
Teaching Transparencies 14: The Taste Buds
HRW Go Site

 One-Stop Planner, Lesson 4.5
 Homework Practice Online

 internet connect
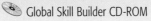

HRW ONLINE RESOURCES

GO TO: go.hrw.com
Then type in a keyword.

TEACHER HOME PAGE
KEYWORD: SY3 Teacher

CHAPTER INTERNET ACTIVITIES
KEYWORD: SY3 PS4
Choose an activity to have students:
- create a drawing or model of the parts of the eye.
- make an oral presentation on the brain and sound processing.
- conduct an Internet scavenger hunt on perception and the senses.

CHAPTER ENRICHMENT LINKS
KEYWORD: SY3 CH4

ONLINE ASSESSMENT
Homework Practice
KEYWORD: SY3 HP4

Standardized Test Prep
KEYWORD: SY3 STP4

Rubrics
KEYWORD: SS Rubrics

CONTENT UPDATES
KEYWORD: SS Content Updates

HOLT PRESENTATION MAKER
KEYWORD: SY3 PPT4

ONLINE READING SUPPORT
KEYWORD: SS Strategies

CURRENT EVENTS
KEYWORD: S3 Current Events

Additional Resources

PRINT RESOURCES FOR TEACHERS
Hubel, D. H. (1988). *Eye, brain, and vision.* New York: Scientific Library.

PRINT RESOURCES FOR STUDENTS
Shepard, R. N. (1990). *Mind sights.* New York: Freeman.
Cytowic, R. G. (1993). *The man who tasted shapes.* New York: Warner Books.

MULTIMEDIA RESOURCES
The enchanted loom: Processing sensory information (VHS). Films for the Humanities & Sciences, P.O. Box 2053, Princeton, NJ 08543-2053.
Sight (VHS). Films for the Humanities & Sciences, P.O. Box 2053, Princeton, NJ 08543-2053.
Smell (VHS). Films for the Humanities & Sciences, P.O. Box 2053, Princeton, NJ 08543-2053.

Chapter Review and Assessment

HRW Go site
REV Chapter 4 Review, pp. 100–101
REV Chapter Review Activities with Answer Key

A Chapter 4 Test (Form A or B)
A Portfolio Assessment Handbook
A Alternative Assessment Handbook

Chapter 4 Test Generator (on the One–Stop Planner)
Global Skill Builder CD-ROM

SENSATION AND PERCEPTION

Introducing Chapter 4

Explain to students that, contrary to popular belief, we have more than five senses. Ask students to name as many senses as they can. Write their answers on the board. Have a student volunteer write down on a piece of paper the senses the class has listed on the chalkboard. After studying Chapter 4, review the answers given.

Sections

Each of the five questions identified on page 76 corresponds to one of these sections.

Chapter 4

SENSATION AND PERCEPTION

Read to Discover

1 In what way do sensation and perception contribute to an understanding of our environment?

2 How does the eye enable vision?

3 How does the ear perceive sound?

4 What are the chemical, skin, and body senses?

5 What are the laws of sensory perception?

Each chapter begins with a vignette, called "A Day in the Life," that relates the information discussed in the chapter to the everyday events in the lives of a group of fictional high school students. The text of the chapter occasionally refers back to the vignette to demonstrate the application of the concept being discussed. An icon marked "A Day in the Life" is placed next to these references.

Copy the following graphic organizer onto the chalkboard, omitting the italicized text. Fill in the columns as you provide an overview of the senses to the class.

Senses					
Vision	*Hearing*	*Smell*	*Touch*	*Taste*	*Body Senses*

A DAY IN THE LIFE

October 15

Linda and Marc were on their first date. They were getting settled in their seats at the movie theater. The movie was about to start, and voices buzzed all around them. Still, Marc did not really hear any of them. He was paying attention to what Linda was saying, and it seemed as if no one else was there at all. The other movie-goers were just gray, colorless shapes in the dim light. Marc hardly even noticed that the popcorn was a little too salty and that the gummy spot under his feet made the soles of his shoes stick to the floor. Instead, he was thinking about how much he liked the smell of Linda's perfume and the touch of her hand, although even these sensations faded into the recesses of Marc's mind as he listened to her speak.

Suddenly a darkened shape said, "Excuse me," and squeezed in front of them to find a seat. A moment later, Marc's toe throbbed with pain, and for the second time in less than a week, Todd was saying, "Oh gee, I'm sorry!" Once again, Todd had accidentally stepped on Marc's foot.

Although Marc was annoyed, he grunted, "It's okay. It's dark in here. I guess you couldn't see." Yet that did not really help his toe, which was still throbbing. However, when Linda asked, "Are you all right, Marc?" her concerned voice practically made the pain in his toe disappear. All of a sudden, he was almost glad the whole accident had happened.

• • •

Like Marc in the movie theater, we all experience the world with our senses. A common belief is that people have five senses: vision, hearing, smell, taste, and touch. But you will learn that people actually have more than five senses. Touch, for example, includes several skin senses—pressure, warmth, cold, and pain. Still other senses tell us the position our body is in without our having to look.

Once we take in information through our senses, we do something with that information to interpret it. What we do depends on many factors—the circumstances, our mood, even our cultural background. Marc, for example, tuned out the background noise in the theater because the only thing he was interested in hearing was Linda's voice. Then, when Todd stepped on his toe, he was both surprised and annoyed. These intense feelings heightened his perception of pain. But just a few seconds later, Linda's concern seemed to drive away the pain.

Psychologists call these two different processes sensation (the feeling) and perception (the interpretation of the feeling). As you read this chapter, you will learn more about these two concepts.

Key Terms

- sensation
- perception
- absolute threshold
- difference threshold
- signal-detection theory
- sensory adaptation
- pupil
- lens
- retina
- photoreceptors
- blind spot
- visual acuity
- complementary
- afterimage
- cochlea
- auditory nerve
- conductive deafness
- sensorineural deafness
- olfactory nerve
- gate theory
- vestibular sense
- kinesthesis
- closure
- proximity
- similarity
- continuity
- common fate
- stroboscopic motion
- monocular cues
- binocular cues
- retinal disparity

WHY PSYCHOLOGY MATTERS

Psychologists have learned much about how people make sense of the world around them. Use CNNfyi.com or other current events sources to learn more about the ways people perceive information.

CNNfyi.com

Section Objective

▶ Distinguish between sensation and perception, and explain how they contribute to an understanding of our environment.

This objective is assessed in the Section Review on page 80 and in the Chapter 4 Review.

Motivator

Tell students that sensation and perception are essential to human communication, learning, and survival. Ask students to write down an example of (1) a situation in which they experienced difficulties as a result of failing to hear, see, taste, smell, or feel something in the environment and of (2) a situation in which they sensed something in the environment but were unable to accurately interpret the sensory information. Encourage students to refer to two different senses in their two examples. Have students share their examples with the class.

Using Truth or Fiction

Each chapter opens with several "Truth or Fiction" statements that relate to the concepts discussed in the chapter. Ask students whether they think each statement is true or false. Answers to each item as well as explanations are provided at appropriate points within the text under the heading "Truth or Fiction Revisited."

For Your Information

Studies of absolute thresholds for various stimuli are complicated by the psychological factor known as response bias. A study participant's response bias is his or her tendency to answer either no or yes when unsure of whether or not there was actually a stimulus. For example, some people taking a hearing test are likely to say yes if they think they might have heard a weak sound, while others will say no unless they are absolutely sure they heard something.

TRUTH OR fiction ?

Read the following statements about psychology. Do you think they are true or false? You will learn whether each statement is true or false as you read the chapter.

- When you look at a rainbow, the wavelength of light determines the colors you see.
- When you mix blue and yellow light, you get green light.
- The smallest bone in your body is in your ear.
- People often lose their sense of taste as they grow older.
- Pinching your arm can help relieve the pain in your toe.
- You have a sense that keeps you upright.

SECTION 1
Sensation and Perception: The Basics

When Todd stepped on Marc's toe, the sensation of pain was registered by sensory neurons in Marc's skin. **Sensation** is the stimulation of sensory receptors and the transmission of sensory information to the central nervous system (the spinal cord and brain). Sensory receptors are located in sensory organs such as the eyes and ears and elsewhere in the body. The stimulation of the senses is automatic. It results from sources of energy like light and sound or from the presence of chemicals, as in smell and taste.

Marc perceived the pain in his brain. **Perception** is the psychological process through which we interpret sensory stimulation. Imagine that you are standing at one end zone of a football field while a play is going on. Some of the players are close and rushing toward you; other players are at the other end of the field. Those players who are far away look very small compared to those players who are barreling down on you. Still, you know that the quarterback, who has just thrown a pass from the other end of the field, is not actually tiny. How do you know? The answer is that you know through experience. Perception reflects learning, expectations, and attitudes.

Stimulation of the senses and the ways in which people interpret that stimulation are affected by several concepts. These concepts include absolute threshold, difference threshold, signal-detection theory, and sensory adaptation.

Absolute Threshold

Have you ever had your hearing tested? If so, try to remember the experience. There you were, sitting in a booth or quiet room with earphones on your head. At first, you heard nothing, and perhaps you began to wonder what was going on. Then suddenly, a beep. You had just discovered your absolute threshold for hearing that kind of sound. **Absolute threshold** is the weakest amount of a stimulus that can be sensed. Even before you heard that first beep, the person testing you was trying different beeps, but you simply could not hear them. The first one you heard was the weakest one you were capable of hearing.

Did you know that dogs can hear certain whistles that people cannot? This is because a dog's absolute threshold for certain sounds is different from that of a human being.

Absolute thresholds for humans have been determined for the senses of vision, hearing, smell, taste, and touch. (See Figure 4.1.) However, the absolute threshold for a particular stimulus can differ from person to person. Some people are more sensitive to certain sensory stimuli than others are. These differences stem from psychological and biological factors.

If absolute thresholds differed much from what they are, we might sense the world very differently. For example, if our ears were more sensitive, we might hear collisions among molecules of air. If our sense of smell was as sensitive as a dog's, we might be able to track down someone just by sniffing a piece of his or her clothing.

Difference Threshold

For us to function well in the world, we need absolute thresholds low enough to see, hear, smell, taste, and feel what is going on around us—but not so low that our senses are overloaded with information we cannot use. We also need to be able to detect small differences between stimuli—what makes one stimulus different from another stimulus. The minimum amount of difference that can be detected between two stimuli is known as the **difference threshold**.

Teaching Section 1

Role-Playing

Organize students into groups of four and assign the following roles: researcher, subject, speaker 1, and speaker 2. The researcher should instruct the subject to pay attention to only one of the speakers. The speakers, positioned on either side of the subject, should give different speeches simultaneously at about the same volume. Afterward, the researcher should ask questions to determine how much of the specified speech the subject heard and whether or not the subject remembers any of the other speech. Have the class discuss how their findings apply to signal-detection theory.

Demonstration

To demonstrate the absolute threshold for taste, bring in five 1-gallon containers filled with water from the same source. In one container, dissolve one-eighth teaspoon of sugar; in the second, dissolve one-fourth teaspoon of sugar; in the third, dissolve one-half teaspoon of sugar; and in the fourth, dissolve one teaspoon of sugar. Add no sugar at all to the fifth container. Then have the students taste the water from each, in random order, and without any discussion. Note the containers the participants think contained some sugar. Discuss the results.

Absolute Thresholds for Humans

SENSE	STIMULUS	RECEPTORS	THRESHOLD
Vision	Electromagnetic energy	Rods and cones in the retina	A candle flame viewed from a distance of about 30 miles on a dark night
Hearing	Sound waves	Hair cells of the inner ear	The ticking of a watch from about 20 feet away in a quiet room
Smell	Chemical substances in the air	Receptor cells in the nose	About one drop of perfume diffused throughout a small house
Taste	Chemical substances in saliva	Taste buds on the tongue	About 1 teaspoon of sugar dissolved in 2 gallons of water
Touch	Pressure on the skin	Nerve endings in the skin	The wing of a fly falling on a cheek from a distance of about 0.4 inch

FIGURE 4.1   *This table shows humans' absolute thresholds for various stimuli and five senses.*

Source: Adapted from "Contemporary Psychophysics," by E. Galanter, 1962, in R. Brown et al. (Eds.), *New Directions in Psychology*, New York: Holt, Rinehart and Winston.

For example, imagine that someone shows you two dark blue paint chips. You may think they are the same color, even if they are slightly different. But now imagine that one of the paint chips is removed and replaced with another chip that is just a bit lighter or darker. Do the two paint chips still seem the same color? No. The smallest amount of difference you can see in order to distinguish between the two shades of blue is your difference threshold. Just as with absolute threshold, people's individual difference thresholds vary slightly.

Signal-Detection Theory

As you might imagine, it is easier to hear a friend talking in a quiet room than in a room where other people are laughing loudly. And when your nose is stuffy from a cold, your dinner may seem to have little flavor. In the first case, the setting has made a difference in your sensation and perception. In the second case, your physical condition has made the difference. **Signal-detection theory** is a method of distinguishing sensory stimuli that takes into account not only their strengths but also

such elements as the setting, your physical state, your mood, and your attitudes.

Signal-detection theory also considers psychological factors such as motivations, expectations, and learning. For example, even if the place where you are now reading is buzzing with distracting signals such as a breeze against your face, the shadow of passing clouds, or the voices of passersby, you will be able to ignore those influences as long as you are motivated to keep reading. Similarly, people who smell perfumes for a living have learned through years of experience how to detect subtle differences others would not be able to smell.

We focus on whatever we consider important. Marc's toe hurt a great deal when Todd stepped on it, but when Linda asked him if he was in pain, her voice was all that interested him. As another example, suppose that you attend a recital at school. A student you do not know plays the piano. Your mind may wander as you listen. But do you think the student's parents let their minds wander? You can be pretty sure that they do not—the performance is much more important to them than it is to other members of the audience.

Closing Section 1

Synthesizing Information

Tell students to create a short story, a miniplay, or a comic strip that demonstrates the following four concepts: absolute threshold, difference threshold, signal-detection theory, and sensory adaptation. Encourage students to use their imaginations but also to depict the concepts in meaningful and accurate ways.

Reviewing Section 1

Have students complete the Section Review questions on page 80.

Section 1 Review: Answers

1. Absolute threshold is the weakest amount of stimulus that can be sensed.

2. Examples of sensory adaptation might include the ability to see figures in a darkened room and the ability to "tune out" noises in the environment, such as street traffic and music.

3. Sensation provides information to the central nervous system about the physical environment, and perception is the process through which people interpret sensory stimulation.

Teaching Transparencies with Teacher's Notes

TRANSPARENCY 11:
The Electromagnetic Spectrum

Section Objective

2

▶ Explain how the eye works to enable vision.

This objective is assessed in the Section Review on page 85 and in the Chapter 4 Review.

The Electromagnetic Spectrum

FIGURE 4.2 *The electromagnetic spectrum is made up of light that is visible to humans and light that is not* *visible to humans. The light that is not visible includes infrared and ultraviolet light.*

Sensory Adaptation

When Marc and Linda first walked into the darkened movie theater, they could see little except the colorless shapes of the other moviegoers. As time passed, they became able to see the faces of people around them and the features of the theater. And if Todd had waited a few minutes before trying to find a seat, his eyes would have adapted to the darkness and he might not have stepped on Marc's toe.

Our sensory systems adapt to a changing environment. **Sensory adaptation** is the process by which we become more sensitive to weak stimuli and less sensitive to unchanging stimuli. As time went on, Marc, Linda, and Todd could see the people around them better—the people were weak stimuli. On the other hand, as we adapt to lying on the beach, we become less aware of the unchanging stimulus of the lapping of the waves. Similarly, city dwellers adapt to the sounds of traffic (unchanging stimuli) except for the occasional car backfire or fire engine siren.

SECTION 1 REVIEW

Homework Practice Online
Keyword: SY3 HP4

1. Define *absolute threshold*.
2. Give two examples of sensory adaptation.
3. **Critical Thinking** *Drawing Inferences and Conclusions* How do sensation and perception affect people's understanding of their environment?

SECTION 2

Vision

Those of us fortunate enough to have good vision usually consider information from vision to be more essential than that from our other senses. No other sense allows us to gather so much information from nearby and distant sources. To understand vision, it is important to know how light works and how our eyes function.

Light

Light is electromagnetic energy. It is described in wavelengths. Not all light is visible to humans. In fact, the light that humans can see makes up only a small part of the spectrum of electromagnetic energy. The wavelengths of cosmic rays are only a fraction of an inch long. The wavelengths of some radio waves extend for miles. The wavelengths of visible light are in between. (See Figure 4.2.)

You have probably seen sunlight broken down into colors as it filters through water vapor—this is what makes a rainbow. Sunlight can also be broken down into colors by means of a glass structure called a prism. The main colors of the spectrum, from longest to shortest wavelengths, are red, orange, yellow, green, blue, indigo, and violet. For generations, people have remembered the order by using the made-up name *Roy G. Biv*, which comes from using the first letter of each of the colors.

Opening Section 2

Motivator

Have a student sit in front of the class and visually fixate on a specific object. Ask the student to identify and name the color of an object that you bring into her or his peripheral vision. Does the student identify the color or the object first? *(The student will be able to identify the object before the color because there are no cones, which are sensitive to color, on the outer part of the retina.)*

Teaching Section 2

Guided Practice

To demonstrate that eye pupil size seems to have an emotional aspect, present students with two nearly identical close-up photographs (or good quality black-and-white photocopies) of the same person's face. Retouch one photo by slightly enlarging the size of the person's pupils. Ask students in which photo the person looks friendlier. After noting students' responses, explain that most people usually feel that the wider open the pupils, the friendlier a person looks. This is because interest in another person usually causes the observer's pupils to widen.

It is true that when you look at a rainbow, the wavelength of light determines the colors you see. The wavelength for red is longer than that for orange, and so on through the spectrum of visible light to violet, which has the shortest wavelength.

The Eye

When you take a picture with a camera, light enters through an opening and is focused onto a sensitive surface—the film. Chemicals on the film are changed by the light and create a lasting impression of the image that entered the camera.

Your eye is very similar. (See Figure 4.3.) As in a camera, light enters the eye and then is projected onto a surface. The amount of light that enters is determined by the size of the opening in the colored part of the eye. This opening is called the **pupil**. When you look into someone's eyes, the black circles you see in the middle are the pupils. They may look solid to you, but actually they are openings.

The size of the pupil adjusts automatically to the amount of light entering the eye. Try the following experiment. With a friend, go into bright light, stay there for a few minutes, then go into a much darker area. Notice how the size of your friend's pupils changes. In the bright light, the pupils become very small. This is because the light is bright enough that the eyes need only a bit of it. In the dark, however, the pupils become very large because they need to let in as much light as possible. Pupil size is also sensitive to our emotions. We can be literally

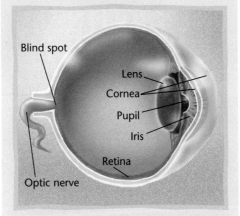

The Human Eye

Blind spot
Lens
Cornea
Pupil
Iris
Retina
Optic nerve

FIGURE 4.3 *In the human eye, light travels through the pupil to the lens and is then reflected onto the retina. The optic nerve sends the visual information to the brain.*

"wide-eyed with fear," meaning that the pupils open widely when we are afraid.

Once light has entered the eye, it encounters the lens. The **lens** adjusts to the distance of objects by changing its thickness. Hold a finger at arm's length and then bring it slowly toward your nose. You will feel tension in the eye as the thickness of the lens adjusts to keep the finger in focus. When people squint to look at something, they are adjusting the thickness of the lenses in their eyes.

These changes project a clear image of the object onto the retina. The **retina** is the sensitive surface in the eye that acts like the film in a camera. However, the retina consists of neurons—not film. Neurons

AS DIRECTOR OF HUMAN RESOURCES I'VE BEEN ASKED TO REDUCE THE COST OF EMPLOYEE BENEFITS.

THE COMPANY WILL NO LONGER PAY FOR EYE-GLASSES. BUT WE WILL SUPPORT A NEW VISION-CORRECTION PROCEDURE.

©1995 United Feature Syndicate, Inc. (NYC)
RADIAL KERATONOMY?
SQUINTING.

DILBERT reprinted by permission of United Feature Syndicate, Inc.

Inform students that, in addition to showing interest, pupils and the eyes as a whole can communicate other important nonverbal messages. Ask students to consider what other emotions or information we show through our eyes. Have students make two-column lists. In one column, they should list three or more eye expressions, and in the other column, they should indicate the emotion or information each expression communicates. *(Possible answers include a person's pupils and/or lids wide open with fear; half-closed lids, indicating boredom; narrowed eyes, indicating anger.)*

Think About It

Answers will vary, but students might note that computers are being used increasingly to help blind people see.

✎ internet connect

TOPIC: Parts of the Human Eye
GO TO: go.hrw.com
KEYWORD: SY4 PS4

Have students access the Internet through the HRW Go site to research parts of the human eye. Ask students to organize the parts of the eye and describe each part's function in a drawing or model. The drawing should distinguish features that function in perception of colors and those that function in perception of light.

PSYCHOLOGY

IN THE WORLD TODAY

Have each student make a list of objects around the school that he or she would program into a computer system designed to help a visually impaired person get around the school. Then have students compare their lists. What did some students forget? Ask students if they think the results indicate how much we take for granted when it comes to our vision and our ability to maneuver.

PSYCHOLOGY

IN THE WORLD TODAY

Using Microchips to See the Light

On the *Star Trek* TV series, Geordi was given a sense of vision by bionic eyes. Are such eyes the stuff of futuristic science fiction or right around the corner? The answer seems to be that they are somewhere in between.

Millions of people around the world suffer from diseases of the retina that cause blindness: macular degeneration and retinitis pigmentosa. In both diseases, the rods and cones in the retina die. Yet much of the other retinal circuitry remain relatively intact. For example, when the ganglion cells are electrically stimulated, they can often generate signals to the visual cortex in the occipital lobe via the optic nerve. A team of researchers led by Dr. John Wyatt, an electrical engineer at M.I.T., and Dr. Joseph Rizzo, a neuro-ophthalmologist at Harvard Medical School, are working on a retinal implant to stimulate the ganglion cells (Eisenberg, 1999).

As silicon chips grow more powerful, researchers are developing microscopic light-sensitive transistors that can be placed on chips and embedded in the retina. The Harvard-M.I.T. group plans a slightly different approach. They intend to use two microchips. They will mount one along with a camera on a pair of glasses. Images will be transmitted wirelessly to the chip embedded in the eye. The chip in the eye will stimulate the functional cells in the retina.

In one experiment, the retinas of blind patients were stimulated by handheld electrodes similar to the tiny chips that will be implanted. Patients reported seeing points of lights, dim outlines, and the shapes of letters. This is not the brilliant technicolor display we have in normal vision, but the abil-

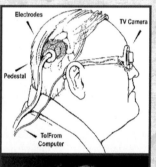

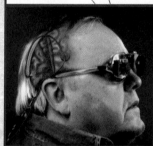

Computer technology will someday help blind people to see.

ity to see changes in traffic lights and the dim outlines of cars and people will create a visible enough world for people who would otherwise see nothing.

Some people have a working visual cortex in the brain, but their optical nerves are not intact. What do researchers have in store for them? One answer is bypassing the eye and optic nerve altogether.

Dr. William Dobelle wired a tiny camera directly into the brain of a blind volunteer, enabling the volunteer to see scattered specks of light and giving the patient a limited ability to perceive objects, such as a two-inch-high letter from a distance of a few feet. The volunteer also located a mannequin in a room, retrieved a black cap that was hanging on a white wall, and placed it on the mannequin's head.

The volunteer wore specially equipped sunglasses. A small pinhole camera was mounted on one lens, and an ultrasonic range finder was mounted on the other. The devices signaled a lightweight computer carried on the hip, which highlighted the edges of the shapes captured by the camera. The computer then instructed a second computer to transmit signals to tiny electrodes implanted on the visual cortex in the volunteer's brain. With exposure to various arrays of light and dark, and practice, the individual begins to organize the specks of light into meaningful displays.

Think About It

Making Generalizations and Predictions What role do you think computer technology will play in helping people to see?

Demonstration

To demonstrate the blind spot to students, have them draw two circles about the size of a dime approximately four inches apart on a piece of paper. Tell students to hold their drawings at arm's length, cover their left eye, and stare at the circle on the left with their right eye. Then direct them to move the drawings slowly toward their face until the circle on the right seems to vanish. The experiment can then be repeated in reverse to demonstrate the blind spot in the other eye.

Assessing Validity

Challenge students to guess how many different shades the average person with normal color vision can distinguish. Write down the range of guesses on the board. Then provide the astonishing answer: about a million. Illustrate this fact to students by bringing in paint samples from a local paint store. Ask the students to arrange the colors from dark to light to show the process of just noticeable difference.

that are sensitive to light are called **photoreceptors**. Once the light hits the photoreceptors, a nerve carries the visual input to the brain. In the brain, the information is relayed to the visual area of the occipital lobe. (See Chapter 3.)

The Blind Spot   Look again at Figure 4.3 and find the point where the optic nerve leaves the eye. When light hits that point, the eye registers nothing because that area lacks photoreceptors. Thus it is called the **blind spot**. We all have one. If we did not, we would never be able to "see" anything—no visual input would reach the brain through the optic nerve for interpretation.

Rods and Cones   Remember how Marc saw only the gray outlines of the other people in the dimly lit movie theater? This was because of the way the photoreceptors in the retina work. There are two kinds of photoreceptors: rods and cones. Rods are sensitive only to the brightness of light. They allow us to see in black and white. Cones provide color vision.

If you are a camera buff, you know that when lighting is low, you get a clearer image with black-and-white film than with color film. In the same way, rods are more sensitive to light than are cones. Therefore, as the lighting grows dim, as in a movie theater when the lights go down, objects lose their color before their outlines fade from view.

Dark and Light Adaptation   When you first enter a movie theater, it may be too dark for you to find a seat. As time passes, however, you come to see the seats and the other people more clearly. This adjustment to lower lighting is called dark adaptation. Your ability to see in low light continues to improve for up to 45 minutes.

But what happens when you first move from the dark into the light? Imagine turning on the lamp next to your bed in the middle of the night. At first, you blink, and it almost hurts, but within only a minute or two, you have adapted. Adaptation to bright light happens much more quickly than adaptation to the dark.

Visual Acuity   The sharpness of vision is called **visual acuity**. Visual acuity is determined by the ability to see visual details (in normal light). When people have their eyes examined, they have to read the letters on a chart like the one shown above. This is the Snellen Vision Chart. It is used to measure

T	E	10
P	V L	7
H C O E		5
H P D N L		4
D V H T L U		3
E V O U C T Y		2
P C Y L H N D V		1

If you have ever had your eyes examined, you probably looked at the Snellen Vision Chart, which is used to measure visual acuity.

visual acuity. If you were to stand 20 feet from the Snellen Chart and could only read the T or the E, we would say that your vision is 20/100. This means that what a person with normal vision could see from a distance of 100 feet away, you could see from no more than 20 feet away. In such a case, you would be nearsighted—you would have to be particularly close to an object to make out its details. A person who is farsighted, on the other hand, needs to be farther away from an object than a person with normal vision to see it clearly.

You may have noticed that older people often hold newspapers or books at more of a distance from their eyes than younger people. As people reach middle age, their lenses become relatively brittle. Therefore, it is more difficult for them to focus, especially on nearby objects. As a result, many older people are farsighted.

Color Vision

The world is a place of brilliant colors—the blue of the sky, the reds and yellows of autumn leaves, the vivid greens of spring. The wavelength of light determines the color. People with normal color vision see any color in the spectrum of visible light.

Cross-Curricular Link: Technology

Point out that several technologies are available to people who are blind, such as specialized computers and computer software. Tell students to learn more about what is available. If possible, students should determine the price, major features, and availability of each item.

Class Discussion

Read the following sentence to the class: "Seeing is believing." Then discuss with the class why we put so much more trust in evidence we have seen than evidence we have heard.

Closing Section 2

Synthesizing Information

Tell students to draw, without referring to the textbook or any other source, a diagram of the human eye. Each part should be labeled by name and function. Have pairs of students correct each other's work.

Reviewing Section 2

Have students complete the Section Review questions on page 85.

Extension

Ask students to research the vision of animals. First, challenge them to find out what colors dogs can see. Which dogs have the greatest visual acuity, and how does this characteristic relate to the specific task(s) for which they were bred? What can students learn about the color vision of bees and other insects? *(Bees are insensitive to red and green but sensitive to yellow, blue, and ultraviolet.)* What can students learn about the sense of smell of dogs, bees, and other creatures, such as fish and snakes? Have students pool their findings.

FIGURE 4.4 *The colors across from each other on the color circle are called complementary colors. What is the complement of green?*

But what about animals? You may be surprised to find out that dogs and cats see far fewer colors than you do but that insects, birds, fish, and reptiles experience a wide variety of colors.

The Color Circle Look at Figure 4.4. What you see is called the color circle. It is the colors of the spectrum bent into a circle. The colors across from each other are called **complementary**. For example, red and green are a complementary pair. If we mix complementary colors together, they form gray. You may have learned in art class that mixing blue and yellow creates green, not gray. But this is true only with *pigments,* or substances such as crayons or paints. Here we are talking about *light,* not about pigments.

TRUTH OR fiction

■ REVISITED ■

It is not true that you get green light by mixing blue light and yellow light. You do get a green pigment when you mix pigments of blue and yellow, but pigments are substances, not light. Mixing blue light and yellow light forms gray.

Cones and Color Vision Cones, one of the two types of photoreceptors in the retina of the eye, enable us to perceive color. Some cones are sensitive to blue, some to green, and some to red. When more than one kind of cone is stimulated at the same time, we perceive other colors of the spectrum, such as yellow and violet.

This is similar to the way color television sets convey colors to the viewer. Although you may not be aware of it, the images you see on a television screen actually consist of thousands of very small dots, called pixels. Each of these dots is either blue, green, or red—the same colors that are perceived by the different types of cones in the eye. There are no yellow, purple, or even black or white dots in the television images. These and other colors are created only through various combinations of blue, green, and red dots.

Afterimages Look at the strangely colored flag in Figure 4.5 for at least half a minute. Then look at a sheet of white paper. What do you see? If your color vision is working properly and if you looked at the flag long enough, you should see a flag composed of the familiar red, white, and blue. The flag you perceive on the white sheet of paper is an afterimage of the first flag. The **afterimage** of a color is its complementary color. You perceive an afterimage when you have viewed a color for a while and then the color is removed. The same holds true for black and white. Staring at one will create an afterimage of the other.

Color Blindness

If you can see the colors of the visible spectrum, you have normal color vision. People who do not have normal color vision are said to be "color blind."

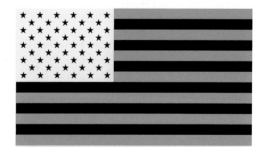

FIGURE 4.5 *Stare at the center of this flag for 30 seconds, then look at a white piece of paper. You should see a more familiar image—the red, white, and blue American flag. The afterimage of a color is that color's complement.*

Section Objective

▶ Describe how the ear perceives sound.

This objective is assessed in the Section Review on page 88 and in the Chapter 4 Review.

Motivator

Discuss with the class the fact that humans generally rely much more on sight than on hearing; nonetheless, our sense of hearing provides us with valuable information. For example, newborn babies, whose vision is underdeveloped, relax when they hear tapes of their mothers' voices. To demonstrate students' abilities to recognize sounds, have the students close their eyes and listen to various sounds that you make (for example, closing a drawer, opening window blinds, and so on). Discuss the results of the demonstration and the accuracy of students' sense of hearing.

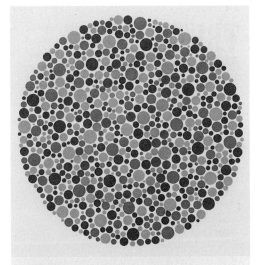

FIGURE 4.6 *This image resembles a test for color blindness. In the actual test, which would be conducted by a trained professional, a person with normal color vision would see an 8, a person with red-green color blindness would see a 3, and a person with total color blindness would see no number.*

These people are partially or totally unable to distinguish color due to an absence of, or malfunction in, the cones. People who are totally color blind are sensitive only to light and dark and see the world as most people do on a black-and-white television set. Total color blindness is rare.

Partial color blindness, on the other hand, is fairly common. People who are partially color blind see some colors but not others. Particularly common is red-green color blindness, in which a person has difficulty seeing shades of red and green. Figure 4.6 shows one of the types of tests that are used to check for color blindness.

SECTION 2 REVIEW

go.hrw.com **Homework Practice Online** Keyword: SY3 HP4

1. What is visible light?
2. What is the retina, and what is its function?
3. Explain how humans are able to see color.
4. **Critical Thinking** *Making Generalizations and Predictions* Imagine that you became completely color blind. How might your life be different from the way it is now? How would you have to adjust? What occupations or hobbies might become difficult for you?

Hearing

Do you know how you are able to hear your phone ringing? a baby crying? leaves rustling? Sound travels through the air in waves. It is caused by changes in air pressure that result from vibration. Anything that makes a sound—the whisper of your voice, the hum of a tuning fork, the strumming of a guitar—causes vibrations. Each of these vibrations is called a cycle or a sound wave. Every sound has its own pitch and loudness.

Pitch

Sound waves can be very fast, occurring many times per second. The pitch of a sound—how high or low the sound is—depends on its frequency, or the number of cycles per second. The more cycles per second, the higher the pitch of a sound.

Try this experiment. Cut a rubber band into two segments—one long, one short—then stretch each one out and twang it. The shorter one has a higher sound, right? In the same way, women's voices usually have a higher pitch than those of men because women's vocal cords tend to be shorter and therefore vibrate at a greater frequency. Similarly, the strings of a violin are shorter and vibrate at a higher frequency than the strings of a cello. Therefore, the violin's sound is higher in pitch than the sound made by the cello.

The human ear can hear sound waves that vary from 20 to 20,000 cycles per second. Many animals, including dogs and dolphins, hear sounds well beyond 20,000 cycles per second. Although we cannot hear them, the sounds emitted by dolphins help them locate objects. The sound pulses echo back from fish and other objects.

Loudness

What is the softest sound you can hear? What is the loudest? The loudness of a sound is determined by the height, or amplitude, of sound waves. The higher the amplitude of the wave, the louder the sound. The loudness of a sound is measured in decibels, a unit that is abbreviated *dB*. Zero dB is considered the threshold of hearing. Zero dB is about as loud as the ticking of a watch 20 feet away in a very quiet room. (See Figure 4.7 on page 86.)

1. Visible light is the portion of the electromagnetic spectrum of wavelengths that can be seen by the human eye.

2. The retina is the light-sensitive surface of the eye. The retina consists of neurons called photoreceptors. When light hits the photoreceptors, the optic nerve carries that visual input to the brain.

3. Photoreceptors called cones enable us to see color. Some cones are sensitive to green, some to blue, and some to red. When more than one kind of photoreceptor is stimulated, we perceive other colors of the spectrum.

4. Answers may include the following: learning where red and green are on a traffic light, enabling the person to respond to the light rather than to the color; remembering specifically where one's car is parked since the person would be unable to locate it by color. Occupations and hobbies that would be difficult for people who are color blind include interior design, fashion consulting, painting, and weaving.

85

Teaching Section 3

Demonstration

To demonstrate the location of sounds, bring to class several simple noisemakers (for example beepers, drumsticks, whistles). Tell students to close their eyes and put their heads down on their desks. Then walk quietly around the classroom. Stop and operate a noisemaker. Then call on one of the students to identify, as precisely as possible, the origin of the sound. Repeat the exercise with each noisemaker. What did students learn about perception of where the noise came from?

Meeting Individual Needs: Gifted Learners

Tell students to study the ways in which hearing and seeing are similar. Point out that both processes involve the body's reception of energy in wave form. To locate the source of a sound, the brain assesses the difference in the amount of time it takes for the sound to reach each ear. Similarly, the brain uses the slight differences in what each eye sees to compute depth and distance. Encourage students to identify and analyze other analogies between sight and hearing.

What's New In Psychology?

Scientists used to think that different neurons in different parts of the brain were responsible for pinpointing the locations of sounds coming from different points in the environment. Recent studies conducted at the University of Florida's Brain Institute suggest something quite different. Middlebrooks believes that a widespread group of neurons work together to track sounds that are coming from all directions. Each of these "panoramic" neurons produces a distinctive sequence of electrical discharges, known as a firing pattern. The brain uses these patterns to help pin down the location of the sound.

Middlebrooks, John C., et al. (1994). A panoramic code for sound location by cortical neurons. *Science, 264.* 842–844.

Cross-Curricular Link: Zoology

A barn owl can identify sounds better than any other living creature. Its ears are slightly asymmetrical, with one ear pointed slightly upward and the other slightly downward. Because of this feature, sounds reach the ears at slightly different times and volumes. By perceiving the difference between the two incoming signals, the owl is able to locate the direction and elevation of its prey.

The Ear

Just as the eye is the human instrument for seeing, the ear is the instrument for sensing all the sounds around us. In fact, the ear is shaped to capture sound waves, to vibrate with them, and to transmit sound to the brain. What we normally think of as the ear is actually the outer ear. We also have a middle ear and an inner ear. (See Figure 4.8.)

The eardrum is the gateway from the outer ear to the middle ear. It is a thin membrane that vibrates when sound waves strike it. As it vibrates, it transmits the sound to three small bones in the middle ear: the hammer, the anvil, and the stirrup. (The stirrup is the smallest bone in the human body.) These bones then also begin to vibrate and transmit sound to the inner ear.

The inner ear consists of the cochlea (KOH-klee-uh). The word *cochlea* comes from the Greek word for "snail." Look at Figure 4.8 again, and you will see why—it is shaped just like the shell of a snail. The **cochlea** is a bony tube that contains fluids as well as neurons that move in response to the vibrations of the fluids. The movement generates neural impulses that are transmitted to the brain via the **auditory nerve**. Within the brain, auditory input is projected onto the hearing areas of the cerebral cortex. (See Chapter 3.)

TRUTH *OR* **fiction** ■ REVISITED ■

It is true that the smallest bone in your body is in your ear. It is the stirrup in your middle ear. The stirrup (along with the hammer and the anvil) vibrates and transmits sound to the inner ear.

Locating Sounds

Did you ever sit in front of a stereo, and for some reason, all the sound seemed to come from one side instead of from straight ahead? What you probably did was adjust the balance knob until the sound seemed equally loud in each ear.

Balancing a stereo set is similar to locating sounds. If a sound seems louder from the right, you think it is coming from the right because you are used to a sound from the right side reaching the right ear first.

But what if a sound comes from directly in front of you, from behind, or from above? All such sounds are equally loud and distant from each ear. So what do you do? Simple—you usually turn your head just a little to determine in which ear the sound increases. If you turn to your right and the

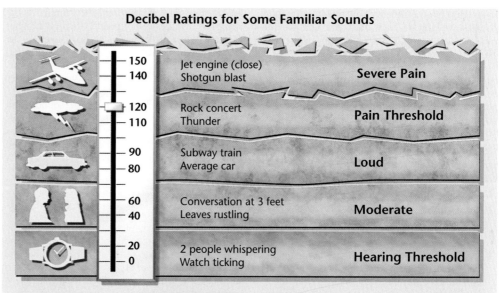

Decibel Ratings for Some Familiar Sounds

150 / 140	Jet engine (close) / Shotgun blast — **Severe Pain**
120 / 110	Rock concert / Thunder — **Pain Threshold**
90 / 80	Subway train / Average car — **Loud**
60 / 40	Conversation at 3 feet / Leaves rustling — **Moderate**
20 / 0	2 people whispering / Watch ticking — **Hearing Threshold**

FIGURE 4.7 *Zero dB is the threshold for hearing. Prolonged exposure to sounds greater than 85 dB will cause some hearing loss. Sounds of 130 dB can cause immediate hearing loss.*

86

Closing Section 3

For Further Research

Have students locate the part(s) of the ear where different kinds of deafness (conductive and sensorineural) originate. How do conductive and sensorineural deafness differ? Have students research the treatments available for both types of deafness.

Summarizing Information

Have students draw from memory a diagram of the outer and inner ear. After they have completed their diagrams, have the students compare them with the diagram on page 87 and then correct any errors in their diagrams.

Reviewing Section 3

Have students complete the Section Review questions on page 88.

The Human Ear

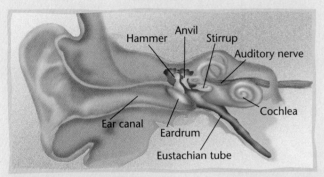

FIGURE 4.8 *Sound enters the outer ear and is funneled to the eardrum. Inside the middle ear, the hammer, anvil, and stirrup vibrate, transmitting the sound to the inner ear.*

loudness increases in your left ear, the sound must be in front of you. Of course, you also use information from vision and other cues in locating the source of sounds. If you hear the roar of jet engines, most of the time you can be fairly certain that the airplane is overhead.

Deafness

Not everyone perceives sound. About 2 million Americans are deaf. Deafness may be inherited or caused by disease, injury, or old age.

Conductive Deafness If we see an older person with a hearing aid, we can assume that he or she is probably suffering from conductive deafness. **Conductive deafness** occurs because of damage to the middle ear. Since this part of the ear amplifies sounds, damage to it prevents people from hearing sounds that are not loud enough. Fortunately, people with conductive deafness are often helped by hearing aids. These aids provide the amplification that the middle ear does not.

Sensorineural Deafness Many people do not perceive sounds of certain frequencies. This is a sign of sensorineural deafness. **Sensorineural deafness** is usually caused by damage to the inner ear. Most often, the neurons in the cochlea are destroyed. Sometimes sensorineural deafness is due to damage to the auditory nerve, either through disease or through prolonged exposure to very loud sounds.

Have you ever attended a high-volume rock concert and left with a ringing sensation in your

ears? This may have meant that neurons had been destroyed in your ears. The same thing can happen to workers who operate certain drilling equipment or drive loud vehicles. The next time you are exposed to loud sounds, remember to cover your ears.

Devices called experimental cochlear implants, or "artificial ears," contain microphones that sense sounds and electronic equipment that stimulates the auditory nerve directly. However, if the auditory nerve itself is damaged, a cochlear implant cannot help.

Deafness in the World Today In recent years, people who are deaf have been able to come more into the mainstream of sensory experience as a result of their own efforts, the efforts of others, and new technology. For example, Heather Whitestone, who lost most of her hearing in infancy, became

Heather Whitestone, Miss America of 1995, lost most of her hearing as an infant.

For Your Information

While most hearing problems involve some sort of hearing loss, tinnitus is an auditory disorder that occurs when an individual hears sounds within her or his own head. Sometimes these sounds can be heard only by the sufferer, but in other cases, the sounds can be detected by an examiner. The sounds can be loud or soft, high or low, and they can be caused by sensorineural hearing loss, ear infections, hypertension, and muscle spasms.

Teaching Transparencies with Teacher's Notes

TRANSPARENCY 13: The Human Ear

internet connect

TOPIC: The Ear and Brain
GO TO: go.hrw.com
KEYWORD: SY3 PS4

Have students access the Internet through the HRW Go site to research how the brain processes sound. Then ask students to create an oral presentation on hearing and sound processing by the ear and brain. Remind students to use proper terminology and audiovisual aids.

4
Section Objective

▶ Identify the chemical, skin, and body senses.

This objective is assessed in the Section Review on page 92 and in the Chapter 4 Review.

Opening Section 4

Motivator

In this section, students will learn about the connection between smell and taste. To demonstrate this, have a blindfolded student volunteer plug his or her nose. Have the student taste a piece of grapefruit and a piece of orange. Point out the fact that both fruits have the same texture. Ask the volunteer if he or she could taste the difference. (NOTE: Before beginning this experiment, ascertain that the volunteer has no food allergies.)

These students at a school for deaf children make the sign for friends *as part of a school performance. More and more people are becoming familiar with the signs of American Sign Language.*

Miss America of 1995. Whitestone is a dancer of classical ballet. She uses the vibrations of the music to dance in rhythm.

Interpreters are often on hand to translate speeches into languages (such as American Sign Language) used by members of the audience who are hearing impaired. More and more schools are offering courses in American Sign Language. Many television shows are now "closed captioned," which means that special decoders make captions of dialogue visible on the screen. And, as you have just read, scientists are always trying to find new ways to counteract damage inside the ear.

SECTION 3 REVIEW

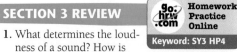
Homework Practice Online
Keyword: SY3 HP4

1. What determines the loudness of a sound? How is loudness measured?
2. Define *eardrum* and explain its function.
3. Describe the two kinds of deafness.
4. **Critical Thinking** *Contrasting* How do the causes of conductive and sensorineural deafness differ?

SECTION 4
Other Senses

Vision and hearing are just two of many human senses. Others are smell, taste, and the skin and body senses. Smell and taste are called the chemical senses. With vision and hearing, physical energy in the form of light and sound waves stimulates our sensory receptors. With smell and taste, however, we sense molecules of substances. The skin detects touch through pressure, temperature, and pain. Body senses alert us to our posture and movement.

Smell

People do not have as strong a sense of smell as many animals. Dogs use seven times as much of the cerebral cortex for smell as people do. Some dogs are used to sniff out drugs or explosives in suitcases or to track lost children or objects.

But smell is important to people too. Without smell, you would not be able to taste as much as you do. For example, if your sense of smell were not

Teaching Section 4

Guided Practice

Have students smell different substances at separate stations around the room. (Create a screen around each of the substances so that students cannot see them.) You can use oranges, cheese, laundry detergent, and so on. Afterward, tell students what substances they were smelling. Then have students discuss the accuracy of their sense of smell.

Independent Practice

Tell students to keep a smell/taste log over a single day. In it, they should list the various smells and tastes they experience during the day and then record, analyze, and evaluate their reactions to these stimuli. Ask students to consider how the senses of smell and taste relate to survival. *(For example, smelling coffee brewing in the morning may not seem like a survival skill, but it demonstrates one's ability to sniff out food in the environment. Perceiving "bad smells," such as those emitted by spoiled food or animal excrement, keeps one away from harmful bacteria.)*

---

working, an onion and an apple would taste very much alike to you.

Odors of substances are detected by receptor neurons high in each nostril. Receptor neurons react when molecules of the substance in the form of a gas come into contact with them. The receptors send information about the odors to the brain via the **olfactory nerve**.

Our sense of smell adapts quickly. In the movie theater, Marc soon lost awareness of Linda's perfume. We adapt rapidly even to annoying odors. This may be fortunate if we are in a locker room. It may not be fortunate if harmful fumes, such as from cars, are present—we may lose awareness of the smoke or fumes even though danger remains. One odor can also be masked by another, which is how air fresheners work.

Taste

Why would your dog gobble up a piece of a candy bar, but your cat turn up its nose at it? Dogs can taste sweetness, but cats cannot.

The four basic taste qualities are sweetness, sourness, saltiness, and bitterness. Do you think that you taste more than these four qualities? What

Humans experience four taste qualities: sweetness, sourness, saltiness, and bitterness.

you are experiencing is the flavor of food, which involves odor, texture, and temperature as well as taste. If you have a cold, for example, food tastes flat because you cannot smell it. The reason older people sometimes complain that their food has little "taste" is usually that they have experienced a loss of the sense of smell, not taste. Thus, they perceive less of the flavor of their food. Older people often spice their food heavily to enhance its flavor.

It is not true that people often lose their sense of taste as they grow older. What older people usually lose is their sense of smell, which is why their food seems to lack flavor.

Taste is sensed through receptor neurons located on taste buds on the tongue. Some people have low sensitivity for sweetness and may have to use twice as much sugar to sweeten their food as others who are more sensitive to sweetness. People who claim to enjoy very bitter foods may actually be "taste blind" to them. Sensitivities to different tastes can be inherited (Bartoshuk, 2000).

By eating hot foods and scraping your tongue, you regularly kill off many taste cells. But you need not be alarmed. Taste cells reproduce rapidly enough to completely renew themselves in a week. The taste system is thus one of the most resilient of all the body's sensory systems. It is very rare for anyone to suffer a complete permanent taste loss.

The Skin Senses

What we normally call touch is better called the skin senses because touch is a combination of pressure, temperature, and pain. Humans have distinct sensory receptors for pressure, temperature, and pain, but some nerve endings may receive more than one type of sensory input. Our skin senses are vitally important to us. Studies have shown that premature infants grow more quickly and stay healthier if they are touched (Field et al., 1986). And older people seem to do better if they have a dog or cat to stroke and cuddle (Pearlman, 1994).

Pressure Your body is covered with hairs, some of them very tiny. Sensory receptors located around the roots of hair cells fire where the skin is touched. Other structures beneath the skin are also sensitive

Class Discussion

Ask students if they ever have food cravings and, if so, for which foods. Then tell students that current research suggests that women are more likely to crave sweet foods with lots of fat, such as chocolate, while men are more prone to craving foods high in protein and fat, such as burgers and lasagna. Scientists have observed the same food preference phenomenon in laboratory animals. Have the class discuss their own food cravings. Was there any split based on gender? Do they think that food cravings are influenced by societal standards?

Role-Playing

Obtain a copy of the play *The Miracle Worker* by William Gibson and locate the scene in which Anne Sullivan teaches Helen Keller the meaning of the word *water* by putting Helen's hand under running water. This dramatic scene is frequently excerpted in literature anthologies. Ask for volunteers to play the roles of Anne and Helen. Then ask the class to discuss the scene. In leading the discussion, emphasize the importance of this moment and the impact it had on the rest of Helen's life.

CASE STUDIES
AND OTHER TRUE STORIES

The easiest words for Helen Keller to learn were words that related to smell, taste, or touch. Ask students what strategies they would use to teach concepts that related to a certain sense that someone lacked. For instance, how would they explain a rainbow to a blind person?

CASE STUDIES
AND OTHER TRUE STORIES

Compensating for Lost Senses: Helen Keller's Story

Most, if not all, of our knowledge of the world comes to us through our senses. What happens, then, if we lose one or more of those senses? Perception may not be lost if other senses can be used to compensate for the missing sense or senses. The life of Helen Keller serves as an excellent example.

Helen Keller was born in Tuscumbia, Alabama, in 1880. She was walking and had just started to learn a few words when suddenly she became very ill. Despite the doctor's prediction that she would die, Keller survived, but she had become both deaf and blind.

It is hard to imagine what it must be like to wake up one day and find nothing but silence and darkness where once you heard sounds and saw objects and people. Not surprisingly, the young Keller became difficult to manage. Fearful, she clung to her mother's apron, and at times she had violent temper tantrums.

When Keller was almost seven, her life changed dramatically. Anne Sullivan arrived in Tuscumbia to teach Keller. Sullivan, who was partially blind herself, had attended the Perkins Institution for the Blind in Boston. Although two operations had restored her eyesight, she understood what it was like to be blind, and she was eager to teach her new pupil.

The situation did not look promising at first. Keller was rude to her new teacher, and she would not sit still to have Sullivan use the manual alphabet. In the manual alphabet, which is still used with people who are deaf and blind, the "speaker" makes the signs right into the hand of the "listener," using the sense of touch to communicate. At first, Sullivan tried the word *doll* when she gave the child a doll as a gift. Keller simply took the present and ran off. Eventually, however, she began to imitate Sullivan. Within days, she signed several words, although she still had some difficulty connecting the words spelled in her hand with the actual objects.

One day, while Sullivan put her pupil's hand under running water, she spelled the word w-a-t-e-r into Keller's palm over and over. Suddenly Keller realized that w-a-t-e-r was the "cool something" that was running over her hand, and a breakthrough had occurred. Within one hour, she learned 30 new words.

From that beginning came a long life of both learning and teaching. The easiest words to learn were those that described objects or things Keller could taste or smell. It was harder for the young girl to understand that her feelings—such as anger and love—also had names.

For the first few years, Sullivan was Keller's only teacher. Keller was soon eager to learn more. At the age of 10, Keller decided that she needed to learn to speak. To do so, she took lessons from a teacher of people who were deaf. Eventually, Keller learned to speak by "hearing" the vibrations made when she placed her fingers on Sullivan's larynx. Keller also learned to "listen" to others speak by putting her middle finger on the speaker's nose, her forefinger on the speaker's lips, and her thumb on the speaker's larynx.

Keller wanted to attend Radcliffe College, but to do so she had to complete regular high school. Sullivan accompanied her to class and signed the lectures into Keller's hand. Keller passed her exams and was admitted to Radcliffe. Later, Keller and Sullivan traveled and lectured around the world. They never rested in their efforts to improve the lives of people with deafness and blindness. Most people who are deaf and blind today agree that Helen Keller, who died in 1968, is a powerful role model.

WHY PSYCHOLOGY MATTERS

Many people have lost the use of one or more of their senses. Use CNNfyi.com or other current events sources to learn more about how people have used other senses to compensate for the loss of one sense. Prepare an oral report describing what you have learned.

Comparing Points of View

Have students compare and contrast their own reactions to temperature, pressure, and pain. They may want to begin by listing some specific stimuli (standing in cold rain, going to sleep in 90-degree heat, receiving a shot of novocaine before having a tooth filled) and then surveying their classmates' reactions to the intensity of the discomfort of each. What generalizations, if any, can be made on the basis of the responses? (For example, is there a correlation between sensitivity to temperature and sensitivity to pain? Are there any clear gender differences in the responses?)

Cooperative Learning

Have students work in pairs to explore kinesthesis—the sense that informs people about the position and motion of parts of their bodies. First, have one student in each pair demonstrate a complex set of movements, such as a dance step, a tai chi chuan movement, or a sports maneuver. Then have the other student try to copy the movement. Next, have the two reverse the demonstrator and learner roles. Afterward, have the students analyze the process of learning to sense where one's own body is and how it is or is not creating a certain movement pattern.

to pressure. Different parts of the body are more sensitive to pressure than others. The fingertips, lips, nose, and cheeks are more sensitive than the shoulders, thighs, and calves.

 The sense of pressure undergoes rapid adaptation. In the movie theater, Marc and Linda held hands, but after a little while they became so used to the feelings of their fingers in each other's hands that they hardly noticed. They had adapted.

Temperature Sensations of temperature are relative. When your body temperature is at a normal 98.6°F, you might perceive another person's skin as being warm. When you are feverish, though, the other person's skin might seem cool.

The receptors for temperature are neurons just beneath the skin. When skin temperature increases because you touch something warm, receptors for warmth fire. Decreases in skin temperature, such as those that occur when you put a cool, moist cloth on your forehead, cause receptors for cold to fire.

We adapt to differences in temperature. Have you ever walked out of an air-conditioned building into the hot sunshine? At first, the heat really hit you, but soon the sensation faded as you adapted to the warmth. In the same way, when you first jump into a swimming pool, the water may seem cold. Yet, after a few moments, the water feels warmer as your body adjusts to it.

Pain When Marc's toe was stepped on, he knew it. Pain told him that something was wrong. Pain is also adaptive—it motivates us to do something to stop it. That is why Marc pulled back his leg.

Headaches, backaches, toothaches—these are only a few of the types of pain most of us experience from time to time. More serious health problems—such as arthritis, cancer, or wounds—also cause pain. Not all areas of the body are equally sensitive to pain. The more pain receptors located in a particular area of our skin, the more sensitive that area is. (See Figure 4.9.)

Distribution of Pain Receptors

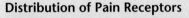
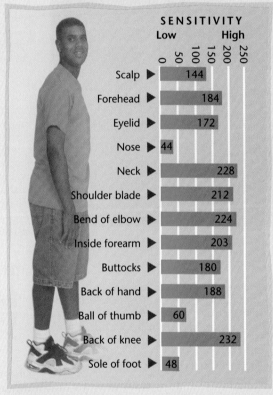

FIGURE 4.9 *Some parts of the body are more sensitive to pressure and pain than others.* **Which part of the body has the fewest pain receptors?**

Source: Strughold, H. (1924). On the density and thresholds in the areas of pain on the epidermis in the various regions of the body. *Z. Biol.,* 80, 367–380. (In German.)

Once a person gets hurt, everything happens very quickly. Pain originates at the point of contact, as with Marc's toe. The pain message is sent from the point of contact to the spinal cord to the thalamus in the brain. Then it is projected to the cerebral cortex, where the person registers the location and severity of the pain. Chemicals called prostaglandins help the body transmit pain messages to the brain. Aspirin and ibuprofen are common pain-fighting drugs that work by curbing production of prostaglandins.

Simple remedies like rubbing and scratching an injured area sometimes help relieve pain. Marc rubbed his toe. Why? One possible answer lies in the gate theory of pain. **Gate theory** suggests that only a certain amount of information can be processed by

Closing Section 4

Meeting Individual Needs: Tactile/Kinesthetic Learners

Place blindfolded students into groups and give each person a walnut. Give them 10 minutes to familiarize themselves with their walnuts. Collect all of the walnuts. Then redistribute them to each group and ask each student to find his or her original walnut.

Organizing Information

Have students make a table listing each of the following senses: sensitivity to pain, pressure, temperature, kinesthesis, and the vestibular sense. Instruct students to indicate how information for each of these senses is received and how the brain uses the information.

Reviewing Section 4

Have students complete the Section Review questions on page 92.

Section 4 Review: Answers

1. Odors are detected by receptor neurons high in each nostril. The receptors send information about the odors to the brain via the olfactory nerve.

2. The vestibular sense tells you whether you are physically upright without actually having to look.

3. smell, taste, skin senses of pressure, temperature, and pain, and the vestibular and kinesthetic body senses

Essay and Research Themes for A. P. Students

Theme 3

Gymnasts rely heavily on their vestibular sense, particularly on the balance beam.

the nervous system at a time. Rubbing or scratching the area transmits sensations to the brain that compete with the pain messages for attention. Thus, many neurons cannot get their pain messages to the brain. It is as if too many calls are flooding a switchboard. The flooding prevents many or all of the calls from getting through.

It is true that pinching your arm can help relieve the pain in your toe. According to the gate theory of pain, the pinching may flood the nervous system with messages so that the news of the pain in your toe does not get through to the brain.

■ REVISITED ■

One of the more fascinating facts in psychology is that many people experience pain in limbs that are no longer there. More than half of combat veterans with amputated limbs report feeling pain in the missing, or "phantom," limbs (Sherman, 1997; Kooijman et al., 2000). In such cases, there is no current tissue damage, but the pain is real. The pain appears to involve activation of nerves in the stump of the missing limb, along with activation of neural circuits that have memories connected with the limb (Melzack, 1997).

Body Senses

Body senses are the senses that people are least aware of. But do not let that fool you. Without them, you would have to pay attention just to stay upright, to lift your legs to go downstairs, or even to put food in your mouth.

The Vestibular Sense Stand up. Now close your eyes. Do you have to look in a mirror to be certain that you are still upright? No, of course not. Your **vestibular sense** tells you whether you are physically upright without your having to use your eyes. Sensory organs located in the ears monitor your body's motion and position in relation to gravity. Your vestibular sense enables you to keep your balance. It tells you whether you are upside down or not and lets you know when you are falling. It also informs you of whether your body is changing speeds, such as in an accelerating automobile.

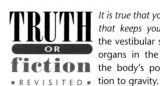

It is true that you have a sense that keeps you upright. It is the vestibular sense. Sensory organs in the ears monitor the body's position in relation to gravity.

■ REVISITED ■

Kinesthesis Ask some friends to close their eyes. Then ask them to touch their noses with their index fingers. How close to their noses did they come? Many of them were probably right on the mark, while others could only come close.

How did they locate their noses? Their eyes were closed, so they could not see their hands. They touched their noses through kinesthesis. **Kinesthesis** is the sense that informs people about the position and motion of their bodies. The word *kinesthesis* comes from the Greek words "to move" (*kinein*) and "perception" (*aisthēsis*). In kinesthesis, sensory information is fed to the brain from sensory organs in the joints, tendons, and muscles.

SECTION 4 REVIEW

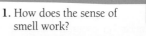

Homework Practice Online
Keyword: SY3 HP4

1. How does the sense of smell work?

2. What is the vestibular sense?

3. **Critical Thinking** *Summarizing* Identify the chemical, skin, and body senses.

Section Objective

▶ Summarize the laws of sensory perception.

This objective is assessed in the Section Review on page 99 and in the Chapter 4 Review.

Opening Section 5

Motivator

Point out to students that understanding what we see requires interpreting the information we receive through our senses. This fact is made clear when we misinterpret or have trouble understanding visual stimuli. Optical illusions may just look like clever tricks, but actually they suggest a lot about how the brain works. Ask students to list different kinds of optical illusions or unclear optical sensations (such as the illustration in Figure 4.12) and then to analyze the reactions people have to these phenomena.

SECTION 5
Perception

Every minute of every day, countless impressions are made on our various senses. Imagine the confusion if we did not find ways to organize all that information. Perception is the way in which we organize or make sense of our sensory impressions.

Rules of Perceptual Organization

Gestalt psychologists applied the principle that "the whole is more than the sum of its parts" to the study of perception. Using this principle, they noted many different ways in which people make sense of sensory information. These ways are called the rules of perceptual organization and include closure, figure-ground perception, proximity, similarity, continuity, and common fate.

Closure   Study Figure 4.10. Do you see random blotches of ink or a dog sniffing the ground? If you perceive the dog, it is not just because of the visual sensations provided by the drawing. Those are actually quite confusing. The pattern is not very clear. Despite the lack of clarity, however, you can still see a dog. Why? The answer is that you are familiar with dogs and that you try to fit the pieces of information into a familiar pattern.

What you are doing with this picture is filling in the blanks. Gestalt psychologists refer to this as the

FIGURE 4.11   *Do you see a vase or the profiles of two faces looking at each other? This figure illustrates the Gestalt principle of figure-ground perception.*

principle of closure. **Closure** is the tendency to perceive a complete or whole figure even when there are gaps in what your senses tell you.

Figure-Ground Perception   Now take a look at Figure 4.11. What do you see? In the center of the drawing, you probably see a vase. If you look again, though, you may see more than a vase. Can you see the two profiles that form the sides of the vase?

This drawing is one of psychologists' favorite illustrations of figure-ground relationships. Figure-ground perception is the perception of figures against a background. When you saw a vase, it was a light-colored figure against a dark background. The profiles, on the other hand, were dark figures against a light background.

We experience figure-ground perception every day. If we look out a window, we may see people, buildings, cars, and streets or perhaps grass, trees, birds, and clouds. We see these objects as figures against a background, such as white clouds against a blue sky or a car in front of a brick building. What we perceive as the figure and what we perceive as the background influence our perception.

Other Rules of Organization   Without reading further, describe Part A of Figure 4.12 on page 94. Did you say that Part A consisted of six lines, or did you say that it was three pairs of lines? If you said three pairs of lines, you were influenced by the **proximity**, or nearness, of some of the lines to each

FIGURE 4.10   *Do you see meaningless ink blotches or a dog sniffing? Although the pattern is unclear, you will probably see a dog because dogs are familiar to you and you fill in the blanks.*

Using Visuals

Poll students to determine how many first saw two faces in Figure 4.12 and how many first saw a vase. Ask what happened after each group managed to see the opposite image. Did they then see both images with equal facility, or did they continue to see one image as the figure and the other as the background?

For Your Information

Synesthesia is a condition in which one type of sensory stimulation creates a perception in another sense—for instance, "hearing" color or "seeing" noise. The most common form appears to be seeing particular colors when certain sounds are heard. While the colors associated with the sounds vary among people with synesthesia, in general, darker colors are perceived in response to lower pitches and brighter colors with higher pitches. Neurologist Richard Cytowic's research indicates that people with synesthesia are typically sensitive, moody, and artistic. Writer Vladimir Nabokov was thought to have synesthesia.

Cytowic, R.E. (1989). Synesthesia and mapping of subjective sensory dimensions. *Neurology, 39.* 849–850.

Teaching Section 5

Demonstration

To demonstrate that the organizational principle of proximity applies to hearing as well as to seeing, tap out the following rhythm with a drumstick or other implement: two rapid beats, pause, two rapid beats, pause, two rapid beats. Ask students to describe the pattern they heard. They will most likely say that they heard three sets of two beats. Point out that they might also have said six beats or even two sets of three beats. It was the proximity of two beats to each other in each set, plus the pause, that made students mentally organize them into three sets.

Applying Ideas

Raise the issue of reporting "the truth" of what one has seen and the fact that sometimes the truth can be misconstrued even though the eyewitness is not intentionally trying to mislead. Describe the example of a criminal trial in which a witness is asked to tell the court her or his observations of a specific event. In light of what the students have learned so far in this chapter about perception, discuss with them how possible it is for a witness to provide information that is strictly factual and objective.

Caption Question: Answer

Answers should reflect an understanding of proximity, similarity, and continuity.

Cross-Curricular Link: History Of Science

Polish astronomer Nicolaus Copernicus (1473–1543) revolutionized Western thought when he published *On the Revolutions of the Celestial Spheres*. In it, he showed that a Sun-centered theory of the solar system explained the movements of the planets far better than the Earth-centered model did. Copernicus argued that the stars were so far away that this apparent change could not be perceived. Thus, Copernicus showed that Earth revolved around the Sun, and thus that the universe was much larger than previously believed.

Teaching Transparencies with Teacher's Notes

TRANSPARENCY 14: Gestalt Laws of Proximity

other. There is no other reason to perceive them in pairs since all of the lines are the same in every other respect.

Now describe Part B of the figure. Did you perceive it as a six-by-six grid or as three columns of *x*'s and three columns of *o*'s? If you said three columns, then you were grouping according to the law of **similarity**, which says that people think of similar objects as belonging together.

What about Part C? Is this a series of half-circles, every other one turned down? Or did you see a wavy line and a straight line? If you saw the wavy line and the straight line, you were probably organizing your perceptions according to the rule of **continuity**. People usually prefer to see smooth, continuous patterns (like lines and waves), not disrupted ones (like the alternating half-circles).

Finally, there is the law of **common fate**. Have you ever noticed how when you see things moving together, you perceive them as *belonging* together? For example, a group of people running in the same direction would appear to have the same purpose. You assume that they are part of the same group and that they are all running to the same place—that they have a common fate.

Perception of Movement

The next time you are in a car or a bus that is stopped at a traffic light, pay attention to what happens when the vehicle in the next lane begins to move forward. Do you think at first that your vehicle, not the other one, is moving? Is it unclear whether your car or bus is moving backward or the other one is moving forward?

To be able to sense movement, humans need to see an object change its position relative to other objects. We all know that Earth is moving, but do we really feel it? To early scientists, whose only instrument for visual observation was the naked eye, it seemed logical that the sun circled Earth. After all, that is what they seemed to be seeing. To observe that it is Earth that moves around the sun, we would have to be somewhere in outer space. We cannot observe it while standing on Earth itself.

So how do you decide which vehicle is moving at the traffic light? One way is to look for objects that you know are stable, like structures on the side of the road—buildings, signs, or trees. If you are steady in relation to them, then your vehicle is not moving. This also sheds light on how participants in events perceive the action from different points of view, physically and psychologically. Those favoring one side over another tend to be biased in their reporting of events. For example, the viewpoint of someone driving a car that runs a red light may differ from that of someone driving a car in another direction.

Stroboscopic Motion

We have been talking about perception of real movement—movement that actually occurs.

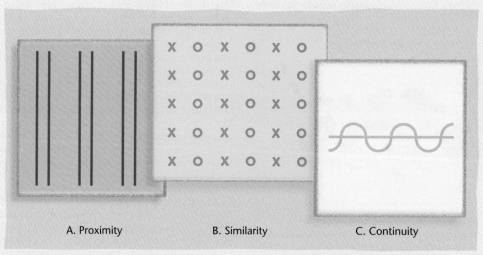

A. Proximity   B. Similarity   C. Continuity

FIGURE 4.12   *How do these drawings illustrate the Gestalt laws of proximity, similarity, and continuity?*

Cooperative Learning

Have pairs of students work together to create two flip books. Both books should show the same person or animal performing the same basic movement, with virtually identical first and last pages in each book. However, while one book should use only 10 pictures to demonstrate the movement from start to finish, the second book should use 20 pictures to demonstrate the same process in more detail. Have the students flip through both books and evaluate the difference that detail makes in creating the illusion of motion.

Predicting Outcomes

Before students read the subsection on depth perception, pose the following questions: If you saw a realistic painting in which some objects, such as trees, were painted in great detail while others were more vague in texture, what would you conclude? If you saw a picture of a number of people at a party and the images of some of the people were complete while the images of others were partially covered up by other people, what would you conclude about the relative distances of the two groups? When students have read the subsection, have them review their predictions.

Psychologists have also studied *illusions* of movement. One such illusion of movement is called stroboscopic motion. In **stroboscopic motion**, the illusion of movement is produced by showing the rapid progression of images or objects that are not moving at all. Have you ever seen one of those little books designed to be flipped through quickly so that the figures on the pages appear to move? These books work because of stroboscopic motion.

Movies work in a similar way. Despite the name *movie*, movies do not consist of images that move. Instead, the audience is shown 16 to 22 pictures, or frames, per second.

In a motion picture, frames of stationary images pass at the rate of about 16 to 22 per second, giving the illusion of motion.

Each frame is just slightly different from the previous one. Showing the frames in rapid succession creates the illusion of movement. Why? Because of the law of continuity, humans prefer to see things as one continuous image. Perception smoothes over the interruptions and fills in the gaps.

Depth Perception

A DAY IN THE LIFE Imagine trying to go through life without being able to judge depth or distance. Like Todd in the theater, you might bump into other people or step on their toes. You would have trouble going up or down stairs without stumbling. Depth, in this case, has little to do with the way people sometimes use the word *deep*. It is not, for instance, the depth of a lake or a hole. Depth here means "distance away." For example, without really thinking about it, you decide how far away a glass of juice is from you. Can you just reach out and pick it up, or do you have to get out of your chair? You perceive the depth of objects through both monocular and binocular cues.

Monocular Cues for Depth Monocular cues need only one eye to be perceived. Artists use monocular cues to create an illusion of depth. These cues create the illusion of three dimensions, or depth, on two-dimensional, or flat, surfaces. Monocular cues cause certain objects to appear more distant from the viewer than others. These cues include perspective, clearness, overlapping, shadow, and texture gradient.

If you take two objects that are exactly the same size and place one of them far away from you and the other nearby, the object that is farther away will stimulate a smaller area of your retina than the one that is near. Even though the objects are the same size, the amount of sensory input from the more distant object is smaller because it is farther away. The distances between far-off objects also appear to be smaller than the same distances between nearby objects. For this reason, the phenomenon known as perspective occurs. Perspective is the tendency to see parallel lines as coming closer together, or converging, as they move away from us. However, experience teaches us that objects that look small when they are far away will seem larger when they are close, even though their size does not actually change. In this way, our perception of a familiar object's size also becomes a cue to its distance from us.

The clearness of an object also helps in telling us how far away it might be. Nearby objects appear to be clearer, and we see more details. Faraway objects seem less clear and less detailed. Thus, the clearer a familiar object seems to be, the closer it is to us.

Overlapping is another monocular cue that tells us which objects are far away and which ones are near. Overlapping is the perceiving of one object as being in front of another. Nearby objects can block our view of more-distant objects. Experience teaches us to perceive partly covered objects as

Cross-Curricular Link: Art

Perspective has not always been a common feature in artists' drawings. Until the 1400s, Western artists represented reality in a flat two-dimensional way. But during the Italian Renaissance, artists learned a technique for portraying three-dimensional reality on a flat surface. The technique was to apply the geometric laws of perspective, in which parallel lines are gradually foreshortened as they move toward a vanishing point. (You may wish to show students some Italian or German painting of the late Middle Ages and then some Renaissance paintings to demonstrate the two ways of depicting reality.)

For Your Information

One's vestibular sense is related to one's visual perception. As a person walks, his or her eyes are continually moving. Yet for the most part, the picture of the world he or she receives remains quite stable rather than constantly jiggling. This stability is accomplished by a reflex system that automatically adjusts for each rotation of the head by an equal and opposite motion of the eyes.

For Further Research

Explain to students that the term *dyslexia* refers to a disturbance in the ability to read or use language. Although there is nothing wrong with their eyesight, dyslexics often do not perceive visual information the same way as people without dyslexia. People with one type of dyslexia habitually reverse the letters of words (for example, reading *saw* for *was*). Have students research the various types of dyslexia and how they are treated. Ask students to present their findings in written reports.

Demonstration

Another way to demonstrate convergence is to lead students through the following exercise: Focus on an object in the distance. Now raise your arm in front of you and hold up one finger. While still focusing on the distant object, close the left eye, then open it, and close the right eye. Note what seems to happen to the finger: it seems to jump to the right. However, if you now focus on the finger instead of on the distant object and again close one eye at a time, something different happens. Now it is the distant object instead of the finger that seems to jump.

96

FIGURE 4.13 *Which circles—the complete circles or those that are partially covered—seem closer to you? Why?*

being farther away than the objects that block them from view. (See Figure 4.13.)

Shadows and highlights also give us information about objects' three-dimensional shapes and where they are placed in relation to the source of light. Look at Figure 4.14. What do you see on the left compared to the right? Your answer probably is that you see a two-dimensional circle on the left and a three-dimensional sphere on the right. What is the difference between the two? The right part of the figure shows a circle with a highlight on its surface and a shadow underneath. Because of these cues, you perceive the highlighted central area to be closest to you.

Still another monocular cue is texture gradient. Texture, of course, is the surface quality and appearance of an object. A gradient is a progressive change. Texture that is farther away from us appears to be denser than texture that is closer, and we see less detail. Therefore, closer objects are perceived as having a more varied texture than objects that are farther away.

The most complex of monocular cues of depth is called motion parallax. It is more complex because, as you have probably guessed by the name, it involves not a stationary picture but the image of something as the viewer moves. Motion parallax is the tendency of objects to seem to move forward or backward depending on how far away they are from the viewer.

If you have the opportunity to take a drive in the countryside, pay attention to what happens to various objects as you move past them. You will notice that distant objects, such as mountains, the Moon,

and stars, appear to move forward with you. Objects at an intermediate distance seem to stand still. Nearby objects, such as roadside markers, rocks, and trees, go by quite rapidly. If you did not know better, you might think that they were moving backward. Through experience, we realize that objects that appear to move with us are at a greater distance than those that pass quickly.

Binocular Cues for Depth Whereas monocular cues can be perceived with just one eye, both eyes are required to perceive **binocular cues** for depth. Two binocular cues for depth are retinal disparity and convergence.

Hold a finger at arm's length. Now slowly bring it closer until it almost touches your nose. If you keep your eyes relaxed as you do this, you will seem to see two fingers. An image of the finger will be projected onto the retina of each eye. Each image will be slightly different because the finger will be seen at different angles. This difference is referred to as **retinal disparity**. The closer your finger comes, the farther apart the "two fingers" appear to be. Thus, the amount of retinal disparity we detect gives us a cue about the depth of an object. However, retinal disparity serves as a cue to depth only for objects that are within a few feet of us, not for objects that are farther away.

The other binocular cue we use is called convergence. Convergence is associated with feelings of tension in the eye muscle. When we try to maintain a single image of the approaching finger, our eyes must turn inward, or converge on it, giving us a cross-eyed look. The closer we feel our eyes moving

FIGURE 4.14 *The addition of a highlight and a shadow gives us the sense that the circle on the right is three-dimensional, or has depth.*

Meeting Individual Needs:
Learners Having Difficulty

To help students grasp the significance of the technical details of this section, suggest that they answer the following questions—in writing—for each phenomenon described (closure, figure-ground perception, perspective, overlapping, and so on). What sensory stimuli is the brain receiving? How does the brain interpret this information? What difference does this make to the way we live or see the world?

Guided Practice

Earlier in the section, paint samples were used to illustrate the number of different hues an average person can distinguish. This time, use several paint samples of the same color. Tape the samples to different parts of the room under different amounts and types of light and adjacent to different-colored backgrounds (for example, one on a dark chalkboard and one on a pale wall). Have students study each sample carefully. Is the color really the same in each sample, or does it vary according to the environment?

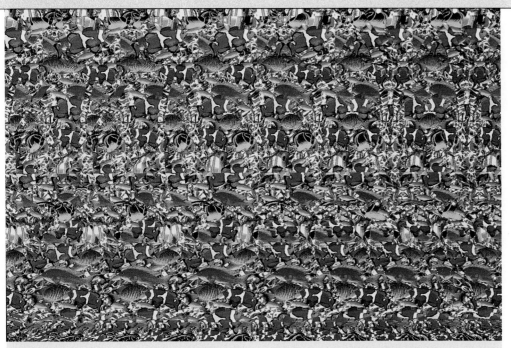

If you look at a Magic Eye® poster in the right way, a three-dimensional image may appear. The image that comes from this poster is of two dolphins, one jumping through a hoop and one in the water.

For Your Information

Research has shown that babies will stare at a new visual stimulus for a much longer period of time than they will at a familiar one or one that closely resembles a familiar visual stimulus. On the basis of this knowledge, scientists devised an experiment to determine if six-month-olds have developed size constancy. Some babies were shown a life-size model of a human head 60 cm away. Then half of them were shown the same model 30 cm away, and half were shown a much smaller model 30 cm away. The babies who were shown the life-size model at a closer distance showed little interest. However, the babies who were shown the smaller model looked at it with interest, as if it was something new—a strong indication that some measure of size constancy is present by the age of six months.

For Your Information

Sensory stimuli that fall below the absolute threshold are called *subliminal*. While an individual may have no conscious awareness of perceiving a subliminal stimulus, there is evidence to suggest that such stimuli are registered on some unconscious level. To illustrate this, researchers flashed an image on a screen so quickly that it was not apparent that there had been an image at all. They then asked

toward each other, the nearer the object they are looking at is. Like retinal disparity, convergence has stronger effects when objects are close.

Have you seen one of those posters that on the surface seems to consist of images of a strange, swirled pattern, but when you stare at the images just the right way, three-dimensional figures pop out at you? Such pictures, which are created by a computer and are known as Magic Eye®, make use of retinal disparity and convergence. Each eye, in fact, sees a slightly different image from the other, and if you can relax your eyes enough, those two images fuse into a three-dimensional picture.

Perceptual Constancies

Imagine that you are just leaving school and that you see your friends waiting for you under a tree some distance away. As you run over to them, they get closer and look larger because, as you have just learned, the image of your friends takes up more and more space on your retina. Why do you not think your friends are literally growing in inches? This would certainly appear to be the case judging from the sensory input. Or consider the problems of

a pet owner who might recognize his or her dog from the side but not from above because the dog's shape would differ from above. The reason you know your friends are not actually getting taller by the second, and the pet owner recognizes the dog from almost every angle, is experience. Each person's experience creates perceptual constancies—constancies of size, color, brightness, and shape.

Size Constancy   The image of a dog seen from a distance of 20 feet occupies about the same amount of space on the retina as an inch-long insect crawling in the palm of the hand. Yet we do not perceive the dog to be as small as the insect. Similarly, we may say that people on the ground look like ants when we are at the top of a tall building, but we know they remain people even if the details of their forms are lost in the distance.

Through experience, people acquire a sense of size constancy. Size constancy is the tendency to perceive an object as being of one size no matter how far away the object is, even though the size of its image on the retina varies with its distance. Through experience, humans learn about perspective—that the same object seen at a great distance

Independent Practice

Ask students to list the four perceptual constancies: constancies of size, color, brightness, and shape. Then have them formulate at least one original example of a situation that demonstrates each constancy. (For example, size constancy would be demonstrated by seeing a house far from the road and knowing that, despite its appearance, it is a normal-sized house; shape constancy would be demonstrated by recognizing a can from all angles, even though it appears to be a rectangle from the side and a circle from the top.)

Applying Information

Organize students into two groups. Provide each group with a photocopy of each illustration contained in this section. Remove the captions from the illustrations. Challenge the students in each group to work together to write a new caption for each item. The caption should explain what phenomenon is being demonstrated (in the correct technical terminology) and how the phenomenon occurs. Score each response for accuracy and completeness. The team with the higher score wins.

the experiment participants to take "wild guesses" at what they had just seen. The participants were often able to describe the object flashed on the screen even though they were unaware that they had seen anything.

Class Discussion

Ask students to describe occasions on which their eyes "played tricks on them." Based on what they have learned in this section, can they guess what caused their confusion?

Section 5 Review: Answers

1. any three of these rules: closure, figure-ground perception, proximity, similarity, continuity, and the law of common fate

2. People perceive motion by their relationship to objects they know are stable and by body sensations. People perceive depth by various monocular and binocular cues.

3. Answers should clearly explain each of the following: size constancy, color constancy, brightness constancy, and shape constancy.

4. What a person sees or hears affects that person's point of view of the event. A person's

98

FIGURE 4.15 *Although the two gray squares are identical, the one on the left is perceived as brighter because it appears against a dark background.*

from the viewer will appear much smaller than when it is nearby.

How do we know that size constancy is something we learn? Some evidence comes from a study of the Mbuti people of Africa, who live in a dense forest. When anthropologist Colin Turnbull (1961) took one of the Mbuti guides out of the forest and onto a wide plain, they happened to see some

buffalo in the distance. The Mbuti guide mistook the buffalo for insects and would not believe Turnbull when he told him otherwise. The reason? Experience. The Mbuti man had seen buffalo before. However, having lived in a dense forest, he was not used to seeing them at great distances. He had therefore not developed size constancy in the way a plains dweller would have.

 Color Constancy Imagine that Marc was wearing a tan sweatshirt and Linda had on a red blouse. Even in the darkened movie theater, Marc and Linda still knew that their shirts were tan and red. Because of their previous experience, they perceived their shirts as remaining tan and red even though both appeared gray in the darkness of the theater. Color constancy is the tendency to perceive objects as keeping their color even though different light might change the appearance of their color.

Brightness Constancy Brightness constancy is the tendency to perceive an object as being equally bright even when the intensity of the light around it changes. Look at Figure 4.15. Does the gray square in the black frame look brighter than the one in the white frame? If it does, it is because we judge the

FIGURE 4.16 *When a door is closed, it looks like a rectangle. When it is open, it is trapezoidal. But because* of shape constancy, we still perceive the door as being rectangular whether it is open or not.

Synthesizing Ideas

Tell interested students to create their own drawings or paintings that use monocular cues to create depth. Challenge students to experiment with a range of such cues. Then encourage them to discuss with their classmates the effectiveness of the monocular cues.

Reviewing Section 5

Have students complete the Section Review questions on page 99.

Extension

There are many excellent books on optical illusions. Students may wish to locate some of these books and share the most interesting illusions with the class. Challenge students to provide a detailed analysis of how and why each optical illusion occurs.

brightness of an object by the brightness of other objects around it. For example, a black object really looks almost gray in very bright sunlight, but we still perceive it as being black because everything else around it is also much brighter.

Shape Constancy Take a glass and look at it from directly above. You see a circle, right? Now move back slightly; it becomes an ellipse. When you look at the glass straight on, the image of the top of it is a line. So why would you still describe the rim of the glass as being a circle? Because of shape constancy— the knowledge that an item has only one shape no matter what angle you view that item from. Figure 4.16 shows another example. A door appears to be a rectangle only when you view it straight on. When you move to the side or open it, the left or right edge comes closer and appears to be larger, changing the retinal image of the door to a trapezoid. Yet because of shape constancy, you continue to think of doors as being rectangular.

Visual Illusions

Do your eyes sometimes "play tricks on you"? Actually, your eyes are not to blame, but your brain's use of perceptual constancies is responsible. Your brain can trick your eye through visual illusions.

Part A of Figure 4.17 shows the Müller-Lyer illusion. Look at the two lines at the top of the illustration. Do you think they are the same length? To most people, the line on the right, with its reversed arrows, looks longer. Why? Again, because of experience. In this culture, we are used to living in rooms in buildings. The line on the right may remind us of how a far corner of a room looks, while the line on the left reminds us of the outside near corner of a building. The rule of size constancy is that if two objects seem to be the same size and one is farther away, the farther object must be larger than it actually seems. How did psychologists come to the conclusion that we are reminded of buildings and rooms in this illusion? Because they found that the illusion does not work

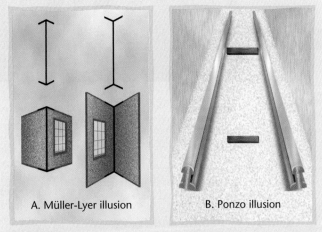

A. Müller-Lyer illusion   B. Ponzo illusion

FIGURE 4.17 *(A) Which line at the top is longer? If you measure them, you will find that they are exactly the same. Notice how the line on the left resembles the near corner of a building and the line on the right looks like the far corner of a room. (B) The two horizontal lines are equally long, but the top line seems longer. Why?*

in cultures that do not live in the same types of structures that we do (Segall, Campbell, & Herskovits, 1966).

Now look at Part B of Figure 4.17, which shows the Ponzo illusion. Which of the two horizontal lines do you think is longer? Do you perceive the top line as being longer? The rule of size constancy may also afford insight into this illusion. Perhaps the converging lines strike you as receding into the distance. If so, you assume from experience that the horizontal line at the top is farther down the track—farther away from you. The rule of size constancy is at work again.

SECTION 5 REVIEW

go.hrw.com **Homework Practice Online** Keyword: SY3 HP4

1. List and explain three rules of perceptual organization.
2. Explain the cues people use to perceive motion and depth.
3. Describe four perceptual constancies.
4. **Critical Thinking** *Analyzing Information* Describe how a person's perceptions affect that person's points of view. What are some examples of bias related to various points of view?

biases can be shaped by the person's point of view: the viewpoint of a driver who runs a red light, for example, may differ from that of a pedestrian who watched the car go through the light.

Caption Question: Answer

Students' answers should demonstrate an understanding of the concept of size constancy.

Chapter 4 Review: Answers

Writing a Summary

See the section subtitles for the main topics in the chapter.

Identifying People and Ideas

1. the stimulation of sensory receptors and the transmission of sensory information to the central nervous system
2. the psychological process through which we interpret sensory stimulation
3. the minimum amount of difference that can be detected between two stimuli
4. the sensitive surface in the eye that acts like the film in a camera
5. deafness caused by damage to the middle ear
6. theory suggesting that only a certain amount of information can be processed by the nervous system at a time

REVIEW AND ASSESSMENT RESOURCES

Technology

▶ Chapter 4 Test Generator (on the One-Stop Planner)

▶ HRW Go site

Reinforcement, Review, and Assessment

▶ Chapter 4 Review, pp. 100–101

▶ Chapter Review Activities with Answer Key

▶ Alternative Assessment Handbook

▶ Portfolio Assessment Handbook Chapter 4 Test (Form A or B)

PSYCHOLOGY PROJECTS

Linking to Community Have an audiologist or an optometrist come to the classroom and discuss the techniques that he or she uses to screen and diagnose hearing or vision problems. Ask the individual to also discuss the following questions:

---

7. rule that people usually prefer to see smooth, continuous patterns, not disrupted ones

8. an illusion of movement produced by showing the rapid progression of images that are not moving at all

9. cue that requires only one eye to be perceived

10. cues that require both eyes to perceive depth

Understanding Main Ideas

1. Sensation is the transmission of sensory information to the central nervous system. Perception is the psychological process by which we interpret sensory stimulation.

2. The pupils become small in bright light because the eyes need only a bit of light. In darkness, they become large to let in more light.

3. Sound waves strike the eardrum, which transmits the vibrations to the middle ear. These vibrations are transferred to the cochlea, which is filled with fluid. Neurons detect the vibrations and relay this information to the brain via the auditory nerve.

4. Smell enhances our sense of taste by enabling us to experience the flavor of foods.

5. Monocular cues (perspective, clearness, overlapping, and light) can be perceived with one eye; binocular cues (retinal disparity and convergence) need both eyes.

Thinking Critically

1. Humans would not pick up important signals from weak stimuli, and pain would remain intense. Life would be intolerable.

Chapter 4 REVIEW

Writing a Summary

Using standard grammar, spelling, sentence structure, and punctuation, summarize the information in this chapter. Consider:
• how sensation and perception differ
• how people see, hear, feel, taste, smell, touch, and otherwise perceive the world around them

Identifying People and Ideas

Identify the following terms or people and use them in appropriate sentences.

1. sensation
2. perception
3. difference threshold
4. retina
5. conductive deafness
6. gate theory
7. continuity
8. stroboscopic motion
9. monocular cue
10. binocular cues

 Understanding Main Ideas

SECTION 1 (pp. 78–80)
1. What is the difference between sensation and perception?

SECTION 2 (pp. 80–85)
2. How do pupils adjust to the amount of light available?

SECTION 3 (pp. 85–88)
3. How does the ear transmit sound to the brain?

SECTION 4 (pp. 88–92)
4. How are smell and taste related?

SECTION 5 (pp. 93–99)
5. What is the difference between monocular cues and binocular cues? Give examples of each.

Thinking Critically

1. Making Generalizations and Predictions What do you think life would be like if human beings lacked sensory adaptation?

2. Analyzing Information What would happen if our eyes were unable to control the amount of light that entered them?

3. Summarizing The process of hearing is considered a chain reaction. Why?

4. Drawing Inferences and Conclusions How might people's perceptions and senses affect their choice of a career?

5. Evaluating Give an example of a situation in which monocular cues could be used to determine how far away an object is.

Writing About Psychology

1. Summarizing Recall an experience in which one of your senses produced such an impact that you still remember it. Write two or three paragraphs to re-create the experience in vivid detail.

2. Analyzing Information With three classmates, take a 10-minute walk outside. Stay together, but do not talk to one another or take any notes. After the walk, divide a sheet of paper into four columns. Write the following headings at the top of each column: *See, Hear, Smell, Feel.* Write down what you experienced during your walk. Compare your list with those of the others in your group. How do people exposed to the same stimuli perceive them differently? Use the graphic organizer below to help you with your chart.

See	Hear	Smell	Feel

- What are the effects of specific auditory and vision problems on learning and behavior?
- What methods are available for correcting auditory and vision problems?
- What are some emotional aspects of the problems?

After the expert has finished her or his presentation, give students the opportunity to ask additional questions.

Cooperative Learning

Explain to students that presenting ideas in a new format is one way to assess how well a person has learned certain concepts. Have students work together to create a simple book on sensation and perception for young children. The book should cover topics such as a delineation of the senses and an explanation of perception. Students should assign themselves different roles: those who brainstorm concepts, those who write the text, and those who illustrate the book.

Building Social Studies Skills

Interpreting Graphs

Study the graph below. Then use the information in the graph to help you answer the questions that follow.

Comparing Senses: Perceptions of Hearing and Seeing

Source: Marks, *The Unity of the Senses*, 1978

1. Which of the senses has a perceived duration of stimulus that is equal to the real duration of stimulus?
   a. sight
   b. hearing
   c. hearing and sight
   d. smell

2. What does this graph reveal about the differences between the senses?

Analyzing Primary Sources

Read the following excerpt, in which Constance Classen discusses the ways different cultures understand the senses. Then answer the questions that follow.

"Different cultures present strikingly different ways of 'making sense' of the world. The Ongee of the Andaman Islands in the South Pacific, for example, live in a world ordered by smell. According to the Ongee, odour is the vital force of the universe and the basis of personal and social identity. Therefore, when an Ongee wishes to refer to 'me,' he or she points to his or her nose, the organ of smell. Likewise, when greeting a friend, an Ongee will ask 'How is your nose?' The primary concern of Ongee culture is to maintain a proper state of olfactory [sense of smell] equilibrium within individuals and within the cosmos."

3. Which of the following statements reflects the argument that Classen makes in the excerpt?
   a. The Ongee are a strange people.
   b. The sense of smell is the sharpest and most accurate sense.
   c. Cultural values shape the way in which people use and understand the senses.
   d. Island peoples are more likely to rely on smell than sight.

4. Which sense do you regard as the most important in your culture? Provide an example to support your answer.

PSYCHOLOGY PROJECTS

Linking to Community

Using Your Observation Skills Conduct an experiment to show the relationship of the senses of taste and smell. Ask several friends to participate. Select four foods that are similar in texture, such as an apple, an onion, a pear, and a potato. Peel and cut the food into pieces. Blindfold the participants and ask them to hold their noses. Guide each person's hand to each bit of food and ask him or her to taste it and guess what it is. Write a report describing how accurately the participants guessed the same foods.

internet connect

Internet Activity: go.hrw.com
KEYWORD: SY3 PS4
Create an activity on sensation and perception to:
- create a drawing or model of the parts of the eye.
- make an oral presentation on the brain and sound processing.
- conduct an Internet scavenger hunt on perception and the senses.

2. The pupils would not automatically get smaller or larger, and too much or too little light would pass through the lenses.

3. Each step in the process causes the next step to occur. The outer ear catches and funnels the sound waves to the eardrum, which vibrates, transmitting the sound waves to the hammer, anvil, and stirrups. These vibrate in turn and transmit the sound waves to the cochlea in the inner ear. The sound waves are transmitted through the fluid-filled cochlea, which contains the neurons that carry the sound impulses to the brain by way of the auditory nerve.

4. A possible answer is that some jobs are better suited for certain senses. For example, a keen sense of hearing is suited to a music teacher or sense of smell to a chef.

5. A possible answer might be the use of overlapping to discern that one car is farther away in a parking lot than another car.

Writing About Psychology

1. Students should explain what made the sensory experience memorable.

2. Students should support their findings about the relationship between taste and smell.

Building Social Studies Skills

1. b

2. Students might note that information from the senses is not necessarily equal or the same as far as reliability.

3. c

4. Students' answers and examples will vary but should place one sense in its cultural context.

101

SENSATION AND PERCEPTION **101**

Consciousness

CHAPTER RESOURCE MANAGER

	Objectives	Pacing Guide		Reproducible and Review Resources
SECTION 1: **The Study of Consciousness** (pp. 104–106)	Analyze the nature of consciousness.	**Regular** 1 day *Block Scheduling Handbook with Team Teaching Strategies, Chapter 5*	**Block Scheduling** 1 day	**E** Research Projects and Activities for Teaching Psychology **RS** Essay and Research Themes for Advanced Placement Students, Theme 4 **REV** Section 1 Review, p. 106
SECTION 2: **Sleep and Dreams** (pp. 106–112)	Describe the stages of sleep and list several sleep problems.	**Regular** 1 day *Block Scheduling Handbook with Team Teaching Strategies, Chapter 5*	**Block Scheduling** 1 day	**PS** Readings and Case Studies, 5 **REV** Section 2 Review, p. 112
SECTION 3: **Meditation, Biofeedback, and Hypnosis** (pp. 112–116)	Explain meditation, biofeed-back, and hypnosis.	**Regular** .5 day *Block Scheduling Handbook with Team Teaching Strategies, Chapter 5*	**Block Scheduling** .5 day	**E** Creating a Psychology Fair, Handout 3, Activity 1 **REV** Section 3 Review, p. 116
SECTION 4: **Drugs and Consciousness** (pp. 116–121)	Describe the ways various kinds of drugs affect consciousness.	**Regular** .5 day *Block Scheduling Handbook with Team Teaching Strategies, Chapter 5*	**Block Scheduling** .5 day	**SM** Mastering Critical Thinking Skills, 5 **REV** Section 4 Review, p. 121

Chapter Resource Key

PS	Primary Sources	**A**	Assessment		Video
RS	Reading Support	**REV**	Review		Internet
E	Enrichment		Transparencies		Holt Presentation Maker Using Microsoft® PowerPoint®
SM	Skills Mastery		CD-ROM		

One-Stop Planner CD–ROM

See the *One-Stop Planner* for a complete list of additional resources for students and teachers.

One-Stop Planner CD–ROM

It's easy to plan lessons, select resources, and print out materials for your students when you use the **One-Stop Planner CD-ROM with Test Generator.**

Technology Resources

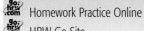 One-Stop Planner, Lesson 5.1
Homework Practice Online
HRW Go Site

 One-Stop Planner, Lesson 5.2
Homework Practice Online
Teaching Transparencies 15: The Stages of Sleep
 Presents Psychology: Slumber Switch
HRW Go Site

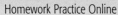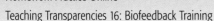 One-Stop Planner, Lesson 5.3
Homework Practice Online
Teaching Transparencies 16: Biofeedback Training
HRW Go Site

 One-Stop Planner, Lesson 5.4
Homework Practice Online

Chapter Review and Assessment

HRW Go site
REV Chapter 5 Review, pp. 122–123
REV Chapter Review Activities with Answer Key

A Chapter 5 Test (Form A or B)
A Portfolio Assessment Handbook
A Alternative Assessment Handbook

 Chapter 5 Test Generator (on the One-Stop Planner)
Global Skill Builder

---

internet connect

HRW ONLINE RESOURCES

GO TO: go.hrw.com
Then type in a keyword.

TEACHER HOME PAGE
KEYWORD: SY3 Teacher

CHAPTER INTERNET ACTIVITIES
KEYWORD: SY3 PS5
Choose an activity to have students:
• make a drawing of the levels and meanings of consciousness.
• create a multimedia display on sleep patterns and dreaming.
• write a research paper on altered states of consciousness.

CHAPTER ENRICHMENT LINKS
KEYWORD: SY3 CH5

ONLINE ASSESSMENT
Homework Practice
KEYWORD: SY3 HP5
Standardized Test Prep
KEYWORD: SY3 STP5
Rubrics
KEYWORD: SS Rubrics

CONTENT UPDATES
KEYWORD: SS Content Updates

HOLT PRESENTATION MAKER
KEYWORD: SY3 PPT5

ONLINE READING SUPPORT
KEYWORD: SS Strategies

CURRENT EVENTS
KEYWORD: S3 Current Events

Additional Resources

PRINT RESOURCES FOR TEACHERS
Benson, H., & Klipper, M. Z. (1975). *The relaxation response.* New York: Avon Books.

Dement, W. C. (1976). *Some must watch while some must sleep: Exploring the world of sleep.* New York: Norton.

Kincher, J. (1994). *Classroom guide to Dreams can help.* Minneapolis, MN: Free Spirit Publishing.

PRINT RESOURCES FOR STUDENTS
Davis, M., Eshelman, E. R., & McKay, M. (1985). *The relaxation and stress reduction workbook* (4th ed.). Oakland, CA: New Harbinger.

Kincher, J. (1988). *Dreams can help: A journal to understanding your dreams and making them work for you.* Minneapolis, MN: Free Spirit Publishing.

MULTIMEDIA RESOURCES
Dynamic concepts in psychology (Videodisc), Films for the Humanities and Sciences, P.O. Box 2053, Princeton, NJ 08543-2053.

Sleep: A prerequisite for health (VHS), Films for the Humanities and Sciences, P.O. Box 2053, Princeton, NJ 08543-2053.

CONSCIOUSNESS

Point out to students that for many years, scientists, including psychologists, thought that it was pointless to study human consciousness because consciousness cannot be directly observed, weighed, or measured. Psychology dealt instead with observable behaviors.

Tell students to imagine that they are researchers who want to study consciousness. Have them pretend to be applying for funding for their project. First, what rationale can they give for wanting to research this topic? Second, what specific questions about consciousness might they begin by asking? Third, how might they actually start to conduct their research—that is, what kinds of experiments might they conduct?

Sections

1 The Study of Consciousness

2 Sleep and Dreams

3 Meditation, Biofeedback, and Hypnosis

4 Drugs and Consciousness

Each of the four questions identified on page 102 corresponds to one of these sections.

5 Chapter
CONSCIOUSNESS

Read to Discover

1 What is consciousness?

2 What are the stages of sleep, and what are several sleep problems?

3 What are meditation, biofeedback, and hypnosis?

4 In what ways do various kinds of drugs affect consciousness?

Each chapter begins with a vignette, called "A Day in the Life," that relates the information discussed in the chapter to the everyday events in the lives of a group of fictional high school students. The text of the chapter occasionally refers back to the vignette to demonstrate the application of the concept being discussed. An icon marked "A Day in the Life" is placed next to these references.

Copy the following graphic organizer onto the chalkboard, omitting the italicized text. Fill in the spaces as you discuss the various meanings of consciousness.

Various Meanings of Consciousness		
A Sense of Self	*Directs Inner Awareness*	*Sensory Awareness*

A DAY IN THE LIFE

November 9

"I had an extremely strange dream last night," Linda said as she, Marc, and Todd were standing around at school waiting for the bell to ring.

"What was it about? Was I in it?" Marc wanted to know.

"Sorry, Marc, you weren't," Linda replied. "Actually, you know who was in it? Nick. And it was weird because it was Nick the way he used to be before he had the drug problem, before he started spacing out all the time. Back when you could talk to him and know that he was actually listening."

The group was silent for a few seconds while they recalled the way Nick used to be. They were all glad his parents had convinced him to go to a treatment center for help.

"But Nick wasn't the only person in my dream," Linda continued. "The thing is, I can't remember who else was there. It was someone I know, but I can't think of who!" She was obviously annoyed.

"Hey, in a movie I saw last weekend, this guy used hypnosis to help a woman remember her dreams," said Todd.

"Did it work?" asked Linda.

"Well, in the movie it did," said Todd. "But I read in a magazine article that you can only be hypnotized if you want to be."

"How did he hypnotize her in the movie?" Linda wanted to know. "What kinds of things did he do?"

"Well, first he got out a chain with something hanging from it. He began to swing it slowly back and forth in front of the woman's eyes, and he told her to concentrate on it. Then he told her that she was getting sleepy, very sleepy, and that her eyelids were getting heavy. Once he'd put her in a trance, he asked her some questions about her dreams, and she was able to answer them. It was amazing."

"Huh," pondered Linda. "Sounds a little creepy to me." Just then the bell rang, and everyone went off to class. Linda never did figure out who else had been in her dream.

. . .

Key Terms

- consciousness
- selective attention
- preconscious
- unconscious
- nonconscious
- altered state of consciousness
- circadian rhythm
- rapid-eye-movement sleep
- insomnia
- night terror
- sleep apnea
- narcolepsy
- meditation
- biofeedback
- hypnosis
- posthypnotic suggestion
- addiction
- depressant
- intoxication
- narcotic
- stimulant
- amphetamine
- hallucination
- delusion
- hallucinogen
- detoxification

Linda's dream, Nick's behavior while on drugs, and Todd's description of hypnotism all have to do with **consciousness**, or awareness of things inside and outside ourselves. Many psychologists believe that we cannot capture the richness of the human experience without talking about consciousness.

You may be fairly certain that you are conscious right now. For example, you are conscious, or aware, that you are reading this page. But what about tonight, when you are asleep? Sleeping and dreaming are related to consciousness. There are also several altered states of consciousness, such as those that occur when a person is in a hypnotic trance or is under the influence of certain drugs. These topics and others that have to do with consciousness will be discussed in this chapter.

Using Key Terms

Explain to students that the key terms can be put into groups according to the major topics to which they relate. Have students try to determine which words belong together and to what larger subject each subgroup relates.

WHY PSYCHOLOGY MATTERS

Psychologists use a variety of techniques to study human consciousness. Use CNNfyi.com or other current events sources to learn more about how psychologists carry out research of human consciousness.

CNNfyi.com

Section Objective 1

▶ Analyze the nature of consciousness.

This objective is assessed in the Section Review on page 106 and in the Chapter 5 Review.

Opening Section 1

Motivator

Challenge students to think about what they already know—or think they know—about consciousness. Have them work in small groups to explore their existing knowledge of this subject. They might begin by listing words related to the concept of consciousness, by writing sentences using the word consciousness, or by attempting to write definitions of the word. Ask each group to identify something they hope to learn or better understand about consciousness after reading this section.

Using Truth Or Fiction

Each chapter opens with several "Truth or Fiction" statements that relate to the concepts discussed in the chapter. Ask students whether they think each statement is true or false. Answers to each item as well as explanations are provided at appropriate points within the text under the heading "Truth or Fiction Revisited."

---

internet connect

TOPIC: The Study of Consciousness

GO TO: go.hrw.com

KEYWORD: SY3 PS5

Have students access the Internet through the HRW Go site to research the meanings and levels of consciousness. Then ask the students to focus on the types of awareness and levels of consciousness, and have them organize their information into a series of drawings or photographs that illustrate the central concepts of the meanings and levels of consciousness.

104

TRUTH OR fiction Read the following statements about psychology. Do you think they are true or false? You will learn whether each statement is true or false as you read the chapter.

- If it were not for cues such as the sunrise and sunset, people would act as if a day were 25 hours long.
- The only time people dream is just before they wake up.
- It is possible to hypnotize any person at any time.
- People who are drunk always know that they are drunk.
- Smoking leads to more deaths in the United States than automobile accidents do.

SECTION 1

The Study of Consciousness

Psychologists have not always thought that consciousness should be part of the study of psychology. In 1904 William James wrote an article titled "Does Consciousness Exist?" In this article, James questioned the value of studying consciousness because he could not think of a scientific way to observe or measure another person's consciousness. His point was that even though we can see other people talking or moving around, we cannot actually measure their consciousness.

John Watson, the founder of behaviorism, agreed with James. In 1913 Watson wrote an article called "Psychology as the Behaviorist Views It." In this article, he stated, "The time seems to have come when psychology must discard all references to consciousness". Watson, like James, questioned whether consciousness could be studied scientifically. He chose instead to focus only on observable behaviors.

Consciousness as a Construct

Not all psychologists dismissed the possibility of studying consciousness. Today many psychologists believe that consciousness can be studied because it can be linked with measurable behaviors, such as talking, and with brain waves.

Consciousness is a psychological construct. Intelligence and emotion are also psychological constructs. None of them can be seen, touched, or measured directly. However, they are known by their effects on behavior and play roles in psychological theories. For example, we can theorize as to how sleep or alcohol affects consciousness and devise ways of testing our theories. When people behave in certain ways, we may conclude that the behaviors result from, say, intelligence even though there is no way to be certain. Although consciousness cannot be seen or touched, it is real enough to most people.

Meanings of Consciousness

Generally speaking, consciousness means awareness. But there is more than one type of awareness. Thus, the term *consciousness* is used in a variety of ways. Sometimes consciousness refers to sensory awareness. At other times, consciousness may mean direct inner awareness. A third use of the term *consciousness* refers to the sense of self that each person experiences.

Consciousness as Sensory Awareness When you see a raindrop glistening on a leaf, when you hear your teacher's voice, or when you smell pizza in the cafeteria, you are *conscious* of all of these sensations around you, including sights, sounds, and smells. Your senses make it possible for you to be aware of your environment. Therefore, one meaning of consciousness is sensory awareness of the environment. In other words, you are conscious, or aware, of things outside yourself.

Focusing on a particular stimulus is referred to as **selective attention.** To pay attention in class, you must screen out the rustling of paper and the scraping of chairs. To get your homework done, you must pay more attention to your assignments than to your hunger pangs or the radio playing in the background. Selective attention makes our senses keener (Basic Behavioral Science Task Force, 1996). We may even be able to pick out the speech of a single person across a room at a party.

We tend to be more conscious of some things than others. We tend to be particularly conscious of sudden changes, as when a cool breeze enters a sweltering room. We also tend to be especially conscious of unusual stimuli—for example, a dog entering the classroom. Intense stimuli—such as bright colors, loud noises, or sharp pains—also tend to get our attention.

Guided Practice

To help students compare consciousness as sensory awareness with consciousness as direct inner awareness, tell them to close their eyes and silently imagine a simple, familiar action, such as sharpening a pencil. Encourage them to imagine the action in logical sequence and minute detail. Then have them open their eyes and actually complete the action they just imagined. Afterward, discuss how their consciousness of the actual and imagined events differed and how they were similar.

Independent Practice

Tell students to find a quiet time in which they can carefully monitor their own states of consciousness. Have them write a description of some of the physical sensations, thoughts, emotions, and external phenomena that registered in their awareness. Later, have small groups of students discuss what percentage of their awareness was focused on external events or sensations and how much was related to inner thoughts and emotions. Did some students focus on inner reality, while others paid more attention to external events?

Consciousness as Direct Inner Awareness

Imagine jumping into a lake or a swimming pool on a hot day. Can you feel the cool, refreshing water all around you? Although this image may be vivid, you did not really experience it. No sensory organs were involved. You are conscious of the image through what psychologists call direct inner awareness.

Anytime you are aware of feeling angry, anytime you remember a best friend you had when you were younger, anytime you think about abstract concepts such as fairness or love, you do so through direct inner awareness. In other words, you do not hear, see, smell, or touch thoughts, images, emotions, or memories. Yet you are still conscious of them. This meaning of consciousness, then, is being aware of things inside yourself.

Consciousness as Sense of Self

Have you ever noticed how young children sometimes refer to themselves by their names? For example, they do not say, "I want milk" but "Taylor wants milk." It is only as they grow older that they begin to understand that they are unique individuals, separate from other people and from their surroundings. From then on, they have a sense of self, no matter how much they or the world around them might change. In some uses of the word, *consciousness* is this sense of self in which we are aware of ourselves and our existence.

Levels of Consciousness

So far, we have discussed only one of the levels of consciousness—the level at which people are aware of something and are aware of their awareness. But many psychologists speak of other levels of consciousness as well. These include the preconscious level, the unconscious level, and the nonconscious level. At these levels of consciousness, awareness is more limited.

The Preconscious Level What if someone asked you what you wore to school yesterday? Or what you did after school? Your class schedule? Your next vacation? Although you were not consciously thinking about any of this information before you were asked about it, you will probably be able to come up with the answers. **Preconscious** ideas are not in your awareness right now, but you could recall them if you had to. You can make these preconscious bits of information conscious simply by directing your inner awareness, or attention, to them.

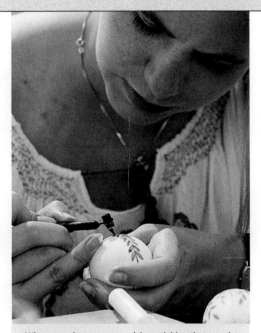

When people are engaged in activities that require close attention to detail, they screen out many sensations to stay focused on the task at hand.

The Unconscious Level Sigmund Freud theorized that people have an unconscious mind. Information stored in the **unconscious** (sometimes called the subconscious) is unavailable to awareness under most circumstances. In other words, this information is hidden. For example, imagine that you are planning to go to a party. Without realizing why, you find yourself continually distracted from getting ready. First, perhaps, you cannot find a pair of shoes. Then maybe you become involved in a lengthy phone call. Can you guess what information was stored in your unconscious? It may be that you did not want to go to the party. But according to Freud's theory this desire to avoid the party was unconscious—you were not aware of it.

Freud believed that certain memories are painful and that some of our impulses, such as aggressiveness, are considered unacceptable. He stated that we use various mental strategies, called defense mechanisms, to push painful or unacceptable ideas out of our consciousness. In this way, we protect ourselves from feelings of anxiety, guilt, and shame. (See Chapter 14.)

The Nonconscious Level Many of our basic biological functions exist on a **nonconscious** level.

Cross-Curricular Link: Philosophy

The great French thinker René Descartes (1596–1650) was an early student of human consciousness. In his search for absolute truth, Descartes eventually concluded that because he had thoughts, he must exist. The awareness of the self (consciousness) was proof that the self existed. This proof—which he stated as, "I think, therefore I am"—was the basis of his philosophy, which still exerts a profound influence on Western thought.

For Your Information

Consciousness of external events is affected by a phenomenon known as selective listening. When multiple auditory stimuli compete for a listener's attention, the listener concentrates on the desired stimuli and filters out the others. For example, a guest at a party can hear the person to whom she or he is speaking, while ignoring the chat of other guests nearby.

Essay and Research Themes for A. P. Students

Theme 4

Closing Section 1

For Further Research

Have students research the classic mind-body problem (i.e., the question of whether human consciousness is a product of the physical body or whether there is a "mind" or "soul" that is somehow distinct from the physical self). Students may want to begin their inquiry by reading about Descartes's conclusions on this subject.

Reviewing Section 1

Have students complete the Section Review questions on page 106.

Extension

Have students return to the beliefs and questions about consciousness that they formulated at the beginning of this section. Have them discuss which beliefs were supported or disproved by information in the section. Which, if any, questions remain unanswered?

Section 1 Review: Answers

1. consciousness, intelligence, and emotion

2. Preconscious level includes information not currently in consciousness but easily retrievable; unconscious level contains information that is unavailable under most circumstances, usually because it is painful or unacceptable; nonconscious level is concerned with body functions that we cannot perceive.

3. Students may suggest that consciousness is an individual experience that cannot be studied by another person; it is a psychological construct that cannot be seen or measured. Other students may say that consciousness can be studied through direct interviews or observation.

Caption Question: Answer

Freud placed irrational wishes on the unconscious level.

Freud's Levels of Consciousness

CONSCIOUS LEVEL
Perceptions
Thoughts

PRECONSCIOUS LEVEL
Memories   Stored knowledge

UNCONSCIOUS LEVEL
Selfish needs   Violent motives
Immoral urges   Fears
Irrational
wishes   Shameful   Unacceptable
                         experiences   desires

FIGURE 5.1 *According to Sigmund Freud, many memories, impulses, and feelings exist below the level of conscious awareness. **On what level did Freud place irrational wishes?***

For example, even if you tried, you could not sense your fingernails growing or the pupils in your eyes adjusting to light. You know that you are breathing in and out, but you cannot actually feel the exchange of carbon dioxide and oxygen. You blink when you step from the dark into the light, but you cannot feel your pupils growing smaller. It may be just as well that these events are nonconscious. After all, how much can a person hope to keep in mind at once?

Altered States of Consciousness

The word *consciousness* sometimes refers to the waking state—the state in which a person is awake. Yet there are also **altered states of consciousness**, in which a person's sense of self or sense of the world changes. When you doze off, you are no longer conscious of what is going on around you. Sleep is one altered state of consciousness. When Nick was under the influence of drugs, he also experienced  altered states of consciousness. Other altered states of consciousness occur through meditation, biofeedback, and hypnosis. The rest of this chapter explores these altered states of consciousness.

A DAY IN THE LIFE

SECTION 1 REVIEW

1. What are three psychological constructs?

2. List and describe three levels of consciousness at which awareness is limited.

3. **Critical Thinking**   *Analyzing Information* Do you think that a person can study or understand the consciousness of another person? Why or why not?

SECTION **2**

Sleep and Dreams

Are you aware that you spend about one third of your life asleep? Why do we sleep? Why do we dream? Why do some of us have trouble getting to sleep or experience nightmares?

Much of how people, animals, and even plants function is governed by **circadian rhythms**, or biological clocks. The word *circadian* comes from the Latin words *circa,* meaning "about," and *dies,* meaning "a day." The circadian rhythms in humans include a sequence of bodily changes, such as those in body

Section Objective

▶ Describe the stages of sleep and list several sleep problems.

This objective is assessed in the Section Review on page 112 and in the Chapter 5 Review.

Opening Section 2

Motivator

Ask students the following questions and record their answers: What time did you go to sleep last night? When did you wake up this morning? Did you have trouble falling asleep? Did you wake up during the night, and if so, why? Do you recall having any dreams or nightmares? Then have students evaluate the results to determine the average number of hours slept; what percentage of the class had sleep problems; and what percentage remembered their dreams. Explain that this section will teach them more about the psychological and physical aspects of sleep.

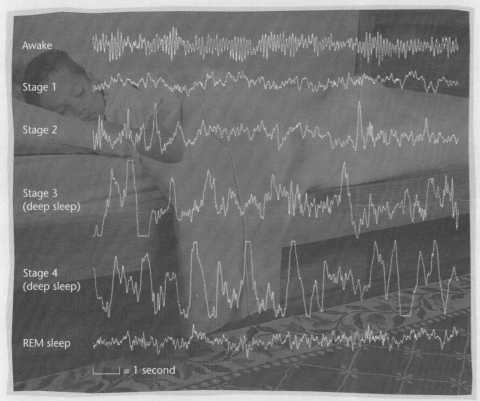

The Stages of Sleep

Awake

Stage 1

Stage 2

Stage 3 (deep sleep)

Stage 4 (deep sleep)

REM sleep

⌐——⌐ = 1 second

FIGURE 5.2   *These are the typical EEG patterns for the stages of sleep. During rapid-eye-movement, or REM, sleep, EEG patterns resemble those of stage 1 sleep. Most people dream or have nightmares during REM sleep.*

What's New In Psychology?

A recent study suggests that eating a carbohydrate snack immediately before taking a nap will make people sleep longer. Researchers think this information could be useful to people who work late shifts, people who have traveled across time zones, and others whose circadian rhythms are out of order and who could benefit from a good nap. Because the study was a small one, however, more research must be conducted before this is proved.

Prevention, Oct. 1995, p. 40.

Teaching Transparencies with Teacher's Notes

TRANSPARENCY 15: The Stages of Sleep

 Technology Resources

CNN. Presents Psychology: Slumber Switch

temperature, blood pressure, and sleepiness and wakefulness, that occurs every 24 hours. The human circadian rhythms usually operate on a 24-hour day. For example, body temperature falls to its lowest point between 3:00 A.M. and 5:00 A.M. each day.

The most-studied circadian rhythm is that of the sleep-wake cycle. Because people normally associate periods of wakefulness and sleep with the rotation of Earth, a full sleep-wake cycle is 24 hours. However, when people are removed from cues that signal day or night (such as clocks, radio or television programs, sunrise, and sunset), their cycle tends to expand to about 25 hours (National Sleep Foundation, 2000). Researchers are unsure why this happens. This and many other issues concerning sleep have been, and continue to be, the subject of much research.

TRUTH OR fiction

■ REVISITED ■

It is true that if it were not for cues such as the sunrise and sunset, people would act as if a day were 25 hours long. Because of Earth's rotation, a day is 24 hours. For reasons not fully understood, however, people may be more suited to a 25-hour day.

The Stages of Sleep

Sleep researchers have discovered that we sleep in stages. (See Figure 5.2.) Sleep stages are defined in terms of brain-wave patterns, which can be measured by an electroencephalograph (EEG). Brain

Teaching Section 2

Meeting Individual Needs: Tactile/Kinesthetic Learners

Have tactile/kinesthetic learners draw a line representing a typical night's sleep pattern. Have them first draw five small boxes in a row and label them Stages 1–4 and REM. Then have them start at the box labeled *Stage 1*, draw a line to the box labeled *Stage 2*, then to stages 3 and 4. Have them, without lifting the pencil, double back to stages 3, 2, and 1 before moving on to a box that represents REM sleep. Have students retrace this pattern four times.

Formulating Hypotheses

Ask students to put themselves in the position of sleep researchers who knew that sleepers produced different patterns of brain activity but did not know whether or how these patterns related to dreaming. Ask students how they would have answered this question. *(The actual researchers who did answer this question in the 1950s, Eugene Aserinsky and Nathaniel Kleitman, wakened research participants when they were having rapid eye movement and when they were not. Eighty percent reported intense dreams during REM sleep; fewer reported vague dreams during non-REM sleep.)*

Classroom Discussion

Ask students how many hours of sleep a night they need to feel rested. Compare these answers with the results of the earlier question about how long they had slept the previous night. Then point out that sleep researcher Mary Carskadon believes that most American teens are sleep deprived. She says they need an average of 9.5 hours of sleep a night but receive an average of only 6.5 to 7.5 hours. Ask students how long they sleep when they can "sleep in." Ask if they think it is possible they are trying to make up for a substantial sleep deficit.

Current Events, Feb. 6, 1995, p. 3.

🖅 internet connect

TOPIC: Sleep and Dreams
GO TO: go.hrw.com
KEYWORD: SY3 PS5

Have students access the Internet through the HRW Go site to research the levels and importance of sleep and dreams. Then ask students to make a multimedia presentation using visual aids and relevant examples to display their research. Ask students to emphasize the importance of sleep to healthy living and the relevance of dreaming.

waves, like other waves, are cyclical, and they vary on the basis of whether we are awake, relaxed, or sleeping. Four different brain-wave patterns are beta waves, alpha waves, theta waves, and delta waves.

When we are awake and alert, the brain emits beta waves, which are short and quick. As we begin to relax and become drowsy, the brain waves slowly move from beta waves to alpha waves, which are a little slower than beta waves. During this relaxed state, we may experience visual images such as flashes of color or sensations such as feeling as if we are falling. This state is followed by five distinct stages of sleep.

Stage 1 is the stage of lightest sleep. As we enter stage 1 sleep, our brain waves slow down from the alpha rhythm to the slower pattern of theta waves. This transition may be accompanied by brief dreamlike images that resemble vivid photographs. Because stage 1 sleep is light, if we are awakened during this stage, we will probably recall these images and feel as if we have not slept at all.

If we are not awakened, we remain in stage 1 sleep no more than 30 to 40 minutes. Then we move into sleep stages 2, 3, and 4. During stages 3 and 4, sleep is deep, and the brain produces delta waves—the slowest of the four patterns. Stage 4 is the stage of deepest sleep, meaning that it is the one during which someone would have the greatest difficulty waking us up.

After perhaps half an hour of stage 4 sleep, we begin a relatively quick journey back to stage 3 to stage 2 to stage 1. About 90 minutes will have passed since we fell asleep. Now something strange happens. Suddenly, we breathe more irregularly,

blood pressure rises, and the heart beats faster. Brain waves become similar to those of stage 1 sleep. Yet this is another stage of sleep—the stage called **rapid-eye-movement sleep**, or REM sleep, because beneath our closed lids, our eyes are moving rapidly. The preceding four stages are known as non-rapid-eye-movement, or NREM, sleep because our eyes do not move as much during them.

During a typical eight-hour night of sleep, most people go through these stages about five times, each of which constitutes one sleep cycle. (See Figure 5.3.) As the night goes on, periods of REM sleep become longer. The final period of REM sleep, toward morning, may last half an hour or longer.

Why Do We Sleep?

People need sleep to help revive the tired body and to build up resistance to infection. Sleep also seems to serve important psychological functions. It may, for example, help us recover from stress. We seem to need more sleep when we have problems in school, with our families and friends, or at work.

What would happen if people forced themselves to go without sleep? In 1964 Randy Gardner, age 17, tried to find out as part of a science project. Under the supervision of a physician, Randy stayed awake almost 11 days. He became irritable, could not focus his eyes, and had speech difficulties and memory lapses. (Because of these types of effects and others that are potentially dangerous, sleep deprivation experiments like Gardner's should be conducted only by trained professionals in laboratory settings.) William Dement, an early sleep

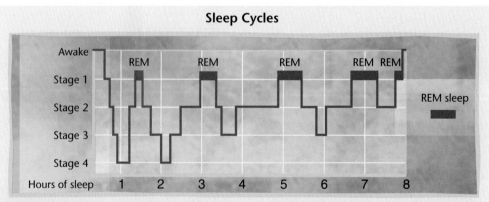

FIGURE 5.3 *This is a typical sleep pattern. Most people go through the cycle five times in eight hours. As the night progresses, stages 3 and 4 become shorter, and REM sleep becomes longer.*

Cooperative Learning

Have students work in pairs to create and administer surveys about dreams. In each pair, one student should be the "writer." He or she should determine exactly what information to collect (for example, how many people dream in color and how many dream in black and white) and then devise questions to elicit the information. The other student, the "interviewer," should determine what population to interview (for example, a mix of people of different ages and both sexes) and should ask the questions and record the answers.

Evaluating Information

After the students have finished administering their survey, have them evaluate their findings. They should summarize the answers to each question. They may want to look for patterns in the answers (for example, does gender or age seem to have any relationship to what kind of dreams people report having). If the data is inconclusive, have students revise and administer the survey again. Finally, have them make an oral report to the class on their findings.

The mystery of dreams has occupied artists, philosophers, and scientists for centuries. Desert Dream, *a painting* by contemporary American artist Michael Parkes, shows *a variety of dreamlike images.*

©1996 Michael Parkes/Steltman Galleries New York. *Desert Dream* oil painting on wood, 110 x 90 cm.

researcher, tracked Gardner's recovery. He found that Gardner slept an extra 6.5 hours for the first three days following the experiment. On the fourth night he slept 2.5 extra hours (Gulevich, Dement, & Johnson, 1966).

In some studies, animals or people have been deprived only of REM sleep. People and animals deprived of REM sleep tend to show what psychologists call REM-rebound. They catch up on their REM sleep by having much more of it when they sleep later on. REM sleep seems to serve particular psychological functions. Animals and people who are deprived of REM sleep learn more slowly than usual. They also forget more rapidly what they have learned (Adler, 1993b; Winson, 1992). Other research findings suggest that REM sleep may help

brain development in infants and "exercise" brain cells in adults (McCarley, 1992).

Dreams

It is during REM sleep that we have the most vivid dreams. Linda's dream, for example, probably occurred while she was in REM sleep. Dreams are a mystery about which philosophers, poets, scientists, and many others have theorized for centuries.

Did you know that dreams can be in black-and-white or in full color? Some dreams seem very realistic. You may have had a dream of going to class and suddenly realizing that there was going to be a

Demonstration

To demonstrate that muscular tension produces psychological tension and vice versa, tell students to tense the muscles in their hands and feet as hard as they can. Afterward, ask them about their feelings. Did they feel "on edge"? Next, ask them to concentrate on a problem or task that is worrying them. Afterward, have them think about the muscles of their necks and faces. How many of the students report that they were frowning, clenching their jaws, or experiencing tension in their upper backs and necks? Point out that mental and physical tension can cause sleep problems.

Role-Playing

Ask three students to role-play a dreamer and two analysts. The "dreamer" should begin by recording a dream (an anonymous other person's real dream might be ideal so as to avoid any personal embarrassment). The dreamer should recall the dream for "analyst 1" while "analyst 2" is out of the room. Analyst 1 should interpret the dream. Then analyst 2 should return to the room, listen to the dream, and also interpret it. Afterward, have the class compare and contrast the two interpretations.

test in the class. You had not studied. You started to panic. Then you woke up. The dream felt very real, and you were relieved to find that it was only a dream after all. Other dreams are disorganized and seem less real.

We may dream every time we are in REM sleep. During REM sleep, dreams are most likely to have clear imagery and plots that make sense, even if some of the events are not realistic. During NREM sleep, plots are vaguer and images more fleeting.

TRUTH *It is not true that the only time people dream is just before they wake up. The most vivid dreams occur during REM sleep, the final part of the sleep cycle. Most people go through the sleep cycle about five times a night.*

OR

fiction

▪ REVISITED ▪

Interestingly, if the events in a person's dream seemed to last 10 minutes, she or he was probably dreaming for 10 minutes. That is, people seem to dream in "real time." Although some dreams involve fantastic adventures, most of the dreams people have—particularly REM-sleep dreams experienced early in the night—are simple extensions of the activities of the day. The characters in dreams are more likely to be friends and neighbors than spies, monsters, or princes. Linda suspected that the other person in her dream was someone she knew, and she was probably right.

Like Linda, we sometimes have difficulty recalling all, or even a few, of the details of our dreams. This may be because we are often unable to hold on to information from one state of consciousness (in this case, sleeping/dreaming) when we move into another (in this case, wakefulness).

The Freudian View Have you ever heard the song "A Dream Is a Wish Your Heart Makes" from the Disney film *Cinderella*? Is it true that your dreams reveal what you really want? Sigmund Freud thought so—he theorized that dreams reflect a person's unconscious wishes and urges—"wishes your heart makes."

However, some unconscious wishes may be unacceptable, perhaps even painful. Those, Freud thought, would be the ones that would most likely appear in dreams, although not always in direct or obvious forms. Freud believed that people dream in

symbols. He thought that these "symbolic" dreams give people a way to deal with painful material that they cannot deal with consciously.

The Biopsychological Approach Some psychologists believe that dreams begin with biological, not psychological, activity. According to this view, during sleep, neurons fire in a part of the brain that controls movement and vision. These neuron bursts are random, and the brain tries to make sense of them. It does so by weaving a story—the dream. When neurons fire in the part of the brain that controls running, for example, we may dream we are running toward or away from something.

The biopsychological approach suggests an explanation for why people tend to dream about events that took place earlier in the day. The most current activity of the brain concerns the events or problems of the day. Thus, the brain uses everyday matters to give structure to the random bursts of neurons during REM sleep.

Today most psychologists caution that there are no hard-and-fast rules for interpreting dreams. And we can never be sure whether a certain interpretation is correct.

Sleep Problems

Even when we need sleep, we may have trouble getting to sleep or sleeping soundly. When these troubles last for long periods of time or become serious, they are considered to be sleep problems.

Insomnia Insomnia is the inability to sleep. The word comes from the Latin *in-*, meaning "not," and *somnus*, meaning "sleep." The most common type of insomnia is difficulty falling asleep. People with insomnia are more likely than others to worry and to have "racing minds" at bedtime. For many people, insomnia comes and goes, increasing during periods of anxiety or tension and decreasing or disappearing during less stressful periods.

People can actually make insomnia worse by *trying* to get to sleep. The effort backfires because it increases tension. We cannot force ourselves to fall asleep. We can only set the stage by lying down and relaxing when we are tired. Yet millions of people go to bed each night dreading the possibility that they will not be able to fall asleep.

Some people use sleeping pills to cope with insomnia, but many psychologists believe that the safest, simplest, most effective ways of overcoming insomnia do not involve medication. Psychologists

Closing Section 2

For Further Research

Have students research the topic of how sleep problems affect health. Aspects of this subject include: the effect of sleep on the production of the hormone serotonin, the evidence that sleep bolsters the immune system, the fact that sleeplessness can lead to paranoia and lack of attentiveness, the digestive problems that can arise from interrupted sleep, and the affects of severe sleep apnea on the cardiovascular system.

Applying Information

Have students write short essays to answer each of the following questions: Which piece of information about sleep and dreams most surprised you? Which piece of information about sleep and dreams do you think is most significant for or applicable to your own life? Explain why.

Reviewing Section 2

Have students complete the Section Review questions on page 112.

---

recommend that people with insomnia try the following techniques:

- Tense the muscles, one at a time, then let the tension go. This helps relax the body.
- Avoid worrying in bed. If worrying persists, get up for a while.
- Establish a regular routine, particularly for getting up and going to sleep each day.
- Use pleasant images or daydreams to relax. These may occur naturally, or people may have to focus on creating them.

Many psychologists also note that occasional insomnia is fairly common and is not necessarily a problem. It becomes a problem only if it continues for long periods of time.

Nightmares and Night Terrors You have probably experienced one or more nightmares in your lifetime. Common nightmares involve snakes or murderers. Some nightmares are specific to a particular activity or profession. For example, the "actor's nightmare" involves being on stage in front of an audience. The dreamer (an actor, naturally) has no idea what play is being presented, much less what any of the lines are.

In the Middle Ages, nightmares were thought to be the work of demons who were sent to make people pay for their sins. Today we know that nightmares, like most other dreams, are generally products of REM sleep. In one study, college students kept dream diaries and reported having an average of two nightmares a month (Wood & Bootzin, 1990). Upsetting events can produce nightmares, as reported in a study of people who experienced the San Francisco earthquake of 1989 (Wood et al., 1992). People who are anxious or depressed are also more likely to have nightmares.

Night terrors (also called sleep terrors) are similar to, but more severe than, nightmares. Dreamers with night terrors feel their hearts racing, and they gasp for air. They may suddenly sit up, talk incoherently, or thrash about. They do not fully wake up. In the morning, they may recall a feeling or an image from the night terror. Unlike the case with nightmares, however, memories of night terror episodes usually are vague.

Night terrors also differ from nightmares in when they occur. Night terrors tend to occur during deep sleep (stages 3 and 4), whereas nightmares occur during REM sleep. Night terrors happen during the first couple of sleep cycles, nightmares more toward morning. Night terrors are most common among

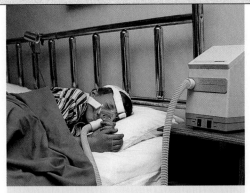

This person with sleep apnea is hooked up to equipment that applies continuous pressure through the nose to keep airways open during sleep.

young children and may reflect immaturity of the nervous system.

Sleepwalking Many children walk in their sleep. Sleepwalkers may roam about almost nightly during stages of deep sleep. They may respond to questions while they are up and about, but when they wake up they typically do not remember what they did or said. Contrary to myth, there is no evidence that sleepwalkers become violent or upset if they are awakened. However, because sleepwalkers are not fully conscious and thus may be prone to accidentally hurting themselves, they should be supervised if possible.

Most children outgrow sleepwalking as they mature. As is true of night terrors, sleepwalking may reflect immaturity of the nervous system.

Sleep Apnea We all have occasional apneas, or interruptions in breathing. **Sleep apnea** is a breathing interruption that occurs during sleep. People with sleep apnea do not automatically start breathing again until they suddenly sit up and gasp for air. Once they begin breathing again, they fall back asleep. They usually do not wake up completely, so they may not even be aware of what has happened during the night. However, they often feel tired during the day.

Sleep apneas occur when a person's air passages are blocked. Thus, they are sometimes accompanied by snoring. A nasal mask that provides a steady air flow can help prevent breathing interruptions.

About 10 million Americans have apnea, and it is associated with obesity as well as snoring. Apnea is more than a sleep problem. It can lead to high blood pressure, heart attacks, and strokes (Lavie et al., 2000; Peppard et al., 2000).

Using Visuals

The nasal mask shown in the photograph on page 111 is one of the devices used to treat sleep apnea. Other devices and techniques include weight-loss programs (for obese people), devices that realign the jaw and keep the airway open at night, and, in extreme cases, surgery.

For Your Information

During REM sleep, the brain is involved in intense activity, as shown on EEGs. However, most of the body's muscular activity comes to a halt during this stage of sleep. Facial and fingertip muscles may continue to twitch, but snoring stops, and the dreamer's legs, arms, and trunk are virtually paralyzed.

111

CONSCIOUSNESS **111**

Section Objective

▶ Explain meditation, biofeedback, and hypnosis.

This objective is assessed in the Section Review on page 116 and in the Chapter 5 Review.

Opening Section 3

Motivator

Ask students what claims they have heard about meditation, biofeedback, or hypnosis. How do they think these activities affect human consciousness? Tell them that in this section, they will learn some of the facts and current theories about meditation, biofeedback, and hypnosis; they will also learn some of the limitations of these activities.

Section 2 Review: Answers

1. Stage 1 is light sleep that produces the alpha waves typical of relaxation. Stages 2, 3, and 4 are deeper. These four stages are non-rapid-eye-movement stages. The final stage is rapid-eye-movement (REM) sleep, when dreams and nightmares occur.

2. Insomnia is the inability to sleep; night terrors are similar to, but more severe than, nightmares; sleepwalking is roaming around during stages of deep sleep without being aware of it; sleep apnea occurs when breathing is interrupted; narcolepsy occurs when people suddenly fall asleep no matter where they are.

3. Nightmares and night terrors are both sleep disturbances. Unlike the case with nightmares, memories of night terrors are vague. Dreamers with night terrors do not fully wake up, dreamers with nightmares do. Night terrors tend to occur during deep sleep, whereas nightmares occur during REM sleep. It might be difficult to differentiate between the two in young children because they may not be able to describe the sensations or determine whether they are fully awake.

Narcolepsy **Narcolepsy** is a rare sleep problem in which people suddenly fall asleep no matter what time it is or where they are. One minute they are awake. The next, their muscles completely relax, and they are in REM sleep. Drug therapy and frequent naps have been used to treat narcolepsy.

Although people usually awaken from an episode of narcolepsy feeling refreshed, such episodes may be dangerous. For example, they can occur while people are driving or operating machinery. No one knows for sure what causes narcolepsy, but it is believed to be a genetic disorder of REM-sleep functioning.

SECTION 2 REVIEW

go.hrw.com **Homework Practice Online** Keyword: SY3 HP5

1. Describe the five stages of sleep.

2. Describe three kinds of sleep problems.

3. **Critical Thinking** *Comparing and Contrasting* How are nightmares and night terrors similar and different? Why might it be difficult to differentiate between the two in a young child?

SECTION 3
Meditation, Biofeedback, and Hypnosis

People who are asleep and dreaming are in an altered state of consciousness. Other altered states

A monk meditates in Thailand. Meditation is important in both Buddhism and Hinduism.

of consciousness occur when we are awake. These states of consciousness can be achieved through meditation, biofeedback, and hypnosis.

Meditation: Narrowing Consciousness

Meditation is a method some people use to try to narrow their consciousness so that the stresses of the outside world fade away. Numerous techniques have been used to accomplish this. The ancient Egyptians gazed upon an oil-burning lamp. The yogis of India stare at an intricate pattern on a vase or carpet. Other meditators repeat pleasing sounds called mantras, such as *om* or *sheereem*, and mentally focus on these sounds.

All of these methods of meditation share a common thread—they focus on a peaceful, repetitive stimulus. This focus helps people narrow their consciousness and become relaxed. By narrowing their consciousness, people can suspend planning, worrying, and other concerns. Meditation is an important part of some religions, such as Buddhism. Some meditators claim that meditation helps them achieve "oneness with the universe," pleasure, or some great insight. These claims have never been scientifically proven, but evidence does suggest that meditation can help people relax. Studies have found that meditation can also help people lower high blood pressure (Alexander et al., 1996; Schneider et al., 1995).

Biofeedback: Feeding Back Information

Biofeedback is a system that provides, or "feeds back," information about something happening in the body. Through biofeedback training, people have learned to control certain bodily functions, such as heart rate. Some people have used biofeedback to learn to create the brain waves produced when relaxing—alpha waves—as a way of coping with tension (Budzynski & Stoyra, 1984). Figure 5.4 shows a biofeedback system designed to record the tension in the forehead muscle of a person who suffers from headaches. As the forehead muscle relaxes, the line on the screen levels off. The patient's task is to keep the line on the screen as level as possible—in other words, the patient needs to keep his or her forehead muscle relaxed. Using biofeedback, people have learned not only to treat tension headaches, but also to lower their heart rates or blood pressure. However, as with

Teaching Section 3

Guided Practice

Have students work together to create a chart comparing and contrasting meditation, biofeedback, and hypnosis. Write the following headings on the board: *Goals, Techniques,* and *Results.* Encourage students to fill in each column with detailed information found in the text.

Independent Practice

Have each student pick one of the three topics from the chart prepared in the Guided Practice activity (meditation, biofeedback, or hypnosis) and research it in the library. Encourage students to look up recent research in newspapers and magazines as well as in reference and other books. Then have students add their findings to the chart.

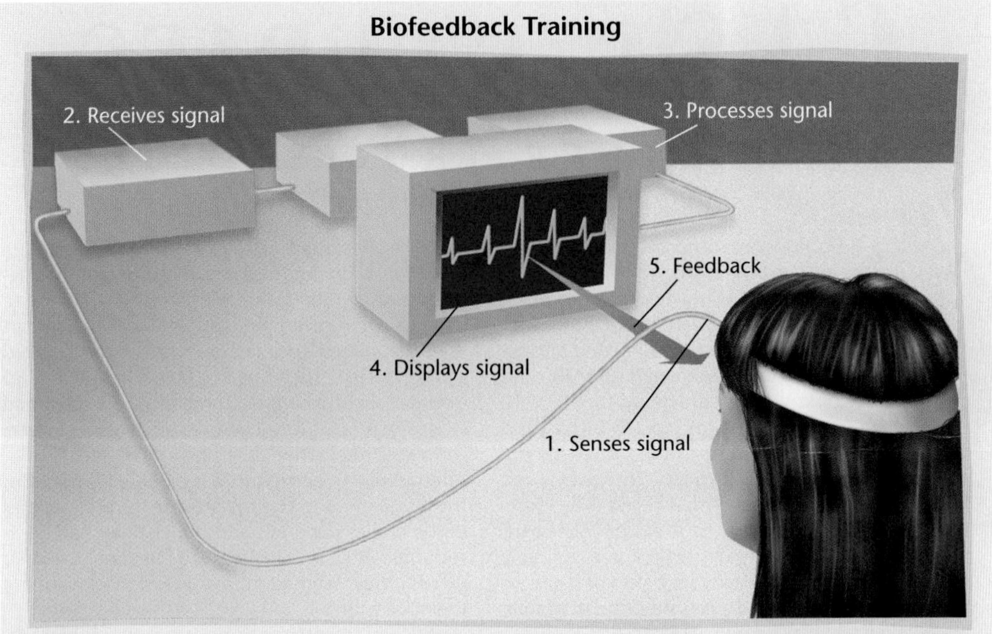

Biofeedback Training
2. Receives signal
3. Processes signal
5. Feedback
4. Displays signal
1. Senses signal

FIGURE 5.4 *By using a biofeedback system to monitor the level of tension in the forehead muscle, a person can learn to control the level of tension and thereby cut down on tension headaches.*

all treatments, biofeedback should be attempted only under the direct supervision of a medical professional.

Hypnosis: Myths and Realities

A DAY IN THE LIFE

Perhaps you have seen movies like the one Todd described to Linda, in which one character hypnotized another. Or perhaps you have seen audience members hypnotized in a magic show. If so, chances are you found that these people seemed unable to open their eyes, could not remember their own names, acted out scenes from childhood, or behaved in other unusual manners. But hypnosis is not always what it seems to be in movies and magic shows.

What Is Hypnosis? The word *hypnosis* is derived from the Greek *hypnos,* meaning "sleep." Some psychologists believe that **hypnosis** is an altered state of consciousness during which people respond to suggestions and behave as though they are in a trance. Other psychologists, however, wonder whether hypnosis truly is an altered state of consciousness. Studies have shown that some of the same effects achieved by hypnosis can also occur without hypnosis. Furthermore, brain-wave patterns (as measured by an EEG) of people in hypnotic states look the same as brain-wave patterns produced in the waking state.

Hypnosis began with the ideas of German physician Franz Mesmer in the late 1700s. Mesmer thought that the universe was connected by forms of magnetism. To cure his patients, he would pass magnets over their bodies. Some of them would fall into a trance, then awaken feeling better. Eventually, scientists decided that Mesmer's so-called cures had little scientific basis.

Hypnotism, however, may have more validity than Mesmer's magnet treatment. Today hypnotism may be used in a variety of ways. For example, some doctors use hypnosis as an anesthetic in certain types of surgery (Montgomery et al., 2000; Lang et al, 2000). Some psychologists use it to help clients reduce anxiety, manage pain, or overcome fears (Pinnell & Corino, 2000). Nevertheless, there is still a great deal about hypnosis that is not understood. Thus, hypnosis should be left in the hands of professionals. Do not attempt hypnotism on your own.

For Your Information

Exercise itself can also lead to an altered state of consciousness. The "runner's high" is a feeling of well-being caused by stimulation of the nervous system and the activation of certain hormones and endorphins. Many individuals report this pleasurable sensation after 30 to 45 minutes of running or jogging.

For Your Information

While individuals can use self-monitoring equipment to exert some control over biological processes, there seem to be serious limitations to the technique of biofeedback. A National Research Council (1988, 1991) team found that subjects could reduce their heart rates or control their body temperatures when resting but not under stressful conditions (when such control would be most useful).

Teaching Transparencies with Teacher's Notes

TRANSPARENCY 16: Biofeedback Training

CASE STUDIES
AND OTHER TRUE STORIES

Have students attempt a simple experiment in biofeedback techniques. Explain to them how to find a strong pulse in the neck or wrist. Have them watch the second hand on a clock and count the number of heartbeats in 6 seconds. Tell them to multiply this number by 10 to get the number of heartbeats per minute. Then have them try, without moving, to lower their heart rates. Discuss the results.

For Further Research

Have interested students research yoga as a method of controlling the autonomic nervous system and other biological functions. Have them first research the traditional claim that advanced yoga practitioners can control their heart rate and body temperature. Then see if they can locate recent research on the effects of yoga on heart rate and other metabolic functions among ordinary practitioners.

internet connect

go hrw .com

TOPIC: Altered States of Consciousness
GO TO: go.hrw.com
KEYWORD: SY3 PS5

Have students access the Internet through the HRW Go site to research the effects of meditation, biofeedback, and hypnosis. Students should emphasize the processes of biofeedback, meditation, and hypnosis and how they influence consciousness. Then ask students to write a research paper. Students should include a works cited page and use standard grammar, spelling, punctuation, and sentence structure.

CASE STUDIES
AND OTHER TRUE STORIES
Taking Psychology to Heart Through Biofeedback

Suppose that someone told you to lift your arm. Could you do it? Of course—all you would have to do is decide to do it. Lifting your arm is an example of *voluntary* behavior. Walking and talking are other examples. You can walk and talk simply by deciding that you are going to.

But suppose someone told you to lower your blood pressure or your heart rate. Could you do *that*? Perhaps, but not directly. To lower your blood pressure, you might eat less salt, lose weight, or lie down and relax. To lower your heart rate, you might sit down and take it easy for a while. But you cannot lower your blood pressure or heart rate directly. Blood pressure and heart rate are *involuntary* forms of behavior.

Or are they?

A few decades ago, psychologists thought they knew the difference between voluntary and involuntary behavior of the body. They thought voluntary behaviors (such as lifting an arm or a leg) were conscious. People could make them happen simply by directing their attention to having them happen. Psychologists thought other behaviors, such as heartbeat and blood pressure, were involuntary. They were automatic. They could not be consciously controlled, at least not on an immediate basis.

Then, in 1969, psychologist Neal E. Miller made an exciting discovery. He was able to train laboratory rats to increase or decrease their heart rates voluntarily. But why would rats do such a thing in the first place? Miller already knew that there is a pleasure center in the hypothalamus of a rat's brain. Whenever a rat was given a small burst of electricity in this center, the rat felt pleasure, and it wanted more.

Because the rats would do whatever they could to continue feeling this pleasure, they quickly learned that whenever they pressed a lever in their cage, they received this bit of pleasure-producing electric shock. Miller's rats pressed this lever to the point of exhaustion.

Miller designed a study to find out what the rats would do for pleasure. He implanted electrodes in the rats' pleasure centers. Then some of the rats were given shocks whenever their heart rates happened to increase. Other rats received shocks when their heart rates happened to decrease. In other words, some rats were rewarded when their heart rates were faster, whereas others were rewarded when their heart rates were slower. After a training session that took only 90 minutes, the rats learned to change their heart rates—either up or down, depending on when they had been rewarded—by as much as 20 percent. In other words, they seemed to be *voluntarily* changing their heart rates.

Miller's research was an example of biofeedback training (BFT). If it could be done with rats, could people, too, control bodily behavior thought to be involuntary? Instead of implanting electrodes in people's brains, researchers used monitors to let people know when, for example, their heart rates were slower. A biofeedback system does not actually control any of the bodily behaviors. Instead, like a mirror, the biofeedback monitor reflects a person's own efforts and enables him or her to see how various voluntary behaviors affect the involuntary ones. For example, a person might be able to observe that breathing slower reduced his or her heart rate. Indeed, some people have learned to control their heart rates using biofeedback.

Studies have shown that biofeedback has numerous other applications. Even people who are paralyzed below the neck can reduce their blood pressure with the help of biofeedback. And biofeedback is moderately effective in reducing the intense pain of migraine headaches and other painful conditions.

WHY PSYCHOLOGY MATTERS

Many people benefit from biofeedback techniques. Use CNNfyi.com or other current events sources to learn more about how researchers are applying biofeedback to improve people's health. Create a brochure that shows what you have learned.

CNNfyi.com

Closing Section 3

Applying Ideas

Have groups of students work together to research the practical applications of hypnosis. Some of the students might try to identify and contact practitioners to learn more about their credentials, methods, and applications (smoking cessation, weight loss, phobias). Some students might research state or national laws or licensing regulations governing the use of hypnosis. Still others might survey friends, family, or neighbors who have tried hypnosis. Have students compile their data in a report.

Reviewing Section 3

Have students complete the Section Review questions on page 116.

Extension

Based on what they have learned, which explanation of hypnosis do students find most convincing? Have those who believe hypnosis is truly an altered state of consciousness debate those who think that people who are hypnotized are playing a game or role.

How Is Hypnosis Achieved? Professional hypnotists may put people in a state of consciousness called a hypnotic trance by asking them to focus on something specific—a spot on the wall, an object held by the hypnotist, or merely the hypnotist's voice. Hypnotists usually suggest that people's arms and legs are becoming warm, heavy, and relaxed. They may also tell people that they are becoming sleepy or are falling asleep. Hypnosis is not sleep, however. People who are sleeping have very different brain waves from people in trances. But hearing the word *sleep* often does help a person enter a hypnotic trance.

People who are easily hypnotized are said to have hypnotic suggestibility. They can focus on the instructions of the hypnotist without getting distracted. Suggestible people also usually *like* the idea of being hypnotized and are not resistant to it. Todd was correct when he told Linda that people can only be hypnotized if they want to be.

A DAY IN THE LIFE

TRUTH OR fiction REVISITED *It is not true that it is possible to hypnotize any person at any time.* People must have a positive attitude toward hypnosis and a willingness to cooperate with the hypnotist for hypnosis to be successful.

How Can We Explain Hypnosis? Psychologists offer various explanations for the behavior of people under hypnosis. According to Freud, hypnotized people permit themselves to return to childish ways of behaving. For instance, they allow themselves to put fantasy and impulse before fact and logic. Therefore, they believe what the hypnotist tells them. They also enjoy becoming passive and waiting for the hypnotist to tell them what to do.

According to another view, called role theory, people who are hypnotized are playing a part as if they are in a play. However, unlike actors in a play, hypnotized people may believe that what they are doing is real. Research suggests that many people in hypnotic trances may *not* be faking it (Kinnunen et al., 1994). Rather, they become engrossed in playing the part of a hypnotized person. They use their imaginations to try to experience what the hypnotist tells them to experience. If they are told that they are blind, for example, and then are handed a book, they

This photograph shows French doctors putting a patient into a trance in the 1890s. Hypnosis gained widespread popularity in the late 1800s.

may think of a white curtain coming down over the page. Then they believe they cannot see or read anything. People with vivid imaginations are especially suggestible.

Is Hypnosis Effective?

Psychologists continue to debate whether hypnosis has a scientific basis. They also continue to research what hypnosis can and cannot do. Some of the research on hypnosis has addressed the effects of hypnosis on memory, on feelings of pain, and on the quitting of habits such as smoking or overeating.

Hypnosis and Memory Police have occasionally used hypnosis to jog the memories of witnesses to a crime. At times this approach has worked with dramatic success. Nevertheless, studies have shown that unhypnotized people are just as likely as hypnotized people to remember details of a crime. More important, hypnotized people are just as likely to make *mistakes* about those details as are others. Many psychologists thus argue that material recalled under hypnosis should not be used as testimony in trials.

One interesting finding about hypnosis and memory has to do with memory of events that occur during the hypnotic trance itself. If so directed by the hypnotist, many people will act as if they do not recall what happened while they were hypnotized (Barber, 2000; Bowers & Woody, 1996). They may not even remember that they were hypnotized at all.

4
Section Objective

► Describe the ways various kinds of drugs affect consciousness.

This objective is assessed in the Section Review on page 121 and in the Chapter 5 Review.

Opening Section 4

Motivator

Have students make a list of questions about the ways in which different drugs affect consciousness. Tell students that this section will discuss the effects drugs have on the human nervous system and human consciousness, the addictive nature of drugs, and the harmful effects of drugs.

Section 3 Review: Answers

1. Meditation is a way of narrowing consciousness to attempt to alleviate the stresses of the outside world.

2. During biofeedback, people are connected to a system that allows them to experience subtle changes in bodily functions, such as heart rate or blood pressure.

3. A possible answer is that because hypnosis does not have a scientific basis, many people—including doctors—are skeptical about using it.

Reprinted with special permission of King Features Syndicate

Hypnosis and Pain Prevention   Under certain circumstances and with careful application, hypnosis has been used to help people prevent feelings of pain (Miller & Bowers, 1993). For example, dentists have used hypnosis successfully to help people avoid feeling pain during certain procedures. Some people are so suggestible that they can even undergo surgery without anesthesia if they are hypnotized and told they feel no pain. On the other hand, some studies have shown that a similar effect can sometimes be achieved through relaxation techniques.

Hypnosis and Quitting Bad Habits   To help someone quit a habit such as overeating or smoking, a therapist may use **posthypnotic suggestion**. In this technique, the therapist gives instructions during hypnosis that are to be carried out after the hypnosis session has ended. Often, psychologists link the habit with something repulsive, something that would make the person feel ill or disgusted. Then whenever that person begins the habit, such as lighting up a cigarette, that sickening image appears in his or her mind. Sometimes hypnotists give more positive posthypnotic suggestions—for example, telling a person that he or she now has the willpower to resist sweets. But the effectiveness of hypnosis for helping people quit smoking is uncertain (Lancaster et al., 2000).

SECTION 3 REVIEW

Homework Practice Online
Keyword: SY3 HP5

1. Define *meditation*.
2. Explain how biofeedback works.
3. **Critical Thinking**   *Drawing Inferences and Conclusions* Why do you think hypnosis is not used more often to relieve pain or help people change habits?

SECTION 4
Drugs and Consciousness

A DAY IN THE LIFE   Linda recalled that Nick had started "spacing out" when he had a drug problem. Some drugs slow down the nervous system, while others spur it into rapid action. Some drugs, such as alcohol and nicotine (the drug found in tobacco), are believed to be connected with serious diseases. Many drugs are addictive. **Addiction** to a drug means that after a person takes that drug for a while, his or her body craves it just to feel normal. Alcohol, nicotine, and many other drugs are considered addictive.

116

Teaching Section 4

Evaluating Ideas

Have students evaluate the images of alcohol consumption as portrayed in the media (advertisements in magazines, television shows, and movies, for example). What impressions of alcohol consumption do the media create? How do these impressions compare with the factual information about alcohol use discussed in this section?

For Further Research

Challenge students to determine when, how, and why the government decided to label cigarettes and alcoholic beverages with warnings that tell consumers of the possible adverse effects of these products. Students may also research how the government limits the advertising of these products.

Drugs also have a number of effects on consciousness. They may distort people's perceptions, change their moods, or cause them to see or hear things that are not real. Categories of drugs that affect consciousness include depressants, stimulants, and hallucinogens.

Depressants

Depressants are drugs that slow the activity of the nervous system. They generally give people a sense of relaxation but can have many negative effects. Depressant drugs include alcohol and narcotics.

Alcohol Few drugs are as widely used in the United States as alcohol. Alcohol is a depressant. Small amounts of alcohol may have little effect, or they may be relaxing. High doses of alcohol can put a person to sleep. Too much alcohol can be lethal, either in the long term or the short term—people have died from drinking too much at one time.

Alcohol also intoxicates. **Intoxication** is another word for drunkenness. The root of the word *intoxication* is *toxic*, which means "poisonous." Intoxication slurs people's speech, blurs their vision, makes them clumsy, and makes it difficult for them to concentrate. They may bump into things or be unable to write. It also affects their judgment. In fact, they may not even realize that they are intoxicated. Therefore, they may try to do things that require a clear mind and good coordination, such as drive a car, when they are incapable of doing these things correctly. Alcohol is involved in more than half of all fatal automobile accidents in the United States.

These Civil War casualties may have been treated with morphine, a painkiller introduced during the war.

TRUTH OR **fiction** ■ REVISITED ■

It is not true that people who are drunk always know that they are drunk. Because intoxication impairs judgment, people who are drunk may believe that they can drive just as well as they can when they are sober.

Some drinkers do things they would not do if they were sober. Why? When intoxicated, people may be less able to focus on the consequences of their behavior. Alcohol can also bring feelings of elation that wash away inhibitions. Furthermore, it provides an excuse for behaviors that sober people know are unwise. Drinkers may place the blame for

their behavior on the alcohol. But, of course, drinkers *choose* to drink. Thus, people remain responsible for actions taken while intoxicated.

Regardless of why people start drinking, regular consumption of alcohol can lead to addiction. Once people become addicted to alcohol, they may continue drinking to avoid withdrawal symptoms such as tension and trembling. Long-term heavy drinking has been linked to liver problems, heart problems, and cancer.

Narcotics The word *narcotic* comes from the Greek *narke*, meaning "numbness" or "stupor." **Narcotics** are addictive depressants that have been used to relieve pain and induce sleep.

Many narcotics—such as morphine, heroin, and codeine—are derived from the opium poppy plant. Morphine is a narcotic that was introduced during the Civil War to deaden the pain from battle wounds. Therefore, addiction to morphine became known as "the soldier's disease."

Heroin, also introduced in the West in the 1800s, was hailed as the "hero" that would cure addiction to morphine. It was named heroin because it made people feel "heroic." This drug, which is now illegal, is a powerful narcotic that can give the user feelings of pleasure. However, coming

For Your Information

Fetal alcohol syndrome (FAS) is the term used to describe a host of problems that can occur in the children of women who drink alcohol during pregnancy. The problems include deformities of the heart, face, kidneys, and fingers. The brain of an infant with FAS is smaller than a normal infant's brain. Fetal alcohol effects can occur if the mother drinks as little as one or two glasses of wine or beer a day during pregnancy.

Class Discussion

Some drugs (such as nicotine and alcohol) are readily available to anyone over a certain age. Others (such as certain narcotics and amphetamines) are available by prescription for certain medical conditions. Still others (such as cocaine) are completely illegal. Have students discuss the rationales for the varying designations of different drugs. Do the differences seem justifiable, or do they seem arbitrary?

117

Demonstration

Locate slides or photographs of healthy lungs and lungs that have been damaged, perhaps by smoking. Point out the physical evidence of lung damage, and describe the symptoms of lung cancer and emphysema. Discuss with students why so many people continue to risk serious health problems despite their awareness of the effects of smoking cigarettes.

Cooperative Learning

Organize students into two groups, "creators" and "reviewers." Have the creators prepare public service messages for teens on the topics of smoking, drug abuse, and alcohol abuse. Their messages may be conveyed through posters, print ads, audiotaped messages, or video spots. Encourage students to be imaginative and to check their facts carefully. Then have the reviewers evaluate the messages. Which messages and presentation methods were most effective? Which did not work? End the activity with a discussion of how best to reach teens on these issues.

For Your Information

Despite recent legislative and corporate efforts to designate no-smoking zones in many public places and to totally ban smoking in others, a recent study reports that 88 percent of all nonsmokers are still exposed to secondhand smoke (CDC, 1996). Researchers concluded this after studying blood samples from more than 10,000 individuals living in 26 states. Many victims of secondhand smoke were unaware of their exposure. Unfortunately, many people exposed to secondhand smoke were children.

off heroin can plunge the user into a deep depression. Furthermore, high doses impair judgment and memory and cause drowsiness and stupor. High doses of heroin can also depress the respiratory system so much that they lead to loss of consciousness, coma, and, in some cases, even death.

The use of heroin can also lead to death indirectly because it is often taken intravenously—that is, injected with a needle into a vein. Sometimes such needles are shared among users. If one user is infected with the virus that causes AIDS, needle sharing can infect other users as well.

People who are addicted to narcotics experience withdrawal symptoms when they try to stop using them. These withdrawal symptoms may include tremors, cramps, chills, rapid heartbeat, insomnia, vomiting, and diarrhea.

Stimulants

Stimulants, in contrast to depressants, increase the activity of the nervous system. They speed up the heart and breathing rate. Stimulants include nicotine, amphetamines, and cocaine.

Nicotine Nicotine, the drug found in tobacco leaves, is one of the most common stimulants. The leaves are usually smoked in the form of cigarettes, cigars, and pipe tobacco. They can also be chewed, as in chewing tobacco.

Nicotine spurs the release of the hormone adrenaline, which causes the heart rate to increase. As a stimulant, nicotine may make people feel more alert and attentive, but research has shown that it does not improve the ability to perform complex tasks, such as solving difficult math problems.

Nicotine reduces the appetite and raises the rate at which the body changes food to energy. For these reasons, some smokers do not try to quit for fear that they will gain weight. But weight gain can be controlled by diet.

Through regular use, people can become addicted to nicotine. In fact, evidence suggests that cigarette smoking is as addictive as the use of heroin. People who stop smoking can experience symptoms such as nervousness, drowsiness, loss of energy, headaches, lightheadedness, insomnia, dizziness, cramps, heart palpitations, tremors, and sweating. Nonetheless, many people have successfully quit smoking.

Smoking has also been associated with serious health risks. All cigarette advertisements and packs sold in the United States carry a message such as:

"Warning: The Surgeon General Has Determined That Cigarette Smoking Is Dangerous to Your Health." Each year, more than 400,000 Americans die from smoking-related diseases. This is more than the number who die from motor-vehicle accidents, abuse of alcohol and all other drugs, suicide, homicide, and AIDS combined.

TRUTH OR fiction ▪ REVISITED ▪ *It is true that smoking leads to more deaths in the United States than automobile accidents do.* In fact, almost one out of every five deaths in the United States is caused by smoking. Lung cancer and heart disease are the most common smoking-related diseases.

Smokers are 12 to 20 times as likely as nonsmokers to die of lung cancer. Moreover, the substances in cigarette smoke have been shown to cause several other kinds of cancer in laboratory animals. Cigarette smoking is also linked to death from heart disease, chronic lung and respiratory diseases, and other illnesses. Pregnant women who smoke risk miscarriage, premature birth, and babies with birth defects. Perhaps due to the risks involved in smoking, the percentage of American adults who smoke has declined from more than 40 percent in the 1960s to less then 25 percent today.

Research indicates that secondhand smoke, the cigarette smoke exhaled by smokers, can even increase the health risk of nonsmokers who inhale it. Secondhand smoke is connected with lung cancer, breathing problems, and other illnesses. It accounts for thousands of deaths per year. Because of the effects of secondhand smoke, smoking has been banned from many public places, such as government buildings, airports, and restaurants.

Amphetamines **Amphetamines** are another kind of stimulant. They are especially known for helping people stay awake and for reducing appetite. Amphetamines are made from the chemical alpha-methyl-beta-phenyl-ethyl-amine, which is a colorless liquid made up of carbon, hydrogen, and nitrogen.

Amphetamines were first used by soldiers during World War II to help them remain awake and alert during the night. Sometimes called "speed" or "uppers," amphetamines can produce feelings of pleasure, especially in high doses.

EXPLORING

DIVERSITY

Multicultural Perspectives on Consciousness

Visions, dreams, meditation, and hallucinations are important parts of many cultures, reflecting the human desire to reach beyond what the senses can directly perceive. The methods for reaching these altered states of consciousness, however, are as diverse as the people who inhabit this planet.

The Aborigines of Australia believe that there are two worlds: the ordinary, physical world and another world called Dreamtime. Ritual songs, dances, stories, and dreams create the Dreamtime world. Frans Hoogland, a Dutchman who lived for 15 years among the Aborigines, described the process: "We start with nothing—a total emptiness—a void. Then we have some singing and dancing. . . . [T]he singing creates the sound and the vibration forms a shape; and the dancing helps solidify it. . . . The process, the Dreaming itself, becomes a reality" (Maybury-Lewis, 1992, pp. 197–202). For the Aborigines, dream and actuality are just different states of the same consciousness.

The Mevlevi, a Muslim sect in Turkey, also use dancing to create an altered state of consciousness. The Mevlevi are known as whirling dervishes because they whirl around until they are in a trance. This trance, they believe, brings them closer to Allah, or God.

Some religions use meditation to achieve an altered state of consciousness. According to the yoga school, a part of Hinduism, every human being consists of two parts. The first is a person's body, mind, and conscious self. The second part is the soul—pure empty consciousness. The yoga school uses certain exercises, including bodily postures, control of breathing, and meditations, to help teach people understanding of their soul.

Accompanied by music, whirling dervishes spin around until they are in a trance.

The followers of Buddhism meditate to achieve a state of enlightenment called *nirvana.* Buddhists believe that nirvana can be achieved through control of the mind, or mental discipline. Certain yoga techniques help followers achieve this control.

People in some cultures use drugs to produce a religious trance. The Inca in the Andean highlands of South America use a drug called yage while a shaman, or holy man, watches them. Once past an initial drug-induced nausea, they begin to hallucinate. The hallucinations range from pleasurable to terrifying. The Inca will endure even the terrifying visions because they believe that terror is something that needs to be overcome in order to gain knowledge, look into the future, and communicate with the spirit world.

The Huichol Indians in central Mexico make a sacred pilgrimage to a place hundreds of miles from their homes. Once they arrive, they fast, pray, dance, and chant. The next day, they hunt for peyote, a strong stimulant that comes from a cactus plant. They then sit with their shaman-priest, talk, eat peyote, and begin to hallucinate. They believe that the hallucinations help them achieve a state of fusion with their ancestors and the universe. The shaman must always be present to help them return from the experience. Many fear that if they stay too long "in paradise," their souls will be lost forever.

Think About It

Analyzing Information In some cultures, people view altered states of consciousness as something to be avoided whenever possible, not something to be sought out. Why do you think some people feel this way?

Cooperative Learning

Organize students into two groups, factual researchers and media critics. Have the factual researchers study the health problems that result from smoking cigarettes. Have the media critics analyze how smoking cigarettes is presented in advertisements. Then have the two groups compare their findings. For example, although smoking is linked to facial wrinkles, the people in the ads are portrayed as young and attractive; also, they are never shown even holding a cigarette.

Summarizing Information

Have students work together to summarize the dangers of all the different drugs they have read about in this section. They may want to place the dangers in categories such as long-term/short-term or physical/psychological. When they have finished, ask them which drugs they think are the most dangerous and why.

120

Various advertising campaigns have helped make people more aware of the dangers of drugs. Posters such as this one encourage people to refuse drugs and enjoy life without them.

Amphetamines can be taken in the form of pills. They can also be injected directly into the veins in the form of liquid methedrine, the strongest form of the drug. People who take large doses of amphetamines may stay awake and "high" for days. Such highs must come to an end, however. People who have been on prolonged highs usually "crash."

That is, they fall into a deep sleep or depression. Some people even commit suicide when crashing. Nick's spaced-out, inattentive behavior may have been the result of his coming down from an amphetamine high.

High doses of amphetamines can cause restlessness, insomnia, loss of appetite, and irritability. They also affect consciousness. For example, people who have taken amphetamines sometimes experience frightening hallucinations. A **hallucination** is a perception of an object or a sound that seems real but is not. One hallucination that people under the influence of amphetamines commonly experience is that bugs are crawling all over them.

Use of amphetamines can also cause the user to have delusions. A **delusion** is a false idea that seems real. If you thought you could fly (without the aid of an airplane), that would be a delusion. Overdoses of amphetamines are sometimes connected with delusions of being in danger or of being chased by someone or something.

Cocaine   Cocaine is a stimulant derived from the leaves of the coca plant, which grows in the tropics of South America. Cocaine produces feelings of pleasure, reduces hunger, deadens pain, and boosts self-confidence. Because cocaine raises blood pressure and decreases the supply of oxygen to the heart while speeding up the heart rate, it can sometimes lead to death.

Cocaine has been used as a painkiller since the early 1800s. It came to the attention of Sigmund Freud in 1884. Freud, then a young neurologist, first used the drug to overcome depression. He even published an article on cocaine called "Song of Praise." But Freud's excitement about cocaine's healing powers was soon cooled by his awareness that the drug was dangerous and addictive.

Overdoses of cocaine can cause symptoms including restlessness, insomnia, trembling, headaches, nausea, convulsions, hallucinations, and delusions. A particularly harmful form of cocaine is known as crack. Crack is very powerful. However, crack is impure, and therefore it is even more dangerous than other forms of cocaine. Because of the strain crack and other forms of cocaine can put on the heart, overdoses of these drugs are sometimes fatal.

Hallucinogens

A **hallucinogen** is a drug that produces hallucinations. In addition, hallucinogens may cause relaxation or feelings of pleasure. However, hallucinogens can also cause feelings of panic. Marijuana and LSD are examples of hallucinogens.

Marijuana   Marijuana is a hallucinogenic drug produced from the leaves of the *cannabis sativa* plant, which grows wild in many parts of the world. Marijuana may produce feelings of relaxation and mild hallucinations. Hashish, or "hash," comes from the sticky part of the plant. Hashish has stronger effects than marijuana.

Marijuana impairs perception and coordination, making it difficult to operate machines, including cars. It also impairs memory and learning. In addition, marijuana can cause anxiety and confusion. It increases the heart rate up to 140 to 150 beats per minute and in some people raises blood pressure. These effects thus pose a particular threat to people with high blood pressure or heart problems.

One hundred years ago, marijuana was used by some people almost the way aspirin is used today—to treat headaches and other minor aches and pains. It could be bought without a prescription in any drugstore. Because it carries a number of health risks, marijuana use and possession are now illegal in most states.

Follow Up

Have students return to the list of drugs and their effects that they made before reading this section. Now that they have completed the section, can they identify any misconceptions they had about drugs? What misconceptions have they heard others voice?

Drawing Conclusions

Ask students what conclusions this section helps them draw about the relationship between the physical body and human consciousness. *(It suggests that human consciousness is affected by physiological factors, and the mind is strongly connected to and influenced by events in the body.)*

Reviewing Section 4

Have students complete the Section Review questions on page 121.

Marijuana has distinct effects on consciousness. People who are very intoxicated with marijuana may think time is passing more slowly than usual. A song might seem to last an hour rather than a few minutes. Some people experience increased consciousness of bodily sensations such as heartbeat. Experiencing visual hallucinations is also fairly common while under the influence of marijuana.

Strong intoxication gives some marijuana smokers frightening experiences. Sometimes marijuana smokers become confused and lose their sense of self—their consciousness of who and where they are. Some fear they will lose themselves forever. Consciousness of a rapid heart rate leads others to fear that their hearts will "run away."

LSD   Lysergic acid diethylamide (LSD) is a hallucinogen. LSD is sometimes simply called acid. It is much stronger than marijuana and can produce intense hallucinations. Some of these hallucinations can be quite bizarre. Users of LSD claim that it expands consciousness and "opens new worlds." Sometimes people are convinced that they have achieved great insights while using LSD. But when its effects wear off, they often are unable to recall or use these "discoveries."

LSD's effects are not predictable. Some LSD experiences are so frightening that the users, in a state of panic and confusion, injure themselves seriously or even commit suicide. In addition, some users of LSD experience lasting side effects. These side effects include memory loss, violent outbursts, nightmares, and feelings of panic.

Another long-term effect of LSD use is the experience of flashbacks. Flashbacks are hallucinations that happen weeks, months, or even years after the LSD was used. Some psychologists believe that flashbacks stem from LSD-induced chemical changes in the brain.

Treatments for Drug Abuse

Treatment for drug abuse varies, depending on the drug abused. Forms of treatment include detoxification, maintenance programs, and therapy. Some people also join support groups.

Detoxification   One form of treatment for drug abuse is detoxification. **Detoxification**, the removal of the harmful substance from the body, is a way of weaning addicts from the drug while restoring their health. This treatment is most commonly used with people addicted to alcohol and narcotics.

Many hospitals have chemical dependency units to help treat drug abusers.

Maintenance Programs   Maintenance programs are sometimes used for people addicted to narcotics. Participants in these programs are given controlled and less dangerous amounts of the drug or some less addictive substitute. This treatment is very controversial because the users never actually become completely free of drugs.

Counseling   Counseling can be conducted either individually or in a group. Both individual and group methods are used for treating stimulant and depressant abuse.

Support Groups   Support groups usually consist of several people who share common experiences, concerns, or problems. These individuals meet in a group setting to provide one another with emotional and moral support. Alcoholics Anonymous is an example of a support group that encourages members to live without drugs—in this case, alcohol—for the rest of their lives.

SECTION 4 REVIEW

go.hrw.com **Homework Practice Online**
Keyword: SY3 HP5

1. Describe the effects of depressants, stimulants, and hallucinogens on consciousness. Give examples of each type of drug.

2. **Critical Thinking** *Evaluating* Do you think people use drugs to heighten consciousness or to escape from it? Explain your answer.

Section 4 Review: Answers

1. Depressants, such as alcohol and narcotics, slow down the nervous system and produce a sense of relaxation; stimulants, such as nicotine, amphetamines, and cocaine, speed up the nervous system and sometimes produce hallucinations and delusions; hallucinogens, such as marijuana and LSD, produce visions (hallucinations).

2. Answers may suggest that when drugs are used as part of a religious ritual, they are intended for heightened consciousness; otherwise, they are probably intended for escape.

Chapter 5 Review: Answers

Writing a Summary
See the section subtitles for the main topics in the chapter.

Identifying People and Ideas

1. awareness of things inside and outside ourselves

2. a state of consciousness in which a person's sense of self or sense of the world changes

3. sleep stage characterized by irregular breathing, increased blood pressure, and faster heart rate

4. the inability to sleep

5. breathing interruption that occurs during sleep

Technology

▶ Chapter 5 Test Generator (on the One-Stop Planner)
▶ HRW Go site

Reinforcement, Review, and Assessment

▶ Chapter 5 Review, pp. 122–123
▶ Chapter Review Activities with Answer Key
▶ Alternative Assessment Handbook
▶ Portfolio Assessment Handbook
▶ Chapter 5 Test (Form A or B)

Linking to Community Have a drug or alcohol counselor or a physician who treats substance abuse visit the class to discuss his or her experience treating patients with addiction problems. Ask the guest to discuss the following questions:

---

6. method some people use to try to narrow their consciousness so that stresses of the outside world fade away

7. a system that provides information about something happening in the body

8. drug that slows the activity of the nervous system

9. drug that increases the activity of the nervous system

10. the removal of a harmful substance from the body

Understanding Main Ideas

1. It means that consciousness cannot be seen, touched, or measured directly.

2. They are the biological rhythms connected with the 24-hour day that govern plant and animal life and influence human behavior, such as sleeping and waking.

3. Alpha waves occur during stage 1 sleep, delta waves during stages 2, 3, and 4. The final stage is REM sleep.

4. It can teach people to control bodily functions that were once thought to be uncontrollable.

5. Depressants (alcohol and narcotics) slow the nervous system, and are addictive. Stimulants (nicotine, amphetamines, and cocaine) increase the activity of the nervous system, may produce hallucinations, and are addictive. Hallucinogens (LSD and marijuana) produce delusions, and have severe side effects.

Thinking Critically

1. During REM sleep people breathe quickly, blood pressure rises, hearts beat faster, eyes move rapidly and dreams occur. During NREM

Chapter 5 REVIEW

Writing a Summary

Using standard grammar, spelling, sentence structure, and punctuation, summarize the information in this chapter. Consider:
• the nature of consciousness, the stages of sleep and possible sleep problems
• the effects of meditation, biofeedback, hypnosis, and drugs on consciousness

Identifying People and Ideas

Identify the following terms or people and use them in appropriate sentences.

1. consciousness
2. altered state of consciousness
3. rapid-eye-movement sleep
4. insomnia
5. sleep apnea
6. meditation
7. biofeedback
8. depressant
9. stimulant
10. detoxification

Understanding Main Ideas

SECTION 1 (pp. 104–106)
1. What does it mean to say that consciousness is a construct?

SECTION 2 (pp. 106–112)
2. What are circadian rhythms, and how do they influence human behavior?
3. What are the five stages of sleep? What brain-wave patterns occur in each stage?

SECTION 3 (pp. 112–116)
4. In what way is biofeedback training useful?

SECTION 4 (pp. 116–121)
5. Describe one of the three major groups of drugs, including their effects and problems.

Thinking Critically

1. **Comparing and Contrasting** How are REM and NREM sleep similar and different?

2. **Drawing Inferences and Conclusions** Why do you think many people use medication to try to overcome insomnia? Why might medication not be an effective cure?

3. **Evaluating** Identify the pros and cons of using biofeedback instead of medication to reduce high blood pressure.

4. **Analyzing Information** Why might some people drink or use other drugs even though they know that the drugs can be harmful?

Writing About Psychology

1. **Making Generalizations and Predictions** Design, but do not actually do, an experiment or survey to study the effects that altered states of consciousness have on sensation and perception. Begin by writing down a question. For example, you might ask, "How do people perceive pain when they are dreaming?" After you have prepared a question, form a hypothesis about the answer to the question. Write a paragraph explaining your hypothesis, then write another paragraph analyzing what results would indicate that your hypothesis was correct.

2. **Summarizing** Create an outline describing the four levels of consciousness. Then, using your outline, write a summary of what you have learned. Use the graphic organizer below to help you with your summary.

Consciousness

- Which substances seem to cause the most serious addictions?
- Which treatments work best with which problems?
- How do patients' attitudes affect their ultimate success in treatment?

Organize students into several groups to research the subject of identifying and coping with sleep problems. They may wish to examine various parenting and self-help books, contact sleep-disorder clinics, their family physicians, or interview individuals who have dealt successfully with sleep problems in their children or themselves. Each group should present its findings in an oral report, with visual aids if necessary.

Building Social Studies Skills

Interpreting Graphs

Study the graph below. Then use the information in the graph to help you answer the questions that follow.

Time Spent Sleeping

Source: Carskadon, *Encyclopedia of Sleep and Dreaming*, 1993

1. How many minutes do most people spend sleeping per night?
   a. less than 300
   b. 420–479
   c. 480–539
   d. more than 600
2. What statement can be made about people who get less than 300 minutes of sleep and people who get more than 600 minutes of sleep?

Analyzing Primary Sources

Read the following excerpt, in which E. Thomas Dowd provides some warnings about selecting a hypnotherapist. Then answer the questions that follow.

❝One should be wary of hypnotists with no formal training in medical, psychological, or other established professions who claim to be able to cure such entrenched [long-term] habits as overeating and smoking in one or two sessions. Such individuals prey on the universal human desire for quick and easy relief from their distress, relief that involves little or no effort on the part of the hypnotized. They take advantage of the common misconception [misunderstanding] that hypnosis is somehow magic in its effects. It takes little time and effort to teach someone how to enter, or help others to enter, a hypnotic trance, but considerably more training and experience to know how to use trance behavior effectively and appropriately.❞

3. Which of the following statements best reflects Dowd's attitudes toward many hypnotists.
   a. Patients seeking assistance should never be hypnotized.
   b. All hypnotists are fakes.
   c. Professionals with proper training can use hypnosis to help patients.
   d. Hypnosis can cure bad habits such as smoking with little effort.
4. According to the excerpt, how does popular misunderstanding of hypnosis lead to misuse of the technique?

PSYCHOLOGY PROJECTS

Cooperative Learning

Creating a Case Study Imagine that a friend tells you the following dream: He is sunbathing on a beach with a friend. Suddenly, other people on the beach begin screaming, and he sees a huge tidal wave. Before he can run, he feels himself being swept away. Working in groups, use the Freudian and biopsychological theories about dream interpretation to analyze the dream. Then write a summary, comparing the interpretations suggested by each approach. Finally, share the analysis with the class.

🖸 internet connect

Internet Activity: go.hrw.com
KEYWORD: SY3 PS5
Choose an activity on consciousness to:
- make a drawing that illustrates the levels and meanings of consciousness.
- create a multimedia display on sleep patterns and dreaming.
- write a research paper on altered states of consciousness.

sleep, eyes do not move as much, brain produce slow delta waves, and any dreams are not as vivid.

2. Medication is a seemingly easy way for people to overcome insomnia. However, it does not get to the root of the problem.

3. Using biofeedback to reduce blood pressure may not be reliable enough if a person has a health risk; however, if the risk is low, it cannot hurt to attempt biofeedback.

4. Students may mention that drug users experience a temporary sense of pleasure, relaxation, or self-confidence.

Writing About Psychology

1. Students' designs should demonstrate an understanding of the proper procedures to follow when studying consciousness. Students' paragraphs should contain a complete analysis and explanation of the results they think they would have received had they actually conducted the experiment.

2. Students' reports should demonstrate an understanding of the four levels of consciousness—awareness, preconscious, unconscious, and nonconscious.

Building Social Studies Skills

1. c
2. Both groups represent a small percentage of the population and make up the extremes of sleep behavior.
3. c
4. Because many people regard hypnosis as "magical," they are willing to pay nonexperts who promise cures that hypnosis cannot provide.

123

UNIT 2 REVIEW

▶ TEACH

Organize students into groups to practice their problem-solving skills. Ask group members to imagine that they have to develop an effective anti-smoking campaign. You might want to suggest another problem of your own choosing. Then have the groups follow the problem-solving process outlined in the simulation to arrive at a solution or plan of action. Each member should participate in the process. Finally, have each group present its solution to the class for evaluation.

▶ EXTEND

Have students review the problem in the Psychology in Action Simulation. Then ask students to imagine that the psychologist's client is suffering from many nightmares and night terrors. Have each group propose a possible cause of the client's sleep problems and a way to help the client. Have volunteers present their problems and solutions to the class. Have other students evaluate each group's proposed solution.

▶ PSYCHOLOGY IN ACTION

Ask each student to create a poster designed to teach the problem-solving process to fellow students in their school. Encourage students to make their posters clear and simple so that other students can easily understand them. In addition, students should strive to make the posters visually pleasing to motivate other students to examine them. Select the best two or three posters and display them in public places in your school.

PSYCHOLOGY IN ACTION

YOU SOLVE THE PROBLEM . . .

How can a psychologist help a client with a sleep disorder?

Complete the following activity in small groups. Imagine that a psychologist has asked your group for advice on helping a client with insomnia. She has asked for a report outlining the best way for her to treat the client.

1. Gather Information. Use your textbook and other resources to find information that might influence your plan of action for preparing the report. Remember that your report must include information that will convince the psychologist that your suggested method should be used. This information might include charts and graphs to show the psychologist which treatment method is most effective. You may want to divide up different parts of the research among group members.

2. List and Consider Options. After reviewing the information you gathered, list and consider the options you might use to help the psychologist choose how to treat her patient. Your final solution to the problem may be easier to reach if you consider as many options as possible. Be sure to record all your options for the preparation of your report.

3. Consider Advantages and Disadvantages. Now consider the advantages and disadvantages of choosing each option. Ask yourselves questions such as,

- What seems to be causing the client's insomnia?
- Is the client taking any medication that might affect his sleeping patterns?

Once you have considered the advantages and disadvantages, record them as notes for use in preparing your report.

4. Choose and Implement a Solution. After considering the advantages and disadvantages, you should choose a solution. Next, plan and create a report that describes how your solution will be implemented. Be sure to make the solution you have chosen very clear.

5. Evaluate the Effectiveness of the Solution. Once you have prepared your report, write a paragraph evaluating how effective your recommendation will be for the psychologist. Explain why you believe that your solution will be more effective than other possible solutions you considered. When you are ready, decide which group members will present which parts of the report. Then take your report to the psychologist (the rest of the class). Good luck!

124

UNIT 3

CHAPTER 6 • *Learning* focuses on the ways behavior can be conditioned and the factors involved in learning.

CHAPTER 7 • *Memory* explores the components of human memory, including kinds of memory, processes of memory, and stages of memory.

CHAPTER 8 • *Thinking and Language* discusses problem-solving, decision-making, and reasoning processes, as well as the role played by language in human thought.

CHAPTER 9 • *Intelligence* presents the theories and measurement of intelligence and explores the various factors that influence intelligence.

Overview

In Unit 3, students will explore the learning and thinking processes of the human mind, including the role of memory, language, and intelligence.

UNIT 3
LEARNING AND COGNITION

▶ Internet Activity

internet connect

go.hrw.com

TOPIC: Education Psychology and Reform
GO TO: go.hrw.com
KEYWORD: SY3 UNIT 3

Have students access the Internet through the HRW Go site to research educational reformers and psychologists of the 1800s and 1900s. Then have the students write a biography of one of the psychologists or reformers featured at the Web site. Students should include information about the person's professional accomplishments, the theories and reforms advocated, and the impact of the theorist's ideas on the education system. Remind students to use standard grammar, spelling, punctuation, and sentence structure in their biographies.

▶ Using Visuals

Ask students to examine the photograph on page 125. Explain that the sculpture shown is *The Thinker* by French sculptor Auguste Rodin. Unlike typical statues of famous people or objects of beauty, *The Thinker* focuses on an idea. Over the years, many people have admired *The Thinker*. Ask students to try to explain the popular response and to tell whether or not they share it.

CHAPTERS

6 *Learning*

7 *Memory*

8 *Thinking and Language*

9 *Intelligence*

125

Learning

CHAPTER RESOURCE MANAGER

	Objectives	Pacing Guide	Reproducible and Review Resources
SECTION 1: **Classical Conditioning** (pp. 128–135)	Explain the principles of classical conditioning.	**Regular** 1 day **Block Scheduling** .5 day *Block Scheduling Handbook with Team Teaching Strategies, Chapter 6*	**SM** Mastering Critical Thinking Skills 6 **REV** Section 1 Review, p. 135
SECTION 2: **Operant Conditioning** (pp. 135–144)	Explain the principles of operant conditioning and describe how they are applied.	**Regular** 1 day **Block Scheduling** .5 day *Block Scheduling Handbook with Team Teaching Strategies, Chapter 6*	**E** Research Projects and Activities for Teaching Psychology **REV** Section 2 Review, p. 144
SECTION 3: **Cognitive Factors in Learning** (pp. 145–147)	Discuss the cognitive factors in learning.	**Regular** 1 day **Block Scheduling** .5 day *Block Scheduling Handbook with Team Teaching Strategies, Chapter 6*	**RS** Essay and Research Themes for Advanced Placement Students, Theme 5 **PS** Readings and Case Studies, 6 **REV** Section 3 Review, p. 147
SECTION 4: **The PQ4R Method: Learning to Learn** (pp. 147–149)	Identify the steps of the PQ4R method of learning.	**Regular** 1 day **Block Scheduling** .5 day *Block Scheduling Handbook with Team Teaching Strategies, Chapter 6*	**SM** Study Skills and Writing Guide, Part 3, Stage 1 **REV** Section 4 Review, p. 149

Chapter Resource Key

PS	Primary Sources	**A**	Assessment		Video
RS	Reading Support	**REV**	Review		Internet
E	Enrichment		Transparencies		Holt Presentation Maker Using Microsoft® PowerPoint®
SM	Skills Mastery		CD-ROM		

One-Stop Planner CD–ROM

See the *One-Stop Planner* for a complete list of additional resources for students and teachers.

One-Stop Planner CD–ROM

It's easy to plan lessons, select resources, and print out materials for your students when you use the **One-Stop Planner CD-ROM with Test Generator.**

Technology Resources

 One-Stop Planner, Lesson 6.1
 Homework Practice Online
 Teaching Transparencies 17: Classical Conditioning
HRW Go Site

 One-Stop Planner, Lesson 6.2
 Homework Practice Online
 Teaching Transparencies 18: Key Concepts in Operant Conditioning
 Teaching Transparencies 19: Schedules of Reinforcement
HRW Go Site

 One-Stop Planner, Lesson 6.3
Homework Practice Online
CNN. Presents Psychology: Influence on Learning: Mice Studies
HRW Go Site

 One-Stop Planner, Lesson 6.4
 Homework Practice Online

Chapter Review and Assessment

 HRW Go site
REV Chapter 6 Review, pp. 150–151
REV Chapter Review Activities with Answer Key

A Chapter 6 Test (Form A or B)
A Portfolio Assessment Handbook
A Alternative Assessment Handbook

 Chapter 6 Test Generator (on the One-Stop Planner)
 Global Skill Builder CD-ROM

---

internet connect

HRW ONLINE RESOURCES

GO TO: go.hrw.com
Then type in a keyword.

TEACHER HOME PAGE
KEYWORD: SY3 Teacher

CHAPTER INTERNET ACTIVITIES
KEYWORD: SY3 PS6
Choose an activity to have students:
• create an exhibit for the "Museum of Classical Conditioning."
• make an action plan using operant conditioning to teach a dog to fetch.
• research the processes of modeling, imitation, and vicarious reinforcement in a classroom.

CHAPTER ENRICHMENT LINKS
KEYWORD: SY3 CH6

ONLINE ASSESSMENT
Homework Practice
KEYWORD: SY3 HP6
Standardized Test Prep
KEYWORD: SY3 STP6
Rubrics
KEYWORD: SS Rubrics

CONTENT UPDATES
KEYWORD: SS Content Updates

HOLT PRESENTATION MAKER
KEYWORD: SY3 PPT6

ONLINE READING SUPPORT
KEYWORD: SS Strategies

CURRENT EVENTS
KEYWORD: S3 Current Events

Additional Resources

PRINT RESOURCES FOR TEACHERS
Bandura, A. (1986). *Social foundations of thought and action.* Englewood Cliffs, NJ: Prentice-Hall.

Bower, G. H., & Hilgard, E. R. (1981). *Theories of learning.* Englewood Cliffs, NJ: Prentice-Hall.

Fernald, L. D. (1989). *Instructor's manual for* **Walden Two** *and walking tour.* New York: Macmillan.

PRINT RESOURCES FOR STUDENTS
Pryor, K. (1984). *Don't shoot the dog! How to improve yourself and others through behavioral training.* New York: Simon & Schuster.

Skinner, B. F. (1948). *Walden two.* New York: Macmillan.

MULTIMEDIA RESOURCES
Learning (VHS). Films for the Humanities & Sciences, P.O. Box 2053, Princeton, NJ 08543-2053.

Pavlov: The conditioned reflex (VHS). Films for the Humanities & Science, P.O. Box 2053, Princeton, NJ 08543-2053.

Dynamic concepts in psychology (Videodisc). Films for the Humanities & Science, P.O. Box 2053, Princeton, NJ 08543-2053.

LEARNING

Ask students how they think the learning process works. Invite them to suggest some factors and variables they think might play a role in learning. The following may serve as idea prompts: observation, past experience, imitation, cultural environment, practice, thinking style, reward, teaching or training, punishment, and questioning. With students, generate and discuss some hypotheses about the role each factor might play in the learning process. Test the hypotheses against students' own experience. Then talk about how people might use these learning factors to affect the behavior of others—for example, in the school setting. Post the discussion notes for reference as students study Chapter 6.

Sections

1 *Classical Conditioning*

2 *Operant Conditioning*

3 *Cognitive Factors in Learning*

4 *The PQ4R Method: Learning to Learn*

Each of the four questions identified on page 126 corresponds to one of these sections.

6 Chapter LEARNING

Read to Discover

1 What are the principles of classical conditioning?

2 How are the principles of operant conditioning applied?

3 What are the cognitive factors in learning?

4 What are the steps of the PQ4R method of learning?

126

Each chapter begins with a vignette, called "A Day in the Life," that relates the information discussed in the chapter to the everyday events in the lives of a group of fictional high school students. The text of the chapter occasionally refers back to the vignette to demonstrate the application of the concept being discussed. An icon marked "A Day in the Life" is placed next to these references.

Copy the following graphic organizer onto the chalkboard, omitting the italicized text. Fill in the circles as you discuss classical conditioning.

Stimulus — **Key Factors of Classical Conditioning** — *Response*

A DAY IN THE LIFE

November 18

Linda, Marc, Dan, and Janet were in the library studying after school. "I don't feel like studying," Marc complained. "Let's shoot some hoops instead."

"Come on," Linda protested. "It's interesting stuff—it's all about how people learn. And don't you want to get a good grade on Thursday's psychology test?"

"Yeah, I suppose," Marc said, playing with his pencil. "But why do we even care about grades anyway? I mean, they're just letters. They don't really *mean* anything."

"Try saying that to the college admissions officers or at a job interview," chimed in Janet. "Even though a grade doesn't mean anything by itself, it means a lot in terms of what it can get you."

"And don't forget the district's new rule—you *have* to get at least a C in order to be on a sports team. Marc, the soccer team can't afford to lose you this year—you *have* to do well in the class," Dan pleaded.

"But what happens if I study a lot and *still* don't do well on the test? That's what happened to me last week on that test in Ms. Kramer's class. I studied for *hours* the night before, and I *still* only got a C on the test. So what's the point in studying if it's not going to help anyway?" asked Marc gloomily.

"There's more to good studying than just memorizing," Linda pointed out. "Hey, why don't we all study together? We can review the chapter and quiz one another. And when we're finished, we can do something fun. Any suggestions?"

Dan made a face. "Anything that doesn't involve eating ice cream. I ate a whole half-gallon of ice cream Monday night, and now the thought of it makes me sick."

"I wasn't thinking about food anyway. How about Marc's idea of playing basketball? Or maybe we could go to a movie," suggested Linda. "But we can't go until we really know the chapter."

"If I knew I'd get to do something fun every time I studied, maybe I'd study more often," Dan reflected thoughtfully.

• • •

Key Terms

- stimulus
- response
- conditioning
- classical conditioning
- unconditioned stimulus
- unconditioned response
- conditioned response
- conditioned stimulus
- taste aversion
- extinction
- spontaneous recovery
- generalization
- discrimination
- flooding
- systematic desensitization
- counterconditioning
- operant conditioning
- reinforcement
- primary reinforcers
- secondary reinforcers
- positive reinforcers
- negative reinforcers
- schedule of reinforcement
- continuous reinforcement
- partial reinforcement
- shaping
- latent learning
- observational learning

Marc, Linda, and the others were studying material about learning. When you hear the word *learning,* you probably think of school—of listening to teachers and studying and taking tests. But people are learning all the time.

Learning is achieved through experience. Anything we are born knowing how to do is not a result of learning. For example, babies do not learn to cry. But people do need experience to learn how to walk, how to speak the languages of their parents and communities, and how to read. The experiences through which we learn all of these things, however, can vary. Sometimes we learn to do things by trying them ourselves; at other times, we learn by watching others or by reading books. This chapter explores several types of learning and the processes involved in each type.

WHY PSYCHOLOGY MATTERS

People learn about their world from the time they are infants. Use **CNNfyi**.com or other current events sources to learn more about how people acquire knowledge.

CNNfyi.com

Section Objective

► Explain the principles of classical conditioning.

This objective is assessed in the Section Review on page 135 and in the Chapter 6 Review.

Opening Section 1

Motivator

Lead students in creating a list of habits and preferences that are part of their daily lives (for example, favorite foods or a daily workout). Write their suggestions on the chalkboard. Challenge them to explore how they acquired these habits and preferences. They might discuss the story behind a particular preference with the class. Tell students that Section 1 offers one explanation for the development of learned habits and preferences.

Using Truth or Fiction

Each chapter opens with several "Truth or Fiction" statements that relate to the concepts discussed in the chapter. Ask students whether they think each statement is true or false. Answers to each item as well as explanations are provided at appropriate points within the text under the heading "Truth or Fiction Revisited."

For Your Information

The concept of association can be traced back to the ancient Greek philosophers Plato and Aristotle. Plato believed that learning relies in large part on associating a new object with existing knowledge of related objects or concepts. Association is integrally linked to recollection or memory. (Memory is more fully discussed in Chapter 7.)

TRUTH OR fiction?

Read the following statements about psychology. Do you think they are true or false? You will learn whether each statement is true or false as you read the chapter.

- Becoming sick from eating a certain food can be a genuine learning experience.
- If you are afraid of snakes, it may help to surround yourself with them.
- Pigeons were used to guide missiles during World War II.
- Negative reinforcement is the same thing as punishment.
- People who watch a lot of violence on television are more likely to be violent themselves than people who watch less violence on television.

SECTION 1

Classical Conditioning

 A DAY IN THE LIFE
Presumably, Linda and her friends were hoping to get a good grade on the psychology test they were studying for. But Marc wanted to know why grades mattered, and it was a good question. After all, people are not born with instinctive attitudes regarding the letters used for grades, such as A and F. So why do most students like As and try to avoid Fs?

As Janet and Dan pointed out by mentioning the relationship between grades and college, jobs, and participation in team sports, grades have meaning because they are associated with other things. Most of us are familiar with this concept of association. Have you ever been listening to the radio and heard a song that was popular a few years ago—maybe a song that you really liked back then? Did you feel a rush of the sensations that you used to feel back when the song was popular?

If so, this reaction was probably a result of associations between the song and the events of the time in your life when the song was popular. In other words, the song served as a stimulus. A **stimulus** is something that produces a reaction, or a **response**, from a person or an animal. In this case, the response consisted of the feelings brought about by hearing the song.

Here is a simple experiment that also demonstrates associations. Think of a food you really like, such as lasagna or enchiladas. Is your mouth watering? If it is, you are experiencing the results of **conditioning**, or learning. Conditioning works through the pairing of different stimuli. In particular, your reaction demonstrates a type of conditioning known as classical conditioning. **Classical conditioning** is a simple form of learning in which one stimulus (in this case, the thought of the food) calls forth the response (your mouth watering) that is usually called forth by another stimulus (the actual food). This occurs when the two stimuli have been associated with each other.

Ivan Pavlov Rings a Bell

Some of the earliest findings about classical conditioning resulted from research somewhat similar to your own experiences in thinking of food. However, that early research was with dogs, not people. Russian physiologist Ivan Pavlov (1849–1936) discovered that dogs, too, learn to associate one thing with another when food is involved.

Does the sight of this pasta make your mouth water? If so, the reaction is a result of classical conditioning.

Teaching Section 1

Meeting Individual Needs: Auditory Learners

Organize the class into pairs to discuss classical conditioning. Have one partner in each pair orally identify the ideas of classical conditioning he or she feels are important. The listening partner should then repeat those ideas in his or her own words and add any significant points the speaker may have omitted. After clarifying any confusion either partner may have, the pair should record their joint explanation of classical conditioning on audiotape.

Analyzing Ideas

Advertisements sometimes make use of conditioning techniques, such as associating a certain brand of detergent with the outdoors to evoke feelings of freshness. Have students suggest examples of ads that use such classical conditioning to sell goods or services.

FIGURE 6.1 *Pavlov strapped dogs into harnesses and collected their saliva in a tube. After several pairings of a bell and meat powder, the dogs learned to salivate at the sound of the bell by itself.*

Cultural Dimensions

Explain the concept of canalization, in which people are conditioned to prefer one stimulus over another because they perceive that stimulus as more satisfying. Because of canalization, people in different cultures are conditioned to various preferences of food, color, and beauty. For example, most people in the United States do not consider insects to be edible, while in certain other cultures insects are considered a delicacy. Have students discuss what preferences they have been conditioned to have.

Class Discussion

Ask students to relate commonplace occurrences that are examples of classical conditioning. To get the discussion started, provide the example of a family pet that runs to the kitchen every time it hears the refrigerator door open. Have volunteers identify the components of classical conditioning in the examples mentioned.

Pavlov did not set out to learn about learning. Rather, he was interested in the relationship between the nervous system and digestion. In particular, Pavlov was studying salivation, or mouthwatering, in dogs. He knew that dogs would salivate if meat was placed on their tongues because saliva aids in the eating and digestion of the meat. In other words, meat on the tongue is a stimulus for the production of saliva.

But Pavlov discovered that the dogs did not always wait until they had received meat to start salivating. For example, they salivated in response to the clinking of food trays. The dogs would also salivate when Pavlov's assistants entered the laboratory. Why? Because the dogs had learned from experience that these events—the clinking of the trays, the arrival of the assistants—meant that food was coming.

At first, Pavlov viewed the dogs' unwanted salivation as a nuisance because it was getting in the way of what he was trying to study. But soon he decided that the "problem" was worth looking into. If the dogs could learn to salivate in response to the clinking of food trays because this clinking was associated with the bringing of meat, could they learn to salivate in response to any stimulus that signaled meat? Pavlov predicted that they could. He set out to show that he could train his dogs to salivate in response to any stimulus he chose.

The stimulus Pavlov chose was the ringing of a bell. He strapped the dogs into harnesses and rang a bell. (See Figure 6.1.) Then about half a second after the bell rang, meat powder was placed on the dogs' tongues. As expected, the dogs salivated in response to the meat powder. Pavlov repeated this process several times.

After several pairings of the meat and the bell, however, Pavlov changed the procedure: he sounded the bell but did not follow the bell with the meat. Yet the dogs salivated anyway—they had learned to salivate in response to the bell alone.

US, UR, CR, and CS: Letters of Learning

The dogs' salivation in response to the bell demonstrates classical conditioning. Terms that are important in understanding classical conditioning include

Instruct learners having difficulty to create flash cards showing the relationship between unconditioned and conditioned stimuli and responses. Students might want to describe the elements of Pavlov's research to trigger their memory of the four terms. Students should use the flash cards for reference during their study of classical conditioning.

Cooperative Learning

Organize the class into small groups. Give each group a different example of classical conditioning. (You might challenge gifted learners to develop their own examples.) Ask each group to draw a diagram of its example in the manner shown in Figure 6.2. One group member should be responsible for the drawing, another for the written explanation, a third for the presentation to the class. After all diagrams have been presented, have students discuss and compare them.

unconditioned stimulus, unconditioned response, conditioned response, and *conditioned stimulus.*

The meat in Pavlov's research was an example of an unconditioned stimulus. An **unconditioned stimulus** (US) is a stimulus that causes a response that is automatic, not learned. That automatic response, in turn, is called an **unconditioned response** (UR). Salivation in response to the meat was an unconditioned response. In other words, the dogs did not *learn* to salivate in response to the meat—they did so naturally, by instinct, because of their biology.

The dogs' salivation in response to the bell was a conditioned response. A **conditioned response** (CR) is a learned response to a stimulus that was previously neutral, or meaningless. In Pavlov's research, the bell was a neutral stimulus. That is, before Pavlov associated it with the meat, it might have made the dogs' ears perk up, but it would not have made the dogs salivate because it had nothing to do with food. Through repeated association with meat, however, the bell became a learned stimulus, or a **conditioned stimulus** (CS), for the response of salivation.

A conditioned response is often the same as or very similar to an unconditioned response. With Pavlov's dogs, for example, salivation in response to the meat was the UR. But salivation in response to the bell was the CR. In other words, salivation was both the UR and the CR. (See Figure 6.2.)

Adapting to the Environment

Classical conditioning helps organisms adapt to their surrounding environment. For example, just as Pavlov's dogs learned that the bell signaled meat, a person's pet dog may learn that the sound of a can opener (CS) means that dog food (US) will soon appear in the dog's bowl. Thus, the dog comes running to the bowl (CR).

Sometimes classical conditioning helps animals and people avoid or deal with danger. For example, a bear cub may learn to associate a particular scent (CS) with the appearance of a dangerous animal (US). The cub can then hide or run away (CR) when it catches the scent. Or a new car owner may hear his or her car alarm go off (CS). Thinking that someone is breaking into the car (US), the car owner calls the police (CR).

Taste Aversions   One form of classical conditioning that can be particularly useful to people is called a taste aversion. A **taste aversion** is a learned avoidance of a particular food. Have you ever eaten a food that made you ill, perhaps because it was spoiled? Did you then stay away from that food for a long time? If so, you had probably developed a taste aversion to it.

Often when foods make us ill, it is because they are unhealthy, even poisonous. A taste aversion helps us avoid these foods by keeping us away from

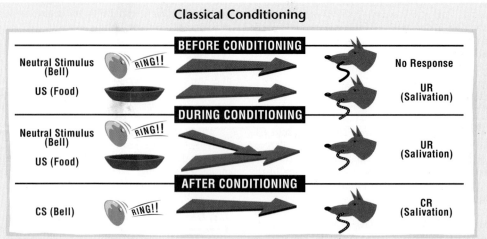

Classical Conditioning

FIGURE 6.2   *Before conditioning, food (US) elicits salivation (UR). The bell (a neutral stimulus at first) elicits no response. Then, during conditioning, the bell precedes* the food. After several repetitions, the bell (now a CS) elicits salivation (CR). **What do US, UR, CS, and CR stand for?**

Identifying Cause and Effect

Review with students the process for creating taste aversions and then extinguishing those aversions. Then invite students to diagram the cause-and-effect relationships in both of the processes. Have students present their diagrams to the class.

For Further Research

Point out to students that the concepts associated with classical conditioning have many practical applications. Have students research ways in which classical conditioning concepts have been used to solve problems. (Use John Garcia's work with coyotes and taste aversion as an example.)

© 1995 Grimmy Inc. Distributed by Tribune Media Services. Reprinted with permission.

A DAY IN THE LIFE them. Psychologists would call Dan's response to eating a half-gallon of ice cream all at one time a taste aversion. Dan had felt nauseated after eating so much ice cream. Ice cream was the unconditioned stimulus (US) that had caused the unconditioned response (UR) of nausea. As a result of his one experience, even the thought of ice cream served as a conditioned stimulus (CS) that made him feel nauseated (CR). The taste aversion was strong. Even though Dan knew that he could probably eat smaller amounts of ice cream safely, the thought of any ice cream at all made him feel ill.

It is useful for people and animals to develop taste aversions readily. With other examples of classical conditioning, an association must be made several times before the conditioned response occurs. Pavlov had to pair the bell with meat several times before the dogs would begin to salivate at the sound of the bell. In taste aversions, however, just one pairing of food and illness may be all that is necessary to create the aversion.

TRUTH *It is true that becoming sick from eating a certain food can be a genuine learning experi-* **OR** *ence. Avoidance of a food* **fiction** *that once caused illness is* ▪ R E V I S I T E D ▪ *called a taste aversion. Taste aversions are a result of classical conditioning.*

Extinction Classical conditioning helps people and animals adapt to their environments. But things can change, and what once was dangerous may no longer be so. What threatens a bear cub may lose its menace once the bear matures. Or the signal for

danger may lose its meaning. A car alarm may be set off so often by accident (such as by a harmless gust of wind) that the car owner no longer rushes to call the police.

When a conditioned stimulus (such as the scent of an animal or a car alarm) is no longer followed by an unconditioned stimulus (a dangerous animal, the car being broken into), it will eventually lose its ability to bring about a conditioned response. In classical conditioning, this is called **extinction**. Extinction occurs when the conditioned stimulus

Researchers used classical conditioning to teach coyotes not to eat sheep by feeding them poisoned lamb meat. Because the poisoned meat made the coyotes sick, they developed a taste aversion to the lamb. Thus, they no longer attacked the livestock, solving an economic problem for many ranchers.

Guided Practice

Give students the opportunity to experience and assess the impact of classical conditioning as you perform the following experiment. Provide each student with a small cup of powdered lemonade. Have students dip a moistened finger into the powder. As you say a signal word, students should place the powdered finger on their tongue. After a few trials, invite students to describe their experiences. *(They should be salivating upon hearing the signal word.)*

Independent Practice

Have students examine the diagram on classical conditioning shown in Figure 6.2. Ask students to reproduce the diagram but to substitute the appropriate components of the powdered-lemonade demonstration for the components of Pavlov's demonstration.

Caption Question: Answer

Without an unconditioned stimulus, a conditioned response will be extinguished.

Cross-Curricular Link: Biology

Point out to students that the first time they hear a song, they may have a strong emotional response to it. When a song loses its ability to evoke that marked response, one has become habituated to it. Behind this adjustment is a biological change. In habituation, there is a decrease in neurotransmitters, the chemicals that carry messages to the brain. The brain, in effect, has learned to ignore the message. In other words, the routes these neurotransmitters had originally created to tell the brain about the song have weakened and become less important. The same concept can work in reverse. When extra neurotransmitters are present, those same brain pathways send a disproportionately strong message to the brain. This process, called sensitization, can lead to some of the fears discussed on page 133.

132

Key Concepts in Classical Conditioning

	Procedure	Result
Classical Conditioning	Before conditioning is begun, an unconditioned stimulus (US) such as meat brings forth an unconditioned response (UR) such as salivation. During conditioning, a neutral stimulus such as a bell is paired with the unconditioned stimulus (US).	The neutral stimulus becomes a conditioned stimulus (CS). The CS (bell) brings forth the CR (salivation).
Example	A child waits for her parents to come home. She hears a car drive up (neutral stimulus). Then her parents come inside (US). She becomes excited (UR) when she sees her parents come in.	After a few repetitions in which hearing the car is followed by her parents' coming in, she becomes excited (CR) when she hears the car drive up (CS).
Related Concepts	Taste aversion, extinction, spontaneous recovery, generalization, discrimination	

FIGURE 6.3 *The more times the unconditioned stimulus is paired with the neutral stimulus, the stronger the neutral stimulus (now the CS) becomes.* **What happens when the conditioned stimulus is presented repeatedly without the unconditioned stimulus?**

(CS) is disconnected from the unconditioned stimulus (US). As a result, the conditioned stimulus (CS) no longer causes the conditioned response (CR) to occur.

Pavlov found that with repeated ringing of the bell (CS) not followed by meat (US), the dogs eventually stopped salivating (CR) when they heard the bell (CS). The dogs had learned that the bell no longer meant that food was on the way. The conditioned response of salivating at the sound of the bell had been extinguished.

Spontaneous Recovery An extinguished response is not necessarily gone forever. In what psychologists have termed **spontaneous recovery**, organisms sometimes display responses that were extinguished earlier. This revival of the response follows a period in which the conditioned stimulus was not presented. For example, after the response of salivating at the sound of the bell had been extinguished in Pavlov's dogs, a day or two passed during which the dogs did not hear the bell at all. After this rest period, the bell was rung again. Even though the salivation response had earlier been extinguished, it was now back. It was, however, a little weaker than it had been when it was in full force—the dogs produced less saliva.

Think again of the song that brought back old feelings. If the song were again to become popular

and you started hearing it every day, you probably would no longer experience the same rush of feelings after hearing it over and over. After all, your life has changed now, and when the song is continually played without actually transporting you into the past, it loses the ability to spark those old feelings—the response has undergone extinction. But if a month passes without your hearing the song at all, the next time you hear it, those old feelings may well return. In other words, they will have been spontaneously recovered.

Generalization and Discrimination Dan's half-gallon of ice cream was probably all one flavor, perhaps chocolate. But Dan did not say, "I can eat any flavor of ice cream except chocolate." Rather, he wanted to avoid ice cream of all flavors. This is called generalization. **Generalization** is the act of responding in the same ways to stimuli that seem to be similar, even if the stimuli are not identical.

In a demonstration of generalization, Pavlov first conditioned a dog to salivate when it was shown a circle. On several occasions, the dog was shown a circle (the CS), then given meat (the US). After several pairings, the dog salivated when presented with only the circle. Pavlov demonstrated that the dog would also salivate in response to the

A DAY IN THE LIFE

Demonstration

Choose a food from the list of foods that students created earlier (page 130). If possible, use a listed food to which many students have a taste aversion. Then conduct a classroom experiment in which pictures of related foods are presented. As a class, explore how closely a pictured food must be to the listed food to produce a taste aversion. Analyze what features distinguish foods to which students have no taste aversion from the listed food.

Applying Information

Have the class discuss generalization and provide examples of it. Make three columns on the board, labeled *Conditioned Stimulus, Conditioned Response,* and *Similar Stimuli.* Have the class tell you what to put in each column for each example. Give the example of the sound of a dental drill making someone cringe. *(Sound of a dental drill: conditioned stimulus; cringing: conditioned response; sounds of other kinds of drills: similar stimuli.)*

sight of many other geometric figures, including ellipses, pentagons, and squares. The more closely the figure resembled a circle, the greater the strength of the response (the more drops of saliva that flowed).

The dog's weaker response to figures that looked less like a circle was an example of discrimination. **Discrimination** is the act of responding differently to stimuli that are not similar to each other. Dan did not want to eat ice cream, but he probably would not have objected to eating other types of food—such as, chocolate pudding. This is because ice cream and pudding are sufficiently different that Dan was able to discriminate them from each other.

Both generalization and discrimination help people and animals adapt to their environments. For example, a bear cub who has a bad experience with a wolf may generalize from that experience that all big furry animals that growl (other than adult bears) should be avoided. On the other hand, the bear cub probably discriminates between the wolf and a mouse. The mouse might be furry, but it is not big and does not growl. Thus, the mouse is not a danger. A child who has been frightened by a dog may generalize and stay away from all dogs. But because of discrimination, the child continues to play with his or her stuffed animals, even the ones that look like dogs.

Applications of Classical Conditioning

Classical conditioning is the means by which stimuli come to serve as signals for other stimuli. It is a major avenue of learning in our daily lives. It also can be used to solve specific problems that people have. For example, classical conditioning can help people overcome their fears of various objects and situations. It can even help children stop wetting their beds.

Flooding and Systematic Desensitization
Many fears—such as fear of heights, of snakes, and of speaking in front of the class—are out of proportion to the harm that could happen. Some people fear looking out of windows in tall buildings, even though they cannot fall. Many people fear snakes, even snakes that are small and nonpoisonous.

Two methods for reducing such fears are based on the principle of extinction. In the method called **flooding**, a person is exposed to the harmless stimulus until fear responses to that stimulus are

People on a roller coaster discriminate between the real danger of an automobile careening out of control and the ride in an amusement park.

extinguished. A person with a fear of heights might look out from a sixth-story window until she or he is no longer upset by it. A person with a fear of snakes might be put in a room with lots of harmless snakes crawling around in the room.

TRUTH OR **fiction** ▪ REVISITED ▪

It is true that if you are afraid of snakes, it may help to surround yourself with them. This is a method of therapy called flooding. In flooding, an application of classical conditioning, a person is exposed to a fear-provoking but harmless stimulus until the fear is extinguished.

Although flooding is usually effective, it tends to be quite unpleasant. When people fear something, forced exposure to it is the last thing they want. For this reason, psychologists usually prefer to use **systematic desensitization** to help people overcome their fears. In this method, people are taught relaxation techniques. Then they are exposed gradually to whatever stimulus they fear while they

CASE STUDIES
AND OTHER TRUE STORIES

Ask students to consider the ethical question posed in the last paragraph of the case study. Was it ethical for Watson and Rayner to repeatedly frighten a small child, ultimately teaching him to fear a previously loved pet? Have student teams use formal debate procedures to explore this question. As they construct their arguments, encourage debaters to consider the value of the research versus the negative impact of its methods.

Closing Section 1

Follow Up

Have students return to the list of daily habits and preferences they made earlier. Challenge them to briefly explain how classical conditioning played a role in creating those personal habits and preferences. Ask students to identify the conditioned and unconditioned stimuli and the response elements in each conditioning process.

Class Discussion

Ask students to recall some of their own childhood fears. Then ask how extinction may have changed those fears. Discuss the fact that as we mature, changing circumstances recondition us. How does this relate to classical conditioning?

internet connect

TOPIC: Classical Conditioning
GO TO: go.hrw.com
KEYWORD: SY3 PS6

Have students access the Internet through the HRW Go site to research Pavlov and classical conditioning. Then ask students to assume the point of view of the curator of the "Museum of Classical Conditioning" and have students plan a museum exhibit on the subject. Students should include information on stimulus and response as well as on the "letters of learning."

CASE STUDIES
AND OTHER TRUE STORIES
The Story of Little Albert

In 1920, psychologists John B. Watson and Rosalie Rayner published an article describing an experiment they had done with an infant named Albert. The experiment had such an impact on the field of psychology that the boy became known as "Little Albert" and the story of the experiment became a classic. Even today, psychologists and psychology students are still familiar with it.

Why do children fear some objects but not others?

What was the experiment? It was a very small but very significant demonstration that emotional reactions such as fears can be acquired through principles of classical conditioning.

Albert was the 11-month-old son of one of Watson's and Rayner's acquaintances. Watson and Rayner observed that Albert did not become easily frightened. They also observed that he had a white laboratory rat for a playmate. To demonstrate that fears can be learned through associations, Watson and Rayner decided to see if they could condition Albert to fear the white rat rather than be amused by it. All they had to do, they reasoned, was pair the rat with something that Albert would find frightening.

What does an 11-month-old instinctively find frightening? Loud, harsh noises—such as the clanging of steel bars. Every time Albert played with the rat, Watson clanged steel bars behind the infant. Sure enough, after seven pairings, Albert showed fear of the rat even when there was no more clanging. The rat had at first brought pleasure to Little Albert. Now, through no fault of its own, it had become a source of fear and trembling. Through association, the animal had taken on the meaning of the jangling, jarring steel bars to Little Albert.

In the terms used in classical conditioning, the clanging of the steel bars was the unconditioned stimulus (US) that led to the unconditioned response (UR) of fear. The rat was the conditioned stimulus (CS) that, through association with the clanging of the bars, also led Albert to feel fear—now the conditioned response (CR).

Little Albert's newfound fear, however, did not stop with the innocent rat. It spread, or generalized, to objects similar in appearance to the rat, such as a rabbit and a fur coat. Because of his experiences with the rat and the steel bars, Albert learned to fear other objects that were white and furry.

Unfortunately, Watson and Rayner never had the chance to help Little Albert overcome his conditioned fear of rats. Therefore, his fear may never have become extinguished. Somewhere out there may be an older man who cringes at the sight not only of rats but also of little girls wearing fluffy sweaters, of small dogs, or maybe even of Santa Claus's beard. Moreover, because the conditioning was carried out at such a tender age, Little Albert—now Big Albert?—may have no idea why he fears these things. He would not remember the original experience.

Was it ethical for Watson and Rayner to experiment on such a small child—especially when the experiment involved repeatedly frightening him and teaching him to fear something that had previously given him pleasure? Today most psychologists would say no, it was not ethical. For this reason, this experiment would never be duplicated today. Psychologists would have to find some other way of demonstrating their theories.

WHY PSYCHOLOGY MATTERS

Some people have difficulty handling their fears of situations or things. Use 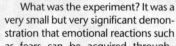 or other current events sources to learn more about how psychologists help people overcome their fears. Create a visual that highlights what you have learned.

CNNfyi.com

Reviewing Section 1

Have students complete the Section Review questions on page 135.

Extension

Have students use what they have learned about classical conditioning to propose a solution to a problem facing your class or school. The problem might involve several students, a school policy, school facilities, or something from the students' own lives.

remain relaxed. For example, people who fear snakes are shown pictures of snakes while they are relaxed. Once they can view pictures of snakes without losing the feeling of relaxation, they are shown some real snakes from a distance. Then, after some more time, the snakes are brought closer, and eventually the people no longer fear snakes. Systematic desensitization takes longer to work than flooding, but it is not as unpleasant.

Counterconditioning Can cookies help children overcome their fears? Perhaps. Early in this century, University of California professors Mary Cover Jones (1924) and Harold Jones reasoned that if fears could be conditioned by painful experiences, perhaps fears could be counterconditioned by pleasant experiences. In **counterconditioning**, a pleasant stimulus is paired repeatedly with a fearful one, counteracting the fear.

The Joneses tried out their idea with a two-year-old boy named Peter, who feared rabbits. The Joneses gradually brought a rabbit closer to Peter while they fed Peter candy and cookies. Peter seemed nervous about the rabbit, but he continued to eat his treat. Gradually, the animal was brought even closer. Eventually, Peter ate treats and petted the rabbit at the same time. Apparently, his pleasure at eating the sweets canceled out his fear of the rabbit. Dentists might caution against overusing this "cookie treatment," however. While it might help children overcome their fears, it might also give them cavities.

The Bell-and-Pad Method for Bed-Wetting By the time children are five or six years old, most of them wake up when their bladders are full. They stop themselves from urinating, which is an automatic response to bladder tension, and go to the bathroom. But some children do not respond to sensations of a full bladder when they are asleep. They remain asleep and often wet their beds.

To help children stop wetting their beds, psychologists came up with the bell-and-pad method. This method teaches children to wake up in response to bladder tension. A child with a bed-wetting tendency sleeps on a special pad placed on his or her bed. When the child starts to urinate, the water content of the urine triggers a bell, and the ringing wakes the child up.

Unlike the case in Pavlov's experiments with the dogs, in which the bell was a conditioned stimulus, the bell in the bell-and-pad method is an unconditioned stimulus (US). That is, it wakes up the child

because of the child's biological makeup; people instinctively wake up when they hear loud noises. Waking up to the bell is the unconditioned response (UR).

Because of repeated pairings, a stimulus that precedes the bell becomes associated with the bell. It also gains the capacity to wake up the child. What is this stimulus? It is the sensation of a full bladder. In this way, bladder tension is the conditioned stimulus (CS) that comes to wake up the child even though the child is asleep during the classical conditioning procedure. Waking up in response to bladder tension is the conditioned response (CR).

After a couple of weeks of using the bell-and-pad method, most children no longer wet their beds. Similar methods have been used to aid in the toilet training of children.

SECTION 1 REVIEW

go.hrw.com
Homework Practice Online
Keyword: SY3 HP6

1. Explain the principles of classical conditioning by describing Pavlov's classic experiment with dogs using the following terms: *unconditioned stimulus, unconditioned response, conditioned response, conditioned stimulus.*

2. Explain what is meant by extinction, spontaneous recovery, generalization, and discrimination in classical conditioning.

3. **Critical Thinking** *Drawing Inferences and Conclusions* Describe and explain learning as an adaptation to the environment.

SECTION 2
Operant Conditioning

In classical conditioning, we learn to associate one stimulus with another. Pavlov's dogs learned to associate a bell with meat. Because of classical conditioning, the response made to one stimulus (for example, meat) is then made in response to the other (for example, the bell).

Classical conditioning, however, is only one type of learning. Another type of learning is operant conditioning. In **operant conditioning**, people and animals learn to do certain things—and not

Section 1 Review: Answers

1. Pavlov noticed that dogs salivated (*unconditioned response*) to various stimuli associated with meat (*unconditioned stimulus*). He then paired the ringing of a bell (*conditioned stimulus*) with the giving of meat. After several repetitions, Pavlov found that the dogs salivated (*conditioned response*) to the sound of the bell.

2. Extinction occurs when the CS is disconnected from the US and no longer causes the CR to occur; spontaneous recovery is the reappearance of an extinguished response; generalization involves responding the same way to similar, but not identical, stimuli; discrimination involves responding differently to stimuli that are not similar.

3. Learning helps organisms function and thrive within their environments. For example, Pavlov's dogs learned that the bell signaled food.

135

Section Objective

▶ Explain the principles of operant conditioning and describe how they are applied.

This objective is assessed in the Section Review on page 144 and in the Chapter 6 Review.

Opening Section 2

Motivator

Draw two columns on the chalkboard, one labeled *Cause* and the other *Effect*. Ask student volunteers to define *cause* and *effect*. Invite additional volunteers to give some examples of cause-and-effect relationships. Explain that the causal relationship is at the heart of operant conditioning. Encourage students to copy the cause-and-effect chart in their notebooks. As students complete their study of Section 2, they can use their charts to track some of the causal relationships discussed in this section.

What's New in Psychology

In psychology, a token economy is the systematic use in a controlled setting of tokens or "points" as reinforcers for behaving appropriately. These tokens can be redeemed for rewards, which may include such things as snacks and television privileges. This system, based on behaviorist concepts such as reinforcement and shaping, has been used with great success in institutions ranging from mental hospitals to schools. A great deal of its success lies in the fact that it reinforces only appropriate behavior; in traditional institutions, staff members often "reward" difficult people with more attention and thus unknowingly reinforce inappropriate behavior.

Class Discussion

Invite students to share examples of the effects of operant conditioning on animals they have encountered. Students might relate stories about their pets, bring in photographs, or describe animal behavior they have seen or read about. You might link this activity to Section 1 by examining the data for examples of classical conditioning as well.

to do others—because of the results of what they do. In other words, they learn from the consequences of their actions. Linda and Janet, for example, had learned that studying would result in good grades. Because they desired good grades, they studied. In operant conditioning, organisms learn to engage in behavior that results in desirable consequences, such as receiving food, an A on a test, or social approval. They also learn to avoid behaviors that result in negative consequences, such as pain or failure.

A DAY IN THE LIFE

In classical conditioning, the conditioned responses are often involuntary biological behaviors, such as salivation or eye blinks. In operant conditioning, however, voluntary responses—behaviors that people and animals have more control over, such as studying—are conditioned.

B. F. Skinner's Idea for the Birds

The ideas behind a secret war weapon that was never built will help us learn more about operant conditioning. The weapon was devised by psychologist B. F. Skinner, and it was called Project Pigeon. During World War II, Skinner proposed training pigeons to guide missiles to targets. The pigeons would be given food pellets for pecking at targets on a screen. Once they had learned to peck at the targets, the pigeons would be placed in missiles. Pecking at similar targets on a screen in the missile would adjust the missile's flight path to hit a real target. However, the pigeon equipment was bulky, and plans for building the missile were abandoned.

TRUTH
OR
fiction
■ R E V I S I T E D ■

It is not true that pigeons were used to guide missiles during World War II. B. F. Skinner, however, proposed that with the proper conditioning, pigeons would be able to guide missiles by pecking at targets on a screen.

Although Project Pigeon was scrapped, the principles of learning Skinner applied to the project are a fine example of operant conditioning. In operant conditioning, an organism learns to do something because of its effects or consequences. Skinner reasoned that if pigeons were rewarded (with food) for pecking at targets, then the pigeons would continue to peck at the targets.

Reinforcement

To study operant behavior, Skinner devised an animal cage that has been dubbed the "Skinner box." A Skinner box is ideal for laboratory experimentation. Treatments can be introduced and removed, and the results can be carefully observed.

In a classic experiment, a rat in a Skinner box was deprived of food. The box was designed so that when a lever inside was pressed, some food pellets would drop into the box. At first, the rat sniffed its way around the box and engaged in random behavior. The rat's first pressing of the lever was accidental. But lo and behold, food appeared.

Soon the rat began to press the lever more frequently. It had learned that pressing the lever would make the food pellets appear. The pellets are thus said to have reinforced the lever-pressing behavior. **Reinforcement** is the process by which a stimulus (in this case, the food) increases the chances that the preceding behavior (in this case, the lever pressing) will occur again. After several reinforced responses, the rat pressed the lever quickly and frequently, until it was no longer hungry.

In operant conditioning, it matters little why the person or animal makes the first response that is reinforced. It can be by chance, as with the rat in the Skinner box, or the person or animal can be physically guided into the response. In training a dog to sit on command, the dog's owner may say, "Sit!" and then push the dog's rear end down. Once sitting, the dog's response might be reinforced with a pat on the dog's head or a food treat.

People, of course, can simply be told what they need to do when they are learning how to do things such as boot up a computer or start a car. In order for the behavior to be reinforced, however, people need to know whether they have made the correct response. If the computer does not turn on or the car lurches and stalls, the learner will probably think he or she has made a mistake and will not repeat the response. But if everything works as it is supposed to, the response will appear to be correct, and the learner will repeat it next time. Knowledge of results is often all the reinforcement that people need to learn new skills.

Types of Reinforcers

The stimulus that encourages a behavior to occur again is called a reinforcer. There are several different types of reinforcers. Reinforcers can be primary or secondary. They can also be positive or negative.

Teaching Section 2

Meeting Individual Needs: Tactile/Kinesthetic Learners

Provide students with detailed information about the features of a Skinner box. Have the students build working models of a Skinner box. Display these in the classroom, and give students an opportunity to demonstrate how each box works.

Predicting Outcomes

Encourage students to restate the concept of operant conditioning. Then challenge them to predict some problems that could arise from applying the theory to humans. Urge students to consider social, educational, and political arenas. How could the ability to control learning in this way be abused? In what ways might an individual's freedom of choice be influenced?

Key Concepts in Operant Conditioning		
	Procedure	**Result**
Operant Conditioning	A behavior is followed by a consequence or reinforcement.	The behavior increases in frequency.
Example	When a child cleans his room, his parents read him a story.	The child cleans his room more often, so as to hear more stories.
Related Concepts	Primary and secondary reinforcers, positive and negative reinforcers, schedules of reinforcement, extinction	

FIGURE 6.4 *In classical conditioning, a neutral stimulus becomes a conditioned stimulus that brings forth the desired behavior. In operant conditioning, on the other hand, reinforcements are used to increase the frequency of the desired behavior from the organism.*

For Your Information

In 1967 a group of young people created a commune in rural Virginia modeled after the utopian community in B.F. Skinner's novel *Walden Two*. The commune, known as Twin Oaks, is based on the idea of using positive reinforcement rather than punitive control to influence the behavior of its members. While many of the more radical practices of the founding members, such as communal child rearing, have proved impractical, the 100-member commune still depends on voluntary cooperation rather than fines or punishments to enforce its work quotas.

Teaching Transparancies with Teacher's Notes

TRANSPARENCY 18: Key Concepts in Operant Conditioning

Primary and Secondary Reinforcers Reinforcers that function due to the biological makeup of the organism are called **primary reinforcers**. Food, water, and adequate warmth are all primary reinforcers. People and animals do not need to be taught to value food, water, and warmth.

The value of **secondary reinforcers**, however, must be learned. Secondary reinforcers initially acquire their value through being paired with established reinforcers. Money, attention, and social approval are all usually secondary reinforcers. Money, for example, is a secondary reinforcer because we have learned that it may be exchanged for primary reinforcers such as food and shelter.

Sometimes secondary reinforcers acquire their value only through a long chain of associations. Janet pointed out that good grades (secondary reinforcers) were important because they could help with college admission or jobs. College admission and jobs (also secondary reinforcers) might lead to money or social approval (other secondary reinforcers). As a result of such a chain of associations, secondary reinforcers—such as good grades—sometimes come to be desired in and of themselves.

Positive and Negative Reinforcers Reinforcers can also be positive or negative. **Positive reinforcers** increase the frequency of the behavior they follow when they are applied. Food, fun activities, and social approval are usually examples of positive reinforcers. In positive reinforcement, a behavior is reinforced because a person (or an animal) receives something he or she wants following the behavior.

Different reinforcers work with different people. For people who enjoy sports, for example, receiving the opportunity to participate in a sport is a positive reinforcer. For people who do not enjoy sports, however, receiving the opportunity to participate in a sport would not be an effective reinforcer. Similarly, what serves as a reinforcer at one time for a person may not be effective at another time for that same person. When a person is hungry, food will work well as a positive reinforcer. But once the person has eaten and is full, food will no longer have an effect.

Unlike with positive reinforcement, with negative reinforcement, a behavior is reinforced because something unwanted *stops* happening or is removed following the behavior. **Negative reinforcers** increase the frequency of the behavior that follows when they are removed. Negative reinforcers are unpleasant in some way. Discomfort, fear, and social disapproval are negative reinforcers.

Daily life is filled with examples of negative reinforcement. When we become too warm in the sun, we move into the shade. When we are tired at the end of the day, we go to sleep. When a food particle is stuck between our teeth, we floss to remove it. And when we have an itch, we often scratch it (even when advised not to do so). All of these situations involve some uncomfortable stimulus—a negative reinforcer—that we act on to make the discomfort disappear. When a specific behavior reduces or

Guided Practice

Have students begin a classroom chart about positive and negative reinforcements. First, allow students 15 minutes to record several examples of operant conditioning from their own lives. Work as a class to record these on the chart under either *Positive Reinforcement* or *Negative Reinforcement*. Then prompt students to write a brief journal entry explaining which type of reinforcement works better for them and why.

Independent Practice

Point out to students that in addition to classical conditioning, many advertisements also use reinforcement to sell their products. A perfume, for example, becomes a secondary reinforcer if purchasers believe it really will lead to the glamorous or romantic life pictured in the ad. Challenge students to analyze print and radio or television advertisements. Have them identify the reinforcers and explain to the class how each is used to sell the advertised product.

Caption Question: Answer

Negative reinforcers increase the behavior they follow when they are removed.

Class Discussion

Skinner recognized the difficulty of identifying the particular reward that will affect a given subject. Ask students what kinds of rewards they like. Do they enjoy material rewards such as money, new CDs, or clothes? Do they use food as a reward? Do they believe that emotional responses, such as praise from a peer, can work as rewards? Discuss the difference between rewards and positive reinforcers, analyzing whether any of the rewards students have identified could work as positive reinforcers.

Reinforcement and Punishment

	Behavior	Result	Change
Positive Reinforcement	Studying	Enjoyment of the material (Positive reinforcer)	Student studies more. (Increase)
Negative Reinforcement	Studying	Decreases fear of doing poorly on test (Negative reinforcer)	Student studies more. (Increase)
Punishment	Littering	Person has to pay fine. (Punishment)	Person stops littering. (Decrease)

FIGURE 6.5 *Both positive and negative reinforcers increase the frequency of a behavior. Punishment, however, is intended to decrease or eliminate a particular behavior.* **Which type of reinforcer increases the behavior when it is removed?**

removes the discomfort, that behavior is reinforced, or strengthened.

A DAY IN THE LIFE

Linda wanted to study for her psychology test in part because she thought the material was interesting. In this case, her interest in the material was a positive reinforcer for her. But Linda was also probably studying because she did not want to do poorly on the test. In this case, fear of doing poorly was a negative reinforcer. She wanted to study because studying would remove her fear of getting a bad grade. In addition, Linda's efforts showed that she understood the importance of monitoring and evaluating her work for timeliness, accuracy, and goal attainment.

Rewards and Punishments

Many people believe that being positively reinforced is the same as being rewarded and that being negatively reinforced is the same as being punished. Yet there are some differences, particularly between negative reinforcement and punishment.

Rewards When Linda suggested that she and her friends do something enjoyable after they finished studying, she was proposing that they give themselves a reward. Rewards, like reinforcers, increase the frequency of a behavior, and some psychologists do use the term *reward* interchangeably with the term *positive reinforcement*. But Skinner preferred the concept of reinforcement to that of reward because the concept of reinforcement can be explained without trying to "get inside the head" of an organism to guess what it will find rewarding. A list of reinforcers is arrived at by observing what kinds of stimuli increase the frequency of a behavior.

Punishments While rewards and positive reinforcers are similar, punishments are quite different from negative reinforcers. Both negative reinforcers and punishments are usually unpleasant. But negative reinforcers increase the frequency of a behavior by being removed. Punishments, on the other hand, are unwanted events that, when they are applied, decrease the frequency of the behavior they follow. (See Figure 6.5.)

TRUTH OR fiction REVISITED

It is not true that negative reinforcement is the same thing as punishment. Both punishments and negative reinforcers are unpleasant, but negative reinforcers encourage a behavior by being removed. Punishments, on the other hand, discourage a behavior by being applied.

Follow Up

Have students return to the cause-and-effect chart they created in the Motivator activity. Help students analyze first a cause-and-effect relationship between a behavior and a reward and then a similar relationship between a behavior and a positive reinforcer. Use the two charts to clarify the difference between rewards and positive reinforcement.

Role-Playing

Have groups of students brainstorm some ways that reinforcement is used in daily life to produce desired behaviors (for instance, obeying traffic laws). Then have the groups role-play the situations that use these reinforcement methods. Invite the remaining students to comment on the effectiveness of the reinforcers. Encourage students to think of alternative methods of reinforcement.

In school districts such as Marc's that tie participation in athletic programs to academic grades, both punishment and negative reinforcement are involved. To the athlete on the team who does not achieve the required grades, being removed from the team is a punishment. But once the student is off the team, the disappointment of being banned from participation is a negative reinforcer. The student may work harder to raise his or her class grades in order to gain permission to rejoin the team, thus ending the disappointment.

Strong punishment can rapidly end undesirable behavior. Yet many psychologists believe that in most cases punishment is not the ideal way to deal with a problem. They point to several reasons for minimizing the use of punishment:

- Punishment does not in itself teach alternate acceptable behavior. A child may learn what not to do in a particular situation but does not learn what to do instead.

- Punishment tends to work only when it is guaranteed. If a behavior is punished some of the time but goes unnoticed the rest of the time, the behavior probably will continue.

- Severely punished people or animals may try to leave the situation rather than change their behavior. For example, psychologists warn that children who are severely punished by their parents may run away from home.

- Punishment can create anger and hostility. A child who is punished may take out such anger on other children.

- Punishment may have broader effects than desired. This can occur when people do not know why they are being punished and what is wanted of them.

- Punishment may be imitated as a way of solving problems. As discussed in the next section, people learn by observing others. Psychologists warn that when children are hit by angry parents, the children may learn not only that they have done something wrong, but also that people hit other people when they are upset. Thus, children who are hit may be more likely to hit others themselves.

- Punishment is sometimes accompanied by unseen benefits that make the behavior more, not less, likely to be repeated. For instance, some children may learn that the most effective way of getting attention from their parents is to misbehave.

Most psychologists believe that it is preferable to reward children for desirable behavior than to punish them for unwanted behavior. For example, parents and other authority figures should pay attention to children, and praise them, when the children are behaving well. If good behavior is taken for granted, and only misbehavior receives attention, misbehavior may be getting reinforced.

Psychologists also point out that children need to be aware of, and capable of performing, the desired behavior. Consider a situation in which parents punish a child for not listening to directions only to find out much later that the child has a hearing problem and could not *hear* the directions.

Schedules of Reinforcement

A major factor in determining how effective a reinforcement will be in bringing about a behavior has to do with the **schedule of reinforcement**—when and how often the reinforcement occurs.

Continuous and Partial Reinforcement Up to now, we primarily have been discussing **continuous reinforcement**, or the reinforcement of a behavior every time the behavior occurs. For

An effective way of encouraging someone to "keep up the good work" is to reward them, as with a prize.

Class Discussion

Have students survey their classmates and families about how parents influence the behavior of their children. Do those surveyed believe a system based on punishment, such as grounding, or a system based on rewards, such as paying the student for every A on his or her report card, works better? Then challenge students to write an editorial for the school or local newspaper supporting either rewards or punishment (or a combination of the two) as a means of influencing behavior. Share and discuss the editorials as a class.

♫ internet connect

TOPIC: Operant Conditioning
GO TO: go.hrw.com
KEYWORD: SY3 PS6

Have students access the Internet through the HRW Go site to conduct research on operant conditioning. Then ask students to draw up a conditioning plan that would teach a dog to fetch the newspaper when it arrives. Students should outline the types of positive and negative reinforcers, punishments and rewards, and reinforcement schedules that would enable the dog to learn this skill. Have students present their plans to the class.

Formulating a Hypothesis

Have students pair off and review the types of reinforcement introduced in this chapter. Have each pair choose a specific behavior and develop a hypothesis about the types and schedules of reinforcement that would work best to modify that behavior. Tell them that later in their study of this section they will have the opportunity to design a reinforcement program to test their hypothesis.

Evaluating Information

Have students review the information about reinforcement schedules and answer the following questions: What are the two basic variables in reinforcement scheduling? How does each variable usually impact the target behavior? *(Two main variables are continuous or partial reinforcement and fixed-interval or variable-interval scheduling; fixed-interval schedules produce predictable rises in responses, while variable-interval schedules produce steadier response rates.)*

Class Discussion

Write the following statement on the chalkboard: "Behaviors learned through partial reinforcement tend to last longer after they are no longer being reinforced than do behaviors learned through continuous reinforcement." Have a student volunteer explain the statement. Then have other student volunteers discuss and clarify any confusion. Finally, challenge the class to develop explanations for this behavioral response.

Teaching Transparencies with Teacher's Notes

TRANSPARENCY 19:
Schedules of Reinforcement

example, the rats in the Skinner box received food every time they pressed the lever. If you walk to a friend's house and your friend is there every time, you will probably continue to go to that same location each time you want to visit your friend because you have always been reinforced for going there. New behaviors are usually learned most rapidly through continuous reinforcement.

It is not, however, always practical or even possible to reinforce a person or an animal for a behavior every single time the behavior occurs. Moreover, a person or animal who is continuously reinforced for a behavior tends to maintain that behavior only as long as the reinforcement is still there. If for some reason the reinforcement stops occurring, the behavior disappears very quickly. For example, if you walk to your friend's house only to find that your friend no longer lives there, you almost certainly will not return to that house again in search of your friend.

The alternative to continuous reinforcement is partial reinforcement. In **partial reinforcement**, a behavior is not reinforced every time it occurs. People who regularly go to the movies may not enjoy every movie they see, for example, but they continue to go to the movies because they enjoy at least *some* of the movies. Behaviors learned through partial reinforcement tend to last longer after they are no longer being reinforced at all than do behaviors learned through continuous reinforcement.

There are two basic categories of partial reinforcement schedules. The first category concerns the amount of time (or interval) that must occur between the reinforcements of a behavior. The second category concerns the number of correct responses that must be made before reinforcement occurs (the ratio of responses to reinforcers).

Interval Schedules If the amount of time—the interval—that must elapse between reinforcements of a behavior is greater than zero seconds, the behavior is on an interval schedule of reinforcement. There are two different types of interval schedules: fixed-interval schedules and variable-interval schedules. These schedules affect how people allocate the persistence and effort they apply to certain tasks.

In a fixed-interval schedule, a fixed amount of time—say, five minutes—must elapse between reinforcements. Suppose a behavior is reinforced at 10:00 A.M. If the behavior is performed at 10:02, it will not be reinforced at that time. However, at 10:05, reinforcement again becomes available and will occur as soon as the behavior is performed. Then the next reinforcement is not available until five minutes later, and so on. Regardless of whether or how often the desired behavior is performed during the interval, it will not be reinforced again until five minutes have elapsed.

The response rate falls off after each reinforcement on a fixed-interval schedule. It then picks up

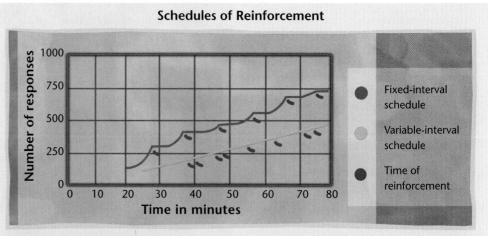

FIGURE 6.6 *This graph shows that the fixed-interval schedule produces increased responses as the time for the reinforcer approaches whereas the variable-interval schedule leads to a relatively steady rate of response.*

Source: Skinner, B. F. (1961). "Teaching machines." Scientific American, Inc.

Ask gifted learners to choose a specific task, skill, or behavior they would like to teach a child. Have them write a detailed, step-by-step explanation of how they would use operant conditioning concepts such as shaping to teach their chosen procedure.

Synthesizing Information

Tell students to write a personal narrative from the point of view of a rat or other research animal involved in an operant conditioning study. Direct students to use their knowledge of the conditioning process and its variables to infer the animal's observations at various points in the study. Narratives should indicate the type of reinforcement schedule in place, including the intervals and the ratios used.

As harvest time draws nearer, the corn farmer begins to check the crop more often. Typically, by late summer, the corn crop will have been completely harvested, and the farmer will not have to check it again until after the next year's replanting. *What type of reinforcement schedule do the corn farmer's actions indicate?*

as the time when reinforcement will be dispensed draws near. For example, in a one-minute fixed-interval schedule, a rat may be reinforced with food the first time it presses the lever after a minute has elapsed since the previous reinforcement. After each reinforcement, the rat's rate of lever pressing slows down, but as a minute approaches, lever pressing increases in frequency. It is as if the rat has learned that it must wait a while before reinforcement is available. Similarly, if you know that your teacher gives a quiz every Friday, you might study only on Thursday nights. After a given week's quiz, you might not study again until the following Thursday. You are on a one-week fixed-interval schedule.

Farmers and gardeners are quite familiar with one-year fixed-interval schedules. If a particular type of fruit ripens only in the spring, for example, the farmer probably will not check to see if the fruit is ripe in the autumn or winter. However, as spring begins, the farmer will probably check more and more frequently to see if the fruit is ripe. Once all the fruit has ripened and been picked, the farmer will stop checking for it until the next spring.

In a variable-interval schedule, varying amounts of time go by between reinforcements. For example, a reinforcement may occur at 10:00, then not again until 10:07 (7-minute interval), then not again until 10:08 (1-minute interval), then not again until 10:20 (12-minute interval). In variable-interval

schedules, the timing of the next reinforcement is unpredictable. Therefore, the response rate is steadier than with fixed-interval schedules. (See Figure 6.6.) If your teacher gives unpredictable pop quizzes, you are likely to do at least some studying fairly regularly because you do not know when the next quiz will be. And if it turns out to be tomorrow, you want to be prepared.

Ratio Schedules   If a desired response is reinforced every time the response occurs, there is a one-to-one (1:1) ratio of response to reinforcement (one response: one reinforcement). If, however, the response must occur more than once in order to be reinforced, there is a higher response-to-reinforcement ratio. For example, if a response must occur five times before being reinforced, the ratio is 5:1. As with interval schedules, there are fixed-ratio schedules and variable-ratio schedules.

In a fixed-ratio schedule, reinforcement is provided after a fixed number of correct responses have been made. The rat in the box would have to press the lever, say, five times, and always exactly five times, in order to receive the food. Some stores use fixed-ratio schedules to encourage people to buy more. A video rental store, for instance, may promise customers a free video rental after payment for five rentals.

With a fixed-ratio schedule, the person or animal tends to try to get its fixed number of responses

Demonstration

Use the following demonstration to highlight the shaping process. Direct several student volunteers to leave the classroom. With the remaining students, choose a target behavior for the volunteers to perform. Simple behaviors such as turning the lights on or off or writing one's name on the chalkboard work best. Work as a class to break down the behavior into steps and to identify a reinforcement signal. Reintroduce the volunteers and experiment with shaping.

Class Discussion

Have students identify problems that might arise when working on fixed-ratio schedules. Provide them with the example of workers who are paid per product made. If students do not identify any problems with fixed-ratio schedules, point out the temptation to shortcut such a system—for example, by sacrificing quality for quantity. Explore the need to balance incentive and reinforcement.

For Your Information

Some behaviorists feel that for gamblers, even losing can be a positive reinforcer because losing is often followed by winning. Moreover, some gamblers seem to have the general belief that their actions are not linked to the results of those actions. This belief, and the willingness to experience either winning *or* losing as a positive reinforcer, often makes gambling a very difficult behavior to extinguish.

"out of the way" as quickly as it can to get to the reward. With the free video rental offer, for example, a customer may rent the five required videos as soon as possible so as to get to the free one sooner. If the ratio is very high, however, it is often less effective, particularly with people.

In a variable-ratio schedule, reinforcement is provided after a variable number of correct responses have been made. Sometimes the rat might have to press the lever 5 times to receive the food; at other times, 8 times; and at still other times, 14 times. The rat cannot predict how many times the lever must be pressed because the number changes each time.

With a variable-ratio schedule, reinforcement can come at any time. This unpredictability maintains a high response rate. Slot machines tend to work on variable-ratio schedules. Even though the players do not know when (or even if) they will win, they continue to drop coins into the machines. And when the players do win, they often continue to play because the next winnings might be just a few lever-pulls away.

Extinction in Operant Conditioning

In operant conditioning, as in classical conditioning, extinction sometimes occurs. In both types of conditioning, extinction occurs because the events that had previously followed a stimulus no longer occur.

In operant conditioning, the extinction of a learned response results from repeated performance of the response without reinforcement. In Skinner's experiment with the rats, lever pressing was followed by—and reinforced by—food. But if a rat presses a lever repeatedly and no food follows, it will eventually stop pressing the lever. The lever-pressing behavior will have been extinguished.

Marc's reluctance to study for the psychology test may have been an example of extinction. The

previous week, he had studied very hard for a test in another class but had done poorly on the test anyway. In other words, his studying behavior had not been reinforced by doing well on the test. As a result, he began to question whether studying was helpful at all. If Linda and the others had not been there to persuade him that it was necessary to study, he might very well not have studied for the psychology test. Marc's studying behavior would have been

extinguished because of the previous week's lack of reinforcement. After a rest period, though, it might have been spontaneously recovered, as in classical conditioning.

Applications of Operant Conditioning

As we have seen, even people who have never had a course in psychology use operant conditioning every day to influence other people. For example, parents frequently use rewards, such as a trip to the park, to encourage children to perform certain tasks, such as cleaning their rooms.

Techniques of operant conditioning also have widespread application in the field of education. Some specific applications of operant conditioning in education include shaping, programmed learning, and classroom discipline.

Shaping   If you have ever tried to teach someone how to do a complex or difficult task, you probably know that the best way to teach the task is to break it up into parts and teach each part separately. When all the parts have been mastered, they can be put together to form the whole. Psychologists call this shaping. **Shaping** is a way of teaching complex behaviors in which one first reinforces small steps in the right direction.

Learning to ride a bicycle, for example, involves the learning of a complex sequence of behaviors and can be accomplished through shaping. First, people must learn to move the bike forward by using the pedals. Then they must learn to balance the bicycle and then to steer it. You may remember when you learned to ride a two-wheeler, or you may have seen a parent help a young child by holding the seat as the child learned to pedal. At first, each of these steps seems difficult, and people must pay close attention to each one. After many repetitions, though, and much praise and reassurance from the instructor, each step—and eventually bicycle riding itself—becomes habitual. Close attention no longer needs to be paid.

Psychologists have used shaping to teach animals some complex behavior patterns. For example, they have trained rats to pedal toy cars by first reinforcing the rats' behavior of turning toward the cars. Next they wait until the rats approach the cars before providing further reinforcement. Then they wait until the rats touch the cars, and so on. In this way, rats have been trained to run up ramps, cross bridges, climb ladders, and the like.

Organize the class into three groups. Challenge the groups to think about other ways technology has affected learning. Have some members of each group research the ways learning has changed during the last ten years. Have other group members use the research to prepare a report that summarizes the group's research and predicts how technology will continue to affect learning.

For Further Research

Tell students that many employees of NASA were inspired to work for the agency because of the lunar missions. Prompt students to identify astronauts, engineers, scientists, or other persons who cite NASA's space missions as an inspiration for their chosen careers. Have the students present brief oral reports that describe the careers of the person they identified.

PSYCHOLOGY
IN THE WORLD TODAY

Technology and Learning

Changes in technology have strongly affected learning. One of the most significant changes is the availability of information on the Internet. Many of the world's libraries and archives can be searched from any computer with online access. The wealth of online information has changed people's behavior in a variety of ways. For example, persons wishing to earn college credit from home can do so by "attending" virtual classes online. Taking classes for credit online reflects one way technology has affected people's growth and development.

Students around the world use computers to learn online.

Thanks to the Internet, medical patients can more easily learn about issues of importance to them. The widespread availability of medical data on the Internet helps people to ask their physicians more informed questions. As a result, many patients are taking more active roles in their own health care.

Advances in technology have enriched the lives of people throughout society. Children now converse online with other children around the world. As children's understanding of other cultures increases, their beliefs about and attitudes toward those cultures changes. Scientific advances have also enriched the lives of disabled and elderly people. Developments in voice technology allow some people who previously could not speak to communicate orally. For example, British physicist Stephen Hawking, who has a motor neuron disease, can speak and write with the help of a voice synthesizer. This technology has helped him remain active in research and teaching. Improvements in medical care have also enhanced the quality of life for many elderly persons.

Scientific and engineering achievements have also expanded people's understanding of the world around them. Research of animal behavior carried out by psychologists and other scientists has increased many people's interest in, and understanding of, the natural world. Knowledge of outer space has similarly increased. The 1969 Moon landing demonstrated the feasibility of lengthy manned space flights. The flight was the culmination of a long-range American goal of landing a human on the Moon, and the mission's success expanded people's belief in the feasibility of space travel. The landing, and subsequent travels to the Moon, inspired many Americans to study science and math.

Space travel had advanced enough by the end of the 1900s that persons other than trained astronauts could travel in space. Interest in space exploration continued to grow as unmanned spacecraft made successful trips to Mars. Vast amounts of information about these voyages have been placed on NASA's Web sites and other sources, sparking further interest in the sciences. In addition, the 1998 flight of then 77-year old U.S. senator John Glenn changed many people's attitudes about what elderly persons could accomplishment with the help of technology.

Think About It

1. *Finding the Main Idea* How have people's attitudes, beliefs, and behaviors been affected by changes in technology?
2. *Analyzing Information* Evaluate the impact of changes in technology on personal growth and development.

Think About It: Answers

1. Changes in technology have, among other things, led people to take classes online, increased understanding of other cultures, and encouraged many people to take a more active role in their own health care.

2. Answers will vary, but students may suggest that changes in technology—such as online learning—have enhanced opportunities for personal growth and development.

Closing Section 2

Applying Information

Have students find the cause-and-effect chart they copied in their notebooks at the beginning of Section 2 and any other charts they completed during their study of this section. Invite students to use these charts as a tool to briefly explain the role of conditioning in each of the causal relationships they have documented. Let other students ask questions regarding the types of reinforcement used in each relationship.

Reviewing Section 2

Have students complete the Section Review questions on page 144.

Extension

Have students analyze and discuss the ways in which video games use the concept of reinforcement to spark and maintain interest.

**Caption Question:
Answer**

Possible steps include using claws to hold the handle.

**Section 2 Review:
Answers**

1. In classical conditioning, learning is involuntary and automatic; in operant conditioning, the organism learns through its own actions.

2. Reinforcement encourages certain behavior, and punishment tends to diminish the behavior. They affect the pace of, or how much, effort is expended in engaging in the activity.

3. the offering of rewards, shaping, programmed learning, and classroom discipline

4. Parents and teachers use rewards (such as a later curfew or good grades) for desired behavior and punishments (removal of privileges or team participation) for undesired behavior. The examples given will vary, depending on students' experiences.

Building on a squirrel's natural tendency to use its paws, this animal was taught to ride a remote-controlled hang glider. **What steps do you think were reinforced to produce this final behavior?**

Programmed Learning B. F. Skinner developed an educational method called programmed learning that is based on shaping. Programmed learning assumes that any task, no matter how complex, can be broken down into small steps. Each step can be shaped individually and combined to form the more complicated whole.

In programmed learning, a device called a teaching machine presents the student with the subject matter in a series of steps, each of which is called a frame. Each frame requires the student to make some kind of response, such as answering a question. The student is immediately informed whether the response was correct. If it was correct, the student goes on to the next frame. If the response was incorrect, the student goes back over that step until he or she learns it correctly.

Teaching machines can be mechanical handheld devices. They can also be books or papers, such as worksheets. These days, however, teaching machines are most likely to be computers that are programmed so that the material can branch off in several different directions, depending on where the student needs the most instruction and practice. The use of computers in learning is called computer-assisted instruction.

Programmed learning does not punish students for making errors. Instead, it reinforces correct responses. Eventually, all students who finish the program earn "100 percent," but they do so at their own pace. The machines are infinitely patient with the learner. They are also highly efficient. Most people, however, believe that teaching machines should not be used to replace human teachers—only to assist them.

Classroom Discipline Sometimes when we think we are reinforcing one behavior, we are actually unknowingly reinforcing the opposite behavior. For instance, teachers who pay attention to students who misbehave may unintentionally give these students greater status in the eyes of some of their classmates (Wentzel, 1994). Some teacher training programs show teachers how to use principles of learning to change students' negative patterns of behavior. In these programs, teachers are taught to pay attention to students when they are behaving appropriately and to ignore their misbehavior as long as the misbehavior is not harmful to themselves or to others. If misbehavior is ignored, or unreinforced, it should become extinct, according to the theory.

Teacher attention and approval may have more influence with elementary school students than with high school students, however. Among some adolescents, peer approval can be more powerful than teacher approval. Peer approval may reinforce misbehavior even when teachers choose to ignore it. Moreover, ignoring adolescents' misbehavior may only encourage other students to become disruptive as well.

Instead of ignoring misbehaving adolescents, therefore, teachers may decide to separate them from the rest of the class or group. Teachers and parents frequently use a technique called time-out to discourage misbehavior. Time-out involves placing students in dull, confining environments for a short period of time, such as 10 minutes, when they misbehave. Students who are isolated cannot obtain the attention of peers or teachers, and no reinforcing activities are available.

SECTION 2 REVIEW

go.hrw.com **Homework Practice Online**
Keyword: SY3 HP6

1. Explain the differences between classical conditioning and operant conditioning.

2. Describe the roles of reinforcement and punishment in determining persistence-and-effort allocation.

3. In what ways are the principles of operant conditioning applied?

4. **Critical Thinking** *Analyzing Information* How do parents and teachers use rewards and punishments to influence children's behavior? Give an example of a reward or punishment that works with some people but not with others.

3
Section Objective

▶ Discuss cognitive factors in learning.

This objective is assessed in the Section Review on page 147 and in the Chapter 6 Review.

Opening Section 3

Motivator

Invite student volunteers to read aloud the questions that open the two subsections in Section 3. Encourage the class to answer the questions through discussion. Then prompt students to share a recently learned skill or item of information with the class. After each student speaks, have the class discuss how the learning took place. What happened to make that all-important understanding "click" into place? Tell students that Section 3 explores some of the ways people select and learn new skills and information.

SECTION **3**

Cognitive Factors in Learning

A DAY IN THE LIFE

If B. F. Skinner had heard Dan speculate that he might study more often if he got to do something enjoyable every time he studied, Skinner probably would have paid little attention. For Skinner, what was important was what organisms actually do, not what they say or think they might do. Skinner was interested only in organisms' behaviors.

Cognitive psychologists, however, are willing to speak about what people and animals know because of learning—not just about what they do. Cognitive psychologists see learning as purposeful, not mechanical. They believe that a person can learn something simply by thinking about it or by watching others. They see people and even some animals as searching for information, weighing evidence, and making decisions. Two kinds of learning that involve cognitive factors are latent learning and observational learning.

Latent Learning

How do you know where objects are in your home, in your school, or in your neighborhood? You probably have a mental picture, or "cognitive map," of the area. Because you are very familiar with your school, for example, you know the locations of your locker, the main office, the cafeteria, the gymnasium, and your psychology classroom. Chances are, no one has reinforced your creation of a mental picture of the school's layout; you have simply created it on your own.

In the past, many psychologists argued that organisms only learn behaviors that are reinforced. Today, however, most psychologists believe that much learning can occur without reinforcement. Support for this view came from the work of E. C. Tolman. Tolman showed that rats will learn about their environments even in the absence of reinforcement. Tolman trained some rats to run through mazes to reach food. Other rats were simply permitted to explore the mazes. They received no food or other rewards. After the unrewarded rats had run around in the mazes for 10 days, food was placed in

a box at the far ends of the mazes. The previously unrewarded explorers reached the food as quickly as the rewarded rats after only one or two reinforced efforts (Tolman & Honzik, 1930).

Tolman concluded that the rats had learned about the layouts of the mazes even when they were unrewarded for their learning. Tolman distinguished between what organisms learn and what they do. Rats would learn about the mazes even when they roamed about without a goal. However, they had no reason to run efficient routes to the far ends of the mazes until they were rewarded for doing so. Therefore, even though they had knowledge of the most rapid routes all along, this knowledge had been hidden, or latent, until the rats had reason to use it—when there was food at the ends. Learning that remains hidden until it is needed is called **latent learning**.

On your way to school each morning, you may pass a particular street corner at which you have never had any reason to stop. But if a friend wants to meet you at that corner on Saturday, you will still know how to get there, even though you may never have stopped there before. This is an example of latent learning.

Observational Learning

How many things have you learned from observing other people, from reading books, and from watching films and television? No doubt you have picked

A mouse will learn its way through a maze even if it is not reinforced with food for turning left or right.

For Your Information

Because of the ways in which our brains organize information, our mental maps are subject to certain flaws. For example, one study (Stevens & Coupe, 1978) documented some of the misconceptions people have about North American geography. Consider the following questions used in the study: Which is farther east, San Diego or Reno? Which is farther north: Seattle or Montreal? The correct answer to each question is the first choice given (be prepared to show doubting students a map of North America). Participants in this study drew on their knowledge about the location of states or countries to help them locate the cities. This study demonstrates our tendency to rely on "higher order" information, which can sometimes lead to faulty reasoning.

Technology Resources

CNN Presents Psychology: Influence on Learning: Mice Studies

Teaching Section 3

Meeting Individual Needs: Visual Learners

Give students a selection of locations with which they are all familiar. Possibilities include the school, town, or neighborhood, a well-known local institution such as a library, or another popular site. Provide recall time, and then challenge students to draw or describe their cognitive map of the site. Invite students to compare and contrast their maps.

Closing Section 3

Classifying Information

Ask students to create a two-column chart with the headings *Latent Learning* and *Observational Learning*. Have them complete the chart with information from Section 3.

Reviewing Section 3

Have students complete the Section Review questions on page 147.

up a few ideas about how to act in certain situations. Certainly, cooking programs on television are based on the premise that people learn by watching or being told how others do things. People also learn to predict likely outcomes of actions by watching others.

Albert Bandura   In his research on social learning, Albert Bandura (1925–) has shown that we acquire knowledge and skills by observing and imitating others (Bandura et al., 1963). Such learning is called **observational learning**. For example, a new student in a class might model his or her behavior after other students. The new student might learn that it is acceptable behavior to speak up in class by watching other students. In learning that classroom discussion is encouraged, the new student has demonstrated the ability to learn by a process known as vicarious reinforcement.

Observational learning accounts for much human learning. Children learn to speak, eat, and play at least partly by observing their parents and others do these things. Modern advertising also uses elements of social learning—people often decide what products they would like to purchase based on advertisements they have seen. You learn to pronounce words in your foreign language class by hearing your teacher pronounce them. We may not always be able to do something perfectly the first time we try it, but if we have watched others do it first, we probably have a head start over people who are coming into it without any previous exposure.

Many people believe that because cartoons are aimed at young children, cartoon violence should be kept to a minimum or eliminated altogether.

The Effects of Media Violence   We learn by observing parents and peers, attending school, reading books, and watching media such as television and films. Television is one of our major sources of informal observational learning. Children are routinely exposed to scenes of violence just by turning on the TV set. If a child watches two to four hours of TV a day, she or he will have seen 8,000 murders and another 100,000 acts of violence by the time she or he has finished elementary school (Eron, 1993). Are G-rated movies safe? Perhaps not. One study found that virtually all G-rated animated films have scenes of violence, with a mean duration of 9 to 10 minutes per film (Yokota & Thompson, 2000). Many video games are also full of violent activity (Anderson & Dill, 2000).

Most health professionals agree that media violence contributes to aggression. A joint statement issued by the American Psychological Association and several medical associations (Holland, 2000) made the following points:

- Media violence supplies *models* of aggressive "skills," which children may learn by watching. Media violence also provides viewers with aggressive *scripts*—that is, ideas about how to behave in situations like those they have observed.

- Children who see a lot of violence are more likely to view violence as an effective way of settling conflicts. Children exposed to violence are more likely to assume that acts of violence are acceptable behavior.

- Viewing violence can lead to emotional desensitization toward violence in real life. It can decrease the likelihood that one will take action on behalf of a victim when violence occurs.

- Viewing violence may lead to real life violence. Children exposed to violent programming at a young age have a higher tendency for violent and aggressive behavior later in life than children who are not so exposed.

TRUTH OR fiction
■ REVISITED ■

It is true that people who watch a lot of violence on television are more likely to be violent themselves, as compared with people who watch less violence on television. People sometimes imitate the behavior they observe in real life and in the media. This is called observational learning.

146

Extension

Interested students might analyze a range of media, including television, films, magazines, books, the Internet, and advertisements to focus on the values demonstrated in these media—that is, the observational learning they offer. Ask students to answer these questions: What might you learn from observing various media? What are some pros and cons in the access young people have to the media?

► Identify the steps of the PQ4R method of learning.

This objective is assessed in the Section Review on page 149 and in the Chapter 6 Review.

Just as observational learning may contribute to violent behavior, it may also be used to prevent it. Television networks, for example, have recently made some attempts to limit the amount of violence in programs intended for children. But it is probably not practical to hope to shield children from all violence—after all, even religious texts, the evening news, and classic works such as Shakespeare's *Macbeth* contain violence. Instead, young people can be informed that the violence they see in the media does not represent the behavior of most people in society. Most people resolve their conflicts without resorting to violence. Children also can be told that the violence they see on TV shows is not real; it involves camera tricks, special effects, and stunts.

A person who has observed a behavior in others does not necessarily begin to display that behavior himself or herself. There is a difference between what people learn and what they do. Of all the children who are exposed to media violence, only a few of them become violent. Furthermore, it may be that people who *choose* to watch violent television programs are more likely to be violent in the first place. It is difficult to prove a cause-and-effect relationship based only on correlation. (See Chapter 2.) If young people consider violence wrong for them, they will probably not be violent, even if they know how to be violent. The same applies to other behaviors as well.

SECTION 3 REVIEW

go.hrw.com **Homework Practice Online**
Keyword: SY3 HP6

1. What cognitive factors are involved in learning?
2. Identify elements of social learning theory in modern advertising.
3. **Critical Thinking** *Summarizing* Describe the processes of modeling and vicarious reinforcement in typical classroom situations.

SECTION 4

The PQ4R Method: Learning to Learn

If you put a sponge in a bathtub, it will soak up the water. Many students assume that simply by attending a course (such as history, biology, or even psychology) they will somehow soak up the subject matter of that course. Not so. Students are not sponges. Courses are not water.

Students learn more when they take an active approach to learning. One such active approach is called the PQ4R method. Based on the work of educational psychologist Francis P. Robinson, the PQ4R method has six steps: Previewing, Questioning, Reading, Reflecting, Reciting, and Reviewing. Following these six steps will help you get the most out of your textbooks.

Preview

Previewing the subject matter in a textbook means getting a general picture of what is covered before you begin reading a chapter. If you are in the library or the bookstore looking at books to decide which ones you would like to read for pleasure, you may flip rapidly through the pages to get some idea of what the books are about. Thumbing through the pages is one way of previewing the material. In fact, many textbooks are designed with devices that encourage students to preview chapters before reading them.

This book, for instance, has Read to Discover chapter questions, Truth-or-Fiction sections, lists of key terms, major and minor section headings in each chapter, section review questions, and chapter reviews. If drama and suspense are your goals, read each chapter page by page. But if learning the material is your aim, it may be more effective to first read the opening chapter questions, skim the pages, and read the questions in the section and chapter reviews.

Familiarity with the overall picture will give you a cognitive map of a chapter. Your map will have many blank areas, but it will have an overall structure. You can fill in the details of the map as you read through the chapter page by page.

Question

Learning is made easier when we have goals in mind, when there is something in particular we want to learn. When we want to learn something, we become active learners.

One way to create goals is to phrase questions about the subject matter in each chapter. You may wonder what is a good way to come up with the questions without reading the chapter first. Look at each heading. Write down all the headings in a notebook. If a book you are reading does not have helpful headings, you might try looking at the first

Section 3 Review: Answers

1. latent learning, observational learning

2. Elements of observational learning are present in modern advertising—people often make purchases based on advertisements they have seen.

3. Answers should reflect the extent to which students' behavior has been affected by witnessing violence.

Readings and Case Studies

Class Discussion

Return to the questions students identified in the Motivator activity on page 145, including those posted on the board. Allow small groups of students to discuss the questions, using brainstorming and section material to construct answers. Have students share and discuss their answers with the whole class.

147

Opening Section 4

Motivator

Without explaining the strategy in detail, initiate a PQ4R approach to Section 4 with students. Begin by asking a volunteer to read the section objective (on page 126), the title, and the subheadings. Have another student describe Figure 6.7 and read its caption. Then challenge students to generate questions about the section on the basis of the foregoing information. Post some of these questions on the chalkboard for later reference.

Teaching Section 4

Synthesizing Information

Point out to students the many applications of PQ4R given in the text. Invite students' comments about the different examples. For example, do they find noting key terms useful, or have they developed other ways to highlight important ideas and concepts? Encourage them to add their own approaches to the 4Rs.

---

sentence of each paragraph instead. Phrase questions as you proceed. With practice, you will develop questioning skills, and your questions will help you grasp the subject matter.

The following questions are based on the major and minor headings at the beginning of this chapter: What is classical conditioning? Who is Ivan Pavlov? (See Figure 6.7.) You may have come up with different questions after reading the headings. Your questions might have been as useful as these, or more useful; there is always more than one "right" question. As you study, you will learn what works for you.

Read

Once you have formulated your questions, read the chapter with the purpose of answering them. A sense of purpose will help you focus on the key points of the material. As you answer each question,

Using PQ4R

I. What is classical conditioning?
   A. Who is Ivan Pavlov?
   B. What do US, UR, CR, and CS mean?
   C. How is adaptation to the environment related to conditioning?
     1. What is a taste aversion?
     2. What is extinction?
     3. What is spontaneous recovery?
     4. How do generalization and discrimination relate to classical conditioning?
   D. What are some applications of classical conditioning?
     1. What are flooding and systematic desensitization?
     2. What is counterconditioning?
     3. How does the bell-and-pad method for bed-wetting work?

FIGURE 6.7 *An actual PQ4R notebook might include a column for answers in addition to the questions.*

you can jot down a few key words in your notebook that will remind you of the answer when you recite and review later. You may find it helpful to keep two columns in your notebook: one column for the questions themselves and the other column for the key words that relate to the answer to each question.

Reflect

Reflecting on subject matter is an important way to understand and remember it. As you are reading, think of examples or create mental images of the subject matter.

One way to reflect is to relate new information to old information. You may remember some facts about B. F. Skinner from Chapter 1, for example. What you learned about him there can serve as a springboard for you to learn about him and about his work in greater detail in this chapter. Take advantage of what you already know.

Another way to reflect is to relate new information to events in your personal life. For instance, you can reflect on classical conditioning by thinking of times when you have experienced it. Then you will find it easier to remember that classical conditioning involves learning through the association of stimuli with each other.

Even if you cannot think of any way to relate the material to your own life, you probably know other people who provide examples of the kinds of behavior discussed throughout this book. To help yourself understand and remember the subject matter of psychology, think of ways in which the behavior of people described in the text and by your teacher is similar to—or different from—the behavior of people you know.

Recite

Do you remember when you learned the alphabet? If you were like many children, you probably learned it by saying it—or singing it to the tune of the "Alphabet Song"—over and over again. This is an example of how reciting something can help a person learn. The same thing can work with your textbook. (You will have to make up your own song, however.)

Once you have read a section and have answered your questions, reciting the answers will help you understand and remember them. You can recite aloud or repeat words silently to yourself. You can also do your reciting alone or with others. Many

Closing Section 4

Drawing Conclusions

Challenge each student to review his or her academic record from the most recent term. Have students write brief descriptions of their study habits for each subject or class. What conclusions can students draw about the success of various study methods?

Applying Information

Working in small groups, have students complete the PQ4R process for Section 1 of this chapter. Encourage them to consider and incorporate any useful strategies suggested by their classmates during the Synthesizing Information activity on page 148.

Reviewing Section 4

Have students complete the Section Review questions on page 149.

---

students learn by quizzing each other with their questions, taking turns reciting the answers. This may have been what Linda had in mind when she suggested that she and her friends study together for the psychology test.

Review

When Marc said that he had been studying for the test in Ms. Kramer's class the night before the test, he may have given the explanation for why he did not do as well on the test as he would have liked. For one thing, learning takes time. That means that we usually have to repeat or reread things before we know them well.

Second, "distributed" learning is more effective than "massed" learning. That is a scientific way of saying what most students already know but that Marc apparently did not: it is more effective to study regularly (to distribute the learning over several days or weeks) than to try to cram just before a test (to mass all the learning at once). Actually, distributed learning usually takes no more work than cramming. But it means that we have to plan ahead and try to stick to some sort of schedule.

Review the material for each subject you are studying according to a reasonably regular schedule, such as once a week. Reviewing leads to relearning, and relearning on a regular schedule is easier than learning something the first time. By reviewing material regularly, we understand and remember it better.

It may seem like a large time commitment to study regularly when there is no apparent immediate need to do so, but it will reduce the amount of time you need to study right before a test. It may also help reduce the amount of anxiety you feel about the test the day before (negative reinforcement) because you know that you have already mastered at least some of the material. And it also helps keep you prepared for pop quizzes.

Once you have set aside enough time to review the material, you will need to figure out what techniques will help you most. One way to review the material is to go back to the questions and key words in your notebook. Cover up the answer column and read the questions in the left column as though they were a quiz. Recite your answers and check them against the key words in the right column. When you forget an answer or get an answer wrong, go back and reread the subject matter in the textbook. (In this technique, your notebook

The PQ4R method helps students take an active approach to learning.

becomes a type of teaching machine used in programmed learning.)

Another way of reviewing the subject matter, as already mentioned, is for you and other classmates to quiz each other. By taking a more active approach to learning, you may find that you are earning higher grades and gaining more pleasure from the learning process.

SECTION 4 REVIEW

go.hrw.com Homework Practice Online
Keyword: SY3 HP6

1. What are the steps in the PQ4R method?

2. What purposes does it serve for a person to reflect on information she or he has read? What purposes does reciting the information out loud serve?

3. **Critical Thinking** *Analyzing Information* Prepare a learning and studying schedule for yourself for one of your classes. Use PQ4R as a basis for the schedule.

Section 4 Review: Answers

1. Steps are preview, question, read, reflect, recite, and review.

2. Reflecting on information helps you to understand it more clearly, and reciting helps you to remember the material for a longer time.

3. Answers should demonstrate an application of the PQ4R elements.

Chapter 6 Review: Answers

Writing a Summary
See the section subtitles for the main topics in the chapter.

Identifying People and Ideas

1. something that produces a reaction

2. a reaction to a stimulus

3. a simple form of learning in which one stimulus comes to call forth a response

4. a learned avoidance of a particular food

5. repeated exposure to a stimulus to extinguish the fear response to the stimulus

6. conditioning in which people or animals learn because of the results of what they do

7. the process by which a stimulus increases the chances that the preceeding behavior will occur again

149

Chapter 6 REVIEW AND ASSESSMENT RESOURCES

Technology
► Chapter 6 Test Generator (on the One-Stop Planner)
► HRW Go site

Reinforcement, Review, and Assessment
► Chapter 6 Review, pp. 150–151
► Chapter Review and Activities Answer Key
► Alternative Assessment Handbook
► Portfolio Assessment Handbook
► Chapter 6 Test (Form A or B)

PSYCHOLOGY PROJECTS

Linking to Community Have students locate programs that help people eliminate such undesirable behaviors as phobias, smoking, alcoholism, or school/job failure. Have them gather information about these programs. They might ask program directors to talk about how they apply the principles discussed in Chapter 6.

---

8. reinforcer designed to increase the frequency of certain behavior

9. a way of teaching complex behaviors in which one first reinforces small steps in the right direction

10. learning achieved by observing and imitating others

Understanding Main Ideas

1. A neutral stimulus is paired with an unconditioned stimulus. The neutral stimulus becomes a conditioned stimulus evoking the desired, or conditioned, response.

2. In a fixed-interval schedule, the same amount of time elapses between each reinforcement. In a fixed-ratio schedule, the person or animal must respond with the desired behavior a fixed number of times before being reinforced.

3. Latent learning may not become apparent until it is needed. Observational learning is acquired by watching someone else.

4. Answers should explain each step of the PQ4R.

Thinking Critically

1. Classical conditioning—the therapist might use the effects of a nauseating drug to make smoking unpleasant. Operant conditioning—the therapist might give a positive reinforcer for not smoking. Cognitive learning—the therapist could appeal to the smoker's intellect by citing the dangers of smoking.

2. In both instances, positive reinforcement strengthens the likelihood that superstitions will be established.

150

Chapter 6 REVIEW

Writing a Summary
Using standard grammar, spelling, sentence structure, and punctuation, summarize the information in this chapter. Consider:
• the principles of classical and operant conditioning
• cognitive factors in learning and the steps of the PQ4R method of learning

Identifying People and Ideas
Identify the following terms or people and use them in appropriate sentences.

1. stimulus
2. response
3. classical conditioning
4. taste aversion
5. flooding
6. operant conditioning
7. reinforcement
8. positive reinforcers
9. shaping
10. observational learning

Understanding Main Ideas

SECTION 1 (pp. 128–135)
1. How do people and animals learn responses through classical conditioning?

SECTION 2 (pp. 135–144)
2. How does a fixed-interval schedule of reinforcement differ from a fixed-ratio schedule?

SECTION 3 (pp. 145–147)
3. What are two types of learning that involve cognitive factors?

SECTION 4 (pp. 147–149)
4. List the six steps of the PQ4R method and explain the purpose of each step.

Thinking Critically

1. **Analyzing Information** How might a therapist help cigarette smokers quit smoking by using each of these types of learning: classical conditioning, operant conditioning, and cognitive learning?

2. **Drawing Inferences and Conclusions** How might the principles of classical conditioning lead to the formation of superstitions? How might the principles of operant conditioning help keep superstitions alive?

3. **Categorizing** Explain how flooding, desensitization, and counterconditioning can help a person overcome a problem. Give one example for each.

4. **Supporting a Point of View** Many psychologists believe that punishment is not the ideal way to change behavior. Do you agree or disagree? Give examples to support your opinion.

Writing About Psychology

1. **Analyzing Information** Use the PQ4R method to create a plan for improving your understanding of the material in this chapter. Create an outline setting forth how you intend to use your plan to achieve your goal of better understanding the chapter. After trying your new system, write a one-page report of your progress. Monitor and evaluate your system for how timely you are able to complete your work, whether your understanding of the material is more accurate, and whether you achieved your goal of better understanding the material.

2. **Making Generalizations and Predictions** People learn about the consequences of courses of action by observing others. Consider what a child might learn from observing an adult who refuses to pay taxes, register to vote, or obey the speed limit. Write a one-page paper predicting the likely outcome of these courses of action. Use the graphic organizer below to help you write your paper.

- What kinds of behaviors does the program address?
- How does the program apply classical and/or operant conditioning to problem behaviors?
- In what ways do program practitioners use latent and observational learning to help participants?

Allow time for students to ask additional questions following each program director's discussion.

Cooperative Learning

Organize the class into several groups. Have students gather information about educational applications for different types of learning. Some students should focus on behavioral issues in the school setting, such as truancy, while others look at instructional issues. Prompt the groups to focus on the different teaching approaches they encountered as well as the problems educators cited and how those problems were addressed. Have students debate the pros and cons of the various approaches.

Building Social Studies Skills

Interpreting Graphs

Study the graph below. Then use the information in the graph to help you answer the questions that follow.

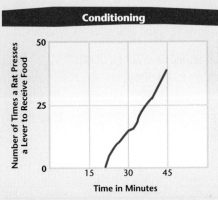

Conditioning

Number of Times a Rat Presses a Lever to Receive Food

Time in Minutes

Source: Blackman, *Operant Conditioning*, 1993

1. What psychological principle does the above graph illustrate?
   a. classical conditioning
   b. operant conditioning
   c. shaping
   d. latent learning

2. What conclusions can you draw from the graph about the rat's behavior and what predictions can be made from the graph?

Analyzing Primary Sources

Read the following excerpt, in which Russian physiologist Ivan Pavlov explains one aspect of the principle of conditioning. Then answer the questions that follow.

"It is pretty evident that under natural conditions the normal animal must respond not only to stimuli which themselves bring immediate benefit or harm, but also to other physical or chemical agencies—waves of sound, light, and the like—which in themselves only *signal* the approach of these stimuli; though it is not the sight and sound of the beast of prey which is in itself harmful to the smaller animal, but its teeth and claws."

3. Which of the following statements best reflects the ideas that Pavlov was trying to convey in the excerpt?
   a. The sight and sound of a beast of prey are unconditioned stimuli.
   b. The sight and sound of a beast of prey are unconditioned responses
   c. The sight and sound of a beast of prey are conditioned stimuli.
   d. The sight and sound of a beast of prey are conditioned responses.

4. According to the excerpt, why must a normal animal respond to the sight and sound of a beast of prey?

PSYCHOLOGY PROJECTS

Cooperative Learning

Reading About Psychology Form a study group with two or three other students in your psychology class. Using material from Chapter 6, practice the recite step of the PQ4R method. Discuss with the other members of the group why this step is helpful. Then make a brief oral report to the rest of the class describing how the recite step helped you learn the material you were studying.

🔲 internet connect

Internet Activity: go.hrw.com
KEYWORD: SY3 PS6
Choose an activity on learning to:
- create an exhibit for "The Museum of Classical Conditioning."
- make an action plan using operant conditioning to teach a dog to fetch.
- research the processes of modeling, imitation, and vicarious reinforcement for a classroom.

go hrw .com

3. In flooding therapy, a person is exposed to a fear-producing stimulus until the fear is overcome. In desensitization, a person is taught relaxation techniques and then exposed to the stimulus. Counter-conditioning pairs a pleasant stimulus with a feared one until the pleasant stimulus overcomes the feared one.

4. Students should give examples to support or refute the idea of using punishment.

Writing About Psychology

1. Students' outlines should reflect an understanding of the PQ4R system, and the reports should note the students' successes or failures in implementing their study plan.

2. Students' papers should discuss how children learn by observation, and how the parent's behavior might influence the child.

Building Social Studies Skills

1. b

2. The rats did not discover that the lever released food pellets for the first 20 minutes or so. After they made that discovery, they consistently pushed the lever in order to receive food.

3. c

4. These sights and sounds serve as conditioned stimuli that lead to responses that protect the normal animal from the dangerous "teeth and claws" of the beast of prey.

Memory

CHAPTER RESOURCE MANAGER

	Objectives	Pacing Guide		Reproducible and Review Resources
SECTION 1: **Three Kinds of Memory** (pp. 154–155)	Compare and contrast the three kinds of memory, and give an example of each kind.	**Regular** 1 day *Block Scheduling Handbook with Team Teaching Strategies, Chapter 7*	**Block Scheduling** .5 day	**SM** Mastering Critical Thinking Skills 7 **REV** Section 1 Review, p. 155
SECTION 2: **Three Processes of Memory** (pp. 155–160)	Explain the three processes of memory.	**Regular** 1 day *Block Scheduling Handbook with Team Teaching Strategies, Chapter 7*	**Block Scheduling** .5 day	**RS** Essay and Research Themes for Advanced Placement Students, Theme 6 **REV** Section 2 Review, p. 160
SECTION 3: **Three Stages of Memory** (pp. 160–166)	Identify the three stages of memory and explain how they are related to each other.	**Regular** 1 day *Block Scheduling Handbook with Team Teaching Strategies, Chapter 7*	**Block Scheduling** .5 day	**PS** Readings and Case Studies, Chapter 7 **REV** Section 3 Review, p. 166
SECTION 4: **Forgetting and Memory Improvement** (pp. 167–173)	Describe the ways memory can be improved.	**Regular** 1 day *Block Scheduling Handbook with Team Teaching Strategies, Chapter 7*	**Block Scheduling** .5 day	**E** Creating a Psychology Fair, Handout 4, Activity 2 **REV** Section 4 Review, p. 173

Chapter Resource Key

PS	Primary Sources	**A**	Assessment		Video
RS	Reading Support	**REV**	Review		Internet
E	Enrichment		Transparencies		Holt Presentation
SM	Skills Mastery		CD-ROM		Maker Using Microsoft® PowerPoint®

 One-Stop Planner CD–ROM

See the *One-Stop Planner* for a complete list of additional resources for students and teachers.

One-Stop Planner CD–ROM

It's easy to plan lessons, select resources, and print out materials for your students when you use the **One-Stop Planner CD-ROM with Test Generator.**

Technology Resources

 One-Stop Planner, Lesson 7.1
 Homework Practice Online
 HRW Go Site

 One-Stop Planner, Lesson 7.2
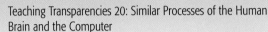 Teaching Transparencies 20: Similar Processes of the Human Brain and the Computer
 Teaching Transparencies 21: Context-Dependent Memories
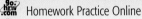 Homework Practice Online
 HRW Go Site

 One-Stop Planner, Lesson 7.3
Homework Practice Online

 One-Stop Planner, Lesson 7.4
 CNN. Presents Psychology: The Brain and Memory
Homework Practice Online
HRW Go Site

Chapter Review and Assessment

 HRW Go site

REV Chapter 7 Review, pp. 174–175

REV Chapter Review Activities with Answer Key

A Chapter 7 Test (Form A or B)

A Portfolio Assessment Handbook

A Alternative Assessment Handbook

Chapter 7 Test Generator (on the One-Stop Planner)

Global Skill Builder CD-ROM

⊿ internet connect

go.hrw.com

HRW ONLINE RESOURCES

GO TO: go.hrw.com
Then type in a keyword.

TEACHER HOME PAGE
 KEYWORD: SY3 Teacher

CHAPTER INTERNET ACTIVITIES
 KEYWORD: SY3 PS7
Choose an activity to have students:
• create a mnemonic device on the types and stages of memory.
• make a flowchart or diagram on memory processes.
• design and test a method of memory improvement.

CHAPTER ENRICHMENT LINKS
 KEYWORD: SY3 CH7

ONLINE ASSESSMENT
 Homework Practice
 KEYWORD: SY3 HP7
 Standardized Test Prep
 KEYWORD: SY3 STP7
 Rubrics
 KEYWORD: SS Rubrics

CONTENT UPDATES
 KEYWORD: SS Content Updates

HOLT PRESENTATION MAKER
 KEYWORD: SY3 PPT7

ONLINE READING SUPPORT
 KEYWORD: SS Strategies

CURRENT EVENTS

Additional Resources

PRINT RESOURCES FOR TEACHERS

Bransford, J. (1984). *The ideal problem solver.* New York: Freeman.

Loftus, E., & Ketcham, K. (1994). *The myth of repressed memory.* New York: St. Martin's.

Rose, S. (1993). *The making of memory: From molecules to mind.* New York: Anchor Books.

Squire, L. (1992). *The encyclopedia of learning and memory.* New York: Macmillan.

PRINT RESOURCES FOR STUDENTS

Baddeley, A. (1993). *Your memory: A user's guide.* London: Prion.

Benne, B. (1988). *WASPLEG and other mnemonics.* Dallas: Taylor.

Loftus, E., & Ketcham, K. (1991). *Witness for the defense.* New York: St. Martin's.

Luria, A. (1987). *The mind of a mnemonist.* Cambridge, MA: Harvard University Press.

MULTIMEDIA RESOURCES

The brain: Learning and memory (Episode 5) (VHS). Films Incorporated, 5547 N. Ravenswood Ave., Chicago, IL 60640-1199.

Memory: Fabric of the mind (VHS). Films for the Humanities & Sciences, P.O. Box 2053, Princeton, NJ 08543-2053.

The nature of memory (VHS). Films for the Humanities & Sciences, P.O. Box 2053, Princeton, NJ 08543-2053.

Neuropsychology (VHS). Films for the Humanities & Sciences, P.O. Box 2053, Princeton, NJ 08543-2053.

MEMORY

Ask students to discuss what memory means to them. What is it? How does it work? What role does it play in their lives and the lives of those around them? Spark the discussion by asking students whether they agree or disagree with the following statement: "Memory is what makes our lives. . . . Without it, we are nothing" (Luis Buñuel, filmmaker). After students discuss their responses to the statement, invite them to contribute other statements about memory. Then challenge students to work independently or in pairs to create their own statements about memory. Have volunteers read their statements to the class for discussion. Tell students that Chapter 7 will introduce them to the psychological perspective on human memory and the flip side of memory—forgetting.

Sections

1 Three Kinds of Memory

2 Three Processes of Memory

3 Three Stages of Memory

4 Forgetting and Memory Improvement

Each of the four questions identified on page 152 corresponds to one of these sections.

7 MEMORY

Chapter

Read to Discover

1 What are the three kinds of memory?

2 What are the three processes of memory?

3 What are the three stages of memory related to?

4 In what ways can memory be improved?

152

Each chapter begins with a vignette, called "A Day in the Life," that relates the information discussed in the chapter to the everyday events in the lives of a group of fictional high school students. The text of the chapter occasionally refers back to the vignette to demonstrate the application of the concept being discussed. An icon marked "A Day in the Life" is placed next to these references.

Copy the following graphic organizer onto the chalkboard, omitting the italicized text. Fill in the circles as you compare and contrast the three types of memory.

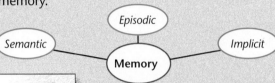

A DAY IN THE LIFE

December 3

"Wow, this song really brings back memories of being in seventh grade," said Linda. She was talking to Marc and Todd at a party Hannah was holding. "Classical conditioning in action, I guess. Hearing it almost makes me feel 13 again. It was so relevant to the things I was feeling then—I used to think Ashley Austin must have written this song just for me."

"Except for one problem," said Todd. "This isn't an Ashley Austin song. It's by . . . I can't think of her name. It starts with an M, . . . Mary? Maria? Something like that. It's on the tip of my tongue."

Marc jumped in. "You're right. Marina Crossley."

At that moment, Dan bounded up and said, "Hey, guess what? I just met the most amazing girl! And she told me her phone number. Quick, before I forget it, someone give me something to write it down on."

While Linda was digging in her bag to find a pencil and a piece of paper, Todd decided to have a little fun with Dan. "What time is it?" he asked him innocently.

"What?" asked Dan in a distracted tone of voice.

"What time is it?" Todd repeated. "Look at your watch."

Dan glanced at his watch. "It's 9:37," he said. By this time, Linda had found a pencil and a scrap of paper and had given them to Dan. He started to write down the number, only to realize that he had forgotten it. He gave Todd a nasty look. "Thanks a lot," Dan said sarcastically. "If you hadn't asked me for the time, I would have remembered the phone number."

"Don't worry, you can look it up in the phone book," said Todd. "That is, assuming you can still remember her *name!*"

Everybody laughed—that is, everybody except Dan, who realized he had, in fact, forgotten her name.

• • •

As Linda, Todd, Marc, and Dan were demonstrating at the party, people use memory all the time. Some things we never seem to forget—visual images such as the faces of family members and friends and basic kinds of information such as the alphabet or simple math. Some of the physical skills we learn, such as walking and swimming, can also last a lifetime.

Much of what is stored in our memory was stored there with no conscious effort on our part. Sometimes it takes only a visual image, a sound, or an odor to bring back a memory. That was what happened when Linda heard the song. It brought back memories of when she was in the seventh grade. Other things in our memory take more effort to store.

This chapter discusses what psychologists have learned about memory. You will read about the "three threes" of memory—the three kinds, the three processes, and the three stages. You will also read about forgetting and learn some ways to improve your memory.

Key Terms

- memory
- episodic memory
- flashbulb memories
- semantic memory
- explicit memory
- implicit memory
- encoding
- storage
- maintenance rehearsal
- elaborative rehearsal
- retrieval
- context-dependent memories
- state-dependent memories
- tip-of-the-tongue phenomenon
- sensory memory
- iconic memory
- eidetic imagery
- echoic memory
- short-term memory
- primacy effect
- recency effect
- chunking
- interference
- long-term memory
- schemas
- recognition
- recall
- relearning
- decay
- infantile amnesia
- anterograde amnesia
- retrograde amnesia

▶ WHY PSYCHOLOGY MATTERS

Everyone remembers significant events in their lives. At the end of this chapter visit **CNNfyi.com** to learn more about psychological research on memory.

CNNfyi.com

Using Key Terms

Explain to students that many of the key terms are compound terms, that is, terms made up of two or more words. Demonstrate to students how to use these words to build meaning. For example, *flashbulb memory* is a memory that works like a flashbulb used with a camera. Encourage students to use this building-block approach to assign meaning to the remaining terms. As students begin reading Chapter 7, direct their attention to the repetition of certain words in the key terms list. Many terms share a word and can be analyzed together. Suggest that students use these repeated words—for example, *memory* or *rehearsal*—to help them build meaning for any terms containing such words.

153

Section Objective

► Compare and contrast the three kinds of memory, and give an example of each kind.

This objective is assessed in the Section Review on page 155 and in the Chapter 7 Review.

Opening Section 1

Motivator

Invite students to brainstorm examples of experiences, general knowledge, and skills they hold in their memory. List the students' responses on the chalkboard. If necessary, guide students to examples of episodic, semantic, and implicit memory. Have students copy the list and put it away for later use. Then explain that there are three kinds of memory, each distinguished by the type of information it contains. Tell students that reading Section 1 will enable them to classify the examples listed on the chalkboard into these three kinds of memory.

TRUTH OR fiction ?

Read the following statements about psychology. Do you think they are true or false? You will learn whether each statement is true or false as you read the chapter.

- Once people learn to ride a bicycle, they probably will never forget how.
- The best way to remember something is to repeat it many times.
- People with photographic memory are rare.
- There is no known limit to how much information you can remember.
- You can remember important events from the first two years of life.
- There are certain tricks you can use to improve your memory.

SECTION 7

Three Kinds of Memory

Look at Figure 7.1. Copy the names of the two objects you see ("eyeglasses" and "hourglass") on a sheet of paper. Do not copy the drawings themselves. Put the sheet of paper aside, but do not discard it. You will need it later in the chapter as a demonstration of one characteristic of memory.

What is memory? **Memory** is the process by which we recollect prior experiences and information and skills learned in the past. There are different kinds of memory. One way to classify memory is according to the different kinds of information it contains: events, general knowledge, and skills.

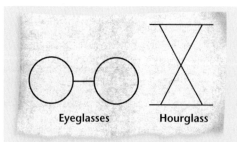

FIGURE 7.1 *Look at these two drawings for a moment. Write the labels of the two drawings on a sheet of paper, then continue reading. You will need the sheet of paper later in this chapter.*

Episodic Memory

Episodic memory is memory of a specific event. The event took place in the person's presence, or the person experienced the event. Your memories of what you ate for dinner last night and of your last quiz are examples of episodic memory.

Some events are so important that it seems as if a flashbulb goes off and we photograph it in every detail. Such memories are called **flashbulb memories**. Linda and Marc would never forget the first time they went out, or the time when they first thought they were in love. Linda would always recall how the sky and the streets and the trees looked different that day. Marc would remember how kind he was to everyone on that day. Both would laugh when they recalled how they were convinced that all of life's problems suddenly seemed solved. But Linda would never laugh when she recalled September 11, 2001.

On that morning, she received a cell phone call that a tower of the World Trade Center in New York City was in flames. She would remember turning on her TV set and watching in horror as the second tower was struck by an airplane and it became clear that terrorism was at work. She would vividly remember the slant of light in her window. She would continue to see the lower part of Manhattan covered with flames, black smoke, and ashen debris after the towers collapsed.

There are several reasons why certain memories become etched in our minds when the "flashbulb" goes off. One reason is the distinctness of the memories. We pay more attention to events that have a special meaning for us. Such events usually arouse powerful feelings. Also, we tend to think about flashbulb memories often, especially if they are positive ones—first love, the birth of a child, or a special accomplishment.

Sometimes places or events make an impression on us—and thus become flashbulb memories—because they are connected to other events that are important at the time, such as a major disaster or tragedy. Then, if we think of the important event later, it will trigger memories of things that were connected to it. Many people have flashbulb memories of the World Trade Center attacks or the explosion of the space shuttle *Challenger* in 1986.

Semantic Memory

General knowledge that people remember is called **semantic memory**. For example, we "remember" that George Washington was the first president of the United States. Unlike with episodic memory, we

Teaching Section 1

Organizing Information

After discussing the three kinds of memory, have students create a three-column chart titled "Three Kinds of Memory." Tell students to label each column with one of the kinds of memory discussed in the section. Then have them complete the chart by supplying a definition, one fact, and two examples for each kind of memory. Have volunteers read items aloud from their charts for other students to identify. Students may wish to keep their charts for later review.

Closing Section 1

Follow Up

Have students retrieve the list of memories from the Motivator activity. Have them create a chart and label each column with one kind of memory. Have them place each item from the list in its proper column on the chart. Review the entries, and have students revise their charts as needed.

Reviewing Section 1

Have students complete the Section Review questions on page 155.

After the attacks, firefighters raised the flag at the World Trade Center site.

instrument, and driving a car are other examples of implicit memory. Once such a skill has been learned, it usually stays with you for many years. Even if you do not use the skill for a long time, you are unlikely to forget it. Once skills have been learned, they tend to stay remembered for many years—perhaps even a lifetime.

It is true that once people learn to ride a bicycle, they probably never will forget how. Once people learn a skill, there is little chance they will ever forget it. Skill memories tend to last, even when they are not used regularly.

SECTION 1 REVIEW

> **go.hrw.com** **Homework Practice Online**
> Keyword: SY3 HP7

1. Describe the three kinds of memory.
2. Explain what flashbulb memories are.
3. **Critical Thinking** *Categorizing* Write down the three kinds of memory you have learned about so far. Next to each, give an example of how you have used that type of memory recently.

usually do not remember *when* we acquired the information in our semantic memory. We probably cannot remember when we first learned about George Washington, for instance.

A DAY IN THE LIFE The memory Marc had at Hannah's party was a semantic memory. He remembered that Marina Crossley wrote the song, not Ashley Austin, as Linda had thought. Most likely, Marc did not remember when he learned that Marina Crossley wrote the song. Still, he remembered correctly that she did.

Here are two more examples of semantic memory. You remember the alphabet, but you probably do not remember where, when, or how you learned it. So, too, you know that humans need oxygen, but you may not recall learning this piece of information. Most of what you have learned in your classes at school has become part of your semantic memory.

Episodic and semantic memories are both examples of **explicit memory**. Things that are *explicit* are clear, or clearly stated or explained. An explicit memory is memory of specific information. That information may be autobiographical (episodic) or refer to general knowledge (semantic).

Implicit Memory

The opposite of explicit is *implicit,* and another kind of memory is **implicit memory**. Things that are implicit are *implied,* or not clearly stated. Implicit memories consist of the skills or procedures you have learned. These skills might include throwing a ball, riding a bicycle, skipping rope, or swimming. Skills such as typing, using a computer, playing a musical

SECTION 2
Three Processes of Memory

Computers and people both process information. Computers use electronic circuits to process the information they receive, while people use their brains. But the processes used by computers and people are very similar. Both computers and people encode, store, and retrieve information.

Encoding

Imagine writing an essay or a story on a computer. You use the keyboard to type information in the form of letters and words. The information is usually stored on a hard drive or a floppy disk. But if you were to put the hard drive or floppy disk under a

Section 1 Review: Answers

1. Episodic memory refers to the memory of a specific event. Semantic memory is the memory of general knowledge. Implicit memory refers to the memory of learned skills or procedures.

2. Flashbulb memory is a kind of episodic memory in which events are remembered in great detail.

3. Students should provide examples of how they recently used episodic, semantic, and implicit memory.

Section Objective

▶ Explain the three processes of memory.

This objective is assessed in the Section Review on page 160 and in the Chapter 7 Review.

Opening Section 2

Motivator

Write the following questions on the chalkboard: What letters do not appear on the telephone keypad? *(Q and Z)* How many sides do most pencils have? *(six)* In what hand does the Statue of Liberty carry the torch? *(right)* Have volunteers answer the questions, then discuss the answers with the class. Point out that we all retain information that we know but fail to recall for some reason. Explain that the memory processes used to absorb information initially and then to store it logically can affect our ability to access that information.

Computers use electronic circuits to process information; humans use their brains. Both use similar processes of encoding, storing, and retrieving information.

microscope, would you be able to see the letters or words you typed? No. This is because the computer changes, or encodes, the information into a form that it can store. **Encoding** is the translation of information into a form in which it can be stored. When people place information in their memory, they, like computers, encode it. For both the computer and the human brain, encoding is the first stage of processing information.

Initially, we receive information through our senses in a physical form—such as light waves or sound waves. When we encode it, we convert the physical stimulation we have received into psychological formats that can be mentally represented. To do so, we use different types of codes.

On a sheet of paper, write this list of letters:

OTTFFSSENT

Look at the letters for 30 seconds and memorize as much of the list as you can in that time. Then continue reading this section to find out which type of code—visual, acoustic, or semantic—you used to remember the letters.

Visual Codes   When you tried to memorize the letters, did you attempt to see them in your mind as a picture? If you did, you used a visual code. That is,

you tried to form a mental picture of the letters in your mind.

Acoustic Codes   Another way that you may have tried to remember the letters might have been to read the list to yourself and repeat it several times. That is, you may have said the letters (either out loud or silently) one after another: O, T, T, and so forth. This way of trying to remember the letters uses an acoustic (or auditory) code. An acoustic code records the letters in your memory as a sequence of sounds.

Semantic Codes   Still another way that you may have tried to remember the list might have been to attempt to make sense of the letters, that is, to figure out what they might mean. For example, you may have noticed that the last four letters spelled the word *sent*. You may then have tried to see if the letters made up a phrase or sentence with the word *sent* in it. The word *semantic* means "relating to meaning," so this type of code is called a semantic code. A semantic code represents information in terms of its meaning. If you tried to figure out a possible meaning for the letters, you were searching for a semantic code.

Another way that you could try to remember the letters by using a semantic code would be to find words that begin with each of the letters in the list and then make up a sentence using those words. Such an approach might result in a sentence that begins "Only Tiny Tots Feel Friendly . . ." By using all 10 letters in a sentence, you would then have to remember only the sentence, not the list of letters.

Yet another way you might use semantic coding to remember the letters would be to use the phrase "other flowers sent" and then make a few changes in the spelling—that is, "OTTher FFlowerS SENT." You would then have to remember the phrase with its "OTTities" (oddities) of spelling!

What you may *not* have realized when you first examined the list is that the letters OTTFFSSENT stand for the first letter of the series of numbers from one (O) through ten (T)—that is, One, Two, Three, Four, Five, Six, Seven, Eight, Nine, Ten. Obviously, if you had known that in the first place, remembering the letters would have been much easier. All you would have had to remember was that the letters were the first letters of the numbers 1 through 10. Remembering this rule would certainly be easier than remembering an apparently meaningless list of 10 letters. By using semantic (meaningful) codes, you can memorize lists of letters and other items more easily and will probably remember them for a longer amount of time than you would otherwise.

Teaching Section 2

Demonstration

To demonstrate the importance of organization in information storage and retrieval, tell students to quickly write down on a sheet of paper the 12 months of the year. Time this exercise, and when all students have finished, tell them how long it took for the class to complete it. Ask students in which type of order they listed the months. *(chronological order)* Have students put away this sheet of paper and take out another one. Then tell them to quickly write down the 12 months in alphabetical order. Discuss why this exercise took much longer to complete.

Applying Ideas

Show students the main menu filing system of a Macintosh or Windows computer operating system. Point out the drive designations, suitcases, folders, and documents. Link these tools to the organizational storage systems of the human brain. Then offer students a range of hypothetical pieces of data. Challenge them to create the necessary filing system to store the data for later retrieval. Have volunteers discuss their filing systems and the reasons they organized the data the way they did.

Storage

After information is encoded, it must be stored. **Storage**, the second process of memory, is the maintenance of encoded information over a period of time. As with encoding, human storage of information is not all that different from a computer's storage of information. With a computer, however, the user must instruct the machine to save information in its memory. Otherwise, it will lose the newly encoded information when the user shuts off the computer. People who want to store new information in their memory use a variety of strategies. These strategies are related closely to the strategies people use for encoding.

Maintenance Rehearsal As Dan found out at

A DAY IN THE LIFE

the party when he tried to remember the phone number of the girl he had met, once we encode information we need to do something more to keep from forgetting it. If you were in a similar situation in which you wanted to remember a name or phone number, how would you do it? One way would be to keep repeating the name or number to yourself to keep it in your memory. If you were concerned that you might forget it before you could write it down, you might need to repeat it several times. Repeating information over and over again to keep from forgetting it is called **maintenance rehearsal**.

The more time spent in rehearsing, or repeating information, the longer the information will be remembered. Actors and actresses know this well. That is why they rehearse their lines again and again until they know them as well as they possibly can. Because maintenance rehearsal does not try to make information meaningful by connecting it to past learning, however, it is a relatively poor way to put information in permanent storage.

Elaborative Rehearsal A more effective and lasting way to remember new information is to make it meaningful by relating it to information you already know well (Woloshyn et al., 1994). This method, called **elaborative rehearsal**, is widely used in education because it has proved to be a much more effective method than maintenance rehearsal. For example, language arts and foreign language teachers recommend elaborative rehearsal when they encourage their students to use new vocabulary words in sentences instead of just repeating individual words by themselves.

TRUTH OR fiction ▪ REVISITED ▪

It is not true that the best way to remember something is to repeat it many times. Usually it is more effective to find a meaning in new information, or to find an application for it, rather than simply to repeat it.

Organizational Systems Memories that you store become organized and arranged in your mind for future use. If you are a fairly organized person, you probably have a place for everything. When you bring items home, you probably do not just throw them on the floor or stick them haphazardly in a closet. You probably sort them and put them in their place. That way you have a better chance of finding them when you need them. You have probably learned from experience that not knowing where items are means that you end up spending a lot of time looking for them when you need them.

In some ways, your memory resembles a vast storehouse of files and file cabinets in which you store what you learn and need to remember. The more you learn, the more files you need and the more elaborate your filing system becomes. When you started attending school, the first facts you learned about American history, for example, may have been about Pocahontas, the Pilgrims, or George Washington. Your first "American history" file probably had only a couple of pieces of information in it.

However, as you progressed and learned more about American history, you had to expand your filing system. As you learned about the presidents, for example, you found new ways to file the information in your memory. You may have filed the presidents in chronological order, that is, in the order in which they held office. In that file you put Washington first, followed by others such as Jefferson, Lincoln, and Theodore Roosevelt. You may also have filed more recent presidents according to the events in American history with which they are associated, such as Franklin Roosevelt with the New Deal and World War II, Richard Nixon with Watergate, and George Bush with the Persian Gulf War.

As your memory develops, it organizes the information you learn into files and then files within files. Your memory organizes the new information it receives into certain groups, or classes, according to common features. For example,

Cross-Curricular Link: Literature

Encourage students to use maintenance rehearsal to memorize a poem, a speech, or dialogue from a play. Have students select a piece of literature and rehearse it until they feel able to deliver it. Have students present the material they selected, and analyze how maintenance rehearsal helped them remember the material.

Cultural Dimensions

In some American Indian cultures, history has been recorded orally. For example, the American Indians who lived in New York during the 1600s and who negotiated treaties with early European settlers passed on the terms of those treaties by means of memory. Each article of a treaty was represented by a different seashell. The shells detailing the treaty were then tied together and displayed in the chief's home. Children able to understand and remember were told by the elders the terms of each shell, or article. Other important aspects of the culture—traditions and legends, for example—were similarly passed down by storytellers, dancers, or singers. Ask students how, if at all, memory processes might be used differently in such a culture. *(People might use acoustic rather than visual codes.)*

Analyzing Information

Have students recall and write down the list of letters they first encountered on page 156: OTTFFSSENT. Ask volunteers to share their lists of letters. How accurate were they? Then have individual students explain how they went about retrieving this information. Note these explanations on the chalkboard. Have students use the explanations to analyze the link between people's information-retrieval method and their original encoding method. Which encoding method seems most effective for the retrieval of information? Why?

Role-Playing

Organize the class into small groups. Assign one student in each group to be the "memory." Give each of the other students a slip of paper that contains information or a familiar saying (such as "time marches on"). Tell the groups to role-play memory at work: the "information" students should read their information to the "memory" student and supply coding clues to help the "memory" later retrieve it. Then, one at a time, the "memory" students should recite their group's information to the class. How accurate were they? Which coding clues were most effective? Why?

The "American history" file in your brain might remind you that Mount Rushmore has the largest figures of any statue in the world and that the faces are those of Washington, Jefferson, Theodore Roosevelt, and Lincoln.

mammals share certain features. They are warm-blooded, and they nurse their young. If you knew that whales are warm-blooded and nurse their young, you probably filed them in your memory as mammals. If you did not know that about them, you might have filed them as fish because they swim and live in the water.

Classes can contain smaller classes and can also be part of a larger class. For example, the class mammals includes monkeys, rats, and other warm-blooded, nursing creatures. At the same time, mammals are part of a larger class—animals. Much of our semantic memory that is stored as we get older and acquire more knowledge is organized into groups or classes.

Filing Errors   Our ability to remember information—even when we are healthy and functioning well—is subject to error. Some memory errors occur because we "file" information incorrectly. Psychologists have discovered that when we classify pieces of information accurately—that is, when we place items in the correct file—we have a much better chance of recalling accurate information about them (Hasselhorn, 1992; Schneider & Bjorklund, 1992). Nevertheless, filing systems are not perfect. Have you ever misplaced a paper? For example, have you ever brought home a science paper and mistakenly filed it in your history folder? Our mental filing systems sometimes make similar errors.

Linda's memory had made a filing mistake. This became evident at the party when she said that Ashley Austin wrote the song that reminded her of being back in the seventh grade. Todd knew the song had not been written by Ashley Austin, but he was unable to remember who did write it. Marc was the one who finally came up with the right answer—Marina Crossley. Linda had apparently put the "wrong label"—Ashley Austin rather than Marina Crossley—on her file of information about the song.

Retrieval

The third memory process is retrieval. **Retrieval** consists of locating stored information and returning it to conscious thought. Retrieving information stored in our memory is like retrieving information stored in a computer. To retrieve information stored in a computer, we have to know the name of the file and the rules for retrieving information. Retrieval of information stored in our memory requires a similar knowledge of proper procedures.

Some information in our memory is so familiar that it is readily available and almost impossible to forget. Examples of this type of information include our own names and those of our friends and family members. But when it comes to trying to remember lines from a play or a mathematical formula, retrieval may be more difficult.

Remember the list of letters discussed earlier in the section? What were they? Write them down now. How did you retrieve them from your memory? The method of retrieval you used might have had to do with the way you encoded them to begin with. If you had encoded the series of letters—OTTFFSSENT—as a three-word phrase ("other flowers sent"), you would try to retrieve the letters by recalling the three words and the rule you needed to use to convert them into the 10 letters. But you might make a mistake. For example, you might recall "other flowers sen**D**" rather than "other flowers sen**T**." Or you might correctly recall "other flowers sent" but then not remember that you have to double the **T**, the **F**, and the **S**.

However, by remembering the semantic code that the letters stand for the numbers 1 through 10, your memory could accurately recall, or retrieve, the letters. Using this semantic code may be more complex than seeing the list in your mind's eye (using a visual code), and it might take you a little longer to reconstruct the list of letters. However, by

Guided Practice

Provide the class with a selection of contextual memory stimuli. These might be photographs of a school or class event or recordings of popular music. Have students suggest the memories each stimulus triggers for them. Then encourage groups of students to compare and contrast their memories with the memories of other people who do not share their context. For example, students might take the various stimuli to classrooms of students at a lower grade level and test the responses of younger students.

Independent Practice

Point out that some context-dependent memories are very personal. They may relate to special places or moments in students' lives. Suggest that students write a short personal narrative about revisiting a person, place, or experience. Narratives should describe the context and the memories it triggered.

using the 1–10 device, you have a much better chance of remembering the letters—and of remembering them for a longer time.

Before reading on, take this very brief spelling quiz: Which of the following words is spelled correctly—*retrieval* or *retreival*? Because you know how the word is pronounced, regardless of how it is spelled, saying the word to yourself (using an acoustic code) will not help you remember the correct spelling, which is retri*e*val. How might you go about remembering the correct spelling? Repeating it over and over (maintenance rehearsal) is certainly one way, and that method might work. However, a much better way would be to remember a spelling rule, such as "*i* before *e* except after *c*," as a semantic code. That rule enables you to reconstruct the correct spelling without having to memorize the order of the letters.

Context-Dependent Memory   Have you ever been to a place that brought back old memories? Perhaps you went back to your elementary school or to a neighborhood where you once lived. The memories that came back to you in that place are called **context-dependent memories**. The context of a memory is the situation in which a person first had the experience being remembered. Such memories are dependent on the place where they were encoded and stored. If you had not returned to the place where your memories were encoded, you probably would not have retrieved them.

A fascinating experiment in context-dependent memory involved some students who belonged to a swimming club. They were asked to memorize lists of words while they were in the water of a pool (Godden & Baddeley, 1975). Other students in the club tried to memorize the lists while they were out of the water. Later, the students who had studied the lists in the water did a better job of remembering them when they were in the water again. Students who had worked on the lists out of the water, on the other hand, remembered more words when they were dry. These findings suggest that the ability to retrieve memories is greater when people are in the place or situation in which they stored the memories to begin with.

Another study of context-dependent memory indicated that students do better on tests when they study for a test in the room where the test will be given (Isarida & Isarida, 1999). If possible, try to do some studying for your tests in the classrooms where you will take the tests. Of course, you should study in a variety of other settings as well to

Context-dependent memories are dependent on the place where they were encoded and stored. This teenager may be remembering childhood friends and the games they played here years ago.

improve your recollection of the material after the tests are over.

When police and lawyers ask witnesses to describe a crime, they ask the witnesses to describe the scene as clearly as possible. By doing this, witnesses are better able to recall details that they might otherwise have forgotten. Police sometimes take witnesses to the scene of the crime in the hope that such visits will improve their memories of what they witnessed.

At Hannah's party, Linda heard the song that brought back memories of being in the seventh grade. Seventh grade was when she heard the song (probably many times), encoded it, and stored it in her memory. Hearing the song again brought back context-dependent memories connected to that earlier period in her life. As Linda put it, "Hearing it almost makes me feel 13 again." In fact, one reason some people like to hear familiar music is that it brings back old and happy memories.

State-Dependent Memory   Not only do people tend to retrieve memories better when they are in the same place they were in when they first stored the memories, but people also retrieve memories

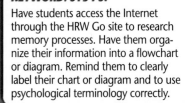
159

Closing Section 2

Summarizing Information

Write the words *Encoding, Storage,* and *Retrieval* on the chalkboard. Ask students to write a short summary of each memory process, explaining its significance to the workings of human memory. Have volunteers read their summaries aloud to the class.

Reviewing Section 2

Have students complete the Section Review questions on page 160.

Section 2 Review: Answers

1. The three processes of memory are encoding, storage, and retrieval.

2. Maintenance rehearsal is a form of memorization that involves repeating information so as not to forget it. Elaborative rehearsal is the relating of new information to information one already knows in order to improve recall of the new information.

3. Memories are organized into mental "files." They are collected into groups that allow us to keep track of the information we have stored.

4. Students should relate a tip-of-the-tongue experience and the steps they took to retrieve the memory.

Essay and Research Themes for A. P. Students

3

Section Objective

▶ Identify the three stages of memory, and explain how they are related to each other.

This objective is assessed in the Section Review on page 166 and in the Chapter 7 Review.

---

better when they are in the same emotional state they were in when they first stored the memories. Memories that are retrieved because the mood in which they were originally encoded is re-created are called **state-dependent memories**. For example, feelings of happiness tend to bring back memories from other times when we were happy, while feelings of sadness can trigger memories from other times when we were sad.

To demonstrate this phenomenon, Gordon Bower (1981) conducted experiments in which study participants were instructed, while in a hypnotic trance, to experience happy or sad moods. Then, while still in the trance, the participants tried to memorize a list of words. People who had studied the list while in a happy mood were better able to recall it when they were put into a happy state again. People who had studied the list while in a sad mood showed better recall when placed back in a sad mood. Bower's explanation of these results is that moods influence memories.

Not only is memory better when people are in the same moods as when the memories were acquired, it is also better when people are in the same states of consciousness. Drugs, for example, alter a person's state of consciousness and thus result in state-dependent memories. (See Chapter 5.) Things that happen to somebody while under the influence of a drug may be remembered most accurately when the person is again under the influence of that drug (Atkinson et al., 1996).

On the Tip of the Tongue At Hannah's party, when Linda said she used to think Ashley Austin wrote the song just for her, Todd knew it was not an Ashley Austin song. However, when he then went on to say who did write it, he could not think of the artist's name. "It's on the tip of my tongue," he said.

As in Todd's experience, memories can sometimes be difficult to retrieve. Either they are not very well organized, or they are incomplete. Trying to retrieve such memories can be highly frustrating. Sometimes we come so close to retrieving information that it seems as though the information is on the "tip of the tongue." Psychologists call this the **tip-of-the-tongue phenomenon**. It is sometimes also referred to as the "feeling-of-knowing experience." You feel you know something. In fact, you are sure you know it. However, you just cannot seem to verbalize it. It is on the tip of your tongue, but that is as far as it goes.

Because the files in our memory have labels, so to speak, that include both the sounds and the meanings of words, we often try to retrieve memories that are on the tip of the tongue by using either acoustic or semantic cues. Sometimes we try to summon up words that are similar in sound or meaning to a word that is on the tip of the tongue. We might make a remark like Todd's: "I can't think of her name. It starts with an M. Mary? Maria? Something like that."

SECTION 2 REVIEW

1. List the three processes of memory.

2. What is the difference between maintenance rehearsal and elaborative rehearsal?

3. How are memories organized?

4. **Critical Thinking** *Analyzing Information* When was the last time you had a tip-of-the-tongue experience? Explain what you did to try to retrieve the memory.

SECTION 3

Three Stages of Memory

We do not store in our memory everything we experience. The world provides us with a rich display of colors, sounds, tastes, and other sources of stimulation, but we can only take in and remember so much. How much of what our senses experience will we encode and remember? That depends on what happens to the information as it flows through each of the three stages of our memory. The three stages of memory are sensory memory, short-term memory (STM), and long-term memory (LTM).

Sensory Memory

Sensory memory is the first stage of memory. It consists of the immediate, initial recording of information that enters through our senses. If we were to see a row of letters or numbers flash briefly on a screen, the memory trace—or impression made on our senses by the image—would last for only a fraction of a second. A memory trace of a visual stimulus held in our sensory memory decays within a second. So if we want to remember it, we have to do something with the information very quickly.

Opening Section 3

Motivator

Have one or more students shine a flashlight against a darkened wall. Ask students who are watching to describe what they see. Then direct the flashlight holder(s) to move the circle of light, first slowly and then more quickly. Again, ask those observing to describe what they see. Help the class understand that their sensory memory vanishes as quickly as the moving light and, like the light, it leaves no visible trace. Explain that Section 3 will help students understand the relationship between this first stage of memory and two longer-term stages of memory.

Teaching Section 3

Evaluating Ideas

Tell students to think about all the sights, sounds, and smells they encounter as they walk to class on a typical morning. Ask them to consider how their lives would be different if these thousands of stimuli were automatically recorded in their memory in vivid detail. Would this be a help or a hindrance to normal, everyday functioning? Why? Then have students evaluate the idea that sensory memory serves as a filter for stimuli that would otherwise overwhelm our senses.

Psychologists believe that all of our senses have sensory registers. The mental pictures we form of visual stimuli are called *icons*. Icons are held in a sensory register called **iconic memory**. Iconic memories are like snapshots. They are accurate, photographic memories. However, these iconic memories are extremely brief—just a fraction of a second. The ability to remember visual stimuli over long periods of time (what most of us think of as photographic memory) is called **eidetic imagery**.

About 5 percent of children have eidetic imagery. They can look at a photograph and remember it in remarkable detail several minutes later. It is as if they were still looking at it (Haber, 1980). This keen ability usually declines with age, however. By adolescence it is nearly gone.

TRUTH OR fiction ■ REVISITED ■

It is true that people with photographic memory are rare. All of us have split-second iconic memories that register in our visual sensory register when we see something. However, what most people usually think of as photographic memory is rare. Some children have the ability to remember what they see in remarkable detail, but that ability usually fades as they become older.

Mental traces of sounds, called *echoes*, are held in a sensory register called **echoic memory**. While icons (memory traces of visual stimuli) are held only for a fraction of a second, echoes can last for several seconds. For this reason, acoustic codes are easier to remember than visual codes. That is, it is easier to remember a spoken list of letters than to try to remember a mental picture of the letters. Saying things to yourself or out loud makes them easier to remember.

Short-Term Memory

If you pay attention to iconic and echoic memories held ever so briefly in a sensory register, you can transfer that information into your **short-term memory**. The information will remain there after the sensory memory trace has faded away. Short-term memory is also called working memory.

A DAY IN THE LIFE At Hannah's party, Dan tried to use his short-term memory to help himself remember the phone number of the girl he had met. After she gave him her number, he converted that echoic memory, which lingered in his sensory register for a few seconds, into his short-term memory. He hoped to keep it there until he could find a piece of paper and write it down.

We use our short-term memory a great deal of the time. Whenever you are thinking about something, it is in your short-term memory. When you are trying to solve a math problem, the elements of the problem are in your short-term, or working, memory. When you meet someone new, you put the person's name in your short-term memory, perhaps by using the name or by repeating it to yourself several times. Similarly, when a teacher assigns homework or changes the date on which a paper is due, you place that information in your short-term memory until you can write it down or store it in long-term memory.

When you are told a new phone number, you can keep it in short-term memory by repeating it over and over. Repeating the number will give you time to look for a pencil and paper. The more times you rehearse a piece of information, the more likely you are to remember it. If you rehearse information often enough, as actors do when they learn lines, you will probably remember it for a long time.

When you look up a number in the phone book and then walk across the room to reach the phone, you try to keep the number in your short-term memory long enough to dial it. You may repeat or rehearse the number on your way across the room

After people look up a phone number, they keep it in short-term memory until it has been dialed.

Cultural Dimensions

Stress to students that actual examples of eidetic imagery are relatively rare. However, in some cultures, specific and extensive memory has proved necessary to survival. For example, in some Eastern European communities, Jews were historically forbidden to practice their religion. Rather than keep religious texts such as the Talmud, Jewish scholars preserved its words entirely by memory. Some modern Talmudic scholars can recall the 20 volumes of the Talmud word for word.

Class Discussion

Tell students to multiply 26 by 8 in their heads. Call on volunteers to supply the answer (208) and to describe the mental steps they used to find the answer. Ask students which stage of memory they used to solve the problem. (short-term memory) Then have students discuss why short-term memory is also called working memory.

Guided Practice

Create a series of 8 random numerical strings. Begin with a string of 4 numbers, increasing each string by 1 number. Present the first string of numbers to students, directing them to remember the numbers in exact order. As students recite the numbers, have them note their correct and incorrect answers. Then discuss with students how to chunk information. Repeat numerical strings 4 through 8 (7 through 11 numbers); this time, instruct students to chunk the numbers. Were students able to improve their accuracy?

Independent Practice

Organize students into pairs. Give each pair of students a copy of the following letter string: XTNTSROTBACEOOKFYI. After a few minutes, one person in each pair should prompt the other to write down as many of the letters as possible. Have students repeat the exercise, first chunking the information into recognizable letter combinations as they memorize it. Partners can retest each other's memory, comparing and contrasting the two trials. *(Chunked letters might read as X TNT SRO TBA CEO OK FYI.)*

to improve your chances of keeping it in your short-term memory. If the number you dial is busy, you can dial it again a few minutes later if you have been able to keep it in your short-term memory. Otherwise, you will have to look it up again.

Information in short-term memory begins to fade rapidly after several seconds. If you want to remember it longer, you need to keep rehearsing the information or take other steps to prevent it from fading. People can sometimes keep visual images in short-term memory. But it is usually better to encode information as sounds so that you can rehearse or repeat the sounds.

At the party, Dan probably would have remembered the phone number of the girl he had just met if he had been able to repeat it until he could write it down. Instead, unable to contain his excitement about meeting her, he stopped to share the good news with his friends. That was Dan's mistake. Talking to Linda and Todd prevented him from rehearsing the number enough times to keep it in his short-term memory.

The Primacy and Recency Effects   When we try to remember a series of letters or numbers, our memories of the first and last items tend to be sharper than our memories of the middle items of the list. The tendency to recall the initial items in a series of items is called the **primacy effect**. (The root *prim-* means "first.") Perhaps we remember the first few items of a series better because, due to their placement early in the list, we have more time to rehearse them than we do for later items. Also, we may remember first items better because our minds are fresher when we first see or hear them.

The tendency to recall the last items in a series is called the **recency effect**. Since the last items in a series are likely to have been perceived and rehearsed most recently, they tend to be fresher in our memory and therefore probably more easily remembered than items in the middle of a series.

Chunking   When we try to keep something in our short-term memory by rehearsing it, it is usually better to organize the information into manageable units that are easy to remember. **Chunking** is the organization of items into familiar or manageable units. Return for a moment to **OTTFFSSENT**. If you tried to remember it letter by letter, there were 10 distinct pieces, or chunks, of information to retain in your short-term memory. When you tried to repeat the list as consisting of 10 meaningless

chunks, you probably had a difficult time. It is not easy to repeat 10 meaningless letters, let alone remember them.

If you tried to encode **OTTFFSSENT** as "other flowers sent" you reduced the number of chunks you needed to remember from 10 to 3. (Of course, you also needed to remember the variations in spelling.) Psychologist George Miller (1956) found that the average person can hold a list of seven items in short-term memory. This, conveniently, is the number of digits in local telephone numbers. Nearly everyone can remember a ZIP code, which is five numbers long. Some people can remember a list of nine items, but very few people can remember more than nine.

Businesses try to obtain telephone numbers with as many zeros or repeated digits as possible because they are easier to remember. For example, 222-2000 is easier for customers to remember than 792-6873. Numbers with zeros and repeated digits contain fewer chunks of information. Alternatively, a business may try to get a telephone number that can be spelled out as a word or phrase (because most digits on the telephone are associated with a set of letters). Thus, people need only remember the word or phrase, not the seven numbers. For instance, a clinic that helped people quit smoking was able to get a telephone number that spelled out the phrase NO SMOKE. This phrase worked well as a semantic code.

How do people remember long-distance telephone numbers? With area codes included, such phone numbers are 10 digits long. Actually, most people do not try to remember the numbers as a series of 10 separate items. They try to remember the area code as a single, separate chunk of information. They become familiar with the area codes of surrounding areas and places where their long-distance friends and relatives live. When they know where someone lives, they sometimes already know and remember the area code.

If you had known that **OTTFFSSENT** stood for the first letters of the numbers 1 through 10, you could have reduced the number of chunks of information you needed to hold in short-term memory from 10 down to 1. That one chunk would have been a single rule: make a list of letters in which each letter is the first letter of the numbers 1 through 10. Of course, your ability to remember the 10 letters rested on the fact that you already knew the numbers 1 through 10 (and how to spell them). But most likely, you learned this information by heart when you were much younger.

Demonstration

As a class, complete the experiment designed by Lloyd and Margaret Peterson to demonstrate the impact of interference on short-term memory. Ask students to memorize a three-letter combination such as WTH. Then have students begin counting backward (silently or quietly) by 3s from 157. Wait about five seconds. Then prompt students to recall the three-letter combination. Note how many can recall it accurately. Have students resume their backward counting. Wait another 20 seconds and test their recall again. Observe and discuss the results.

Meeting Individual Needs: Learners with Limited English Proficiency

Students with limited English proficiency may have difficulty with the vocabulary in the text. Tell students to use the following steps to learn the meanings of unfamiliar words: (1) Carefully read the sentence or paragraph surrounding the word for clues to meaning. (2) Study the word for a familiar base word. Then define the prefixes and suffixes to build a complete meaning. (3) Find dictionary definitions and note these for ongoing reference.

Three Stages of Memory

Rehearsal

Sensory input

Sensory registers

Attention

Rehearsal

Storage

Retrieval

Sensory Memory   **Short-Term Memory**   **Long-Term Memory**

FIGURE 7.2 *Psychologists have identified three stages of memory. Outside stimuli first enter sensory memory. Here most stimuli are soon forgotten. Certain pieces of information—those to which attention is paid—enter short-term memory, where they remain if they are rehearsed. Information that is not rehearsed is forgotten. Information needed for future use is stored in long-term memory, where it can be retrieved when necessary.*

Interference   Short-term memory is like a shelf that holds only so much. Once a shelf is full, you cannot put something on it without shoving something else off. Only a limited amount of information at a time can be retained in short-term memory. **Interference** occurs when new information appears in short-term memory and takes the place of what is already there.

A classic experiment by Lloyd and Margaret Peterson (1959) showed how new information can cause problems with what is stored in short-term memory. The Petersons asked college students to remember three-letter combinations, such as ZBT. Because most students can remember seven chunks of information, this task was fairly easy. Nearly 100 percent of the students could recall the three-letter sequences when asked to repeat them immediately. But then the Petersons asked the students to count backward from a number such as 142 by threes (142, 139, 136, 133, and so forth). After a certain amount of time passed, the students were then asked to stop counting backward and to report the letters they had been asked to remember. After only three seconds of this interference, the percentage of students who could recall their letters dropped by about half. After 18 seconds had elapsed, practically nobody could recall the letters. The numbers that entered the students' short-term memory while they were counting backward had displaced the letters in nearly all cases.

A DAY IN THE LIFE   Interference was what happened to Dan at Hannah's party. His conversation with Linda and Todd, especially when Todd asked him the time, interfered with his short-term memory of the phone number. When Dan looked at his watch and told Todd it was 9:37, it was as if the new numbers bumped the old numbers off the shelf of his short-term memory.

Short-term memory is very useful, but it is only a temporary solution to the problem of remembering information. It allows us just enough time to find a way to store the information more permanently. Short-term memory is the bridge between sensory memory and long-term memory.

Long-Term Memory

Long-term memory is the third, and final, stage of memory of information. (Figure 7.2 shows all three stages of memory.) If you want to remember something more than just briefly, you have to take certain steps to store it in your long-term memory. Mechanical repetition (maintenance rehearsal) is one way of transferring information from short-term memory to long-term memory. Relating new

Using Visuals

Direct students' attention to Figure 7.2. Point out that the path of memories is somewhat like a road map or a maze. If you take a wrong turn, you may end up at a dead end. For memory information, that dead end means forgetting.

Cross-Curricular Link: Science and Technology

In ancient times, memory skills were critical to education, religion, law, and the arts. These subjects were preserved mainly through word of mouth, and people with good memories had special status. Today, technology often replaces the need for human memory. Information is stored in printed material and on computers, videodiscs, and so on. Household appliances such as telephones, television sets, and coffeemakers have a sort of built-in memory. You no longer have to remember your friends' telephone numbers because some telephones do it for you. Have students suggest other examples of memory-saving technology. Then ask them to consider how such technology may affect people's memory skills over several generations.

Cooperative Learning

Organize students into pairs. Ask the partners to prompt each other's memory. One partner can start with an everyday topic such as the school cafeteria menu. The other student should recall as much as possible about that topic. As the partners continue to trigger each other's memory, have them also measure each other's memory capacity (the number of memories recalled for a given topic). Ask students whether they remembered more about topics that interested them than about those that did not.

Meeting Individual Needs: Learners Having Difficulty

The "three threes" of memory (three kinds, three processes, three stages) may be confusing to some students. To help these students differentiate among the various concepts, have them make a series of flash cards about memory. Students should write a term or concept on one side of an index card and write a definition or description on the other side. After students have finished making their flash cards, they can take turns testing each other on the material.

Journal Activity

Discuss with students the idea that we reconstruct our memories through our own personal viewpoints. Tell students to explore this idea further by writing a journal entry about an experience shared with a friend or family member. Then have them interview that person and record his or her memory of the same experience. How do the memories differ, both in the record of events and in the emotional mark left behind?

Cross-Curricular Link: Biology

Tell students that human memory involves several parts of the brain. The frontal lobes, located in the cerebral cortex, help humans conceive and plan actions. The thalamus receives all incoming information from the senses (except for the sense of smell, which is received by the olfactory nerve in the nose) and encodes it into memory language. Without the thalamus, new information cannot be understood and stored. Information then is passed through the limbic system, where the hippocampus helps us recall spatial relationships and the amygdala helps us access memories created by the senses (including smell) and links memories and emotions.

164

information to information that you already know (elaborative rehearsal) is another.

New information is constantly being transferred into your long-term memory. Your long-term memory already contains far more information than an encyclopedia or a computer's hard drive. It holds names, dates, places, the memory of how you kidded around with the student in front of you in second grade, and the expression on your mother's face when you gave her the picture you drew of her in fourth grade. Your long-term memory contains more words, pictures, sounds, smells, tastes, and touches than you could count.

When Linda heard the song at the party, it brought back images and feelings stored in her long-term memory. The song reminded her of being back in the seventh grade. Had she been asked to reminisce about what she remembered, she probably could have talked for a long time about many of the feelings and experiences she had when she was 13, with all their rich sights, sounds, smells, and even tastes.

Capacity of Memory Our long-term memory holds the equivalent of vast numbers of videos and films of our lifetime of experience. All of them are in color (as long as we can perceive color). They also come with stereo sound (as long as we can hear), with smells, tastes, and touches thrown in. This light and sound show will never fit on any stage. But all of it is contained comfortably within our long-term memory. And there is room for more, much more. How much more? Psychologists have yet to discover a limit to how much can be stored in a person's long-term memory.

It is true that there is no known limit to how much information a person can remember. There seems to be no restriction on the capacity of long-term memory.

■ R E V I S I T E D ■

Although there is apparently no limit to how much we can remember, we do not store all of our experiences permanently. Not everything that reaches our short-term memory is transferred to our long-term memory. Our memory is limited by the amount of attention we pay to things. We are more likely to remember the things that capture our attention. If we are distracted or uninvolved with what is occurring around us, we are not going to remember as much as we will if we are interested and paying attention. The memories we have stored in our long-term memory are the incidents and experiences that have had the greatest impact on us.

Memory as Reconstructive Some psychologists once thought that nearly all the perceptions and ideas people had were stored permanently in their memory. Supporters of this view often pointed to the work of Wilder Penfield (1969), a brain surgeon. Many of Penfield's patients reported that they had experienced images that felt like memories when parts of their brain were stimulated electrically during surgery. From this information, some observers inferred that experiences become a physical part of the brain and that proper stimulation can cause people to remember them.

Today psychologists recognize that electrical stimulation of the brain does not bring about the accurate replay of memories. Memory expert Elizabeth Loftus, for example, notes that the memories stimulated by Penfield's instruments had little in the way of detail and were often factually incorrect (Loftus, 1983; Loftus & Loftus, 1980).

We now know that memories are not recorded and played back like videos or movies. Rather, they are reconstructed from the bits and pieces of our experience. When we reconstruct our memories, we tend to shape them according to the personal and individual ways in which we view the world. Thus, we tend to remember things in accordance with our beliefs and needs. That is, we put our own personal stamp on our memories. This is one of the reasons brothers and sisters can have differing memories of the same family events. Each sibling has interpreted the information differently.

Schemas The mental representations that we form of the world by organizing bits of information into knowledge are called **schemas**. To understand better what is meant by a schema, take out the sheet of paper on which you wrote the names of the objects you saw in Figure 7.1. Without looking back at Figure 7.1, draw the items on your sheet of paper. Try to make your drawings as similar to the originals as you can. (But again, no peeking!)

Now turn to Figure 7.3 on page 166. Are your drawings more similar to those in Group 1 or those in Group 2? Because of the labels you had already written on the sheet of paper, your drawings probably look more like the ones in Group 1. The labels

For Further Research

Challenge students to learn more about the legal safeguards already in place to allow for the imperfections of human memory. For example, what cautions can judges give to juries about eyewitness testimony? Can a defendant be convicted on the testimony of one eyewitness? How do U.S. laws on this subject compare with those of other countries? Students may report their findings either orally or in a brief written report.

To demonstrate the topic of eyewitness testimony, have students recruit a volunteer audience from outside the class. Ask your students to stage a "crime," complete with props and costumes. Then experiment with the different lineups described on page 165. Students might also role-play a mock courtroom scene in which audience volunteers are questioned about what they have witnessed. Instruct student "lawyers" to slant some of their questions, and have students analyze the varying witness responses.

PSYCHOLOGY

IN THE WORLD TODAY

Can We Trust Eyewitness Testimony?

Jean Piaget, the renowned child psychologist, described an attempt to kidnap him from his baby carriage along the Champs-Élysées in Paris. He portrayed the excited people, the scrapes on the face of the nurse who rescued him, the police officer's baton, and the escape of the kidnapper. Although Piaget's memories were clear, they were false. Years later, the nurse admitted that she had made up the tale.

Can eyewitness testimony be trusted? Is the testimony of eyewitnesses any more factual than that of Piaget? Legal professionals are concerned about the accuracy of our memories as reflected in eyewitness testimony (Wells et al., 2000). Misidentification of suspects "creates a double horror: The wrong person is devastated by this personal tragedy, and the real criminal is still out on the streets" (Loftus, 1993, p. 550).

One problem with eyewitness testimony is that the words chosen by a lawyer interviewing a witness can influence the reconstruction of memories (Wells et al., 2000). For example, as in the experiment described on page 166, a lawyer might ask the witness, "How fast was the car going when it *smashed* into the other car?" In such a case, the car might be reported as going faster than if the question had been: "How fast was the car going when the accident occurred?" (Loftus & Palmer, 1974). Could the use of the word *smashed* bias the witness? What about jurors who heard the word *smashed*? Would they assume that the driver had been reckless?

Children tend to be more suggestible witnesses than adults, and preschoolers are more suggestible than older children (Ceci & Bruck, 1993). But when questioned carefully, even young children may be able to provide accurate and useful testimony (Ceci & Bruck, 1993).

There are cases in which the memories of eyewitnesses have been "refreshed" by hypnosis. But hypnosis does more than enhance memories; it can

Even when witnesses believe they are telling the truth, their memories may be inaccurate.

also distort them (Loftus, 1994). Witnesses may accept suggestions made by the hypnotist as their own memories. Witnesses may report false memories obtained through hypnosis as forcefully as if they were real (Loftus, 1994).

There are also problems in the identification of criminals by eyewitnesses. Witnesses may pay more attention to the suspect's clothing than to more important characteristics such as facial features, height, and weight. In one experiment, viewers of a videotaped crime incorrectly identified a man as the criminal because he wore the eyeglasses and T-shirt that had been worn by the actual criminal on the tape (Sanders, 1984).

Other problems with eyewitness testimony include the following:

- Identification of suspects is less accurate when suspects belong to ethnic or racial groups that differ from that of the witness (Egeth, 1993).
- Identification of suspects is confused when interrogators make misleading suggestions (Loftus, 1997).
- Witnesses are seen as more believable when they claim to be certain in their testimony, but there is little evidence that such claims are accurate (Wells et al., 2000).

There are thus many problems with eyewitness testimony. Yet even Elizabeth Loftus (1993), who has extensively studied the accuracy of eyewitness testimony, agrees that it is a valuable tool in the courtroom. After all, identifications made by eyewitnesses are frequently correct, and what, Loftus asks, is the alternative? If we were to prevent eyewitnesses from testifying, how many criminals would go free?

Think About It

Drawing Inferences and Conclusions How do you think eyewitness testimony could be made more reliable?

Cross-Curricular Link: Literature

Have students work with a librarian to locate mystery novels containing eyewitness testimony. Some possibilities are the works of P. D. James, Edna Buchanan, and Jonathan Ross. Ask students to take turns reading sections aloud. Then have the class discuss if and how the literature reflects the factual information presented on page 165.

Think About It: Answer

Students may support suggestions already made in the feature. For example, eyewitness testimony is more reliable when it is confirmed by other witnesses, and testimony tends to be more accurate when witnesses can describe what happened in their own words rather than being influenced by their questioners. Students may also offer ideas of their own.

Readings and Case Studies

Closing Section 3

Interpreting Information

Have students fill out index cards for each of the three memory stages. Ask them to write a short paragraph summarizing each concept. Then prompt students to list two to three personal experiences that exemplify each of the three stages of memory.

Reviewing Section 3

Have students complete the Section Review questions on page 166.

Extension

To demonstrate the idea that people construct memories that "fit" the facts or stimuli at hand, have students try the following experiment with several family members or friends. Tell students to ask their participants to remember this list of words: *bed, night, snore, wake, dream, comfort, snooze, tired, slumber, nap, rest.* Students should record the number of participants who remembered the entire list. They should then note how many participants included the word sleep in their lists. Point out that most people include this word in their memory because it "fits" with the others.

Section 3 Review: Answers

1. Sensory memory is the immediate recording of information we get from our senses; short-term memory is the bridge between sensory memory and long-term memory; long-term memory contains a vast amount of information that we want or need to remember for a longer period of time.

2. Sensory registers record information from the senses and briefly hold it as memory traces in the sensory memory. If memory traces are given attention, they are transferred to short-term memory. Through maintenance rehearsal or elaborative rehearsal, information is stored more permanently in long-term memory.

3. A possible answer might be meeting someone for the first time after having been told something about that person, and then having certain expectations about him or her.

served as schemas for the drawing—they helped you mentally represent the objects. When you drew the items, you did not draw them exactly from memory. Rather, you drew them to fit the schemas. Therefore, you did not recall them exactly. You reconstructed them from your ideas about what eyeglasses and hourglasses look like. People who have been told that the initial drawings are of a dumbbell and a table, on the other hand, reconstruct drawings more similar to those in Group 2 (Carmichael et al., 1932).

Elizabeth Loftus and J. C. Palmer (1974) conducted a classic experiment on the role of schemas in memory. They showed people a film of a car crash. Then they asked them to complete questionnaires about the film. One question asked for an estimate of how fast the cars were going when they collided. However, the phrasing of the question differed for different participants. Some participants were asked how fast the cars were going when they "hit" each other. Other participants were asked how fast the cars were going when they "smashed" into each other.

The participants who had been asked how fast the cars were going when they "hit" each other estimated an average speed of 34 miles per hour. Those who had seen the word "smashed," on the other hand, estimated an average speed of 41 miles per hour. In other words, which schema people used—"hit" or "smashed"—influenced how they mentally reconstructed the crash.

The participants were questioned again a week later. They were asked if they had seen any broken glass. There was no broken glass in the film; thus, a yes answer was incorrect. Of participants who had been told that the cars had hit each other, 14 percent incorrectly said yes, there was broken glass. However, 32 percent of those who had been told that the cars had smashed into each other—more than twice the percentage of the other group—incorrectly reported seeing broken glass. Schemas influence both the ways we perceive things and the ways our memories store what we perceive.

SECTION 3 REVIEW

1. What are the three stages of memory?

2. How does information move through each of the three stages of memory?

3. **Critical Thinking** *Analyzing Information* Give an example of a situation in which a schema might distort a person's memory.

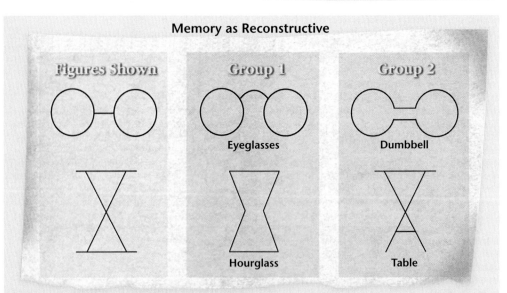

FIGURE 7.3 *Are your drawings more like those in Group 1 or those in Group 2? Although you may not have recalled the drawings exactly, you reconstructed them from a schema, or mental representation. Your drawings were probably more like those in Group 1 because of the labels you copied from Figure 7.1.*

Section Objective

▶ Describe the ways memory can be improved.

This objective is assessed in the Section Review on page 173 and in the Chapter 7 Review.

Opening Section 4

Motivator

Ask students to note, for a one-week period, every time they realize they have forgotten something, such as a homework assignment, an important telephone call, or their gym clothes. At the end of the week, ask for volunteers to share their lists. Emphasize that we all forget information every day. In fact, forgetting is an important part of memory. We need to forget information for various reasons. Still, we can learn to remember the facts and experiences we most want and need to retain. Encourage students to read Section 4 with this goal in mind.

SECTION 4

Forgetting and Memory Improvement

Forgetting is the flip side of memory. Forgetting may seem simple enough. If you do not think about something, you forget it, right? Not really. It is not that simple.

Forgetting can occur at any one of the three stages of memory—sensory, short-term, or long-term memory. Information encoded in sensory memory decays almost immediately unless you pay attention to it and transfer it into short-term memory. A memory trace in a visual sensory register decays in less than a second, and a sound recorded in echoic memory lasts no more than a few seconds.

Information in short-term memory does not last much longer. It will disappear after 10 or 12 seconds unless you find a way to transfer it into your long-term memory. As Dan found out at the party, information stored in short-term memory is lost when it is displaced, or crowded out, by new information.

Information in long-term memory also can be lost. Because long-term memory holds such vast amounts of material and the material is represented in an abstract form, forgetting and other memory errors (such as recalling information incorrectly) occur. Sometimes new information becomes mixed with material you already know. Old learning can interfere with new learning. For example, if you study a new foreign language, your knowledge of a language you already know or are studying at the same time can interfere with your new learning. This is more likely to happen if the languages are somewhat similar.

Consider the example of French, Spanish, and Italian. All three are closely related to each other because they are all based on Latin, the language of the ancient Romans. French, Spanish, Italian, and Latin have similar roots and spellings. Anyone who has ever tried to learn two or more of these languages, especially at the same time, knows how easy it is to confuse them.

Basic Memory Tasks

Do you know what DAL, RIK, and KAX are? They are nonsense syllables, or meaningless sets of two

In long-term memory, old learning can interfere with new learning. If you try to learn more than one foreign language at a time, especially similar ones such as the Romance languages, you might become confused.

consonants with a vowel in the middle. Nonsense syllables provide psychologists with a way to measure three basic memory tasks: recognition, recall, and relearning.

The first researcher to use nonsense syllables to study memory and forgetting was German psychologist Hermann Ebbinghaus (1850–1909). Today his experiments are regarded as the first scientific study of forgetting, and psychologists continue to use nonsense syllables in their studies. Because nonsense syllables are meaningless, remembering them depends on acoustic coding (saying them out loud or in one's mind) and mechanical repetition (maintenance rehearsal). These tasks play a part in recognition, recall, and relearning.

Recognition   One of the three basic memory tasks is **recognition**, which involves identifying objects or events that have been encountered before. It is the easiest of the memory tasks. That is why multiple-choice tests are often considered easier than other tests. In a multiple-choice test, you need only recognize the right answer. You do not have to come up with the answer on your own.

In some experiments on recognition, psychologists ask people to read a list of nonsense syllables. The participants then read a second list of nonsense syllables and are asked whether they recognize any syllables in the second list as having appeared in the first list. In this instance, forgetting is defined as failure to recognize a nonsense syllable that had been read before.

Teaching Section 4

Cooperative Learning

Organize the class into two groups. Have the members of one group recall the names of the seven dwarfs (from *Snow White and the Seven Dwarfs*). Give the second group the following list: Grouchy, Gabby, Fearful, Sleepy, Pop, Smiley, Jumpy, Hopeful, Shy, Droopy, Dopey, Wishful, Puffy, Dumpy, Sneezy, Lazy, Wheezy, Doc, Grumpy, Bashful, Cheerful, Shorty, Happy, and Stubborn. Ask the members of this group to identify the names of the seven dwarfs. Students may find that it was easier to recognize the names from a list than to recall the names with no prompting.

Applying Information

To help the class understand the value of paired associates to the recall of information, pair students who speak a second language with those who do not. Challenge the pairs to construct meaningful links between words in the two languages. If your class lacks sufficient second-language speakers, create solely English-speaking pairs. Give them a list of words and definitions from another language such as Spanish or French. Have volunteers discuss their paired associates with the class and explain how the linkages between the words help them recall the second language.

Class Discussion

Review with students the 1975 study by Bahrick and his colleagues. Then have students discuss why it is easier to remember people's faces than it is to remember their names. (*Remembering a face is a task of recognition, whereas attaching a name to that face involves the more complex task of recall.*)

Using Visuals

Tell students to try Ebbinghaus's recall experiment and then add their own results to the chart shown in Figure 7.4.

internet connect

TOPIC: Memory Enhancement
GO TO: go.hrw.com
KEYWORD: SY3 PS7

Have students access the Internet through the HRW Go site to research the stages and methods of memory improvement. Then ask them to design a method of improvement based on their research, and then test it on groups of students to measure the effects of their method on memory enhancement.

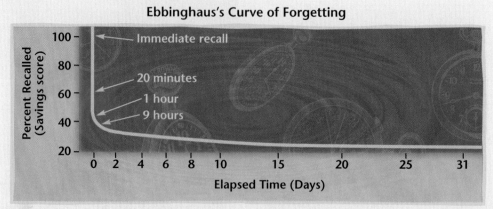

Ebbinghaus's Curve of Forgetting

Percent Recalled (Savings score) vs *Elapsed Time (Days)*

Immediate recall — 20 minutes — 1 hour — 9 hours

FIGURE 7.4 *Ebbinghaus found that people's ability to recall lists of words dropped sharply during the first hour after learning. After the first hour, however, losses then became more gradual.*

A classic study by Harry Bahrick and his colleagues (1975) examined recognition using a different technique. Bahrick took pictures from the yearbooks of high school graduates and mixed them in with four times as many photos of strangers. Recent graduates correctly picked out their former classmates 90 percent of the time. Graduates who had been out of school for 40 years recognized their former schoolmates less often, but not by too much—they recognized them 75 percent of the time. Keep in mind that only one photo in five was actually of a former schoolmate. Thus, if the graduates had been guessing, they would have picked out former schoolmates only 20 percent of the time. The participants recognized the photos of their former classmates far more easily than they recalled their classmates' names. The study showed that the ability of people to recognize familiar faces remains strong and lasting.

Recall The second memory task is recall. To **recall** something means to bring it back to mind. In recall, you do not simply recognize whether you have come across something before. Rather, you try to reconstruct it in your mind.

Hermann Ebbinghaus sometimes studied his own recall ability. For example, he would read a list of nonsense syllables aloud to himself while a metronome (an instrument that marks exact time) was ticking. He would then see how many nonsense syllables he could recall from memory. After reading through his list one time, Ebbinghaus could typically recall seven nonsense syllables. As noted earlier, this is the number of items most people can keep in short-term memory.

If a person memorizes a list of nonsense syllables or words and is asked to repeat the list immediately, there is generally no memory loss. But the ability to recall the list drops dramatically within an hour after learning it. In fact, about half of the nonsense syllables or words on the list are forgotten within the first hour. After that first hour, memory loss becomes more gradual. For instance, the amount of material a person remembers is cut in half again in about a month. The person continues to forget as time goes on, but the rate of forgetting slows down considerably. (See Figure 7.4.)

Psychologists also use paired associates to measure recall. Paired associates are lists of nonsense syllables, as shown in Figure 7.5. In this method, people read a list pair by pair. Later they are given the first member in each pair and are asked to recall the other one. That is, the people try to retrieve one syllable with the other serving as the cue.

Learning the vocabulary of a foreign language is something like learning paired associates. For example, a student studying Spanish might try to remember a Spanish word by pairing it with an English word that has a similar meaning. The student could most easily remember that the Spanish word *mano* means "hand" by creating a meaningful link between the words. She or he could do that by remembering that to do something *manually* is to do it by *hand*. Otherwise, the only way to remember the foreign word is by mechanical repetition (maintenance rehearsal).

Demonstration

Demonstrate Ebbinghaus's finding that relearning facts or skills is faster and easier than learning them for the first time. Invite students to cite skills that they have learned in the past year, such as how to browse the Internet. For each skill on the list, organize students according to those who know this skill and those who do not. Those who know it will relearn it, while those who do not know it will learn it for the first time. Record and then compare the times necessary for each group to remember the information. Have students discuss the results.

Taking a Stand

Present the topic of repressed memories, telling students that the topic has prompted much heated debate among contemporary psychologists. Have students conduct library research to learn more about both sides of the debate. Then organize volunteers for a panel discussion. Challenge the panel to consider whether the repression of memories actually does occur, and if not, why not.

Relearning   The third basic memory task is **relearning**. Sometimes we do not remember things we once knew. For example, people who have been out of school for 25 years might not remember the algebraic formulas they learned when they were in high school. However, they could probably relearn them very quickly if someone showed them how to use them again. With some study and effort we can usually relearn fairly rapidly things we once knew but have forgotten.

Ebbinghaus (1885) used nonsense syllables to study relearning and other memory tasks. First, he would record how many repetitions a particular person needed to memorize a list of nonsense syllables. Then, after a few months had passed, Ebbinghaus would check on the person again. Typically, the person could not recall or even recognize the list of nonsense syllables that she or he had memorized. However, Ebbinghaus found that the person was able to relearn the list more quickly than she or he had learned it the first time.

Different Kinds of Forgetting

Much of the time, forgetting is due to interference or decay. As you have already learned, interference occurs when new information shoves aside or disrupts what has been placed in memory. **Decay**—the fading away of a memory—is similar to a burning candle. The candle burns down until it goes out. Both decay and interference are part of normal forgetting. They occur when memory traces fade from sensory or short-term memory. Memory loss also occurs in long-term memory when something that has been stored there cannot be retrieved. However, there are more extreme kinds of forgetting.

Repression

According to Sigmund Freud, the founder of psychoanalytic theory, we sometimes forget things on purpose without even knowing we are doing it. Some memories may be so painful and unpleasant that they make us feel anxiety, guilt, or shame. To protect ourselves from such disturbing memories, said Freud, we forget them by pushing them out of our consciousness. Freud called this kind of forgetting *repression*. For example, a person might forget to go to a dentist appointment because he or she expects the experience to be unpleasant. However, the extent to which repression occurs—and even *whether* repression occurs—is controversial in contemporary psychology.

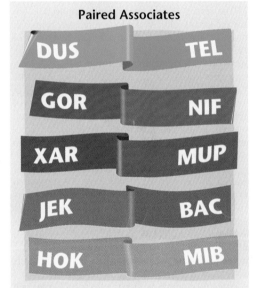

Paired Associates

DUS — TEL
GOR — NIF
XAR — MUP
JEK — BAC
HOK — MIB

FIGURE 7.5   *Psychologists often use paired associates, such as those shown here, to measure recall. The task is to recall the second syllable in the pair when given the first syllable as a cue.*

Amnesia

Psychoanalysts believe that repression is responsible for a rare but severe kind of forgetting called dissociative amnesia. Amnesia is severe memory loss caused by brain injury, shock, fatigue, illness, or repression. Dissociative amnesia is thought to be caused by psychological trauma (an extremely upsetting experience or series of experiences). Other kinds of amnesia include infantile amnesia, anterograde amnesia, and retrograde amnesia.

Infantile Amnesia   Some people think that they can remember special events that took place in their infancy, but they cannot. After many years of hearing his patients talk about their childhoods, Freud found that they could not remember things that had happened to them before the age of three. This forgetting of early events is called **infantile amnesia**.

People who think that they can remember their birth have probably constructed the memory from other memories. For example, they may remember being told about their birth by a parent or another family member. Or they may remember the birth of a younger sibling and then use that information to create a memory of their own birth.

Class Discussion

Tell students the story of S. A man with an extraordinary memory, S remembered huge amounts of information in astonishing detail. To demonstrate his ability, S memorized lengthy lists and other essentially irrelevant information. Because of his memory skills, however, he could not forget this information. It plagued him, popping into his head and distracting him from his daily activities. He finally achieved some relief by imagining he was erasing the information from a chalkboard. Have students comment on the story and discuss the implications of having such a vast memory.

Journal Activity

Direct students to write a short description of their earliest memory, including as much detail as possible, in their journals. Without asking students to share the actual memory, have them discuss whether they think they have really *remembered* the event or have instead constructed the memory from other information sources.

169

Meeting Individual Needs: Gifted Learners

Many psychologists believe that children learn how to remember as they mature. For example, at age three, a child begins to place memories within a recognizable routine, such as having a bath every night. Have gifted learners research the growth of memory skills in young children. Tell them to use this information to make a time line showing the progression of memory development over time.

Predicting Outcomes

Have each student write a "case review" for a hypothetical patient suffering from amnesia. Tell students that their case reviews should include the following information: descriptive information about the patient (age and sex); cause of the amnesia; type and amount of memory loss; duration of the problem; and prognosis (likelihood that memories will be regained). Have volunteers present their case reviews to the class. Encourage the class to comment on the case reviews and to ask the presenters for additional details about their cases.

For Your Information

Some people who have suffered from encephalitis (brain inflammation) experience amnesia. It seems that the amnesia is caused not by the disease itself but by the high fever and reduced oxygen flow that result from the inflammation.

What's New in Psychology?

Many people today worry that they will develop Alzheimer's disease, a progressive brain disease that destroys memory and other brain functions. Current research suggests that some memory loss is a normal part of aging. This kind of memory loss is called age-associated memory impairment, or AAMI. In a 1993 survey by the Dana Foundation of New York, 67 percent of the adults questioned reported experiencing some memory loss. There are many explanations for AAMI, including the general slowing down of physical and mental functions over time. One test to distinguish AAMI from more worrisome memory loss is to ask who is concerned about it, you or the people around you? People with normal memory loss, such as AAMI, will recognize their declining abilities.

The reason people have infantile amnesia is not that the events happened a long time ago. People in their 70s and 80s have many precise memories of their life between the ages of 6 and 10, even though the events they remember occurred 60 or 70 years earlier. College freshmen, meanwhile, have difficulty remembering events that occurred before the age of 6, even though these events occurred only 13 or 14 years earlier (Wetzler & Sweeney, 1986). Thus, failure to recall events from infancy or early childhood is not simply a matter of gradually forgetting information over many years.

Freud explained infantile amnesia in terms of repression. He believed that young children often have aggressive and sexual feelings toward their parents but that they forget these feelings as they get older. However, repression may not be the reason, or at least the only reason, people forget events from their earliest years. The fact that people tend to forget boring and bland events from their early childhoods casts doubt on Freud's theory.

Infantile amnesia probably reflects biological and cognitive factors. For example, a part of the brain (the hippocampus) that is involved in the storage of memories does not become mature until we are about two years old (Squire, 1993, 1996). Also, myelination of brain pathways is incomplete for the first few years, so memory formation remains somewhat inefficient.

There are also cognitive reasons for infantile amnesia:

- Infants are not particularly interested in remembering the past year (Neisser, 1993).
- Infants, unlike older children and adults, tend not to weave episodes together into meaningful stories of their lives. Information about specific episodes thus tends to be lost.
- Infants do not make reliable use of language to symbolize or classify events. Their ability to encode sensory input is therefore limited.

. . . .

TRUTH OR fiction
■ REVISITED ■

It is not true that you can remember important events from the first two years of life. Apparent infant memories are reconstructed and probably inaccurate. Many factors contribute to and help explain this memory loss during the first two years of life.

. . . .

Note that infantile amnesia refers to memory of specific events (episodic memory). We certainly learn and remember many other things during infancy and early childhood using semantic and implicit memory. For example, we learn who our parents are and learn to have strong feelings for them. We learn and remember the language spoken at home. We learn how to encourage other people to care for us. We learn how to get from one part of the home to another. We remember such information and skills quite well.

Anterograde Amnesia Trauma to the brain caused by a blow to the head, electric shock, or brain surgery can cause memory loss of events that took place both before and after the trauma. Memory loss from trauma that prevents a person from forming new memories is called **anterograde amnesia**. Certain kinds of brain damage, such as damage to the hippocampus, have been linked to anterograde amnesia (Corkin et al., 1985; Squire et al., 1984).

Retrograde Amnesia In **retrograde amnesia**, people forget the period leading up to a traumatic event. For example, many people who are injured in auto accidents do not remember that they were in the car before the accident. Similarly, athletes who are knocked unconscious during a game often have no memory of what happened before the play in which they were injured. Some cannot even remember starting the game.

In the most severe cases of retrograde amnesia, the person cannot remember a period of several *years* prior to the traumatic incident. One man with retrograde amnesia received a head injury in a motorcycle accident (Baddeley, 1982). When he woke up after the accident, he had no memory of anything that had happened since he was 11 years old. As a matter of fact, he thought that he was still 11. Over a period of months, he regained much of his memory, but he never did remember what happened just before the accident.

Improving Memory

Memory can be improved, and there are specific ways to go about improving it. As a result of studies of memory and forgetting, psychologists have been able to identify different strategies people can use to improve their memory. Some of the methods they recommend are discussed in the rest of this section. You may find them helpful.

Drill and Practice One basic way to remember information is by going over it again and again, that

For Further Research

There are many causes of memory loss in addition to those cited in the chapter. Direct students to research some of these causes, choosing from such general topics as disease, drug use, aging, or injury. Encourage students to include a selection of case studies in a short oral report explaining how one or more factors can cause memory loss.

Ask students to consider how occupational therapists might help H.M. use his remaining skills productively. Challenge students to develop a list of skills that H.M. could effectively learn and remember. Then have students brainstorm some occupations H.M. might be able to undertake and some strategies he might use to accommodate his memory failings in daily life activities.

CASE STUDIES
AND OTHER TRUE STORIES

The Case of H.M.

Studies of people who have undergone brain surgery to reduce epileptic seizures have helped provide a clearer picture of the relationship between amnesia and damage to certain parts of the brain. In the operations, which are now performed only rarely, the patients had one or both of their temporal lobes surgically removed to stop the epileptic seizures. One of the most famous of these cases was that of a man known by his initials: H.M.

H.M. suffered from severe epileptic seizures beginning at the age of 16. His seizures became worse as he reached adulthood. By the time he was 27, he could no longer function at work or live a normal life. At that point, he agreed to undergo surgery to reduce the rate and severity of the seizures. Surgery was performed to remove part of his hippocampus.

Following the operation, H.M.'s personality and mental functioning seemed to be normal. However, as time went on, it became increasingly difficult for him to process new information. His memory of events during the year leading up to the operation was weak, and his ability to learn and store new information was almost nonexistent. For example, two years after the surgery, H.M. thought he was still 27 years old. His memory was so poor that he forgot something as soon as he was distracted from rehearsing it.

When he moved with his family to a new home, he could not remember his new address or how to reach his new home. When his uncle died, he expressed appropriate grief at the loss. However, he then began asking about his uncle and wanting to know why he did not visit. Each time he was told that his uncle was dead, H.M. grieved as if he were hearing the information for the first time.

The formal testing that was done on H.M. showed that he could remember verbal information for as long as 15 minutes if he was allowed to rehearse it. However, it soon became clear that H.M.'s operation had caused him to lose the ability to transfer information from his short-term memory to his long-term memory. As soon as his short-term memory capacity reached its limit, or he was distracted from the rehearsing he had to do to keep new information in his short-term memory, he would forget the information. His capacity to remember nonverbal material was even more impaired. With or without distractions, he forgot even simple figures, such as circles, squares, and triangles.

Despite this severe memory loss, H.M. retained a limited capacity to learn, although the learning process was very slow and difficult. For example, H.M. had to exert great effort to learn to navigate a very short visual maze. What took most people only a couple of trials to master took H.M. 155 trials. Surprisingly, a week after he did so, H.M. remembered what he had painstakingly learned. Two years later he still retained some of what he had learned. At that time, it took him only 39 trials to relearn his way through the maze (116 fewer trials than he had needed to learn it originally).

H.M. showed learning ability in other situations as well. When he was asked to trace the drawing of a star by looking at its reflection in a mirror, he completed the task successfully. Not only did he draw the star as well as other people do, but his ability to retain what he had learned was also normal. For example, on the second and third days, he performed as well on the first trial of the day as he had on the last trial of the day before. That was evidence that there was no memory loss from day to day. Apparently, the operation he had did not significantly impair his ability to retain motor skills even though his ability to transfer information from short-term memory into long-term memory was impaired.

WHY PSYCHOLOGY MATTERS

Many psychologists focus their research on how memory functions and how people's memories can be improved. Use CNNfyi.com or other current events sources to learn more about research into memory. Create a flyer that describes what you have learned.

CNNfyi.com

Class Discussion

Tell students that brain surgery has been performed in the past to treat mental as well as physical illnesses. Ask students whether they would support brain surgery for the severely mentally ill, even if this surgery would cause memory loss.

Cross-Curricular Link: Art

Have students consider how their lives would change if they were suddenly faced with a situation similar to that of H.M. Then have them create a piece of art that conveys the emotions and experiences of a person who suffers severe memory loss. The art may take the form of a poem, song, dance, painting, sketch, or short story. Have volunteers display or perform their art for the class and then discuss it.

Technology Resources

CNN Presents Psychology: The Brain and Memory

Guided Practice

Tell students to think of 10 locations in their home, choosing them in the order in which a person could easily move from location to location. Then give students a list of 10 items commonly found in a classroom, such as a chalkboard, an eraser, and a pencil. Tell students to imagine one of these items in each of the 10 locations. If the first item is a paper clip, for example, students might imagine a huge paper clip serving as a door knocker. After students do this for each of the 10 items, have them mentally walk through their house and recall the list of 10 items. How many were able to recall the entire list?

Independent Practice

Have students develop procedures for using unusual associations to remember information in their other classes. For example, a student taking a government course who must remember the executive departments of the federal government might suggest associating the departments with various pieces of playground equipment. In this instance, the Department of Defense might be remembered as two soldiers playing on a seesaw. After students have developed their procedures, ask volunteers to describe their unusual associations to the rest of the class.

JUMP START reprinted by permission of United Feature Syndicate, Inc.

is, by repetition, or drill and practice. Repetition is one fairly effective way to transfer information from sensory memory to short-term memory and from short-term memory to long-term memory.

Mechanical repetition may sound boring. Nevertheless, it was by repetition that we all learned the alphabet and how to count. We can memorize the spellings and meanings of new vocabulary words by repeating them over and over again. Math students can memorize formulas by writing and rewriting them. They can then use their time on tests to figure out how to use the formulas rather than spending time trying to remember what they are.

You can remember facts in social studies and other courses by pairing different pieces of information with each other and then drilling yourself on the connections between the items. This is what flash cards do. Use flash cards and write each word or phrase from the pair on a different side of a card. For example, write, "The U.S. president during the Persian Gulf War" on one side of the card and "George Bush" on the other. If you make a set of flash cards and then go over them again and again, drilling yourself on the information, eventually you will know it by heart.

You can use this method to learn new vocabulary words as well. Put the words on one side of the cards and the definitions on the other, and then test yourself both ways. You can read the definitions first and see if you know the words that go with them. Then you can read the words and see if you can remember their definitions. You might then want to go on to practice using the words in sentences. If you rehearse what you have learned by going through this procedure with the cards at regular intervals, including just before a test, you should do well on the test.

Douglas Herrmann (1991) has some advice about how to remember the names of people you meet. He recommends using the names right away. This will help you remember them later. If you are introduced to a new person, for example, say his or her name aloud when you are introduced. Instead of saying, "Glad to meet you," say, "Glad to meet you, Sam." You can also use his or her name in a question, such as, "Where do you live, Sam?" As you continue to talk, use the person's name some more. You might find it even more helpful, says Herrmann, to write the name down, if you can, at the end of the conversation. If you need to remember the names of several different people you meet, you may want to write down a brief description of each person next to the listing of the person's name.

 At Hannah's party, Dan concentrated so hard on remembering the telephone number of the girl he had met that he ended up forgetting her name as well as her number. He forgot her number because he did not write it down soon enough while it was still in his short-term memory. He then forgot her name, too, because he was so confident he would remember it that he did not bother to rehearse it sufficiently to keep it in his short-term memory.

Relate to Things You Already Know Relating new information to what you already know (elaborative rehearsal) is not as mechanical and repetitious as drill and practice (maintenance rehearsal). Relating new information to what you already know requires you to think more deeply about the new information (Willoughby et al., 1994). As a result, you may remember the new information better.

There are many situations in which elaborative rehearsal can be helpful. For example, if you were trying to remember the spelling of the word *retrieve*, you would probably do it by recalling the rule "*i* before *e* except after *c*." But then how would you remember the spelling of the word *weird*, which does not follow

Closing Section 4

Organizing Information

Ask students to create a chart listing the main reasons for forgetting. Then have them pair the reasons for forgetting with the mnemonic devices most likely to counteract the forgetting. Ask students to write a brief explanation of the links they have made.

Reviewing Section 4

Have students complete the Section Review questions on page 173.

Extension

Tell students to imagine they are reporters for the school newspaper. Have them use what they have learned in the section to write an article for the newspaper explaining how mnemonic devices can be used as tools to improve memory. Have volunteers read their articles to the class for discussion. Some students may wish to submit their articles to the school newspaper for publication consideration.

---

the rule? One way would be to use elaborative rehearsal on the word by recalling that it does not follow the "i before e" rule because it's a "weird" word.

Learning to expand our knowledge by relating new information to things we already know begins early. For instance, children learn that a lion is like a house cat, only bigger and more dangerous.

Form Unusual Associations It is sometimes easier to remember a piece of information if you can make an unusual or even humorous association between that piece of information and something else. That will make it stand out from ordinary things and thus help you recall it. For example, suppose that you wanted to memorize the symbol for the chemical element tin. You could remember that *Sn* is the symbol for tin by thinking of a *sn*ake in a *tin* can. The more unusual the association, the more effective it will probably be.

Sometimes people can enhance memory by forming a group of unusual associations. Suppose that you need to buy groceries but do not have time to write out a shopping list. How will you remember what items to buy? First, think of a group of related images, such as the parts of your body. Then picture each dish you plan to cook as hanging from a different body part. For example, you might envision lasagna hanging off your left shoulder. When you are at the supermarket, mentally go through the body parts you have designated and see what is connected to each one. When you get to the left shoulder and envision the lasagna, tick off the items you want to buy in order to make the lasagna: lasagna noodles, tomato paste, mozzarella cheese, and so forth.

Construct Links Constructing links between items is another way elaborative rehearsal can help improve memory. You may find it easier to remember vocabulary words from a foreign language if you construct a meaningful link between each foreign word and its English equivalent (Atkinson, 1975). One way to create such a link is to find part of the foreign word and construct a sentence or phrase that includes that part of the word in English. For example, suppose that you are trying to remember that a *peso* (PAY-soh) is a unit of Mexican money. You might note that *peso* contains the letters *pe*, and then construct the following sentence: "*Pe*ople pay with money." Then, when you come across the word *peso*, you recognize the *pe* and retrieve the sentence that serves as the link. From that sentence, you can then reconstruct the meaning of the word *peso* as "a unit of money."

Use Mnemonic Devices All these methods for improving memory are called *mnemonics* (ni-MAH-niks). Mnemonic devices are systems for remembering information. Such devices usually combine chunks of information into a format, such as an acronym, phrase, or jingle. For example, many psychology students have used the acronym *Roy G. Biv* to remember the colors of the spectrum (*r*ed, *o*range, *y*ellow, *g*reen, *b*lue, *i*ndigo, and *v*iolet).

In biology, you can remember that dromedary camels have one hump, whereas Bactrian camels have two humps. How? Just turn the uppercase letters D and B on their sides and count the "humps" in each one. In geography, the acronym HOMES stands for the Great Lakes: *H*uron, *O*ntario, *M*ichigan, *E*rie, and *S*uperior.

Douglas Herrmann (1991) recommends using a mnemonic device to remember the name of someone new. He suggests that you make up a little rhyme that uses the name. For example, suppose the name of the girl Dan met at the party was Kate. When he stopped talking to her, he might have made up this rhyme: "I've met my next date; her name is Kate." However, he wanted to remember her telephone number as well as her name. Since poetry and telephone numbers do not mix very well, a poem would not have been much help in this case.

TRUTH **OR** **fiction** ■ REVISITED ■ *It is true that there are certain tricks you can use to improve your memory. Such tricks are called mnemonic devices. These devices provide people with systems for remembering information.*

SECTION 4 REVIEW

1. Explain how psychologists use nonsense syllables to study both memorization and forgetting.

2. How can memory be improved?

3. What are the differences between infantile, anterograde, and retrograde amnesia?

4. **Critical Thinking** *Drawing Inferences and Conclusions* How can you test whether you really remember something that happened in early childhood?

Section 4 Review: Answers

1. They measure the difference between remembered and forgotten information.

2. By drilling and practicing, relating to things one already knows, forming unusual associations, constructing links, and using mnemonic devices.

3. Infantile amnesia is the inability to remember events from early childhood; anterograde amnesia is the inability to form new memories after a traumatic event; retrograde amnesia involves the loss of memories leading up to the traumatic event.

4. Students can ask family members or others who knew them as infants for confirmation of the memory.

Chapter 7 Review: Answers

Writing a Summary

See the section subtitles for the main topics in the chapter.

Identifying People and Ideas

1. the process by which we recollect prior experiences

2. general knowledge that people remember

3. the locating of stored information and returning it to conscious thought

Chapter 7 REVIEW AND ASSESSMENT RESOURCES

Technology
▶ Chapter 7 Test Generator (on the One-Stop Planner)
▶ HRW Go site

Reinforcement, Review, and Assessment
▶ Chapter 7 Review, pp. 174–175
▶ Chapter Review Activities with Answer Key
▶ Alternative Assessment Handbook
▶ Portfolio Assessment Handbook
▶ Chapter 7 Test (Form A or B)

PSYCHOLOGY PROJECTS

Linking to Community Invite a neurologist to talk with the class about memory loss and how it can be treated. You might consider another health-care practitioner who works with people who have Alzheimer's disease. If possible, locate an individual who has coped with memory loss. Following are some questions students

---

4. the first stage of memory
5. the tendency to recall the initial items in a series of items
6. the tendency to recall the last items in a series
7. the act of bringing something back to mind
8. the process of relearning something once known but forgotten
9. the forgetting of events occurring before the age of three
10. the forgetting of the period leading up to a traumatic event

Understanding Main Ideas

1. A flashbulb memory is like a photograph in that the event is remembered instantly and in great detail.

2. Maintenance rehearsal (repeating information over and over) and elaborative rehearsal (relating information to something already known) are strategies for storing information.

3. Icons are mental pictures formed from visual stimuli. Icons are held in iconic memory.

4. Mnemonics are devices such as acronyms, phrases, and jingles that help improve memory; one example is Roy G. Biv.

Thinking Critically

1. The types are, respectively, semantic, episodic, and procedural.

2. Family members might have different memories because people reconstruct their memories according to their individual ways of viewing the world.

Chapter 7 REVIEW

Writing a Summary

Using standard grammar, spelling, sentence structure, and punctuation, summarize the information in this chapter. Consider:
• the kinds, processes, and stages of memory
• how memory can be improved

Identifying People and Ideas

Identify the following terms or people and use them in appropriate sentences.

1. memory
2. semantic memory
3. retrieval
4. sensory memory
5. primacy effect
6. recency effect
7. recall
8. relearning
9. infantile amnesia
10. retrograde amnesia

Understanding Main Ideas

SECTION 1 (pp. 154–155)
1. How is a flashbulb memory like a photograph?

SECTION 2 (pp. 155–160)
2. What are maintenance rehearsal and elaborative rehearsal?

SECTION 3 (pp. 160–166)
3. What are icons, and where are they held?

SECTION 4 (pp. 167–173)
4. What are mnemonics? Give an example.

Thinking Critically

1. **Categorizing** Name the type of memory involved in each of the following situations: (a) You can recite the capitals of every U.S. state. (b) You and your friends laugh every time you think about the fun you had last summer. (c) You know how to program a VCR to tape your favorite TV show.

2. **Contrasting** Why might you and another family member have different memories of the same vacation?

3. **Analyzing Information** Which type of forgetting is usually to blame when people cannot find their car keys?

4. **Drawing Inferences and Conclusions** If you were asked to identify all the students in a photo of your third-grade class, which memory task would be involved? Why might the task be easier if you were supplied with a list of their names?

5. **Analyzing Information** Give several reasons why you may be unable to recall your fifth birthday.

Writing About Psychology

1. **Comparing** Interview a person who must memorize a great deal of information to perform a task or job well. For example, you might interview a classmate who acts in school plays or a person who works for the U.S. postal service. Ask the person what techniques he or she uses to memorize material. Compare these techniques with information you read in this chapter. Write up your findings in a "helpful tips" column for the school newspaper.

2. **Analyzing Information** Ask your parents or older adults to describe where they were and what they were doing when they heard the news of some shocking event, such as the assassination of President John F. Kennedy or the explosion of the space shuttle *Challenger*. Ask them to describe details surrounding the event, such as what they were doing or who else was with them. Write a one-page report describing what the person remembers. Be sure to note what kind of memory the person is demonstrating. Use the graphic organizer below to help you write your report.

Memories of Event —— Type of Memory

174

may wish to ask the presenter(s).

- How are Alzheimer's disease and other types of memory loss diagnosed? How are the types differentiated?
- What techniques are used to help people with memory loss recover their memory or adapt to its loss?
- What emotional or psychological issues arise as a result of memory loss, both for the sufferer and for those around him or her?

Cooperative Learning

Tell students that the class will be creating a memory exhibit for the school. Organize the class into four groups. Each group will be responsible for presenting the material from one section of Chapter 7. Within the groups, students should be organized to work on research, graphics, oral presentations, or role-plays. Encourage all groups to conduct library research for additional information on their topics. Have the groups present their memory exhibits to the school community.

Building Social Studies Skills

Interpreting Graphs

Study the bar graph below. Then use the information in the graph to help you answer the questions that follow.

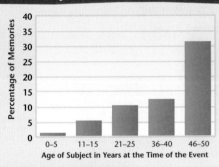

The Memory of Events from a Person's Life

Source: Bjork and Bjork, *Memory*, 1996

1. Which of the following statements best reflects the information contained in the bar graph?
   a. The highest percentage of memories is of events from the recent past.
   b. The percentage of memories increases consistently as one moves from childhood to older age.
   c. People have no memories of early childhood.
   d. Adolescence is the time when most memories are formed.
2. From a psychological perspective, what unusual or interesting information does the graph reveal?

Analyzing Primary Sources

Read the following excerpt from a poem written by American poet Emily Dickinson. Then answer the questions that follow.

"The Brain—is wider than the sky—
For—put them side by side—
The one the other will contain
With ease—and You—beside—

The Brain is deeper than the sea—
For—hold them—Blue to Blue—
The one the other will absorb—
As Sponges—Buckets—do—"

3. Which of the following statements reflects one meaning of Dickinson's poem?
   a. The human brain is a surprisingly large organism.
   b. The world does not exist outside of human thought.
   c. The functioning of the human brain is a mystery that only poetry is capable of explaining.
   d. The human brain is able to "contain" the world around us through memory and thought.
4. Why, according to Dickinson, is the brain "wider than the sky" and "deeper than the sea"?

PSYCHOLOGY PROJECTS

Cooperative Learning

Using Your Observation Skills Working in groups, conduct an experiment on the primacy and recency effects. Make up a list of 15 items. Have everyone in the group show a copy of the list to friends, and then see how many items the friends can remember and write down. Pool your findings and, calculate what percentage of participants were able to recall the first item, the second item, and so on. Make a line graph of the results. Does the graph demonstrate the primacy and recency effects?

internet connect

Internet Activity: go.hrw.com
KEYWORD: SY3 PS7

Choose an activity on memory to:
- create a mnemonic device on the types and stages of memory.
- make a flowchart or diagram on memory processes.
- design and test a method of memory improvement.

go hrw .com

3. Forgetting where one put one's car keys is usually a function of decay. The problem is common because information in short-term memory lasts only a few seconds.

4. It would involve recall or mental reconstruction. A list would make identification easier because the names would cue recognition.

5. Reasons may include: interference, ineffective encoding and storage techniques at the time of the event, or ineffective retrieval techniques, repression, or infantile amnesia.

6. Students should suggest three mnemonic devices and explain how they could be used to remember information in the chapter.

Writing About Psychology

1. Students' newspaper columns should include information from the textbook and from interviews.

2. Students are studying flashbulb memory. People are able to recall where they were because the event was so surprising and significant.

Building Social Studies Skills

1. b
2. Students' answers will vary, but many students will note the dramatic increase in the percentage of memories from events beginning in a person's 40s.
3. d
4. Dickinson argues that the human brain has the capacity to understand, or at least capture, the vastness of the natural world.

Thinking and Language

CHAPTER RESOURCE MANAGER

Objectives	Pacing Guide	Reproducible and Review Resources
SECTION 1: **What Is Thinking?** (pp. 178–179)	Explain the role that symbols, concepts, and prototypes play as units of thought.	**Regular** 1 day **Block Scheduling** .5 day *Block Scheduling Handbook with Team Teaching Strategies, Chapter 8*	**PS** Readings and Case Studies, Chapter 8 **SM** Mastering Critical Thinking Skills 8 **REV** Section 1 Review, p. 179
SECTION 2: **Problem Solving** (pp. 179–188)	Describe several methods people use to solve problems and identify obstacles to problem solving.	**Regular** 1 day **Block Scheduling** .5 day *Block Scheduling Handbook with Team Teaching Strategies, Chapter 8*	**RS** Essay and Research Themes for Advanced Placement Students, Theme 7 **REV** Section 2 Review, p. 188
SECTION 3: **Reasoning** (pp. 189–191)	Differentiate between deductive reasoning and inductive reasoning.	**Regular** 1 day **Block Scheduling** .5 day *Block Scheduling Handbook with Team Teaching Strategies, Chapter 8*	**E** Research Projects and Activities for Teaching Psychology **REV** Section 3 Review, p. 191
SECTION 4: **Decision Making and Judgment** (pp. 191–195)	Analyze the strategies used in decision making.	**Regular** 1 day **Block Scheduling** .5 day *Block Scheduling Handbook with Team Teaching Strategies, Chapter 8*	**E** Creating a Psychology Fair, Activity 3 **REV** Section 4 Review, p. 195
SECTION 5: **Language** (pp. 195–201)	Identify the basic elements of language and summarize the stages of language development.	**Regular** 1 day **Block Scheduling** .5 day *Block Scheduling Handbook with Team Teaching Strategies, Chapter 8*	**SM** Study Skills and Writing Guide, Part 3, Stage 2 **REV** Section 5 Review, p. 201

Chapter Resource Key

PS Primary Sources	**A** Assessment	Video
RS Reading Support	**REV** Review	Internet
E Enrichment	Transparencies	Holt Presentation Maker Using Microsoft® PowerPoint®
SM Skills Mastery	CD-ROM	

 One-Stop Planner CD–ROM

See the *One-Stop Planner* for a complete list of additional resources for students and teachers.

 **One-Stop** Planner CD–ROM

It's easy to plan lessons, select resources, and print out materials for your students when you use the ***One-Stop Planner CD-ROM with Test Generator.***

Technology Resources

 One-Stop Planner, Lesson 8.1
Homework Practice Online

 One-Stop Planner, Lesson 8.2
Homework Practice Online
HRW Go Site

 One-Stop Planner, Lesson 8.3
Homework Practice Online
Teaching Transparencies: Transparencies 22 and 23

 One-Stop Planner, Lesson 8.4
Homework Practice Online
HRW Go Site

 One-Stop Planner, Lesson 8.5
Homework Practice Online
 Presents Psychology: Baby Language
HRW Go Site

Chapter Review and Assessment

 HRW Go site

REV Chapter 8 Review, pp. 202–203

REV Chapter Review Activities with Answer Key

A Chapter 8 Test (Form A or B)

A Portfolio Assessment Handbook

A Alternative Assessment Handbook

 Chapter 8 Test Generator (on the One–Stop Planner)

Global Skill Builder CD-ROM

↗ internet connect

HRW ONLINE RESOURCES

GO TO: go.hrw.com
Then type in a keyword.

TEACHER HOME PAGE
KEYWORD: SY3 Teacher

CHAPTER INTERNET ACTIVITIES
KEYWORD: SY3 PS8
Choose an activity on thinking and language to have students:
• write a short analysis of their own methods of solving problems.
• role-play a conflict resolution process that uses persuasion, compromise, debate, and negotiation.
• research and evaluate theories of language acquisition and development.

CHAPTER ENRICHMENT LINKS
KEYWORD: SY3 CH8

ONLINE ASSESSMENT
Homework Practice
KEYWORD: SY3 HP8
Standardized Test Prep
KEYWORD: SY3 STP8
Rubrics
KEYWORD: SS Rubrics

CONTENT UPDATES
KEYWORD: SS Content Updates

HOLT PRESENTATION MAKER
KEYWORD: SY3 PPT8

ONLINE READING SUPPORT
KEYWORD: SS Strategies

CURRENT EVENTS
KEYWORD: S3 Current Events

Additional Resources

PRINT RESOURCES FOR TEACHERS

Baron, N. (1992). *Growing up with language.* Reading, MA: Addison-Wesley.

Halpern, D. (1989). *Thought and knowledge: An introduction to critical thinking.* Hillsdale, NJ: Erlbaum.

Mayer, R. (1992). *Thinking, problem solving, cognition* (2nd ed.). New York: Freeman.

Restak, R. M. (1994). *The modular brain.* New York: Scribner's.

PRINT RESOURCES FOR STUDENTS

Adams, J. L. (1986). *Conceptual blockbusting: A guide to better ideas* (3rd ed.). Reading, MA: Addison-Wesley.

Barrett, S. L. (1992). *It's all in your head.* Minneapolis, MN: Free Spirit.

Schaller, S. (1991). *A man without words.* Berkeley: University of California Press.

MULTIMEDIA RESOURCES

The brain: The two brains (Episode 6) (VHS). Films Incorporated, 5547 N. Ravenswood Ave., Chicago, IL 60640-1199.

Avoiding conflict: Dispute resolution without violence (VHS). Films for the Humanities & Sciences, P.O. Box 2053, Princeton, NJ 08543-2053.

How the human mind works: Patricia Smith Churchland (VHS). Films for the Humanities & Sciences, P.O. Box 2053, Princeton, NJ 08543-2053.

Neuropsychology (VHS). Films for the Humanities & Sciences, P.O. Box 2053, Princeton, NJ 08543-2053.

THINKING AND LANGUAGE

Introducing Chapter 8

Write the following questions on the chalkboard:

► What is the sum of 362 and 499? *(861)*

► You found Brand A soup on aisle 10 of your grocery store. How will you find Brand B soup?

► College X and College Z both offer you a scholarship. How will you choose which college to attend?

Have students answer the questions. Then read aloud the definition of *thinking* on page 178. Tell students that while they used thinking to answer all three questions, each of the questions required a different type of thinking *(problem solving, reasoning, and decision making, respectively)*. Then tell students that they will learn more about thought processes and these types of thinking by reading Chapter 8.

Sections

1 **What Is Thinking?**

2 **Problem Solving**

3 **Reasoning**

4 **Decision Making and Judgment**

5 **Language**

Each of the five questions identified on page 176 corresponds to one of these sections.

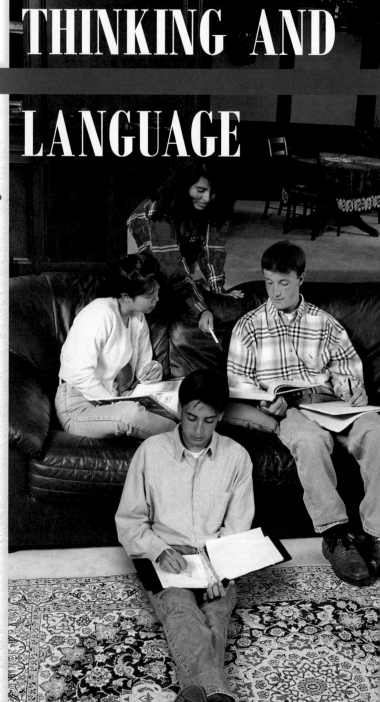

Chapter 8 THINKING AND LANGUAGE

Read to Discover

1 What are the three units of thought?

2 What steps can be used to solve problems?

3 How do deductive reasoning and inductive reasoning differ?

4 What strategies can be used in decision making?

5 What are the basic elements of language?

Each chapter begins with a vignette, called "A Day in the Life," that relates the information discussed in the chapter to the everyday events in the lives of a group of fictional high school students. The text of the chapter occasionally refers back to the vignette to demonstrate the application of the concept being discussed. An icon marked "A Day in the Life" is placed next to these references.

Copy the following graphic organizer onto the chalkboard, omitting the italicized text. Fill in the circles as you introduce the topic of thinking.

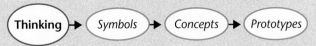

Thinking → Symbols → Concepts → Prototypes

A DAY IN THE LIFE

December 14

"I can*not* figure out this trig problem!" Dan sighed. He, Marc, Linda, and Hannah were studying. "This is so frustrating!"

"I know what you mean," replied Hannah. "I'm stumped on this crossword puzzle assignment for world history. Here's one of the clues: 'The _____ Republic.' Five letters, C _ _ C H. What could that be?"

After a brief pause, Linda blurted out, "The *Czech* Republic!"

"Oh, of course. The CZ was throwing me off," stated Hannah.

Dan smiled and said, "Very good, Linda. Now does someone want to help with my trig problem?"

"I have problems of my own to solve," said Marc. "Like whether to take Japanese or creative writing next semester. Hannah, how hard will Japanese be?"

"How should I know?" she asked.

"Because you speak Korean, right? Korea and Japan are pretty near each other, so I figured the languages would be similar."

"As far as I know, Korean and Japanese are completely different."

"Oh. That's no help, then. Well, either way, I have to figure out how to tell Mr. Hochberg I'm not taking computer science, which is what *he* suggested I take." Mr. Hochberg is the school's guidance counselor.

"Mr. Hochberg will understand. When I talked to him last year about what courses to take, he was very open to my ideas," said Linda.

"Oh!" Dan exclaimed. "I just figured out the trig problem. Weird. I had stopped thinking about it."

"I think we should all stop thinking about studying for a moment," Linda stated. "Tonight is my night to cook dinner for my family. What am I going to make?"

"How about making macaroni and cheese?" Dan suggested.

"Had it last night," said Linda.

"Tacos?" put in Hannah.

"My sister doesn't eat red meat," Linda replied.

"Chicken stew?" Marc proposed.

"I don't have all the ingredients."

"So go to the store and get them!" the other three said together.

"I guess I could do that," Linda reflected. "That sounds like a pretty good idea, come to think of it."

• • •

This chapter is about thinking. When you are awake, you are probably thinking nearly all the time. But the type of thinking you are doing may vary from moment to moment. You may be solving a problem, such as Dan's math problem, Hannah's crossword puzzle, or Linda's dinner dilemma. Or you may be reasoning—using information to draw a conclusion. Or perhaps you are making a decision, such as Marc's decision about which course to take. Problem solving, reasoning, and decision making are three types of thinking explored in this chapter. And because thinking often relies on language, this chapter also deals with language.

Key Terms

- thinking
- symbol
- concept
- prototype
- algorithm
- heuristic
- difference reduction
- means-end analysis
- incubation effect
- mental set
- functional fixedness
- convergent thinking
- divergent thinking
- reasoning
- deductive reasoning
- premise
- inductive reasoning
- confirmation bias
- representativeness heuristic
- availability heuristic
- anchoring heuristic
- framing effect
- language
- phoneme
- morpheme
- syntax
- semantics
- overregularization
- language acquisition device

► WHY PSYCHOLOGY MATTERS

Psychologists study the relationship between thinking and language. Use CNNfyi.com or other current events sources to learn more about research on how thinking and language interrelate.

CNNfyi.com

Using Key Terms

Before students begin to read the chapter, have them sketch out a series of word webs in their journals. They can begin with words found in each chapter objective. For example, one web might have the word *reasoning* in the center circle and related terms in circles flowing out from this center. Tell students that as they encounter each term in their reading, they should enter a definition in the appropriate circle. They can also rearrange the webs if necessary to show various word relationships.

Using Visuals

Have students examine the photograph on page 176. Ask them to consider how this photograph relates to the chapter topic—thinking and language. Then have them read "A Day in the Life" on page 177. Ask them how the questions facing the characters in the narrative are similar to the questions they answered in the Introducing Chapter 8 activity.

Section Objective

▶ Explain the role that symbols, concepts, and prototypes play as units of thought.

This objective is assessed in the Section Review on page 179 and in the Chapter 8 Review.

Opening Section 1

Motivator

Write the word *dog* on the chalkboard and tell students to make a mental picture of a dog. Ask them what type of dog they pictured and write the responses on the chalkboard. Next ask students how they know a type (of dog) is a dog and not a bird. *(Students should mention how dogs and birds differ.)* Then have them explain why they pictured this particular type of dog. Tell students that they have just illustrated three units of thought: symbols, concepts, and prototypes. Ask them to keep this exercise in mind as they read Section 1.

Using Truth or Fiction

Each chapter opens with several "Truth or Fiction" statements that relate to the concepts discussed in the chapter. Ask students whether they think each statement is true or false. Answers to each item as well as explanations are provided at appropriate points within the text under the heading "Truth or Fiction Revisited."

Class Discussion

To clarify students' understanding of symbols, direct their attention to an American flag. Ask them what this flag means to Americans. *(Students might mention country, loyalty, patriotism, and so on.)* Remind students that the flag stands for these ideals and is not the ideal itself. Then ask students to suggest symbols that are indicative of their school and to explain what these symbols mean to them. Have students discuss how human communication would be different if human thought processes did not include the use of symbols.

Readings and Case Studies

TRUTH OR fiction

Read the following statements about psychology. Do you think they are true or false? You will learn whether each statement is true or false as you read the chapter.

- The most reliable way of solving a problem correctly is not always the best way of solving it.
- If you do not see the answer to a problem right away, you will probably not be able to solve it.
- Scientists can never prove for certain that their theories are true.
- Most people easily change their opinions when presented with convincing arguments.
- Once a child learns the correct form of a word, he or she will never use the incorrect form.

SECTION 1

What Is Thinking?

Thinking is the mental activity that is involved in the understanding, processing, and communicating of information. But how is all this accomplished? Thinking is made possible through the use of symbols, concepts, and prototypes. These are all units of thought.

Symbols

When we think, we use symbols to represent the things about which we are thinking. A **symbol** is an object or an act that stands for something else. As you are probably aware, symbols are a part of our daily lives. Your school mascot and the American flag are both examples of symbols. Different types of symbols are found in mathematics. Plus and minus

signs, for example, are both symbols: the plus sign signifies "add," and the minus sign signifies "subtract." Dan probably was all too familiar with various mathematics symbols from his trigonometry class.

Letters and words are also symbols. After all, a word actually stands for something else—it is not the thing itself. For example, the word *plate* is not itself a plate—it only refers to an object that is called a plate in English.

Even your mental images are a type of symbol. If you picture a dog in your mind, that image stands

Shown here is the Greek letter psi—the symbol of the American Psychological Association.

for a dog, but of course it is not itself a dog. If it were not for symbols, we would be unable to think about things that were not present.

Concepts

What do dogs, horses, and elephants have in common? You may say that they are all animals, or perhaps you may say that they are all mammals. When we think, we tend to mentally group together objects, events, or ideas that have similar characteristics, as dogs, horses, and elephants do. Such a grouping is called a **concept**. "Animal" and "mammal" are both examples of concepts.

Much thinking involves categorizing new items and manipulating the relationships among them. Think of a new kind of animal, for instance—just make one up. What makes it an animal? You have used the concept "animal" to create a new item that fits into the "animal" category. Now imagine your new animal in a tree eating a piece of fruit. You are thinking about relationships among concepts (your animal, the tree, and the fruit).

People organize concepts in hierarchies, series of levels that go from broad to narrow. As we saw above, dogs, horses, and elephants can be grouped both as animals and as mammals. The "animal" concept is higher up in the hierarchy than is the "mammal" concept because it is broader, or contains more elements. Sparrows, goldfish, and spiders are all animals, but they are not mammals.

People learn concepts through experience. Simple concepts such as "ball" and "vegetable" are taught by means of examples. We point to a baseball or a basketball and say, "Ball" or "This is a ball" to a child. We point to broccoli or carrots and say, "Eat your vegetables." Communication of the meaning of abstract concepts such as fairness, beauty, and goodness may require detailed explanations, a variety of personal experiences, and many examples. Even then, people may still disagree about what is fair, beautiful, or good.

Prototypes

Often when we think about a concept, we have an image in our minds of a particular example of that concept, even though a concept is a category and

Closing Section 1

Interpreting Information

Organize the class into three groups and assign each group one of the following topics: symbols, concepts, prototypes. Have the members of each group work together to draw a comic strip that illustrates how people use this unit of thought in their daily lives.

Reviewing Section 1

Have students complete the Section Review questions on page 179.

Section Objective

▶ Describe several methods people use to solve problems, and identify obstacles to problem solving.

This objective is assessed in the Section Review on page 188 and in the Chapter 8 Review.

---

contains many different examples. For instance, picture a shoe in your mind. What does the shoe you pictured look like? Does it have shoelaces, straps, or neither? Does it have a heel, or is it flat-soled?

The shoe you imagined was a **prototype**—an example of a concept that best exemplifies that concept. A prototype does not have to be an actual, experienced example, such as a particular shoe you have seen. Instead, a prototype can be more like an average of all experienced examples. You may never have seen a shoe that looks exactly like your shoe prototype, but your prototype probably contains elements of many different shoes you have seen.

Which do you think is a better example of a shoe: a loafer or a slipper? You probably said a loafer. Why? Because a loafer is probably closer to your "shoe" prototype than is a slipper. Most people think of shoes as items that are worn outside or in public, and slippers usually are worn only around the house. But a slipper is a type of shoe.

Even though there are many, many different types of shoes, you probably picture only one type when you hear the word shoe. *What you picture is your prototype of a shoe.*

SECTION 1 REVIEW

Homework Practice Online
go.hrw.com
Keyword: SY3 HP8

1. Define *thinking*.
2. List and describe three units of thought.
3. **Critical Thinking** *Drawing Inferences and Conclusions* Is a concept a type of symbol? Why or why not?

SECTION **2**

Problem Solving

A DAY IN THE LIFE

People solve many different kinds of problems. Some, such as Dan's trigonometry problem, are in math and science. In such cases, people often use formulas and scientific facts to solve the problems. For example, they may need to know the formula for the area of a circle or how many protons oxygen contains.

Other problems concern fitting things into a busy schedule or paying for what we need. Such problems are best solved by budgeting. Still other problems are social problems, such as how Marc should approach Mr. Hochberg about his choice of an elective for next semester. How should Marc tell Mr. Hochberg that he really wants to take Japanese or creative writing rather than computer science?

Solving problems involves a series of processes including analyzing the problem, breaking it into component parts, and establishing goals. Intermediate goals address parts of the problem that must be solved to arrive at the terminal goal—that is, the final solution to the problem.

Figure 8.1 on the next page shows some more problems. Try to solve them now. If you have difficulty with any of them, do not worry—you will learn the answers as you read.

Algorithms and Heuristics

In many cases, people do not go straight from a problem to its solution in one giant leap. Rather, they move toward the solution in a series of steps. Ideally, each step taken moves the problem solver closer to the solution. But how do people know what steps to take? If they do not know the solution, how can they know where to start?

Through experience, people know that different types of problems must be approached in different ways. By simply identifying the type of problem it is, people have an idea of which method to use—which steps to take—in solving the problem.

Algorithms Some types of problems are best approached with the use of an algorithm. An **algorithm** is a specific procedure that, when used

179

Opening Section 2

Motivator

Ask students to describe the kinds of problems they generally enjoy solving. For example, some people like to solve word search puzzles, while others prefer more abstract, thought-provoking problems. Encourage students to examine the six problems on page 180 for ideas. Then have the class discuss how the various types of problems on this page differ and what features they have in common.

Teaching Section 2

Meeting Individual Needs: Tactile/Kinesthetic Learners

Encourage tactile/kinesthetic learners to sketch out some of the problems on page 180 before they attempt to solve them. They might draw Naomi's house, the street, and the house where the party is being held. Using small objects to represent the girls and the umbrella, they could then test various solutions. These students also might benefit from handling and manipulating the actual objects mentioned in some of the problems (such as problems D and E).

Caption Questions: Answers

A. Two of the girls must take the umbrella and cross together, leaving one behind. Then one of the first two must return with the umbrella to Naomi's home to retrieve the third girl.

B. Weak rays should be sent from several points to meet at the tumor site. Each ray is gentle enough to leave normal tissue unharmed, but together they are intense enough to destroy the tumor.

C. The lines connecting the four dots must extend beyond the dots.

D. Tack the box of matches to the wall and then use it to support the candle.

E. Tie the safety scissors to one of the strings, then set the string swinging. As you hold the free string, grab the swinging string and then tie the two together.

F. You do not bury survivors. This is a trick question.

Six Problems to Solve

A Naomi, Marquita, and Kim are planning to go to a party, and they want to prepare for the party together. The party is across the street from Naomi's home, so the three meet there an hour before the party. When, at the end of the hour, they are ready to go to the party, they discover that it has started to rain heavily. None of them wants to get wet because they are all wearing nice clothing. Unfortunately, they only have one umbrella for the three of them, and the umbrella is big enough to protect only two people from the rain. How can all three of them get to the party without becoming drenched?

B Imagine that you are a doctor. One of your patients has a stomach tumor that must be destroyed if the patient is to live. Certain rays will destroy the tumor if they are intense enough. To reach the tumor, however, the rays need to pass through the healthy tissue that surrounds it, and at the intensity needed to destroy the tumor, the rays will also destroy the healthy tissue. How can you use the rays to destroy the tumor without damaging the healthy tissue? (Adapted from Duncker, 1945)

C Copy this dot formation on a sheet of tracing paper. Then connect all four dots with two straight lines without lifting your pencil from the paper.

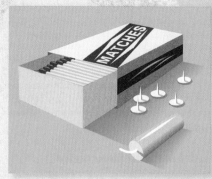

D Imagine that you are in a room with a candle, a box of matches, and some thumbtacks. Your task is to use these objects to attach the candle to the wall. How do you do it? (Adapted from Duncker, 1945)

E Imagine that you are in a room in which two strings are hanging from the ceiling. Your task is to tie the two strings together, but they are so far apart that you cannot reach both of them at the same time. The only other object in the room is a pair of safety scissors. How can you tie the strings together? (Adapted from Maier, 1931)

F An airplane crashes on the border of Mexico and the United States. Where do you bury the survivors?

FIGURE 8.1 *Try solving these problems. You will learn the answers as you read the section.*

Comparing and Contrasting Information

Have students make a chart that compares and contrasts algorithms and heuristics. Students should list the features, advantages, and disadvantages of each approach. Then ask students which approach they should use to do each of the following: build a model airplane *(algorithms)*; find an unfamiliar address without a map *(heuristics)*; play a game of chess *(heuristics)*; bake a cake *(algorithms)*; convert today's temperature from Fahrenheit to Celsius *(algorithms)*. Have students explain their answers.

For Further Research

Tell students that computers are used today as tools for problem solving. For example, computers can be used to quickly test each missing letter in a crossword puzzle word. Ask students to conduct library research on computer-assisted problem solving. Have students focus their research on the following questions: What can computers do to help humans solve problems? How are computers limited in their problem-solving capabilities? In what ways is this technology expected to improve in the future? Have students present their findings in a short written report.

properly and in the right circumstances, will always lead to the solution of a problem.

Formulas are examples of algorithms. If you know the radius (*r*) of a circle and you want to find the area (*A*) of that circle, you can apply the formula $A = \pi r^2$ to get the correct answer. As long as you know the formula and how to use it correctly, you need know nothing else to solve the problem.

Many algorithms are more complex and time-consuming than simple formulas, however. One such complex algorithm is called a systematic search. In a systematic search, each possible solution to a problem is tried and tested according to a certain set of rules.

People who do crossword puzzles regularly know of several heuristics that often help lead to solutions quickly. For example, if a word ends in G, the previous two letters are often I and N.

A DAY IN THE LIFE For example, suppose that you, like Hannah, are working on a crossword puzzle. You are trying to fill in a word for which you have all but one letter—say, C L _ F F. Using a systematic search, you would try putting every letter of the alphabet, starting with A, in that blank middle space until you found the letter that formed a word that fit the clue. In other words, first you would try C L A F F, then you would try C L B F F, then C L C F F, and so on, until you came to the right letter, which would probably be an I (C L I F F). It might take some time, but as long as you had all the other letters in the word correct and as long as you were able to recognize the word once you found it, this method would be guaranteed to work.

Heuristics While algorithms are guaranteed to work, they are not always practical. Suppose, for example, that you were missing not one, but two letters of your crossword puzzle word—C _ _ F F. In order to have success with the systematic search, not only would you have to try every letter of the alphabet in each of the two spaces, but you would have to fill in one of them with a placeholder while you tried letter after letter in the other space.

In other words, first you would have to fill the first blank space with an A, then you would have to run through all 26 letters in the second blank space. And when that did not work, you would have to try

a B in the first space, and then run through all the letters *again* in the second space. By the time you arrived at C L I F F, you would have already run through 294 other possible solutions.

Needless to say, although this algorithm would eventually lead to success, it would not be a very efficient way to do a crossword puzzle, nor would it be very interesting or rewarding. This is why, for many types of problems, people use heuristics rather than algorithms. **Heuristics** are rules of thumb that often, but not always, help us find the solution to a problem. They are shortcuts.

In the first crossword puzzle problem, where only one letter is missing, you probably would use the following heuristic: in a five-letter word in which four of the letters are consonants, the fifth letter will be a vowel. Thus, instead of trying *eight* possible combinations before you arrived at the letter I, you would try only *two*: A and E (the only vowels that precede I). In the second crossword puzzle problem, in which two letters are missing, a heuristic might involve deciding that certain letters of the alphabet (B, C, D, F, and so on) would be unlikely to follow the first letter C, and thus you would not even try them as possibilities. Rather, you might focus on the letters that you know are likely to follow C.

Heuristics are faster than algorithms, but they are not as reliable. For example, we might forget that if C is the first letter of a word, the letter L (a

Identifying Cause and Effect

Tell students that children about 18 to 24 months of age begin to use mental "trial and error" techniques to understand their surroundings. Have students discuss how mental trial and error could broaden a child's horizons, and ask students to identify the possible effects of these mental trials on learning. Then have students identify instances in which they used trial and error to solve a difficult problem. When later faced with a similar problem, were they able to solve it more quickly?

Role-Playing

Discuss with students the fact that a common problem facing teenagers is conflict with parents or other adult authority figures. Invite students to consider some of the problem-solving methods described in the section. Then challenge small groups of students to adapt these methods to hypothetical conflicts with parents or other authority figures. Finally, have each group role-play solutions to a typical conflict by using one or more of the problem-solving methods. Have the class critique each solution.

consonant rather than a vowel) might be the second. And in some circumstances, we might miss some more unusual words. This is probably what happened to Hannah with **C _ _ C H.** She did not try a **Z** in the first blank space because the letter **Z** usually does not directly follow the letter **C.** As Hannah put it, "The **CZ** was throwing me off." Thus, she was unable to come up with the word **C Z E C H.**

• • • • • • • • • •

TRUTH OR **fiction** ▪ R E V I S I T E D ▪

It is true that the most reliable way of solving a problem correctly is not always the best way of solving it. Algorithms are guaranteed to lead to the solution eventually, but they can be time-consuming. Heuristics are less reliable, but when they do work, they lead to solutions more quickly than do algorithms.

• • • • • • • • • • • • • •

Problem-Solving Methods

Algorithms and heuristics are general approaches to problem solving. There are also specific methods of problem solving. Systematic searching, which we have already discussed, is one of these methods. Others include trial and error, difference reduction, means-end analysis, working backward, and use of analogy.

Trial and Error Sometimes we have little choice but to resort to trial and error in solving a problem. We know what our goal is, but we have absolutely no idea how to reach it, and all we can do is try different things and see what happens with each one until we arrive at our goal more or less by chance. Trial and error is somewhat similar to systematic searching, except that it is more haphazard and less reliable. In trial and error, we often do not keep track of which possibilities we have already tried.

If you have ever tried to work on a complicated maze puzzle, you probably found that the only thing you could do was just to pick one possible route and see where it took you. When you hit a dead end, you came back and tried something else. In other words, you used trial and error—trying one thing until it is proved to be an error.

Difference Reduction In a method called **difference reduction**, we identify our goal, where

we are in relation to it, and the direction we must go to move closer to it. In other words, we want to *reduce the difference* between our present situation (problem unsolved) and our desired situation (problem solved).

Suppose you are standing blindfolded on the side of a hill. Your goal is to get to the top of the hill, but because you cannot see, you do not know which way to go. So what do you do? You take a step. If you feel yourself moving downward, then you know that you are going the wrong way and that you must change direction. But if you feel a pull in your legs that means you are moving upward, you know you are getting closer to the top of the hill. You have identified which direction to go in to move closer to your goal.

The difference-reduction method is a heuristic, however, and thus is not always reliable. Sometimes we may think we have reached our goal when we have not. Suppose that the hillside levels off for a bit and then continues upward to the top, for instance. You may think you have reached the top when you arrive at this level place, and you may stop there. You do not know that there is more hill ahead.

Furthermore, sometimes we have to take what seems to be a step away from our goal in order to

This woman will probably use trial and error to figure out which key is the correct one.

Cooperative Learning

Organize the class into six groups and assign each group one of the problem-solving methods discussed in the section. Have the members of each group work together to write a script for a scene similar to that featured in this chapter's opening vignette. The script should focus on a hypothetical problem facing the group and how group members use their assigned method to reach a solution. Then ask each group to dramatize its script for the class. Have class members identify the problem-solving method being used and evaluate its effectiveness.

Meeting Individual Needs:
Learners Having Difficulty

For learners having difficulty understanding the various problem-solving methods, help them break down each method into steps. One way to do this would be to have students walk through the difference-reduction example described on page 182. Alternatively, guide students in creating graphic organizers for each method. Then ask them to complete their organizers with real-life examples or examples from the textbook.

achieve that goal. For example, to straighten up your desk, you might have to take everything out of the drawers first, to organize the contents—even though this would seem to be a step in the wrong direction (since at first, things will become messier rather than neater). Similarly, what seems to be moving us closer to a goal may actually be moving us farther away.

Problem A in Figure 8.1 highlights some of the pitfalls of the difference-reduction method. In order for Naomi, Marquita, and Kim to get to the party dry, two of them (say, Marquita and Kim) must cross the street to the party first, leaving the third one (Naomi) back at Naomi's home. But then either Marquita or Kim must *leave* the party and go back with the umbrella for Naomi. In other words, they must temporarily increase, rather than decrease, the difference between the goal (all three of them at the party) and their present situation (two of them at the party but one of them not). One of the two currently at the party must temporarily leave the party.

Means-End Analysis Another heuristic problem-solving technique is called means-end analysis.

In **means-end analysis**, we know that certain things we can do (means) will have certain results (ends). If the stew Linda is making for dinner seems bland, adding pepper will probably help. Adding water probably will not.

As with the difference-reduction method, means-end analysis aims to reduce the difference between where we are and where we want to be. But means-end analysis goes beyond difference reduction in its awareness that a particular action will have a particular effect. Whereas the difference-reduction user asks, "What direction must I move in to get from here to there?" the means-end-analysis user asks, "What can I do to get there?"

Those who use means-end-analysis often break a problem down into parts and then try to solve each part individually, recognizing that solving each of the parts will contribute to solving the entire problem. We do this all the time without realizing it.

When people set out to cook or bake something, they use means-end analysis to break the task down into individual steps.

Once Linda had decided to make chicken stew for dinner, for example, she first had to identify the ingredients she needed. Then she had to figure out how to obtain these ingredients—a trip to the grocery store seemed necessary. Next, she had to figure out which store to go to, how to get there, how to find what she needed once she arrived at the store, and how to pay for what she bought. Finally, she had to figure out how to put the ingredients together in the way that would yield the taste and flavor she was trying to achieve—in other words, she had to do the actual cooking. Each of these steps was one means toward the end of serving chicken stew for dinner.

Working Backward Related to means-end analysis is the technique known as working backward. As in means-end analysis, working backward involves breaking a problem down into parts and then dealing with each part individually. In working backward, however, the problem solver starts by examining the final goal, then works back from the final goal to the present position to determine the best course of action.

This method is particularly useful when we know what we want to accomplish but are not sure how best to begin. Working backward helps ensure that we start off on the right path and avoid having to retrace our steps if we discover that the path we have chosen does not lead where we want to be.

For Your Information

Experts in a field usually find it easier than beginners to solve problems related to their field. This is partly because of their experience with the material. However, a second factor relates to the way that experts chunk information. Experts are able to think in larger chunks of information because the smaller chunks included in these larger ones are already known and therefore need no further thought. The ability to think in large chunks helps experts recognize patterns, retrieve schemas from long-term memory, and eliminate unworkable problem-solving strategies to quickly arrive at practical solutions. Have volunteers discuss instances when they and a person with considerably more knowledge in a particular area were trying to solve a problem related to that area. Who was able to solve the problem more quickly? How was this done?

Meeting Individual Needs:
Gifted Learners

Invite gifted learners to research the problem-solving methods used by some of history's great thinkers. Suggest that they focus on a particular subject area or on one particular culture. Specific thinkers might include Sir Isaac Newton, Albert Einstein, Friedrich Kekule von Stradonitz, or Euclid. Encourage students to look for examples of the problem-solving approaches employed by these great thinkers and to present their findings in a short oral report.

Analyzing Ideas

Tell students that analogies always include four parts and that the relationship between the first two parts is the same as the relationship between the second two parts. Clarify this idea by using the following example: Coat is to closet as car is to ____. *(garage)* Have students create other examples. Then tell students that standardized tests such as the SAT often include analogies. Have them analyze why this problem-solving method figures so prominently in standardized tests.

Class Discussion

Link the concept of insight to humor by recalling the common response to a joke: "Oh, I get it!" Explain that in humor the teller presents a situation or a problem for the listener to understand. The listener follows the story or the joke in search of sense. When the surprise conclusion arrives, it becomes a sudden insight into the problem. The listener notices some fact or twist of language that changes the whole structure of the problem and leads to the punch line. To demonstrate this link, have volunteers share some favorite jokes (caution them not to use inappropriate humor). Have students discuss their responses to the jokes.

For Your Information

Great thinkers have experienced insight in all kinds of places (besides the bathtub, as in the case of Archimedes). For example, scientist Friedrich Kekule von Stradonitz (1829–1896) solved a critical chemistry problem in his sleep. He dreamed the solution! The composer Ludwig van Beethoven is said to have experienced musical insights while riding in a carriage.

Suppose that you need to cross a stream that has no bridge and is too wide to leap across. There is, however, a series of stepping-stones that you can use to cross the stream. If you start by selecting one stone near your side of the bank, then select another stone to step to from there, and so on, you may find yourself ending up at a stone that is too far away from the opposite bank (your destination) for it to be useful.

A better approach might be to work backward from the opposite bank. Start off by identifying the stone that is nearest the opposite bank. Then find the stone that is nearest to that one, and so on, working back to your own side of the stream. This way you can avoid getting stuck in the middle of the stream with no place to go except back.

Analogies   People also solve some problems by analogy. An analogy is a similarity between two or more items, events, or situations. Linda, for example, saw an analogy between her situation last year, when she went to talk to Mr. Hochberg about what courses to take, and Marc's situation this year.

When people have successfully solved one problem, they may try to use the same approach in solving another problem if it is similar enough to the first one. For example, if you observe that studying early and getting a good night's rest helps you do well on a test for one class, you may try that technique again the next time you have a test, even if the next test is in a different class. Many analogies, however, are much less obvious, and the trick is to find one that works.

Problem B in Figure 8.1 (the ray-tumor problem) is not an easy one, and people typically have difficulty solving it. However, when they are provided with a story to use as an analogy, they often can solve the problem (Gick & Holyoak, 1980). Such a story might be as follows:

A dangerous group of terrorists barricaded themselves in a building in the middle of a town. Government officials considered it necessary to capture the terrorists, even though the operation would require a large force of agents to storm the building. Furthermore, the terrorists had planted mines on all of the streets that led to the building. If the entire force passed over any one of the streets, the mines would explode, killing not only the agents but also the people who lived in the surrounding area. Thus, the officials decided to divide the force into smaller units and send each unit on

a different street leading to the building. Timing was arranged so that all of the units arrived at the building at the same time, and the terrorists were captured.

(If you still cannot figure out the solution to the problem in Figure 8.1B, refer to Figure 8.2.)

A famous example of problem solving by analogy involves the ancient Greek scientist Archimedes (ahr-kuh-MEE-deez). As legend has it, Archimedes had been trying to find a way of measuring the volume of the king's crown, but the crown's irregular shape made it difficult, and Archimedes could not figure out what to do.

One day, as Archimedes climbed into his bath, some water overflowed from the filled tub onto the floor. Suddenly, Archimedes saw an analogy between what had just happened and the crown problem he was working on, and the solution to the problem came to him. He could measure the volume of the crown by placing it in a water-filled bowl and then collecting and measuring the amount of water that overflowed. Archimedes had realized that the volume of water displaced by an object

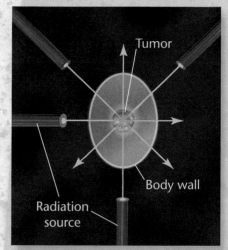

Solution to Figure 8.1B

Tumor

Body wall

Radiation source

FIGURE 8.2 *Weak rays sent from several points meet at the tumor site. Radiation will be intense at this site, thereby destroying the tumor. But because the rays are weak individually, healthy tissue surrounding the tumor will not be damaged.*

At first, the chimpanzee cannot reach the bananas hanging from the ceiling. After some time has passed, however, the chimpanzee experiences a "flash of insight." *The chimp suddenly stacks the boxes, climbs up on them, and reaches the fruit. What does it mean to say that a problem has been solved by insight?*

equals the volume of the object—whether the object is a human body or a king's crown. He was said to be so happy that he shouted "Eureka!" which means, "I have found it."

Insight and Incubation

Not only was Archimedes' experience an example of problem solving by analogy, it was also an example of insight, or sudden understanding. Usually we solve a problem by breaking it down into steps. Sometimes, however, we seem to arrive at the solution to a problem all of a sudden, as Archimedes did. Often we have little conscious awareness of how we found the solution—it just seems to come to us on its own.

Have you ever pondered a problem for a while, then had the solution come to you suddenly? Did it seem to come in a flash? This is what seemed to

A DAY IN THE LIFE happen to Dan, with his trig problem—suddenly he just knew how to solve it. When this happens, we have experienced insight. Often we express our delight and surprise by exclaiming "Aha!" or something similar. As a result, experiences of insight are also known as "Aha!" experiences.

Psychologist Wolfgang Köhler pioneered studies into this type of experience. During World War I, Köhler was marooned on one of the Canary Islands, off the northwest coast of Africa. While stranded,

Köhler worked with a colony of chimpanzees that the Prussian Academy of Science kept there. His research with these animals demonstrated to him that much learning is achieved by insight.

In one of Köhler's experiments, a chimpanzee was placed in a room in which some bananas were hanging from the ceiling. The chimp clearly wanted the bananas and tried to reach them by jumping. But the bananas were too high up to be reached this way. The chimp walked around, looked at the bananas, walked around some more, noticed some boxes that were also in the room, and sat down for a while. The chimp seemed to be doing nothing related to the problem of reaching the bananas. Then, all of a sudden, the chimp got up, stacked the boxes, and climbed up on them to reach the bananas. Apparently, the chimp had suddenly seen the situation in a new way. That is, the chimp had had a flash of insight.

Köhler's findings suggested that animals and people set up problems in their minds and play with them until they are solved. Once the parts of the problem fit together in the right way, the solution seems to come in a flash.

Sometimes, as with Dan and his trig problem and also as with Köhler's chimp and the bananas, we need to get away from a problem for a while before a solution comes to us. When we arrive at the solution to a problem when we have not even been consciously working on the problem, we have experienced the **incubation effect**. An incubator warms

Demonstration

To demonstrate the concept of mental set, organize 12 volunteers in three lines of four students each. Tell the students at the head of each line that when they hear the word *go*, they are to hop to the back of the classroom and then return to their seats. (Make sure there is enough room first.) Then say, "Ready, set, go!" as quickly as you can. Do this for the first three groups. When you get to the last group, say "Ready, set," but do not say "go." How many members of the group started to hop? Have the class discuss why this occurred.

Meeting Individual Needs:
Visual Learners

To help visual learners understand the concept of mental set, have them work with the school librarian to locate problems similar to the one solved in Figure 8.4 on page 187. Tell these students to work with the problems and their solutions until they feel comfortable enough to demonstrate them in class. Then have the students challenge the class with the problems, provide solutions as needed, and explain why mental set may have made the problems difficult to solve.

Caption Question: Answer

In each case, fill Jar B completely. Pour water from Jar B to fill Jar A. Then pour more water from Jar B to fill Jar C. Empty Jar C and fill it again with water from Jar B.

For Your Information

Experiments have shown that people's thinking becomes more fixed the more they want to solve a problem. It is as if their strong motivation to solve the problem brings with it unchangeable preconceptions about the elements in the problem.

internet connect

TOPIC: How Do You Solve Problems?

GO TO: go.hrw.com
KEYWORD: SY3 PS8

Have students access the Internet through the HRW Go site to research problem solving and problem-solving methods. Ask students to think of the ways in which they might solve a typical problem. Then have them write a short analysis of how they use algorithms, heuristics, and other problem-solving methods discussed in the chapter.

PROBLEM	JAR A	JAR B	JAR C	GOAL
1	21	127	3	100
2	14	163	25	99
3	18	43	10	5
4	9	42	6	21
5	20	59	4	31
6	23	49	3	20

FIGURE 8.3 *For each of the six problems, how can you use some combination of the amounts of water (shown here in ounces) in Jars A, B, and C—and a tap—to obtain the precise number of ounces of water indicated as the goal in the column at the far right? The jars have no markings on them.*

Source: Adapted from *Rigidity of Behavior* (p. 109) by Abraham S. Luchins and Edith H. Luchins, 1959, Eugene: University of Oregon Press.

eggs so that they will hatch. Incubation in problem solving means standing back from a problem for a period of time while some unconscious process within us continues to work on it. Later, the answer may occur to us in a flash—it will have "hatched" on its own.

Because of the incubation effect, psychologists sometimes recommend that people take a break from work on a difficult problem. After taking such a break, they may come back to the problem refreshed, and a new point of view or approach may have incubated (Azar, 1995).

TRUTH OR fiction
■ REVISITED ■

It is not true that if you do not see the answer to a problem right away, you will probably not be able to solve it. In fact, it is common for people to have greater success in solving a problem if they go away from it for a little while. This is called the incubation effect.

Obstacles to Problem Solving

Sometimes we have trouble finding the solution to a problem simply because the problem is difficult or perhaps because we have little experience in solving that type of problem. At other times, particular obstacles get in our way of solving a problem. Two of these obstacles are known as mental set and functional fixedness.

Mental Set As we know from our discussion on problem solving by analogy, people often try to solve new problems in ways that worked for similar problems. The tendency to respond to a new problem with an approach that was successfully used with similar problems is called **mental set**. While mental set can sometimes help us solve a problem, it can also sometimes get in the way.

Take a moment to work out each of the six problems in Figure 8.3. You have three jars—A, B, and C. They each hold the amount of water you see in the figure. For example, for Problem 1, Jar A holds 21 ounces of water, Jar B holds 127 ounces of water, and Jar C holds 3 ounces. Your goal for Problem 1 is to get 100 ounces. You can fill or empty any of the three jars as many times as you wish.

How did you solve the six problems? You probably discovered that one formula—B – A – 2C—works for all six problems. However, if you are like most people, you did not realize that the final problem, Problem 6, can be solved much more simply, using the formula A – C. Because of your work on problems 1 through 5, you had a mental set on the B – A – 2C formula. In this case, your mental set allowed you to solve the problem, but it prevented you from using the most efficient method. In other cases, mental set may block a person from solving a problem altogether.

For example, were you able to solve Problem C in Figure 8.1? If not, mental set may have been responsible. From past experience, you probably perceived the four dots as the corners of a quadrilateral, and thus it may not have occurred to

Guided Practice

Remind students that creativity requires divergent thinking—the consideration of many possible solutions to a problem. Tell students that one way psychologists test creativity is with a remote associates test. A remote associate is a word that links a set of three apparently unrelated words. For example, an associated word for the set wall-girl-May is *flower* (wallflower, flower girl, *Mayflower*). Have students provide sets of words for *party* and for *paper. (Answers may include birthday-animal-favor and wall-clip-news.)* Ask students how their answers reflect divergent thinking.

Independent Practice

Ask students to develop a remote associates test containing five sets of words. Each set should include three apparently unrelated words that can be linked by a remote associate. Tell students to write their sets of words on one side of a sheet of paper and the corresponding remote associates on the other side of the paper. When students have completed their tests, have volunteers present their sets of words to the class. Have students suggest the remote associates. How successful were they? Did students suggest associates not noted by the writers?

you that the lines could go beyond the dots. (See Figure 8.4.)

Functional Fixedness Another obstacle to problem solving is called functional fixedness. **Functional fixedness** is the tendency to think of an object as being useful only for the function that the object is usually used for.

Problems D and E in Figure 8.1 are challenging because of functional fixedness. In Problem D, the solution is to tack the box of matches to the wall and then use it to support the candle. (See Figure 8.5.) But people have trouble arriving at this solution because they think of the box as a container and not as something they can actually use. In other words, they are fixed on the function of the box as a container because that is usually what it is.

Similarly, in Problem E in Figure 8.1, the solution is to tie the safety scissors to one of the strings and then to set the string swinging so that it will reach you as you hold the other string. (See Figure 8.6). But again, most people are fixed on the function of the scissors as something to cut with, not as a weight to make the string swing.

Problem Solving and Creativity

Functional fixedness can often be overcome by creativity—the ability to come up with new or unusual ways of solving a problem. Thinking of the box of matches as a support platform rather than as a container, for example, is creative; this is not how matchboxes are usually used.

Creativity requires divergent thinking rather than convergent thinking (Guilford, 1967). With **convergent thinking**, thought is limited to available facts. One tries to narrow one's thinking to find the single best solution. With **divergent thinking**, however, one associates more freely to the various elements of a problem. One follows "leads" that run in various directions; perhaps one of them will lead to the solution unexpectedly. Linda may have used divergent thinking when she helped Hannah figure out the correct answer in the crossword puzzle. And Marc almost certainly will find divergent thinking useful if he decides to take creative writing next semester.

Successful problem solving may require both divergent and convergent thinking. At first, divergent thinking produces many possible solutions. Convergent thinking is then used to select the most probable solutions and to reject the others.

Solutions to Figures 8.1C, D, and E

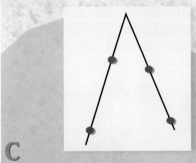

C

FIGURE 8.4 *The lines connecting the four dots must extend beyond the dots.*

D

FIGURE 8.5 *To solve this problem, you have to overcome functional fixedness and think of the box as a platform, not a container.*

E

FIGURE 8.6 *To solve this problem, tie the safety scissors to one of the strings and set the string swinging. Then catch the swinging string.*

Journal Activity

One way to overcome functional fixedness is to practice overturning preconceptions. Tell students to think of some common items around their homes or classrooms. Then challenge them to list all the ways (especially unusual ways) in which they might use each object.

What's New in Psychology?

Some business firms today are using the psychology of problem solving to train more creative workers and managers. For example, in the 1990s Suzanne Merritt of the Polaroid Corporation ran workshops in which participants played word games, conduct hands-on written and tactile exercises, and use other techniques to bring creativity to a problem and its solution. According to Merritt, people can learn to be better problem solvers through creative discovery: "Discovery is looking at the same things as everyone else and seeing something different."

Closing Section 2

Evaluating Ideas

Write the following statement on the chalkboard: No problem in life is too big to solve if you use the correct problem-solving method. Ask students if they support or contest this statement and have them explain why.

Reviewing Section 2

Have students complete the Section Review questions on page 188.

Extension

Emphasize that the problem-solving methods discussed in this section can and should be applied to real-life problems. Encourage students, working independently or in pairs, to identify some local problems currently facing your community. Then have them proceed through the ABCDEs of problem solving in search of solutions. Have students present their work in the form of a letter to a local official, offering advice on how to solve one of the community's problems.

The ABCDEs of Problem Solving

What is the best way to solve a problem? Some psychologists advise following these steps:

A: *A*ssess the problem.

B: *B*rainstorm approaches to the problem.

C: *C*hoose the approach that seems most likely to work.

D: *D*o it—try the most likely approach.

E: *E*valuate the results.

Assessing the Problem   Assessing a problem means examining its parts and making sure that you understand it. Often the first assessment we make about a problem is the *type* of problem it is.

Did you figure out the answer to the question in Figure 8.1F? The answer, of course, is that you don't bury the survivors anywhere at all—the survivors are still alive. But many listeners get this problem wrong, suggesting answers such as, "In their hometowns." (Try this riddle on your friends!)

The reason that most people get this problem wrong when they first hear it is that they have assessed it incorrectly. They assess it to be a *political* problem; they hear the word *border* and assume that the problem has to do with territorial concerns. People who give the correct answer, however, have assessed it to be a trick question. They look for the trick (the word *survivor*) and find it.

Brainstorming Approaches   Brainstorming is the free, spontaneous production of possible approaches or solutions to a problem. Often brainstorming is done in a group; people are free to call

A DAY IN THE LIFE

out ideas as they think of them. When Dan, Hannah, and Marc were trying to help Linda figure out what to make for dinner, they brainstormed. That is, they called out ideas as the ideas occurred to them.

Brainstorming can also be done individually. It helps to have a sheet of paper handy so that you can jot down your ideas as they occur to you.

With brainstorming, anything goes. The more ideas, the better. The purpose of brainstorming is to encourage creativity; brainstorming stimulates a large number of ideas, even wild ideas. The more ideas that are suggested, the more likely one of them is to help solve the problem. With Linda, it took a few tries, but eventually she found a dinner idea that seemed possible.

Choosing an Approach   Once a number of possible approaches have been proposed through brainstorming, the problem solver must choose which approach to take and which course of action to follow. The choice is made on the basis of which approach seems most likely to work.

Doing the Problem   Once the approach has been chosen, the next step is to actually do the problem—to try out the approach.

Evaluating the Results   The final step in problem solving is evaluating the results. Has the goal been achieved? Does the end point make sense? Has the problem been solved? If not, we must figure out what went wrong. Did we assess the problem incorrectly? Did we choose the wrong approach or carry it out incorrectly? We may need to go back and repeat any or all of the earlier steps of the problem-solving process.

A group of people may find a "brainstorming session" to be a productive way of accomplishing a task.

SECTION 2 REVIEW

go.hrw.com **Homework Practice Online**
Keyword: SY3 HP8

1. What is the primary advantage of using heuristics rather than algorithms in solving problems? What is the primary disadvantage?

2. What are the steps of problem solving?

3. **Critical Thinking**   *Analyzing Information* Describe the relationship between, and sequence of, intermediate goals and terminal goals.

Section Objective

▶ Differentiate between deductive reasoning and inductive reasoning.

This objective is assessed in the Section Review on page 191 and in the Chapter 8 Review.

Opening Section 3

Motivator

Bring the game Clue® (or some other mystery-based game) to class or arrange for one or more of the students to do so. Explain the game to the class and have volunteers play the game while the rest of the class watches. When the game is over, have the winner explain how he or she used the information collected during the game to reach the correct conclusions. Then tell the class that Section 3 explores two important ways that people use information to reach conclusions—deductive reasoning and inductive reasoning.

SECTION **3**

Reasoning

A DAY IN THE LIFE

When Marc was trying to figure out how hard it would be to learn Japanese, he assumed that Japanese and Korean were similar. Thus, he also assumed that Hannah, who spoke Korean, would be able to tell him how difficult Japanese would be to learn. Whether Marc knew it or not, he had used reasoning in his thought process. **Reasoning** is the use of information to reach conclusions. There are two main types of reasoning: deductive reasoning and inductive reasoning.

Deductive Reasoning

In **deductive reasoning**, the conclusion is true if the premises are true. A **premise** is an idea or statement that provides the basic information that allows us to draw conclusions. Here is an example of deductive reasoning:

1. South Korea is in Asia.
2. The city of Seoul is in South Korea.
3. Therefore, Seoul is in Asia.

The first two statements of this example are the premises, while the third statement is the conclusion. The conclusion is said to be *deduced* from the premises; if South Korea is in Asia and Seoul is in South Korea, then Seoul must be in Asia. (See Figure 8.7A.)

In deductive reasoning, the conclusion is always true when the premises are true. However, if the premises are incorrect, then the conclusion may be incorrect as well. Marc's reasoning about Japanese and Korean went as follows:

1. Countries that are near each other have similar languages.
2. Japan and Korea are near each other.
3. Therefore, Japan and Korea have similar languages.

Logically, Marc's reasoning was sound. He made a statement about a category (countries that are near each other), then he assigned something (Japan and Korea) to the category. He was right to assume that whatever was true for the category as a whole would be true for members of the category. (See Figure 8.7B.) But his first premise—that countries that are near each other have similar languages—was faulty. Countries that are near each other do not necessarily have similar languages. Thus, Marc's conclusion was incorrect. Japan and Korea are near each other, but their languages are not very similar.

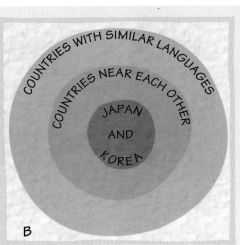

FIGURE 8.7 *Venn diagrams such as these use circles to show simple relationships among sets. Overlapping regions show the intersection of sets. (A) This diagram illustrates the Seoul–South Korea–Asia deductive reasoning. If South Korea is in Asia and Seoul is in South Korea, then Seoul is in Asia. (B) In deductive reasoning, if the premises are incorrect, the conclusion may be incorrect as well. Marc's first premise, that countries near each other have similar languages, was faulty. Thus, his conclusion that Japanese and Korean are similar was incorrect.*

Teaching Section 3

Demonstration

To demonstrate confirmation bias, write the numbers 2, 4, and 6 on the chalkboard. Ask them to develop three number groups that follow the rule of your example (three numbers in increasing order of magnitude). Each time students assemble three-number sequences, ask them what rule is being demonstrated. *(Some may say start with any number and then add 2.)* At the conclusion of the exercise, guide students to see that they chose examples to prove their hypotheses rather than examples that might disprove the hypotheses.

Taking a Stand

Call students' attention to "Truth or Fiction Revisited" on page 191. Have a volunteer read the feature aloud to the class. Then write the following statement on the chalkboard: In science, it is just as important to disprove theories as it is to find support for them. Have students debate this idea and explain why they agree or disagree with it.

Cultural Dimensions

Sometimes an approach to a problem only appears to be a solution. People then develop unsubstantiated beliefs about the approach. For example, if you did well on your history test after eating oatmeal for breakfast, you might conclude that the oatmeal caused the success. Thereafter, you might always eat oatmeal on test mornings. This phenomenon may help explain some of the traditions, customs, and superstitions found in various cultures. Have students research their own culture or another that interests them to find examples of this phenomenon. Have students share their findings with the class.

Teaching Transparencies with Teacher's Notes

TRANSPARENCY 23: Inductive Reasoning

Inductive Reasoning

In deductive reasoning, we usually start out with a general statement or principle and reason down to specifics that fit that statement or principle. In **inductive reasoning**, on the other hand, we reason from individual cases or particular facts to reach a general conclusion.

In inductive reasoning, the conclusion is sometimes wrong, even when the premises are correct. Marc's assumption that countries that are near each other have similar languages was probably based on inductive reasoning. His thinking may have been:

1. Spain and Portugal are near each other, and they have similar languages.
2. Sweden, Denmark, and Norway are near each other, and they all have similar languages.
3. Therefore, countries that are near each other have similar languages.

But just because *some* countries that are near each other have similar languages, this does not mean that *all* countries that are near each other do. (See Figure 8.8.) In effect, Marc's statement that countries that are near each other have similar languages was really only a hypothesis, or an educated guess, rather than a conclusion. And Hannah proved the hypothesis wrong—Japan and Korea are near each other yet do not have similar languages.

Assume for a moment that Marc's hypothesis was correct—that countries that are near each other have similar languages. How could Marc have proved that hypothesis? Only with great difficulty—by comparing the languages of every single country in the world and showing that *all* countries that are near each other have similar languages. However, it was quite easy to prove that Marc's hypothesis was *wrong*—by providing only one example of countries that are near each other and have different languages.

It is often impossible to prove an assumption reached by inductive reasoning to be true. We can only prove it false. But people often fail to realize this. As a result, they seek to prove, or confirm, their hypotheses rather than disprove them. This tendency is called **confirmation bias**.

Even though inductive reasoning does not allow us to be certain that our assumptions are correct, we use inductive reasoning all the time. And until we prove a hypothesis false, we assume it to be true. For example, if we have read two books by a particular author and enjoyed both books, we conclude that a third book by the same author also will be enjoyable. Until we find a book by that author that we do not enjoy, we will probably go on reading that author's books. Inductive conclusions do not follow logically from premises, as deductive conclusions

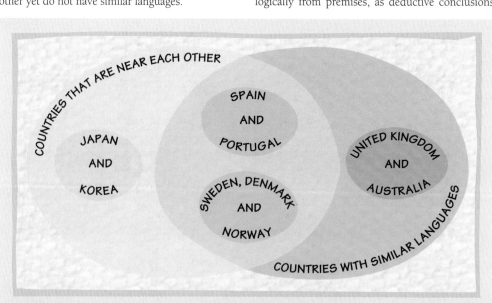

FIGURE 8.8 *In inductive reasoning, the conclusion can be wrong even when the premises are correct.* *Some, but not all, countries that are near each other have similar languages.*

Interpreting Information

Have students create study cards for both inductive and deductive reasoning. Cards should contain a definition of the reasoning approach and at least two examples. Invite students to exchange cards, offering comments on clarity and accuracy.

Reviewing Section 3

Have students complete the Section Review questions on page 191.

Section Objective

▶ Analyze the strategies used in decision making.

This objective is assessed in the Section Review on page 195 and in the Chapter 8 Review.

---

do. Yet they are accurate often enough that we can rely on them in our daily lives.

Most sciences, including psychology, rely on inductive reasoning. Scientists gather specific pieces of information, and then they come up with general theories that explain the information. However, no matter how much information scientists have to support a particular theory, they can never know for sure if the theory is true for all times and all situations. There might still be some information not yet collected that would prove the theory false.

TRUTH OR fiction
■ R E V I S I T E D ■

It is true that scientists can never prove for certain that their theories are true. They can only gather evidence that supports their theories. On the other hand, it *is* possible to prove a theory false.

SECTION 3 REVIEW

go.hrw.com Homework Practice Online
Keyword: SY3 HP8

1. What is reasoning?
2. Define *premise*. What role do premises play in deductive reasoning?
3. **Critical Thinking** *Contrasting* In what ways do deductive and inductive reasoning differ?

SECTION 4

Decision Making and Judgment

Life is filled with decisions. Most of these decisions are fairly minor in the general scheme of things. Should we take an umbrella with us when we go out or leave it at home? Should we walk or take the bus? Which route should we take to school or work?

Other decisions, of course, are relatively major. Should we go to college or get a job right after high school? What career do we want to pursue? Which political candidates should we vote for? People use a variety of methods to make decisions. Some methods are more effective than others.

Weighing the Pluses and Minuses

Making decisions means choosing among goals or courses of action to reach goals. When we are making careful decisions, we weigh the pluses and minuses of each possible course of action. We think about the importance of our goals and our abilities to overcome the obstacles in our paths. To make good decisions, we often need to gather more information about our goals. We also need to learn more about our abilities to attain our goals.

The use of a balance sheet—a listing of various reasons for or against making a particular choice—can help us make sure that we have considered the information available to us. A balance sheet might be a list of the pluses and the minuses of taking an action. For example, if you are trying to decide whether to participate in a certain extracurricular activity, you might make a list of the advantages (such as gaining experience and having fun) and the disadvantages (such as losing time that might be needed for studying) of doing so.

A balance sheet can also be useful when a person is trying to decide between two or more alternatives. Listing all the alternatives and the reasons for each one may help the person visualize which of the alternatives is the better course of action. The balance sheet may also help indicate areas where more information is needed.

When Marc was trying to decide whether to take creative writing or Japanese, it might have helped him to put together a balance sheet listing the potential benefits of each class. After he had completed the list, he could have based his decision on which option appeared to have greater rewards. Or he might have discovered that there was still some information he needed to collect before he could make an informed decision. (See Figure 8.9 on page 192.)

Shortcuts in Decision Making and Judgment

Weighing the pluses and minuses may be the best thing to do whenever we want to be sure to make the right decision. But weighing the pluses and minuses can be time-consuming and is not always practical. Furthermore, in order to weigh the pluses and minuses, we need to know what they are, and often we have to make decisions based on somewhat limited information. In such cases, we use heuristics. That is, we take shortcuts.

🔲 **internet** connect

TOPIC: Conflict Resolution and Decision Making
GO TO: go.hrw.com
KEYWORD: SY3 PS8
Have students access the Internet through the HRW Go site to research decision-making and conflict-resolution processes. Ask them to think of typical decisions a teenager might make that could result in conflict among people or groups. Then have the students role-play a conflict resolution process that uses persuasion, compromise, debate, and negotiation.

Opening Section 4

Motivator

Ask students to record in their journals some difficult decisions they made in the recent past. Invite volunteers to share some of those decisions in a class discussion. Have students discuss what made those decisions difficult. Explain that Section 4 analyzes the effectiveness of various approaches to decision making.

Teaching Section 4

Cooperative Learning

Organize the class into groups of three or four. Challenge each group to develop a list of difficult decisions facing teenagers. They might draw from the decisions discussed in the Motivator activity or from additional brainstorming. Encourage groups to focus on decisions that all group members can consider. Once a single decision is chosen, each group member should create a balance sheet to assess the pros and cons of each choice. Reassemble the groups and have the students evaluate their information and make a final group decision.

Using Visuals

Tell students to imagine that they must decide between taking a part-time job after school and working on the school newspaper, both of which they really want to do. Have students create a balance sheet similar to the one shown in Figure 8.9. Then have students discuss the usefulness of the balance-sheet approach in making decisions.

What's New in Psychology?

A study reported in the *Journal of the American Medical Association* found that many Americans use irrational methods to make decisions concerning their medical care. Instead of considering statistical or factual information, they rely on what the neighbor down the street did in a similar situation. In other words, they use a representativeness heuristic that does not necessarily fit the decision being made.

Redelmeier et al. (1993). Understanding patients' decisions. *Journal of the American Medical Association.* 72–76.

Reasons for Taking Japanese	Reasons for Taking Creative Writing
Learn about a different culture.	Gain greater skills in writing.
Prepare for travel to a foreign country.	Writing skills may be more practical than Japanese.
Impressive for college and job applications.	Also impressive for college and job applications.
Fear of not being able to come up with creative ideas to write about in creative writing.	Foreign languages have always been difficult for me, and Japanese might be even more difficult.

Information Still Needed to Finalize Decision

- Does my schedule allow for the time when each class is offered?
- If I take Japanese now, can I continue to study it later?
- Exactly what types of writing will I be able to learn in creative writing?

FIGURE 8.9 *Constructing a balance sheet can sometimes help us make decisions.*

The Representativeness Heuristic Imagine that you are taking a true-false quiz. The quiz has six items. Which of the following answer sequences (T stands for true and F stands for false) do you think is most likely to appear on the quiz?

T T T T T T

F F F T T T

T F F T F T

You probably said the third one. Why? For one thing, you know that six "trues" in a row are unlikely (assuming your teacher is not trying to play games with you). Second, you probably assume that your teacher wrote a quiz that had a random mix of true and false answers. The sequence T F F T F T looks random. The T T T T T T and F F F T T T sequences do not. Most people would thus select the T F F T F T sequence because it looks *representative*. It seems to represent a random sequence.

Based on the **representativeness heuristic**, people make decisions about a sample according to the population that the sample appears to represent. In all the true-false quizzes and tests you have ever taken—in other words, in the entire population of true-false tests you have seen—more answer sequences have looked like the third one (on your sample quiz) than like either of the other two. Thus, the third answer sequence best *represents* the type of sequence you have come to expect, based on all of your previous experiences with true-false tests.

The representativeness heuristic can be misleading, however. Assuming that your teacher really has written a quiz with a random mix of true and false answers—with a 50-50 chance of either a true or a false answer on any given quiz item—each of the three sequences listed above is *equally likely*. For each item, the chance that the answer will be true is

Even if you flip "heads" 20 times in a row, the chance that you will flip it the next time is still 50 percent.

Analyzing Information

Have students experiment with the true-false example described on pages 192 and 193. Using classmates or other students (perhaps from another grade level), student researchers should develop and administer a short true-false quiz. Questions should be arranged in a random sequence of true and false answers. Let students repeat the testing several times, each time resequencing the questions. Ask students to use the results to analyze the relationship between representativeness and decision making.

Identifying Cause and Effect

Remind students that people tend to overestimate the occurrence of plane crashes and acts of violence because these events are well publicized and hence come readily to mind. Ask students to think of other catastrophic events whose occurrence people tend to overestimate. *(Students may mention shark attacks or being struck by lightning.)* For each event mentioned, have students determine how the availability heuristic may affect people's decision making. *(For example, people who believe the probability of being bitten by a shark is high may refuse to swim in the ocean.)*

one in two, just as the chance that the answer will be false is also one in two. The likelihood of attaining *any* specific sequence—whether T T T T T or T F F T F T, say—is the same (1 in 64, in fact).

It is true that the likelihood of attaining a random-looking answer sequence is greater than that of attaining a nonrandom-looking sequence. But that is because there are a greater number of random-looking sequences than of nonrandom-looking sequences—out of 64 possible sequences, most of them look random. For example, T F F T F T, F T F T T F, and T T F T F F all look random. But the likelihood of attaining any *one* sequence—whether it looks random or not—is the same as that of attaining any other sequence.

So what does this have to do with decision making? Well, imagine taking that quiz again. Suppose that you know the answers to the first five items and that they are all true. But the sixth item has you stumped, and you have to guess at the answer. Do you guess true, which would mean six "trues" in a row? Or do you guess false because you figure that it is unlikely that six "trues" in a row would occur? The temptation may be strong to go with the "false." But if the answers were assigned randomly, it really doesn't matter. Regardless of the answers to the previous five items, the answer to the final item has a 50-50 chance of being true and a 50-50 chance of being false. You might as well flip a coin.

The Availability Heuristic People also make decisions on the basis of information that is available to them in their immediate consciousness. This is called the **availability heuristic**.

For example, what percentage of the students at your school would you estimate are involved in extracurricular activities? Unless you go to a very small school, your answer to this question will probably reflect your personal knowledge of students who do, and do not, participate in extracurricular activities. Knowledge of these individuals is available to you. Rather than going out of your way to find out whether all the students you do *not* know participate in activities, you base your answer on what you already know.

Thus, if most of the students you know participate in extracurricular activities, you may think that most of the students in the school as a whole do too. But this is not necessarily true—the sample of students you know may not be representative of all students in the school.

Events that are more recent or better publicized than others also tend to be more available. For

A student's estimate of how many students play football could be biased by how many of the student's friends play the sport.

example, whenever a plane crashes, the event is very well publicized. Car accidents, however, cause far more deaths than airplane crashes in the United States. But because of the publicity given to the airplane crashes, people are more likely to fear flying than they are to fear driving. They overestimate the risk of flying and underestimate the risk of driving.

The media also tends to focus on acts of violence, such as murder. As a result, people tend to overestimate the amount of violence in the United States (Silver et al., 1994).

The Anchoring Heuristic Another shortcut that people sometimes take in making decisions is called the anchoring heuristic. When using the **anchoring heuristic**, people make decisions based on certain ideas or standards they hold, ideas or standards that serve as an anchor for them. For example, people often decide to go along with the things they learn early in life. Early learning serves as an anchor in thinking.

If you have grown up in a family in which everyone else votes in elections, you probably expect to

Closing Section 4

For Further Research

Have students conduct library research to learn more about the methods advertisers use to sway the decision making of consumers toward particular products. What strategies do advertisers use to catch the attention of consumers? How do advertisers determine what words will attract consumers? What roles do humor and dramatic appeal play in consumer decision making? How does the government protect consumers against dishonest advertising? Students should present their findings in short oral reports.

Drawing Conclusions

Ask students to rank each of the decision-making methods discussed in the section in order of its effectiveness, from most effective to least effective. Then have students explain what people can do to avoid the least effective methods and to become discerning decision makers.

Reviewing Section 4

Have students complete the Section Review questions on page 195.

page 195.

Class Discussion

Have the class discuss why the anchoring heuristic can have both positive and negative effects on decision making. Ask students why some people are reluctant to change their initial presumptions, even in light of information to the contrary.

Cross-Curricular Link: Civics and Government

Remind students that politicians as well as advertisers use the framing effect to sway people to their point of view. Then have students discuss why it is important for voters in a democratic nation such as the United States to be aware of how politicians use the framing effect.

Journal Activity

Ask students to note in their journals instances when they were overconfident about their decisions, even when they were wrong. Have students analyze why they held so tightly to their decisions.

194

vote too. That expectation is an anchor in your life. Beliefs about politics, religion, and way of life are common anchors. When something happens that makes people question the beliefs they have grown up with, they may change their beliefs a bit. But most people change only reluctantly.

When people form judgments or make estimates, they begin with an initial view, called a presumption. The initial view serves as the anchor. As they receive additional information, they make adjustments. But such adjustments are often difficult for people to make, and sometimes people are unwilling to make them.

The Framing Effect

Suppose that once Linda arrived at the store, she "chickened out" of making chicken stew from scratch and decided instead to buy canned stew. She noticed that there were two brands to choose from. One brand called the stew "zesty" and "hearty." The other brand simply contained the name of the stew. As far as Linda could tell, the two brands were identical in every other respect. Which one do you think Linda decided to buy? Probably the zesty, hearty one.

The way information is presented, or framed—such as on product labels—can affect our decisions.

If so, this decision was based on the framing effect. The **framing effect** refers to the way in which wording affects decision making. Advertisers try to use the framing effect to get people to decide to buy a particular product. They are very careful in choosing what words to put on a product. Foods with fewer calories, for example, are advertised as being "light," not "thin." A "thin" food does not sound as appetizing as a "light" food.

Advertisers are not the only people who use the framing effect to their advantage. Political groups also are very aware of the framing effect. Most political groups, for example, pick names that sound positive—they know that people are more likely to support a cause that they feel good about rather than a cause that merely opposes something. This is why groups are usually "pro" something rather than "anti" something.

Experienced parents, too, know all about the framing effect, particularly when dealing with very young children. They know that they have to choose their words carefully to encourage the children to give the desired responses. Thus, when parents want the child to take a bath, they might say, "Mr. Duck is waiting for you in the tub!" and not "You'll be cleaner after your bath."

Overconfidence

People tend to have a great deal of confidence in their decisions, whether the decisions are right or wrong (Gigerenzer et al., 1991; Lundeberg et al., 1994). For instance, many students refuse to change their opinions about how well they did on a test they have just taken even when other students point out that their answers were wrong. Likewise, have you ever known anyone who kept unrealistic confidence in a baseball team, even though the team was far behind in the standings?

There are a number of reasons why people tend to be overconfident, even when they are wrong:

- People are often unaware of how flimsy their supporting evidence is.
- People tend to pay attention to examples that confirm their opinions and to ignore examples that do not.
- People tend to bring about things they believe in. If students believe that they are capable of getting an A on next week's test, for example, they are more likely to study for the test and prepare for it in ways that might just help get them that A.

▶ Identify the basic elements of language and summarize the stages of language development.

This objective is assessed in the Section Review on page 201 and in the Chapter 8 Review.

Tell students to imagine they need to communicate with visitors from another planet. Ask them how they would tell the visitors what they were thinking. What clues or cues would students use to understand what the visitors were thinking? Invite students to suggest some methods for communicating. These methods might include drawing pictures, making gestures, or role-playing emotions. Ask students to consider whether these methods constitute language. Explain that Section 5 will define language and outline key connections between thinking and language.

- Even when people are told that they tend to be overconfident in their decisions, they usually do not make use of this information (Gigerenzer et al., 1991).

TRUTH OR fiction ■ REVISITED ■

It is not true that most people easily change their opinions when presented with convincing arguments. To the contrary, people tend to stick to their opinions even when they are presented with evidence that suggests that they might be wrong.

SECTION 4 REVIEW

go.hrw.com **Homework Practice Online** Keyword: SY3 HP8

1. What is the main drawback of basing decisions on the availability heuristic?

2. Give two reasons why people tend to be overconfident about their decisions.

3. **Critical Thinking** *Summarizing* What are several strategies that can be used in decision making?

SECTION 5

Language

Language is the communication of ideas through symbols that are arranged according to rules of grammar. Language makes it possible for people to share knowledge. People can use language to describe what they ate for breakfast or what they thought of the movie they just saw. They can use language to set down the learning of past generations and store it for people who will live hundreds or even thousands of years in the future. Language also permits people to use the eyes and ears of other people to learn more than they ever could from their own individual experiences.

The Basic Elements of Language

Languages contain three basic elements: phonemes (sounds), morphemes (basic units of meaning), and syntax (grammar). Combinations of these units create the words, phrases, and sentences that people use to communicate ideas.

Phonemes The basic sounds of a language are called **phonemes**. (Languages that do not consist of sounds, such as American Sign Language, do not have phonemes.) There are 26 letters in the English alphabet, but there are many more than 26 phonemes. Phonemes include consonants, such as the *d* and *g* in *dog*. They also include vowels, such as the *o* in *dog* and the *o* in *no*. Even though *no* and *dog* each contain an *o*, the *o* sound is different in each word, and thus the two *o* sounds are two different phonemes. Other phonemes in the English language cannot be represented by a single letter—for example, the sound *sh*.

English contains some phonemes and phoneme distinctions that are not found in other languages. French has no equivalent for the English *th*, for example, which is why native French speakers often use a *z* sound to approximate the *th* in an English word: "Zee book is on zee table." Chinese does not distinguish between a *p* sound and a *b* sound; Japanese does not distinguish between *r* and *l*.

Morphemes The units of meaning in a language are called **morphemes**. Morphemes are made up of phonemes. Some morphemes, such as *car* and *bike,* are words in and of themselves. Other morphemes are prefixes (for example *pre*, which means "before"), while still others are suffixes (for example, *-ness* and *-ence*). Many words use combinations of morphemes. English uses morphemes such as *z* and *s* to make objects plural. Adding the *z* morpheme to *car* makes the word plural; adding the *s* morpheme to *bike* makes it plural.

In English, the past tense of regular verbs is formed by adding the *ed* morpheme to the end of the present-tense verb. The past tenses of *walk* and *talk,* for example, are *walked* and *talked*. Verbs such as *to be, to run,* and *to think* do not follow this rule, however. Thus they are considered irregular verbs.

Syntax The way in which words are arranged to make phrases and sentences is **syntax**. The rules for word order are the grammar of a language. English syntax usually follows the pattern of subject, verb, and object of the verb. For example:

Linda (subject)→cooked (verb)→dinner (object).

Many other languages have a different word order. Whereas in English the verb usually goes in

Cultural Dimensions

Infants' brains develop in part as a function of what they are exposed to. With language, this means that the phonemes an infant hears over and over are mapped in the brain. Special receivers are created in the brain's auditory area to "hear" these phonemes. These receivers are grouped by the similarity of the phonemes. Thus, babies hearing English phonemes will separate the areas used to hear *ra* and *la*. Babies hearing Japanese, a language that does not distinguish between *l* and *r*, will not create the same distinctions.

Teaching Section 5

Guided Practice

Organize the class into large groups. Tell the groups to break down a short sentence, such as "Bob walked home," into phonemes and to assign the various phonemes to different group members. Have the members of each group stand and say their phonemes aloud for the class. Then tell the "phonemes" to group themselves into morphemes. Finally, have the group members arrange themselves and perform their sentence in such a way that the syntax of the sentence will be incorrect. Have the class rearrange the group members to achieve the correct syntax.

Independent Practice

Ask students to create a three-column chart titled "Basic Elements of Language." Tell students to label each column with one of the basic elements of language discussed in the text. Have them complete their charts by supplying a definition, two facts, and two examples for each element. Then have students write a paragraph explaining how people combine these basic elements to communicate ideas.

the middle of the sentence, between the subject and the object, in German the verb often is placed at the end of a sentence. In the vast majority of languages, however, the subject precedes the object. And in no languages does the object appear first in a sentence (Slobin, 1983).

Semantics

Compare these two sentences:

It will be a long time before dinner is served.

The members of Linda's family long for a tasty dinner.

In the first sentence, *long* is an adjective. The sentence means that there is still much time before dinner. In the second sentence, on the other hand, *long* is a part of a verb—"to long for." The word *long* has more than one meaning.

The study of meaning is called **semantics**. Semantics involves the relationship between language and the things depicted in the language. Words that sound alike, such as *right* and *write,* can have different meanings, depending on how they

This infant may coo to indicate satisfaction at being fed. Cooing is a form of verbal expression that precedes the development of actual language.

are used. So can words that are spelled alike, as we saw with *long.*

How a sentence is structured also affects meaning. Compare these two sentences:

Linda's chicken is ready to eat.

Linda's family is ready to eat.

The first sentence probably means that Linda has prepared the chicken and that it is ready to be eaten. The second sentence looks similar, but it most likely means that Linda's family is hungry—that the members of her family want to eat as soon as possible.

Sentences have a surface structure and a deep structure. The surface structure is what you see, the actual words of a sentence. Both "ready to eat" sentences have the same surface structure. The deep structure of a sentence is its deeper meaning, the message the speaker is trying to communicate. The "ready to eat" sentences differ in meaning.

Some sentences, such as "Make me a sandwich," have an unclear surface structure—you cannot be certain of the deep structure based on the surface structure. If you ask someone with a sense of humor to make you a sandwich, don't be surprised if the reply is, "Poof! You're a sandwich!"

The Stages of Language Development

Children develop language in a sequence of steps. The sequence is the same for nearly all children. It begins with crying, cooing, and babbling, then moves into the learning of words, and finally, the learning of grammar.

Crying, Cooing, and Babbling Crying, cooing, and babbling are not considered true language because they do not use symbols with specific meanings. Nevertheless, crying is a highly effective form of verbal expression for newborn infants—it usually gets the attention of caregivers.

During their second month, babies begin to coo. Coos are vowel-like and resemble "oohs" and "ahs." Cooing seems to express feelings of pleasure. Tired, hungry babies do not coo. Cries and coos can communicate discomfort, hunger, or enjoyment of being rocked, held, or fed.

At about six months of age, infants begin to babble. Unlike crying and cooing, babbling has the sounds of speech. Babies often babble consonant and vowel combinations, as in *ba, gaz* even the

EXPLORING
DIVERSITY

Language and Culture

Nearly all humans are born with the capacity to learn language. But the languages used in different cultures vary widely.

List 10 basic colors. Would it surprise you to know that the Dani, a people who live in New Guinea, have only two words for colors: *mili,* used to describe dark, cool shades, and *mola* for bright, warm shades?

You might think that any word in one language can be translated into another language, but this is not true. Many languages contain words that have no direct equivalent in other languages. The Arabic language contains more than 250 words for camel. The Hanunoo people of the Philippines have some 90 words for rice. And the Inuit, who live near the Arctic, have many terms describing different types and conditions of snow.

According to the Whorfian hypothesis (named after its originator, Benjamin Whorf), differences such as these indicate that language determines how people perceive the world. In other words, someone who has many words for snow actually perceives snow differently than someone who only has one word for snow.

Most research evidence, however, does not support the Whorfian hypothesis. The Inuit may have many different words for snow, but that does not mean that they perceive snow differently from other people. Rather, because snow is a basic part of their daily existence, the Inuit may have more of a need and more of a use for several snow terms than do people who have less exposure to snow.

Vocabulary is only one of the ways in which languages differ. Languages also differ from each other in the phonemes, or sounds, they use. The Spanish rolled *r,* for example, does not appear in English and is difficult for some native English speakers to pronounce. Similarly, German contains some vowel sounds (such as *ä, ö,* and *ü*) that are not generally used in English. One Khoisan language of southern Africa contains four different clicking sounds. And in some languages, even the pitch or tone of the speaker's voice can change the meaning of a word.

Think About It

Drawing Inferences and Conclusions Think of an item that Americans use many different words to identify. What does the large number of words indicate about the importance of the item in American culture?

Class Discussion

Spark a class debate on the Whorfian hypothesis by asking students to respond to the following question: If the English language did not contain a future tense, would you still be able to imagine yourself as an adult? Lead students to understand that while language influences thought, it does not restrict thought.

Think About It: Answer

Items will vary, but students should state that the large number of words used to identify the item indicates that the item figures prominently in American culture.

internet connect

TOPIC: Language Acquisition and Development
GO TO: go.hrw.com
KEYWORD: SY3 PS8

Have students access the Internet through the HRW Go site to research language acquisition and theories of language development. Then ask students to create an illustrated and annotated chart to display their information. Students should evaluate theories of language acquisition and development and specify the theories' strengths and weaknesses.

Calvin and Hobbes
by Bill Watterson

Formulating Hypotheses

Have volunteers create a time line on the chalkboard that shows the steps involved in language development and the ages at which they occur. Explain that although all children pass through the same sequence of steps, they may do so at very different rates. Thus, while the progression shown on the time line is quite common, it is not true for all children. Even in the same family, one child may speak in complete sentences at 18 months while another speaks only a few words at 30 months. Challenge students to formulate some hypotheses to explain these differences.

Cooperative Learning

Organize the class into small groups. Tell the members of each group to work together to create a comic strip that illustrates some aspect of grammar development in young children. Have the groups present their comic strips to the class and explain how they relate to the principles presented in the textbook. Students may wish to group their comic strips according to developmental stage and create a bulletin-board display titled "The Development of Grammar."

Journal Activity

Tell students to imagine that they awaken one day to find that everyone around them speaks a different language. Have them make an entry in their journal describing the feelings and emotions evoked by not being able to communicate effectively with others. Have them link these feelings to those probably experienced by young children who cannot yet communicate their thoughts clearly or effectively.

Cultural Dimensions

Despite the fact that all babies around the world babble similar sounds, they soon begin to acquire the language of those around them. Estimates suggest that there are between 4,000 and 10,000 distinct languages spoken in the world today, with the number of dialects estimated to be between 20,000 and 50,000. Even though so many different tongues are spoken around the world, there are certain commonalities. For example, in almost every language the word for mother begins with an m sound—one of the first phonemes a baby can pronounce.

highly valued *mama* and *dada*. At first, however, combinations with actual meaning, such as *mama* and *dada*, are purely coincidental.

Crying, cooing, and babbling are basic human abilities. Children from cultures whose languages sound different all babble similar sounds, including sounds they have not heard. In fact, children babble phonemes found in languages spoken around the world. By 9 or 10 months of age, however, children pick out and repeat the phonemes used by the people around them. Other phonemes start to drop away.

Babies understand much of what other people are saying before they can talk. They demonstrate understanding with their actions and gestures.

Words, Words, Words   After babbling comes the learning of words—the start of true language. Most children acquire new words slowly at first. After they speak their first word, it may take another three or four months before they have a 10-word vocabulary. By about 18 months of age, children are saying about two dozen words. Most early words are nouns—names for things. Research indicates that reading to children increases their vocabulary.

Studies have shown that reading to children can increase their vocabulary.

It is thus a good idea for parents to pull out the storybooks and read to their children (Arnold et al., 1994; Robbins & Ehri, 1994).

Children sometimes overreach—they try to talk about more things than they have words for. Often they extend the meanings of words to refer to things for which they do not have words. This behavior is called overextension. For example, if a child sees a cow but does not know the word *cow*, she or he might call the cow a doggie.

Development of Grammar   The first things children say are usually brief, but they have the meanings of sentences. That is, these utterances have a grammar. Even one word can express a complete thought, such as "Sit!" Children just starting to use language use only the words essential to communicating their meaning.

Sometimes a word will have more than one meaning, depending on the circumstances. For example, *doggie* can mean "There is a dog," "That stuffed animal looks like my dog," or "I want you to give me the dog!" Most children readily teach their parents what they mean with their utterances. They are delighted when parents do as requested and may howl when they do not.

As they approach their second birthday, most children begin to use two-word sentences. "That doggie" might seem like just a phrase but is really a sentence in which *is* and *a* are implied: "That (is) (a) doggie." Two-word utterances such as this appear at about the same time in all languages (Slobin, 1983).

Even brief two-word utterances show understanding of grammar. A child who wants his or her mother to sit in a chair says, "Sit chair," not "chair sit." Similarly, the child says, "my doggy," not "doggy my," to show possession. "Mommy go" means Mommy is leaving. "Go Mommy" expresses the desire to have Mommy leave.

Between the ages of two and three, children's sentences expand to include missing words. They add articles (*a, an, the*), conjunctions (*and, but, or*), possessive and demonstrative adjectives (*your, her, that*), pronouns (*she, him, it*), and prepositions (*in, on, over, around, under, through*).

One interesting aspect of how children learn grammar has to do with irregular words. As you know, English has many irregular verbs and nouns. For example, the past tense of *am* is *was*, the past tense of *sit* is *sat*, and the plural of *child* is *children*. Children first learn irregular words by imitating their parents. Two-year-olds often use them correctly. But then a seemingly odd thing happens.

Even though the children have used these words correctly, they soon begin to use them incorrectly (Kuczaj, 1982). What has happened?

What has happened is that they have learned the rules for forming the past tense and plurals (in English, adding *d* or *ed* morphemes to make a word past tense and adding *s* or *z* morphemes to form plurals). Once they have learned these rules, they begin to make errors. For example, three- to five-year-olds may be more likely to say, "I runned away" than "I ran away." They are likely to talk about the "gooses" and "sheeps" they "seed" on the farm.

They make these errors because they have applied the normal rules to all words, even the words for which the rules do not work. This is called **overregularization**. Although it may seem like a bad thing when children begin to incorrectly use words that they previously used correctly, overregularization represents an advance in the development of grammar. And in another year or two, children will learn the correct forms of the irregular words as well as the regular ones, and overregularization will stop.

TRUTH *OR* **fiction** ▪ R E V I S I T E D ▪

It is not true that once a child learns the correct form of a word, he or she will never use the incorrect form. Because of overregularization of the rules of grammar, children often begin to use words incorrectly that they once used correctly. However, the errors are only temporary.

How Do We Learn Language?

Billions of children have acquired the languages of their parents and have then proceeded to hand them down to their own children. In this manner, languages pass, with small changes, from generation to generation. How are languages learned? Both heredity and environment play a role.

Hereditary Influences Many psychologists believe that people have a natural tendency to acquire language. Linguist Noam Chomsky and some other researchers refer to this tendency as a **language acquisition device** (LAD). These researchers assert that humans have a LAD. Animals do not.

The LAD enables the brain to understand and use grammar. It enables people to turn ideas into sentences (Pinker, 1990, 1994). People may not be

ready for chemistry and algebra until high school, but the LAD makes people most capable of acquiring language between about 18 to 24 months of age and puberty (Lenneberg, 1967). One- and two-year-olds seem to learn languages with ease. In many cases, they learn more than one language.

Environmental Influences People may have an inborn ability to learn language, but environmental influences are important as well. Learning theorists claim that language learning is similar to other kinds of learned behavior (Gleason & Ratner, 1993). Children learn language, at least in part, by observing and imitating other people. For example, all children babble. But during the first year, children start to babble the sounds they hear around them more often and drop other sounds.

Bilingualism

A DAY IN THE LIFE Hannah speaks both Korean and English. She most likely learned Korean at home and English in school, in other public places, and from English-speaking friends. Because she learned English very early, Hannah

It is becoming increasingly common in the United States to see signs in public places printed in several different languages.

Have students summarize the research findings presented in the feature. Then initiate a discussion of the research by asking students to respond to the following questions: How does the evidence from these research studies support the conclusion that language is a function of humans alone? If future research were to discover that chimps actually can use language, what would be the implications for the way humans view themselves and their place among the other species on the planet?

For Further Research

Play recordings of a mynah bird for the class. *(Recordings of animal sounds are available in many public libraries.)* Ask students to report what they hear. Then have them conduct library research to learn how mynah birds are able to reproduce sounds that are similar to human speech. Have students present their findings in oral reports to the class. Have the class discuss why bird "speech" does not constitute language.

Cross-Curricular Link: Biology

Human language is produced in a very different way than are animal sounds or even nonlanguage human sounds. This is due, in part, to a biological difference in brain function. In chimps and other primates, sounds are controlled by the limbic system. This area of the brain is linked more to emotion and, in fact, controls human sounds such as sobbing and laughing. Spoken language in humans is controlled by a different area of the brain—the cerebral cortex.

CASE STUDIES
AND OTHER TRUE STORIES

Washoe and Kanzi: Chimps with Language?

Language is one of the things that sets people apart from other creatures. Sure, parrots can say a few words like "Polly wants a cracker." And your dog may respond to commands such as "Sit!" But animals cannot use language.

Or can they?

Over the past few decades, various researchers have made a number of attempts to teach language to chimpanzees (the animal that is biologically most similar to humans) and to other apes. One of the earliest efforts was aimed at getting a chimp to speak human words. But several years of work that yielded few positive results led to the conclusion that chimps cannot produce verbal speech (Hayes, 1951). Just because chimps cannot talk, however, does not necessarily mean that they are incapable of understanding language. Subsequent efforts therefore focused instead on teaching chimps to use symbols, such as those of American Sign Language (ASL).

Washoe, a female chimpanzee raised by Beatrice and Allen Gardner (1980), was one of the first chimps reported to use language. By the age of 5, Washoe could use more than 100 ASL signs. These included signs for actions *(come, give, tickle),* objects *(apple, flower, toothbrush),* and even for more abstract concepts such as *more.*

Moreover, Washoe could combine the signs to form simple sentences. The sentences were similar to those of two-year-old children: "More tickle," "More banana," "More milk." As time passed, Washoe signed longer sentences such as "Please sweet drink" and "Give me toothbrush hurry." However, Washoe had trouble with word order. One day she might sign, "Come give me toothbrush." The next she might sign, "Hurry toothbrush give me." Even one-year-old children use correct syntax more consistently.

Can chimps use language?

Psychologist Sue Savage-Rumbaugh and her colleagues (1993) had somewhat better luck in terms of grammar with a bonobo, or pygmy chimpanzee, named Kanzi. Kanzi learned several hundred words and to correctly respond to commands in which these words were put together in ways that Kanzi had not previously heard. For example, he knew the words *dog, bite,* and *snake.* When Kanzi was given a stuffed dog and a stuffed snake and asked to "make the dog bite the snake," he put the snake to the dog's mouth, even though he had never before heard this sentence. Kanzi's grammatical ability, however, never surpassed that of the average two-and-a-half-year-old child.

So the question remains: Can chimps use language? The answer seems to hinge on the definition of language. It seems clear that chimps and even some other types of apes can learn to use signs and symbols and can follow some commands given to them. So if this is considered language, then yes, chimps can use language.

Most psychologists, however, use a more restrictive definition of language: the combination of symbols into original, grammatical sentences. If we use originality and mastery of grammar as the standards for defining language, there is little question that chimps fall short. For now, at least, the theory that language belongs to humans alone remains standing.

WHY PSYCHOLOGY MATTERS

Psychologists and other scientists study how animals communicate. Use CNNfyi.com or other current events sources to learn more about scientific research of animals' ability to communicate. Create a pamphlet describing what you have learned.

CNNfyi.com

Closing Section 5

Synthesizing Information

Have students use what they learned in this section to write diary entries about a hypothetical child's language development. Tell students to write from the perspective of a parent or a caregiver recording anecdotal observations of the child's maturing language skills.

Reviewing Section 5

Have students complete the Section Review questions on page 201.

Extension

Prompt students to survey the school and the community to determine what languages are spoken in your area. Languages should be divided into first language and other language categories. Have students organize their findings in a chart. If students choose to, they may research the immigration patterns in your community that have contributed to their findings.

speaks it with no accent. Her parents, who learned English as adults, do have accents. If Marc decides to study Japanese, he will probably never be able to speak it without an American accent. He could become perfectly fluent, yet never speak it without an accent.

In general, the earlier in life a person learns a second language, the more likely the person is to become fluent in it and sound like a native speaker (Snow, 1993). This fact lends support to the theory that there is a period in life—a portion of childhood—during which language acquisition is easiest and most effective.

Although many people in the United States speak only one language, the number of people who (like Hannah) are bilingual, or speak two languages, is growing. In this respect the United States is becoming more similar to many other parts of the world. Many people throughout the world speak two or more languages. A number of countries have minority populations whose languages differ from the national tongue. A large percentage of Europeans are taught English and the languages of neighboring nations. Consider the Netherlands. Dutch is the native language, but children are also taught French, German, and English in the public schools.

For more than 40 million people in the United States, English is a second language. Spanish, French, Chinese, Russian, or Arabic is spoken in the home and, perhaps, in the neighborhood.

A century ago it was widely believed that children reared in bilingual homes would be slowed in their cognitive and language development. It was thought that people who knew two languages were crowding their mental abilities because cognitive capacity is limited (Lambert, 1990). However, the U.S. Bureau of the Census reports that more than 75 percent of Americans who first spoke another language in the home also speak English "well" or "very well." Moreover, a careful analysis of older studies in bilingualism shows that the bilingual children often lived in poor families and had little education. Yet these bilingual children were compared to middle-class children who spoke English. In addition, achievement and intelligence tests were given in English, which was the second language of the bilingual children (Reynolds, 1991). Lack of education and poor testing methods, rather than bilingualism, accounted for the apparent differences in achievement and intelligence.

Today most psychologists believe that it is good for children's cognitive development to be bilingual. Knowledge of more than one language expands children's awareness of different cultures and broadens their outlooks on life (Cavaliere, 1996). For example, bilingual children are more likely to understand that the symbols used in language are arbitrary. Children who speak only English are more likely to think that the word *dog* is somehow connected with the nature of the animal. Bilingual children therefore have somewhat more cognitive flexibility. Learning a second language has been shown to increase children's expertise in their first (native) language. Research evidence reveals that learning French enhances knowledge of the structure of English among Canadian children whose native language is English (Lambert et al., 1991).

Many students in the United States are learning, or already know, more than one language.

SECTION 5 REVIEW

go.hrw.com — Homework Practice Online
Keyword: SY3 HP8

1. Identify and explain the three basic elements of language.

2. Define *overextension* and *overregularization*.

3. **Critical Thinking** *Finding the Main Idea* How do research findings about bilingualism indicate that language acquisition involves both environmental and hereditary influences?

Section 5 Review: Answers

1. The elements are: phonemes (the basic sounds of language), morphemes (the units of meaning), and syntax (the way words are arranged to form sentences or phrases).

2. Overextension is the tendency to extend the meanings of words to refer to things for which one does not have words. Overregularization is the tendency to apply the rules of grammar to all words.

3. Environmental influences are important because language is similar to other learned behaviors and children learn language by imitating those around them. In terms of heredity, there is a time during childhood when language acquisition occurs more easily than during any other period.

Chapter 8 Review: Answers

Writing a Summary

See the section subtitles for the main topics in the chapter.

Identifying People and Ideas

1. an object or an act that stands for something else

Technology

► Chapter 8 Test Generator (on the One-Stop Planner)

► HRW Go site

Reinforcement, Review, and Assessment

► Chapter 8 Review, pp. 202–203

► Chapter Review and Activities with Answer Key

► Alternative Assessment Handbook

► Portfolio Assessment Handbook

► Chapter 8 Test (Form A or B)

PSYCHOLOGY PROJECTS

Linking to Community Have students work independently or in groups to develop community or school resources that focus on problem-solving and decision-making techniques. These might be after-school courses, pamphlets for distribution by community groups, seminars given at the

---

2. a mental grouping of objects, events, or ideas that have similar characteristics

3. an example of a concept that best exemplifies the concept

4. the tendency to respond to new problems with an approach successfully used with similar problems

5. the tendency to see an object as useful only for its most familiar function

6. the use of information to reach conclusions

7. the attempt to prove rather than disprove a hypothesis

8. a heuristic used to make a decision based on information learned early in life

9. a basic sound of language

10. the study of meaning

Understanding Main Ideas

1. Prototypes provide people with a basic idea of a particular concept.

2. Algorithms provide specific ways to solve problems.

3. Confirmation bias is the attempt to prove rather than disprove a hypothesis. It affects inductive reasoning.

4. People use the representativeness heuristic when they make a decision based on what they have come to expect; they use the availability heuristic when they make a decision based only on available information; they use the anchoring heuristic when they make a decision based on information learned early in life.

5. It is an inborn tendency to acquire language.

202

Chapter 8 REVIEW

Writing a Summary

Using standard grammar, spelling, sentence structure, and punctuation, summarize the information in this chapter. Consider:
• how people solve problems and make decisions
• the basic elements of language, and deductive and inductive reasoning

Identifying People and Ideas

Identify the following terms or people and use them in appropriate sentences.

1. symbol
2. concept
3. prototype
4. mental set
5. functional fixedness

6. reasoning
7. confirmation bias
8. anchoring
9. phoneme
10. semantics

Understanding Main Ideas

SECTION 1 (pp. 178–179)
1. How do prototypes help people understand concepts?

SECTION 2 (pp. 179–188)
2. What is the purpose of an algorithm?

SECTION 3 (pp. 189–191)
3. What is confirmation bias, and which type of reasoning does it affect?

SECTION 4 (pp. 191–195)
4. How do people use each of the following shortcuts to make a decision: the representativeness heuristic, the availability heuristic, and the anchoring heuristic.

SECTION 5 (pp. 195–201)
5. What is a language acquisition device?

Thinking Critically

1. Drawing Inferences and Conclusions How could a child be taught the meaning of an abstract concept such as honesty?

2. Evaluating Explain how mental set might occasionally help problem solving rather than hinder it.

3. Analyzing Information Imagine that you are driving to a strange town to visit a friend. Using the ABCDEs of problem solving, explain how you would plan your trip.

4. Categorizing In addition to using words and sentences to communicate, human beings use sounds, symbols, gestures, and other means to communicate. Give five examples of how people communicate without using words, and the type of communication they use.

5. Supporting a Point of View Give reasons to support or reject a proposal to teach world languages in elementary schools.

Writing About Psychology

1. Analyzing Information Go to the library to find information about the development of language skills in young children. Write a one-page paper explaining why children are often able to learn more than one language with relative ease.

2. Evaluating Think of a problem facing your school or community for which there are two or more possible solutions or courses of action. On a sheet of paper, create a "balance sheet" listing each possible course of action and its pros and cons. Write a brief report explaining what your decision is, how you reached that decision, and how the balance sheet helped you arrive at your decision. Be sure to use standard grammar, spelling, sentence structure, and punctuation. Use the graphic organizer below to help you with your report.

Balance Sheet	
Pros	Cons

local library, or even corporate training programs. The following questions may be useful in designing the features of each resource:

- What are some problems and decisions that each target audience is likely to encounter?
- What will be the goals of the resources?
- What techniques will best help each specific target group solve problems and make decisions more effectively?

Cooperative Learning

Organize the class into groups of three. Tell students that language development is a critical component of effective thinking and communication. Have students research the importance of language and critical thinking skills in the current educational and job arenas. Then have the groups consider how the requirements of these areas may be changing and what may be causing the changes. Finally, have each group draft a position statement about the need for language and critical thinking curricula at various educational stages.

Building Social Studies Skills

Interpreting Graphs

Study the bar graph below. Then use the information in the graph to help you answer the questions that follow.

Acquisition of Language Skills by Young Children

Age in Months

First words · Vocabulary increase · Sentences

Language Achievement

Source: Damon (Ed.), *Handbook of Child Psychology*, 1998

1. Which of the following statements best reflects the information given in the graph?
   a. A child who does not use words by its 12th month has a problem with language skills.
   b. A child who does not speak until its 17th month will not use sentences until it is 32 months old.
   c. All children experience a dramatic increase in vocabulary by their 8th month.
   d. Some children begin using sentences as early as their 18th month.
2. What conclusions can you draw from this graph about children and language development?

Analyzing Primary Sources

Read the following excerpt, in which psychologist Alan Lesgold discusses the role that problem solving plays in daily life. Then answer the questions that follow.

“Problem solving is a major human activity in our high-technology society. Many of the jobs currently available are characterized by the problem solving they require. Doctors have to solve the problem of what is causing their patients' symptoms. Auto mechanics have to determine why cars don't run properly. Counselors often perceive either their role, the client's role, or both as one of solving certain life problems. The political process, on both an international and a domestic level, is driven by the need to solve complex problems. College students have to schedule courses, jobs, and study time. Almost every aspect of daily life seems to involve problem solving.”

3. Which of the following statements best reflects the meaning of the excerpt?
   a. Only professionals such as doctors and mechanics use problem-solving skills.
   b. Problems make daily life difficult for almost everyone.
   c. For most people, problem solving requires a college education.
   d. Problem solving is a regular activity used by many people every day in modern society.
4. According to the excerpt, why are problem-solving skills essential in today's society?

PSYCHOLOGY PROJECTS

Cooperative Learning

Applying Psychology With several of your classmates, play a popular board game. Team up with one other person in the group and play as partners. Decide together how you will make your moves. At the end of the game, have each set of partners give examples of the thought processes they used to make their moves during the game. You may want to discuss with the class how prior familiarity with the game helped or hindered your strategy.

internet connect

Internet Activity: go.hrw.com
KEYWORD: SY3 PS8
Choose an activity on thinking and language to:
- write a short analysis of your own methods of solving problems.
- role-play a conflict resolution process that uses persuasion, compromise, debate, and negotiation.
- research and evaluate theories of language acquisition and development.

go.hrw.com

Thinking Critically

1. Students' suggestions may include reading stories about honest characters or rewarding the child for honest behavior.
2. Mental set may encourage people to be more persistent when searching for solutions to problems.
3. Students should explain how they would plan their trip using the ABCDE problem-solving method.
4. Students might mention such means as winks, hand waves, nods, laughter, and frowns.
5. Students who support the proposal may point to the ease with which young children can learn foreign languages; those who reject the proposal may suggest that too many other subjects must already compete for limited teaching time.

Writing About Psychology

1. Students' papers should note that a language acquisition device helps small children learn other languages.
2. Possible problems facing schools and communities include violence in schools, crime, and pollution.

Building Social Studies Skills

1. d
2. Development of language skills can vary greatly from child to child. One child may just be using its first words, while another of the same age may be on the verge of using sentences.
3. d
4. In a modern, high-tech society, people from all walks of life regularly use problem-solving skills.

Intelligence

CHAPTER RESOURCE MANAGER

Objectives	Pacing Guide		Reproducible and Review Resources
SECTION 1: **What Is Intelligence?** (pp. 206–210)	Define intelligence and explain the various theories of intelligence.	**Regular** 1 day **Block Scheduling** .5 day *Block Scheduling Handbook with Team Teaching Strategies, Chapter 9*	**E** Research Projects and Activities for Teaching Psychology **REV** Section 1 Review, p. 210
SECTION 2: **Measurement of Intelligence** (pp. 211–215)	Describe how the various types of intelligence tests differ.	**Regular** 1 day **Block Scheduling** .5 day *Block Scheduling Handbook with Team Teaching Strategies, Chapter 9*	**PS** Readings and Case Studies, Chapter 9 **SM** Mastering Critical Thinking Skills 9 **REV** Section 2 Review, p. 215
SECTION 3: **Differences in Intelligence** (pp. 215–218)	Identify the characteristics of mental retardation and of giftedness, and explain the relationship between giftedness and creativity.	**Regular** 1 day **Block Scheduling** .5 day *Block Scheduling Handbook with Team Teaching Strategies, Chapter 9*	**RS** Essay and Research Themes for Advanced Placement Students, Theme 8 **REV** Section 3 Review, p. 218
SECTION 4: **What Influences Intelligence?** (pp. 218–221)	Explain how heredity and the environment influence intelligence.	**Regular** 1 day **Block Scheduling** .5 day *Block Scheduling Handbook with Team Teaching Strategies, Chapter 9*	**E** Creating a Psychology Fair, Handout 6, Activity 4 **REV** Section 4 Review, p. 221

Chapter Resource Key

PS	Primary Sources	**A**	Assessment		Video
RS	Reading Support	**REV**	Review		Internet
E	Enrichment		Transparencies		Holt Presentation Maker Using Microsoft® PowerPoint®
SM	Skills Mastery		CD-ROM		

 One-Stop Planner CD–ROM

See the *One-Stop Planner* for a complete list of additional resources for students and teachers.

One-Stop Planner CD–ROM

It's easy to plan lessons, select resources, and print out materials for your students when you use the **One-Stop Planner CD-ROM with Test Generator.**

Technology Resources

 One-Stop Planner, Lesson 9.1
 Homework Practice Online
Teaching Transparencies 24: Sternberg's Triarchic Model
 HRW Go Site

 One-Stop Planner, Lesson 9.2
 Homework Practice Online
HRW Go Site

 One-Stop Planner, Lesson 9.3
Homework Practice Online
Teaching Transparencies 25: Distribution of IQ Scores
CNN Presents Psychology: Elephant Smarts

 One-Stop Planner, Lesson 9.4
 Homework Practice Online
HRW Go Site

Chapter Review and Assessment

 HRW Go site
REV Chapter 9 Review, pp. 222–223
REV Chapter Review Activities with Answer Key

A Chapter 9 Test (Form A or B)
A Portfolio Assessment Handbook
A Alternative Assessment Handbook

Chapter 9 Test Generator (on the One-Stop Planner)
Global Skill Builder CD-ROM

☑ internet connect

HRW ONLINE RESOURCES

GO TO: go.hrw.com
Then type in a keyword.

TEACHER HOME PAGE
KEYWORD: SY3 Teacher

CHAPTER INTERNET ACTIVITIES
KEYWORD: SY3 PS9
Choose an activity to have students:
• research theories of intelligence.
• write a report on the concept of "transformed score" as it applies to intelligence quotient (IQ) scores, and define and differentiate reliability and validity.
• design a program that has a positive impact on intelligence.

CHAPTER ENRICHMENT LINKS
KEYWORD: SY3 CH9

ONLINE ASSESSMENT
Homework Practice
KEYWORD: SY3 HP9

Standardized Test Prep
KEYWORD: SY3 STP9

Rubrics
KEYWORD: SS Rubrics

CONTENT UPDATES
KEYWORD: SS Content Updates

HOLT PRESENTATION MAKER
KEYWORD: SY3 PPT9

ONLINE READING SUPPORT
KEYWORD: SS Strategies

CURRENT EVENTS
KEYWORD: S3 Current Events

Additional Resources

PRINT RESOURCES FOR TEACHERS

Gardner, H. (1983). *Frames of mind: The theory of multiple intelligences.* New York: Basic Books.

Mensh, E., and Mensh, H. (1991). *The I.Q. mythology.* Carbondale: Southern Illinois University Press.

Sternberg, R. (1988). *The triarchic mind.* New York: Viking Press.

PRINT RESOURCES FOR STUDENTS

Gardner, H. (1993). *Creating minds.* New York: Basic Books.

Goleman, D. (1995). *Emotional intelligence.* New York: Bantam Books.

Treffert, D. (1989). *Extraordinary people: Understanding savant syndrome.* New York: Ballantine Books.

MULTIMEDIA RESOURCES

Nature & nurture (VHS). Films for the Humanities & Sciences, P.O. Box 2053, Princeton, NJ 08543-2053.

The nature of human nature (VHS). Films for the Humanities & Sciences, P.O. Box 2053, Princeton, NJ 08543-2053.

Neuropsychology (VHS). Films for the Humanities & Sciences, P.O. Box 2053, Princeton, NJ 08543-2053.

The special child: Maximizing limited potential (VHS). Films for the Humanities & Sciences, P.O. Box 2053, Princeton, NJ 08543-2053.

INTELLIGENCE

Introducing Chapter 9

Ask students to provide examples of people from historical and contemporary times who are considered to have been or to be extraordinarily intelligent. Write the names of these people on the chalkboard, and have students explain why these people are considered intelligent. Then write the following questions on the chalkboard: What is intelligence? What factors are involved in intelligence? Give students 10 minutes to write a response to these questions and then have volunteers read their responses aloud. Record some of the commonly held views on the chalkboard. Ask students to relate these views to the names on the chalkboard. Then tell students that while psychologists can provide a definition of intelligence, there are actually many theories about what factors are involved in intelligence. Tell students that Chapter 9 will introduce them to the psychological perspectives on intelligence.

Sections

Each of the four questions identified on page 204 corresponds to one of these sections.

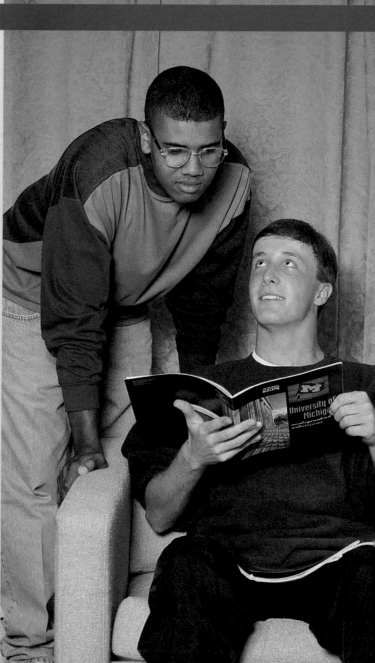

Chapter 9 INTELLIGENCE

Read to Discover

1 How is intelligence defined, and what are the various theories of intelligence?

2 How do the various types of intelligence tests differ?

3 What are the characteristics of mental retardation and of giftedness?

4 How do heredity and the environment influence intelligence?

Each chapter begins with a vignette, called "A Day in the Life," that relates the information discussed in the chapter to the everyday events in the lives of a group of fictional high school students. The text of the chapter occasionally refers back to the vignette to demonstrate the application of the concept being discussed. An icon marked "A Day in the Life" is placed next to these references.

Copy the following graphic organizer onto the chalkboard, omitting the italicized text. Fill in the circles as you provide an overview of the senses to the class.

What Is Intelligence? ← *Intelligence* / *Achievement*

A DAY IN THE LIFE

January 8

Todd and Dan were at Todd's house after school. Todd had decided to go to college six months ago and had already begun applying. Dan, on the other hand, had not decided what he wanted to do. He noticed some of Todd's college catalogs sitting on the table and began looking through them.

"Todd, what made you decide to go to college?" Dan asked.

"I'm not really sure. I've always done well in school, and I love studying science. Why do you ask?"

"I don't know. I've just always wondered if I'm intelligent enough for college," Dan replied. "My older brother seems to get good grades without any effort at all, but I have to work hard for every A or B that I get. And we both have the same parents and have had the same upbringing."

"Yeah, but you and your brother aren't identical. You two only share some of the same genes, and you've had different experiences, especially in school," Todd said. "Plus, don't you think there might be different types of intelligence?"

"How so?" Dan asked.

"Well, have you ever heard Hannah play the violin?"

"Of course I have," Dan replied. "She's great at it."

"Right. Hannah has a special ability to read the music and play the right notes. You're the same way with sports, and you have great communication and people skills."

"But those are talents, not *intelligence*," Dan replied. "Talent is different from intelligence."

"Maybe," Todd pondered. "But I think any kind of learning ability is a type of intelligence."

"Okay then, what if I don't have enough learning ability to go to college? Don't they have some sort of test to tell you if you have enough intelligence for college?" Dan asked.

"I don't know," Todd replied honestly. "When I was younger I took some sort of intelligence test for placement. But I doubt that there are tests to tell you if you're intelligent enough for college. Why don't you talk to Mr. Hochberg, the guidance counselor?"

"I guess I could do that," Dan said. "Thanks, Todd."

"No problem. Hey, I have to work hard for every A that I get, too."

Intelligence is one characteristic that sets humans apart from other forms of life. Intelligence permits us to adapt to changing conditions and to challenge our physical limitations—to move faster and higher than any other animal. The human ability to think about abstract ideas, such as space and time, also sets us apart from all other species. Intelligence has even expanded our senses, enabling us to invent microscopes and telescopes to see things too small or distant for the naked eye to detect. This chapter examines how intelligence is defined and measured. It also discusses differences in intelligence and considers the factors that influence intelligence.

Key Terms

- achievement
- intelligence
- mental age
- intelligence quotient
- transformed score
- reliability
- test-retest reliability
- validity
- mental retardation
- gifted
- creativity
- heritability

WHY PSYCHOLOGY MATTERS

Psychologists have developed a number of ways to measure intelligence. Use **CNNfyi.com** or other current events sources to learn more about research on human intelligence.

CNNfyi.com

Using Key Terms

Write on the chalkboard the titles of the four sections that make up Chapter 9. Under each section title, write the key terms found in that section. Ask students to use the Glossary at the back of the book to find a definition for each of the terms in the chapter. Then have students write short paragraphs explaining how the terms found in each section relate to the section title. Ask volunteers to share their paragraphs with the class for discussion.

Section Objective

▶ Define intelligence, and explain the various theories of intelligence.

This objective is assessed in the Section Review on page 210 and in the Chapter 9 Review.

Using Truth or Fiction

Each chapter opens with several "Truth or Fiction" statements that relate to the concepts discussed in the chapter. Ask students whether they think each statement is true or false. Answers to each item as well as explanations are provided at appropriate points within the text under the heading "Truth or Fiction Revisited."

Journal Activity

Encourage students to consider their own type of intelligence. Ask them to record the ways in which they feel "smart" or "not so smart." Remind students to include nonacademic areas and to note both their strengths and their weaknesses.

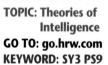

■ internet connect

TOPIC: Theories of Intelligence
GO TO: go.hrw.com
KEYWORD: SY3 PS9

Have students access the Internet through the HRW Go site to research theories of intelligence. Then have students organize their research into a news or radio broadcast that outlines the strengths and weaknesses of the main theories of intelligence.

Opening Section 1

Motivator

Before students read Section 1, tell them to imagine that they are members of a committee organized to select the World's Most Intelligent Person. Their job is to create a profile of that person that can be used as a guideline in the final selection process. Tell students that their profiles should include traits, abilities, and accomplishments commonly associated with highly intelligent people. Ask volunteers to read their profiles aloud. After students have read Section 1, have them explain how, if at all, they would revise their profiles.

TRUTH OR fiction?

Read the following statements about psychology. Do you think they are true or false? You will learn whether each statement is true or false as you read the chapter.

- There may be more than one kind of intelligence.
- Two children can answer exactly the same items on an intelligence test correctly, yet one may have an above-average IQ and the other may have a below-average IQ.
- When we think we will not succeed at something, we may not try as hard as we can.
- Intellectually gifted people are by definition highly creative.
- Preschool programs have long-term benefits for the children who attend them.

SECTION 1

What Is Intelligence?

A DAY IN THE LIFE

Todd and Dan raised many interesting points about the nature of intelligence. People can be very intelligent and not know a lot because they have not studied. People can also know a lot because they have worked hard, even if their intelligence is not particularly high. But what exactly is intelligence?

Some people, like Todd, have very strong science or math skills. Others, such as Hannah, are talented in music or art. Still others, including Dan, have the ability to get along well with other people. Are all of these abilities signs of intelligence? Are *any* of them? How many factors are involved in intelligence? Throughout human history, many philosophers and scientists have speculated about the answers to these questions.

Intelligence Versus Achievement

According to psychologists, one thing intelligence is *not* is achievement. **Achievement** refers to knowledge and skills gained from experience. In other words, achievement focuses on the things that you know and can do. Thus, achievement involves specific content, such as Spanish, calculus, history, psychology, biology, art, or music. The relationship between achievement and experience is obvious. If

you have spent a lot of time reading about the Civil War, for example, then you will probably do well on a test about that period in U.S. history. You will have gained knowledge on the subject of the Civil War. But if you were tested on the Revolutionary War instead, you might not do as well. That would be because you had more content knowledge of the Civil War.

Although intelligence is not the same as achievement, intelligence can provide the *basis* for achievement. Intelligence makes achievement possible by giving people the ability to learn. Todd pointed this out when he suggested that intelligence might be involved in Hannah's abilities to read music and to play the right notes on her violin.

Now we know what intelligence is *not*. But what is it? **Intelligence** can be defined as the abilities to learn from experience, to think rationally, and to deal effectively with others. Within that general definition, however, psychologists have a number of differing theories about what exactly makes up intelligence.

Spearman's Two-Factor Theory

Nearly 100 years ago, British psychologist Charles Spearman suggested that all the behaviors we consider to be intelligent have a common underlying factor. He labeled this factor *g*, which stands for "general intelligence." The *g* factor represents the abilities to reason and to solve problems. Spearman noted that people who do well in one area usually do well in others. Yet even the most capable people are relatively better at some things than at others—writing and music rather than math, for example. For this reason, he suggested that specific, or *s*, factors account for particular abilities.

Thurstone's Theory of Primary Mental Abilities

American psychologist Louis Thurstone believed that eight separate factors make up intelligence. He called them primary mental abilities. These primary mental abilities are as follows:

- visual and spatial ability (the ability to picture shapes and spatial relationships)
- perceptual speed (the ability to understand perceptual information rapidly and to see the similarities and differences between stimuli)
- numerical ability (the ability to calculate and recall numbers)

Teaching Section 1

Meeting Individual Needs: Learners Having Difficulty

Some students may have difficulty keeping track of the many theories presented in the section. Suggest that they create a chart in which they list the main features of each theory of intelligence. Tell students to include in their charts the name of the theory, the name of the persons associated with the theory, key terms, factors of intelligence, and any examples that might help them remember each theory. Students should add to the chart as needed.

Cooperative Learning

Organize the class into small groups and assign each group one of the kinds of intelligence included in Gardner's theory of multiple intelligences. Tell the groups that they are to write and perform a short skit demonstrating their assigned kind of intelligence. After students have presented their skits, have them discuss why it is that people can be strong in some types of intelligence and weak in others. Also have them debate whether exceptional abilities in the musical-rhythmic and bodily-kinesthetic areas should be considered intelligence or talent.

Thurstone would probably suggest that architects excel in visual and spatial ability.

- verbal meaning (knowledge of the meanings of words)
- memory (the ability to recall information, such as words and sentences)
- word fluency (the ability to think of words quickly for such tasks as rhyming or doing crossword puzzles)
- deductive reasoning (the ability to derive examples from general rules)
- inductive reasoning (the ability to derive general rules from examples)

Thurstone believed that people can be high in one factor and low in another. For example, someone may have high word fluency—meaning that she or he can find words that rhyme with one another—but be poor at solving math problems (Thurstone & Thurstone, 1963).

Gardner's Theory of Multiple Intelligences

Contemporary psychologist Howard Gardner (1983, 1993; Gardner & Hatch, 1989) believes that intelligence has a broader base and that there are actually several different kinds of intelligence within us:

- linguistic intelligence
- logical-mathematical intelligence
- visual-spatial intelligence
- bodily-kinesthetic intelligence
- musical-rhythmic intelligence
- interpersonal intelligence (insight into one's own inner feelings)
- intrapersonal intelligence (sensitivity to other people's feelings)

A DAY IN THE LIFE

Gardner refers to each of these as "an intelligence" because they are very different from one another. He also believes that each kind of intelligence is based in different areas of the brain. Gardner's theory might help to explain why Dan responds well to other people but might not get the highest grades in school.

Some of Gardner's "intelligences," such as language ability, math ability, and spatial-relations skills, are similar to those proposed by other theorists, including Thurstone. A major difference between Gardner's and Thurstone's theories, however, is that Thurstone believed that the eight factors he identified, when taken together, make up intelligence. Gardner, on the other hand, proposes that the different intelligences are independent of each other.

According to Gardner's theory, people can possess various kinds of intelligence. These skaters probably have highly developed bodily-kinesthetic intelligence.

Cross-Curricular Link: History

Another theory of intelligence, called phrenology, was popular during the 1800s. Phrenology was pioneered by physician and scientist Franz Joseph Gall and his colleague Johann Spurzheim. The underlying assumption of the theory was that there is a relationship between the physical shape of a person's skull and that person's mental capabilities. People of the 1800s would have their head shapes evaluated in order to determine their mental strengths and weaknesses. Although phrenology was dismissed fairly quickly, Gall is noted for being the first scientist to recognize that various brain functions are located under different regions of the skull.

207

Guided Practice

Create a three-column chart on the chalkboard. Label the columns *Theories, Strengths,* and *Weaknesses*. In the first column, list the various theories of intelligence discussed in this section. Then have students identify the strengths and weaknesses of each theory. Write their suggestions in the appropriate column. Then have students debate which of the theories of intelligence most adequately explains the question of what makes up intelligence.

Independent Practice

Have students use what they learned in the Guided Practice activity to write a letter of support to the psychologist whose theory they believe best explains intelligence. In their letters, students should tell the theorist why this particular theory makes a more convincing case than the other theories of intelligence. Tell students to support their reasoning with examples. Have volunteers read their letters aloud to the class.

Teaching Transparencies with Teacher's Notes

TRANSPARENCY 24:
Sternberg's Triarchic Model

According to Gardner, a person can be a great mathematician or composer but be average in self-insight or in interpersonal relationships. Gardner would probably say that Todd, Dan, and Hannah are each intelligent in their own way. Todd has strong scientific ability. Dan, as an athlete, has highly developed bodily-kinesthetic skills. And Hannah undoubtedly has special musical ability.

Furthermore, according to Gardner, the various intelligences exist side by side within each person but vary in intensity. They can also change over time. They are simply intellectual "potentials" that can be tapped given the right environment (Gardner, 1995).

Critics of Gardner's views think that exceptional abilities in the musical or bodily-kinesthetic areas are not really part of intelligence at all. They argue that those skills are talents and that being talented is not the same thing as being intelligent (Neisser et al., 1996). Dan, too, made this distinction when he asserted that talent and intelligence are two different things.

Sternberg's Triarchic Theory

While Gardner talks about separate and distinct intelligences, psychologist Robert Sternberg (1995) believes that different kinds of intelligences all work together. He has created a three-level, or *triarchic*,

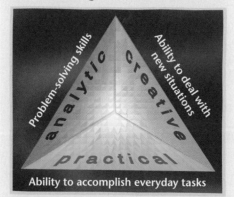

FIGURE 9.1 *According to Sternberg, intelligence has three parts: the analytic part that enables us to solve problems, the creative part that allows us to deal with new situations, and the practical part that makes it possible for us to perform everyday tasks. We often use more than one of these parts simultaneously.*

model of intelligence. (See Figure 9.1.) According to Sternberg, intelligence includes analytic, creative, and practical abilities. Analytic intelligence involves the ability to solve problems. Creative intelligence involves the ability to deal with new situations. Practical intelligence involves the ability to accomplish everyday tasks.

Often, we must use more than one of these three types of intelligence at the same time. For example, if you were doing an experiment for an upcoming social studies or science fair, you would use practical intelligence to plan your time and materials to do the project. You would use your analytic intelligence to interpret the results of the experiment and draw conclusions. You would also use creativity to design the display for your project.

It is true that there may be more than one kind of intelligence. Both Gardner's and Sternberg's theories discuss the existence of different kinds of intelligences.

■ REVISITED ■

Emotional Intelligence

Psychologist Daniel Goleman (1995) is interested in why smart people are not always as successful as might be expected. He proposes yet another kind of intelligence: emotional intelligence. Emotional intelligence, says Goleman, consists of five factors that are involved in success in school or on the job:

■ Self-awareness (the ability to recognize our own feelings). If we know when we are happy, sad, or angry, we are better able to cope with our feelings.

■ Mood management (the ability to distract oneself from an uncomfortable feeling). Although we may not be able to prevent feelings of anger or sadness, we do have some control over how long the feelings last. Rather than dwell on bad feelings, we can distract ourselves and make changes to reduce the likelihood that we will find ourselves in the same situation again.

■ Self-motivation (the ability to move ahead with confidence and enthusiasm). People who are self-motivators sometimes accomplish more than people who obtain higher scores on intelligence tests. (Intelligence tests are discussed later in this chapter.)

PSYCHOLOGY
IN THE WORLD TODAY

Artificial Intelligence

In 1997 the reigning world champion chess player Gary Kasparov pitted his skills against an IBM computer known as Deep Blue. The event was captured live on an IBM Web site, where millions of chess fans logged on to watch the match. In two previous matches, Kasparov had beaten the best artificial intelligence IBM could muster. But this match would be different. In the sixth game a tired Kasparov accidentally reversed two steps in a well-known defensive maneuver. Deep Blue immediately took advantage of the situation by killing Kasparov's queen. After just 19 moves Kasparov admitted defeat.

Kasparov versus the computer

Artificial intelligence (AI) is a broad field that involves the creation and development of "intelligent machines." These machines include industrial robots and computers such as the one that played chess with Gary Kasparov. Chess-playing computers are considered *expert systems*—computer programs that specialize in some particular field. Expert systems have been created not only to play chess but also to aid in medical diagnosis, the drilling of oil wells, and the mining of minerals.

But are these programs anything like human intelligence? Not really. For one thing, expert systems are very limited in their information. Prescriptive computer programs for psychologists are created by human experts who tell programmers all they know about their particular field. Then all the possible psychological symptoms—for depression, for example—and combinations of symptoms are included in the program. Under those limited conditions, the computer does well enough. But it is restricted by what it "knows," which is what it has been "told" by the programmer.

The human brain is a complicated machine. We may not be able to calculate numbers as quickly as a computer can, but we can deal with complex ideas and problems with remarkable ability. That is because our brains use what is known as "parallel processing." In other words, our thoughts analyze several different aspects of a problem at once. A computer, on the other hand, uses serial processing. The computer analyzes only one step at a time. Humans use serial processing, too, but parallel processing is what gives us the decided edge. Even highly sophisticated robots have difficulty moving with speed because it takes them so long to serially analyze all the stimuli necessary for coordinated motion.

Will we ever be able to create a computer or robot that thinks like the human brain? It does not seem likely anytime soon. Despite its electronic brainpower, AI is simply no match for human intelligence. Powerful computers can handle many problems and vast amounts of information. But they do not have the insights, intuitions, and creativity that humans have. They follow commands very well, but they have no originality. These limitations become quickly evident when, for instance, computers are asked to write poetry or compose music.

THINK ABOUT IT

Drawing Inferences and Conclusions If you were creating a new expert system of your own, in what area would it be? To whom would you go for expertise? What sort of problems can you anticipate?

Closing Section 1

Role-Playing

Select five volunteers to participate in a Meeting of the Minds panel discussion. Tell each of the volunteers to assume the role of one of the five theorists discussed in Section 1. Tell the rest of the class to imagine that they are journalists on assignment to cover the panel discussion. Have the journalists prepare a list of questions about intelligence that they think their readers would like answered. Then have the journalists pose their questions to the theorists, and have the theorists debate the answers based on their own theories.

Applying Information

Have students use what they have learned in this section and in the Role-Playing activity to write a newspaper article about theories of intelligence. Ask volunteers to read their articles aloud and have the class serve as newspaper editors to edit the articles for accuracy and completeness.

Reviewing Section 1

Have students complete the Section Review questions on page 210.

Section 1 Review: Answers

1. Achievement refers to knowledge and skills gained from experience. Achievement involves specific content areas (or accomplishments). Intelligence, on the other hand, involves the capacity to learn.

2. Spearman suggested that people have general intelligence and specific intelligence. Thurstone asserted that eight separate factors made up intelligence. Gardner believes that intelligence has a broader base and that people have several different kinds of intelligence. Sternberg argues that all intelligences work together in a way that can best be understood in a three-level model of intelligence.

3. Answers will vary. One possible occupation is editor. According to Spearman's theory, an editor would need specific writing and editing ability; Thurstone's theory points to high verbal meaning and word fluency; Gardner's theory points to language ability; Sternberg would list both analytic and creative abilities; all of Goleman's factors undoubtedly would help ensure success in any occupation.

Emotional intelligence includes mood management and people skills, qualities possessed by many airline flight attendants.

- Impulse control (the ability to delay pleasure until the task at hand has been accomplished). A student who resists the temptation to watch television until her or his homework is done may do better in school than a student who puts off homework until later.

- People skills (the ability to empathize, understand, communicate, and cooperate with others). People skills help us get along with others, and getting along with others helps us in school and on the job.

A DAY IN THE LIFE As Todd pointed out, Dan has exceptional people skills. According to Goleman's theory, Dan would be characterized as emotionally intelligent. Goleman's view has captured the interest of many psychologists and educators. However, research studies still need to be done to confirm Goleman's ideas.

Links Between Different Types of Intelligences

As you have read, a number of psychologists believe that there are several different kinds of intelligences. But what, if any, relationship exists between these different intelligences? Are they totally separate, or are some types of intelligence somehow linked to other types? Research suggests that there may in fact be some links.

Hannah has studied the violin since early childhood. What has been happening in Hannah's mind as she learned to play the violin? Has she learned about the music of composers like Mozart and Beethoven? Certainly. Has she gained self-confidence and performance skills when she plays at recitals? Absolutely. But according to recent psychological research, Hannah may also have been enhancing her spatial reasoning ability.

A study done by the research team of Frances Rauscher, Gordon Shaw, and Katherine Ky (1993) has suggested links between musical- and spatial-reasoning ability. According to the researchers, listening to 10 minutes of a Mozart piano sonata on several occasions enhanced college students' scores on spatial-reasoning items on tests they were given.

A follow-up study done by the same group (1994) recruited 19 children ranging from three to four years old. The researchers gave the children eight months of music lessons, including singing and playing a keyboard. Another 15 children served as a control group—they received no music lessons. After the music course was completed, the researchers gave all of the children a task in which they had to put pieces of a puzzle together to form a complete object. The scores of the 19 children who had had the lessons significantly exceeded those of the 15 children who had not received the training in music.

How can we explain these results? How can listening to music or training in music enhance spatial reasoning ability? One view is that the parts of the brain that are involved in music overlap with the parts involved in other cognitive functions, such as spatial reasoning (Blakeslee, 1995). Musical training thus might help develop the connections between nerve cells in these parts of the brain. The beneficial changes in the nervous system may help children in geometry, art and design, and geography. The changes may even help people fit suitcases into the trunk of a car (Martin, 1994).

SECTION 1 REVIEW

go.hrw.com Homework Practice Online
Keyword: SY3 HP9

1. What is the difference between achievement and intelligence?

2. Describe the various theories of intelligence.

3. **Critical Thinking** *Evaluating* Choose an occupation that interests you. List the types of intelligence, as outlined by any of the theories in this section, that a person should possess to succeed in that occupation.

Section Objective

▶ Describe how the various types of intelligence tests differ.

This objective is assessed in the Section Review on page 215 and in the Chapter 9 Review.

Motivator

Invite an educational psychologist to visit your classroom to discuss intelligence tests. Before the visit, work with students to develop a list of questions they would like answered. Here are some possibilities: How are intelligence tests developed? How have intelligence tests changed over the years? How do test developers ensure that tests are reliable and valid? What types of intelligence tests are used by schools, the government, and employers? Advise the psychologist of the students' interests so that he or she can appropriately direct the discussion.

SECTION 2

Measurement of Intelligence

A DAY IN THE LIFE

You have probably taken many tests throughout your school career. Some of the tests you have taken or will take are achievement tests—they show what you have learned. Other tests are aptitude tests, which are intended to predict your ability to learn new skills. There are also tests that are designed to measure intelligence. The most widely used intelligence tests are the Stanford-Binet Intelligence Scale and the Wechsler scales. These are probably the types of tests Todd was given when he was younger.

The Stanford-Binet Scale

In the early 1900s, leaders of the French public school system were interested in finding a test that could identify children who were likely to need special educational attention. In response, French psychologist Alfred Binet devised the first modern intelligence test. The original version of the test was first used in 1905.

Binet assumed that intelligence increased with age. Thus, Binet's test contained questions for children of different age levels. (See Figure 9.2.) Older children were expected to answer more difficult questions. Children earned "months" of credit for correct answers.

Binet's test yielded a score called a mental age. A child's mental age is not the same thing as his or her chronological age. **Mental age** (MA) shows the intellectual level at which a child is functioning. For

Typical Items on the Stanford-Binet Intelligence Scale

Age Level	Item 1	Item 2
2 years	Children know basic vocabulary words. When the examiner says, "Show me the eyes" (or ears), they can point to the proper parts of a doll.	Children can match a model by building a tower made up of four blocks.
4 years	Children show language and classifying ability by filling in a missing word: "Brother is a boy; sister is a ____."	Children show general understanding by answering questions such as: "Why do people have telephones?"
9 years	Children can point out absurdities. For example: "She dug up a coin dated 544 B.C. What is silly about that?"	Children show increased language ability, as shown by answering: "Can you tell me a number that rhymes with *gate*?"
Adult	Adults show knowledge of the meanings of words and conceptual thinking by correctly explaining the differences between word pairs such as "sickness and misery," "house and home," and "integrity and prestige."	Adults show spatial skills by correctly answering questions such as: "If a car turned to the right to head north, in what direction was it heading before it turned?"

FIGURE 9.2 *These items are similar to those that appear on the Stanford-Binet Intelligence Scale. The test includes tasks for age levels from two to adulthood. The* test produces an intelligence quotient, or IQ, that reflects the relationship between a person's mental age and his or her chronological age.

Note: Adapted from Stanford-Binet Intelligence Scale.

Teaching Section 2

Demonstration

To demonstrate how psychologists calculate the intelligence quotient, write the following equation on the chalkboard: IQ = MA/CA x 100. Ask students to supply pairs of mental ages and chronological ages. Write these pairs on the chalkboard. Use the equation to calculate IQs for several pairs of numbers. Then ask volunteers to come to the chalkboard and calculate IQs for the remainder of the pairs. When all pairs have been calculated, have students indicate which IQs are above average and which are below average.

Applying Ideas

Discuss with students the fact that there are different learning styles and that some people are visual learners, some are auditory learners, some are tactile/ kinesthetic learners, and so on. Ask students why written intelligence tests might be difficult for people with certain learning styles. Then have students work as a group to devise other testing approaches that might better take into account the variety of learning styles. Ask students to describe testing experiences that have been successful for them.

internet connect

TOPIC: Reliability, Validity, and Scoring on IQ Tests
GO TO: go.hrw.com
KEYWORD: SY3 PS9

Have students access the Internet through the HRW Go site to research the methods, reliability, and validity of tests employed to measure intelligence. Have students write a report in which they define and differentiate reliability and validity, define the concept of "transformed score" as it applies to intelligence quotient (IQ) scores, and outline the issues with intelligence tests.

example, a child with an MA of six is functioning, intellectually, like the typical six-year-old, even if the child is not six years old. An MA of nine is above average for a seven-year-old. The same MA of nine is below average for an 11-year-old.

In 1916 Binet's test was brought to the United States and revised by Louis Terman of Stanford University. For this reason, the test became known as the Stanford-Binet Intelligence Scale (SBIS).

The version of the test used today provides an intelligence quotient, not an MA. An **intelligence quotient** (IQ) is a number that reflects the relationship between a child's mental age and his or her actual, or chronological, age (CA).

The IQ is a *quotient* because we use division to obtain the number. The IQ was initially computed using the formula IQ = (mental age divided by chronological age) × 100, or

$$IQ = \frac{\text{Mental Age (MA)}}{\text{Chronological Age (CA)}} \times 100$$

A child with an MA of nine and a CA of nine would thus have an IQ of 100. Children who answer test items as competently as older children have IQs above 100. For example, an 8-year-old who does as well as the average 10-year-old will attain an IQ of 125. Children who do not do as well as typical children their age attain IQ scores below 100. In other words, people who do better than average for their age attain IQ scores above 100. People who score below average attain scores below 100. The intelligence quotient is an example of a **transformed score**—that is, any score that has been changed from a raw score in a systematic way. Psychologists transform raw scores so that test results can be more easily compared.

An adult takes one of the performance subtests of the Wechsler scales.

TRUTH OR fiction

REVISITED

It is true that two children can answer exactly the same items on an intelligence test correctly, yet their scores may differ significantly. This happens when the children taking the test are different ages.

The Wechsler Scales

The Stanford-Binet is the "classic" individual intelligence test. Today, however, David Wechsler's scales are more widely used (Watkins et al., 1995). Wechsler developed intelligence tests for children

and adults. The most widely used test is the revised Wechsler Adult Intelligence Scale (WAIS-R).

The Wechsler scales consist of several subtests. (See Figure 9.3.) Each subtest measures a different intellectual skill. Some of Wechsler's subtests measure verbal skills. Others assess performance skills. In general, verbal subtests involve words and ideas; performance subtests focus on spatial relations. Both verbal and performance subtests require reasoning ability. The Wechsler scales reveal relative strengths and weaknesses as well as overall intellectual functioning.

The Wechsler scales differ from the Stanford-Binet test in several important ways. The Wechsler scales do not use the concept of mental age, although they still use the term IQ. The Stanford-Binet test measures verbal ability, whereas the Wechsler scales measure both verbal and nonverbal abilities. Because the Wechsler tests yield three scores (verbal, nonverbal, and combined), they can be used to identify particular learning disabilities. For example, if an individual's verbal score is significantly lower than his or her nonverbal score, this might indicate a reading disability.

Scores on the Wechsler tests are based on a comparison of a person's answers with the answers of others in the same age group. The average score for any age level is 100. About 50 percent of scores fall within a broad range of 90 to 110. About 2 percent of people who take the tests score above 130, and about 2 percent score below 70.

Cooperative Learning

Organize the class into groups, and assign each group one of the subtests shown in Figure 9.3. Tell the groups to develop new items similar to the ones shown in their subtest that would be appropriate for people in their age group. After the groups have completed the assignment, have them present their items to the class, discuss what type(s) of intelligence the items are designed to assess and explain how the items could be tested for reliability and validity. Then have the class discuss how the Wechsler scales differ from the Stanford-Binet test.

For Further Research

Tell students that Binet and Wechsler are not the only people ever to construct intelligence tests. Have students conduct library research to find other examples of tests that have been used to measure intelligence. Tell students to compare and contrast these tests with the ones devised by Binet and Wechsler. Have students present their findings in a written report. Ask students to include some sample items from the tests they find in their report and to state their points of view concerning the validity of each test as a measure of intelligence.

Typical Subtests from the Wechsler Scales

VERBAL SUBTESTS

General Information
1. How many wings does a bird have?
2. How many nickels make a dime?
3. What is steam made of?
4. Who wrote *Tom Sawyer*?
5. What is pepper?

General Comprehension
1. What should you do if you see someone forget his book when he leaves a restaurant?
2. What is the advantage of keeping money in a bank?
3. Why is copper often used in electrical wires?

Vocabulary
This test consists simply of asking, "What is a_____?" or "What does _____ mean?" The words cover a wide range of difficulty.

Similarities
1. In what way are a lion and a tiger alike?
2. In what way are a saw and a hammer alike?
3. In what way are an hour and a week alike?
4. In what way are a circle and a triangle alike?

Arithmetic
1. Sam had three pieces of candy and Joe gave him four more. How many pieces of candy did Sam have altogether?
2. Three women divided 18 golf balls equally among themselves. How many golf balls did each person receive?
3. If two buttons cost 15¢, what will be the cost of a dozen buttons?

PERFORMANCE SUBTESTS

Digit Symbol
The test taker is asked to learn to associate meaningless figures with numbers.

Block Design
The test taker is asked to copy pictures of geometric designs using multicolored blocks.

Picture Completion
The test taker is asked to identify what is missing from a picture such as this one.

Picture Arrangement
The test taker is asked to arrange pictures such as these in a sequence so that they tell a story.

FIGURE 9.3 *These items are similar to those on the revised Wechsler Adult Intelligence Scale (WAIS-R). The WAIS-R contains several subtests; some measure verbal ability, and others measure performance. The WAIS-R is now more widely used than the classic Stanford-Binet Intelligence Scale. Because the Wechsler tests place more emphasis on performance than does the Stanford-Binet, they are not as likely to put less verbally oriented people at a disadvantage.*

Closing Section 2

Analyzing Ideas

After reviewing the issue of test bias, ask students to develop some test questions that would be biased against people from their parents' age group. For example, questions regarding current popular slang or dress styles might be difficult for their parents to answer. Ask them also to develop some test items that would be easy for their parents to answer but difficult for students to answer. Then have students analyze why an intelligence test that gives an unfair advantage to one particular group is not an effective test of intelligence.

Reviewing Section 2

Have students complete the Section Review questions on page 215.

Extension

Ask students to review current periodicals to find articles containing tips and suggestions for boosting brainpower. Have students summarize these articles and produce a booklet to share with the class. Have the class evaluate the likely effectiveness of the suggestions.

Reliability and Validity

Before psychologists accept intelligence tests (or other types of psychological tests), the tests must meet two criteria: they must be *reliable* and *valid*.

Test Reliability Imagine that every time you measured the width of your desk with a tape measure, it showed a different result. If this happened, we would say that the tape measure was an unreliable form of measurement. The **reliability** of a test refers to its consistency. A test or any other method of assessment is reliable if it gives highly similar scores every time it is used. A reliable intelligence test should obtain similar IQ scores for the same individual on different testing occasions.

There are different ways of showing a test's reliability. One of the most common is called test-retest reliability. **Test-retest reliability** is determined by comparing scores earned by the same person on the same test taken at different times. The Stanford-Binet and Wechsler tests are both highly reliable. For example, if you took the Stanford-Binet in your first year of high school and again in your senior year, your IQ score would probably be nearly the same the second time as it was the first.

Keep in mind that "nearly the same" does not mean "identical." Scores for the same person from different testing occasions may vary somewhat for a variety of reasons. For one reason, a person may be more motivated or attentive one day than another. For a second reason, we may improve our scores from one testing to another because we have become familiar with the test format. For another reason, intelligence is not a fixed item—it varies over time. Some intellectual skills may increase with education; some may decline with age, injury, or various health problems.

Test Validity A test has **validity** if it measures what it is supposed to measure. To see whether a test is valid, test scores are compared with outside standards or norms. A proper standard for checking the validity of a musical aptitude test might be the ability to learn to play a musical instrument. Tests of musical aptitude therefore should predict ability to learn to play a musical instrument.

What standards might be used to check the validity of intelligence tests? Most people agree that intelligence plays a role in academic success. Intelligence test scores should therefore predict school grades. They do so moderately well (Sattler, 1988). Intelligence is also thought to contribute, in part, to

job success. Scores on intelligence tests have been shown to predict adult occupational status reasonably well (McCall, 1977). Thus, these intelligence tests seem to be reasonably valid. However, because there is considerable disagreement about what intelligence is, some psychologists believe that it is difficult to make definitive statements about the validity of IQ tests.

Problems with Intelligence Tests

Intelligence tests are not perfect. Some test takers do better than others, but not necessarily because they are more intelligent. Other factors—such as education or economic background—can make a difference. For example, on average, lower-income children attain IQ scores that are 10 to 15 points lower than those of middle- and upper-income children (Taylor & Richards, 1991). This may be because they have not had the opportunities to acquire the skills that help raise scores on intelligence tests.

Motivation to do well also contributes to performance on intelligence tests (Collier, 1994). Faced with frequent failure, a person begins to expect to fail and so does not try to succeed. Such a person may think, "Why make the effort when it won't make any difference?" For this reason, some children expect to fail, which affects their motivation to try their best (Tharp, 1991).

TRUTH OR fiction
■ REVISITED ■

It is true that when we think we will not succeed at something, we may not try as hard as we can. We believe that trying will not make a difference anyway.

Some intelligence tests have been criticized for being culturally biased (Helms, 1992). A test that is culturally biased would give an advantage to a particular group. Cultural bias is expressed in several ways. First of all, the words and concepts used on the test might be those used every day by members of one group but not by members of other groups. As a result, some test takers would perform less well on such a test because they might not understand the meanings of some questions or might interpret questions in a way the test makers did not anticipate. Second, questions might be biased toward certain problem-solving methods.

► Identify the characteristics of mental retardation and giftedness.

This objective is assessed in the Section Review on page 218 and in the Chapter 9 Review.

Opening Section 3

Motivator

Initiate a class discussion about an educational policy called *mainstreaming* (inclusion). Explain to students that at various times in recent history, American schools have either separated students according to their abilities or included students of varied abilities in the same classroom. Point out that the debate involves students of gifted ability as well as those facing special challenges. Ask students how they think the issue should be addressed, both in their school and in general.

In theory, tests that are free from cultural bias ought to be possible. The challenge is for test makers to develop questions that test the appropriate skills while taking cultural differences into account.

SECTION 2 REVIEW

Homework Practice Online
Keyword: SY3 HP9

1. What is an IQ?

2. Using the Stanford-Binet Scale, what would be the intelligence quotient of a child with an MA of 11 and a CA of 11?

3. How do test reliability and test validity differ?

4. **Critical Thinking** *Comparing and Contrasting* How are the Stanford-Binet Intelligence Scale and the Wechsler scales similar and different?

SECTION 3

Differences in Intelligence

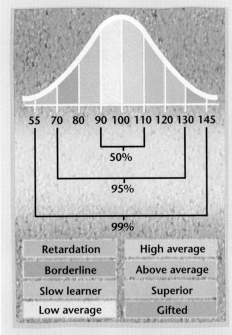

Distribution of IQ Scores

55 70 80 90 100 110 120 130 145

50%

95%

99%

Retardation	High average
Borderline	Above average
Slow learner	Superior
Low average	Gifted

FIGURE 9.4 *Psychologists refer to this bell-shaped curve as a normal curve. Normal curves display the distribution of many traits, including intelligence as measured by IQ tests. The average IQ score is 100. About 50 percent of scores fall within the broad average range from 90 to 110.*

A DAY IN THE LIFE Despite the limits of intelligence tests, they do have some uses, as Todd recalled. One of the primary functions of intelligence tests is to help identify people whose intelligence is out of the ordinary—at either end of the scale. The average IQ score is 100. About half of the people in the United States attain scores in the broad average range from 90 to 110. Nearly 95 percent attain scores between 70 and 130. (See Figure 9.4.)

But what about the other 5 percent? People who attain IQ scores of 70 or below are defined by psychologists as having mental retardation. People who attain scores of 130 or above are regarded as gifted.

Mental Retardation

While having an IQ score at or below 70 is the technical definition of **mental retardation**, there are other indicators of mental retardation as well. According to the American Association on Mental Retardation, mental retardation is also associated with problems in communication, taking care of oneself, social skills, use of leisure time, travel in the community, self-direction, personal hygiene, and vocational training (Michaelson, 1993). There are several levels of mental retardation.

Mild Retardation About 80 percent of people with retardation are classified as mildly retarded, with an IQ ranging from 50 to 70. Such people often are not obviously retarded, but as children they have more difficulty than most other children in learning to walk, in feeding themselves, and in learning to talk. Most children with mild retardation are able to learn to read and do arithmetic. As adults, they often are able to take care of themselves and hold jobs. They may, however, need occasional guidance and support when under unusual social or economic stress.

Moderate Retardation People with an IQ of between 35 and 49 have moderate retardation. They can learn to speak, to feed and dress themselves, to take care of their own hygiene, and to work under supportive conditions, as in sheltered workshops. They usually do not learn to read or

Section 2 Review: Answers

1. An IQ is a number that reflects the relationship between a person's mental age and chronological age.

2. The IQ would be 100.

3. The reliability of a test is its ability to give consistent results time after time; the validity of a test is its ability to measure what it is supposed to measure.

4. The Stanford-Binet uses mental age and chronological age to compute IQ; the Wechsler scales compare answers to those of others in the same age group. The Stanford-Binet measures verbal ability; the Wechsler scales measure verbal and performance skills.

Teaching Transparencies with Teacher's Notes

TRANSPARENCY 25: Distribution of IQ Scores

215

Teaching Section 3

Guided Practice

Create on the chalkboard a three-column chart titled "Mental Retardation." Label the column heads *Level of Retardation, IQ,* and *Description.* In the first column, list the four levels of retardation, from mild retardation to profound retardation. Ask volunteers to complete the chart by providing the IQ ranges for each level of retardation and a description of the general abilities of people who fall within each IQ range. Have students make a copy of the chart for later review.

Independent Practice

Tell students to imagine that they are members of a national association dedicated to protecting the rights of people with mental retardation. Further, tell them that they have been invited to speak at a congressional hearing being held to gather information on mental retardation and the needs of people with such retardation. Have students prepare a draft of the speech they will present at the hearing. Ask volunteers to read their speeches aloud to the class.

Class Discussion

Tell students that severe mental retardation can be caused by environmental factors in a child's early life, such as exposure to lead-based paints. Moreover, living under severely reduced socioeconomic circumstances has been linked to certain milder forms of retardation. Thus, a child who is not exposed to music, art, books, trips to new and different places, and a supportive educational setting may be prevented from functioning at or developing his or her innate intelligence level. Ask students to suggest ways to address these "reversible" causes of mild mental retardation.

Cross-Curricular Link: History

Share with students information about Leonardo da Vinci. Explain that he was a person who used his intellectual gifts in very creative ways. For example, he designed mechanical inventions such as the aerial screw on which the modern helicopter is based. Da Vinci was also a great artist and painter. His life and accomplishments clearly demonstrate that people can be gifted in both intellectual and artistic fields.

216

---

solve math problems. Children with Down syndrome are most likely to be classified in the moderately retarded range. (See Chapter 3.) Although adults with moderate retardation are usually not capable of self-maintenance, they can participate in simple recreation and travel alone in familiar places.

Severe Retardation People with severe mental retardation—IQs of 20 to 34—usually require constant supervision. They may have some understanding of speech and be able to respond. Although they can perform daily routines and repetitive activities, they need continuing direction in a protective environment. Some children in this category can respond to training in some basic self-help tasks, such as self-feeding.

Profound Retardation People with profound retardation—IQs below 20—barely communicate. They may show basic emotional responses, but they cannot feed or dress themselves and are dependent on other people for their care throughout their lives.

Causes of Retardation Retardation can be caused by any of several factors. Accidents that result in brain damage and difficulties during childbirth can cause retardation. Pregnant women who abuse alcohol or drugs, are malnourished, or who have other health problems may give birth to children who are mentally retarded. Retardation also can be caused by genetic disorders or abnormalities, such as Down syndrome.

Most doctors today recommend that pregnant women exercise to remain healthy, thereby increasing chances of giving birth to a healthy child.

Although they sometimes need guidance, most people with mental retardation can perform a variety of tasks.

Giftedness

Technically speaking, people who are gifted have IQ scores of 130 or above. However, giftedness (like retardation) may be more than just a matter of IQ. In general, to be **gifted** is to possess outstanding talent or to show the potential for performing at remarkably high levels of accomplishment when compared with other people of the same age, experience, or environment.

Some researchers believe that motivation and creativity contribute to giftedness (Renzulli, 1986). Others emphasize the importance of insight (Davidson, 1986). And many educators consider children with outstanding abilities to be gifted. The abilities can be in specific areas such as music, language arts, mathematics, or science. Children may be gifted in terms of leadership abilities or creativity, or they may exhibit excellence in the visual or performing arts. On the basis of research and experience, educators generally recognize the importance of identifying gifted children early and providing them with rich, varied learning opportunities to help them develop their potential.

Creativity

Giftedness is often linked with creativity. **Creativity** is the ability to invent new solutions to problems or to create original or ingenious materials. Although creativity may be a part of giftedness, a person can

For Further Research

Invite students to learn more about one of the seven people Howard Gardner studied in developing his theory of the exceptional creator. Encourage students to conduct library research, view the artwork and performance work of Pablo Picasso and Martha Graham if these people are chosen, and read the writings of their chosen person. Have students present their findings in a written report. In addition to presenting an overall picture of their chosen person, students should explain how the person fits Gardner's EC criteria.

CASE STUDIES
AND OTHER TRUE STORIES

CASE STUDIES
AND OTHER TRUE STORIES

The Exceptional Creator

Harvard psychologist Howard Gardner believes that there are several kinds of intelligences. He decided to study some of the most creative people of the 1900s. In 1993 Gardner published his findings in a book titled *Creating Minds*. In it, Gardner described the characteristics and circumstances that shaped the lives and work of seven major figures: Sigmund Freud, Albert Einstein, Pablo Picasso, Igor Stravinsky, T. S. Eliot, Martha Graham, and Mohandas Gandhi. Each of these people was outstanding in his or her field, and each one also happens to represent one of the intelligences in Gardner's theory.

Dancer Martha Graham had bodily-kinesthetic intelligence.

Sigmund Freud, as you know, was a famous psychologist whose intelligence provided insight into his own deepest feelings. Albert Einstein, the physicist who established the theory of relativity, had a special ability in math. Pablo Picasso—a sculptor and potter as well as a painter—had outstanding spatial-relations intelligence. Igor Stravinsky, a composer, had extraordinary musical ability. T. S. Eliot, a poet, had linguistic intelligence. Martha Graham, a dancer, had special body-kinesthetic intelligence. Mohandas Gandhi possessed exceptional sensitivity to the feelings and needs of others, which helped him to become an influential leader in India.

Using the information he learned about these creative people, Gardner then developed EC. *EC* stands for Exceptional Creator, an imaginary person who combines the common characteristics of creators. The characteristics are as follows:

- EC comes from outside a major city but not so far removed that she is uninformed.
- EC's family is neither wealthy nor poor but is reasonably comfortable.
- EC's upbringing was fairly strict, and her closest friend is outside her immediate family.

- EC's family is not especially educated, but they value learning and achievement.
- EC discovered her talent at an early age.
- As an adult, EC feels the need to test herself against others in her field, and she moves to the city.
- Once she makes a major breakthrough in her field, EC becomes isolated from her peers.
- EC works nearly all the time and constantly makes tremendous demands on herself.
- EC is self-confident, stubborn, and able to deal with adversity.
- EC has a second major breakthrough in her field about 10 years after the first.
- EC lives a long time, gains many followers, and continues to make contributions in her field until her death.

Most of the famous creators had to struggle to win acceptance for their ideas. When acceptance came too easily, some even made a special effort to be unconventional because they felt it made them more creative.

Gardner admits that his seven people do not represent all cultures or all time periods in history. Also, one cannot expect each and every one of the characteristics to be true for all creative individuals. Even for his seven case studies, there were always differences between them and the imaginary EC. However, Gardner believes that quite a few of the details still hold true.

WHY PSYCHOLOGY MATTERS

Many exceptionally creative people have changed the way people think about the arts, politics, and science. Use CNNfyi.com or other current events sources to learn more about the contributions of an exceptionally creative person. Create a mural illustrating that person's achievements.

CNNfyi.com

Journal Activity

Remind students that most of the exceptional creators Gardner studied had to struggle to have their ideas accepted and that some believed their unconventionality made them more creative. Have students consider this information. Then ask them to comment in their journals on the relationship between creativity and unconventionality.

Essay and Research Themes for A. P. Students

Theme 8

Technology Resources

 CNN. Presents Psychology: Elephant Smarts

Closing Section 3

Evaluating Information

Have students brainstorm a list of careers in which creativity is the primary criterion for success. Note their responses on the chalkboard. Have students use the list to evaluate the following statement: A person can be highly creative without being gifted.

Reviewing Section 3

Have students complete the Section Review questions on page 218.

Extension

Leslie Lemke is the savant on whom Dustin Hoffman based his well-known performance in the film *Rain Man*. Lemke, who has multiple disabilities (including blindness) and did not speak until the age of 25, is amazingly gifted in the area of music. Able to play a piece on the piano after just one hearing, Lemke now gives concerts and has begun composing. Discuss any questions students have about savants. Then encourage them to research the life of Leslie Lemke or another savant and share their findings with the class.

A child who is exceptionally talented at something is often called a prodigy. One well-known prodigy was Wolfgang Amadeus Mozart, who began performing music at the age of six.

It is not true that intellectually gifted people are by definition highly creative. Gifted people are more likely to be creative than are people of average intelligence. However, not all highly intelligent people are highly creative.

SECTION 3 REVIEW

Homework Practice Online Keyword: SY3 HP9

1. Define *mental retardation*.

2. What characteristics do gifted people share?

3. **Critical Thinking** *Drawing Inferences and Conclusions* If highly creative students are not always easily identified as highly intelligent students, how can teachers make sure that they identify students with high creativity and help them reach their potential?

be highly creative without being gifted. In fact, a person can even be substantially below average in intelligence and yet have very high creativity.

English psychiatrist Lorna Selfe (1978) identified one such person, a girl named Nadia. Nadia had diminished mental skills and could not speak. However, she had a remarkable talent for drawing, and her creative ability was indisputable. Nadia was an idiot savant—a person who has mental retardation or autism yet exhibits extraordinary skill, even brilliance, in a particular field.

Research suggests that highly intelligent people are more likely than the average person to be particularly creative. Yet just as a high level of creativity does not guarantee high intelligence, high intelligence does not guarantee high creativity (Simonton, 2000; Sternberg, 2001). For example, a Canadian study of gifted children (ages 9 to 11) found that they generally were more creative than children who were average in intelligence. However, this was only true for the group as a whole. Some of the gifted individuals were no more creative than the children who were average in intelligence (Kershner & Ledger, 1985).

SECTION 4

What Influences Intelligence?

A DAY IN THE LIFE How could Dan's older brother get good grades without any apparent effort while Dan has to study hard for his grades? Why do some people seem to be more intelligent than others? To what extent is it possible to improve a person's intelligence? In order to address these questions, it is necessary to determine from where intelligence comes. Are people born with it, or do they acquire it during their lifetime?

Many psychologists believe that both heredity and environment influence intelligence. Mark Snyderman and Stanley Rothman (1987, 1990) surveyed a sample of 1,020 psychologists and educational specialists and found the following:

- Forty-five percent believe that differences in IQ scores among people reflect both genetic and environmental factors.

- Fifteen percent believe that these differences reflect environmental factors alone.

Section Objective

▶ Explain how heredity and the environment influence intelligence.

This objective is assessed in the Section Review on page 221 and in the Chapter 9 Review.

Opening Section 4

Motivator

Take an informal survey of the students by asking for a show of hands in response to the following questions: How many students think IQ is determined by genetics? How many students think IQ is determined by environment? How many students think IQ is determined by both heredity and environment? Then have a volunteer read the bulleted text on page 219. Tell students that, in this section, they will read about some of the factors that influence intelligence.

- One percent believe that intelligence is determined entirely by genetic factors.
- Twenty-four percent believe that there is not enough research information to support any particular opinion.

In the case of Dan and his brother, it would be difficult to research the reasons for their differences. As Dan himself pointed out, they both have the same parents, and they grew up with similar upbringings. Thus, their differences could not easily be attributed either to heredity or environment alone. Psychologists have, however, been able to conduct some studies on the roles of nature and nurture in the development of intelligence.

Genetic Influences on Intelligence

Are all people born with the same amount of intelligence? How do genetic factors influence the level of intelligence we have? Researchers who study the genetic factors in intelligence have used kinship studies and adoptee studies to explore questions such as these.

Kinship Studies If genetic factors are involved in intelligence, then closely related people should be more alike in terms of IQ scores than distantly related or unrelated people. For this reason, psychologists have studied IQ scores of related people. Identical twins have often been used in these studies. Because they have exactly the same genetic makeup, their test scores should be identical if intelligence is solely inherited. Any difference in scores means that other factors are also involved.

Thomas Bouchard and his colleagues (1990) compiled the results of more than 100 studies on the relationship between heredity and IQ. They found that the IQ scores of identical twins are more similar than those of any other group of people. This finding holds true even when the twins are reared apart and therefore in different environments. Similarities in IQ scores between pairs of fraternal twins, other brothers or sisters, and parents and children are moderate. Similarities in IQ between children and foster parents and between cousins are weak. What does all this mean? It means that genes do seem to play some role in intelligence. But how great a role does inheritance play?

Heritability is the extent to which variations in a trait from person to person can be explained by genetic factors. Most studies suggest that the heritability of intelligence is between 40 percent and 60

percent (Neisser et al., 1996; Bouchard et al., 1990). That is, about half of the differences in IQ scores among people can be accounted for by heredity.

Adoptee Studies Some studies have compared the IQ scores of adopted children to those of their biological parents and their adoptive parents (Coon et al., 1990). If children are separated from their biological parents at early ages but their IQ scores remain very similar to those of their biological parents, it is probably because of genetic influences. On the other hand, if the IQ scores of the adopted children are more like those of their adoptive parents, it is probably because of environmental influences. Most studies of adopted children have found that their IQ scores are more like those of the biological parents than those of the adoptive parents (Baker et al., 1983; Horn, 1983; Scarr & Weinberg, 1983). Thus, there seems to be further evidence of heredity's role in intelligence.

Psychologists Diana Baumrind (1993) and Jacquelyne Jackson (1993), however, argue that an overemphasis on heredity can undermine parental and educational efforts to help children learn. Parents and educators are most effective when they believe their efforts will improve

Kinship studies have shown moderate similarities in IQ scores between parents and children.

Journal Activity

Before students read Section 4, have them write a paragraph in their journals explaining why they answered the questions in the Motivator activity on page 219 the way they did. After students have read the section, have them reread their journal paragraphs and explain why they would or would not change their answers to the questions.

⏵ internet connect

TOPIC: Influences on Intelligence
GO TO: go.hrw.com
KEYWORD: SY3 PS9

Have students access the Internet through the HRW Go site to research genetic and environmental influences on intelligence. Then ask students to imagine they are applying for a grant to fund a program that they believe will positively impact intelligence for children and adults. Have students design a program that takes into account what psychologists have learned about intelligence, and then have them describe it in a grant proposal.

Teaching Section 4

Comparing and Contrasting Information

Ask students to create a two-column chart titled "Influences on Intelligence." Tell them to label one column *Genetic Influences* and the other column *Environmental Influences*. Have students complete their charts by comparing and contrasting the evidence presented in the textbook for both types of influences. Then have volunteers debate the following question: Which has a greater influence on intelligence—heredity or environment?

Cooperative Learning

Organize the class into groups of three or four. Refer students to the bulleted list on page 220 showing factors that contribute to high levels of intellectual functioning in children. For each factor listed, have groups brainstorm several ways that the factor can be translated into real-life experiences. *(For example, concerning the factor of parents' involvement in their children's activities, students may suggest that parents attend their children's recitals or athletic games.)* Have each group present its ideas to the class.

For Your Information

Explain the concept of evolutionary psychology: Early human beings developed the aspects of their intelligence that were useful and necessary in their living situation. Then through marriage, particular intelligence levels and styles became more concentrated. For example, people would choose partners with similar cognitive abilities. Children of these similarly intelligent parents would most likely have those attributes as well. After discussing the evolutionary psychology concept, ask students how it supports or contradicts the heredity and environment approaches to intelligence.

Class Discussion

Discuss with students the range of materials—books, toys, music, and so on—available to parents and child-care professionals for the intellectual stimulation of young children. Show some of these materials if possible. Ask students to discuss other kinds of materials that might be useful in developing young minds. *(Students may suggest board games, word games, and number games.)*

children's knowledge and skills. Because parents and educators cannot change children's genetic codes, it is useful for them to assume that effective parenting and teaching can make a difference.

Environmental Influences on Intelligence

Bouchard and his colleagues (1990) found that for each type of kinship, from identical twins to parents and children, IQ scores are more alike for pairs of people who were reared together than for pairs who were reared apart. This result holds for identical twins, other brothers and sisters, and even people who are unrelated. These findings suggest that environmental factors also affect intelligence. A variety of studies have examined the influence of home environment, parenting style, schooling, and other environmental factors on intelligence.

Home and Parenting   Studies have shown that home environment and styles of parenting influence the development of intelligence (Coon et al., 1990; Olson et al., 1992; Steinberg et al., 1992). The following factors apparently contribute to high levels of intellectual functioning in children:

- The parents are emotionally and verbally responsive to their children's needs.
- The parents provide enjoyable and educational toys.
- The parents are involved in their children's activities.
- The parents provide varied daily experiences during the preschool years.
- The home environment is well organized and safe (Bradley et al., 1989).
- The children are encouraged to be independent—to make their own decisions and solve their own problems whenever possible (McGowan & Johnson, 1984).

Preschool Programs   Many preschool programs are designed to provide young children with enriched early experiences. These experiences are intended to develop intelligence and prepare children for school. Many such programs exist, but one program is particularly well known. That program is Head Start. Begun in 1965, Head Start was designed to give economically disadvantaged children a better start in school.

Communities throughout the United States operate Head Start centers under the guidance and funding of the U.S. Department of Health and Human Services. Parental involvement is an important feature of Head Start. This program includes health, education, and social services for participating children and their families. In local Head Start centers, children become familiar with books. They also play word and number games; work with puzzles, drawing materials, toy animals, and dolls; and interact with teachers in a school-like setting.

Preschool programs such as Head Start have been shown to increase the IQ scores, achievement test scores, and academic skills of participants (Barnett & Escobar, 1990; Zigler, 1999). Preschool programs also appear to have long-term benefits. Graduates of these programs are less likely to repeat a grade or be placed in classes for slow learners. They are more likely to finish high school, attend college, and earn high incomes. Participation in such programs even decreases the likelihood of juvenile delinquency and reliance on welfare programs (Schweinhart & Weikart, 1993; Zigler et al., 1992).

Children in Head Start centers, such as this one in New Mexico, receive educational opportunities that otherwise might not be available to them.

Closing Section 4

Demonstration

To demonstrate the effect of environmental factors on intelligence, arrange for the class to visit a Head Start center, a workshop for people with mental retardation, or a senior citizens center. Have students prepare a list of questions about the program to ask the teachers or supervisors of the program. Following the visit, lead a classroom discussion based on the students' observations and the answers to their questions. Have students evaluate the effectiveness of the program in terms of providing intellectual stimulation.

Synthesizing Ideas

Organize the class into groups. Ask each group to develop a list of things they can do to ensure that they function at peak intelligence through middle and late adulthood. Have the groups combine their lists with illustrations and create a pamphlet titled "Intelligence: Use It or Lose It."

Reviewing Section 4

Have students complete the Section Review questions on page 221.

TRUTH OR fiction ∎ REVISITED ∎

It is true that preschool programs have long-term benefits for the children who attend them. Graduates of preschool programs are less likely to be held back in school and are more likely to graduate from high school, attend college, and earn high incomes.

Adults and Intelligence

Psychologists are also concerned about factors that affect intelligence among adults, especially older adults. Older people show some drop-off in intelligence as measured by scores on intelligence tests. The decline is usually most notable in timed test questions—questions that must be answered within a certain amount of time (Schaie, 1994; Schaie & Willis, 1991). On the other hand, vocabulary skills can continue to expand for a lifetime.

Biological changes contribute to some of the decline. However, older people who retain their health have very high levels of intellectual functioning (Schaie, 1994). One study, conducted in Seattle, has been following intellectual changes in adults for nearly 40 years. The Seattle study has found that intellectual functioning in older people is linked to several environmental factors (Schaie, 1993, 1994):

- level of income
- level of education
- a history of stimulating jobs
- intact family life
- attendance at cultural events, travel, and reading
- marriage to a spouse with a high level of intellectual functioning
- a flexible personality

In general, the more of these factors that are present in people's lives and the higher and stronger the factors are, the higher the level of intellectual functioning.

A DAY IN THE LIFE

All things considered, intellectual functioning in people of all ages appears to reflect many genetic, physical, personal, and social factors. Todd clearly understood this when he reminded Dan that although Dan and

Remaining active may help older adults continue to function intellectually at a high level.

his brother share the same parents and similar upbringings, they still have some different genes and have had different experiences, such as in school.

The fact that a person's genetically determined intellectual potential cannot be predicted makes it difficult to resolve the debate about the roles that genetics and environment play in intelligence. However, no matter what genes a person may have inherited, that person's intelligence is not fixed or unchangeable. People such as Hannah, Dan, and Todd can, depending on their education and other factors, improve their intellectual functioning. Genetic factors give each person a range of possibilities. The environment influences the expression of these possibilities. Intelligence remains a complex concept that challenges psychologists, educators, and many others.

SECTION 4 REVIEW

go.hrw.com **Homework Practice Online** Keyword: SY3 HP9

1. What evidence suggests that genetic factors play a role in intelligence?

2. What are three environmental factors that affect intelligence?

3. **Critical Thinking** *Analyzing Information* Describe three activities that you think would provide preschool children with an important skill or would enrich their lives.

Technology

▶ Chapter 9 Test Generator (on the One-Stop Planner)

▶ HRW Go site

Reinforcement, Review, and Assessment

▶ Chapter 9 Review, pp. 222–223

▶ Chapter Review and Activities with Answer Key

▶ Alternative Assessment Handbook

▶ Portfolio Assessment Handbook

▶ Chapter 9 Test (Form A or B)

PSYCHOLOGY PROJECTS

Linking to Community Invite an educational psychologist to your classroom. Ask this professional to share his or her views about intelligence and its elements and applications with the class. Here are some issues for discussion:

■ What role does intelligence testing have in schools and in the workplace?

---

3. the intellectual level at which a child functions

4. any score that has been changed from the raw score in a systematic way

5. the consistency of a test

6. reliability determined by comparing scores earned by the same person on the same test taken at different times

7. an indication of whether a test measures what it is supposed to measure

8. to possess outstanding talent or to show the potential for performing at remarkably high levels of accomplishment

9. the ability to invent new solutions to problems or to create original or ingenious materials

10. the extent to which variations in a trait from person to person can be explained by genetic factors

Understanding Main Ideas

1. Intelligence makes achievement possible.

2. Thurstone believes that intelligence is made up of nine mental abilities; Gardner suggests seven different intelligences.

3. Wechsler scales give a verbal score, a non-verbal score, and a combined score; they can be used to assess IQ in non-English-speaking people and to diagnose learning disabilities.

4. People with moderate retardation can be taught to speak, to care for their physical needs, and to work in a safe environment; people with profound retardation may not speak and may need help eating and dressing; gifted people have above-average

---

Chapter **9** REVIEW

Writing a Summary

Using standard grammar, spelling, sentence structure, and punctuation, summarize the information in this chapter. Consider:
• the types of intelligences and intelligence tests
• mental retardation, giftedness, creativity, and the roles that heredity and environment play in intelligence

Identifying People and Ideas

Identify the following terms or people and use them in appropriate sentences.

1. achievement
2. intelligence
3. mental age
4. transformed score
5. reliability
6. test-retest reliability
7. validity
8. gifted
9. creativity
10. heritability

Understanding Main Ideas

SECTION 1 (pp. 206–210)

1. What is the relationship between achievement and intelligence?

2. Contrast Louis Thurstone's theory of intelligence with that of Howard Gardner.

SECTION 2 (pp. 211–215)

3. Why are the Wechsler scales more widely used than the Stanford-Binet test?

SECTION 3 (pp. 215–218)

4. Give one characteristic of each of the following individuals: a person with moderate mental retardation, a person with profound mental retardation, a gifted person, a creative person.

SECTION 4 (pp. 218–221)

5. What have kinship and adoptee studies revealed about the genetic role in intelligence?

Thinking Critically

1. **Supporting a Point of View** Which theory of intelligence do you think is the most accurate? Use specific examples to explain your answer.

2. **Evaluating** Other than vocabulary and problem-solving methods, what else might cause intelligence tests to be culturally biased?

3. **Summarizing** List some examples of steps parents and educators can take to encourage highly creative children.

4. **Drawing Inferences and Conclusions** How might a person boost his or her score on an intelligence test?

5. **Analyzing Information** What are three activities that could help someone who is age 70 or older maintain a high level of intellectual functioning?

Writing About Psychology

1. **Drawing Inferences and Conclusions** Write a report describing the criteria you would use to select the most intelligent students for a student body hall of fame. You might want to compare your criteria with those prepared by other members of the class.

2. **Analyzing Information** Go to the library to find information about Gardner's "intelligences." Prepare brief biographies of three people who appear to exhibit one such intelligence. Be sure to use standard grammar, spelling, sentence structure, and punctuation. Use the graphic organizer below to help you write your biographies.

Person and Intelligence Type	Person and Intelligence Type	Person and Intelligence Type

- What are some ways that parents and educators can help a student develop his or her intelligence?

- Do schools test for IQ scores? Does knowledge of their IQ scores affect students' performance?

- How did schools in the past deal with children who fall into different extremes of intelligence?

Building Social Studies Skills

Interpreting Graphs

Study the bar graph below. Then use the information in the graph to help you answer the questions that follow.

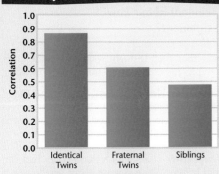

Similarity of IQ Scores Among Relatives

Source: Bouchard and McGue, *Genetic and Environmental Influences on Adult Personality*, 1981

1. Which statement best reflects the information presented in the graph?
   a. There is a significant correlation between IQ levels and how closely people are related.
   b. There is no relation between IQ levels and how closely people are related.
   c. A higher correlation between IQ levels exists between siblings than between identical twins.
   d. A higher correlation between IQ levels exists between fraternal twins than between identical twins.

2. What does the information in this graph suggest about the effect heredity has on intelligence?

Analyzing Primary Sources

Read the following excerpt, in which a group of psychologists discuss the use of intelligence tests. Then answer the questions that follow.

"Critics . . . often stress the political history of IQ testing in the United States. . . . They highlight the use of IQ tests in the early to mid-twentieth century to . . . restrict immigration and defend segregation. . . . Based on this history, many dismiss testing. We do not take this approach, for two reasons. First, . . . testing in other countries shows that it is really a history of the *decisions* people made about how to use tests. In the United States, IQ tests were made for discriminatory purposes, but elsewhere, like Great Britain, liberal reformers used similar tests to find promising lower-class children and provide them with opportunities. Second, IQ and similar tests are widely used by educators and employers as gatekeeping mechanisms to determine who will or will not obtain scarce positions. It is highly unlikely that such tests will be discarded simply because people used them badly in the past."

3. Which of the following statements best reflects the meaning of the excerpt?
   a. The use of IQ tests must be abandoned entirely.
   b. Because people continue to use IQ tests, psychologists must continue to study and improve testing methods.
   c. British psychologists are superior to American psychologists.
   d. People today would never misuse an IQ test.

4. According to the excerpt, how have IQ tests been used in the past to benefit people?

mental ability and may have special talents; creative people can devise new ideas and ways of doing things.

5. Studies show that closely related people are closer in IQ than unrelated people. Other studies show that adoptees are closer in IQ to biological parents than to adoptive parents.

Thinking Critically

1. Answers will vary but should include examples.

2. Tests may be biased in the kinds of situations they present. For example, a sailing question may be outside an inner-city dwellers experience.

3. Parents could expose creative children to art and music; educators might nurture creative students with assignments that elicit creativity rather than promote intelligence.

4. Familiarity with the types of test questions and diligent study might boost an IQ score.

5. Activities might include sharing experiences and discussing books.

Writing About Psychology

1. Lists should include criteria beyond IQ or grade point average.

2. Students should connect the intelligences to well-known people.

Building Social Studies Skills

1. a

2. A significant link between heredity and intelligence.

3. b

4. British psychologists used the exam to identify capable children who would otherwise not have had opportunities because of their social and economic backgrounds.

PSYCHOLOGY PROJECTS

Cooperative Learning

Research in Psychology Fetal alcohol syndrome (FAS) is a cause of mental retardation. Work with a group to find out more about FAS. Then make a poster warning about the dangers of drinking alcohol during pregnancy. As you work on the project, keep in mind that members of your group should act in accordance with acceptable behavior to maintain group cohesion. Be sure to meet regularly and support the group. When your group has finished the poster, display it in the classroom.

internet connect

Internet Activity: go.hrw.com
KEYWORD: SY3 PS9
Choose an activity on intelligence to:
- make a news broadcast on theories of intelligence.
- write a report on the concept of "transformed score" as it applies to IQ scores and define and differentiate reliability and validity.
- design a program that has a positive impact on intelligence.

223

UNIT 3 REVIEW

► TEACH

Organize students into groups to practice their conflict-resolution skills. Have each group consider a conflict that might arise between a teenager and a parent, such as a disagreement about what movies the parent allows the teen to see.

► PSYCHOLOGY IN ACTION

Pair students and have each pair create a chart or a table of the ways that conflicts can be resolved. Have the pairs present their charts or tables to the class, then call on volunteers to share additional ways that conflicts can be resolved.

Ask the groups to follow the four-step process outlined in the Psychology in Action Simulation to resolve the conflict. Have one member of each group present their conflict-resolution process to the class.

► EXTEND

Have students review the Psychology in Action Simulation. Then organize them into groups and have each group develop a

plan to complete the class assignment. Next, have the groups prepare for a debate on the best way to complete the class assignment by listing as many arguments as they can both for and against the idea that they have proposed. Finally, have each group hold practice debates in which some members argue for the group's plan and others argue against it.

PSYCHOLOGY IN ACTION

YOU RESOLVE THE CONFLICT . . .

How can people settle a disagreement about how to complete a class assignment?

Complete the following activity in small groups. Imagine that two of your friends are having a disagreement about how to complete a class assignment. Prepare a presentation outlining ways to resolve the conflict.

1. Consider Persuasion. Encourage your friends to try to persuade one another to come around to the other's point of view. To help your friends come up with persuasive arguments for their side, list the reasons why they hold the positions that they do. Then rank each reason in order of persuasiveness. Finally, urge your friends to present the most persuasive reasons to one another in an effort to sway the other to his or her point of view.

2. Compromise. Explain to your friends that sometimes compromise is necessary to resolve a conflict. Tell them that each will have to give up something to reach an agreement. Consider what they would be willing to give up to resolve their disagreement. Then encourage your friends to meet and discuss what they would be willing to give up to reach an agreement.

3. Debate the Issue. Suggest to your friends that they hold a debate. Gather information about the advantages and disadvantages of each side of their disagreement. Ask questions such as,

- Has one friend worked on this type of assignment before?
- Has one of the friends already researched the assignment and thus gained a stronger understanding of how it should be carried out?

Then consider having your friends prepare flash cards outlining the best arguments they can come up with in support of their side. Finally, hold the

debate. Your friends might want to include charts and graphs to better demonstrate their positions.

4. Consider Negotiation. Urge your friends to begin negotiations about the conflict. Suggest that they meet to discuss their positions and what they would be willing to agree upon. Tell them that perhaps by working together to resolve the conflict, they will arrive at a solution that neither had considered before. When you are ready, decide who in your group will make which part of the presentation. Then make your presentation to the class. Good luck!

UNIT 4

Overview

In Unit 4, students will trace the path of human development from infancy through childhood, adolescence, adulthood, and finally death.

CHAPTER 10 • *Infancy and Childhood* describes the physical and social developments that occur during infancy and childhood and discusses the major theories of infant and child development.

CHAPTER 11 • *Adolescence* identifies the physical and psychological changes that occur during adolescence and discusses social development, identity formation, and the challenges facing adolescents in modern society.

CHAPTER 12 • *Adulthood* addresses the physical changes, emotional concerns, and developmental tasks that accompany each stage of adult development.

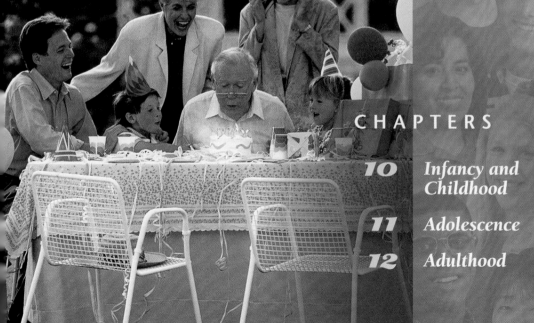

UNIT 4
DEVELOPMENT

CHAPTERS

10   *Infancy and Childhood*

11   *Adolescence*

12   *Adulthood*

▶ Internet Activity

internet connect

go.hrw.com

TOPIC: Psychological Development
GO TO: go.hrw.com
KEYWORD: SY3 UNIT 4

Have students access the Internet through the HRW Go site to research human psychological development. Then ask students to take the point of view of a person writing a series of journal or diary entries from early childhood to older adulthood. Have the students write a series of entries that could have been written at different stages of the person's life. Remind students that their entries should reflect concerns and psychological development appropriate to the age of the hypothetical person.

▶ Using Visuals

Ask students to examine the photograph on this page. Have them describe the people in it, noting the approximate age of each. Then explain that Unit 4 focuses on human development from infancy through adolescence and adulthood.

Infancy and Childhood

CHAPTER RESOURCE MANAGER

	Objectives	Pacing Guide		Reproducible and Review Resources
SECTION 1: The Study of Development (pp. 228–230)	Explain the major theories of development.	**Regular** 1 day	**Block Scheduling** .5 day	**SM** Mastering Critical Thinking Skills 10 **REV** Section 1 Review, p. 230
		Block Scheduling Handbook with Team Teaching Strategies, Chapter 10		
SECTION 2: Physical Development (pp. 230–233)	Describe the physical development that occurs during infancy.	**Regular** 1 day	**Block Scheduling** .5 day	**REV** Section 2 Review, p. 233
		Block Scheduling Handbook with Team Teaching Strategies, Chapter 10		
SECTION 3: Social Development (pp. 233–241)	Describe the social development of infants and children.	**Regular** .5 day	**Block Scheduling** .5 day	**E** Research Projects and Activities for Teaching Psychology **RS** Essay and Research Themes for Advanced Placement Students, Theme 9 **REV** Section 3 Review, p. 241
		Block Scheduling Handbook with Team Teaching Strategies, Chapter 10		
SECTION 4: Cognitive Development (pp. 241–247)	Identify the stages in Piaget's theory of cognitive development and in Kohlberg's theory of moral development.	**Regular** .5 day	**Block Scheduling** .5 day	**PS** Readings and Case Studies, Chapter 10 **REV** Section 4 Review, p. 247
		Block Scheduling Handbook with Team Teaching Strategies, Chapter 10		

Chapter Resource Key

PS	Primary Sources	**A**	Assessment		Video	
RS	Reading Support	**REV**	Review		Internet	
E	Enrichment		Transparencies		Holt Presentation	
SM	Skills Mastery		CD-ROM		Maker Using Microsoft® PowerPoint®	

  One-Stop Planner CD–ROM

See the *One-Stop Planner* for a complete list of additional resources for students and teachers.

One-Stop Planner CD–ROM

It's easy to plan lessons, select resources, and print out materials for your students when you use the *One-Stop Planner CD-ROM with Test Generator.*

Technology Resources

 One-Stop Planner, Lesson 10.1
Homework Practice Online
HRW Go Site

One-Stop Planner, Lesson 10.2
Homework Practice Online
HRW Go Site

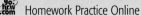 One-Stop Planner, Lesson 10.3
Homework Practice Online
Teaching Transparency 26: Styles of Parenting
CNN. Presents Psychology: Child Development

One-Stop Planner, Lesson 10.4
Homework Practice Online
HRW Go Site

Chapter Review and Assessment

 HRW Go site

REV Chapter 10 Review,
pp. 248–249

REV Chapter Review Activities
with Answer Key

A Chapter 10 Test
(Form A or B)

A Portfolio Assessment
Handbook

A Alternative Assessment
Handbook

Chapter 10 Test Generator (on the
One-Stop Planner)

Global Skill Builder CD-ROM

internet connect

HRW ONLINE RESOURCES

GO TO: go.hrw.com
Then type in a keyword.

TEACHER HOME PAGE
  KEYWORD: SY3 Teacher

CHAPTER INTERNET ACTIVITIES
  KEYWORD: SY3 PS10
  Choose an activity on infancy and childhood to:
  • write a report on the role of nature and nurture in development.
  • create an annotated time line on human physical development.
  • create a multimedia presentation on social and cognitive development in children and infants.

CHAPTER ENRICHMENT LINKS
  KEYWORD: SY3 CH10

ONLINE ASSESSMENT
  Homework Practice
  KEYWORD: SY3 HP10
  Standardized Test Prep
  KEYWORD: SY3 STP10
  Rubrics
  KEYWORD: SS Rubrics

CONTENT UPDATES
  KEYWORD: SS Content Updates

HOLT PRESENTATION MAKER
  KEYWORD: SY3 PPT10

ONLINE READING SUPPORT
  KEYWORD: SS Strategies

CURRENT EVENTS
  KEYWORD: S3 Current Events

Additional Resources

PRINT RESOURCES FOR TEACHERS
Edelman, M. W. (1992). *The measure of our success: A letter to my children and yours.* Boston: Beacon Press.

Elkind, D. (1979). *The child and society.* New York: Oxford University Press.

Kagan, J. (1984). *The nature of the child.* New York: Basic Books.

PRINT RESOURCES FOR STUDENTS
Axline, V. (1964). *Dibs in search of self.* New York: Ballantine Books.

Brazelton, T. (1992). *Touchpoints.* Reading, MA: Addison-Wesley.

Erikson, E. (1963). *Childhood and society.* New York: Norton.

MULTIMEDIA RESOURCES
Child development (VHS/Videodisc). Films for the Humanities & Sciences, P.O. Box 2053, Princeton, NJ 08543-2053.

The development of self (VHS). Films for the Humanities & Sciences, P.O. Box 2053, Princeton, NJ 08543-2053.

Childhood physical abuse (VHS). Films for the Humanities & Sciences, P.O. Box 2053, Princeton, NJ 08543-2053.

INFANCY AND CHILDHOOD

Introducing Chapter 10

Review with students what they learned in Chapter 9 about the roles of heredity and environment in intellectual development. Then have students write short paragraphs in response to the following questions:

▶ What roles do heredity and environment play in the physical development of young children?

▶ What roles do heredity and environment play in the social development of young children?

▶ What roles do heredity and environment play in the cognitive development of young children?

Have students save their responses and review them after studying Chapter 10.

Sections

1 **The Study of Development**

2 **Physical Development**

3 **Social Development**

4 **Cognitive Development**

Each of the four questions identified on page 226 corresponds to one of these sections.

10 Chapter

INFANCY AND CHILDHOOD

Read to Discover

1 What are the major theories of development?

2 How do infants develop physically?

3 What are some of the ways infants and children develop socially?

4 What are the stages in Piaget's theory of cognitive development and in Kohlberg's theory of moral development?

Each chapter begins with a vignette, called "A Day in the Life," that relates the information discussed in the chapter to the everyday events in the lives of a group of fictional high school students. The text of the chapter occasionally refers back to the vignette to demonstrate the application of the concept being discussed. An icon marked "A Day in the Life" is placed next to these references.

Copy the following graphic organizer onto the chalkboard, omitting the italicized text. Fill in the spaces as you introduce the topic of infancy and childhood.

| Nature | *Nurture* | ⟷ | Stages | *Continuity* |

A DAY IN THE LIFE

January 28

Hannah and her friends were having a discussion with Hannah's three-year-old brother, Eddie. "Why does it get dark outside?" Hannah asked him.

"'Cause I go to sleep," Eddie answered emphatically.

"Why does the sun rise?" Todd asked Eddie.

"'Cause I get up!" Eddie said.

"And why does the sun move in the sky?" Linda asked, taking a turn.

Eddie thought for a moment, "To follow me!" he answered as he scampered off to play with Dan.

"He's really something else," Marc grinned. "It's like he thinks the world revolves just around him."

"You should see some of the other things he does," Hannah said. "The other day, I showed him two rows of pennies. There were five pennies in each row. But in the first row, the pennies were half an inch apart. In the second row, they were two inches apart. I asked Eddie which row had more pennies."

"Bet I know his answer," said Marc. "The longer row, right?"

"Right. But then I asked him to count both rows, which he did, and

he counted five pennies in each row. Then I asked him again which row had more pennies. He pointed to the second row again!"

"Makes you wonder how his mind works, doesn't it?" asked Marc.

"He's grown so fast," Hannah replied after a bit. "Not so long ago, he couldn't even sit by himself, then he suddenly started crawling, then standing, then he was walking. Now just look at him go."

"I remember last year when all he wanted to do was stay next to his mother or you," Todd said. "Now all he wants to do is go and explore."

"Yeah," remembered Hannah, laughing. "He used to tug on my leg until I'd pick him up. Now he's so big, I can hardly lift him."

"Bet your parents are spoiling him rotten," said Marc.

"Actually, they're pretty strict. They say it's better for kids."

"Really?" asked Marc. "I don't believe that. I bet it's better just to love them a lot."

Hannah thought for a moment. "Parents can be strict and still love their kids."

"Well," Marc replied, "Eddie is turning out great. Guess your parents are doing something right."

. . .

Hannah and her friends had discovered that Eddie's view of the world was very different from theirs. Psychologists know that preschool children such as Eddie do not think like adults—or like teenagers. Children's thinking is truly in a class of its own. Psychologists know this because they have studied people of all ages—throughout the life span. This chapter is about two stages in the life span: infancy, the stage of life that lasts from birth until the second birthday, and childhood, the stage that follows infancy and spans the period from the second birthday to the beginning of adolescence.

Key Terms

- developmental psychology
- maturation
- critical period
- reflex
- infancy
- childhood
- attachment
- stranger anxiety
- separation anxiety
- contact comfort
- imprinting
- authoritative
- authoritarian
- self-esteem
- unconditional positive regard
- conditional positive regard
- assimilation
- accommodation
- sensorimotor stage
- object permanence
- preoperational stage
- conservation
- egocentrism
- concrete-operational stage
- formal-operational stage
- preconventional moral reasoning
- conventional moral reasoning
- postconventional moral reasoning

WHY PSYCHOLOGY MATTERS

Psychologists researched how people grow and develop. Use **CNNfyi**.com or other current events sources to learn more about how people change as they age.

CNNfyi.com

Using Key Terms

Have students create flash cards for the key terms in this chapter. Students should begin by noting on each card a possible definition of a term. Encourage them to use a variety of vocabulary strategies, such as analyzing word roots. Then have students exchange their cards with a partner, discussing and clarifying each other's definitions. Finally, urge students to look up the words in the Glossary at the back of the book and make the necessary corrections to their flash cards.

Journal Activity

After students have read "A Day in the Life," ask them to consider the thinking processes of siblings who are of preschool age or other preschool-age children they know. Ask them to write a paragraph in their journals providing evidence to support the textbook statement that the thinking of preschool children "is truly in a class of its own."

227

Section Objective

▶ Explain the major theories of development.

This objective is assessed in the Section Review on page 230 and in the Chapter 10 Review.

Motivator

Distribute long sheets of paper. Tell students to hold the paper horizontally and to draw two lines from side to side. Have them write the word *Birth* at the start of each line and the words *Beginning of Adolescence* at the end. One of these lifelines will track the major developmental milestones discussed in Chapter 10. The other lifeline, which may remain private, will record parallel events from students' own lives. Students might include key events such as learning to ride a bicycle and learning to read. Students should add milestones to both lifelines during their study of Chapter 10.

Using Truth or Fiction

Each chapter opens with several "Truth or Fiction" statements that relate to the concepts discussed in the chapter. Ask students whether they think each statement is true or false. Answers to each item as well as explanations are provided at appropriate points within the text under the heading "Truth or Fiction Revisited."

Class Discussion

Before students read Section 1, have them brainstorm reasons why psychologists might be interested in studying young children and why learning about young children might help students learn more about themselves.

Cultural Dimensions

The field of developmental psychology has evolved differently in various cultures. Psychologists in Great Britain, for example, did not focus on human development until well after American psychologists had begun to do so. Today British work in the field is viewed as a moderating influence between American developmental psychology (very experimental) and the European approach (less experimental).

228

TRUTH or fiction ?

Read the following statements about psychology. Do you think they are true or false? You will learn whether each statement is true or false as you read the chapter.

- Most babies triple their birth weights by the time they reach their first birthdays.
- Newborn babies would rather be held by their mothers than by other people.
- Baby geese become attached to the first moving object that they see—even if the object is a human being.
- Most abused children become child abusers themselves when they grow up.
- Children's self-esteem tends to decrease as they go through elementary school.

SECTION 1

The Study of Development

Developmental psychology is the field in which psychologists study how people grow and change throughout the life span—from conception, through infancy, childhood, adolescence, and adulthood, and until death. Psychologists are interested in studying the two stages discussed in this chapter—infancy and childhood—for many reasons. One is that early childhood experiences affect people as adolescents and adults. Another is that by studying early stages of development, psychologists can learn about developmental problems, what causes them, and how to treat them. For example, why do some children have low self-esteem? Psychologists can also learn about what types of experiences in infancy and childhood foster healthy and well-adjusted children and adults.

Studying development is also interesting in and of itself. Eddie's thinking would fascinate psychologists just as it intrigued Hannah and her friends. Developmental psychologists study not only people of different ages but also different types of development. These include physical development, social development, and cognitive development.

A DAY IN THE LIFE

Because developmental psychologists study people across the life span, they are interested in seeing how people change over time. Psychologists use two methods to study change: the longitudinal method and the cross-sectional method. Using the longitudinal method, developmental researchers select a group of participants and then observe that same group for a period of time, often years or even decades. Because the longitudinal method is very time-consuming (and also expensive), psychologists often use the cross-sectional method instead. Using this method, researchers select a sample that includes people of different ages. They then compare the participants in the different age groups. (See Chapter 2.)

Developmental psychologists are concerned with two general issues. The first involves the ways in which heredity and environmental influences contribute to human development. The second issue involves whether development occurs gradually or in stages.

The Roles of Nature and Nurture

Psychologists have long debated the extent to which human behavior is determined by heredity (nature) or environment (nurture). This debate has been particularly relevant to the study of development. Some aspects of behavior originate in the genes people inherit from their parents. In other words, certain kinds of behavior are biologically "programmed" to develop as long as children receive

This infant will not learn to walk until she is biologically ready to walk. The point at which such readiness will occur is influenced by heredity.

Teaching Section 1

Taking a Stand

Review with students the controversy over the roles played by heredity and environment in human development. Then have students debate the contention of philosopher John Locke that the mind of a newborn infant is like a "blank slate" on which the infant's experiences will be written. Have students on both sides of the debate provide evidence to support their reasoning.

Meeting Individual Needs: Visual Learners

Visual learners may find it easier to grasp the differences between the stages and continuity approaches to development if these approaches are presented graphically. Suggest that these students create drawings or charts for each approach, using the staircase and hill models described in the textbook. Students should fill in information and examples about each approach as they read the chapter.

SOURCE: PEANUTS © copyright 1996. Reprinted by permission of United Feature Syndicate, Inc.

adequate nutrition and social experience. Researchers use kinship studies, including studies of twins, to learn about the influence of heredity on human development. (See Chapter 3.)

In the field of human development, heredity manifests itself primarily in the process called maturation. **Maturation** is the automatic and sequential process of development that results from genetic signals. For instance, because of maturation, infants generally sit up before they crawl, crawl before they stand, and stand before they walk. This sequence happens automatically and on its own genetically determined timetable. No matter how much one might try to teach these skills to infants, they will not do these things until they are "ready."

This concept of "readiness" relates to an important term in the study of development: critical period. A **critical period** is a stage or point in development during which a person or animal is best suited to learn a particular skill or behavior pattern. For example, much research suggests that there may be a critical period for language development in humans. Young children seem to learn language more easily than older children and adults.

Psychologist Arnold Gesell (1880–1961) proposed that maturation played the most important role in development. He focused on many areas of development, including physical and social development. Behavioral psychologists, such as John Watson, took a different view from Gesell's. Behaviorism originated in the 1600s with English

philosopher John Locke, who believed that the mind of the infant is like a *tabula rasa* (Latin for "blank slate"). That is, when an infant is born, her or his mind is like a blank slate on which the infant's experiences will be written. In this view, "nurture"—or the environment—will have the greatest effect on the newborn's development.

Watson and other behaviorists presented environmental explanations for behavior. They thought that the influence of nurture was much stronger than that of nature. The influences of nurture, or the environment, are found in factors such as nutrition, family background, culture, and learning experiences in the home, community, and school.

Today nearly all psychologists would agree that both nature and nurture play key roles in children's development. For example, while few psychologists today believe that maturation plays the major role in *all* areas of development, they certainly think it is central in some, such as physical development and motor development.

Stages Versus Continuity

Another topic of debate among psychologists is whether human development occurs primarily in stages or as a continuous process. In other words, is development like climbing a set of stairs to reach the top (each stair being a distinct level), or is it like walking up an inclined plane or hill (a gradual increase up to the top, without distinct levels)?

Journal Activity

Ask students to think about the concept of maturational readiness and how it applies to their own lives. Have them consider times when they tried but failed to acquire a skill only to succeed easily at a later time. For example, perhaps a parent tried to teach them how to tie their shoes at the age of four. While they struggled and probably failed at age four, they learned the skill with ease when taught it again at age five or six. Ask students to write about such an experience in their journals. Afterward, have students discuss the importance of matching skills instruction to a child's level of maturation.

internet connect

TOPIC: Human Development
GO TO: go.hrw.com
KEYWORD: SY3 PS10

Have students access the Internet through the HRW Go site to research human development. Then have them organize their information in the form of an oral report to given in front of the class. Make sure that the students include information regarding environmental influences as well as genetic factors in development.

Closing Section 1

Organizing Information

Ask students to create a two-column chart titled "Stages Versus Continuity in Human Development." Have them complete the chart by noting the arguments and theorists on both sides of the debate. Also have students provide examples of both types of development.

Reviewing Section 1

Have students complete the Section Review questions on page 230.

A stage, like one step in a staircase, is a period or a level in the development process that is distinct from other levels. Certain aspects of physical development appear to take place in stages. For example, Eddie and most other young children go through sitting, crawling, standing, and walking stages—in that order. When people move from one stage to another, their bodies and behavior can change dramatically.

A DAY IN THE LIFE

Maturational theorists, such as Gesell, generally believe that most development occurs in stages. Rapid changes usher in dramatically new kinds of behavior, causing entry into the next stage. For instance, when an infant's legs become strong enough to support him or her, the infant stands and soon begins to walk. A new stage of life has begun—from infant to toddler.

One of the most famous stage theorists was Jean Piaget. His field was cognitive development, and he would have said that Eddie's self-centered way of thinking reflected his cognitive stage of development. Piaget would have further noted that Eddie's thinking would change dramatically when he entered the next stage of cognitive development.

Not all psychologists, however, agree that development occurs in stages. For example, J. H. Flavell and his colleagues (2002) argue that cognitive development is a gradual process. According to Flavell, cognitive development is an example of continuous development, which, like walking up a slope, happens slowly and gradually. For instance, the effects of learning cause gradual changes, such as the addition of new words to a child's vocabulary.

Continuous development can occur almost unnoticed. A child's steady growth in weight and height from the ages of about 2 to 11 years is an example of continuous development that happens so gradually we usually are not aware of the changes as they are occuring.

However, it is not always clear whether development occurs in stages or in a steady progression. Psychologists continue to debate the issue.

SECTION 1 REVIEW

go.hrw.com **Homework Practice Online** Keyword: SY3 HP10

1. Define *maturation*.

2. Describe the major theories of human development.

3. **Critical Thinking** *Analyzing Information* What is one kind of development that appears to be gradual?

A newborn enters the world possessing certain physical characteristics and equipped with certain abilities. For example, an infant is born measuring a certain length and weighing a certain amount. Both height and weight will increase with time and nourishment. The infant is also born with certain reflexes. A **reflex** is an involuntary reaction or response, such as swallowing. Some of these reflexes the infant keeps; others such as sucking disappear when they are no longer needed. Changes in reflexes and gains in height and weight are examples of physical development. Motor development and perceptual development are other examples.

Height and Weight

Babies grow at an amazing rate, but the most dramatic gains in height and weight occur even before an infant's birth. During the first eight weeks of the mother's pregnancy, the tiny embryo in the mother's uterus develops fingers, toes, eyes, ears, a nose, a mouth, a heart, and a circulatory system. At eight weeks, the 1 1/2-inch-long embryo becomes a fetus. During the fetal stage (which lasts until birth), the organs of the various body systems, such as the

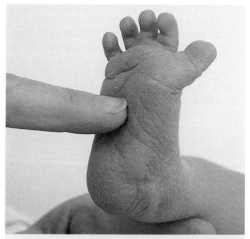

Most babies are born with the Babinski reflex, which means that they fan out their toes when the soles of their feet are touched.

Section Objective

▶ Describe the physical development that occurs during infancy.

This objective is assessed in the Section Review on page 233 and in the Chapter 10 Review.

Opening Section 2

Motivator

Ask student volunteers to bring in a collection of baby pictures from their own infancy and childhood. Have students organize the pictures in chronological order from youngest to oldest. Discuss the physical changes shown in the pictures of each student. Help students use the pictures to make generalizations about the physical changes that occur in children. Tell them that Section 2 will discuss some of those physical developments.

Teaching Section 2

Assessing Validity

Have students interview the parent of a young child about the approximate ages of the child when key milestones in motor development appeared—when the child turned over from stomach to back, sat, crawled, stood, and walked. Have students record the child's development on a time line. Using a different color ink, students should record the ages given in the text for acquisition of the same skills. Have students compare the ages on their time lines. Did the development of the child whose development they tracked fall in the range of norms given in the text?

respiratory system, develop to the point at which they can sustain the life of the baby after he or she is born.

During the nine months of pregnancy, the embryo develops from a nearly microscopic cell to a baby about 20 inches in length. A newborn weighs a billion or more times what it weighed at conception.

During **infancy**—the period from birth to the age of two years—dramatic gains continue in height and weight. Infants usually double their birth weight in about five months and triple it by one year. They grow about 10 inches in height in the first year. During the second year, infants generally gain another four to six inches in height and another four to seven pounds in weight.

TRUTH OR fiction ▪ REVISITED ▪

It is true that most babies triple their birth weights by the time they reach their first birthdays. Babies make dramatic gains in weight and height during their first two years.

After infancy comes **childhood**, the period from two years old to adolescence. Following the second birthday, children gain on average two to three inches and four to six pounds each year until they reach the start of adolescence.

Motor Development

It might seem that, at first, babies are just bundles of reflexes and random movements. Soon, however, as their muscles and nervous systems mature, newborns' random movements are replaced by purposeful motor activity. The development of purposeful movement is called motor development. Milestones in infants' and children's motor development are shown in Figure 10.1.

Motor development usually proceeds in stages. Almost all babies roll over before they sit up unsupported, and they crawl before they walk. When Hannah talked about Eddie growing so fast, she was describing the different stages of his motor development: from sitting to crawling to standing to walking.

A DAY IN THE LIFE

The point at which these various behaviors occur, however, is different from infant to infant and even from culture to culture. For example, in Uganda, infants usually walk before they are 10

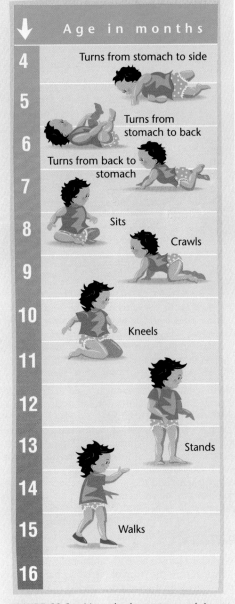

Motor Development in Infancy

Age in months

4 — Turns from stomach to side

5

6 — Turns from stomach to back

Turns from back to stomach

7

8 — Sits

Crawls

9

10 — Kneels

11

12

13 — Stands

14

15 — Walks

16

FIGURE 10.1 *Motor development proceeds in an orderly sequence. At birth, an infant's behavior is reflexive. During the first six months, the brain and body mature to enable crawling and, later on, walking. The ages shown here are approximate.*

Class Discussion

Tell students that health care professionals in the United States routinely assign newborn babies what is called an Apgar score one minute after birth and again four minutes later. The Apgar score, named for American physician Virginia Apgar, is a scaled rating of a newborn's physical condition based on five measures: heart rate, respiration, muscle tone, color, and reflexive responsiveness. Have students speculate on why it is important for health care professionals to know a newborn's Apgar score.

Using Visuals

Ask a volunteer to read aloud the caption accompanying Figure 10.1. Point out that motor development is sequential but may vary in timing from child to child. Have students survey parents or older family members about the students' motor development. Have students record the ages at which they acquired each of the motor skills shown in Figure 10.1.

Cooperative Learning

Review with students the American and Ugandan child-rearing practices that influence when children in those cultures begin to walk. Then organize the class into small groups. Direct the students in each group to research child-rearing practices in other cultures or in the United States at earlier periods in history. Ask the groups to present their findings in an oral report accompanied by graphics and illustrations. Have the class discuss the impact of these practices on children's motor development.

Demonstration

Invite the parent of a newborn baby to come to class to demonstrate some of the baby's reflexes for the students. Have students take turns placing a finger against the baby's palm (grasping reflex) and touching the soles of the baby's feet (Babinski reflex). Also ask the parent to demonstrate the baby's Moro, or startle, reflex. Following the demonstration, have students discuss how and why the maturation process brings about changes in a child's reflexes.

Cultural factors can influence when certain stages of motor development occur. Infants in some African countries, who spend much of their time being carried upright on their parents' backs, walk (on average) earlier than American infants.

months old, whereas in the United States, babies often do not start walking until around one year of age (Frankenberg et al., 1992). Why might this be? Perhaps because, while American babies spend much of their time lying in cribs, Ugandan babies spend much of their time being carried on their parents' backs. This contact with the parents, the sense of movement, and the upright position the babies maintain as they are being carried may help them learn to walk earlier (Bril, 1986).

Reflexes

Soon after a baby is born, the doctor or nurse places a finger against the palm of the baby's hand. Babies are not told how to respond and do not "know" what to do, of course. Even so, they usually grasp the finger firmly. Grasping is a reflex. Reflexes are inborn, not learned, and they occur automatically, without thinking.

Some reflexes are essential to our survival. Breathing is such a reflex. Although it is a reflex, we

can also breathe consciously if we wish—slowly or quickly, deeply or shallowly. The breathing reflex works for a lifetime. Sneezing, coughing, yawning, blinking, and many other reflexes also continue for a lifetime.

Rooting is another reflex that babies are born with. Because of the rooting reflex, babies turn toward stimuli that touch their cheeks or the corners of their mouths. Once infants locate the source of a stimulus, they automatically begin sucking and swallowing. The sucking and swallowing reflexes are essential to an infant's survival; without them, newborns would not eat. Babies reflexively suck objects that touch their lips and reflexively swallow food in their mouths.

Babies also reflexively withdraw from painful stimuli. They pull up their legs and arch their backs in response to sudden sounds or bumps. This is known as the Moro, or startle, reflex. Babies also raise their big toes when the soles of their feet are touched, a behavior that is called the Babinski reflex. They also eliminate wastes by reflex.

As children develop, many reflexes, such as rooting and sucking, disappear. Other reflexes, such as swallowing, remain. And some reflexes, such as elimination of wastes, come under voluntary control. These changes are all part of the maturation process.

Perceptual Development

Imagine what the world must seem like to a newborn. Prior to birth, the baby has spent several months in a warm, wet, dark place. Now suddenly, it finds itself in a bright, noisy world full of sensory stimuli. Perceptual development is the process by which infants learn to make sense of the sights, sounds, tastes, and other sensations to which they are exposed.

Infants tend to prefer new and interesting stimuli. They seem to be "preprogrammed" to survey their environment and to learn about it. For example, a study by Robert Fantz (1961) found that two-month-old infants preferred pictures of the human face to any other pictures, such as newsprint, a bull's-eye, or colored disks without patterns.

Researchers have, however, discovered that infants' perceptual preferences are influenced by their age. For example, 5- to 10-week-old babies look longest at patterns that are fairly complex. It does not matter whether the pattern looks like a human face. What most interests them is the variety and complexity of the pattern. At this age, eyesight

232

Role-Playing

Organize the class into five groups and assign each group one of the five senses: sight, sound, smell, taste, and touch. Tell the members of each group that they are to write and role-play a short skit that demonstrates an infant's ability to perceive the assigned sense. Characters in the skits should include, but need not be limited to, parents and infants. After the groups have presented their skits, have representatives from each group describe to the class the aspects of perceptual development portrayed in the skits.

Summarizing Information

Have students demonstrate their understanding of the section's content by writing a short paragraph that summarizes each subsection: Height and Weight, Motor Development, Reflexes, and Perceptual Development. Ask for student volunteers to read their paragraphs aloud.

Reviewing Section 2

Have students complete the Section Review questions on page 233.

is not fully developed, so infants prefer to look at the most complex things they are capable of seeing reasonably well. By 15 to 20 weeks, patterns begin to matter. Babies then begin to stare longer at face-like patterns (Haaf et al., 1983).

These studies illustrate how nature and nurture work together. At first, infants seem to have an inborn preference for moderately complex visual stimuli. That is a result of nature. Their preference for human faces seems to appear only after they have had some experience with people. That results from the interaction of nature with nurture.

Other studies have focused on depth perception in infants. In some of these studies, researchers use what has become known as the "visual cliff." The visual cliff is a special structure, a portion of which has a surface that looks like a checkerboard. Another portion is a sheet of glass with a checkerboard pattern a few feet below it. It creates the illusion of a drop-off of a few feet—like a cliff.

One classic study with the visual cliff found that very young infants seem to be unafraid (as indicated by heart rate) when they are placed face down on the edge of the apparent drop-off. By nine months, however, infants respond with fear to the drop-off (Campos et al., 1970). Another classic study found that by the time infants learn to crawl, most of them will refuse to move onto the glass portion even when their mothers call them from the other side (Walk & Gibson, 1961). Perhaps crawling and exploring the world have taught the older infants that drop-offs are dangerous. Experience may have contributed to their ability to perceive depth. (See Chapter 4.)

Vision, of course, is only one type of perception. In general, infants' hearing is much better developed at birth than is their eyesight. When it comes to hearing, most newborns stop whatever they are doing to turn toward unusual sounds. They respond more to high-pitched sounds than to low-pitched ones, although they seem to be soothed by the sounds of someone singing softly or speaking in a low-pitched tone (Papousek et al., 1991). No wonder parents often sing lullabies to help their infants go to sleep.

Newborns immediately distinguish strong odors. They spit, stick out their tongues, and wrinkle their noses at pungent odors (as the rest of us do). But they smile and show licking motions in response to the sweet smells of chocolate, strawberry, and vanilla. They also like sweet-tasting liquid but refuse to suck salty or bitter liquids. A "sweet tooth" is of human nature.

This visual cliff has a glass-covered drop-off. It is used in experiments to test the depth perception of infants. Most infants who can crawl refuse to cross the part that appears to be a cliff even if their mothers call them.

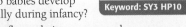

SECTION 2 REVIEW

Homework Practice Online
go.hrw.com
Keyword: SY3 HP10

1. How do babies develop physically during infancy?
2. Define *reflex* and give two examples.
3. Describe the purpose of research studies that use the visual cliff.
4. **Critical Thinking** *Drawing Inferences and Conclusions* Why are reflexes necessary for an infant's survival?

SECTION 3
Social Development

Social development involves the ways in which infants and children learn to relate to other people. For example, infants usually can be comforted by being held, and they soon respond to their mothers' voices. At first, they might cling to their mothers, but after a few months they venture out to explore the world and to make contact with strangers. Infants tend to play with toys by themselves, even when other children are around. As they grow older, however, they begin to play with others. All of these changes are part of social development.

Class Discussion

Have students discuss any ethical concerns they might have about the visual-cliff studies. Spark the discussion by asking students to respond to the following questions: Do you think it is ethical to use infants in studies that might cause them to feel fear? Do the benefits of such studies outweigh the possible costs to the infants?

Section 2 Review: Answers

1. Infants' height and weight increase rapidly. Their muscles and nervous systems soon develop, allowing them to crawl, walk, and generally act more purposefully.

2. A reflex is an involuntary reaction or response; examples include swallowing, sucking, the Babinski reflex, and the Moro reflex.

3. The visual cliff is used to test infants' depth perception.

4. If babies did not have reflexes such as breathing, sucking, and swallowing, they would not know how to breathe and eat.

233

Section Objective

▶ Describe the social development of infants and children.

This objective is assessed in the Section Review on page 241 and in the Chapter 10 Review.

Opening Section 3

Motivator

Ask students to tell about their social interactions with babies and young children. For example, some students may have younger siblings or relatives living with them. Others may baby-sit, work as lifeguards, or work with children in some other capacity. Have students describe their interactions with these young people. In what ways is communication with young children different from communication with peers and adults? List the students' comments on the chalkboard for reference during the study of this section.

Many important factors affect social development. Such factors include attachment, parenting styles, child care, child abuse and neglect (for some children), and self-esteem.

Attachment

Feelings of **attachment** are the emotional ties that form between people. Feelings of attachment keep people together. Because infants are basically helpless and are totally dependent on others to fulfill their needs, feelings of attachment are essential to their survival.

A DAY IN THE LIFE

Infants and children try to stay in contact with the people to whom they are attached. That may be why Eddie used to tug on Hannah's pant leg.

Development of Attachment Psychologist Mary Ainsworth studied attachment in infants around the world (Ainsworth & Bowlby, 1991). What she observed in every place she studied was that, at first, infants prefer being held or even just being with someone—anyone—over being alone. By about four months of age, however, infants develop specific attachments to their main caregivers—usually their mothers. This attachment grows stronger by six to seven months. Once they reach this point, infants and children try to maintain contact with their mothers and cry or complain when they are separated.

TRUTH OR fiction
■ REVISITED ■

It is not true that newborn babies would rather be held by their mothers than by other people. It takes a number of months for infants to become attached to specific people.

By the age of about eight months, some infants develop a fear of strangers. This fear is known as **stranger anxiety**. Infants who experience stranger anxiety cry and reach for their parents if they are near strangers. Their anxiety is somewhat less if the person to whom they are attached is holding them (Thompson & Limber, 1990). The closer they are to the strangers, however, the more upset they become (Boccia & Campos, 1989). They are most distressed when the strangers actually touch them.

At about the same age, infants may also develop separation anxiety. **Separation anxiety** causes infants to cry or behave in other ways that indicate distress if their mothers leave them. Why do infants become so attached to their primary caregivers? Research suggests that at least two factors are involved: contact comfort and imprinting.

Contact Comfort For a long time, psychologists thought that infants became attached to those who fed them. But then psychologist Harry F. Harlow observed that infant monkeys without mothers or companions became attached to pieces of cloth in their cages—even though, of course, the pieces of cloth did not provide food. The monkeys held on to their pieces of cloth and were upset when the cloth was taken away. Harlow conducted several experiments to find out why, and what types of objects to which the monkeys would and would not become attached (Harlow, 1959).

In one study, Harlow placed infant monkeys in cages, each of which had two "mother" objects. One object was made from wire and held a baby bottle. The other, which had no bottle, was made of soft terry cloth. The monkeys spent most of their time clinging to their cloth "mother," even though it did not feed them. Harlow thus concluded that the monkeys had a basic need for **contact comfort**, which is the instinctual need to touch and be

Newborn infants can usually be comforted by being held. They prefer their mothers' voices to those of other women from the time they are a few days old.

Teaching Section 3

Interpreting Ideas

After discussing attachment and contact comfort, have students write an imaginative short story about a world in which all newborns are raised by robots in a separate facility. Ask volunteers to read their stories aloud to the class. Tell students to think about the following questions as they listen to each story: How is the world depicted in the story different from the world in which you now live? How would your life be different if you had been raised in such a world? Then have students discuss their reactions to the stories.

Meeting Individual Needs: Gifted Learners

Remind students that there is no known critical period for attachment in humans. Have gifted students research methods recommended by psychologists for forming attachments between parents and newly adopted children who are past infancy. How are these methods related to the ways in which attachment is formed between biological parents and their infants? Have students share their findings with the class.

In Harlow's study of the importance of contact comfort, monkeys spent most of their time with their cloth "mother" even though it did not feed them.

moving object they see. The moving object is said to become imprinted on the infant animal. **Imprinting** is the process by which some animals form immediate attachments during a critical period.

Researchers have shown that animals can become imprinted on some rather unusual objects. Using imprinting, researcher Konrad Lorenz (1937) acquired a family of goslings for himself. How did he do it? He was present when the goslings hatched, and he then allowed them to follow him. The critical period for imprinting in geese and some other animals begins when they can first move about on their own. Lorenz's "family" followed him wherever he went. They ran to him when they were frightened. They honked loudly when he left them alone—just as human infants cry when they are left by the people to whom they are attached.

TRUTH OR fiction

■ REVISITED ■

It is true that baby geese become attached to the first moving object that they see— even if the object is a human being. This is called imprinting. Imprinting is what caused baby geese to become attached to Konrad Lorenz, as if he were their mother.

touched by something soft, such as skin or fur. This need seems to be even stronger than the need for food. In other words, the monkeys and perhaps human babies may cling to their mothers because of the need for contact comfort rather than just because they are hungry. Based on such findings, researchers have concluded that attachment grows more from bodily contact than from feeding.

Bonds of attachment between mothers and infants also appear to provide a secure base from which the infants can explore their environments. Harlow and Zimmerman (1959) placed toys, such as stuffed bears and wooden insects, in cages with infant monkeys. Some of the cages had wire "mothers," and the others had terry cloth "mothers." The monkeys who were alone or with wire mothers cringed in fear as long as the bears or insects were in the cage. Infant monkeys in cages with terry cloth mothers, on the other hand, cringed for a while but eventually began to explore the bears or insects. The terry cloth mothers apparently gave the infant monkeys a sense of security that enabled them to explore the world around them.

Imprinting For many animals, attachment is an instinct. Instinctive behavior develops during a critical period shortly after birth. Ducks, geese, and some other animals become attached to the first

Imprinting involves animals forming attachments during a critical period. Konrad Lorenz was present when these goslings hatched. Because he was the first moving object they perceived and could follow, they became attached to him.

235

Cooperative Learning

Organize students into groups of four. Have each group brainstorm a hypothetical incident between a parent and a child (for example, the child takes a candy bar from the display at the supermarket checkout line). Have each member of the group analyze the incident from one of the four parenting-style combinations: warm-permissive, warm-strict, cold-permissive, and cold-strict. What would be each parent's likely reaction to the situation? What are some possible effects on the child of the parent's reaction?

Evaluating Ideas

Have students use library resources to locate historical quotations that focus on child rearing. Have volunteers read their quotations aloud and have the class relate each quotation to the styles of parenting discussed in the section. Then conduct a class discussion in which students evaluate how valid each of the viewpoints expressed is in today's society. Ask students to write their own quotations about child rearing that they would like to see appear in a book of familiar quotations. What parenting styles are reflected in the students' quotations?

Although the development of attachment may also be instinctive in people (Ainsworth & Bowlby, 1991), human attachments develop somewhat differently than attachments among ducks and geese. For example, children do not imprint on the first person they see or are held by. For humans, it takes several months before infants become attached to their main caregivers. There is also no known critical period for attachment in humans. Children can become strongly attached to their adoptive parents even when they are adopted after infancy.

Secure Versus Insecure Attachment When mothers or other primary caregivers are affectionate and reliable, infants usually become securely attached (Cox et al., 1992). Infants with secure attachment are very bonded to their caregivers. They cry or protest if the parent or caregiver leaves them. When the caregiver returns, the infants welcome that person back and are happy again.

When caregivers are unresponsive or unreliable, the infants are usually insecurely attached. They often do not seem to mind when the caregivers leave them. When the caregivers return, the infants make little or no effort to seek contact with them. Some insecure infants may cry when picked up, as if they are angry with the caregiver (Ainsworth, 1973, 1979; Ainsworth et al., 1978).

Secure infants may mature into secure children. Secure children are happier, friendlier, and more cooperative with parents and teachers than insecure children are. They get along better with other children than insecure children do (Belsky et al., 1991; Thompson, 1991a). Secure children are also less likely to misbehave and more likely to do well in school than insecure children (Lyons-Ruth et al., 1993; Youngblade & Belsky, 1992).

Styles of Parenting

Styles of parenting differ along two separate dimensions. One dimension is warmth-coldness; the other is strictness-permissiveness (Baumrind, 1991a, 1991b; MacDonald, 1992). Warm parents can be either strict or permissive, as can cold parents.

Warm or Cold? Warm parents show a great deal of affection to their children. For example, they hug and kiss them and often smile at them. They show their children that they are happy to have them and enjoy their company. Cold parents may not be as affectionate toward their children or appear to enjoy them as much.

Research suggests that children fare better when their parents are warm to them (Dix, 1991). The children of warm parents are more likely to be well adjusted. They are also more likely to develop a conscience—a sense of moral goodness or a sense of responsibility when they do wrong (MacDonald, 1992; Miller et al., 1993). Children of cold parents, on the other hand, are usually more interested in escaping punishment than in doing the right thing for its own sake.

Strict or Permissive? If you have younger brothers and sisters, you probably know that children do many things that anger or annoy other people. For example, they may make noise when other people are trying to sleep or concentrate on a difficult task. Sometimes they make messes. Children may also engage in behaviors that are unhealthy to themselves. They may have poor eating habits or watch too much television. They may neglect their schoolwork or play with dangerous objects.

Some parents are extremely strict when it comes to such behaviors. They impose many rules and supervise their children closely. Permissive parents, on the other hand, impose fewer rules and watch their children less closely. Permissive parents tend to be less concerned about neatness and cleanliness than are strict parents.

Parents may be strict or permissive for different reasons. Some extremely strict parents cannot tolerate disorder. Others fear that their children will run wild and get into trouble if they are not taught self-discipline. Some parents are permissive because they believe that children need freedom to express themselves if they are to become independent. Other parents are permissive because they are less concerned or have little time to monitor their children's activities. Without clear and consistent guidance, these children may become confused about which behaviors are acceptable and which are not.

Strictness can have positive and negative results, depending on how it is used. Strictness is not necessarily the same as meanness—as Hannah pointed out, parents can be strict but still love their children. Research suggests that consistent and firm enforcement of rules can foster achievement and self-control, especially when combined with warmth and support (Putallaz & Heflin, 1990). But physical punishment or constant interference may lead to disobedience and poor grades in school (Olson et al., 1992; Westerman, 1990).

Guided Practice

Create a two-column chart on the chalkboard and title the chart "Nonparent Child Care." Label the column on the left *Positive Effects* and label the column on the right *Negative Effects*. Then have students identify both the positive effects and the negative effects of nonparent child care on children. Write their suggestions in the appropriate column. Then have students write a paragraph summarizing what research studies have found about the effects of nonparent child care on children's social development. Have volunteers read their paragraphs aloud.

Independent Practice

Tell students to imagine that they are psychologists who have been asked to create a set of guidelines for child care facilities in your community. The purpose of the guidelines is to help child care facilities maximize the positive effects of nonparent child care on children and minimize the negative effects. Tell students that their guidelines should address both the organization of the child care facility and the interaction of the child care workers with the children. Have volunteers present their guidelines to the class for discussion.

Authoritative (meaning with authority) parents combine warmth with positive kinds of strictness. The children of authoritative parents are often more independent and achievement oriented than other children. They also feel better about themselves (Baumrind, 1991b; Dumas & LaFreniere, 1993). Parental demands for responsible behavior combined with affection and support usually pay off. Apparently, Hannah's parents knew this, and were raising Eddie with both strictness and warmth.

Be careful not to confuse the term *authoritative* with the word *authoritarian,* which means "favoring unquestioning obedience." **Authoritarian** parents believe in obedience for its own sake. They have strict guidelines that they expect their children to follow without question. Often they are rejecting and cold. Children of authoritarian parents may become either resistant to other people or dependent on them (Baumrind, 1989). They generally do not do as well in school as children of authoritative parents. They also tend to be less friendly and less spontaneous (DeKovic & Janssens, 1992; Maccoby & Martin, 1983).

Child Care

In the United States today, most parents—both fathers and mothers—work outside the home. More than half of mothers of children younger than one year of age are working mothers (Erel et al., 2000). For this reason, millions of preschoolers are cared for in day-care facilities. Parents and psychologists are concerned about the effects of day care on the development of children.

The effects of day care depend in part on the quality of the day-care center. One study found that children in day-care centers with many learning resources, many caregivers, and a good deal of individual attention did as well on cognitive and language tests as children who remained in the home

Styles of Parenting

Demanding
Possessive
Controlling
Dictatorial
Antagonistic

Supportive
Protective
Affectionate
Flexible
Caring

Strict

Cold

Most Parents

Warm

Neglecting
Indifferent
Careless
Negligent
Detached

Lenient
Democratic
Inconsistent
Overindulgent

Permissive

FIGURE 10.2 *Styles of parenting can be classified along the dimensions of warm-cold and strict-permissive. Both dimensions are continuums, and most parents do not lie at the extremes but cluster in the middle.*

with their mother (Azar, 1997). A Swedish study actually found that on tests of math and language skills, children in the best day-care centers outperformed children who remained in the home (Broberg et al., 1997).

Studies of the effects of day care on parent-child attachment have yielded mixed results. Children in full-time day care show less distress when their mothers leave them and are less likely to seek out their mother when they return. Some psychologists worry that this distancing from the mother could mean that the child is insecurely attached (Belsky, 1990). But other psychologists suggest that children may simply be adapting to repeated separations from and reunions with their mothers (Field, 1991; Lamb et al., 1992; Thompson, 1991b).

Day care seems to have mixed effects on other aspects of children's social development. First, the positive: children in day care are more likely to share their toys and be independent, self-confident, and outgoing (Clarke-Stewart, 1991; Field, 1991).

Cross-Curricular Link: Sociology

Tell students that the number of two-earner families in the United States has risen dramatically in recent decades. Have students conduct library research to learn how American companies are changing to accommodate the needs of working parents. Students may also wish to explore and graphically illustrate the steady rise, since World War II, in the number of American women who work outside the home. The *Statistical Abstract of the United States* and *The World Almanac and Book of Facts* are useful sources for this exercise.

Teaching Transparencies with Teacher's Notes

TRANSPARENCY 26: Styles of Parenting

Essay and Research Themes for A. P. Students

Theme 9

PSYCHOLOGY

IN THE WORLD TODAY

To show how the concept of fatherhood has changed over time, have students interview a father who is more than 50 years of age and one who is under 30. Students should compile a list of questions that will elicit each father's views on parenting. Students might want to ask what each man thinks is the ideal amount of time to spend with his children or whose responsibility it is to take a sick child to the doctor. Students should then compare and contrast the two interviews in a brief report.

Debating Ideas

Tell students that many people consider parenting to be the most difficult job in the world, yet there are no formal avenues for teaching people how to be effective parents. Then ask each student to write two formal statements, one on the importance of being an effective father and one on the importance of being an effective mother. Have volunteers read their statements to the class for discussion. Then have students debate the following statement: Parenting classes should be a requirement for graduation from all high schools in the United States.

For Your Information

According to the U.S. Census Bureau, between 1977 and 1988 about 15 percent of children were cared for during the day by their fathers. In 1991 this figure rose to 20 percent. Then in 1993 the percentage of fathers caring for their children at home fell to 16 percent. The Census Bureau links the change to economic factors. Unemployment was high during the early 1990s, and many men found themselves out of work and available at home. As the number of jobs increased toward the mid-1990s, these men went back to work, and their children often went to day care.

Think About It: Answer

Fathers would benefit from taking an active role in rearing their children by developing a closer relationship with them and by earning the satisfaction that comes from knowing they have done their best to be effective parents.

PSYCHOLOGY

IN THE WORLD TODAY

The Importance of Being a Father

With many mothers returning to the workplace after the birth of their babies, fathers are becoming more actively involved in the rearing of children than ever before in American culture. In fact, six-month-old infants are generally just as attached to their fathers as they are to their mothers.

Although fathers are as good as mothers at such things as bottle-feeding, once the baby comes home, the mother is usually still the one who does most of the caregiving. Caregiving includes feeding, diapering, and bathing infants. So if men generally do not spend the time they have with their children in caregiving, what is it they do? Most fathers play—and they are usually very good at it.

The way fathers play with their children turns out to be very different from the way mothers play. Whereas mothers usually use toys or word games, fathers tend to play in a rough-and-tumble way. They bounce and lift their children. They move their arms and legs (Parke, 1981). Psychologists have discovered that as infants grow, they come to prefer those sorts of games. By the time most children are 30 months old, they often are more cooperative, excited, and interested in play with their fathers than with their mothers (Clarke-Stewart, 1978).

But do fathers make a difference in the development of their children? They most certainly do. A father's involvement has an effect in at least two major areas: social development and cognitive develoment. Socially, children whose fathers play with them tend to be more popular and have better relationships with their peers (MacDonald & Parke, 1984). During physical play with their fathers, children learn to figure out other people's emotions and expressions and to regulate

Fathers tend to play with children in a rough-and-tumble way.

their own emotions. Therefore, fathers help teach them how to get along with their friends and other people. Children whose fathers are involved with them also generally grow up to be more empathic (Koestner et al., 1990). Empathy is the ability to understand another person's point of view and imagine what that person might be feeling.

When it comes to cognitive development, a father's influence is most noticeable in boys. If a boy has a close relationship with his father, he often does better at solving problems and taking cognitive tests (Radin, 1981).

Because of the influence fathers have on their children's development, psychologists have argued that a parental leave of absence from work for fathers is very important. Other changes in the workplace, such as shorter workweeks and flexible hours, may make it easier for both parents to spend time with their children (Parke, 1981). And in 1993, Congress passed the Family and Medical Leave Act. This legislation enables new parents to take 12 weeks of unpaid leave. Still, most fathers do not take advantage of this. Some of them simply cannot afford to go without pay for that long. Others may worry that their employers will think they are not committed enough to their jobs if they take time off.

This may change over time. In Sweden, where both parents are guaranteed parental leave, over 40 percent of fathers take time off from their jobs to be with their newborn children. In the 1970s this figure was only 2 percent.

THINK ABOUT IT

Drawing Inferences and Conclusions How might it benefit fathers to take an active role in rearing their children?

For Further Research

Point out to students that violence against children has not always been viewed by Americans as a serious social issue. Nor has everyone always agreed on what behaviors constitute child abuse. Have interested students research the changes in American society's views on child abuse during this century. Also have students research the short-term and long-term effects of child abuse on children. Ask students to present their findings in a written report.

Meeting Individual Needs: Learners with Limited English Proficiency

To help students with limited English proficiency understand the sensitive issue of child abuse, ask them to point out any words or terms in the section that they do not understand. Then direct them to the psychology dictionaries and encyclopedias that are available for reference and clarification. Have them look up difficult terms and concepts, and then clarify any that are still unclear.

However, some studies have found that children in day care are less cooperative and more aggressive than are other children (Vandell & Corasaniti, 1990). Perhaps some children in day care do not receive the individual attention or resources they need. When they are placed in a competitive situation, they become more aggressive to try to meet their needs. Yet some psychologists interpret the greater aggressiveness of children in day care as a sign of independence rather than social maladjustment.

All in all, it would appear that nonparental care in itself may not affect child development very much (Erel et al., 2000). The quality of care seems to be more important than who provides it.

Child Abuse and Neglect

Most parents are kind and loving to their children. Yet child abuse—physical or psychological—is widespread. The incidence of child abuse is seriously underreported because children themselves often do not go to the authorities and abusive parents sometimes try to protect one another. It is estimated that nearly 3 million children in the United States are neglected or abused by their parents or other caregivers each year (Herman-Giddens et al., 1999). More than half a million of them suffer serious injuries, and thousands die.

Physical child abuse refers to a physical assault of a child. Neglect is failure to give a child adequate food, shelter, clothing, emotional support, or schooling. More health problems and deaths result from neglect than from abuse (Hamby & Finkelhor, 2000; Hashima & Finkelhor, 1999).

Why do some parents abuse or neglect their children? Psychologists have found the following factors to be associated with child abuse or neglect:

- stress, particularly the stresses of unemployment and poverty (Lewin, 1995; Trickett et al., 1991)
- a history of child abuse in at least one parent's family of origin
- acceptance of violence as a way of coping with stress
- lack of attachment to the child
- substance abuse
- rigid attitudes about child rearing (Belsky, 1993; Kaplan, 1991).

Studies show that children who are abused run a higher risk of developing psychological problems than children who did not grow up in an abusive environment. For example, they tend to be unsure of themselves. They are thus less likely than other children to venture out to explore the world around them (Aber & Allen, 1987). They are more likely to suffer from a variety of psychological problems such as anxiety, depression, and low self-esteem (Wagner, 1997). They are less likely to be close to their peers and more likely to engage in aggressive behavior (DeAngelis, 1997; Parker & Herrera, 1996; Rothbart & Ahadi, 1994). As adults, they are more likely to act in violent ways toward their dates or spouses (Malinosky-Rummell & Hansen, 1993).

Child abuse tends to run in families (Ertem et al., 2000). There are many possible reasons for this pattern. For one thing, children may imitate their parents' behavior. If children see their parents coping with feelings of anger through violence, they are likely to do the same. They are less likely to seek other ways of coping, such as humor, verbal expression of negative feelings, deep breathing, or silently "counting to 10" before reacting, thus giving the feelings of anger time to subside.

Children also often adopt their parents' strict ideas about discipline. Abused children may come to see severe punishment as normal. As a result, when they have children of their own, they may continue the pattern of abuse and neglect.

This pattern does not mean, however, that all people who were abused as children will in turn become abusers themselves. Most children who are victims of abuse do not later abuse their own children (Kaufman & Zigler, 1989). One study found that mothers who had been abused as children but who were able to break the cycle of abuse with their own children were likely to have received emotional support from a nonabusive adult during childhood. They were also likely to have participated in therapy and to have a nonabusive mate (Egeland et al., 1988).

TRUTH *OR* **fiction** ▪ R E V I S I T E D ▪

It is not true that most abused children become child abusers themselves when they grow up. Although some children of abuse do become abusers, most do not.

Cross-Curricular Link: Political Science

Child advocates, parents' rights groups, and government are at odds over how much authority parents should have over their children. State agencies and child advocates favor intervention to limit parental authority where child abuse is suspected. Parental rights' groups want to keep authority within the family. Have students find out about the laws in your state that protect children.

For Your Information

Tell students that there are many ways children and young adults can seek help to end abuse. Talking with trusted adults—such as teachers, religious or school counselors, coaches, or friends—is one option. In addition, many communities have telephone hot lines and other services available for victims of abuse. Have groups of students research the options available in your community for victims of abuse and report back to the class.

Closing Section 3

Role-Playing

Organize students into groups of three. Tell group members that they are to role-play two parents and a child. Each group is to develop a hypothetical situation involving the interaction of all three members (such as a discussion of the child's report card). Each group should role-play its scene twice, once with the parents showing unconditional positive regard and once with them showing conditional positive regard. After all groups have presented their role-plays, have students discuss the effects of parental reactions on children's self-esteem.

Follow Up

Ask students to retrieve the lifelines they began in the Motivator activity on page 228. Have them add information about the social development of infants and young children to both their general and personal lifelines.

Reviewing Section 3

Have students complete the Section Review questions on page 241.

Self-Esteem

The development of self-esteem begins in early childhood. **Self-esteem** is the value or worth that people attach to themselves. Self-esteem is important because it helps to protect people against the stresses and struggles of life. Although everyone experiences failure now and then, high self-esteem gives people the confidence to know that they can overcome their difficulties.

Influences on Self-Esteem What factors influence self-esteem? Secure attachment plays a major role. Young children who are securely attached to their parents are more likely to have high self-esteem (Cassidy, 1988).

The ways in which parents react to their children can also make a difference. Research suggests that authoritative parenting contributes to high self-esteem in children (Baumrind, 1991). Children with high self-esteem tend to be close to their parents because their parents are loving and involved in their lives. Their parents also teach and expect appropriate behavior and thus encourage them to become competent individuals.

Psychologist Carl Rogers noted that there are two types of support parents can give to their children—unconditional positive regard or conditional positive regard. **Unconditional positive regard** means that parents love and accept their children for who they are—no matter how they behave. Children who receive unconditional positive regard usually develop high self-esteem. They know that even if they do something wrong or inappropriate, they are still worthwhile as people.

On the other hand, children who receive conditional positive regard may have lower self-esteem. **Conditional positive regard** means that parents show their love only when the children behave in certain acceptable ways. Children who receive conditional positive regard may feel worthwhile only when they are doing what their parents (or other authority figures) want them to do.

Once these children grow up, they often continue to seek the approval of other people. Excessive need for approval from other people is linked to low self-esteem (Ellis & Dryden, 1987). It is unrealistic for people to expect everyone to like and respect them. If they understand that it is natural for others to not always appreciate them, they may have higher self-esteem in the long run.

A sense of competence also increases self-esteem. By the age of about four, children begin to

When children are encouraged and given the means to develop skills, such as tending a garden, their self-esteem may rise.

judge themselves according to their cognitive, physical, and social competence (Harter, 1990). Children who know that they are good at something usually have higher self-esteem than others. Children may feel good about themselves if they are good at puzzles or counting (cognitive skills), if they are good at tying their shoelaces or swinging (physical skills), or if they have friends (social skills).

Both heredity and environment play a role in individual differences in skills. Some people are more physically coordinated than others and therefore naturally good at sports. Other people may take lessons and train to improve their athletic abilities. Part of becoming competent is setting realistic goals. Warmth and encouragement from parents and teachers can help children reach high levels of competence and self-esteem.

Gender and Self-Esteem By the ages of five to seven, children begin to value themselves on the basis of their physical appearance and performance in school. Once in grade school, girls tend to display greater competence in the areas of reading and general academic skills. Boys tend to display competence in math and physical skills (Eccles et al., 1993; Marsh et al., 1991). (See Chapter 9.)

Does this mean that girls are genetically better in reading and boys better in math and sports? No. It may be that the reason girls and boys show greater competence, and thus higher self-esteem, in these areas is that people around them have suggested that this is what girls and boys are *supposed* to be good at. For example, girls predict that they will do

Extension

Have students visit a local toy store and examine 10 toys or games for preschool children. Ask students to list the toys or games that show only boys on the packaging, those that show only girls, and those that show both boys and girls. In class, have students compile their findings to make three master lists, one for each category. Use the lists as the basis for a class discussion on gender expectations. How do such expectations affect the self-esteem of boys and girls? How do gender expectations become self-fulfilling prophecies?

4
Section Objective

▶ Identify the stages in Piaget's theory of cognitive development and in Kohlberg's theory of moral development.

This objective is assessed in the Section Review on page 247 and in the Chapter 10 Review.

---

better on tasks that are considered "feminine," and boys predict better performance for themselves when tasks are labeled "masculine" (Lips, 1993). When people feel they will do well at a particular task, they often do. People generally live up to the expectations that they have for themselves and that others have for them. Such expectations often become self-fulfilling prophecies.

Age and Self-Esteem   Children gain in competence as they grow older. Through experience they learn more skills and become better at them. Even so, their self-esteem tends to decline during the elementary school years. Self-esteem seems to reach a low point at about age 12 or 13 and increases again during adolescence (Harter, 1990; Pomerantz et al., 1993). How can we explain this pattern?

It appears that young children, such as Hannah's brother Eddie, assume that others see them as they see themselves. Thus, if they like themselves, they assume that other people like them too. As children develop, however, they begin to realize that some people might not see them the way they see themselves. They also begin to compare themselves to their peers. If they see themselves as less competent in some areas, their self-esteem may decrease.

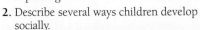

It is true that children's self-esteem tends to decrease as they go through elementary school. As children develop and mature, they begin to compare themselves to others of the same age. Sometimes they feel they do not measure up to their peers.

SECTION 3 REVIEW

go.hrw.com | Homework Practice Online
Keyword: SY3 HP10

1. Define the terms *attachment, contact comfort,* and *imprinting.*

2. Describe several ways children develop socially.

3. **Critical Thinking** *Evaluating* What are three things you think parents and teachers can do to help children keep self-esteem high throughout the school years?

SECTION 4
Cognitive Development

In addition to social development, psychologists are interested in studying cognitive development, or the development of people's thought processes. Two psychologists who are famous for their work on children's cognitive development are Jean Piaget and Lawrence Kohlberg.

Piaget's Theory of Cognitive Development

Jean Piaget

When Jean Piaget (1896–1980) was in his early 20s, he was employed at the Binet Institute in Paris. At the institute he worked on the Binet intelligence test, trying out potential test questions on children.

Before long, Piaget realized that the children he questioned gave certain types of wrong answers and that these wrong answers fit patterns from child to child. Piaget was so interested in these patterns that the study of children's thinking became his life's work.

Assimilation and Accommodation   Piaget believed that human beings organize new information in two ways: through assimilation and through accommodation. **Assimilation** is the process by which new information is placed into categories that already exist. For example, a child might know the word *doggie* because the family has a pet collie. If that child sees a Great Dane on the street and says "doggie," she or he has assimilated the new information about the Great Dane into the category "dog"—even though the Great Dane looks and may act differently from the collie familiar to the child.

If the same child sees a cat and says "doggie" again, some adults most likely will correct the child. Through such corrections, the child will learn that the category "dog" does not apply to cats and that a new category is needed. This adjustment is an example of **accommodation**—a change brought about because of new information.

Section 3 Review: Answers

1. Attachment refers to the emotional ties that form between people; contact comfort is the need to touch and be touched by something soft, such as skin or fur; imprinting is the process by which some infant animals form immediate attachments during a critical period of development.

2. Several factors affect how children learn to relate to others, including attachment parenting styles, child care, and self-esteem.

3. Answers may include giving praise when it is due, focusing on the talents of each child, helping children accept themselves, and helping children overcome gender expectations.

Motivator

Review with students the information on cognitive factors in learning that they read about in Section 3 of Chapter 6. Ask students to speculate on how these factors might apply to child development, noting, for example, the ways in which observational learning influences a child's behavior. Have students suggest questions about the role of cognition in child development. Write their suggestions on the chalkboard, and encourage them to read Section 4 with these questions in mind.

Demonstration

Use the following activity to demonstrate the concepts of assimilation and accommodation. Hold up a pen and ask students to develop a definition of a pen. Write this definition on the chalkboard. Then show students a variety of other pens. With each new example, ask students whether it fits the definition on the chalkboard (assimilation) or whether the definition needs to be altered or refined (accommodation). Then have students use the activity to explain how children organize new information.

Cross-Curricular Link: Literature

Have students read *Diary of a Baby* by Daniel N. Stern (New York: Basic Books, 1990), which should be available in a local library or bookstore. The book contains sections written in diary format from a baby's perspective with accompanying explanatory text. Ask students to relate the diary entries to Piaget's developmental stages. If multiple copies are difficult to obtain, you may want to have students read sections of the book aloud.

For Your Information

Within the sensorimotor stage of cognitive development, there are six shorter substages: (1) first month, when actions are mostly reflexive; (2) 1 to 4 months, when babies can choose to repeat reflex actions; (3) 4 to 8 months, when babies can repeat learned actions; (4) 8 to 12 months, when babies can imitate simple actions; (5) 12 to 18 months, when toddlers physically try to solve problems but cannot imagine workable solutions; and (6) 18 to 24 months, when babies begin to think about problem solutions.

Object permanence means understanding that objects exist even when they are out of sight. This toddler realizes that his brother still exists even when he is hidden behind the cushions.

Piaget theorized that children's thinking develops in a sequence of stages. Some children are more advanced than others at a given age. However, the developmental sequence is the same for everyone. Piaget identified four stages in the sequence: sensorimotor, preoperational, concrete operational, and formal operational.

The Sensorimotor Stage The behavior of newborns is mainly reflexive. They are capable only of responding to their environment and cannot initiate behavior. Instead of acting, infants react. By about one month of age, however, infants begin to act with purpose. As they coordinate vision with touch, for example, they will look at objects they are holding.

The first stage of cognitive development is characterized mainly by learning to coordinate sensation and perception with motor activity. Infants begin to understand that there is a relationship between their physical movements and the results they sense and perceive. That is why Piaget called this stage the **sensorimotor stage**.

Infants who are three and four months old are fascinated by their own hands and legs. They are easily amused by watching themselves open and close their fists. If they hear an interesting sound, such as a rattle, they might do something to sustain the sound. By four to eight months, infants are

exploring cause-and-effect relationships. They might, for example, hit mobiles that hang over their cribs so that the mobiles will move.

Perhaps you have heard the expression "Out of sight, out of mind." Before infants are six months old, objects out of their sight are truly out of their minds. The infants do not realize that objects out of sight still exist. They might stare at a stuffed animal, but if you were to put the stuffed animal behind a piece of paper, they would not look behind the paper or reach to find it. By eight months to a year, however, infants understand that things that have been taken away still exist. For example, a 10-month-old child probably would search for a stuffed animal that was hidden behind a screen. Piaget called this **object permanence**—the understanding that objects exist even when they cannot be seen or touched.

According to Piaget's theory, object permanence occurs because infants are able to hold an idea in mind. For instance, they learn that "stuffed animal" is a soft, fuzzy object. They can mentally picture a stuffed animal even when it is no longer in view. Therefore, they know to look for it when it is hidden behind a screen.

The Preoperational Stage The sensorimotor stage ends at about the age of two years, when children begin to use words and symbols (language) to represent objects. At this point, children enter the **preoperational stage**.

As we saw with Eddie, preoperational thinking is very different from more mature forms of thinking. Children's views of the world are different from those of adolescents and adults. For example, preoperational thinking is one-dimensional. In other words, preoperational children can see only one aspect of a situation at a time.

This one-dimensional thinking is most evident in the fact that in the preoperational stage children do not understand the law of **conservation**. The law says that key properties of substances, such as their weight, volume, and number, stay the same even if their shape or arrangement are changed. That is, the basic properties are *conserved*. Children in the preoperational stage cannot comprehend all the aspects at once, so they focus only on the most obvious one—the way a substance looks.

When preoperational children are shown two identical tall, thin glasses of water, each filled to the same level, they know that both glasses hold the

242

Assessing Validity

Have each student interview a child in the preoperational stage of cognitive development (ages two to seven). Students should ask the child five questions—such as, Why is the sky blue?—and record the child's answers. Students may develop their own questions or use the questions shown in Figure 10.3 on page 244. Ask volunteers to read their questions and the children's responses in class. Have students discuss their findings. Do the children's responses support Piaget's theory? How do the responses reflect egocentrism?

Meeting Individual Needs: Learners Having Difficulty

Some students may have difficulty recalling and identifying the various stages in Piaget's theory of cognitive development. Ask these students to create a study card for each developmental stage. On each card, students should note the name of the stage, the general age range of children who fall into the particular stage, and a description of the cognitive characteristics of the stage. Then have students organize the cards in developmental order.

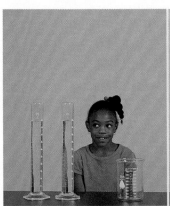

In the first photograph, the child looks at two tall glasses filled to the same level and understands that both glasses contain the same amount of liquid. In the second photograph, the child watches as the liquid from one of the tall glasses is emptied into a shorter glass. In the third photograph, the child indicates a belief that the tall glass that is still full contains more liquid than the short one simply because the taller glass looks larger.

Class Discussion

Have students consider the roles of heredity and environment in relation to the development of cognitive skills in children. Does Piaget's theory place greater emphasis on nature or nurture? *(nature)* What role does maturation play in cognitive development? *(Maturation makes possible increasingly complex thinking.)* Also have students discuss how teaching materials and teaching styles at various grade levels differ to take into account different levels of cognitive maturity.

same amount of water. However, if water from one of the tall glasses is poured into a short, squat glass, the children say that the other tall glass contains more liquid than the short one. They say this even if they have *watched* the water being poured. Because they can focus only on what they are seeing at a given moment—and on one dimension at a time—they incorrectly think that the tall glass now contains more water than the short glass. Their thinking is that it looks as if there is less water in the short glass (because the water level is lower) and therefore it must be so. Children in the preoperational stage do not realize that increases in one dimension (such as width) can make up for decreases in another (such as height).

 Eddie—who at three years of age is in the preoperational stage—did not understand the law of conservation, as demonstrated by Hannah's experiment with the five pennies. Eddie insisted that the row of five pennies that were farther apart had more pennies in it than the row in which the pennies were close together. He said so even when Hannah had him count the pennies in both rows, which he did correctly.

Another characteristic of children in the preoperational stage is **egocentrism**—the inability to see another person's point of view. Remember how Eddie thought it became dark because he went to sleep and that the sun rose because he woke up? Preoperational children assume that other people see the world just as they do. They cannot imagine

that things might happen to others that do not happen to them. They think that the world exists to meet their needs. Egocentrism is a consequence of the preoperational child's one-dimensional thinking. Egocentrism is not the same as selfishness. When a preschooler sits down in front of the television set blocking everyone else's view, he or she is not being rude. The child simply thinks you can see exactly what he or she can see.

Preoperational children are also artificialistic and animistic. They think that natural events such as rain and thunder are made by people (artificialism). They also think objects such as the sun and the moon are alive and conscious (animism).

The Concrete-Operational Stage Most children enter the **concrete-operational stage** at about the age of seven. In this stage, children begin to show signs of adult thinking. Yet they are logical only when they think about specific objects, not about abstract ideas. Their thinking is still grounded mostly in concrete experiences. This is one reason why many teachers assign them hands-on projects. Seeing, touching, and manipulating objects often help concrete-operational children understand abstract concepts.

Children at the concrete-operational stage can focus on two dimensions of a problem at the same time. For this reason, they understand the laws of conservation. They understand that a short, wide glass might contain the same amount of water as a tall, thin glass. They can focus on both the height

Cooperative Learning

Tell students that many day care facilities and preschools base their curricula on Piaget's theory. Organize students into groups of three. Have one student identify day care facilities and preschools in your community. The second student should contact each facility to find out if its curriculum is based on Piaget's theory or on another developmental approach. The third student should create a chart on which to display the group's findings. Have students use their charts to discuss the impact of Piaget's theory on preschool education.

Synthesizing Information

Have each student choose one of Piaget's theoretical stages that interests him or her and use the information in the textbook to develop a one-paragraph anecdote about a child at that stage. Students may use situations from their own experience or create a fictional child and situation. Students may present their anecdotes in written or oral form.

Using Visuals

Direct students' attention to Figure 10.3, noting that it addresses only Piaget's preoperational stage. Ask students to extend the chart to include some questions and typical answers for children in the concrete-operational stage.

For Your Information

One alternative to Piaget's view suggests that babies know on a primitive level that they are like other humans. As they observe those around them, the babies add to their knowledge. They develop more specific ideas about how to think and act like other humans.

internet connect

TOPIC: Social Development

GO TO: go.hrw.com

KEYWORD: SY3 PS10

Have students access the Internet through the HRW Go site to research social development and Piaget's theories of cognitive development in children. Then have students prepare a multimedia presentation on their research. Students should include information about attachment, separation anxiety, and thinking patterns outlined by Piaget.

Examples of Preoperational Thought

Kind of Thinking	Sample Questions	Typical Answers
Egocentric *(thinking that the world exists to meet one's own needs)*	Why does it get dark out?	So I can go to sleep.
	Why does the sun shine?	To keep me warm.
	Why is there snow?	For me to play in.
	Why is grass green?	Because that's my favorite color.
	What are TV sets for?	To watch my favorite shows and cartoons.
Animistic *(thinking that inanimate objects are alive and conscious)*	Why do trees have leaves?	To keep them warm.
	Why do stars twinkle?	Because they're happy and cheerful.
	Why does the sun move in the sky?	To follow children and hear what they say.
	Where do boats go at night?	They sleep like we do.
Artificialistic *(thinking that natural things and events are made by people)*	Why is the sky blue?	Somebody painted it.
	What is the wind?	A man blowing.
	What causes thunder?	A man grumbling.
	What makes it rain?	Somebody emptying a watering can.

FIGURE 10.3 *The second stage of Piaget's theory of cognitive development is the preoperational stage. At about two years of age, the child begins to use words and symbols to represent things. Thinking tends to be one-dimensional, however. The child believes that the world exists to meet his or her needs.*

and the width of the glasses at the same time. They can therefore recognize that a gain in width compensates for a loss in height. Similarly, in a few years, Eddie will conserve numbers. He will understand that the two rows have the same numbers of pennies in them, even though one row is longer because the pennies are spaced farther apart.

Concrete-operational children are less egocentric than children in earlier stages. They can see the world from another person's point of view. They understand that people may see things differently because they have different experiences or are in different situations.

The Formal-Operational Stage The final cognitive stage in Piaget's theory begins at about puberty and represents cognitive maturity. It is the **formal-operational stage**.

People in the formal-operational stage think abstractly. They realize that ideas can be compared and classified mentally just as objects can. For example, they understand what is meant by the unknown quantity x in algebra. They can work on geometry problems about lines, triangles, and squares without concerning themselves with how the problems relate to the real world. They can also deduce rules of behavior from moral principles. They focus on many aspects of a situation simultaneously when reasoning and solving problems.

During the formal-operational stage, people are capable of dealing with hypothetical situations. They realize that they may be able to control the outcome of a situation in several different ways. Therefore, if one approach to solving a problem does not work, they will try another. They think ahead, imagining the results of different courses of action before they decide on a particular one.

Criticism of Piaget's Theories Over the years, a number of psychologists have questioned the accuracy of Piaget's views. Some believe his methods caused him to underestimate the abilities of children. Recent research using different methodology indicates that preschoolers are less egocentric

CASE STUDIES
AND OTHER TRUE STORIES

Organize the class into pairs. Have one member of the pair tell John's story and Henry's story to both a 6-year-old and a 12-year-old (after securing permission from the children's parents). Have that same student then question the children using the same questions posed by Piaget. The other student should record the interactions (again, after securing permission). In class, have each pair analyze the responses. Did students obtain the same results as Piaget? Then ask students to explain why subjective reasoning is a sign of cognitive maturity.

For Further Research

Jean Piaget was just one of many psychologists who have conducted research in the field of child development. Other researchers have focused on various aspects of development, including the emotional development of children. Have students gather information about the work of one of the following researchers: Lev Vygotsky, Carolyn Saarni, Nancy Eisenberg, Susanne Denham, Jackie Gnepp, Susan Harter, or Paul Harris. Have students present their findings in a short written or oral report.

CASE STUDIES
AND OTHER TRUE STORIES

The Story of the Cups

Adults do not usually blame people for breaking things by accident. But Jean Piaget discovered that preoperational children differ greatly from adults in their reactions to accidents. He studied their reasoning by telling them stories and then asking them questions about the stories. Here are two stories Piaget used (adapted from Piaget, 1932, pp.125–130):

John's Story   A little boy, who was called John, was in his room. He was called to dinner. He went downstairs to the dining room. However, behind the dining-room door, which was closed, was a chair, and on the chair was a tray holding 15 cups. John did not know what was behind the door when he pushed open the door. The door knocked against the tray. Bang went the 15 cups and they all broke.

Henry's Story   Once there was a little boy named Henry. One day when his mother was out, Henry tried to reach some jam in the cupboard. He climbed onto a chair and stretched out his arm. But the jam jar was too high up and he could not reach it. But while Henry was trying to reach the jar, he knocked over a cup. The cup fell to the floor and broke.

After Piaget told the stories, he asked the children some questions. The dialogue typically went as follows when the listener was six years old:

Piaget: *Have you understood these stories? Let me hear you tell them.*

Child: *A little child was called in to dinner. There were 15 plates on a tray. He didn't know. He opens the door and he breaks the 15 plates.*

Piaget: *. . . And now the second story?*

Child: *There was a child. [He] wanted to go and get some jam. He gets onto a chair. His arm catches onto a cup, and it gets broken.*

Piaget: *Are those children both naughty, or is one not so naughty as the other?*

Child: *Both just as naughty.*

Piaget: *Would you punish them the same?*

Child: *No. The one who broke 15 plates.*

Piaget: *And why would you punish the other one . . . less?*

Child: *The first one broke lots of things, the other fewer.*

Piaget: *How would you punish them?*

Child: *The one who broke the 15 cups, two slaps. The other one, one slap.*

Piaget said that this kind of reasoning was based on objective responsibility. This means that younger children focus only on the amount of damage done. The greater the damage, the greater the punishment. Intentions do not matter.

With older children, however, the dialogue went differently:

Piaget: *Which is the naughtiest?*

Child: *The second, the one who wanted to take the jam pot, because he wanted to take something without asking.*

Piaget: *Did he [actually get the jam]?*

Child: *No.*

Piaget: *Was he the naughtiest all the same?*

Child: *Yes.*

Piaget: *And the first [child]?*

Child: *It wasn't his fault. He didn't do it on purpose.*

This kind of response, typical of older children, Piaget called reasoning by subjective responsibility. It means that older children take the intentions of wrongdoers into consideration.

Primary Source Note

Description of Change: excerpted

Rationale: excerpted to focus on main idea

Journal Activity

Have students recall a time in their childhood when they accidentally broke something. Ask them to write about the incident in their journals. What were the circumstances? For example, were they throwing a ball in the house despite a warning not to do so? How did their parents react to the breakage? How important to their parents was the intention behind the misdeed?

Guided Practice

Ask a volunteer to explain what a moral dilemma is. Have students propose a moral dilemma similar to the one Heinz faced. Write the dilemma on the chalkboard. Then have students explain how people in each of Kohlberg's six stages of moral development might respond to the dilemma. Also have students explain how the reasoning process underlying each stage contributes to the type of response. Finally, have students copy the chart on page 247, add a third column, headed *Example,* and fill in the column with the responses from this activity.

Independent Practice

Have students work in pairs to test Kohlberg's theory of moral development. Suggest that students tell the moral dilemma posed in the Guided Practice activity to several people selected from different age groups. After telling the story to each participant, students should ask how the person could solve the problem and why he or she chose this approach. After students have completed their survey, have them review and divide the responses into Kohlberg's stages of moral development. How closely do the responses match the examples in their charts?

Primary Source Note

Description of Change: excerpted

Rationale: excerpted to focus on main idea

Cross-Curricular Link: Literature

Have students choose a favorite book from early childhood. Ask them to reread the book and determine which of Kohlberg's stages of moral development appears to influence the behavior of each character. Have volunteers discuss their findings with the class, and have the class discuss how children's literature seeks to teach children right from wrong.

Readings and Case Studies

Kohlberg's Theory of Moral Development

Psychologist Lawrence Kohlberg (1927–87) devised a cognitive theory about the development of children's moral reasoning. Kohlberg used the following story in his research:

A woman was near death from a special kind of cancer. There was one drug that the doctors thought might save her. It was a form of radium that a pharmacist in the same town had recently discovered. The drug was expensive to make, but the pharmacist was charging 10 times what the drug cost him to make. He paid $200 for the radium and charged $2,000 for a small dose of the drug. The sick woman's husband, Heinz, went to everyone he knew to borrow the money, but he could raise only about $1,000—half the amount he needed. He told the pharmacist that his wife was dying and asked him to sell it cheaper or let him pay later. But the pharmacist rejected the man's plea saying that he had discovered the drug and intended to make money from it. Heinz became desperate and broke into the man's store to steal the drug for his wife. (Adapted from Kohlberg, 1969, p. 379.)

Should Heinz have stolen the drug? Was he right or wrong? Kohlberg believed that there was no simple answer. Heinz was involved in what Kohlberg called a moral dilemma. In this case, laws against stealing contradicted Heinz's strong human desire to save his wife's life.

Kohlberg was not particularly interested in whether children thought Heinz was right or wrong to steal the drug. More important to Kohlberg were the reasons why children thought Heinz should or should not steal the drug. People arrive at answers for different reasons. Kohlberg classified these reasons according to levels of moral development.

Kohlberg, like Piaget, was a stage theorist. He believed that the stages of moral development always follow a specific sequence. People do not skip any stages or go backward. Children advance at different rates, however, and not everyone reaches the highest stage. Kohlberg theorized that there are three levels of moral development and two stages within each level.

than Piaget's research suggested. Some psychologists also assert that several cognitive skills appear to develop more continuously than Piaget thought. Nonetheless, his theories are still respected.

The Preconventional Level   According to Kohlberg, through the age of nine, most children are at the preconventional level of moral development. Children who use **preconventional moral reasoning** base their judgments on the consequences of behavior.

In stage 1, children believe that what is "good" is what helps one avoid punishment. Therefore, children at stage 1 would argue that Heinz was wrong because he would be caught for stealing and sent to jail.

At stage 2, "good" is what satisfies a person's needs. Stage 2 reasoning holds that Heinz was right to steal the drug because his wife needed it.

The Conventional Level   People who are at the level of **conventional moral reasoning** make judgments in terms of whether an act conforms to conventional standards of right and wrong. These standards derive from the family, religion, and society at large.

At stage 3, "good" is what meets one's needs and the expectations of other people. Moral behavior is what most people would do in a given situation. According to stage 3 reasoning, Heinz should steal the drug because a good and loving husband would do whatever he could to save the life of his wife. But stage 3 reasoning might also maintain that Heinz should not steal the drug because good people do not steal. Both conclusions show conventional thinking. Kohlberg found stage 3 moral judgments most often among 13-year-olds.

Stage 4 moral judgments are based on maintaining the social order. People in this stage have high regard for authority. Stage 4 reasoning might insist that breaking the law for any reason sets a bad example and undermines the social order. Stage 4 judgments occurred most often among 16-year-olds (Kohlberg, 1963).

The Postconventional Level   Reasoning based on a person's own moral standards of goodness is called **postconventional moral reasoning**. Here, moral judgments reflect one's personal values, not conventional standards.

Stage 5 reasoning recognizes that laws represent agreed-upon procedures, that laws have value, and that they should not be violated without good reason. But laws cannot bind the individual in exceptional circumstances. Stage 5 reasoning might suggest that it is right for Heinz to steal the drug, even though it is against the law, because the needs of his wife have created an exceptional situation.

Comparing and Contrasting Ideas

Have students compare and contrast Piaget's theory of cognitive development with Kohlberg's theory of moral development. Encourage students to use a graphic organizer such as a Venn diagram to identify similarities and differences between the two theories.

Reviewing Section 4

Have students complete the Section Review questions on page 247.

Extension

Challenge students to test the gender bias some people believe exists in Kohlberg's theory of moral development. Students should survey an equal number of males and females of the same age about the moral dilemma posed in the story of Heinz on page 246. Ask students to report whether their survey supports or contradicts the gender-bias criticism leveled against Kohlberg's theory and why.

Kohlberg's Stages of Moral Development

Stage	Moral Reasoning Goal	What Is Right?
preconventional level		
1	Avoiding punishment	Doing what is necessary to avoid punishment
2	Satisfying needs	Doing what is necessary to satisfy one's needs
conventional level		
3	Winning approval	Seeking and maintaining the approval of others using conventional standards of right and wrong
4	Law and order	Moral judgments based on maintaining social order High regard for authority
postconventional level		
5	Social order	Obedience to accepted laws Judgments based on personal values
6	Universal ethics	Morality of individual conscience, not necessarily in agreement with others

FIGURE 10.4 *According to Lawrence Kohlberg, people's moral development follows a specific sequence. Not every person reaches the highest stage.*

Stage 6 reasoning regards acts that support the values of human life, justice, and dignity as moral and good. People at stage 6 rely on their own consciences. They do not necessarily obey laws or agree with other people's opinions. Using stage 6 reasoning, a person might argue that the pharmacist was acting out of greed and that survival is more important than profit. Therefore, Heinz had a moral right to steal the drug to save his wife's life. Postconventional moral reasoning rarely occurs before adolescence and is found most often in adults.

Bias in Kohlberg's Theory Some studies have found that according to Kohlberg's stages, boys appear to reason at higher levels of moral development than do girls. Does this mean that boys are morally superior to girls? No. It may mean instead that Kohlberg's stages and scoring system were biased to favor males.

Psychologist Carol Gilligan argues that the differences between boys and girls are created because of what adults teach children about how they should behave as boys or girls (1982; Gilligan et al., 1989). For example, girls are often taught to consider the needs of others over simple right or wrong. Therefore, a girl might worry that both stealing the drug and letting Heinz's wife die are wrong. Such reasoning—involving empathy for others—would be classified as stage 3.

Boys, however, are often taught to argue logically rather than with empathy. Therefore, a boy might set up an equation to prove that life has greater value than property. This would be considered reasoning at stage 5 or even stage 6.

Gilligan suggests, however, that girls' reasoning is at as high a level as that of boys. Girls have, in fact, thought about the same kinds of issues boys considered. In the end, they have chosen to be empathetic, not because their thinking is simpler, but because it is very complex—and because of what they have been taught is appropriate for girls. Shortly before his death in 1987, Kohlberg had begun to correct the gender bias in his theory.

SECTION 4 REVIEW

go.hrw.com **Homework Practice Online**
Keyword: SY3 HP10

1. Identify and briefly describe Piaget's four stages of cognitive development.

2. List the three levels of moral development, as theorized by Kohlberg.

3. **Critical Thinking** *Comparing* In what way are Piaget's preoperational stage and Kohlberg's stage 2 similar?

Technology

► Chapter 10 Test Generator (on the One-Stop Planner)

► HRW Go site

Reinforcement, Review, and Assessment

► Chapter 10 Review, pp. 248–249

► Chapter Review and Activities Answer Key

► Alternative Assessment Handbook

► Portfolio Assessment Handbook

► Chapter 10 Test (Form A or B)

PSYCHOLOGY PROJECTS

Linking to Community Invite several health care workers who work in neonatal intensive care units to visit your classroom. Ask your visitors to briefly describe their jobs and to discuss the importance of human contact during the first few months of life.

---

5. infants' distress at separation from their mothers

6. the process by which some animals form immediate attachments during a critical period

7. the process by which new information is placed into categories that already exist

8. the understanding that objects exist even when they cannot be seen or touched

9. developmental stage in which children begin to show signs of adult thinking

10. moral-reasoning level at which moral judgments reflect one's personal values, not conventional standards

Understanding Main Ideas

1. The main focus is on how people grow and change.

2. Motor development occurs as infants' nervous systems mature. They are better able to engage in purposeful activities such as crawling and walking.

3. An authoritarian parent sets rigid rules, demanding obedience for its own sake; an authoritative parent also demands responsible behavior but in the context of a warm, loving relationship.

4. Object permanence occurs because the infant is able to hold an idea in mind.

5. Key properties of substances stay the same even if their shape or arrangement is changed.

Thinking Critically

1. Maturational factors include the development of visual acuity, eye-hand coordination, and the ability to

Chapter 10 REVIEW

Writing a Summary

Using standard grammar, spelling, sentence structure, and punctuation, summarize the information in this chapter. Consider:
• how people develop physically and socially
• cognitive and moral development

Identifying People and Ideas

Identify the following terms or people and use them in appropriate sentences.

1. developmental psychology
2. maturation
3. attachment
4. stranger anxiety
5. separation anxiety
6. imprinting
7. assimilation
8. object permanence
9. concrete-operational stage
10. postconventional moral reasoning

Understanding Main Ideas

SECTION 1 (pp. 228–230)
1. What is the main focus of developmental psychology?

SECTION 2 (pp. 230–233)
2. Describe motor development in infants.

SECTION 3 (pp. 233–241)
3. How does an authoritarian parenting style differ from an authoritative parenting style?

SECTION 4 (pp. 241–247)
4. According to Piaget, what allows object permanence to occur?
5. What is meant by the law of conservation in developmental psychology?

Thinking Critically

1. Evaluating Why might a child's learning to read be the result of both maturation and nurture?

2. Summarizing How do infants unknowingly encourage warmth and affection from their caregivers?

3. Drawing Inferences and Conclusions Provide an example of how cognitive development occurs gradually.

4. Analyzing Information How might a child's physical development influence his or her social development?

5. Categorizing Describe how each of the following types of parents might react to their child drawing a picture on the wall with crayons: a warm-permissive parent, a warm-strict parent, a cold-permissive parent, a cold-strict parent.

Writing About Psychology

1. Analyzing Information Use the library to find more information about Piaget's theories of child development. Then create an annotated time line that provides examples of growth and development of children based on cognitive theories.

2. Evaluating Write a one-page paper that evaluates theories of human development. Note the strengths and weaknesses of each theory. Be sure to use standard grammar, spelling, sentence structure, and punctuation. Use the graphic organizer below to help you write your paper.

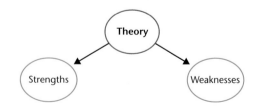

Questions for discussion should include the following:

- How do health-care workers ensure that hospitalized babies receive contact comfort? What happens to babies who do not receive this comfort?

- How do health-care workers help hospitalized babies form attachments to their parents?

- What genetic and environmental factors cause some babies to need early hospitalization?

Cooperative Learning

Challenge students to develop an ideal child care program. Organize students into groups of four, and have them compile a list of developmental issues they would expect to see addressed in a child care facility. Two group members should create a floor plan or layout of the facility, identifying special equipment and showing its location. The other two should then develop a schedule of activities for a typical day. Have representatives from each group present their group's materials to the class for discussion.

Building Social Studies Skills

Interpreting Graphs

Study the graph below. Then use the information in the graph to help you answer the questions that follow.

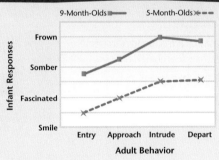

Responses of Infants to the Presence of a Strange Adult

9-Month-Olds ▬▬ 5-Month-Olds ✕ ▬ ✕

(y-axis, top to bottom: Frown, Somber, Fascinated, Smile; label: Infant Responses)
(x-axis: Entry, Approach, Intrude, Depart; label: Adult Behavior)

Source: Ruff and Rothbart, *Attention in Early Development*, 1996

1. Which of the following statements can be drawn from the information found in the graph?
   a. Five-month-old infants are afraid of strange adults.
   b. Infant responses to strangers do not change markedly between the ages of five months and nine months.
   c. Infants cannot tell the difference between family members and strangers.
   d. Nine-month-old infants respond differently to strangers than do five-month-old infants.

2. What conclusions can you draw about infant development based on the information in the graph?

Analyzing Primary Sources

Read the following excerpt, in which Swiss psychologist Jean Piaget considers the role of curiosity in child development. Then answer the questions that follow.

❝As sense organs . . . widen an organism's field of activity, then biological needs take on an aspect of implicit curiosity which keeps growing and flourishing. We see it already in primates, for example. Chimpanzees demonstrate intellectual curiosity.

For example, once when one of my children was in his playpen . . . I held out an object to him horizontally, so that if he tried to pull it towards himself, it was blocked by the rails of the playpen. He tried various positions, and finally got it in, but he got it in by chance, and he wasn't satisfied. He put it back outside the playpen and tried to do it again, and continued until he understood how he had to turn it to get it through the rails. He wasn't satisfied just to succeed. He wasn't satisfied until he understood how it worked.❞

3. According to Piaget's theory of cognitive development, at what stage was the child in the playpen?
   a. sensorimotor
   b. preoperational
   c. concrete-operational
   d. formal-operational

4. According to the excerpt, what role did curiosity play in the child's development?

distinguish and produce sounds; environmental factors include access to reading materials and adults who encourage reading.

2. Infants smile, laugh, and coo in response to their caregivers.

3. Showing a preoperational or concrete-operational child involved in abstract thinking would indicate that cognitive development occurs gradually.

4. A child who is taller than average might become a "leader" for that group of children.

5. A warm-permissive parent would be affectionate and applaud the child's artistic ability; a warm-strict parent would be affectionate but also discipline the child; a cold-permissive parent would be distant and ignore the child's behavior; and a cold-strict parent would be distant and punish the child.

Writing About Psychology

1. Students' time lines should reflect an understanding of Piaget's theoretical stages of cognitive growth.

2. Students' papers should reflect an understanding of Piaget's and Kohlberg's theories, as well as criticisms of those theories.

Building Social Studies Skills

1. d

2. As infants grow older, they become more hesitant and suspicious about the behavior of people whom they do not know.

3. a

4. The child's curiosity led him to explore the cause-and-effect relationship between the object and the position of his body.

PSYCHOLOGY PROJECTS

Cooperative Learning

Research in Psychology Working in small groups, construct a scenario in which a moral judgment must be made. Have one person write out the scenario and make a copy for each group member. Consider how people belonging to different age groups will respond to the scenario. Then have each member read the situation to a young child, an adolescent, and an adult, and record their responses. Evaluate the responses and compare them with Kohlberg's levels and stages of moral development.

🎵 **internet** connect

Internet Activity: go.hrw.com
KEYWORD: SY3 PS10
Choose an activity on infancy and childhood to:
- write a report on the role of nature and nurture in development.
- create an annotated time line on human physical development.
- create a multimedia presentation on social and cognitive development in children and infants.

go.hrw.com

249

Adolescence

CHAPTER RESOURCE MANAGER

	Objectives	Pacing Guide	Reproducible and Review Resources
SECTION 1: **Physical Development** (pp. 252–254)	Identify the physical changes that occur in males and females during adolescence, and examine the psychological effects of these changes.	**Regular** 1 day **Block Scheduling** .5 day *Block Scheduling Handbook with Team Teaching Strategies, Chapter 11*	**PS** Readings and Case Studies, Chapter 11 **REV** Section 1 Review, p. 254
SECTION 2: **Social Development** (pp. 256–259)	Describe the role that parents and peers play in the lives of adolescents.	**Regular** 1 day **Block Scheduling** .5 day *Block Scheduling Handbook with Team Teaching Strategies, Chapter 11*	**E** Creating a Psychology Fair, Handout 7, Activity 5 **REV** Section 2 Review, p. 259
SECTION 3: **Identity Formation** (pp. 260–264)	Define identity formation, and describe the four categories of adolescent identity status.	**Regular** 1.5 day **Block Scheduling** .5 day *Block Scheduling Handbook with Team Teaching Strategies, Chapter 11*	**E** Research Projects and Activities for Teaching Psychology **REV** Section 3 Review, p. 264
SECTION 4: **Challenges of Adolescence** (pp. 264–269)	Describe some of the important challenges that adolescents face in today's society.	**Regular** 1.5 day **Block Scheduling** .5 day *Block Scheduling Handbook with Team Teaching Strategies, Chapter 11*	**SM** Study Skills and Writing Guide, Part 3, Stage 3 **REV** Section 4 Review, p. 269

Chapter Resource Key

PS	Primary Sources	**A**	Assessment		Video
RS	Reading Support	**REV**	Review		Internet
E	Enrichment		Transparencies		Holt Presentation Maker Using Microsoft® PowerPoint®
SM	Skills Mastery		CD-ROM		

One-Stop Planner CD–ROM

See the *One-Stop Planner* for a complete list of additional resources for students and teachers.

One-Stop Planner CD–ROM

It's easy to plan lessons, select resources, and print out materials for your students when you use the **One-Stop Planner CD-ROM with Test Generator.**

Technology Resources

 One-Stop Planner, Lesson 11.1
  Homework Practice Online
Teaching Transparencies 27: Average Growth Rates for Boys and Girls from Childhood Through Adolescence
 HRW Go Site

 One-Stop Planner, Lesson 11.2
 Homework Practice Online

 One-Stop Planner, Lesson 11.3
 Homework Practice Online
 HRW Go Site

 One-Stop Planner, Lesson 11.4
 Homework Practice Online
 CNN. Presents Psychology: Eating Disorders
 HRW Go Site

internet connect

HRW ONLINE RESOURCES

GO TO: go.hrw.com
Then type in a keyword.

TEACHER HOME PAGE
 KEYWORD: SY3 Teacher

CHAPTER INTERNET ACTIVITIES
 KEYWORD: SY3 PS11
Choose an activity to have students:
- create a mural or collage on rites of passage and the physical environment.
- make a 3D model illustrating identity formation.
- create a pamphlet on challenges faced by adolescents.

CHAPTER ENRICHMENT LINKS
 KEYWORD: SY3 CH11

ONLINE ASSESSMENT
 Homework Practice
  KEYWORD: SY3 HP11
 Standardized Test Prep
  KEYWORD: SY3 STP11
 Rubrics
  KEYWORD: SS Rubrics

CONTENT UPDATES
 KEYWORD: SS Content Updates

HOLT PRESENTATION MAKER
 KEYWORD: SY3 PPT11

ONLINE READING SUPPORT
 KEYWORD: SS Strategies

CURRENT EVENTS
 KEYWORD: S3 Current Events

Additional Resources

PRINT RESOURCES FOR TEACHERS
Eagle, C., & Colman, C. (1993). *All that she can be.* New York: Simon & Schuster.

Erikson, E. (1968). *Identity: Youth and crisis.* New York: Norton.

Lerner, R. (1993). *Early adolescence: Perspectives on research, policy, and intervention.* Hillsdale, NJ: Erlbaum.

PRINT RESOURCES FOR STUDENTS
Guest, J. (1992). *Ordinary people.* New York: Viking Penguin.

Levenkron, S. (1989). *The best little girl in the world.* New York : Warner Books.

Woititz, J. (1990). *Adult children of alcoholics.* Deerfield Beach, FL: Health Communications.

MULTIMEDIA RESOURCES
Eating disorders (VHS). Films for the Humanities & Sciences, P.O. Box 2053, Princeton, NJ 08543-2053.

Under the influence: An interactive look at alcohol (CD-ROM). Cambridge Educational, P.O. Box 2153, Dept. DC15, Charleston, WV 25328-2153.

Chapter Review and Assessment

 HRW Go site
REV Chapter 11 Review, pp. 270–271
REV Chapter Review Activities with Answer Key

A Chapter 11 Test (Form A or B)
A Portfolio Assessment Handbook
A Alternative Assessment Handbook

Chapter 11 Test Generator (on the One-Stop Planner)
Global Skill Builder CD-ROM

ADOLESCENCE

Introducing Chapter 11

Prior to assigning the reading of Chapter 11, write the following questions on the chalkboard:

▶ What does it mean to be an adolescent?

▶ How is your relationship with your peers different from your relationship with your parents?

▶ What are your greatest fears at this stage in life?

▶ What are the most significant challenges facing teenagers today?

Have students write short answers to these questions and use the answers as the basis for a class discussion on adolescence as a stage in human development.

Sections

1 **Physical Development**

2 **Social Development**

3 **Identity Formation**

4 **Challenges of Adolescence**

Each of the four questions identified on page 250 corresponds to one of these sections.

11 Chapter ADOLESCENCE

Read to Discover

1 How do males and females change physically during adolescence, and what are the psychological effects of these changes?

2 What role do parents and peers play in the lives of adolescents?

3 What is identity formation, and what are the four categories of adolescent identity status?

4 What are some of the challenges that adolescents face in today's society?

Each chapter begins with a vignette, called "A Day in the Life," that relates the information discussed in the chapter to the everyday events in the lives of a group of fictional high school students. The text of the chapter occasionally refers back to the vignette to demonstrate the application of the concept being discussed. An icon marked "A Day in the Life" is placed next to these references.

 Copy the following graphic organizer onto the chalkboard, omitting the italicized text. Fill in the spaces as you introduce the topic of adolescence.

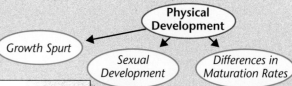

Physical Development
Growth Spurt
Sexual Development
Differences in Maturation Rates

A DAY IN THE LIFE

February 12

 Linda and Hannah feel very much a part of their circle of friends, which they often refer to as "the group." They are friendly with classmates outside the group, but when it comes to discussing the people and ideas they care about most, they talk to each other more than to anybody else except their parents. When they were concerned about Nick and his problems with drugs and alcohol, they could always talk to each other about it.

As it turned out, Nick wasn't the only one of their classmates they were concerned about. Linda and Hannah were eating lunch one day when Linda asked Hannah quietly, "Can I tell you something?"

"Sure," said Hannah. "Don't tell me Marc actually did something wrong. I thought he was supposed to be *perfect.*"

Linda laughed. "Hardly. No, Marc is wonderful." Her expression turned serious. "It's about Annie."

"Oh, Annie," said Hannah. "I bet I know what you're going to say."

They both liked Annie although she wasn't really a part of their group. She was a bright, quiet girl, well liked by her teachers—and everyone else for that matter.

"I'm worried about her," said Linda. "She keeps losing weight."

"I know," said Hannah.

"You've noticed too?" Linda asked with concern.

"How can you not notice it?" replied Hannah.

"She says she's on a diet. But she looks like a skeleton."

"I know," Hannah responded. "She's been skipping gym a lot too. I asked her when she was going to stop dieting. She said her weight was nearly where she wanted it to be and that she had never felt better."

"I don't know," said Linda. "Something's not right. Maybe I should talk to my parents about it. They might know how to help her."

"You're right," said Hannah. "We really should do something."

• • •

This chapter is about adolescence—the time between childhood and adulthood. For many teenagers, adolescence can be a rich and fulfilling time of life. Close friendships may develop. New opportunities to learn and grow present themselves. Most teenagers look to the future and see it as a time of hope and promise. However, adolescence can also be a confusing and difficult period. Rapid physical growth and sexual development bring dramatic changes. Teenagers must define who they are and what they stand for as they begin to establish identities as young adults. Even though they may be old enough to reproduce and be as big, or bigger, than their parents, adolescents sometimes feel they are treated like "big children." At other times, they must make adult decisions when they do not feel ready to make them. This chapter explores the physical changes that occur during adolescence, adolescent social development and identity formation, and the special challenges of adolescence.

Key Terms

- adolescent growth spurt
- puberty
- primary sex characteristics
- secondary sex characteristics
- menarche
- cliques
- crowds
- identity crisis
- identity status
- identity moratorium
- identity foreclosure
- identity diffusion
- identity achievement
- anorexia nervosa
- bulimia nervosa
- juvenile delinquency
- status offenses

WHY PSYCHOLOGY MATTERS

Psychologists and other researchers study how people change during adolescence. Use **CNNfyi.com** or other current events sources to learn more about how people develop psychologically during adolescence.

CNNfyi.com

Using Key Terms

Call students' attention to the six key terms that contain the word *identity.* Point out that these key terms are clearly linked in some way. Have students create a word web with *identity* in the center circle. Six circles should surround the center circle, each connected to the center circle by a line. Have students write one of the "identity" key terms in each of the six surrounding circles. As students encounter each key term in the textbook, have them write a brief definition in the circle containing that key term.

Journal Activity

Before students read Chapter 11, have them write in their journals a list of questions about adolescence they hope will be answered by reading the chapter. After students have read the chapter, have them review their lists and note any questions that might still be unanswered. Invite students to discuss these remaining questions with you, their parents or guardians, or the school psychologist.

251

Section Objective

▶ Identify the physical changes that occur in males and females during adolescence, and examine the psychological effects of these changes.

This objective is assessed in the Section Review on page 254 and in the Chapter 11 Review.

Opening Section 1

Motivator

Tell students to imagine what their lives would be like if adolescence were not considered a separate stage of development. Ask them to respond to the following question: How would your life be different from what it is today if people were considered to be adults at the age of 13? After students have responded, tell them that adolescence as a separate stage in the life cycle is a relatively recent concept. Have them read Section 1 to learn how the concept of adolescence came to be and about the physical changes that accompany adolescence.

Using Truth or Fiction

Each chapter opens with several "Truth or Fiction" statements that relate to the concepts discussed in the chapter. Ask students whether they think each statement is true or false. Answers to each item as well as explanations are provided at appropriate points within the text under the heading "Truth or Fiction Revisited."

Class Discussion

Have a student volunteer read aloud the first two paragraphs of Section 1. Ask students to speculate on why the transition from childhood to adulthood has changed in this way. Have students discuss the following questions: Why does the transition remain brief and early in some developing countries today? How does delayed adulthood in Western society affect young people? Does this delay make it easier or more difficult for adolescents to move into adulthood?

Readings and Case Studies

TRUTH **OR** **fiction**

Read the following statements about psychology. Do you think they are true or false? You will learn whether each statement is true or false as you read the chapter.

- Boys begin their adolescent growth spurt before girls do.
- Boys who mature early have certain advantages over their peers.
- Adolescents are in a constant state of rebellion against their parents.
- Girls are more likely than boys to have close friendships.
- Many adolescents follow the example of their peers in matters of clothing, hairstyles, speech patterns, and musical tastes.
- Excessive dieting may be a sign that a person has an eating disorder.

SECTION 1

Physical Development

In earlier times in Western societies (and in some developing countries today), the period of transition from childhood to adulthood was very brief. Most people took over the responsibilities of adulthood—going to work, caring for children, and so on—shortly after they reached sexual maturity. The transition to adulthood was often marked by an elaborate ceremony that symbolized the passage from childhood to adulthood.

In the 1900s, however, all that has changed. In Western societies, required education has been extended, and the status and duties of adulthood have been delayed. As a result, adolescence has come to cover most of the teen years. Today the period known as adolescence is sometimes subdivided into smaller categories. These categories include early adolescence (ages 11 through 14), middle adolescence (15 through 18), and late adolescence (18 through 21).

The biological changes that occur during adolescence are greater than those of any other time of life, with the exception of infancy. In some ways, however, the changes in adolescence are more dramatic than those that occur in infancy—unlike infants, adolescents are aware of the changes that

are taking place and of what the changes mean. But no teenager can ever be quite sure how all these physical changes will turn out. There are many variables to consider. Different adolescents begin their growth spurts at different ages, and they grow at different rates. Even the different parts of an adolescent's body grow at different rates. Most adolescents can only wonder about the final shape and size of their body.

The Adolescent Growth Spurt

During adolescence the stable growth patterns in height and weight that mark early and middle childhood come to an end. Stability is replaced by an abrupt burst of growth. This **adolescent growth spurt** usually lasts two to three years. During this time of rapid growth, most adolescents grow 8 to 12 inches in height.

Girls begin the adolescent growth spurt earlier than boys. The growth spurt usually begins in girls at about the age of 10 or 11 and in boys about 2 years later. As a result, girls tend to be taller and heavier than boys during early adolescence. Then, during middle adolescence, most boys catch up and grow taller than their female classmates. However, the exact time when this growth will occur for any individual—boy or girl—is difficult to predict (Rathus, 2003).

TRUTH **OR** **fiction** ■ REVISITED ■

It is not true that boys begin their adolescent growth spurt before girls do. Most boys begin their spurt at about 12 or 13 years of age, two years later than most girls.

A DAY IN THE LIFE

By the time Linda entered her senior year of high school, she had been at her full height for about four years. At the same time, Marc had been at his full height for only about two years. In eighth grade, when Marc first noticed Linda, she was taller than he was. But then he caught up and passed Linda in height. His voice deepened, and by the time they were juniors, they seemed to be more or less equal in their level of physical maturity.

This period of sudden adolescent growth can be awkward for both boys and girls because different parts of their bodies grow and mature at different

Cooperative Learning

Organize the class into small groups. Have each group review the textbook material on the adolescent growth spurt and sexual development. Then challenge each group to research the changing nutritional and fitness needs of growing teenagers. Have the groups use their findings to prepare a brochure titled "Health and Fitness During the Teenage Years." Brochures should include written text, drawings, and charts and graphs. Display the brochures in class, and allow students time to examine them.

Meeting Individual Needs: Learners Having Difficulty

Some students may not understand the difference between puberty and adolescence. Explain that puberty is a phase of biological development that involves the physical changes that enable a person to reproduce. Adolescence, on the other hand, is a stage of psychological development that occurs between puberty and adulthood. Have students review the textbook and list characteristics of both terms.

rates. For example, hands and feet may grow before arms and legs do. This growth spurt may cause adolescents to feel as if their hands or feet are too big or to worry that they "just don't look right."

Although some teenagers may feel that they look awkward, they tend to be well coordinated during adolescence. As adolescents become older and complete the growth spurt, their bodies usually reach their correct proportions. Once this has happened, the seeming awkwardness of the early teens becomes a thing of the past. Some psychologists believe that only a small percentage of adolescents—no more than about 15 percent—have difficulty adjusting to the adolescent growth spurt (Petersen, 1987).

Sexual Development

Adolescence begins with the onset of puberty. **Puberty** refers to the specific developmental changes that lead to the ability to reproduce. This biological stage of development ends when physical growth does.

During puberty the reproductive organs of both males and females develop and dramatically change the body of an adolescent. Characteristics that are directly involved in reproduction are called **primary sex characteristics**. Other characteristics that are not directly involved in reproduction—called **secondary sex characteristics**—also develop during puberty. These characteristics include the growth of hair on certain parts of the body, the deepening of the voice in males, and the rounding of the hips and breasts in females.

These changes are linked to changes in hormone levels. All hormones are present in children of both sexes from birth. During puberty, however, boys begin to produce higher levels of some hormones, while girls begin to produce higher levels of other hormones.

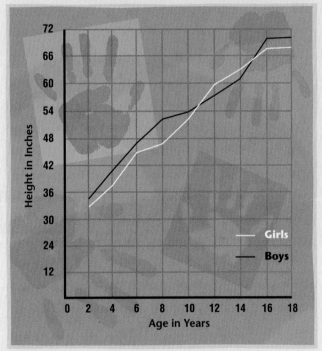

Average Growth Rates for Boys and Girls from Childhood Through Adolescence

FIGURE 11.1 *Throughout childhood, girls and boys are similar in height, with boys being slightly taller. At puberty, girls surge ahead for a short time. At about age 14, boys surge back ahead of girls.*

Source: Tanner, J.M. (1978). *Fetus into man: Physical growth from conception to maturity.* Cambridge, MA: Harvard University Press. (p. 118)

Changes in Males In boys, hormones from the pituitary gland cause the testes to increase output of the hormone testosterone. This causes boys' sexual organs to grow, their voices to deepen, and hair to grow on their faces and later on their chests. During the period of rapid growth, boys develop broader shoulders and thicker bodies. They also develop more muscle tissue and larger hearts and lungs.

Changes in Females In girls, hormones from the pituitary gland stimulate the ovaries to secrete more estrogen. Estrogen spurs the growth of breast tissue and supportive tissue in the hips and buttocks. As a result, the pelvic region widens and the hips become rounder. Girls also produce small amounts of androgens, which are similar to testosterone, in the adrenal glands. Androgens stimulate

Closing Section 1

For Further Research

The role of hormones in physical development is complex. Challenge students to learn more about hormones. They might focus on one of the hormones mentioned in the textbook, such as testosterone or estrogen. Students should write a brief report identifying the hormone and explaining where in the body it is produced, its effects on the body at various ages, and the problems that may result from the production of too much or too little of the hormone.

Applying Information

Point out that physical changes are easier to deal with when one knows what to expect. Have students create an informational pamphlet that will prepare preteens for the physical changes they will soon be experiencing. Have volunteers share their pamphlets with the class.

Reviewing Section 1

Have students complete the Section 1 Review questions on page 254.

Section 1 Review: Answers

1. Characteristics include an 8- to 12-inch growth in height; a growth-spurt duration of 2 to 3 years; and earlier growth for girls than for boys.

2. Boys experience deepening of the voice, growth of body hair and sexual organs, and increased muscle tissue; girls experience menstruation, the rounding of hips and breasts, and the growth of pubic and underarm hair.

3. One possible effect might be continuing to feel self-conscious about their bodies even after other teens have caught up with them.

Adolescents develop physically at different rates. Both early- and late-maturing adolescents may experience difficulties associated with their rates of development, but these problems usually fade over time.

the growth of pubic and underarm hair. Estrogen and androgens work together to spur the growth of the female sex organs.

The production of estrogen, which becomes cyclical in puberty, regulates the menstrual cycle. The first menstruation, or **menarche**, is a major life event for most girls, and most societies consider it the beginning of womanhood. It usually occurs between the ages of 11 and 14.

Differences in Maturation Rates

Some adolescents reach physical maturity at a relatively early age, while others reach it later. Research suggests that boys who mature early have certain advantages over boys who mature later (Alsaker, 1992). They tend to be more popular and to be leaders within their circle of friends. Their greater size and strength may give them a competitive edge in sports. They also tend to be more self-assured and relaxed. Because they have matured early, they no longer need to worry about maturing later than their peers. This may boost their self-esteem.

However, boys who mature early physically are not necessarily more mature than their peers in some other ways, such as in how they approach and handle problems. Also, coaches, friends, and others may pressure them to perform beyond their abilities. They may not be prepared to live up to the expectations of others (Kutner, 1993). Boys who mature early may even be more likely than other boys to engage in types of problem behaviors (Andersson & Magnusson, 1990).

Furthermore, although early-maturing boys may have some advantages over their peers who develop later, these advantages fade over time. In fact, some longitudinal studies indicate that boys who mature later show better adjustment as adults than boys who mature early (Livson & Peskin, 1972). Of course, not all early maturing boys have problems, either as adolescents or as adults.

> **TRUTH OR fiction**
> ■ R E V I S I T E D ■
>
> It is true that boys who mature early have certain advantages over their peers. For example, they tend to be more popular and self-assured than their peers. However, early maturity may also carry certain disadvantages.

Early maturation is somewhat different for girls. Girls who mature early may feel awkward because they are taller than their classmates, both male and female. They may be teased about their height. Early maturing girls may be tempted to associate with older teens, even when they are not emotionally ready for such associations. Moreover, older boys may assume that these girls are more mature than they really are and may expect them or pressure them to do things they do not want to do.

Needless to say, not all girls who mature early encounter problems. In any case, the differences between early and late-maturing girls usually do not last long. Once their peers catch up to them, the issue of differences in maturity generally disappears (Simmons & Blyth, 1987).

SECTION 1 REVIEW

Homework Practice Online
Keyword: SY3 HP11

1. List three characteristics of the adolescent growth spurt.

2. What physical changes occur in males during puberty? in females?

3. **Critical Thinking** *Finding the Main Idea* Identify some long-term effects of early maturation for girls and for boys.

EXPLORING
DIVERSITY

Rites of Passage

A rite of passage is a ceremony that marks a person's entrance into a new stage of life. Rites of passage include ceremonies such as baptism, graduation, and marriage. For many Americans, rites of passage such as school graduations and weddings signify the end of one period of life and the beginning of another.

Most rites of passage are characterized by three stages. In the first stage, the participant is separated from his or her previous status. The next stage is a transitional stage in which the participant learns the behavior and ideas appropriate to his or her new status. In some African societies, for example, boys who are on the verge of adulthood are separated from others for days or even months while they learn tribal traditions and skills. After the completion of the second stage, the participant is formally admitted into his or her new status. This is often marked by an elaborate ceremony.

People often pass through the stages of a rite of passage as a group. For example, in many graduation ceremonies in the United States, the graduating students sit together in a special area separated from their families and friends. The walk across the stage to receive their diploma symbolizes the transition from student to graduate. In some ceremonies, in which the graduates wear academic caps and gowns, they move the tassels on the caps from one side to the other to signify their entrance into the society of graduates.

Many cultures have special ceremonies to mark young people's passage from childhood to adulthood. In some societies, teenagers celebrate certain birthdays as rites of passage. For example,

In some Hispanic cultures, a girl's 15th birthday marks her passage into adulthood.

the 15th birthday is an important occasion for many Hispanic girls. It is celebrated by the girl, her family, and community members in an event called the *quinceañera*. A ceremony, usually in a church, is followed by a party.

Jewish adolescents mark their entrance into the adult religious community in a ceremony called (for boys) a bar mitzvah, which means "son of the commandment," or (for girls) a bat mitzvah, which means "daughter of the commandment." When a Jewish child reaches age 13, he or she is expected to observe the religious customs and obligations of Jewish adulthood. After much preparation, Jewish teens show what they have learned about Judaism.

Several Christian traditions—including Roman Catholicism, Eastern Orthodox, Lutheranism, and Episcopalianism—also have an initiation ceremony. It is called a confirmation, and it confers full adult membership in the church. At the confirmation service, young people renew, or confirm, promises made for them at baptism.

For many American teenagers, rites of passage are neither formal nor religious. Rather, they are a series of "first" events that signify assuming more responsibility and receiving adult treatment. Obtaining one's driver's license is one example. Getting one's first after-school job is another.

Think About It

Analyzing Information Besides the examples mentioned above, what are some other rites of passage for adolescents in the United States?

255

Section Objective

▶ Describe the role that parents and peers generally play in the lives of adolescents.

This objective is assessed in the Section Review on page 259 and in the Chapter 11 Review.

Opening Section 2

Motivator

Acknowledge to students that adolescence has the reputation for being a difficult time of life. Adolescents are often seen as battling with parents or teachers and struggling against negative peer pressure. Section 2 suggests that adolescence also includes many positive interactions with parents and peers. Before students read the section, have them identify three positive features in their own relationships with parents, teachers, and friends. Encourage them to keep these positive features in mind as they read the section.

Journal Activity

Building on the Motivator activity, ask students to write a letter (in their journals) to their parents or guardians identifying both positive and negative aspects of the relationship. Remind students that they need not share these letters unless they want to.

For Your Information

Adolescence is known to be a time of emotional upheaval, but often this upheaval is experienced by parents of teenagers as well. As their children become more independent and gain more interests outside the family, many parents feel a sense of loss. Some parents even experience an identity crisis because they had defined themselves solely by their role as a parent. According to Betty and Raymond Fish, authors of *A Parent's Guide to Letting Go* (White Hall, VA: Betterway Publications, 1988), it is common for parents to mourn the loss of the child the teenager once was while at the same time appreciate the person the teenager has become.

SECTION 2

Social Development

About 100 years ago, G. Stanley Hall, the founder of the American Psychological Association, described adolescence as a time of *Sturm und Drang*. These are German words that mean "storm and stress." Hall attributed the conflicts and distress some adolescents experience to biological changes.

Research suggests that the hormonal changes of adolescence do have some effect on the activity levels, mood swings, and aggressive tendencies of many adolescents. However, contemporary studies suggest that cultural and social influences may have more of an effect on adolescent behavior than hormones do (Buchanan et al., 1992).

Adolescence is a psychological concept as well as a biological concept. Psychologically, the adolescent period ends when people become adults and take on adult responsibilities. How long adolescence lasts varies with each individual. For some people, adolescence may be quite extended; for others, it is quite short. For example, when a teenager finds himself or herself caring for family members, financially supporting the family, or assuming other significant responsibilities, adolescence for that individual has probably been quite short, at least in the psychological sense.

Certainly, adolescence can be a challenging time of life. Some teenagers may experience difficulties at home or at school that lead to psychological and social problems. Nonetheless, the vast majority of teenagers face the many challenges of adolescence and cope with them successfully. They form new friendships, increase their knowledge, build their self-esteem, and develop personal and social skills that enable them to become successful and competent adults.

Relationships with Parents

During adolescence, parent-child relationships undergo redefinition. However, the picture of adolescence as a state of constant rebellion against parents and society is exaggerated. The truth is that most of the changes that occur during adolescence are positive rather than negative (Collins, 1990; Steinberg, 1991).

As adolescents strive to become more independent from their parents, however, some conflicts may arise. This striving for greater freedom often results in bickering, especially in early adolescence (Smetana & Gaines, 1999). Conflicts typically center on such issues as homework, chores, money, appearance, curfews, and dating (Galambos & Turner, 1999). Arguments sometimes arise when adolescents maintain that personal choices, such as those that have to do with clothes and friends, should be made by them, not their parents (Smetana et al., 1991).

The adolescent quest for independence may lead to less time spent with family, greater emotional attachment to people who are not family members, and more activities outside the home. In one study, children ranging in age from 9 to 15 carried electronic pagers for a week so that when signaled they could report to researchers what they were doing and with whom (Larson & Richards, 1991). The study showed that the older the children were, the less time they spent with their families. The 15-year-olds spent only half as much time with their families as the 9-year-olds. For the older boys in the study, time spent with the family tended to be replaced by time spent alone. The older girls, on the other hand, tended to divide the time they spent away from their families between friends and solitude.

Greater independence from parents does not necessarily mean that adolescents withdraw emotionally from their parents or fall completely under the influence of their peers. Most adolescents continue to love, respect, and feel loyalty toward their parents (Montemayor & Flannery, 1991).

 Linda and Hannah spent less time with their parents than they did when they were younger. They also talked to each other more than they did to either one of their parents. Still, they continued to love their parents and depend on them for emotional support. Adolescents who feel close to their parents tend to show greater self-reliance and independence than those who are distant from their parents. Adolescents who retain close ties with parents also tend to fare better in school and have fewer adjustment problems (Davey, 1993; Papini & Roggman, 1992; Steinberg, 1991).

Despite a certain amount of parent-adolescent conflict, parents and adolescents usually share similar social, political, religious, and economic views (Paikoff & Collins, 1991). For example, adolescents tend to share the religion of one or both of their parents. Rarely will a teenager break completely with his or her family and adopt a different

Teaching Section 2

Taking a Stand

Organize the class into debate teams of no more than six students. Teams should debate one of the following statements: Parents and adolescents usually share similar social, political, religious, and economic views; or, Choices about clothes, friends, and personal habits should be made by adolescents, not by their parents. Encourage students to use formal debate rules, including a statement-and-rebuttal period for each team. Then have students discuss why young people strive to become more independent from their parents during adolescence.

Demonstration

Give students the chance to test the textbook statement that adolescents spend less time with their families than do younger children. Have students record the amount of time they spend with their families each day during a one-week period. Ask them also to record the same information for a younger sibling or friend. In class, tally the results, and have students find the average time spent with families for the class as a whole and for their younger siblings. Does the demonstration support or contradict the textbook statement?

What's New in Psychology?

Remind students of what they learned in Chapter 10 about the authoritative parenting style. Explain that recent research suggests that an authoritative parenting style is especially effective in moderating negative peer pressure. According to the study, teenagers with authoritative parents are more influenced by high-achieving friends and less influenced by drug-using friends than are teens with less authoritative parents. The combination of control and warmth gives adolescents a sense of security while allowing them the freedom to mature in a loving environment.

Mounts, N. S., & Steinberg, L. (1995) "An ecological analysis of peer influence on adolescent grade point average and drug use." *Developmental Psychology, 31.* 915–922.

religion. Therefore, while there are frequent parent-adolescent differences of opinion about behavior and rules of conduct, conflict between the generations on broader issues is less common.

TRUTH OR fiction ▪ REVISITED ▪

It is not true that adolescents are in a constant state of rebellion against their parents. While there may be conflict with parents about family rules, most adolescents are in agreement with their parents about broader issues.

Adolescents tend to interact with their mothers more than they do with their fathers. Most adolescents also see their mothers as more supportive than their fathers, as knowing them better, and as more likely to tolerate their opinions (Collins & Russell, 1991; Noller & Callan, 1990). Teenagers are also more likely to seek and follow advice from their mothers than from their fathers (Greene & Grimsley, 1991).

Relationships with Peers

The transition from childhood to adolescence involves an increase in the importance of peers. While most adolescents maintain good relations with parents, peers become more important in terms of influence and emotional support. For example, fourth-graders consider parents to be their most frequent providers of emotional and social support. If something upsetting happens at school, they are more likely to discuss it with their parents than with anybody else. However, by seventh grade, friends of the same gender are generally seen as providing more support than parents (Furman & Buhrmester, 1992).

Adolescent Friendships Friendship is a very important part of adolescence. Most adolescents tend to have one or two "best friends," but they have other good friends as well. Linda and Hannah probably considered themselves to be best friends, but they had other friends too, such as Annie. Adolescents may spend several

A DAY IN THE LIFE

257

Guided Practice

Create on the chalkboard a three-column chart titled "Adolescent Friendships." Label the columns *Purposes of Friendship, Characteristics of Friends,* and *Gender Differences in Friendship.* Have students supply information from the textbook about adolescent friendships while you write the information in the appropriate column. Then have students write a short paragraph explaining why friendship is a very important part of adolescence.

Independent Practice

Have each student interview several young children (7 to 10 years old) and several older teenagers (16 to 18 years old). Tell the interviewers to ask the participants in both groups the following question: How would you describe a good friend? In class, have students review the responses given by the participants and compare the responses of the young children with those given by the teenagers. Have students discuss their findings in class.

258

Friends begin to take on greater importance during adolescence. Although most teenagers maintain loving relationships with their parents, they spend more time with friends, either in person or on the phone. Friendships provide adolescents with support and understanding and boost self-esteem.

hours a day with their friends (Hartup, 1993). When teenagers are not actually with their friends, they are often speaking with them on the telephone.

Friendships serve many purposes for adolescents. One teen girl described her best friend this way: "I can tell her things and she helps me talk. And she doesn't laugh at me if I do something weird—she accepts me for who I am" (Berndt & Perry, 1990, p. 269).

Adolescents also value loyalty as a key aspect of friendship. They say that true friends "stick up for you in a fight" and do not "talk about you behind your back" (Berndt & Perry, 1990, p. 269). In other words, having friends means more to adolescents than just having people to spend time with. Close friends provide support and understanding, strengthen one's ability to be a caring person, and contribute to self-esteem.

Adolescents usually choose friends who are similar to themselves in age, background, educational goals, and attitudes toward drinking, drug use, and sexual activity (Hartup, 1993; Youniss & Haynie, 1992). In addition, adolescents' closest friends are usually of their own sex (Hartup, 1993). The friendships of adolescent girls tend to be closer than those of boys (Berndt & Perry, 1990; Manke, 1993). Girls are more likely than boys to share their secrets, personal problems, and innermost feelings. While boys also have close friendships, they tend to spend time together in larger, less intimate groups. These gender differences in patterns of friendship continue into adulthood (Dindia & Allen, 1992).

TRUTH
OR
fiction
■ R E V I S I T E D ■

It is true that girls are more likely than boys to have close friendships. Boys seem to be more comfortable spending time with friends in larger, less intimate groups.

Cliques and Crowds Adolescents not only have close friends; they also tend to belong to one or more larger peer groups. **Cliques** are peer groups of 5 to 10 people who spend a great deal of time with one another, sharing activities and confidences. Larger groups of people who do not spend as much time together but share attitudes and group identity are called **crowds**.

A DAY IN THE LIFE

Marc, Linda, Hannah, Todd, Dan, Janet, and a few others were members of a clique, which they called "the group." Adolescent cliques often include members of both sexes, which may lead to romantic relationships such as the one between Marc and Linda. Most young people also belong to a larger crowd with whom they go to parties, play basketball or baseball, and participate in other activities.

Some adolescents join certain cliques in their search for the stability and sense of belonging that come from being part of such a group. They may imitate their peers' speech and adopt some of their values. Teens in the same clique may follow similar fads in the way they dress or style their hair. They and the other members of the group may even become intolerant of "outsiders"—people not in the group.

Peer Influences Parents often worry that their adolescent children's needs for peer approval will influence them to engage in risky or unacceptable behavior. However, the assumption that parents and peers often pull an adolescent in different directions does not seem to be borne out by reality. In fact, parental and peer influences often coincide to some degree (Brown et al., 1993; Youniss & Haynie, 1992). For example, research suggests that peers are more likely to urge adolescents to work for good grades and complete high school than they are to try to involve them in drug abuse, sexual activity, or delinquency (Brown et al., 1993).

Closing Section 2

Synthesizing Information

Have students write an imaginative short story titled "The Perfect First Date." Ask volunteers to read their stories aloud to the class for discussion. How do the stories reflect the information in the textbook about dating and romantic relationships?

Reviewing Section 2

Have students complete the Section Review questions on page 259.

Extension

Ask students to conduct library research to learn about dating and courtship patterns in other cultures or in the United States at an earlier period in time. Have the students give oral presentations of their findings in class. Have the class compare and contrast these findings with the dating patterns found among U.S. teenagers today.

Studies show that while girls are more likely to develop close, personal relationships with a couple of other girls, boys are more likely to spend time in a larger group. Girls are also more likely to spend their time together talking and sharing thoughts and feelings, while boys are more likely to engage in an activity, such as a sport.

Nevertheless, adolescents are influenced by their parents and peers in different ways. Adolescents are more likely to follow their peers in terms of dress, hairstyles, speech patterns, and taste in music (Camarena, 1991). However, they are more likely to agree with their parents on issues such as moral values and educational and career goals (Savin-Williams & Berndt, 1990).

TRUTH OR fiction *It is true that many adolescents follow the example of their peers in matters of clothing, hairstyles, speech patterns, and musical tastes.* ■ REVISITED ■ However, they are likely to agree with their parents on important and broader issues, such as morality and educational goals.

In early adolescence, peer pressure is relatively weak, but it increases in middle adolescence, peaking at about the age of 15. Peer pressure seems to decrease after the age of 17 (Brown et al., 1993; Youniss & Haynie, 1992). Adolescents are strongly influenced by their peers for several reasons. They seek the approval of their peers and feel better about themselves when they receive it. Peers provide standards by which adolescents can measure their behavior as they grow more independent of their parents (Foster-Clark & Blyth, 1991). Also, because peers may share some of the same feelings, they can provide support in times of difficulty.

Dating and Romantic Relationships Many people begin dating during adolescence. Dating usually develops in stages (Padgham & Blyth, 1991). During the first stage, adolescents place themselves in situations where they will probably meet peers of the other sex—for example, at after-school events. In the next stage, adolescents participate in group dating, such as joining a mixed group at the movies. Finally, they may pair off as couples for traditional dating.

People date for several reasons. Obviously, people may date simply because they enjoy spending time with somebody they like. But dating may also help adolescents learn how to relate positively to other people. Furthermore, dating may help prepare adolescents for the more serious courtship activities that come later in life.

Among younger adolescents, dating relationships tend to be casual and short-lived. But in later adolescence, relationships tend to be more stable and committed (Feiring, 1993). As 18-year-olds, Marc and Linda were most likely thinking in terms of trust, commitment to each other, and honesty.

SECTION 2 REVIEW

go.hrw.com **Homework Practice Online** Keyword: SY3 HP11

1. In what ways does a teen's relationship with his or her parents change during adolescence? How does it stay the same?

2. Suggest two reasons why adolescents are influenced by their peers.

3. What are the three stages of dating?

4. **Critical Thinking** *Evaluating* Why might adolescence be considered a time of "storm and stress"?

▶ Define identity formation, and describe the four categories of adolescent identity status.

This objective is assessed in the Section Review on page 264 and in the Chapter 11 Review.

Motivator

Ask students to define the term *identity* and to suggest how people go about forming their identities. List responses on the chalkboard. *(Students may say that people form their identities on the basis of their beliefs, actions, points of view, and so on.)* Then explain that identity formation is a psychological process that, according to some psychologists, is the main task of adolescence. Tell students that Section 3 examines identity formation in detail. Encourage them to amend the chalkboard definition of *identity* as they read the section.

Class Discussion

Ask students to consider what types of educational and career decisions await them at this stage in their lives. Discuss with students how they might use formal-operational thinking to address these questions. Ask them to consider why abstract thinking is so important to making these kinds of decisions. *(It would be difficult for teenagers to make decisions about options they have never experienced if they did not have the ability to analyze hypothetical situations.)*

Journal Activity

Remind students that adolescent identity is achieved when different "selves" are brought together into a unified and consistent sense of self. Then have students write *Who Am I?* on a blank page in their journals. Under the heading, students should describe how they think their parents, their teachers, and their peers view them. Which of the views is closest to the way they see themselves? How close are they to identity achievement?

SECTION **3**

Identity Formation

Psychoanalyst Erik Erikson maintained that the journey of life consists of eight stages. (See Chapter 14.) At each stage, there is a task that must be mastered in order for healthy development to continue. Erikson said that young children must deal with issues of trust, autonomy (self-government), and initiative (taking the lead). Once children begin school, their main task becomes the development of competence, which is the sense that they can learn and achieve.

According to Erikson, the main task of the adolescent stage is the search for identity—a sense of who one is and what one stands for. Adolescents seek to identify their beliefs, their values, and their life goals. They also need to identify the areas in which they agree and disagree with parents, teachers, and friends.

Identity Development

According to Erikson, the task of establishing one's identity is accomplished mainly by choosing and developing a commitment to a particular role or

Investigating various career options at a career fair might be one step toward developing an identity, according to Erikson.

occupation in life. Accomplishing this task may also involve developing one's own political and religious beliefs.

To find an identity that is comfortable, adolescents may experiment with different values, beliefs, roles, and relationships. They may try out different "selves" in different situations. For example, the way they behave with their friends may be quite different from the way they behave with their parents. Adolescents who take on these different roles may sometimes wonder which one of their selves is the "real" one. Adolescent identity is achieved when different selves are brought together into a unified and consistent sense of self (Conger, 1978).

Erikson believed that teens who do not succeed in forging an identity may become confused about who they really are and what they want to do in life. They may have difficulty making commitments and may drift from situation to situation. Since they do not create a solid sense of self, they may remain overly dependent on the opinions of others.

One key aspect of adolescent identity development is what Erikson called an identity crisis. An **identity crisis** is a turning point in a person's development when the person examines his or her values and makes or changes decisions about life roles. Should I go to college? Which one? What type of job should I look for? What career is right for me? Adolescents can feel overwhelmed by the choices that lie before them and the decisions they must make (Crain, 2000).

Chapter 10 discussed Piaget's four stages of cognitive development. The final stage is the formal-operational stage. It generally begins at puberty and continues through adulthood. Formal-operational thinking involves abstract thinking, such as hypothetical situations. It enables people to find reasonable solutions to problems and to predict the possible consequences of the decisions they make. Formal-operational thinking helps adolescents make important life choices. Because their thinking is no longer tied to concrete experience, adolescents can evaluate the options available to them even though they may not have personally experienced them (Kahlbaugh & Haviland, 1991).

Identity Status

According to psychologist James Marcia (1966, 1993), the adolescent identity crisis arises as teenagers face decisions about their future work, moral standards, religious commitment, or political orientation. Marcia studied the different ways that

CASE STUDIES
AND OTHER TRUE STORIES

Working Teens

In the United States today, more teenagers than ever before are working. Three out of every four high school juniors and seniors hold part-time jobs. The majority of parents and psychologists have supported the idea of teenage employment in the belief that having a part-time job prepares teenagers for adult life and teaches them self-reliance, money management, and the value of hard work. Several panels in the 1970s and 1980s suggested that many of the problems of modern adolescents, including crime, substance abuse, and lack of motivation, could be cured if teens were more actively involved in the working world. Just how does holding a job affect an adolescent?

Research indicates that having a part-time job may help teenagers develop a sense of independence. They may no longer have to rely on their parents for spending money, nor are they as accountable to their parents for how they spend the money they make (Greenberger & Steinberg, 1986). Taking a part-time job can thus be beneficial for teens as they strive to become independent from their parents. Erik Erikson believed that independence from one's parents is an important step in identity development.

However, part-time employment of adolescents may have some drawbacks. Psychologists Ellen Greenberger and Laurence Steinberg (1986) argue that in order for a work experience to be beneficial for teenagers, it should teach them skills or knowledge valuable for adult life. In the past, adolescents worked primarily in farming, factories, or skilled trades and crafts. But today the majority of teens work in food-service and sales jobs. These jobs often do not teach teenage workers specific skills for their future professions as many jobs of the past did. Nor do they give workers much responsibility. There is little room for ambition and little reward for putting in extra effort. As a result of these conditions, teenage employees often develop a negative attitude about work and about its ability to lead to self-fulfillment. Instead of gaining respect for work,

teenagers with part-time jobs often come to see work as a necessary evil with no worth in and of itself.

Greenberger and Steinberg also believe that for work to be valuable, it should fill a financial need of the teenager's family, the community, or the teen's own future. But the majority of teens today work to supply themselves with "extras" rather than to help support their families or to save for a long-term goal, such as a college education. Because most teens tend to spend their paychecks on luxury items such as CDs and designer clothing, they may develop an unrealistic view of money. Instead of learning the hard reality of life—that for many people there is little money left over after paying for rent, groceries, and utilities—teens may become accustomed to spending most of their income on nonnecessities.

Perhaps the biggest concern for many people is the effect that working has on teens' grades. While some studies have indicated that students who work excessive hours do worse in school than their nonworking counterparts (Lillydahl, 1995; Steinberg, 1993), evidence suggests that students who have jobs but work fewer than 13.5 hours per week actually do *better* in school than those who do not work (Lillydahl, 1995).

To work or not to work? There is no easy answer. Each teenager and his or her parents should examine the issues—necessity, goals, grades, and time—before deciding. However, many teenagers can benefit from the working experience, especially if they keep school a top priority, avoid working too many hours, save part of the money earned toward future education, and continue to participate in other activities.

WHY PSYCHOLOGY MATTERS

Psychologists study the effects of work on teenagers. Use CNNfyi.com or other current events sources to learn more about working teens. Create a poster noting the benefits and drawbacks of teen employment.

CNNfyi.com

internet connect
go.hrw.com

Teaching Section 3

Role-Playing

Give each student a slip of paper on which one of James Marcia's four categories of identity status is written. Then present the class with a number of hypothetical decision-making situations. For example, have students decide what they will do during the summer. Tell students to respond to the situations as someone in their identity status category would. As each student responds, the other students should identify the category being presented.

Interpreting Ideas

Write the following headings on the chalkboard: *Identity Moratorium, Identity Foreclosure, Identity Diffusion,* and *Identity Achievement.* Have students supply names of characters from movies or from television programs who exemplify one of the four identity status categories. Students should supply a rationale for their responses. Write students' suggestions under the appropriate heading. Then have students compare and contrast the characteristics of the four categories.

Cross-Curricular Link: History

Until the 1800s it was common for boys as young as nine years old to leave home to seek employment or apprenticeships. Girls who did not seek employment typically left the household a few years later than their male counterparts, usually to marry. By the mid-1800s, however, the concept of adolescence as we know it today had become firmly established in middle- and upper-income homes in Western societies. Educators advised parents that adolescence was the time when children most needed parental guidance to protect them from the corruption and temptations of the adult world. As a result, parents began to keep their children home until well into their teens and even into their 20s.

Journal Activity

Have students review the four identity status categories. In a private journal entry, students should note which category they are in right now and their reasons for choosing that category.

adolescents handle commitment and cope with the adolescent identity crisis. He concluded that there are four categories of adolescent **identity status**, or reaction patterns and processes. Adolescents do not remain in a single one of these categories throughout their entire adolescence, nor do they proceed through them in a particular order. Rather, they move in and out of the various categories, from one to another. The four categories are identity moratorium, identity foreclosure, identity diffusion, and identity achievement. (See Figure 11.2.)

Identity Moratorium   A moratorium is a "time out" period. Teens experiencing what Marcia termed **identity moratorium** delay making commitments about important questions. They are actively exploring various alternatives in an attempt to forge their identity. They may even experiment with different behaviors and personalities. Adolescents experimenting with different ways of life in their search for an identity may adopt distinctive ways of dressing or behaving. For example, they may cut or style their hair in a particular way. Or they might adopt a special article of clothing as their "trademark."

Adolescents who remain in moratorium longer than other teens may become somewhat anxious as they struggle to find anchors in an unstable world (Patterson et al., 1992). But for most high school students in moratorium who say, "I don't know what I want to do," it is enough to know that they are heading in a general direction even if they do not know where their journey will end. They may end up attending college, joining the armed services, or doing something completely different to reach their final goals. It is not unusual for young people to actively explore their life alternatives for a decade or more.

Identity Foreclosure   To avoid an identity crisis, adolescents in the **identity foreclosure** category make a commitment that forecloses (or shuts out) other possibilities. These adolescents make a definite commitment, but the commitment is based on the suggestions of others rather than on their own choices. They adopt a belief system or a plan of action without closely examining whether it is right for them. They may simply follow the model set by their parents, peers, teachers, or other authority figures in order to avoid uncertainty. For example, an adolescent who is "foreclosed" might decide to become a lawyer because one or both parents are lawyers. Adolescents in identity foreclosure tend to

be inflexible and intolerant of people who do not share their views and commitments (Berzonsky et al., 1993; Marcia, 1991).

Although following a path recommended by a respected adult eliminates the need to make some hard choices, some adolescents become foreclosed too early. After they find themselves dissatisfied with the direction of their lives, they may switch to the moratorium category. For instance, the adolescent who has chosen to be a lawyer simply because both parents are lawyers may discover in law school, or even after becoming a lawyer, that being a lawyer is not really what he or she wants to do. The individual may then enter moratorium to reassess life goals and to decide whether to make a career change.

Identity Diffusion   Adolescents in the category of **identity diffusion** seem to be constantly searching for meaning in life and for identity because they have not committed themselves to a set of personal beliefs or an occupational path. They tend to wander about without goals or interests and seem to live from crisis to crisis.

Identity diffusion is characteristic of children in middle school and early high school. However, if it continues into the 11th and 12th grades, identity diffusion can lead to an "I don't care" attitude. Some adolescents in this category become angry and rebellious. They may reject socially accepted beliefs, values, and goals (Archer & Waterman, 1990; Marcia, 1991).

Identity Achievement   Adolescents in the **identity achievement** category have coped with crises and have explored options. They have then committed themselves to occupational directions and have made decisions about important life questions. Although they have experienced an identity crisis, they have emerged from it with a solid set of beliefs or with a life plan. The plan might be to pursue a course of study that leads to a particular career. Identity-achieved teens tend to have feelings of well-being, high self-esteem, and self-acceptance. They are capable of setting goals and working toward attaining them (Berzonsky et al., 1993; Waterman, 1992). A teenager who decides to become a veterinarian or a businessperson, for example, may choose courses in high school or take an after-school job with that goal in mind.

Many young people do not reach identity achievement until well after high school. It is normal to change majors in college and to change

Closing Section 3

Meeting Individual Needs: Gifted Learners

Have gifted students read more about Erik Erikson's ideas on identity formation, particularly as they relate to the relationship between gender and identity formation. Then ask students to write an essay suggesting ways in which Erikson's theories might be adjusted to accommodate the greater equality of opportunities and expectations that young men and women face today. Have volunteers read their essays aloud for class discussion.

Synthesizing Information

Ask students to write fictional or real-life anecdotes about adolescents in each of the four identity status categories. Each anecdote should center on an important commitment concerning career, education, or values. Have volunteers read their anecdotes to the class.

Reviewing Section 3

Have students complete the Section Review questions on page 264.

Marcia's Adolescent Identity Status Categories

Identity Status	Characteristics	Example
Identity Moratorium	Searching for identity; Exploring various alternatives; Delaying making commitments	"I don't know what I want to do when I graduate, so I'm going to apply to college and for jobs. Then I'll decide which would be best for me."
Identity Foreclosure	Conforming; Accepting identity and values from childhood; Choosing to identify with others rather than self; Making commitments and adopting plans without self-examination; Becoming inflexible	"Everyone in my family has gone into the military after high school, so that's what I'm planning to do."
Identity Diffusion	Making no commitment; Doing no soul-searching; Wandering without goals; Becoming angry and rebellious	"I really have no idea what I'll do after graduation. I'll just have to see what happens."
Identity Achievement	Exploring options; Committing self to direction in life and occupation; Finding own identity	"I'm going to start college in the fall. My parents wanted me to go into the family business after I graduated, but I decided that what I really want to do is go to school and become a scientist."

FIGURE 11.2 *By studying how teenagers handle commitment and cope with the adolescent identity crisis, psychologist James Marcia identified four adolescent identity status categories.*

Using Visuals

Discuss Figure 11.2 with students, clarifying if necessary the characteristics of each identity status category. Then have students collect additional examples from the textbook to fit each of the categories.

Cultural Dimensions

Suggest to students that they read *New Kids on the Block: Oral Histories of Immigrant Teens,* edited by Janet Bode (New York: Franklin Watts, 1989). Explain that the oral histories in this collection address the struggles young immigrants face as they work to create new lives and to find an identity for themselves in the United States. Discuss how the stories reflect the added challenge to identity formation of being faced with two often-conflicting sets of cultural values.

careers. Such changes, which may even be made several times, do not necessarily mean that these people are indecisive or that they have made wrong decisions. The changes may simply mean that these individuals are continuing to actively explore their options. College, vocational training, and jobs are broadening experiences that expose people to new ways of life, career possibilities, and belief systems. It is common to adjust one's personal goals and beliefs as one matures and views the world from a new or broader perspective.

Gender and Ethnicity in Identity Formation

All adolescents struggle at some point with issues concerning who they are and what they stand for. However, the nature of the struggle is somewhat different for males and females and for adolescents from different ethnic backgrounds.

Gender and Identity Formation According to Erik Erikson's theory, identity development during adolescence means embracing a philosophy of life and a commitment to a career. However, his views of the development of identity were intended to apply primarily to boys (Archer, 1992; Patterson et al., 1992).

Erikson believed that people develop the capacity to form intimate relationships in the young adult stage of development. He also believed that the development of interpersonal relationships was more important than occupational issues and values to women's identity. Erikson, like Sigmund Freud,

ADOLESCENCE **263**

Extension

Have students conduct library research to learn how much time per day and per week employed husbands and wives each devote to child-rearing and home-maintenance tasks. Ask students to display this information in a bar graph and to write a caption for the bar graph describing their findings. Then have students discuss the relationship between their findings and identity formation in adolescent males and females.

4
Section Objective

▶ Describe some of the important challenges that adolescents face in today's society.

This objective is assessed in the Section Review on page 269 and in the Chapter 11 Review.

Section 3 Review: Answers

1. An identity crisis is a critical turning point in one's social development—a time when major decisions must be made about one's life goals and direction.

2. The four categories are identity moratorium (delaying commitment), identity foreclosure (making an early and unwavering commitment), identity diffusion (soul-searching or wandering without commitment), and identity achievement (commitment made after a period of soul-searching).

3. Students who feel pressure to make life decisions will probably agree that identity formation is the most important task of adolescence. Others may feel comfortable letting their identities evolve.

The cultural heroes for adolescents from ethnic minority groups are often not as well known in other groups in society. Some, however—such as professional basketball player Hakeem Olajuwon—are quite well known and respected.

believed that women's identities were intimately connected with their roles as wives and mothers. Men's identities, on the other hand, were not assumed to depend on their roles as husbands and fathers (Patterson et al., 1992).

Today many women work outside the home. Research shows that female adolescents are now more apt to approach identity formation like male adolescents (Archer, 1992). The concern of female adolescents about occupational plans is now about equal to that of males. However, there is a difference. Female adolescents also express concern about how they will balance the day-to-day demands of work and family life (Archer, 1992). Their concern is well founded. Despite their involvement in the workplace, women in the United States still bear most of the responsibility for rearing the children and maintaining the home (Archer, 1991).

Ethnicity and Identity Formation Identity formation is often more complicated for adolescents from ethnic minority groups (Collins, 2000; Phinney, 2000). These adolescents may be faced with two sets of cultural values: those of their ethnic group and those of the larger society (Phinney, 2000; Phinney & Devich Navarro, 1997). When these values are in conflict, minority adolescents need to reconcile the differences and, frequently, decide where they stand.

Prejudice and discrimination can also contribute to the problems faced by adolescents from ethnic minority groups as they strive to forge a sense of identity. For example, the cultural heroes for these adolescents may not be recognized by members of other groups in society.

Adolescents whose father and mother are from different cultural backgrounds must also wrestle with balancing two cultural heritages (Collins, 2000; Phinney, 2000). Parents from different ethnic groups may decide to spend their lives together, but their values sometimes do not dwell contentedly side by side in the minds of their children. As a result, the children may experience some emotional conflict.

SECTION 3 REVIEW

Homework Practice Online
Keyword: SY3 HP11

1. What is an identity crisis?
2. Briefly describe the four adolescent identity status categories.
3. **Critical Thinking** *Supporting a Point of View* Do you agree that the main task of adolescence is the formation of identity? Why or why not?

SECTION 4
Challenges of Adolescence

A DAY IN THE LIFE

Adolescence is a rewarding time of life for many young people. Close friendships, such as the one between Hannah and Linda, develop. So do romantic relationships, such as that of Linda and Marc. While there are important choices to be made, the future seems exciting. Yet, for some, adolescence is a difficult time.

Some adolescents have problems that seem too large to handle. Nearly all teenagers know classmates who have school or family problems. Adolescents who are not accepted by their peers often experience loneliness and feelings of low self-esteem. Concerns about getting a good job, being able to support family members, and being accepted into college can be highly stressful.

Some young people, such as Annie, may develop an eating disorder. Others, such as Nick, may abuse alcohol or other drugs. Still others may turn to crime and acts of mischief. Tragically, a few take their own lives.

Opening Section 4

Motivator

Have students work together in small groups to create collages about being a teenager in today's society. Students may use pictures and articles from magazines and newspapers as well as photographs and other items. Encourage students to portray both positive and negative aspects. Display the finished posters in the classroom, and allow students time to examine them. Have students discuss the posters. What do the posters say about the challenges of being a teenager in today's society?

Teaching Section 4

For Further Research

Have interested students conduct further research on eating disorders. Possibilities for research include the warning signs of eating disorders, methods of therapy used, and available support groups and hot lines for people experiencing eating disorders. Have students present their findings to the class in the form of oral reports. Students may wish to prepare charts and graphs to accompany their reports.

Eating Disorders

The adolescent growth spurt makes it especially important that teenagers receive adequate nutrition. The average girl needs about 2,200 calories a day, and the average boy needs about 3,000 (Ekvall, 1993). Adolescents also need sufficient protein, carbohydrates, fiber, vitamins, and minerals in their diet. Teens who primarily eat foods such as hamburgers, pizza, potato chips, and candy may not be getting the nutrients their growing bodies need.

Adolescents who develop eating disorders get neither the calories nor the nutrients their bodies need. Some, such as Annie, literally starve themselves. Eating disorders affect many teenagers and young adults, especially females. More attention has been focused on eating disorders in recent years. The two main types of eating disorders are anorexia nervosa and bulimia nervosa.

Anorexia Nervosa   In the United States the typical person with anorexia or bulimia is a young white woman of higher socioeconomic status. **Anorexia nervosa** is a life-threatening disorder characterized by self-starvation and a distorted body image. Adolescents with anorexia usually weigh less than 85 percent of what would be considered a healthy weight. By and large, eating disorders afflict women during adolescence and young adulthood (Heatherton et al., 1997; Winzelberg et al., 2000). Women with anorexia greatly outnumber men with the disorder.

In the typical pattern, an adolescent girl notices some weight gain and decides that it must come off. But even after she loses the "excess" weight, dieting—and, often, exercise—continue at a fever pitch. They persist even after she reaches an average weight, even after family members and others have told her that she is losing too much. Girls with anorexia usually deny that they are wasting away. Their body image is distorted (Williamson et al., 1993; Winzelberg et al., 2000). They focus on remaining pockets of fat—which may be nonexistent—while others see them as "skin and bones."

Many girls with anorexia become obsessed with food. They engross themselves in cookbooks, take on the family shopping chores, and prepare elaborate dinners—for others.

Women with anorexia may lose 25 percent or more of their body weight in a year. Their overall health declines. A British study found that for many women, anorexia is a prolonged problem. Of women

contacted 21 years after being hospitalized for the problem, only half had fully recovered (Zipfel et al., 2000). About 4 to 5 percent of women with anorexia die from causes related to the problem, such as weakness or imbalances in body chemistry.

TRUTH OR fiction REVISITED   It is true that excessive dieting may be a sign that a person has an eating disorder. Anorexia nervosa is an eating disorder characterized by self-starvation and a distorted body image. It can be life-threatening.

Bulimia Nervosa   **Bulimia nervosa** is characterized by recurrent cycles of binge eating followed by dramatic measures to eliminate food, such as vomiting. Binge eating frequently follows a pattern of severe dieting (Lowe et al., 1996). As with anorexia, the great majority of people with bulimia are female. In addition to vomiting, girls may seek to compensate for what they have eaten by fasting, strict dieting, and vigorous exercise. Girls with bulimia tend to be perfectionists about their body shape and weight (Joiner et al., 1997).

Origins of Anorexia Nervosa and Bulimia Nervosa   To understand anorexia and bulimia, let us return to the fact that so many more women than men develop these problems. Theorists account for the gender gap in different ways. Some psychodynamic theorists suggest that anorexia represents a woman's effort to return to a stage before puberty. Anorexia allows her to avoid growing up, separating from her family, and taking on adult responsibilities.

But the cultural aspects of eating disorders seem to be more important. Young people with eating disorders are often attempting to conform to an ideal body shape. Popular fashion models represent that ideal: they are 9 percent taller and 16 percent slimmer than the average woman (Williams, 1992). For most women, that 16 percent is at least 16 pounds. The feminine ideal has been becoming slimmer and slimmer. For example, winners of the Miss America contest have been getting thinner over the years. Since the beginning of the pageant in 1922, the annual winner of the contest has become taller but is 12 pounds lighter in weight. In the late 1920s, her height-to-weight ratio was what the World Health Organization (WHO) considers to be "normal" today (Rubinstein & Caballero, 2000). But in recent years, Miss America

Meeting Individual Needs: Learners with Limited English Proficiency

As LEP students discuss the issue of substance abuse, it is important to clarify terms and concepts. Explain to students that many drugs have legitimate medicinal uses. Distinguish medicinal drug use from substance abuse. Substance abuse involves using illegal drugs, using drugs for pleasure, or self-medicating without professional guidance. Point out the importance of following professional and parental advice when using drugs for medicinal purposes.

Demonstration

Invite a speaker from a local drug- and alcohol-abuse prevention program to make a presentation to the class. Rather than have the speaker give the usual program about the dangers of drugs and alcohol, ask him or her to explain the methods used to reach teenagers, the programs that seem to be most effective, and why these programs work. Have students prepare questions for the speaker ahead of time.

What's New in Psychology?

According to a study by Mary Ann Marrazzi, a combination of medication and psychotherapy can help anorexics and bulimics recover. The researcher used the drug naltrexone to reduce the bulimics' urge to binge and to help anorexics stop losing weight. One theory behind the effectiveness of the medication is that some people may become addicted to the "high" produced by brain chemicals called opioids, which are released during self-starvation. Naltrexone helps break the addiction by blocking the brain's opioid receptors.

Marrazzi, M. A. (1995). "Naltrexone use in treatment of anorexia nervosa and bulimia nervosa." *International Clinical Psychopharmacology, 10.* 163–172.

For Your Information

Addictions and eating disorders may be linked to genetics, but environment also plays an important role. Not everyone who has a genetic inclination will develop an addiction, and not everyone who has an addiction problem is genetically predisposed.

Anorexia nervosa and bulimia nervosa are much more common in adolescent girls than in boys, but boys can suffer from these disorders as well. Wrestlers are more likely to develop eating disorders than boys in general because their sport demands that they stay in a certain weight class during wrestling season.

has become "undernourished" according to the WHO's standards. As the feminine cultural ideal grows thinner, women with average or heavier-than-average figures feel more and more pressure to slim down (Winzelberg et al., 2000).

Many men with eating disorders are involved in sports or jobs that require them to retain a certain weight, such as wrestling, dancing, and modeling (Goode, 2000). Men are more likely than women to control their weight through intense exercise. Like women, men are under social pressure to conform to an ideal body image—one that builds their upper bodies and trims their abdomens (Goode, 2000).

Families also play a role in eating disorders. Parents of adolescent girls with eating disorders are relatively more likely to have problems with eating and dieting themselves, to think that their daughters should lose weight, and to consider their daughters to be unattractive (Baker et al., 2000; Pike & Rodin, 1991). Some researchers speculate that adolescents may develop eating disorders as a way of coping with feelings of loneliness and alienation they experience in the home.

Some cases of anorexia nervosa may even reflect exaggerated efforts to remain healthy by avoiding intake of fat and cholesterol, which are widely publicized as risk factors for heart problems. For example, a 15-year-old boy developed anorexia nervosa after his grandfather—a heavy man who enjoyed steak and deep-fried vegetables—died from a heart attack while he and the boy were playing checkers (Markel, 2000).

Anorexia nervosa and bulimia nervosa both tend to run in families (Strober et al., 2000). Researchers have found evidence pointing to genetic factors involving perfectionism as increasing the risk of these disorders (Kaye et al., 2000). Even so, they believe there is a role for cultural influences (Wade et al., 2000). Perhaps genetic factors contribute to a perfectionistic personality and then cultural and family influences direct the perfectionism toward concern about body shape (Baker et al., 2000).

Treatment Whatever the causes, eating disorders are a severe health problem, and people who have them require professional assistance to overcome them. Often a school psychologist or counselor can suggest possible courses of action.

Sometimes health professionals will give students with eating disorders a choice—either to enter a treatment program (where their caloric intake is closely monitored) or to remain in school as long as they stop losing weight and receive counseling. They may have to see a psychologist on a regular basis and have their weight checked weekly. Treatment for eating disorders is often a long and difficult process. Many issues are often involved, including some that have nothing to do with food.

Substance Abuse

Substance abuse usually begins with experimentation in adolescence (Chassin et al., 2000). Why do adolescents experiment with drugs? Reasons include curiosity, response to peer pressure, parental abuse, rebelliousness, escape from boredom or pressure, and looking for excitement or pleasure (Finn et al., 2000; Wills et al., 2000).

A government survey of more than 15,000 teenagers across the United States found that use of drugs and cigarettes increased over the 1990s, despite public education campaigns about the risks (Centers for Disease Control, 2000). Cigarette smoking was up slightly, with 35 percent of teenagers reporting lighting up in the previous month. The number of teens who reported smoking marijuana in the previous month nearly doubled from about 15 percent in 1991 to 27 percent in 1999. Self-reported cocaine use also doubled in the same period, from about 2 percent to 4 percent. Alcohol is used at least occasionally by the majority of high school and college students (Johnston et al., 2000). Drinking in early adolescence is a risk factor for alcohol abuse later in life (DeWit et al., 2000).

Cooperative Learning

Organize students into groups of four to develop prevention programs addressing one of the challenges of adolescence. Two students should gather information about existing prevention programs, each focusing on either the program's structure or its effectiveness. The other two students should research the shortcomings of various programs and brainstorm approaches that avoid these pitfalls. Direct the two pairs to exchange information and work together to outline a proposed prevention program. Have the class critique the groups' proposals.

Evaluating Information

Have students locate and bring to class magazine articles that give advice to parents on how to handle a problem of adolescence, such as drinking, anorexia, or delinquency. Ask students to summarize the articles and evaluate them in terms of clarity, substance, and effectiveness. Have volunteers read their summaries to the class. Is the advice given to parents on how to handle the problem realistic? Is the article's portrayal of teenagers accurate? How closely does the article parallel the information given in the textbook?

Adolescents often try alcohol and other substances because their peers recommend them or their parents use them. Adolescents also frequently turn to alcohol and other substances as a way of coping with stress (Armeli et al., 2000). In the short term, use of a substance may win the approval of peers or have a positive effect on one's mood. It may also reduce unpleasant sensations such as anxiety and tension (Bonin et al., 2000; Swendsen et al., 2000). But binge drinking—that is, having five or more drinks in a row—and long-term drinking are connected to aggressive behavior, poor grades, and accidents (Vik et al., 2000; Wilgoren, 2000). Alcohol is involved in about half of the fatal automobile accidents in the United States.

Some 430,000 Americans die from smoking-related diseases each year, including lung cancer, emphysema, and heart attacks (American Lung Association, 2000). Cocaine narrows blood vessels, thickens the blood, and quickens the heart rate. These events have caused the sudden deaths of a number of athletes who used cocaine to try to boost their performance and self-confidence (Moliterno et al., 1994). Marijuana contains more tars than cigarette smoke—a factor in lung cancer. Marijuana also elevates one's heart rate and blood pressure. Marijuana can also make it more difficult to retain information—that is, it can make it more difficult to learn both in and out of school (Sullivan, 2000). All in all, these substances cause many more problems than they solve.

Regular use of alcohol and some other substances—particularly nicotine, cocaine, barbiturates, and heroin—can cause teenagers, such as Linda's and Janet's friend Nick, to become addicted to them. Addicts experience intense cravings for the substances when their effects have worn off. They usually have to take more and more of the substance to achieve the same effects they once obtained with a small amount. The substance may eventually take control of the person's life.

Treatment Withdrawing from alcohol and other drugs can be a physically and psychologically painful experience for people of any age. After someone such as Nick is admitted to a hospital or a treatment center, the first step in his or her treatment is detoxification—the removal of the toxic, or poisonous, substance from the body. During this

Peer counseling is a valuable way of preventing substance abuse in teenagers. Scare tactics by adults can often backfire by making students more curious. Teenagers may be more willing to believe the warnings of other students who have actually used illegal substances.

process, the person is gradually and carefully taken off the drug. Both medical treatment and emotional support are very important to help the individual through the process.

Another important aspect of the treatment of adolescents with substance abuse problems is psychological in nature. Therapists can help young people understand the meaning of their drug use. For example, they can learn to recognize that they might be using drugs or alcohol to avoid facing the difficult issues in their lives: How are they doing in school? How are their relationships with their family? How do they feel about themselves? Therapy can help teenagers recognize that low self-esteem may be at the root of their problems.

Drug Prevention Most school drug-prevention programs are aimed at stopping the use of so-called gateway drugs. These drugs include alcohol, cigarettes, and marijuana. They are called gateway drugs because they are typically tried first—before teenagers "open the gate" to more powerful drugs, such as heroin and cocaine.

Research on the effectiveness of prevention programs shows mixed results. Attempts to scare students by warning them about the dangerous consequences of using drugs can backfire, possibly because scare tactics can arouse their curiosity and disbelief (Kazdin, 1993). Peer counseling is often effective because students are generally more willing to believe other students who have actually

Using Visuals

Direct students' attention to the photograph on page 267 showing teen peer counseling. Tell students that DARE (Drug Abuse Resistance Education) is a program that uses peer counselors to teach young people to avoid substance abuse. DARE also uses teen counselors to educate children in elementary schools. This program—and others like it—offers teenagers an important way to make a positive contribution to the fight against substance abuse.

Class Discussion

Ask students to consider how alcohol is presented in the media and through advertising. *(Some may say that it is shown as fun and glamorous, with the dangers glossed over.)* Have them discuss which of the psychological concepts they have learned might be utilized in a media and advertising campaign against alcohol abuse. *(peer pressure, conditioning)*

Guided Practice

Direct students' attention to the bulleted list of factors (on page 268) that contribute to the likelihood of teenage pregnancy. Ask for a student volunteer to read the list aloud. For each item in the list, have students discuss ways in which young people might go about eliminating or alleviating the situation. For example, students might suggest ways to improve communication with parents, ways to obtain help for emotional problems, or ways to deal with peer pressure. Then have students discuss the consequences of teenage pregnancy.

Independent Practice

Have students use what they learned in the Guided Practice activity to write a letter to the editor of their local newspaper. In their letters, students should suggest what individuals, groups, and government officials can do to reduce the number of teenage pregnancies in their state or community. Students should also explain how teenage pregnancies affect individuals and society. Have volunteers read their letters aloud to the class. Some students may wish to submit their letters to the editor of the school or local newspaper.

In the United States, many babies are born to teenage mothers every year. Rearing a child is always challenging, even without the additional burdens teen parents usually face, such as a lack of money, education, and emotional maturity.

used the substances they are being warned against (Hawkins et al., 1992; Perry, 1991).

Sexuality

Many adolescents struggle with issues of how and when to express their sexual feelings. But they receive mixed messages. Their bodies may be giving them a powerful "go-ahead" signal at the same time that their parents and other adults are advising them of the dangers of early sexual relationships and encouraging them to practice abstinence. Yet other messages may come from media images—models in advertisements, television shows that revolve around sex, and popular songs with lyrics that contain powerful sexual messages. Many teenagers may assume that sexual activity is more widespread among their peers than it actually is. The truth is, however, that many adolescents are not sexually active.

People today often start dating and "going steady" at a younger age than people of earlier times. Adolescents who begin dating early are more likely to engage in sexual relations during high school (Brooks-Gunn & Furstenberg, 1989; Miller et al., 1986). About 10 percent of American girls between the ages of 15 and 19 become pregnant each year. This amounts to more than 900,000 pregnancies a year.

Teenage pregnancies can be devastating for adolescent mothers, their children, and society at large. Life for many teenage mothers is an uphill struggle. Teenage mothers are more likely to live in poverty and lack hope for their futures than teenagers of the same age who do not have children (Desmond, 1994; Grogger & Bronars, 1993). Half of all adolescent mothers quit school and go on welfare (Kantrowitz, 1990). Few receive financial or emotional help from the fathers of their children. The fathers—sometimes also adolescents—often cannot support themselves, much less a family. Most adolescents share the view that teenage parenthood is very undesirable (Moore & Stief, 1992).

Several factors contribute to the likelihood of teenage pregnancy (Rathus, 2003). These include the following:

- problematic relationships with parents or rebellion against parents
- emotional problems, such as feelings of emptiness or loneliness
- problems in school or lack of educational or vocational goals
- societal loosening of traditional prohibitions against adolescent sexuality and the portrayal of sexual themes in the media
- pressure from peers who are engaging in sexual activity
- misunderstanding or lack of knowledge about reproduction

Some adolescent girls intentionally become pregnant to try to strengthen relationships with their boyfriends or to fill an emotional void by having a child. However, the relationships with the fathers usually come to an end. Premature motherhood tends to make emotional problems worse, not better. It also has serious implications for the offspring. Teen mothers are more likely to give birth to premature babies and to babies who are below average in weight (Osofsky et al. 1988).

Juvenile Delinquency

The term **juvenile delinquency** refers to many illegal activities committed by children or adolescents. The most extreme acts of delinquency include

Closing Section 4

Applying Information

Ask students to imagine that they are parents of a teenager. Using what they have learned in this section, how would they handle their teenager who is using drugs? is skipping school? has an eating disorder?

Reviewing Section 4

Have students complete the Section Review questions on page 269.

Extension

Have students interview parents, grandparents, or other adults about what life was like for teenagers of earlier generations. Tell students to tape-record (with permission) the interviews or to take careful notes. Have students write summaries of their interviews, and ask volunteers to read their summaries aloud. Then have students consider whether it is more difficult to be a teenager today than it was in earlier times. Why or why not?

robbery, rape, and homicide, which are considered criminal acts regardless of the age of the offender. Less serious offenses, known as **status offenses**, are illegal only when they are committed by minors. Status offenses include truancy (unexcused absence from school), drinking, smoking, and running away from home.

Some people assume that teenagers from poor neighborhoods are more likely to break the law than other teens. However, this is not true. Research shows that low income is not a factor (Hinshaw, 1992; Zigler et al., 1992). Another common belief is that children whose mothers work outside the home are more likely to engage in delinquent behavior. Once again, research shows that this is not the case (Silverstein, 1991).

Many delinquent acts do not lead to arrest and prosecution but still have other serious consequences for the delinquent teenager. Status offenses tend to be handled by school officials, social workers, parents, and other such authorities. When adolescents *are* arrested and prosecuted, they are often referred to mental-health agencies and are not formally labeled as delinquents. Nonetheless, between 25 percent and 30 percent of the serious crimes in the United States are committed by teenagers under the age of 18.

Factors that contribute to juvenile delinquency are similar to those that contribute to substance abuse. They include the following:

- low self-esteem and feelings of alienation (Krueger et al., 1993)
- lack of affection, lax and ineffective discipline, and use of severe physical punishment in the home (Kopera-Frye et al., 1993)
- behavior problems that began at an early age (Brook et al., 1993)
- poor grades and lack of educational or vocational goals (Zigler et al., 1992)
- pressure from peers who engage in delinquent behavior (Etaugh & Rathus, 1995)
- having a parent or sibling who has been convicted of criminal behavior (Butterfield, 1992)

Avoiding Problems

Most adolescents who have clear educational and vocational goals manage to steer clear of problems. Adolescents who fear the onset of a particular problem are usually better off if they can talk things over with a trusted adult—a parent or another relative, a teacher, or a guidance counselor.

The most successful programs for dealing with juvenile delinquency try to address potential problems early. Many counselors focus their efforts on reducing school violence.

Unfortunately, many troubled adolescents do not get into programs developed to deal with juvenile delinquency until after the delinquent behavior pattern has become well established. At that late date, it is more difficult to help them. The most successful delinquency-prevention programs are those that address the potential problems early. These programs provide classes and support groups for parents, make home visits to families, and provide other effective services. And they encourage parents to become involved in the activities of their children both in and out of school.

Research shows that children who participate in prevention programs do better in school and are more likely to graduate from high school, go to college, and work at a steady job. They also seem less inclined to commit crimes (Zigler et al., 1992).

SECTION 4 REVIEW
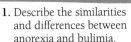 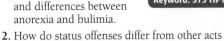
Homework Practice Online
Keyword: SY3 HP11

1. Describe the similarities and differences between anorexia and bulimia.
2. How do status offenses differ from other acts of delinquency?
3. List three factors that contribute to juvenile delinquency.
4. **Critical Thinking** *Categorizing* List several types of challenges faced by adolescents today.

Section 4 Review: Answers

1. Anorexia and bulimia are both eating disorders that primarily afflict adolescent girls. Anorexia is self-starvation brought on by excessive dieting; bulimia involves cycles of eating binges followed by purging.

2. Status offenses differ from other acts of delinquency because they are only illegal when committed by a minor.

3. Factors that contribute to juvenile delinquency include early behavior problems, low self-esteem, poor grades, parental neglect, abuse at home, and peer pressure.

4. Challenges include dealing with eating disorders, substance abuse, and juvenile delinquency.

Chapter 11 Review: Answers

Writing a Summary

See the section subtitles for the main topics in the chapter.

Identifying People and Ideas

1. the developmental changes that lead to the ability to reproduce
2. characteristics that are directly involved in reproduction
3. the first menstruation

Chapter 11 REVIEW AND ASSESSMENT RESOURCES

Technology
▶ Chapter 11 Test Generator (on the One-Stop Planner)
▶ HRW Go site

Reinforcement, Review, and Assessment
▶ Chapter 11 Review, pp. 270–271
▶ Chapter Review and Activities with Answer Key
▶ Alternative Assessment Handbook
▶ Portfolio Assessment Handbook
▶ Chapter 11 Test (Form A or B)

PSYCHOLOGY PROJECTS

Linking to Community Invite a selection of professionals who deal with adolescent problems to visit your class. Possible visitors might include a physician or a nurse, a psychotherapist, a drug or eating-disorder counselor, and a social worker. Invite each visitor to tell the class about his or her work with adolescents. Students may want to ask

---

4. peer groups who spend a great deal of time together

5. a turning point in a person's development when he or she makes decisions or changes about life roles

6. Shutting out other possibilities to avoid an identity crisis.

7. a category in which adolescents have coped with crises and have explored options

8. a life-threatening disorder characterized by self-starvation and a distorted body image

9. illegal activities committed by children or adolescents

10. less serious offenses that are illegal only when committed by minors

Understanding Main Ideas

1. Some adolescents feel awkward because their body parts grow at different rates and their peers may be in a different growth stage.

2. They are likely to follow peers in dress, hairstyles, and speech.

3. It means to have a solid sense of who you are and what you value.

4. A person might take time out from making a commitment to explore alternatives.

5. Detoxification involves removing the chemicals from the body, usually under the care of health-care personnel who provide medical and emotional support.

Thinking Critically

1. Most adolescents do not need to support their families; there are laws against child labor; there are mandatory education laws.

Chapter 11 REVIEW

Writing a Summary

Using standard grammar, spelling, sentence structure, and punctuation, summarize the information in this chapter. Consider:
• physical and psychological changes that occur during adolescence, and the role parents and peers play in a teen's life
• how teens form identity, and what challenges they face today

Identifying People and Ideas

Identify the following terms or people and use them in appropriate sentences.

1. puberty
2. primary sex characteristics
3. menarche
4. cliques
5. identity crisis
6. identity foreclosure
7. identity achievement
8. anorexia nervosa
9. juvenile delinquency
10. status offenses

Understanding Main Ideas

SECTION 1 (pp. 252–254)
1. Why do some adolescents feel awkward during the adolescent growth spurt?

SECTION 2 (pp. 256–259)
2. How is the behavior of adolescents influenced by fads and peers?

SECTION 3 (pp. 260–264)
3. What does it mean to find one's identity?
4. How is the concept of moratorium related to finding an identity?

SECTION 4 (pp. 264–269)
5. Describe the detoxification process in the treatment of substance abuse.

Thinking Critically

1. **Drawing Inferences and Conclusions** Why do you think adolescence has become prolonged in Western societies?

---

2. **Categorizing** List several types of peer relationships that develop during adolescence. What are some of the advantages and disadvantages of these types of relationships?

3. **Summarizing** What factors might help a teenager in his or her search for identity?

4. **Contrasting** Other than physical changes, how does adolescence differ for boys and girls?

5. **Evaluating** Why might peer counseling be an effective way of helping teenagers deal with the challenges of adolescence?

Writing About Psychology

1. **Evaluating** Read a short story or novel that features an adolescent as its main character. (Ask your school librarian or English teacher for suggestions on appropriate books.) As you read, try to connect the character to information you learned in this chapter about adolescent development and the challenges of adolescence. For example, is the character having an identity crisis? Is the character dealing with negative peer pressure? Write a profile of the character exploring these issues.

2. **Analyzing Information** Imagine that you are the writer of a newspaper column in which you answer letters from teens seeking advice. Think of a problem or concern that a teen might have. Compose a letter to "Dear (your name)" briefly describing the background of the problem. Then write a response that suggests a way to deal with the situation. Read your letter and response to the class. Use the graphic organizer below to help you write your letter and response.

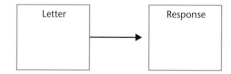

questions such as the following:

- What are the most common problems you see in your work?

- What approach(es) do you find most effective in helping adolescents who are struggling with problems?

- How are young people involved in developing their own treatment or support programs? How are parents involved? How can teens find out about such programs?

Cooperative Learning

Tell students that it is important that teenagers be able to communicate successfully with others to navigate the developmental changes of adolescence. One way to share information is through a teen-generated publication. Groups of four should begin by brainstorming a focus for the publication. Each group should include an editor, two writers, and a designer. Final versions should be completed on a computer, if possible, or with typed text and hand-drawn illustrations. When the publications are complete, post them in the classroom.

Building Social Studies Skills

Interpreting Charts

Study the chart below. Then use the information in the chart to help you answer the questions that follow.

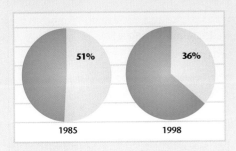

Percent of Adolescents Who Have Smoked Cigarettes

51% — 1985
36% — 1998

Source: U.S. Bureau of the Census, 2000

1. Which of the following statements can be made using information from the chart above?

   a. Cigarette smoking among teenagers increased consistently between 1985 and 1998.

   b. Cigarette smoking among teenagers declined from 1985 to 1998.

   c. Very few American adolescents smoke cigarettes.

   d. Adolescent use of cigarettes increased slightly between 1985 and 1990.

2. How might a psychologist use this information to assist in creating an effective antismoking program?

Analyzing Primary Sources

Read the following excerpt, in which several psychologists explain adolescence as a stage of life. Then answer the questions that follow.

"How do we best characterize adolescence? Until recently, psychologists regarded it primarily in terms of age-related stress and crisis. Traditional psychoanalytic theory assumed that crisis is inevitable when adolescents, made particularly vulnerable to stressors by the biological changes of puberty, strive to develop self-identity and ego strength needed to deal with . . . adult roles. . . . Most researchers today argue that difficulties or problems presenting themselves during adolescence should not be considered solely in terms of their disruptive nature and their contribution to crisis and storm, but also with regard to the coping responses they evoke in the young people concerned. The focus is on coping rather than crisis."

3. Which of the following statements best reflects the authors' viewpoint?

   a. Adolescence is a time of crisis.

   b. Adolescents cannot cope with crises in their lives without professional help.

   c. The manner in which psychologists understood adolescence in the past was completely wrong.

   d. Psychologists are changing the way in which they view adolescence.

4. In view of the authors' argument, what skills would be most valuable to a person during adolescence?

PSYCHOLOGY PROJECTS

Cooperative Learning

Research in Psychology Working in small groups, survey the contents of several recent teen magazines. Identify the types of articles, features, and advertisements that appear most frequently. Discuss the overall message these magazines send to teenagers. Also consider whether the material appearing in the magazines is representative of the issues students at your high school face. Have one person in your group report your findings to the class.

internet connect

Internet Activity: go.hrw.com
KEYWORD: SY3 PS11

Choose an activity on adolescence to:
- write a report describing rites of passage.
- make a 3D model illustrating identity formation.
- create a pamphlet on challenges faced by adolescents.

go.hrw.com

---

2. Friendships, cliques, crowds, and dating relationships develop during adolescence. Advantages include security and emotional support; disadvantages include peer pressure and exclusivity.

3. Formal-operational thinking, experimenting with various roles, decision-making practice, feedback from others, and a confidant can all help teenagers find their identities.

4. Girls have more intimate friendships than do boys, who spend more time in larger, less intimate groups; girls are more susceptible to eating disorders, while boys are more likely to use drugs and engage in delinquent behavior.

5. Teenagers may feel more comfortable talking with their peers than with adults, assuming that peers have faced similar situations.

Writing About Psychology

1. Students may profile a character growing up as a member of an ethnic group, having romantic problems, or coping with parents' divorce.

2. Letters will vary but should reflect a reasoned consideration of a problem.

Building Social Studies Skills

1. b

2. Students' answers will vary but might note that psychologists could try to determine why cigarette use has declined, and use those methods to help further reduce cigarette smoking.

3. d

4. Adolescents would benefit from skills that teach young people to cope with crises.

271

Adulthood

CHAPTER RESOURCE MANAGER

Objectives	Pacing Guide		Reproducible and Review Resources

SECTION 1:
Young Adulthood
(pp. 274–280)

List the characteristics and issues of young adulthood.

Regular 1 day	**Block Scheduling** .5 day

Block Scheduling Handbook with Team Teaching Strategies, Chapter 12

E Research Projects and Activities for Teaching Psychology

REV Section 1 Review, p. 280

SECTION 2:
Middle Adulthood
(pp. 280–284)

Describe the changes that occur and issues that are faced in middle adulthood.

Regular 1 day	**Block Scheduling** .5 day

Block Scheduling Handbook with Team Teaching Strategies, Chapter 12

PS Readings and Case Studies, Chapter 12

E Creating a Psychology Fair, Handout 8, Activity 6

REV Section 2 Review, p. 284

SECTION 3:
Late Adulthood
(pp. 284–291)

Explain how people's lives change in late adulthood.

Regular 1 day	**Block Scheduling** .5 day

Block Scheduling Handbook with Team Teaching Strategies, Chapter 12

SM Mastering Critical Thinking Skills 12

REV Section 3 Review, p. 291

SECTION 4:
Death and Dying
(pp. 291–293)

Explain the attitudes and issues related to death and dying.

Regular 1 day	**Block Scheduling** .5 day

Block Scheduling Handbook with Team Teaching Strategies, Chapter 12

RS Essay and Research Themes for Advanced Placement Students, Theme 10

REV Section 4 Review, p. 293

Chapter Resource Key

PS	Primary Sources	**A**	Assessment	Video	
RS	Reading Support	**REV**	Review	Internet	
E	Enrichment		Transparencies	Holt Presentation Maker Using Microsoft® PowerPoint®	
SM	Skills Mastery		CD-ROM		

 One-Stop Planner CD–ROM

See the *One-Stop Planner* for a complete list of additional resources for students and teachers.

 **One-Stop** Planner CD–ROM

It's easy to plan lessons, select resources, and print out materials for your students when you use the *One-Stop Planner CD-ROM with Test Generator.*

Technology Resources

 One-Stop Planner, Lesson 12.1
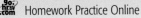 Homework Practice Online
 HRW Go Site

 One-Stop Planner, Lesson 12.2
 Homework Practice Online
 Teaching Transparencies 28: Developmental Tasks of Young Adulthood
 HRW Go Site

 One-Stop Planner, Lesson 12.3
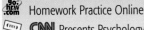 Homework Practice Online
CNN Presents Psychology: Keeping Young
 HRW Go Site

 One-Stop Planner, Lesson 12.4
 Homework Practice Online

Chapter Review and Assessment

 HRW Go site
REV Chapter 12 Review, pp. 294–295
REV Chapter Review Activities with Answer Key

A Chapter 12 Test (Form A or B)
A Portfolio Assessment Handbook
A Alternative Assessment Handbook

Chapter 12 Test Generator (on the One-Stop Planner)
Global Skill Builder CD-ROM

 **internet** connect

HRW ONLINE RESOURCES

GO TO: go.hrw.com
Then type in a keyword.

TEACHER HOME PAGE
  KEYWORD: SY3 Teacher

CHAPTER INTERNET ACTIVITIES
  KEYWORD: SY3 PS12
  Choose an activity on adulthood to:
  • create a product or advertisement applying various perspectives of motivation to target young adults.
  • write a newspaper article on the challenges of middle adulthood.
  • conduct a poll or interview regarding the joys and challenges of late adulthood.

CHAPTER ENRICHMENT LINKS
  KEYWORD: SY3 CH12

ONLINE ASSESSMENT
  Homework Practice
  KEYWORD: SY3 HP12

  Standardized Test Prep
  KEYWORD: SY3 STP12

  Rubrics
  KEYWORD: SS Rubrics

CONTENT UPDATES
  KEYWORD: SS Content Updates

HOLT PRESENTATION MAKER
  KEYWORD: SY3 PPT12

ONLINE READING SUPPORT
  KEYWORD: SS Strategies

CURRENT EVENTS
  KEYWORD: S3 Current Events

Additional Resources

PRINT RESOURCES FOR TEACHERS

Levinson, D. (1978). *The seasons of a man's life.* New York: Knopf.

Levinson, D. (1996). *The seasons of a woman's life.* New York: Knopf.

Maddox, G. (Ed.). (1987). *The encyclopedia of aging.* New York: Springer.

PRINT RESOURCES FOR STUDENTS

Doress-Worters, P. B., & Siegal, D. L. (1987). *The new ourselves, growing older.* New York: Touchstone.

Engel, M. L. (1994). *Divorce help sourcebook.* Detroit: Visible Ink Press.

Grollman, E. A. (1990). *Talking about death.* Boston: Beacon.

MULTIMEDIA RESOURCES

Aging well (VHS). Films for the Humanities & Sciences, P.O. Box 2053, Princeton, NJ 08543-2053.

Children of divorce (VHS). Films for the Humanities & Sciences, P.O. Box 2053, Princeton, NJ 08543-2053.

When parents grow old (VHS). Learning Corporation of America, 1350 Avenue of the Americas, New York, NY 10019.

271b

ADULTHOOD

Prior to assigning the reading of Chapter 12, write the following statement on the chalkboard: *Development is a process that continues throughout one's lifetime.* Next write the following headings on the chalkboard: *Young Adulthood (ages 20 to 40), Middle Adulthood (ages 40 to 65), and Late Adulthood (ages 65 and over).* Under each heading, make a column for males and a column for females. Ask students to suggest 10 or so new experiences or tasks that are common to each age category. Some experiences or tasks will apply to males, others will apply to females, and many will apply to both. Write students' responses under the appropriate headings. Use the lists as the basis for a class discussion about development as a process that continues throughout one's lifetime.

Sections

1 Young Adulthood

2 Middle Adulthood

3 Late Adulthood

4 Death and Dying

Each of the four questions identified on page 272 corresponds to one of these sections.

Chapter 12 ADULTHOOD

Read to Discover

1 What are the characteristics and issues of young adulthood?

2 What are the changes that occur and the issues that are faced in middle adulthood?

3 How do people's lives change in late adulthood?

4 What are the attitudes and issues related to death and dying?

272

Each chapter begins with a vignette, called "A Day in the Life," that relates the information discussed in the chapter to the everyday events in the lives of a group of fictional high school students. The text of the chapter occasionally refers back to the vignette to demonstrate the application of the concept being discussed. An icon marked "A Day in the Life" is placed next to these references.

Copy the following graphic organizer onto the chalkboard, omitting the italicized text. Fill in the spaces as you introduce the topic of adulthood.

Young Adulthood		
Reassessment	*Settling Down*	*Marriage and Intimate Relationships*

A DAY IN THE LIFE

February 22

Marc and Linda had decided to volunteer at the local residential community for senior citizens. They had just finished for the day and were comparing experiences while they waited for the bus.

"So what did you do today?" asked Marc.

"I visited with the patients in the nursing home," said Linda. "At first it was upsetting because it reminded me of visiting my grandmother in the hospice before she died. I didn't think I'd ever get over missing her, but I guess I've adjusted."

"That must have been hard," Marc sympathized.

"I used to love spending time with my grandmother," Linda mused. "She would always think of fun things for us to do. Until she got sick, she was very energetic."

"She sounds like the people I met today," said Marc. "I was helping some of the people who live in their own apartments over by the recreation center. There was a man there in his late 70s who was doing yard work. He told me that he walks about five miles every day—he says that regular exercise keeps him

healthy. I hope I'm as fit as he is when I'm that age."

"My dad will be happy to hear about him," said Linda. "When Dad turned 40, he began worrying about aging. He started doing all these things he'd never done before, like exercising and taking classes. It's funny, but I really think he's actually happier now than he was when he was younger."

"That's fantastic," said Marc. "Turning 40 seems to make people really think about their lives."

"Yeah," answered Linda. "Janet said that when her parents hit their 40s, they finally realized how unhappy they were with each other."

"How's Janet been doing since her parents' divorce, by the way?" asked Marc.

"Well, it was really hard for her at first, but she's basically fine now. In fact, she told me she feels closer than ever to her mom."

Marc and Linda were both silent for a moment.

"Do you realize we'll be in our 20s soon?" asked Linda.

"I know. We'll be on our own then—we'll be independent," said Marc, obviously anticipating the arrival of that day.

⋯

Marc and Linda had just been confronted with what it means to be an adult, grow older, and eventually die. Development is a process that continues throughout one's lifetime. Many theorists believe that adult development, like childhood and adolescence, follows certain stages. Others believe that there is no "standard" life cycle with predictable life stages. Nowadays, people are living longer and, in some ways, are freer than ever to make their own life choices. The adult years are generally divided into three broad stages: young adulthood, middle adulthood, and late adulthood.

Key Terms

- patriarchy
- generativity
- midlife transition
- midlife crisis
- empty-nest syndrome
- menopause
- programmed theories
- cellular damage theories
- free radical
- cross-linking
- dementia
- senile dementia
- Alzheimer's disease
- ego integrity
- hospice
- euthanasia
- living wills
- bereaved

WHY PSYCHOLOGY MATTERS

People face many changes and issues as they age. Use **CNNfyi.com** or other current events sources to learn more about how psychologists study and classify the changes that occur during life.

CNNfyi.com

Using Key Terms

Ask students to find a definition for each of the key terms in the chapter, using either the Glossary or Chapter 12. Then have students use these definitions to prepare a set of riddles with the key terms as answers. For example, "I am a period of reassessment that comes during the midlife transition. What am I?" *(midlife crisis)* Tell students to write their riddles on one side of a sheet of paper and the answers on the other side. Have students exchange their completed sets of riddles, then answer them. You may wish to instruct students to keep their riddles for later review.

Journal Activity

After students have read the "A Day in the Life" vignette, ask them to write in their journals about what being independent means to them. What do they hope their lives will be like when they are in their 20s? What are their dreams? What are their fears?

Section Objective

▶ List the characteristics and issues of young adulthood.

This objective is assessed in the Section Review on page 280 and in the Chapter 12 Review.

Opening Section 1

Motivator

Point out to students that young adulthood—from about age 20 to about age 40—is the life stage they will shortly enter. Urge students to think about their expectations for these years. In a brief essay that may be either shared or kept private, have students describe what they think they will be like as young adults. They might list goals they hope to achieve, questions they want to find answers to, or ways they will contribute to their family and community. Ask student volunteers to share their thoughts in a class discussion.

Using Truth or Fiction

Each chapter opens with several "Truth or Fiction" statements that relate to the concepts discussed in the chapter. Ask students whether they think each statement is true or false. Answers to each item as well as explanations are provided at appropriate points within the text under the heading "Truth or Fiction Revisited."

Class Discussion

Briefly discuss the gender differences described in the text. Ask students what differences they perceive between the goals and priorities of young adult men and women. Do students' experiences support or contradict the studies cited in the text? Are these differences the result of heredity or environment? Have students provide examples to support their reasoning.

TRUTH OR fiction?

Read the following statements about psychology. Do you think they are true or false? You will learn whether each statement is true or false as you read the chapter.

- Many people in their 30s completely change the lives they created for themselves in their 20s.
- People in the United States have been marrying later than people did a few generations ago.
- Romantic love is a relatively new reason for marrying.
- Most parents feel a great sense of loss and loneliness when the youngest child leaves home.
- It is good for older people not to exercise.
- Everyone who lives long enough will eventually become senile.

SECTION 1

Young Adulthood

Young adulthood, also called early adulthood, covers a span of approximately 20 years—from about age 20 to about age 40. Most people reach their physical peak in their 20s. During their 20s and early 30s, they are faster, stronger, better coordinated, and have more endurance than they have ever had or will ever have again. Many people also are at the height of their cognitive powers during this period (Baltes, 1997).

Young adulthood is characterized by a desire to try new ways of doing things and by changing relationships with parents. In their late teens and early 20s, some people assume that they must live the way their parents do if they want to succeed in life. Some also assume that their parents will always be there to rescue them if their plans fail. As time passes, however, young adults learn to become independent and to take responsibility for themselves and the decisions they make.

Studies indicate that, in the United States, becoming independent from parental authority is a

A DAY IN THE LIFE

key goal of development for most young adult men (Guisinger & Blatt, 1994). Although Marc is still in high school, his remark anticipating independence indicates that he, too, shares this goal. Women are generally less

concerned with seeing themselves as separate, independent individuals. They tend to be more interested in creating relationships with others (Gilligan et al., 1990, 1991; Jordan et al., 1991). Of course, these are generalizations only; many women in their 20s become independent and focus on their development as individuals (Helson, 1993). The creation and maintenance of relationships are also important concerns for many men.

Reassessment

Adults in their 20s often believe they have chosen the course in life that is exactly right for them. As they reach their 30s, however, they often reevaluate the decisions they have made in an effort to determine whether their chosen course is really the one that is right for them. Levinson (1978, 1996) has labeled the period of the late 20s and early 30s the "age 30 transition." For many young adults, this is a time to reassess earlier choices. People often ask themselves, "Why am I doing this?" or "Where is my life going?" Sometimes they find that the life paths they chose in their 20s are no longer the paths they truly want to follow.

This period of reassessment may bring about major life changes. Some people change jobs or start new careers. Many single people feel that this is the time to find a mate. People who have been working in the home, perhaps raising children, may feel the urge to find a job outside the home. Couples who are without children may now think about starting a family (Sheehy, 1995).

TRUTH OR fiction ▪ REVISITED ▪

It is true that many people in their 30s completely change the lives they created for themselves in their 20s. During their late 20s and early 30s, many young adults undertake a major reassessment of their lives. Sometimes this reassessment leads to major life changes.

Women in particular may find themselves reassessing their lives in their 30s. Some women in their 30s begin to think about the biological changes that lie ahead. Many women become concerned about how many childbearing years they have left, especially if they have not already had children. Furthermore, during their early 30s, many women begin to feel that they have been controlled

Teaching Section 1

Guided Practice

Create on the chalkboard a three-column chart titled "Young Adulthood." Label the three columns *Reassessment, Settling Down,* and *Marriage and Intimate Relationships.* Have students supply information from the textbook about these areas of young adulthood while you write the information in the appropriate column. Then have students write a short paragraph summarizing the characteristics of young adulthood as a developmental stage in the life cycle.

Independent Practice

Ask students to assume the roles of persons in their middle thirties. Have them use information from the chart in the Guided Practice activity to write a letter to a friend they have not seen since graduation from high school. In their letters, students should tell the friend what they have been doing since high school and what their lives are like now. Have volunteers read their letters aloud to the class.

by others and that they have never had the chance to shape their own lives (Helson & Moane, 1987). Today, as in years past, it is still mostly women who take care of family and household chores. As a result, women in the workforce may feel overwhelmed by the double duties of caring for their families and maintaining jobs.

In addition, research suggests that some working women have mixed feelings about success on the job. Even though the great majority of women are in the workplace, some still feel they must sacrifice their family lives to advance their careers. Although working men also have less time to spend with their families, many people still consider it more acceptable for men to work long hours than for women to do the same (Levinson, 1996).

Settling Down

After the upheaval of the early 30s, the mid- to late 30s are often characterized by settling down or "planting roots" (Levinson, 1978). People in their 30s may increase the financial and emotional investments they make in their lives. Many have been employed long enough to gain promotions and pay raises. They often become more focused on advancing their careers and gaining stability in their personal lives.

Figure 12.1 on page 276 lists some of the developmental tasks of young adulthood. Not every individual necessarily experiences all of these tasks. Nor does every young adult follow them in a particular order. For example, many people today choose to remain single or to postpone or forgo having and rearing children.

Marriage and Intimate Relationships

An important part of adolescence and young adulthood is the development of an identity—who you are and what you stand for (your values). Identity brings the personal stability that is needed to form lasting relationships. (See Chapter 11.) According to Erik Erikson (1963), one of the key tasks of young adulthood is the forming of relationships.

Relationships can be difficult to sustain when one or both of the people involved lack personal stability, which may be one reason why teenage marriages suffer a higher divorce rate than adult marriages. However, young adults who have developed a firm sense of identity during adolescence may be ready to join their lives with those of other

It is not unusual for women to feel torn between their obligations to their jobs and to their families. Many women still have the primary responsibility for taking care of the family and home in addition to working full-time.

people through friendships and marriage. Erikson believed that people who do not develop intimate relationships may risk falling into a pattern of isolation and loneliness. An intimate relationship is not necessarily a physical relationship. Rather, it is a trusting, close friendship with another person in which one can be honest without fear of rejection.

In the United States, 75 percent to 80 percent of people get married at least once (Marital Status, 1998). However, more people have been delaying marriage in recent decades to pursue educational and career goals. Therefore, the median age of marriage has risen in the past 30 years from about 23 to 27 for men and from about 21 to 25 for women (Marital Status, 1998).

TRUTH OR fiction ■ REVISITED ■

It is true that people in the United States have been marrying later than people did a few generations ago. Many people now wait until they have finished college or have their careers under way before they marry.

Journal Activity

Suggest that students write about their thoughts concerning marriage. What do they think is the likelihood that they will marry? What do they think is the ideal age to get married? What social, emotional, and intellectual needs do they expect marriage to fulfill?

Classifying Information

Have students begin a chart to record and analyze Erikson's developmental tasks in various life stages. Instruct students to label the columns *Important Tasks* and *Psychological Challenges*. Have them label the rows *Adolescence, Young Adulthood, Middle Adulthood,* and *Late Adulthood.* Students should fill in the first column with Erikson's developmental tasks. They should use the text and their own analysis to fill in the second column. Have students complete the Adolescence row (drawing from Chapter 11) and the Young Adulthood row at this time.

Making Decisions

Have students discuss the research findings concerning factors that influence people in their choice of a spouse. Ask students to respond to the following questions: What might be the advantages and disadvantages of marrying someone who has characteristics similar to your own? What might be the advantages and disadvantages of marrying someone who has characteristics different from your own? Then have students consider which of the following sayings is true of marriage: "Opposites attract" or "Birds of a feather flock together."

History of Marriage In most Western societies, men have traditionally played the dominant role in marriage as well as in the larger society. This system is known as a **patriarchy**. Over the past several decades, however, this situation has changed, and spouses are now more likely to be considered equal partners in marriage.

Marital roles in modern society are still changing. Some couples continue to adhere to roles in which the husband is the breadwinner and the wife is the homemaker. Other couples have begun to share, and even sometimes reverse, these roles. And many single or divorced individuals are alone responsible for fulfilling these roles.

In the United States today, most people marry primarily for love. The concept of romantic love as a reason for marriage, however, did not become widespread in Western societies until the 1800s. In the 1600s and 1700s, most marriages were arranged by the parents of the bride and groom, generally on the basis of how the marriage would benefit the two families. This practice permitted the orderly transferring of wealth from one family to another and from one generation to the next. Another purpose of marriage was to provide a stable home life in which to have and rear children.

Developmental Tasks of Young Adulthood

- Exploring adult roles
- Becoming independent
- Developing intimate relationships
- Adjusting to living with another person
- Starting a family and becoming a parent
- Assuming the responsibilities of managing a home
- Beginning a career or a job
- Assuming some responsibilities in the larger community—for example, participating in local government or religious organizations
- Creating a social network of friends and co-workers

FIGURE 12.1 *Erikson believed that each stage of life has its own developmental tasks. This chart lists some of the tasks associated with young adulthood. Not all young adults experience all of these tasks, nor do they experience them in a particular order.*

TRUTH OR fiction ▪ R E V I S I T E D ▪ *It is true that romantic love is a relatively new reason for marrying. Historically, marriage was seen as an institution for rearing children and for providing for the transferring of wealth from one generation to another. Marriage was not viewed as an expression of romantic love.*

Today, however, companionship and intimacy are central goals in most marriages. Marriage generally provides feelings of security and opportunities to share experiences and ideas with someone special. A *New York Times* poll found that the great majority of people in the United States still see marriage as permanent. The poll asked, "If you got married today, would you expect to stay married for the rest of your life, or not?" Some 86 percent of respondents said yes (Eggers, 2000).

Choosing Spouses Unlike in times past, in which marriages were arranged by the family, today young people in the United States typically select their own mates. Parents may, however, have at least some degree of influence over the choice.

People are also influenced in their marital decisions by factors such as ethnicity, level of education, social class, and religion. Generally, people marry others who are similar to themselves. For example, Americans tend to marry people who are from the same geographic area and social class—perhaps because they are more likely to meet such people in the first place.

People in the United States rarely marry people of different races or socioeconomic classes. According to the U.S. Census Bureau, only 2 percent of U.S. marriages are interracial. More than 90 percent of married couples are of the same religion. Similarity in attitudes and tastes is a key contributor to attraction and intimate relationships (Laumann et al., 1994; Singh & Ho, 2000; Watson et al., 2000).

Cooperative Learning

Organize the class into pairs. Have the pairs interview parents, grandparents, or other older adults about their perceptions of the ideal mate and the ideal marriage. One student in the pair should conduct the interview while the other one takes notes or otherwise records the interview (caution students first to secure the permission of the participants). Ask each pair to create a love story from the findings of the interview. In class, have the pairs present their love stories aloud. Then have the class group the stories into categories.

Ask students to determine which love stories are presented most frequently in the media. Have them work independently to examine both print and other media (including songs) for examples. Additionally, ask students to note love stories they find in their media study that are not described in the textbook feature. Challenge students to describe and label two of these love stories, using labels other than Sternberg's "fantasy" story and "gardening" story. Have students present their findings to the class for discussion.

READINGS IN

PSYCHOLOGY

LOVE STORIES

Some couples seem perfectly happy. Then suddenly, to the surprise of all their friends, they divorce. Other couples seem to fight all the time and constantly complain about each other. Yet they stay married. Why does this happen? That is the question psychologist Robert Sternberg asked himself. After interviewing many people he formed the theory that "love is a story."

Sternberg maintains in his article "Love Stories" (1996) that through the interaction of our personalities and the environment, we create stories about love, which we then try to fulfill. Various potential spouses fit these stories to a greater or lesser degree. According to Sternberg, marriages tend to last when the partners fulfill the roles they have created for themselves in their love stories.

Sternberg explains how we develop these stories and why they are very different from culture to culture:

The stories we invent draw on elements from our experience of living in the world—from the fairy stories we heard as young children, from the models of love relationships we observe around us in parents and relatives, from television and movies, from conversations with other people about their relationships, and so on. (p. 62)

According to Sternberg, love is not just a single story. He has come up with 24 model stories but cautions that there are probably many more. Two of Sternberg's stories are the "fantasy" story and the "gardening" story. The fantasy story is similar to a fairy tale. A woman who has a fantasy story expects her mate to be a "knight in shining armor" to protect her from danger. A man with a fantasy story expects his mate to be a "princess." The potential for the success of such a union depends on how much the people expect the fantasy to continue. If their expectations are too high, they may become disappointed.

In the "gardening" story, both partners tend and nurture the relationship as they would a beautiful rose. According to Sternberg, this relationship has potential for success as long as the partners continue to tend the "garden" (marriage).

Although people have created these stories, they are not aware that they have done so. Sternberg suggests what happens when we meet a person who might be a potential partner:

. . . if our story is a fantasy story then the slot we want to fill is reserved for a knight or princess. . . . Thus . . . we are attracted to a person who (we think) can fill a slot in our story line and we will stay attracted as long as the person continues to fill the slot. (pp. 71–72)

If the potential mate does not meet our story ideals, we probably will not even consider him or her, but if the person comes close, we might fall in love. What matters more than the individual story itself is that both partners believe in the same story. That is what is needed for the success of the union, as stated in the following excerpt:

Love stories have complementary roles. We look for someone who shares our story or who at least has a compatible story that can more or less fit it. (p. 69)

Sternberg's story theory might explain why some people stay with abusive partners:

Abused individuals might stay with partners not only for reasons of finances or fear, but because they truly believe—perhaps from what they have seen as children or in movies—that abuse is part of love. (p. 73)

It is possible that both people in an abusive relationship share a terrible story—that love includes hurt and abuse. And stories, explains Sternberg, are hard to change or break.

Think About It

Categorizing What might be some other common love stories? Give three examples and explain what kinds of roles people would play in those stories.

Many wedding ceremonies blend modern and traditional customs.

People also tend to choose marriage partners who are near their own age (Michael et al., 1994). This is especially true for couples who marry in early adulthood. People who meet in school and then marry each other tend to be similar in age. Most bridegrooms are about two to five years older than the women they are marrying (Buss, 1994). People who marry later in life or who remarry after being divorced or widowed are less likely to select partners who are as close in age.

Marriages between similar people may have a greater chance at survival because the partners probably share many of the same values and attitudes (Michael et al., 1994). Dissimilar couples, however, can work to overcome the differences that divide them by developing shared interests and mutual respect. Evidence that similarity between spouses is beneficial in the long run—the entire course of the marriage—remains somewhat limited (Karney & Bradbury, 1995).

Divorce

A DAY IN THE LIFE

Although most couples get married because they are in love, about half of the marriages in the United States—such as the one between Janet's parents—end in divorce (Carrère et al., 2000). The divorce rate rose steadily throughout most of the last century before leveling off in the 1980s. More than one quarter of children live in single-parent households (USBC, 1998).

Reasons for Divorce Why is divorce such a common occurrence when most couples believe in marrying for life? One reason may be that obtaining a divorce has become easier than it used to be. Many states now have "no-fault" divorce laws. That means that a judge can grant a divorce without having one or both partners blaming the other. If both partners agree on issues of child custody, financial support, and the distribution of the couple's assets, the marriage is legally dissolved.

The increased economic independence of women also may have contributed to the rise in the divorce rate. Just 30 years ago, most women were homemakers with little or no work experience outside the home. Because there were relatively few opportunities for women to enter the paid workforce at that time, many women probably doubted whether they would be able to support themselves and their children on their own. Thus, they may have been inclined to remain in troubled marriages because they perceived that they had no realistic alternative. Today, however, more women have jobs outside the home and are therefore more likely to have the economic independence that makes it easier for them to break away.

Increasingly high expectations may also have made divorce more likely. Today many couples expect marriage to be constantly gratifying—and to be easy. Relationships, however, require work and commitment. Some couples no longer feel committed enough to the marriage to try to make it work. Of course, there are numerous other reasons why people get divorced, including spouse abuse, child abuse, infidelity, strains brought about by illness or financial hardship, and an inability to communicate effectively (Carrère et al., 2000; Gottman et al., 1998).

The Costs of Divorce Divorce has many financial and emotional costs. When a household splits, the financial resources, such as income and property, are usually divided. Often, neither partner can afford to maintain the standard of living he or she had while married. A woman who does not have an established career may find herself struggling to compete with younger, more experienced workers as she enters the workforce.

Women generally are granted custody of the couple's children. Thus, divorced mothers often face the primary responsibility for rearing the children and

For Further Research

Suggest that students look at some of the books on divorce that are currently available, such as *Divorce Help Sourcebook* and *Helping Children of Divorce*. Students should report to the class about how divorce affects both parents and children and what divorcing couples can do to minimize the emotional, financial, and practical difficulties of the divorce process for all family members.

Role-Playing

Select two groups of volunteers to participate in a Public Forum panel discussion. Tell one group to imagine they are psychologists who believe that parents in unhappy marriages should stay together for the sake of the children. Tell the other group to imagine they are psychologists who believe that living with parents who are in constant conflict is more harmful to children than divorce. Have the rest of the class play an audience of concerned parents who have come to hear the psychologists debate the issue and to ask questions of them.

may need to increase income to make ends meet. These responsibilities can be extremely stressful. Divorced fathers, meanwhile, may find it difficult to pay child support and alimony—financial support paid to a former spouse.

Divorce can lead to feelings of failure, loneliness, fears about the future, and depression. Married people—especially happily married people—are usually better able to cope with the stresses of life, perhaps because they lend each other emotional support. Divorced and separated people have higher rates of physical and psychological disorders than do married people (Nevid et al., 2000).

Yet, for some people, divorce is a time of personal growth and renewal. When partners are convinced they cannot save their marriage, divorce may enable them to establish new and more rewarding lives. Despite the difficulties in adjusting to a divorce, most divorced people eventually recover. The majority remarry. Yet research suggests that remarriages are even more likely than first marriages to end in divorce (USBC, 1998). This may be because divorced people—having set a precedent by ending their first marriage—are inclined to leave a troubled second marriage fairly quickly. People in first-time marriages, on the other hand, may be more inclined to persist even if the marriage is difficult. In addition, many divorced people who remarry have alimony and child-support obligations that often place a financial strain on their new marriages.

 The Children of Divorce Divorce can be difficult for the children, even when they are almost adults, as Janet was, when their parents get divorced. Research shows that the children of divorced people are more likely to have behavioral problems, engage in substance abuse, and earn lower grades in school (O'Connor et al., 2000). Sometimes a stepfamily introduces new family relationships. Parents may have to work more to support the family financially and have less time for the children. Nevertheless, like Janet, most children overcome an initial period of stress and eventually stop doubting their ability to adjust to their new situation. Boys have greater problems than girls in adjusting to parental conflict or divorce, such as conduct problems at school and increased anxiety and dependence (Grych & Fincham, 1993; Holden & Ritchie, 1991).

It also seems that it is not so much parental separation that affects the children as the breakdown in the quality of parenting that often follows separation (Erel & Burman, 1995). Clarke-Stewart and

her colleagues (2000) analyzed data from the National Institute of Child Health and Human Development Study of Early Child Care to examine the effects of marital separation on children during the first three years of life. The families studied included nearly 100 separated or divorced mothers and a comparison group of 170 two-parent families. In general, the children in the two-parent families obtained higher scores on achievement and ability tests, showed more social skills, and experienced fewer problems and greater security. However, when the researchers considered the mothers' levels of education and income, the differences between the children in one-parent versus two-parent families became less significant. Thus, the psychological development of the children in this study was not affected by parental separation or divorce. Instead, the children's psychological development was related to the mother's income, level of education, and well-being. The results of this study suggest that children may fare better in homes with well-adjusted mothers than in homes with constantly bickering parents. In order to protect the children, psychologists usually advise parents who are getting divorced to

- try to agree on how they will interact with the children (for example, how to handle a situation where a child asks a parent for something after the other parent has said no),
- help each other maintain a good parent-child relationship, and
- avoid criticizing each other to or in front of the children.

Some people believe that parents in unhappy marriages should stay together for the sake of the children. While divorce can take its toll on children, so can living in a household with parents who are in constant conflict with each other.

For Your Information

Like the rest of American society, schools have had to adapt to the rising divorce rate in this country. The Family Educational Rights and Privacy Act requires that schools give full access to children's records to either parent, regardless of the custody arrangements (presuming neither parent has been barred from involvement by the courts). If both parents ask, then both must also receive all notices, information, report cards, and so on. Parent-teacher conferences should also include both parents, either separately or together.

Journal Activity

Encourage students to write in their journals about divorce as they have either experienced it in their own family or witnessed it in another family. Remind them that these journal writings are private. Urge students to examine the impact of divorce on all members of the family.

279

Closing Section 1

Synthesizing Information

Tell students to create a short story, one-act play, or comic strip that illustrates the key tasks of young adulthood. Remind them to include concepts discussed in the section.

Reviewing Section 1

Have students complete the Section Review questions on page 280.

▶ Describe the changes that occur and issues that are faced in middle adulthood.

This objective is assessed in the Section Review on page 284 and in the Chapter 12 Review.

Section 1 Review: Answers

1. Issues and characteristics for young adults include reassessment of what course in life they have chosen, an urge to settle down when in their thirties, and the formation of marriage and intimate relationships.

2. Erikson believed that people who do not develop such relationships may retreat into isolation and loneliness.

3. Students who agree may cite economic reasons or the need for stability in children's lives. Students who disagree may cite the parents' right to be happy or the stresses on children who are raised in troubled marriages.

Cross-Curricular Link: Art

Ask students to speculate on what their lives will be like when they enter middle adulthood. Then have them create a piece of art that symbolizes the life they hope to have at age 40. Art may take the form of a poem, song, dance, painting, sculpture, sketch, or short story. Have volunteers display and discuss or perform their art for the class. Then have students discuss what they can do now to help themselves achieve their long-term goals.

280

Should parents in conflict stay together for the sake of the children? There is no easy answer to this question. Although divorce can have negative effects on children, so do marital conflicts. Marital conflict or fighting is also connected with serious psychological distress in children and adolescents. Marital conflicts make relationships between parents and children more difficult and are also connected with later conflict in the children's marriages.

SECTION 1 REVIEW

Homework Practice Online
go.hrw.com
Keyword: SY3 HP12

1. List some of the issues and characteristics of young adulthood.

2. According to Erikson, what are the risks for people who do not develop intimate relationships during young adulthood?

3. **Critical Thinking** *Supporting a Point of View* Do you agree or disagree with the following statement: "Parents in conflict should remain together for the sake of the children"? Provide evidence to support your answer.

SECTION 2
Middle Adulthood

Middle adulthood spans the years from 40 to 65. By age 40, most people have begun to lose some of the strength, coordination, and stamina they had in their 20s and 30s. This decline in physical ability is generally so gradual that it is hardly noticeable. It is often only of concern to people who rely on physical fitness for their livelihoods or interests. However, middle adulthood can also be the time when many people first *begin* to work on developing their physical potential, as Linda's father did when he was 40. Even someone who has been inactive for years might decide at 45 to train for a marathon. People who work at their conditioning can maintain excellent health and strength throughout middle adulthood.

Generativity

Figure 12.2 on page 281 summarizes some of the developmental tasks of middle adulthood, according to Erik Erikson. Erikson believed that the greatest challenge for middle-aged adults is **generativity**—the ability to

create, originate, and produce. According to Erikson, generativity adds meaning to the lives of adults, and it helps them to maintain and enhance their self-esteem.

Adults can be creative, or generative, in various areas of their lives, such as their career, their family, and their community. People in middle adulthood are often also in positions in which they can exercise a particularly important influence on the world around them. As experienced workers, they may improve methods and relationships in the workplace. As parents, they guide the next generation. As voters and residents, they can help make their communities safer, friendlier places. Erikson also believed that adults who are not generative become stagnant. Stagnation—lack of advancement or development—can result in feelings of emptiness and meaninglessness.

Transition

Some psychologists have noted that many people experience a midlife transition around the ages of 40 to 45. The **midlife transition** is a period in middle adulthood when people's perspectives change in a major way. Some adults in their 40s are struck with the dramatic realization that they have lived about half their lives. They see themselves as being at a turning point. Previously, they had probably thought of their ages mostly in terms of how many years had elapsed since their birth. Once the midlife transition occurs, however, they begin to think of their ages in terms of how many years they may have left.

People in their 30s may still think of themselves as the older sibling of brothers or sisters in their 20s. Then, in their early 40s, a critical event often occurs. It may be a serious illness, a change at work, the death of a friend or a parent, or even just losing at basketball to one's child. Whatever the event, it triggers a 40-year-old's realization that he or she has made a generational shift. For example, the death of a parent may mean that the 40-year-old is now the head of the family. Similarly, losing at basketball to one's child may trigger the realization that "I'm not a kid anymore."

Women tend to undergo their midlife transitions about five years earlier than men do, at about age 35 instead of 40 (Reinke et al., 1985; Sheehy, 1995). What makes the mid-30s so special for women? For some women, 35 is about the age when they have sent their youngest child off to grade school, an event that can illustrate that their children are

Opening Section 2

Motivator

Explain that middle adulthood—from age 40 to age 65—is the time when most adults achieve the most for their families and communities and in their careers. Invite students to speculate on what the joys and challenges of this phase of life might be. For example, adults may be achieving career success or feeling stress from too many commitments. Record some of the ideas on the chalkboard. Then tell students that they will learn more about the rewards and challenges of middle adulthood by reading Section 2.

Teaching Section 2

Demonstration

Have students assess the validity of Erikson's list of developmental tasks of middle adulthood. Ask students to turn Figure 12.2 into a questionnaire to give to adults aged 40 to 65. Tell students to have the adults rate the importance of each task on a scale of 1 to 5, with 5 being "very important" and 1 being "not at all important." Have the class collate the data. Does it confirm Erikson's list? You might also have students discuss which tasks were consistently ranked the most or the least important. How do students explain these responses?

quickly growing up. Many women, of course, are not finished (or have not begun) having children by the age of 35, and for women who become pregnant at age 35 or older, doctors advise routine fetal testing for Down syndrome and other chromosomal disorders. (See Chapter 3.) Thirty-five is often also the age at which women are given a baseline mammogram—a specialized X ray for early detection of breast cancer—and are considered at greater risk for various types of cancer. These are all events that can cause women to reflect on their age and mortality.

With the thought that their lives may be close to half over, many people—men and women—come face-to-face with their limitations. They may acknowledge that dreams they had when they were younger may never be realized. For instance, they probably will never be a professional baseball player, a movie star, or president of the United States. People begin to adjust to the idea that they are growing older. For some adults, entering midlife may trigger a sense of urgency—a "last chance" to do certain things.

Midlife Crisis or Age of Mastery? In some people, the midlife transition triggers a second period of reassessment, often referred to as a **midlife crisis**. The middle-aged professional who sees younger people advancing at a faster rate may become seriously depressed. The parent with two or three teenagers may feel less needed by her or his children. Both may feel trapped and think they have lost their purpose in life.

The concept of the midlife crisis has often been treated as something generally negative. It suggests that people are overwhelmed by the crushing realities and the limits of their lives. Yet journalist Gail Sheehy (1995) is quite positive about the years from 45 to 65. She calls these years the "age of mastery."

Sheehy maintains that during these years, people are frequently at the height of their creative and productive powers. In many cases, they need only

Developmental Tasks of Middle Adulthood

- Helping one's children make the transition from home life to the outside world

- Strengthening one's relationship with one's spouse

- Helping make the world a better place by assuming leadership roles in social and civic activities

- Achieving mastery in one's career

- Adjusting to the physical changes that occur in middle age

- Making decisions about how to spend one's "second adulthood"

- Pursuing one's passions

- Coping with one's aging parents

FIGURE 12.2 *Earlier in the chapter you read a list of what Erikson believed are the developmental tasks of young adulthood. Erikson also believed that middle adulthood has its own developmental tasks. The focus of these tasks is on improving one's quality of life and strengthening relationships, both personal and in the community.*

find new outlets for their talents and experience. Therefore, Sheehy believes, the key task for middle-aged adults is to decide what they will do with the remainder of their lives. Because people are living longer than people did in previous generations, most American adults have 30 to 40 healthy years left after they reach middle adulthood. Men and women can continue to have fulfilling lives if they find careers, hobbies, or other activities that bring satisfaction and if they pursue these newfound interests wholeheartedly.

"Middlescence" But how do people go about recognizing and finding these interests? The term *middlescence* is sometimes used to describe a period of searching that in some ways resembles adolescence. Both middlescence and adolescence are periods of transition. Just as a key task of adolescence is the formation of identity in becoming an adult, middlescence involves a search for a *new* identity, or a *second* adulthood.

By the time they reach their early 40s, women have already dealt with some of the fears and

Applying Ideas

Ask students to choose a fictional character from a book or movie who is going through a midlife crisis. Have them write a short essay analyzing the character's behavior and attitudes in terms of the concepts discussed in this section. Students should also be able to describe how the character resolved his or her midlife crisis. Have volunteers read their essays aloud to the class for discussion.

Role-Playing

Organize students into groups of three, and tell the students in each group to assume the role of a mother, a father, and a grown child who has returned home for a visit. Tell the groups that they are to write and perform two versions of a scene from that visit: one version in which one or both parents are experiencing empty-nest syndrome, and one version in which neither parent is experiencing empty-nest syndrome. After the groups perform their scenes, have students discuss which version seems to be more indicative of parents today.

internet connect

TOPIC: Middle Adulthood
GO TO: go.hrw.com
KEYWORD: SY3 PS12

Have students access the Internet through the HRW Go site to research psychological factors of middle adulthood. Then have students write a newspaper article in which they apply the concepts of transition, explain the factors involved in midlife crisis, "middlescence", empty nest syndrome, and menopause. Students should use standard grammar, spelling, punctuation, and sentence structure in their articles.

FRANK & ERNEST ® by Bob Thaves

FRANK & ERNEST reprinted by permission of Newspaper Enterprise Association, Inc.

uncertainties that are only just starting to confront men (Helson 1993). As women emerge from middlescence in their 40s and 50s, they frequently experience a renewed sense of self. Many women in this age group feel confident and secure. They extend their interests. For example, they may become more involved in their communities. They are committed to what they are doing and feel productive, effective, and empowered.

The Empty-Nest Syndrome

In the past, psychologists placed great emphasis on the so-called empty-nest syndrome. **Empty-nest syndrome** is the term applied to the feelings of emptiness and loss mothers and fathers sometimes feel after the children have left home to establish their own lives. For mothers who have never worked outside the home, it can be particularly difficult to adjust to the departure of the children

While parents do encounter some adjustment problems when their youngest child leaves home, many actually experience a new sense of freedom.

whose upbringings have been a full-time job. After years of being totally committed to being a wife and mother, some women seem to lose their sense of purpose and become depressed after their children go out on their own.

Contemporary research findings, however, reveal a much more optimistic picture. Once the "nest" is empty, many women report that they are happier with their marriages and other aspects of their lives. Many women mention positive changes, such as greater peace of mind, self-confidence, and personal stability (Helson et al., 1995). Many middle-aged women become more self-assertive and achievement oriented. Furthermore, most women whose children have left home are already employed. With more energy and time to spend outside the home, many women become more influential in politics and careers. Many others return to school. And although there may be some problems of adjustment once children leave, those problems affect both parents, not just mothers.

TRUTH OR fiction ■ REVISITED ■

It is not true that most parents feel a great sense of loss and loneliness when the youngest child leaves home. Instead, many parents experience a new sense of opportunity.

There is much variation, of course. Some people in middle age feel hopeless and drained. But often middle age is a time of increased freedom. Many people have been successful enough to be free of financial worries. Many begin to travel extensively. They may have the leisure time to take up new hobbies or explore old interests. Therefore, middle age

Meeting Individual Needs: Gifted Learners

Have gifted students research the biology of aging as it applies to people in middle adulthood. Direct students to use the information to create two flowcharts showing the major physical changes middle-aged men and women experience. Flowcharts should focus on the sequence of physical changes and the cause-and-effect relationships involved in those changes. Have students display and discuss their charts.

Applying Information

Review with students the myths and realities about menopause outlined in Figure 12.3. Then tell students to conduct library research to locate an article on menopause in a current popular magazine such as *Redbook, Woman's Day,* or *Ms.* magazine. Have students write a summary of the article and evaluate the article in terms of the myths and realities of menopause. Does the article present a realistic picture of menopause, or does it perpetuate the myths? Have volunteers present their summaries and evaluations in a brief written report.

does not need to be a painful period. Rather, it can be a time to enjoy new freedoms and opportunities for self-development.

Menopause

Menopause, the end of menstruation, usually occurs in a woman's late 40s or early 50s, although it can occur earlier or later. It is caused by a decrease in the secretion of the hormones estrogen and progesterone. After menopause, a woman no longer produces egg cells that can be fertilized. Other body changes also occur. Breast tissue decreases, and the skin becomes less elastic. There may also be a loss in bone density that can lead to brittle bones—a condition called osteoporosis.

In some women, the hormonal changes of menopause may cause discomfort, such as hot flashes—sudden sensations of warmth, often accompanied by reddening and sweating, fatigue, and mood swings. However, in most cases, these symptoms are relatively mild. Some women cope with the more severe changes of menopause with hormone-replacement therapy—taking doses of hormones to replace those the body no longer produces.

The psychological meaning of menopause to a woman is often more important than the physical changes she experiences. Some women feel that they have become less attractive or even that they are losing their identity as women. These women are likely to be more distressed by menopause than those who do not have such feelings (Rathus et al., 2000). Women who feel that their primary purpose in life was birthing and rearing children are also likely to find menopause stressful.

Figure 12.3 highlights some myths and realities about menopause. Notice that all the myths are negative. The reality, however, is often positive. For

Myths and Realities About Menopause

Myth	Reality
Menopause is abnormal.	Menopause is a normal development in women's lives.
Doctors consider menopause to be a disease.	Not so. Menopause is now conceptualized as a "deficiency syndrome" because of the drop-offs in estrogen and progesterone.
After menopause, women need estrogen-replacement therapy.	Not necessarily. Some estrogen is still produced by the adrenal glands and other parts of the body. Estrogen-replacement therapy is recommended only occasionally.
Menopause is accompanied by depression and anxiety.	Not necessarily. Much of a woman's response to menopause reflects its psychological aspects rather than biological changes.
At menopause, women suffer crippling hot flashes.	Not necessarily. Many women do not experience any hot flashes. Women who do experience them usually find them mild.
Menopause ends a woman's sex drive.	Not at all. In fact, many women feel a renewal of sexual interest.
A woman's general level of activity is lower after menopause.	Not so. Many women report having more energy after menopause.

FIGURE 12.3 *The left-hand side of this table shows several of the myths about menopause. The realities of menopause are shown on the right-hand side. Why do you suppose people have so many misconceptions about menopause? How might these misconceptions influence the way menopausal women are treated?*

For Your Information

Hormone replacement therapy (HRT) is intended to counteract the major discomforts of menopause some women experience. In addition, HRT can help women avoid some of the physical problems that may occur after menopause. For example, HRT slows bone loss, reducing the risk of osteoporosis. HRT can also keep cholesterol at healthy levels, lowering the risk of heart disease. While many women can benefit from HRT, a few, such as those with certain types of cancer, should not use HRT.

Caption Question: Answer

Students may say that many people are uncomfortable discussing physical changes that are linked to human sexuality. When people do not have all the facts, information can become distorted. People who have misconceptions about menopause may treat menopausal women as if they have a disease or are emotionally and mentally unbalanced.

Closing Section 2

Follow Up

Have students retrieve the charts they began in the Classifying Information activity on page 276. Tell students to use information from Section 2 to fill in the Middle Adulthood row on their charts.

Reviewing Section 2

Have students complete the Section Review questions on page 284.

Extension

Have students conduct library research and create a line graph titled "Life Expectancy of U.S. Men and Women, 1900–2000." Tell students that their graphs should contain two lines, one for men and one for women, and should show life expectancy in 20-year intervals from 1900 to 2000. The *Statistical Abstract of the United States* and *Historical Statistics of the United States* are useful sources of data. Have students write a paragraph comparing the life expectancies of men and women and offering explanations for the differences.

Section 2 Review: Answers

1. According to Erikson, generativity adds meaning to the lives of adults and enhances and maintains their self-esteem.

2. Changes and issues include generativity, transition, the empty-nest syndrome, and menopause.

3. Some students may argue that middle age is a time of crisis because of the reassessment and searching common during this period.

Teaching Transparencies with Teacher's Notes

TRANSPARENCY 28: Developmental Tasks of Young Adulthood

---

example, many women report having more energy —not less—after menopause.

When someone is referred to as "menopausal," it is usually the mood swings and increased irritability that are being talked about. Unfortunately, this oversimplifies what menopause is all about for women, and it also reinforces the stereotype of menopause as a time when women are not in control of their emotions. Such stereotypes and myths often do not have anything to do with the biology or psychology of aging.

Do men undergo menopause? The quick answer is "of course not," since men have never menstruated. Yet occasionally one hears of a so-called male menopause. Men do experience a hormone decline. At about age 40 or 50, testosterone levels in men begin to decline. They may fall to one third or one half of their peak levels by age 80 (Brody, 1995c). However, this is a gradual drop-off. It does not resemble the sharp plunge in estrogen levels that women experience.

The decline in a man's testosterone level may be connected with such other age-related changes as loss of strength, weight gain, reduced energy, and decreased fertility. Some of these changes, however, could just as well be due to a gradual loss of the human growth hormone rather than a diminishing testosterone level.

SECTION 2 REVIEW

go.hrw.com
Homework Practice Online
Keyword: SY3 HP12

1. How does generativity contribute to a healthy middle adulthood?

2. List some of the changes that occur and issues that are faced in middle adulthood.

3. **Critical Thinking** *Evaluating* Do you think middle age is a time of crisis or a period of new opportunities? Explain your answer.

SECTION 3
Late Adulthood

Age 65 marks the beginning of late adulthood. People are living longer than ever before. In 1900 only one American in thirty was over 65. By the year 2020 nearly one American in five will be age 65 or older (Longer, 1997).

Some people view the later years as the beginning of the end of life, but they can be much more. In fact, the later years provide many opportunities for self-fulfillment. John Glenn served as a member of the space shuttle crew when he was 77; comedian George Burns performed his comedy routines into his late 90s.

Physical Changes

Many physical changes take place in late adulthood. Wrinkles and skin folds occur as the skin becomes less elastic. Some of the senses become less sharp. In general, older people do not see and hear as well as younger people. A decline in the sense of smell leads many older people to add more spices to their food for flavor. The reflexes and the reaction time of older people also tend to be a little slower than those of younger people.

A few of the physical changes cause health problems. For example, as bones become more brittle, they fracture more easily, and the risk is greater that they will break if the person falls. As people grow older, their immune systems also become less effective as a barrier against disease.

However, older adults can do many things to maintain their health, strength, and energy levels.

Many people continue to learn new skills and lead active lives well into late adulthood.

Section Objective

▶ Explain how people's lives change in late adulthood.

This objective is assessed in the Section Review on page 291 and in the Chapter 12 Review.

Opening Section 3

Motivator

Acknowledge to students that many Americans have stereotypical views of older adults. Invite students to suggest what some of these stereotypes might be. List students' suggestions on the chalkboard, and have them make a copy of the list. Then have students prepare a chart, similar to the one shown in Figure 12.3, titled "Myths and Realities of Late Adulthood." Have them write the list of stereotypes in the column labeled *Myths.* Tell students to fill in the column labeled *Realities* after reading Section 3.

A DAY IN THE LIFE

Regular exercise and a healthful diet can contribute to making older adults feel well and also help them fight disease. The man whom Marc met doing yard work is a good example of the benefits of exercise.

Exercise helps people maintain flexibility and fitness at any age—including the years of late adulthood. Because brittle bones and stiff joints are part of the aging process, many older people may prefer walking and swimming to more weight-bearing exercises such as running and bicycling. The latter activities tend to cause more stress on bones and joints (Pena & Bricklin, 1990).

TRUTH OR fiction
■ REVISITED ■

It is not true that it is good for older people *not* to exercise. Exercise helps people maintain flexibility and fitness at any age. Many older adults enjoy walking and swimming.

Why Do People Age?

Why do some people seem to age faster than others? Many scientists hope that by understanding the process of aging, we may eventually be able to slow it down or even reverse some of its negative effects. Theories of aging fall into two categories: programmed theories and cellular damage theories.

Programmed Theories   The developmental theories that maintain that aging is the result of genetics are called **programmed theories**. These theories of aging view people as having biological clocks that move forward at a predetermined pace. Studies show that people whose parents lived long lives are more likely to have long lives themselves. This suggests that genetics plays a significant role in the length of one's life.

Heredity influences our cells, our hormones, and our immune systems. The cells in our bodies divide and repair themselves only a specific number of times. After that, they become inactive and eventually die. Some researchers believe that the limitation on the number of times a cell can divide is less important than the fact that the cells are aging. As they age, cells become less able to repair themselves. This makes people vulnerable to diseases that involve cellular breakdown, such as cancer (Lehrman, 1995).

Exercise is beneficial at every stage of life, especially late adulthood. Regular exercise can help older people stay healthy, flexible, and energetic.

Heredity also affects our hormones. Hormonal changes in later life may leave the body more vulnerable to certain health problems, such as diabetes, osteoporosis, and heart disease. Researchers are investigating the possible role of certain hormones—such as melatonin and the human growth hormone—in the aging process.

In addition, heredity influences the immune system. According to programmed theories, genetics may predetermine the decline in our immune systems. Such a decline makes the body less able to fight off disease.

Cellular Damage Theories   In contrast to programmed theories, **cellular damage theories** of aging suggest that cells malfunction as a result of damage, not heredity. The damage may come from internal body changes or from external causes, such as trauma or toxins.

The cells in our bodies are affected by the environment. If they are exposed to poisons or cancer-causing agents for long periods of time, they become less able to repair themselves and more vulnerable to disease. As time passes, cells and vital organs are worn down, like machines whose parts eventually wear out from constant use.

Some scientists blame free radicals for damage to our bodies. **Free radicals** are unstable molecules in our bodies. They are normally produced as a by-product of digestion. They may also be produced by exposure to environmental agents, including

Cross-Curricular Link: Biology

Researchers have discovered the gene that causes Werner's syndrome, a rare disease that causes premature aging. Symptoms of the syndrome include gray hair in the teens and cataracts and wrinkles in the twenties. The discovery of this gene is of particular interest to scientists who study aging because it may provide clues to the genetic basis of normal aging. The discovery lends support to theories of programmed aging.

internet connect
go.hrw.com

TOPIC: Late Adulthood
GO TO: go.hrw.com
KEYWORD: SY3 PS12

Have students access the Internet through the HRW Go site to research the physical, cognitive, and social changes of late adulthood. Ask students to design a poll or series of interview questions based upon their research, and conduct the poll or interview people in this age group. Students should organize their findings and discuss them with the class.

Teaching Section 3

Demonstration

To help students understand some of the physical changes that occur during the aging process, have them simulate some of the experiences of late adulthood. For example, they might place cotton in their ears to experience hearing loss (being careful to stay in a safe area while doing so), remove their own corrective eyeglasses or wear an old pair of scratched sunglasses to experience vision loss, or try to take coins out of a change purse while wearing gloves to experience loss of manual dexterity. Have students discuss the experience.

Cooperative Learning

Remind students of the list of stereotypes about older adults suggested by the class in the Motivator activity on page 285. Then organize the class into small groups. Ask half of the groups to create posters illustrating stereotypes about late adulthood. Ask the other half to create posters illustrating realities of late adulthood. Have the groups use their posters to create a classroom or hallway display titled "Myths and Realities of Late Adulthood."

Late adulthood can be a time of creativity and self-fulfillment.

ultraviolet light, air pollution, pesticides, and even extreme heat. According to this view, aging occurs because free radicals accumulate in the body. These molecules eventually damage cells, causing people to age faster and to become vulnerable to various diseases (Hayflick, 1994; Lehrman, 1995).

Another cause of aging may be **cross-linking**. According to this view, proteins within a cell bind together, toughening body tissues. This toughening eventually leads to the breakdown of various bodily processes and causes aging (Lamb, 1993).

Aging is a complex biological process. It may not be due to a single cause. It may not be explainable by a single theory. Aging may result from a combination of the processes described here, or it may involve factors we are not even aware of yet. For these reasons, researchers continue to study the aging process.

Cognitive Changes

Cognitive development is also affected by aging. Cognitive development in adulthood has many aspects—creativity, memory functioning, and intelligence. People can be creative for a lifetime. At the age of 80, Merce Cunningham choreographed a dance that made use of computer-generated images

(Teachout, 2000). Pablo Picasso was still painting quite exciting canvases in his 90s, and Grandma Moses did not begin painting until she was 78. Architect Frank Lloyd Wright designed New York City's innovative Guggenheim Museum when he was 89 years old.

Although people can lead creative lives throughout old age, memory ability does decline with age. It is common for older people to have trouble recalling the names of things or people. Memory lapses can be embarrassing, and older people sometimes lose confidence in their memory (Cavanaugh & Green, 1990). But declines in memory are not usually as great as people assume, and they can sometimes be reversed (Villa & Abeles, 2000). Memory tests usually measure ability to recall meaningless information. Older people show better memory in areas in which they can apply their special experiences to new challenges (Graf, 1990). For example, who would do a better job of learning and remembering how to solve problems in chemistry—a young expert in history or a retired chemistry teacher?

All in all, most older people do quite well intellectually. Late adulthood is a time to discover new skills and ways of thinking. Unfortunately, some older people do have cognitive problems, such as senile dementia and Alzheimer's disease.

Senile Dementia The serious loss of cognitive functioning is called **dementia**. People with dementia show major losses in memory. They may also have speech problems or be unable to perform simple tasks, such as tying their shoes or buttoning a shirt, even if they are physically able to perform such tasks. They may also have difficulty concentrating or making plans.

Dementia that occurs after the age of 65 is called **senile dementia**. Only a minority of older people have senile dementia, sometimes called senility. Most cases occur in people over the age of 80 (Nevid et al., 2000).

TRUTH OR fiction
■ REVISITED ■

It is not true that everyone who lives long enough will eventually become senile. Senile dementia (sometimes called senility) is not an automatic result of aging.

Evaluating Ideas

Have students locate historical and contemporary quotations that focus on late adulthood. Ask volunteers to read their quotations aloud, and have the class evaluate each quotation in terms of the information presented in the text. Do the quotations perpetuate myths, or do they provide a realistic portrayal of late adulthood? Have students use information from the text to write their own quotations. Ask them to discuss how learning about late adulthood has changed their views of what their own lives will be like when they are old.

Analyzing Information

Have students analyze an evening's worth of television commercials. Instruct them to record the number of commercials shown, the number of commercials that contain older adults, and the types of products advertised in the commercials that contain older adults. Tell students to use this information to write a paragraph analyzing how advertisers characterize the period of late adulthood. Have volunteers read their paragraphs aloud to the class, and have the class debate the validity of the characterizations.

Alzheimer's Disease **Alzheimer's disease** is a progressive form of mental deterioration that affects about 10 percent of people over the age of 65 and nearly half of those over the age of 85 (Katzman, 2000). Although Alzheimer's is connected with aging, it is a disease and not a normal part of aging (Haan, 2000).

Alzheimer's disease is characterized by general, gradual deterioration in mental processes such as memory, language, and problem solving. As the disease progresses, people may fail to recognize familiar faces or forget their names. Eventually, people with Alzheimer's disease become helpless. They become unable to communicate or walk and require help eating.

Alzheimer's disease is characterized by reduced levels of the neurotransmitter acetylcholine (ACh) and by the buildup of a sticky plaque in the brain. The plaque is formed from fragments of a body protein (Cotman, 2000; Frangione, 2000). Normally, the immune system prevents the buildup of this plaque, but the immune system does not do its job effectively in the case of people with Alzheimer's disease. One form of drug therapy is aimed at boosting ACh levels by slowing its breakdown. This approach achieves modest benefits with many people. Another approach to the treatment of Alzheimer's is the development of a vaccine made of a harmful protein that will help the immune system to better attack the plaque (Schenk, 2000).

Vascular Dementia Another common kind of dementia is vascular dementia. Vascular dementia can be caused by the bursting of a blood vessel in the brain (as during a stroke) or by a decrease in the blood supply to the brain. Such a decrease happens when fatty deposits collect in the blood vessels that go to the brain. The deposits cause the blood vessels to narrow, impeding the blood flow. Various infections can also cause dementia.

Social Changes

In addition to physical and cognitive changes, aging also involves many social changes. People have to make decisions about their retirement, how much time to spend with their children and grandchildren, and where they should live.

Retirement Many people dream of retirement, the period when they no longer need to wake up early in the morning and go to work. Other people dread the idea of retirement, wondering what they will do with all their free time. In many cases, retirement is voluntary. But people in some jobs, including teachers in most school systems, must retire when they reach a certain age, usually 65 or 70. In other cases, older people find themselves forced out of jobs because of discrimination or for other reasons related to age.

Some people turn their attention to leisure activities when they retire. Others continue in part-time work, either paid or voluntary. Research indicates that there may be some common experiences involving retirement (Atchley, 1991). When people first retire, they often undergo a "honeymoon" phase. They feel very positive about their newfound freedom, and they do many of the things they had dreamed about doing once they had the time. During this honeymoon period, people are often quite busy.

After a while, however, many people become disillusioned with retirement. Their schedules slow down, and they discover that the things they had fantasized about are less stimulating than they had thought they would be. Retirement can also place stress on a marriage because spouses may suddenly be spending a great deal more time together than they ever have before. As people encounter such experiences, they tend to develop a more realistic view of retirement. They may join volunteer groups and participate more in community activities. Sometimes elderly persons begin entirely new careers—painting or writing, for example. In general, people establish a new routine, and stability sets in.

Grandparenthood Grandparents often have more relaxed relationships with their grandchildren than they had with their children. Their perspectives may have become broader as they have grown older. Many have become more tolerant and understanding over the years. And because they do not usually have to shoulder the major responsibility for the grandchildren, grandparents usually can enjoy them. Because of a variety of circumstances, increasing numbers of grandparents are in fact taking on the major responsibility for raising their grandchildren.

A DAY IN THE LIFE Grandparents are frequently valued by their children for the roles they play with the grandchildren. For example, retired grandparents who live nearby can help baby-sit. Grandparents also often serve as special sources of wisdom and love for grandchildren, as Linda remembered about her own grandmother.

For many older adults, balancing a need for independence with a need to stay involved with their

For Your Information

Community programs can help older adults adjust to retirement. For example, a foster-grandparents program creates links that help retired adults feel connected to young people in the community. There are some programs in which youngsters from grade school through high school teach computer skills to older adults. These programs help dispel stereotypes among the younger generation about the abilities of older adults.

Cultural Dimensions

In some cultures, it is traditional for grandparents to live with their children and grandchildren in a multigenerational household, regardless of health or economic circumstances. If any students live in a multigenerational household, ask them to share their experiences. While some of these cultural traditions have faded in American society, some families in the United States are once again living in multigenerational households because of economic necessity. In fact, about 4 percent of American households include three or more generations.

Guided Practice

Create on the chalkboard a five-column chart titled "Successful Aging." Label the columns *Ego Integrity, Adjustment, Reshaping Life, Outlook,* and *Self-Challenge.* Have students supply information from the textbook about the characteristics of successful aging while you write the information in the appropriate column. Then have students write a short essay summarizing what people can do to ensure that they age successfully. Have students read their essays aloud to the class for discussion.

Independent Practice

Have students use what they have learned to write a slogan for each of the five columns on the chart in the Guided Practice activity. For example, a slogan for the Ego Integrity column might be "Letting go does not mean giving up." Have students combine their slogans with illustrations to create a banner that carries the title "Age Successfully!" Have students display and compare their banners, and discuss them with the class.

To grandchildren, grandparents often serve as a source of love and understanding—and enjoyment.

children and grandchildren is an important job. How often older adults see the children and grandchildren and whether they have the right to make "suggestions" become key issues. Although many older people worry that their families might no longer want them around, they are not usually rejected by their children. Most older people see or talk to their children regularly (Berger, 1994).

Living Arrangements   Some Americans hold certain stereotypes about older people's living arrangements. One stereotype portrays older people living with their children. Another has them in nursing homes and other institutions (Stock, 1995). Still another stereotype is that older people buy condominiums or move to retirement communities in areas with warmer climates.

Most older people are independent. Many of them are financially secure and own their own homes. It is true that nearly 30 percent of older people will spend some time in a nursing home (Kemper & Murtaugh, 1991). However, the populations of nursing homes usually consist of people who are 80 or older.

Most older people also remain in their hometowns rather than moving to other areas of the United States. They prefer to live in familiar surroundings where they have social and cultural ties (U.S. Bureau of the Census, 1995).

Successful Aging

Some people age more successfully than others. Psychologists have found that "successful agers" have several characteristics that can inspire all people to lead more enjoyable and productive lives.

Ego Integrity   Erik Erikson (1963) believed that people in late adulthood, like those in other stages of life, face certain developmental tasks. (See Figure 12.4 on page 290.) He believed that one challenge facing people in late adulthood is the maintenance of **ego integrity**—the belief that life is meaningful and worthwhile even when physical abilities are not what they used to be. A person with ego integrity is able to accept his or her approaching death with composure.

People spend most of their lives developing relationships and gathering possessions. Erikson believed that ego integrity enables people to let go of relationships and objects as the end of life approaches. Older people who do not maintain ego integrity risk falling into despair because they feel as if they are losing everything that matters to them. Ego integrity is connected with the wisdom to accept that one's life span is limited and to realize that nothing will last forever. Successful agers have this wisdom.

Aging and Adjustment   Most people in their 70s report being largely satisfied with their lives (Margoshes, 1995). Despite the physical changes that occur with aging, more than 75 percent rate their health as good or excellent.

Older people tend to be more satisfied with their lives when they are in good health and when they are financially secure. In fact, there is a correlation between socioeconomic status and health (Leary, 1995). Economically disadvantaged people at any age are more likely to report ill health than people of higher socioeconomic status. People who are financially secure are usually able to afford better health care and preventive services. They tend to worry less, and thus their stress is reduced. It may also be true that throughout life, people who are healthy are able to work harder and earn higher incomes. Most older people have some degree of financial security, but about 10 percent of people age 65 or older do live below the poverty line.

Among older people, as among younger people, a strong connection exists between social support and personal well-being. Social support is provided by various relationships. Spouses, children, and

Remind students that each life stage gives people certain strengths, which they can use to enhance their career, family life, or community. Have students analyze the stories of Pablo Picasso, Mother Teresa, and Thurgood Marshall. What strengths or characteristics of early adulthood did they bring to their careers during their early years? *(endurance, stamina)* What strengths of middle and late adulthood did they bring? *(creativity, wisdom, experience)*

For Further Research

Have students conduct library research to find additional examples of older adults who are or were highly creative and productive. Ask them to compile their findings in a proposed table of contents for a biographical anthology of older achievers. Encourage students to examine many fields, such as the arts, community service, politics, education, medicine, science, and literature. Have students choose one person from their table of contents and write a biographical sketch similar to the ones included on page 289.

CASE STUDIES
AND OTHER TRUE STORIES

Making the Most of Late Adulthood

Late adulthood does not mean the end of achievement. In fact, many people reach the height of their productivity and accomplishments in late adulthood. Three people who have proved just how valuable the contributions of older people can be are Pablo Picasso, Mother Teresa, and Thurgood Marshall.

Pablo Picasso (1881–1973)

Many people consider Pablo Picasso to be the most influential artist of the 1900s. This Spanish-born artist experimented with various styles of painting, sculpture, and ceramics. His innovative art styles were sometimes viewed with surprise, even horror, as so often happens when something different is introduced. Throughout Picasso's life and career, he never stopped trying new things. The last major exhibition of his work during his own lifetime was mounted in 1973, when he was in his 90s. As with earlier shows, the public was once again surprised by the newness of his artistic vision. Many of the works in this exhibit were early expressions of a style that came to dominate the art of the early 1980s. Picasso never stopped working. He died in his sleep. Next to his bed was a bundle of crayons—placed there in case he woke with an inspiration. As he once said: "The painter never finishes . . . you can never write 'The End.'"

Mother Teresa (1910–1997)

Mother Teresa became a nun when she was only 18 years old. Known as Sister Teresa early on, she found herself in India teaching the daughters of middle-class Indians. Then one day she received what she referred to as "a call within a call." She believed that God wanted her to serve only the poorest people, the dying, and the homeless for the rest of her life. She left the convent with only the clothes she was wearing. In 1948 Sister Teresa opened her first school. Two years later, she founded the Order of the Missionaries of Charity, a congregation of women dedicated to helping poor people. She established schools and opened health centers for the care of the blind, the elderly, the sick, and the dying. In 1989, when she was 79, Mother Teresa suffered a heart attack and, soon after, resigned as head of the order. But by the end of 1990, she had returned to her post in India. Although Mother Teresa was a small, frail-looking woman, old age did little to weaken her. At the time she returned to the order, the Missionaries of Charity had more than 3,000 nuns.

Thurgood Marshall (1908–1993)

Thurgood Marshall was another extremely influential figure whose contributions continued throughout his life. He first made his mark as a young lawyer when he became the lead attorney for the National Association for the Advancement of Colored People (NAACP). Although it was often dangerous to do so, Marshall traveled across the country urging the courts to protect the constitutional rights of African Americans. He became famous for his leading work on the *Brown* v. *Board of Education of Topeka* case, which resulted in the historic 1954 Supreme Court ruling that segregation in the nation's public schools is unconstitutional.

In 1967 Marshall was appointed to the Supreme Court, the first African American to receive such an appointment. He worked to end political, economic, and social injustices in this country. Despite several serious illnesses, he continued to serve, noting that he had "a lifetime appointment." However, during his 80s, Marshall's health declined, and he retired from the bench in 1991. He will always be remembered for his strong convictions, especially regarding civil rights.

▶ WHY PSYCHOLOGY MATTERS

Many people lead productive and creative lives well into late adulthood. Use **CNNfyi.com** or other current events sources to learn more about elderly persons who continue to contribute to their communities. Write a brief biography of one such person.

CNNfyi.com

Cross-Curricular Link: Art

An artist's work is sometimes discussed in terms of "periods"—stylistic stages representing certain times in the artist's life. Picasso's later work, for example, had a different artistic vision than work he created in his earlier periods. Show students some books containing photographs or color plates of Picasso's work, and point out the various periods of his work. Have students compare these periods and suggest any evidence in the work of the life stage that Picasso was in when he produced a particular piece of art.

Journal Activity

Have students write about someone they know who is a role model for successful aging. What characteristics or traits do students find most admirable about this person?

Technology Resources

CNN Presents Psychology: Keeping Young

Closing Section 3

Synthesizing Information

Remind students that social support is important at every age. Have students compare social support in young adulthood with such support in late adulthood. Also have them fill in the Late Adulthood portion of the chart begun in the Classifying Information activity on page 276.

Reviewing Section 3

Have students complete the Section Review questions on page 291.

Extension

Have students research an organization or association dedicated to improving the lives of older Americans. Some possibilities include the American Association of Retired Persons (AARP), the Gray Panthers, and the National Council on Aging. Have students find out about the history of the organization, its goals and functions, and its membership. Students may wish to write to the organization and request any available literature it might have. Have students present their findings in a written report.

Section 3 Review:
Answers

1. physical changes such as a decline in the ability to see and hear, cognitive changes such as memory loss, and social changes such as retirement

2. Ego integrity helps older adults maintain the belief that life is meaningful even as physical abilities decline. Ego integrity also helps older people let go of their possessions and relationships as the end of life approaches.

3. Students may suggest such aids as a chart to track medication schedules, a list of telephone numbers to be kept in one's wallet or purse, and a handy map marked with frequently visited places.

Developmental Tasks of Late Adulthood

- Adjusting to physical changes and keeping (or becoming) physically active

- Maintaining concern about other people so that one does not become preoccupied with one's own physical changes

- Shifting interests from work to retirement or leisure activity

- Adjusting to changes in financial status

- Establishing fulfilling living arrangements

- Learning to live with one's husband or wife in retirement (in that both spouses may now be together much of the time)

- Adjusting to the illness or the death of one's husband or wife

FIGURE 12.4 *Erikson also believed that late adulthood has its own particular developmental tasks. Acceptance and adjustment are primary tasks at this time in life.*

Paul and Margret Baltes (1995) noted that successful agers no longer try to compete with younger people in certain activities, such as athletics or business. Rather, they focus on matters that allow them to maintain a sense of personal control. They also try to find ways to make up for losses in some of their abilities. If their memories are not quite what they used to be, they may make notes or use other types of reminders. If their senses are no longer as sharp as they once were, they use devices such as hearing aids or eyeglasses. Some older people even develop creative solutions to their problems. The great pianist Arthur Rubinstein performed well into his 80s, even after he had lost much of his speed. To make up for this lack, he would slow down as he approached a passage in the music that required him to play faster. In this way, he gave the impression of speed during the more rapid passages (Margoshes, 1995).

friends may all provide social support, helping out in both practical and emotional ways when necessary. This may help explain the research finding that older couples generally are happier than older single or widowed people (Berger, 1994). Once couples are retired, they tend to spend more time together. Their relationships thus take on greater importance in their lives. When one spouse dies, however, children often are able to give needed support to the surviving spouse.

Reshaping One's Life Another component of successful aging is reshaping one's life to focus on what is important. Laura Carstensen's (1995) research on people aged 70 and above revealed that successful agers formulate specific goals that bring them satisfaction. For example, rather than becoming involved with many different causes or hobbies, they may focus on one particular interest. Successful agers may have less time left than people in earlier stages of adulthood, but they tend to spend it more wisely (Garfinkel, 1995).

A Positive Outlook A positive outlook is another component of successful aging. For example, some older people blame their occasional aches and pains on specific causes, such as a cold. Others simply blame old age itself. Not surprisingly, those who attribute their problems to specific causes are more optimistic that they will get better. Thus, they have a more positive outlook or attitude.

Researcher William Rakowski (1995) followed 1,400 people aged 70 and above who had common health problems, such as aches and pains. He found that those who blamed the problems on aging were more likely to die sooner than those who blamed the problems on specific factors.

Self-Challenge Yet another component of successful aging is challenging oneself. Many people look forward to late adulthood as a time when they can rest from life's challenges. However, sitting back and allowing the world to pass by is a prescription for becoming passive and for not living life to its fullest extent.

Section Objective

▶ Explain the attitudes and issues related to death and dying.

This objective is assessed in the Section Review on page 293 and in the Chapter 12 Review.

Opening Section 4

Motivator

Invite a student volunteer to read aloud the subsection titles from Section 4. Point out that death and dying are subjects many people are uncomfortable discussing. In addition, individuals from different cultures have various beliefs about death that they may hold very strongly. Encourage students to be sensitive to each other's views and beliefs. Additionally, urge students to use their journals to record any questions, comments, or concerns they feel uncomfortable sharing in class.

This view was confirmed in a study conducted by Curt Sandman and Francis Crinella (1995). They randomly assigned 175 participants, whose average age was 72, either to a foster-grandparent program or to a control group. They then followed the participants for 10 years. As compared to people in the control group, the foster grandparents faced greater physical challenges, such as walking a few miles each day. They also had new social experiences by getting to know the children and their families. The results of the study showed that people in the foster-grandparent program improved their overall cognitive functioning, including their memories. They even slept more soundly.

Withdrawing from life and avoiding challenges is clearly not the route to well-being and good health for older people. Focusing on what is important, maintaining a positive attitude, and accepting new challenges are as important for older people as for younger people.

SECTION 3 REVIEW

Homework Practice Online
go.hrw.com
Keyword: SY3 HP12

1. What are some changes people face in late adulthood?

2. Why is ego integrity an important part of healthy aging?

3. **Critical Thinking** *Analyzing Information* Many older people experience memory losses. What are some ways older people can keep track of their medication and remember important telephone numbers or directions to the doctor's office?

SECTION 4
Death and Dying

We all must face death at some point in our lives. Yet most of us seem to want to turn away from such a thought. According to psychiatrist Elisabeth Kübler-Ross (1969), the subject of death is often avoided. We seem to do all kinds of things to avoid confronting the reality of death. For example, prior to burial, cosmetics are used to make the deceased person look as if he or she is asleep.

Because death often brings sadness, some people send their children away to friends or relatives so that they need not face the sadness and anxiety around the home. Children may be prevented from visiting dying grandparents. But part of healing after a death is having the chance to say good-bye. Therefore, some psychologists suggest that trying to protect children by keeping them away from a dying loved one may actually make it harder for them to cope with their grief.

Stages of Dying

Kübler-Ross (1969) worked with people who had terminal illnesses. An illness is terminal when it seems certain to lead to death. Some types of cancers are terminal illnesses. Kübler-Ross theorized that there are five stages through which many dying people pass. She believed that many older people have similar feelings when they suspect that death is near, even if they have not been diagnosed with a terminal illness. The stages are as follows:

1. *Denial.* For example, the dying person might think, "It can't be me. The doctor's diagnosis must be wrong."

2. *Anger.* People in this stage might think, "It's unfair. Why me?"

3. *Bargaining.* For instance, "I'll be kinder if I can just live to see my grandson graduate."

4. *Depression.* The person may despair and wonder, "What's the use of living another day?"

5. *Acceptance.* The person reasons, "I've had a good life. I'm ready to die."

Kübler-Ross's theory has met with considerable criticism. Some psychologists, such as Edwin Shneidman (1984), agree that many terminally ill people have the kinds of feelings described by Kübler-Ross. But Shneidman has not found that the feelings follow a particular sequence. Shneidman finds that people faced with approaching death show a variety of reactions. Some people have quickly shifting emotions that range from rage to surrender, from envying the young and healthy to yearning for the end. Some people accept death more easily; others feel despair. Still others feel terror. People's reactions to dying reflect their unique personalities and their philosophies of life.

Another problem with Kübler-Ross's theory is that it may tempt family members and health professionals to ignore the uniqueness of each individual's experiences at the end of life. If a dying person is angry or in despair, people may think that it is just a stage and not pay close attention to the dying

Cross-Curricular Link: Literature

For centuries, writers have struggled in their work to make sense of death. Have students read and report on one of the following works: *The Dead* by James Joyce, *Death Be Not Proud* by John Donne, *A Separate Peace* by John Knowles, *Sadako and the Thousand Paper Cranes* by Eleanor Coerr, or *A Death in the Family* by James Agee. You might also wish to have students discuss any songs or poems with which they are familiar that focus on death and dying.

Journal Activity

Have students explore death and their feelings about it in a brief journal entry. Suggest that students focus their writing on these questions: What is death? What is your greatest fear about dying? How would you want others to describe you after your death? Stress that these writings will remain private.

Teaching Section 4

Comparing and Contrasting Information

Create a two-column chart on the chalkboard. Label one column *Hospitals* and the other column *Hospices*. Have students list the characteristics of each location as a place where dying people spend their final days. Write students' suggestions under the appropriate heading. Then have students compare and contrast hospitals with hospices and explain how hospices contribute to a more humane and dignified death.

Taking a Stand

Tell students that assisted suicide is a form of euthanasia in which a doctor or other individual assists a dying person in committing suicide. One controversial activist for assisted suicide is Dr. Jack Kevorkian, who has assisted in a number of suicides. Challenge students to consider the issue of assisted suicide and to develop a position for or against the practice. Encourage them to research both sides of the controversy. Give students time to prepare and then organize teams to debate the issue.

Class Discussion

Discuss with students the difficulties encountered in balancing the emotional needs of a dying person with those of his or her family. Ask students if they think a dying person should receive pain medication even at the risk of becoming addicted. How might one evaluate an individual's desire to know all the details about his or her terminal condition?

For Your Information

The hospice approach to dying is perhaps best understood through the derivation of the word *hospice*. The word comes from the Latin root *hospes,* meaning both "guest" and "host." Thus, a hospice (the host) takes care of the patient (the guest). During the Middle Ages, monks and nuns gave shelter and solace to sick or weary travelers. Modern hospice care, which began in Great Britain in 1967, gained rapid acceptance as an alternative to hospital care for terminally ill patients. Today there are more than 2,500 hospices in the United States.

An alternative to hospitals, hospices are homelike places where dying people and their families are given the physical and emotional support to help them cope with terminal illness.

person's feelings. In addition, people might try to encourage the dying person to work through the sequence of stages in the belief that by doing so the dying person will reach the acceptance stage sooner. However, what a dying person may really need is to be treated as a living individual with hopes and feelings, not as someone undergoing predictable stages of behavior.

Dying with Dignity

Dying people, like other people, need security, self-confidence, and dignity. Dying people may also need relief from pain. One controversial issue is whether terminally ill individuals should be given painkilling drugs, such as narcotics, that are highly addictive. Physicians usually try to balance the patient's need for relief from severe and constant pain against the dangers of such drugs. However, some people feel that to worry about addiction does not make sense when a person is going to die soon.

Dying people, perhaps even more than other people, need to feel cared for and supported. Therefore, it is helpful for family members to encourage a dying person to talk about his or her feelings. Sometimes it is enough just to spend quiet time with the person—to let the person know that he or she is not alone. Family members and others also can help by assisting with the financial and legal arrangements to pay for medical care and distribution of property. The knowledge that one's final wishes will be carried out can help the dying person gain a sense of peace and completion.

Some dying people want to know all the details regarding their situation; others do not. Therefore, it is important for family members and health professionals to understand the extent of the person's need for details. It is also important to give the person accurate information about what she or he can expect to experience in terms of pain and loss of body functions and control. Old and dying people should not be treated like infants, but as adults who have dignity and a right to know what is going to happen to them.

The Hospice Alternative Linda mentioned that her grandmother had been in a hospice. A **hospice** is a homelike place where dying people and their families are given the physical and emotional support to help them cope with terminal illness. Unlike hospitals, hospices do not restrict visiting hours. Family members and friends work with trained staff to provide physical comfort and emotional support. Hospice care may be given in the patient's own home by visiting hospice workers.

In a hospital, rules determine a patient's treatment—usually the patient has little say in the matter. In a hospice, however, dying people are allowed more control over their lives. They are encouraged to make decisions about their diets, activities, and medication. Relatives and friends often remain in contact with the hospice staff to cope with their own feelings of grief after the person has died.

Euthanasia The term **euthanasia** comes from the Greek language and means "easy death" (*eu* means "well"; *thanatos* means "death"). Euthanasia—also called mercy killing—is another controversial issue regarding death and dying.

Some physicians may consider euthanasia when they are absolutely convinced that there is no hope for a person's recovery, such as when a person has been in a coma for a long time or when the pain of a terminal illness is so severe and constant as to be unbearable. Euthanasia is illegal in most states.

Opponents of euthanasia argue that no one has the right to take—or to help another person take—a life, even one's own life. Opponents also maintain that new medications and therapies are continually being developed and that a person who feels today that death is the most desirable option may feel more optimistic tomorrow or next week. In other words, the pain and suffering may be temporary, but death is permanent.

Closing Section 4

Evaluating Information

Point out to students that in Western culture, traditional signs of mourning, such as wearing black clothing for a year following the death of a close relative, have declined and almost disappeared. Ask students to consider whether this decline in observance of such rituals helps or hinders the bereavement process. *(Some students may say that the decline is helpful because people are freer to develop their own ways of dealing with grief, whereas others may say that the rituals give people guidelines for handling their grief.)*

Identifying Cause and Effect

Point out to students that only about 100 years ago, most people died at home. Many were prepared for burial by their relatives. Ask students to analyze how the movement of the dying to hospitals and hospices and the growth of the funeral industry have influenced Americans' views about death.

Reviewing Section 4

Have students complete the Section Review questions on page 293.

The Living Will   Many people today write **living wills** to avoid being kept alive by artificial support systems (such as respirators) when there is no hope for recovery. The living will is a legal document.

A living will is intended to spare people the perceived indignity and cost of being kept alive when there is no hope of survival and to spare their families from having to make the decision to remove a loved one from an artificial life-support system. The idea is that once the person has died, the family members can grieve and move on with their lives. Of course, whether to have a living will is a choice that each individual must make.

The Funeral

The funeral is a traditional way for a community to acknowledge that one of its members has died. The rituals of the funeral also provide a framework for what to do and how to act when a family member or friend has died.

The specific kind of funeral chosen usually reflects religious beliefs and cultural customs. Some funeral services tie a person's death to the ongoing progression of time and the universe. Various professionals, such as undertakers and religious leaders, can be especially helpful when a family's grief adds to the difficulty of making decisions concerning the final arrangements for the deceased.

Funerals are a way of saying good-bye. But they accomplish much more. As the deceased is physically removed and prepared for burial or cremation, his or her body is both physically and symbolically separated from the living. In some religions and cultures, the transition is slow. Some customs provide periods of time during which mourners may view the body and meet with family members.

Funerals also provide a way to remember and celebrate the life of the deceased. Many funerals include a eulogy—a speech praising the person who has just died. Finally, there is the burial or the cremation of the body. This is when family and friends physically let go of the person who has died.

Bereavement

 A DAY IN THE LIFE   Linda was sad when her grandmother died, but she may also have felt a sense of relief that her suffering was finally over. Such feelings of relief often seem disturbing, but they are rather common. The people who are left behind are said to be **bereaved**, which means mourning

Different cultures deal with death in different ways. Most cultures have rituals to commemorate the life and passing of the deceased. Here, a New Orleans jazz band is featured in a funeral procession known as a wake.

over something or someone precious who has been taken away. People who are bereaved may have feelings of sadness and loneliness, numbness, anger, and even relief. When the dying person suffers greatly, family members may feel they have reached the limits of their ability to be helpful. Therefore, it is normal for them to feel a certain amount of relief when death finally comes.

Some bereaved people may join support groups or seek professional help in dealing with their grief. With or without such help, most bereaved people eventually recover from their losses. They may never forget the person they have lost, but they usually become less preoccupied by the loss itself. They resume their lives at home and at work. They may always miss the person who died, but most of the time they are able to resume normal functioning. Sometimes the survivors grow in compassion because of their loss and gain a deeper appreciation of the value of life.

SECTION 4 REVIEW   go.hrw.com **Homework Practice Online**   Keyword: SY3 HP12

1. List two or three ways that people tend to try to push aside death rather than face it.

2. Identify three ways in which hospice care differs from hospital care.

3. **Critical Thinking** *Sequencing* List in order the five stages of death and dying in Kübler-Ross's theory.

Section 4 Review: Answers

1. Possible answers include avoiding speaking about death and dying; keeping terminally ill patients alive by artificial means; and using euphemisms for death, such as "passed away" or "gone," instead of more explicit terms.

2. Unlike hospitals, hospices do not restrict visiting hours; family and friends are included in planning and providing care; a dying person is allowed control over the care he or she receives, including making decisions about diet, activities, and medication.

3. The five stages are denial, anger, bargaining, depression, and acceptance.

Chapter 12 Review: Answers

Writing a Summary
See the section subtitles for the main topics in the chapter.

Identifying People and Ideas
1. system in which men play the dominant role in marriage and society
2. the ability to create, originate, and produce
3. a period of reassessment occurring during midlife
4. feelings of emptiness and loss that mothers and fathers experience after children have left home

293

Chapter 12 REVIEW AND ASSESSMENT RESOURCES

Technology
► Chapter 12 Test Generator (on the One-Stop Planner)
► HRW Go site

Reinforcement, Review, and Assessment
► Chapter 12 Review, pp. 294–295
► Chapter Review and Activities with Answer Key
► Alternative Assessment Handbook
► Portfolio Assessment Handbook
► Chapter 12 Test (Form A or B)

PSYCHOLOGY PROJECTS

Linking to Community Invite a gerontologist or a representative from a local hospice to speak to the class about the concept of death with dignity. Some questions students may wish to ask the speaker include the following:

---

5. the end of menstruation
6. theories that cells malfunction as a result of damage rather than heredity
7. dementia occurring after the age of 65
8. a progressive form of mental deterioration that affects elderly persons
9. a homelike place where dying people and their families are given the physical and emotional support to help them cope with terminal illness
10. legal documents expressing a person's intention to refuse medical treatment if the person becomes terminally ill and unable to communicate such a refusal

Understanding Main Ideas

1. Factors include age, ethnicity, education, social class, and religion.
2. Both describe a period in which people search for identity.
3. It helps older adults maintain the belief that life is meaningful and helps them let go of their possessions and relationships as the end of life nears.
4. They might spend time with the person, help with legal or financial concerns, provide requested information, carry out final wishes, or encourage the person to discuss his or her feelings.

Thinking Critically

1. Students may mention middlescence and the fact that middle-aged people may search for new identities and interests.

Chapter 12 REVIEW

Writing a Summary

Using standard grammar, spelling, sentence structure, and punctuation, summarize the information in this chapter. Consider:
• the issues faced by persons in young and middle adulthood
• issues of importance to elderly persons, and how people cope with issues related to death and dying

Identifying People and Ideas

Identify the following terms or people and use them in appropriate sentences.

1. patriarchy
2. generativity
3. midlife crisis
4. empty-nest syndrome
5. menopause
6. cellular damage theories
7. senile dementia
8. Alzheimer's disease
9. hospice
10. living wills

Understanding Main Ideas

SECTION 1 (pp. 274–280)
1. What factors typically influence a young adult's choice of a spouse?

SECTION 2 (pp. 280–284)
2. In what ways are middlescence and adolescence similar?

SECTION 3 (pp. 284–291)
3. Why is maintaining ego integrity important for older adults?

SECTION 4 (pp. 291–293)
4. List two ways in which family members and friends can help a dying person.

Thinking Critically

1. **Evaluating** Why do you think large numbers of middle-aged adults enroll in classes and programs offered by community organizations, schools, and colleges?

2. **Making Generalizations and Predictions** How could the concept of free radicals be used in a campaign to discourage teenagers from using drugs and alcohol?

3. **Analyzing Information** What strengths might workers in the different stages of adulthood bring to a business?

4. **Drawing Inferences and Conclusions** What steps might a young person take to prepare for a successful late adulthood?

5. **Categorizing** What are the advantages and disadvantages of classifying adult development into stages?

Writing About Psychology

1. **Summarizing** Read about the marriage or funeral customs in a different culture or during an earlier time in history. As you read, look for answers to the following questions: What people play important roles in the customs? What is the basis of the customs? How have the customs changed over time, if at all, and what has led to the changes? Write a brief report summarizing your findings.

2. **Categorizing** Create a two-page dialogue between the following fictional characters: a 25-year-old, his or her 50-year-old parent, and his or her 75-year-old grandparent. In the dialogue, have the characters discuss some of the challenges each of them is facing and the methods each character is using to face the challenges. Use the graphic organizer below to help you with your dialogue.

25-year-old	50-year-old	75-year-old

- When and how did the concept of death with dignity emerge?
- Is the number of hospices in the United States likely to increase as the baby-boom generation continues to age?
- What kind of training do hospice workers need?
- Why is doctor-assisted suicide such a controversial issue?
- Are living wills legally enforceable?

Building Social Studies Skills

Interpreting Graphs

Study the graph below. Then use the information in the graph to help you answer the questions that follow.

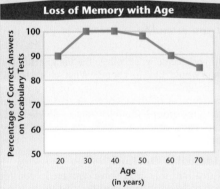

Loss of Memory with Age

Source: Light and Burke, (eds.), Language, Memory, and Aging, 1988

1. Which of the following statements accurately uses the information found in the graph?
   a. The younger a person is, the better that person will perform on a vocabulary test.
   b. A person's age is never a factor in performance on vocabulary exams.
   c. People in their 20s and 30s are most able to write well.
   d. Performance on vocabulary tests declines after age 40.
2. How might a psychologist explain the improvement in scores that takes place during the period from 20 years of age to 30 years of age?

Analyzing Primary Sources

Read the following excerpt from *On Death and Dying,* in which Dr. Elisabeth Kübler-Ross discusses the behavior of a dying patient. Then answer the questions that follow.

"Another patient was in utmost pain and discomfort, unable to go home because of her dependence on injections for pain relief. She had a son who proceeded with his plans to get married, as the patient had wished. She was very sad to think that she would be unable to attend this big day, for he was her oldest and favorite child. . . . She had made all sorts of promises if she could only live long enough to attend this marriage. The day preceding the wedding she left the hospital as an elegant lady. Nobody would have believed her real condition. She was the 'happiest woman in the whole world' and looked radiant. . . . I will never forget the moment when she returned to the hospital. She looked tired and somewhat exhausted and—before I could say hello—said, "Now don't forget I have another son!""

3. According to Kübler-Ross's stages of dying, which stage had the patient in the excerpt reached?
   a. denial
   b. anger
   c. bargaining
   d. depression
4. Why do you think that the patient in the excerpt thought it important to tell Kübler-Ross that she had another son?

PSYCHOLOGY PROJECTS

Linking to Community

Using Interviewing Skills Working with a partner, create a chart or other visual that summarizes the physical, mental, and social characteristics and issues of young adulthood, middle adulthood, and late adulthood. Start off by filling in the visual with information from the chapter. Then interview people in each of the three stages to build on what you have already filled in. When your visual is completed, present your chart to the class.

📶 **internet** connect

Internet Activity: go.hrw.com
KEYWORD: SY3 PS12

Choose an activity on adulthood to:
- create a product or advertisement applying various perspectives of motivation to target young adults.
- write a newspaper article on the challenges of middle adulthood.
- conduct a poll or interview regarding the joys and challenges of late adulthood.

UNIT 4 REVIEW

▶ TEACH

Have students review the Case Studies feature on page 261. Organize students into small groups and have each group decide whether it is in teenagers' best interests to take part-time jobs. Have students review the four-step process provided in the Psychology in Action simulation while arriving at their decision. Ask the groups to prepare presentations outlining how they arrived at their decision. Have one student from each group present the group's decision to the rest of the class.

▶ EXTEND

Have students review the Psychology in Action Simulation. Then ask them to research the course offerings of different colleges. Have students use the decision-making steps provided in the simulation to decide which courses they would be most interested in taking. Ask the students to note the results of their decision-making processes in their journals.

▶ PSYCHOLOGY IN ACTION

As an extension of the simulation activity, have each student write an essay expressing what characteristics he or she would want in a college. Remind students to use standard grammar, spelling, sentence structure, and punctuation. Have volunteers present their essays to the class.

UNIT 4

PSYCHOLOGY IN ACTION

YOU MAKE THE DECISION . . .

Which college should you attend?

Complete the following activity in small cooperative groups. Your group is looking for information about a number of colleges to help the members of the group decide which one they would like to attend. Work together to prepare a flyer that describes one of the colleges that a member of your group would like to attend.

1. Gather Information. Use your textbook and other resources to find information that might help you decide what college the members of your group would like to attend. What characteristics are the group members looking for in a college? What type of information about colleges is available to the group? You may want to divide up different parts of the research among the various members of the group.

2. Identify Options. After reviewing the information that you have gathered, consider which college has characteristics that the members of your group find appealing. Your final decision may be easier to reach if you consider as many options as possible. Be sure to record the options your group has identified for your flyer.

3. Predict Consequences. Now take each option you and the members of your group came up with and consider how each college might meet the needs of each group member. Ask yourself questions such as,

- Does this college offer a major in the group member's area of interest?
- Is this college affordable?

Once you have predicted the consequences of each option your group has identified, record them as notes for your flyer.

4. Take Action to Implement Your Decision. After you have considered your options, you should create your flyer. Be sure that your flyer makes your decision about what college to attend very clear. You will need to support your decision by including information you gathered and by explaining why you rejected other options. You may want to create charts or graphs to support your decision. When you are ready, decide who in your group will present the flyer. Then make your presentation to the class. Good luck!

UNIT 5

Overview

In Unit 5, students will learn about various aspects of the human personality, including how and why a person experiences emotions, the theories and psychological tests related to personality development, and the effect of cultural gender roles on an individual's attitudes and behavior.

CHAPTER 13 • *Motivation and Emotion* focuses on the various theories explaining how and why people experience various emotions.

CHAPTER 14 • *Theories of Personality* explores the different theoretical explanations for the development of the human personality.

CHAPTER 15 • *Psychological Tests* explains the various means psychologists use to assess personality.

CHAPTER 16 • *Gender Roles* reviews the evolution of gender roles, and addresses the impact these expectations have on an individual's emotional and behavioral development.

UNIT 5

PERSONALITY

▶ Internet Activity

internet connect

go.hrw.com

TOPIC: Personality Development: The Game
GO TO: go.hrw.com
KEYWORD: SY3 UNIT 5

Have students access the Internet through the HRW Go site to research factors relating to the development of personality. Organize students into groups and have them apply their research by creating a board game simulating the various factors and theories involved in personality development. Groups should create rules, a playing board, and any other items required for their game. The game should integrate information from their research and reflect the positive and negative forces involved in the development of personality.

▶ Using Visuals

Have students look at the photograph on page 297. How do they think this photograph relates to personality? Then explain that this unit focuses on how an individual's emotions, personality, and gender govern his or her behavior and attitudes.

CHAPTERS

297

Motivation and Emotion

CHAPTER RESOURCE MANAGER

	Objectives	Pacing Guide		Reproducible and Review Resources
SECTION 1: **The Psychology of Motivation** (pp. 300–302)	List and explain four theories of motivation.	**Regular** 1 day *Block Scheduling Handbook with Team Teaching Strategies, Chapter 13*	**Block Scheduling** .5 day	**PS** Readings and Case Studies, Chapter 13 **SM** Study Skills and Writing Guide, Part 3, Stage 4 **REV** Section 1 Review, p. 302
SECTION 2: **Biological Needs: Focus on Hunger** (pp. 303–306)	Describe the hunger drive, and analyze the causes of obesity.	**Regular** 1 day *Block Scheduling Handbook with Team Teaching Strategies, Chapter 13*	**Block Scheduling** .5 day	**E** Creating a Psychology Fair, Activity 7 **REV** Section 2 Review, p. 306
SECTION 3: **Psychological Needs** (pp. 306–311)	Explain stimulus motives, the balance theory, and achievement motivation.	**Regular** 1 day *Block Scheduling Handbook with Team Teaching Strategies, Chapter 13*	**Block Scheduling** .5 day	**SM** Mastering Critical Thinking Skills 13 **REV** Section 3 Review, p. 311
SECTION 4: **Emotions** (pp. 311–316)	Explain how psychologists describe emotion.	**Regular** 1 day *Block Scheduling Handbook with Team Teaching Strategies, Chapter 13*	**Block Scheduling** .5 day	**E** Research Projects and Activities for Teaching Psychology **RS** Essay and Research Themes for Advanced Placement Students, Theme 11 **REV** Section 4 Review, p. 316

Chapter Resource Key

PS	Primary Sources	**A**	Assessment
RS	Reading Support	**REV**	Review
E	Enrichment		Transparencies
SM	Skills Mastery		CD-ROM

 Video

 Internet

 Holt Presentation Maker Using Microsoft® PowerPoint®

 One-Stop Planner CD–ROM

See the *One-Stop Planner* for a complete list of additional resources for students and teachers.

One-Stop Planner CD–ROM

It's easy to plan lessons, select resources, and print out materials for your students when you use the *One-Stop Planner CD-ROM with Test Generator.*

Technology Resources

 One-Stop Planner, Lesson 13.1
 Homework Practice Online
 Teaching Transparencies 29: Maslow's Theory of the Hierarchy of Needs
 HRW Go Site

 One-Stop Planner, Lesson 13.2
 Homework Practice Online
 CNN. Presents Psychology: The Hunger Drive: Skinny Pigs
 HRW Go Site

 One-Stop Planner, Lesson 13.3
 Homework Practice Online
 HRW Go Site

 One-Stop Planner, Lesson 13.4
Homework Practice Online

Chapter Review and Assessment

 HRW Go site

REV Chapter 13 Review, pp. 318–319

REV Chapter Review Activities with Answer Key

A Chapter 13 Test (Form A or B)

A Portfolio Assessment Handbook

A Alternative Assessment Handbook

Chapter 13 Test Generator (on the One-Stop Planner)

Global Skill Builder CD-ROM

---

internet connect

HRW ONLINE RESOURCES

GO TO: go.hrw.com
Then type in a keyword.

TEACHER HOME PAGE
KEYWORD: SY3 Teacher

CHAPTER INTERNET ACTIVITIES
KEYWORD: SY3 PS13
Choose an activity on motivation and emotion to:
- create a comic strip or set of drawings to illustrate cognitive consistency, balance theory, or cognitive-dissonance theory.
- apply various perspectives of motivation to a given economic situation.
- create a brochure of psychological and biological aspects of obesity.

CHAPTER ENRICHMENT LINKS
KEYWORD: SY3 CH13

ONLINE ASSESSMENT
Homework Practice
KEYWORD: SY3 HP13
Standardized Test Prep
KEYWORD: SY3 STP13
Rubrics
KEYWORD: SS Rubrics

CONTENT UPDATES
KEYWORD: SS Content Updates

HOLT PRESENTATION MAKER
KEYWORD: SY3 PPT13

ONLINE READING SUPPORT
KEYWORD: SS Strategies

CURRENT EVENTS
KEYWORD: S3 Current Events

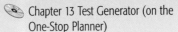

Additional Resources

PRINT RESOURCES FOR TEACHERS
Csikszentmihalyi, M. (1990). *Flow.* New York: Harper & Row.

Logue, A. W. (1993). *The psychology of eating and drinking* (2nd ed.). New York: W. H. Freeman.

Myers, D. (1992). *The pursuit of happiness.* New York: Morrow.

Tavris, C. (1989). *Anger: The misunderstood emotion.* New York: Touchstone Books.

PRINT RESOURCES FOR STUDENTS
Carson, J., & Hatfield, E. (1991). *Psychology of emotion and stress.* Fort Worth, TX: Holt, Rinehart and Winston.

Frankl, V. (1984). *Man's search for meaning.* New York: Touchstone Books.

Geisel, T. S., and Geisel, A. (1990). *Oh the places you'll go!* New York: Random House.

MULTIMEDIA RESOURCES
Masks: How we hide our emotions (VHS). Social Studies School Service, 10200 Jefferson Boulevard, Room 33, P.O. Box 802, Culver City, CA 90232-0802.

Self-fulfillment: Becoming the person you want to be (VHS). Social Studies School Service, 10200 Jefferson Boulevard, Room 33, P.O. Box 802, Culver City, CA 90232-0802.

A separate peace (VHS). Social Studies School Service, 10200 Jefferson Boulevard, Room 33, P.O. Box 802, Culver City, CA 90232-0802.

MOTIVATION AND EMOTION

Point out to students that psychology, like other scientific fields, involves the study of causes and effects. Ask students to consider the inner causes and the inner effects of human actions. Pick a simple, universal action such as eating. What are some of the inner causes that motivate a person to eat? Do people eat strictly because of biological needs, or does eating also fulfill some psychological or social need? What are the effects of eating—both physical and emotional? Explain that in this chapter students will learn more about the nature of human motivation and emotion. Tell students that they will also learn about theories that have been proposed to explain these interrelated concepts.

Sections

1 **The Psychology of Motivation**

2 **Biological Needs: Focus on Hunger**

3 **Psychological Needs**

4 **Emotions**

Each of the four questions identified on page 298 corresponds to one of these sections.

Chapter 13

MOTIVATION AND EMOTION

Read to Discover

1 What are the four theories of motivation?

2 What is the hunger drive, and what are the causes of obesity?

3 What are the stimulus motives, the balance theory, and achievement motivation?

4 How do psychologists describe emotion?

298

Each chapter begins with a vignette, called "A Day in the Life," that relates the information discussed in the chapter to the everyday events in the lives of a group of fictional high school students. The text of the chapter occasionally refers back to the vignette to demonstrate the application of the concept being discussed. An icon marked "A Day in the Life" is placed next to these references.

Copy the following graphic organizer onto the chalkboard, omitting the italicized text. Fill in the circles as you introduce the psychology of motivation.

Psychology of Motivation

Needs   *Drives*   *Theories of Motivation*

A DAY IN THE LIFE

March 8

Hannah, Todd, and Dan gathered at Hannah's house after school to study. Hannah was trying to work on her psychology assignment, but she could not seem to concentrate.

"Hannah, what are you thinking about?" Todd finally asked. "Every time I look at you, you're staring off into space and smiling."

"I'm sorry. I just can't stop thinking about my violin recital last night. I played better than I ever had in a recital before."

"I'm glad I was there to see it. You were great," Dan said.

"Thanks!" Hannah replied with enthusiasm. "At first, I was really nervous, but once I started playing, I was fine. Of course, it really helped that you, Marc, and Linda were all there with my parents. For some reason, I was so much more confident because I knew that all of you were in the audience."

"I really wish I could have been there," Todd commented, "but I had to study for that advanced biology test I had today."

Hannah knew how much Todd enjoyed studying science. "Don't

worry about it," Hannah said. "You love science. And you need to do well in biology if you're going to get that scholarship."

"You'll have to try to go to the next recital, though, Todd. Hannah is really good," Dan added. "Hey, wasn't Janet going to study with us this afternoon?"

"She'll be here later," Hannah answered. "She wanted to stop by the recreation center after school. The youth group is planning a hiking trip and, knowing Janet, she'll probably be the first person to sign up. That is, of course, if she can fit it into her schedule."

Everyone laughed because they knew Hannah was right. Whenever Janet was not working at her part-time job or studying for her classes, she was outdoors playing basketball or riding her mountain bike.

Just then, Eddie, Hannah's three-year-old brother, came wandering into the room. "Hannah, I'm hungry," he announced as he walked over to sit with Dan.

Dan loved spending time with Eddie, so he welcomed the opportunity to take a study break. "You know what, Eddie?" Dan said. "I'm hungry too. Let's have a snack."

Key Terms

- motive
- need
- drives
- instincts
- homeostasis
- self-actualization
- obese
- stimulus motives
- sensory deprivation
- achievement motivation
- performance goals
- learning goals
- extrinsic rewards
- intrinsic rewards
- cognitive consistency
- balance theory
- imbalance
- nonbalance
- cognitive-dissonance theory
- affiliation
- emotions
- opponent-process theory

WHY PSYCHOLOGY MATTERS

A number of forces influence human motivation. Use **CNNfyi.com** or other current events sources to learn more about what motivates people to take action.

CNNfyi.com

Why does Todd push himself to study advanced biology when he could be relaxing in front of the television set or outside playing ball? Why does Hannah spend hours, days, and weeks of her free time practicing the violin for a 40-minute recital? Is the elation Hannah feels after her recital worth the anxiety she felt on stage? The answers to these questions involve motivation (the elusive feelings that make us do the things we do) and emotions (the responses generated by certain situations). In this chapter, we will examine the ways in which our emotions lead us to behave in certain ways.

Using Key Terms

Have students prepare a matching test using the key terms and their definitions, found in the Glossary or in Chapter 13. Students should write their test items on one side of a sheet of paper and the answers to the test items on the other side of the paper. Then have students exchange their papers and complete the tests. Have students keep their papers for later review.

Journal Activity

After students have read the "A Day in the Life" vignette, ask them to think about some past goal or aim they pushed themselves to achieve. Have them write in their journals about that goal and why they considered the goal an important one to achieve. Did they have to give up anything to reach the goal? Ask them also to write about how they felt when they achieved the goal or failed to achieve it.

299

Section Objective

▶ List and explain four theories of motivation.

This objective is assessed in the Section Review on page 302 and in the Chapter 13 Review.

Opening Section 1

Motivator

Have students provide examples of activities they performed the previous day. Write these activities on the chalkboard. For each activity listed, ask students to supply the reason why they performed the activity. Organize these reasons under headings labeled *Biological Reasons* and *Psychological Reasons*. Then tell students that people have both biological and psychological needs and that it is those needs that motivate people to act. Have students read Section 1 to learn about the theories of motivation.

Using Truth or Fiction

Each chapter opens with several "Truth or Fiction" statements that relate to the concepts discussed in the chapter. Ask students whether they think each statement is true or false. Answers to each item as well as explanations are provided at appropriate points within the text under the heading "Truth or Fiction Revisited."

Class Discussion

Ask students to think about the important psychological needs that people have. Have students describe these needs and then analyze the cultural, familial, and personal forces that might give rise to these needs.

Readings and Case Studies

TRUTH OR fiction ? Read the following statements about psychology. Do you think they are true or false? You will learn whether each statement is true or false as you read the chapter.

- Robins and other birds have to learn the songs that are characteristic of their species.
- The major trigger of the hunger drive is hunger pangs in the stomach.
- "Getting away from it all" by being in a place away from all sensory input is relaxing.
- When people feel anxious, they want to be alone.

The Psychology of Motivation

Why do many people like to travel to faraway places or to try new foods? The answer to this question—and other questions about why people do the things they do—relates to motivation. A **motive** is a stimulus that moves a person to behave in ways designed to accomplish a specific goal. Motives are considered theoretical states because they cannot be seen or measured directly. Psychologists assume that people and other organisms are motivated when they observe the people trying to reach their goals. The psychology of motivation deals with the *whys* of behavior.

Needs

When psychologists speak of motives, they also often speak of needs. A **need** is a condition in which we require something we lack. People have both biological and psychological needs. People fulfill biological needs to survive. Examples of biological needs include the need for oxygen and food. Some biological needs such as for food or sleep occur in part because of physical deprivation. That is, people feel hungry or sleepy when they have not eaten or slept for a while.

Achievement, self-esteem, a sense of belonging, and social approval are examples of psychological needs. Like biological needs, psychological needs motivate people to accomplish certain goals. However, psychological needs differ from biological

needs in two important ways. First, psychological needs are not necessarily based on deprivation. A person with a need to achieve an A on a test may already be an honor-roll student. Second, unlike biological needs, which are inborn, psychological needs may be learned. People possess common biological characteristics, thus they have similar physical needs. For example, all people must eat to survive, therefore all people need food. However, people have different psychological needs because they learn from a variety of experiences. Psychological needs are shaped by culture and learning, so people's psychological needs differ markedly. For example, some people prefer vegetarian diets because they believe it is morally wrong to kill animals for food.

Drives

Biological needs and psychological needs give rise to **drives**—the forces that motivate an organism to take action. The biological need for food gives rise to the hunger drive. The biological need for water gives rise to the thirst drive.

Although hunger and thirst are aroused by biological needs, the *experience* of them is psychological. The longer we are deprived of something such as food or water, the stronger our drive becomes. For example, our hunger drive is stronger 6 hours after eating than it is 20 minutes after eating.

Theories of Motivation

Psychologists agree that motives prompt behavior, but they are not in agreement about the nature of motivation. The leading theories of motivation are instinct theory, drive-reduction theory, humanistic theory, and sociocultural theory.

Instinct Theory   Behavior patterns that are genetically transmitted from generation to generation are known as **instincts**. Sometimes they are called fixed-action patterns. Researchers have discovered that many animals are born to act in certain ways in certain situations. Studies have shown that birds acquire the songs characteristic of their species largely by instinct (Marler, 1991).

Siamese fighting fish reared in isolation also display instinctive behavior. Males fan their fins and gills in the typical threatening posture when other males are introduced into their tanks. Similarly, bees perform an instinctive "dance" to relay the location of food to other bees (Moffett, 1990).

Teaching Section 1

Guided Practice

List on the chalkboard each of the needs included in Maslow's hierarchy of needs. For each item on the list, have students provide examples of ways in which people could go about satisfying that need. Write these suggestions on the chalkboard. Then have students evaluate Maslow's theory of the hierarchy of needs. Under what circumstances would the need for personal growth outweigh basic needs? Why is it that some people show no interest in satisfying higher-level needs? How effective is Maslow's theory in explaining human motivation?

Independent Practice

Tell students to imagine that they have been shipwrecked alone on a desert island, with little chance for rescue. Have them write a series of short diary entries about life on the island. In the diary entries, students should describe how they go about satisfying the needs listed in Maslow's hierarchy of needs. Have volunteers read their diary entries aloud to the class. Which needs would students satisfy first? How would satisfying these needs help the castaways satisfy the higher needs in the hierarchy?

Certain behavior patterns are largely instinctive and do not have to be learned. Birds raised in isolation will build nests characteristic of their species, despite the fact that they were never taught how to do this by other members of the species.

TRUTH OR fiction
■ REVISITED ■

It is not true that robins and other birds have to learn the songs that are characteristic of their species. These songs are largely inborn, or instinctive, not learned.

At one time, psychologists believed that human behavior, like that of animals, is instinctive. In the late 1800s and early 1900s, psychologists William James (1890) and William McDougall (1908) argued that people have instincts that foster survival and social behavior. Today, however, most psychologists do not believe that human behavior is primarily motivated by instinct. If a behavior pattern is instinctive, they argue, it must be found throughout a species. However, there is so much variation in the way people behave that much of human behavior is unlikely to be instinctive.

Drive-Reduction Theory Psychologist Clark Hull formulated the drive-reduction theory in the 1930s. Drive-reduction theory is based on learning as well as motivation. According to this theory, people and animals experience a drive arising from a need as an unpleasant tension. They learn to do whatever will reduce that tension by reducing the drive, such as eating to reduce their hunger drive.

Some drives, such as hunger, are caused by biological needs, which are inborn. Other drives, such as a drive for money, are learned from experience. According to drive-reduction theory, people will try to reduce these learned drives, just as they try to reduce biological drives.

Basic drives, such as hunger, motivate us to restore an internal state of equilibrium, or balance. The tendency to maintain this state of equilibrium in the body is called **homeostasis**. Homeostasis works like a thermostat. When room temperature drops below a certain point—called the set point—the heat comes on. The heat stays on until the set point is reached. Similarly, according to the theory, when people are hungry, they will eat until they reach a level at which they are no longer hungry.

Drive-reduction theory seems to apply to many biological drives, including hunger and thirst. Yet people sometimes eat when they are not hungry. They also often act to increase rather than decrease the tension they experience. For example, some people enjoy riding roller coasters and driving fast cars. Yet these activities *increase* rather than decrease the tension they experience. Clearly, drive-reduction theory does not explain all motivation.

Humanistic Theory Humanistic psychologists argue that instinct theory and drive-reduction theory suggest that human behavior is mechanical and directed only toward surviving and reducing tension. According to humanistic psychologists, however, people are also motivated by the conscious desire for personal growth and artistic fulfillment. In fact, they argue, sometimes our drive to fulfill such needs outweighs our drive to meet more basic needs. For example, some people seek artistic or political goals, even though they may have difficulty affording food or may have to give up a certain level of comfort or security to achieve their goals. Some artists, musicians, and writers commit themselves to their artistic goals even when they are unable to make a living by doing so.

Abraham Maslow, one of the pioneers of humanistic psychology, pointed out that some people are willing to tolerate pain, hunger, and other kinds of tension to achieve their artistic or political goals. Hannah undoubtedly spent countless hours practicing the violin and learning new songs. Humanistic theory would suggest that her desire to achieve artistic fulfillment was worth sacrificing other desirable activities, such as spending time with her friends.

A DAY IN THE LIFE

Cross-Curricular Link: Economics

Explain that insurance underwriters analyze the risks involved in supplying insurance to various categories of individuals. Economist Mark B. Valenziano suggests that a new system be used to rate applicants for disability insurance. Rather than using the traditional system of rating risk according to occupation, Valenziano suggests testing applicants' inner motivation and using the results to determine risk. The idea behind the suggestion is that a highly motivated person is less likely to file a disability claim than is a poorly motivated person.

Valenziano, Mark B. (Feb. 20, 1995). Consider rating DI with motivational classes. *National Underwriter, Life and Health–Financial Services Edition.* 16.

⑅ internet connect

TOPIC: Theories of Motivation
GO TO: go.hrw.com
KEYWORD: SY3 PS13

Have students access the Internet through the HRW Go site to research theories of motivation presented in the textbook. Then tell students to imagine they are buying a car, creating a personal budget, or choosing a job, and then have the students write a paragraph analyzing how the decision could be predicted or interpreted depending upon which theory of motivation is applied to the situation.

301

Closing Section 1

Taking a Stand

Review with students what they have learned about the various theories of motivation included in Section 1. Which theory do they think most persuasively explains human motivation? Have students argue their positions in brief debates or in oral reports.

Reviewing Section 1

Have students complete the Section Review questions on page 302.

Extension

Have students look through newspapers and magazines to locate a variety of product advertisements. Tell them to analyze the advertisements in terms of which needs the advertisements are promising to satisfy. How do such advertisements go about attempting to motivate people to buy certain products? How persuasive are such advertisements? How successful are these products in satisfying human needs? Have students discuss their findings in class.

Caption Question: Answer

Answers will vary but should be based on sound reasoning.

Section 1 Review: Answers

1. A motive is a stimulus that moves us to behave in ways designed to accomplish a specific goal; a need is a condition in which we require something we lack; a drive is a force that arouses action.

2. The four theories are instinct theory (behavior patterns are genetically transmitted), drive-reduction theory (people act to reduce drives and their associated tensions), humanistic theory (people act out of the desire for growth and fulfillment beyond basic survival needs), and sociocultural theory (individual needs and motives are influenced by culture and society).

3. Those who support the theory may say that in times of crisis, most people worry less about higher-level needs and more about survival. Those who refute the theory may say that even impoverished individuals are motivated by higher needs such as esteem.

302

Maslow claimed that people strive to fulfill their capacity for self-actualization. The term **self-actualization** refers to the need to become what one believes he or she is capable of being. The desire to fulfill oneself takes one past the point of just satisfying one's physical needs. Maslow believed that striving to become something or to do something meaningful in one's life is as essential to human well-being as food.

Maslow (1970) organized human needs into a hierarchy—a ranking of items in order of importance. (See Figure 13.1.) At the bottom of the hierarchy are biological needs. The need for self-actualization is at the top. Maslow believed that once a person's needs are satisfied at one level, the person will try to satisfy needs at the next higher level. For example, once food and drink have satisfied a person's biological needs, that person will then seek means to satisfy safety needs, such as the needs for shelter and security. Maslow believed that people rise naturally through the levels of this hierarchy as long as they do not encounter overwhelming obstacles along the way. Many people seek self-actualization through work, hobbies, and aesthetic experiences such as music, art, and poetry.

Critics of Maslow's hierarchy of needs argue that it does not apply to everyone (Neher, 1991). For example, some people show little interest in satisfying higher-level needs such as achievement and social recognition, even after their biological and safety needs have been met. But, one might ask, does their apparent lack of interest stem from not being motivated to seek achievement or from having met with overwhelming obstacles?

Sociocultural Theory Sociocultural theorists argue that even if basic drives such as hunger are inborn, cultural experiences and factors influence the behavior that people use to satisfy those drives. The foods people eat and the way they eat those

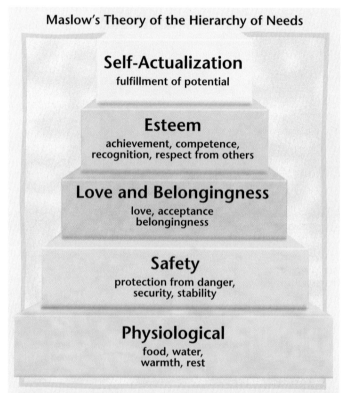

Maslow's Theory of the Hierarchy of Needs

Self-Actualization
fulfillment of potential

Esteem
achievement, competence, recognition, respect from others

Love and Belongingness
love, acceptance belongingness

Safety
protection from danger, security, stability

Physiological
food, water, warmth, rest

FIGURE 13.1 *Maslow believed that people begin to fulfill higher psychological needs (such as achievement) only after their basic survival needs (such as hunger and thirst) have been at least partially met.* **Do you agree or disagree?**

foods are shaped by culture. Cultural experience affects whether people prefer hot dogs or tacos, coffee or tea, apples or pineapples. Cultural experiences also affect whether people prefer kissing lips or rubbing noses to express feelings of affection.

SECTION 1 REVIEW

1. Define the following terms: *motive, need,* and *drive.*

2. Briefly summarize the four leading theories of motivation.

3. **Critical Thinking** *Supporting a Point of View* Maslow believed that people seek to satisfy basic survival needs before they seek to satisfy higher psychological needs. Use specific examples to argue for or against Maslow's theory of the hierarchy of needs.

► Describe the hunger drive, and analyze the causes of obesity.

This objective is assessed in the Section Review on page 306 and in the Chapter 13 Review.

Opening Section 2

Motivator

Discuss with students their feelings of hunger. Ask questions about how exercise, fatigue, and illness affect their appetites. What kinds of food satisfy their hunger, and what kinds do not satisfy their hunger? How do emotional factors, such as stress or unhappiness, affect their appetites? How do cultural expectations make them more or less hungry? List on the chalkboard some of the factors that make people feel hungry. Discuss with students any patterns that emerge from the list. Tell them that Section 2 focuses on hunger.

SECTION 2

Biological Needs: Focus on Hunger

Biological needs are based mainly on body tissue needs, such as the needs for food, water, air, temperature regulation, and pain avoidance. However, even basic biological needs can be complex because they involve psychological as well as physiological factors. People need food to survive, but food can mean much more than mere survival. Food can be a symbol of the closeness of the family or group of friends, or it can be something to make a stranger feel welcome. Food can also be part of a pleasurable social experience with others. For example, when Dan took time out from studying for his class to share a snack with Hannah's little brother Eddie, it was an enjoyable break for both of them.

The Hunger Drive

Hunger is regulated by both biological and psychological factors. In this section, we will look at the mechanisms in the body that are involved in the hunger drive. We will also examine the psychological influences that are involved in hunger.

The Role of the Mouth   The acts of chewing and swallowing provide certain sensations that help satisfy the hunger drive, as shown by "sham feeding" research with dogs. In a classic research experiment, tubes were implanted in dogs' throats so that the food they swallowed was dropped out of their bodies instead of moving into their stomachs (Janowitz & Grossman, 1949). Nevertheless, the dogs stopped feeding after a brief period. Based on the finding of this and other studies, researchers have concluded that chewing and swallowing apparently help reduce feelings of hunger in animals as well as in people.

The hunger drive is usually satisfied when the body digests food and the nutrients in the food enter the bloodstream. However, this takes time. Chewing and swallowing help let the body know that its hunger drive is being satisfied, thus saving us from eating more than is needed. Still, it is wise to stop eating *before* feeling completely full because it takes time for the digestive tract to metabolize

Although food is a basic biological need, it can also be part of a pleasurable social experience with others.

food and provide signals to the brain that the need for food has been satisfied.

The Role of the Stomach   It was once believed that the growls and contractions (called hunger pangs) of an empty stomach were the cause of hunger. Researchers did, in fact, find that when a person is hungry, his or her stomach does contract. However, they also found that the stomach contracts at other times as well (Cannon, 1939). Furthermore, people who have surgery to remove their stomachs still experience hunger. Thus, the researchers concluded that hunger pangs felt in the stomach play a role in hunger but are not the main factor involved in signaling hunger.

The Hypothalamus   The level of sugar in the blood and the part of the brain known as the hypothalamus are key influences on feelings of hunger. When people have not eaten for a while, their blood sugar level drops. Information about the sugar level is then communicated to the hypothalamus, which is known to be involved in the regulation of body temperature and various aspects of psychological motivation and emotion.

Researchers have learned more about how the hypothalamus functions through research conducted with laboratory animals. In these studies, researchers implanted electrodes on the hypothalami and observed the effects on the animals' behavior. They

303

Teaching Section 2

Cooperative Learning

Organize the class into groups, and have each group research and analyze a popular weight-control plan. Tell students that they may use plans from magazines or books or choose a nationally known plan, such as Weight Watchers®. In their analyses, the groups should determine if and how the plans address the biological and psychological influences on hunger. Groups should also analyze the plans according to the criteria for a sound weight-control program given on page 305. What are the strengths of the plan? What are its weaknesses?

Demonstration

Bring to class some cereal, bread, cooked pasta, bowls, plates, a measuring cup, and a scale. Ask volunteers to measure what they consider a reasonable amount of these foods for one day. Then point out that according to the U.S. Department of Agriculture, one should eat 6 to 11 servings of grains a day. A serving is 1 slice of bread, 1/2 cup of cooked pasta, or 1 ounce of ready-to-eat cereal. Weigh and measure the volunteers' portions. Does the evidence support the frequently made claim that Americans tend to eat large portions?

Researchers have discovered that a part of the hypothalamus, called the ventromedial hypothalamus (VMH), serves as a "stop-eating" center. When this portion of the hypothalamus is destroyed, the rat will continue to eat until it is several times its normal weight. Eventually, the rat's food intake will level off enough to simply maintain the rat's higher weight; that is, the rat will no longer continue to gain weight.

found that the side of the hypothalamus, called the lateral hypothalamus (LH), appears to function as a "start-eating" center. If the LH is electrically stimulated, the rat will begin to eat, even if it has just finished eating a large meal (Miller, 1995). Conversely, if a lesion is made in the LH, the rat may stop eating altogether and eventually die of starvation if it is not force-fed.

The underside of the hypothalamus, called the ventromedial hypothalamus (VMH), apparently functions as a "stop-eating" center. When this center is electrically stimulated, the rat will stop eating. When this part of the hypothalamus is destroyed, the rat will continue to eat until it is several times its normal weight. The damage to the VMH interferes with the rat's ability to recognize that its hunger has been fulfilled and the rat simply continues to nibble. Eventually, the rat's eating will level off and the rat will maintain the higher weight (Miller, 1995).

Psychological Influences Many biological factors affect the hunger drive. However, this is only part of the story. In human beings, psychological as well as biological factors affect feelings of hunger. For example, we usually eat more when we are in the presence of other people than when we are alone (Zajonc, 1965). Dan did not realize he was hungry until Eddie mentioned that he was hungry. Eddie, therefore, acted as a psychological influence on Dan's hunger drive.

Learning that certain amounts of food or drink will produce a feeling of well-being and relaxation can cause people to eat and drink when they feel upset. For example, they may develop the habit of eating and drinking at the first sign of pressure or anxiety as a way to fend off feeling any negative emotions. People with a tendency to eat compulsively or drink alcohol excessively need to be alert to this tendency. Likewise, parents should consider whether it is wise to give children food as a reward for doing something good. Rewarding with food can cause a child to grow up associating food with parental approval, perhaps leading to dietary problems in later life.

Obesity

More than half the adults in the United States are overweight, and 18 percent are **obese**—that is, they weigh more than 30 percent above their recommended weight. Being overweight is an increasing problem in the United States. For example, 38 percent of Californians were overweight in 1984, compared with 45 percent in 1990 and 53 percent in 1999 ("Californians losing fight," 2000).

Obese people encounter more than their fair share of illnesses, including heart disease, stroke, diabetes, gall bladder disease, gout, respiratory problems, even certain kinds of cancer. It has been estimated that 300,000 people in the United States

Closing Section 2

Taking a Stand

Have students write a short paragraph summarizing what is known about the causes of obesity. Then have students use this information to debate whether heredity or environment plays a greater role in influencing obesity.

Reviewing Section 2

Have students complete the Section Review questions on page 306.

Extension

Have students choose a culture other than that of the United States or an earlier time period in American history. Ask students to research body image, food, hunger, and eating in that culture or historical period. Have students determine that culture's or time period's attitude toward food and eating, types of food eaten, and view of the ideal body type for men and for women. Tell students to compare the findings from that culture or time period to current U.S. attitudes and behaviors. Have students report their findings to the class in a brief oral report.

Source: HAGAR THE HORRIBLE reprinted with special permission of King Features Syndicate.

die each year because of health problems related to excess weight and inactivity. Weight control is elusive for most obese people. They regain most of the weight they have lost, even when they have dieted successfully (Jeffery et al., 2000).

Losing Weight Psychologists have worked with other professionals to devise strategies to help overweight people lose weight. However, not everyone who is a few pounds overweight should be trying to slim down. For example, women in the United States today are often under social pressure to conform to an unnaturally slender feminine ideal. As a result, they tend to set unrealistic weight-loss goals (Sarwer & Madden, 1999).

Any teenager who considers going on a diet should proceed with caution because adolescents need a good deal of nourishment—perhaps more than any other age group. Adolescents should discuss the benefits and hazards of dieting with their parents and with a health professional, such as a doctor or school nurse.

A sound diet is one that is sensible, realistic, and well planned. Healthful weight-control programs do not involve fad diets such as fasting, eliminating carbohydrates, or eating excessive amounts of one particular food. Instead, they involve changes in lifestyle that include improving nutritional knowledge, decreasing caloric intake, exercising, and substituting healthful foods for harmful foods.

Most people in the United States eat too much fat and not enough fruits and vegetables. Fast foods like french fries, hamburgers, muffins, and candy tend to be particularly high in fat. Eating foods that are low in fat sets a good precedent for a lifetime of healthful eating. It is good for the heart and can also help in losing weight. Losing weight means "burning" or using more calories than you eat. Foods that are high in fat also tend to be high in calories. Nutritional knowledge helps people manage their consumption of food to take in fewer calories. Taking in fewer calories does not just mean eating smaller portions. It means switching to some lower-calorie foods—relying more on fresh, unsweetened fruits and vegetables (eating apples rather than apple pie), fish and poultry, and skim milk and cheese. It means cutting down on butter, margarine, oils, and sugar.

The same foods that help control weight—whole grains, fruits, and vegetables—also tend to be high in vitamins and fiber and low in fats. Such foods therefore may also reduce the risk of heart disease, cancer, and other illnesses.

Dieting plus exercise is more effective than dieting alone for shedding pounds and keeping them off. Exercise burns calories and builds muscle tissue, which metabolizes more calories than fatty tissue does.

Causes of Obesity Why are so many people obese? As with the hunger drive in general, both biological and psychological factors appear to contribute to obesity. Obesity seems to run in families. But does this mean that it is inherited? Not necessarily. For example, obese parents may simply encourage their children to overeat by having fattening foods around the house and by setting an example. However, research suggests that heredity plays a major role in obesity (Friedman & Brownell, 1995). One study showed that adopted children tend to more closely resemble their biological parents than their adoptive parents in terms of body weight (Stunkard et al., 1990).

Section Objective

► Explain stimulus motives, the balance theory, and achievement motivation.

This objective is assessed in the Section Review on page 311 and in the Chapter 13 Review.

Section 2 Review: Answers

1. the urge to eat, arising from the need to supply the body with food

2. People with a certain gene may not be aware that they are eating too much; genes also determine the number of fat cells a person has.

3. As the body begins to lose weight, it signals the brain and triggers the hunger drive. Also, the body often reacts to stress (such as the stress of a diet) by craving more to eat.

Opening Section 3

Motivator

Tell students to imagine a hypothetical individual whose every physical need has been satisfied. The person is adequately fed, clothed, and sheltered and feels no physical pain. Ask students to consider what psychological needs the person might experience. Write students' suggestions on the chalkboard, and ask students to consider how these psychological needs might motivate this person to behave. Then tell students that they will read about psychological needs in Section 3.

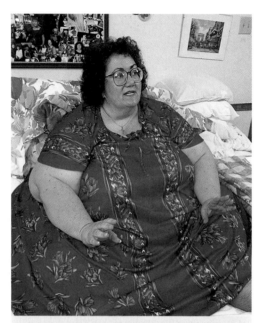

Obese people are more likely to suffer from such health problems as heart disease, diabetes, gout, poor respiratory systems, and some types of cancer than are their slimmer counterparts.

One of the ways in which heredity may contribute to obesity is that certain people with a particular gene may not receive the biological signal that they have eaten enough to sustain them (Lindpaintner, 1995). Thus, they end up eating more than they need to.

Genes also help determine the number of fat cells a person has. People with a greater number of fat cells feel hungry sooner than people with fewer fat cells, even if they are of the same weight. When overweight people take off extra pounds, they do not reduce the number of fat cells in their body. Instead, the fat cells shrink. As they shrink, they signal the brain, triggering the hunger drive. For this reason, many people who lose weight complain that they feel hungry all the time.

People metabolize food—or burn calories—at different rates and in accordance with the amount of muscle and fat in their bodies. Since fatty tissue converts food to energy more slowly than muscle does, people with more body fat metabolize food more slowly than people who weigh the same but have a lower percentage of body fat. Men tend to have more muscle and less fat in their bodies than

women. The average man is approximately 40 percent muscle and 15 percent fat. The average woman is 23 percent muscle and 25 percent fat. Therefore, men tend to burn calories more quickly than women of the same weight. For this reason, men generally are able to lose weight more easily than women, and they can usually eat more than women can without putting on extra pounds.

Psychological factors also play a role in obesity. For example, people tend to eat more when they are under stress or experiencing certain negative emotions, such as anxiety (Cools et al., 1992; Greeno & Wing, 1994). Ironically, the stress of trying to diet can make some people want to eat even more.

Personal circumstances also affect people's ability to control their weight. For example, many people tend to overeat and ignore their diets when they are attending family gatherings, watching television, or experiencing tension at school, home, or at work (Drapkin et al., 1995).

SECTION 2 REVIEW

1. What is the hunger drive?

2. What is the relationship between heredity and obesity?

3. **Critical Thinking** *Analyzing Information* How might dieting actually cause the body to resist efforts to lose weight?

SECTION 3

Psychological Needs

Human beings and other organisms are motivated to reduce the tension or stimulation caused by biological drives such as hunger or thirst. The hungry person who "has a bite to eat" wants to reduce the feeling of being hungry. However, we experience psychological needs as well as biological needs. Some psychological needs motivate us to reduce tension or stimulation. Other psychological needs actually lead us to increase the amount of stimulation we experience.

Stimulus Motives

Desires for stimulation are called **stimulus motives**. Stimulus motives include sensory stimulation, activity, exploration, and manipulation of the environment. Some stimulus motives have clear

Teaching Section 3

Demonstration

Bring to class several pairs of thick gloves, earplugs, and cloths that can be used as blindfolds. Ask for volunteers to demonstrate the effects of sensory deprivation. Have the volunteers wear the gloves, earplugs, and blindfolds and sit in chairs at the back of the classroom for a period of 15 minutes. Instruct the volunteers not to move. Afterward, have the volunteers describe their thoughts and bodily sensations to the class. Ask them how long they think they would have lasted in the sensory deprivation experiment at McGill University.

Cooperative Learning

Organize the class into groups. Have the members of each group formulate a hypothesis about why some people become sensation seekers—people who need high levels of sensation. Ask group members to decide which research method could best be used to test the hypothesis, and have them develop a written rationale for their choice. Have the groups present their hypotheses and rationales to the class. Ask the class to critique each group's method in terms of its advantages and disadvantages and to suggest other methods that might be more efficient.

---

survival value. Human beings and other organisms who are motivated to explore and manipulate their environments are more likely to survive (Keller & Boigs, 1991). Learning about one's surroundings increases usable information concerning resources and potential dangers. Manipulation allows people to change the environment in useful ways, thereby increasing and enhancing their chances of survival.

Sensory Deprivation During the 1950s, several student volunteers at McGill University in Montreal were paid $20 a day for participating in an experiment in which they did nothing—literally nothing. They were blindfolded and placed in small rooms (Bexton et al., 1954). Their arms were bandaged so that they could feel no tactile sensations (sensations of touch), and they could hear nothing except the dull hum of the air-conditioner. The intention of the experiment was to see how people would react to an absence of stimulation, a state referred to as **sensory deprivation**.

With nothing to do, some of the students slept. Those who remained awake began to feel bored and irritable. As the hours passed, the students felt more and more uncomfortable. Some reported having hallucinations. The study was scheduled to last for several days, but many students quit during the first day despite the monetary incentive and the desire to help in the research. Most of those who completed the study felt they had been through a terrible ordeal and, for several days after the experiment, found it difficult to concentrate on even simple matters. They reported feeling extreme boredom and disorientation for some time. The experiment demonstrated the importance of sensory stimulation to human beings.

TRUTH OR fiction ■ REVISITED ■

It is not true that "getting away from it all" by being in a place away from all sensory input is relaxing. The sensory deprivation experiments conducted at McGill University were shown to be very stressful to the participants.

Desire for Sensory Stimulation All people seek sensory stimulation, but it is clear that some need it more than others. Some people like being couch potatoes. They enjoy sitting and relaxing in front of a television set whenever possible. Other people prefer more active lifestyles. They are not happy

unless they are out running or tossing a ball around.

A DAY IN THE LIFE

As Dan noted, Janet was always on the run. She seemed to be happiest when she was hiking or riding her mountain bike. Many psychologists would call Janet a sensation seeker. A sensation seeker is somebody who regularly seeks out thrilling activities such as riding mountain bikes, roller coasters, or even skydiving. They feel at their best when they are doing something active or adventurous.

It is not clear why some people seek high levels of sensation and others prefer lower levels. Inborn factors may play a role. So may learning experiences. For example, a child or adolescent whose parents ride motorcycles or skydive will be exposed to these activities at an early age. He or she may be inclined to want to try these activities.

Exploration and Manipulation

Anybody who has ever had the experience of bringing home a new cat knows that the animal's first reaction to totally new surroundings is to show anxiety. The frightened cat may hide under a bed or in a closet. However, eventually, the cat will feel adventurous enough to take a few tentative steps out. Then it will begin exploring its new surroundings. Within a few days, the cat will probably have explored every corner of the house. In this respect,

Some people are more motivated to seek stimulation than others. These people are called sensation seekers.

Have students write about their own need for sensory stimulation. Do they seek high levels of sensation, or do they prefer relatively low levels? Do they think this preference is inborn or learned?

Uncontrolled wandering is a common and dangerous behavior among patients with Alzheimer's disease. Geriatric expert Mary Lucero suggests that Alzheimer's disease patients wander because they are frustrated in their need to explore the environment. A study funded by the National Institute on Aging examined ways of providing sensory stimulation to patients with varying degrees of dementia. Results suggest that individuals in the early stages of dementia can perform familiar tasks, while individuals in later stages need very simple objects to handle.

Lucero, Mary. (Feb. 28, 1993). Sensory stimulation allows nursing staff to manage dementia wanderers. *Brown University Long-Term Care Quality Letter.* 1.

Meeting Individual Needs: Tactile/Kinesthetic Learners

Obtain several infant and toddler toys and bring them to class. Have tactile/kinesthetic learners hold and manipulate the toys and analyze the various kinds of sensory and cognitive stimulation they provide. Then have students discuss how the lack of stimulating objects in the environment might affect the development of infants and young children. You may wish to provide a real-life example by discussing how the lack of stimulation has affected children living in orphanages in Romania.

For Further Research

Many famous and successful individuals have had high achievement motivation. Have students conduct research into the lives of individuals who have made their marks in a variety of fields, such as science, business, politics, and the arts. Encourage students to locate direct quotations in which these individuals explain how and why they were motivated to achieve their goals. Have students present their findings in short oral reports. Then have students discuss the advantages and disadvantages of taking risks in the pursuit of one's goals.

Both animals and humans seem to have a need to explore objects in their environments.

cats and people appear to behave in similar ways. Most people are also motivated to explore their immediate surroundings.

Once people and animals become sufficiently comfortable with their environment, they seek novel stimulation. That is, they seek new and varied experiences. For example, researchers have shown that laboratory rats who are not terribly hungry usually choose to explore unfamiliar parts of mazes rather than to head down familiar alleys directly to a food reward (Wilkie et al., 1992). Studies have also shown that monkeys learn to manipulate gadgets for the reward of being able to observe novel stimulation (Harlow et al., 1950).

Do people and animals explore and manipulate their environment because these activities help them meet their needs for food and safety? Or do they explore and manipulate these objects simply for the sake of novel stimulation? Many psychologists believe that exploration and manipulation are reinforcing in and of themselves. Monkeys appear to enjoy "monkeying around" with gadgets. If you leave mechanical devices in their presence, the monkeys will learn how to manipulate them without any reward other than the pleasure of doing so (Harlow et al., 1950).

Many human infants will play endlessly with "busy boxes"—boards or boxes with pieces that move, honk, squeak, rattle, and buzz. Most children seem to find pleasure in playing with new gadgets and discovering interesting new activities. This seems to support the view of psychologists who see the desire for novel stimulation as natural to both people and animals.

Achievement Motivation

People who are driven to get ahead, to tackle challenging situations, and to meet high personal standards of success are said to have high **achievement motivation**. For example, students who demonstrate high achievement motivation will work on difficult test items until they find the answer or run out of time. These students tend to earn higher grades than students with equal abilities but lower achievement motivation (Allen et al., 1992).

Adults with high achievement motivation may strive to move ahead in their careers. They may set challenging goals for themselves, broaden their skills, or simply recognize and take advantage of opportunities presented to them. Adults with high achievement motivation are more likely to be promoted and earn high salaries than less motivated people with similar opportunities. Research shows that people with high achievement motivation enjoy personal challenges and are willing to take moderate risks to achieve their goals (McClelland, 1965).

Types of Goals Achievement motivation can be fueled by different sources (Dweck, 1990). For some students, performance goals may be the reason for their achievement motivation. **Performance goals** are specific goals such as gaining admission to college, earning the approval of parents or teachers, or even simply avoiding criticism. It was a performance goal—winning the science scholarship—that motivated Todd to study advanced biology.

A DAY IN THE LIFE

Evaluating Ideas

Review with students the four styles of parenting discussed in Chapter 10. Then organize students into groups of four. Have each group brainstorm a hypothetical interaction between a parent and a child that could affect the child's achievement motivation. Have each group member analyze the interaction in terms of one of the four parenting-style combinations: warm-permissive, warm-strict, cold-permissive, and cold-strict. What are some possible effects of this type of interaction on the child's achievement motivation?

Role-Playing

Organize the class into small groups to create and perform short skits in which an individual is facing a situation that produces cognitive dissonance. Group members should decide among themselves who will write, direct, and perform the skit. Tell the groups that each skit should end with a resolution that allows the main character to reestablish cognitive consistency. Have the groups perform their skits for the class. Ask the class to critique each skit for conceptual accuracy.

Other students are driven mainly by learning goals. For some students, learning for learning's sake is the most powerful motivator. We call such motivators **learning goals**. People who demonstrate high achievement motivation may be influenced by more than one type of goal. For example, in addition to striving to win the scholarship, Todd enjoyed studying science.

Performance goals are usually satisfied by external or extrinsic rewards. **Extrinsic rewards** include good grades, a good income, and respect from others. On the other hand, learning goals are usually satisfied by internal or **intrinsic rewards**, such as self-satisfaction.

Development of Achievement Motivation
Where does achievement motivation come from? Parents and caregivers certainly play a crucial role. Their attitude toward achievement is instrumental in developing a child's motivation.

Research suggests that children with learning goals often have parents who encourage them to be persistent, to enjoy schoolwork, and to find their own ways to solve problems whenever possible (Ginsburg & Bronstein, 1993; Gottfried et al., 1994). Such parents create opportunities to expose their children to new and stimulating experiences. Parents of children with performance goals, on the other hand, are often more likely to reward their children with toys or money for good grades and to punish them for poor grades.

Achievement motivation can come from a variety of sources. This graduate's motivation probably includes earning the approval of parents.

Research also shows that parents of children with high achievement motivation tend to be generous with their praise when their children do well. Such parents are also less critical of their children when they do poorly (Ginsburg & Bronstein, 1993; Gottfried et al., 1994). The children themselves set high personal standards and relate their feelings of self-worth to their achievements (Dweck, 1990; Ginsburg & Bronstein, 1993).

Making Things Fit

The stimulus motives we have been discussing are examples of psychological needs aimed at increasing our level of stimulation. However, many psychological needs are aimed at reducing stimulation or tension, especially in interactions with other people. These types of psychological needs are based on people's need to maintain a balance between their personal beliefs, actions, and thoughts.

Cognitive Consistency   Cognitive theorists, such as Leon Festinger (1957) and Sandra Bem (1993), maintain that people are motivated to achieve **cognitive consistency**. That is, they seek to think and behave in a way that fits what they believe and how others expect them to think and behave. According to Festinger, people are primarily motivated to behave according to their beliefs. Therefore, a person who is politically liberal would find it difficult to support a conservative candidate. According to Bem, most girls and boys try to behave in ways that are consistent with what people expect of females and males in their society.

Most people prefer that the "pieces" of their lives fit together. They seek out as friends those who have values and interests similar to their own. As they grow older, most people try to find a set of beliefs that will help them understand the world in which they live. Most people feel better when the important relationships in their lives are stable and orderly. Two theories that address this need to create cognitive consistency are balance theory and cognitive-dissonance theory.

Balance Theory   According to **balance theory**, people need to organize their perceptions, opinions, and beliefs in a harmonious manner (Heider, 1958). They want to maintain a cognitive balance by holding consistent views and by being with people who share their beliefs and values. When the people we like share our attitudes, there is a state of balance that gives us a feeling that all is well.

What's New in Psychology?

In many school systems, students are not allowed to participate in sports if their grades fall below a certain average. Unfortunately, "no pass, no play" rules cause many academically challenged students to lose motivation altogether. To help solve this problem, Joel Kirsch, president of the American Sports Institute, created a program called PASS (Promoting Achievement in School through Sports). PASS is a program in which students attend a daily class that teaches them such things as concentration, balance, relaxation, and flexibility—skills needed for both sports and academics. PASS has helped many students improve their motivation, raise their grades, and regain their sports eligibility.

Journal Activity

Have students evaluate their own achievement motivation. Encourage them to distinguish between learning goals and performance goals and to include vivid anecdotes to illustrate this dimension of their personalities.

Closing Section 3

Applying Ideas

Have pairs of students research balance theory by creating a questionnaire designed to determine respondents' interests, beliefs, and values. (One student can devise the questions—subject to the teacher's review for appropriateness; the other can administer it.) Have the pairs administer the survey to classmates and then analyze the results. Do the answers of respondents who are close friends show more similarity than the answers of acquaintances? Have students discuss their findings.

Reviewing Section 3

Have students complete the Section Review questions on page 311.

Extension

Invite groups of students to test the hypotheses about sensation seekers they developed in the Cooperative Learning activity on page 307. Review their research designs for feasibility before they begin. Afterward, have students discuss what they learned.

Cross-Curricular Link: Political Science

The concept of cognitive consistency also applies to the world of politics. When evaluating the extent to which televised presidential debates influenced viewers' attitudes, psychologists determined that voters who already were committed to one candidate generally rated that candidate as the "winner" in a debate. Apparently, committed viewers decided to "register" only the behaviors that supported their existing views.

Class Discussion

Ask students to identify and discuss the differences that they could tolerate in a friendship and the differences that would make them question the feasibility of continuing the friendship.

A DAY IN THE LIFE

Hannah, Todd, Dan, Janet, Marc, and Linda are all very good friends. But why is this group of friends so close? According to balance theory, they have probably discovered that they share many of the same values, interests, and beliefs. Balance theory also suggests that, when we care about a person, we tend to share her or his interests. For example, prior to meeting Hannah, Dan may not have been very interested in attending a classical violin recital. However, because of his friendship with Hannah, he was introduced to, and developed positive feelings about, the things she liked.

Psychologists note that people who have strong feelings for each other, as Marc and Linda do, might be very upset to discover a major area of disagreement (Orive, 1988). Such a disharmony would place them in a state of **imbalance**. When someone we care about disagrees with us, an uncomfortable state of imbalance arises. We may attempt to end the uncomfortable state by trying to persuade the other person to change his or her attitude or by changing our feelings about the other person.

Relationships can usually survive disagreements about such things as different tastes in food or a difference of opinion about a movie. However, more basic conflicts such as over religion, politics, or personal values can create a state of imbalance.

When we dislike certain people or have no feelings toward them one way or another, their attitudes are not of much interest to us. Because we do not care about them, we are not greatly affected by the disharmony between their views and ours. We can be said to be in a state of **nonbalance**. Unlike imbalance, which tends to upset people, nonbalance usually leaves people feeling indifferent (Newcomb, 1981).

Cognitive-Dissonance Theory Why do people find a state of imbalance uncomfortable? The answer is that most people want their thoughts and attitudes (cognitions) to be consistent with their actions. Awareness that our cognitions are inconsistent (dissonant) with our behavior is unpleasant. It causes an inner tension, which can be uncomfortable. According to **cognitive-dissonance theory**, people are motivated to reduce this inconsistency (Festinger, 1957; Festinger & Carlsmith, 1959).

Classic research on cognitive dissonance was conducted by Leon Festinger and James Carlsmith (1959). Participants in their experiment were divided into two groups. The people in one group

were paid $20 to tell another person that a boring task—such as turning pegs—was interesting. The people in the second group were paid $1 to say that it was interesting. Afterward, the participants were asked to express their own feelings about the task. The people who received $1 rated the task *more* interesting than the people who were paid $20.

According to cognitive-dissonance theory, this occurred because the people who received $1 felt an inconsistency—a dissonance—between their cognition ("That was a boring task") and their action ("I just told someone that task was interesting"). The people who received $20 could easily justify lying about how they really felt about the task because doing so was worthwhile, financially. The people who received just $1 could not use that excuse. Instead, they changed their attitude about the task. By convincing themselves that the task was more interesting than it really was, they were able to reduce the inconsistency between their cognition and their action.

What happens when two people in a relationship disagree about a key issue, such as religion? A strong disagreement about an important issue can injure or even end a relationship. Cognitive-dissonance theory suggests that people having such a basic disagreement may seek to reduce the dissonance by trying to pretend that the differences between them are unimportant or even by denying that the differences exist. They may avoid thinking about those differences and put off dealing with them as long as possible.

Affiliation

Of course, if we never dealt with other people we would not need to worry about balance or cognitive dissonance. However, humans are social beings who have a need to be with other people. The desire to join with others and be part of something larger than oneself is called **affiliation**. The desire to affiliate is what prompts people to make friends, join groups, and participate in activities with others rather than by oneself. During adolescence, the motive for affiliation with one's peers is particularly strong. It is a time of life when one discovers the extent to which peers provide emotional support, useful advice, and pleasurable company.

Affiliation motivation helps keep families, groups, and nations together. However, some people are so strongly motivated to affiliate that they find it painful to be by themselves. Sometimes a strong need to affiliate may be a sign of anxiety.

Section Objective

▶ Explain how psychologists describe emotion.

This objective is assessed in the Section Review on page 316 and in the Chapter 13 Review.

Opening Section 4

Motivator

Ask a volunteer to read aloud the definition of *emotion* found on page 311. Then have students list as many emotions as they can in two minutes. Write these emotions on the chalkboard. Then have students try to group together similar emotions. (For example, irritation and rage are both forms of anger.) How many core emotions have they pointed out? Tell students that they will learn about the psychological perspective on emotions in Section 4, including the nature of emotions and theories of emotion.

Psychologist Stanley Schachter (1959) showed how anxiety increases the desire to affiliate. In a classic study, he manipulated people's anxiety levels. He told one group of people that they would be given painful electric shocks. He told another group of people that they would be given mild electric shocks. All participants were then asked to wait for the shock apparatus to be set up. They were given the choice of waiting alone or waiting in a room with other participants.

The majority (63 percent) of those who expected the painful shock chose to wait with other participants. In contrast, only one third of those who expected the mild shock chose to wait with other participants. Schachter concluded that anxiety tends to cause people to want to affiliate with other people.

TRUTH
OR
fiction
▪ REVISITED ▪

It is not true that when people feel anxious, they want to be alone. A classic experiment by Stanley Schachter found that the more anxious the participants were, the more they wanted to be with other participants.

In general, individuals are motivated to make friends and participate in activities with others. This desire to join with others is known as affiliation motivation.

SECTION 3 REVIEW

go. hrw .com Homework Practice Online
Keyword: SY3 HP13

1. What are stimulus motives?

2. Define *balance, imbalance,* and *nonbalance* in terms of balance theory.

3. **Critical Thinking** *Summarizing* What is achievement motivation, and where does it come from?

SECTION 4

Emotions

Anxiety and elation are two commonly experienced emotions. **Emotions** are states of feeling. For most people, positive emotions such as happiness and love make life worth living. Persistent negative emotions such as fear and sadness can make life difficult.

Some emotions arise in response to a situation. At her violin recital, Hannah was anxious because she was uncertain about her ability to perform. Emotions can also motivate behavior. When Hannah remembered that her friends and family were in the audience, she felt their support and played with great confidence.

The Nature of Emotions

Emotions have biological, cognitive, and behavioral components. Strong emotions spark activity in the autonomic nervous system (LeDoux, 1997). For example, anxiety triggers activity of the sympathetic division of the autonomic nervous system. (See Chapter 3.) When people are anxious, their hearts race. They breathe rapidly, sweat heavily, and tense their muscles. The cognitive component of anxiety—the idea that something terrible might happen—may lead a person to try to escape from the situation. But where do emotions come from, and how many does the average person experience?

The ancient Chinese believed that there are four inborn (instinctive) human emotions: happiness, anger, sorrow, and fear (Carlson & Hatfield, 1992). Behaviorist John B. Watson (1924) believed that there are three instinctive emotions: fear, rage, and love. In 1932 psychologist Katherine Bridges proposed that people are born with one basic emotion: general excitement. This excitement then divides into other emotions as children develop.

Section 3 Review: Answers

1. They are motives that increase the desire of an organism to seek stimulation.

2. A state of cognitive balance exists when one's views are consistent, one's beliefs and behaviors match, and one shares the company of people who have similar views and values. Major disagreements with other people who are important to us can create a state of imbalance. Disharmony with those to whom we are indifferent, however, creates a state of nonbalance.

3. Achievement motivation is the drive to get ahead, to tackle challenging situations, and to meet high personal standards. Parents and caregivers usually play a crucial role in establishing a person's achievement motivation.

Cross-Curricular Link: Physiology

Emotions can have physiological components. Have students research and report on what happens to people physically when they experience emotions such as happiness, anger, sorrow, and fear.

311

Teaching Section 4

Guided Practice

Review with students the information on emotions and facial expressions found on this page. Ask them to evaluate the textbook statement that facial expressions are probably inborn and expressed in similar ways around the world. Then have students examine the photographs on page 315 and write down an answer to the caption question. Have students share their answers with the class. How similar were the students' responses? Have students discuss possible reasons for this similarity.

Independent Practice

Have each student show the photographs on page 315 to 10 people and record the responses of the participants to the caption question. In class, have volunteers tally the results. Use the results as the basis of a class discussion on the universality of emotions and facial expressions.

For Your Information

Happiness may be determined at least in part by genetics. Identical twins tend to share feelings of well-being regardless of whether they were raised together or apart, and regardless of their circumstances in life.

Cultural Dimensions

Because anger is potentially so dangerous, different cultures have their own ways of controlling and directing angry feelings. Among people whose lives are very precarious, such as the Kung of the Kalahari Desert and the Utku Eskimo, violent anger is almost never expressed. The Kapauku Papuans of Irian Jaya, however, use ritual displays of rage to enforce social rules about marriage and property.

Journal Activity

Have students write about the degree to which they display their emotions to other people. Which emotion seems to be predominant in their interactions with other people? What role, if any, does their gender play in their display of emotions?

Psychologist Carroll Izard (1984, 1990, 1994) suggests that all the emotions that people experience are present and distinct at birth. However, they do not all show up at once. Instead, they emerge as the child develops.

Many psychologists support Izard's view. In fact, they have found that infants show many emotions at ages earlier than those suggested by Bridges. In one study, the mothers of three-month-old babies were interviewed (Johnson et al., 1982). Results of the study revealed that 99 percent of the mothers reported that their babies showed curiosity; 95 percent of the mothers reported that the babies displayed joy; 84 percent, anger; 74 percent, surprise; and 58 percent, fear.

Questions concerning how many emotions there are, how they develop, and how they affect our lives remain unanswered (Fischer et al., 1990). Two emotions of great importance to most people, however, are happiness and anger.

Happiness William James (1902) said that the motive behind everything that people do is "how to gain, how to keep, how to recover happiness." Certainly our state of happiness or unhappiness affects nearly everything we do as well as our perception of our surroundings. People who are happy think the world is a happier, safer place (Johnson & Tversky, 1983), make decisions more readily (Isen & Means, 1983), and report greater satisfaction with their lives (Schwarz & Clore, 1983) than do people who are unhappy. When a person is unhappy, gloom seems to settle over everything he or she does. When his or her mood brightens, everything seems better—school, work, relationships, and self-image (Isen et al., 1987; Izard, 1989). It seems that happiness and unhappiness create their own momentum. When we feel good, the world looks good. But when we are feeling low, nothing seems to go right.

Moreover, many studies have found that the happier we are, the more likely we are to help others. When good things happen that lift our mood, we are more likely to volunteer our time to help other people (Khanna & Rathee, 1992).

Anger Anger is a common response to an insult or an attack. Anger can often make a person seem out of control. Angry people may even seek revenge. The ancient Roman poet Horace called anger "a short madness."

What makes people angry? In one study, participants were asked to keep a record of their experiences with anger (Averill, 1983). Most of the participants reported becoming at least moderately angry several times a week, while others became angry several times a day. Usually the anger was directed against someone close—a friend or family member—and over some alleged offense, especially if the act seemed deliberate or thoughtless. However, small annoyances such as a loud noise, an unpleasant odor, or an accidental injury can also make a person angry.

What is an effective way to handle anger? Hold it in? Lash out at the offender? The participants in Averill's study reported that when they became angry they tended to react by being assertive rather than hostile. Their anger frequently prompted them to discuss the situation with the offending person, thus easing the unpleasant feelings. Such controlled reactions are almost always more effective at reducing anger than hostile outbursts or suppression of the feelings of anger.

Facial Expressions

We often rely on the practice of "reading" people's faces. We can tell when people are happy from their smiles. We can see when they are fearful from their open mouths and the look in their eyes. We can read people's expressions and know when they are sad or surprised. Are these facial expressions of emotion instinctive, or do people learn to show these expressions to signify certain emotions on the basis of their cultural settings?

Cross-cultural evidence suggests that facial expressions are probably inborn. The ways in which many specific emotions are expressed appear to be the same around the world (Rinn, 1991). Certain facial expressions seem to suggest the same emotions in all people (Brown, 1991; Buss, 1992; Ekman, 1992, Izard, 1994). Smiling appears to be a universal sign of friendliness and approval. Baring the teeth may be a universal sign of anger. Charles Darwin, the evolution theorist, believed that the universal recognition of facial expressions had survival value by communicating motivation. For example, facial expressions could signal whether a group of approaching strangers were friendly or hostile.

In a classic study by Paul Ekman, people from around the world were asked to identify the emotions that were being expressed in a series of photographs. (The photos were of people showing anger, disgust, fear, happiness, sadness, and surprise.) Researchers interviewed people ranging

PSYCHOLOGY

IN THE WORLD TODAY

PSYCHOLOGY

IN THE WORLD TODAY

Is It Possible to Detect Lies?

For better or worse, lying is a part of life. A *New York Times* poll found that 60 percent of adults in the United States believe that it is sometimes necessary to lie, especially to protect people's feelings (Smiley, 2000). Some students lie about why they have not completed assignments. Research shows that the great majority of people lie to their boyfriends or girlfriends—most often about other relationships (Rowatt et al., 1999; Saxe, 1991). People also lie about their qualifications to obtain jobs, and some people lie when they deny guilt for crimes.

People's facial expressions often offer clues to whether or not they are telling the truth, but some people can lie with a straight face—or a smile. As Shakespeare wrote in his play *Hamlet*: "One may smile, and smile, and be a villain." The use of devices to try to detect lies has a long history. The Bedouin people of the Arabian Peninsula used to make parties involved in conflict lick a hot iron. They concluded that the one whose tongue was burned was lying. The ancient Chinese had a somewhat similar lie detection method. A person suspected of lying was made to chew rice powder and then spit it out. If the powder was dry, the suspect was judged to be guilty. The Chinese technique is, in fact, consistent with modern psychological knowledge. Anxiety about being caught in a lie is linked to activity of the sympathetic division of the autonomic nervous system. One sign of sympathetic activity is lack of saliva, or dryness in the mouth. The emotions of fear and guilt are linked to sympathetic activity, and so both of them are connected with dryness in the mouth.

In modern times, the close connection between emotions and the nervous system has led to the creation of devices called polygraphs, or lie detectors. The assumption behind the lie detector is that when somebody tells a lie, his or her body reacts in a way that can be detected with particularly sensitive equipment. Lie detectors detect something, but do they detect specific emotional responses that mean that the person is lying?

Modern lie detectors measure several signs of sympathetic activity while a witness or suspect is being questioned. These indicators include heart rate, blood pressure, rate of breathing, and perspiration. However, questions have been raised about the accuracy of assessing truth or fiction in this way (Saxe & Ben-Shakhar, 1999).

The American Polygraph Association claims that the use of the polygraph is 85 percent to 95 percent accurate. However, critics find polygraph testing to be less accurate and claim that it is sensitive to more than lies (Saxe & Ben-Shakhar, 1999). Factors such as tense muscles, drugs, and previous experience with polygraph tests can reduce their accuracy. In one experiment, people were able to reduce the accuracy of polygraph-based judgments to about 50 percent by biting their tongue to produce pain or by pressing their toes against the floor to tense muscles while being interviewed (Honts et al., 1985).

Psychologists William Iacono and David Lykken (1997) conducted a mail survey of members of the Society for Psychophysical Research and the American Psychological Association to see how much faith the members of these organizations put in polygraph testing. Response rates were high—91 percent and 74 percent, respectively. Most of the people who responded to the survey agreed on the following:

- Polygraph lie detection is not theoretically sound.
- Claims of the accuracy of polygraph testing are exaggerated.
- People can easily learn to beat the test.
- Polygraph results should not be admitted as evidence in courts of law.

It appears that no specific pattern of bodily responses pinpoints lying (Iacono & Lykken, 1997; Saxe & Ben-Shakhar, 1999). Because of problems in accuracy, results of polygraph examinations are not admitted as evidence in many courts.

Think About It

Supporting a Point of View Do you think lie detector tests are an accurate way to determine whether someone is lying? Why or why not?

Demonstration

Write down the names of various emotions on index cards. Hand each card to a volunteer and have that student try to act out the emotion without using any speech or sounds. Have the rest of the class guess which emotion is being demonstrated. Keep track of correct and incorrect guesses. Are some emotions easier to "read" than others? Are any pairs or groups of emotions easily confused? If so, which ones?

Meeting Individual Needs: Visual Learners

Have visual learners collect photographs that show the various emotions described in the textbook. Tell them to group pictures of the same emotions together. Then, as a way to help students translate visual information into verbal information, have them write a paragraph on each basic expression, describing the components of that expression.

Essay and Research Themes for A. P. Students

Theme 11

Many psychologists believe that all the emotions people experience are present at birth and that they emerge as the child develops.

from college students at a European university to tribal members in the remote highlands of New Guinea. All groups, including the New Guineans, who had had almost no contact with Americans or Europeans, agreed on the emotion that was being portrayed in each photograph (Ekman, 1982; Ekman & Friesen, 1984).

Theories of Emotion

Emotions are states of feeling that influence thought and behavior. People respond emotionally to events and situations in a variety of ways. Psychologists have different theories about what emotions are, where they come from, and how they operate.

The Opponent-Process Theory   According to the **opponent-process theory**, originated by psychologist Richard Solomon, emotions often come in pairs, with one emotion being followed by its opposite. That is, one emotion—for example, extreme happiness—tends to be followed by feelings that are opposite—for example, extreme sadness—rather than by a neutral feeling (Kimble, 1994; Solomon, 1980). Solomon and his colleague J. D. Corbitt (1974) suggested that people are inclined to

maintain balance in their emotional lives. When this balance is upset by a strong emotional response to a particular situation, an opponent process, or an opposite emotional response, occurs and eventually restores the balance.

Although Hannah had practiced in preparation for her recital, she was anxious when she went on stage. Once she began to play, however, and focused on the music, her anxiety disappeared and was replaced by tremendous relief, even elation. The first emotion (anxiety) was followed by its opposite (relief). At the end of the performance, when she drew her bow across the strings for the final time, she knew she had played the piece very well.

The Commonsense Approach   You and most of your classmates would probably agree with a "commonsense approach" to emotions. According to this view, when something happens to a person in a certain situation, the person quickly interprets the situation. The interpretation triggers body sensations that signal a feeling, or emotion. The emotion, in turn, triggers a behavior. For example, a person who is walking down the street and encounters a large stray dog may sense that he or she is in danger. That person then feels anxious (body sensation) and quickly turns down the nearest side street to avoid the dog (behavior).

Many psychologists agree that thoughts (appraisal of the situation) come before our feelings and behavior (Lazarus, 1991). They maintain that people's appraisals of their situations are the keys to emotional response. That is, people's thoughts, feelings, and behavior are strongly intertwined, and their thoughts to some degree determine their emotional and behavioral responses.

Other psychologists, however, believe that it is important to understand the biology of emotion. According to these psychologists, the activities of the nervous system and hormones play a more important role in determining emotion than what people are thinking about their situations (Izard, 1984; Zajonc, 1984). Some psychologists even believe that people's behavior determines their thoughts and feelings. Three important theories of emotion are the James-Lange theory, the Cannon-Bard theory, and the theory of cognitive appraisal.

The James-Lange Theory   About 100 years ago, William James suggested that people's emotions follow, rather than cause, their behavioral

Organizing Information

Create on the chalkboard a four-column chart titled "Theories of Emotion." Label the columns *Opponent-Process, James-Lange, Cannon-Bard,* and *Cognitive Appraisal.* Have students complete the chart by identifying the main ideas, strengths, and weaknesses of each theory. Also ask students to provide examples to illustrate each theory. Have students make a copy of the completed chart to review as they study Section 4.

Applying Information

Tell students to recall a recent occasion on which they felt a strong emotion. Have them write a detailed description of the event, the emotion, and the thoughts they experienced. Encourage students to describe each event, thought, and sensation in the order in which it occurred. Then have students determine which theory of emotion best explains their particular experience.

reactions to their situations. That is, people act first and then react emotionally according to the way they acted. For example, a person crossing the street who looks up and sees a truck bearing down acts first to get out of the way, then feels fright. James would say that the emotions of fear and panic are the *result* of jumping out of the way of the truck, not the cause of the action. This theory was also proposed by the Danish biologist Karl G. Lange at about the same time. Hence, it is called the James-Lange theory of emotion.

According to James and Lange, certain situations trigger reactions, called instinctive bodily response patterns. These patterns include specific feelings and behaviors. For example, a physical threat can trigger one of two instinctive response patterns: fighting or fleeing from the situation. According to this view, people who would meet the threat by fighting would experience the emotion of anger *because* (and only *after*) they acted aggressively. People who would meet the threat by fleeing would experience the emotion of fear *because* (and *after*) they ran away from the situation. In other words, their behavior would come first, followed by the emotion that fit the behavior.

The James-Lange theory suggests that people can change their feelings by changing their behavior. Changing one's behavior to change one's feelings is an approach used in behavior therapy, a method that has been employed to treat certain psychological disorders. (See Chapter 19.)

The James-Lange theory has been criticized, however, because it downplays the role of human cognition. This theory views the cognitive appraisal of a situation as having little or no role in determining human behavior. The James-Lange theory also minimizes the role of personal values and choice as factors in human behavior.

The Cannon-Bard Theory Walter Cannon (1927) and Philip Bard (1934) suggested that emotions *accompany* the bodily responses that are aroused by an external stimulus. According to the Cannon-Bard theory, a situation triggers an external stimulus that is processed by the brain. The brain then stimulates bodily changes and cognitive activity (the experience of the emotion) simultaneously. Emotions are not produced by the bodily responses.

The central question raised by the Cannon-Bard theory is whether bodily responses and emotions do in fact occur at the same time. In some cases, it seems they do not. For example, pain or a threat may trigger bodily responses (such as rapid heartbeat) in someone before that person begins to experience distress or fear. Also, people who manage a "narrow escape" from a dangerous situation often become quite upset and shaken afterward, when they have had a chance to consider what might have happened to them. In such situations it seems that a two-stage reaction is involved—the bodily response is followed by the emotional reaction.

The Theory of Cognitive Appraisal Other theoretical approaches to emotion have focused on cognitive factors. One such theory argues that all emotions have basically similar bodily response patterns (Schachter & Singer, 1962). That is, the body reacts in physically similar ways even though different emotions are being experienced. This theory, called the theory of cognitive appraisal, maintains that the way people label an emotion depends largely on their cognitive appraisal of the situation.

Cross-Curricular Link: Drama

The job of actors is to simulate emotions they are not actually feeling. The better the actor, the more convincing the simulation. Actors may draw on personal experiences to portray emotions, yet there is a difference between "real" emotion and "dramatic" emotion that is obvious both to the audience and to the actors. Have students discuss this difference.

Class Discussion

Tell students that Charles Darwin proposed a theory of emotion in his work *The Expression of the Emotions in Man and Animals.* In this work, Darwin argued that emotions are a product of evolution and that they developed because they aided in survival. Ask students if they agree with Darwin. Why or why not? If so, what would be the survival value of emotions such as love, hate, anger, fear, and sorrow?

Caption Question: Answer

The emotions expressed are— from left to right—happiness, anger, surprise, and fear.

Studies indicate that the facial expressions of basic emotions, such as anger, disgust, happiness, fear, sadness, and surprise, are universally recognized. What emotions do you think are being expressed in these four photographs?

Closing Section 4

Taking a Stand

Have students write an essay on the theory of emotion they find most persuasive. Students should explain why this theory provides the best explanation for emotions. Encourage students to use their own observations to support or criticize the theories discussed in this section.

Reviewing Section 4

Have students complete the Section Review questions on page 316.

Extension

Bring to the classroom several dictionaries of quotations and collections of poetry. Have students look up key words pertaining to emotions in the indexes and read aloud the quotations or selections. What insights did the writers of these selections have into such emotions as love, sorrow, and hatred? Do their insights correspond with the findings of psychologists? How did the writers most likely obtain their "data"? Have students choose an emotion and write their own quotations or poems about that emotion.

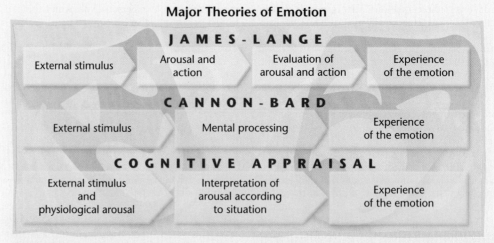

FIGURE 13.2 *According to the James-Lange theory, emotions follow the evaluation of a bodily response. The Cannon-Bard theory maintains that bodily response and emotion occur simultaneously. The cognitive appraisal theory states that emotion is the result of the individual's evaluation of a situation.*

The cognitive appraisal that occurs is based on many factors. These factors include the person's analysis of the situation and the ways other people are reacting in the same situation. When other people are involved in the same situation, an individual will look at the way they are reacting and then compare his or her reaction to theirs to arrive at what seems to be the right response.

Critics of the theory of cognitive appraisal point out that studies designed to support the theory often yield different results when repeated (Ekman, 1993). In science, research studies must be replicated with the same methods used and similar results obtained. Since several studies designed to prove cognitive appraisal theory produced different results, some psychologists have questioned the theory's validity.

Evaluation of the Theories The theory of cognitive appraisal is quite different from the James-Lange theory. The James-Lange theory asserts that each emotion has distinct and easily recognized bodily sensations. The theory of cognitive appraisal asserts that all emotions are rooted in common bodily sensations but argues that we label these sensations differently according to the situation. The truth may lie somewhere in between.

In summary, it is possible that the bodily response patterns of different emotions are more distinct than Schachter and Singer suggested, but

are not as distinct as James and Lange suggested. In addition, research with PET scans suggests that different emotions involve different parts of the brain (Goleman, 1995). Furthermore, lack of control over our emotions and ignorance of what is happening to us appear to be distressing experiences (Zimbardo et al., 1993). Thus, it seems that our cognitive appraisals of our situations do affect our emotional responses but not to the extent envisioned by some cognitive-appraisal theorists.

People are complex, thinking beings who evaluate information both from their personal situations and from their bodily responses to their situations. Most likely, they process information from both sources to label their emotions and to decide what action to take. No one theory of emotion we have discussed applies to all people in all situations. That may not be a bad thing. People's emotions are not as easily understood or manipulated as some theorists have believed.

SECTION 4 REVIEW

go.hrw.com   **Homework Practice Online**   Keyword: SY3 HP13

1. Identify three theories of emotion, and describe how each of the theories explains where emotions come from.

2. **Critical Thinking** *Analyzing Information* How have photographs of faces been used to prove the universality of emotions?

For Further Research

To clarify what occurred in the Schachter-Singer experiment, have volunteers act out the parts of the three groups—the participants, the researchers, and the different types of confederates. Have the volunteers reenact the experiment (simulating, of course, the injections of adrenaline and the inactive substance). Then have students explain how the experiment supports the contention of Schachter and Singer that emotion is the result of the individual's evaluation of a situation.

Have students conduct library research to learn about the effects of adrenaline, caffeine, and other stimulants on the body and on emotions. Have students present their findings in the form of written reports. Students may wish to create charts, graphs, and illustrations to accompany their reports.

CASE STUDIES
AND OTHER TRUE STORIES

The Schachter-Singer Experiment

A classic experiment by Stanley Schachter and Jerome Singer (1962) showed that similar bodily responses can be labeled differently, depending on a person's situation. Participants were told that the purpose of the study was to examine the effects of a particular vitamin on eyesight.

Half of the participants were given an injection of adrenaline, a hormone that activates the autonomic nervous system. The other half—the control group—was given an injection of an inactive solution that had no effect on behavior. None of the participants were aware of the type of injection they received.

The participants in the group who received adrenaline were organized into three smaller groups. Group 1 was told nothing about the side effects of the adrenaline. Group 2 was told that the substance would cause itching and numbness. Group 3 was told that the injection would increase the activity of their nervous systems.

After the participants were given their injections, they were taken to a reception room and asked to wait, in pairs, for their "vision test." The participants did not know that the person with whom they were paired was a confederate—someone who was "in" on the experiment. The participants believed that the confederates had received the same injection they had. The confederates exhibited behavior that the participants would believe was caused by the injection.

Some of the participants were paired with confederates who acted in a happy-go-lucky manner. They joked, danced around, and made paper airplanes out of their questionnaires. Another set complained bitterly as they filled out their questionnaires. Some of them tore up the questionnaires and stormed out of the room. The researchers observed the reactions of the participants through a one-way mirror.

People in groups 1 and 2, who did not have accurate information about the effects of the injection, tended to imitate the confederates. Those exposed to the happy-go-lucky confederates acted happy and relaxed. Those paired with the angry confederates also tended to be angry and upset. The participants in group 3 (who had been told the truth) and the members of the control group were relatively uninfluenced by the behavior of the confederates.

Schachter and Singer concluded that those in groups 1 and 2, who felt aroused by the adrenaline injection but had no accurate information with which to interpret their bodily reactions, looked to the confederates for behavioral cues to better understand their reactions. These participants then felt happy or angry, depending on how their confederates were behaving.

The participants in group 3, who were accurately informed about their adrenaline injection, expected arousal from the injection without any particular accompanying emotions. They watched as their confederates acted either happy or angry. They did not imitate the confederates because they had no reason to expect happiness or anger to be one of the consequences of receiving their adrenaline injection. Likewise, the participants in the control group were not inclined to imitate the behavior of the confederates. Since they had not been given adrenaline, they had no reactions that needed to be explained.

The experiment suggested those participants who had no way to interpret their reaction to the injection began feeling and acting the way they had been prompted. The experiment supports Schachter and Singer's theory that the body reacts in physically similar ways even though different emotions are being experienced. It also suggests that we interpret our emotions according to the behavior of those around us.

> ### WHY PSYCHOLOGY MATTERS
>
> Psychologists study the ways that a person's behavior affects others. Use CNN**fyi**.com or other current events sources to learn more about how people influence one another through their behavior. Create a chart noting in what ways people's behavior is influenced by others.
>
> CNN**fyi**.com

Have students think about how they might have responded if they had been participants in the Schachter-Singer experiment. Have them write in their journals about how easily their emotions are manipulated by others. Do they tend to interpret their own emotions according to the emotions of others around them? Do they cry while watching sad movies? Do they laugh louder than usual when people around them are also laughing?

Chapter 13 Review: Answers

Writing a Summary

See the section subtitles for the main topics in the chapter.

Identifying People and Ideas

1. a stimulus that moves a person to behave in ways designed to accomplish a certain goal

2. behavior patterns that are genetically transmitted

3. weighing more than 30 percent above one's recommended weight

4. desires for stimulation

5. a condition in which there is no stimulation present

6. external rewards

7. a state in which a person thinks and behaves in a way that fits what they believe

8. theory stating that people need to organize their perceptions, opinions, and beliefs in a harmonious manner

Technology

► Chapter 13 Test Generator (on the One-Stop Planner)

► HRW Go site

Reinforcement, Review, and Assessment

► Chapter 13 Review, pp. 318–319

► Chapter Review and Activities with Answer Key

► Alternative Assessment Handbook

► Portfolio Assessment Handbook

► Chapter 13 Test (Form A or B)

PSYCHOLOGY PROJECTS

Linking to Community Ask a nutritionist, dietitian, or sports psychologist to speak to the class about the nutritional needs of teenagers. The following are some questions you might like the speaker to address:

■ What are the daily caloric and nutritional needs of teenage boys and girls?

---

9. the desire to join with others and be part of something larger than oneself

10. states of feeling

Understanding Main Ideas

1. Biological needs (food, water) are inborn and common to all people; psychological needs (achievement, self-esteem, belonging) are not necessarily based on deprivation, and they differ among people.

2. Knowledge of nutrition helps people get essential nutrients while reducing caloric intake.

3. Stimulus motives include sensory stimulation, activity, exploration, and manipulation of the environment; by prompting humans to interact with the environment, these motives help ensure survival.

4. The term is *opponent process*.

Thinking Critically

1. For behavior to be instinctive, it must be found among all people, and human motivation varies among people.

2. Drive-reduction theorists might say risk takers are satisfying their drive for stimulation; humanistic theorists might say they are seeking self-actualization; instinct theorists would say they have an inborn need for excitement; sociocultural theorists would say they learned to be risk takers.

3. It is an important concept because it enables researchers to explore the importance of outside stimuli to the maintenance of psychological well-being. Responses will vary.

Chapter 13 REVIEW

 Writing a Summary

Using standard grammar, spelling, sentence structure, and punctuation, summarize the information in this chapter. Consider:
• theories of motivation and the causes of obesity
• stimulus and achievement motives, and theories of emotion

 Identifying People and Ideas

Identify the following terms or people and use them in appropriate sentences.

1. motive
2. instincts
3. obese
4. stimulus motives
5. sensory deprivation
6. extrinsic rewards
7. cognitive consistency
8. balance theory
9. affiliation
10. emotions

 Understanding Main Ideas

SECTION 1 (pp. 300–302)
1. How do biological and psychological needs differ?

SECTION 2 (pp. 303–306)
2. Why is knowledge of nutrition important as a strategy for weight loss?

SECTION 3 (pp. 306–311)
3. What are two examples of stimulus motives, and why are they important?

SECTION 4 (pp. 311–316)
4. What term explains why a person might feel "on top of the world" one day and "down in the dumps" another day?

 Thinking Critically

1. Drawing Inferences and Conclusions Why is the instinct theory not used to explain human motivation?

2. Comparing and Contrasting How do the different theories of motivation explain why some people engage in high-risk behavior while other people prefer to avoid potentially dangerous situations?

3. Evaluating Why is sensory deprivation an important concept in the study of human motivation and emotion?

4. Analyzing Information List an example of the James-Lange and Cannon-Bard theories of emotion.

Writing About Psychology

1. Supporting a Point of View Imagine that a local school board is contemplating cutting all high school sports and extracurricular activities. Money, school officials say, should be spent on essentials such as books and equipment, teachers' salaries, and building maintenance. Write a letter to the school board in which you argue in favor of retaining extracurricular activities. Use your knowledge of humanistic theory of motivation to support your point of view.

2. Analyzing Information Identify a person in your school or community who has worked hard to achieve a specific goal. Interview that person and try to determine the motivation behind his or her success. Also find out if the person gave up anything or had to overcome obstacles to achieve his or her goal. Write a brief report summarizing your findings. Be sure to use standard grammar, spelling, sentence structure, and punctuation. Use the graphic organizer below to help you write your report.

Motivation → Obstacles → Goal

What type of foods might a well-balanced meal for a teenager include?

- How successful are weight-control programs? What types of weight-control programs should people avoid?

- What are the physical, intellectual, and psychological effects of poor nutrition?

Have pairs of students work together to record human motivations and emotions. Have them choose an occasion or place at which they can make observations. Each partner should take separate notes about people's behavior, and speculate about the motivations and emotions behind the behavior. Did the partners attribute similar motivations and emotions to the people they observed, or did they have different ideas about the motivations and emotions behind the behavior? Have the students relate their findings to the theories presented in the textbook.

Building Social Studies Skills

Interpreting Charts

Study the chart below. Then use the information in the chart to help you answer the questions that follow.

Percentage of Overweight Individuals Among U.S. Adolescents

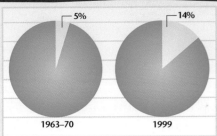

5%   14%

1963–70   1999

Source: U.S. Surgeon General, 2001 Report on Overweight and Obesity

1. Which of the following statements can be drawn from the information presented in the chart above?
   a. Children are more obese than any other age group in American society.
   b. Diseases caused by obesity are leading killers of young people.
   c. Obesity is on the rise among young people in the United States.
   d. The United States leads the world in the number of obese children.

2. What cultural factors might psychologists point to in an effort to explain the information in the chart?

Analyzing Primary Sources

Read the following excerpt, in which Abraham Maslow describes people who are psychologically healthy. Then answer the questions that follow.

"It would convey the wrong impression to say that they are self-satisfied. What we must say rather is that they can take the frailties and sins, weaknesses, and evils of human nature in the same unquestioning spirit with which one accepts the characteristics of nature. One does not complain about water because it is wet, or about rocks because they are hard, or about trees because they are green. As the child looks out upon the world with wide, uncritical, undemanding, innocent eyes, simply noting and observing what is the case, without either arguing the matter or demanding that it be otherwise, so does the self-actualizing person tend to look upon human nature in himself and in others."

1. With which of the following statements would Maslow most likely agree?
   a. Self-actualized people see human nature as it is, not as they want it to be.
   b. Self-actualized people behave like children.
   c. Self-actualized people like to go on nature hikes.
   d. Self-actualization requires people to try to change themselves and the world around them.

2. Drawing upon information in the excerpt, what is Maslow's concept of human nature?

4. Jumping out of the way of a car and then feeling fear as a result of the action supports the James-Lange theory. Realizing that one may be ill and feeling fear as a result of the realization supports the theory of cognitive appraisal.

Writing About Psychology

1. Humanistic theory argues that humans have a need for growth, fulfillment, and self-actualization. For many students, extracurricular activities are the means to reaching these goals.

2. Examples might include a person with a disability who competes in sports despite the time and the struggle involved or a person who gave up a lucrative job to do community service.

Building Social Studies Skills

1. c

2. Students' answers will vary, but might point to poor diet caused by increased access to junk foods, or lack of exercise as a result of an increase in the amount of time spent watching television or playing video games.

3. a

4. According to Maslow, human nature is at times weak and frail; however, students should note that the self-actualizing person represents the best of human nature, accepting nature for what it is.

PSYCHOLOGY PROJECTS

Cooperative Learning

Applying Psychology Working in small groups, prepare a chart about the four theories of motivation (Instinct Theory, Drive-Reduction Theory, Humanistic Theory, and Sociocultural Theory). Apply the various perspectives of motivation to a given economic situation. For example, you might want to consider the choice of car to purchase, personal budget priorities, and the choice of job. Present your chart to the class.

internet connect

Internet Activity: go.hrw.com
KEYWORD: SY3 PS13
Choose an activity on motivation and emotion to:
- create a comic strip to show cognitive consistency, balance, or cognitive-dissonance theory.
- apply various perspectives of motivation to a given economic situation.
- create a brochure that illustrates psychological and biological aspects of obesity.

go hrw com

319

Theories of Personality

CHAPTER RESOURCE MANAGER

	Objectives	Pacing Guide		Reproducible and Review Resources
SECTION 1: **The Trait Approach** (pp. 322–324)	Explain the main features and limitations of the trait theory of personality.	**Regular** 1 day *Block Scheduling Handbook with Team Teaching Strategies, Chapter 14*	**Block Scheduling** .5 day	**RS** Essay and Research Themes for Advanced Placement Students, Theme 12 **REV** Section 1 Review, p. 324
SECTION 2: **The Psychoanalytic Approach** (pp. 324–332)	Describe the impact of the psychoanalytic theory of personality and how the theory has been modified since Sigmund Freud.	**Regular** 1 day *Block Scheduling Handbook with Team Teaching Strategies, Chapter 14*	**Block Scheduling** .5 day	**E** Research Projects and Activities for Teaching Psychology **PS** Readings and Case Studies, Chapter 14 **REV** Section 2 Review, p. 332
SECTION 3: **The Learning Approach** (pp. 332–334)	Describe what learning theorists believe are the influences on and motivations for behavior.	**Regular** 1 day *Block Scheduling Handbook with Team Teaching Strategies, Chapter 14*	**Block Scheduling** .5 day	**SM** Mastering Critical Thinking Skills 14 **REV** Section 3 Review, p. 334
SECTION 4: **The Humanistic Approach** (pp. 334–337)	Explain how the humanistic approach views the role of the self and free choice in shaping behavior.	**Regular** 1 day *Block Scheduling Handbook with Team Teaching Strategies, Chapter 14*	**Block Scheduling** .5 day	**E** Creating a Psychology Fair, Activity 8 **REV** Section 4 Review, p. 337
SECTION 5: **The Sociocultural Approach** (pp. 337–339)	Discuss how the sociocultural approach views the importance of ethnicity, gender, culture, and socioeconomic status in the development of personality.	**Regular** 1 day *Block Scheduling Handbook with Team Teaching Strategies, Chapter 14*	**Block Scheduling** .5 day	**REV** Section 5 Review, p. 339

Chapter Resource Key

PS	Primary Sources	**A**	Assessment
RS	Reading Support	**REV**	Review
E	Enrichment		Transparencies
SM	Skills Mastery		CD-ROM

 Video

 Internet

 Holt Presentation Maker Using Microsoft® PowerPoint®

 One-Stop Planner CD–ROM

See the *One-Stop Planner* for a complete list of additional resources for students and teachers.

One-Stop Planner CD–ROM

It's easy to plan lessons, select resources, and print out materials for your students when you use the **One-Stop Planner CD-ROM with Test Generator.**

Technology Resources

 One-Stop Planner, Lesson 14.1
 Homework Practice Online
 HRW Go Site

 One-Stop Planner, Lesson 14.2
 Homework Practice Online

 One-Stop Planner, Lesson 14.3
Homework Practice Online

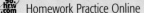

One-Stop Planner, Lesson 14.4
Homework Practice Online
HRW Go Site

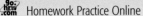

One-Stop Planner, Lesson 14.5
Teaching Transparencies 30: The Self in Relation to Others from the Individualist and Collectivist Perspectives
Homework Practice Online
CNN. Presents Psychology: Type D Personality
HRW Go Site

Chapter Review and Assessment

 HRW Go site
REV Chapter 14 Review, pp. 340–341
REV Chapter Review Activities with Answer Key

A Chapter 14 Test (Form A or B)
A Portfolio Assessment Handbook
A Alternative Assessment Handbook

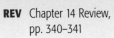 Chapter 14 Test Generator (on the One–Stop Planner)
Global Skill Builder CD-ROM

---

internet connect

HRW ONLINE RESOURCES

GO TO: go.hrw.com
Then type in a keyword.

TEACHER HOME PAGE
KEYWORD: SY3 Teacher

CHAPTER INTERNET ACTIVITIES
KEYWORD: SY3 PS14
Choose an activity on theories of personality to:
• create a theoretical profile of a noted personality theorist.
• identify elements of social-learning theory in modern advertising.
• write a dinner party conversation that could occur among theorists of different approaches to personality.

CHAPTER ENRICHMENT LINKS
KEYWORD: SY3 CH14

ONLINE ASSESSMENT
Homework Practice
KEYWORD: SY3 HP14

Standardized Test Prep
KEYWORD: SY3 STP14

Rubrics
KEYWORD: SS Rubrics

CONTENT UPDATES
KEYWORD: SS Content Updates

HOLT PRESENTATION MAKER
KEYWORD: SY3 PPT14

ONLINE READING SUPPORT
KEYWORD: SS Strategies

CURRENT EVENTS
KEYWORD: S3 Current Events

Additional Resources

PRINT RESOURCES FOR TEACHERS
Bennett, E. A. (1983). *What Jung really said.* New York: Schocken Books.

Bjork, D. W. (1993). *B. F. Skinner.* New York: Basic Books.

Brenner, C. (1973). *An elementary textbook of psychoanalysis.* New York: Anchor Books.

PRINT RESOURCES FOR STUDENTS
Feldman, R., & Feinman, J. (1992). *Who you are: Personality and its development.* New York: Franklin Watts.

Rogers, C. (1995). *A way of being.* Boston: Houghton Mifflin.

Skinner, B. F. (1976). *Walden two.* New York: Macmillan.

MULTIMEDIA RESOURCES
Carl Gustav Jung: An introduction (VHS). Films for the Humanities & Sciences, P.O. Box 2053, Princeton, NJ 08543-2053.

Discovering who you are: Theories of personality (VHS). Social Studies School Service, 10200 Jefferson Boulevard, Room 33, P.O. Box 802, Culver City, CA 90232-0802.

Freud: The greatest thinkers (VHS). Social Studies School Service, 10200 Jefferson Boulevard, Room 33, P.O. Box 802, Culver City, CA 90232-0802.

THEORIES OF PERSONALITY

Introducing Chapter 14

People both inside and outside the field of psychology tend to agree that each human being has a unique personality. Psychologists disagree, however, about how human personality develops and how best to differentiate among various types of personalities. Have students think of two celebrities who have very different personalities. Then have the class work together to compare and contrast the two individuals. You may want to have students create a Venn diagram to show the features that are similar and those that are different. Next, pose the following questions: Why do you think these individuals have such different personalities? What factors in their biological makeup, cultural background, gender, childhood experiences, and/or personal choices have made them who they are? Finally, tell students that Chapter 14 will introduce them to various theories of personality.

Sections

1 **The Trait Approach**

2 **The Psychoanalytic Approach**

3 **The Learning Approach**

4 **The Humanistic Approach**

5 **The Sociocultural Approach**

Each of the five questions identified on page 320 corresponds to one of these sections.

Chapter 14 THEORIES OF PERSONALITY

Read to Discover

1 What are the main features and limitations of the trait theory of personality?

2 What impact has the psychoanalytic theory of personality had, and how has the theory been modified since Freud's time?

3 What do learning theorists believe are the influences on and motivations for behavior?

4 How does the humanistic approach view the role of the self and free choice in shaping behavior?

5 How does the sociocultural approach view the importance of ethnicity, gender, culture, and socioeconomic status in the development of personality?

Each chapter begins with a vignette, called "A Day in the Life," that relates the information discussed in the chapter to the everyday events in the lives of a group of fictional high school students. The text of the chapter occasionally refers back to the vignette to demonstrate the application of the concept being discussed. An icon marked "A Day in the Life" is placed next to these references.

Copy the following graphic organizer onto the chalkboard, omitting the italicized text. Fill in the spaces as you introduce the trait approach to personality.

The Trait Approach	
Hippocrates Gordon Allport *Hans Eysenck*	*Five-Factor Model*

A DAY IN THE LIFE

March 19

Janet and Todd were having lunch together, and Todd, as usual, kept joking around. "Hey, Janet, look! Over there," Todd said as he stole one of her pretzels.

"I can't believe you're still pulling that same joke," Janet laughed.

"Well, I can't believe you're still falling for it," joked Todd. "You are so gullible."

"I'm not gullible; I'm just trusting," Janet said laughing. Just then Hannah came running up.

"Janet, Todd—I'm so glad I found you both. I have the best news!" Hannah was talking so fast they could barely understand her.

"Hannah, calm down a second. What's going on?" Janet asked.

"Mr. Hochberg just called me into his office because he said he had some news for me. Remember my violin recital last week?" Hannah asked, still trying to talk slowly. "Well, there was an arts foundation representative there, and she offered me a performing arts scholarship to

almost any college I choose!"

"Hannah, that's great!" Janet exclaimed. "I always knew you could do it. Where do you think you'll go?"

"Well, I'm thinking about going to the same school where my brother goes. He loves it there. He said that there's a large Korean population. My parents have always raised us both to understand our heritage, but it will be really cool to meet lots of other people with the same background."

"Have you told your parents yet?" Todd asked.

"No, not yet. I want to tell them at the same time, and they're both at work right now," Hannah answered. "It would make them so happy if my brother and I were at the same school. It means a lot to them that we keep the family together as much as possible."

"Well, Hannah, congratulations," said Todd. "But you have to promise that you won't forget about us when you become a famous violinist!"

"Don't be silly," Hannah smiled. "Would I do a thing like that?"

• • •

Would Hannah do a thing like that? What influences the things people do and do not do? Some people might say that the answer is found in personality. But what exactly is personality? When people think of a person's personality, they usually think of the person's most striking characteristics, as in an "assertive personality" or an "artistic personality." Psychologists define **personality** as the patterns of feelings, motives, and behavior that set people apart from one another.

Psychologists seek to describe personality characteristics and to explain how personality develops. They try to predict how different people will respond to life's demands. In this chapter, we explore five approaches to the study of personality: trait theory, psychoanalytic theory, learning theory, humanistic theory, and sociocultural theory.

Key Terms

- personality
- trait
- introverts
- extroverts
- id
- ego
- superego
- defense mechanisms
- repression
- rationalization
- displacement
- regression
- projection
- reaction formation
- denial
- sublimation
- collective unconscious
- archetypes
- inferiority complex
- socialization
- self-concept
- congruence
- acculturation

▶ WHY PSYCHOLOGY MATTERS

Psychologists have long studied the development of human personality. Use **CNNfyi.com** or other current events sources to learn more about the study of personality development.

CNNfyi.com

321

7
Section Objective

▶ Explain the main features and limitations of the trait theory of personality.

This objective is assessed in the Section Review on page 324 and in the Chapter 14 Review.

Using Truth or Fiction

Each chapter opens with several "Truth or Fiction" statements that relate to the concepts discussed in the chapter. Ask students whether they think each statement is true or false. Answers to each item as well as explanations are provided at appropriate points within the text under the heading "Truth or Fiction Revisited."

Cross-Curricular Link: History

Although Hippocrates' theory of the four basic humors was incorrect, some of his other ideas were far ahead of their time. Born about 460 B.C., Hippocrates lived in an age when most people thought illness was caused by demons or magic. Hippocrates believed that poor hygiene and malnutrition cause disease. He studied diseases carefully and taught his methods to other physicians. He was competent at setting broken bones and at surgery. He strongly believed that physicians have a moral responsibility to their patients. Physicians today still take the Hippocratic oath, in which they promise to practice medicine in an ethical and caring way.

322

Opening Section 1

Motivator

Write the words *shy* and *outgoing* on the chalkboard. Explain that these are two basic personality traits. Then read aloud the textbook definition of the word *trait*. Ask volunteers to list some of their own personality traits and explain why they consider these traits to be reasonably consistent. Tell students that while trait theorists believe that traits form the basis of personality, they disagree on how individuals come to possess certain traits and not others. Then have students read Section 1 to learn about the trait approach to personality.

TRUTH OR fiction ?

Read the following statements about psychology. Do you think they are true or false? You will learn whether each statement is true or false as you read the chapter.

- People can lose feeling in their hands or legs even though nothing is medically wrong with them.
- According to Freud's theory, biting one's fingernails and smoking cigarettes are signs of early childhood conflicts.
- According to Jung, people can remember things that never happened to them personally.
- All psychologists believe that humans have free will to make their own choices in life.
- Psychologists feel that culture, gender, and ethnicity are important in personality development.

SECTION 1
The Trait Approach

A **trait** is an aspect of personality that is considered to be reasonably stable. We assume that a person has certain traits based on how the person behaves. If you describe a friend as shy, it may be because you have seen your friend looking anxious and trying to escape social encounters. Traits are assumed to account for consistent behavior in different situations. You would probably expect your shy friend to act withdrawn in most social situations. Todd, on the other hand, was constantly making jokes with his friends. Therefore, we might conclude that being outgoing and being humorous are two of Todd's personality traits. But if Todd made jokes only around his friends, we would not consider him to have these traits.

Trait theorists have generally assumed that traits are somehow fixed or unchanging. However, the question of where traits come from has been pondered through the ages.

Hippocrates

An early answer to where traits come from was offered by the ancient Greek physician Hippocrates. The ancient Greeks believed that the body contains fluids called humors. Hippocrates suggested that traits are a result of different combinations of these bodily fluids.

Hippocrates believed that there are four basic fluids, or humors, in the body:

- yellow bile, which was associated with a choleric, or quick-tempered, disposition
- blood, which was connected with a sanguine, or warm and cheerful, temperament
- phlegm, which was linked with a phlegmatic, or sluggish and cool, disposition
- black bile, which was associated with a melancholic, thoughtful temperament

Certain diseases and disorders were believed to reflect a lack of balance in these humors. Methods such as bloodletting (the removal of blood from the body) and vomiting were recommended to restore the balance of fluids and one's health. Although there is no scientific evidence for Hippocrates' biological theory, the terms based on his ideas remain in use today. A cheerful person, for example, may still be called sanguine.

Gordon Allport

In the 1930s, psychologist Gordon Allport (1897–1967) searched through a dictionary to find every term that could describe a person (Allport & Odbert, 1936). He cataloged some 18,000 human traits from a search through lists of descriptive words. Some of the words, such as *short* and *brunette,* describe physical traits. Others, such as *shy* and *emotional,* describe behavioral traits. Still others, such as *honest,* concern morality.

Allport assumed that traits can be inherited and that they are fixed in the nervous system. He conducted thorough and detailed studies of individuals, noting their outstanding traits as well as their behaviors. Allport's research led him to conclude that traits are the building blocks of personality. He believed that a person's behavior is a product of his or her particular combination of traits (Allport, 1937, 1961, 1965, 1966).

Hans Eysenck

British psychologist Hans J. Eysenck (1916–1997) focused on the relationships between two personality dimensions: introversion-extroversion and emotional stability-instability. **Introverts** tend to be imaginative and to look inward rather than to other people for their ideas and energy. **Extroverts**, on the other hand, tend to be active and self-expressive and gain energy from interaction with other people. The contrast between introversion and extroversion was first pro-

Teaching Section 1

Guided Practice

Ask students to create a list of words describing moods and a list describing traits. Write their suggestions on the chalkboard as you discuss the differences between these two concepts. Remind students that moods come and go, but traits are enduring.

Independent Practice

Ask students to create a cartoon or comic strip in which the characters exhibit traits discussed in the chapter. You may want to have the students post their work in the class.

Have students find out more about the trait approach by studying Gordon Allport or Hans Eysenck. Students should be able to find a number of similarities and differences between these two scientists.

The Five-Factor Model

Factor	Name	Traits
I	Extroversion	Contrasts talkativeness, assertiveness, and activity with silence, passivity, reserve
II	Agreeableness	Contrasts kindness, trust, and warmth with hostility, selfishness, and distrust
III	Conscientiousness	Contrasts organization, thoroughness, and reliability with carelessness, negligence, and unreliability
IV	Emotional Stability-Instability	Contrasts reliability and coping ability with nervousness, moodiness, and sensitivity to negative events
V	Openness to Experience	Contrasts imagination, curiosity, and creativity with shallowness and lack of perceptiveness

FIGURE 14.1 *The Five-Factor Model may be useful for helping people who suffer from a variety of psychological disorders.*

posed by Carl Jung, whom you will read about later in this chapter. Stable people are usually reliable, composed, and rational. Unstable people can be agitated and unpredictable.

Eysenck cataloged various personality traits according to where those traits appear within the dimensions of introversion-extroversion and emotional stability-instability. (See Figure 14.2 on page 324.) For instance, an anxious person might be highly introverted and emotionally unstable. A reckless or impulsive person might be highly extroverted and unstable (Eysenck, 1953).

Eysenck's scheme is similar to the one suggested by Hippocrates. According to Eysenck's dimensions, the choleric type would be extroverted and unstable; the sanguine type, extroverted and stable; the phlegmatic type, introverted and stable; and the melancholic type, introverted and unstable.

The Five-Factor Model

The "big five" may sound like a description of a basketball team. In psychology, however, the term refers to recent research suggesting that there may be five basic personality factors. These include the two found by Eysenck—extroversion and emotional stability—along with conscientiousness, agreeableness, and openness to experience (See Figure 14.1). Many personality theorists, particularly Robert McCrae and Paul T. Costa, Jr., have helped in the development of the Five-Factor Model. Cross-cultural research has found that these five factors appear to define the personality structure of American, German, Portuguese, Jewish, Chinese, Korean, and Japanese people (McCrae & Costa, 1997). A study of more than 5,000 German, British, Spanish, Czech, and Turkish people suggests that the factors are related to people's basic temperaments, which are considered to be largely inborn (McCrae et al., 2000). The researchers interpreted the results to suggest that our personalities tend to mature rather than be shaped by environmental conditions, although the expression of personality traits is certainly affected by culture. For example, a person who is "basically" open to new experience is likely to behave less openly in a restrictive society than in an open society.

A great deal of research is currently underway on the Five-Factor Model. There are hundreds of studies relating scores on the five factors, according to a psychological test constructed by Costa and McCrae (the NEO Five-Factor Inventory™), with various behavior patterns, psychological problems, and kinds of personalities. For example, consider driving. Research shows that people who are given more traffic tickets and who get into more accidents tend to score lower on the factor of agreeableness than do others (Cellar et al., 2000). In other words, it is safer to share the freeway with agreeable people. People who get along with nearly everybody tend to score low on conscientiousness—that is,

Journal Activity

Have students write an entry about the aspect of their own personality they like best and the trait they would most like to change. Have them include examples of how each trait helps or hurts them.

Class Discussion

Have students apply the concepts of introversion and extroversion to well-known characters from movies, television shows, or familiar books. How do these aspects of personality affect behavior?

internet connect

TOPIC: Social-Learning Theory and Advertising
GO TO: go.hrw.com
KEYWORD: SY3 PS14

Have students access the Internet through the HRW Go site to research social-learning theory and to identify elements of social-learning theory in modern advertising. Then have students choose an advertisement and make a short presentation regarding how social-learning theory is integrated into the message and content of the advertisement they have chosen.

Closing Section 1

Applying Ideas

Review with students the four personality types suggested by Hippocrates and the two personality dimensions suggested by Eysenck. Then have students write a description of each of the following hypothetical people: someone who is extroverted and unstable, someone who is extroverted and stable, someone who is introverted and stable, and someone who is introverted and unstable. Have students read their descriptions aloud for class discussion. Then have students explain how Eysenck's scheme is similar to the one proposed by Hippocrates.

Classifying Information

Give students index cards on which you have listed the basic personality types or traits according to Hippocrates, Eysenck, and the psychologists who support the "big five" theory. Then have students sort the cards according to the theory to which each belongs.

Reviewing Section 1

Have students complete the Section Review questions on page 324.

Section 1 Review: Answers

1. Main features include a focus on cataloging traits, examining where traits come from, and which traits are predominant.

2. The "big five" personality factors are extroversion, emotional stability-instability, conscientiousness, agreeableness, and openness to experience-closed.

3. Limitations may include pigeonholing people according to oversimplified characteristics.

Essay and Research Themes for A. P. Students

Theme 12

Eysenck's Personality Dimensions

| Sanguine | STABLE | Phlegmatic |

| EXTROVERTED | | INTROVERTED |

Sanguine — Sociable, Outgoing, Talkative, Responsive, Easygoing, Lively, Carefree

Phlegmatic — Calm, Reliable, Controlled, Peaceful, Thoughtful, Careful, Passive

Choleric — Aggressive, Excitable, Changeable, Impulsive, Optimistic, Touchy, Restless

Melancholic — Quiet, Unsociable, Pessimistic, Sober, Rigid, Anxious, Moody

| | UNSTABLE | |
| Choleric | | Melancholic |

FIGURE 14.2 *This diagram shows how closely Eysenck's personality dimensions relate to the four personality types identified by Hippocrates.*

they do not examine other people too closely, and high on agreeableness—they tend to go along with what other people want (Bernardin et al., 2000).

The Five-Factor Model also has been used to study politics. For example, studies in the United States (Butler, 2000), Belgium, and Poland (van Hiel et al., 2000) show that people who are authoritarians or dictators tend to score low on openness to experience—that is, they do not want people reading too much or watching the news too much.

Researchers are also studying the way in which the five factors are connected with the ways in which people interact with their friends and families (e.g., Wan et al., 2000; Wintre & Sugar, 2000). In the field of psychological problems, researchers are studying links between the five factors and a variety of disorders. These include anxiety disorders (Clarke et al., 1994), thinking that one is ill when there is no medical basis for the belief (Cox et al., 2000), depression and suicide attempts (Duberstein et al., 2000), schizophrenia (Gurrera et al., 2000), and personality

disorders (Widiger & Costa, 1994). The Five-Factor Model helps in describing these disorders. It remains to be seen how well the model will enable psychologists to explain the disorders, and control them—that is, prevent them or help people who develop them.

Psychologists continue to disagree about which personality factors are the most basic. However, nearly all psychologists would agree that the "big five" personality dimensions are important in defining a person's psychological makeup. Moreover, a person's position along these dimensions tends to be established at an early age and then remains stable through life.

Evaluation of the Trait Approach

One shortcoming of the trait approach is that it describes personality but does not explain where traits come from. The efforts of Allport and other trait theorists to link personality traits to biological factors have not been successful. Today trait theory focuses on describing traits rather than tracing their origins or investigating how people with certain traits can change for the better.

The work of trait theorists has, however, had a number of practical applications. In suggesting that there are links between personalities, abilities, and interests, trait theorists have alerted us to the value of matching people to educational programs and jobs on the basis of their personality traits.

SECTION 1 REVIEW

go.hrw.com — **Homework Practice Online** — Keyword: SY3 HP14

1. List the main features of the trait theory of personality.

2. List the "big five" personality factors.

3. **Critical Thinking** *Evaluating* What are the limitations of the trait theory?

SECTION **2**

The Psychoanalytic Approach

The psychoanalytic approach to personality teaches that all people—even the most well-adjusted—undergo inner struggles. According to this approach, people are born with certain biological drives such as aggression, sex, and the need for

Section Objective

▶ Describe the impact of the psychoanalytic theory of personality and how the theory has been modified since Sigmund Freud.

This objective is assessed in the Section Review on page 332 and in the Chapter 14 Review.

Motivator

Survey students to find out how many of them have at least some familiarity with the following images or concepts: a client lying on a psychiatrist's couch and recounting his or her dreams, the idea of unconscious fears and wishes, the terms *Oedipus complex* and *Electra complex,* the idea of "Freudian slips." Explain that in Section 2 they will learn where these concepts originated and how they have affected our view of psychological development.

superiority. These drives, however, may come into conflict with laws, social norms, and moral codes that have previously been internalized. At any moment, a person's behavior, thoughts, and emotions represent the outcome of inner contests between the opposing forces of drives and rules.

Sigmund Freud

The "inner conflict" approach to personality theory owes its origin to Sigmund Freud (1856–1939). Freud was trained as a physician. Early in his practice in Vienna, Austria, he was astounded to find that some people had lost feeling in a hand or had become paralyzed in the legs even though nothing was medically wrong with them. When Freud interviewed these individuals, he found that many things in their lives were making them very angry or anxious. Yet they refused to recognize their emotional or social problems. They were at the mercy of very powerful inner emotions, yet on the surface they seemed calm.

It is true that people can lose feeling in their hands or legs even though nothing is medically wrong with them. Sigmund Freud directly observed such ailments.

Freud believed that conscious ideas and feelings occupy only a small part of the mind. Many of people's deepest thoughts, fears, and urges remain out of their awareness. These urges are pushed into an unconscious part of the mind.

One way in which Freud explored the unconscious is through psychoanalysis. In psychoanalysis, people are encouraged to talk about anything that pops into their minds. They do so in a comfortable and relaxed setting. The people Freud observed—those who had lost feeling in their hands or legs—regained much of their functioning when they talked about the things that were on their minds. For this reason, psychoanalysis has been called a "talking cure."

Freud also explored the unconscious through dream analysis. He believed that people experience unconscious wishes in their dreams—often in disguised form. Freud would ask people to record their dreams upon waking. He would then help them explore the dreams' possible hidden meanings.

In psychoanalysis, the client is made comfortable, usually on a couch similar to Freud's original couch, which is shown here.

Another technique that Freud used was hypnosis. He felt that people in a hypnotic state had better access to their unconscious thoughts. Freud eventually abandoned hypnosis, however, because many people later denied the things they said when they were in a hypnotic state.

Id, Ego, and Superego

Freud believed that the mind has three basic psychological structures: the id, the ego, and the superego. The id is like the stereotypical two-year-old: "I want what I want, and I want it now." The **id** represents basic drives such as hunger. It demands pleasure through instant gratification and pays no attention to laws, social customs, or the needs of others. It follows what Freud called the *pleasure principle*—the urge for an immediate release of energy or emotion that will bring personal gratification, relief, or pleasure.

According to Freud, the id is present at birth. The **ego**, however, develops because a child's demands for instant gratification cannot be met or because meeting these demands may be harmful. Freud wrote that the ego "stands for reason and good sense" (1964). It is guided by the *reality principle*—the understanding that in the real world we cannot always get what we want.

Cross-Curricular Link: Biology

One of the clues that alerted Freud and his colleagues to the fact that inner emotions could cause the symptoms of paralysis were reports of such symptoms that made no biological sense. Several patients reported "glove anesthesia"—a loss of sensation in the hand just below the wrist. Physicians knew that if the nerves governing sensation in the hand were damaged, feeling also would be lost above the wrist. Therefore, they had to search for another explanation.

Cultural Dimensions

For historical and cultural reasons, different psychological theories have become popular in different parts of the world. Psychoanalysis is one of the major influences on Latin American psychology, especially in Argentina, where psychology has traditionally been taught by physicians who have been trained in Freudian psychoanalysis.

Role-Playing

Select three volunteers to play the role of the id, the ego, and the superego. Have other students suggest ideas for moral dilemmas in which the ego is caught between the conflicting demands of the id and the superego. Have the three students improvise dialogue to dramatize this conflict. (Remind students that the three structures are psychological constructs and that this dialogue theoretically takes place in the mind.) Then have students consider how the outcome would differ if the id or the superego were the dominant structure.

Meeting Individual Needs: Tactile/Kinesthetic Learners

Ask tactile/kinesthetic learners to make three sketches: one that represents the id, one that represents the ego, and one that represents the superego. Have the students display their sketches and explain why they depicted the three psychological structures the way they did. Also have students explain the relationship between the three structures and their connection to the following principles: the pleasure principle, the reality principle, and the moral principle.

Calvin and Hobbes
by Bill Watterson

SOURCE: CALVIN & HOBBES copyright Bill Watterson. Distributed by Universal Press Syndicate. Reprinted with permission. All rights reserved.

The ego seeks to satisfy the appetites of the id in ways that are consistent with reality. For example, the id lets you know that you are hungry, but the ego lets you know that certain ways of satisfying your hunger—such as cooking a hamburger—are more appropriate than others—such as eating raw hamburger. The ego also provides the conscious sense of self. Activities such as planning dinner and studying for a test are functions of the ego.

Although most of the ego is conscious, some of its business is carried out unconsciously. For instance, the ego acts as a censor that screens out the wild impulses of the id. When the ego senses that indecent or improper impulses are rising into awareness, it tries to repress them.

The third psychological structure Freud formulated is the **superego**. The superego develops throughout early childhood. It functions according to the *moral principle*. By incorporating the standards and values of parents and members of the community, the superego provides us with our moral sense. The superego acts as the conscience and floods the ego with feelings of guilt and shame when we think or do something that society defines as wrong.

The ego does not have an easy job. It is caught between the conflicting messages of the id and the superego. For example, the id may urge, "You want to go out with your friends. Don't study now!" while the superego warns, "You have to study or you will not pass the test." According to Freud, people with healthy egos—and thus healthy personalities—find ways to balance the id's demands and the superego's warnings. In this case, the healthy ego would probably conclude, "Study now, and after you do well on the test, you can spend time with your friends."

Defense Mechanisms

According to Freud, **defense mechanisms** are methods the ego uses to avoid recognizing ideas or emotions that may cause personal anxiety. These defenses operate unconsciously.

Repression One of the main Freudian defense mechanisms is repression. **Repression** removes anxiety-causing ideas from conscious awareness by pushing them into the unconscious. To explain repression, Freud compared people's personalities to teakettles. Primitive urges such as aggression seek expression just like steam tries to escape from a boiling kettle. But acknowledging these urges would cause a person serious feelings of guilt, anxiety, and shame. Thus, the urges are repressed to keep the lid on the boiling kettle.

Repression, however, is not always successful. When enough steam builds up inside, the teakettle pops its lid. When people "pop their lids," the results are outbursts of anger and the development of other psychological and emotional problems.

Rationalization Other defense mechanisms protect us from unacceptable ideas in a different manner. They do not completely repress such ideas, but they distort them in one way or another. One such defense mechanism is **rationalization**—the use of self-deception to justify unacceptable behaviors or ideas. For instance, a student who cheats during a test may explain, "I only cheated on a couple of questions—I knew most of the material."

Displacement According to Freudian theorists, **displacement** is defined as the transfer of an idea or

Synthesizing Information

Have students write down two examples to illustrate each defense mechanism discussed in the section. Ask the class to review the examples and then to select the best ones. Organize students into groups of three and assign each group one of the selected examples. Have each group produce a visual, such as a comic strip or poster, to illustrate the assigned example. Also ask each group to write a caption to accompany the visual. Have representatives from the groups display and discuss their materials.

Cooperative Learning

Organize the class into eight groups, and assign each group one of the defense mechanisms discussed in the section. Tell the members of each group that they are to write and perform a short skit that focuses on the use of their assigned defense mechanism. After each group has performed its skit, have the class try to determine which defense mechanism was portrayed in the skit. Then have the class discuss the benefits and drawbacks of using defense mechanisms in daily life.

impulse from a threatening or unsuitable object to a less threatening object. For example, a football player who is yelled at by his coach may go home and yell at his little brother.

Regression   Freud believed that when an individual is under a great deal of stress he or she will return to behavior that is characteristic of an earlier stage of development. He termed this behavior **regression**. For example, an adolescent may pout and refuse to speak to her parents when forbidden to go out with friends. Similarly, an adult may become highly dependent on his parents following the breakup of his own marriage.

Projection   A motion picture projector thrusts an image outward onto a screen. Freud believed that people sometimes deal with unacceptable impulses by projecting these impulses outward onto other people. In other words, people see *their own* faults in other people. For example, hostile people, unable to think of *themselves* as hostile, may accuse other people of hostility. As a result of this **projection**, they may think of the world as a dangerous place.

Reaction Formation   People who use the defense of **reaction formation** act contrary to their genuine feelings in order to keep their true feelings hidden. A person who is angry with a coworker may behave in a "sickly sweet" manner toward that coworker. Someone who is unconsciously attracted to another person may keep the impulses out of mind by being mean to that person.

Denial   In the mechanism of **denial**, a person refuses to accept the reality of anything that is bad or upsetting. For example, people who smoke cigarettes may ignore the risks of lung cancer and heart disease from smoking because they think, "It can't happen to me."

Sublimation   Freud also believed that individuals can channel their basic impulses into socially acceptable behavior through a process called **sublimation**. For example, a hostile student may channel aggressive impulses into contact sports.

Effects of Defense Mechanisms   According to Freud, when used in moderation, defense mechanisms may be normal and even useful to protect people from painful feelings such as anxiety, guilt, and shame. Such defense mechanisms become unhealthy, he said, when they lead a person to ignore the underlying issues causing those feelings. However, Freud also noted that a person with a strong and healthy ego is able to balance the id and the superego without the use of such mechanisms. Therefore, the use of defense mechanisms may indicate the presence of inner conflict or personal anxiety.

Stages of Development

Freud believed that an individual's personality develops through a series of five stages. These stages of development begin at birth and continue to shape human personality through adolescence. He believed that people instinctively seek to preserve and extend life. He also thought that these instinctive efforts to survive are aided by a psychological energy he labeled libido. (*Libido* is the Latin word for "desire.")

Freud organized psychological development into five periods: oral, anal, phallic, latent, and genital. Children were said to encounter conflicts during each stage. If the conflicts were not resolved, Freud believed that the child might become fixated, or stuck, at an early stage of development. The child would then carry that stage's traits into adulthood. Thus, Freud believed that an adult's psychological problems might actually stem from unresolved childhood conflicts.

The Oral Stage   In Freud's theory, psychological development begins in the first year of life. He noted that infants are continually exploring their

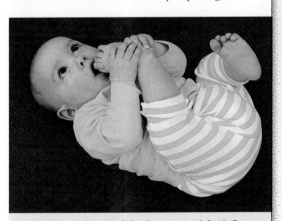

During the oral stage of development, an infant's first reaction to many objects is often to suck on them.

Journal Activity

Have students write in their journals about the defense mechanism or mechanisms they seem to use most often. Under what circumstances do they use the defense mechanism(s)? How does the use of each defense mechanism help or hinder their interactions with other people? How does the use of each defense mechanism affect their self-concept? Remind students that journal writings are private.

Cross-Curricular Link: Music

Tell students to listen closely to the lyrics of some of their favorite songs for examples of defense mechanisms in action. Have students play their songs in class or read the lyrics aloud and explain how they illustrate the use of defense mechanisms. Which defense mechanisms seem to be most commonly used? Does the use of a defense mechanism make a song more personal to listeners and help them identify with it?

CASE STUDIES
AND OTHER TRUE STORIES

Review the case of Hans and Freud's theories about Hans's behavior. Remind students that many of Freud's critics do not believe that the Oedipus and Electra complexes really exist. Have students evaluate Freud's theories and explain why they agree or disagree with the critics. What other explanations might students offer for Hans's behavior? Write these explanations on the chalkboard. Then have students write a brief case study of Hans based on the explanation they find most credible.

Meeting Individual Needs: Auditory Learners

Have students locate English-language synopses of the Greek plays about Oedipus and Electra and read them aloud. Then have auditory learners explain the plays in their own words and relate them to the Oedipus and Electra theories proposed by Freud. Ask students to consider whether these ancient stories apply to human experience generally or only to certain cultures, such as American culture.

CASE STUDIES
AND OTHER TRUE STORIES
The Case of Little Hans: A Mystery in Vienna

Five-year-old Hans lived in turn-of-the-century Vienna, a flourishing capital of music and the arts. But Hans was afraid—afraid that horses were biting people in the streets. He was terrified that he would be bitten himself if he left his house. In 1908, the boy's father, distressed about Hans's fears, turned to Sigmund Freud for advice. One year later, Freud wrote a lengthy case history about Hans. It would become one of the most celebrated cases in psychology.

Freud came to believe that Hans did not fear horses because of anything the horses might do. Instead, Hans feared what horses symbolized, or represented, to him. According to Freud, horses represented Hans's father. As Freud studied Hans, he came to believe that Hans was hostile toward his father and that he *projected* this hostility onto the horses. Thus, he fantasized that his father—the horse—was hostile toward him. Hans's fear of being bitten by horses symbolized his unconscious fear of his father.

Why would Hans feel hostility and fear toward his father? Freud related these feelings to two aspects of the phallic stage: the strong desire a child has for the parent of the other sex and the jealousy the child has toward the parent of the same sex. In other words, little boys may expect to marry their mothers when they grow up, and little girls may expect to marry their fathers.

Such feelings toward parents would be difficult for children to handle if they were consciously aware of the feelings of aggression. For this reason, Freud believed that these feelings were repressed and would remain unconscious. Their influence would be felt, however, and the child would seek approval from the parent of the other sex and have hostility toward the parent of the same sex.

Freud labeled this conflict the *Oedipus complex* in boys. Oedipus was a legendary Greek king who unknowingly killed his father and married his mother. Freud said that similar feelings in girls give rise to the *Electra complex*. According to the famous Greek play, Electra was the daughter of King Agamemnon. She longed for him after his death and sought revenge on his slayers—her mother and her mother's lover. Thus, the Oedipus and Electra complexes relate to feelings of desire for the parent of the other sex. They also both involve resentment toward the parent of the same sex.

Freud theorized that the Oedipus and Electra complexes are normally resolved by the time children are five or six years old. Hans overcame his fear of horses by age six. Freud believed that Hans had coped with his fear of his father by surrendering the wish to possess his mother. The father then ceased to be his rival in love, and Hans no longer had a reason to be hostile toward his father. Hans' projection of his hostile impulses was no longer necessary. Therefore, he no longer viewed horses, which represented his father, as being dangerous.

Hans not only repressed his hostility toward his father. He also started to identify with his father. He began to assume his father's behavior and attitudes. Freud believed that people try to become like the people they fear so that they will be accepted by them and will no longer need to fear them. Identification leads boys to assume the behavior of men and to bring inward, or internalize, their fathers' values. Similarly, identification leads girls to assume the behavior of women and to internalize their mothers' values. Identification is an indication that the Oedipus and Electra complexes have been resolved.

As celebrated as this case has been, Freud's theories on the matter have been widely criticized. Many psychologists believe that the Oedipus and Electra complexes do not really exist and that of all of Freud's theories, these are the weakest.

WHY PSYCHOLOGY MATTERS

Psychologists use a variety of techniques to help children cope with the world. Use CNN fyi.com or other current events sources to learn more about the types of counseling available to children. Write a brief summary of what you have learned.

CNN fyi.com

To demonstrate the prevalence of what Freud termed the oral fixation, have the class make a list of oral behaviors such as chewing gum, smoking, eating when not hungry, biting one's nails, chewing one's lip or the inside of one's mouth, and so on. Then have each student unobtrusively observe a group of students or adults for 15 minutes and note the number of times people engage in these behaviors. In class, have a volunteer tally the results. Use the results as the basis for a class discussion on the oral stage of development.

Use the following activity to have pairs of students explore some of Jung's examples of archetypes. Have one student in each pair call out a character from a fairy tale, legend, or myth and the other student in the pair respond with the name of the archetype this character represents (such as young hero or wicked witch). Then have the students switch roles. Ask the pairs to evaluate Jung's contention that archetypes represent the accumulated experience of all human beings. Have students explain how they arrived at their conclusions.

world by picking up objects and putting those objects into their mouths. Infants also receive their main source of pleasure—food—with their mouths. For these reasons, Freud termed the first stage of development the oral stage. He theorized that the infant's survival is dependent on the attention of adults. A child whose caretakers do not meet his or her needs during this stage may become fixated at the oral stage. Some examples of this fixation might include smoking, overeating, excessive talking, and nail biting. In addition, as an adult, such a person might be inclined to have clinging, dependent interpersonal relationships.

TRUTH OR fiction ▪ REVISITED ▪

It is true that according to Freud's theory, biting one's fingernails and smoking cigarettes are signs of early childhood conflicts. Such behavior might reflect fixation at the oral stage of development.

The Anal Stage   According to Freud, the anal stage occurs between the ages of one and a half and two and a half. During this stage, children learn that they can control their own bodily functions, and the general issue of self-control becomes a vital issue to children. Conflict during the anal stage can lead to two sets of adult personality traits. So-called anal-retentive traits involve an excessive use of self-control. They include perfectionism and excessive needs for order and cleanliness. People with anal-expulsive traits, on the other hand, are less restrained and may be careless and messy.

The Phallic Stage   The third year of life marks the beginning of the phallic stage. Young girls and boys begin to discover the physical differences between the two sexes and become more focused on their own bodies. Children may also develop strong attachments to the parent of the opposite sex. At the same time, they may view the same-sex parent as a rival for the other parent's affections. Freud argued that the complex emotions of the phallic stage can lead to several psychological disorders later in life, including depression, excessive guilt, and anxiety.

The Latency Stage   By the age of five or six, Freud believed, children would have been in conflict with their parents for several years. At this

Pictured here is a mandala, the symbol Carl Jung used to represent the collective nature, or oneness, of human experience.

point, they would retreat from the conflict and repress all aggressive urges. In so doing, they would enter the latency stage. *Latent* means "hidden," and during the latency period, impulses and emotions remain hidden, or unconscious.

The Genital Stage   Freud wrote that people enter the final stage of psychological development, or the genital stage, at puberty. The adolescent does not generally encounter any new psychological conflicts during this period but does become more aware of his or her own gender identity. Instead, the conflicts of the early development stages resurface.

Carl Jung

Sigmund Freud had several intellectual heirs. The best known of these theorists was Carl Jung (1875–1961). Jung was a Swiss psychiatrist who had been a colleague of Freud's. He fell into disfavor with Freud, however, when he developed his own psychoanalytic theory—known as *analytic psychology*—which places a greater emphasis on the influences of mysticism and religion on human behavior.

Jung, like Freud, was intrigued by unconscious processes. But he dramatically altered Freud's theory of these processes. Jung believed that people

Ask students whether the discussion of Freud's psychological stages of human development makes them embarrassed or uncomfortable. Explain that many of Freud's peers felt the same way. According to Freud, resistance to his theories was strong because many people found the theories to be disturbing. Discuss the fact that the exploration of psychology sometimes requires the student to focus on material that can be embarrassing or disturbing and that the sensitivity and privacy of others should be respected.

Ask students to examine the photograph of the mandala shown on this page. Have students describe the mandala and speculate on why Jung chose it to represent the collective nature of human experience.

For Further Research

To illustrate the influence of Jung's theories on popular culture, have students do a search of literature in bookstores, *Books in Print,* and reviews of articles in magazines and newspapers. Have them look up relevant terms such as *Jung, collective unconscious, dream analysis,* and *archetype.* Also have them see if they can find actual books on dream interpretation or books on mythic archetypes, such as the popular *Women Who Run with the Wolves: Myths and Stories of the Wild Woman Archetype* by Jungian analyst Clarissa Pinkola Estés.

Taking a Stand

Jung, Adler, and Horney all had more optimistic views of human nature than did Freud. While Freud tended to see individuals as condemned to act out the results of early childhood experiences with little understanding, many of his followers saw human beings as more self-aware and in control of their lives. Ask students where they stand on this fundamental question: Are humans mostly driven by unconscious forces or are they "creative selves" capable of healing and growing?

The deity is an example of an archetype. Although most cultures believe in deities, specific forms vary. Shown here are sculptures of the Aztec god Quetzalcoatl (left) and the Hindu god Rama (right).

TRUTH OR fiction
■ R E V I S I T E D ■

It is true that according to Jung, people can remember things that never happened to them personally. Jung believed that in addition to individual memory, all human beings share a collective unconscious in which we carry a store of some primitive concepts. He called these concepts archetypes.

Jung believed that every person's conscious sense of self can be characterized by four functions of the mind—thinking, feeling, intuition, and sensation. He argued that all four of these elements exist in every individual's unconscious. However, an individual can be identified by the function that becomes his or her primary form of expression. He thought that people could form healthy personalities by bringing together, or integrating, these conscious elements with the collective unconscious archetypes. His name for this integrating process is *individuation.*

Many psychologists consider Jung's theory of the collective unconscious to be mystical and unscientific. But Jungian theory has developed a tremendous following among the general public. Many people enter Jungian analysis to examine their dreams and to work toward individuation. Scholars explore the use of archetypical symbols as they appear in literature and the arts. In addition, Jung's focus on myth has made his theory very popular with those interested in the study of religion.

Alfred Adler

Alfred Adler (1870–1937) was another follower of Freudian psychoanalysis. Adler believed that people are basically motivated by a need to overcome feelings of inferiority. To describe these feelings of inadequacy and insecurity, Adler coined the term **inferiority complex**.

In some people, Adler theorized, feelings of inferiority may be based on physical problems and the need to compensate for them (Adler, 1927). This theory may have developed in part from Adler's own attempts to overcome repeated bouts of illness. As a child, Adler was crippled by a disease called rickets and suffered from pneumonia.

Physical problems are not the only source of feelings of inferiority, according to Adler. He believed that all of us have some feelings of inferiority

have not only a personal unconscious that stores material that has been forgotten or repressed but also an inherited collective unconscious. According to Jung, the **collective unconscious** is a store of human concepts shared by all people across all cultures (Jung, 1917, 1936).

The structural components of the collective unconscious are basic, primitive concepts, called archetypes. **Archetypes** are ideas and images of the accumulated experience of all human beings. Examples of archetypes include the supreme being, the young hero, the fertile and nurturing mother, the wise old man, the hostile brother, and even fairy godmothers, wicked witches, and themes of rebirth or resurrection. Jung found that each of these concepts appears in some form across most cultures and religions (Jung, 1936).

Jung argued that although these images remain unconscious, they often appear to us as figures in our dreams. He declared that these images influence our thoughts and feelings and that they help form a foundation on which personality develops. Despite his interest in the collective unconscious, Jung granted more importance to conscious thoughts than Freud did. Jung believed that one archetype is the sense of self. According to Jung, the self is a unifying force of personality that gives people direction and provides a sense of completeness.

Role-Playing

Select two groups of volunteers to participate in a Meeting of the Minds panel discussion. Tell one group to imagine that they are psychoanalysts trained by Freud. Tell the other group to imagine that they are psychoanalysts trained by Erikson. Have the two groups explain their views on psychological development to the class. Then have the groups debate which theory of psychological development—Freud's or Erikson's—better explains personality. Ask the class to evaluate the contributions made by both theories to our understanding of personality.

Comparing and Contrasting Points of View

Have students construct a matrix that compares and contrasts the various psychoanalytic theories in terms of the following issues: past and present, determinism versus free will, nature versus nurture, and the role of childhood.

Reviewing Section 2

Have students complete the Section Review questions on page 332.

because of our small size as children. He thought that these feelings give rise to a drive for superiority. Adler also introduced the term *sibling rivalry* to describe the jealousies that are often found among brothers and sisters.

Adler, like Jung, believed that self-awareness plays a major role in the formation of personality. Adler spoke of a creative self. The creative self is self-aware and strives to overcome obstacles and develop the individual's unique potential. President Theodore Roosevelt exemplified this personality. Roosevelt was a frail child who became not only president but also a strong and robust man. Similarly, football quarterback Boomer Esiason, who suffered from juvenile arthritis, overcame his disease to become a professional athlete.

Karen Horney

Karen Horney (HAWR-ny), who lived from 1885 to 1952, agreed with Freud that childhood experiences play a major role in the development of adult personality. She believed that the greatest influences on personality are social relationships.

Horney, like Freud, saw parent-child relationships to be of paramount importance (Horney, 1937). Small children are completely dependent. When their parents treat them with indifference or harshness, children develop feelings of insecurity that Horney termed *basic anxiety*. Because children also resent neglectful parents, Horney theorized that feelings of hostility would accompany the anxiety. Horney agreed with Freud that children would repress rather than express feelings of hostility because they would fear driving their parents away. In contrast to Freud, however, she also believed that genuine and consistent love could temper the effects of even the most painful childhoods.

Erik Erikson

Like Horney, Erik Erikson (1902–1994) believed that social relationships are the most important factors in personality development (Erikson, 1950). He placed great emphasis on the general emotional climate of the mother-infant relationship. Erikson also granted more powers to the ego than Freud had allowed. According to Freud's theory, people may think that they are making choices, but they may only be rationalizing the compromises forced upon them by inner conflict. According to Erikson's theory, however, people are entirely capable of making real and meaningful choices.

Erikson, like Freud, devised a developmental theory of personality. Erikson, however, expanded on Freud's five stages of development and formulated a psychosocial theory of development consisting of eight stages. Whereas Freud's developmental theory ends with adolescence, Erikson's includes the changing concerns of adulthood.

Erikson named his stages after the traits people might develop during each of them. (See Figure 14.3 on page 332.) For example, the first stage of psychosocial development is named the stage of trust versus mistrust. A warm, loving relationship with the mother (and others) during infancy may lead to a sense of basic trust in people and in the world. Janet, for example, had always maintained a very close relationship with her mother. Erikson's theories would indicate that Janet's trusting personality may have been a result of that warm relationship.

A cold, unfulfilling relationship may generate a broad sense of mistrust, which could damage the formation of relationships for a lifetime unless it is resolved successfully. Erikson believed that most people maintain a blend of trust and mistrust.

Evaluation of the Psychoanalytic Approach

Although psychoanalytic concepts such as libido and id strike many psychologists as unscientific today, Freud was an important champion of the idea that human personality and behavior are subject to scientific analysis. In Freud's day, serious psychological problems were still commonly seen as signs of weakness or so-called craziness. Freud's thinking contributed greatly to the development of compassion for people with psychological disorders.

Psychoanalytic theory also focused the attention of scientists and therapists on the far-reaching effects of childhood events. Freud and Erikson suggested that early childhood traumas can affect us for a lifetime. Psychoanalytic theorists have heightened society's awareness of the emotional needs of children.

Freud also helped us recognize that sexual and aggressive urges are common. He pointed out that there is a difference between recognizing these urges and acting on them. He realized that our thinking may be distorted by our efforts to avoid anxiety and guilt. And he devised an influential method of psychotherapy, which is described in Chapter 19.

Journal Activity

Tell students to think about their early childhoods. Have them write in their journals about times when they felt insecure or experienced what Horney called basic anxiety. What was the source of the anxiety? Also have them consider Horney's contention that genuine and consistent love can temper the effects of even the most painful childhoods. Do students agree or disagree? Why?

Section Objective

► Describe what learning theorists believe are the influences on and motivations for behavior.

This objective is assessed in the Section Review on page 334 and in the Chapter 14 Review.

Opening Section 3

Motivator

Have students recall and discuss what they learned in Chapter 1 about the learning perspective. Tell them to use this prior knowledge to write a brief paragraph predicting what learning theorists might say about human personality development. Have volunteers read their paragraphs aloud for class discussion. After students have read Section 3, have them review their paragraphs and revise them as needed.

Section 2 Review: Answers

1. The id represents basic drives such as hunger and demands instant gratification; the ego represents reason and seeks to satisfy the id's demands in a rational way; the superego represents the moral sense.

2. Freud has had a number of intellectual heirs, and his ideas have strongly influenced psychology. He was an important champion of the idea that human personality and behavior should be subject to scientific analysis.

3. Unlike Freud, Horney believed that the effects of a painful childhood could be overcome through love; Jung believed in the collective as well as the personal unconscious and granted more importance to conscious thoughts than did Freud.

4. Later practitioners of psychoanalysis placed less emphasis on unconscious motives and more emphasis on social relationships.

Erik Erikson's Stages of Psychosocial Development

Infancy (0–1)	Early childhood (2–3)	Preschool years (4–5)	Grammar school years (6–12)
Trust versus mistrust	Autonomy versus shame and doubt	Initiative versus guilt	Industry versus inferiority
Coming to trust the mother and the environment—to associate surroundings with feelings of inner goodness	Developing the wish to make choices and the self-control to exercise choice	Adding planning and "attacking" to choice; becoming active and on the move	Becoming eagerly absorbed in skills, tasks, and productivity; mastering the fundamentals of technology

FIGURE 14.3 *Erik Erikson believed that social relationships are the most important factors in personality development. Shown here are the eight stages of Erikson's theory of psychosocial development.*

Psychoanalytic theories—particularly the views of Freud—have, however, been criticized on many counts. Even followers of Freud argued that he placed too much emphasis on unconscious motives and neglected the importance of social relationships. Opponents of Freud's theories also assert that people consciously seek self-enhancement and intellectual pleasures and do not merely try to gratify the dark demands of the id.

Critics have also questioned Freud's method of gathering evidence from clinical sessions (Hergenhahn, 2000). Using this method, therapists may subtly influence clients to say what the therapists expect to hear. Also, Freud and many other psychoanalytic theorists gathered their evidence only from case studies of white, middle-class individuals who had sought help for their psychological problems. These individuals may not have provided the most representative sample of the general population. (See Chapter 2.)

SECTION 2 REVIEW

go.hrw.com Homework Practice Online
Keyword: SY3 HP14

1. Define the terms *id*, *ego*, and *superego*.
2. Trace the impact of Freud's theory.
3. How do the psychoanalytic theories of Jung and Horney disagree with the theories presented by Freud?
4. **Critical Thinking** *Summarizing* In what ways has the psychoanalytic theory of personality been modified since Freud?

SECTION 3

The Learning Approach

A DAY IN THE LIFE

Some personality theorists might assume that Todd's sense of humor was largely a learned behavior. They might explain that Todd made jokes because he had learned that he would somehow be rewarded or positively reinforced for such behavior. Janet's laughter and obvious amusement would be examples of such positive reinforcement. Other theorists might suggest that Todd had learned to be comical by observing the behavior of other humorous people.

The two psychological approaches that might offer such explanations are, respectively, behaviorism and social-learning theory. Both are branches of a broader school of psychological thought called the learning approach.

Behaviorism

John B. Watson claimed that external forces or influences—not internal influences such as traits or inner conflict—largely shape people's preferences and behavior (Watson, 1924). In the 1930s, Watson's approach was taken up by B. F. Skinner. Skinner agreed that we should pay attention to how organisms behave and avoid trying to see within people's minds. Skinner also emphasized the effects of reinforcement on behavior (Skinner, 1938). (See Chapter 6.)

Teaching Section 3

Demonstration

Without first explaining that your actions are part of the lesson, ask a student to do some sort of minor task for you (perhaps to open a window or bring you something). Do this at a time when the class is paying close attention to you. When the student complies, be very appreciative. (If the student does not comply immediately, show strong disapproval.) Then ask students how your actions and the customs of the school combined to make the student do what you wanted him or her to do. Have students relate the exercise to social-learning theory.

Closing Section 3

Summarizing Information

Assign students further research into the careers and theories of Watson, Skinner, and Bandura. Have students summarize their findings in brief oral reports. Also have students prepare written handouts containing an outline of their research findings.

Reviewing Section 3

Have students complete the Section Review questions on page 334.

Have students complete the Section Review questions on page 334.

Adolescence (13–18)	Young adulthood (19–30)	Middle adulthood	Late adulthood
Identity versus role diffusion	Intimacy versus isolation	Generativity versus stagnation	Integrity versus despair
Connecting skills and social roles to formation of career objectives	Committing the self to another; engaging in sexual love	Needing to be needed; guiding and encouraging the younger generation; being creative	Accepting the timing and placing of one's own life cycle; achieving wisdom and dignity

Most of us assume that our wants originate within us. But Watson and Skinner largely discarded ideas of personal freedom, choice, and self-direction. Skinner suggested that environmental influences, such as parental approval and social custom, condition or shape us into wanting some things and not wanting others. **Socialization** is the process by which people learn the socially desirable behaviors of their particular culture and adopt them as part of their personalities.

In his 1948 novel, *Walden Two*, Skinner described a utopian (or ideal) society in which people are happy and content because every member of the society contributes to, and receives the benefits of, the society. They have been socialized from early childhood to help other people and society at large. Because of childhood socialization, people in the fictional community want to be decent, kind, and unselfish. They see their actions as a result of their own free will. According to Skinner, however, no one is really free. We may think of ourselves as being free because we can go after what we want and get it. But in Skinner's view, we are shaped into wanting what is good for society at an early age.

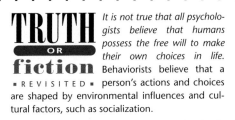

TRUTH or fiction ▪ REVISITED ▪

It is not true that all psychologists believe that humans possess the free will to make their own choices in life. Behaviorists believe that a person's actions and choices are shaped by environmental influences and cultural factors, such as socialization.

Social-Learning Theory

Social-learning theory is a contemporary view of learning that is advocated by Albert Bandura and other psychologists. Social-learning theorists focus on the importance of learning by observation and on the role of the cognitive processes that produce individual differences (Bandura, 1986).

Unlike behaviorists, who believe that people are at the mercy of their environment, social-learning theorists argue that people can act intentionally to influence the environment. To behaviorists, learning is the mechanical result of reinforcement. To social-learning theorists, on the other hand, people engage in purposeful learning. Individuals seek to learn about their environment and have a certain degree of control over reinforcement. Observational learning extends to reading about others or watching them in media such as television and film.

According to social-learning theorists, behavior is not based solely on what is learned from observation. Internal variables also influence how we act in certain situations. These internal factors include the following:

- *Skills:* Skills include a person's physical and social abilities.
- *Values:* The value we put on the outcome of a certain behavior affects how we act. For example, if you value good grades, you will study.
- *Goals:* We regulate ourselves by setting goals. Once the goal is set, we plan the most effective way to achieve it.
- *Expectations:* Expectations are predictions of what will happen in certain situations.

Class Discussion

Have students evaluate Skinner's belief that environmental influences condition or shape behavior. Ask students to supply examples of the kinds of positive reinforcers that people receive at different points in their lives. (For example, young children might receive hugs; older children might receive treats or money for especially good behavior; adults receive promotions and social standing for behaving in certain ways.)

For Your Information

B. F. Skinner believed that both positive and negative reinforcement influence human (and animal) behavior. Positive reinforcement, such as food, would increase the likelihood of a certain behavior, while negative reinforcement would decrease the likelihood of a behavior. Skinner learned, however, that punishment can have a paradoxical effect. Sometimes a person will eliminate an undesirable behavior as long as the punisher is present or nearby and then increase the behavior when the punisher disappears—as if to make up for lost time!

► Explain how the humanistic approach views the role of the self and free choice in shaping behavior.

This objective is assessed in the Section Review on page 337 and in the Chapter 14 Review.

Opening Section 4

Motivator

Look through some art books and find two portraits of individuals set against interesting backgrounds (a building's interior, a beautiful landscape, a factory). Select one portrait in which the person dominates the painting, in both size and placement. Select another in which the person's surroundings seem equally, or maybe even more, important. Have students discuss what the two portraits suggest about different views of the relationship between person and environment. Tell students that in Section 4 they will learn how humanists view this relationship.

Many behavior theorists believe that environmental factors, such as parental approval, condition us to exhibit certain behaviors and not others.

- *Self-efficacy expectations:* This term, coined by Bandura (1989), refers to beliefs people have about themselves. For example, if you believe that you are a good public speaker, you will be motivated to speak before the class assembly. People with high self-efficacy expectations are also more likely to persist at difficult tasks.

Evaluation of the Learning Approach

What are the strengths and weaknesses of learning theories? Learning theorists have made key contributions to the understanding of behavior, but their theories have left some psychologists dissatisfied. Psychoanalytic theorists and trait theorists focus on internal variables such as unconscious conflict and traits to explain behavior. Learning theorists emphasize the influence of environmental conditions on behavior. They have shown that people learn to do things because of reinforcements.

Behaviorism is limited in its ability to explain personality. Behaviorism does not describe, explain, or even suggest the richness of inner human experience. Behaviorism does not deal with thoughts, feelings, and people's complex inner maps of the world. Social-learning theory does deal with these issues. But critics of social-learning theory argue that it has not come up with satisfying explanations for the development of traits or accounted for self-awareness. Also, social-learning theory—like behaviorism—may not pay enough attention to the role genetic variation plays in determining individual differences in behavior.

SECTION 3 REVIEW

Homework Practice Online
Keyword: SY3 HP14

1. According to behaviorism, what is the main influence on how people act?

2. Many students strive to get good grades. How would social-learning theorists explain this behavior? How would behaviorists explain it?

3. **Critical Thinking** *Supporting a Point of View* Do you agree with the behaviorist view that true personal freedom does not exist? Why or why not?

SECTION 4

The Humanistic Approach

Behaviorists argue that psychologists should not attempt to study self-awareness. Humanists, on the other hand, begin with the assumption that self-awareness is the very core of humanity. They focus on people's pursuits of self-fulfillment and ethical conduct. To humanistic psychologists, people are truly free to do as they choose with their lives. Moreover, because people are free to choose, they are responsible for the choices that they make.

Abraham Maslow

Humanistic psychologist Abraham Maslow (1908–1970) believed that humans are separated from lower animals because they recognize their desire to achieve self-actualization—to reach their full potential. (See Chapter 13.) He also believed that because people are unique, they must follow their own paths to self-actualization. However, accomplishing this requires taking risks. Maslow argued that people who stick to what is tried and true may find their lives boring and predictable. Although Hannah was very close to her

A DAY IN THE LIFE

friends, she realized that she possessed a unique musical ability. According to Maslow's theory, Hannah's willingness to pursue her talent and her courage to go away to college were factors in her search for self-actualization.

Teaching Section 4

Guided Practice

Work with students to create several scenarios that demonstrate Carl Rogers's theory about self-concept and congruence. Help students get started by describing a fictional person who has a certain self-concept. For example, "Anne sees herself as strong and outspoken." Then have students suggest two separate experiences for Anne: one that is consistent with her self-concept and one that is inconsistent. According to Rogers, how would these two separate experiences affect Anne?

Independent Practice

Tell students to assume the role of one of the fictional people developed in the Guided Practice activity. Then have each student write two letters to a friend or relative. One letter should describe a recent experience that was consistent with the person's self-concept. The other letter should describe a recent experience that was inconsistent with the person's self-concept. Both letters should describe how the experience made the person feel. Have volunteers read their letters aloud. Then have students evaluate Rogers's theory of self-concept and congruence in relation to these letters.

Carl Rogers

Carl Rogers (1902–1987), another advocate of the humanistic approach, believed that people are to some degree the conscious architects of their own personalities. In Rogers's view, people shape their personalities through free choice and action (Rogers, 1961, 1977). Because Rogers's theory revolves around people's sense of self, it is termed *self theory*.

Rogers placed great emphasis on the human ability to derive a **self-concept**, a view of oneself as an individual. He also believed that the self is concerned with recognizing personal values and establishing a sense of one's relationships to other people. The self is the center of each person's experience, an ongoing sense of who and what one is. It provides the experience of being human in the world and it is the guiding principle behind both personality and behavior.

The Self-Concept and Congruence Our self-concepts are made up of our impressions of ourselves and our evaluations of our adequacy. Rogers believed that the key to happiness and healthy adjustment is **congruence**, or consistency between one's self-concept and one's experience. For example, if you consider yourself to be outgoing and friendly, this self-concept will be reinforced if you have good relationships with other people. This will probably lead to feelings of happiness and a sense that your self-concept is accurate. If, however, you have difficulty getting along with others, the inconsistency between your self-concept and your experience will probably cause you to feel anxious or troubled.

Self-Esteem and Positive Regard Rogers assumed that we all develop a need for self-esteem. Self-esteem is belief in oneself, or self-respect. At first, self-esteem reflects the esteem in which others hold us. As discussed in Chapter 10, parents help children develop self-esteem when they show them unconditional positive regard. Parents show unconditional positive regard when they accept children as they are, regardless of the children's behavior at the moment.

Parents show children conditional positive regard if they accept children only when they behave in a desired manner. Conditional positive regard may lead children to think that they are worthwhile only if they behave in certain ways.

Humanistic psychologists believe that each of us has a unique potential. Therefore, children who think that they are worthwhile only if they behave in certain ways will end up being disappointed in themselves. Humanistic psychologists believe that we cannot fully live up to the wishes of others and also remain true to ourselves.

The expression of the self does not always have to lead to conflict. Rogers was optimistic about human nature. He believed that we hurt others or act in antisocial ways only when we are frustrated in our efforts to develop our potential. When parents and others are loving and tolerant of the ways in which we are different, we, too, are loving.

However, Rogers believed that children in some families learn that it is bad to have ideas of their own, especially about political, religious, or sexual matters. When they perceive their parents' disapproval, they may come to see themselves as rebels and label their feelings as selfish, wrong, or evil. If they wish to retain a consistent self-concept and self-esteem, they may have to deny many of their genuine feelings. They may, in a sense, have to disown parts of themselves.

According to Rogers's theory, the path to self-actualization requires getting in touch with our

Carl Rogers argued that people shape their personalities through free choice and action. He believed that it is important for individuals to recognize their personal values and to establish a sense of their relationships with other people.

For Your Information

There is a strong similarity between Rogers's theories and those of Carl Jung. Both psychologists believed in a partnership with their clients. In addition, both saw therapy as a journey toward wholeness and a deeper understanding of the self. Both theorists were more optimistic about human nature than was Freud.

internet connect

TOPIC: Theoretical Profile: Personality
GO TO: go.hrw.com
KEYWORD: SY3 PS14

Have students access the Internet through the HRW Go site to research the theories and viewpoints of important personality theorists. Then ask students to create a theoretical profile of one of the psychologists presented in the chapter. Students should trace the impact of associationism, psychodynamic (Freudian) thinking, behaviorism, and humanism on current thinking in psychology. Students should also use standard grammar, spelling, punctuation, and sentence structure in their profiles.

335

After students have read the feature, ask them to consider which theorist, Watson or Rogers, better explains human development. Then select two groups of volunteers to debate the views of Watson and Rogers. Allow the members of each group time to meet and organize their arguments. After the debate, have the class evaluate the contributions of each theorist to our understanding of human development. Also ask students whether the debate influenced them to change their views on which theorist is better able to explain development.

Interpreting Ideas

Rogers used the image of a plant surviving crashing waves to express his view of human nature. Have students choose one of the other theorists discussed in this chapter and create their own vivid metaphor (based on nature, sports, or anything else they choose) to express that theorist's view of human personality. Have volunteers read their work aloud to the class and have the class try to determine which theorists were chosen.

Primary Source Note

Description of Change: excerpted, bracketed

Rationale: excerpted to focus on main idea; bracketed to clarify meaning

Cross-Curricular Link: Art

Tell half of the students to imagine that they have been raised according to behaviorist principles. Tell the other half to imagine that they have been raised according to humanist principles. Then have students create a piece of art that depicts what their upbringing has been like. Art may take the form of a poem, song, dance, painting, sketch, or short story. Have volunteers from each group display or perform their art for the class. Have the class discuss how the focus of the art from the two groups differs.

Think About It: Answers

1. Students who believe that a person can be trained to become what is desired of him or her should support their views using the behaviorist approach. Students who do not believe this should support their views using the humanist approach.

2. Students should use sound reasoning and examples to support their point of view.

WATSON AND ROGERS:
At Opposite Ends of the Theory Spectrum

The theories of behaviorist John B. Watson and humanist Carl Rogers are at opposite ends of the theoretical spectrum. Consider Watson's challenge to the field of psychology in his influential 1924 book, *Behaviorism*:

> Give me a dozen healthy infants, well-formed, and my own specified world to bring them up in and I'll guarantee to take any one at random and train him to become any type of specialist I might suggest—doctor, lawyer, merchant-chief and, yes, even beggar-man and thief, regardless of his talents, penchants, tendencies, abilities, vocations, and the race of his ancestors. (1924, p. 82)

With these words, Watson stated the classic behaviorist belief: Regardless of who we think we really are inside, we can be totally molded, or conditioned, by external stimuli. Our belief in individual choice is just an illusion.

Carl Rogers had a very different view of the freedom and dignity of the individual human being. He summarized this view in a 1974 article:

> My experience in therapy and in groups makes it impossible for me to deny the reality and significance of human choice. To me it is not an illusion that man is to some degree the architect of himself. (1974, p. 119)

About 10 years before writing this article, Rogers described an experience that helped confirm his conviction that life is more than a reaction to environmental forces:

> During a vacation weekend some months ago I was standing on a headland [piece of ground jutting out over water] overlooking one of the rugged coves which dot the coastline of northern California. Several large rock outcroppings were at the mouth of the cove, and these received the full force of the great Pacific combers [waves] which, beating upon them, broke into mountains of spray before surging into the cliff-lined shore. As I watched the waves breaking over these large rocks in the distance, I noticed with surprise what appeared to be a tiny palm tree on the rocks, no more than two or three feet high, taking the pounding of the breakers. Through my binoculars I saw that these were some type of seaweed, with a slender "trunk" topped off with a head of leaves. . . . In the interval between the waves it seemed clear that this fragile, erect, top-heavy plant would be utterly crushed and broken by the next breaker. When the wave crunched down upon it, the trunk bent almost flat, the leaves were whipped into a straight line by the torrent of the water, yet the moment the wave had passed, here was the plant again, erect, tough, resilient. It seemed incredible that it was able to take this incessant [never-ending] pounding hour after hour, day after night, week after week, for all I know, year after year, and all the time nourishing itself, extending itself, reproducing itself; in short, maintaining and enhancing itself in this process which, in our shorthand, we call growth. Here in this palmlike seaweed was the tenacity of life, the forward thrust of life, the ability to push into an incredibly hostile environment and not only hold its own, but to adapt, develop, become itself. (1963, pp. 1–2)

Rogers used this vivid metaphor to express the humanistic belief that living things, including people, struggle on, attempting in the toughest of conditions to actualize themselves.

Think About It

1. **Supporting a Point of View** Do you believe that anyone, regardless of ability, can be trained to become, say, a doctor, lawyer, or musician? Why or why not?

2. **Evaluating** Do you believe, like Rogers, that each individual takes charge of his or her environment? Explain your answer.

Organizing Information

Have each student create a two-column chart titled "Humanistic Approach." Have them label one column *Strengths* and the other column *Weaknesses*. After students have filled in their charts, have them write a paragraph assessing the ability of the humanistic approach to explain personality.

Reviewing Section 4

Have students complete the Section Review questions on page 337.

Extension

Have students conduct library research to find books and magazine articles on child rearing. Tell students to skim these materials and look for tips on how to help young children realize their full potential. Have students list as many of these tips as they can find. In class, have students read their lists aloud. Which of the tips listed reflect the humanistic approach to personality? Have students determine how well accepted the humanistic approach is in popular culture.

genuine feelings and acting on them. This is the goal of person-centered therapy, Rogers's method of psychotherapy. (See Chapter 19.)

Evaluation of the Humanistic Approach

For most animals, to be alive is to move, to eat, to breathe, and to reproduce. However, humanistic psychologists feel that humans are not merely animals. They believe that for human beings, an essential aspect of life is conscious experience—the sense of one's self as progressing through space and time. Humanists grant consciousness a key role in our daily lives. This focus on conscious experience is one reason that humanistic theories have tremendous popular appeal.

Another reason for their popularity is that they stress human freedom. Psychoanalytic theories see us largely as products of our childhoods. Learning theories, to some degree, see us as products of circumstances. Both theories argue that our sense of freedom is merely an illusion. Humanistic theorists, however, say that our freedom is real.

The primary strength of the humanistic theories—their focus on conscious experience—is also their main weakness. Conscious experience is private and subjective. Therefore, some psychologists question the soundness of framing theories in terms of consciousness (Liebert & Spiegler, 1982). Others, however, believe that the science of psychology can afford to relax its methods somewhat if loosening them will help it address the richness of human experience (Bevan & Kessel, 1994).

Critics also note that humanistic theories, like learning theories, have little to say about the development of traits and personality types. Humanistic theorists assume that we are all unique, but they do not predict the sorts of traits, abilities, and interests we will develop.

SECTION 4 REVIEW

go.hrw.com **Homework Practice Online** Keyword: SY3 HP14

1. Summarize Rogers's concept of congruence.

2. Trace the impact of humanism on current thinking in psychology.

3. **Critical Thinking** *Finding the Main Idea* According to the humanistic approach, what is the role of self and free choice in shaping human behavior?

SECTION 5

The Sociocultural Approach

The sociocultural perspective focuses on the roles of ethnicity, gender, and culture in the formation of personality. Hannah was raised by parents who had grown up in South Korea. She was also comfortable in an American school with her American friends. Sociocultural theorists would argue that her family and her environmental influences were key factors in the development of Hannah's personality.

Individualism Versus Collectivism

One aspect of culture that sociocultural theorists focus on is the level of individualism or collectivism in a society. Individualism is a trait valued by many people in the United States and in many European nations. Individualists tend to define themselves in terms of their personal identities. They usually give priority to their personal goals. When asked to complete the statement "I am . . . ," they are likely to respond in terms of their own personality traits or occupations. For example, they are likely to say, "I am outgoing" or "I am a nurse" (Triandis, 1990).

Collectivists, such as those pictured here, tend to define themselves in terms of the groups to which they belong. They often give priority to the goals of the group over their own individual needs.

Section 4 Review: Answers

1. Congruence is the concept of a match between one's self-image and one's experience. According to Rogers, a healthy and relaxed self-image results from a high degree of congruence.

2. Humanistic theories have had tremendous popular appeal, but these theories suffer from their inability to objectively study conscious experience. Some psychologists therefore question the soundness of framing theories in terms of consciousness.

3. Humanists believe that people have the freedom (to some degree) to create their own personalities.

Technology Resources

CNN. Presents Psychology: Type D Personality

5
Section Objective

▶ Discuss how the sociocultural approach views the importance of ethnicity, gender, culture, and socioeconomic status in the development of personality.

This objective is assessed in the Section Review on page 339 and in the Chapter 14 Review.

Opening Section 5

Motivator

Have students provide examples of television programs that depict a mix of characters of different ethnicities, genders, cultures, or socioeconomic backgrounds. List these programs on the chalkboard. For each program listed, have students explain how these sociocultural factors affect the personalities, self-concepts, and behavior of the various characters portrayed in the program. Ask students if they think the portrayals reflect reality. Then tell students they will learn about the sociocultural approach to personality in Section 5.

Journal Activity

Have students complete the statement "I am . . ." Challenge them to complete it with 10 to 20 different endings. Then have students classify each completed statement as either collectivist or individualist. Which type of statement appears more frequently?

Teaching Transparencies with Teacher's Notes

TRANSPARENCY 30:
The Self in Relation to Others from the Individualist and Collectivist Perspectives

internet connect

TOPIC: Invite a Theorist to Dinner
GO TO: go.hrw.com
KEYWORD: SY3 PS14

Have students access the Internet through the HRW Go site to research theories of personality presented in the textbook. Then ask them to imagine they have invited representatives of each approach to dinner and to write a sketch or perform a skit illustrating conversations that might take place. Students' dialogues can be humorous or serious, but it must include references to students' research for full credit.

338

The Self in Relation to Others from the Individualist and Collectivist Perspectives

FIGURE 14.4 *An individualist sees the self as separate from other people. A collectivist, on the other hand, sees the self as complete only in terms of his or her relationships to other people.*

Based on Markus & Kitayama, 1991.

In contrast, many people from Africa, Asia, and Central and South America tend to be more collectivistic. (See Figure 14.4.) Collectivists tend to define themselves in terms of the groups to which they belong and often give priority to the goals of their group. They feel complete only in terms of their social relationships with others (Markus & Kitayama, 1991). When asked to complete the statement "I am . . . ," they are likely to respond in terms of their families, religion, or nation. For example, they are likely to say, "I am a father," "I am a Buddhist," or "I am Japanese" (Draguns, 1988; Triandis, 1994).

The Western capitalist system fosters individualism. It assumes that individuals are entitled to amass personal fortunes if they have the drive and ability to do so. The individualist perspective is found in the self-reliant heroes in Western entertainment—from Clint Eastwood's gritty cowboys to the character Belle in the Disney film *Beauty and the Beast*. The traditional writings of many non-Western cultures, on the other hand, have praised people who put the well-being of the group ahead of their personal ambitions.

There are, of course, conflicting ideals—as well as individual differences—within cultures. In the United States, for example, children are taught to share with other children as well as to be "Number One." But on the whole, the contrast between the individualist Western world and the more collectivist nations of other parts of the world is a generally reliable measure of some personality differences between individuals from these regions.

Sociocultural Factors and the Self

According to sociocultural theorists, social and cultural factors also affect the self-concept and self-esteem of the individual. Carl Rogers noted that our self-concepts tend to reflect how we believe other people see us. Members of ethnic groups who have been subjected to discrimination and poverty may have poorer self-concepts and lower self-esteem than people who have not experienced discrimination and poverty (Greene, 1993; Lewis-Fernández & Kleinman, 1994). Similarly, members of ethnic groups that have traditionally held power in society are likely to have a positive sense of self because they share in the expectations of personal achievement and respect that are typically given to members of such groups.

In some cases, however, things are not so simple. Many women in the United States, particularly white women, are unhappy with their appearance. This is in part because the current media ideal is

Closing Section 5

Applying Ideas

Have students devise questionnaires that explore the connection between sociocultural factors and the sense of self. After reviewing the questionnaires, have students administer them to a small group of volunteers and then analyze the results.

Reviewing Section 5

Have students complete the Section Review questions on page 339.

Extension

Have students interview a friend, parent, grandparent, or other adult who has immigrated to the United States about what it was like to move to the United States from another country. What cultural differences did the person encounter? What was the most difficult part of the acculturation process? What was the easiest part of the acculturation process? What customs of the person's country of origin does the person retain? Have students present their findings to the class in the form of an oral report.

---

found in female models who are on average 9 percent taller and 16 percent slimmer than the average woman in the United States (Williams, 1992). But a survey by the American Association of University Women (1992) found that African American girls are likely to be happier with their appearances than white girls are. Sixty-five percent of African American elementary-school girls said they were happy with the way they were, as compared with 55 percent of white girls. Among high school students, 58 percent of African American girls remained happy with the way they were, as compared with only 22 percent of white girls.

How do sociocultural theorists explain this difference? It appears that African American girls are taught that there is nothing wrong with them if they do not match the ideals of the majority culture. They come to believe that if the world treats them negatively, it is because of prejudice, not because of who they really are or what they do (Williams, 1992). White girls, on the other hand, may be more likely to look inward and blame themselves for not attaining the unreachable ideal.

Acculturation and Self-Esteem

Personalities are influenced by more than personal traits and learning experiences. They are also influenced by cultural settings. Hannah belonged to a traditional Korean family. At school, however, she was exposed daily to values that are in some ways unique to the United States.

Acculturation is the process of adapting to a new or different culture. People who immigrate to the United States undergo acculturation. If they come from Africa, Asia, or Latin America, they are likely to find that differences in language are only the tip of the iceberg of cultural differences.

Acculturation takes various patterns. Some immigrants become completely assimilated, or absorbed, into the culture of the area to which they move. They may stop using both the language and customs of their country of origin. Others choose to maintain separation. They retain the language and customs of their country of origin and never become completely comfortable with those of their adopted country. Still others become bicultural. That is, they successfully integrate both sets of customs and values.

Research suggests that people who are bicultural have the highest self-esteem (Phinney et al., 1992). For example, Mexican Americans who are fluent in

English are more likely to be emotionally stable than Mexican Americans who do not speak English as well (Salgado de Snyder et al., 1990). Adopting the ways of the new society without giving up a supportive cultural tradition and a sense of ethnic identity apparently helps people function most effectively. According to the sociocultural approach, Hannah's musical and educational success and her high self-esteem may have been results of her ability to balance her Korean heritage with her cultural surroundings in the United States.

It is true that psychologists feel that culture, gender, and ethnicity are important in personality development. Sociocultural theorists believe that all of these factors contribute in some way to the development of personality.

Evaluation of the Sociocultural Approach

The sociocultural perspective provides valuable insights into the roles of ethnicity, gender, culture, and socioeconomic status in personality formation. Sociocultural factors are external forces that are internalized and affect all of us. They run through us deeply, touching many aspects of our personalities. Without reference to sociocultural factors, we may be able to understand generalities about behavior and mental processes. We cannot, however, understand how individuals think, behave, and feel about themselves within a given cultural setting. The sociocultural perspective also enhances our sensitivity to cultural differences and allows us to appreciate much of the richness of human behavior.

SECTION 5 REVIEW

Homework Practice Online
Keyword: SY3 HP14

1. Explain the difference between individualism and collectivist perspectives on personality.

2. What is acculturation and how can it affect self-esteem?

3. **Critical Thinking** *Analyzing Information* According to the sociocultural approach, what role do ethnicity, gender, culture, and socioeconomic status play in the development of personality?

Technology
▶ Chapter 14 Test Generator (on the One-Stop Planner)
▶ HRW Go site

Reinforcement, Review, and Assessment
▶ Chapter 14 Review, pp. 340–341
▶ Chapter Review and Activities with Answer Key
▶ Alternative Assessment Handbook
▶ Portfolio Assessment Handbook
▶ Chapter 14 Test (Form A or B)

Linking to Community Invite a clinical, educational, school, or other type of psychologist from the community to visit the classroom and discuss the theory of personality he or she finds most persuasive. Ask the psychologist to discuss the following:

6. removes anxiety-causing ideas from conscious awareness by pushing them into the unconscious

7. returning to an early stage of development

8. believed that social relationships are the most important factors in personality development

9. consistency between one's self-concept and one's experience

10. the process of adapting to a new or different culture

Understanding Main Ideas

1. Traits may include careful, passive, rigid, moody, and impulsive.

2. Erikson's stages of psychosocial development include trust versus mistrust, autonomy versus shame and doubt, initiative versus guilt, industry versus inferiority, identity versus role diffusion, intimacy versus isolation, generativity versus stagnation, and integrity versus despair.

3. Behaviorism has had a strong influence on current thinking in psychology, but its influence has been somewhat limited because it does not acknowledge inner human experience

4. According to Rogers, a healthy and relaxed self-image results from a high degree of congruence.

5. Individualists define themselves in terms of achievement or personality; collectivists define themselves in terms of their families, religions, or nations.

Thinking Critically

1. Students should describe a situation in which self-awareness would be helpful, such as deciding between college and a job.

14 REVIEW
Chapter

Writing a Summary

Using standard grammar, spelling, sentence structure, and punctuation, summarize the information in this chapter. Consider:
• the main features of the trait and psychoanalytic theories of personality
• how behaviorists, learning theorists, humanists, and socioculturalists view the development of personality

Identifying People and Ideas

Identify the following terms or people and use them in appropriate sentences.

1. personality
2. trait
3. introverts
4. id
5. defense mechanisms

6. repression
7. regression
8. Erik Erikson
9. congruence
10. acculturation

Understanding Main Ideas

SECTION 1 (pp. 322–324)
1. What are five examples of personality traits?

SECTION 2 (pp. 324–332)
2. Describe Erikson's stages of psychosocial development.

SECTION 3 (pp. 332–334)
3. What is the impact of behaviorism on current thinking in psychology?

SECTION 4 (pp. 334–337)
4. How is congruence related to a person's self concept?

SECTION 5 (pp. 337–339)
5. What are examples of behaviors that would indicate whether a person is more individualistic or collectivistic?

Thinking Critically

1. **Analyzing Information** Describe a situation where an awareness of one's own traits and abilities might help in making important decisions.

2. **Making Generalizations and Predictions** What do you think would happen to society if people's minds had an id but not an ego or superego?

3. **Supporting a Point of View** Which do you think has a greater effect on people's behavior: the socialization received as children (nurture) or the natural instincts and feelings people are simply born with (nature)? Explain your answer.

4. **Categorizing** What are two positive and two negative aspects of individualism and of collectivism?

Writing About Psychology

1. **Evaluating** Prepare a fact sheet in which you evaluate the various perspectives of human learning. Be sure to specify the strengths and weaknesses of each.

2. **Categorizing** Write a report that gives examples of growth and development based on social-learning theories and behavioral theories. Be sure to use standard grammar, spelling, sentence structure, and punctuation. Use the graphic organizer below to help you write your report.

Social-Learning Theories	Behavioral Theories

- How does this theory fit with the observations you have made in your practice of psychology?

- In what ways do other theories not coincide as well with your observations?

- What, if any, limitations do you perceive in your preferred theory of personality?

Cooperative Learning

Organize students into groups of three or four. Tell them to explore popular print media for theories of personality (including astrological explanations). Have students discuss the degree of scientific evidence for the various theories. Then have them try to find parallels between the explanations they found in books and magazines and the explanations discussed in this chapter. Have students theorize about why the effort to classify human personality is so interesting and yet so puzzling.

Building Social Studies Skills

Interpreting Graphs

Study the graph below. Then use the information in the graph to help you answer the questions that follow.

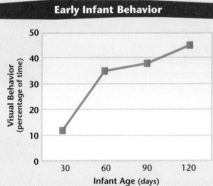

Early Infant Behavior

Source: Mischel, *Introduction to Personality*, 1986

1. Which of the following statements is supported by the information presented in the graph?

   a. Hearing is the primary means infants use to learn about the world.

   b. Infant use of visual behavior decreases with age.

   c. Infants do not rely upon other senses as much as they do visual behavior.

   d. Infant use of visual behavior increases with age.

2. How might a psychologist use this graph to criticize Freud's stages of development?

Analyzing Primary Sources

Read the following excerpt, in which psychologist Alfred Adler discusses why he believes people strive for superiority. Then answer the questions that follow.

"Now I began to see clearly in every psychical phenomenon the striving for *superiority*. It runs parallel to physical growth. It is an intrinsic necessity of life itself. It lies at the root of all solutions of life's problems, and is manifested in the way in which we meet these problems. All our functions follow its direction. . . . Willing, thinking, talking, seeking after rest, after pleasure, learning, understanding, work and love, betoken [show] the essence of this eternal melody. Whether one thinks or acts more wisely or less, one always moves along the lines of that upward tendency. In our right and wrong conceptions of life and its problems, in the successful or the unsuccessful solution of any question, this striving for perfection is uninterruptedly at work."

3. How does Adler define "striving for superiority" in this excerpt?

   a. attempting to achieve dominance over other people

   b. the effort to reach perfection

   c. trying to exercise complete control over one's environment

   d. receiving attention and praise from one's peers

4. How might a behaviorist such as John B. Watson have responded to Adler's arguments in this excerpt?

2. Students may suggest that such a society would be violent and chaotic.

3. Some students may argue that socialization has the greater effect because our internal values are formed through socialization; others may say that people's freedom of choice can overcome socialization.

4. Positive aspects of individualism include freedom of choice and self-reliance; negative aspects include greed and selfishness. Positive aspects of collectivism include a sense of community and empathy for weaker group members; negative aspects include a lack of initiative and a tendency to ostracize outsiders.

Writing About Psychology

1. Students' papers should reflect an understanding of the different perspectives of human learning.

2. Students should provide examples that reflect an understanding of social-learning theories and behaviorist theories.

Building Social Studies Skills

1. d

2. The graph shows that children rely increasingly on visual behavior during that stage Freud called the oral stage.

3. b

4. Students' answers will vary but should note that behaviorists would argue that Adler's "striving for superiority" was merely a matter of environmental influences affecting some individuals, including Adler.

PSYCHOLOGY PROJECTS

Cooperative Learning

Writing About Psychology With a classmate, write a skit that shows someone using one of the defense mechanisms mentioned in the chapter. Act out your skit for the class, and have students guess which defense mechanism you are portraying. As a class, discuss situations in which defense mechanisms might be helpful and times when they might be harmful.

internet connect

Internet Activity: go.hrw.com
KEYWORD: SY3 PS14
Choose an activity on theories of personality to:
- create a theoretical profile of a noted personality theorist.
- identify elements of social-learning theory in modern advertising.
- write a dinner party conversation that could occur among theorists of different approaches to personality.

Psychological Tests

CHAPTER RESOURCE MANAGER

Objectives	Pacing Guide	Reproducible and Review Resources
SECTION 1: What Are Psychological Tests? (pp. 344–347)	List the purposes and characteristics of psychological tests.	**Regular** 1 day **Block Scheduling** .5 day *Block Scheduling Handbook with Team Teaching Strategies, Chapter 15*	**E** Creating a Psychology Fair, Handout 5, Activity 9 **REV** Section 1 Review, p. 347
SECTION 2: Measuring Achievement, Abilities, and Interests (pp. 347–350)	Explain how achievement tests, aptitude tests, and interest inventories are used.	**Regular** 1 day **Block Scheduling** .5 day *Block Scheduling Handbook with Team Teaching Strategies, Chapter 15*	**PS** Readings and Case Studies, Chapter 15 **SM** Study Skills and Writing Guide, Part 3, Stage 5 **REV** Section 2 Review, p. 350
SECTION 3: Personality Tests (pp. 350–355)	Identify the two kinds of personality tests and discuss their uses.	**Regular** 1 day **Block Scheduling** .5 day *Block Scheduling Handbook with Team Teaching Strategies, Chapter 15*	**SM** Mastering Critical Thinking Skills 15 **RS** Essay and Research Themes for Advanced Placement Students, Theme 13 **REV** Section 3 Review, p. 355
SECTION 4: Taking Tests (pp. 355–359)	Identify strategies for taking tests and ways to avoid test anxiety.	**Regular** 1 day **Block Scheduling** .5 day *Block Scheduling Handbook with Team Teaching Strategies, Chapter 15*	**E** Research Projects and Activities for Teaching Psychology **REV** Section 4 Review, p. 359

Chapter Resource Key

PS Primary Sources	**A** Assessment	Video
RS Reading Support	**REV** Review	Internet
E Enrichment	Transparencies	Holt Presentation Maker Using Microsoft® PowerPoint®
SM Skills Mastery	CD-ROM	

 One-Stop Planner CD–ROM

See the *One-Stop Planner* for a complete list of additional resources for students and teachers.

 **One-Stop** Planner CD–ROM

It's easy to plan lessons, select resources, and print out materials for your students when you use the *One-Stop Planner CD-ROM with Test Generator.*

Technology Resources

 One-Stop Planner, Lesson 15.1
 Homework Practice Online
 Teaching Transparency 31: Woman Gesturing
 HRW Go Site

 One-Stop Planner, Lesson 15.2
 Homework Practice Online
 CNN. Presents Psychology: The Debate over Standardized Testing
 HRW Go Site

 One-Stop Planner, Lesson 15.3
 Homework Practice Online
 HRW Go Site

 One-Stop Planner, Lesson 15.4
 Homework Practice Online
Teaching Transparency 32: Test Anxiety

Chapter Review and Assessment

 HRW Go site
REV Chapter 15 Review, pp. 360–361
REV Chapter Review Activities with Answer Key

A Chapter 15 Test (Form A or B)
A Portfolio Assessment Handbook
A Alternative Assessment Handbook

Chapter 15 Test Generator (on the One-Stop Planner)
Global Skill Builder CD-ROM

---

internet connect

HRW ONLINE RESOURCES

GO TO: go.hrw.com
Then type in a keyword.

TEACHER HOME PAGE
KEYWORD: SY3 Teacher

CHAPTER INTERNET ACTIVITIES
KEYWORD: SY3 PS15
Choose an activity on psychological tests to:
• define the concept of "transformed score" and explain percentile grade equivalent scores.
• write a report on psychological testing.
• design questions for a personality test.

CHAPTER ENRICHMENT LINKS
KEYWORD: SY3 CH15

ONLINE ASSESSMENT
Homework Practice
KEYWORD: SY3 HP15
Standardized Test Prep
KEYWORD: SY3 STP15
Rubrics
KEYWORD: SS Rubrics

CONTENT UPDATES
KEYWORD: SS Content Updates

HOLT PRESENTATION MAKER
KEYWORD: SY3 PPT15

ONLINE READING SUPPORT
KEYWORD: SS Strategies

CURRENT EVENTS
KEYWORD: S3 Current Events

Additional Resources

PRINT RESOURCES FOR TEACHERS
Anastasi, A. (1988). *Psychological testing* (6th ed.). New York: Macmillan.

Buck, J. (1992). *House-tree-person projective drawing technique: Manual and interpretive guide.* Los Angeles: Western Psychological Services.

Kleinmuntz, B. (1985). *Personality and psychological assessment.* Malabar, FL: Krieger.

PRINT RESOURCES FOR STUDENTS
Aero, R., & Weiner, E. (1981). *The mind test.* New York: Morrow.

Aiken, L. (1989). *Assessment of personality.* Needham Heights, MA: Allyn and Bacon.

Geisinger, K. (1992). *Psychological testing of Hispanics.* Washington, DC: American Psychological Association.

MULTIMEDIA RESOURCES
Evaluating personality: From inkblots to intuition (VHS). Social Studies School Service, 10200 Jefferson Boulevard, Room 33, P.O. Box 802, Culver City, CA 90232-0802.

Effective study strategies (Videodisc). Library Video Company, P.O. Box 1110, Bala Cynwyd, PA 19004 (610-667-0200).

Your personal trainer for the SAT (CD-ROM). Davidson and Associates, Inc., 19840 Pioneer Ave., Torrance, CA 90503 (1-800-545-7677).

PSYCHOLOGICAL TESTS

Have students brainstorm all the different types of tests they can think of, such as blood tests, driving tests, soil or water tests, battery tests, and academic tests. Point out that the purpose of most tests is to measure something—the level of cholesterol in a person's blood, for example, or how much students have learned in a given subject area. Ask them what they think each test they named measures. Tell students that psychologists also use tests. Then ask students what they think psychologists might be interested in measuring. After students have had a chance to respond, tell them that the psychological tests discussed in Chapter 15 measure achievement, abilities, interests, or personality traits. There are also tests that measure intelligence. Lead students in a discussion of the uses that may be found for each type of test.

Sections

Each of the four questions identified on page 342 corresponds to one of these sections.

15
Chapter
PSYCHOLOGICAL TESTS

Read to Discover

1 What are the purposes and characteristics of psychological tests?

2 How are achievement tests, aptitude tests, and interest inventories used?

3 What are the two kinds of personality tests, and what are their uses?

4 What are some strategies for taking tests and for avoiding test anxiety?

Each chapter begins with a vignette, called "A Day in the Life," that relates the information discussed in the chapter to the everyday events in the lives of a group of fictional high school students. The text of the chapter occasionally refers back to the vignette to demonstrate the application of the concept being discussed. An icon marked "A Day in the Life" is placed next to these references.

 Copy the following graphic organizer onto the chalkboard, omitting the italicized text. Fill in the spaces as you introduce the trait approach to personality.

Psychological Tests	
Uses of	*Features*

A DAY IN THE LIFE

April 2

 Marc and Todd were meeting Dan in the library to study for a history test. When they found him, he was reading something intently.

"Hi, Dan. What are you reading?" Todd asked curiously.

"Oh hi, guys," Dan answered. "I met with the guidance counselor, Mr. Hochberg, yesterday because I'm still having trouble figuring out what I want to do after high school. He asked me to take some tests, and now I'm trying to make sense of the results."

"Don't we take enough tests in school already?" Marc asked.

"These weren't *regular* school tests. Some tested my interests, and others looked at my aptitudes."

"I took some of those tests last year," Todd said. "I'd always known that I liked studying living things, but Mr. Hochberg showed me types of jobs I could pursue if I really took my biology courses seriously."

"So, Dan, what did your tests show?" Marc asked.

"Well, according to one of these tests, I have good communication skills and relate well to people. Both of those qualities are listed under guidance counselor and teacher."

"Guys, we really should start studying for this history test," Todd reminded them.

Suddenly Marc looked panicked. "I wish you hadn't reminded me."

"What's wrong?" Todd asked.

"I just don't like taking tests," Marc answered. "I get so nervous, and no matter how much I study, I always seem to draw a blank when I actually sit down to take the test."

"No one likes tests," Dan said.

"But I think I get more upset than most people. I know it's weird, but sometimes I get so nervous that I can't even think straight, even if I've studied enough."

Todd looked rather concerned about his friend. "Why don't you try talking to your teachers or maybe even to Mr. Hochberg? They might at least be able to give you some advice about how to study or how to concentrate during the actual test."

"I guess it's worth a try."

• • •

As Dan discovered, there are many different kinds of psychological tests. In Chapter 9, you learned about one kind of psychological test: intelligence tests. The psychological tests that will be discussed in this chapter are achievement tests, aptitude and interest tests, and personality tests.

Tests to determine how much students have learned are called achievement tests. Mr. Hochberg gave Dan a test for special aptitudes and interests to help find out whether he is suited for certain occupations.

There are also tests that identify the psychological traits that make up a person's personality. Therefore, tests that measure psychological traits are also known as personality tests. Personality tests measure almost every known personality trait. Some tests measure a dozen or more traits at one time.

Key Terms

- behavior-rating scales
- self-reports
- standardized test
- validity scales
- norms
- norm group
- achievement tests
- aptitude tests
- vocational interest inventories
- forced-choice format
- objective tests
- projective tests
- open-ended format
- cognitive restructuring

WHY PSYCHOLOGY MATTERS

Psychologists use a variety of tests to assess human abilities and attitudes. Use CNNfyi.com or other current events sources to learn more about psychological tests.

CNNfyi.com

Using Key Terms

Have students use the Glossary or Chapter 15 to find definitions for the key terms in the list and rephrase the definitions in their own words. Then have students exchange the rephrased definitions with a partner to determine if the partner can recognize the terms from the definitions. Encourage partners to discuss any rephrased definitions they think are ambiguous or incorrect to help clarify their understanding of the terms.

Journal Activity

After students have read the "A Day in the Life" vignette, have them write in their journals about any psychological or personality tests they have taken in popular magazines. What personality traits or psychological components were these tests attempting to assess? Why are psychological tests in magazines so appealing to readers? How scientific do students consider these tests to be?

Section Objective

▶ List the purpose and characteristics of psychological tests.

This objective is assessed in the Section Review on page 347 and in the Chapter 15 Review.

Opening Section 1

Motivator

Have students write a paragraph about their favorite TV show. Without letting the others know, give half the students additional and very specific instructions about what to include. Read some of the paragraphs aloud without revealing who wrote them. Point out how the content of the paragraphs reflects differences in the instructions given. Tell students that this is why tests must be standardized—administered and scored the same way every time—if they are to be accurate. Note that in Section 1 students will learn about this and other features of psychological tests.

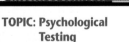

internet connect

TOPIC: Psychological Testing
GO TO: go.hrw.com
KEYWORD: SY3 PS15

Have students access the Internet through the HRW Go site to research different types of psychological testing. Then ask students to write a report. As an extension, ask students to include a paragraph in their report on whether they took one of the tests mentioned in the chapter, their opinions on its validity and reliability, and their feelings on standardized testing in general.

TRUTH OR fiction? Read the following statements about psychology. Do you think they are true or false? You will learn whether each statement is true or false as you read the chapter.

- Psychologists can always tell whether a person has told the truth on a personality test.
- Some tests measure only aptitude.
- Psychologists agree that the Rorschach inkblot test is a reliable method for determining psychological health.
- You should always go with your first guess on a multiple-choice test.
- The longer your answer to an essay question, the better your score on that question is likely to be.

SECTION 1
What Are Psychological Tests?

Psychological tests assess abilities, feelings, attitudes, and behaviors. The responses a person gives on test items help psychologists predict a person's future behavior.

Psychological tests are hardly a new invention. It appears that over 2,500 years ago, during the golden age of Greece, people were selected for government service on the basis of psychological tests (Matarazzo, 1990). Those early tests measured physical as well as mental abilities. Evidence also suggests that psychological tests were used to select civil-service employees some 2,000 years ago in China (Bowman, 1989). The Chinese tests measured verbal and mathematical abilities as well as knowledge of law and geography.

Modern researchers have been using various types of psychological tests for about 100 years. Francis Galton, James Cattell, Alfred Binet, and other psychologists began constructing modern psychological tests in the late 1800s.

Uses of Psychological Tests

Psychological tests can be used to help people make important decisions. Tests can help indicate whether a person is suited for a certain line of work, for a particular class in school, or for medication to reduce agitation (Saccuzzo, 1994). Intelligence tests are often used to indicate whether children are likely to profit from special kinds of educational experiences. Transformed score tests such as the Scholastic Assessment Test (SAT) are used to help determine whether students are likely to succeed in college. As part of their admissions process, college admissions personnel also often ask high school teachers and guidance counselors to rate applicants on scales that measure such traits as willingness to work hard and cooperativeness.

More specialized tests are used to measure students' prospects for success in graduate schools such as business, law, and medical schools. Many graduate schools use the Graduate Record Examination (GRE). Similarly, medical schools use the Medical College Admission Test (MCAT).

Some psychological tests measure behavior directly. For example, **behavior-rating scales** are used to measure behavior in such places as classrooms and hospitals. With behavior-rating scales, trained observers may check off each occurrence of a specific behavior within a certain amount of time, say, 15 minutes. For example, an observer might count how many times a person gestures while talking to someone else. This might be a measure of how outgoing the person is.

Behavior-rating scales are growing in popularity today, particularly for use with children (Kamphaus et al., 2000). However, most psychological tests rely on people's **self-reports** about their attitudes, feelings, and behavior.

Features of Psychological Tests

Psychological tests are sometimes frightening for the test takers and sometimes misleading for the evaluators. Tests such as the SAT can be particularly scary because the results on a test taken on one day can seem nearly as important as the grades earned over several years. The results can be misleading because a person may be ill or distracted on the day of the test and not perform as well as he or she might on another day.

For a psychological test to be useful and reasonably accurate, it has to have certain features, or characteristics. It has to be standardized, it has to show reliability and validity, and it has to have norms for scoring.

Standardization A **standardized test** is one that is administered and scored the same way every time. Psychologists and educators are trained in how to administer and score standardized tests accurately. For example, the two most widely used

Teaching Section 1

Role-Playing

To demonstrate how subtle variations in the administration of a standardized test can affect performance, ask pairs of students to role-play test givers administering exams to test takers. All test givers should read exactly the same directions to test takers but, through the use of facial expressions and body language, convey varying degrees of interest, encouragement, and support. After several pairs have played their roles, ask the class how they think the differences they observed in test-giver behavior might affect test-taker performance.

Cooperative Learning

To clarify the concept of validity scales, have each student write six true-false statements designed to elicit the same information about a person but in different ways. For example, one statement might be "I love animals," and another might be "I'd rather go to the arcade than to the zoo." Have students exchange their statements with a classmate and then to write responses to the items they receive in turn. Tell them to respond to some of the statements honestly and to others dishonestly. Ask students to exchange responses and to try to detect the deception.

Some psychological tests measure behavior directly by means of behavior-rating scales. With these scales, trained observers count the number of times a specific behavior occurs in a certain amount of time. For example, an observer might count how many times a person gestures during a conversation.

intelligence tests, the Stanford-Binet and Wechsler, are given individually. All test administrators are trained to ask the same questions in the same way. They also receive training in how to score the tests and interpret those scores.

Other tests such as the SAT are given to thousands of students at a time. All students receive the same instructions, and computers grade most of the answers. Essay questions on a standardized test are not graded by a computer. However, instructions for administrators on how to score essay questions are very clear and precise. This helps ensure that the same criteria will be used to score essay questions regardless of who is doing the scoring.

Reliability and Validity In Chapter 9, you learned that the *reliability* of a measure is its consistency. That is, an individual's score on a test should be the same or very nearly the same every time the individual takes that test. Test-retest reliability is demonstrated when a person receives similar scores on the same test taken on different occasions. *Validity* refers to the extent to which a test measures what it is intended to measure and predicts what it is intended to predict.

Test results can be distorted when people answer in ways they think will please the interviewer. People have also been known to exaggerate

their problems on personality tests as a way to get attention. In addition, people may answer in the way they think is "correct," even if there are no objectively right or wrong answers. To avoid such distortion, some psychological tests have validity scales built into them.

Validity scales involve questions that, if answered in a certain way, let the psychologist know that the test taker is not answering the test questions honestly. Validity scales always depend on the answers to many interlinking questions. For example, there may be several test items on which a psychologist would expect to see a pattern of similar answers. If no such pattern is found, those answers, taken together, may indicate that the test taker is not answering the questions honestly. Validity scales are often quite helpful. However, they are not foolproof.

It is not true that psychologists can always tell whether a person has told the truth on a personality test. Validity scales help, but they cannot indicate with certainty whether a test taker has answered questions honestly.

In general, the tests you take in your classes are not psychological tests, and most are not constructed scientifically. Still, these tests should also be reliable and valid. Generally speaking, the longer a test is, the more valid it is. (Would you rather have your grade on a math test depend on solving just one problem, or would you prefer it to be based on your solutions to 10 or 20 problems?) Marc

believes that the scores he receives on tests he takes in class are often not a valid measure of what he knows. He argues that the tests do not really measure what he has learned because his nervousness interferes with his ability to perform well.

Using Visuals

Ask students what they think the person in the photograph on page 345 might be feeling, based on her facial expression and body language. Have them consider how much communication might be missed if she were to write her statements on paper rather than convey them in person, as in the photograph. Point out that this is one of the limitations of pencil-and-paper psychological tests.

For Your Information

Some experts question the validity of IQ tests as general measures of intelligence. They believe that most IQ tests measure only one type of ability—analytic ability—and that there are other important abilities, such as creativity and practical skills, that the tests do not measure. Although students who do well on IQ tests are likely to score high on academic tests, they may not have the creativity or practical skills needed to succeed in college.

Teaching Transparencies with Teacher's Notes

TRANSPARENCY 31: Woman Gesturing

PSYCHOLOGY
IN THE WORLD TODAY

Arrange for interested students to participate in a CASPER interview, being sure to keep their test results confidential. After students have completed the interview, ask them how they felt when they were taking the test. Was it easier to "talk" to a computer than it would have been to talk to a psychologist? Also ask them how they feel about the results of their interview. Do they think the results are valid, given what they know about themselves?

Closing Section 1

Synthesizing Information

Have students write a short essay that explains how standardization, reliability, validity, and norms contribute to the development of a useful and accurate psychological test. Ask volunteers to read their essays aloud to the class.

Reviewing Section 1

Have students complete the Section Review questions on page 347.

For Your Information

Computers can be used not only to administer tests, such as the CASPER interview, but also to help students prepare for tests such as the SAT and the ACT. Many test preparation programs are now available. Some offer detailed tutorials; others offer customized study plans. Most contain hundreds of practice questions that familiarize students with a particular test and help reduce test anxiety. In addition, such programs are upbeat and fun, making test preparation an enjoyable experience for students.

Think About It: Answer

Possible problems in diagnosis might be difficulty in including every possible symptom or diagnosis in a computer program and the inability of a computer to read such nonverbal cues as body language and facial expression. During treatment, a computer cannot provide empathy and emotional support, which can be important components of psychotherapy.

PSYCHOLOGY
IN THE WORLD TODAY

Would You Tell Your Problems to a Computer?

Imagine you have been feeling tense lately and are wondering what is causing the tension. You decide to consult a psychologist. When you arrive at the psychologist's office, you are instructed to sit in a room with a computer that asks you several personal questions.

The fact is that computers have been "interviewing" people for more than 20 years. One computer program currently in use for this purpose is CASPER. CASPER stands for Computerized Assessment System for Psychotherapy Evaluation and Research. A CASPER interview lasts about 30 minutes. CASPER explores a wide variety of topics, including family relationships, social activities, overall life satisfaction, and specific behavior patterns that may be suggestive of physical and psychological disorders.

A CASPER interview

Questions and possible responses are displayed on the monitor. To answer a question, the test taker presses a number on the computer keyboard. CASPER then follows up with additional questions. For example, if you report difficulty sleeping, CASPER will inquire whether sleep has become a key problem. CASPER asks whether the sleep problem is "something causing you great personal distress or interfering with your daily functioning" (Farrell et al., 1987). If the answer is yes, the computer will explore further by asking more questions.

How well do people respond to being interviewed by a computer? Research shows that people find the computer program user-friendly. They also find that they are able to complete CASPER interviews with little difficulty. In fact, most people like the computerized interview (Bloom, 1992; Farrell et al., 1987). This is especially true for younger, better-educated people who are experienced with computers (Spinhoven et al., 1993).

People also seem to report more problems to CASPER than they do to a real, live psychologist. Why? Some people seem to prefer "speaking" with an impersonal computer to speaking with a person, who might disagree with or judge them.

Computer diagnostic programs apparently offer some advantages over human interviewers (Farrell et al., 1987):

- Standardization seems to be easier and more consistent. Computers can be programmed to ask specific questions in a prescribed sequence.
- People may be less embarrassed about reporting personal matters to a computer. Computers make no emotional or judgmental responses.
- Use of the computer for purposes of diagnosis frees clinicians to spend more of their time doing psychotherapy.

As computer programs become more sophisticated, they are also likely to become more accurate at diagnosis and better able to identify unusual problems. Because of its memory, a computer can also easily connect a person's complaints to similar cases and thus make the choice of treatment easier for the therapist.

A review of the research in computer diagnosis suggests that some computer programs are as capable of obtaining pertinent information from a client and arriving at an accurate diagnosis as trained clinicians (Bloom, 1992). Computer programs seem to be the wave of the future. Sophisticated diagnostic and treatment programs continue to be developed.

Think About It

Making Generalizations and Predictions What possible problems do you think might occur with computer diagnosis and treatment?

Extension

Have students conduct library research to learn about the history and development of the Scholastic Assessment Test (explain that it once was called the Scholastic Aptitude Test). When was the SAT first used? How and why was it developed? How were the norms established? How has the test changed over time? How is it scored? How have scores on the SAT changed over time? What controversies have surrounded its use? Have students present their findings in a written report. Students may wish to create charts and graphs to accompany their reports.

2 Section Objective

▶ Explain how achievement tests, aptitude tests, and interest inventories are used.

This objective is assessed in the Section Review on page 350 and in the Chapter 15 Review.

Norms Psychological tests are usually scored by comparing an individual's score to the norm. **Norms** are established standards of performance. They are designed to tell test administrators which scores are average, high, or low.

Norms for a test are usually established by administering the test to a large group of people who are similar to those for whom the test is intended. This group of test takers is called the **norm group**.

Imagine you are asked to create a psychological test for elementary school students. The tests would need to ask questions appropriate to the age of the children. You would establish the norm by administering the test to thousands of elementary school students of the same age or grade level. This would be your norm group. The average score of the norm group would become the norm for that particular test, and the scores of all other children taking the test in the future would be compared to that norm.

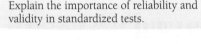

Achievement tests are given to most elementary and middle school students every year to assess basic skills such as reading and math.

A DAY IN THE LIFE The history test Dan, Marc, and Todd were studying for was an achievement test. Throughout elementary and middle school, most students' basic skills are tested every year. They are tested in science, reading, math, and many other subject areas.

In high school, most students are tested repeatedly on their achievements in each of their courses. Factors such as intelligence and motivation play a role in achievement, but so does learning. For example, it should come as no surprise that students taking Spanish will have higher scores on a Spanish achievement test than students who are not taking Spanish, even though they may be equal in intelligence and motivation.

College students who wish to go to graduate school may be required to take standardized achievement tests in their major field of study—Spanish, political science, math, or psychology, for example. The tests are designed to determine whether the students have enough knowledge in the specific area to succeed in graduate school.

SECTION 2
Measuring Achievement, Abilities, and Interests

Achievement tests, aptitude tests, and tests of interests are all closely related. Most of the tests that you have taken in your classes at school have probably been achievement tests. There are also tests that measure people's abilities, or aptitudes. Still other tests help people identify their interests. Dan and his friends had been taking achievement tests for many years. Then when Dan was having difficulty deciding on a college major, Mr. Hochberg focused on testing Dan's abilities and interests.

Achievement Tests

Achievement tests measure people's skills and the knowledge they have in specific academic areas.

Aptitude Tests

Achievement tests measure a narrow range of skills. Intelligence tests, on the other hand, measure overall learning ability. Aptitude tests fall somewhere in

Opening Section 2

Motivator

Ask students if they recall being asked as young children, "What do you want to be when you grow up?" Did they respond by naming one of only a few different occupations they knew about, such as firefighter or ballet dancer? Now they know there are many more occupations from which to choose. In fact, they may feel overwhelmed by the number of choices. Tell them that the tests discussed in Section 2 can help narrow the career choices most suitable for them by assessing their abilities, skills, and interests.

Teaching Section 2

Applying Ideas

Have students brainstorm ways to assess achievement that do not depend on typical pencil-and-paper tests. Possibilities might include applying knowledge to the solution of practical problems, teaching concepts or skills to other students, preparing test questions, or writing research reports that require a basic command of the subject. Which type of assessment do they think would be most useful? Why?

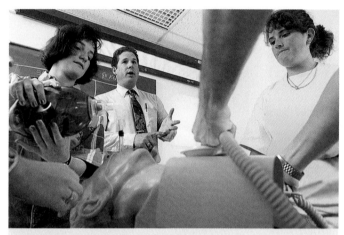

The Medical College Admission Test (MCAT) is an aptitude test that can help predict how well students will do in medical school. Aptitude tests are broader than intelligence tests but narrower than achievement tests.

between. Aptitude tests measure more specific abilities or skills than intelligence tests but broader ones than achievement tests. **Aptitude tests** are generally used to determine whether a person is likely to do well in a given field of work or study.

The Scholastic Assessment Test is a general aptitude test. It is used to predict how well students are likely to do in college. The Law School Admission Test and the Medical College Admission Test are more specialized. They use percentile grade equivalent scores—the percent of scores at or below any given score—to predict how well students will do in law school and medical school, respectively. For example, success in medical school depends heavily on the ability to understand chemistry and biology. Therefore, the MCAT has many questions relating to these subjects.

Distinguishing Between Achievement and Aptitude

Sometimes it is difficult to distinguish between an achievement test and an aptitude test. Aptitude tests are intended to measure potential for learning in a specific area. An aptitude test is usually given to a person before that person has had any training in a specific area. It is used to predict how well the person will do in that area after receiving training. However, current abilities and future success are often based on past achievements. For example, the SAT is intended to measure the ability to do well in college, but it is given in specific languages. Therefore, the ability to do well on the SAT depends

on achievements in English (or the language in which the individual takes the test).

Moreover, the SAT consists of verbal and quantitative parts. The verbal sections rely heavily on vocabulary—that is, knowledge of the meaning of words. The quantitative part relies heavily on mathematical knowledge. Skill in these areas—knowledge of vocabulary and mathematics—depends on the amount one has learned or achieved. However, because performance on the SAT does not depend on one specific course, the SAT used to be called the Scholastic *Aptitude* Test. Recently, however, in recognition of the role that achievement plays in the SAT, the test was renamed the Scholastic *Assessment* Test.

It may be that there is no such thing as a "pure" aptitude test. All aptitude tests rely on some kind of prior achievement.

TRUTH
OR
fiction
■ REVISITED ■

It is not true that some tests measure only aptitude. All aptitude tests rely on some kind of achievement. In recognition of this fact, the Scholastic Aptitude Test was renamed the Scholastic Assessment Test.

Vocational Interest Inventories

A DAY IN THE LIFE

When Dan was having difficulty deciding what to do after high school, Mr. Hochberg gave him some tests to help him figure out what his interests were. People usually perform better in jobs that interest them. Moreover, people who share interests with those who are successful in a given job are more likely to succeed in that job. Thus, many psychologists and educators use **vocational interest inventories** to help people determine whether their interests are similar to those of people in various lines of work. Two widely used interest inventories are the Kuder™ Preference Records and the Strong-Campbell Interest Inventory.

Guided Practice

Point out that vocational interest inventories help people focus on career-related interests but that knowledge of interests alone is insufficient for making wise career choices. Aptitudes and other factors are also important. Ask students to provide examples of aptitudes they think might be important for particular careers. Then ask the class if they can think of any other factors that may influence career choices. Possibilities include educational requirements, salaries, and employment opportunities.

Independent Practice

Have pairs of students interview people in various career fields about the reasons they chose their careers. One student in each pair should conduct the interview while the other student notes the responses. After the interviews are completed, ask the pairs to deduce from the information that they gathered what other factors, besides aptitudes and interests, may influence career choices. Have the pairs share their findings with the rest of the class.

Kuder™ Preference Records Mr. Hochberg may have given Dan a test called a Kuder Preference Record. This test has a **forced-choice format**, which means that the test taker is forced to choose one of the answers, even if none of them seems to fit his or her interests precisely. For example, test takers are asked to indicate which of a group of activities they like most and which they like least. They are not allowed to answer "none of the above."

The Kuder asks test takers to choose between activities such as the following:

a. hiking in the forest
b. giving someone advice
c. playing a musical instrument

The results are scored to show how much the person appears to be interested in areas such as science, music, art, literature, and outdoor work.

Strong-Campbell Interest Inventory People taking a Kuder test can see where their interests lie and which areas they might want to look into for employment opportunities. Obviously, a person who repeatedly indicates a preference for music-related activities is showing a definite interest in music. The Strong-Campbell Interest Inventory is not as obvious or direct. It includes many different kinds of items.

The Strong-Campbell compares the test taker's interests with the interests of people who enjoy and are successful in various kinds of work. For example, if most successful accountants enjoy reading and solving puzzles, then a test taker who indicates these same preferences might also be a successful accountant. Therefore, the content of the test questions themselves may not be as important as the combinations of interests the test taker shares with people in certain occupations.

Evaluation of Interest Inventories Interest inventories are of great value to students such as Dan who do not have specific career goals. There are over 20,000 different occupations in the United States, and the task of trying to select one can be overwhelming to people who are unclear about their interests. Interest inventories can help point people in a direction they might find fulfilling.

On the other hand, interest in an area does not necessarily mean that one has the ability, or aptitude, to succeed in that area. Therefore, it is usually desirable to make vocational choices on the basis of one's abilities as well as one's interests.

No important life decisions should be made on the basis of a single psychological test. Tests provide only one source of information about an individual, and no test is perfectly reliable. Teachers' and counselors' personal knowledge of an individual should also be taken into account. People may also believe that the results of a single test may not be an accurate reflection of who they are.

Dan was pleased with the outcome of his interest test because it seemed to fit his own image of himself. If his test results had seemed wrong to him, it would be unwise for him to follow the directions suggested by the test results. For example, suppose the test showed that Dan likes outdoor activities, which suggests a career that includes working outdoors. Dan enjoys hiking and boating *occasionally*, but he also knows that he would dislike

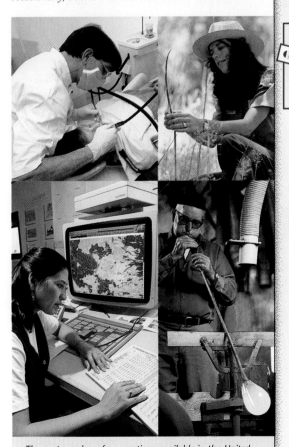

The vast number of occupations available in the United States can make it difficult to know which career to pursue. Vocational interest inventories are often used to help people narrow down their career possibilities.

Journal Activity

Arrange for interested students to take either the Kuder™ Preference Records or the Strong-Campbell Interest Inventory. Have students write down their test results and how they feel about them. Do they think the results reflect their strongest interests? Do they have other interests that do not show up in the results?

Technology Resources

 CNN. Presents Psychology: The Debate over Standardized Tests

Readings and Case Studies

Closing Section 2

Summarizing Information

Have students summarize the similarities and differences between achievement tests and aptitude tests and between the Kuder Preference Records and the Strong-Campbell Interest Inventory. Then ask them to identify specific uses of each type of test.

Reviewing Section 2

Have students complete the Section Review questions on page 350.

Section 2 Review: Answers

1. Achievement tests measure skills and knowledge in specific areas. Aptitude tests measure the potential for learning.

2. The purpose is to match test takers' interests with possible careers.

3. Achievement tests measure people's skills and the knowledge that they have in specific academic areas. Aptitude tests measure more specific abilities or skills than intelligence tests but broader ones than achievement tests. Vocational interest inventories help people determine whether their interests are similar to those of people in various lines of work.

For Your Information

A psychologist's theoretical background influences which type of personality test he or she prefers to use. Trait theorists tend to prefer objective paper-and-pencil tests such as the MMPI-2™ and the CPI. Projective tests, which tend to reflect the workings of the unconscious mind, are more typically used by people trained in psychoanalysis. Behaviorists prefer to use behavioral assessments such as behavior-rating scales and self-reports to assess personality.

350

3
Section Objective

▶ Identify the two kinds of personality tests and discuss their uses.

This objective is assessed in the Section Review on page 355 and in the Chapter 15 Review.

having to work outside all day and every day. He would have to carefully consider the test results in light of what he knows about himself. Taking additional interest tests might provide a clearer picture of the kind of career he would enjoy.

SECTION 2 REVIEW

go.hrw.com **Homework Practice Online** Keyword: SY3 HP15

1. What is the difference between an achievement test and an aptitude test?

2. What is the purpose of vocational interest inventories?

3. **Critical Thinking** *Summarizing* In what ways are achievement tests, aptitude tests, and interest inventories used?

SECTION 3
Personality Tests

An individual's personality consists of his or her characteristics, habits, preferences, and moods. Psychologists use personality tests to describe and measure various aspects of people's personalities. Sometimes, they also use personality tests to help diagnose psychological problems and disorders. There are two kinds of personality tests: objective tests and projective tests.

Objective Tests

Objective tests present test takers with a standardized group of test items in the form of a questionnaire. The Minnesota Multiphasic Personality Inventory® (MMPI®) and the California Psychological Inventory™ (CPI™), discussed below, are examples of objective personality tests. Sometimes test takers are limited to a specific choice of answers—true or false, for example. Sometimes test takers are asked to select the preferred answer from groups of three. In either case, though, the test takers must choose from a list of answers provided for them.

Minnesota Multiphasic Personality Inventory

The MMPI is the psychological test most widely used in clinical work (Helmes & Reddon, 1993; Watkins et al., 1995) and in research that requires measurement of personality traits. First developed

The results of the MMPI-2 can alert a psychologist to the possibility that the test taker may be suffering from a psychological disorder, such as depression. Most psychologists believe that the MMPI-2 scores should be supplemented and confirmed by interviews and observation.

in the late 1930s, the MMPI was intended for use by clinical and counseling psychologists to help diagnose psychological problems in people. A revised version of the test (the MMPI-2™) was released in 1989.

The MMPI-2 contains 567 items presented in a true-false format. Psychologists can score the MMPI-2 by hand, but they usually score it by computer. Computers generate reports by comparing the individual's score to group norms stored in the computer's memory. While the computer is certainly an objective (unbiased) scorer, most psychologists believe that the scores should be supplemented and confirmed by interviews and observation.

The MMPI-2 is organized into 10 clinical scales, up to 8 validity scales, and numerous subscales. The clinical scales reveal psychological problems. (See Figure 15.1) They also indicate whether people have stereotypical masculine or feminine interests and whether they are outgoing or shy.

To create the clinical scales of the MMPI-2, the designers interviewed people who had already been diagnosed with various psychological disorders. A test-item bank of several hundred items was derived from questions often asked in clinical interviews.

Motivator

Show the class a Rorschach inkblot and ask them to write down what it resembles to them. Collect their anonymous responses, and read several to the class. Point out some of the ways in which the responses vary. Tell students that differences in what people see in an inkblot may reflect differences in personality. Add that the Rorschach inkblot test is just one of several tests discussed in Section 3 that are used to measure various aspects of people's personalities.

Analyzing Information

To help students grasp the essential differences between objective and projective personality tests, ask them to find evidence in the textbook to support the claim that objective tests are standardized whereas projective tests are not. Students should point out that the forced-choice responses on objective tests can be scored in exactly the same way for each test taker. In contrast, the open-ended responses in projective personality tests are rated subjectively and may be interpreted differently by different raters.

Commonly Used Validity and Clinical Scales of the Revised Minnesota Multiphasic Personality Inventory (MMPI-2™)

	Scale	Abbreviation	Possible Interpretations
Validity Scales	Cannot say	?	Corresponds to number of items left unanswered
	Lie	L	Lies or is highly conventional
	Infrequency	F	Exaggerates complaints or answers items haphazardly
	Correction	K	Denies problems
Clinical Scales	Hypochondriasis	Hs	Has bodily concerns and complaints
	Depression	D	Is depressed, guilty; has feelings of guilt and helplessness
	Conversion hysteria	Hy	Reacts to stress by developing physical symptoms; lacks insight
	Psychopathic deviate	Pd	Is immoral, in conflict with the law; has stormy relationships
	Masculinity-Femininity	Mf	High scores suggest interests and behavior patterns considered stereotypical of the other gender
	Paranoia	Pa	Is suspicious and resentful, highly cynical about human nature
	Psychasthenia	Pt	Is anxious, worried, high-strung
	Schizophrenia	Sc	Is confused, disorganized, disoriented; has bizarre ideas
	Hypomania	Ma	Is energetic, restless, active, easily bored
	Social introversion	Si	Is introverted, timid, shy; lacks self-confidence

FIGURE 15.1 *The MMPI-2 is the most widely used psychological test in clinical work. Although originally intended for use by psychologists to diagnose psychological disorders, it has now become the most widely used instrument of personality measurement in psychological research. This list describes the specific disorders that the MMPI-2 typically assesses.*

Using Visuals

Tell students that the validity scales of the MMPI-2, shown in Figure 15.1, are used to assess whether test results are valid for a particular test taker. In this context, validity indicates whether the test taker understood the questions and answered them truthfully. Explain to students that the validity scales do not reflect whether the MMPI-2 is a valid test in general—that is, whether it actually measures what it is intended to measure, which is personality traits.

Class Discussion

Point out that the MMPI-2 was designed originally as an instrument for diagnosing psychological disorders; this is why its clinical scales are based on the responses of people already diagnosed with various disorders. Tell students that the MMPI-2 is also used to measure personality traits in people who do not have psychological problems. Have students discuss whether it is appropriate to use the MMPI-2 for this purpose. Why or why not?

Meeting Individual Needs:
Gifted Learners

Ask gifted students to research the evolution of the Minnesota Multiphasic Personality Inventory. The students should find answers to such questions as how the MMPI-2 differs from the MMPI, why the changes were made, and what advantages the newer version is believed to have over the original test. Ask the students to share what they have learned with the rest of the class.

Applying Information

Tell students that the MMPI-2 and the CPI are both objective personality tests, differing primarily in the specific items they include: items in the MMPI-2 focus on pathology; those in the CPI on normality. Explain that in practice the MMPI-2 is more useful for diagnosing current psychological problems, while the CPI is better for identifying relatively permanent features of people's personalities. Have students give examples of situations for which each type of test might be better suited.

Cultural Dimensions

Tell students that cultural differences may influence how people perceive Rorschach inkblots. In Morocco, for example, psychologically healthy individuals given the Rorschach test tend to focus on small details—even the tiny specks—in the inkblots. In the United States and Europe, this type of response might be interpreted as a sign of a serious psychological disorder. Emphasize that knowing an individual's cultural background is crucial for proper interpretation of the Rorschach test.

Caption Question:
Answer

Point out to the class that what they see in the inkblot shown in Figure 15.2 depends on many factors, including which part of the inkblot they focus on. Have them focus on just the white areas at the bottom. Do they see something different now than they did at first?

Here are some of the true-false items:

My father was a good man. **T F**
I am seldom troubled by headaches. **T F**
My hands and feet are usually warm enough. **T F**
I have never done anything dangerous for the thrill of it. **T F**
I work under a great deal of tension. **T F**

People with various psychological disorders, such as depression or schizophrenia, will answer certain questions in predictable ways. For example, a person suffering from depression might answer "true" to such questions as "I often feel sad for no reason" or "Sometimes I think life simply isn't worth living." These test items are then placed on scales to measure the presence of psychological disorders in other people. If a person taking the test answers the questions in ways that are similar to people who are known to have a particular psychological disorder, the psychologist administering the test is alerted to the possible presence of that disorder.

The validity scales are designed to detect distorted answers, misunderstood items, or an uncooperative test taker. For example, people with high "T" scores may answer questions in a way that makes them seem excessively moral or well behaved. Such people might answer the item "I never get angry" with "true." People with high "F" scores have a tendency to exaggerate complaints, or they may be trying to get attention by giving seemingly bizarre answers. (See Figure 15.1.)

However, there are questions concerning the usefulness of the validity scales (Helmes & Reddon, 1993). For example, people with serious psychological disorders may indeed see the world in an unusual way. Therefore, if they obtain high F-scale scores, it may be because of their problems and not because they are exaggerating their situation.

California Psychological Inventory Because the MMPI-2 was designed to diagnose and classify psychological disorders, some psychologists prefer not to use it to measure the personality traits of "normal" clients. Many of these psychologists instead use the California Psychological Inventory, or CPI. The format of the CPI is similar to that of the MMPI-2, but it is designed to measure 15 "normal" personality traits, such as dominance, sociability, responsibility, and tolerance.

In many ways, the CPI is a much more valid instrument than the MMPI-2, even though it is not as widely used as the latter test. The norm group for the CPI is much larger than that for the MMPI-2,

and greater care was taken in controlling for factors such as age, socioeconomic status, and geographic location. Furthermore, the CPI has a much higher test-retest reliability than the MMPI-2 and seems to be a better predictor of such things as school and job success, leadership, and reactions to stress (Ross, 1987).

Projective Tests

Projective tests, unlike objective tests, have no clearly specified answers. Such tests use an **open-ended format**. People are presented with ambiguous stimuli such as inkblots, drawings of vague shapes, or pictures of people engaged in various activities. The test takers are then asked to report what the stimuli represent to them. They might also be asked to tell stories about the stimuli. Since the inkblots or drawings are open to interpretation, it is thought that people's interpretations of the pictures reveal something about their personalities. The Rorschach (RAWR-shahk) inkblot test and the Thematic Apperception Test (TAT) are two examples of widely used projective tests.

Rorschach Inkblot Test Have you heard of a personality test that asks people to tell what a drawing or an inkblot looks like? There are actually a number of such personality tests. The Rorschach inkblot test is the best known of them. The Rorschach is named after its originator, Swiss psychiatrist Hermann Rorschach (1884–1922).

A Rorschach Inkblot

FIGURE 15.2 *While there is no "correct" response to a Rorschach inkblot test, certain answers are more in keeping than others with the features of the blot. What do you see?*

352

CASE STUDIES
AND OTHER TRUE STORIES

Tell students that career counselors use both the interest inventories that were described in the previous section and the Myers-Briggs Type Indicator (MBTI®) that is described in this feature. Ask students how the two types of tests differ. Specifically, what does each type of test measure, and how are the results typically used? Which type of test do students think is better for matching people to suitable occupations and why?

Interpreting Information

List on the chalkboard a variety of occupations that are familiar to students—for example, doctor, lawyer, teacher, store clerk, firefighter, taxi driver, and actor. Have students decide which set of four traits from the MBTI dimensions—extroversion or introversion, sensation or intuition, thinking or feeling, and judging or perceiving—would best suit someone for each occupation. Ask students to justify their decisions.

CASE STUDIES
AND OTHER TRUE STORIES

What Personality Type Are You?

Have you ever wondered how you or someone else would classify your personality? Whether you are an extrovert or an introvert? Whether you are logical or emotional?

Many people like to find out about themselves—to identify their characteristics and personalities. One of the most popular tests for that purpose is the Myers-Briggs Type Indicator® (MBTI®). Isabel Briggs Myers and her mother, Katharine Cook Briggs, began designing a personality test in the 1940s. Their goal was to create an objective test that would help employers hire the people who were best suited for particular kinds of jobs. Even today, the MBTI is popular in career and business counseling.

The MBTI is based on the personality theory of psychologist Carl Jung, who was one of Sigmund Freud's students. Jung believed that there are different personality types and that how a person acts in certain situations is based on the person's personality type. He also suggested that a person's personality preferences are present early in life and become more apparent as the person matures.

Each year, approximately 2 million people take the MBTI. The MBTI items are in forced-choice format. Typical questions include the following:

1. Which rules you more?
   (a) your head
   (b) your heart
2. At a party, do you
   (a) interact with many, including strangers?
   (b) interact with a few, known to you?

After choosing between (a) and (b) answers for 126 questions, the test taker's preferences are evaluated along four dimensions. The dimensions are extroversion versus introversion (E vs. I); sensing versus intuition (S vs. N); thinking versus feeling (T vs. F); and judging versus perceiving (J vs. P). Preferences may be classified as strong, moderate, or weak. The stronger one's preference along a dimension, the more one will exhibit the characteristics of that dimension.

Each preference is characterized by a particular way of seeing, or responding to, situations and other people. For example, extroverted people enjoy interacting with others, while introverted people prefer solitary activities. Intuitive people value creativity, while sensation-oriented people prefer practicality. Thinking people prefer to be logical and analytical when making decisions, while the decision-making process for feeling people relies more on interpersonal involvement and subjective values. Judgers typically prefer an environment that is ordered and structured, while perceivers tend to be more flexible and spontaneous.

The total possible combinations add up to 16 types, such as INTJ, ISFP, ESTJ, ENFP, and so on. In theory, each person is one of those 16 types. According to people who support the MBTI's results, how an individual sees the world and how he or she behaves can be predicted on the basis of the person's personality type.

The MBTI has received its share of criticism. One criticism has been that a person's type changes over time. Although Myers, Briggs, and Jung believed that an adult is one type and one type only, that appears to be untrue. The MBTI does not pass the test-retest standards for reliability.

Since the same test taker often obtains different results each time he or she takes the test, the MBTI cannot be considered an accurate predictor of behavior. In addition, the MBTI seems to label people in a prejudicial way.

For these and other reasons, a National Academy of Sciences Study has concluded that the Myers-Briggs Type Indicator is not useful in career counseling programs—at least not until further research proves otherwise.

WHY PSYCHOLOGY MATTERS

Many employers use psychological tests to screen potential employees. Use CNNfyi.com or other current events sources to learn more about these types of tests. Write a report supporting or opposing the use of such tests.

CNNfyi.com

For Your Information

With the publication of the third edition of the *Diagnostic and Statistical Manual of Mental Disorders* (DSM-III) in 1980, personality disorders were recognized for the first time as a separate category of psychological disorders. Since then, psychologists have struggled to distinguish between normal and pathological personality traits. Most experts have concluded that normal and pathological personality traits differ in degree rather than in kind.

Demonstration

Have students make inkblots similar to the ones used in the Rorschach test by putting a drop of ink or food coloring in the middle of a sheet of plain white paper, folding the paper in half, and pressing the two sides together. Show some of the inkblots to the class and ask a few volunteers to describe what they think the inkblots resemble. Discuss students' responses in terms of location, determinants, content, and form level to demonstrate how psychologists interpret people's answers on the Rorschach test.

For Further Research

Have students research the history and development of the Thematic Apperception Test (TAT). Some questions students may wish to explore include how and why the test was developed, for whom the test was originally intended, what is included in the test, how the test meets the standards of a valid and reliable test, and how the test is interpreted. Have students present their findings in oral reports to the class. Some students may wish to make sketches of actual TAT cards to show to the class.

Interestingly, Rorschach's nickname as an adolescent was Klex, which means "inkblot" in German (Allison et al., 1988).

Figure 15.2 on page 352 shows a Rorschach inkblot. If you were taking the test, a psychologist would hand you a card with the inkblot and ask you what it looks like or what it could be. Because the Rorschach is a projective test, there is no list of clearly defined answers from which to choose. Instead, test takers provide their own responses to each inkblot. However, some answers are more in keeping than others with the features of the blot.

Look again at Figure 15.2. It could be a bat or a flying insect. It also could be an animal with a pointed face. It could be a jack-o'-lantern or many other things. But answers such as "diseased lungs" or "the devil in flames" are not readily suggested by the features of the blot. Therefore, a pattern of responses such as these is more likely than other patterns to suggest the presence of a personality disorder in the test taker.

Many attempts have been made to standardize the Rorschach. People's responses to the cards are usually interpreted according to factors such as location, determinants, content, and form level.

- *Location* is the part of the blot to which the person responds. Does he or she respond to the whole card or to a detail of the card?
- *Determinants* include features of the blot such as shading, texture, or color. People who are highly influenced by the texture and color are thought to be more emotional than those who do not focus on these aspects of the blot. Answers that incorporate many features of the blot are thought to reflect high intelligence.
- *Content* refers to the precise object the test taker reports seeing. Is he or she seeing a bat, a jack-o'-lantern, or a human figure?
- *Form level* indicates whether the answer is in keeping with the actual shape of the blot. Generally speaking, answers that fit the shape of the blot suggest that the individual sees the world the way most people do. (Some psychological disorders, such as schizophrenia, are characterized by bizarre perceptions.)

Supporters of the Rorschach test claim that it provides useful information that might not be obtained elsewhere. However, some researchers raise serious questions about the reliability and validity of the test. Because no two professionals interpret Rorschach responses in quite the same way, they argue that the test results can be arbitrary or biased to support the professional's point of view.

TRUTH OR fiction
■ REVISITED ■

It is not true that psychologists agree that the Rorschach inkblot test is a reliable method for determining psychological health. Many psychologists are skeptical about the Rorschach. They argue that the test is not reliable because the results depend too much on the interpretation of the professional giving the test.

Thematic Apperception Test The Thematic Apperception Test, or TAT, was developed in the 1930s by psychologists Henry Murray and Christiana Morgan at Harvard University. It is widely used in clinical practice and in motivation research (Watkins et al., 1995).

The TAT consists of drawings such as the one shown in Figure 15.3. These drawings, like the Rorschach inkblots, invite a variety of interpreta-

Thematic Apperception Test (TAT)

FIGURE 15.3 *Like the Rorschach inkblots, the TAT can invite a variety of interpretations. Test takers are asked to create a story for a variety of cards similar to the one pictured. From the responses, trained psychologists can derive achievement motivation scores.*

Closing Section 3

Evaluating Information

Ask students to write six statements summing up what they believe are the most important points in this section. Then have them rewrite the statements as true-false questions and use them to quiz a partner. Do the partners agree on which points are most important?

Reviewing Section 3

Have students complete the Section Review questions on page 355.

Section Objective

▶ Identify strategies for taking tests and ways to avoid test anxiety.

This objective is assessed in the Section Review on page 359 and in the Chapter 15 Review.

---

tions. As with the Rorschach, test takers are given the cards one at a time. They are then asked to create a story for each card. For example, people are asked what might have led to the scene depicted on the card, what the person (or people) in the picture is (are) doing, and how the story will end.

The idea behind the TAT is that people's needs and values emerge from the stories they tell. This can be especially true of attitudes toward other people, such as parents and romantic partners. The TAT is also used to measure achievement motivation. As you learned in Chapter 13, achievement motivation refers to the desire to do one's best and to realize one's goals.

For example, a TAT card may show an image of two women. However, it may be unclear exactly what their connection is. Are they mother and daughter? Do they have a close relationship? Are they friends? Here are two stories that could be told about this card:

Story 1   The mother and daughter are both annoyed. They dislike family gatherings. They have little in common and have nothing to say to one another, so they avoid even making eye contact. They are anxious for the awkward moment to be over.

Story 2   The mother and daughter are enjoying a quiet moment together. As they've gotten older, they don't have as much time to spend with one another. But they've remained close and have shared many special times. They feel lucky to have each other's support and love.

Psychologists are trained to derive attitudes and achievement motivation scores from stories such as these. As you might have guessed, the second story suggests a more positive attitude and achievement motivation than the first story.

Studying in a group can often be helpful. Members of the study group can pool their knowledge and take turns quizzing each other.

SECTION 4

Taking Tests

Many students think, "I know the material from my classes, but I just don't do well on tests." Sometimes they are right. But often they are wrong. When students are sure that they know something but cannot quite retrieve it—when it seems to be on the tip of their tongues—it may be that they did not learn it as well as they think they did. That is, some students have trouble on tests because they do not know the subject matter well enough, or they do not know it as well as they think they know it. For them, much of the cure lies in developing better study habits. (See Chapter 6.)

Some students, however, do know the material and yet they still perform poorly on tests. This section offers some general tips on taking tests, as well as specific ways of coping with certain types of test questions. Finally, the section analyzes the subject of test anxiety.

Tips for Taking Tests

Teachers generally determine the types of tests they give and when they give them. Midterm and final exams are usually a matter of school or department policy. And standardized tests, such as the SAT, are scheduled for certain dates throughout the year. You might think you have little control over the tests you take, but in reality there are many things students can do to help take charge of tests.

SECTION 3 REVIEW

Homework Practice Online
Keyword: SY3 HP15

1. What is the function of the validity scales in the MMPI-2?

2. How are the two types of personality tests used?

3. **Critical Thinking**   *Supporting a Point of View*   Because there are no standardized criteria for scoring answers on projective tests such as the Rorschach and the TAT, how accurate do you think they are? Support your answer.

Section 3 Review: Answers

1. The validity scales serve to alert test givers to the possibility of dishonesty or exaggeration on the part of test takers.

2. Psychologists use personality tests to describe and measure various aspects of people's personalities.

3. Some students may say that standardization is one of the criteria for an accurate test, so projective tests may not be accurate. Other students may say that people who have psychological disorders are likely to give such unusual responses on projective tests that it would be clear they have psychological problems, even in the absence of standardized criteria for scoring their responses.

For Your Information

A psychometrician is a person who specializes in the theory and/or practice of administering, scoring, and interpreting the results of psychological tests. Have interested students research the training and skills required to become a psychometrician and report back to the class.

355

Opening Section 4

Motivator

Write the following open-ended statement on the chalkboard: I don't like taking tests because . . . Ask several volunteers to complete the statement. Then generalize by saying that many people do not like taking tests and that some people, such as Marc in the "A Day in the Life" vignette, have test anxiety, or worry excessively over taking tests. Tell students that in Section 4 they will learn about a number of ways to make test taking less stressful and to improve test-taking success.

Journal Activity

The next time students have an upcoming test, encourage them to follow the preparation tips given on pages 356–357. Advise them to start preparing several days before the test. Have them use their journals to write down all the general information they need to study, such as the types of questions to be asked and the topics to be covered. Students should then write out a plan for studying the material. Have them keep a record of how closely they followed their plans, and have students refer back to their plans after they receive their graded tests. Can students identify what did and did not work for them?

Teaching Transparencies with Teacher's Notes

TRANSPARENCY 32:
Test Anxiety

Teaching Section 4

Demonstration

Explain to students that both multiple-choice and true-false questions are objective questions. Have students rewrite the two multiple-choice questions on page 356 as true-false items. For example, item 1 might be rewritten as, "The Kuder Preference Records is an aptitude test." Point out that answering each type of question requires essentially the same information. Have students determine how the information required for these objective questions differs from information that might be needed to answer an essay question about the Kuder Preference Records.

Gather Information Learn where and when the next test will be given. Find out about the types of questions that will be asked and the topics you should study. Most teachers and other test administrators do not mind being asked questions. Some teachers may say that "everything" will be on the test, but others may offer specific information about what they consider important.

In addition, ask students who have already taken the course where test questions tend to come from. Do they tend to come from the textbook or from class notes?

Practice Plan regular study periods. Use your reading assignments and class notes to create test questions that might be similar to those on the exam. Practice answering these test items with the members of your study group. Define key terms on your practice test. Outline the answers to possible essay questions. Try to answer all the questions and exercises in your textbook—even the ones that were not assigned as homework. Some of them may appear on the test. Even if they do not appear on it, they will provide useful practice.

Make the most of your study group. Pool your knowledge. Quiz one another and read the answers to your essay questions aloud. This is a good way to prepare yourself for writing the essays on the actual test. In the process, you will probably discover the areas that need further study.

Be Test-Wise Small oversights can cause you problems on a test. For example, be sure you read the directions carefully and follow them precisely.

Bring the right equipment to tests. Avoid asking your teacher for a pen or a pencil during a test. Doing so communicates a message that you are not prepared for the test and that you do not take the course seriously.

Be sure your pencils are sharpened or that your pens have blue or black ink. Have some loose-leaf paper available, if only to use as scrap paper. Ask your teacher if you may use a pocket dictionary to check your spelling on essays. Teachers may also let you bring calculators and formulas to science tests.

Multiple-Choice Questions

Multiple-choice items are commonly used on many types of tests. They are used in standardized tests, such as the SAT, and they are also used in classroom quizzes and exams. Educators tend psychologists often use multiple-choice questions because they

encourage the student to focus on the right answer (and reject the wrong ones). They can also be graded quickly and objectively.

Below are two sample multiple-choice questions that might appear on a test for this chapter:

1. The Kuder Preference Record is a(n)
   (a) achievement test.
   (b) aptitude test.
   (c) vocational interest inventory.
   (d) personality test.
2. Which of the following tests is an objective personality test?
   (a) the Thematic Apperception Test
   (b) the Minnesota Multiphasic Personality Inventory
   (c) the Standard Assessment Test
   (d) the Rorschach inkblot test

Here are some hints for doing well on multiple-choice tests:

- *Try to answer the question before you look at the choices.* When you see "Kuder Preference Record," turn it into a question: "What is the Kuder Preference Record?" If you can describe the test to yourself, it will be easy to select the correct choice.

- *Consider every possible choice.* The last choice may read "All of the above." If you have time, find a coherent reason for eliminating each choice you reject.

- *Look for answers that are opposites.* When you see two answers that are opposite in meaning, one of them is likely to be the correct choice.

- *Look for the best choice listed.* It may be that no choice is perfect, but one choice is probably better than the others.

- *Mark difficult questions so that you can come back to them later.* Do not let a tough question eat up your time.

- *Guess only when the odds of gaining points outweigh the odds of losing points.* For example, always guess when there is no penalty for wrong answers. But if full credit is subtracted for wrong answers and you have no idea which is the correct choice, do not guess.

- *Change your answer if you think you have made a mistake.* It is only a myth that you should go with your first hunch. Your hunch could be wrong, and by looking at the question again, you may come up with the right answer.

Meeting Individual Needs: Learners with Limited English Proficiency

True-false questions can be difficult for students with limited English proficiency because the wording of the items is very important. Devise several true-false items covering material in one chapter section, and guide students in using the hints to decide whether each item is true or false. For example, "The Kuder Preference Records is a projective test with a forced-choice format." Ask students what is true and false about the statement. Can the statement as a whole be true?

Cooperative Learning

Organize the class into small groups, and have each group write four questions covering the material from any one paragraph in the chapter. The groups should write one of each type of question described in Section 4. Have the groups exchange questions and then try to answer them. Ask volunteers to read aloud questions they think are particularly good examples of each type. Lead students in discussing which type of question seems best suited for particular types of material. How might students use this knowledge when preparing for exams?

By staying relaxed and keeping certain rules of thumb in mind, students can improve their scores on a variety of types of tests. The most important rule of thumb is to study thoroughly.

TRUTH OR fiction ▪ REVISITED ▪

It is not true that you should always go with your first guess on a multiple-choice test. If you believe that you have made an error, you should change your answer. Often people arrive at the correct answer after thinking about the answer again.

True-False Questions

True-false questions can be tricky. After all, if half the questions are true and half are false, you could earn a grade of 50 percent simply by guessing. Below are two sample true-false questions that might appear on a test for this chapter:

1. The Minnesota Multiphasic Personality Inventory (MMPI-2) is a subjective personality test used in clinical work.
2. All psychologists consider the Rorschach inkblot test to be a valid measure for determining psychological health.

The following pointers can help you maximize your performance on true-false items:

- *For the item to be true, every part of it must be true.* If one part is false, then the entire item must be false. The question about the MMPI-2 correctly identifies it as a personality test used in clinical work, but it is an objective test, not a subjective test. Therefore, the answer to this question would be "false."
- *Be wary of items that use absolutes such as* all, always, *or* never. These items are usually false. Since only some, not all, psychologists consider the Rorschach to be a valid measure of psychological health, the answer to the second question would be "false."
- *Items that provide more information and are longer than others tend to be true.*

Keep in mind that these are only rules of thumb, however. They are not foolproof instructions. Your best strategy is still to study thoroughly and know the answers on your own.

Short-Answer Questions

Short-answer items ask the test taker to give a brief response to a question. Here are some sample short-answer questions:

1. What is an achievement test?
2. What is the difference between an objective test and a projective test?

Here are some pointers for responding to short-answer questions:

- *Answer in brief but complete sentences.* For example, the answer to the first question might be phrased as follows: "An achievement test measures a person's skill or knowledge in a specific subject or field of study."
- *Include significant terms in your answer.* In the answer to question 1, the significant terms would include *skill, knowledge, subject,* and *field of study.*
- *Use detail if time and space allow.* A detail added to the answer might be the following: "An achievement test is used to determine how much knowledge a person has acquired in a particular subject."

Essay Questions

The first step in answering an essay question is making certain you have understood the question. When students do not understand the question, the answer may draw comments such as the following: "Strays from the question" or "Nicely written, but misses the point."

Using Visuals

Point out to the class how good the student in the photograph on page 357 seems to feel after earning a high score on a test. Tell students that such emotional rewards can serve as positive reinforcement for good study habits. Have students relate this type of reinforcement to the process of operant conditioning that they learned about in Chapter 6.

Cross-Curricular Link: Art/Literature

Have students draw a poster or write a poem promoting good study and test-taking habits. Ask volunteers to discuss their posters or poems. Display these materials in the classroom.

Class Discussion

Initiate a discussion of ways to improve performance on multiple-choice tests. Ask the class to read the hints listed on page 356 and then try to apply them to the two sample multiple-choice questions that precede the hints. Have students discuss which hints work best and why. Which ones do they already use? Can they think of others? Write their suggestions on the chalkboard. Have students copy the list in their journals and refer to it as needed.

Guided Practice

To put the material on test anxiety into a broader psychological framework, tell students that cognitive restructuring is a method of cognitive therapy, which they will read about in Chapter 19. Explain that cognitive therapists help people with anxiety, depression, and similar problems by helping them understand that their feelings may be based on faulty assumptions or thought processes. Ask the class to explain why a thought such as "I know I'm going to flunk this exam" is likely to be based on faulty ways of thinking.

Independent Practice

Have pairs of students write monologues that demonstrate cognitive restructuring. One student in each pair should write negative statements about an upcoming exam, such as "I know I'll forget the dates of all the battles" or "It's impossible for me to remember formulas." The other student in each pair should then write corresponding positive statements, such as "I know I'll remember all the dates (or formulas) if I review them every day this week." Ask volunteers to share their monologues with the class for discussion.

Using Visuals

Call students' attention to the chart on page 358. Discuss how important guiding words such as those shown in the chart are in structuring the direction an essay should take. Because guiding words establish the focus of an essay, it is important that students have a clear understanding of what these guiding words mean. For each guiding word in the chart, have a volunteer define the word, create an essay question using that word, and answer the essay question. Make sure that students understand the sometimes subtle differences between the guiding words.

Guiding Words Found in Essay Questions

Analyze	Identify
Compare	Illustrate
Contrast	Interpret
Criticize	Justify
Define	List
Describe	Prove
Discuss	State
Enumerate	Support
Evaluate	Trace
Explain	

FIGURE 15.4 *The first step in answering an essay question is to make sure that you understand the question. Look for key words such as those in the list above to guide your answer.*

Read the directions carefully and look for key words to guide your answer. Figure 15.4 lists some of these key words. Ignoring them increases the chances that you will omit important points from your answer.

Before beginning to write your essay, make a quick outline on a piece of scrap paper to help you organize your thoughts. The outline should help you keep track of the main points you wish to make in your answer. Mark where you will start and where you will end. Jot down key terms that represent ideas you wish to expand on in your essay. If you run out of time before you complete the essay, attach the outline to show where you were headed. It may help your grade (and it certainly will not hurt it).

Express your strongest ideas first. When you lead with the concepts you know best, you build a foundation for presenting a strong argument.

How long should your essay be? A good rule of thumb is "Don't count words; just answer the question." Teachers will reward you for being right on the mark as long as you have provided sufficient support for your argument.

TRUTH **OR** **fiction** ■ REVISITED ■ *It is not true that the longer your answer to an essay question is, the better your score on that question is likely to be.* Essay questions are graded on how completely and accurately you have covered the main points of the topic, regardless of how long the answer is.

Test Anxiety

A DAY IN THE LIFE Like Marc, some students become anxious before and during exams. The anxiety they experience consists of feelings of dread and foreboding. They may sense that something terrible—though they may not know what—is going to happen. Test anxiety ranges from increased tension to actual physical symptoms, such as rapid breathing, pounding heartbeat, light-headedness or dizziness, nausea, and diarrhea.

Anxiety may be very uncomfortable, but it is not always a bad thing. It is normal to feel somewhat anxious as a test approaches. Anxiety shows that we understand the importance of the occasion and that failure may have serious consequences. Test anxiety

The test anxiety that many students feel before and during a test can often be overcome by being prepared and thinking positively.

Closing Section 4

Synthesizing Information

Ask students to synthesize the material in this section by explaining how poor preparation for tests can lead to test anxiety. Also have them outline steps for improving test preparedness.

Reviewing Section 4

Have students complete the Section Review questions on page 359.

Extension

Have students apply the tips they learned in this section to preparing for the SAT. How would they prepare themselves for the exam without becoming too anxious? How would they study and practice the content of the exam? What would they do during the exam to ensure that they were working at peak performance? Have students create a one-page plan that addresses these questions. Also have students explain why they consider their plans to be feasible and efficient.

For those who suffer from test anxiety, practicing cognitive restructuring can eventually result in better grades.

reflects the thoughts of students before and during the test. Such thoughts might include the following:

- "I study as hard as I can, but my mind just blanks when the tests are distributed."
- "What's wrong with me? I know the material, but I just can't take tests."
- "I just know I'm going to flunk."
- "I wish I could get out of here. I wish the test was over."
- "I'm not going to have enough time to finish."

Test-anxious students allow these thoughts and self-doubts to distract them, preventing them from focusing on the test itself.

The good news, however, is that test anxiety can be overcome. The ways of handling test anxiety include being prepared, overlearning, and changing the way one thinks about tests. Changing the way one thinks about tests can also change the way in which one's body responds to test situations.

Be Prepared One way to overcome test anxiety is to be prepared. Actors who have thoroughly memorized their lines may still be anxious when they hear their cue, but they are less likely to forget the line they have to speak. If you study carefully and review the material regularly, you can be confident that you will recall what you have learned.

Review the material regularly before a test and avoid cramming. Learning takes time. Studying a reasonable amount every day is far more effective than cramming suddenly the night before. You can

begin to cope with possible test anxiety right from the beginning of the semester—by planning a regular study schedule and sticking to it.

Overlearn Overlearning means reviewing the material over and over, even after you think you have mastered it. Overlearning accomplishes two objectives: remembering the subject matter longer and building confidence. Overlearning makes you realize, "I *really* know this stuff!"

Think Helpful Thoughts What if you are well prepared for tests and still make yourself anxious with self-defeating thoughts? There are strategies for ending upsetting thoughts and focusing on the task at hand—the test.

What are the negative thoughts that occur to you at test-taking times? Write them down. Once you are aware of these negative thoughts, you can replace them with positive ones. For example, replace "I'm probably going to fail this test" with "I'm prepared for this test, and I know I'll do well."

This method of coping is called cognitive restructuring. **Cognitive restructuring** means consciously changing the thoughts one has in a particular situation. Cognitive restructuring consists of the following four steps:

1. Identify self-defeating thoughts, paying special attention to the ones that seem exaggerated.
2. Replace self-defeating thoughts with positive and encouraging messages to yourself.
3. Imagine yourself in the testing situation and practice positive thinking.
4. Reward yourself for thinking positively.

If you consistently practice cognitive restructuring, chances are you will begin to see a change for the better. Eventually, you will become less anxious and more confident about taking tests. Your grades may reflect the changes.

SECTION 4 REVIEW

Homework Practice Online
Keyword: SY3 HP15

1. How does making an outline help one answer an essay question more effectively?
2. List the four steps of cognitive restructuring to cope with test anxiety.
3. **Critical Thinking** *Identifying Cause and Effect* What type of stress do some students feel before or during tests, and how might this stress affect their scores?

Section 4 Review: Answers

1. Making an outline can help you organize your thoughts and keep track of the main points you wish to make in your answer. It can also let the grader know where you were headed with an answer you did not have time to finish.

2. The four steps of cognitive restructuring are identifying self-defeating thoughts, replacing these thoughts with helpful thoughts, practicing positive thinking while imagining the testing situation, and rewarding yourself for thinking positively.

3. Some students feel anxious before tests. Test anxiety can have a negative effect on their scores.

Chapter 15 Review: Answers

Writing a Summary

See the section subtitles for the main topics in the chapter.

Identifying People and Ideas

1. tests that measure behavior in such places as classrooms and hospitals

2. reports in which people comment on their own attitudes, feelings, and behavior

359

15 REVIEW AND ASSESSMENT RESOURCES

Technology
▶ Chapter 15 Test Generator (on the One-Stop Planner)
▶ HRW Go site

Reinforcement, Review, and Assessment
▶ Chapter 15 Review, pp. 360–361
▶ Chapter Review and Activities with Answer Key
▶ Alternative Assessment Handbook
▶ Portfolio Assessment Handbook
▶ Chapter 15 Test (Form A or B)

PSYCHOLOGY PROJECTS

Linking to Community Invite a psychologist from the community to talk to the class about the types of psychological testing that are used in his or her practice. If possible, have the psychologist bring sample tests to share with the class. Ask the guest to discuss the following questions:

---

3. a test that is administered and scored the same way every time

4. established standards of performance

5. a test that measures people's skills and the knowledge they have in specific academic areas

6. tests generally used to determine whether a person is likely to do well in a given field of work or study

7. format in which the test taker is forced to choose one of several answers, even if none of them seem to fit his or her interests precisely

8. a test with no clearly specified answers

9. a test format that is ambiguous

10. changing the thoughts one has in a particular situation

Understanding Main Ideas

1. Two examples are the SAT and the GRE.

2. Aptitude tests are generally used to determine whether a person is likely to do well in a given field of work.

3. They were based on the answers of people already diagnosed with particular psychological disorders.

4. Cognitive restructuring might help a student with test anxiety.

Thinking Critically

1. Missing just one item on a test of only a few items can result in a low score, even when test takers know most of the material.

2. Interest inventories do not necessarily reflect abilities, and free-time

---

15 REVIEW

Chapter

Writing a Summary

Using standard grammar, spelling, sentence structure, and punctuation, summarize the information in this chapter. Consider:
• the purposes, characteristics, and types of psychological tests
• strategies for taking tests and avoiding test anxiety

Identifying People and Ideas

Identify the following terms or people and use them in appropriate sentences.

1. behavior-rating scales
2. self-reports
3. standardized test
4. norms
5. achievement tests
6. aptitude tests
7. forced-choice format
8. projective tests
9. open-ended format
10. cognitive restructuring

Understanding Main Ideas

SECTION 1 (pp. 344–347)
1. What are two examples of transformed score tests used by schools?

SECTION 2 (pp. 347–350)
2. How are aptitude tests generally used?

SECTION 3 (pp. 350–355)
3. How were the clinical scales of the Minnesota Multiphasic Personality Inventory (MMPI) originally created?

SECTION 4 (pp. 355–359)
4. What steps might a student take to overcome test anxiety?

Thinking Critically

1. Evaluating Why is a longer test generally more valid and reliable?

2. Analyzing Information Why is it important not to depend too much on the results of interest inventories?

3. Supporting a Point of View Do you think it is possible for psychologists to accurately measure a person's personality using only multiple-choice and true-false questions? Explain your answer.

4. Categorizing What are the advantages and disadvantages of using self-reports, rather than observing behavior, to measure personality?

5. Drawing Inferences and Conclusions Why do you think people in the same occupation often share the same interests, even outside interests not directly related to their jobs?

Writing About Psychology

1. Analyzing Information Popular magazines often include tests or self-inventories that claim to measure such diverse qualities as one's ability to handle money or how happy one's marriage is. Look through magazines at home or in the library and then create an outline that describes the test. Consider the following questions as you prepare your outline: What does the test claim to measure? Do you think it has any scientific validity? Why or why not? Why do you think these tests are so prevalent? Briefly present your outline to the class. As a class, discuss the kinds of issues these tests seem to focus on.

2. Supporting a Point of View The importance and the validity of the Scholastic Assessment Test (SAT) have been a subject of debate for the past several years. Research some of the issues surrounding the SAT. Write an essay stating your position on the use of the SAT as a part of the college admission process. Be sure to include references to your research to support your position. Use the graphic organizer below to help you write your essay.

(For) ◀— Use of the SAT —▶ (Against)

- What kind of tests do you administer?

- Why do you give those kinds of tests?

- Do you administer tests (such as the SAT) that are designed to predict how well students will do in college?

Building Social Studies Skills

Interpreting Graphs

Study the graph below. Then use the information in the graph to help you answer the questions that follow.

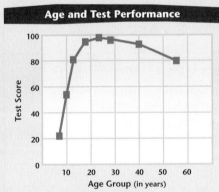

Age and Test Performance

Source: Sundberg, *Assessment of Persons*, 1977

1. Which of the following statements accurately reflects the information in the graph?
   a. Most 20 year-old test takers do not perform as well as most 10 year-old test takers.
   b. Growing older causes a decline in test performance.
   c. Performance on tests gradually declines after age 10.
   d. Test scores improve dramatically during adolescence.

2. What areas of research might this graph lead psychologists to investigate?

Analyzing Primary Sources

Read the following excerpt, in which Theodora Abel considers the issue of culture and testing. Then answer the questions that follow.

"On the island of Montserrat in the Caribbean until recently there was no electricity, nor windowpanes in homes, and no motion picture houses, so that the idea of switching on lights, breaking windowpanes and replacing them, or knowing what to do in case of fire in a theater (items on various tests) would not have made much sense to children. At least these phenomena would not have had the same impact as they would if the children had had direct experience of them. Non-familiarity with the kind of stimuli presented or the kind of performance expected (looking at ink-blots, copying block designs, tracing through mazes, making up plots and stories) can cause test results to be incorrectly interpreted unless the psychologist takes these factors into account. "

3. Which statement best reflects Abel's argument?
   a. Psychologists must be aware of cultural differences between groups when administering tests.
   b. People from poor backgrounds rarely do well on assessment tests.
   c. Cultural differences have no effect on psychological tests.
   d. Testing is an inherently flawed process and should be abandoned.

4. According to the excerpt, how can the test design itself lead to problems for test takers?

PSYCHOLOGY PROJECTS

Cooperative Learning

Applying Psychology With a partner, review the tips on taking tests that are discussed in this chapter. Decide on a visual—such as a booklet, flyer, or poster—that gives advice to other students about how to take tests. Be sure that the visual clearly illustrates the test–taking advice that you want to convey to your classmates.

internet connect

Internet Activity: go.hrw.com
KEYWORD: SY3 PS15

Choose an activity on psychological tests to:
- define the concept of "transformed score" and explain percentile grade equivalent scores.
- write a report that describes psychological testing.
- design questions for a personality test.

Gender Roles

CHAPTER RESOURCE MANAGER

Objectives	Pacing Guide		Reproducible and Review Resources

SECTION 1: What are Gender Roles? (pp. 364–365)

Define gender roles and gender stereotypes, and explain the difference between the two terms.

Regular 1 day | **Block Scheduling** .5 day

Block Scheduling Handbook with Team Teaching Strategies, Chapter 16

E Research Projects and Activities for Teaching Psychology

REV Section 1 Review, p. 365

SECTION 2: Gender Differences (pp. 366–371)

Describe gender differences in cognitive abilities, personality, and behavior.

Regular 1 day | **Block Scheduling** .5 day

Block Scheduling Handbook with Team Teaching Strategies, Chapter 16

E Creating a Psychology Fair, Activity 10

REV Section 2 Review, p. 371

SECTION 3: Gender Typing (pp. 372–377)

Define gender typing, and discuss several theories that explain how it may occur.

Regular 1 day | **Block Scheduling** .5 day

Block Scheduling Handbook with Team Teaching Strategies, Chapter 16

SM Mastering Critical Thinking Skills 16

RS Essay and Research Themes for Advanced Placement Students, Theme 14

REV Section 3 Review, p. 377

SECTION 4: Variation in Gender Roles (pp. 377–379)

Explain how gender roles have changed over time, and identify the ways in which they can vary from culture to culture.

Regular 1 day | **Block Scheduling** .5 day

Block Scheduling Handbook with Team Teaching Strategies, Chapter 16

PS Readings and Case Studies, Chapter 16

REV Section 4 Review, p. 379

Chapter Resource Key

PS Primary Sources
RS Reading Support
E Enrichment
SM Skills Mastery

A Assessment
REV Review
Transparencies
CD-ROM

 Video
 Internet
 Holt Presentation Maker Using Microsoft® PowerPoint®

 One-Stop Planner CD–ROM

See the *One-Stop Planner* for a complete list of additional resources for students and teachers.

One-Stop Planner CD-ROM

It's easy to plan lessons, select resources, and print out materials for your students when you use the **One-Stop Planner CD-ROM with Test Generator.**

Technology Resources

 One-Stop Planner, Lesson 16.1
 Homework Practice Online
 CNN. Presents Psychology: Gender Roles
 HRW Go Site

 One-Stop Planner, Lesson 16.2
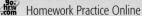 Homework Practice Online

 One-Stop Planner, Lesson 16.3
 Homework Practice Online
 Teaching Transparencies 33: Modeling Behavior
 HRW Go Site

 One-Stop Planner, Lesson 16.4
 Homework Practice Online
 HRW Go Site

Chapter Review and Assessment

HRW Go site
REV Chapter 16 Review, pp. 380–381
REV Chapter Review Activities with Answer Key

A Chapter 16 Test (Form A or B)
A Portfolio Assessment Handbook
A Alternative Assessment Handbook

Chapter 16 Test Generator (on the One-Stop Planner)
Global Skill Builder CD-ROM

⏎ internet connect

HRW ONLINE RESOURCES

GO TO: go.hrw.com
Then type in a keyword.

TEACHER HOME PAGE
  KEYWORD: SY3 Teacher

CHAPTER INTERNET ACTIVITIES
  KEYWORD: SY3 PS16
  Choose an activity on gender roles to have students:
  • create a poster illustrating gender roles and the way in which roles are reinforced by mass media.
  • write a "help wanted" ad and research gender roles of the past.
  • make a chart outlining theories of gender typing.

CHAPTER ENRICHMENT LINKS
  KEYWORD: SY3 CH16

ONLINE ASSESSMENT
  Homework Practice
  KEYWORD: SY3 HP16
  Standardized Test Prep
  KEYWORD: SY3 STP16
  Rubrics
  KEYWORD: SS Rubrics

CONTENT UPDATES
  KEYWORD: SS Content Updates

HOLT PRESENTATION MAKER
  KEYWORD: SY3 PPT16

ONLINE READING SUPPORT
  KEYWORD: SS Strategies

CURRENT EVENTS
  KEYWORD: S3 Current Events

Additional Resources

PRINT RESOURCES FOR TEACHERS

Goffman, E. (1976). *Gender advertisements.* New York: Harper & Row.

Lonner, W., & Malpas, E. (Eds.). (1994). *Psychology and culture.* Needham Heights, MA: Allyn & Bacon.

Unger, R., & Crawford, M. (1992). *Women and gender.* New York: McGraw-Hill.

PRINT RESOURCES FOR STUDENTS

Doyle, J. (1989). *The male experience.* Dubuque, IA: W. C. Brown.

Eagle, C., & Colman, C. (1993). *All that she can be.* New York: Simon & Schuster.

Hyde, J. S. (1991). *Half the human experience.* Lexington, MA: D. C. Heath.

Tannen, D. (1990). *You just don't understand: Women and men in conversation.* New York: Morrow.

MULTIMEDIA RESOURCES

Gender and communication (VHS). Social Studies School Service, 10200 Jefferson Boulevard, Room 33, P.O. Box 802, Culver City, CA 90232-0802.

Sex and gender (VHS). Social Studies School Service, 10200 Jefferson Boulevard, Room 33, P.O. Box 802, Culver City, CA 90232-0802.

Sexual stereotypes in media: Superman and the bride (VHS). Films for the Humanities & Sciences, P.O. Box 2053, Princeton, NJ 08543-2053.

GENDER ROLES

Introducing Chapter 16

Tell students to write two sentences as quickly as possible, writing down the first thoughts that come into their heads. The first sentence should begin, "The girl . . ."; and the second sentence should begin "The boy . . ." Have students read their sentence pairs aloud. Compare and contrast the roles assigned to the girls with those assigned to the boys in the various sentences. Group the sentences in which the subjects play similar roles. Ask students whether they can make any generalizations about how they tend to see the roles of males versus those of females. What percentage of the males in the sentences perform activities traditionally associated with males? What percentage of the females perform traditional female activities? Then tell students that Chapter 16 examines traditional and changing gender roles.

Sections

Each of the four questions identified on page 362 corresponds to one of these sections.

16 Chapter

GENDER ROLES

Read to Discover

1 What are gender roles and gender stereotypes, and how do they differ?

2 How have some studies indicated gender differences in cognitive abilities, personality, and behavior?

3 What is gender typing, and what are several theories that explain how it may occur?

4 How have gender roles changed over time, and in what ways can they vary from culture to culture?

Each chapter begins with a vignette, called "A Day in the Life," that relates the information discussed in the chapter to the everyday events in the lives of a group of fictional high school students. The text of the chapter occasionally refers back to the vignette to demonstrate the application of the concept being discussed. An icon marked "A Day in the Life" is placed next to these references.

Copy the following graphic organizer onto the chalkboard as you introduce the topic of gender roles.

(Gender Roles) ◄——► (Gender Stereotypes)

A DAY IN THE LIFE

April 23

Marc, Janet, Dan, and Linda were at the recreation center following their school's annual career day. Suddenly, they were all thinking about their futures.

"What's wrong, Dan?" Janet asked. She had noticed that Dan seemed exceptionally quiet.

"This career fair just made me realize that I still don't know for sure what I want to do after graduation. I'm afraid that if I don't make some decisions I may end up just like my Uncle John," Dan said.

"Uncle John was laid off from his job, and my Aunt Debbie had to go to work to support the family. Now she's making more money than Uncle John ever did."

"That's great, isn't it?" Linda said.

"It should be, but ever since Aunt Debbie went to work, my uncle is always upset. I think he can't accept that my aunt is making more money than he did. All I know is, when I'm older I want to have a good career so I can support my family."

"Are you saying you wouldn't want your wife to work outside the home?" Janet asked defensively.

"It's not that I wouldn't *want* her to work. I just feel that she shouldn't *have* to work. I should be able to support her and our family."

"I don't understand that attitude," Linda said. "My parents both work, and usually they both help around the house. But when my grandparents visit from Mexico, my dad won't be caught doing any housework. I guess he doesn't want his parents to see him doing work they still consider 'women's work.'"

"Some people don't realize that times change," Janet responded. "Ever since my parents' divorce, my mom has had to work nights and take care of the house during the day. She still manages to have time for me, though. She's been great."

"I plan to have a career," Linda said. "I've always wanted to do something with math—maybe engineering or architecture."

Grinning, Linda turned to Marc and asked, "So, Marc, what would you think about staying at home while your wife went to work?"

• • •

Dan's uncle was having a hard time accepting his wife's new role, but she also was having a difficult time. She worked all day at her job and then had to take care of the home. She also had to deal with her husband's feelings of frustration and depression. Her husband was normally a good and generous person, but he was feeling trapped by his beliefs about the kinds of behavior that are appropriate for men and for women.

Some people, such as Dan's uncle, believe that a woman's place is in the home with the children and that a man's place is on the job, working to support them. Other people believe that a wide range of behaviors is appropriate for men and women. This chapter explores these and other beliefs about what it means to be male and what it means to be female.

Key Terms

- gender
- gender roles
- gender stereotypes
- nurturance
- gender typing
- lateralization
- modeling
- gender schema

WHY PSYCHOLOGY MATTERS

Gender roles often differ significantly from culture to culture. Use CNNfyi.com or other current events sources to learn more about gender roles in different cultures around the world.

CNNfyi.com

Using Key Terms

Before students read the chapter, have them write down each key vocabulary term. As students read Chapter 16, have them rephrase the definition of each key term in their own words and create an original sentence to illustrate the meaning of the term. Challenge students to find examples of the use of some of these key terms in newspaper or magazine articles.

Journal Activity

Before students read Chapter 16, have them write a paragraph in their journals describing what they believe are the roles of men and women. After students have read the chapter, have them reread their paragraphs and consider whether their beliefs about the roles of men and women have changed. Have them write a paragraph explaining why they would or would not now revise their earlier paragraphs.

Section Objective

▶ Define gender roles and gender stereotypes, and explain the difference between the two terms.

This objective is assessed in the Section Review on page 365 and in the Chapter 16 Review.

Opening Section 1

Motivator

List the following personality traits on the chalkboard: independent, helpful, hostile, and kind. Have students rate themselves on each trait, using a scale from 1 to 5 (with 1 being the lowest rating and 5 being the highest rating). Then have students rate women as a group and men as a group on each trait. How do students' ratings of themselves as individuals compare with their ratings of their gender group? Have students keep their ratings to discuss after reading Section 1.

Using Truth or Fiction

Each chapter opens with several "Truth or Fiction" statements that relate to the concepts discussed in the chapter. Ask students whether they think each statement is true or false. Answers to each item as well as explanations are provided at appropriate points within the text under the heading "Truth or Fiction Revisited."

TOPIC: Gender Roles
GO TO: go.hrw.com
KEYWORD: SY3 PS16

Have students access the Internet through the HRW Go site to research variation in gender roles through time. Then ask students to create a poster that illustrates how gender roles have changed over the last century, the impact on individuals and society, and how gender roles are transmitted through media.

Technology Resources

 CNN. Presents Psychology: Gender Roles

Read the following statements about psychology. Do you think they are true or false? You will learn whether each statement is true or false as you read the chapter.

- Men generally demonstrate more aggressive behavior than women.
- Women tend to be more talkative than men.
- The qualities men look for in a potential mate are different from the qualities women look for.
- Boys and girls are treated in much the same way until about age three.
- Much of the behavior we think of as typical male or female behavior we are not born with but learn from other members of our culture.

SECTION 1

What Are Gender Roles?

We all have physical characteristics that make us different from other people. Height, hair color, eye color, and many other physical traits help to differentiate who we are. Possibly the most fundamental physical characteristic of any human being is his or her gender. **Gender** refers to the sex of an individual, either male or female. Like hair color and eye color, gender is a biological trait that is fixed by the genes before birth.

Gender Roles

Closely related to the concept of gender is the idea of **gender roles**—widely accepted societal expectations about how males and females should behave. Gender roles define what is considered to be appropriate masculine and feminine behavior in a particular culture.

 When Dan explained that he thought he should be able to support his wife and family, he was expressing his belief in the type of behavior that he considered appropriate for men in American society. That is, he was adhering to a gender role.

Unlike gender itself, gender roles are not genetically determined. Rather, gender roles appear to be a product of both biological and social factors.

Gender Trait Stereotypes Around the World

Stereotypes of Males	Stereotypes of Females
Active	Affectionate
Adventurous	Appreciative
Aggressive	Cautious
Arrogant	Changeable
Autocratic	Charming
Capable	Complicated
Coarse	Dependent
Conceited	Dreamy
Confident	Emotional
Courageous	Excitable
Cruel	Faultfinding
Determined	Fearful
Disorderly	Fickle
Enterprising	Foolish
Hardheaded	Forgiving
Individualistic	Fussy
Inventive	Gentle
Loud	Imaginative
Obnoxious	Modest
Opinionated	Nervous
Pleasure-seeking	Patient
Precise	Pleasant
Quick	Self-pitying
Rational	Sensitive
Realistic	Sentimental
Reckless	Sexy
Resourceful	Softhearted
Rigid	Sophisticated
Robust	Submissive
Sharp-witted	Suggestible
Show-off	Superstitious
Steady	Talkative
Stern	Timid
Stingy	Touchy
Tough	Unambitious
Unscrupulous	Understanding
	Unstable
	Weak
	Worrying

FIGURE 16.1 *Psychologists John Williams and Deborah Best (1994, p. 193, Table 1) found that people in 30 nations around the world tended to agree on the nature of masculine and feminine gender trait stereotypes.*

Teaching Section 1

Role-Playing

Give pairs of students a simple scenario to act out for the class (e.g., grocery shopping, having an argument, getting lost while driving). Have one student in each pair play the female role and the other the male role (not necessarily according to their own sex). Tell the students to act out the scene in a stereotypically male or female way. Following the role-play, have the students explain how the behavior they portrayed is stereotypical. Have the class compare the stereotypes with the reality of modern-day gender roles.

Closing Section 1

Follow Up

Tell students to retrieve the ratings they compiled in the Motivator activity on page 364. Have them compare their ratings with the findings of the study discussed on page 365. Do their ratings also find that gender differences are much smaller than stereotypes suggest?

Reviewing Section 1

Have students complete the Section Review questions on page 365.

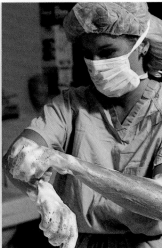

Many kinds of work that people do today can be done equally well by men and women. As an increased number of women have entered the workforce, gender roles have become less rigid. **How might this affect future generations?**

Although one speaks of "playing a role," people do not *play* gender roles in the same way that they play roles on the stage. That is to say, they do not usually see themselves as pretending to be someone they are not. Instead, for most people, gender roles are simply a part of who they are and how they see themselves.

Gender Stereotypes

Gender roles can become so rigid that they develop into **gender stereotypes**, which are fixed and oversimplified beliefs about the ways in which men and women ought to behave. Many gender stereotypes in the United States are linked to the traditional view of men as breadwinners and women as homemakers. In our society, people tend to see the feminine gender stereotypes as warm, emotional, dependent, gentle, helpful, mild, patient, submissive, and interested in the arts. The typical masculine gender stereotype is perceived as independent, competitive, tough, protective, logical, and competent at business, math, and science. Women are traditionally expected to care for the children and cook the meals. Cross-cultural studies confirm that these gender role stereotypes are widespread. (See Figure 16.1.) For example, in their survey of 30 countries, John Williams and Deborah Best

(1994) found that men are more likely to be judged to be active, adventurous, aggressive, arrogant, and autocratic. Women are more likely to be seen as fault finding, fearful, fickle, foolish, and fussy.

Even emotions are stereotyped. Subjects in one study believed that women more often than men experienced the emotions of sadness, fear, and sympathy (Plant et al., 2000). But they thought that men were more likely to feel anger and pride.

Gender stereotypes have tended to keep women in the home. Educational opportunities for women have traditionally been more limited. Today many jobs are still stereotyped as primarily for women—for example, nursing and teaching in elementary school. However, large numbers of women have entered some professions previously limited to men, such as medicine and law.

SECTION 1 REVIEW

Homework Practice Online
Keyword: SY3 HP16

1. Define *gender, gender role,* and *gender stereotype*.

2. **Critical Thinking** *Contrasting* In what ways do *gender roles* and *gender stereotypes* differ?

Section Objective

▶ Describe gender differences in cognitive abilities, personality, and behavior.

This objective is assessed in the Section Review on page 371 and in the Chapter 16 Review.

Opening Section 2

Motivator

Ask students what measurable cognitive and behavioral differences they think can be found between males and females. Write their responses on the chalkboard. For each difference listed, ask students to supply evidence to support their beliefs. Then have students consider whether each difference listed is biologically based or learned through experience. Tell them that in Section 2 they will read about gender differences and what research has discovered about the origins of these differences.

For Your Information

Gender differences in behavior have been observed in very young infants. Just a few hours after birth, females are more sensitive to touch than males. Female infants are more disturbed by loud noises than male infants and also seem to respond more to adults who are talking to them than do males. At the age of about four months, most baby girls can distinguish photographs of people they know from photographs of strangers; baby boys generally cannot.

Class Discussion

Have students discuss whether or not their personal experiences and observations support the statement that girls generally outperform boys in computation in elementary school, whereas males tend to outperform females in mathematics in high school. How would students account for this change?

SECTION 2

Gender Differences

What kinds of differences actually exist between men and women? There are obvious physical differences between the sexes, but other, less obvious differences between men and women also seem to exist. These include differences in cognitive, or intellectual, abilities and differences in personality and behavior. As we shall see, psychologists disagree about whether these differences are biologically based or learned through experience.

It is important to note that *group* differences between men and women in certain traits and abilities says nothing about the differences among *individual* men and women. In fact, there is greater variation within each gender group than there is between the average man and the average woman.

Physical Differences

Several physical differences between the sexes are usually apparent because males and females differ in both primary and secondary sex characteristics. Primary sex characteristics refer to the organs of the reproductive system. For example, women have ovaries and men have testes. Secondary sex characteristics include such traits as deeper voices and greater amounts of facial hair in men and smaller body size and wider hips in women. These traits are controlled by sex hormones, which, in turn, are determined by genes.

Differences in Cognitive Abilities

It was once believed that men were more intelligent than women because they had greater knowledge of world affairs and skill in science and industry. Although men could demonstrate greater knowledge and skill in these areas, this did not reflect differences in intelligence. Rather, it merely reflected the exclusion of women from world affairs, science, and industry. Assessments of intelligence do not show overall gender differences in cognitive abilities (Halpern & LaMay, 2000). However, reviews of the research suggest that girls are somewhat superior to boys in verbal abilities, such as the ability to make up sentences and paragraphs, the ability to find

words that are similar in meaning to other words, spelling, knowledge of foreign languages, and pronunciations (Halpern, 1997).

Girls seem to acquire language somewhat faster than boys do. Also, in the United States far more boys than girls have reading problems, ranging from reading below grade level to severe learning disabilities (Halpern, 1997; Neisser et al., 1996). Men headed for college seem to catch up in verbal skills.

On the other hand, men seem to be somewhat superior in the ability to manipulate visual images held in memory. Psychological tests of spatial ability assess skills such as finding figures embedded within larger designs and mentally rotating figures in space (See Figure 16.2.) Men apparently excel in visual-spatial abilities of the sort used in mathematics, science, and even map reading (Grön et al., 2000; Halpern & LaMay, 2000). One study compared the navigation strategies of 90 male and 104 female college students (Dabbs et al., 1998). In giving directions, college men more often referred to miles and directional coordinates in terms of north, south, east, and west. College women were more likely to refer to landmarks and turns to the right or left.

Studies in the United States and elsewhere find that men generally obtain higher scores on mathematics tests than women (Beller & Gafni, 2000; Gallagher et al., 2000; Halpern & LaMay, 2000). Females excel in computational ability in elementary school, however. Males excel in

The gender gap in mathematical abilities seems to be closing, as more females are enrolling in advanced mathematics courses.

Teaching Section 2

Meeting Individual Needs: Learners Having Difficulty

Some students may have difficulty understanding that there is greater variation in cognitive abilities within each gender group than there is between the average male and the average female. Explain that while the average of all the boys' scores on a mathematics test may be slightly higher than the average of all the girls' scores, there will be many boys and many girls who score both far higher and far lower than either average. Use hypothetical test scores to clarify this concept.

Demonstration

Organize the class into two groups, according to gender. Have each group perform the visual-spatial tests shown in Figure 16.2 on page 367. Do the males in the class tend to outperform the females? If so, by what degree? Then have the class discuss how early socialization patterns may encourage the development of mathematical and visual-spatial abilities in males and verbal abilities in females.

Visual-Spatial Tests

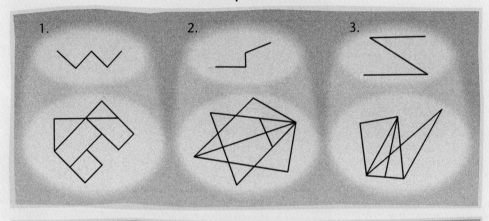

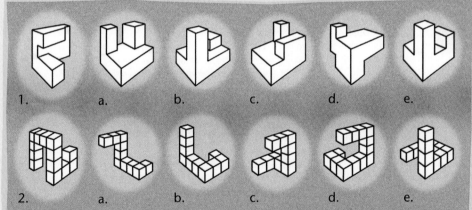

FIGURE 16.2 *Two items commonly used to measure visual-spatial abilities are the embedded-figures test, which requires one to find a geometric shape embedded in a more complex design, and the mental rotation test, which requires one to imagine how a shape would change in appearance as it moved through space.*

Class Discussion

Encourage students to discuss the many ways in which individuals tend not to practice skills for which they believe they have little "natural" ability. Ask them to find and provide examples of people in history or contemporary times who overcame this reluctance and became adept at something (such as a sport) after much determination, hard work, and practice.

For Your Information

There are a number of male/female differences in vision. According to Anne Moir and David Jessel, women tend to see better in the dark; men see better in bright light. Men have a better awareness of depth and perspective. However, women have wider peripheral vision because they have more receptor rods and cones in the retina and thus receive a broader band of visual stimuli.

Moir, A., & Jessel, D. (1991). *Brain sex: The real difference between men and women.* New York: Dell. 18.

mathematical problem solving in high school and college. Boys generally outperform girls on the mathematics section of the Scholastic Assessment Test (SAT).

These gender differences do appear to exist, at least for the time being. However, psychologists note the following:

- In most cases, the differences are small. Differences in verbal, math, and visual-spatial abilities also appear to be narrowing as more women pursue course work in fields that had beeen typically preserved for men. More girls such as Linda are continuing to excel in

mathematics. As Linda noted, her interest in mathematics could lead to a career in engineering or architecture—two fields previously dominated by men.
- These gender differences are *group* differences. There is greater variation in these skills between individuals *within* the groups than between men and women (Maccoby, 1990). That is, there may be a greater difference in, say, verbal skills between two women than between a woman and a man. Millions of women outdistance the "average" man in math and spatial abilities.

Bring to the classroom a number of advertisements for children's games and toys from children's magazines, parents' magazines, toy or children's catalogs, and advertising circulars. Ask students to examine the advertisements and discuss the ways in which the games and toys are designed and marketed to appeal to one sex or the other. Then have the students analyze the skills and/or attitudes that the games or toys are likely to develop in the children who play with them.

Instruct students to watch an hour or so of children's television programming (perhaps on Saturday morning). Have them take careful notes during the programs and use their observations to answer the following questions: Which sex appears most often in the programs? What types of cognitive and physical skills does each sex display? What types of activities do members of each sex engage in? Then have the students analyze the attitudes that the programs are likely to foster in the children who watch them. Ask volunteers to discuss their findings in class.

Caption Question: Answer

Participation in sports gives girls the opportunity to practice visual-spatial skills, such as hand-eye coordination, thus leading to enhanced abilities in this area.

Cross-Curricular Link: History

Although women have generally been viewed as less courageous and aggressive than men, history has many examples of female bravery and aggression. During the English civil wars of the 1600s, many observers were shocked by the behavior of some of the women of the time. The Countess of Portland, for example, offered to be the first to fire a cannon instead of surrendering to the enemy.

- Some differences may largely reflect cultural influences. In our culture spatial and mathematics abilities are stereotyped as masculine. Women who are given just a few hours of training in spatial skills—for example, rotating geometric figures or studying floor plans—perform at least as well as men on tests of these skills (Baenninger & Elenteny, 1997; Lawton & Morrin, 1999).

Differences in Personality and Behavior

Many notable gender differences are found in both personality and behavior. Women, for example, tend to exceed men in demonstrating trust and **nurturance**, or affectionate care and attention. Men, on the other hand, tend to exceed women in such traits as assertiveness and tough-mindedness. Other gender differences in personality and behavior include differences in levels of aggression, communication styles, and traits desired in a mate (Feingold, 1994).

Aggression   In most cultures, it is primarily the men who fight in war and compete in sports and games. This is, in part, because men tend to be physically larger and stronger than women, as previously mentioned. Yet men may be more suited to these activities for another reason as well—their generally higher level of aggression.

Most psychological studies of aggression have found that men tend to be more aggressive than women (Eagly & Wood, 1991; Knight et al., 1996). Not only are men more likely than women to act aggressively, particularly if provoked, but they are also more likely to use physical forms of aggression, such as hitting and shoving. Women act aggressively less often, and when they do, they tend to use indirect forms of aggression. For example, if provoked by a friend or an acquaintance, a woman is more likely to ignore or end her relationship with that person than to hit her or him (Bjorkqvist et al., 1992; Lagerspetz et al., 1988).

Women's sports have become increasingly popular. In the past, however, sporting activities were primarily reserved for men. *How might participation in sports help girls improve their visual-spatial skills?*

TRUTH OR fiction
■ REVISITED ■

It is true that men generally demonstrate more aggressive behavior than women do. According to several studies, men are also more likely than women to be physical in the expression of their aggression.

Although it is clear that men tend to be more aggressive than women, the origins of this gender difference are not as clear. Some experts believe that gender differences in aggression are primarily due to biological differences between men and women (Baron & Richardson, 1994). For example, aggressive behavior has been linked with high levels of testosterone (Berman et al., 1993; Olweus, 1986). One theory suggests that, among early humans, more aggressive men were more successful at winning mates than were less aggressive men. According to this theory, the result was that genes for aggression were more likely to be passed on to following generations (Baron & Richardson, 1994).

Although biology may help explain gender differences in aggression, it is likely that the

368

For Further Research

Organize the class into groups. Have the members of each group write and perform two skits: one based on the story of Nancy and Josh discussed in the feature and one in which Josh presents his friend's visit to Nancy without upsetting her. After the groups have performed their skits, have students discuss how the communication styles portrayed in the two skits differ. Also have students speculate on how each communication style is likely to affect Josh and Nancy's relationship over time.

Have interested students obtain copies of Deborah Tannen's book *You Just Don't Understand,* read it, and summarize various chapters. Students can present oral reports on the chapters they read. You may wish to have the class as a whole debate some of Tannen's hypothesis about gender differences.

READINGS IN

PSYCHOLOGY

GENDER DIFFERENCES IN INTIMACY AND INDEPENDENCE

In her book *You Just Don't Understand* (1990), psychologist Deborah Tannen discusses the human needs for intimacy and independence. Although males and females both need intimacy and independence, Tannen believes that women tend to focus on the former and men on the latter. The difference, Tannen argues, rests on how men and women interact with the world around them and how they view relationships. The difference can lead to problems in communication between men and women.

According to Tannen, most women tend to live in a world of connection with others. They negotiate complex networks of friendship, try to reach consensus, minimize differences, and avoid the appearance of superiority because this tends to highlight differences. Intimacy with others is key for individuals with this view of relationships.

In contrast, Tannen sees the majority of men as living in a world of status, where they must establish their own place in a hierarchy of others. Here independence is key. This is because telling others what to do is a primary means of increasing status. Taking orders from others, on the other hand, is a mark of low status.

These differing perspectives of the two sexes can lead women and men to interpret and react to the same situation in very different ways. Tannen provides the example of a couple, Nancy and Josh, to illustrate how these differing views of relationships create problems in communication.

Nancy and Josh When Josh's old high school buddy called him at work and said he would be in town on business the following month, Josh invited him to stay for the weekend. That evening he informed Nancy that they were going to have a houseguest and that he and his buddy would be going out together like they did in high school.

When Josh told Nancy about the plans he had made, she was upset. Nancy reminded Josh that she was going to be away on business the week before his buddy's visit. The Friday night that Josh

would be out with his buddy would be her first night home. What upset Nancy the most, however, was that Josh had made the plans on his own and only later informed her of them rather than discussing them with her first.

Nancy would never have made plans, even for an evening, let alone a whole weekend, without first checking with Josh. She could not understand why Josh did not show her the same courtesy and consideration that she would show him. When she protested, Josh responded, "I can't say to my friend, 'I have to ask my wife for permission'!"

To Josh, checking with his wife means seeking permission, and that, in turn, implies that he is not independent and free to act on his own. It would make him feel like a child. To Nancy, checking with her husband has nothing to do with permission. She thinks husbands and wives should discuss their plans with each other because their lives are connected and the actions of one have consequences for the other. Not only does Nancy not mind telling someone, "I have to check with Josh," but on the contrary, she likes it. It makes her feel good to know and to show that her life is connected with another's.

Conclusion Nancy and Josh were more upset about the incidents described above, as well as by others like them, than seemed warranted. This is because the incident reflected basic gender differences in how they view the world of relationships. Nancy was upset because she sensed a failure of connectedness and intimacy in her relationship with Josh. Josh was upset because he felt as though Nancy was trying to control him and limit his independence.

Think About It

Identifying Cause and Effect How do the perspectives of men and women differ, and how do these differences affect communication between men and women?

Primary Source Note

Description of Change: excerpted

Rationale: excerpted to focus on main idea

Journal Activity

Have students write in their journals about an incident or situation that they interpreted very differently than did someone of the opposite sex. Also have students analyze why the difference in interpretation may have occurred. Does the analysis tend to support Tannen's hypothesis about gender differences?

Think About It: Answer

According to Tannen, men place greater value on independence, while women place a higher value on intimacy. This difference can cause communication problems—for example, when a certain behavior or statement signals heightened intimacy to a woman but a lowered level of independence to a man.

Cooperative Learning

Organize students into pairs of one female and one male. Have the male student in each pair write down ways in which he believes, has observed, or has heard that females are socialized to be less assertive and aggressive than males. Have the female student in each pair write down ways in which she believes that males are raised to be more aggressive and assertive than females. Then have the partners exchange, critique, and discuss each other's lists.

Demonstration

Prior to a class discussion, secretly arrange for one student to record the number and approximate duration of the spoken contributions of the male students and those of the female students. (To conceal the nature of the experiment, you may wish to announce that the student is taking minutes of the content of the discussion.) Then have the recorder present the data to the group for analysis. How does the data support or refute the notion that males tend to dominate classroom discussions?

What's New in Psychology?

Early research consistently showed that women's self-confidence was lower than men's. However, a 1992 survey of male and female managers found no significant difference in the self-confidence of the two groups. Top-level managers were more confident than middle managers, regardless of gender, and both male and female managers reported they felt more self-confident at work than at home.

Koberg, C., et al. (1992). Gender and hierarchical level coalignment with managers' self-confidence. *Psychology, 29.* 50.

Cross-Curricular Link: Biology

The behavior of rats is influenced by hormones. Male rats usually learn how to run through a maze more quickly than female rats. This is presumably because male rats have better spatial skills. However, if a female rat is given injections of the male hormone testosterone, she will run through a maze as quickly as a male.

370

*All of these predominantly male sports are based on aggressive behavior: hockey in Canada, judo in Japan, rugby in England, and boxing in the United States. **Why do men tend to dominate aggressive sports?***

differences are also at least partly due to predominant male and female gender roles (Eagly & Steffen, 1986). In many societies, men are expected and socialized, or taught through the influence of social pressures, to be tougher, more assertive, and more aggressive than women (Eagly, 1987).

Communication Styles A common gender stereotype is that of the "strong, silent" man. Many people believe that women talk more than men do, but some research suggests that the opposite is actually true. Although girls tend to be more talkative than boys during early childhood, by the time they enter school, boys usually dominate classroom discussions (Sadker & Sadker, 1994). Indeed, as girls mature, they do less of the talking in most mixed-sex groups. By adulthood, men generally spend more time talking than women do in many situations. Men are also more likely to introduce new topics and to interrupt others (Rathus, 2003).

TRUTH OR fiction ▪ REVISITED ▪

It is not true that women tend to be more talkative than men. Girls may be more talkative when they are young, but as they mature, they generally talk less than men do.

Men tend to talk less than women do about their feelings and personal experiences (Dindia & Allen, 1992). Women often talk with other women—mothers, sisters, roommates, and friends—about intimate matters. Men talk about intimate matters much less often. When they do discuss personal matters, they generally do so with women rather than with other men, perhaps because women tend to be better at using and understanding nonverbal communication (Hall, 1978, 1984). Women are also more likely to offer understanding and support (Hall, 1984; Reisman, 1990). Dan, for example, was experiencing several issues that he was having difficulty working through. Rather than discuss these issues with Marc, he chose to confide in Janet.

A DAY IN THE LIFE

Whether these gender differences in communication styles are biologically based or socially learned is still unclear. Male and female children tend to be treated differently from birth in both the number and nature of verbal and nonverbal communications directed toward them.

Mate Selection Many physical features, such as cleanliness, good complexion, clear eyes, strong teeth and healthy hair, firm muscle tone, and a steady gait, are found to be universally appealing to both genders (Buss, 1999). However, studies on mate selection find that men tend to

Closing Section 2

Analyzing Information

Have students review the material in Section 2 and make a list of all of the gender differences discussed. Then have them indicate whether these differences seem to be biological, cultural, or a mix of the two.

Reviewing Section 2

Have students complete the Section Review questions on page 371.

Extension

Have groups of students interview pediatricians, child psychologists, and/or experienced day-care providers about gender differences in the development, abilities, interests, and behavior of babies and young children. Encourage students to ask these professionals for examples of differences that seem to be innate and examples of differences that seem to be encouraged by parents or other adults. Have the groups report their findings to the class.

Section 2 Review: Answers

1. Students may refer to the study that found that, although males seem to have superior visual-spatial skills, females who had been given just three hours of training in rotating geometric figures did just as well as male students at these tasks.

2. The hormone has been linked to aggressive behavior is testosterone.

3. Examples may include a boy who is encouraged to play an aggressive sport such as football, a female toddler who is strongly reprimanded for grabbing or hitting, and children who are exposed to movies and books in which females are submissive and males are aggressive.

be more swayed than women by a partner's physical appearance. Women tend to place greater emphasis than men on traits such as professional status, consideration, dependability, kindness, and fondness for children (Buss, 1994; Feingold, 1992). In a survey of more than 13,000 people in the United States, psychologist Susan Sprecher and her colleagues asked a series of questions relating to characteristics that people find appealing in a mate. Questions included how willing a person would be to marry someone who was older, younger, of a different religion, unlikely to hold a steady job, and not good-looking. Each item was answered by choosing a number on a 7-point scale on which 1 meant "not at all" and 7 meant "very willing." Women were more willing than men to marry someone who was not good-looking, but they were less willing to marry someone who was unlikely to hold a steady job.

Some psychologists believe that men and women originally valued different characteristics in potential mates because they are the traits that help ensure successful reproduction (Buss, 1994; Feingold, 1992; Fisher, 1992). However, this explanation cannot be proved conclusively. Gender differences in socialization may also influence which traits men and women look for in a mate. Regardless of the cause, however, the differences between the sexes in the traits they consider important in a mate are real, and they can be found in many different cultures (Buss, 1989).

TRUTH OR fiction

REVISITED

It is true that the qualities men look for in a potential mate are different from the qualities women look for. Men tend to focus more on the physical attractiveness of potential mates, whereas women tend to place greater emphasis on personal qualities, such as kindness.

As discussed earlier, actual differences in cognitive abilities, personality, and behavior are quite small and may be diminishing. Furthermore, many differences between men and women appear to be due largely to environmental influences and cultural expectations and not to inborn biological differences between men and women.

SECTION 2 REVIEW

go.hrw.com **Homework Practice Online**
Keyword: SY3 HP16

1. What evidence suggests that gender differences in cognitive abilities are at least partly due to differences in boys' and girls' life experiences?

2. What hormone is linked to aggressive behavior?

3. **Critical Thinking** *Analyzing Information* Give three examples of ways that children might be socialized to be more or less aggressive.

Section Objective

▶ Define gender typing, and discuss several theories that explain how it may occur.

This objective is assessed in the Section Review on page 377 and in the Chapter 16 Review.

Opening Section 3

Motivator

Have students brainstorm some of the possible ways in which gender differences may arise. List students' suggestions on the chalkboard, and lead students in a discussion of each suggestion. Have students copy the final list in their notebooks. Then tell them that in Section 3 they will read about various theories concerning the development of gender roles. Encourage students to refer to their copied list as they read and to classify the items on the list according to the various theories.

For Your Information

If it were not for the secretion of the hormone testosterone in the developing fetus roughly six weeks after conception, all fetuses would develop into females.

Class Discussion

Ask female students what they think are the advantages of being a male, and ask male students what they think are the advantages of being a female. Lead the class in a discussion about the accuracy of these perceived advantages.

internet connect

TOPIC: Gender Typing
GO TO: go.hrw.com
KEYWORD: SY3 PS16

Have students access the Internet through the HRW Go site to research gender typing. Then have students create a chart in which they outline biological and psychological theories, the role of reinforcement, and evidence supporting each theory. As an extension, ask students to explain which theories seem most credible to them and their reasoning behind their opinions.

SECTION 3

Gender Typing

As you have learned, differences do exist between the genders. If these differences are not based solely on biological factors, however, how do they develop into gender roles? As in many areas of psychology, several different theories have been proposed to explain gender role development, which is also known as **gender typing**.

Research has shown that children as young as two and a half years of age have begun to develop ideas about traits and behaviors they consider characteristic of males and females (Rathus, 2003). These findings suggest that gender typing takes place at an early age. Exactly how and why gender roles develop, however, is a subject of considerable debate among psychologists. A number of theories have been proposed to explain gender typing. These theories fall into two general categories: those that explain gender typing as a biological process and those that explain it as a psychological process.

Biological Views

Biological views of gender typing focus on the impact of such factors as genes and hormones in the development of gender-related behavior.

Genetics Most biologists believe that genes for traits that help individuals survive and reproduce tend to be passed on to future generations. Some psychologists have argued that the traits that ensured the survival and reproductive success of early humans made early men successful hunters and warriors and early women successful child rearers (Buss, 2000). For men, these would have included such traits as good visual-spatial skills and aggression. For women, such traits would have included good nonverbal communication skills and nurturance. According to the theory, genes for these traits would have been passed on to future generations, and the traits would eventually come to characterize humans as a species.

The genetic view of gender role origins is highly controversial. Critics argue that a person's biological makeup does not predetermine how that person will behave. Instead, they point to cross-cultural research that suggests that gender roles are largely learned and not inherited (Mead, 1935). In their view, genes are important determinants of physical traits such as strength, but complex social behaviors such as aggression involve learning and cultural influences as well as heredity.

Hormones Some psychologists believe that gender typing occurs because men and women differ in the organization and functioning of their brains. According to this view, sex hormones sculpt the brains of men and women differently before birth. To understand this theory, some background on brain structure and function is necessary.

The two hemispheres, or right and left sides, of the brain are somewhat specialized to carry out different functions. In most people, the right hemisphere tends to be better specialized to perform visual-spatial tasks, whereas the left hemisphere tends to be better specialized to perform verbal tasks. This does not imply a strict division of roles, because neither hemisphere is solely responsible for any cognitive abilities. However, some cognitive tasks appear to be performed more quickly and efficiently by one hemisphere than by the other (Bradshaw et al., 1981). (See Chapter 3.)

This specialization of the two sides of the brain is called **lateralization**. Lateralization occurs during fetal development and is apparently influenced by sex hormones. Thus, lateralization may occur somewhat differently in boys and girls, resulting in some gender differences in brain organization and function (Collaer & Hines, 1995; Tan, 1994).

There is some evidence to suggest that testosterone leads to relatively greater growth of the right hemisphere as compared with the left hemisphere (Grimshaw et al., 1995). This evidence is consistent with research that indicates that females tend to show less lateralization than males (Grön et al., 2000). Taken together, these studies could help explain why males seem to be better at visual-spatial tasks, which tend to be processed by the right hemisphere, and why females seem to be better at verbal tasks, which tend to be processed by the left hemisphere of the brain.

Some psychologists also believe that gender typing may be a result of subtle prenatal changes to the brain caused by sex hormones. These psychologists suggest that boys' inclinations toward aggression and rough-and-tumble play, for example, might also be due to the influence of testosterone on the brains of developing male fetuses (Collaer & Hines, 1995). The results of these and other ways that "masculine" and "feminine" brains in young children are thought to differ are shown in Figure 16.3.

Meeting Individual Needs: Visual Learners

To help visual learners understand the problems with Freud's psychoanalytic theory as an explanation of gender typing, make and compare two simple time lines. One time line should show child development between the ages of three and five according to Freud. The other time line should show current research on gender typing from infancy through age three.

Cooperative Learning

Have pairs of students research gender typing in infants and toddlers. One student in each pair should interview parents of young children about such topics as the children's toy preferences, levels of independence, and levels of aggression. The other student should carefully note or record the responses. Both students should work together to develop the interview questions and to analyze the findings. Instruct the pairs to write up their findings and analyses in short reports to share with the class.

Psychological Views

Although many psychologists believe that genes and sex hormones play some role in gender typing (Money, 1987), others believe that psychological processes play a more important role. Among the psychological theories that have been suggested to explain how gender typing comes about are psychoanalytic theory, social-learning theory, and gender-schema theory.

Psychoanalytic Theory Sigmund Freud's psychoanalytic theory argues that gender typing can be explained in terms of gender identification. According to Freud, boys come to identify with their fathers and girls with their mothers. This occurs between the ages of three and five.

At the beginning of this period, Freud argued, children seek the attention of the parent of the opposite sex and perceive the parent of the same sex as a rival for that attention. By the end of the period, however, children no longer feel this way and instead identify with the parent of the same sex. (See Chapter 14.)

According to Freud, it is through this process of identification with the same-sex parent that a child comes to develop the behaviors that are associated with his or her own sex. The child internalizes the standards of the same-sex parent and eventually adopts that parent as a role model for behavior.

There are several problems with Freud's psychoanalytic theory, one of the most apparent being the age at which gender typing occurs. According to Freud, the complex feelings that children have for the parent of the opposite sex are not resolved until children reach age five. However, as noted previously, children tend to display gender typing much earlier. Even in infancy, boys have been found in some studies to be more independent than girls. Also, between the ages of one and three, many girls appear to show preferences for dolls and soft toys, whereas many boys,

on the other hand, prefer hard transportation toys (Rathus, 2003).

Although Freud's theory has been criticized for this and other reasons, it laid the foundation for other theories that better fit the facts as we now know them. In particular, social-learning theory was influenced by Freud's emphasis on the importance of role models and learning by imitation (Beal, 1994).

Social-Learning Theory According to social-learning theory, gender role behavior, like other behavior, is acquired through two different learning processes—reinforcement and modeling.

Reinforcement occurs when a behavior has favorable consequences. Because it is rewarded, the behavior is more likely to be repeated. In contrast, behaviors that are not rewarded and behaviors that are punished are less likely to be repeated, because they are not reinforced. (See Chapter 6.)

Social-learning theorists argue that reinforcement of appropriate gender role behavior starts very early. Almost from the moment of birth, the way

Some Possible Differences Between Male and Female Preschoolers in Brain Organization and Function

Male preschoolers	Female preschoolers
Prefer blocks and building	Prefer playing with living things
Build high structures	Build long and low structures
Are indifferent to newcomers	Greet newcomers
Prefer stories of adventure	Prefer stories about relationships
Play more competitive games (e.g., tag)	Play less competitive games (e.g., hopscotch)
Are better visual-spatial learners	Are better auditory learners

FIGURE 16.3 *Some psychologists believe that the presence of prenatal sex hormones contributes to the development of male-differentiated brains and female-differentiated brains. This difference can affect the behavior of males and females, even those of preschool age.*

Source: Moir, A., & Jessel, D. (1991). *Brain Sex.* New York: Carol Publishing/Lyle Stuart.

Cultural Dimensions

According to Freud, a little boy has hostile feelings toward his father because he is jealous of his father's sexual involvement with the boy's mother. However, among the Trobriand Islanders of the Pacific, little boys do not exhibit hostile feelings toward their fathers. In the Trobriand Islander culture, fathers play with their children but have no authority over their behavior. Instead, the disciplinarian is the mother's brother. Young boys often become angry with their uncles—not because the boys are jealous of them but because the boys resent their uncles for telling them what to do. This phenomenon suggests that Freud's theory about childhood development was imperfect because it was based on his observations of his own culture rather than a wider knowledge of human beings.

Guided Practice

Have students work together to brainstorm a list of the ways that people go about trying to get their own way, win an argument, or get something they want from another person. Then have students classify the techniques into two broad categories: aggressive actions and nonaggressive actions. Have students discuss which of these techniques tend to be used more often by males and which tend to be used more often by females. Ask students to supply evidence to support their responses and to relate their responses to social-learning theory.

Independent Practice

Have students watch popular television shows or movies and separately rate how often the male and the female characters in the dramatizations use persuasion versus more aggressive means of getting what they want. In class, ask volunteers to tally the results of the individual ratings. Have students use the results as the basis of a class discussion on gender differences in aggression. Also have students debate whether aggression as portrayed on television serves as a model for gender differences or merely reflects those differences.

Freud believed that children model gender-typed behaviors after their parent of the same sex. He termed this process identification.

babies are treated may depend on their sex. When children are old enough to understand language, parents and others begin to instruct them about how they are expected to behave. Parents tend to talk and read more to baby girls, for example, and fathers often engage in more rough-and-tumble play with boys (Jacklin et al., 1984).

TRUTH OR fiction ▪ REVISITED ▪

It is not true that boys and girls are treated in much the same way until about age three. Studies have shown that gender-typed treatment of children begins at a very early age. Thus, gender differences in the behavior of very young children are not necessarily due to biological differences between boys and girls.

Parents are also likely to reward children for behavior they consider appropriate for their gender and punish, or at least fail to reward, them for behavior they consider inappropriate. For example, studies have found that parents tend to react positively when their children play with toys considered appropriate for their gender. On the other hand, parents often react negatively when children play with toys considered inappropriate for their gender. Fathers especially are likely to react negatively when their sons play with toys considered more

appropriate for girls, such as dolls. They may frown, make sarcastic comments, and even physically separate the child from the toy (Langlois & Downs, 1980). Girls, however, are less likely to receive negative reactions from their fathers for playing with toys considered more appropriate for boys, such as trucks (Siegal, 1987).

From an early age, boys are also more likely to be given toy cars, toy guns, and athletic equipment. Girls, on the other hand, are more likely to receive dolls and other soft toys (Smith & Daglish, 1977). When playing with their children at home, parents also tend to reach first for toys considered appropriate for the child's sex, even when the child owns toys that are generally considered appropriate for both sexes (Eisenberg et al., 1985; Schau et al., 1980).

Aggression provides a good example of how behavior is learned through reinforcement. In one study (Fagot et al., 1985), one-year-old boys and girls were found to be equally likely to use aggressive actions, such as pushing or grabbing, in order to obtain what they wanted. They were also equally likely to use communication, such as whining or gesturing. However, adults' reactions to their efforts varied greatly, depending on the children's sex. The adults tended to respond positively when the girls tried to communicate and solve the dispute in a nonaggressive manner but showed little response when the boys did. On the other hand, the adults tended to ignore aggression in the girls and respond positively to it in the boys.

Not surprisingly, by age two the girls in the study no longer acted aggressively. They had apparently learned through reinforcement to communicate their wants verbally. The boys had learned the opposite lesson, and their level of aggression remained high. As a result of such differences in reinforcement, girls tend to develop more anxiety about aggression and greater inhibitions against displaying it (Maccoby & Jacklin, 1974).

Even in the absence of reinforcement, social learning can occur through observation and imitation of others. This process is known as **modeling**. Children learn about both male and female gender

CASE STUDIES
AND OTHER TRUE STORIES

Have students view one or more syndicated television programs from the 1950s or the 1960s (such as *Father Knows Best, Ozzie and Harriet, The Donna Reed Show,* or *Leave It to Beaver*). Instruct students to write a short essay that compares and contrasts the gender-role expectations evident in these programs with the gender-role expectations found in television programs today. Have volunteers read their essays aloud to the class for discussion.

Cooperative Learning

Organize students into small groups. Challenge each group to develop scenarios for children's television programs and commercial advertisements that promote nonsexist attitudes. (The groups may describe their television programs in brief outlines, or they may create storyboards for commercials.) Ask representatives from the groups to share their work with the class. Have the class determine which approaches seem most feasible and effective.

CASE STUDIES
AND OTHER TRUE STORIES
What Children Learn from Television

What do Sonic the Hedgehog and Spiderman have in common—aside from millions of young fans? The answer is that they are male creatures. Almost every study in the past 20 years of children's television shows has found that many shows have all-male casts and that among shows with characters of both sexes, males outnumber females at least two or three to one (Comstock & Paik, 1991; Huston et al., 1992).

Television—and other popular media, such as books, comics, magazines, radio, and film—often portrays women and men in traditional gender roles (DeBell, 1993; Kortenhaus & Demarest, 1993; Signorielli, 1990). Female characters on television are often portrayed as less active than males and more likely to follow the directions of others (especially male characters). The activities of female characters also have less impact on the outcome of stories than do those of males. Male characters are more likely to conceive and carry out plans and to be aggressive, dominant, and authoritative. These gender role images have not changed much over the past couple of decades (DeBell, 1993).

Television commercials also support gender role stereotypes. Even though men and women now appear equally often in prime-time commercials, women are more likely to be seen inside the home, advertising domestic products. Men continue to provide 90 percent of the narratives (known as voice-overs) in commercials, conveying the idea that men are more authoritative and knowledgeable (Bretl & Cantor, 1988; DeBell, 1993; Lovdal, 1989).

Not surprisingly, the more time children spend watching television, the more likely they are to hold stereotypical ideas about masculine and feminine behavior (Comstock & Paik, 1991; Huston et al., 1992). Some researchers found that children who watched cartoons in which characters adopted stereotypical gender roles were more likely than children who watched nonstereotyped gender role behavior to describe men and women according to the stereotypes. The same authors also found that children who were shown girls in nonstereotyped roles, such as building a clubhouse, held stereotypical attitudes less strongly afterward.

There is some evidence that the impact of television on children's stereotypes is lessened if children are raised by adults with more flexible views of gender roles. In one study, third graders were classified as either high, medium, or low stereotyped on the basis of their tendency to prefer activities considered typically masculine or feminine (List et al., 1983). The children were then shown two films, one of a woman in traditional roles (those of wife and mother) and one of a woman in nontraditional roles (those of physician and army officer). Children low in gender role stereotyping later recalled details about both films equally, whereas children high in gender role stereotyping recalled more about the film showing the woman in traditional roles.

Television has a powerful potential to influence children's attitudes about appropriate gender role behaviors. Critics of gender stereotyping argue that if producers could be more strongly encouraged to eliminate gender role stereotypes from television shows and commercials, sexism in American society could decrease substantially.

WHY PSYCHOLOGY MATTERS

Psychologists have extensively studied how television and other media affect children. Use **CNNfyi.com** or other current events sources to learn more about these types of studies. Write a brief paper summarizing the key aspects of what you have learned.

CNNfyi.com

Invite students to research gender role expectations in another culture, such as those in Russia, China, or Japan. Have students compare gender-role expectations in their chosen culture with those found in the United States. How are they similar? How do they differ? How are these expectations taught? Have students report their findings to the class.

Essay and Research Themes for A. P. Students

Theme 14

Closing Section 3

Evaluating Information

Ask students to identify the evidence they found most significant and persuasive for both the biological and the psychological explanations of gender typing. Have them discuss the reasons for their choices.

Reviewing Section 3

Have students complete the Section Review questions on page 377.

Extension

Ask students to locate information about the number and variety of athletic opportunities for girls in their school in the past. Suggest that students examine old yearbooks or old administrative records (with permission from current administrators) or interview teachers and former students. Then have students pool their findings and discuss how athletic opportunities for girls have changed over time and what might account for these changes.

role behavior by observing the behavior of the males and females with whom they commonly interact. However, the children are more likely to model, or imitate, individuals, particularly parents, who are of the same sex as themselves. Children are also more likely to be positively reinforced for imitating the behavior of the parent of the same sex (Golombok & Fivush, 1994).

Observational learning and imitation were illustrated in a classic experiment by David Perry and Kay Bussey (1979). In their study, eight- and nine-year-old boys and girls watched adult models indicate their preferences for one of the items in each of 16 different pairs of items. The adults chose among such pairs as toy cows versus toy horses and oranges versus apples. The children in the study did not realize that the adults' preferences were purely arbitrary. When the children were asked to indicate their own preferences for the items in the pairs, the boys' choices matched the adult men's choices 14 out of 16 times, and the girls' choices matched the adult women's choices 13 out of 16 times. Thus, both boys and girls tended to model their behavior after role models of their own sex, even though the behavior was arbitrary and unrelated to gender.

A DAY IN THE LIFE

If gender roles are learned, as social-learning theory suggests, then they should be flexible, or capable of changing. Indeed, there are indications that this is the case. Today, as more women are working outside the home,

gender roles seem to be changing. Janet's mother is a good example. After Janet's parents divorced, her mother took on the role of wage earner in addition to her roles as parent and homemaker. Another indication of gender role change is that parents are more likely now than in the past to encourage their daughters to play sports and follow careers. They are also more likely to encourage their sons to be nurturing and cooperative.

Gender-Schema Theory   Social-learning theory has made important contributions to our understanding of how reinforcement and modeling promote gender-typed behavior. A related but somewhat different view of gender typing is provided by gender-schema theory. According to this theory, children themselves play an active role in developing gender-appropriate behavior. Children form their own concepts about gender and then shape their behavior so that it conforms to their gender concepts.

Specifically, children develop a gender schema in order to organize their perceptions of the world (Bowes & Goodnow, 1996). A **gender schema** is a cluster of physical qualities, behaviors, and personality traits associated with one sex or the other. It is argued that because society places so much emphasis on gender, children organize their perceptions along gender lines.

Gender-schema theorists suggest that as soon as children learn whether they are boys or girls, they begin to seek information concerning gender-typed traits. Even very young children start to mentally group people of the same sex according to the traits they believe are representative of that gender.

Once their gender schema is formed, children strive to live up to it. They begin to judge themselves according to the traits they believe are relevant to their sex, using their gender schema as a standard for comparison. In so doing, children blend their developing self-concepts with the prominent gender schema of their culture. For example, boys may react aggressively when provoked because they perceive that is what society expects males to

Children may be less likely to adopt traditional gender behaviors if they are allowed to play freely with both masculine and feminine toys.

Section Objective

► Explain how gender roles have changed over time, and identify the ways in which they can vary from culture to culture.

This objective is assessed in the Section Review on page 379 and in the Chapter 16 Review.

Motivator

Have students think about the gender roles with which they are familiar. Ask them to consider ways in which gender roles have changed since their parents were teens. List students' responses on the chalkboard. For each suggestion listed, ask students to offer an explanation for why the gender role has changed. Then tell students that not only can gender roles change over time, but they can also vary from culture to culture. Have students read Section 4 to learn about these variations in gender roles.

---

do. Girls, on the other hand, may try to cooperate because they perceive that society expects such behavior from females.

Across both genders, children's self-esteem depends in part on how similar their own personalities, behaviors, and physical appearances are to those of the prominent gender schema of their culture. In other words, boys who see themselves as fitting their culture's idea of masculinity are more likely to develop higher self-esteem than boys who do not. Similarly, girls who see themselves as fitting their culture's idea of femininity are more likely to develop higher self-esteem than girls who do not (Bem, 1993).

Children's gender schema also determines how important particular traits are to them. Consider the dimensions of strength-weakness and kindness-cruelty. Children are likely to learn that the strength-weakness dimension is more important to males, whereas the kindness-cruelty dimension is more important to females. Thus, a boy is more likely to be concerned about how strong he is, whereas a girl is more likely to be concerned about being kind.

In summary, both biological and psychological views of gender typing can help us understand why males and females behave as they do. This is because differences in gender roles are likely to be influenced by differences in biology, life experiences, and cultural expectations. All of these factors appear to play some role in determining how individual males and females behave.

Regardless of how gender typing occurs, it should not be viewed as an inevitable process. In early human societies, it may have seemed appropriate for males and females to have very different roles. Today, however, many people believe that these strict gender roles no longer suit our contemporary way of life.

Source: ZIGGY copyright 1995 Ziggy & Friends, Inc. Distributed by Universal Press Syndicate. Reprinted with permission. All rights reserved.

SECTION 4

Variation in Gender Roles

Both social-learning theory and gender-schema theory proposes that learning plays the key part in gender role development. They suggest that gender roles are not inborn or fixed at birth but may vary from person to person. Indeed, as the increasing participation of women in activities long considered appropriate only for men—business, sports, and politics, to name a few—demonstrates, gender roles have changed dramatically over time. Research has also shown that gender roles can vary from culture to culture. In other words, what is considered gender-appropriate behavior in one society may be viewed differently in another cultural setting.

Variation Through Time

In the past, gender roles were more distinct and rigid than they are today. There were distinct female and male worlds that were clearly set apart from each other. Throughout most of history, women in many parts of the world were expected to be the

SECTION 3 REVIEW

go.hrw.com | **Homework Practice Online**
Keyword: SY3 HP16

1. Why do some theorists believe that brain lateralization leads to gender-typed behaviors and abilities?

2. Give an example to show how reinforcement could influence the types of toys children choose to play with.

3. **Critical Thinking** *Supporting a Point of View* What role do you think television might play in the development of a child's gender schema? Give examples to support your answer.

1. Because lateralization is influenced by sex hormones, some researchers think it may occur differently in boys and girls. Evidence also shows that males tend to perform better at visual-spatial tasks and females at certain verbal tasks, which are processed by different hemispheres of the brain.

2. Boys are more likely to be given action toys, while girls tend to be given dolls and soft toys. Boys tend to be discouraged from playing with toys that are considered to be "girls'" toys.

3. By showing women in more domestic and supportive roles and men in more independent, active, decision-making roles, television may develop the gender schema of young viewers along traditional gender-role lines. Examples will vary.

Teaching Section 4

Debating Ideas

Remind students that women's roles have expanded greatly over the past several decades and that a majority of women now work outside the home. Then organize volunteers into two opposing groups to debate the following statement: Men should take equal responsibility for home-maintenance and child-care tasks. Following the debate, have students evaluate the arguments made by both sides in the debate.

Analyzing Ideas

Have students survey two-career couples to find out how much time they spend on household tasks. Students should first brainstorm a list of household tasks and then ask selected couples to monitor their time spent on the tasks for a specified period of time (perhaps a week). Students should analyze the responses to determine whether there are gender-role differences in the types of tasks women and men generally do and in the amount of time women and men spend doing household tasks. Have students display their findings in a graph or a chart.

Cultural Dimensions

In the Soviet Union of the 1980s, the problems faced by working mothers reached nightmarish proportions. The average working mother spent 40 hours a week on such domestic tasks as laundry, shopping, and food preparation, while her husband spent fewer than 5 hours on such tasks.

internet connect

TOPIC: Gender Roles in the Past
GO TO: go.hrw.com
KEYWORD: SY3 PS16

Access the Internet through the HRW Go site to find additional information about lives and gender roles assigned to people in the United States in the 1700s or 1800s. Then use the information to write a "help wanted" ad for a man and woman for that place and time.

Readings and Case Studies

In the 1950s most American families lived on one income. It was typical then for the husband to work outside the home and the wife to stay home and care for the house and family.

homemakers and child rearers, and men were expected to be the providers for and protectors of women and children.

These differences in gender roles were based in part on the different biological characteristics of the two sexes. Women were more restricted in their activity and mobility by childbearing and the need to nurse their young children. In the earliest human societies, women typically stayed home and assumed responsibility for the homemaking and child-rearing chores. Men, being larger, stronger, and biologically less tied to childbearing and rearing, were considered better suited for hunting and similar activities. These roles remained largely unchanged until quite recently.

Just a generation or two ago, the accepted pattern was for a woman to marry, stay at home, and care for the house and children. She was expected to put the needs of her husband and children ahead of her own. The idea that a woman should put her own career or personal ambitions ahead of marriage

and raising a family was not very widespread. According to the dominant ideas of the time concerning gender roles, the ideal woman was the devoted wife who kept a clean house and had dinner waiting when her husband returned from work.

Over the past several decades, women in the United States have entered the workforce in increasing numbers. Today many women work outside the home because they enjoy the financial rewards and the social and intellectual stimulation their jobs provide. In other instances, economic conditions have led women into the workplace. Many working women are single mothers; others work because their families cannot afford to live on the husband's income alone. In some families, the wife works to support the family while the husband remains at home, either by choice or because he is unable to find a job.

Not surprisingly, male and female gender roles in the United States are much more flexible today than they were just a few decades ago. In many marriages, for example, husbands and wives share household chores, child rearing, and wage earning equally (Goodnow & Bowes, 1994). This is the case

A DAY IN THE LIFE with Linda's parents. As Linda noted, her father, like an increasing number of men in American society, is willing to take on at least some of the tasks that were once performed almost solely by women.

In contemporary American society, women often balance two full-time jobs—their careers and motherhood.

Identifying Cause and Effect

Ask students to determine why women's roles have changed over the past several decades and what effects these changes have had on our society. Also have students speculate on the societal effects that would be brought about by an expansion of men's roles.

Reviewing Section 4

Have students complete the Section Review questions on page 379.

Extension

Have students locate information in books, magazines, and other sources about the ways in which male and female roles have been perceived during various historical time periods and in various locations. Have them summarize and present their findings, including visual information where appropriate. Lead the class in a discussion of the variety of roles that have existed.

Both men and women of Arapesh society were taught from birth that aggressive behavior is unacceptable.

However, most women who work outside the home are still expected to retain traditional feminine gender roles in the household (Crosby & Jaskar, 1993; Deaux & Lewis, 1983). Dan's Aunt Debbie is a good example. In addition to her outside work, she is expected to maintain the household and care for the children.

Cultural Variation

Gender roles not only vary through time, but they also vary from culture to culture. A famous study by anthropologist Margaret Mead (1935) explored this issue. In the 1930s, Mead studied three different groups of people—the Mundugumor, the Arapesh, and the Tchambuli—on the South Pacific island of New Guinea.

According to Mead, the Mundugumor were a warlike people, and both men and women were very aggressive. Mundugumor women looked down on bearing and rearing children because this interfered with their ability to go to battle. In contrast, the neighboring Arapesh were a gentle and peaceful culture. In this group, both men and women played an equal role in caring for the children and maintaining the land.

The Tchambuli differed from both the Mundugumor and Arapesh in their gender roles. Mead reported that their behavior was the opposite of traditional gender roles in the United States. Tchambuli men spent most of their time caring for children, gossiping, bickering, primping, and haggling over prices. Tchambuli women, on the other hand, spent most of their time catching the fish that made up the bulk of the Tchambuli diet. Tchambuli women also kept their heads shaved, disliked wearing ornaments, and were more aggressive than the men.

Margaret Mead's interpretation of her New Guinea study has been criticized as being too subjective, or biased by her personal views concerning gender roles (Errington & Gewertz, 1987). However, the data Mead collected suggests that what is considered to be appropriate behavior for men and women can differ from one culture to another. Thus, the data may support the claim that many gender differences are learned, not inborn.

· · · · · · · · · · · · · · · · · · · ·

TRUTH OR **fiction** ▪ REVISITED ▪

It is true that much of the behavior we think of as typical male or female behavior we are not born with but learn from other members of our culture. Because gender roles differ from culture to culture, it is likely that they are learned and not the result of inborn traits.

· · · · · · · · · · · · · · · · · · · ·

A DAY IN THE LIFE

Linda's father grew up in a culture in which the roles of men and women were strictly defined. His parents supported these roles. In his own marriage, however, he adopted a less stereotypical role. Clearly, gender roles are not only learned but can be unlearned as well.

SECTION 4 REVIEW

go. hrw .com Homework Practice Online
Keyword: SY3 HP16

1. What biological factors have been suggested to explain the historic division between male and female gender roles?

2. How have gender roles in the United States changed in the past few decades?

3. **Critical Thinking** *Comparing and Contrasting* Describe how gender roles can vary from culture to culture.

379

Technology

► Chapter 16 Test Generator (on the One-Stop Planner)

► HRW Go site

Reinforcement, Review, and Assessment

► Chapter 16 Review, pp. 380–381

► Chapter Review and Activities with Answer Key

► Alternative Assessment Handbook

► Portfolio Assessment Handbook

► Chapter 16 Test (Form A or B)

Linking to Community Invite a number of women from your community who work in traditionally male-dominated occupations (lawyers, doctors, engineers, judges, and so on) to hold a panel discussion in your classroom about how career opportunities for women and men are changing as

---

4. affectionate care and attention

5. psychologist who has researched the different ways men and women communicate

6. gender-role development

7. the specialization of both sides of the brain

8. social learning that occurs through observation and imitation of others

9. a cluster of physical qualities, behaviors, and personality traits associated with one sex or the other

10. anthropologist who carried out studies of different cultures in the South Pacific

Understanding Main Ideas

1. Examples of change include more men staying at home to raise their children and more women working outside the home.

2. Men tend to talk more than women, but discuss intimate matters less often than do women.

3. Children are reinforced for exhibiting behaviors that adults think are gender-appropriate. Children also model the behavior of adults of the same sex.

4. Women are now freer to pursue careers than they once were.

Thinking Critically

1. Students should cite differences between gender roles now and in the past.

2. Answers will vary, but students might say that studies will show less differences between the genders.

Chapter
16 REVIEW

Writing a Summary

Using standard grammar, spelling, sentence structure, and punctuation, summarize the information in this chapter. Consider:

• gender roles and stereotypes, and how men and women differ in cognitive abilities, personality, and behavior

• gender typing, and how gender roles have changed over time

Identifying People and Ideas

Identify the following terms or people and use them in appropriate sentences.

1. gender
2. gender roles
3. gender stereotypes
4. nurturance
5. Deborah Tannen
6. gender typing
7. lateralization
8. modeling
9. gender schema
10. Margaret Mead

Understanding Main Ideas

SECTION 1 (pp. 364–365)

1. How have gender roles in the United States changed over the past few decades?

SECTION 2 (pp. 366–371)

2. What are two differences in the typical communication styles of men and women?

SECTION 3 (pp. 372–377)

3. What roles do reinforcement and modeling play in gender typing?

SECTION 4 (pp. 377–379)

4. How has the entrance of large numbers of women into the workforce affected current expectations concerning women's roles?

Thinking Critically

1. **Drawing Inferences and Conclusions** What evidence suggests that gender roles are in a state of transition?

2. **Making Generalizations and Predictions** How might the results of gender role studies change as more women work outside the home?

3. **Evaluating** Why do you think the increase in the number of women in the workplace has helped change gender stereotypes in the United States?

4. **Categorizing** List the advantages and disadvantages that you might think would exist for girls educated in female-only classes.

Writing About Psychology

1. **Comparing and Contrasting** Go to the library to learn more about psychological views of gender typing. Write a one-page report comparing and contrasting the various theories. Be sure to use standard grammar, spelling, sentence structure, and punctuation.

2. **Categorizing** Create a detailed chart listing actual gender differences between men and women as well as the stereotyped differences between them. Cite evidence that supports or refutes each difference shown in the chart. Use the graphic organizer below to help you complete your chart.

Gender Differences	
Actual Differences	Stereotyped Differences

perceptions about gender roles change. Ask the panel to discuss the reasons why they chose their occupations and any discriminatory obstacles that they had to overcome in achieving their goals.

Building Social Studies Skills

Interpreting Graphs

Study the bar graph below. Then use the information in the graph to help you answer the questions that follow.

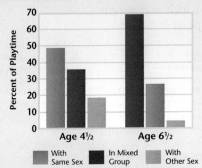

Gender and Play Behavior in Children

Percent of Playtime

Age 4½   Age 6½

■ With Same Sex   ■ In Mixed Group   ■ With Other Sex

Source: Maccoby, *The Two Sexes*, 1998

1. Which of the following statements best reflects the information presented in the graph?
   a. Children rarely play with members of the opposite sex.
   b. Mixed-group play declines dramatically during the early years of childhood.
   c. As children grow older, they play less with members of the opposite sex.
   d. Boys are less willing to play with girls than girls are willing to play with boys.

2. What questions might this graph raise in the mind of a psychologist?

Analyzing Primary Sources

Read the following excerpt from *The Two Sexes: Growing Up Apart, Coming Together,* in which Eleanor Maccoby explains the ways in which parents influence gender roles. Then answer the questions that follow.

❝In a study done in the 1970s, parents got their first view of their newborn infant through a hospital window, and were asked to describe the child. Although the infant boys and girls in this study did not differ on objective measures of size or activity, parents saw their infant sons as robust, strong, alert, and large-featured, while they saw daughters as fine-featured, small, delicate, and 'soft.' (Rubin, Provenzano, and Luria, 1974). These parental reactions seemed to indicate that, from the very beginning, the way parents perceived their infants was strongly biased by their expectations about femaleness and maleness.❞

3. Which of the following statements best reflects Maccoby's point of view?
   a. Parental biases influence a child's perception of self from the day of birth.
   b. Fathers are more biased in their expectations for their children than mothers are.
   c. Parental bias plays a minimal role in a child's development.
   d. Many parents are biased in their perceptions of their children from birth.

4. How else might this study have been conducted to learn more about parental expectations?

3. The increase in the number of women in the workplace gives evidence that women have skills they were once thought to lack.

4. Girls in such classes would be less likely to have their self-esteem lowered by more assertive male classmates but would be less likely to become familiar and comfortable with boys.

Writing About Psychology

1. Reports should reflect an understanding of psychoanalytic theory, social-learning theory, and gender-schema theory.

2. Charts should list actual and stereotypical differences and include evidence supporting or refuting each difference.

Building Social Studies Skills

1. c

2. Students' answers will vary but might include whether boys or girls are most reluctant to play with members of the opposite sex, or if the nature of mixed play changes over time.

3. d

4. Answers will vary, but parents could be shown a child and asked to evaluate it in male and female terms before learning if it is a boy or a girl. Parents would then later be shown the same child and told its gender. Psychologists would note if their perception of the child changed with the new information.

PSYCHOLOGY PROJECTS

Linking to Community

Using Surveys With several of your classmates, carry out a survey to assess gender stereotypes in your community. Work together as a group to brainstorm a list of questions and develop a questionnaire that will reveal how people think about men and women and what behaviors they think are appropriate for each. Then work individually to interview at least three or four people. Include people from a wide range of ages. Summarize the results in an oral report to the class.

♫ **internet** connect

Internet Activity: go.hrw.com
KEYWORD: SY3 PS16

Choose an activity on gender roles to:
- create a poster illustrating gender roles and how roles are reinforced by the media.
- research gender roles of the past and create a pamphlet showing how contemporary roles differ from those in the past.
- make a chart outlining theories of gender typing.

go.hrw.com

UNIT 5 REVIEW

▶ TEACH

Have students review the tips for taking tests in chapter 15. Then organize students into small groups. Have the groups build on the tips given in chapter 15 by brainstorming ways to achieve higher test scores. Ask each group to prepare a list of their ideas and choose one person to present their ideas to the rest of the class.

▶ EXTEND

Divide the class into three groups. Have the groups use the textbook and other resources to research test-taking strategies. Then have the groups incorporate the problem-solving skills outlined in the Psychology in Action Simulation to develop a presentation detailing the techniques they have found to improve test scores. Have volunteers from each group present their group's findings to the class for evaluation.

▶ PSYCHOLOGY IN ACTION

Ask students to imagine that they are forming a new club at their school. Have each student designate a focus for his or her club. Then have students use the problem-solving skills outlined in the simulation to develop a plan of action for encouraging other students to join their clubs. Each student should create a flowchart showing the process he or she went through to develop a plan of action for attracting members. Have volunteers present their flowcharts to the class.

UNIT 5

PSYCHOLOGY IN ACTION

YOU SOLVE THE PROBLEM . . .

How can a psychologist learn which motivation theory explains a certain type of behavior?

Complete the following activity in small cooperative groups. Imagine that a psychologist has requested your help in studying why people act in certain ways. Choose a behavior to be studied, and help the psychologist determine which motivation theory best explains the behavior. He has asked you to prepare a report outlining the solution to this problem.

1. Gather Information. Use your textbook and other resources to find information that will help your group prepare the report. Remember that your report must include information that will convince the psychologist which motivation theory best explains the behavior. This information might include charts and graphs to show the psy-

chologist. You may want to divide up different parts of the research among members of the group.

2. List and Consider Options. After reviewing the information you have gathered, list and consider the theories that you might suggest to the psychologist. Your final solution to the problem may be easier to reach if you consider as many options as possible. Be sure to record the options you have considered for the preparation of your report.

3. Consider Advantages and Disadvantages. Now consider the advantages and disadvantages of each option. Ask questions such as,

- Does the patient's behavior seem to be driven only by biological needs?
- Is the patient's behavior motivated by a desire for personal growth?

Once you have considered the advantages and disadvantages, record them as notes for use in preparing your report.

4. Choose and Implement a Solution. After considering the advantages and disadvantages, you should choose a theory. Next, plan and create a report that describes how your solution will be implemented. Be sure that your report makes your solution very clear.

5. Evaluate the Effectiveness of the Solution. Once you have prepared your report, write a paragraph evaluating how effective your recommendation will be for the psychologist. Explain why you believe that your solution will be more effective than other possible solutions you considered. When you are ready, decide which group members will present which parts of the report. Then take your report to the psychologist (the rest of the class). Good luck!

UNIT 6

CHAPTER 17 • *Stress and Health* describes the effect stress has on physical and psychological health, and identifies ways that people can better cope with stress.

CHAPTER 18 • *Psychological Disorders* explains the causes and symptoms of various types psychological disorders.

CHAPTER 19 • *Methods of Therapy* focuses on the various treatment methods available to people suffering from psychological disorders, including methods of psychotherapy and biological therapy.

Overview

In Unit 6, students will learn about various aspects of physical and psychological health, including how an individual's health is related to stress, the various types of psychological illness, and the treatment methods that attempt to improve an individual's psychological well-being.

UNIT 6
HEALTH AND ADJUSTMENT

CHAPTERS

17   *Stress and Health*

18   *Psychological Disorders*

19   *Methods of Therapy*

▶ Internet Activity

internet connect   go.hrw.com

TOPIC: Psychological Trading Cards
GO TO: go.hrw.com
KEYWORD: SY3 UNIT 6

Have students access the Internet through the HRW Go site to research psychological health and adjustment. Then have students create a set of trading cards that profile a common psychological disorder, issue in mental health, or treatment method. Trading cards should have a photograph or symbol for the topic on one side and information or statistics regarding the topic on the other. Encourage students to be creative. Students may want to model the format of their trading cars on baseball, football, or other collectible trading cards.

▶ Using Visuals

Have students look at the picture on page 383. How do they think this image may be related to the focus of Unit 6—stress, health, and adjustment.

Stress and Health

CHAPTER RESOURCE MANAGER

	Objectives	Pacing Guide		Reproducible and Review Resources
SECTION 1: **What Is Stress?** (pp. 386–392)	Describe some of the main causes of stress.	**Regular** 1 day	**Block Scheduling** .5 day	E Research Projects and Activities for Teaching Psychology
		Block Scheduling Handbook with Team Teaching Strategies, Chapter 17		REV Section 1 Review, p. 392
SECTION 2: **Responses to Stress** (pp. 392–395)	Identify the factors that determine one's responses to stress.	**Regular** 1 day	**Block Scheduling** .5 day	RS Essay and Research Themes for Advanced Placement Students, Theme 15
		Block Scheduling Handbook with Team Teaching Strategies, Chapter 17		REV Section 2 Review, p. 395
SECTION 3: **Physical Effects of Stress** (pp. 395–397)	Explain the general adaptation syndrome, and describe the effects of stress on the immune system.	**Regular** 1 day	**Block Scheduling** .5 day	SM Mastering Critical Thinking Skills 17
		Block Scheduling Handbook with Team Teaching Strategies, Chapter 17		REV Section 3 Review, p. 397
SECTION 4: **Psychological Factors and Health** (pp. 398–402)	Identify the ways in which psychological factors contribute to headaches, heart disease, and cancer.	**Regular** 1 day	**Block Scheduling** .5 day	REV Section 4 Review, p. 402
		Block Scheduling Handbook with Team Teaching Strategies, Chapter 17		
SECTION 5: **Ways of Coping with Stress** (pp. 403–405)	Describe some ways in which people cope with stress.	**Regular** 1 day	**Block Scheduling** .5 day	PS Readings and Case Studies, Chapter 17
		Block Scheduling Handbook with Team Teaching Strategies, Chapter 17		REV Section 5 Review, p. 405

Chapter Resource Key

PS	Primary Sources	**A**	Assessment		Video	
RS	Reading Support	**REV**	Review		Internet	
E	Enrichment		Transparencies		Holt Presentation Maker Using Microsoft® PowerPoint®	
SM	Skills Mastery		CD-ROM			

One-Stop Planner CD–ROM

See the *One-Stop Planner* for a complete list of additional resources for students and teachers.

One-Stop Planner CD–ROM

It's easy to plan lessons, select resources, and print out materials for your students when you use the **One-Stop Planner CD-ROM with Test Generator.**

Technology Resources

 One-Stop Planner, Lesson 17.1
 Homework Practice Online
 Teaching Transparencies 34: The Four Types of Conflict
 HRW Go Site

 One-Stop Planner, Lesson 17.2
 Homework Practice Online
 CNN Presents Psychology: Stress, who needs it

 One-Stop Planner, Lesson 17.3
 Homework Practice Online
 Teaching Transparencies 35: The Fight-or-Flight Response
 HRW Go Site

 One-Stop Planner, Lesson 17.4
 Homework Practice Online
 HRW Go Site

 One-Stop Planner, Lesson 17.5
 Homework Practice Online
 Teaching Transparencies 36: Incidence of Heart Attack and Levels of Physical Activity

Chapter Review and Assessment

 HRW Go site
REV Chapter 17 Review, pp. 406–407
REV Chapter Review Activities with Answer Key

A Chapter 17 Test (Form A or B)
A Portfolio Assessment Handbook
A Alternative Assessment Handbook

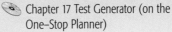 Chapter 17 Test Generator (on the One–Stop Planner)
 Global Skill Builder CD-ROM

---

internet connect

HRW ONLINE RESOURCES

GO TO: go.hrw.com
Then type in a keyword.

TEACHER HOME PAGE
KEYWORD: SY3 Teacher

CHAPTER INTERNET ACTIVITIES
KEYWORD: SY3 PS17
Choose an activity on stress and health to have students:
• create a newspaper on avoiding stress.
• research the impact of stress on everyday life.
• create case studies regarding psychological factors and health.

CHAPTER ENRICHMENT LINKS
KEYWORD: SY3 CH17

ONLINE ASSESSMENT
Homework Practice
KEYWORD: SY3 HP17

Standardized Test Prep
KEYWORD: SY3 STP17

Rubrics
KEYWORD: SS Rubrics

CONTENT UPDATES
KEYWORD: SS Content Updates

HOLT PRESENTATION MAKER
KEYWORD: SY3 PPT17

ONLINE READING SUPPORT
KEYWORD: SS Strategies

CURRENT EVENTS
KEYWORD: S3 Current Events

Additional Resources

PRINT RESOURCES FOR TEACHERS
Boon, T. (1993). Teaching the immune system to fight cancer. *Scientific American, 266*(3), 82–89.

Rodin, J. (1992). *Body traps.* New York: Morrow.

Seligman, M. (1998). *Learned optimism.* New York: Pocket Books.

PRINT RESOURCES FOR STUDENTS
Hipp, E. (1995). *Fighting invisible tigers: A stress management guide for teens.* New York: Free Spirit.

Wilson, N. (1990). *Teenagers and stress.* New York: PPI Publishing.

MULTIMEDIA RESOURCES
Student stress: Coping with academic pressures (VHS). Human Relations Media, 175 Tompkins Ave. Pleasantville, NY 10570 1-800-431-2050.

Teenagers, stress, and how to cope (VHS). Sunburst Communications, Inc., 101 Castleton St. Pleasantville, NY 10570 1-800-431-1934.

Teens dealing with stress (VHS). RMI Media Productions, Inc., 1365 N. Winchester St. Olathe, KS 66061 1-800-745-5480.

STRESS AND HEALTH

Remind students that the teenage years are often stressful because they are a time of enormous changes—emotional, physical, mental, and social. Ask students to provide examples of specific changes that teenagers typically experience. Possible responses may include developing the physical attributes of an adult, dating for the first time, taking on more responsibilities at home, getting a part-time job, choosing a career, and deciding which college to attend. Then tell the class that stress can have a negative impact on people's health. Add that in Chapter 17 students will learn more about what causes stress, how stress can affect them, and what they can do to manage the stress in their lives.

Sections

Each of the five questions identified on page 384 corresponds to one of these sections.

17
Chapter

STRESS AND HEALTH

Read to Discover

1 What are some of the main causes of stress?

2 What are the factors that determine one's responses to stress?

3 What is the general adaptation syndrome, and how does stress affect the immune system?

4 How can psychological factors contribute to headaches, heart disease, and cancer?

5 In what ways can people cope with stress?

384

Each chapter begins with a vignette, called "A Day in the Life," that relates the information discussed in the chapter to the everyday events in the lives of a group of fictional high school students. The text of the chapter occasionally refers back to the vignette to demonstrate the application of the concept being discussed. An icon marked "A Day in the Life" is placed next to these references.

Copy the following graphic organizer onto the chalkboard, omitting the italicized text. Fill in the circles as you introduce the topic of stress.

A DAY IN THE LIFE

May 6

Linda, Marc, and Janet were relaxing after a frantic day at school when they saw Todd rush by. Until recently, Todd was the one person they knew who never seemed to be stressed out.

"Hey, Todd," Marc called out. "Slow down a second. Why are you in such a hurry?"

"Sorry, guys. I really can't talk," Todd answered. "I have to get this scholarship application to Mr. Hochberg, then I have to finish my biology project. Then my dad and I are going to sit down and decide what college I should go to."

"Stay and talk with us for a second," Janet suggested. "You have time to get the application to Mr. Hochberg. And, Todd, you really shouldn't be so stressed. You've already been accepted by almost every college you applied to."

"I know I was accepted, but now I have to decide which one I want to go to. And what if I don't get this scholarship . . . ? Oh, my headache's coming back again."

"Todd, you're going to make yourself sick if you don't calm down a little," Linda warned.

"Thanks for worrying, but I'll be fine," Todd insisted.

"Don't you remember when my dad got sick last year?" Marc reminded Todd. "My dad always seemed like the healthiest guy in the world. Then he got so stressed over work that he started having serious heart problems."

"He's right, Todd," Janet added. "I don't want you to get sick."

"I know, but I have to decide what school to attend, I have to finish my homework, and I'm still working at my part-time job. These aren't things I can just ignore."

"We just want you to find a way to take it easy. We're worried about you," Linda told him.

"Well, I'm open to suggestions if you have any ideas," Todd said as he tried to smile.

"Okay, then," Janet said suddenly. "Why don't you and I play a little basketball tonight? It'll take your mind off things, and the exercise will make you feel better."

"Okay, you're on," said Todd smiling. "Now may I go to Mr. Hochberg's office?"

"Sure," laughed Janet, "but I hope it won't add to your stress when I beat you at basketball."

• • •

With some help from his friends, Todd recognized that he was stressed out and needed to ease up on himself. Many young people and adults alike experience a great deal of stress. This chapter is about the relationship between stress and health. We will explore the many sources of stress and some specific behavior patterns that contribute to stress. We then will look at the psychological factors associated with stress, the body's response to stress, and the effect of stress on one's health. Finally, we will examine the various ways in which people cope with stress.

Key Terms

- stress
- eustress
- distress
- stressor
- approach-approach conflict
- avoidance-avoidance conflict
- approach-avoidance conflict
- multiple approach-avoidance conflict
- self-efficacy expectation
- general adaptation syndrome
- migraine headache
- defensive coping
- active coping

WHY PSYCHOLOGY MATTERS

Psychologists help people deal with the stress of daily life. Use CNNfyi.com or other current events sources to learn more about how psychologists and other professionals help people cope with stress.

CNNfyi.com

Using Key Terms

Organize the class into three groups and assign four terms to each group, keeping the terms in the same sequence as they appear in the list. Have the groups find definitions for their terms in the text or in the Glossary, brainstorm examples of the terms, and determine how the terms are related to one another. When all three groups have completed the task, ask them to share their work.

Class Discussion

Write the term *Stressor* on the chalkboard and then link it with an arrow to the term *Stress.* Tell students that a stressor is anything that causes stress. Ask them to identify the stressors in Todd's life. Record their answers under the word *Stressor* on the chalkboard. What other stressors can they think of that might affect teenagers? Record these as well. Then have students rank the stressors in the list. Point out that becoming aware of significant stressors in their lives is important for reducing the amount of stress they experience.

17

Section Objective

▶ Describe some of the main causes of stress.

This objective is assessed in the Section Review on page 392 and in the Chapter 17 Review.

Opening Section 1

Motivator

Generate a discussion of what stress means to students in the class by writing on the chalkboard, "When I am stressed out, I . . ." Ask volunteers to complete the sentence. Possible responses might include "sweat a lot," "eat junk food," "can't sleep," and "get sick." After students have responded, ask them to give examples of some of the things that they find stressful. Tell the students that they will learn more about stress and its causes by reading Section 1.

Using Truth or Fiction

Each chapter opens with several "Truth or Fiction" statements that relate to the concepts discussed in the chapter. Ask students whether they think each statement is true or false. Answers to each item as well as explanations are provided at appropriate points within the text under the heading "Truth or Fiction Revisited."

Using Visuals

Point out that Figure 17.1 shows that more than half the college students who seek counseling do so because of stress. Also point out that several of the other reasons college students seek counseling are stressors themselves. The transition to the career world, for example, is a major life change, and financial problems are one of many potential daily hassles. Ask volunteers to interview your school psychologist or guidance counselor about the types of stressors high school students experience and to report this information back to the class.

TRUTH OR fiction ?

Read the following statements about psychology. Do you think they are true or false? You will learn whether each statement is true or false as you read the chapter.

- Changes are stressful, even when those changes are for the better.
- Laughter can help people cope with stress.
- Few people are exposed to microorganisms that cause disease.
- Many people develop cancerous cells but do not become ill from them.

SECTION 1

What Is Stress?

In physics, stress is defined as pressure, or a force. Examples of physical stress include tons of rock crushing the earth or water pressing against a dam. Psychological forces, or stresses, can "crush" and "press" people. People may feel crushed by the burden of making an important decision, or they may feel pressed by a lack of time in which to complete a major task.

In psychology, **stress** is the arousal of one's mind and body in response to demands made upon them. Stress forces an organism to adapt, to cope, to adjust. There are different sources of stress, including frustration, daily hassles, life changes, and conflict. Furthermore, the word *stress* is used differently by different psychologists. Some psychologists describe stress as an event that causes tension. Others describe stress as a person's response to a disturbing event. Still others define stress as a person's perception of an event.

Not all stress is bad. Stress can increase sharpness and motivation and can keep people alert and involved. This kind of positive stress is called **eustress**. Positive stress can be a sign that a person is taking on a challenge or trying to reach a goal. For example, you might experience eustress as you participate in a classroom activity, whether you are leading or following the activity.

Negative stress—called **distress**—is linked to intense pressure or anxiety that can have severe psychological and physical effects. When stress becomes too severe or prolonged, it can strain

Students' Reasons for Seeking Counseling

REASON REPORTED	PERCENT REPORTING REASON
Stress, anxiety, nervousness	51
Romantic relationships	47
Low self-esteem, self-confidence	42
Depression	41
Family relationships	37
Academic problems, grades	29
Transition to the career world	25
Loneliness	25
Financial problems	24

FIGURE 17.1 *This table lists some of the reasons college students give for seeking counseling.*

Source: Data are from "College Youth Haunted by Increased Pressures" by B. Murray, 1996, *APA Monitor*, 26 (4), 47.

people's ability to adjust to various situations. Negative stress can dampen people's moods and impair their ability to experience pleasure. Negative stress can even harm the body.

High school and college students often experience stress that is related to family problems, relationships, pressures at school, loneliness, and general nervousness. In fact, stress is one of the main reasons that college students seek help at college counseling centers (Murray, 1996). Figure 17.1 lists a number of the reasons students give for seeking counseling.

Sources of Stress

The event or situation that produces stress is called a **stressor**. However, what is a stressor for one person may not be a stressor for another. For example, two people might react to a long bus trip quite

386

Teaching Section 1

Demonstration

Bring a large, wide-mouthed jar or fishbowl to class. Place a marble in the bottom of the jar or bowl. Give several students a pair of chopsticks, dowels, or similar utensils, and have the students try to remove the marble. Students will quickly realize that this is a difficult and frustrating task. Point out that many difficult situations are frustrating and that frustration is a common cause of stress. Have students provide some examples of situations that might produce frustration and stress.

Summarizing Information

Ask students to keep a list of the daily hassles (as described in the text) in their own lives over the next few days. At the end of the established time period, have students summarize the types of daily hassles that affect them most, such as time-pressure hassles, environmental hassles, or work hassles. Then have students explain how identifying the most common hassles in their lives can help them learn how to avoid such situations or minimize their effects.

differently. For one it might be a relaxing vacation, while for another person it could be stressful and unpleasant. However, some stressors are common to most people. For example, a loud, continuous drilling noise outside one's window would be irritating to just about everyone.

When stressors and stresses pile up on each other, we can reach a point where we have difficulty coping. To avoid reaching that point, it is important to recognize some of the causes of stress.

Frustration One of the most common sources of stress is frustration—being blocked from obtaining a goal. Examples include being delayed from keeping an appointment, lacking enough money to buy an item we need or want, or forgetting something important. Sometimes life seems full of frustrations. Although many frustrations are minor, the more serious ones can be extremely stressful—for example, working for weeks on an important project, only to lose it and have to create it all over again.

Daily Hassles The everyday frustrations we all experience are called daily hassles. They come in different forms, but they have one thing in common—they all create stress. When daily hassles become severe or frequent enough, they can threaten a person's well-being. Psychologist Richard Lazarus and his colleagues (1985) found that there are eight main types of hassles:

- household hassles, including preparing meals, cleaning, shopping, and mowing the lawn
- health hassles, including illness, anxiety about medical or dental treatment, and the side effects of medications
- time-pressure hassles, including the feeling that there are too many things to do, too many responsibilities, and not enough time to do what needs to be done
- inner-concern hassles, including feelings of low self-esteem and loneliness
- environmental hassles, including noise, crowding, pollution, traffic, and crime
- financial hassles, including concerns about paying current bills, repaying loans, and saving for the future
- work hassles, including unhappiness with one's job and problems with coworkers
- future-security hassles, including concerns about job security, taxes, investments, and retirement income

These hassles can result in feelings of tension, nervousness, worry, and sadness.

Life Changes British writer Samuel Johnson wrote, "Change is not made without inconvenience, even from worse to better." Next year, when Todd goes to college, he will be living away from home for the first time. Right now, he may not know where he is going or even where he wants to go. He is, however, undergoing a major life change.

Life changes—such as moving, serious illness, or a death in the family—are another source of stress. Life changes differ from daily hassles in two important ways: (1) All hassles are annoying or irritating, but many life changes go "from worse to better." That is, they are positive and desirable changes. (2) Hassles occur regularly, often on a daily basis; life changes tend to happen less frequently, often after a long, stable period of little or no change.

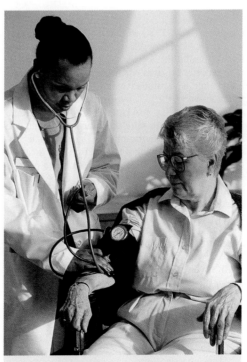

Daily hassles, such as anxiety about medical tests, can create stress. When daily hassles become severe enough, they may threaten a person's well-being.

Primary Source Note

Description of Change: excerpted

Rationale: excerpted to focus on main idea

Class Discussion

Remind students that even positive changes in a person's life can cause stress. Have students discuss and evaluate this statement, explaining why they agree or disagree with it. Then have them provide examples of positive life changes that can produce stress.

internet connect

TOPIC: Avoiding Stress
GO TO: go.hrw.com
KEYWORD: SY3 PS17

Access the Internet through the HRW Go site to research the types of conflicts and events that lead to stress. Then have students write a newspaper article regarding the issues related to stress and how it can be avoided. Ask students to be sure to include the types of conflicts and events that lead to stress.

Some students may have difficulty distinguishing between types of conflict. Tell them that the term *approach* refers to a decision that is attractive, that "pulls" the person to it, such as going to a movie with friends. In contrast, *avoidance* refers to a decision that is unattractive, that "pushes" the person away from it, such as going to the dentist. Have students work through several examples of conflicts to identify both their attractive and unattractive aspects.

Role-Playing

Organize volunteers into four small groups, and assign each group one of the four types of conflict discussed in this section. Tell the members of each group that they are to write (or improvise) and perform for the class a short skit depicting their assigned type of conflict situation. After the groups have performed their skits, have audience members rank the types of conflict situations from least stressful to most stressful and discuss what people can do to make difficult decisions less stressful.

Some people cope with the stress and confusion of making decisions by listing the pros and cons of each possible alternative.

Even new and positive events in a person's life can cause stress. For example, a high-school senior who is looking forward to enlisting in the armed forces, joining the workforce, or attending college may experience stress when preparation for such a life change is combined with schoolwork, a part-time job, social life, or other responsibilities.

Researchers Thomas Holmes and Richard Rahe (1967) attempted to rank the effects of various life changes according to the amount of stress each produced. These life changes ranged from the death of a spouse to less upsetting events, such as a change in sleeping or eating habits and going on a vacation. The researchers asked people to rate each of the life changes on a scale of 1 to 100 in terms of how much stress they experienced and how much adjustment they needed to make. They used the figures they collected to create the Social Readjustment Rating Scale. (See Figure 17.2.)

Even life changes that are enjoyable can produce stress because they require a certain amount of adjustment. According to Holmes and Rahe, too much of a good thing can even make a person ill. Too many life changes, even good ones, can cause stress that leads to headaches, high blood pressure, accidents, and other health problems.

Daily hassles and life changes—especially unpleasant ones—influence the quality of a person's life. They can cause a person to worry excessively and can dampen his or her spirits. Stressors can also lead to health problems that range from minor athletic injuries to serious illnesses, such as heart disease (Kanner et al., 1981; Smith et al., 1990; Stewart et al., 1994). Holmes and Rahe found that people who experienced many life changes within a year's time were much more likely to develop medical problems than those who did not.

TRUTH
OR
fiction
■ REVISITED ■

It is true that changes are stressful, even when those changes are for the better. Changes that improve one's situation can cause stress because, like negative stressors and life changes, they also require adjustment.

Conflict Another source of stress is conflict, being pulled in two or more directions by opposing forces or motives. Conflict can be frustrating, especially when a person is facing a difficult decision.

A DAY IN THE LIFE

For example, Todd had been accepted by several colleges, and he had to decide which college he wanted to attend. The pressure to make the right choice only adds to the stress involved in making such a major decision.

A person thinking about going to college or entering the armed services may feel conflicting emotions. He or she may be excited about the prospect of learning new information and developing new skills for the future. However, college is expensive, and a person who plans to attend college must think about how to pay for it. A young person may be reluctant to accumulate a large debt through college loans that will take many years to repay. The person may also have mixed feelings about leaving his or her home and friends.

Psychologists have identified four types of conflicts (Moir & Jessel, 1991). These are approach-approach conflicts, avoidance-avoidance conflicts, approach-avoidance conflicts, and multiple approach-avoidance conflicts. (See Figure 17.3 on page 390.)

An **approach-approach conflict** is the least stressful type of conflict because the choices are positive. In this situation, each of the goals is both desirable and within reach. Since Todd was accepted by several colleges, he was faced with an approach-approach conflict because he had to choose which college to attend.

An approach-approach conflict is usually resolved by making a decision. However, after the decision is made, the person may still have

Cooperative Learning

Point out that the scale shown on page 389 was developed in the 1960s. Remind students that many changes have occurred in U.S. society since then—for example, the AIDS epidemic, a rise in the number of single-parent families. Organize the class into small groups, and have each group identify ways to update the 1967 scale. Are any items on the scale less important today? Should any items be added? Ask the groups to modify the scale and post their revisions in the classroom for comment by other students.

Predicting Outcomes

Review with students what they learned in Chapter 16 about gender differences. Then ask students to predict how the major life events shown in Figure 17.2 might affect men and women differently. Have students justify their answers. You may wish to have volunteers debate the various responses given by students.

Social Readjustment Rating Scale

Rank	Life Event	Mean Value	Rank	Life Event	Mean Value
1	Death of spouse	100	22	Change in responsibilities at work	29
2	Divorce	73	23	Son or daughter leaving home	29
3	Marital separation	65	24	Trouble with in-laws	29
4	Jail term	63	25	Outstanding personal achievement	28
5	Death of close family member	63	26	Spouse begins or stops work	26
6	Personal injury or illness	53	27	Beginning or ending school	26
7	Marriage	50	28	Change in living conditions	24
8	Fired at work	47	29	Revision of personal habits	24
9	Marital reconciliation	45	30	Trouble with boss	23
10	Retirement	45	31	Change in work conditions	20
11	Change in health of family member	44	32	Change in residence	20
12	Pregnancy	40	33	Change in schools	20
13	Sexual difficulties	39	34	Change in recreation	19
14	Gain of new family member	39	35	Change in church activities	19
15	Business readjustment	39	36	Change in social activities	18
16	Change in financial state	38	37	Mortgage or loans less than $10,000	17
17	Death of close friend	37	38	Change in sleeping habits	16
18	Change to different line of work	36	39	Change in number of family get-togethers	15
19	Change in number of arguments with spouse	35	40	Change in eating habits	15
20	Mortgage over $10,000	31	41	Vacation	13
21	Foreclosure of mortgage or loan	30	42	Christmas	12
			43	Minor violations of the law	11

FIGURE 17.2 *Researchers Thomas Holmes and Richard Rahe created the Social Readjustment Rating Scale to rank the effects of various life changes according to the amount of stress each produces. Since its creation in 1967, it has been revised and expanded by several other researchers.*

Reprinted with permission from T. H. Holmes and R. H. Rahe (1967). The social readjustment rating scale. *Journal of Psychosomatic Research,* 11, 213–218.

Using Visuals

Call students' attention to items 25, 41, and 42 in Figure 17.2. Although most people would think of these as happy or positive events, these events may nonetheless be stressful. Ask the class to think of reasons why these events might be stressful to some people.

Cultural Dimensions

Holmes and Rahe, the psychologists who developed the Social Readjustment Rating Scale, asked people from various cultures to rank the major life events shown in Figure 17.2 in order of their seriousness and the amount of individual adjustment they require. The researchers found that Japanese, Western European, African American, and Mexican American samples of people all agreed on the impact of these life events.

Guided Practice

Copy the first two columns of Figure 17.3 on the chalkboard. Review the four types of conflict, and make sure students understand how the types differ. Point out that what all of the conflicts have in common is that they can be resolved by making a decision. Ask students to provide examples of decisions teenagers commonly make. Which type of conflict is involved in each decision? Do all students agree? Why or why not? List the agreed-on examples in a third column labeled *Examples*. Have students copy down the final chart.

Independent Practice

Organize students into pairs, and have the partners write a dialogue between two hypothetical friends who are discussing a decision that is stressful to one of them. Ask a few of the pairs to read their dialogues to the rest of the class. Ask the other students to identify which type of conflict is involved in each decision. What do students think would be the best way to resolve each conflict?

The Four Types of Conflict

Type of Conflict	Definition	Example
Approach-approach	A choice between two equally attractive alternatives	Choosing between cake and ice cream for dessert
Avoidance-avoidance	A choice between two equally unattractive alternatives	Going to the dentist or letting a toothache get worse
Approach-avoidance	A choice of whether or not to do something when part of the situation is attractive but the other is not	Deciding whether or not to buy a new CD player because it will cost a lot of money
Multiple approach-avoidance	A choice between alternatives that have both good and bad aspects	Deciding to stay at home to study for a test or to go out to the movies with friends

FIGURE 17.3 *Conflict, the feeling that you are being pulled in two or more directions by opposing forces or motives, can be a source of stress. Psychologists have identified four types of conflict.*

persistent self-doubts about whether he or she has made the right decision. The decision maker may not feel settled until he or she is in the new situation and knows that things are working out. For example, even after Todd talks with his father and decides which college he will attend, he may still feel uncertain until he settles into his dorm, meets his roommates, and begins classes.

An **avoidance-avoidance conflict** is more stressful. People in this type of conflict are forced to choose "the lesser of two evils"—that is, to choose between two unsatisfactory alternatives. People are motivated to avoid each of two negative goals, but the problem is that avoiding one requires approaching the other. For example, a student may be faced with the choice of dropping a course in which he or she is doing poorly and may receive a failing grade. However, by dropping the course, the student will not have enough credits to graduate. Both alternatives have a negative side.

A single goal can produce both approach and avoidance motives. This is called an **approach-avoidance conflict**. People face an approach-avoidance conflict when a choice is both good and bad at the same time. For Todd, it might be a college that has an excellent reputation and exactly the program he is looking for, but the college is very far away and visiting home will be difficult and costly.

The most complex form of conflict is a **multiple approach-avoidance conflict**. In this kind of conflict, each of several alternative courses of action has its advantages and disadvantages. Todd may face this type of conflict when he has to decide which college courses to take. The factors he will consider may include his level of interest in the subject, the reputation of the teacher, the usefulness of the course to his overall plan, and the difficulty of the course (does he have the educational background necessary to succeed).

When making a decision about what to eat in a restaurant, you might have to decide between food that is healthful but not very tasty, tasty food that is not very healthful, and food that is both tasty and healthful but is too expensive. In such a situation, you would be faced with a multiple approach-avoidance conflict.

When conflicting motives are strong, people may encounter high levels of stress and confusion about what course of action to choose. They need to make a decision to reduce the stress, yet decision making itself can be quite stressful, especially when there is no clear right choice. Some people cope with such difficult decisions by making a two-column list, jotting down all the reasons for and against a particular choice. The thought that goes into making the list sometimes helps people decide what to do.

CASE STUDIES
AND OTHER TRUE STORIES

Ask students to create a graphic illustration to explain Ellis's A-B-C approach. Under a schematic that links "activating events" via "beliefs" to "consequences," have students list several potentially stressful events, irrational beliefs about the events, and feelings one might have as a consequence of those beliefs. Ask volunteers to present their work to the class and discuss how the beliefs might be modified to reduce the stress of the consequences.

Demonstration

To demonstrate how irrational beliefs can be changed, choose several of the beliefs from page 391 and rephrase them as more rational statements. For example, Irrational Belief 2 might be rephrased as "I will always try my best, but I know that no one is perfect." Then have students suggest situations common to teens and state both an irrational and a rational belief for each situation. For example, an irrational belief about a low test score might be "Now I'll never pass this course"; a rational belief, "Next time, I'll study harder and do better."

CASE STUDIES
AND OTHER TRUE STORIES

Ten Doorways to Distress

According to psychologist Albert Ellis, people's beliefs about events, as well as the events themselves, can be stressful. For example, a student who suddenly finds out she must move with her family to another state may feel a great deal of stress as she wonders how her life will change. Although the move itself may be stressful, anticipating the change and worrying about possible consequences may prove even more stressful.

Ellis uses an A-B-C approach when looking at each situation. For example, moving to another state is an activating event (A). The consequence (C) is stress. Between the activating event (A) and the consequence (C) lie beliefs (B). These beliefs may include such thoughts as "I may not be able to make friends in my new school." Anxieties about the future are normal and to be expected. However, according to Ellis, people tend to have some irrational beliefs that can lead to both depression and stress. He calls these beliefs "personal doorways to distress" because they create problems themselves and, at the same time, aggravate problems from other sources.

Ellis has identified some of these unrealistic expectations and beliefs, which are described below.

Irrational Belief 1: I must have sincere love and approval just about all the time from the people who are important to me.

Irrational Belief 2: I must prove myself to be thoroughly adept at something important. (This belief is called perfectionism.)

Irrational Belief 3: Things have to go the way I want them to go. Life is awful when I can't have my first choice in everything.

Irrational Belief 4: Other people must treat me fairly and justly. When people act unfairly or unethically, they are bad.

Irrational Belief 5: When I see something that is dangerous or makes me afraid, I must concentrate on it and become upset.

Irrational Belief 6: People and things should turn out better than they do. It is terrible when I do not find quick solutions to life's hassles.

Irrational Belief 7: My emotional misery stems from outside pressures that I have little or no ability to control. Unless these pressures change, I am going to have to stay stressed out.

Irrational Belief 8: It is easier to evade life's responsibilities and problems than to face them and try to work them out.

Irrational Belief 9: My past influenced me immensely and must therefore continue to determine the way I feel and act today.

Irrational Belief 10: I can achieve happiness by staying on my present path or by just enjoying myself from day to day.

In the case of the first irrational belief, for example, Ellis finds it understandable that people want the approval of others. However, he thinks it is irrational for them to believe that they cannot survive without it. The belief invites disappointment since it is unrealistic to expect approval all the time. Ellis allows that childhood experiences often explain where such beliefs come from. He also notes, however, that to retain those beliefs can cause much unhappiness. Challenging and changing irrational beliefs is an effective way to reduce stress.

Primary Source Note

Description of Change: excerpted

Rationale: excerpted to focus on main idea

For Your Information

Like Albert Ellis, Dean Ornish, director of the Preventive Medicine Research Institute in Sausalito, California, believes that it is not so much the events in life that are stressful but how one thinks about them. Ornish advises people who are troubled by stressful thoughts to practice meditation, which involves focusing on a single word or phrase. According to Ornish, this helps clear the mind of the worrying that makes events seem more stressful. The benefits of meditation seem to last well beyond the meditation session itself.

WHY PSYCHOLOGY MATTERS

Change can be stressful. Use CNNfyi.com or other current events sources to learn more about how people can help control stress by dealing constructively with changes in their lives. Prepare a brochure that gives people tips on how to deal with stress.

CNNfyi.com

Closing Section 1

Organizing Information

Have students create a three-column chart titled "Five Types of Stressors." Ask them to label the columns *Causes of Stress, Definitions,* and *Examples*. Have students complete their charts with the needed information, exchange them with a partner, and discuss any points of disagreement.

Reviewing Section 1

Have students complete the Section Review questions on page 392.

Section 1 Review: Answers

1. Daily hassles are minor frustrations; life changes are major events.

2. Causes include frustration, daily hassles, and life changes.

3. Students may say that type A people create stress by trying to do too much, working at a rapid pace, and being impatient and dissatisfied with their performance.

Section Objective

▶ Identify the factors that determine one's responses to stress.

This objective is assessed in the Section Review on page 395 and in the Chapter 17 Review.

Here is a classic example of a type A personality—highly driven, intense, and impatient.

Personality Types

Some people actually create their own stress. Psychologists have classified people into two basic personality types: type A (intense) and type B (laid-back). Type A people are always on the go; they put pressure on themselves and thus are constantly under stress. They are highly driven, competitive, and impatient. Type A people always feel rushed and pressured because they operate at full speed and become annoyed when there is even the slightest delay. They are irritable when they have to wait in line. Type A people never seem to have enough time, especially since they often try to do several things at once. They walk, eat, and talk faster than other people, and they are generally quick to become angry.

Type B people, in contrast, are more relaxed. They are more patient, do not become angry as easily, and are typically less driven than type A people. While type A people often earn more money than type B people do, type A people pay a high price for their success. They must live with the heightened stress they create for themselves. Research shows that type A personalities run a much greater health risk than type B people. If they do not loosen up and relax, but instead continue their type A behavior, they are in greater danger of suffering coronary heart disease.

SECTION 1 REVIEW

Homework Practice Online Keyword: SY3 HP17

1. What are the differences between daily hassles and life changes?

2. List the main causes of stress.

3. **Critical Thinking** *Supporting a Point of View* Do you agree that some people create their own stress through type A behavior? Explain your answer.

SECTION 2
Responses to Stress

Psychological factors play an important role in people's responses to stress. People with different types of personalities respond to stress in different ways (Vaillant, 1994). People who are more relaxed and free of conflict are less likely than others to become sick when they do experience prolonged stress (Holahan & Moos, 1990).

The stress of an event depends largely on what the event means to the person involved (Whitehead, 1994). Going to college is important to Todd, but leaving home and being away from his family and friends also means a great deal to him. Moving can be a positive or a negative event, depending on whether one moves to where one wants to be and on the difficulties of packing, unpacking, and paying for the move. Even

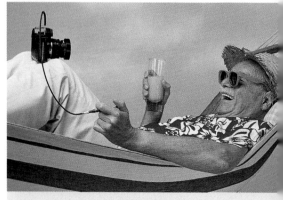

In contrast to type A individuals, those with type B personalities tend to be more relaxed, less ambitious, and more patient.

Opening Section 2

Motivator

Announce that you are giving a pop quiz today. Ask students to take out a sheet of paper, allowing them plenty of time to react to the idea of the quiz. Then explain that there is no quiz—you were simply conducting an experiment. Ask volunteers to discuss their initial reactions to the news of the quiz. How stressful was the news? How stressful would it be if they knew they had a week to prepare for a quiz? Explain that the predictability of events and how well prepared people are to deal with them influence how much stress the events cause.

Teaching Section 2

Cooperative Learning

Organize students into pairs. Then present each pair with a different potentially stressful event or situation. Have one partner describe how someone with psychological hardiness might respond to the event or situation. Then have the other partner describe how someone lacking psychological hardiness might respond. Ask partners to share how they felt giving their responses. (The partner giving the "hardiness" response probably felt more secure and confident than his or her partner.)

a positive move, such as moving to a larger house, creates some stress. However, a negative move, such as an eviction, is much more stressful because of the fear, anxiety, anger, and depression it can trigger.

Biological factors also account for some of the differences in people's responses to stress. Research suggests that some people inherit the tendency to develop certain health problems under stress. Yet most people can do things to influence or reduce the effects of their stress. Factors that influence the effects of stress include self-efficacy expectations, psychological hardiness, a sense of humor, predictability, and social support.

Self-Efficacy Expectations

Do you remember the story "The Little Engine That Could"? In an effort to pull a heavy load up a great hill, the engine repeated to itself, "I think I can, I think I can . . ." The engine succeeded because of its self-efficacy expectations. **Self-efficacy expectations** are the beliefs people have that they can accomplish goals that they set for themselves. The goal might be to write a persuasive essay, dunk a basketball, or learn to solve math problems. Believing one can do it helps one reach the goal.

Self-efficacy expectations are closely related to self-confidence. Self-confidence affects people's abilities to withstand stress (Basic Behavioral Science Task Force, 1996; Maciejewski et al., 2000). For example, when people are in frightening situations, self-confidence reduces the level of adrenaline in the bloodstream (Bandura et al., 1985). As a result, people are less likely to experience panic and nervousness. People with more self-confidence—a strong belief that they can handle difficult situations—are also less likely than those with less self-confidence to be upset by stress. In other words, a self-confident person is more likely to keep cool under pressure.

Psychological Hardiness

Psychological hardiness is a personality characteristic that helps people withstand stress. The research on psychological hardiness is based on the pioneering work of Suzanne Kobasa and her colleagues (1994). They studied business executives who were able to resist illness despite heavy workloads and stress. The researchers found that these psychologically hardy executives differed from other executives in three important ways:

- Commitment. The hardy executives were highly committed to their jobs; they believed

A child who develops strong self-efficacy expectations will probably have a greater sense of self-confidence as an adult.

that their work was meaningful, though it was also demanding and stressful; they regarded their stress as a source of motivation rather than as something that was victimizing them.

- Challenge. The hardy executives sought out challenges; they preferred change to stability even though change required adjustment; they regarded change as interesting rather than threatening.

- Control. The hardy executives viewed themselves as being in control of their lives and able to influence and control the rewards and punishments they received; they did not feel helpless in the face of the forces that were involved in shaping their lives.

Other researchers have also found that believing that one is in control of one's situation tends to enhance one's ability to withstand stress (Folkman & Moskowitz, 2000; Tennen & Affleck, 2000).

Sense of Humor

When Janet jokingly hinted that she would beat Todd at basketball, she instinctively knew that humor was what the situation needed. Do you remember the old saying "Laughter is the best medicine"? The idea that

Class Discussion

Lead the class in a discussion about self-esteem and stress. Initiate the discussion by asking students how self-esteem is related to self-efficacy expectations and to psychological hardiness. *(People with high self-esteem believe in themselves; they are confident that they can accomplish their goals and deal with whatever challenges come their way.)* Ask the class to summarize the discussion by giving examples of how someone with high self-esteem and someone with low self-esteem might respond to the same stressor.

What's New in Psychology?

It may not be the ambition and impatience of type A people that leads to heart disease but rather their hostility. According to a study reported in the July/August 1995 issue of *Health* magazine, physicians who had scored high in hostility on a personality test taken in medical school were four to five times more likely to develop heart disease over the next few decades than physicians who had scored low in hostility.

Closing Section 2

Interpreting Information

Ask students to write a short dialogue between two hypothetical friends, one of whom is experiencing stress, that illustrates several ways of providing social support—such as expressing concern, offering financial or other help, or just socializing. Have volunteers read their dialogues to the class. Ask the class to suggest other ways the characters in the dialogues might provide social support for someone who is experiencing stress.

Synthesizing Information

Have students write a character profile of a person who responds well in stressful situations because he or she has self-efficacy expectations, psychological hardiness, a sense of humor, and social support. How might this person behave? How might others respond to this person?

Reviewing Section 2

Have students complete the Section Review questions on page 395.

Both scientific studies and anecdotal evidence suggest that humor has positive effects on one's health.

humor lightens the burdens of life is one that dates back to ancient times. One study found that students who had a sense of humor and saw humor in difficult situations experienced less stress than students who were not able to find humor in the same situations (Martin & Lefcourt, 1983).

Research suggests that emotional responses, such as happiness and even anger, may have beneficial effects on the immune system as well (Kemeny, 1993). Since humor and laughter are connected with feelings of happiness, they probably really are good "medicine" for the body. In *Anatomy of an Illness as Perceived by the Patient*, Norman Cousins (1979) reported his experience with a painful illness that is similar to arthritis. He found that laughing at Marx Brothers movies eased his pain. Laughter also helped him sleep better. He believed that it even reduced the painful inflammation of his joints.

TRUTH OR fiction

■ REVISITED ■

It is true that laughter can help people cope with stress. Research studies and the personal experiences of many people suggest that laughter is healthy and can actually reduce certain physical symptoms.

Predictability

The ability to predict a stressor seems to reduce the amount of stress it causes. Predictability allows people to brace themselves for an event and, in many cases, to plan various ways to cope with it. Since having control of the situation helps reduce stress, having prior information about the expected stressor gives people a feeling that they will be able to deal with it. For example, ill people who ask about the medical procedures they will undergo and the pain they will experience tend to cope with the stress better than ill people who do not know what to expect (Ludwick-Rosenthal & Neufeld, 1993).

Social Support

The presence and interest of other people provide the social support that helps people cope with stress. Todd's friends realized he was under stress and tried to find ways to help him cope with it. Like psychological hardiness, social support helps insulate people from the effects of stress (Folkman & Moskowitz, 2000a; Uchino et al., 1996). People who lack social skills and spend most of their time alone seem more likely to develop infectious diseases when they are under stress (Cohen & Williamson, 1991).

There are several ways to provide social support to people who are under stress.

- Express your concern by listening to people's problems and offering sympathy, understanding, and reassurance.
- Provide physical relief by offering the material support and services that help people adjust to stress—for example, financial assistance, food, and temporary shelter.
- Offer information, including advice, that helps people cope with stress.
- Provide feedback to help people understand or make sense of what they have experienced.
- Socialize, which includes talking, playing, or just being with the people who are under stress. While this may not directly solve people's problems, it helps them feel less isolated.

Research clearly suggests the value of social support. For example, older people who have social support recover more rapidly from physical problems than older people who have no support (Wilcox et al., 1994). People who have buddies who help them begin an exercise program are more

Extension

Suggest to students that they gain firsthand experience in the benefits of social support by serving as volunteers at places where people tend especially to be in need of such support, such as nursing homes, hospitals, or homeless shelters. Have students detail their experiences in a series of

3
Section Objective

journal entries to share with the class. Ask students to focus on the ways in which social support helps people cope with stressful situations.

▶ Explain the general adaptation syndrome, and describe the effects of stress on the immune system.

---

likely than others to stay with the activity (Gruder et al., 1993; Nides et al., 1995). Social support also appears to shield people and help them recover from feelings of depression (Holahan et al., 1995; Lewinsohn et al., 1994; McLeod et al., 1992).

Social support helps many immigrants to cope with the stresses of adapting to life in the United States. For example, social support helped children cope with the stresses of Hurricane Andrew and helped Chinese villagers cope with a major earthquake (Wang et al., 2000). Social support also helps people remain healthy and in good spirits when caring for other people who have serious health problems.

SECTION 2 REVIEW

go.hrw.com **Homework Practice Online**
Keyword: SY3 HP17

1. What is psychological hardiness?

2. Describe five kinds of social support.

3. **Critical Thinking** *Summarizing* What types of factors determine one's response to stress?

SECTION 3

Physical Effects of Stress

How is it that daily hassles, life changes, conflict, and other sources of stress often make people ill? Stress researcher Hans Selye (1976) suggested that the body under stress is like a clock with an alarm that does not shut off.

The General Adaptation Syndrome

Selye observed that different stressful situations each produced similar responses by the body. Whether the source of stress was a financial problem, a physical threat, or a bacterial invasion, the body's response was the same. Selye labeled this response the **general adaptation syndrome** (GAS). The GAS has three stages: an alarm reaction, a resistance stage, and an exhaustion stage.

The Alarm Reaction The alarm reaction is initiated when a stressor is perceived. This reaction mobilizes the body for defensive action. In the early 1900s, physiologist Walter Cannon described this alarm system as the fight-or-flight reaction.

Animals and human beings experience this fight-or-flight reaction in similar ways. Consider an

When an animal is confronted by a stressor, it prepares itself for defensive action. **During which stage of the GAS does this occur?**

animal's reaction when a stranger approaches or when the animal notices some other change in its environment that signals possible danger. A person might react the same way. Imagine that as you are about to go to sleep, you hear a loud noise in another room. Like the animal, you also become alert to your environment and sensitive to any sight, sound, or other stimulus around you that might indicate danger. Your body is in a state of high alert. Your heart is beating faster, your breathing is quicker, and your muscles are tense. Your body is in the fight-or-flight mode that occurs when danger is perceived to be present.

During the alarm reaction, the sympathetic nervous system is activated (Gallucci et al., 1993). (See Chapter 3.) This produces a flood of stress hormones, including adrenaline, noradrenaline, adrenocorticotropic hormone (ACTH), and corticosteroids. These hormones act in different ways to prepare the body to deal with the stressor.

Adrenaline and noradrenaline arouse the body to help it cope with threats and stress. They do this by speeding up the heart rate and causing the liver to release glucose (sugar), which provides energy for the body under stress. Corticosteroids and ACTH protect the body from allergic reactions (such as difficulty breathing). They also produce an inflammation that increases circulation to the part of the body that may be injured. Finally, they send

---

Caption Question: Answer

This objective is assessed in the Section Review on page 397 and in the Chapter 17 Review.

Section 2 Review: Answers

An animal prepares itself for defensive action during the alarm reaction.

1. Psychological hardiness is a personality characteristic that helps people withstand stress.

2. Five kinds of social support are expressing concern, providing physical relief, offering information, providing feedback, and socializing.

3. Factors include self-efficacy expectations, psychological hardiness, sense of humor, predictability, and social support.

Technology Resources

CNN. Presents Psychology: Stress, who needs it

Opening Section 3

Motivator

Spark students' interest in the GAS by telling them how Hans Selye stumbled on the link between stress and disease. In his early days, Selye was an inexperienced lab worker who sometimes dropped his lab rats and had to chase them around the room. Noticing that the rats he chased developed ulcers, Selye investigated further and concluded that the stress he caused the rats by chasing them depressed their immune systems and led to ulcers. Tell students that the GAS describes how any type of prolonged stress can depress the immune system and cause illness.

Teaching Section 3

Meeting Individual Needs: Visual Learners

To help visual learners understand the general adaptation syndrome, have them create graphs, flowcharts, and/or drawings to illustrate each of the three stages included in the GAS. Also have them write a caption that summarizes the features of the three stages. Display their best efforts in the classroom to help other students gain a better understanding of the GAS.

Teaching Transparencies with Teacher's Notes

TRANSPARENCY 35:
The Fight-or-Flight Response

🎵 internet connect

TOPIC: Physical Effects of Stress

GO TO: go.hrw.com
KEYWORD: SY3 PS17

Have students access the Internet through the HRW Go site and research the physical effects of stress. Then ask students to assume the point of view of the Associate Director of Research on the Physical Effects of Stress for the APA and prepare a report for a Congressional committee investigating the physical effects of stress on individuals. Tell students to summarize the latest research and to recommend a course of action to the Congressional committee.

The Fight-or-Flight Response

- Air passages widen to allow more air intake
- Hair stands on end
- Level of blood sugar increases
- Heart rate increases
- Muscles tighten up
- Blood pressure rises
- Senses sharpen and become more alert
- Steroids and adrenaline are secreted

GRRRR!

FIGURE 17.4 *When a person first perceives a stressor, the body initiates an alarm reaction, which mobilizes the body for defensive action. This reaction is known as the fight-or-flight response.*

white blood cells to the injury to fight off invading germs. Some of the changes that occur as a result of the alarm reaction are shown in Figure 17.4. Once the stressor or threat is removed, the body returns to its previous state.

The Resistance Stage If the alarm reaction mobilizes the body and the stressor is not removed, people enter the resistance stage of the GAS. During this stage, people attempt to find a way to cope with the stressor to avoid being overwhelmed by their negative reactions to the stressor. Hormones are still being released but at lower levels than in the alarm reaction stage. The body tries to regain its lost energy, repair damage, and restore balance. However, at this stage, people may still feel enough of a strain to continue to experience some physical symptoms.

The Exhaustion Stage If the stressor is still not removed, people may enter the exhaustion stage of the GAS. The capacity to resist stress varies from person to person, but everyone eventually becomes

exhausted when severe stressors persist. At this stage, the adrenal and other glands activated by the fight-or-flight reaction can no longer continue to secrete hormones. People's muscles become worn out. Their heart and breathing rates slow down.

As the resources available to combat stress become depleted, people reach a breaking point. Continued stress during the exhaustion stage may cause people to develop health problems ranging from allergies and hives to ulcers and heart disease—and even death.

Effects of Stress on the Immune System

Stress also affects the body's ability to cope with disease. Research shows that chronic stress suppresses the activity of the body's immune system (Coe, 1993; Delhanty et al., 1996; O'Leary, 1990).

The Immune System You might think that some people, luckily, are not exposed to the kinds of organisms that cause serious health problems.

Closing Section 3

Summarizing Ideas

Ask students to write a paragraph summarizing how reactions associated with the general adaptation syndrome can interfere with the normal functioning of the immune system. Have volunteers read their paragraphs aloud to the class for discussion.

Reviewing Section 3

Have students complete the Section Review questions on page 397.

Extension

Ask students to locate and read research reports that show a link between a major life event (such as the death of a close family member) and the risk of becoming ill. Have them share what they learn with the rest of the class in a brief oral or written report. Students' reports should include a description of how the two variables—stress and disease—were measured in each of the research reports they read.

This marathon runner has probably entered the exhaustion stage, during which the adrenal gland and other glands that were activated by the alarm reaction can no longer continue to secrete hormones and the runner's muscles become worn out.

Actually, that is not true. Most people are exposed to a great variety of disease-causing organisms. However, an intact immune system manages to fight off most of them.

How does the immune system fight against disease? The immune system prevents disease by producing white blood cells that destroy disease-causing microorganisms (bacteria, fungi, and viruses), worn-out body cells, and cells that have become malignant (cancerous). White blood cells engage in "search-and-destroy missions." They first recognize and then destroy foreign bodies and unhealthy cells.

Some white blood cells produce antibodies—chemicals that attach to harmful cells and microorganisms, marking them for destruction. Other white blood cells destroy the foreign bodies by surrounding and digesting them. The immune system "remembers" these invaders and maintains antibodies in the bloodstream to fight them, often for years.

TRUTH OR fiction

■ REVISITED ■

It is not true that few people are exposed to the microorganisms that cause disease. Most people are continuously exposed to a great variety of disease-causing microorganisms. However, a healthy immune system produces white blood cells that fight off most of them.

Stress and the Immune System One of the reasons that stress eventually exhausts people is that it stimulates their bodies to produce steroids, which suppress the functioning of the immune system. Persistent secretion of steroids interferes with the formation of antibodies, which are crucial in fighting germs. In the case of some serious diseases, such as cancer, the added stress that results from having a life-threatening disease contributes to the suppression of the immune system, thus leading to further health problems (Andersen et al., 1994).

A study of dental students showed the effects of stress on the immune system (Jemmott et al., 1983). To test the functioning of each student's immune system, researchers measured the level of antibodies in the students' saliva at different times during the school year. The lower the level of antibodies, the lower a person's immune-system functioning.

Students showed lower immune-system functioning during more stressful school periods than during the periods immediately after vacations. The study also showed that students with many friends had healthier immune systems than students with fewer friends. The study suggests that social support may have been a factor in insulating some students from the detrimental effects of stress.

Other studies have found that the stress of examinations weakens the capacity of the immune system to combat certain viruses, such as the Epstein-Barr virus, which causes fatigue and other health problems (Glaser et al., 1991, 1993). In another study researchers found that training aimed at improving coping skills and relaxation techniques improved the functioning of the immune systems of the participants (Glaser et al., 1991).

These studies prove that stress causes the immune system to function less effectively. They also indicate that social support, which reduces stress, makes the immune system function better.

SECTION 3 REVIEW

go.hrw.com **Homework Practice Online**
Keyword: SY3 HP17

1. List and describe the three stages of the general adaptation syndrome.

2. How does the immune system protect people against disease?

3. **Critical Thinking** *Analyzing Information* What advice for maintaining his or her immune system would you give to a student who was in a high-stress situation?

Section Objective

▶ Identify the ways in which psychological factors contribute to headaches, heart disease, and cancer.

This objective is assessed in the Section Review on page 402 and in the Chapter 17 Review.

Opening Section 4

Motivator

Tell the class the following anecdote. One day, a student with a cold accidentally sneezed in the faces of two classmates. Two days later, one came down with a bad cold but the other did not, even though both had equal exposure to the cold virus. Ask students how they would explain this outcome. Then tell them that psychological factors—such as attitudes, patterns of behavior, and depression—can affect how susceptible people are to illness. In this section, students will learn about the role of such factors in headaches, heart disease, and cancer.

Cross-Curricular Link: Health

It has been estimated that stress accounts for between 60 and 90 percent of all visits to a doctor's office. Some of the conditions that stress is known to cause or worsen include asthma, chronic pain, cardiac arrhythmia, insomnia, anxiety disorders, panic attacks, depression, infertility, and premenstrual syndrome.

internet connect

TOPIC: Psychological Factors in Health
GO TO: go.hrw.com
KEYWORD: SY3 PS17

Have students access the Internet through the HRW Go site to research the study of psychological factors and health. Than have students organize their information in the form of hypothetical case studies to be delivered in front of the class. Make sure that the students include case studies regarding headaches as well as heart disease.

SECTION 4

Psychological Factors and Health

Why do some people develop cancer or have heart attacks? Why do others seem immune to these health problems? Why do some people seem to fall prey to just about everything that is going around, while others ride out the longest winters with hardly a sniffle?

Biological factors play an important role in physical illness. For example, family history of a particular disease can certainly increase a person's susceptibility to that disease. Other biological factors that are involved in the development of illness include exposure to disease-causing microorganisms, inoculations against certain diseases, accidents and injuries, and age.

A family history of health problems, such as heart disease and cancer, may tempt some people to assume there is little they can do to influence their health. But one's family history (or genetic inheritance) merely suggests a potential for developing an illness. Health writer Jane Brody (1995) noted that a bad family medical history should not be considered a sign of doom. She noted that, instead, it should be welcomed as an opportunity to keep the harmful genes from expressing themselves.

 Prolonged stress may have caused Marc's father to develop heart problems. This does not necessarily mean, however, that Marc will develop similar health problems. Instead, it has helped Marc to recognize how harmful stress can be and prompted him to take steps to manage the stress in his own life—and advise his friend Todd to do the same.

While biological factors are important, many health problems are affected by psychological factors, such as one's attitudes and patterns of behavior (Ader, 1993; Salovey et al., 2000). Psychological states of anxiety and depression can impair the functioning of the immune system and make people all the more vulnerable to physical health problems (Penninx et al., 1998; Salovey et al., 2000).

Health psychology is concerned with the relationship between psychological factors and the prevention and treatment of physical illness (Taylor, 1990). In recent years, health psychologists have been exploring the various ways in which states of mind influence physical well-being. Because of the growing recognition of the link between psychological factors and health, an estimated 3,500 psychologists are now on the faculties of medical schools (Matarazzo, 1993; Wiggins, 1994).

This section examines the interrelationship of biological and psychological factors in the development and treatment of three fairly common health problems: headaches, heart disease, and cancer. Health psychologists have made important contributions to the understanding and treatment of all three of these medical problems.

Headaches

Among the most common stress-related health problems are headaches. People under stress will sometimes get a headache as a direct result of feeling tense. Todd felt a headache developing as he was trying to deal with the stress of getting his scholarship application in on time. It is estimated that 20 percent of Americans experience intense stress-induced headaches such as the one Todd suffered.

Headaches are among the most common stress-related health problems. They can be treated with medicine and various behavioral methods, such as progressive relaxation and biofeedback.

Teaching Section 4

Guided Practice

Point out to the class that cause-and-effect relationships between variables can be two-way. Draw a schematic on the chalkboard that consists of a two-way arrow connecting the terms *stress* and *illness,* indicating that stress can be both a cause and an effect of illness. Ask students to describe how stress contributes to each of the three illnesses discussed in this section: headache, heart disease, and cancer. Then ask students to describe how each of these illnesses can in turn cause additional stress.

Independent Practice

Have students interview friends, teachers, and family members about how they feel when they have headaches and what they think causes their headaches. Can the students identify signs of stress as both the cause and the effect of headaches in the responses of the people interviewed? Ask students to share the findings of their interviews with the rest of the class.

Types of Headaches There are several types of headaches. The most frequent kind is the muscle-tension headache. When people are under stress, the muscles in their shoulders, neck, forehead, and scalp tend to tighten up. Prolonged stress can lead to prolonged muscle contraction, which causes muscle-tension headaches. Such headaches usually come on gradually. They are characterized by dull, steady pain on both sides of the head and by feelings of tightness or pressure.

The next most common kind of headache is the **migraine headache.** Migraine headaches usually have a sudden onset and are identified by severe throbbing pain on one side of the head. Migraines affect 1 American in 10. They may last for hours or days. Some people have warning "auras" before attacks. These warnings include visual distortions or the perception of unusual odors. The migraines themselves may be accompanied by sensitivity to light, loss of appetite, nausea, vomiting, loss of balance, and changes in mood. Brain imaging suggests that when something triggers a migraine, neurons at the back of the brain fire in waves that ripple across the top of the head then down to the brainstem, which has many pain centers.

Triggers for migraines include barometric pressure, pollen, some drugs, monosodium glutamate—better known as MSG, a chemical often used to enhance the flavor of food. Other triggers are aged cheese and the hormonal changes connected with menstruation (Mulvihill, 2000).

Psychological factors also trigger or worsen migraines. For example, the type A behavior pattern apparently contributes to migraines. In one study, 53 percent of people who had migraine headaches showed the type A behavior pattern, compared with 23 percent of people who had muscle-tension headaches (Rappaport et al., 1988). Another study compared 26 women who had regular migraines with women who did not get migraines. The migraine sufferers were more sensitive to pain, more self-critical, more likely to believe that stress and pain were awful things, and less likely to seek social support when they were under stress (Hassinger et al., 1999).

Regardless of the source of the headache, people can unwittingly propel themselves into a vicious cycle. Headache pain is a stressor that can lead to an increase in, rather than a relaxing of, muscle tension in the neck, shoulders, scalp, and face.

Treatment Aspirin, acetaminophen, and many prescription drugs are used to fight headache pain.

Some inhibit the production of the prostaglandins that help initiate transmission of pain messages to the brain. Newer prescription drugs can help prevent many migraines. Behavioral methods can also help. Progressive relaxation focuses on decreasing muscle tension and has been shown to be highly effective in relieving muscle-tension headaches. Biofeedback training has also helped many people with migraine headaches. However, these methods should only be attempted under the supervision of a trained health-care professional.

Heart Disease

Nearly half the deaths in the United States each year are caused by heart disease (American Heart Association, 2000), making it a major national health problem. Marc's father is just one of the people who have developed heart disease. There are many risk factors associated with heart disease.

- *Family history (genetics).* People with a family history of heart disease are more likely than others to develop heart disease themselves (American Heart Association, 2000).
- *Physical conditions.* Obesity, high serum cholesterol levels, and hypertension all contribute to heart disease. About one American in five has hypertension—abnormally high blood pressure. Although there appears to be a genetic component to hypertension (Levy et al., 2000; Williams et al., 2000), many other factors are also involved. These factors include smoking, obesity, and excessive salt in one's diet. Blood pressure also rises when people become angry or are on guard against threats (Suls et al., 1995).
- *Patterns of consumption.* Heavy drinking, smoking, overeating, and eating food high in cholesterol can also contribute to heart disease (Stampfer et al., 2000). Smoking, for example, raises the level of cholesterol in the blood and weakens the walls of blood vessels (Bartecchi et al., 1994).
- *Type A behavior.* People who exhibit type A behavior are more likely than people who exhibit type B behavior to develop heart disease (Thoresen & Powell, 1992).
- *Anger and hostility.* A constant need to control angry and hostile impulses increases the risk of developing heart disease (Birks & Roger, 2000; Richards et al., 2000).

Class Discussion

Have students review the risk factors associated with heart disease, shown on pages 399 and 401. Point out that a majority of the factors are preventable. Ask students to speculate on why many Americans continue to ignore the health risks associated with unhealthy habits and behavior, including a diet high in fat and type A behavior. As a class, brainstorm ideas for changing Americans' unhealthy habits. (Students may suggest a campaign similar to the anti-smoking advertisements.)

For Your Information

For decades, members of the medical profession believed that women were at far lower risk for heart disease than men. Thus, simply being male was considered a risk factor for heart disease. Although many people still think of heart disease as primarily a male problem, recent research indicates that this is not the case. Heart disease is the number one cause of death for women as well as men, although women tend to develop cardiovascular problems later in life than men do.

For Further Research

Have students conduct library research to find information about the role heredity plays in the development of serious diseases such as cancer and heart disease. Also have students find out what people who have a hereditary disposition for these types of diseases can do to lower their probability of contracting a serious disease. What behavioral changes do experts recommend? What psychological changes do they recommend? Have students present their findings in a written report.

Point out that in studies of cause and effect, variables representing presumed causes are often treated as independent variables and those representing presumed effects as dependent variables. The researchers then study how variation in the independent variables influences the dependent variables. Have students identify the independent (*diet*) and dependent (*health status*) variables in Campbell's study.

Primary Source Note

Description of Change: excerpted

Rationale: excerpted to focus on main idea

Cultural Dimensions

There are gender as well as cultural differences in heart disease, yet until the late 1980s most large-scale studies of heart disease included only men as subjects. Researchers now know that cardiovascular diseases, their risk factors, and the drugs used to treat them do not always affect both sexes in the same way. Consider the following: Women are more likely than men to die in the first year following a heart attack; the link between a high-fat diet and heart disease is not as strong for women as it is for men; and some blood pressure medications are much less effective for women than for men.

Think About It: Answer

Students are likely to suggest decreasing the amount of meat and dairy products in the diet and increasing the amount of vegetables, legumes, and grains.

EXPLORING
DIVERSITY

Cultural Differences in Diet and Health

How important is an individual's diet to his or her health? In their search for evidence about the relationship between diet and health, researchers often look at Asian countries, where rates for cancer, heart disease, and other degenerative diseases are considerably lower than in Western nations.

Research indicates that death rates from cancer and heart disease are relatively high in Western nations such as the Netherlands, Denmark, the United Kingdom, Canada, and the United States, where people eat foods with a high fat content (Cohen, 1987). Death rates from cancer, heart disease, and other serious conditions are lower in Asian nations such as Thailand, the Philippines, Japan, and China, where the consumption of fat is lower.

Studies have shown that the difference has more to do with diet than with race. For example, the diets of Japanese Americans are similar in fat content to those of other Americans—and so are their death rates from cancer. Because of dietary differences, Japanese American men living in California and Hawaii are also much more likely to become overweight than Japanese men who live in Japan (Curb & Marcus, 1991).

One of the most extensive nutrition research projects ever undertaken was conducted by T. Colin Campbell, professor of nutritional biochemistry at Cornell University, and colleagues from China and Oxford Universities. Begun in 1983, the China Diet and Health Study used the vast population of China to study the relationship between

The low-fat diet in many Asian countries has been linked to lower rates of cancer, heart disease, and other degenerative diseases than the rates in Western countries.

dietary intake and health. Beginning in 1983, the study collected information about the eating habits and health records of thousands of people in 65 Chinese provinces. The researchers studied the kinds of foods eaten, examined medical records, took blood samples, and made other tests on thousands of rural Chinese.

In 1991, Campbell's team published an 896-page report containing their initial findings, which they are continuing to analyze and add to as the study progresses. So far, the researchers have found that the Chinese consume far greater amounts of rice and other grains, vegetables, and legumes (beans and peas) than Americans do. They also found that Asian diets are much lower in protein than the average American diet. On average, Asians eat far less meat and dairy products than Americans do. The Chinese plant-based diets were found to be much more healthful because they consist of significantly less fat and animal protein.

The preliminary conclusion of this ongoing study is that the Chinese diet of good-quality plant foods is preventing a wide range of degenerative diseases. "Our study suggests," says Campbell, "that the closer one approaches a total plant food diet, the greater the health benefits."

Think About It

Analyzing Information What are some positive dietary changes that Americans could make to ensure longer and healthier lives?

- *Job strain.* Overtime work, assembly-line labor, and exposure to conflicting demands on the job can all contribute to heart disease (Jenkins, 1988).
- *Lack of exercise.* People who do not get regular exercise are more likely to suffer from coronary heart disease than those who do exercise regularly (Stampfer et al., 2000).

Once heart disease has been diagnosed, various medical treatments, such as surgery and medication, are available. However, people can also benefit from behavioral changes that reduce the risks of heart disease. Among these behavioral changes are the following:

- Quitting smoking. The links between smoking and heart disease (and lung cancer) make quitting smoking the single best way to reduce the risks of serious health problems.
- Controlling weight. Maintaining a healthy weight appropriate to one's body proportions, not being either overweight or underweight, can help reduce the risk of heart disease.
- Reducing hypertension. Relaxation training, meditation, exercise, weight control, and a reduction in the intake of salt all help control blood pressure.
- Lowering serum cholesterol levels. Behavioral methods for lowering cholesterol include cutting down on foods high in cholesterol and saturated fats and exercising regularly (Stampfer et al., 2000).
- Changing type A behavior patterns. Learning to slow down and relax can decrease the risk of heart attacks. This is especially true for people who exhibit type A behavior and who have had previous heart attacks (Friedman & Ulmer, 1984; Roskies et al., 1986).
- Exercising regularly. A sustained program of exercise protects people from heart disease (Stampfer et al., 2000). People should consult their physicians before beginning an exercise program.

Cancer

Cancer is a disease that involves the rapid and abnormal growth of malignant cells. Cancerous cells can take root anywhere—for example, in the blood, skin, digestive tract, lungs, or reproductive organs. If not controlled early, cancer cells can spread and establish masses, or tumors, elsewhere in the body. People actually develop cancer cells frequently, but the immune system normally succeeds in destroying them. Individuals whose immune systems are weakened by physical or psychological factors appear to be more likely candidates than others for getting cancer (Azar, 1996).

TRUTH OR fiction
■ REVISITED ■

It is true that many people develop cancerous cells but do not become ill from them. A strong immune system regularly rids the body of such cells. A weakened immune system has a more difficult time destroying them.

Risk Factors People may inherit a tendency to develop certain kinds of cancer. The genes involved may remove the normal controls on cell division, allowing cancer cells to multiply wildly (Lichtenstein et al., 2000). Certain kinds of behavior also increase the risk of cancer. These behaviors include smoking, sunbathing (ultraviolet light can cause skin cancer), and eating animal fats (Bartecchi et al., 1994; Willett et al., 1990). Substances in cigarette smoke may damage the genes that would otherwise block the development of many types of cancers. Psychological problems such as prolonged anxiety and depression may also heighten the risk of cancer (Penninx et al., 1998; Salovey et al., 2000).

Research suggests that stress may be an additional risk factor for the development of cancer. In one study, researchers separated mice into one of two groups. One group was regularly subjected to stressful conditions, while the other group was not. The immune systems of the mice in the group that was exposed to stressful conditions showed a reduced ability to kill cancer cells compared to the mice that were not exposed to stressful conditions (Kandil & Borysenko, 1987). Other experiments with animals have suggested that once cancer has taken root, stress can affect the course of its development (Visintainer et al., 1982).

In one study, researcher V. Riley (1981) examined the effects of a cancer-causing virus that can be passed from female mice to their nursing

401

Closing Section 4

Classifying Information

Ask students to identify factors that increase people's risk of both heart disease and cancer, the two major killers of men and women in the United States today. Which of the risk factors can be reduced by making behavioral changes?

Reviewing Section 4

Have students complete the Section Review questions on page 402.

Extension

Have students research and report on some of the alternative approaches to the treatment of serious illness (for example, acupuncture, macrobiotic diets, meditation). Ask students to find out how these treatments are used, why people use them, and how the medical community views such treatments. Also have students learn why the proponents of alternative medicine consider these types of treatments to be of value. Have students present their findings to the class for discussion.

Section 4 Review: Answers

1. Attitudes, patterns of behavior, and levels of anxiety and depression may contribute to headaches, heart disease, and cancer.

2. Stress might weaken the ability of the immune system to destroy cancer cells.

3. Psychological can help people modify unhealthy attitudes and behavior patterns and manage stress.

offspring. The virus usually produces breast cancer in 80 percent of the female offspring by the time they have reached the age of 400 days.

Riley placed one group of female offspring that had been infected with the virus into a stressful environment with loud noises and unpleasant odors. She placed another group in a less stressful environment. By the age of 400 days, 92 percent of the female mice in the stressful environment had developed breast cancer, as compared with 7 percent of those in the other group. The mice that underwent stress also had increased levels of steroids that suppress the functioning of the immune system.

However, by the time another 200 days had elapsed, the mice that had been placed in the non-stressful environment showed about the same incidence of cancer as those that had experienced the stressful environment. Exposure to stress seemed to hasten the development of cancer in the mice infected with the cancer-causing virus. Nevertheless, the absence of stress did not prevent mice placed in a less stressful atmosphere from ultimately developing cancer as well.

Psychological Aspects People with cancer must cope with the many biological aspects of their illness, ranging from possible weakness and pain to the side effects of their medications. They also face many psychological effects of cancer. Anxiety about the medical treatment itself and about the possible approach of death are common psychological effects of cancer. Additionally, severe depression and feelings of vulnerability often accompany the diagnosis of cancer (Jacox et al., 1994).

Many people who are diagnosed with cancer are also burdened by the necessity of dealing with the insensitivity of others. Other people may actually criticize the person with the illness for feeling sorry for himself or herself or for "giving up" the fight against the disease (Andersen et al., 1994; Rosenthal, 1993).

Painful side effects sometimes accompany the treatment for certain types of cancer. For example, nausea frequently accompanies chemotherapy. People receiving chemotherapy are sometimes taught relaxation and guided imagery techniques, which have been shown to significantly reduce the nausea and vomiting associated with chemotherapy (Burish et al., 1987).

Studies with children and adolescents who have cancer have found that playing video games also reduces the discomfort of chemotherapy (Kolko &

Rickard-Figueroa, 1985; Redd et al., 1987). By allowing the children to focus their attention on battling computer-generated enemies, such games help keep the children distracted from the discomfort caused by the treatment.

Cancer requires medical treatment, and in some cases there are too few available treatment options. However, the attitudes people have about their cancer do seem to make a difference. A 10-year follow-up of women with breast cancer found a significantly higher survival rate among women who met their diagnosis with a "fighting spirit" rather than with resignation (Pettingale et al., 1985). A desire to fight the illness is apparently a key component of successful treatment. Social support also increases the survival rate of people who have cancer (Sleek, 1995).

Psychologists have found that the feelings of hopelessness that sometimes accompany the diagnosis of cancer may hinder recovery because they can suppress the person's immune system (Brody, 1994; Levy et al., 1985). Hospitalization itself is stressful because it removes people from the familiar surroundings of home and the sources of social support. Furthermore, being in the hospital and subject to hospital routines—for any reason—reduces one's sense of control.

In some cases, there may not be a great deal that a person with cancer can do to affect the eventual outcome of the disease. However, there are numerous ways to reduce the risk of developing cancer. The most effective way is to avoid behavioral risk factors for cancer by reducing the intake of fats and increasing the intake of fruits and vegetables (Mevkens, 1990; Willett et al., 1990). Limiting the amount of stress one is exposed to and having regular medical checkups are also vital factors in the reduction of the risk of developing cancer.

SECTION 4 REVIEW

go.hrw.com
Homework Practice Online
Keyword: SY3 HP17

1. What psychological factors contribute to headaches, heart disease, and cancer?

2. Explain how stress might affect the progression of cancer.

3. **Critical Thinking** *Summarizing* How can psychological methods be used to help people prevent or deal effectively with health problems?

Section Objective

▶ Describe some ways in which people cope with stress.

This objective is assessed in the Section Review on page 405 and in the Chapter 17 Review.

Motivator

On the chalkboard, draw a flowchart that shows the alternatives one can take in coping with a stressor: change the environment to remove the stressor (active coping), change the response to the stressor so it is no longer harmful (active coping), or reduce the immediate effects of the stressor (defensive coping). Give students an example of a stressor, such as a conflict with a friend, and ask them to provide examples of each way of coping. Tell them that in Section 5 they will learn more about ways of coping with stress.

SECTION 5

Ways of Coping with Stress

Because stress harms people's physical and psychological well-being, it is important to know how to cope with or reduce the stress in one's life. In this section we consider various ways of handling stress, including defensive coping and active coping.

Defensive Coping

Defensive coping is one way to reduce the immediate effects of a stressor, but it is probably not the most desirable way. Defensive coping may involve socially unacceptable behavior (substance abuse or aggression), running away from one's problems (withdrawal), or self-deception (use of defense mechanisms).

Defensive coping may give people time to gather their resources, but it does not eliminate the source of stress or improve the effectiveness of one's response to stress. In fact, in the long run, defensive methods are self-defeating and usually harmful.

Some people use aggression to cope with stressful situations. However, aggressive behavior can often increase conflict rather than resolve it.

Substance Abuse Some adolescents and adults use alcohol, tranquilizers, and other drugs to try to reduce feelings of stress (Wills et al., 1996). People may become psychologically dependent on these substances as they try to decrease their awareness of stress or to disguise what has become, for them, an unpleasant reality. That dependence only makes a problem worse because it makes people less able and less willing to deal with it.

Aggression Some people use aggression and violence to cope with stressful situations, such as those that involve feelings of frustration or a difference of opinion with another person. However, violence rarely, if ever, provides solutions to people's problems. In fact, aggressive behavior often heightens interpersonal conflict because it may motivate an injured party to seek revenge.

Withdrawal Some people withdraw from a stressful situation because they are frightened, feel helpless, or believe that any decision they make will be a mistake. Withdrawal can be emotional (loss of interest in life, turning away from friends and family), or it can be physical (moving to a new location to avoid dealing with an old problem).

Suicide Suicide is the ultimate form of withdrawal. Some people experience so much stress and feel so hopeless about solving their problems that they believe the only way out is to commit suicide. Of course, suicide does not solve or reduce problems. It usually only increases the pain of those who are left to deal with its aftermath.

Defense Mechanisms Sigmund Freud believed that defense mechanisms protect the ego from anxiety that may be produced by an awareness of unacceptable ideas or impulses. (See Chapter 14.) Defense mechanisms become problematic when they are the only means used to cope with stress.

Active Coping

Active coping involves changing the environment or situation (in socially acceptable ways) to remove stressors or changing one's response to stress so that stressors are no longer harmful. Todd was actively coping with the stressors in his life by submitting his scholarship application, talking with his father about his college selection, and completing his biology project.

Teaching Section 5

Interpreting Ideas

Describe several situations to the class in which an individual's stressful thoughts are creating additional stress. For example, a teenager might be hesitating outside the gym where a dance is being held, thinking, "I can't go in there—no one will dance with me, and I'll look like a fool." For each situation, ask students to suggest calming thoughts that might help reduce the stress the individual is feeling. For example, instead of having self-defeating thoughts, the teenager outside the gym might think, "I'll bet half the kids in there are as nervous as I am."

Role-Playing

Organize the class into small groups. Tell the members of each group that they are to write and perform a short skit about a group of friends, one of whose stressful thoughts are interfering with his or her ability to deal with a stressful situation. The members of the group are to help this person recognize his or her stressful thoughts and suggest ways that the person can change them. After each group has performed its skit for the class, have the class critique the skit and suggest additional approaches to the solution of the problem.

Section 5 Review: Answers

1. Defensive coping does not eliminate the source of the stress or improve one's ability to cope with it. In contrast, active coping reduces the effects of the stressor by changing the environment in a socially acceptable way.

2. Stressful thoughts increase the amount of stress people experience.

3. Methods of defensive coping become harmful when they cause problems. For example, drugs and alcohol do not solve problems; they are likely to be worse than the original stressors.

Changing Stressful Thoughts

Stressful Thoughts	Calming Thoughts
"I feel like I'm losing control."	"This is painful and upsetting, but I don't have to go to pieces."
"This will never end."	"This will come to an end even if it's hard to see it right now."
"How can I go out there? I'll look like a fool."	"So you're not perfect. That doesn't mean that you're going to look stupid. And so what if someone thinks you look stupid? You can live with that too. Just stop worrying and have some fun."
"My heart is beating so fast. I feel like it's about to leap out of my chest."	"Calm down—hearts don't leap out of chests. Stop and think! Distract yourself. Breathe slowly, in and out."
"There's nothing I can do!"	"Stop and think—just because you can't come up with a solution right now doesn't mean there's nothing you can do. Take it one minute at a time. Breathe easy."

FIGURE 17.5 *Some people think stressful thoughts, which increases the stress they experience. People can actively cope with stress by becoming aware of these thought patterns and changing them.*

Sometimes stressors cannot be reduced, eliminated, or changed. In such cases, active coping involves adjusting to the stressors by reducing their impact. When Janet suggested playing basketball with Todd, she was trying to help him soften the effect of the stressors he was experiencing. Some methods of active coping include changing stressful thoughts, relaxing, and strengthening one's ability to withstand stress through exercise.

Changing Stressful Thoughts   Have you ever had any of these thoughts?

"I feel like I'm losing control."

"This will never end."

"How can I go out there? I'll look like a fool."

"My heart is beating so fast. I feel like it's about to leap out of my chest."

"There's nothing I can do!"

Each of these thoughts increases the amount of stress people experience. However, people who have stressful thoughts can learn to recognize and change them before becoming overwhelmed by them. Through careful study, people can learn to identify self-defeating thoughts. Whenever a person feels tense or anxious, he or she should pay close attention to such thoughts and transform them into calming ones. (See Figure 17.5.) A sign that this is working is evident when the person begins to automatically have calming thoughts rather than stressful ones.

Relaxation   Stress can cause strong bodily reactions, such as muscle tension, rapid breathing, high blood pressure, sweating, and a rapid heart rate. These reactions are signs that something is wrong. They prompt people to survey the situation and try to make things right. Psychologists and other researchers have developed a number of methods for reducing the bodily changes that are brought on by stress. These methods include meditation, biofeedback, and progressive relaxation. (See Chapter 5.)

Progressive relaxation helps lower stress in the body by reducing muscle tension. Reducing tension also affects the heart and breathing rates. Progressive relaxation teaches people how to relax by having them purposely tense a specific muscle group and then relax it. This process of tensing and then relaxing helps people develop awareness of muscle tension and distinguish between feelings of tension and feelings of relaxation. For example, a person can experience muscle relaxation in the arms while leaning back in a reclining chair by first tightening one fist, then the other, and gradually increasing the pressure (Wolpe & Lazarus, 1966).

Changing stressful thoughts and lowering the level of bodily reactions to stress reduce the effects of stressors and give the person more time to develop a plan for effective action. When there is no way to reduce or eliminate the stressors, thinking calming thoughts and relaxing the body will increase the ability to endure stress.

Closing Section 5

Evaluating Information

Ask students to write six statements summing up what they believe are the most important points in this section. Then have them rewrite the statements as true-false questions and use them to quiz a partner. Do the partners agree on which points are most important?

Reviewing Section 5

Have students complete the Section Review questions on page 405.

Extension

Suggest that students engage in some type of stress-reducing physical exercise, such as walking, jogging, or bicycle riding, for a period of one week. Have students keep a journal of the thoughts and emotions they experience during each exercise period. At the end of the week, have the students write a paragraph about the benefits they think they received from the exercise. Ask volunteers to read their paragraphs to the class. Encourage students to make this exercise program part of their daily routine.

Exercise Exercise fosters physical health, enhances people's psychological well-being, and helps people cope with stress (Jonsdottir et al., 2000; Tkachuk & Martin, 1999). Janet knew that. That is why she suggested to Todd that they play basketball. Other kinds of stress-reducing exercise include activities such as running and jogging, running in place, brisk walking, swimming, bicycle riding, jumping rope, and playing team sports.

Sustained physical activity reduces the incidence of heart attacks (Stampfer et al., 2000). In one long-term research project, Paffenbarger and his colleagues (1993) studied 17,000 people. They

Incidence of Heart Attacks and Level of Physical Activity

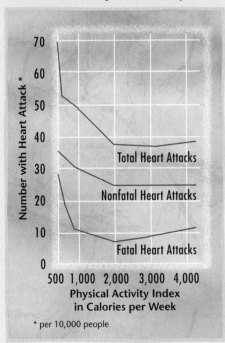

FIGURE 17.6 *Research suggests that sustained physical activity reduces the incidence of heart attacks. In one study, researchers (1993) correlated the incidence of heart attacks with the level of physical activity. Their results showed a decline in the incidence of heart attacks as the activity level rose. The decline seemed to level off at the activity level of burning approximately 2,000 calories a week.*

Source: Paffenbarger et al. (1993). *New England Journal of Medicine, 328,* 538–545.

Exercise is one of the most effective ways to control stress and maintain physical and psychological well-being.

examined the relationship between the incidence of heart attacks and the levels of physical activity in the people they studied. As shown in Figure 17.6, the incidence of heart attacks began declining when the physical activity level rose to that of burning as few as 500 calories a week.

Inactive people run the highest risk of heart attacks. People who burn at least 2,000 calories a week through physical activity live two years longer, on average, than less active people. Sustained exercise also appears to strengthen the functioning of the immune system (Jonsdottir et al., 2000; Tkachuk & Martin, 1999).

SECTION 5 REVIEW

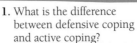

Keyword: SY3 HP17

1. What is the difference between defensive coping and active coping?
2. How do people's thoughts affect the amount of stress they experience?
3. **Critical Thinking** *Drawing Inferences and Conclusions* How can methods of defensive coping become harmful rather than helpful?

Teaching Transparencies with Teacher's Notes

TRANSPARENCY 36: Incidence of Heart Attack and Levels of Physical Activity

Chapter 17 Review: Answers

Writing a Summary
See the section subtitles for the main topics in the chapter.

Identifying People and Ideas
1. the arousal of one's mind and body in response to demands made upon them
2. positive stress
3. negative stress
4. an event or situation that produces stress
5. conflict in which a person is forced to choose between two unsatisfactory alternatives
6. conflict in which each of several alternatives has advantages and disadvantages
7. beliefs people have that they can accomplish goals that they set for themselves
8. the body's similar responses to different types of stresses

405

Technology
▶ Chapter 17 Test Generator (on the One-Stop Planner)
▶ HRW Go site

Reinforcement, Review, and Assessment
▶ Chapter 17 Review, pp. 406–407
▶ Chapter Review and Activities with Answer Key
▶ Alternative Assessment Handbook
▶ Portfolio Assessment Handbook
▶ Chapter 17 Test (Form A or B)

PSYCHOLOGY PROJECTS

Linking to Community Invite a community practitioner in aerobic exercise to show the class how his or her specialty helps people cope with stress. Ask the practitioner to demonstrate some of the techniques used and to explain why they lead to relaxation and reduced feelings of

---

9. a way to reduce the immediate effects of a stressor

10. coping that involved changing the environment or situation to remove stressors, or changing one's response to stress so that stressors are no longer harmful

Understanding Main Ideas

1. Eustress can keep people stay alert and involved.

2. Self-efficacy expectations are closely related to self-confidence. Self-confidence helps people handle stress.

3. The general adaptation syndrome is the body's typical response to stress.

4. Methods include progressive relaxation and biofeedback.

5. Defensive coping includes substance abuse, aggression, withdrawal, suicide, and defense mechanisms; active coping includes changing stressful thoughts, relaxing, and exercising.

Thinking Critically

1. Overeating is defensive coping; leaving early and lying down while listening to music are active coping.

2. Students may say that insurance companies should not charge higher rates for people under stress because stress is difficult to measure and because there are many behaviors that put people at high risk for health problems, such as lack of exercise or unhealthy diets.

Chapter 17 REVIEW

Writing a Summary

Using standard grammar, spelling, sentence structure, and punctuation, summarize the information in this chapter. Consider:
• the causes of stress and the general adaptation syndrome
• the effects of stress on health, and the ways people try to cope with stress

Identifying People and Ideas

Identify the following terms or people and use them in appropriate sentences.

1. stress
2. eustress
3. distress
4. stressor
5. avoidance-avoidance conflict
6. multiple approach-avoidance conflict
7. self-efficacy expectation
8. general adaptation syndrome
9. defensive coping
10. active coping

Understanding Main Ideas

SECTION 1 (pp. 386–392)
1. What are the benefits of eustress?

SECTION 2 (pp. 392–395)
2. How do self-efficacy expectations affect the way a person responds to stress?

SECTION 3 (pp. 395–397)
3. What is the general adaptation syndrome?

SECTION 4 (pp. 398–402)
4. What are some behavioral methods for reducing the pain of headaches?

SECTION 5 (pp. 403–405)
5. List two defensive coping methods and two active coping methods.

Thinking Critically

1. Categorizing Which of the following reactions to stress are defensive coping and which are active coping: overeating, leaving for work early to avoid rush-hour traffic, lying down while listening to music?

2. Supporting a Point of View Should companies that provide health and life insurance be allowed to charge higher rates to people under high levels of stress? Support your answer.

3. Analyzing Information Under what circumstances might eustress help a person perform better?

4. Summarizing What are three behavioral changes that help reduce the risk of heart disease?

Writing About Psychology

1. Analyzing Information Research how stress in the workplace, along with other stress, can affect a person's health and well-being. What kinds of situations contribute to job stress? How do employers try to deal with job stress? Write a report summarizing your findings.

2. Comparing and Contrasting Reread the chapter's section on type A and type B personalities. Think of famous people (present or past) or fictional characters that exemplify either type of personality. Write a paragraph to explain each choice. Be sure to use standard grammar, spelling, sentence structure, and punctuation. Use the graphic organizer below to help you write your paragraph.

stress. Also ask the practitioner to identify the major reasons people come to his or her sessions. How many are looking for help in coping with stress or stress-related problems? Point out to students that not all relaxation or stress-reducing techniques work for everyone.

Cooperative Learning

Organize the class into groups. Assign each group one of the following types of situations: a frustration, such as failing a test; a daily hassle, such as riding a crowded bus for an hour each way between school and home; or a life change, such as moving. Then have the groups write a skit showing why the situation is stressful and illustrating one or more active ways of coping with the stress. Ask the groups to present their skits to the class. Then ask the class to suggest alternative active ways of dealing with the situations.

Building Social Studies Skills

Interpreting Graphs

Study the graph below. Then use the information in the graph to help you answer the questions that follow.

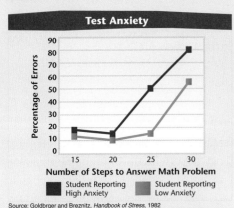

Test Anxiety

Percentage of Errors (y-axis): 0, 10, 20, 30, 40, 50, 60, 70, 80, 90

Number of Steps to Answer Math Problem (x-axis): 15, 20, 25, 30

■ Student Reporting High Anxiety
■ Student Reporting Low Anxiety

Source: Goldbrger and Breznitz, *Handbook of Stress*, 1982

1. Which statement is the best conclusion that can be made from the information in the graph?
   a. Students with low anxiety levels are more intelligent than those with high anxiety levels.
   b. Anxiety levels play an unimportant role in the testing process.
   c. Psychologists should take test anxiety into account when assessing test performance.
   d. Students with high anxiety levels will never do well in math.

2. Which factors played a role in causing the greatest number of errors?

Analyzing Primary Sources

Read the following excerpt, in which Anne Petersen and Ralph Spiga look at school as one of the sources of adolescent stress. Then answer the questions that follow.

❝Indeed, the school may provide major stress during the adolescent years. In early adolescence, young people in our society move from a single classroom, with one teacher and the same group of classmates, into a middle school or junior high school, where they pass from class to class, most often with different teachers and different students. For many young people, this transition may be smooth, but for others it appears to be untimely and stressful. . . . Little research has focused on the transition from eighth or ninth grade into senior high school. Research with early adolescents, however, would suggest that this change also involves stress.❞

3. According to this excerpt, what is a key source of school-related stress for adolescents?
   a. greater demands placed on students at higher-grade levels
   b. fear of being unpopular
   c. meeting new teachers
   d. the change in the students' routine and environment

4. Using material from this excerpt, offer ideas as to how educators can make school less stressful for adolescents.

3. Answers will vary, but students might say that eustress helps motivate them to study more and earn better grades.

4. Changes include quitting smoking, controlling body weight, and exercising.

Writing About Psychology

1. Students' reports should reflect current research on stress in the workplace and what companies are doing to reduce job-related stress.

2. Students should be able to cite some examples of type A and type B personalities and support their choices.

Building Social Studies Skills

1. c

2. High anxiety levels and a greater number of steps required to solve a problem led to more errors.

3. d

4. Students' answers will vary, but educators might reduce the number of class changes, try to keep the same students in classes that change, or other such ideas to reduce stress at school.

PSYCHOLOGY PROJECTS

Cooperative Learning

Using Your Observation Skills The Social Readjustment Rating Scale (shown on page 389) focuses primarily on life changes experienced by adults. In small groups, create a social readjustment scale for teens. Make a list of 20 events and assign a rating to each item on the basis of a consensus of group members. Post the completed scales in the classroom. Join in a class discussion of the similarities and differences between the scales. Participate in the discussion as a leader and as a follower.

☑ internet connect

Internet Activity: go.hrw.com
KEYWORD: SY3 PS17

Choose an activity on stress and health to:
- create a newspaper that discusses how to cope with stress.
- research the impact of stress on everyday life.
- create case studies regarding psychological factors and health.

go. hrw .com

407

Psychological Disorders

CHAPTER RESOURCE MANAGER

	Objectives	Pacing Guide		Reproducible and Review Resources
SECTION 1: **What Are Psychological Disorders?** (pp. 410–415)	Describe the basis for classifying psychological disorders.	**Regular** .5 day *Block Scheduling Handbook with Team Teaching Strategies, Chapter 18*	**Block Scheduling** .5 day	**E** Research Projects and Activities for Teaching Psychology **RS** Essay and Research Themes for Advanced Placement Students 16 **REV** Section 1 Review, p. 415
SECTION 2: **Anxiety Disorders** (pp. 415–419)	Describe the anxiety disorders.	**Regular** 1 day *Block Scheduling Handbook with Team Teaching Strategies, Chapter 18*	**Block Scheduling** .5 day	**SM** Mastering Critical Thinking Skills 18 **REV** Section 2 Review, p. 419
SECTION 3: **Dissociative Disorders** (pp. 420–421)	Describe the four dissociative disorders.	**Regular** 1 day *Block Scheduling Handbook with Team Teaching Strategies, Chapter 18*	**Block Scheduling** .5 day	**SM** Study Skills and Writing Guide, Part 3, Stage 6 **REV** Section 3 Review, p. 421
SECTION 4: **Somatoform Disorders** (pp. 421–422)	Explain how the two somatoform disorders differ.	**Regular** 1 day *Block Scheduling Handbook with Team Teaching Strategies, Chapter 18*	**Block Scheduling** .5 day	**REV** Section 4 Review, p. 422
SECTION 5: **Mood Disorders** (pp. 423–426)	Describe how psychologists attempt to explain mood disorders.	**Regular** 1 day *Block Scheduling Handbook with Team Teaching Strategies, Chapter 18*	**Block Scheduling** .5 day	**PS** Readings and Case Studies 18 **REV** Section 5 Review, p. 426
SECTION 6: **Schizophrenia** (pp. 426–429)	Describe the subtypes of schizophrenia.	**Regular** 1 day *Block Scheduling Handbook with Team Teaching Strategies, Chapter 18*	**Block Scheduling** .5 day	**REV** Section 6 Review, p. 429
SECTION 7: **Personality Disorders** (pp. 429–431)	Distinguish personality disorders from other psychological disorders.	**Regular** .5 day *Block Scheduling Handbook with Team Teaching Strategies, Chapter 18*	**Block Scheduling** .5 day	**REV** Section 7 Review, p. 431

Chapter Resource Key

PS	Primary Sources	**A**	Assessment		Video
RS	Reading Support	**REV**	Review		Internet
E	Enrichment		Transparencies		Holt Presentation Maker Using Microsoft® PowerPoint®
SM	Skills Mastery		CD-ROM		

 One-Stop Planner CD–ROM

See the *One-Stop Planner* for a complete list of additional resources for students and teachers.

One-Stop Planner CD–ROM

It's easy to plan lessons, select resources, and print out materials for your students when you use the *One-Stop Planner CD-ROM with Test Generator.*

Technology Resources

 One-Stop Planner, Lesson 18.1
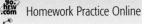 Homework Practice Online
Teaching Transparencies 37: Anxiety Disorders

 One-Stop Planner, Lesson 18.2
 Homework Practice Online
 HRW Go site

 One-Stop Planner, Lesson 18.3
CNN. Presents Psychology: September 11, 2001: A Turning Point in History
 Homework Practice Online

 One-Stop Planner, Lesson 18.4
Homework Practice Online

 One-Stop Planner, Lesson 18.5
 Homework Practice Online
HRW Go site

 One-Stop Planner, Lesson 18.6
CNN. Presents Psychology: Living with Schizophrenia
 Homework Practice Online
 HRW Go site

 One-Stop Planner, Lesson 18.7
 Homework Practice Online

Chapter Review and Assessment

 HRW Go site
REV Chapter 18 Review, pp. 432–433
REV Chapter Review Activities with Answer Key

A Chapter 18 Test (Form A or B)
A Portfolio Assessment Handbook
A Alternative Assessment Handbook

 Chapter 18 Test Generator (on the One–Stop Planner)
Global Skill Builder CD-ROM

---

internet connect

HRW ONLINE RESOURCES

GO TO: go.hrw.com
Then type in a keyword.

TEACHER HOME PAGE
KEYWORD: SY3 Teacher

CHAPTER INTERNET ACTIVITIES
KEYWORD: SY3 PS18
Choose an activity on psychological disorders to have students:
- create a profile and treatment regimen for an anxiety patient.
- write an article on teenage depression.
- outline the latest theories and treatments for schizophrenia.

CHAPTER ENRICHMENT LINKS
KEYWORD: SY3 PS18

ONLINE ASSESSMENT
Homework Practice
KEYWORD: SY3 HP18
Standardized Test Prep
KEYWORD: SY3 STP18
Rubrics
KEYWORD: SS Rubrics

CONTENT UPDATES
KEYWORD: SS Content Updates

HOLT PRESENTATION MAKER
KEYWORD: SY3 PPT18

ONLINE READING SUPPORT
KEYWORD: SS Strategies

CURRENT EVENTS
KEYWORD: SS3 Current Events

Additional Resources

PRINT RESOURCES FOR TEACHERS
Caplan, P. J. (1995). *They say you're crazy: How the world's most powerful psychiatrists decide who's normal.* Reading, MA: Addison-Wesley.
Duke, P. (1992). *A brilliant madness: Living with manic-depressive illness.* New York: Bantam.
Levenkron, S. (1991). *Obsessive-compulsive disorders.* New York: Warner Books.

PRINT RESOURCES FOR STUDENTS
Green, H. (1964). *I never promised you a rose garden.* New York: New American Library.
Kesey, K. (1962). *One flew over the cuckoo's nest.* New York: Viking.
Styron, W. (1990). *Darkness visible: A memoir of madness.* New York: Random House.

MULTIMEDIA RESOURCES
Depression: Beyond the darkness (VHS). Social Studies School Service, 10200 Jefferson Boulevard, Room 33, P.O. Box 802, Culver City, CA 90232-0802.
Schizophrenia: Removing the veil (VHS). Social Studies School Service, 10200 Jefferson Boulevard, Room 33, P.O. Box 802, Culver City, CA 90232-0802.
The three faces of Eve (VHS). Social Studies School Service, 10200 Jefferson Boulevard, Room 33, P.O. Box 802, Culver City, CA 90232-0802.

PSYCHOLOGICAL DISORDERS

Introducing Chapter 18

Prior to assigning the reading of Chapter 18, have students write short answers to the following questions:

▶ How do "abnormal" thoughts and behaviors differ from "normal" thoughts and behaviors?

▶ Do most psychological disorders have biological causes or environmental causes?

▶ What types of psychological disorders are there?

Have students save their responses and review them after studying Chapter 18. Tell students that they, like medical students who study physical illnesses, may be tempted to see in themselves some of the symptoms they will read about. Caution students against this natural tendency toward self-diagnosis.

Each of the seven questions identified on page 408 corresponds to one of these sections.

18 Chapter

PSYCHOLOGICAL DISORDERS

Read to Discover

1 What is the basis for classifying psychological disorders?

2 What are anxiety disorders?

3 What are the four dissociative disorders?

4 How do the two most common somatoform disorders differ?

5 How do psychologists attempt to explain mood disorders?

6 What are the subtypes of schizophrenia?

7 How do personality disorders differ from other psychological disorders?

Each chapter begins with a vignette, called "A Day in the Life," that relates the information discussed in the chapter to the everyday events in the lives of a group of fictional high school students. The text of the chapter occasionally refers back to the vignette to demonstrate the application of the concept being discussed. An icon marked "A Day in the Life" is placed next to these references.

Copy the following graphic organizer onto the chalkboard. Ask students to briefly discuss the importance of these three steps in understanding psychological disorders.

Identifying — Psychological Disorders — Symptoms / Classifying

A DAY IN THE LIFE

May 16

Janet was at home studying in her bedroom when the phone rang. "Hello?" she answered.

"Hey, Janet, it's me—Dan. Can you talk for a minute?"

Janet and Dan had been friends for years, and she could always tell when he sounded sad. "Of course I can. What's up?" Janet answered, trying to sound positive.

"It's Michelle again," Dan said.

About a year ago, Dan's older sister, Michelle, had been diagnosed with a serious psychological disorder called schizophrenia. Michelle was 23 years old and lived with her husband, Jeff, in a small house in the country. Accepting the fact that Michelle had a psychological disorder had been difficult for Dan. At first, he didn't talk about it with anyone outside his family. Then, after a while, he began confiding in Janet.

"It's so hard sometimes," Dan said sadly. "I really thought she was going to be okay after the doctors finally diagnosed and started treating her last year."

"Did something happen?" Janet asked, genuinely concerned.

"Well, I hadn't seen her in weeks

because Jeff was the only person she would talk to. I finally saw her tonight, and I could tell that something was happening again. She always seems so distracted. It's like she's listening to something only she can hear."

"Has she been taking the medicine that the doctor prescribed?" Janet asked.

"I don't know for sure," Dan answered. "I asked her about it tonight, but she got really defensive. She kept saying that I was trying to confuse her, and then she insisted that Jeff take her home."

"I'm sorry, Dan. I wish there were something I could do," Janet responded sympathetically.

"Thanks," Dan said. "It really helps to be able to talk to someone. At least I'm handling it a lot better than my parents are. My mom thinks that somehow it's her fault—like it is hereditary or Michelle caught it as a baby."

"Do the doctors have any idea how she *did* get it?" Janet asked.

"Not really," Dan said. "They have a bunch of different theories, but I don't think they know for sure. I'm just hoping that somehow they'll figure out exactly what's wrong so they'll be able to really help her."

"Me, too," Janet replied softly.

• • •

Dan's sister, Michelle, has schizophrenia, a serious psychological disorder that causes her to hear things that others cannot hear and, in general, often to lose touch with reality. Most psychological disorders are less serious than schizophrenia, but they still may cause great distress for affected individuals and their families and friends. This chapter describes several types of psychological disorders, including schizophrenia. The treatment of psychological disorders is the focus of Chapter 19.

Key Terms

- psychological disorders
- culture-bound syndromes
- anxiety
- phobia
- simple phobia
- social phobia
- panic attack
- agoraphobia
- obsessions
- compulsions
- post-traumatic stress disorder
- dissociation
- depersonalization
- somatization
- depression
- bipolar disorder
- mania
- schizophrenia
- catatonic stupor

WHY PSYCHOLOGY MATTERS

Psychologists help people deal with psychological disorders. Use **CNNfyi.com** or other current events sources to learn more about how psychologists and other professionals help people cope with disorders.

CNNfyi.com

409

Estimates suggest that about one out of every three people in the United States will experience a psychological disorder at some point in life.

Section Objective

7

▶ Explain the basis for classifying psychological disorders.

This objective is assessed in the Section Review on page 415 and in the Chapter 18 Review.

Opening Section 1

Motivator

Challenge students to determine what criteria are used to distinguish "abnormal" or disordered psychological thoughts and behavior from "normal" thoughts and behavior. Ask volunteers to read the answers they wrote in response to the first question in the Introducing Chapter 18 activity on page 408. List on the chalkboard the criteria mentioned in the responses. Tell students that Section 1 will help clarify the distinction between normal and abnormal thoughts and behavior and explain how psychologists classify various psychological disorders.

Using Truth or Fiction

Each chapter opens with several "Truth or Fiction" statements that relate to the concepts discussed in the chapter. Ask students whether they think each statement is true or false. Answers to each item as well as explanations are provided at appropriate points within the text under the heading "Truth or Fiction Revisited."

Cultural Dimensions

Distinguishing between abnormal and normal, or unacceptable and acceptable, behavior is influenced by cultural expectations. For example, most people would find it distressing or suspicious if a stranger stood "too close" to them. However, the appropriate distance differs from culture to culture. For example, in Japan the appropriate distance is 40 inches apart; in some Arab countries, however, the appropriate distance is less than 32 inches apart.

TRUTH OR fiction?

Read the following statements about psychology. Do you think they are true or false? You will learn whether each statement is true or false as you read the chapter.

- Very few people are actually affected by psychological disorders.
- People sometimes forget a very traumatic event as a way of coping with the psychological stress of the trauma.
- People whose illnesses are "all in their heads" do not really have symptoms of disease.
- Depression is the most common type of psychological disorder.
- Some people do not feel guilty, even when they commit serious crimes.

SECTION 7

What Are Psychological Disorders?

Psychology is the scientific study of behavior and mental processes. **Psychological disorders** are behavior patterns or mental processes that cause serious personal suffering or interfere with a person's ability to cope with everyday life.

Many people believe that psychological disorders are uncommon, affecting relatively few individuals. It is true that the great majority of people are never admitted to mental hospitals, and most people never seek the help of psychologists or psychiatrists. And although many people have relatives they consider eccentric, few people have family members they consider to be truly abnormal.

Estimates suggest, however, that almost one third of the adults in the United States have experienced some type of psychological disorder (Goldstein et al., 1986). In addition to the many people with substance abuse problems, 23 percent of people in the United States experience some type of psychological disorder in their lifetime. In any given month, the figure is approximately 13 percent (Regier, 1993). As Dan's family discovered, psychological disorders can affect almost anyone.

TRUTH OR fiction ▪ REVISITED ▪

It is not true that very few people are actually affected by psychological disorders. Millions of people are affected by psychological disorders during their lifetimes.

Identifying Psychological Disorders

Deciding whether particular behaviors, thoughts, or feelings are "normal" or "abnormal" can be difficult. What is normal is often equated with what is average for the majority of people. Using this definition of normality, deviation from the majority becomes the primary criterion for abnormality.

People with psychological disorders usually do not differ much from "normal" people. In fact, the primary difference is the simple exaggeration of certain behaviors or mental processes. For example, laughing is a normal and healthy response to humorous situations. However, someone who laughs all the time, even in very inappropriate situations, might be considered abnormal.

Symptoms of Psychological Disorders

Several behavior patterns and mental processes may suggest that an individual has a psychological

Teaching Section 1

Guided Practice

Write on the chalkboard the following four criteria used in determining the presence of a psychological disorder: *Typicality, Maladaptivity, Emotional Discomfort,* and *Socially Unacceptable Behavior.* For each criterion listed, have a volunteer explain how it is used to determine whether behavior is suggestive of a psychological disorder. Then have students brainstorm examples of behaviors that would fall under each criterion. List these under their proper headings on the chalkboard, and have students make a copy of the lists.

Independent Practice

Remind students that not all behavior can easily be categorized as normal or abnormal. Ask students to examine the lists of behaviors developed in the Guided Practice activity. For each behavior listed, have them write down two situations—one in which the behavior would be viewed as normal and one in which the behavior would be viewed as abnormal. *(For example, crying uncontrollably would be a normal reaction to the death of a loved one; it would be an abnormal reaction to losing a pen.)* Have volunteers read their paired items aloud for discussion.

disorder. The word *suggest* is important here because diagnosing an individual with a psychological disorder is often difficult, and diagnoses are not always simple or straightforward.

However, psychologists generally use several criteria to determine whether a person's behavior indicates the presence of a psychological disorder. These criteria include how typical the behavior is of people in general, whether the behavior is maladaptive, whether the behavior causes the individual emotional discomfort, and whether the behavior is socially unacceptable.

Typicality As previously noted, the normality of a behavior or mental process is often determined by the degree to which it is average, or typical, of the behavior or mental processes of the majority of people. There are, however, problems with defining normality in terms of what is typical of most people. The fact that a behavior is not typical of most people does not mean it is abnormal. Scientific and artistic geniuses, such as Marie Curie and Pablo Picasso, certainly are not typical of people in general. That does not mean, however, that such people are abnormal.

Maladaptivity Many psychologists believe that what makes a behavior abnormal is the fact that it is maladaptive (Coleman et al., 1984). That is, the behavior impairs an individual's ability to function adequately in everyday life. Behavior that causes misery and distress rather than happiness and fulfillment may be considered maladaptive. Alcohol abuse is one such behavior. Alcohol abuse often has strong negative effects on the drinker's health, work, and family life. Abuse of alcohol may discourage the drinker from seeking healthier solutions to the problem of anxiety as well as create additional problems of its own.

Behavior that is hazardous to oneself or to others may also be considered maladaptive. This type of maladaptive behavior may include threatening or attempting suicide as well as threatening or attacking other people.

It is important to note that most people who commit violent crimes do not have psychological disorders. This is because most criminals are fully aware of what they are doing. That is, they know that their behavior is illegal and that they can be held responsible for it. Equally important, the majority of people with psychological disorders, even severe psychological disorders, are not violent or dangerous.

Emotional Discomfort Psychological disorders such as anxiety and depression cause most people great emotional discomfort. For example, people who are depressed often suffer feelings of helplessness, hopelessness, worthlessness, guilt, and extreme sadness. They may lose interest in virtually everything they once enjoyed and believe that life is no longer worth living. Such feelings are so stressful that they may lead the affected individual to consider suicide. Thus, severe emotional discomfort may be a sign of a psychological disorder.

Socially Unacceptable Behavior Behavior that violates a society's accepted norms may also be an indication of a psychological disorder. However, whether a behavior is socially unacceptable may depend on the particular society or culture in which it occurs. What is considered normal behavior in one culture may be considered abnormal in another. Therefore, the cultural context of a behavior must be taken into account before deciding that the behavior indicates a psychological disorder.

The importance of culture is demonstrated by **culture-bound syndromes**, clusters of symptoms that define or describe an illness. Many behaviors associated with culture-bound syndromes would be considered abnormal by people who are unaware of the syndrome's cultural context. For example, many people in Middle Eastern cultures believe that certain inappropriate behaviors, such as banging one's head, are due to possession of the body by a spirit. In the United States, such a belief would likely be considered a sign of a serious psychological disorder. However, in the cultural context of some areas in the Middle East, spirit possession is considered to be a rational explanation for certain types of behavior, and the affected individual is not thought to have a psychological disorder. There are many examples of culture-bound syndromes, some of which are listed in Figure 18.1 on page 413.

Classifying Psychological Disorders

Most psychologists believe that it is important to have a widely agreed upon classification of psychological disorders. Unless there is agreement about how to classify psychological disorders, it is difficult to know how many people have a given disorder or what other factors, such as socioeconomic status, heredity, or gender differences, may be associated with it. It is also important to classify psychological disorders so that individuals can be correctly diagnosed and treated.

Cross-Curricular Link: History

Point out that what a culture considers to be unacceptable or abnormal behavior may change over time. During much of the 1800s, for example, some people thought that runaway slaves suffered from a mental illness called drapetomania (after the Greek words for "runaway" and "madness"). Today the effort to escape the bonds of slavery would be seen as heroic. Challenge students to provide examples of behaviors that once were considered socially unacceptable but are more widely acceptable today *(tattooing, men wearing earrings, women working outside the home).* Have students discuss why a society's views of acceptable and unacceptable behavior may change over time.

CASE STUDIES
AND OTHER TRUE STORIES

Have students research the case of Daniel M'Naghten and re-create the case in the form of a mock trial. Assign volunteers to play the following roles: M'Naghten, defense attorneys, prosecuting attorneys, the judge, witnesses for the defense and for the prosecution, and jury members. Following the conclusion of the mock trial, have students discuss whether the use of the insanity defense was justifiable in this case and how the outcome of the case might have been different if the insanity defense had not been used.

Cooperative Learning

Organize the class into five groups, and assign each group one of the following categories of people: police officers, attorneys, judges, psychologists, private citizens. Tell group members that they are to interview people in their assigned category concerning the use of the insanity plea. Interviews should focus around this central question: Does the insanity plea allow people to "get away with" crimes? Have the class discuss how and why the opinions of the interviewees differ.

For Your Information

Some students might argue that the existence of the "temporary insanity" plea contradicts the textbook statement that "according to the law, one cannot be just a little insane." Remind students that the M'Naghten Rule refers to a condition of insanity "at the time of committing a criminal act." In other words, the accused person is judged to have been either sane or insane at the time he or she committed the crime.

Essay and Research Themes for A. P. Students

Theme 16

CASE STUDIES
AND OTHER TRUE STORIES
Not Guilty by Reason of Insanity

The vast majority of people with mental illnesses are not dangerous to others. Some, however, do commit crimes. Many people have been found not guilty of serious crimes—even murder—"by reason of insanity." Typically, they are sent to psychiatric institutions instead of prison. They may be released when they are judged no longer to be a threat to others.

John Hinckley's lawyers used the insanity defense at his trial.

A well-known use of the insanity plea occurred in the case of John Hinckley, the man who attempted to assassinate President Ronald Reagan in 1981. Not only did Hinckley attempt to murder the president, but he did so in front of millions of television witnesses. Nevertheless, Hinckley was found not guilty by reason of insanity after expert witnesses testified that he had schizophrenia. Rather than being sent to prison, Hinckley was committed to a psychiatric institution.

In using an insanity defense, lawyers apply a modified version of the M'Naghten Rule, which states that if it can be proved that at the time of committing a criminal act a person either did not understand the nature of the act or did not know that it was wrong, then the person is insane and not responsible for the act.

The M'Naghten Rule goes back to 1843, when a Scotsman named Daniel M'Naghten was found not guilty of murder by reason of insanity. M'Naghten had tried to kill the British prime minister, Sir Robert Peel, because he had delusions that Peel was persecuting him. In the assassination attempt, Peel's secretary was killed. However, the court found M'Naghten not guilty of murder, stating that he was insane and thus not responsible for his criminal act.

Typically, when an accused person pleads insanity, prosecuting attorneys try to demonstrate that the accused was sane at the time of the crime, while the defense tries to prove that the accused was not sane. Both rely on the testimony of expert witnesses, usually psychologists or psychiatrists, who have interviewed the accused after the crime or who have previous knowledge of the accused.

Many people worry that criminals are literally "getting away with murder" because of the insanity defense. However, the defense is actually used in just 1 percent of felony cases and is unsuccessful in three fourths of those. Recent reforms have made it more difficult to use the insanity plea successfully. For example:

- In many states, to be considered insane the accused now must be diagnosed with a severe psychological disorder.

- The burden of proof has been shifted from the prosecution to the defense. It is now up to the defense to prove the accused was insane.

- Some states have gone even further and abolished the insanity plea altogether.

Insanity is a legal concept, not a psychological one, and to be legally useful, it must be all or nothing—one is either sane or insane. In reality, most psychological disorders are a matter of degree. The distinction is important. One can be just a little depressed, for example, but according to the law, one cannot be just a little insane. Because of its all-or-nothing nature, deciding on someone's sanity can be a very difficult decision to make.

WHY PSYCHOLOGY MATTERS

Psychologists and legal scholars still debate the best way to deal with criminal defendants who claim insanity. Use CNNfyi.com or other current events sources to learn more about how the American justice system handles people suffering from psychological disorders. Present an oral report of what you have learned to the class.

CNNfyi.com

For Further Research

Interested students may delve further into the symptoms and the official psychological recognition of post-traumatic stress disorder. Some students may wish to focus on the experiences of the Vietnam veterans who were found to suffer from post-traumatic stress disorder. Other students may wish to focus on other groups (refugees, rape victims, victims of natural disasters) who show signs of PTSD or on why PTSD was added to the DSM. Have students present their findings in short oral reports.

Meeting Individual Needs: Learners Having Difficulty

Some students may have difficulty understanding the difference between classifying disorders according to their presumed causes and classifying them according to their observable signs and symptoms. Provide the following analogy. A descriptive approach to the common cold would be to list the symptoms—runny nose, sneezing. An analysis of the cause of the common cold would include references to cold-causing viruses and how they affect the body.

The most widely used classification system for psychological disorders is the DSM, or *Diagnostic and Statistical Manual of Mental Disorders*, published by the American Psychiatric Association. The most recent version of the manual, the DSM-IV-TR™, which was published in 1994, recognizes 18 different categories of psychological disorders, many of which are shown in Figure 18.2 on page 414.

It is important to note that the classification of psychological disorders shown in Figure 18.2 is significantly different from earlier classifications. Until 1980, when the third edition of the DSM was published, psychological disorders were classified on the basis of their presumed causes. For many decades, the most widely accepted causes were those suggested by Freud's psychoanalytic theory.

Many psychologists criticized early versions of the DSM because very diverse psychological disorders were grouped together under the labels "neuroses" and "psychoses." As a result, beginning with the DSM-III in 1980, psychological disorders have been categorized on the basis of observable signs and symptoms rather than presumed causes.

The DSM is subject to ongoing revision. New categories are added and old ones deleted as knowledge of psychological disorders increases. For example, post-traumatic stress disorder was added to the DSM only after the Vietnam War, when many soldiers were found to suffer from the disorder.

The remainder of this chapter focuses on six major types of psychological disorders as classified by the DSM-IV: anxiety disorders, dissociative disorders, somatoform disorders, mood disorders, schizophrenia, and personality disorders. Many symptoms are simply exaggerations of normal thoughts, feelings, or behaviors. These symptoms do not necessarily indicate a psychological disorder. Psychological disorders can only be diagnosed by a skilled professional after careful evaluation.

Some Culture-Bound Syndromes

Latah
Malaysia and elsewhere:
hypersensitivity to sudden fright, often with nonsense mimicking of others; trance-like behavior

Hwa-byung
Korea:
panic, depression, or other symptoms believed to be due to the suppression of anger

Zar
Middle East:
shouting, laughing, head banging, or other inappropriate behavior that is believed to be caused by possession of the body by a spirit

Susto
Latino groups in the United States and the Caribbean:
unhappiness and illness following a frightening event that is believed to cause the soul to leave the body

Ghost sickness
Native Americans in the United States:
bad dreams, hallucinations, fainting, and other symptoms believed to be due to preoccupation with death and the dead

Mal de ojo
Mediterranean and elsewhere:
sufferers, mostly children, are believed to be under the influence of an "evil eye," causing fitful sleep, crying, and sickness

FIGURE 18.1 *Several patterns of abnormal behavior are recognized in specific cultures and may or may not be linked to an official category of psychological disorder. Listed here are a few of these culture-bound syndromes.* ***Why is it important to consider the cultural context of a behavior before classifying it as a psychological disorder?***

Source: Adapted from the DSM-IV-TR, 2000.

Class Discussion

Point out that many disorders involve exaggerations of common behaviors. Have students discuss why it is important that a formal diagnosis of a suspected disorder be made by a trained professional rather than by a nonprofessional knowledgeable in the study of psychology. *(Many nonprofessionals have some knowledge of psychology, just as they have some knowledge of physical illnesses. However, in the cases of both mental and physical health, the issues are too complex and important to leave in the hands of amateurs.)*

Caption Question: Answer

It is important to consider the cultural context of a behavior before classifying it as a psychological disorder because different cultures have different customs and different views of normal and abnormal behavior.

Closing Section 1

Evaluating Ideas

Have students write a paragraph summarizing how the criteria for classifying psychological disorders have changed over time. Ask volunteers to read their paragraphs aloud to the class. Then have students discuss whether the fact that a classification system is subject to ongoing revision affects its present-day value as a tool of science.

Reviewing Section 1

Have students complete the Section Review questions on page 415.

Extension

Have interested students locate earlier versions of the *Diagnostic and Statistical Manual of Mental Disorders* and bring them to class. Instruct small groups of students to compare earlier and later versions of the DSM and to identify and describe specific differences.

Categories of Psychological Disorders in the DSM-IV™

Category	Disorder	Category	Disorder
Disorders Usually First Diagnosed in Infancy, Childhood, or Adolescence	Mental Retardation, Reading Disorder, Autistic Disorder	Sexual and Gender Identity Disorders	Sexual Dysfunctions, Paraphilias, Gender Identity Disorders
Delirium, Dementia, and Amnestic and Other Cognitive Disorders	Substance Intoxication, Delirium, Alzheimer's Disease	Sleep Disorders	Primary Insomnia, Sleepwalking Disorder
Substance-Related Disorders	Caffeine-Related Disorders, Hallucinogen-Related Disorders, Nicotine-Related Disorders	Impulsive-Control Disorders Not Elsewhere Classified	Kleptomania, Pyromania
		Adjustment Disorders	With Depressed Mood, with Anxiety
Schizophrenia and Other Psychotic Disorders	Paranoid Schizophrenia, Disorganized Schizophrenia, Catatonic Schizophrenia	Personality Disorders	Paranoid Personality Disorder, Schizoid Personality Disorder, Dependent Personality Disorder, Antisocial Personality Disorder
Mood Disorders	Major Depressive Disorder, Bipolar Disorder	Eating Disorders	Anorexia Nervosa, Bulimia Nervosa
Anxiety Disorders	Phobias, Panic Disorder, Generalized Anxiety, Obsessive-Compulsive Disorder, Acute and Post-Traumatic Stress Disorders	Conditions That May Be a Focus of Clinical Attention	Non-compliance with Treatment, Malingering, Academic or Occupational Problem
Somatoform Disorders	Conversion Disorder, Hypochondriasis	Additional Codes	Unspecified Mental Disorder (nonpsychotic disorders)
Dissociative Disorders	Dissociative Amnesia, Dissociative Identity Disorder, Dissociative Fugue, Depersonalization		

FIGURE 18.2 *The most widely used classification system for psychological disorders is found in the* Diagnostic and Statistical Manual of Mental Disorders *(DSM). The most recent version is called the DSM-IV-TR.*

Source: Adapted from the DSM-IV, 1994.

Section Objective

► Distinguish among the anxiety disorders, and outline the theories that explain them.

This objective is assessed in the Section Review on page 419 and in the Chapter 18 Review.

Opening Section 2

Motivator

Ask a volunteer to read aloud the definition of *anxiety* given on page 415. Then ask students to locate the category *Anxiety Disorders* in the chart on page 414 and identify the examples contained within that category. Write these examples on the chalkboard. Ask students to speculate on why these disorders are grouped under the category *Anxiety Disorders* and how they relate to the definition of anxiety. Tell students that they will learn the answers to these questions by reading Section 2.

SECTION 1 REVIEW

1. Identify three problems with defining normal behavior as the behavior displayed by the majority of people.
2. How have the criteria for the classification of psychological disorders been arranged since 1980?
3. **Critical Thinking** *Categorizing* Give an example of a feeling or a behavior that would be considered normal in one circumstance but might be considered a sign of a psychological disorder in another circumstance.

SECTION 2

Anxiety Disorders

Anxiety refers to a general state of dread or uneasiness that occurs in response to a vague or imagined danger. It differs from fear, which is a response to a real danger or threat. Anxiety is typically characterized by nervousness, inability to relax, and concern about losing control. Physical signs and symptoms of anxiety may include trembling, sweating, rapid heart rate, shortness of breath, increased blood pressure, flushed face, and feelings of faintness or light-headedness. All are the result of overactivity of the sympathetic branch of the autonomic nervous system. (See Chapter 3.)

Everyone feels anxious at times—for example, before a big game or an important test. In such situations, feeling anxious or worried is an appropriate response that does not indicate a psychological disorder. However, some people feel anxious all or most of the time, or their anxiety is out of proportion to the situation provoking it. Such anxiety may interfere with effective living, the achievement of desired goals, life satisfaction, and emotional comfort. When these problems occur, anxiety is considered a sign of a psychological disorder. Anxiety-based disorders are among the most common of all psychological disorders in the United States (Gorman et al., 1989).

Types of Anxiety Disorders

Anxiety disorders classified in the DSM-IV include phobic disorder, panic disorder, generalized anxiety disorder, obsessive-compulsive disorder, and stress disorders. A description of each follows.

Phobic Disorder The word **phobia** derives from the Greek root *phobos*, which means "fear." **Simple phobia**, which is the most common of all the anxiety disorders, refers to a persistent excessive or irrational fear of a particular object or situation. To be diagnosed as a phobic disorder, the fear must lead to avoidance behavior that interferes with the affected person's normal life.

Almost any object or situation may lead to a phobic reaction. Several phobias, however, are especially common. The most common include:

- zoophobia: a fear of animals
- claustrophobia: a fear of enclosed spaces
- acrophobia: a fear of heights
- arachnophobia: a fear of spiders

Other relatively common phobias include fear of storms, blood, snakes, dental procedures, driving, and air travel.

When people with simple phobias are confronted with the object or situation they fear, they are likely to feel extremely anxious. As a result, they tend to avoid what they fear. For example, someone with hematophobia (a fear of blood) might avoid needed medical treatment. Someone with aviaphobia (a fear of air travel) might turn down a job

This person is waiting anxiously to be interviewed for a job. **What situations make you feel anxious?**

Section 1 Review: Answers

1. Problems include the following: the behavior of the majority is not always wise or healthy; some atypical behaviors are eccentric rather than indicative of a disorder; people with psychological disorders usually do not differ much from people who are "normal."

2. The criteria have changed from presumed causes to observable signs and symptoms.

3. Answers will vary. One possible answer is that feeling grief would be a normal response to the death of a friend but an abnormal reaction to getting a pimple.

Caption Question: Answer

Answers will vary, but students should identify situations that make them feel the emotional and/or physical symptoms characteristic of anxiety. Remind students that everyone feels anxious at times and that these feelings do not necessarily indicate the presence of a psychological disorder.

Teaching Section 2

Meeting Individual Needs: Auditory Learners

Have auditory learners work as a group to research the proper names for as many phobias as they can locate. In class, have them read aloud the proper name of each phobia and identify the object of the phobia. (*Examples include hydrophobia: fear of water; brontophobia: fear of thunder and lightning; ergophobia: fear of work.*) Students may be amused by some of the more unusual phobias, but lead them to understand that almost any object or situation may lead to a phobic reaction in certain individuals.

Role-Playing

Organize the class into small groups. Tell the members of each group that they are to write and perform a scenario demonstrating a simple phobia, social phobia, panic disorder, or agoraphobia. Also instruct group members to include in their scenario the use of avoidance behavior to mask or manage fear. After the groups have completed their role-playing, have the class discuss the ways in which anxiety disorders affect people's work and social life.

*Someone with agoraphobia or panic disorder would be likely to avoid this crowded shopping mall. **Why might these disorders lead to similar avoidance behaviors?***

promotion because the new position involves air travel. Thus, although most people with simple phobias never seek treatment for their disorders, a simple phobia can seriously disrupt a person's life.

Social phobia is characterized by persistent fear of social situations in which one might be exposed to the close scrutiny of others and thus be observed doing something embarrassing or humiliating. Some people with social phobias fear all social situations; others fear specific situations, such as public speaking, eating in public, or dating.

People with social phobias generally try to avoid the situations they fear. They may invent excuses to avoid going to parties or other social gatherings, for example. If avoidance is impossible, the situations are likely to cause great anxiety. In addition, the avoidance behavior itself may greatly interfere with work and social life.

Panic Disorder and Agoraphobia People with panic disorder have recurring and unexpected panic attacks. A **panic attack** is a relatively short period of intense fear or discomfort, characterized by shortness of breath, dizziness, rapid heart rate, trembling or shaking, sweating, choking, nausea, or other distressing physical symptoms. It may last from a few minutes to a few hours. People having a panic attack may believe they are dying or "going crazy." Not surprisingly, they usually have persistent fears of another attack.

For most people who suffer panic disorder, attacks have no apparent cause. However, many people with panic disorder also have agoraphobia. **Agoraphobia** is a fear of being in places or situations in which escape may be difficult or impossible. People with agoraphobia may be especially afraid of crowded public places such as movie theaters, shopping malls, buses, or trains.

Agoraphobia is a common phobia among adults. In fact, according to the DSM-IV, people with one or both disorders make up about 50 to 80 percent of the phobic individuals seen in clinical practice.

Most people with agoraphobia have panic attacks when they cannot avoid the situations they fear. They are afraid they will have a panic attack in a public place, where they will be humiliated or unable to obtain help. Panic disorder and agoraphobia both lead to avoidance behaviors. These behaviors can range from avoiding crowded places to never leaving home at all. Thus, these phobias can be very serious.

Generalized Anxiety Disorder According to the DSM-IV, generalized anxiety disorder (GAD) is an excessive or unrealistic worry about life circumstances that lasts for at least six months. The worries must be present during most of that time in order to warrant a diagnosis of GAD. Typically, the worries focus on finances, work, interpersonal problems, accidents, or illness.

GAD is one of the most common anxiety disorders, yet few people seek psychological treatment for it because it does not differ, except in intensity and duration, from the normal worries of everyday life. It is difficult to distinguish GAD from other anxiety disorders, and many people with GAD have other anxiety disorders as well, most often phobic disorders (Barlow et al., 1986).

Obsessive-Compulsive Disorder Among the most acute of the anxiety disorders is obsessive-compulsive disorder (OCD). **Obsessions** are unwanted thoughts, ideas, or mental images that occur over and over again. They are often senseless or repulsive, and most people with obsessions try to ignore or suppress them. The majority of people with obsessions also practice compulsions, which may reduce the anxiety their obsessions produce. **Compulsions** are repetitive ritual behaviors, often involving checking or cleaning something.

Demonstration

Bring to class a sanitizing lotion or a container of moist towelettes used to clean the hands and face. During the class session, clean your hands each time you touch something, such as chalk, a book, an eraser, and so on. When students comment on your actions, tell them that you do not want to catch any germs. After a few more hand cleanings, ask students to explain how your behavior demonstrated both the mental and physical components of obsessive-compulsive disorder. Make sure that students understand the difference between obsessions and compulsions.

Applying Ideas

Before instructing students to read the textbook explanations of anxiety disorders, found on page 419, ask them to suggest their own explanations. Encourage students to consider the disorders from the various psychological perspectives they have learned about (psychoanalytic theory, cognitive theory, learning theory, and so on). Then have them compare their ideas with the explanations given on page 419. Ask volunteers to discuss which theory they believe best explains anxiety disorders and why.

The following examples are typical of people with OCD. One person is obsessed every night with doubts that he has locked the doors and windows before going to bed. He feels driven to compulsively check and recheck every door and window in the house, perhaps dozens of times. Only then can he relax and go to sleep. In another example, a team of researchers reported the case of a woman who was obsessed with the idea that she would pick up germs from nearly everything she touched. She compulsively washed her hands over and over again, sometimes as many as 500 times a day (Davison & Neale, 1990).

People who experience obsessions are usually aware that the obsessions are unjustified (March et al., 1989; Rapoport, 1989; Swedo et al., 1989). This distinguishes obsessions from delusions. Although obsessions are a sign of a less serious psychological disorder than delusions, they still can make people feel extremely anxious, and they can seriously interfere with daily life. Compulsions may alleviate some of the anxiety associated with obsessions, but the compulsions themselves are time-consuming and usually create additional interference with daily life.

Constant organizing and cleaning are common compulsions in people who experience obsessive-compulsive disorder.

Stress Disorders   Stress disorders include post-traumatic stress disorder (PTSD) and acute stress disorder. The two disorders have similar symptoms, but they differ in how quickly they occur after the traumatic event that triggers the disorder. They also differ in how long they last.

Post-traumatic stress disorder refers to intense, persistent feelings of anxiety that are caused by an experience so traumatic that it would produce stress in almost anyone. Experiences that may produce PTSD include rape, severe child abuse, assault, severe accident, airplane crash, natural disasters, and war atrocities. It appears to be a common syndrome in people who have experienced extensive trauma. For example, more than one third of the victims of Hurricane Andrew in 1992 developed PTSD (Ironson, 1993).

People who suffer from PTSD may exhibit any or all of the following symptoms (American Psychiatric Association, 2000):

- flashbacks, which are mental reexperiences of the actual trauma
- nightmares or other unwelcome thoughts about the trauma
- numbness of feelings
- avoidance of stimuli associated with the trauma
- increased tension, which may lead to sleep disturbances, irritability, poor concentration, and similar problems

The symptoms may occur six months or more after the traumatic event, and they may last for years or even decades. The more severe the trauma, the worse the symptoms tend to be.

Acute stress disorder is a short-term disorder with symptoms similar to those of PTSD. Also like PTSD, acute stress disorder follows a traumatic event. However, unlike with PTSD, the symptoms occur immediately or at most within a month of the event. The anxiety also lasts a shorter time—from a few days to a few weeks. Not everyone who experiences a trauma, however, will develop PTSD or acute stress disorder.

Explaining Anxiety Disorders

Several different explanations for anxiety disorders have been suggested. As is true for most of the psychological disorders discussed in this chapter, the explanations fall into two general categories: psychological views and biological views.

Cross-Curricular Link: History

The disorder known today as post-traumatic stress disorder was in the past known by several different names (combat exhaustion, war neurosis, and shell shock, for example) associated with the psychological trauma of war. The term *shell shock* was introduced during World War I by a British medical officer named Frederick Mott. Mott believed that the soldiers' psychological symptoms were caused by tiny brain hemorrhages from the concussion of nearby exploding shells. This theory was abandoned, though, when it was realized that many people suffering symptoms had not been near areas of blasting. Following World War II, the American Psychiatric Association used the term *gross stress reaction* to describe psychological symptoms of trauma from war as well as from civilian exposure to catastrophes such as tornadoes and flooding. Today post-traumatic stress disorder describes the symptoms associated with exposure to trauma.

Class Discussion

Have students discuss the ways in which anxiety disorders interfere with daily life. Which disorders are probably the most disruptive? Why?

For Further Research

Many people around the world have been victims of terrorist attacks. Challenge students to find accounts of people who have survived such an attack. Have the students research how the person was affected by the terrorist activity, and what the person has done to cope with the psychological shock of the attack.

Have students read the feature and then describe the types of stress and anxiety that many Americans felt after the attacks of September 11, 2001. Ask the students to consider how these symptoms might be similar to or different from those experienced by persons who survive a natural disaster such as a flood, earthquake, or tornado.

Think About It: Answer

Methods of dealing with unsettling events include seeking social support of family and friends and limiting exposure to the disturbing images related to the attacks.

Technology Resources

CNN Presents Psychology: September 11, 2001: A Turning Point in History

---

PSYCHOLOGY
IN THE WORLD TODAY

Terrorism and Anxiety

The September 11, 2001, terrorist attacks shocked people in the United States and around the world. The scale, surprise, and violence of the attacks provoked a wide variety of psychological responses both in those who survived the attacks and those who followed the events through the media.

Shortly after the attacks, many people were stunned. The reality of the attacks began to sink in as television stations repeatedly played images of the World Trade Center towers ablaze and collapsing, the Pentagon burning, and of the airplane crash site in Pennsylvania. Fears that more attacks were imminent quickly spread across the United States. Meanwhile, people desperately sought information about friends and relatives who worked in or near the World Trade Center towers and the Pentagon. The confusion and lack of information shortly after the attacks resulted in anxiety and frustration for many people.

After the initial shock of the attacks passed, people across the nation began to feel new anxieties as they struggled to cope with what had happened. New York City residents—particularly those who worked in or near the World Trade Center on September 11—grieved and experienced a range of unsettling and disturbing feelings. Some workers relived the fear they felt the day of the attacks every time they passed by "ground zero" on their way to work. Others were gripped with passing moments of fear whenever an airplane would pass overhead.

People in New York City and throughout the United States experienced other reactions as well. Many people reported unusually vivid and terrifying dreams related to the terrorist attacks. For example, one woman in Oregon dreamed she was trapped in a World Trade Center tower when it was hit by an airplane. A person in California

President George W. Bush met with rescue personnel after the attacks.

dreamed of a beautiful bald eagle that was suddenly transformed into a snarling bird with glowing red eyes.

Some people who experienced terrifying dreams were suffering from the crippling anxiety of post-traumatic stress disorder. People with this disorder may have sleep problems, irritable outbursts, and difficulty concentrating on their work. Many people continued to experience intrusive memories for weeks and months after the attacks. Others experienced flashbacks—the sudden feeling that the events were happening again. These sudden feelings were prompted by a variety of sights and sounds. Sirens, television images, tall buildings, and construction crews sparked anxiety in many people. These flashbacks and memories reflected the difficult struggle people were having to regain their emotional balance.

People tried to cope with the stress of the terrorist attacks in a number of ways. Many took the advice of psychologists who recommended that they limit their exposure to the horrific images of the attacks and that they seek social support among families and friends. Church membership grew after the attacks. Others flew flags at half staff or held quiet vigils to remember the victims and their families. Many people participated in the national day of mourning called for by President George W. Bush. In these ways, people across the nation tried to restore their sense of security.

Think About It

Analyzing Information What were some ways that people tried to deal with unsettling events such as the terrorist attacks of September 11, 2001?

Closing Section 2

Summarizing Information

Have students create a two-column chart summarizing the psychological and biological explanations of anxiety disorders. Then have students write a paragraph discussing which explanation they believe best explains anxiety disorders and why.

Reviewing Section 2

Have students complete the Section Review questions on page 419.

Extension

Have students collect first-person accounts of experiences with phobias, panic disorder, post-traumatic stress disorder, or other anxiety disorders. They can find these in books or in magazine and newspaper articles or by interviewing people they know. Have students share these accounts in class. Remind them that if they are sharing the experiences of people they know, they should respect each person's privacy by not identifying him or her.

Psychological Views For anxiety disorders, as well as the other disorders discussed later in this chapter, psychoanalytic views are presented even though they are no longer widely accepted. These views are included because they influenced later theories and had a major impact on the classification of psychological disorders until recently, as discussed earlier.

According to psychoanalytic theory, anxiety is the result of "forbidden" childhood urges that have been repressed, or hidden from consciousness (Freud, 1936). If repressed urges do surface, psychoanalysts argue, they may do so as obsessions and eventually lead to compulsive behaviors. For example, if one is trying to repress "dirty" sexual thoughts, then repetitive hand washing may help relieve some of the anxiety.

Learning theorists believe that phobias are conditioned, or learned, in childhood. This may occur when a child experiences a traumatic event—such as being lost in a crowd or frightened by a bad storm—or when a child observes phobic behavior in other people (Bandura, 1986). If a parent screams or faints when a child picks up a spider, for example, the child may learn that spiders are things to be feared and develop a fear of them. Learning theorists argue that such conditioned phobias may remain long after the experiences that produced them have been forgotten.

Learning theorists also believe that people will learn to reduce their anxiety by avoiding the situations that make them anxious (Gorman et al., 1989). For example, a student who feels anxious speaking in front of others in class may learn to keep quiet because it reduces his or her feelings of anxiety. However, by intentionally avoiding the anxiety-producing behavior, the student has no chance to learn other ways of coping with or unlearning the anxiety. As a result, the anxiety may worsen or be generalized to other situations that involve speaking in front of others.

Cognitive theorists, on the other hand, believe that people make themselves feel anxious by responding negatively to most situations and coming to believe they are helpless to control what happens to them. This creates great anxiety.

Biological Views Research indicates that heredity may play a role in most psychological disorders, including anxiety disorders. For example, one study showed that if one of a pair of identical twins exhibited an anxiety disorder, there was a 45 percent chance that the other twin would also exhibit the dis-

order. This was true even of twins raised in different families. By contrast, the chances of fraternal twins both developing anxiety disorders was only about 15 percent (Torgersen, 1983). Similarly, adopted children are more likely to have an anxiety disorder if a biological parent has one than if an adoptive parent does. Both types of studies suggest that genes play at least some role in the development of anxiety disorders.

How did genes get involved? Some psychologists believe that people are genetically inclined to fear things that were threats to their ancestors (Mineka, 1991). These psychologists argue that people who rapidly acquired strong fears of real dangers—such as large animals, snakes, heights, and sharp objects—would be more likely to survive and reproduce. To the extent that the tendency to develop such fears is controlled by genes, they conclude, the tendency would be passed on to future generations, causing the disorders to be relatively common today.

Interaction of Factors Some cases of anxiety disorder may reflect the interaction of biological and psychological factors. People with panic disorder, for example, may have a biologically based tendency to overreact psychologically to physical sensations (Ciesielski et al., 1981; Turner et al., 1985). The initial physical symptoms of panic—such as rapid heart rate and shortness of breath—cause these people to react with fear, leading to even worse panic symptoms. They may think they are having a heart attack and experience severe psychological stress. Anxiety about having another panic attack becomes a psychological disorder itself— one that originated in a biological reaction.

Regardless of their cause, anxiety disorders are both common and disabling. In serious cases, they lead to tremendous restrictions and limitations in lifestyle, relationships, and work. They can also lead to great personal distress. Fortunately, most people who suffer from anxiety disorder respond well to treatment, which is covered in Chapter 19.

SECTION 2 REVIEW

go.hrw.com **Homework Practice Online**
Keyword: SY3 HP18

1. How does anxiety differ from fear?

2. Describe the relationship between panic disorder and agoraphobia.

3. **Critical Thinking** *Analyzing Information* Explain why studies of twins are important for determining whether a disorder has a biological basis.

Journal Activity

Have students write in their journals about any avoidance behavior they use to reduce their anxiety about particular situations or objects. Ask them to consider how facing an anxiety-producing situation or object rather than avoiding it might help them overcome their feelings of anxiety.

Section 2 Review: Answers

1. Anxiety is a dread or uneasiness over a vague or imagined threat or danger. Fear is a similar feeling but one that occurs in response to a real threat or danger.

2. People with panic disorder often have agoraphobia as well. They are afraid they will have a panic attack where they will be humiliated or unable to flee or to get help.

3. Identical twins have the same genetic makeup. Therefore, if a disorder shows up in one twin, it is expected to show up in the other.

SECTION 3

Dissociative Disorders

Dissociation refers to the separation of certain personality components or mental processes from conscious thought. In some situations, dissociation is normal. Someone may be so engrossed in reading a book or watching a television program, for example, that he is unaware that his name is being called. Someone else may become so involved in watching the road that she misses the sign for her exit on the highway. Perhaps the most common form of normal dissociation is daydreaming, in which the person's thoughts may be "a million miles away." In each of these cases, dissociation usually does not indicate a psychological disorder.

However, when dissociation occurs as a way to avoid stressful events or feelings, it is considered to be a sign of a psychological disorder. People with dissociative disorders may lose their memory of a particular event or even forget their identity. It is believed that dissociation occurs when individuals are faced with urges or experiences that are very stressful. By dissociating, they are able to remove themselves from the source of stress and lessen their feelings of anxiety.

There are no current statistics on the prevalence of dissociative disorders. In part, this is because the DSM-IV classifies them somewhat differently than they were classified in the past. However, dissociation is a common psychological symptom.

Types of Dissociative Disorders

In the DSM-IV, the dissociative disorders are classified as dissociative amnesia, dissociative fugue, dissociative identity disorder, and depersonalization disorder. These disorders are described next.

Dissociative Amnesia Formerly called psychogenic amnesia, dissociative amnesia is characterized by a sudden loss of memory, usually following a particularly stressful or traumatic event. A person experiencing dissociative amnesia typically cannot remember any events that occurred for a certain period of time surrounding the traumatic event. Less commonly, a person may forget all prior experiences and may be unable to remember his or her name, recognize friends and family, or recall important personal information. Dissociative amnesia may last for just a few hours, or it may persist for

years. Memory is likely to return just as suddenly as it was lost, and the amnesia rarely recurs.

The term *psychogenic* means "psychological in origin." Dissociative amnesia cannot be explained biologically—as the result of a head injury, for example. Most often, a traumatic event, such as witnessing a serious accident, precedes the amnesia. Not surprisingly, the incidence of dissociative amnesia rises markedly during wartime and crises such as natural disasters.

TRUTH OR fiction ▪ REVISITED ▪ *It is true that people sometimes forget a very traumatic event as a way of coping with the psychological stress of the trauma. This occurrence is called dissociative amnesia.*

Dissociative Fugue Dissociative fugue—previously called psychogenic fugue—is characterized not only by forgetting personal information and past events but also by suddenly relocating from home or work and taking on a new identity. Like dissociative amnesia, dissociative fugue usually follows a traumatic event that is psychologically very stressful. It is reported most frequently during wartime and natural disasters.

When individuals with dissociative fugue travel away from their home or workplace, they may take on a new name, residence, and occupation. They may become socially active in their new identity and not appear to be ill in any way. When the fugue comes to an end, they no longer remember what happened during the fugue state.

Dissociative Identity Disorder Formerly called multiple personality disorder, dissociative identity disorder involves the existence of two or more personalities within a single individual. The various personalities may or may not be aware of the others, and at least two of the personalities take turns controlling the individual's behavior.

Each personality is likely to be different from the others in several ways, including in such observable traits as voice, facial expressions, and handedness, as well as self-perceived age, gender, and physical characteristics. The personalities may even have different allergies and eyeglass prescriptions. They may also behave very differently from one another.

People who are diagnosed with dissociative identity disorder usually were severely abused in

Applying Information

Have students use what they have learned in Section 3 to write a 10-item true-false quiz on dissociative disorders. Tell them to write their questions on one side of a separate sheet of paper and the answers on the other side. Then have students exchange papers and complete the quizzes.

Reviewing Section 3

Have students complete the Section Review questions on page 421.

Section Objective

▶ Explain somatization, and list the symptoms of two somatoform disorders.

This objective is assessed in the Section Review on page 422 and in the Chapter 18 Review.

---

childhood. They typically suffered severe physical, sexual, and/or psychological abuse (Spanos, 1994). Less often, dissociative identity disorder is preceded by other types of trauma.

Depersonalization Disorder Depersonalization refers to feelings of detachment from one's mental processes or body. People with this disorder describe feeling as though they are outside their bodies, observing themselves at a distance.

Depersonalization is a common symptom of other psychological disorders in addition to being a disorder in its own right. After depression and anxiety, it is the most common complaint among psychiatric patients. Like the other dissociative disorders, depersonalization disorder is likely to be preceded by a stressful event.

Explaining Dissociative Disorders

Dissociative disorders have been explained primarily by psychological views. According to psychoanalytic theory, people dissociate in order to repress unacceptable urges. In dissociative amnesia or fugue, for example, the person forgets the disturbing urges. In dissociative identity disorder, the person expresses undesirable urges by developing other personalities that can take responsibility for them. In depersonalization, the person goes outside the self, away from the turmoil within.

According to learning theorists, individuals with dissociative disorders have learned not to think about disturbing events in order to avoid feelings of guilt, shame, or pain. They dissociate themselves from the stressful events by selectively forgetting them. This is reinforced by the reduced anxiety they feel when the trauma is forgotten.

Neither cognitive nor biological theorists have offered a complete explanation for dissociative disorders. At present, there is no convincing evidence that either biological or genetic factors play a role in the development of dissociative disorders.

SECTION 3 REVIEW

go.hrw.com Homework Practice Online
Keyword: SY3 HP18

1. Describe the four dissociative disorders.
2. **Critical Thinking** *Evaluating* In some cultures, people are encouraged to go into trancelike states. Should this type of dissociation be considered a sign of a psychological disorder? Why or why not?

SECTION 4

Somatoform Disorders

Somatization, which comes from the Greek word for "body," refers to the expression of psychological distress through physical symptoms. People with somatoform disorders have psychological problems (such as depression) but experience inexplicable physical symptoms (such as paralysis).

It is important to distinguish between somatoform disorders and malingering, or the conscious attempt to "fake" an illness in order to avoid work, school, or other responsibilities. People with somatoform disorders do not intentionally fake their illnesses. They honestly feel pain or believe they cannot move their limbs.

TRUTH OR fiction

■ REVISITED ■

It is not true that people whose illnesses are "all in their heads" do not really have symptoms of a disease. Although psychological in origin, the physical symptoms of somatoform disorders are very real to the people who experience them.

Reliable statistics on the incidence of somatoform disorders are not available. Many diagnoses of somatoform illness later prove to be incorrect when patients are found to have medical illnesses that account for their symptoms. On the other hand, cases of somatoform disorders may go undiagnosed because of the focus on physical, as opposed to psychological, symptoms.

Types of Somatoform Disorders

The DSM-IV identifies six types of somatoform disorders. The two most common are conversion disorder and hypochondriasis. The symptoms of these two disorders are described below and summarized in Figure 18.3 on page 422.

Conversion Disorder People with conversion disorder experience a change in or loss of physical functioning in a major part of the body for which there is no known medical explanation. For example, they may suddenly develop the inability to see at night or to move their legs, even though no

---

Opening Section 4

Motivator

Explain to students that the term *somatoform* comes from the Greek word *soma,* meaning "body." Then ask students what they think somatoform disorders might involve. Have students write down their responses and refer to them after reading this section.

Closing Section 4

Analyzing Information

Have students examine Figure 18.3 and analyze the ways in which conversion disorder differs from hypochondriasis. Then have students explain why both disorders are included in the category of somatoform disorders.

Reviewing Section 4

Have students complete the Section Review questions on page 422.

Class Discussion

Point out that some people with conversion disorder may have "glove anesthesia," the loss of sensation in the hand and wrist. Psychologists consider this to be of psychogenic rather than organic origin because there is no combination of neural fibers that serve this area of the body and no other. Have students discuss how psychologists might explain glove anesthesia.

Section 4 Review: Answers

1. Malingering is the conscious faking of an illness to avoid work. In somatization, symptoms are actually experienced; in malingering, they are not.

2. Conversion disorder is characterized by a sudden and severe loss of physical functioning that has no medical explanation. Hypochondriasis is the unhealthy fear of having a serious illness.

3. Learning theorists view behavior as the result of modeling and reinforcement. Thus, they might explain that a person who receives attention only after complaining of physical symptoms may learn to express psychological discomfort as physical symptoms.

422

medical explanation can be found for their sudden physical disability. These behaviors are not, however, intentionally produced. That is, the person is not faking it.

Conversion disorder is further complicated because many people who experience conversion disorder show little concern about their symptoms, no matter how serious or unusual those symptoms may be. This lack of concern about the symptoms may help in the diagnosis of conversion disorder.

Hypochondriasis Also called hypochondria, hypochondriasis is defined as a person's unrealistic preoccupation with thoughts that he or she has a serious disease. People with hypochondriasis become absorbed by minor physical symptoms and sensations, convinced that the symptoms indicate a serious medical illness. These people maintain their erroneous beliefs despite reassurances from doctors that there is nothing physically wrong with them. Some people with hypochondriasis visit doctor after doctor, seeking the one physician who will find the cause of their symptoms.

Explaining Somatoform Disorders

Explanations for somatoform disorders in general, and specifically conversion disorder or hypochondriasis, are primarily psychological. According to psychoanalytic theory, somatoform disorders occur when individuals repress emotions associated with forbidden urges and instead express them symbolically in physical symptoms. The physical symptoms thus represent a compromise between the unconscious need to express feelings and the fear of actually expressing them.

More recently, other psychologists have argued that people with conversion disorder "convert" psychological stress into actual medical problems. For example, a fighter pilot may lose the ability to see at night as a response to the great anxiety he feels

Two Examples of Somatoform Disorders

Type	Characteristics
Conversion Disorder	Sudden and severe loss of physical functioning, as in blindness or paralysis, despite the fact that no medical explanation can be found for the physical symptoms; usually characterized by the person's apparent lack of concern about his or her physical symptoms
Hypochondriasis	An unhealthy fear of having, or the unsubstantiated belief that one has, a serious disease; characterized by the person's misinterpretation of his or her normal bodily symptoms or functions

FIGURE 18.3 *People with somatoform disorders have psychological problems that express themselves in physical symptoms. There is, however, no known medical basis for the physical symptoms. The two most prevalent of the somatoform disorders are conversion disorder and hypochondriasis, the symptoms of which are described here.*

Source: Adapted from the DSM-IV, 1994.

about flying nighttime bombing missions. Another individual may suffer paralysis of the legs after nearly being in a car accident.

Some behavioral theorists have suggested that somatoform symptoms can serve as a reinforcer if they successfully allow a person to escape from anxiety. There are also some indications that biological or genetic factors may play a role in the development of somatoform disorders (Kellner, 1990).

SECTION 4 REVIEW

1. Define malingering. How does somatization differ from malingering?

2. How do conversion disorder and hypochondriasis differ?

3. **Critical Thinking** *Analyzing Information* How do you think learning theorists might explain somatoform disorders? Do you agree with this type of explanation? Why or why not?

Section Objective

▶ Identify several theories that attempt to explain mood disorders.

This objective is assessed in the Section Review on page 426 and in the Chapter 18 Review.

Motivator

Ask students to write yes or no on a separate sheet of paper in response to the following question: Have you ever known anyone who had overwhelming feelings of sadness or hopelessness for no apparent reason? Collect the papers and tally the number of yes responses. Point out that mood disorders are quite common and that it is important that everyone understand the signs and symptoms of these disorders. Tell students that mood disorders are the focus of Section 5.

FRANK & ERNEST® by Bob Thaves

Source: FRANK & ERNEST reprinted by permission of Newspaper Enterprise Association, Inc.

Using Visuals

Have students examine the comic strip on this page. Ask them what they find amusing about it. Then have students explain why hypochondriasis is not a source of amusement to the people who have the disorder.

Cross-Curricular Link: Health

Research shows that depression has a negative effect on physical health. It weakens the immune system, making people more susceptible to illness.

SECTION 5

Mood Disorders

Most people have mood changes that reflect the normal ups and downs of daily life. They feel down when things go wrong, such as failing an important test, and they feel up when good things happen, such as when their team wins a championship. Dan felt down when his sister's condition worsened. Janet noted that Dan was depressed, but she also realized that Dan's mood was a normal reaction to his situation.

Some people, however, experience mood changes that seem inappropriate for or inconsistent with the situations to which they are responding. These people feel sad when things are going well, or they feel elated for no apparent reason. People who have abnormal moods such as these may have a mood disorder.

Mood disorders fall into two general categories. **Depression** typically involves feelings of helplessness, hopelessness, worthlessness, guilt, and great sadness. **Bipolar disorder** involves a cycle of mood changes from depression to wild elation and back again.

Mood disorders—particularly depression—are very common psychological disorders. In any six-month period, about 8 percent of women and 4 percent of men are likely to be diagnosed with some form of depression (Myers et al., 1984).

Types of Mood Disorders

The DSM-IV classifies mood disorders into several different types of depressive and bipolar disorders. These are summarized in Figure 18.4 on page 424.

Major Depression Depression is by far the most common of all the psychological disorders. It has been estimated that depression affects more than 100 million people worldwide and that between 8 and 18 percent of the general population will experience depression in their lifetime (Boyd & Weissman, 1982).

TRUTH OR fiction ▪ REVISITED ▪

It is true that depression is the most common type of psychological disorder. At least 8 percent of the general population will experience depression.

According to the DSM-IV, major depression is diagnosed when an individual experiences at least five of the following nine symptoms of depression:

▪ persistent depressed mood for most of the day

▪ loss of interest or pleasure in all, or almost all, activities

▪ significant weight loss or gain due to changes in appetite

▪ sleeping more or less than usual

▪ speeding up or slowing down of physical and emotional reactions

▪ fatigue or loss of energy

▪ feelings of worthlessness or unfounded guilt

▪ reduced ability to concentrate or make meaningful decisions

▪ recurrent thoughts of death or suicide

For a diagnosis of major depression to be made, at least one of the individual's five symptoms must be one of the first two symptoms in the list.

◪ internet connect

TOPIC: Mood Disorders
GO TO: go.hrw.com
KEYWORD: SY3 PS18

Have students access the Internet through the HRW Go site to research depression among teenagers today. Then ask students to write an article about teenage depression for your school newspaper or newsletter. Ask students to describe the major symptoms of depression, and to explain the causes in a way that classmates, teachers, and parents can understand. As an extension, ask the class if they believe teenagers are more likely to become depressed today than in the past.

Teaching Section 5

Demonstration

Bring to class a book containing the paintings of Edvard Munch. Show students some of his self-portraits and some of the portraits of his family, such as the painting titled *Death in the Sickroom*. Have students discuss the sense of depression that permeates many of Munch's paintings. You may also want students to discuss the meaning of the following quotation from his writings: "Sickness and insanity and death were the black angels that hovered over my cradle and have since followed me throughout my life."

Cooperative Learning

Have pairs of students review the symptoms and effects of depression and bipolar disorder. One student should name a symptom and the other should match it to the appropriate disorder. Remind students that some symptoms may be typical of both disorders.

Additionally, the symptoms must be present for at least two weeks, and occur nearly every day during that period (American Psychiatric Association, 2000).

Severely depressed individuals may become consumed by feelings of worthlessness or guilt. Severe depression calls for immediate treatment—as many as 15 percent of severely depressed individuals eventually commit suicide (Hirschfield & Goodwin, 1988).

Bipolar Disorder   Formerly called manic depression, bipolar disorder is characterized by dramatic ups and downs in mood. Periods of **mania**, or extreme excitement characterized by hyperactivity and chaotic behavior, can change into depression very quickly and for no apparent reason.

The manic phase is characterized by a mood that is persistently and abnormally elevated. In some people, however, this phase may be characterized by irritability instead of elation. Manic moods are also characterized by at least some of the following traits:

- inflated self-esteem
- inability to sit still or sleep restfully
- pressure to keep talking and switching from topic to topic
- racing thoughts (referred to as "flight of ideas")
- difficulty concentrating

Individuals in the manic phase may appear highly excited and act silly or argumentative. In severe cases, they may have delusions (beliefs that have no basis in reality) about their own superior abilities or about others being jealous of them. They may also experience hallucinations (sensory perceptions that occur in the absence of sensory stimuli) such as hearing imaginary voices or seeing things that are not really there. These individuals may also engage in impulsive behaviors, such as going on wild spending sprees, quitting their jobs to pursue wild dreams, or making foolish business

Irrational, Depressing Thoughts and Rational Alternatives

Irrational Depressing Thought	Rational Alternative
"There's nothing I can do."	"I can't think of anything to do right now, but if I work at it, I may."
"I'm no good."	"I did something I regret, but that doesn't make me evil or worthless as a person."
"This is absolutely awful."	"This is pretty bad, but it's not the end of the world."
"I just don't have the brains for this course."	"I guess I really need to go back over the basics in the course. Who can I turn to for help?"
"I just can't believe I did something so terrible!"	"That was a bad experience. Well, I won't be likely to try that again soon."
"I can't imagine ever feeling right."	"This is painful, but if I try to work it through step by step, I'll probably see my way out of it eventually."

FIGURE 18.4 *Psychologists point out that many of us create or worsen feelings of depression through irrational thoughts. We can make mountains out of molehills and make it seem as if we cannot change things for the better. This figure shows the kinds of thoughts that can be depressing, and the kinds of more realistic thoughts that make it possible for people to take charge of their lives.*

investments. Thus, the manic phase of bipolar disorder can be very disruptive to an individual's life.

Explaining Mood Disorders

Psychological and biological theories have been proposed to explain why such a large number of people experience mood disorders, particularly depression. These theories are explained here.

Psychological Views   The psychoanalytic view of depression is that some people are prone to depression because they suffered a real or imagined loss of a loved object or person in childhood. According to this view, the child feels anger toward the lost object or person but, instead of expressing the anger, internalizes it and directs it toward himself or herself. This leads to feelings of guilt and loss of self-esteem, which in turn lead to depression.

Learning theorists have suggested other explanations for depression. Some believe that *learned helplessness* makes people prone to depression. Psychologist Martin Seligman (1975) demonstrated the concept of learned helplessness in a classic experiment in which he taught dogs that they were

Classifying Information

Review the ways people explain life events, discussed on page 425. Ask students to provide examples of situations that do not work out (e.g., failing to get a desired job, throwing a party nobody enjoys). For each example, have students write six possible ways to explain the event. Ask volunteers to read aloud their explanations, and have students determine whether the explanations are internal or external, stable or unstable, global or specific. Then have students identify which explanations are more likely to be used by people who are depressed.

Synthesizing Information

Have students summarize the symptoms and possible causes of depression and bipolar disorder. Have them write their summaries on index cards. Then have the class work together to create a final version that is as concise and as complete as possible.

Reviewing Section

Have students complete the Section Review questions on page 426.

---

helpless to escape from electric shock. First, he placed a barrier in the dogs' cage to prevent them from leaving when shocks were administered. Later the barrier was removed. However, when shocks were again administered, the dogs made no effort to escape. They had apparently learned there was nothing they could do to prevent the pain.

This helpless behavior has been compared to the helplessness often seen in people who are depressed. Learning theorists argue that people prone to depression have learned through experience to believe that previous events in their lives were out of their control. This leads them to expect that future events will be out of their control as well. As a result, whenever a negative event occurs, these people feel helpless, and this leads to depression.

In contrast, cognitive theorists have suggested that some people are prone to depression because of their habitual style of explaining life events. According to this view, people assign different types of explanations to most events—internal or external, stable or unstable, and global or specific. These attributional styles affect people's self-esteem and self-efficacy. These styles also relate to expectancy—what people expect based on prior experiences. Suppose, for example, that someone goes on a date that does not work out. Different ways to explain this might include the following:

- "I really messed up" (internal explanation, places blame on self).
- "Some people just don't get along" (external explanation, places the blame elsewhere).
- "It's my personality" (stable explanation, suggests problem cannot be changed).
- "It was my head cold" (unstable explanation, suggests problem is temporary).
- "I have no idea what to do when I'm with other people" (global explanation, suggests problem is too large to deal with).
- "I have difficulty making small talk" (specific explanation, suggests problem is small enough to be manageable).

Research shows that people who are depressed are more likely than other people to explain their failures on internal, stable, and global causes—causes they feel helpless to change. Cognitive theorists argue that such explanations give rise to feelings of helplessness, which in turn lead to depression. Dan's hope that the doctors would find a treatable (unstable, specific) cause for Michelle's disorder would be considered a healthy outlook.

Another cognitive theory was proposed by Aaron Beck (1976), who suggested that people who are depressed have a negative view of themselves, their experiences, and their future. According to Beck, this is because people who are depressed have negative self-schemas, developed from negative experiences in early childhood. This leads them to filter out positive information and perceive negative information as more negative than it really is. Such negativity, Beck argued, makes people prone to depression.

Biological Views Other researchers have investigated biological factors in mood disorders. Mood disorders, like anxiety disorders, tend to occur more often in the close relatives of affected individuals than they do in the general population (Rose, 1995; Wachtel, 1994). Between 20 and 25 percent of people with mood disorders have a family member who is affected by a similar disorder (Hirschfeld & Goodwin, 1988). Moreover, identical twins of affected individuals are more likely to be affected than fraternal twins (Goodwin & Jamison, 1990). These studies seem to indicate that mood disorders have a genetic basis.

Scientists believe that two neurotransmitters, or chemical messengers, in the brain—serotonin and noradrenaline—may at least partly explain the connection between genes and mood. Serotonin and noradrenaline both play a role in mood regulation (Cooper et al., 1991; Michels & Marzuk, 1993). Low levels, or deficiencies, of serotonin may create a tendency toward mood disorders in general. Deficiencies of serotonin *combined* with deficiencies of noradrenaline, however, may be linked to depression specifically. These findings have been important in the development of drug therapy for the treatment of mood disorders. (See Chapter 19.)

Biological and Psychological Factors Many cases of depression may reflect the interaction of biological factors such as neurotransmitter levels and psychological factors such as learned helplessness. This has been demonstrated with laboratory animals. Seligman (1975) and Weiss (1982) found that dogs that learned they were helpless to escape electric shocks also had less noradrenaline activity in their brains. Helplessness is thus linked to specific neurotransmitter deficiencies. The relationship may result in a vicious cycle. A depressing situation may slow down the activity of noradrenaline in the brain; in turn, the chemical changes may then worsen the depression.

Class Discussion

Have students debate whether individuals, through willpower and positive thinking, can control tendencies toward depression, or whether biological factors and circumstances outside individuals' control cause some individuals to be depressed no matter what they do. Make sure students use sound reasoning to support their arguments.

Cultural Dimensions

According to a study by the World Health Organization, people throughout the world experience the same mental health problems, even though they may give different names to the same set of symptoms. This runs counter to the view of many anthropologists that people of different cultures experience different symptoms.

Patel, T. (March 25, 1995). Depression feels the same the whole world over. *New Scientist*. 10.

Readings and Case Studies

A DAY IN THE LIFE

Section Objective

▶ Describe the subtypes and causes of schizophrenia.

This objective is assessed in the Section Review on page 429 and in the Chapter 18 Review.

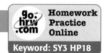

Opening Section 6

Motivator

Tell students that Section 6 focuses on schizophrenia, usually considered the most serious of the psychological disorders. Also tell them that the word *schizophrenia* literally means a "schism" or "splitting" between the functions of feeling, or emotion, and the functions of thinking, or thought processes. The result is a loss of contact with reality. Ask students to speculate how a loss of contact with reality might affect the daily functioning of someone suffering from schizophrenia.

Section 5 Review: Answers

1. Depression is recurrent or chronic feelings of sadness, worthlessness, or guilt. Bipolar disorder is cyclical changes from depression to mania and back again.

2. Symptoms include the following: persistent depressed mood, loss of interest in most activities, weight loss due to changes in appetite, disrupted sleep patterns, changes in physical and emotional reactions, fatigue, feelings of worthlessness or guilt, inability to concentrate or make decisions, and recurring thoughts of death.

3. Self-esteem, self-efficacy, and expectancy are all affected by how people explain events that occur in their lives.

SECTION 5 REVIEW

Homework Practice Online
Keyword: SY3 HP18

1. What is the difference between depression and bipolar disorder?

2. List five symptoms of major depression.

3. **Critical Thinking** *Summarizing* Describe and explain self-esteem, self-efficacy, and expectancy from the perspective of attribution theory.

SECTION 6

Schizophrenia

Schizophrenia, usually considered the most serious of the psychological disorders, is characterized by loss of contact with reality. Schizophrenia can be very disabling, and even lead to the affected person's inability to function independently. Typically, schizophrenia first appears in young adulthood, but it may occur at other ages. Although it usually develops gradually, it can also appear suddenly. Schizophrenia can now be treated more effectively, although if untreated it can worsen over time.

The most obvious symptoms of schizophrenia include hallucinations, delusions, and thought disorders. In most cases, the hallucinations are auditory—voices may tell the individual what to do or comment on the individual's behavior. This is what Dan's sister Michelle experienced. Sometimes the voices may tell the individual to harm herself or himself or others.

Individuals with schizophrenia may experience delusions of grandeur—beliefs that they are superior to other people. For example, such individuals may believe that they are famous or on a special mission to save the world. Sometimes the delusions are of persecution. For example, a person with schizophrenia might believe that he or she is being pursued by the CIA, FBI, or some other government agency. Other delusions may include beliefs that one has committed unpardonable sins or even that one does not really exist.

Thought disorders involve problems in the organization or the content of mental processes. The thoughts of a person with schizophrenia may skip from topic to topic in an apparently illogical way. This is reflected in the person's speech, which sounds disorganized and confused. A person with schizophrenia may also repeat the same word or phrase over and over, repeat words or phrases that another person has spoken, or invent new words.

People with schizophrenia experience other symptoms that result in a decreased ability to function. These symptoms include social withdrawal, loss of social skills, and loss of normal emotional responsiveness. Some people with schizophrenia may even go into a **catatonic stupor**—an immobile, expressionless, comalike state.

Understandably, these symptoms cause tremendous stress to individuals with schizophrenia and their families. It has been estimated that as many as 20 percent of people with schizophrenia attempt suicide and that 10 percent actually do kill themselves (Caldwell & Gottesman, 1990).

Schizophrenia is found in all cultures and has been recognized for several thousand years. A large number of people have schizophrenia—an estimated 2 million in the United States alone (Regier, 1993).

Types of Schizophrenia

Individuals with schizophrenia vary greatly in the symptoms they exhibit, although virtually all have thought disorders. Most people with schizophrenia exhibit a combination of symptoms.

The disturbed thoughts of people with schizophrenia sometimes appears in their artwork and in their speech.

Teaching Section 6

Interpreting Information

Have each student write a "case study" for a hypothetical person with one of the types of schizophrenia discussed in the section. Tell students that their case studies should include the following information: descriptive information about the person (age and sex), symptomatology (physical and emotional), and duration of the disorder. Have volunteers present their case studies to the class, and have class members "diagnose" which type of schizophrenia each hypothetical individual has.

Role-Playing

Organize the class into small groups, and have the groups reread the "A Day in the Life" vignette for this chapter. Then tell the members of each group that they are to write and perform a conversation among a group of close friends, one of whom has a family member diagnosed with one of the types of schizophrenia discussed in this section. After the groups have presented their role-playing, have the class discuss why schizophrenia causes emotional distress not only for the affected individuals but also for their family members and friends.

The DSM-IV classification of schizophrenia and other psychotic disorders is based primarily on the duration and recurrence of symptoms. The types of schizophrenia include paranoid, disorganized, and catatonic schizophrenia.

Paranoid Schizophrenia People with paranoid schizophrenia have delusions or frequent auditory hallucinations, all relating to a single theme. These people may have delusions of grandeur, persecution, or jealousy. For example, an individual with paranoid schizophrenia may be convinced that people have been plotting against him or her even when there is no evidence of such.

Dan's sister, Michelle, was distrustful of everyone except her husband. She even accused Dan of trying to confuse her when he asked how she was feeling. Although people with this type of schizophrenia tend to have less disordered thoughts and bizarre behavior than do people with other types of schizophrenia, they may be agitated, confused, and afraid.

Disorganized Schizophrenia People with disorganized schizophrenia are incoherent in their thought and speech and disorganized in their behavior. They usually have delusions or hallucinations as well, but these tend to be fragmentary and unconnected, unlike the more ordered and systematic delusions of those with paranoid schizophrenia.

People with disorganized schizophrenia are also either emotionless or show inappropriate emotions. Typically, they act silly and giddy, and they tend to giggle and speak nonsense. They may neglect their appearance and hygiene and even lose control of their bladders and bowels.

The following case description (adapted from Spitzer et al., 1988, pp.137–138) illustrates several symptoms of disorganized schizophrenia. A 40-year-old man was brought to the hospital by his mother, who reported that she was afraid of him. It was his twelfth hospitalization. The man was dressed in a tattered overcoat, a baseball cap, and house slippers. He spoke with a childlike quality and walked with exaggerated movements. His emotions ranged from anger (hurling obscenities) to silliness (giggling for no apparent reason).

Schizophrenia and other serious psychological disorders affect many people in the United States and around the world.

Since stopping his medication about a month prior to his hospitalization, the man had been hearing voices and looking and acting more bizarre. He told the interviewer that he had been "eating wires and lighting fires." His speech was generally incoherent and consisted frequently of rhymes.

Catatonic Schizophrenia The most obvious symptom of catatonic schizophrenia is disturbance of movement. Activity may slow to a stupor and then suddenly switch to agitation. Individuals with this disorder may hold unusual, uncomfortable body positions for long periods of time, even after their arms and legs swell and stiffen. They may also exhibit waxy flexibility, a condition in which other people can mold them into strange poses that they continue to hold for hours.

Taking a Stand

Ask volunteers to summarize the evidence suggesting that biological factors are involved in schizophrenia. Ask other volunteers to summarize the psychological explanations of schizophrenia. Then have students debate whether psychological views or biological views offer a more complete and convincing explanation of schizophrenia.

Comparing and Contrasting Information

Have students make a chart in which they compare and contrast the symptoms of the three types of schizophrenia discussed in Section 6.

Reviewing Section 6

Have students complete the Section Review questions on page 429.

Individuals with catatonic schizophrenia may hold unusual positions for hours. Many of these people alternate between periods of immobility and periods of frenzied physical activity.

Explaining Schizophrenia

Many different theories have been proposed to explain schizophrenia. These theories include both psychological and biological views.

Psychological Views According to the psychoanalytic perspective, schizophrenia is the result of the overwhelming of the ego by urges from the id. The urges threaten the ego and cause intense conflict. In response, the individual regresses to an early phase of the oral stage of development in which the infant has not yet learned that it is separate from the mother. (See Chapter 14.) In this condition, fantasies become confused with reality, leading to hallucinations and delusions. Like many psychoanalytic theories, this one has fallen into disfavor over the years.

Other psychological views focus on the family environment as the root of schizophrenia. One such theory suggests that a family environment in which a parent frequently expresses intense emotions and has a pushy, critical attitude puts children at risk of developing schizophrenia (Leff & Vaughn, 1985). It is possible, however, that such a family environment may only increase the chances of relapse in individuals who have schizophrenia. That is to say the family environment does not actually *produce* schizophrenia.

Biological Views Schizophrenia appears to be a brain disorder, and many studies have been done to determine how the brains of schizophrenic people differ from those of other people. One avenue of brain research connects the major problems found in schizophrenia—problems in attention, memory, abstract thinking, and language—with differences in the frontal part of the brain. Schizophrenic people have smaller brains than other people and, in particular, a smaller frontal region (Selemon, 2000). Research suggests that the difficulties may reflect a loss of synapses, the structures that connect neurons and make it possible for neurons to communicate with one another (Glantz & Lewis, 2000; Selemon, 2000).

What might cause the loss of synapses? Research evidence suggests that there are three biological risk factors for schizophrenia: heredity, complications during pregnancy and birth, and birth during winter (Carpenter & Buchanan, 1994). Schizophrenia, like many other psychological disorders, runs in families, a view to which Dan's mother had alluded (Cannon et al., 1998; Kendler et al., 1997). People with schizophrenia constitute about 1 percent of the population. However, children with one parent who has been diagnosed as schizophrenic have about a 10 percent chance of being diagnosed as schizophrenic themselves. Children with two such parents have about a 35 to 40 percent chance of being so (Gottesman, 1991; Straube & Oades, 1992). When one identical twin has schizophrenia, the other has about a 40 to 50 percent chance of being diagnosed with it. Many studies have been carried out to try to isolate the gene or genes involved in schizophrenia. Some studies have found locations for multiple genes on several chromosomes. Recent research suggests that particular genes may provide the vulnerability to schizophrenia (Brzustowicz et al., 2000).

Many people with schizophrenia have experienced complications during pregnancy and birth (Rosso et al., 2000). For example, the mothers of many people with schizophrenia had influenza during the sixth or seventh month of pregnancy (C. E. Barr, et al., 1990). People with the disease are also somewhat more likely to have been born during the winter than would be predicted by chance (Carpenter & Buchanan, 1994). Maternal starvation has also been related to schizophrenia (Susser & Lin, 1992). These biological risk factors suggest that schizophrenia involves abnormal prenatal brain development.

Section Objective

▶ Distinguish personality disorders from other psychological disorders.

This objective is assessed in the Section Review on page 431 and in the Chapter 18 Review.

Opening Section 7

Motivator

Ask students to think of all the psychological disorders they have studied thus far in this chapter. Then ask if they can think of any other psychological problems that would seriously interfere with an individual's ability to live a productive and enjoyable life. Explain that this final section will discuss a number of such psychological problems, known as personality disorders.

Problems in the central nervous system may involve neurotransmitters as well as brain structures, and research has focused on one particular neurotransmitter: dopamine (Carpenter & Buchanan, 1994). According to the dopamine theory of schizophrenia, people with schizophrenia *use* more dopamine than other people do, although they may not *produce* more of it. Why? They may have more dopamine receptors in the brain than other people, or their dopamine receptors may be hyperactive (Davis et al., 1991).

A Multifactorial Model of Schizophrenia
The multifactorial model of schizophrenia illustrates how several biological and psychological factors may interact in the development of the disorder. In this model, genetic factors create a vulnerability, or susceptibility, to schizophrenia. Among people who are genetically vulnerable, other factors, such as trauma during birth, may lead to brain injury and the subsequent development of schizophrenia. Once the disorder develops, its course may be negatively affected by the family environment.

The model also suggests that environmental factors alone are not enough to lead to the

development of schizophrenia. Thus, people who are not genetically vulnerable are unlikely to develop the disorder, regardless of the environmental risk factors to which they are exposed.

SECTION 6 REVIEW

Homework Practice Online
go.hrw.com
Keyword: SY3 HP18

1. List four symptoms of schizophrenia.
2. How does paranoid schizophrenia differ from disorganized schizophrenia?
3. **Critical Thinking** *Drawing Inferences and Conclusions* Explain why a multifactorial model of schizophrenia may help in explaining the disorder.

S E C T I O N 7

Personality Disorders

Personality disorders are patterns of inflexible traits that disrupt social life or work and/or distress the affected individual. They usually show up by late adolescence and affect all aspects of the individual's personality, including thought processes, emotions, and behavior.

It is important to note the distinction between personality disorders and other psychological disorders that they may resemble. Psychological disorders, such as schizophrenia or phobic disorder, for example, are episodes of illness that an individual experiences. They can be distinguished from the individual's personality. In contrast, personality disorders are enduring traits that are major components of the individual's personality.

Antisocial personality disorder, described in detail below, is the only personality disorder for which there are data on prevalence. The estimates as to the number of affected individuals vary widely—from less than 1 percent to almost 10 percent of the population (Robins, 1987).

Types of Personality Disorders

Figure 18.6 on page 430 shows the DSM-IV classification of personality disorders. Four of these personality disorders—paranoid, schizoid, antisocial, and avoidant—are described next.

Multifactorial Model of Schizophrenia

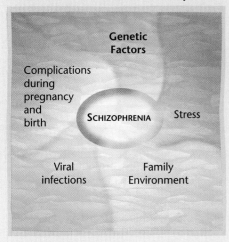

Genetic Factors

Complications during pregnancy and birth

SCHIZOPHRENIA

Stress

Viral infections

Family Environment

FIGURE 18.5 *This model reflects several biological and psychological factors that may interact in the development of schizophrenia.*

Source: Adapted from the DSM-IV-TR, 2000.

Teaching Section 7

Guided Practice

Write on the chalkboard the following four headings: *Paranoid Personality, Schizoid Personality, Antisocial Personality, Avoidant Personality.* Ask students to provide symptoms of people who have each of these types of personality disorders. Write each symptom under its proper heading. Then have students think of television shows and films they have seen and books they have read that contain characters who might have personality disorders. Ask the students to name each character and explain how the character shows symptoms of a personality disorder.

Independent Practice

Ask students to use what they have learned in the Guided Practice activity to write a one-act play, a poem, or a short story that portrays a character who has a personality disorder. Students should present their work to the class, either orally or visually. Have members of the class determine which personality disorder is being depicted.

Paranoid Personality Disorder   People with paranoid personality disorder tend to be distrustful and suspicious of others and to interpret others' motives as harmful or evil. They tend to perceive other people's behavior as threatening or insulting, even when it is not. They are difficult to get along with—argumentative, yet cold and aloof. Not surprisingly, these people often lead isolated lives.

Unlike individuals with paranoid schizophrenia, people with paranoid personality disorder are not confused about reality. However, their view of reality is distorted, and they are unlikely to see their mistrust and suspicions as unfounded or abnormal.

Schizoid Personality Disorder   People with schizoid personality disorder have no interest in relationships with other people. They also lack normal emotional responsiveness. They do not have tender feelings for, or become attached to, other people. Thus, people with schizoid personalities tend to be loners, with few if any friends.

These symptoms are similar to some of the symptoms of schizophrenia. Unlike people with schizophrenia, however, people with schizoid personality disorder do not have delusions or hallucinations. They stay in touch with reality.

Antisocial Personality Disorder   People with antisocial personality disorder show a persistent behavior pattern of disregard for, and violation of, the rights of others. Typically, they do not feel guilt or remorse for their antisocial behaviors, and they continue the behaviors despite the threat of social rejection and punishment.

It is true that some people do not feel guilty, even when they have committed serious crimes. Such people are likely to experience antisocial personality disorder.

In childhood and early adolescence, a person with antisocial personality disorder may run away from home, hurt other people or animals, lie, or steal. In adulthood, the person may be aggressive and reckless, have a hard time holding a job, fail to pay bills and debts, or break the law.

Avoidant Personality Disorder   People with avoidant personality disorder desire relationships with other people, but they are prevented from forming these relationships by tremendous fear of the disapproval of others. Thus, they act shy and withdrawn in social situations, always afraid they will say or do something foolish or embarrassing.

Personality Disorders and Their Characteristics

Type	Characteristics
Paranoid	Suspiciousness and distrust about others' motives
Schizoid	Detachment from social relationships
Schizotypal	Acute discomfort in close relationships, eccentricities of behavior
Antisocial	Disregard of the rights of others
Borderline	Instability in interpersonal relationships and self-image
Histrionic	Excessive emotionality, need for attention
Narcissistic	Grandiosity, need for admiration, lack of empathy
Avoidant	Social inhibition, feelings of inadequacy
Dependent	Submissive, clinging
Obsessive-Compulsive	Obsession with orderliness, perfectionism, and control

FIGURE 18.6 *Personality disorders are inflexible and lasting patterns of behavior that hamper social functioning. Listed here are the 10 specific personality disorders and their main characteristics.*

Source: Adapted from the DSM-IV, 1994.

Closing Section 7
Assessing Validity

Organize the class into small groups. Ask half of the groups each to devise a research study that could be used to test the validity of a psychological explanation for personality disorders. Have the other half of the groups each devise a research study that could be used to test the validity of a biological explanation for personality disorders. Ask representatives from the groups to discuss their proposed research studies with the class, and have the class critique each study.

Reviewing Section 7

Have students complete the Section Review questions on page 431.

Extension

Have students research one of the disorders listed in Figure 18.6 and *not* discussed in the text. Ask students to prepare a written description of the disorder to share with the class. Also have students explain why the disorder is classified as a personality disorder.

This teen seems to want to join the fun but holds back out of fear of looking foolish. *If he had a personality disorder, how could you tell if it was avoidant personality disorder or social phobia?*

The symptoms of avoidant personality disorder are similar to those of social phobia, and people with avoidant personality disorder virtually always have social phobias as well. However, not all people who have social phobias have avoidant personality disorder. The latter seems to be a more severe and all-encompassing condition.

Explaining Personality Disorders

Most personality disorders were not classified until 1980, with the publication of the third edition of the DSM. However, the concept of personality disorders is not new, and both psychological and biological theories have been suggested to explain certain types of personality disorders.

Psychological Views Freud's psychoanalytic theory regarding the antisocial personality type states that a lack of guilt underlies the antisocial personality. This lack of guilt is due to a problem in the development of the conscience, or superego. Research has found that children who are rejected by adults and harshly punished rather than treated with affection tend to lack a sense of guilt.

Some learning theorists have suggested that childhood experiences "teach" children how to relate to other people. If children are not reinforced

for good behavior and only receive attention when they behave badly, they may learn antisocial behaviors. Such behaviors may persist into adulthood. Other learning theorists maintain that antisocial personality disorder develops when a child lacks appropriate role models and when the role models they encounter act aggressively (Millon, 1981).

Cognitive theorists have argued that antisocial adolescents tend to see other people's behavior as threatening, even when it is not. They use this faulty interpretation of other people's actions to justify their own antisocial behavior (Lochman & Dodge, 1994).

Biological Views Genetic factors are apparently involved in some personality disorders. For example, antisocial personality disorder tends to run in families. Adoptee studies reveal higher incidence of antisocial behavior among the biological parents than among the adoptive relatives of individuals with the disorder (DiLalla & Gottesman, 1991).

The genetics of antisocial personal disorder may involve the frontal part of the brain, an area that is connected with emotional responses. There is some evidence that people with antisocial personality disorder have fewer neurons in the frontal part of the brain than other people (Damasio, 2000; Raine et al., 2000). The fewer neurons could make the nervous system less responsive. As a result, such people would be less likely to show guilt for their misdeeds and to learn to fear punishment. But a biological factor is unlikely by itself to cause the development of an antisocial personality (Rutter, 1997).

Although the origins of personality disorders are still unresolved, treatment of these disorders is more straightforward. Methods of treatment for the psychological disorders discussed in this chapter are the focus of Chapter 19.

SECTION 7 REVIEW

go. hrw .com **Homework Practice Online**
Keyword: SY3 HP18

1. What is the major difference between personality disorders and other psychological disorders they may resemble?
2. Describe three behaviors of an individual with avoidant personality disorder.
3. **Critical Thinking** *Evaluating* Why do you think people with antisocial personality disorder are often more difficult to treat than people with other types of personality disorders?

Chapter 18 Review: Answers

Writing a Summary

See the section subtitles for the main topics in the chapter.

Identifying People and Ideas

1. behavior patterns or mental processes that cause serious personal suffering or interfere with a person's ability to cope with everyday life
2. a general state of dread or uneasiness that occurs in response to a vague or imagined danger
3. a persistent or irrational fear
4. a relatively short period of intense fear or discomfort, characterized by shortness of breath, dizziness, rapid heart rate, trembling, or other physical symptoms
5. a separation of some personality components or mental processes from conscious thought
6. detachment from one's mental processes or body
7. a mood disorder involving feelings of helplessness, hopelessness, worthlessness, guilt, or great sadness
8. a mood disorder involving a cycle of mood changes from depression to mania and back again
9. wild elation
10. psychological disorder characterized by a loss of contact with reality

Understanding Main Ideas

1. by observable signs and symptoms
2. a persistent, irrational fear of a particular object or situation

431

Technology

▶ Chapter 18 Test Generator (on the One-Stop Planner)

▶ HRW Go site

Reinforcement, Review, and Assessment

▶ Chapter 18 Review, pp. 432–433

▶ Chapter Review and Activities with Answer Key

▶ Alternative Assessment Handbook

▶ Portfolio Assessment Handbook

▶ Chapter 18 Test (Form A or B)

PSYCHOLOGY PROJECTS

Linking to Community Invite a clinical psychologist, a psychiatrist, or another psychiatric facility professional to visit the classroom. Tell the visitor that the students have prepared case studies on hypothetical individuals who have psychological disorders and will present the case studies to

---

3. dissociative amnesia—sudden loss of memory, usually following a traumatic event; dissociative fugue—loss of memory combined with relocating from home or work and assuming a new identity; dissociative identity disorder—existence of two or more personalities within a single individual; depersonalization disorder—feelings of detachment from one's mental processes or body

4. psychological problems, combined with inexplicable physical symptoms such as paralysis or pain

5. psychological—some people may be prone to depression because they suffered a real or imagined loss of a loved object or person in childhood, and they direct anger toward that object or person toward themselves; biological—neurotransmitters in the brain may at least partly explain why some people suffer from depression

6. it appears to be a brain disorder that is related to several biological risk factors: heredity, complications during pregnancy and birth, and birth during winter

7. A personality disorder influences virtually all of a person's behavior and thought. Other psychological disorders tend to be discrete episodes of illness that can be distinguished from a person's usual behavior.

Thinking Critically

1. They are self-defeating because they reduce the person's anxiety only for a little while, if at all; and they interfere with daily life.

Chapter 18 REVIEW

Writing a Summary

Using standard grammar, spelling, sentence structure, and punctuation, summarize the information in this chapter. Consider:
- anxiety disorders, dissociative disorders, and somatoform disorders
- mood disorders, schizophrenia, and how to distinguish personality disorders from other psychological disorders

Identifying People and Ideas

Identify the following terms or individuals and explain their significance.

1. psychological disorders
2. anxiety
3. phobia
4. panic attack
5. dissociation
6. depersonalization
7. depression
8. bipolar disorder
9. mania
10. schizophrenia

Understanding Main Ideas

SECTION 1 (pp. 410–15)
1. How are psychological disorders classified?

SECTION 2 (pp. 415–19)
2. What is a phobic disorder?

SECTION 3 (pp. 420–21)
3. Describe the types of dissociative disorders.

SECTION 4 (pp. 421–22)
4. What are the symptoms of somataform disorders?

SECTION 5 (pp. 423–26)
5. What are the psychological and biological views of depression?

SECTION 6 (pp. 426–29)
6. What are the causes of schizophrenia?

SECTION 7 (pp. 429–31)
7. How can personality disorders be distinguished from other psychological disorders?

Thinking Critically

1. **Analyzing Information** Explain why compulsions might be considered self-defeating behaviors.

2. **Drawing Inferences and Conclusions** Why might dissociative identity disorder be confused with schizophrenia?

3. **Comparing** What do dissociative disorders have in common with stress disorders?

4. **Contrasting** What are the differences between schizoid personality disorder and avoidant personality disorder?

5. **Evaluating** Psychological disorders and physical disorders can be classified by their causes or their symptoms. Use examples of physical disorders, such as the common cold, to demonstrate these two approaches to classifying disease.

Writing About Psychology

1. **Analyzing Information** Research information about a psychological disorder that is not covered in this chapter, such as histrionic personality disorder, alcohol abuse disorder, or anorexia nervosa. Make sure the information is up-to-date and based on the DSM-IV classification of the disorder. Then write a report that includes a description of the disorder's symptoms, estimates of how common it is, and what theories have been proposed to explain it.

2. **Sequencing** Go to the library to learn more about the history of schizophrenia, from Hippocrates to the 2000s. Then summarize your findings in an annotated time line that shows how schizophrenia has been perceived at different times. Share your time line with the rest of the class, and explain how changing perceptions of schizophrenia influenced the way affected individuals were treated by society. Use the graphic organizer below to help you create your time line.

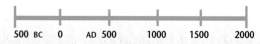

the visitor for review. One at a time, have volunteers read or discuss the case studies they prepared for the Interpreting Information activity (see p. 427). Ask the visitor to critique each case study for accuracy and objectivity and to offer other possible diagnoses and explanations. Encourage the visitor to challenge the students by asking for additional information on their hypothetical individuals.

(see p. 427)

Cooperative Learning

Organize the class into six groups, and assign each group one of the categories of psychological disorders discussed in the chapter. Direct them to prepare a panel discussion, including text and visuals, about their assigned disorder. Have the students conduct library research on their assigned topic to ensure that they have a thorough and accurate understanding of the disorder. Invite members of the class to ask questions of the panelists.

Building Social Studies Skills

Interpreting Graphs

Study the bar graph below. Then use the information in the graph to help you answer the questions that follow.

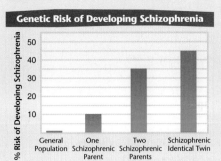

Genetic Risk of Developing Schizophrenia

% Risk of Developing Schizophrenia

Categories: General Population, One Schizophrenic Parent, Two Schizophrenic Parents, Schizophrenic Identical Twin

Sources: Gottesman, 1991; Brzustowicz et al., 2000

1. What in the graph might suggest the existence of a biological link among people who have schizophrenia?
   a. The comparatively low number of schizophrenia sufferers among the general population.
   b. A child of one schizophrenic parent has a higher risk of becoming schizophrenic than a child of a schizophrenic mother and father.
   c. A person who has schizophrenic parents or a schizophrenic twin is much more likely to have schizophrenia than a member of the general population.
   d. The comparatively high number of schizophrenia sufferers among the general population.

2. How many more times likely is a person with a schizophrenic identical twin to have schizophrenia than a member of the general population?

Analyzing Primary Sources

Read the following excerpt, in which psychologist Theodore Millon describes the difficulties that have arisen in studying depression. Then answer the questions that follow.

" The history of depression in its manifold forms has been known to humankind since earliest recorded history. It has remained an enigma, however. The overt manifestations of the disorder are obvious. . . . Yet its underlying causes and shifting expressions are debated to the present time, as evident in intense discussions during the most recent DSM . . . formulations. . . . Is there an irritable, explosive component associated with it, does it wax and wane, is there a continuous chronic state with moments of greater and lesser intensity, is it an adaptive reaction to life circumstances, or a constitutionally based temperament with genetic origins? Through the ages, clinicians, theorists, and empiricists have sought answers to questions such as these. "

3. Which of the following statements best describes Millon's point of view?
   a. Depression shares many symptoms with mania.
   b. The causes of depression are easy to discover.
   c. Clinicians and theorists are in agreement as to the causes of depression.
   d. The causes of depression are still debated by psychologists.

4. According to this excerpt, what challenges do psychologists face in treating depression?

PSYCHOLOGY PROJECTS

Cooperative Learning

Research in Psychology Work with a small group of other students to research psychological theories that attempt to explain depression, including psychoanalytic, biological learning, and cognitive theories. Summarize arguments for and against each of the theories. Then select one student to represent each of the theories in a debate in front of the rest of the class. After the debate, ask volunteers from the class to state which theory they agree with and why.

🔲 internet connect

Internet Activity: go.hrw.com
KEYWORD: SY3 PS18

Choose an activity on psychological disorders to:
- create a profile and treatment regimen for an anxiety patient.
- write an article on teenage depression.
- outline the latest theories and treatments for schizophrenia.

go.hrw.com

2. A person with bipolar disorder may have delusions, hallucinations, and the appearance of disordered thoughts, all of which are associated with schizophrenia.

3. Both types typically are triggered by a very stressful event, and both may involve forgetting.

4. Both disorders involve avoidance of social situations and relationships. However, people with schizoid personality disorder have no interest in personal relationships, while people with avoidant personality disorder want relationships but fear them.

5. Classified by cause, colds would be grouped with other viral illnesses and hay fever with other allergies. Classified by symptoms, colds and hay fever would be grouped together.

Writing About Psychology

1. Reports should contain the same types of information regardless of the disorder chosen, including symptoms, prevalence, and causes.

2. Students should understand the relationship between perceptions of schizophrenia and the treatment of schizophrenics by society.

Building Social Studies Skills

1. c
2. 45 times
3. d
4. The causes of depression are not always clear and could be biologically based or stem from the person's life experiences.

Methods of Therapy

CHAPTER RESOURCE MANAGER

	Objectives	Pacing Guide		Reproducible and Review Resources
SECTION 1: **What Is Therapy?** (pp. 436–440)	Define psychotherapy, and list the advantages of each method of psychotherapy.	**Regular** 1 day *Block Scheduling Handbook with Team Teaching Strategies, Chapter 19*	**Block Scheduling** .5 day	**SM** Mastering Critical Thinking Skills 19 **REV** Section 1 Review, p. 440
SECTION 2: **The Psychoanalytic Approach** (pp. 441–444)	Describe the major techniques of psychoanalysis.	**Regular** 1 day *Block Scheduling Handbook with Team Teaching Strategies, Chapter 19*	**Block Scheduling** .5 day	**REV** Section 2 Review, p. 444
SECTION 3: **The Humanistic Approach** (pp. 444–446)	Identify the primary goals and methods of humanistic therapy.	**Regular** .5 day *Block Scheduling Handbook with Team Teaching Strategies, Chapter 19*	**Block Scheduling** .5 day	**E** Research Projects and Activities for Teaching Psychology **REV** Section 3 Review, p. 446
SECTION 4: **Cognitive Therapy and Behavior Therapy** (pp. 446–451)	Describe how cognitive and behavior therapists try to help people.	**Regular** 1 day *Block Scheduling Handbook with Team Teaching Strategies, Chapter 19*	**Block Scheduling** .5 day	**PS** Readings and Case Studies, Chapter 19 **REV** Section 4 Review, p. 451
SECTION 5: **Biological Therapy** (pp. 451–453)	Describe the three major biological treatments for psychological disorders.	**Regular** .5 day *Block Scheduling Handbook with Team Teaching Strategies, Chapter 19*	**Block Scheduling** .5 day	**REV** Section 5 Review, p. 453

Chapter Resource Key

PS	Primary Sources	**A**	Assessment		Video
RS	Reading Support	**REV**	Review		Internet
E	Enrichment		Transparencies		Holt Presentation Maker Using Microsoft® PowerPoint®
SM	Skills Mastery		CD–ROM		

One-Stop Planner CD–ROM

See the *One-Stop Planner* for a complete list of additional resources for students and teachers.

One-Stop Planner CD–ROM

It's easy to plan lessons, select resources, and print out materials for your students when you use the **One-Stop Planner CD-ROM with Test Generator.**

Technology Resources

 One-Stop Planner, Lesson 19.1
Homework Practice Online

 One-Stop Planner, Lesson 19.2
Homework Practice Online

 One-Stop Planner, Lesson 19.3
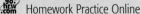 Homework Practice Online
HRW Go Site

 One-Stop Planner, Lesson 19.4
 Homework Practice Online
 Teaching Transparencies 38: Cognitive Model of Depression
 CNN Presents Psychology: Technology and New Therapies
HRW Go Site

 One-Stop Planner, Lesson 19.5
 Homework Practice Online
 HRW Go Site

Chapter Review and Assessment

 HRW Go site

REV Chapter 19 Review,
pp. 454–455

REV Chapter Review Activities
with Answer Key

A Chapter 19 Test
(Form A or B)

A Portfolio Assessment
Handbook

A Alternative Assessment
Handbook

Chapter 19 Test Generator (on the
One–Stop Planner)

Global Skill Builder CD-ROM

---

internet connect

HRW ONLINE RESOURCES

GO TO: go.hrw.com
Then type in a keyword.

TEACHER HOME PAGE
KEYWORD: SY3 Teacher

CHAPTER INTERNET ACTIVITIES
KEYWORD: SY3 PS19
Choose an activity on methods of therapy to have students:
• make a series of drawings illustrating the principles of humanistic therapy.
• create a graphic organizer for cognitive and behavior therapy.
• create a chart tracing changes in biological therapy over the years.

CHAPTER ENRICHMENT LINKS
KEYWORD: SY3 CH19

ONLINE ASSESSMENT
Homework Practice
KEYWORD: SY3 HP19

Standardized Test Prep
KEYWORD: SY3 STP19

Rubrics
KEYWORD: SS Rubrics

CONTENT UPDATES
KEYWORD: SS Content Updates

HOLT PRESENTATION MAKER
KEYWORD: SY3 PPT19

ONLINE READING SUPPORT
KEYWORD: SS Strategies

CURRENT EVENTS
KEYWORD: S3 Current Events

Additional Resources

PRINT RESOURCES FOR TEACHERS
Atkinson, D., Morten, G., & Morten, S. D. (1993). *Counseling American minorities.* Dubuque, IA: Brown & Benchmark.

Bergin, A., & Garfield, S. (Eds.). (1994). *Handbook of psychotherapy and behavior change.* New York: Wiley.

Corsini, R. (1991). *Five therapists and one client.* Itasca, IL: Peacock.

PRINT RESOURCES FOR STUDENTS
Dawes, R. (1994). *House of cards: Psychology and psychotherapy built on myth.* New York: Free Press.

Ehrenberg, O., & Ehrenberg, M. (1986). *The psychotherapy maze.* Northvale, NJ: Aronson.

Engler, J., & Goleman, D. (1992). *The consumer's guide to psychotherapy.* New York: Simon & Schuster.

MULTIMEDIA RESOURCES
Depression: Beating the blues (VHS or 16mm). Filmmakers Library, 124 East 40th Street, Number 901, New York, NY 10016.

Psychotherapy (VHS). CRM Films, L. P., 2215 Faraday Avenue, Suite A, Carlsbad, CA 92008.

Seeking help: But where? (VHS). RMI Media Productions, Inc., 1365 North Winchester, Olathe, KS 66061.

METHODS OF THERAPY

Review with students the various types of psychological disorders described in Chapter 18. Remind the class that different schools of psychology attribute different causes to the various disorders—ranging from the repression of urges (psychoanalytic theory) to the reinforcement of behaviors (learning theory). Point out that different schools of psychology also take correspondingly different approaches to the treatment of psychological disorders—ranging from helping people identify and come to terms with repressed urges to reinforcing positive rather than negative behaviors. Tell students they will learn about these and other methods of therapy in this chapter.

Sections

Each of the five questions identified on page 434 corresponds to one of these sections.

Chapter 19

METHODS OF THERAPY

Read to Discover

1 What is psychotherapy, and what are the advantages of each method of psychotherapy?

2 What are the major techniques of psychoanalysis?

3 What are the primary goals and methods of humanistic therapy?

4 How do cognitive and behavior therapists try to help people?

5 What are the three major biological treatments for psychological disorders?

Each chapter begins with a vignette, called "A Day in the Life," that relates the information discussed in the chapter to the everyday events in the lives of a group of fictional high school students. The text of the chapter occasionally refers back to the vignette to demonstrate the application of the concept being discussed. An icon marked "A Day in the Life" is placed next to these references.

Copy the following graphic organizer onto the chalkboard, omitting the italicized text. Fill in the boxes as you discuss the methods of psychotherapy.

Methods of Psychotherapy			
Psychoanalysis	*Humanistic*	*Cognitive and Behavioral*	*Biological*

A DAY IN THE LIFE

May 25

"Hey, Janet, what's up?" Dan asked.

"Not much. I'm on my way to the library to study with Marc and Linda for Friday's history test," Janet replied.

"Marc is studying for a test that's three days away?" Dan joked. "I thought he always waited until the last minute."

"That's what I thought too," Janet laughed. "Marc said that he talked to his mom and to one of his teachers because he used to get so nervous when he took tests. Whatever they said seems to be working. He still doesn't enjoy studying, but he isn't dreading tests like he used to. So, what are you up to?"

"I'm just looking over the college brochures that Mr. Hochberg gave me. I asked him what I should major in in college, but he keeps telling me that I have to decide for myself."

"Any ideas?" Janet asked.

"I'm still leaning toward counseling, especially lately," Dan said.

"Why lately?" Janet asked.

"I guess it has something to do with everything my family has been going through with Michelle." (Michelle, Dan's sister, had been diagnosed with schizophrenia.)

"How is she doing?" Janet asked.

"Better," Dan said. "She's taking her medication and she started seeing the psychiatrist again."

"That's good. You seem to be feeling better too," Janet noted.

"I really am. Can I tell you something, just between us?" Dan asked.

"Of course you can," Janet assured him. "What's up?"

"Well, my parents and I started going to therapy too. The psychologist we're seeing is trying to help us deal with Michelle's disorder."

"That's great," Janet said. "But Dan, you really don't have to worry about people finding out that you're seeing a therapist. You know, my mom and I went to talk with someone after she and my dad got divorced. It was good just to talk to someone about what I was feeling."

"I guess you're right," Dan agreed. "Thanks, Janet."

• • •

Chapter 18 explored the many different types of psychological disorders, from anxiety, such as Marc suffered before tests, to schizophrenia which afflicts Dan's sister, Michelle. In this chapter, we will look at the various treatments, or therapies, for such problems.

Methods for treating psychological problems and disorders fall into two general categories: psychological methods, or methods of psychotherapy, and biological methods. The methods of psychotherapy aim to change the thought processes, feelings, or behavior of the individual. They are based on psychological principles. In contrast, biological therapies attempt to alleviate psychological problems by affecting the nervous system in some way. This chapter examines several different methods of therapy for psychological problems, including both psychological and biological methods.

Key Terms

- psychotherapy
- self-help group
- encounter group
- free association
- resistance
- dream analysis
- manifest content
- latent content
- transference
- humanistic therapy
- person-centered therapy
- nondirective therapy
- active listening
- rational-emotive behavior therapy
- aversive conditioning
- token economy
- successive approximations
- antianxiety drug
- antidepressant drug
- lithium
- antipsychotic drug
- electroconvulsive therapy
- psychosurgery
- prefrontal lobotomy

WHY PSYCHOLOGY MATTERS

Each year, many people seek professional help in dealing with problems. Use CNNfyi.com or other current events sources to learn more about how psychologists and other mental health professionals provide counseling.

CNNfyi.com

Using Key Terms

Have students find definitions for each of the key terms, either in the Glossary or in Chapter 19. Then have them use the definitions as clues in a word-search puzzle that incorporates at least 15 of the key terms. When students have finished creating their puzzles, have them exchange papers and try to find the hidden words. Students may wish to keep their puzzles for later review.

Class Discussion

Before having students read the chapter, have them discuss any preconceptions they might have about psychotherapy and about therapists. You may wish to spark the discussion by asking students what they think of when they hear the word *psychotherapy*. If this question elicits negative responses, remind students of Janet's remark to Dan at the end of the "A Day in the Life" vignette. Guide students to see that seeking help for psychological problems is just as important as seeking help for physical problems.

435

Section Objective

▶ Define psychotherapy, and list the advantages of each method of psychotherapy.

This objective is assessed in the Section Review on page 440 and in the Chapter 19 Review.

Opening Section 1

Motivator

List on the chalkboard some psychological problems that might affect teens, such as shyness, test anxiety, or depression. Ask students where a teen could seek help for each problem. After they have responded, name any sources of help they failed to mention, including nonprofessional sources. Tell students that in Section 1 they will learn more about where people with psychological problems can go for help.

Using Truth or Fiction

Each chapter opens with several "Truth or Fiction" statements that relate to the concepts discussed in the chapter. Ask students whether they think each statement is true or false. Answers to each item as well as explanations are provided at appropriate points within the text under the heading "Truth or Fiction Revisited."

For Your Information

At any given time in the United States, an estimated 50 million adults suffer from some type of psychological disorder. However, fewer than one third of them receive professional help for their problems.

TRUTH OR fiction?

Read the following statements about psychology. Do you think they are true or false? You will learn whether each statement is true or false as you read the chapter.

- Just believing they will improve helps some people recover from psychological disorders.
- It is always preferable to see a therapist alone rather than in a group.
- Some therapists analyze people's dreams.
- People should avoid relating to their therapist as a parent or other authority figure.
- People's reactions to life events are based not on the events themselves but on their ways of thinking about the events.
- Severe depression is sometimes treated by passing an electric current through the brain.

The development of a trusting relationship between client and therapist is one way that psychotherapy helps people with psychological problems.

SECTION 1

What Is Therapy?

Therapy is a general term for the variety of approaches that mental health professionals use to treat psychological problems and disorders. Although there are many types of therapy, all approaches fall into two basic categories: psychologically based therapy and biologically based therapy. Psychologically based therapy, known as **psychotherapy**, involves verbal interactions between a trained professional and a person—usually called the client or patient—who is seeking help for a psychological problem. Biologically based therapies involve the use of drugs or other medical procedures to treat psychological disorders.

Achieving the Goals of Psychotherapy

Although the various methods of psychotherapy use different approaches, they all seek to help troubled individuals. They do this by giving individuals hope for recovery; helping individuals gain insights or new perspectives on their problems; and providing the individual with a caring, trusting relationship with a mental health professional.

Providing people hope for recovery is very important because most people who seek therapy

have problems they believe they cannot handle alone. They may have low self-esteem and lack the confidence to recognize that their situation can improve. Just the belief that therapy will help them is enough to put many people on the road to recovery. This is called the placebo effect.

TRUTH OR fiction ■ REVISITED ■

It is true that just believing they will improve helps some people recover from psychological disorders. This is called the placebo effect. Belief in recovery increases their confidence and helps people become motivated to become well.

Helping the individual gain insight or a new perspective is important because many psychological problems are the result of negative outlooks and misinterpretations. For example, someone who is depressed is likely to have poor self-esteem. This person may be able to see only the negative side of every situation and may feel responsible for that negativity. Changing this individual's outlook and perceptions may help to relieve the depressed mood and to improve his or her self-esteem.

Providing a caring, trusting relationship is important because people with psychological problems often feel isolated, afraid, and distrustful of others. Psychotherapy encourages individuals to

Analyzing Ideas

Remind students of the role that social support plays in helping people cope with stress, or have them review this material in Chapter 17. Then ask students to compare the therapist-client relationship with the relationship a person might have with a close friend or family member. In what ways are the two relationships similar? In what ways are they different? Point out that the support offered by a therapist in a trusting relationship is an important aspect of psychotherapy.

Cooperative Learning

Organize the class into several small groups. Have each group research local sources of psychological help for problems that teens commonly face, such as relationship problems, eating disorders, or substance abuse. Then have the groups create posters that convey the most important information about each problem in a way that will attract the attention of other teens. Arrange to have the posters displayed in areas of the school where large numbers of students are likely to see them.

talk freely about their uncomfortable feelings and problems. Therefore, a trusting relationship with the therapist is essential to the process. Establishing such a relationship between client and therapist is a key goal of psychotherapy.

In addition to providing hope, a new perspective, and a trusting relationship, all psychotherapy methods share the goal of bringing about changes in the individuals who are seeking help. In the case of an individual who is depressed, for example, the psychotherapist tries to help the client develop a more positive outlook and higher self-esteem. In the case of a person experiencing a phobia, the psychotherapist helps the individual become desensitized, or less likely to react, to the object of fear.

The most commonly used methods of psychotherapy are psychoanalysis, humanistic therapy, cognitive therapy, and behavior therapy. Figure 19.1 summarizes the main features of these methods.

Each method of psychotherapy has a different goal and different ways of achieving that goal. Some psychotherapists use just one method. Others use an eclectic approach; that is, they choose from a variety of methods, depending on what works best for the individual client. Which method is the most effective often depends on the nature of the psychological problem (Beutler, 1991; Shoham-Salomon, 1991; Snow, 1991).

This raises the issue of the effectiveness of psychotherapy in general. Although some people find that psychotherapy does not help them, many people seem to benefit from it. However, it is difficult to know how those who benefit would have done in the absence of treatment. Some people feel better about themselves as time goes on, even without treatment; others find solutions to problems on their own. Nonetheless, research on the effectiveness of psychotherapy is encouraging (Barlow, 1996; Shadish et al., 2000).

Psychotherapy in Practice

Many types of professionals are involved in the treatment of psychological problems and disorders. (See Figure 19.2 on page 438.) However, it is primarily psychologists, psychiatrists, and social workers who practice psychotherapy.

Types of Mental Health Professionals Counseling psychologists generally treat people with less serious psychological problems, such as adjustment problems. These psychologists often work in schools and other educational institutions, where they counsel people about their personal problems. Clinical psychologists help people with psychological problems adjust to the demands of life. Their clients' problems may range from anxiety to loss of motivation. Many clinical psychologists work in hospitals or clinics, while others work in private practice.

For Your Information

According to a report in the November 1995 issue of *Consumer Reports,* a survey of people in therapy found that those who started out feeling the worst seemed to show the most improvement. More than half of those who said that they had felt "very poor" at the start of therapy reported that therapy made them feel much better, and another third reported that therapy helped them to some extent. Almost everyone surveyed—regardless of the initial severity of their problems—said that therapy had given them at least some relief.

Using Visuals

Call students' attention to Figure 19.1. Ask them to look for similarities and differences between the various methods of psychotherapy shown in the chart. How are all of the methods alike? How are they different? Which methods seem most similar to one another? Have students explain their answers.

Commonly Used Methods of Psychotherapy

Method	Goals	Key Techniques
Psychoanalysis	To replace avoidant behavior with coping behavior; to reduce inappropriate feelings of anxiety and guilt	Free association; dream analysis; analysis of the transference relationship
Humanistic Therapy	To remove obstacles in the path of self-actualization	Active listening; unconditional positive regard
Cognitive Therapy	To replace irrational, self-defeating attitudes and beliefs with rational, self-enhancing attitudes and beliefs	Encouraging clients to challenge irrational beliefs and replace them with rational beliefs; teaching clients to evaluate their beliefs and attitudes rationally
Behavior Therapy	To replace maladaptive, self-defeating behavior with adaptive, self-enhancing behavior	Systematic desensitization; modeling; aversive conditioning; operant conditioning

FIGURE 19.1 *The key techniques of commonly used methods of psychotherapy are shown here.*

For Further Research

Have students choose one of the professions shown in Figure 19.2 or another type of psychotherapy profession that interests them and research that profession as a possible future career. In their research, students should seek such information as educational and training requirements, average salary, and work settings. Sources students might find useful include the *Occupational Outlook Handbook* and the *Encyclopedia of Careers and Vocational Guidance*. After students complete their research, have them hold a Psychotherapy Career Day in class.

Synthesizing Information

Have students use what they are learning in Section 1 and in the For Further Research activity to write a job advertisement for a professional involved in the treatment of psychological problems and disorders. Tell students to specify in their advertisements what the nature of the job will be but not to specify which type of professional is sought. Have volunteers read their advertisements to the class, and have the class try to determine which type of psychotherapy professional could best fulfill the duties of the job.

Journal Activity

Have students write in their journals about the personal qualities they think would be important in a psychotherapist. For example, would it be more important for a therapist to be compassionate or objective? Should a therapist be talkative or reserved?

Using Visuals

Call students' attention to Figure 19.2. Tell them that educational and licensing requirements may vary from state to state. Have students research their state's educational and licensing requirements for the various types of mental-health professionals listed in the figure. Then have them use the information to modify Figure 19.2 so that it applies specifically to their state.

438

Psychiatrists are medical doctors and many have private practices. As medical doctors, psychiatrists are the only mental health professionals who can prescribe medication and administer other types of biological therapy.

Other professionals who help people with psychological problems include psychiatric social workers and psychiatric nurses. Both have special training in psychology and usually work with other medical or mental health professionals. Psychiatric social workers may also practice psychotherapy.

Teachers, guidance counselors, clergy, and family doctors may also help individuals with psychological problems. Although such professionals may have little formal training in psychology, they are often the people troubled individuals turn to first for help. Marc, for example, went to his teacher for advice on dealing with his test anxiety, and Dan asked his guidance counselor for help in making a career decision.

A DAY IN THE LIFE

Selecting the Right Professional   Those seeking help for a psychological problem should familiarize themselves with the various practitioners and the type of treatment each offers. One way that people can gain that type of information is to ask the following questions:

- What is the professional's field? For example, people with psychological problems should see people who belong to a recognized profession, such as psychology, psychiatry, medicine, social work, or nursing.

- What degrees does the professional hold? Psychiatrists have medical degrees; psychologists usually have doctoral degrees; and social workers usually have master's degrees. The

Professionals Involved in the Treatment of Psychological Problems and Disorders

Type of Professional	Typical Education/Training	Usual Role
Counseling psychologist	Master's degree or Ph.D. (doctor of philosophy) in counseling psychology	Works in educational institutions, such as colleges and high schools, or in businesses; usually refers clients with serious problems to a clinical psychologist
Clinical psychologist	Ph.D. in psychology	Works in hospitals and clinics; assists and treats people with psychological problems
Psychiatrist	M.D. with a specialization in psychiatry and postgraduate training in abnormal behavior	Able to prescribe medicine and perform operations
Psychiatric social worker	Master's degree in social work with additional practical training and two years of graduate-level courses in psychology	Counsels people with everyday personal and family problems
Psychiatric nurse	Standard nursing license with advanced training in psychology	Dispenses medicine and acts as a contact person between counseling sessions

FIGURE 19.2   *Several types of professionals practice psychotherapy. A few of the various kinds of therapists are listed here along with the training they receive and descriptions of the work they do.*

Role-Playing

Ask small groups of volunteers to role-play consumers who are "shopping" for the best professional help for a particular psychological problem. Students should act out either telephone conversations or preliminary meetings with at least two different professionals. Students should ask for the information they need to make an informed decision about therapy. Following the role-plays, have students suggest other types of information the role-players might have requested in order to be well-informed consumers.

Demonstration

To suggest the possible advantages of group therapy, pose the same open-ended problem to several students as individuals and to the rest of the class as a group. Ask both the individual students and the group to brainstorm as many solutions to the problem as possible. However, have the individuals each work alone while group members brainstorm together in another room. After 10 minutes, bring the entire class together to share ideas. Was the group able to think of more solutions than the students working alone? Why or why not?

appropriate degrees help ensure that the professional is properly trained.

- Is the professional licensed by the state? All states require licensing of psychologists and psychiatrists. Some states also require the licensing of social workers and nurses. To be issued a state license, professionals must pass exams or demonstrate expertise and knowledge in other ways.
- What are the therapist's plans for treatment, and how long will treatment likely take? There is considerable variation in the nature and duration of treatment for different methods of psychotherapy. For example, traditional psychoanalysis tends to take longer than other psychotherapy methods. The individual should know in advance what to expect from the treatment method.
- What is the estimated cost of treatment? Psychotherapy can be expensive, and it is not always covered by health insurance plans. Although cost should not have to be the deciding factor in choosing a therapist, for some people, it must be.

People in group therapy usually sit in a circle as they share their thoughts and feelings. A therapist is usually present to guide and facilitate the discussion.

Individual Versus Group Therapy

Methods of psychotherapy are practiced either with individuals or in groups. Frequently, people who seek help for psychological problems have a choice between individual and group therapy. To make the best choice, it is important to be aware of the advantages of each type.

Advantages of Individual Therapy Some people do better with individual therapy because they need more personal attention than they would receive as part of a group. Moreover, some people feel uncomfortable talking about their problems in front of other people. These individuals are likely to talk more openly and freely if they are alone with their therapist.

Advantages of Group Therapy Group therapy can, however, have certain advantages over individual therapy. In fact, many people who begin

seeing a therapist individually eventually switch to group therapy.

One advantage of group therapy is that it helps individuals realize that they are not alone. People can see other group members struggling with problems similar to their own. Members of the group can often benefit from the insights gained by other group members who have gone through similar struggles. Group members can support each other because they all have had similar experiences—they have "been there" themselves. Group therapy also gives individuals a chance to practice coping and other social skills in a supportive environment.

One of the most significant advantages of group therapy is that it shows individuals that therapy can work. People see other members of the group recovering, and this gives them hope of recovery for themselves.

From a practical standpoint, group therapy enables the therapist to work with several people at once. In addition, it often allows a therapist to immediately see people who might otherwise have to be placed on a waiting list to receive individual help. It is also more affordable for clients because they share the cost of the therapist's time.

TRUTH **OR** **fiction** ■ REVISITED ■

It is not true that it is always preferable to see a therapist alone rather than in a group. In group therapy, members of the group can provide support and understanding and serve as role models for each other.

Cultural Dimensions

Point out to the class that the therapy group shown in the photograph on page 439 is composed of people who differ from one another in sex, age, and ethnicity. Ask students to imagine another group—one in which everyone is of the same sex, age, and ethnicity. Which group do they think would be more effective for group therapy? Why?

Class Discussion

Ask the class to discuss the advantages and disadvantages of group therapy for specific psychological problems, such as depression, various phobias, schizophrenia, or antisocial personality disorder. Are certain disorders better suited than others for group therapy?

Closing Section 1

Making Decisions

Assign each student one of the psychological problems described in Chapter 18, such as hypochondriasis, obsessive-compulsive disorder, or depression. Then have students write a paragraph describing which type of professional they think could most effectively treat the disorder and whether they think individual or group therapy would be more effective. Ask volunteers to share their paragraphs with the class. Do other students agree with the decisions made about treatment? Why or why not?

Reviewing Section 1

Have students complete the Section Review questions on page 440.

Extension

Ask interested students to research the history of psychotherapy and summarize the information in a time line. Have students share their completed time lines with the rest of the class for discussion.

In family therapy, the therapist often can help family members see problems in their relationships more clearly.

Types of Group Therapy There are several types of group therapy. These include couples therapy, family therapy, and therapy for people who are dealing with similar problems, such as an eating disorder or the loss of a loved one.

Couples therapy tries to help two people improve or find more satisfaction in their relationship with each other. In particular, it helps them communicate more effectively by helping them learn new ways to listen to each other and to express their feelings (Rathus & Sanderson, 1999). Such therapy also helps couples discover healthy ways to resolve conflicts and handle intense emotions.

Family therapy aims to help troubled families by improving communication and relations among family members. It also seeks to promote the family's emotional growth (Prochaska & Norcross, 1999). Family therapy is based on the assumption that the lives of family members are so intertwined that the family as a whole is likely to suffer when one member has a problem. A parent may be addicted to alcohol, for example, and become abusive when intoxicated. The abuse may lead to low self-esteem, anxiety, and depression in other family members. Dan's family provides another example. They sought family

A DAY IN THE LIFE

therapy to help them cope with Michelle's schizophrenia. Janet and her mother also sought family therapy to help them adjust to the divorce.

Self-help groups are composed of people who share the same problem, such as overeating, drug addiction, or compulsive gambling. Members of a self-help group meet regularly—often without a therapist—to discuss their problem, share solutions, and give and receive support. One of the best-known self-help groups is Alcoholics Anonymous (AA). AA has served as a developmental model for many other self-help programs.

Encounter groups differ from these other kinds of groups. They are composed of strangers who do not necessarily share a common problem. In fact, encounter group members do not necessarily have psychological problems at all. Encounter groups are sometimes made up of people who simply desire emotional growth.

Encounter groups promote emotional growth by helping group members become more aware of their own feelings and the feelings of others. Under the guidance of a leader, group members share their feelings through role-playing and other group techniques. The fact that group members are strangers makes it easier for some people to reveal their private feelings in an encounter group. However, other people are often unprepared for the intense emotions they experience in encounter therapy. For this and other reasons, encounter groups are somewhat controversial and less popular today than they were in the 1960s and 1970s.

SECTION 1 REVIEW

go.hrw.com
Homework Practice Online
Keyword: SY3 HP19

1. What is psychotherapy?
2. What questions should one ask when selecting a psychotherapist?
3. **Critical Thinking** *Evaluating* What are the advantages of each type of psychotherapy?

Section Objective

▶ Describe the major techniques of psychoanalysis.

This objective is assessed in the Section Review on page 444 and in the Chapter 19 Review.

Motivator

Read aloud a list of words for common objects, situations, events, and relationships. After each word, ask students to write down whatever comes to mind, no matter how silly, embarrassing, or trivial it seems. Point out to students that Freud called this psychoanalytic technique free association and believed that it could help bring clients' unconscious thoughts into consciousness, where they could be dealt with openly. Tell students that they will learn more about free association and other psychoanalytic techniques in Section 2.

SECTION 2

The Psychoanalytic Approach

Psychoanalysis, the model of therapy developed by Sigmund Freud, literally means "analysis of the psyche (mind)." Psychoanalysis was the first formal method of psychotherapy used in Western countries. For many years, it was the only method used. In recent decades, however, it has become less popular (Arlow, 1989).

As you may recall from Chapter 14, Freud believed that most of people's psychological problems originate in early childhood experiences and inner conflicts. These conflicts can cause people to develop unconscious sexual and aggressive urges that, in turn, cause anxiety. According to Freud, guilt occurs when the urges enter conscious thought or when the individual acts upon them. Guilt also leads to more anxiety. For example, someone may experience feelings of anxiety and guilt caused by repressed rage toward a parent.

Psychoanalysts try to reduce anxiety and guilt by helping clients become aware of the unconscious thoughts and feelings that are believed to be at the root of their problems. Psychoanalysts call this self-awareness *insight*. Once insight has been gained, clients can use the knowledge to resolve the problems that arise in their daily lives. Some of the techniques psychoanalysts use to help clients gain insight include free association, dream analysis, and transference.

Free Association The primary technique of psychoanalysis is **free association**. In free association, the analyst asks the client to relax and then to say whatever comes to mind. Free association developed from Freud's early use of hypnosis to tap into his clients' unconscious thoughts and feelings. The use of free association instead of hypnosis enables the client to participate more actively in the analysis.

The topic of the free association might be a memory, dream, fantasy, or recent event. The analyst may say nothing, occasionally ask a question, or attempt to lead the client in a particular direction. The assumption is that, as long as the client associates freely, unconscious thoughts and feelings will "break through" and show up in what the client says. The client is encouraged to say whatever

comes to mind, no matter how trivial, embarrassing, or painful the ideas may seem. In fact, psychoanalysts believe that the more hesitant the patient is to say something, the more likely it is that the hesitancy reflects an unconscious thought or feeling.

Resistance is the term psychoanalysts use to refer to a client's hesitancy or unwillingness to discuss issues raised during free association. An experienced psychoanalyst can recognize a client's resistance. It may occur when the client makes a joking remark about a serious subject, for example, or when the client changes the subject entirely. Resistance is believed to reflect a defense mechanism, such as the repression or denial of painful feelings. (See Chapter 14.)

The role of the analyst in free association is to point out the types of things the client is saying—or resisting saying—and to help the client interpret the meaning of the utterances or lack thereof. Psychoanalysts believe that free association allows the client to express troubling, unconscious thoughts and feelings in a safe environment where those thoughts and feelings may be explored. Through such means, clients are thought to gain insight into their problems.

Dream Analysis Freud believed that dreams express unconscious thoughts and feelings. He called them the "royal road into the unconscious." In a technique called **dream analysis**, the analyst interprets the content of clients' dreams to unlock these unconscious thoughts and feelings.

Freud also distinguished between the manifest and latent content of dreams (Freud, 1952). **Manifest content** refers to the actual content of the dream as it is remembered by the client. **Latent content** refers to the hidden meaning in the dream, which the therapist interprets from the manifest content. For example, a client may dream about falling from a mountain and being unable to grab anything to break his fall (manifest content). The therapist might interpret the dream to mean that the client has repressed feelings that his life is out of control (latent content).

TRUTH
OR
fiction
■ REVISITED ■

It is true that some therapists analyze people's dreams. Most psychoanalysts believe that dreams are an expression of unconscious thoughts and feelings.

Journal Activity

Ask students to write in their journals about a time when they made a joking remark about a serious subject or tried to focus attention away from a serious subject. Did the resistance reflect a defense mechanism? If so, which one, and why did the student use it? (Remind students that their journal writings are private.)

What's New in Psychology?

Talk about "talk" therapy! Just as you can order a pizza or a pair of jeans by telephone, now you can also talk to a therapist by telephone. Although professional therapists disagree on the value of telephone therapy, proponents argue that it fulfills a real need. Most people who take advantage of telephone therapy would not otherwise receive treatment because they live in rural areas, are homebound, or want strict anonymity. Telephone therapy may cost as little as $1 a minute.

Guided Practice

To help students appreciate the significance of transference, point out that according to the psychoanalytic approach, the way in which individuals perceive the world, including the people in it, is shaped by their earlier experiences. A teen might expect his gym teacher to make fun of his awkwardness, for example, because that is what his father has always done. Ask students to suggest other examples of ways in which relationships with parents might affect a person's expectations about other people in positions of authority.

Independent Practice

Have students work in pairs to write two dialogues: one between a student and a parent; and the other between the same student and a coach, teacher, principal, police officer, employer, or another person in a position of authority. The dialogues should demonstrate how people tend to transfer feelings and expectations—both good and bad—from parents to other authority figures. Ask volunteers to read their dialogues aloud, and have the class try to identify any examples of transference.

For Your Information

Psychoanalysts use the term *catharsis* to describe the release of emotional stresses (guilt, tension, anxiety) that occurs when unconscious or repressed feelings, ideas, wishes, or memories are brought into consciousness. Tell students that the term comes from a Greek word meaning "purification" or "purging."

Class Discussion

Lead the class in a discussion of the types of clients and problems that are best suited for treatment with psychoanalysis. Spark the discussion by asking students to describe a client who would *not* benefit from psychoanalysis. *(a person with limited verbal skills, a person who has a limited education, a person with schizophrenia)* Have students conclude the discussion by making general recommendations for the use of psychoanalytic treatment.

Traditionally, psychoanalysis was conducted with the patient lying on a couch and the analyst sitting out of the patient's line of vision in order to be less of a distraction. Today psychoanalysis is often conducted with patient and analyst sitting face-to-face.

Transference As analysis proceeds, many clients begin to view their relationship with their analyst as being similar to one they have or had with another important person in their lives, often a parent. They experience similar feelings toward the analyst and expect the analyst to feel and behave as the other person did. In other words, the client is transferring feelings and expectations from one person to another. This process is called **transference**.

Psychoanalysts make use of transference to help the client express and analyze unconscious feelings he or she has toward that other important person. In fact, establishing a transference relationship is a major goal of psychoanalysis. Psychoanalysts believe that transference exposes unresolved problems in earlier relationships. The client can then work through these problems, with the help of the analyst, in order to solve similar problems in current relationships.

TRUTH OR fiction
■ REVISITED ■

It is not true that people should avoid relating to their therapist as a parent or other authority figure. People in psychoanalysis are often encouraged to relate to their therapist in this way.

The following example makes the concept of transference easier to understand. Consider a client who has repressed feelings of anger toward her mother because of her mother's cold, critical attitude toward her throughout her childhood. During the course of psychoanalysis, the client transfers the unconscious anger at her mother to the therapist. She falls into patterns of interaction with the therapist that are characteristic of her relationship with her mother.

The therapist, however, does not react as the client's mother would. Instead, he or she remains neutral and helps the patient examine her feelings. Through this process, the client gains insight into her relationship with her mother and how it affects her current relationships. The client begins to understand, for example, that problems with her boss at work may stem from unconscious and unresolved feelings of anger toward her mother.

Evaluation of Psychoanalysis Many psychologists believe that Freud placed too much emphasis on sexual and aggressive urges. Some argue that he underestimated the importance of conscious ideas and changes in behavior. Despite these criticisms, however, a classic review of dozens of studies concluded that people who had received psychoanalysis showed greater well-being than 70 to 75 percent of those who had not received treatment (Smith & Glass, 1977). Psychoanalysis has proved especially useful in the treatment of anxiety, mild depression, and difficulty in handling social relationships. However, it is generally not useful for the treatment of major depression, bipolar disorder, or schizophrenia (Melle & Friis, 1991).

The techniques of traditional psychoanalysis often require clients to meet with their analyst four or five times a week, for a period of months or years. For some clients, this provides a supportive, long-term relationship that fosters emotional growth and insight. For others, however, the cost of therapy in time, money, and emotional distress is too great to make psychoanalysis a real option.

Psychoanalysis does not work for everyone. For example, it is not the most effective type of psychotherapy for individuals who are less verbal or who have limited educational background. Psychoanalysis also is not useful for people who are too seriously disturbed to gain insight into their problems. For example, a person with schizophrenia may lose touch with reality. Such an individual is unlikely to be able to gain the insight needed for effective psychoanalytic treatment.

CASE STUDIES
AND OTHER TRUE STORIES

Ask students to identify evidence of transference and resistance in the excerpt quoted in the feature. *(Evidence of transference is the client saying, "I've never felt comfortable when thinking of myself outdoing you." Evidence of resistance is the client looking distressed and changing the subject.)* Then have students analyze why transference is believed to be an effective technique for helping clients work through psychological problems.

Meeting Individual Needs: Gifted Learners

Ask gifted students to create a verbal exchange between a client and a psychoanalyst that demonstrates the development of a transference relationship. Have volunteers read their dialogues to the rest of the class. Ask students to explain how the therapist is trying to establish transference. What evidence is there that transference has occurred?

CASE STUDIES
AND OTHER TRUE STORIES

The Transference Relationship

To develop and resolve a transference relationship between client and analyst may take years. The following excerpt (Silverman, 1984) from a therapy session shows how an analyst focuses on the client's feelings for him. The analyst is thus encouraging the development of a transference relationship.

Client: I have been feeling weak and tired. I saw my doctor yesterday and he said there's nothing . . . wrong.

Analyst: Does anything come to mind in relation to weak and tired feelings?

Client: I'm thinking of the way you looked last year after you came out of the hospital. [The client was referring to a hospitalization (of the analyst) during which treatment sessions were suspended.]

Analyst: Do you recall how you felt when you saw me looking that way?

Client: It made me upset, even guilty.

Analyst: But why guilty?

Client: I'm not sure why I said that. There was nothing to feel guilty about.

Analyst: Perhaps you had other feelings.

Client: Well, it's true that at one point I felt faintly pleased that I was young and vigorous and you seemed to be going downhill. . . .

Analyst: Perhaps . . . you imagined I felt bad because you were going uphill while I was going down.

Source: BIZARRO copyright 1995 Dan Piraro. Reprinted with permission of UNIVERSAL PRESS SYNDICATE. All rights reserved.

Client: That feels correct. . . . [The client looks distressed and then goes off on another topic.]

Analyst: Clearly you're not very comfortable when you contrast your state with mine. . . .

Client: Well, you know I've never felt comfortable when thinking of myself outdoing you in any way. And when it comes to our states of health, the idea is particularly distressing.

Analyst: I wonder now if the weak and tired feelings that you spoke about earlier in the session aren't related to what we're discussing now. . . . Perhaps you felt that you were making me ill again with your wishes and thus you had to punish yourself by making yourself ill.

By the end of the excerpt, the analyst is interpreting the client's feelings in typical Freudian terms: hidden urges (wishing the father were sick and weak) are transferred to the analyst; these urges lead in turn to guilt and anxiety ("you had to punish yourself by making yourself ill"). In this way, the transference relationship helped the client gain an awareness of his unconscious feelings of rivalry toward his father.

> ### WHY PSYCHOLOGY MATTERS
> Psychoanalysis is just one therapy technique. Use CNNfyi.com or other current events sources to learn more about different types of counseling. Write a brief report outlining the types of counseling that are available.
>
> CNNfyi.com

Primary Source Note

Description of Change: excerpted, bracketed

Rationale: excerpted to focus on main idea; bracketed to clarify meaning

Cultural Dimensions

The treatment of psychological problems in other cultures differs in several ways from Western psychoanalysis. One of the major differences is the relationship between client and therapist or healer. Whereas the Western psychoanalyst tries to establish a warm, caring relationship with the client in order to encourage transference, traditional healers in many other cultures take on the role of a charismatic and powerful religious figure. The impersonal nature of this role discourages the development of a transference relationship between client and healer.

443

Evaluating Ideas

Ask students to demonstrate their understanding of psychoanalytic therapy by explaining in a paragraph the rationale behind each of the three techniques discussed in Section 2: free association, dream analysis, and transference. Then have students evaluate each technique.

Reviewing Section 2

Have students complete the Section Review questions on page 444.

Cross-Curricular Link: Mathematics

Have students compare the cost of a typical course of traditional psychoanalysis with that of brief psychoanalysis, assuming that an hour of treatment costs $100 in each case.

Section 2 Review: Answers

1. The techniques are free association (client explores unconscious thoughts and feelings with help from the therapist); dream analysis (therapist interprets client's dreams to unlock unconscious thoughts and feelings); and transference (client transfers feelings and expectations about a person to the therapist and examines them with the therapist's guidance).

2. Unconscious thoughts and feelings can lead people to have faulty expectations about others, which interfere with relationships.

3
Section Objective

▶ Identify the primary goals and methods of humanistic therapy.

This objective is assessed in the Section Review on page 446 and in the Chapter 19 Review.

Brief Psychoanalysis Over the past several decades, shorter terms of psychoanalysis have become more common. In traditional psychoanalysis, a client and therapist may meet almost daily over the course of several years. By contrast, in brief psychoanalysis, client and analyst typically meet just 10 to 20 times over the course of a few months to a year. The shorter duration of treatment makes brief psychoanalysis available to a wider range of people (Prochaska & Norcross, 1999).

The techniques used in brief psychoanalysis are generally the same techniques that are used in traditional psychoanalysis. The primary difference between the two approaches is that brief psychoanalysis has a more limited focus. Whereas traditional psychoanalysis examines the client's entire personality, brief psychoanalysis concentrates on fixing a specific problem. For brief psychoanalysis to be effective, clients usually must be highly motivated and actively involved in applying the insights gained in therapy to the events in their lives.

SECTION 2 REVIEW

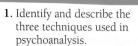
go.hrw.com **Homework Practice Online**
Keyword: SY3 HP19

1. Identify and describe the three techniques used in psychoanalysis.

2. **Critical Thinking** *Drawing Inferences and Conclusions* According to psychoanalytic theory, what effect do unconscious thoughts and feelings have on a person's ability to form meaningful personal relationships?

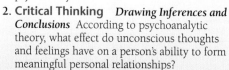

SECTION 3
The Humanistic Approach

The primary goal of **humanistic therapy** is to help individuals reach their full potential. It does this by helping individuals develop self-awareness and self-acceptance. The method assumes that most people are basically good and have a natural tendency to strive for self-actualization—that is, to become all that they are capable of being. The method also assumes that people with psychological problems merely need help tapping their inner resources so that they can grow and reach their full potential. Among the several types of humanistic therapy, person-centered therapy is the most widely used.

Person-Centered Therapy **Person-centered therapy** was developed in the early 1950s by psychologist Carl Rogers. According to Rogers, psychological problems arise when people stop being true to themselves and instead act as others want or expect them to act (Rogers, 1986). The role of therapy is to help clients find their true selves and realize their unique potential.

Person-centered therapy is sometimes called client-centered therapy. The use of the term *client* instead of *patient* reflects the status given to individuals seeking help. Clients are seen as equals in a working relationship with the therapist rather than as inferiors who are ill. Clients are encouraged to take the lead in therapy, talking openly about whatever may be troubling them. This method is called **nondirective therapy** because it is not directed by the therapist. The therapist's role is to act as a mirror, reflecting clients' thoughts and feelings back so that the clients can see themselves more clearly.

Techniques of Person-Centered Therapy **Active listening** is a widely used communication technique in which the listener repeats, rephrases, and asks for clarification of the statements made by the speaker. Facial expressions and body language are also important. The goal is to convey to the speaker that his or her words are being heard and that his or her thoughts and feelings are being understood.

The therapist also must remain nonjudgmental, accepting, and supportive, regardless of what the client says, providing what Rogers calls *unconditional positive regard.* The acceptance and support of the therapist help the client accept himself or herself and his or her true feelings. Self-esteem also rises, giving the client the confidence to make his or her own choices, take responsibility for those decisions, and form healthy relationships.

Other Applications Person-centered therapy is practiced widely by school and college counselors. It not only helps students deal with anxiety, depression, and other psychological problems but also helps students make decisions. Counselors try to provide a supportive atmosphere in which students feel free to explore alternatives and make their own choices. Dan's school counselor, Mr. Hochberg, is not a psychologist, but he took a person-centered approach in helping Dan decide on a career. He helped Dan identify options, but he did not make a decision for him.

A DAY IN THE LIFE

Opening Section 3

Motivator

Ask a volunteer to pretend that he or she is a client and you are a therapist. Have the volunteer talk about a hypothetical problem and describe his or her thoughts and feelings about it. Demonstrate active listening while the "client" talks. Following the demonstration, explain what active listening is, and ask students to describe how you used active listening during the "therapy session." Tell students that active listening is one technique used in humanistic therapy, which they will read about in Section 3.

EXPLORING
DIVERSITY

Tell students that, whereas depression may be expressed as the loss of one's soul in Latin America, in Arab cultures it is more likely to be expressed as body aches and pains. Ask students to speculate on how a depressed person from an Arab culture might be diagnosed and treated if the therapist were not aware of this cultural difference. Then have students explain why cultural variations must be taken into account when attempting to diagnose and treat psychological disorders.

EXPLORING
DIVERSITY

Therapy and Culture

Increasingly in the United States, people who seek help for psychological disorders come from a wide range of cultures. This has led to a growing awareness on the part of therapists that culture is a significant factor in the diagnosis and treatment of psychological disorders. People differ in how they describe or even experience problems such as anxiety and depression. Their ideas about psychological disorders—and in some cases even the disorders themselves—are influenced by their culture.

The relevance of culture to the diagnosis and treatment of psychological disorders is illustrated by the case of a woman, originally from Ecuador, who was taken to a psychiatric hospital in the United States by her relatives. The woman seemed to be seriously disturbed. She was listless and withdrawn, complaining only that she had "lost her soul" (Goleman, 1995c).

Many therapists probably would have diagnosed the woman with schizophrenia and labeled as a delusion her belief that she had lost her soul. However, the psychiatrist who interviewed the woman at the hospital was familiar with her cultural background. He recognized the woman's "soul loss" as a symptom of *susto*.

Susto is a term used only in Latin American cultures. The condition is believed to occur when a person's soul is captured by spirits and taken from the body. The condition often develops after a frightening or stressful event, such as a serious injury or the death of a loved one. The symptoms of *susto* include loss of appetite, loss of weight, listlessness, apathy, and withdrawal from normal activities. Do these symptoms sound familiar?

The symptoms of susto *include loss of appetite, listlessness, and apathy.*

They should—they are also the symptoms of what Western psychiatrists call depression.

In the case of the Ecuadoran woman, the psychiatrist determined that her problem had started when a close relative in Ecuador had died unexpectedly. In her grief, the woman had developed all the typical symptoms of *susto*. In Western psychiatric terms, the woman was depressed. However, the psychiatrist did not prescribe antidepressants, as he might have for some other depressed patients. Instead, he decided on a form of therapy that was culturally more relevant.

In Ecuador, a mourning ceremony would have been held to help family members adjust to the loss of the loved one. Therefore, with the help of the woman's family, the therapist arranged a mourning ceremony to help the woman confront and accept the death of her relative. Openly mourning the death in a supportive circle of family and friends was apparently what the woman needed to begin healing from her loss and recovering from her depression. Soon her symptoms had improved and she was functioning normally again.

This example illustrates the relevance of culture to therapy. Clearly, both the diagnosis and the treatment of psychological disorders should take into account a person's cultural background.

Think About It

Making Generalizations and Predictions What do you think might have happened to the woman from Ecuador if she had been diagnosed incorrectly with schizophrenia?

Think About It: Answer

If the woman from Ecuador had been diagnosed incorrectly, she might have been hospitalized and given unnecessary medication. This would have further isolated her from family and friends and worsened her condition.

internet connect

TOPIC: Humanistic Psychotherapy
GO TO: go.hrw.com
KEYWORD: SY3 PS19

Have students access the Internet through the HRW Go site to research the theories of Carl Rogers and the humanistic approach to psychotherapy. Then ask students to create a series of drawings or diagrams that illustrate the main components of humanistic psychotherapy. Student drawings should illustrate the principles of person-centered therapy, active listening, other humanistic applications of therapy, and contrast this approach with other psychological techniques.

445

Closing Section 3

Predicting Outcomes

Ask students to predict the effect that unconditional positive regard by a therapist is likely to have on a client with low self-esteem. *(The acceptance and support of the therapist are likely to help the client accept and like himself or herself better, leading to higher self-esteem.)*

Reviewing Section 3

Have students complete the Section Review questions on page 446.

4

Section Objective

▶ Describe how cognitive and behavior therapists try to help people.

This objective is assessed in the Section Review on page 451 and in the Chapter 19 Review.

Section 3 Review: Answers

1. In person-centered therapy, clients receive help finding their true selves and realizing their unique potential. In this type of therapy, called nondirective therapy, the client is seen as an equal of the therapist.

2. The goal of active listening is to convey to the speaker that his or her words are being heard and that his or her thoughts and feelings are being understood.

3. Person-centered therapists try to help clients reach their full potential by allowing clients to lead the therapy in a supportive, accepting environment.

Teaching Transparencies with Teacher's Notes

TRANSPARENCY 38: Cognitive Model of Depression

446

Evaluation of Humanistic Therapy In a review of several studies, nearly three fourths of people obtaining person-centered therapy showed greater well-being, on average, than people who did not receive therapy (Smith & Glass, 1977). Like psychoanalysis, person-centered therapy seems to be most helpful for well-educated, motivated people. Humanistic therapy in general works best for people who experience anxiety, mild depression, or problems in their social relationships. However, it is ineffective for people who have major depression, bipolar disorder, or schizophrenia.

SECTION 3 REVIEW

Homework Practice Online
Keyword: SY3 HP19

1. Describe the methods of humanistic therapy.
2. What is the goal of active listening?
3. **Critical Thinking** *Analyzing Information* What role does the therapist play in person-centered therapy?

SECTION **4**

Cognitive Therapy and Behavior Therapy

Cognitive therapy and behavior therapy are considered together because both methods share the same goal—to help clients develop new ways of thinking and behaving. Both cognitive and behavior therapists encourage the clients to focus on their thoughts and actions. Advocates of these two theories contend that only by modifying self-defeating thoughts and behavior patterns will the client truly be able to solve his or her own problems. Thus, the aim of these therapies is to eliminate troubling emotions or behaviors rather than to help patients gain insight into the underlying cause of their problems, which is a key goal of psychoanalysis and humanistic therapy.

Cognitive Model of Depression

"Oh well, there's always next year."

"I'm a failure. I'm no good."

FIGURE 19.3 *Cognitive psychologists believe that some people develop ways of thinking that can lead to emotional and behavioral problems. In this example, we will call the person on the left Person A and the person on the right Person B. A's positive thinking gives him the motivation to keep practicing and to try to make the team. B's negative thinking leads to depression, feelings of worthlessness, and a reluctance to try again.*

Opening Section 4

Motivator

Ask the students to pretend that they have just heard a funny joke and to laugh heartily. After they have laughed for at least a full minute, ask them how they feel. Do they feel better, more relaxed, happier? Chances are they do because even pretending to laugh has therapeutic effects. Tell the class that, in general, changing behaviors and thoughts often can make a big difference in the way a person feels. Point out that this is the rationale underlying the types of therapy they will read about in Section 4.

Teaching Section 4

Cooperative Learning

Organize the class into groups, and have each group prepare a list of events that are frustrating or depressing (such as failing a test). For each event, have group members identify faulty assumptions that might lead people to react in a negative way. ("Failing a test means I will never amount to anything.") Then ask group members to rewrite the faulty assumptions as more emotionally healthy ones. ("If I fail a test, it means I must study harder next time.") Have each group share its work and relate the work to the goals of cognitive therapy.

Cognitive Therapy

The aim of cognitive therapy is to help people learn to think about their problems in more productive ways. Cognitive psychologists focus on the beliefs, attitudes, and thought processes that create and compound their clients' problems (Beck, 1993; Ellis, 1995). They believe that some people develop ways of thinking that are illogical or based on faulty assumptions. Such ways of thinking can lead to emotional and behavioral problems for these people. This idea is illustrated in Figure 19.3 on page 446.

Figure 19.3 shows how two different individuals, whom we will call Person A and Person B, react to the same event—being rejected for the swim team. Person A has a positive, logical way of thinking. His ability to look forward gives him the motivation to continue practicing and to try again next year. Person B's negative way of thinking, on the other hand, leads to feelings of worthlessness and depression. It is highly unlikely that Person B will continue practicing, let alone try out for the team again next year.

- - - - - - - - - - - - - - - -

TRUTH
OR
fiction
■ REVISITED ■

It is true that people's reactions to life events are based not on the events themselves but on their ways of thinking about the events. This is why cognitive therapists try to help people who are having emotional problems change the ways that they think.

- - - - - - - - - - - - - - - -

Cognitive therapists help people change their ways of thinking. These therapists also try to help people develop more realistic and logical ways of thinking. Cognitive psychologists argue that once people have changed their ways of thinking, they become more capable of solving their emotional and behavioral problems.

The two most widely used cognitive therapy methods are rational-emotive therapy and psychiatrist Aaron Beck's model of therapy, sometimes called cognitive restructuring therapy. Both of these methods aim at modifying people's ways of thinking as a means of improving their emotional health. However, the two methods differ somewhat in the aspects of thinking they maintain must be changed and in the approach they take to bring about those changes.

Rational-Emotive Behavior Therapy First developed by psychologist Albert Ellis in the 1950s, **rational-emotive behavior therapy** (REBT) is based on Ellis's belief that people are basically logical in their thinking and actions. However, the assumptions upon which they base their thinking or actions are sometimes incorrect. According to Ellis, people may develop emotional problems when they base their behavior on these faulty assumptions (Ellis & Dryden, 1996).

An example of a commonly held false assumption that leads to emotional problems is "I must do everything perfectly." People who believe they must do everything perfectly in order to be happy must also believe that if they are unhappy, it is because they did something imperfectly. Thus, their unhappiness is their own fault. In addition, no matter how hard these people try, they are unlikely to be able to live up to their own unrealistically high standard of perfection. It is easy to see why belief in this false assumption could lead a person to experience anxiety or severe depression.

People are often unaware of their false assumptions even though the assumptions influence their conscious thoughts and actions. The role of the therapist in REBT is first to identify and then to challenge the false assumptions. To teach individuals to think more realistically, REBT therapists use techniques such as role-playing and modeling. Role-playing helps individuals see how their assumptions affect their relationships. Modeling is used to show individuals other, more realistic assumptions they might adopt.

Individuals in rational-emotive behavior therapy may also receive homework assignments. For example, they may be asked to read relevant literature, listen to tapes of psychotherapy sessions, or carry out experiments designed to test their assumptions. The more faithfully patients complete their homework, the more likely it is that their therapy will succeed (Ellis & Dryden, 1996).

Beck's Cognitive Therapy Another form of cognitive therapy was introduced in the 1960s by psychiatrist Aaron Beck. In contrast to REBT's focus on faulty assumptions, the focus of Beck's cognitive therapy is on restructuring illogical thought processes. Beck (1993) has noted several types of illogical thought processes that may lead to emotional problems, particularly depression. Some of these include the following:

- *Arbitrary inference*, or drawing conclusions for which there is no evidence. For example, when a teacher passes a student in the hall and

Journal Activity

Ask students to record their thoughts and feelings in response to frustrating or depressing events that occur to them over the next several days. Then have them identify the assumptions underlying their thoughts and feelings. Encourage them to question the validity of their assumptions. Which assumptions do they think are valid? Are there any that they think are false? How could the false assumptions be changed to make them more realistic?

Cross-Curricular Link: Drama

A therapy technique called *psychodrama*, developed in the 1930s by psychiatrist Jacob L. Moreno, allows clients to role-play troubling situations in their lives, often on an actual stage and with other members of their therapy group. Clients play themselves or assume the role of a significant person in their lives, such as a parent. The technique helps people face deep-seated conflicts and express emotions in the relatively safe and protected environment of the therapeutic "stage."

Meeting Individual Needs: Learners with Limited English Proficiency

Students with limited English proficiency may have difficulty distinguishing the various types of illogical thought processes Beck identified. Help them gain a better understanding of these thought processes by giving them additional examples and having them identify the thought process involved in each example. Then ask students to provide examples of each type of illogical thought process. Correct any errors.

Interpreting Ideas

Have the class brainstorm problems teenagers commonly face that they think would be well suited for treatment using behavior therapy. *(Possibilities may include different types of phobias, drug abuse or other self-destructive behaviors, or various kinds of compulsions.)* Ask students to explain why they think each problem could be helped by behavior therapy.

Class Discussion

Have students discuss why some psychologists believe that cognitive therapy is successful in treating depression. Guide them to conclude that depression is sometimes caused by faulty thinking or unrealistic expectations and that the aim of cognitive therapy is to help people find more productive ways of thinking.

internet connect

TOPIC: Cognitive and Behavior Therapy
GO TO: go.hrw.com
KEYWORD: SY3 PS19

Have students access the Internet through the HRW Go site to research the various types of cognitive and behavior therapy. Then ask students to create a graphic organizer in which they outline the various types of therapy in this category as well as the role of conditioning.

Technology Resources

CNN. Presents Psychology: Technology and New Therapies

does not smile, the student may arbitrarily conclude that the teacher is planning to fail her.

- *Selective abstraction,* or drawing conclusions about a situation or event on the basis of a single detail and misinterpreting or ignoring other details that would lead to a different conclusion. For example, a person may look at his reflection in a mirror, but instead of feeling happy about his good features—say, a handsome smile and a muscular build—all he notices is the small blemish on his chin.

- *Overgeneralization,* or drawing a general conclusion from a single experience. For example, a person may conclude that she is worthless because she failed one test.

Instead of confronting and challenging clients about the errors in their ways of thinking, as the REBT therapist does, the therapist using Beck's approach gently guides clients in testing the logic of their own thought processes and developing more logical ways of thinking. One technique for doing this is to train clients to observe and record their thoughts in response to the events of daily life. Therapists can later review events with clients and help them see the illogical thought processes that are causing them emotional problems.

Evaluation of Cognitive Therapy Cognitive therapy tends to be a short-term method, making it a realistic option for more people than traditional psychoanalysis. Clients generally meet with their therapist once a week for 15 to 25 weeks.

Studies of cognitive therapy show that modifying irrational beliefs of the type described by Albert Ellis helps people with problems such as anxiety and depression. Modifying self-defeating beliefs of the sort outlined by Aaron Beck also frequently alleviates anxiety and depression (Robins & Hayes, 1993; Whisman et al., 1991). Cognitive therapy has also helped people with personality disorders (Beck & Freeman, 1990).

Cognitive therapy is helpful with people with major depression who had been considered responsive only to medicine and other kinds of biological therapies. Many studies show that cognitive therapy is as effective or even more effective than antidepressant medication (Antonuccio, 1995; Muñoz et al., 1994). For one thing, cognitive therapy provides coping skills that reduce the risk of recurrence of depression once treatment ends. A combination of cognitive therapy and antidepressant medication may be superior to either treatment

A person who has a phobia of snakes may seek behavior therapy as a means of confronting and overcoming the phobia. According to behavior theorists, a client who fears snakes can be counterconditioned to react to snakes in a relaxed manner.

alone in the case of people with persistent depression (Keller et al., 2000).

Behavior Therapy

The goal of behavior therapy, which is also called *behavior modification,* is to help people develop more adaptive behavior. Some people seek behavior therapy to eliminate undesirable behaviors, such as overeating or smoking. Others seek behavior therapy to acquire desirable behaviors, such as the skills needed to develop healthy social relationships or confront phobias.

Behaviorists believe that both desirable and undesirable behaviors are largely learned and that people with psychological problems have learned unhealthy ways of behaving. The aim of behavior therapy is to teach people more desirable (or healthier) ways of behaving. To behaviorists, the reasons for the undesirable behavior are unimportant. Changing the behavior is what matters. For example, in Marc's case, changing his study habits led to a decrease in his test anxiety, but it did not help him understand why he had test anxiety in the first place.

Many behavioral techniques fall into two categories: counterconditioning, which helps people to unlearn undesirable behaviors, and operant conditioning, which helps in the learning of desirable

Guided Practice

Demonstrate systematic desensitization with a volunteer "client" from the class. Ask the volunteer to pretend that he or she has a phobia, such as a fear of flying or a fear of heights. Show the client pictures of increasingly frightening stimuli relating to the phobia while demonstrating how a therapist would help the client relax. Then have the class evaluate systematic desensitization as a therapeutic technique and suggest other fears that might be conquered through the use of systematic desensitization.

Independent Practice

Tell students to imagine that they are psychotherapists specializing in behavior therapy. Have them write a series of "case notes" describing the desensitization treatment of a hypothetical client with a phobia. In their case notes, students should provide the following information: background information on the client, type of phobia and symptoms leading to a diagnosis of phobic disorder, course of treatment (methods used and client's reactions to treatment), and prognosis. Have volunteers read their case notes aloud to the class for discussion.

behaviors. The choice of behavioral techniques for an individual client depends largely on the nature of the individual's psychological disorder.

Counterconditioning If undesirable behaviors are conditioned, or learned through reinforcement, then presumably they can be unlearned, or counterconditioned. Counterconditioning pairs the stimulus that triggers an unwanted behavior (such as fear of spiders) with a new, more desirable behavior. (See Chapter 6.) For example, a client who reacts with fear to spiders can be counterconditioned to respond to spiders in a relaxed manner instead. Counterconditioning techniques include systematic desensitization, modeling, and aversive conditioning.

Systematic desensitization was developed by psychiatrist Joseph Wolpe in the 1950s as a treatment for phobias and other anxiety disorders. The assumption underlying systematic desensitization is that a person cannot feel anxious and relaxed at the same time. The therapist therefore trains the client to relax in the presence of an anxiety-producing situation (Wolpe, 1990).

This is done in a systematic way. First, the therapist teaches the client how to relax completely. Once this has been accomplished, the therapist gradually exposes the client to the object or situation that causes the phobic response. For a person who fears spiders, the therapist might first ask the person to simply imagine a spider. If the thought of a spider makes the client feel anxious, the client is told to stop thinking about the spider and relax again. This is done repeatedly until the thought of a spider no longer causes anxiety.

Gradually, the stimulus is increased—the person might be shown pictures of spiders, asked to hold a toy spider, and eventually asked to handle a real spider. In each case, the person is trained to respond with relaxation until the stimulus no longer provokes anxiety.

Systematic desensitization may be combined with other counterconditioning measures, such as modeling and aversive conditioning. Modeling involves observational learning. The client observes and then imitates the therapist or another person coping with the feared object or situation. For the person with a fear of spiders, the therapist might ask the person to observe someone calmly watching a spider make a web. The client would then be encouraged to behave in the same way.

Aversive conditioning is, essentially, the opposite of systematic desensitization. In aversive conditioning, the therapist replaces a positive

*Someone who has a fear of water may gradually lose that fear through the behavior therapy technique of systematic desensitization. Once a person has overcome the fear of water, she may actually enjoy the experience of swimming. **What other fears might be overcome through systematic desensitization?***

What's New in Psychology?

A new way to treat people with phobias is on the horizon, and it shows promise of being very effective. Psychologist Ralph Lamson has introduced virtual reality as a treatment method for people with acrophobia, or fear of heights. Lamson's clients put on a virtual-reality helmet that allows them to enter a virtual environment in which they can safely confront their fears. They can walk a narrow plank high above the ground or cross a suspension bridge spanning a body of water, among other frightening feats—all without leaving the safety of their therapist's office. More than 90 percent of Lamson's clients have noticed a significant decline in their fear of heights. Lamson is now at work on similar virtual therapies for claustrophobia and agoraphobia.

Nadis, S. (1995). Virtual therapy: A little bit of electronic vertigo may cure the acrophobe. *Omni, 17,* 20.

Caption Question: Answer

Other fears might include fear of social situations, enclosed spaces, blood, dogs, and insects.

Applying Ideas

Have class members work together to develop a token economy for their school to improve student behavior in the halls and classrooms. Students should come to agreement on the specific behaviors that would be rewarded, the tokens that would be used, the real rewards for which the tokens could be exchanged, and a way to make the system financially self-sustaining. After students have finalized their system, ask whether they think it would work in their school. How could they find out?

Demonstration

Demonstrate the concept of successive approximations by making a model of this process on the chalkboard. First, draw a staircase with 10 steps to represent 10 successive goals a person must accomplish to change a behavior, such as better controlling his or her anger. Write the overall goal at the top of the stairs. Then ask the class to fill in each step, starting at the bottom, with increasingly challenging goals to help a person reach the overall goal. Also have students suggest how the achievement of each goal could be rewarded.

response to a stimulus with a negative response. For example, for a person who wants to stop smoking, the therapist might replace the pleasant feelings associated with smoking with unpleasant ones. The person might be asked to smoke several cigarettes at once through a device that holds two or more cigarettes. This overexposure to cigarette smoke makes smoking an unpleasant experience. With repetition, the person may come to avoid smoking.

People who learn more desirable behaviors through counterconditioning often experience a boost in their self-esteem as well. Furthermore, by confronting, challenging, and overcoming their fears or bad habits, such people will increase their opportunity to lead less restrictive lives.

Operant Conditioning The behavioral technique of operant conditioning is based on the assumption that behavior that is reinforced tends to be repeated, whereas behavior that is not reinforced tends to be extinguished. Behavioral therapists reinforce desirable behaviors with rewards and at the same time withhold reinforcement for undesirable behaviors. In other words, therapists teach clients in a given situation, or antecedent, to behave in a certain way to achieve a desired consequence. The rewards for desirable behavior might be praise or treats, for example, depending on the client and the setting. For Marc, reducing his test anxiety may be all the reward he needs to motivate him to continue his new study habits.

Operant conditioning has sometimes proved effective in more severe cases, such as schizophrenia and childhood autism, that were previously resistant to other types of treatment. Operant conditioning is often used in institutional settings, such as mental hospitals. In such settings, the therapist may set up a system of rewards, called a **token economy**. When people in these settings begin to demonstrate appropriate behavior, they are rewarded with a plastic coin or token. The tokens can be accumulated and exchanged for real rewards, such as snacks, extra television time, a trip to town, or a private room.

The staff at one mental hospital used operant conditioning to convince withdrawn schizophrenic patients to eat their meals (Ayllon & Haughton, 1962). The more the staff coaxed the patients to eat—sometimes even hand-feeding them—the worse the problem became. The extra attention from the staff was apparently reinforcing the patients' lack of cooperation: the greater the refusal to eat, the more attention the patients received.

The solution was to stop reinforcing the uncooperative behavior and instead reinforce cooperative behavior. Patients who arrived late at the dining hall were locked out, and hospital staff were prevented from helping patients at mealtime. Thus, uncooperative behavior was no longer rewarded with extra attention. Only those who cooperated received food. As a result, the uncooperative patients quickly changed their eating habits.

Sometimes people find it difficult to adopt a new behavior all at once, finding it easier to change their behavior gradually. Another method of operant conditioning, called successive approximations, is useful in such situations. The term **successive approximations** refers to a series of behaviors that gradually become more similar to a target behavior. Through reinforcement of behaviors at each stage, the target behavior is finally achieved.

The technique of successive approximations is best understood by considering an example. Suppose a student wants to increase his studying

Aversive Versus Operant Conditioning

	Aversive	**Operant**
Goal	End maladaptive (harmful) behavior	Encourage adaptive behavior, or end maladaptive behavior
Technique	Associate the maladaptive behavior with aversive (painful) stimulation	Reinforce adaptive behavior, or avoid reinforcement of maladaptive behavior
Rationale	Associating a goal with aversive stimulation makes the goal aversive	Reinforcement increases the frequency of behavior, and lack of reinforcement extinguishes behavior

FIGURE 19.4 *Operant conditioning applies reinforcement to increase the frequency of desirable behavior and withholds reinforcement to extinguish undesirable behavior. Aversive conditioning makes use of punishment to make a once-desired goal unpleasant.*

Synthesizing Ideas

Ask students to create a four-column chart in which they compare and contrast the types of therapy that would be offered to a phobic client by a cognitive therapist, a behavior therapist, a psychoanalyst, and a humanistic psychologist. Have volunteers discuss their charts.

Reviewing Section 4

Have students complete the Section Review questions on page 451.

Section Objective

▶ Describe the three major biological treatments for psychological disorders.

This objective is assessed in the Section Review on page 453 and in the Chapter 19 Review.

---

time to two hours a day. However, he is not used to studying that long and cannot maintain his concentration for more than half an hour at a time. Instead of trying to study for two hours the first day, he studies for half an hour and then gives himself a small reward, such as shooting baskets or watching television for 15 minutes. Each night he adds five minutes to his study time, and each time he meets his new goal he reinforces his behavior with a small reward. Within a few weeks, through successive approximations, he reaches his goal of studying for two hours a day.

The relationship between antecedents, behavior, and consequences can be seen when operant conditioning is used for social skills training. People with severe psychological problems may lack social skills because of isolation and social withdrawal. In fact, lacking the social skills needed for independent living is one of the major symptoms of schizophrenia. A therapist might assist a client by teaching him or her to say "hello" in a friendly way when meeting someone. This technique would help the client function more comfortably in society—that is, it would help the client achieve a desired consequence.

Behavior therapists help people build their social skills by advising clients on their behavior, modeling effective behaviors, and encouraging clients to practice effective behaviors. Such techniques have proved successful in helping students build social relationships. They have also been used to help people with severe psychological disorders. With social skills training, a person who otherwise would be dependent on others might be able to hold a job and live on her or his own.

Evaluation of Behavior Therapy Behavior therapy tends to be somewhat more effective overall than psychoanalysis or person-centered therapy. It is also a short-term therapy, sometimes bringing about lasting results in just a few months.

Behavior therapy is especially effective for well-defined problems such as phobias, post-traumatic stress disorder, and compulsions (Borkovec & Costello, 1993; Thom et al., 2000). It has also helped many people overcome depression, social problems, and problems with self-control (as in quitting smoking or drinking). In addition, behavior therapy has proved very useful for managing the care of people living in institutions, including people with schizophrenia and people with mental retardation (Spreat & Behar, 1994).

Behavior therapy is less useful for some other disorders. For example, it is not usually effective for

treating the thought disorder of schizophrenia (Wolpe, 1990).

SECTION 4 REVIEW

go.hrw.com
Homework Practice Online
Keyword: SY3 HP19

1. Identify related antecedents, behavior, and consequences in a provided behavioral situation.

2. What is aversive conditioning?

3. **Critical Thinking** *Summarizing* What techniques do cognitive and behavior therapists use to help people?

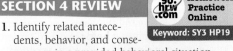

Biological Therapy

The methods of psychotherapy described so far rely on verbal interactions between the psychotherapist and the individual seeking help. As you have seen, psychotherapists may give their clients emotional support, advice, and help in understanding and changing their thoughts and behaviors.

Biological therapy, on the other hand, relies on methods such as medication, electric shock, and even surgery to help people with psychological disorders. All of these biological methods affect the brain in some way.

Because these treatments are medical in nature, they must be administered or prescribed by psychiatrists or other physicians. Psychologists do not prescribe drugs or administer biological treatments, but they may help decide whether a certain kind of biological therapy is appropriate for the treatment of a particular individual.

Drug Therapy

Drug therapy is the most widely used biological treatment for psychological disorders. It works well for several different problems. Four major types of medication are commonly used: antianxiety drugs, antidepressant drugs, lithium, and antipsychotic drugs. All of these medications can be obtained only with a prescription.

Antianxiety Drugs Also called minor tranquilizers, **antianxiety drugs** are used as an outpatient treatment to help people with anxiety disorders or panic attacks. (See Chapter 18.) They are also prescribed for people who are experiencing serious distress or tension in their lives.

Section 4 Review: Answers

1. For example, a behavioral therapist could teach a client who is meeting someone new (antecedent) to say "hello" in a friendly way (behavior) to achieve social approval (the desired consequence).

2. Aversive conditioning is a behavior-modification technique in which the therapist replaces a positive response to a stimulus with a negative one. It is the opposite of systematic desensitization, in which the client gradually learns to cope with increasingly frightening stimuli.

3. Cognitive therapists use rational-emotive therapy, and Beck's cognitive restructuring therapy. Behavioral therapists use counter-conditioning and operant conditioning.

Motivator

Ask students to identify the types of treatment they use for various physical illnesses, such as headaches, upset stomachs, and colds. They probably will name various forms of drug therapy. Tell them that drugs and other forms of biological therapy are also important in the treatment of some psychological disorders, especially mood disorders and schizophrenia. Add that in Section 5 they will learn more about drug therapy and other types of biological therapy for psychological disorders.

Drawing Conclusions

Controlling the symptoms of schizophrenia with medication often allows those with schizophrenia to lead more normal lives. They can live more independently—even hold jobs—and maintain better social relationships. Ask the class what effect these outcomes of drug therapy might have on the emotional well-being and prognosis of people with schizophrenia. *(Greater independence and better social relationships increase self-esteem and social support, both of which are likely to have a positive effect on emotional health and the control of schizophrenia.)*

Class Discussion

ITo put the chapter in a broader context, tell the class that the way in which a society views people with psychological disorders varies from time to time and from place to place. For example, people with aberrant behavior have been viewed as witches or creatures possessed by evil spirits but also as harmless eccentrics or gifted healers. Have students discuss how a society's views about people with psychological disorders might affect how these people are treated. How are people with psychological disorders viewed and treated in American society today?

Antianxiety drugs work by depressing the activity of the nervous system. They lower the heart rate and respiration rate. They also decrease feelings of nervousness and tension. Although antianxiety medications help control the symptoms of anxiety, they are not a permanent cure for anxiety disorders. Thus, most people use them for a short period of time (Shader & Greenblatt, 1993). The longer a person takes an antianxiety medication, the less effective the drug may become. Higher doses may be needed in order to achieve the same effect.

The major side effects of antianxiety medications are feelings of fatigue (Shader & Greenblatt, 1993). It is also possible to become dependent on antianxiety drugs. People who are dependent on these drugs may lose the ability to face the stresses and strains of everyday life without them.

Antidepressant Drugs   People who suffer from major depression are often treated with **antidepressant drugs**. Antidepressant drugs are also sometimes used in the treatment of eating disorders and panic disorder (Craighead & Agras, 1991).

Antidepressants work by increasing the amount of one or both of the neurotransmitters norepinephrine (noradrenaline) and serotonin. They tend to be most helpful in reducing the physical symptoms of depression. They increase activity levels and reduce the severity of eating and sleeping problems.

In order to work effectively, antidepressant medications must build up in the body to a certain level. This may take anywhere from several days to a few weeks. Severely depressed people who are at risk of suicide are sometimes hospitalized until the medication reaches the level required to improve their depressed mood. This is to prevent them from taking an overdose, which could be lethal. In addition, antidepressants sometimes have negative side effects, such as escalated heart rate and excessive weight gain (Sleek, 1996). For these and other reasons, some psychologists believe that antidepressant medications should be reserved for people who fail to respond to psychotherapy.

Lithium   The ancient Greeks and Romans may have been the first people to use the metal **lithium** to treat psychological disorders. They discovered that mineral water helped many people with what is now called bipolar disorder. (See Chapter 18.) It has been speculated that the mineral water may have contained lithium.

Today lithium carbonate, a salt of the metal lithium, is given in tablet form to help people with bipolar disorder. Lithium seems to flatten out their cycles of mania and depression. How lithium does this is not completely understood, although it is known to affect the functioning of several neurotransmitters (Price & Heninger, 1994).

Lithium may have side effects such as shakiness, memory impairment, and excessive thirst (Price & Heninger, 1994). Memory problems are reported to be the major reason that people stop using the drug.

Antipsychotic Drugs   People with schizophrenia, such as Dan's sister, are likely to be prescribed **antipsychotic drugs**, also called major tranquilizers.

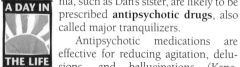
A DAY IN THE LIFE

Antipsychotic medications are effective for reducing agitation, delusions, and hallucinations (Kane, 1996). Their use has enabled many thousands of people with schizophrenia to live outside of mental hospitals and even to hold jobs.

Schizophrenia is associated with high levels of dopamine activity. (See Chapter 18.) Antipsychotic medications are thought to work by blocking the activity of dopamine in the brain. Unfortunately, prolonged use of these medications can lead to problems in balance and coordination and produce tremors and twitches (Kane, 1996).

Electroconvulsive Therapy

Electroconvulsive therapy (ECT), commonly called electric-shock therapy, was introduced as a treatment for psychological disorders in the 1930s by Italian psychiatrists Ugo Cerletti and Lucio Bini. Before ECT is given, anesthesia is administered to render the person unconscious throughout the procedure. Then an electric current is passed through the person's brain. The electric current produces convulsions (violent involuntary contractions of muscles) throughout the body. In some cases, muscle relaxant drugs are given to prevent injury during the convulsions.

When ECT was first introduced, it was used for many psychological disorders, including schizophrenia. However, once antipsychotic drugs became available, ECT was used much less often. In fact, in 1990 the American Psychiatric Association recommended that ECT be used primarily for people with major depression who do not respond to antidepressant drugs.

ECT is controversial for many reasons. For one thing, many professionals are distressed by the thought of passing an electric shock through a

Summarizing Information

Ask the class to create a chart on the chalkboard that summarizes the major use(s) and side effects of each type of biological therapy discussed in this section. Ask a volunteer to record the information as the rest of the class supplies it.

Reviewing Section 5

Have students complete the Section Review questions on page 453.

Extension

Have interested students research the role that institutionalization has played in the treatment of people with psychological disorders. Have them address the reasons for, and conditions of, institutionalization and how these have changed over time. Ask students to report back to the class with the results of their research.

---

patient's head and producing convulsions. There are also side effects, including memory problems (Lisanby et al., 2000; Weiner, 2000). However, research suggests that for most people, cognitive impairment tends to be temporary. One study followed up on 10 adolescents who had received ECT an average of three and a half years earlier. Six of the ten had complained of memory impairment immediately after treatment, but only one complained of continued problems at the follow-up. Nevertheless, psychological tests did not reveal any differences in cognitive functioning between severely depressed adolescents who had received ECT and others who had not (Cohen et al., 2000). Despite the controversies surrounding ECT, it appears to help many people who do not respond to antidepressant drugs (Thase & Kupfer, 1996).

TRUTH OR fiction
■ REVISITED ■

It is true that severe depression is sometimes treated by passing an electric current through the brain. This is called electroconvulsive therapy. It is a biological treatment used primarily for patients with severe depression who do not respond to antidepressants.

Psychosurgery

Psychosurgery is brain surgery that is performed to treat psychological disorders. The best-known technique, **prefrontal lobotomy**, has been used to reduce the agitation and violence of people with severe psychological disorders.

The method was developed by Portuguese neurologist António Egas Moniz in the 1930s. The procedure involves cutting nerve pathways in the brain between the prefrontal lobes and the thalamus. (See Chapter 3.) However, the treatment produces several serious side effects, including distractibility, reduced learning ability, overeating, apathy, social withdrawal, seizures, reduced creativity, and occasionally even death.

Not surprisingly, prefrontal lobotomy is an even more controversial procedure than ECT. The original rationale behind the surgery has been challenged, and early success rates are now known to have been exaggerated (Valenstein, 1986). Because of the side effects of the surgery and the availability of antipsychotic drugs, prefrontal lobotomies are now performed only rarely.

When a person with severe depression fails to respond to medications, electroconvulsive therapy may be considered. It is a drastic treatment that is used only in extreme cases.

Drug therapies, and to a limited extent ECT, seem to be effective for some psychological disorders that do not respond to psychotherapy. It is important to realize, however, that medications and electric shocks cannot help a person develop more rational ways of thinking or solve relationship problems. Changes such as these are likely to require psychotherapy.

SECTION 5 REVIEW

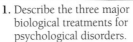

Homework Practice Online
Keyword: SY3 HP19

1. Describe the three major biological treatments for psychological disorders.
2. Explain why electroconvulsive therapy is a controversial treatment for psychological disorders.
3. **Critical Thinking** *Categorizing* Describe the type of biological therapy that might be prescribed for each of the following: panic disorder, bipolar disorder, schizophrenia, and severe depression.

453

Technology
- ► Chapter 19 Test Generator (on the One-Stop Planner)
- ► HRW Go site

Reinforcement, Review, and Assessment
- ► Chapter 19 Review, pp. 454–455
- ► Chapter Review and Activities with Answer Key
- ► Alternative Assessment Handbook
- ► Portfolio Assessment Handbook
- ► Chapter 19 Test (Form A or B)

PSYCHOLOGY PROJECTS

Linking to Community Invite at least two different types of psychotherapists from the community to speak to the class. Include, for example, a psychologist, a psychiatrist, and a psychiatric nurse or social worker. Ask the therapists to discuss their field of specialization and the training they

relax and then to say whatever comes to mind

4. the hidden meaning in a dream

5. therapy intended to help individuals reach their full potential

6. communication technique in which the listener repeats, rephrases, and asks for clarification of the statements made by the speaker

7. therapy in which a positive response to a stimulus is replaced with a negative response

8. a system of rewards set up to encourage people to demonstrate appropriate behavior

9. drugs prescribed to help people with anxiety disorders

10. brain surgery performed to treat psychological disorders

Understanding Main Ideas

1. They give people hope for recovery, a new perspective, and a caring relationship.

2. Manifest content is the dream as recalled by the dreamer; latent content is the hidden meaning as seen by the analyst.

3. Answers should describe a client who develops a relationship with his or her therapist that is similar to an earlier relationship.

4. The goal is to help people realize their potential.

5. In systematic desensitization, the client learns to relax while facing gradually more frightening stimuli; in aversive conditioning, the stimulus is paired with a negative response.

6. It has serious side effects, is not well understood, and may not be as effective as once thought. It is used for severe depression that does not respond to drug therapy.

Chapter 19 REVIEW

Writing a Summary

Using standard grammar, spelling, sentence structure, and punctuation, summarize the information in this chapter. Consider:
- the methods and goals of psychotherapy
- humanistic, cognitive, and behavioral therapies, and biological therapies for psychological disorders

Identifying People and Ideas

Identify the following terms or people and use them in appropriate sentences.

1. psychotherapy
2. encounter group
3. free association
4. latent content
5. humanistic therapy
6. active listening
7. aversive conditioning
8. token economy
9. antianxiety drug
10. psychosurgery

Understanding Main Ideas

SECTION 1 (pp. 436–440)

1. In what ways do all methods of psychotherapy help troubled individuals?

SECTION 2 (pp. 441–444)

2. What is the difference between the manifest content and the latent content of dreams?

3. Give an example of a transference relationship. Why might a therapist encourage the formation of such a relationship?

SECTION 3 (pp. 444–446)

4. What is the primary goal of humanistic therapy?

SECTION 4 (pp. 446–451)

5. List and describe two counterconditioning techniques.

SECTION 5 (pp. 451–453)

6. When do therapists use electroconvulsive therapy, and why is it a controversial form of treatment?

Thinking Critically

1. **Summarizing** Why did Freud think that free association can reveal unconscious thoughts and feelings?

2. **Drawing Inferences and Conclusions** How could belief in the assumption "I must be loved by everyone to be happy" lead to unreasonable expectations and feelings of depression?

3. **Analyzing Information** Other than examples given in the text, what is an example of the use of systematic desensitization?

4. **Contrasting** What are the advantages of treating depression with cognitive therapy instead of with antidepressant drugs?

Writing About Psychology

1. **Summarizing** Research how the social and cultural conditions of Sigmund Freud's time influenced his ideas about the causes of psychological problems. Think about how Freud's era differed from the present. How did conditions then influence Freud's ideas? Write a brief summary of what you have learned.

2. **Comparing and Contrasting** In addition to person-centered therapy, there are other types of humanistic therapy. Three of these are existential therapy, Gestalt therapy, and transactional analysis. Read more about these other types of humanistic therapy, then write a report of their similarities and differences. Use the graphic organizer below to help you write your report.

Existential	Gestalt	Transactional

received. Also have them discuss their approach to therapy, describe the techniques they use, and identify the types of disorders they most commonly treat. Ask the therapists to share what they find most satisfying and most stressful about their work.

Make copies of several case studies from books on abnormal psychology. The type of disorder should be apparent from the information provided. Next, organize the class into small groups, and assign each group a different therapeutic approach. The groups should describe the specific goals of their form of therapy, the treatment techniques they would use, the roles that the therapist and the client would play, and how long they expect treatment to take. Then lead a class discussion about which treatment would be most effective in each case.

Building Social Studies Skills

Interpreting Graphs

Study the graph below. Then use the information in the graph to help you answer the questions that follow.

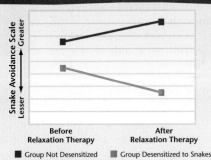

The Effect of Desensitization and Therapy on Persons with a Phobia of Snakes

Snake Avoidance Scale (Lesser ↕ Greater)

Before Relaxation Therapy — After Relaxation Therapy

■ Group Not Desensitized   ■ Group Desensitized to Snakes

Source: Rachman, *Phobias*, 1968

1. Which of the following statements best reflects the information presented in the graph?
   a. Relaxation therapy worked best when used with desensitization.
   b. Relaxation therapy was useless in helping people with phobias.
   c. Some people feared snakes no matter what therapy or help they received.
   d. Desensitization rarely helps people with phobias.
2. Using information from this graph, what general statements can be made about relaxation therapy and the treatment of phobias?

Analyzing Primary Sources

Read the following excerpt from *The Story of Psychology*, in which Morton Hunt describes aspects of psychologist Aaron Beck's personal life. Then answer the questions that follow.

"As a child, he had had a series of operations, and from then on the sight of blood would make him feel faint. By the time he reached his teens he decided to defeat the phobia. 'One of the reasons I went into medicine was to confront my fear,' he has said, and in his first year in medical school he made himself watch operations from the amphitheater and in his second year elected to be a surgical assistant. By making himself experience blood as a normal phenomenon, he dispelled his fear. Later in life he similarly tackled a fear of tunnels, manifested as involuntary shallow breathing and faintness (he attributes the phobia to a childhood fear of suffocation caused by a bad bout of whooping cough). He got rid of the fear by pointing out to himself repeatedly that the symptoms would show up even before he entered a tunnel."

3. Which method of therapy did Beck use to end his phobia of blood?
   a. psychoanalysis
   b. cognitive therapy
   c. behavior therapy
   d. biological therapy
4. Use Beck's experiences and his method of cognitive therapy to explain how personal background can shape a psychologist's views.

PSYCHOLOGY PROJECTS

Cooperative Learning

Writing About Psychology With a partner, write a skit showing how a client and a person-centered therapist might interact. First, select a suitable problem based on the text. Then write dialogue and descriptions for body language and facial expressions that illustrate active listening and unconditional positive regard. Rehearse the skit, and then present it to the rest of the class. After performing the skit, ask the class to identify examples of active listening and unconditional positive regard from the skit.

Internet Activity: go.hrw.com
KEYWORD: SY3 PS19
Choose an activity on methods of therapy to:
- make a series of drawings illustrating the principles of humanistic therapy.
- create a graphic organizer for cognitive and behavior therapy.
- create a chart tracing changes in biological therapy over the years.

Thinking Critically

1. He believed unconscious thoughts and feelings break through during free association and show up in what people say or resist saying.

2. People with such thoughts may also believe that if they are unhappy, it is because they are unlovable. Such thoughts can lead to depression.

3. An example is to train someone with a fear of germs to relax by having the person touch doorknobs, then shake hands with other people, and finally handle dirt.

4. Cognitive therapy improves coping skills that can reduce the risk of depression returning once treatment ends; it also has no negative side effects.

Writing About Psychology

1. Summaries should note that Freud's emphasis on repressed sexual urges reflected a social and cultural environment in which sexuality was repressed.

2. Reports should indicate that all three therapies help people achieve self-determination but in different ways.

Building Social Studies Skills

1. a
2. Relaxation therapy was useful only when used with desensitization; when used alone, it was not only ineffective but also led to increased problems for patients who had a phobia about snakes.
3. c
4. Students should note that cognitive therapy focuses on eliminating illogical thoughts such as those that Beck had as a young man.

455

UNIT 6 REVIEW

▶ TEACH

Ask students to examine several newspapers, magazines, or other news sources to collect four to five examples of disagreements among people. The disagreements may concern a variety of topics, such as labor disputes, negotiations between parties to a lawsuit, or two nations that have a border dispute. Have the students work together in groups to create posters that outline ways the parties in the news sources could work to resolve their disagreements. Suggest that the students either include a brief summary of the conflict on the poster or paste the article directly on their creation. Have one person from each group explain the group's poster to the class. Display the posters in the classroom.

▶ PSYCHOLOGY IN ACTION

Have students review the simulation's steps of conflict resolution. Ask the students to search the textbook or other sources for examples of the four steps. Have students prepare a chart with the following headings: *Persuasion, Compromise, Debate* and *Negotiation.* Have students list at least one example under each step.

▶ EXTEND

Have students review the discussion of sources of stress in chapter 17. Point out that conflict is a major source of stress for many people. Ask the groups to think of examples of conflict that cause stress. Have the groups use the conflict-resolution process outlined in the simulation to develop a plan for resolving the conflict. Have each group present its plan to the class.

UNIT 6

PSYCHOLOGY IN ACTION

YOU RESOLVE THE CONFLICT . . .

*How could two people settle a disagreement
in order to reduce stress in their lives?*

Complete the following activity in small groups. Imagine that two of your friends are having a disagreement about the best way to prepare for an upcoming test. Both friends are very distressed by their disagreement, but they are unsure how they can go about resolving the situation. Prepare a presentation outlining ways to help your friends.

1. Consider Persuasion. Encourage your friends to try to persuade one another to come around to the other's point of view. To help your friends come up with persuasive arguments for their side, list reasons why they have the points of view that they do. Then rank each reason in order of persuasiveness. Finally, urge your friends to present the most persuasive reasons to one another in an effort to sway the other to his or her point of view.

2. Compromise. Explain to your friends that sometimes compromise is necessary to resolve a conflict. Tell them that each of them will have to give up something in order to reach an agreement. Have them consider what they would be willing to give up to resolve their disagreement. Then encourage your friends to get together to discuss a compromise that they could both agree to.

3. Debate the Issue. Suggest to your friends that they hold a debate. Tell them to gather information about the advantages and disadvantages of each side of their disagreement. Ask questions such as,

- Should your friends have one cram session the night before the test?

- Should your friends study a little each night during the week leading up to the test?

Then consider having your friends prepare flash cards outlining the best arguments that they can come up with in support of their side. Finally, hold the debate. Your friends might want to include charts, graphs, or other visuals to better demonstrate their positions.

4. Consider Negotiation. Urge your friends to negotiate their conflict. Have them meet to discuss their positions and what they would be willing to agree to. Tell them that perhaps by working together to resolve the conflict, they will arrive at a solution that neither had considered before. Have your group decide who will prepare which part of the presentation. Then make your presentation to the class. Good luck!

UNIT 7

Overview

In Unit 7 students will be introduced to the field of social psychology, including how our attitudes affect the way we see the world and the people in it, and the various factors that promote and inhibit attraction, conformity, obedience, aggression, and altruism.

CHAPTER 20 • *Social Cognition* examines the ways that people think and act in certain situations. This chapter examines such issues as attitudes, persuasion, attraction, and love.

CHAPTER 21 • *Social Interaction* focuses on the impact group interaction has on the behavior and attitudes of individuals, including the individual's tendency toward conformity, obedience, aggression, and altruism.

UNIT 7
SOCIAL PSYCHOLOGY

Habitat for Humanity

HABITAT FOR HUMANITY
Los Angeles

Jimmy Carter Work Project

Is The New Home Of:

▶ Internet Activity

internet connect

TOPIC: How Objective is the News?
GO TO: go.hrw.com
KEYWORD: SY3 UNIT 7
Have students access the Internet through the HRW Go site to research bias, subjectivity, and the use of statistics in news reporting. Then have students make a group presentation that examines issues in news reporting, explains and illustrates cautions related to interpreting statistics in news stories, and outlines the problems for people trying to understand complex issues covered by mainstream media outlets. Students should list specific ways in which statistics can be distorted.

▶ Using Visuals

Ask students to look closely at the photograph on page 457. Challenge students to list the many benefits of volunteering. Lead students to see the less obvious benefits, such as getting to know and work with a person of a different race or ethnicity and thus perhaps break down preconceived stereotypes.

CHAPTERS

20 *Social Cognition*

21 *Social Interaction*

Social Cognition

CHAPTER RESOURCE MANAGER

Objectives	Pacing Guide	Reproducible and Review Resources
SECTION 1: **Attitudes** (pp. 460–462) Define attitudes, and explain how they develop.	**Regular** .5 day **Block Scheduling** .5 day *Block Scheduling Handbook with Team Teaching Strategies, Chapter 20*	**PS** Readings and Case Studies, Chapter 20 **REV** Section 1 Review, p. 462
SECTION 2: **Persuasion** (pp. 462–465) Describe the influence of persuasion on people's attitudes and behavior.	**Regular** .5 day **Block Scheduling** .5 day *Block Scheduling Handbook with Team Teaching Strategies, Chapter 20*	**E** Research Projects and Activities for Teaching Psychology **REV** Section 2 Review, p. 465
SECTION 3: **Prejudice** (pp. 465–468) Identify causes of prejudice and ways that it can be overcome.	**Regular** 1 day **Block Scheduling** .5 day *Block Scheduling Handbook with Team Teaching Strategies, Chapter 20*	**SM** Mastering Critical Thinking Skills 20 **REV** Section 3 Review, p. 468
SECTION 4: **Social Perception** (pp. 468–472) List factors that influence our perceptions of other people, and explain how people use various forms of nonverbal communication.	**Regular** 1 day **Block Scheduling** .5 day *Block Scheduling Handbook with Team Teaching Strategies, Chapter 20*	**REV** Section 4 Review, p. 472
SECTION 5: **Interpersonal Attraction** (pp. 472–475) Describe the role of attraction in friendships and love relationships.	**Regular** 1 day **Block Scheduling** .5 day *Block Scheduling Handbook with Team Teaching Strategies, Chapter 20*	**RS** Essay and Research Themes for A. P. Students, Theme 17 **REV** Section 5 Review, p. 475

Chapter Resource Key

PS	Primary Sources	**A**	Assessment		Video	
RS	Reading Support	**REV**	Review		Internet	
E	Enrichment		Transparencies		Holt Presentation Maker Using Microsoft® PowerPoint®	
SM	Skills Mastery		CD-ROM			

One-Stop Planner CD–ROM

See the *One-Stop Planner* for a complete list of additional resources for students and teachers.

One-Stop Planner CD-ROM

It's easy to plan lessons, select resources, and print out materials for your students when you use the **One-Stop Planner CD-ROM with Test Generator.**

Technology Resources

 One-Stop Planner, Lesson 20.1
 Homework Practice Online
 Teaching Transparencies 39: The Relationship Between Attitudes and Behavior
 HRW Go Site

 One-Stop Planner, Lesson 20.2
 Homework Practice Online
 Teaching Transparencies 40: Save the Children Advertisement
 HRW Go Site

 One-Stop Planner, Lesson 20.3
 Homework Practice Online
 HRW Go Site

 One-Stop Planner, Lesson 20.4
 Homework Practice Online
 CNN Presents Psychology: School Violence Prevention Programs

 One-Stop Planner, Lesson 20.5
 Homework Practice Online

Chapter Review and Assessment

 HRW Go site
REV Chapter 20 Review, pp. 476–477
REV Chapter Review Activities with Answer Key

A Alternative Assessment Handbook
A Portfolio Assessment Handbook
A Chapter 20 Test (Form A or B)

Chapter 20 Test Generator (on the One–Stop Planner)
Global Skill Builder CD-ROM

---

internet connect

HRW ONLINE RESOURCES

GO TO: go.hrw.com
Then type in a keyword.

TEACHER HOME PAGE
KEYWORD: SY3 Teacher

CHAPTER INTERNET ACTIVITIES
KEYWORD: SY3 PS20
Choose an activity on social cognition to:
• create an annotated display on attitudes and behavior.
• design an advertisement employing methods of persuasion.
• create a theoretical profile analyzing prejudice and bias.

CHAPTER ENRICHMENT LINKS
KEYWORD: SY3 CH20

ONLINE ASSESSMENT
Homework Practice
KEYWORD: SY3 HP20
Standardized Test Prep
KEYWORD: SY3 STP20
Rubrics
KEYWORD: SS Rubrics

CONTENT UPDATES
KEYWORD: SS Content Updates

HOLT PRESENTATION MAKER
KEYWORD: SY3 PPT20

ONLINE READING SUPPORT
KEYWORD: SS Strategies

CURRENT EVENTS
KEYWORD: S3 Current Events

Additional Resources

PRINT RESOURCES FOR TEACHERS

Ciadini, R. (1993). *Influence: Science and practice* (3rd ed.). New York: HarperCollins.

Feldman, R., & Rime, B. (1991). *Fundamentals of nonverbal behavior.* Cambridge, England: Cambridge University Press.

Gamson, W., Fireman, B., & Rytina, S. (1982). *Encounters with unjust authority.* Homewood, IL: Dorsey Press.

Turner, J. (1991). *Social influence.* Pacific Grove, CA: Brooks-Cole.

PRINT RESOURCES FOR STUDENTS

Aronson, E. (1992). *The social animal.* New York: W. H. Freeman.

Duvall, L. (1994). *Respecting our differences: A guide to getting along in a changing world.* Minneapolis, MN: Free Spirit.

MULTIMEDIA RESOURCES

Body language: An introduction to non-verbal communication (VHS). Social Studies School Service, 10200 Jefferson Boulevard, Room 33, P.O. Box 802, Culver City, CA 90232-0802.

The psychology of neo-Nazism: Another journey by train to Auschwitz (VHS). Films for the Humanities & Sciences, P.O. Box 2053, Princeton, NJ 08543-2053.

The unbiased mind: Four obstacles to clear thinking (VHS). Social Studies School Service, 10200 Jefferson Boulevard, Room 33, P.O. Box 802, Culver City, CA 90232-0802.

SOCIAL COGNITION

Introducing Chapter 20

Write the following quotation on the chalkboard: "No man is an island." Ask students to discuss what the quotation means to them. When no more responses are forthcoming, explain that the quotation comes from a sermon by the English poet and clergyman John Donne and refers to the fact that no person lives in isolation from the rest of humankind, but rather all people are interconnected and affected by one another. In essence, people have and need social relationships. Then challenge students to work independently or in pairs to create their own quotations about the human need for social relationships. Have volunteers read their quotations to the class for discussion. Tell students that Chapter 20 focuses on social cognition, the way that people think and act in social situations.

Sections

1 Attitudes

2 Persuasion

3 Prejudice

4 Social Perception

5 Interpersonal Attraction

Each of the five questions identified on page 458 corresponds to one of these sections.

20
Chapter
SOCIAL COGNITION

Read to Discover

1 What are attitudes, and how do they develop?

2 How does persuasion affect people's attitudes and behavior?

3 What are the causes of prejudice, and how can it be overcome?

4 What factors influence our perceptions of other people, and how do people use various forms of nonverbal communication?

5 What role does attraction play in friendships and love relationships?

Each chapter begins with a vignette, called "A Day in the Life," that relates the information discussed in the chapter to the everyday events in the lives of a group of fictional high school students. The text of the chapter occasionally refers back to the vignette to demonstrate the application of the concept being discussed. An icon marked "A Day in the Life" is placed next to these references.

Copy the following graphic organizer onto the chalkboard as you discuss the relationship between attitudes and behavior.

Attitudes ⟷ Behavior

A DAY IN THE LIFE

June 4

On Saturday morning Marc was in a complete panic when he called Linda at home. That night, Marc was to have dinner with Linda's entire family—grandparents and all—and he was really nervous.

"Why are you so nervous?" Linda asked with a smile. "You know how much my parents like you."

"I know," Marc said, "but have you forgotten their attitude toward me at first? They didn't like me very much. I finally convinced your parents that I'm a good guy—now I have to go through the same thing with your grandparents."

"Marc, my parents first met you when we were six years old. When we started dating this year, they only remembered you from when we were little kids. Now that they know you better, they really like you," Linda tried to assure him.

"But what about your grandparents?" Marc said. "I really want them to like me the first time I meet them. What if I still come across as that same clumsy kid?"

"You'll be fine," Linda said. "Just relax, and I'll see you at six o'clock. I have to go now—I promised Hannah I'd help her out this afternoon."

"Okay," Marc sighed. Somehow Linda had managed to calm his fears. "What are you and Hannah doing today?" he asked. For the first time all morning, he was able to think about something other than the upcoming dinner.

"Remember how that representative from the performing arts foundation offered her a scholarship? Well, she has to pass an interview before they'll give her the scholarship, and I promised her that I'd help her prepare for it," Linda said.

"What are you going to help her with?" Marc asked.

"Well, she's been practicing the types of things she wants to say in the interview, and she wants to try them out on me first. She also wants me to help her decide what she should wear for the interview," Linda explained.

"Oh no!" Marc suddenly exclaimed in panic.

"What's wrong?" Linda asked.

"What am I going to wear to dinner tonight?"

Linda just laughed. "Really, Marc, I think you're taking this first impression thing a little too seriously."

. . .

Both Marc and Hannah want to make a good impression on other people. Their concern about how other people see them is one of the major aspects of the field of social psychology referred to as social cognition, which is the subject of this chapter.

Social cognition refers to the way people think and act in social situations. It is concerned not only with first impressions but also with attitudes, persuasion, attraction, and love. These and other aspects of social cognition are the focus of this chapter.

Key Terms

- attitude
- cognitive evaluation
- cognitive anchor
- persuasion
- central route
- peripheral route
- two-sided argument
- emotional appeal
- sales resistance
- prejudice
- discrimination
- scapegoat
- social perception
- primacy effect
- recency effect
- attribution theory
- actor-observer bias
- fundamental attribution error
- self-serving bias
- attraction
- matching hypothesis
- reciprocity
- triangular model of love
- intimacy
- passion
- commitment

WHY PSYCHOLOGY MATTERS

Psychologists study the way people think and act in social situations. Use **CNNfyi.com** or other current events sources to learn more about the study of social cognition.

CNNfyi.com

Using Key Terms

Write on the chalkboard the titles of the five sections that make up Chapter 20. Under each section title, write the key terms found in that section. Ask students to use the Glossary at the back of the book to find a definition for each of the terms in the chapter. Then have students write short paragraphs explaining how the terms found in each section relate to the section title. Ask volunteers to share their paragraphs with the class for discussion.

Journal Activity

After students have read the "A Day in the Life" vignette, have them write in their journals about a time when they worried about whether they would make a good first impression on someone. Why were they concerned about how this person would view them? What did they do to ensure a good first impression? How did they feel about the encounter—did they put forth their "true self" or "put on an act"? Did they accomplish the goal of making a good first impression?

459

7

Section Objective

► Define attitudes, and explain how they are acquired and how they are related to behavior.

This objective is assessed in the Section Review on page 462 and in the Chapter 20 Review.

Motivator

Ask a volunteer to read aloud the definition of the term *attitudes,* found on page 460. Then write on the chalkboard the following terms and phrases: *Education, Earning money, Prejudice, Helping others,* and *Marriage.* Ask students to jot down some notes about their attitudes regarding these matters. Have volunteers discuss how they developed their attitudes and how the attitudes affect their lives. Then explain why attitudes, the focus of Section 1, are an important aspect of social cognition.

Using Truth or Fiction

Each chapter opens with several "Truth or Fiction" statements that relate to the concepts discussed in the chapter. Ask students whether they think each statement is true or false. Answers to each item as well as explanations are provided at appropriate points within the text under the heading "Truth or Fiction Revisited."

Class Discussion

Have students discuss how easy or how difficult they find it to persuade other people to change their attitudes. Do people tend to hold firmly to their attitudes, or are their attitudes easily changed? Why?

Readings and Case Studies

TRUTH OR fiction ?

Read the following statements about psychology. Do you think they are true or false? You will learn whether each statement is true or false as you read the chapter.

- People's attitudes are always consistent with their behavior.
- Showing television commercials over and over reduces their effectiveness.
- People who are victims of prejudice usually feel empathy for others who are victims of prejudice.
- Our first impressions of other people tend to have lasting effects on our relationships with them.
- When it comes to choosing a partner or friend, "opposites attract."

SECTION 1

Attitudes

Attitudes are beliefs and feelings about objects, people, and events that can affect how people behave in certain situations. A person's attitude about strangers, for example, can influence how that person feels and behaves around people he or she does not know. If a person believes that strangers are dangerous, that person is likely to feel afraid around strangers and may try to avoid situations where he or she is likely to meet new people. On the other hand, if a person believes that strangers are people just like him or her, that person is more likely to feel open to strangers and try to know them better.

Attitudes are a major aspect of social cognition. In fact, our attitudes may be the primary motivator for how we behave and how we view the world.

Attitudes are such an important aspect of our psychological lives because they foster strong emotions, such as love or hate (Petty et al., 1997). Attitudes can also vary greatly. A person belonging to a particular cultural group may have attitudes that have been shaped by the traditional physical environment of that group.

Under certain circumstances, a person's attitudes can change. They tend to remain stable, however, unless that person is strongly encouraged to change them. This section examines several aspects of attitudes—how they develop, how they affect behavior, and how behavior affects them.

How Attitudes Develop

People often have attitudes about things they have never experienced directly. People may be opposed to war or capital punishment, for example, even though they have no personal experience of either event. Where do such attitudes come from?

Attitudes develop in a variety of ways. Conditioning, observational learning, cognitive evaluation, and the use of cognitive anchors all play roles in the development of attitudes.

Conditioning   Learning through conditioning plays an important role in acquiring attitudes. Children are often reinforced for saying and doing things that are consistent with the attitudes held by their parents, teachers, and other authority figures. For example, parents who believe that it is important to share with others may praise, or reinforce, a child who shares a toy with a friend. Through such conditioning, the child acquires an attitude about the importance of sharing.

Observational Learning   People also acquire attitudes by observing other people. For example, teens may observe that classmates who dress, talk, or act in certain ways seem to be admired by their peers. These teens may adopt the same ways of dressing, talking, or acting because they have learned through observation that doing so might lead to acceptance and approval.

People who act with kindness and generosity toward others—such as the teens pictured here—may come to like other people better.

Teaching Section 1

Cognitive Evaluation People often evaluate evidence and form beliefs on the basis of their evaluations. This process, which is known as **cognitive evaluation**, also plays a role in the development of attitudes. People evaluate evidence that comes from many sources. Part of the process of cognitive evaluation is learning to examine data carefully. For example, when looking at statistics provided in a news story, a viewer should consider issues such as whether the statistics were gathered properly, and what audience is being targeted by the story. A news story providing statistics indicating that seat belt use provides little protection in a car accident should be viewed skeptically.

People are especially likely to evaluate evidence if they think they will have to justify their attitudes to other people (Tetlock, 1983). For example, a teen who wants a part-time job after school may evaluate the evidence about working if he knows he will have to justify it to his parents. He may ask friends who have part-time jobs how they handle the extra responsibility and still do their schoolwork.

Cognitive evaluation was involved in Linda's parents' change in attitude toward Marc. At first, Linda's parents did not especially like Marc, an attitude that was based on their knowledge of him as a child who misbehaved. Once they came to know the teenage Marc, however, they formed a more positive attitude toward him.

Cognitive Anchors A person's earliest attitudes tend to serve as **cognitive anchors**, or persistent beliefs that shape the ways in which he or she sees the world and interprets events. Cognitive anchors tend to keep a person's attitudes from changing. Attitudes that emerge later in life may be rejected if they differ greatly from a person's cognitive anchors (Petty et al., 1999; Wood, 2000).

Attitudes and Behavior

The definition of *attitudes* suggests that people's behaviors are always consistent with their attitudes. However, the link between attitudes and behavior is not always strong (Eagly & Chaiken, 1993). In fact, people often behave in ways that contradict their attitudes. For example, many people know that smoking cigarettes and drinking alcohol excessively are harmful to their health, yet they still smoke and drink excessively. Likewise, most people realize that it is dangerous and illegal to drink and drive, yet some do it just the same (Stacy et al., 1994).

These children are learning an attitude of patriotism, which may serve as a cognitive anchor later in life.

When Behavior Follows Attitudes People are more likely to behave in accordance with their attitudes if the attitudes are specifically tied to the behaviors. For example, someone who believes that aerobic exercise is necessary to prevent heart disease is more likely to exercise regularly than someone who believes that only a healthy lifestyle is important for good health. Similarly, strong attitudes are better predictors of behavior than weak attitudes (Petty et al., 1997). Students who believe strongly in the value of hard work, for example, may be more likely to study than students who believe less strongly in the benefits of hard work.

People are also more likely to behave in accordance with their attitudes when they have a vested interest, or a personal stake, in the outcome of a behavior (Crano, 1997). People are more likely to go to the polls and vote on an issue, for example, if the issue affects them directly. That is one reason why issues such as tax reform often have high voter turnouts.

Attitudes are more likely to guide behavior when people are aware of them, particularly if the attitudes are put into words and spoken (Fazio, 1990; Krosnick, 1989). Verbalizing and repeating an attitude makes it come to mind quickly, and attitudes that come to mind quickly are more likely to influence how people act (Fazio, 1990). People are

Closing Section 1

Interpreting Information

Have students create a set of diagrams to show the possible relationships between various attitudes and behaviors. Have them use boxed phrases and directional arrows to show how specific attitudes lead to certain behaviors and vice versa. Discuss the diagrams in class.

Reviewing Section 1

Have students complete the Section Review questions on page 462.

Extension

Ask students to examine the various media to determine some of the major social attitudes that dominate popular culture today. They should bring in clippings from the print media and notes, sketches, or videotapes/audiotapes from the broadcast media. Some students may want to focus their searches on particular attitudes (such as attitudes toward women or minorities in television and popular music). Have students share and discuss their findings with the rest of the class.

also more likely to be aware of attitudes that affect them emotionally (Wu & Shaffer, 1987). Someone who loves animals is likely to be aware of his attitude about animal rights, for example. Likewise, someone who is angered by destruction of the environment is likely to be aware of her attitudes about recycling and conservation.

When Attitudes Follow Behavior   Most of the time attitudes come first and behavior follows (Petty et al., 1997, 1999). However, sometimes the reverse is true. In some situations, attitudes follow behavior.

Attitudes are especially likely to follow behavior when people are encouraged to behave in ways that go against their attitudes. In such situations, people may suffer cognitive dissonance, an uncomfortable feeling of tension that may accompany a contradiction between attitudes and behaviors (Festinger, 1957). In order to reduce the tension they feel, people may try to justify their behavior and gradually change their attitudes to fit their acts.

As an example, in one experiment, people were asked to argue in favor of something they did not believe in. Doing so made them feel very uncomfortable, and they eventually modified their

attitudes to bring them more in line with their arguments (Cialdini, 1993).

It is not true that people's attitudes are always consistent with their behavior. People can also change their attitudes to make them consistent with their behavior.

Although the patterns may change, one thing is certain—attitudes and behavior influence each other. As Figure 20.1 shows, people tend to act as they believe, but they may also come to believe as they act.

SECTION 1 REVIEW

go.hrw.com **Homework Practice Online** Keyword: SY3 HP20

1. What do psychologists mean by *attitude*, and how do attitudes develop?

2. Why should people be cautious when using statistics from news stories or information from other sources?

3. **Critical Thinking**   *Drawing Inferences and Conclusions*   In what ways do people adjust their behavior to fit various situations?

The Relationship Between Attitudes and Behavior

FIGURE 20.1   *Behavior usually follows attitudes, but attitudes can follow behavior when people behave in ways that go against their attitudes.*

SECTION 2

Persuasion

Attitudes tend to remain constant unless people are strongly motivated to change them. People may change their attitudes because they are persuaded to do so. **Persuasion** is a direct attempt to influence other people's attitudes or views. Parents, for example, may try to persuade their children to adopt the same values that they hold. Children, on the other hand, may try to persuade their parents to allow them more freedoms and privileges.

A DAY IN THE LIFE

Both Marc and Hannah want to persuade others to have a favorable impression of them. Both are hoping to influence people by the way they will dress for two important occasions—Hannah's interview with the performing arts foundation and Marc's first meeting with Linda's grandparents.

Section Objective

▶ Describe the influence of persuasion on people's attitudes and behavior.

This objective is assessed in the Section Review on page 465 and in the Chapter 20 Review.

Opening Section 2

Motivator

Bring in a variety of persuasive messages pulled from magazines, newspapers, advertising circulars, merchandise catalogs, and political mailings. Circulate these materials among the students, and ask what goal all of them have in common. *(to persuade)* Point out that persuasive messages are everywhere and that it is important for people to understand and evaluate these messages. Tell students that they will learn about persuasion in Section 2. After students have read Section 2, have them explain how they were persuaded to read the section.

Methods of Persuasion

There are two basic ways to persuade people: via the central route and via the peripheral route (Petty et al., 1997). The most persuasive messages use both routes.

The **central route** uses evidence and logical arguments to persuade people (Eagly & Chaiken, 1993). Advertisements might point out the superior quality of a product or a service—the superior taste and nutritional content of a breakfast cereal, for example. Similarly, a parent might use statistics on bicycle accidents and injuries to persuade a child to wear a safety helmet.

The **peripheral route** is indirect. It attempts to associate objects, people, or events with positive or negative cues. For example, an advertisement for athletic shoes might feature a famous athlete. A public service announcement for staying in school might feature an admired actor. The aim is to influence people to associate their positive feelings for the famous individual with the product or the message that is being endorsed.

In the central route, the message itself is most important. In the peripheral route, other factors, including the messenger, the situation, and the nature of the audience, are also important. Each of these aspects of persuasion is considered in turn.

Politicians try to persuade people to vote for them. Yet it is not always clear which route is being used—the central route or the peripheral route. Which route do you think politicians use most often?

The Message

Research shows that repeated exposure to a stimulus eventually results in a more favorable attitude toward that stimulus. For example, studies have found that people respond more favorably to abstract art (Heingartner & Hall, 1974) or classical music (Smith & Dorfman, 1975) after being repeatedly exposed to it.

Advertisers, political candidates, and others who want to persuade people use repetition to encourage people to adopt a favorable attitude toward their product or ideas. Many television commercials are repeated over and over so that potential consumers will react favorably to the products—and buy them—when they see these items in the store. One might think that such repetition would offend or annoy viewers (and to some extent it does), but research suggests that commercials are more effective when they are repeated regularly (Haugtvedt et al., 1994). Similarly, political candidates who appear regularly in television commercials tend to receive more votes than candidates who appear less often in commercials (Grush, 1980).

TRUTH *OR* **fiction** ▪ REVISITED ▪ *It is not true that showing television commercials over and over reduces their effectiveness. In fact, studies have shown that the more often a commercial is repeated, the more likely it is to be persuasive.*

In addition to being presented frequently, the persuasive message can be presented in ways that are especially effective. Two-sided arguments tend to be more effective than one-sided arguments, especially when the audience is uncertain about its position on the issue (Jacks & Devine, 2000). Emotional appeals are also very effective.

Two-Sided Arguments One of the most persuasive types of messages is the **two-sided argument**, in which people present not only their side of the argument but also the opposition's side. The purpose is to discredit the opposition's views. For example, a cereal advertiser admits that its brand of cereal is not as sweet as competing brands and then explains how the less sweet taste is evidence that the product is more nutritious. Admitting weaknesses in this way also makes the message seem more honest (Bridgwater, 1982).

Caption Question: Answer

Students' answers should demonstrate that they understand the distinction between the central and peripheral routes. Ask students to provide examples and reasoning to justify which route they think politicians use more frequently.

⎘ internet connect

TOPIC: Persuasion
GO TO: go.hrw.com
KEYWORD: SY3 PS20
Have students access the Internet through the HRW Go site to research methods of persuasion and overcoming bias. Then have students design a series of advertisements that account for factors in persuasion such as emotional appeals, situation patterns, and the interplay among the message, messenger, and audience. Encourage students to share their advertisements with the class.

Teaching Section 2

Demonstration

Have students locate and bring to class examples of advertisements that demonstrate the elements of persuasion discussed in the section, such as two-sided arguments and the use of persuasive "messengers." Have students present their examples in class and explain the techniques used in each *(Possible example: a car ad that includes an endorsement by a former race car driver who is portrayed as an automotive expert).* Then organize the class into groups, and have each group design a campaign to persuade potential school dropouts to stay in school.

Closing Section 2

Analyzing Ideas

Bring to class a print message related to an emotional issue, such as food and clothing drives to help homeless people during the holidays. Have students analyze the elements (both verbal and visual) of the emotional appeal. Ask students how such appeals affect them.

Reviewing Section 2

Have students complete the Section Review questions on page 465.

Emotional Appeals   Another effective way to present a persuasive message is to appeal to the audience's emotions. **Emotional appeals** persuade by arousing such feelings as loyalty, desire, or fear rather than by convincing through evidence and logic. Thus, an emotional appeal is a peripheral route in persuasion.

Arousing fear is a particularly effective method of persuasion. Smokers are more likely to be convinced to quit smoking, for example, when they are presented with frightening photos of blackened lungs rather than dry, unemotional statistics on lung cancer. In general, appeals based on fear tend to be most effective when they are strong, when the audience believes them, and when the audience believes it can avoid the danger by changing its behavior (Eagly & Chaiken, 1993).

The Messenger

Some people are more persuasive than others. Research (Hennigan et al., 1982; Mackie et al., 1990; Wilder, 1990) shows that people are persuasive if they are

- experts. This makes the audience more likely to follow their advice.
- trustworthy. This makes the audience more likely to believe what they say.
- physically attractive. This makes the audience more likely to pay attention to them.
- similar to their audience in ethnicity, age, and other physical characteristics. People are more likely to imitate others who appear similar to themselves.

Messengers who stand to gain from their persuasive efforts are less likely than others to be effective. For example, if the president of a company says his or her company's product is the best one on the market, people are generally less likely to be persuaded by his or her arguments.

The Situation

When a person is in a good mood, he or she is less likely to evaluate messages carefully (Petty et al., 1991; Schwarz et al., 1991). As a result, people tend to be more receptive to persuasion when they are feeling good. Thus, putting people in a good mood—with a compliment, for example—tends to boost the acceptance of persuasive messages.

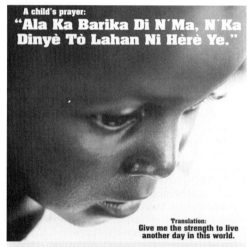

A child's prayer:
"Ala Ka Barika Di N´Ma, N´Ka Dinyè Tò Lahan Ni Hèrè Ye."

Translation:
Give me the strength to live another day in this world.

Advertisements such as this one are meant to appeal to the emotions of the audience rather than to convince them through logic.

The Audience

Most messages are aimed at a specific audience. A political candidate is trying to reach the voters in his or her district, for example. Differences in age, sex, and other characteristics of the intended audience influence how the message should be delivered to be most persuasive. Emotional appeals may work better with children, for example, whereas logic may be more effective with adults (Kunkel & Roberts, 1991).

Saying No to Persuasive Messages

Some people are less easily persuaded than others. For example, some people have developed an attitude called **sales resistance**. People possessing sales resistance have no trouble turning down requests to buy products or services. Other people have little or no sales resistance. They find it difficult to refuse a sales pitch or other types of requests.

Research suggests that two personality factors may be involved in sales resistance—self-esteem and social anxiety (Rhodes & Wood, 1992; Santee & Maslach, 1982). People who find it easy to refuse requests tend to have high self-esteem and low social anxiety. They believe in themselves, stand up for what they want, and are not overly concerned about what other people think of them.

People who find it difficult to say no, on the other hand, are likely to have lower self-esteem and

Section Objective

▶ Identify causes of prejudice and ways that it can be overcome.

This objective is assessed in the Section Review on page 468 and in the Chapter 20 Review.

Motivator

Write the term *prejudice* on the chalkboard. Give students a minute or two to jot down words or images that this term brings to mind. Then ask students to explain how prejudice relates to social cognition and to speculate on how being the focus of prejudice affects people's daily lives and the way in which they view themselves and others. Tell students that in Section 3 they will learn about the causes of prejudice and how prejudice can be overcome.

greater social anxiety. They may worry what salespeople will think of them, for example, or be concerned that the people requesting donations will be insulted if they refused to give. Such people may also believe they should help others rather than act self-centered (Schwartz & Gottman, 1976).

People with low self-esteem and high social anxiety are likely to be easily persuaded in situations other than sales and donations. For example, they may be more easily persuaded to engage in activities that go against their attitudes, beliefs, and values, such as using alcohol or other drugs.

SECTION 2 REVIEW

Homework Practice Online
go.hrw.com
Keyword: SY3 HP20

1. In what ways does persuasion affect people's attitudes and behavior?

2. What characteristics would you expect to find in an individual with sales resistance?

3. **Critical Thinking** *Categorizing* List the different types of advertising, and give examples of ways an advertiser might use persuasion to sell a car.

SECTION 3

Prejudice

A type of attitude that causes a great deal of harm is prejudice. **Prejudice**—a generalized attitude toward a specific group of people—literally means "prejudgment." People who are prejudiced judge other people on the basis of their group membership rather than as individuals. People who are prejudiced may decide, for example, that one person is deceitful because he or she belongs to a particular ethnic group or that another person is highly intelligent because that individual belongs to another ethnic group. Prejudicial attitudes such as these are based on stereotypes.

Stereotypes

Stereotypes are unchanging, oversimplified, and usually distorted beliefs about groups of people. People tend to develop or adopt stereotypes as a way to organize information about their social world (Azar, 2002; Langlois et al., 2000). Stereotypes make it easier for people to interpret the behavior of others, even though the interpretations

For decades, black South Africans were discriminated against by the ruling white minority. A series of political reforms in the early 1990s, however, brought about the official end of apartheid. By mid 1994, black South Africans were able for the first time to vote in elections.

are often wrong. For example, if we expect an older man to be sexist because a sexist attitude is part of our stereotype of older males, then we are more likely to interpret his words and deeds as sexist.

Another reason people tend to develop stereotypes is because they assume that those who are different from themselves are similar to each other in many ways (Mussweiler & Bodenhausen, 2002). Traits seen in some members of a group are incorrectly assumed to characterize all members of the group. An Asian American may think, for example, that all European Americans or all African Americans have similar personality traits, behavior patterns, or attitudes.

Stereotypes are harmful because they ignore people's individual natures and assign traits to them on the basis of the groups to which they belong. One of the many problems with stereotyping is that the traits assigned are usually negative. However, stereotypes can also include positive traits—such as the belief that members of a particular group are hard workers.

Stereotypes limit possibilities by discouraging the expression of the full range of an individual's talents, interests, and feelings. Even positive stereotypes can be harmful because they may put pressure on people to live up to unrealistic expectations.

Discrimination

Prejudice often leads to negative behavior in the form of discrimination. **Discrimination** refers to

Section 2 Review: Answers

1. Persuasion—through the central route and the peripheral route—can change people's attitudes and behavior.

2. An individual with sales resistance usually has high self-esteem and low social anxiety. The person is likely to believe in herself or himself, stand up for what she or he wants, and not be overly concerned with what other people think of her or him.

3. Examples may include the following: The advertiser may present evidence that the car gets better gas mileage than the competitor's car (central route), or the advertiser may attempt to associate its car with a positive cue, such as a successful businessperson or a well-known performer (peripheral route).

Teaching Section 3

Guided Practice

Guide students in creating on the chalkboard a flowchart that depicts the cause-and-effect relationships surrounding prejudice and discrimination. First draw a column of five boxes on the chalkboard, and to their right (centered on the column), write the term *Prejudice*. Next have volunteers fill in the boxes with the various causes of prejudice and draw arrows connecting the boxes with the term. Then ask other volunteers to complete the flowchart by depicting graphically the effects of prejudice. Have students discuss the flowchart.

Independent Practice

Tell students to imagine that they have been invited to address the assembly of a local elementary school on the causes and effects of prejudice. Have students use what they learned in the Guided Practice activity to write a draft of the speech they will present to the children at the elementary school. Caution students to keep in mind the vocabulary level of elementary school children. After students have completed their drafts, have volunteers "rehearse" their speeches by reading them aloud for the class.

Cross-Curricular Link: Literature

Suggest to students that they read Ralph Ellison's *Invisible Man*, Richard Wright's *Black Boy*, Anne Frank's *The Diary of a Young Girl*, or other classic works of literature that focus on prejudice and discrimination.

internet connect

TOPIC: Bias and Prejudice
GO TO: go.hrw.com
KEYWORD: SY3 PS20

Have students access the Internet through the HRW Go site to research the causes and types of discrimination, prejudice, and bias. Then have students create a theoretical profile that defines and gives examples of bias related to various points of view and outlines how and why prejudice occurs, how it manifests itself, and how it can be overcome.

the unfair treatment of individuals because they are members of a particular group. For example, people may be denied jobs, housing, voting privileges, or other rights because of their skin color, sex, or religion. Victims of discrimination may begin to see themselves as inferior. Thus, they are likely to have low self-esteem (Bohon et al., 1993). People with low self-esteem tend to have low expectations for themselves, thus reducing their chances for success.

Causes of Prejudice

Why are some people prejudiced and others are not? Psychologists and other researchers have studied the origins of prejudice and have found many potential causes.

Exaggerating Differences One reason some people are prejudiced is that they exaggerate how different others are from themselves. People tend to prefer (as friends and acquaintances) those who are similar to themselves and who share their attitudes. People who differ in one or several ways—in skin color or religion, for example—are often assumed to have attitudes and customs that are more different than they really are.

Justifying Economic Status People also tend to develop prejudice against those who are not in the same economic group. Those in higher socioeconomic groups often justify their own economic superiority by assuming that people who have a lower economic status are inferior to them. They may believe that people who are worse off than themselves work less hard or are less motivated to succeed. Such beliefs may be used as an excuse for—and thus help maintain—existing injustices.

Social Learning Children, like adults, acquire many attitudes from other people. They are especially likely to acquire the attitudes of their parents. Children tend to imitate their parents, and parents often reinforce their children when they do. In this way, parents who are prejudiced often pass along their prejudicial attitudes to their children.

Victimization Sometimes people who are the victims of prejudice feel empathy for others who are discriminated against. However, this is not always the case. In fact, some victims of prejudice try to gain a sense of power and pride by asserting their superiority over people that are even worse off than themselves (Van Brunt, 1994). Thus, victimization may lead to further prejudice.

It is not true that people who are victims of prejudice usually feel empathy for others who are victims of prejudice. Instead, they may discriminate against others in an effort to feel better about themselves.

Scapegoating A **scapegoat** is an individual or group that is blamed for the problems of others because the real cause of the problems is either too complex, too powerful, or too remote to be confronted. The term *scapegoating* refers to aggression against the group that has been made the target.

The scapegoat group is likely to have certain characteristics that make it a safe and highly visible target. Typically, scapegoats are people who are too weak to defend themselves or who choose not to return the attack. They are also likely to stand out because of their differences from majority groups.

Probably the best-known and most extreme example of scapegoating is the victimization of European Jews in the 1930s and 1940s. Nazi dictator Adolf Hitler blamed Jewish people for Germany's serious economic troubles. Under Hitler's leadership, millions of Jews were killed.

Intergroup contact can reduce feelings of prejudice by giving people the opportunity to work together and come to know each other as individuals.

CASE STUDIES
AND OTHER TRUE STORIES

To help students better comprehend W. E. B. Du Bois' story and its emotional impact, have them rewrite the story using contemporary words and phrasing. Have students read their versions aloud to a partner and make any necessary changes. Ask volunteers to read their final versions aloud. Then have students analyze why laws designed to end discrimination in a society do not always put an end to prejudice and injustice.

Demonstration

To demonstrate the effects of prejudice, tell students that new studies have shown that brown-eyed people are smarter than blue-eyed people and that students learn better when grouped by eye color. Then move brown-eyed students to one side of the room and blue-eyed people to the other side. Take every opportunity to call on and praise brown-eyed students and to criticize blue-eyed students. After 20 minutes, tell the class that such findings have not been made and explain the nature of the demonstration. Have volunteers from both groups describe how they felt.

CASE STUDIES
AND OTHER TRUE STORIES
Being Black in America

W. E. B. Du Bois was one of the most influential educators, writers, and social leaders in American history. A child of mixed European and African ancestry, he was born in Massachusetts in 1868, just five years after President Abraham Lincoln issued the Emancipation Proclamation.

After earning a Ph.D. from Harvard University, he became active in the movement to gain equality for African Americans and became a prominent member of the National Association for the Advancement of Colored People (NAACP). He died in 1963 at the height of the civil rights movement—a movement he helped to foster and one that inspired millions of Americans to call for equality and freedom.

In 1903 Du Bois published a classic work titled *The Souls of Black Folk.* The book is partly autobiographical, and in the following excerpt, Du Bois reveals how he felt when he first learned, as a schoolboy, that he was "different from the others" and "shut out from their world." The incident may seem trivial, but it had a profound effect on him for the rest of his life.

W. E. B. Du Bois

It is in the early days of rollicking boyhood that the revelation first bursts upon one, all in a day, as it were. I remember well when the shadow swept across me. I was a little thing, away up in the hills of New England. . . . In a wee wooden schoolhouse, something put it into the boys' and girls' heads to buy gorgeous visiting-cards—ten cents a package—and exchange. The exchange was merry, till one girl, a tall newcomer, refused my card. . . . Then it dawned upon me with a certain suddenness that I was different from the others; or like, mayhap, in heart and life and longing, but shut out from their world by a vast veil. I had thereafter no desire to tear down that veil, to creep through; I held all beyond it in common contempt, and lived above it in a region of blue sky and great wandering shadows. That sky was bluest when I could beat my mates at examination-time, or beat them at a foot-race. . . . Alas, with the years all this fine contempt began how to fade; for the words I longed for, and all their dazzling opportunities, were theirs, not mine. But they should not keep these prizes, I said; some, all, I would wrest from them. Just how I would do it I could never decide: by reading law, by healing the sick, by telling the wonderful tales that swam in my head—some way. With other black boys the strife was not so fiercely sunny: their youth shrank into tasteless sycophancy [fawning], or into silent hatred of the pale world about them and mocking distrust of everything white; or wasted itself in a bitter cry, Why did God make me an outcast and a stranger in mine own house?

The U.S. government has passed many laws against discrimination, and considerable progress in race relations has been achieved since Du Bois published *The Souls of Black Folk.* However, attitudes of racial prejudice still exist. The NAACP and other groups continue to work to eliminate discrimination in American society.

WHY PSYCHOLOGY MATTERS

Many Americans are working to end discrimination in society. Use **CNNfyi.com** or other current events sources to learn more about civil rights efforts. Create a poster illustrating these efforts.

CNNfyi.com

Primary Source Note

Description of Change: excerpted, bracketed

Rationale: excerpted to focus on main idea; bracketed to clarify meaning

Class Discussion

Allow students ample time to discuss the Demonstration activity. Did the brown-eyed students begin to feel superior to the blue-eyed students? Did the blue-eyed students begin to feel inferior, angry, or hurt? How might the self-images of the blue-eyed students be affected if they had to face this discrimination every day? What other harmful effects might such discrimination have?

Closing Section 3

Synthesizing Information

Have students write a short essay describing the damage that results from prejudice—both to the individuals against whom prejudice is directed and to society as a whole. Ask volunteers to read their essays aloud to the class for discussion.

Reviewing Section 3

Have students complete the Section Review questions on page 468.

Section 3 Review: Answers

1. Prejudice is a generalized negative attitude toward a specific group of people. Discrimination is unfair treatment of people because they are members of a particular group.

2. Causes include exaggerating differences between oneself and others, assuming others are inferior because they are not as well off as oneself, learning through observation and reinforcement, asserting one's superiority over those who are less well off, and scapegoating.

3. Possibilities include speaking out when others show prejudice, setting an example of tolerance for others, and working toward common goals in groups of people with various racial, gender, or ethnic backgrounds.

Journal Activity

Tell students to think about the people they consider to be their closest friends. Have students write in their journals about a time when they had an unfavorable first impression of one of these people but later changed their minds about that person and became good friends. What made students change their opinions?

468

4 Section Objective

▶ List factors that influence our perceptions of other people, and explain how people use various forms of nonverbal communication.

This objective is assessed in the Section Review on page 472 and in the Chapter 20 Review.

Overcoming Prejudice

Although prejudice is difficult to overcome, it can be done. Increased contact among members of different groups is one of the best ways for people to develop less prejudicial attitudes. For example, when people work together to achieve common goals, they are likely to learn about one another as individuals, and this may weaken the stereotypes.

On an individual level, one can reduce prejudice by speaking up when other people act or talk in ways that reflect prejudicial attitudes. Individuals can also set an example of tolerance and understanding for others by their own words and actions.

Finally, prejudicial attitudes do not have to lead to discriminatory behavior. A person who is prejudiced can make a conscious effort to treat other people courteously and fairly, regardless of the groups to which they belong. This, in turn, may help reduce the person's own prejudicial attitudes.

SECTION 3 REVIEW

Homework Practice Online
Keyword: SY3 HP20

1. Explain the difference between prejudice and discrimination.
2. Identify several causes of prejudice.
3. **Critical Thinking** *Summarizing* Identify three ways people can help reduce prejudice in their communities.

SECTION 4
Social Perception

Social perception refers to the ways in which people perceive one another. Social perception affects the attitudes people form toward others. For example, Marc believed that if he made a negative first impression on Linda's grandparents, it would be difficult to change their opinion of him later. He assumed that first impressions have a lasting effect on people's attitudes toward others. As you will see in this section, Marc was right.

Primacy and Recency Effects

People often wear their best clothes to job interviews. Likewise, defense attorneys encourage their clients to be well dressed when they are in the courtroom and within view of the jury. The reason? People think that their first impressions of other people are accurate (Gleitman et al., 1997), and first impressions are often based on how a person looks. The tendency for people to form opinions of others on the basis of first impressions is called the **primacy effect**.

First impressions are important because they may have lasting effects on our relationships with others. If our first impression of a new acquaintance is negative because the person appears to be self-centered, for example, then we are unlikely to want to know the person better. However, if our first impression is positive—the person seems friendly and interesting—then we are more likely to want to develop a relationship with that person.

How people interpret the future behavior of others is also influenced by their first impressions. For example, someone who impresses us as intelligent and well educated is more likely to be taken seriously in future encounters than someone who comes across as superficial and silly.

TRUTH OR fiction ▪ REVISITED ▪ *It is true that our first impressions of other people tend to have lasting effects on our relationships with them. This is because people often interpret another person's future behavior in light of their first impressions.*

The **recency effect** occurs when people change their opinions of others on the basis of recent interactions instead of holding on to their first impressions. This is what happened with Linda's parents and Marc. Linda's parents' first impression of him was of a rude and misbehaving six-year-old. After they got to know Marc as a teen, however, they saw him in a more positive light and changed their attitude toward him.

Attribution Theory

People often explain the behavior of others differently from the way in which they explain their own behavior. According to **attribution theory**, people tend to explain behavior in terms of either dispositional, or personality, factors or in terms of situational, or external, factors. For example, suppose you meet someone at a party who seems reluctant

PSYCHOLOGY
IN THE WORLD TODAY

Organize the class into groups. Have the members of each group work together to create and present a 60-second commercial on the harmful effects of prejudice and ways that prejudice can be overcome. Tell the groups that their commercials should contain both oral text and visual materials. After all presentations have been made, have students speculate on how a world without prejudice would be different from the world in which we now live.

Meeting Individual Needs: Auditory Learners

Have auditory learners work together to locate historical and contemporary quotations that focus on the need for tolerance of individual and group differences. Have these learners read the quotations aloud to the class and explain how the quotations speak against prejudice. Then have the class work in pairs to create their own quotations that could work to break down stereotypes and reduce prejudice.

PSYCHOLOGY
IN THE WORLD TODAY

What Can Be Done About Prejudice?

Prejudice is not just an abstract concept that affects people other than ourselves. Prejudice dwells within us. In fact, people are often unaware of their own prejudices because such attitudes tend to be deep-seated. Thus, overcoming prejudice can be difficult. What can you do to help reduce prejudice?

Speak Out Against Prejudice Even people who do not have feelings of prejudice themselves often do little to counter the prejudice of others. They may say nothing when they hear another person make a sexist joke or an ethnic slur. They may do nothing when their club or other organization denies admission to people of other racial or religious groups.

By saying and doing nothing when they encounter prejudice, people appear to be condoning, or excusing, the prejudicial words or actions. Therefore, it is important to speak out against prejudice as well as to show an attitude of tolerance in one's own words and actions.

Break Down Stereotypes Prejudice is based on stereotypes. Thus, one of the best ways to combat prejudice is to break down stereotypes. The more contact we have with people of other races, ethnic groups, or religions, the more aware we become that these groups are made up of individuals who are not only different from one another but also similar to ourselves in many ways. Through intergroup contact, we are likely to learn that people of the same skin color, for example, differ from one another in a variety of ways, including language, values, abilities, religious beliefs, and interests.

Intergroup contact is especially effective at breaking down stereotypes and reducing prejudicial attitudes when individuals work cooperatively to achieve common goals. Playing together on the same sports team, working together on a class project, or working side by side on the school yearbook are examples of cooperative efforts that can foster increased understanding and tolerance of others.

If individuals share similar backgrounds, intergroup contact is even more effective at breaking down stereotypes and reducing prejudice. People who have the same socioeconomic background, religious beliefs, or level of education, for example, are more likely to have the same values. Shared values, in turn, promote liking and openness toward others.

Intergroup contact is generally more effective when it is informal. Informal contacts, such as sitting together in the school cafeteria or hanging out together at the mall, encourage people to get to know one another as individuals. In contrast, more formal contacts, such as participating in the same class debate or attending the same religious service, allow people to maintain their distance from one another.

Brief contacts are also less likely to produce lasting changes in stereotypes and prejudicial attitudes than contacts that last longer periods of time. Chatting with a stranger on a bus, for example, is not likely to bring about a permanent change in attitudes toward the group that the stranger represents. However, working in chemistry lab throughout the school year with a lab partner who belongs to a different group may better break down stereotypes and reduce prejudice in society.

Combat Discrimination Even when people's attitudes of prejudice cannot be changed, it is still possible to combat discrimination. Discrimination on the basis of sex, religion, race, or disability is against the law. Thus, people who are discriminated against can seek legal remedies to stop the discrimination.

Think About It

Analyzing Information Give examples of ways not mentioned in the feature that students might work together in or out of school to break down their own stereotypes and reduce their prejudices toward others.

Think About It: Answer

Answers will vary, but students should discuss ways that they can overcome their own prejudice toward others by breaking down the stereotypes that they hold.

Technology Resources

 CNN. Presents Psychology: School Violence Prevention Programs

Opening Section 4

Motivator

Ask students if they sometimes think that others have the wrong impression of them or that they have misjudged other people. Explain that both of these problems stem from faulty social perception. Read aloud the definition of the term *social perception* on page 468. Then tell students that after reading Section 4, they will have a better understanding of how social perception works.

Teaching Section 4

Cooperative Learning

Have pairs of students conduct an experiment in first impressions. Have them go together to a public place, such as a library or shopping mall. Instruct one member of each pair to dress in an outfit that would look very neat and attractive to adults and the other member to dress in a way that looks messy and unkempt. Tell the pairs to singly approach librarians or other people, seeking help or information. Have them note and record the adults' reactions. Ask students to share and discuss their findings in class.

Caption Question: Answer

Students will probably say that they would be more likely to pick up the professionally dressed man because he looks better able to pay his fare.

What's New in Psychology?

A recent study by Dartmouth University psychologists Carol Barr and Robert Kleck suggests that a common problem in social perception is that individuals tend to think that their facial expressions communicate far more emotion than they actually do. One partner in a couple may think he or she is signaling disgust or annoyance to the other when in fact his or her face has not revealed that at all. The discrepancy between what we think our faces show and what they actually show seems greater for negative emotion. Fortunately, people can more effectively communicate through facial expression when they consciously work at it.

Barr, C., & Kleck, R. (Sept./Oct. 1995). Do we know what we show? *Psychology Today*. 14.

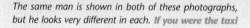

The same man is shown in both of these photographs, but he looks very different in each. **If you were the taxi** **driver, whom would you be more likely to pick up? How does this relate to the concept of social perception?**

to talk to other people. You may assume that this person is either shy or conceited. This would be a dispositional attribution. On the other hand, you may assume that this person is usually friendly but simply does not know anyone at the party. This would be a situational attribution.

Actor-Observer Bias For the most part, people tend to attribute the behavior of others to dispositional, or internal, factors and to attribute their own behavior to situational, or external, factors. This tendency is called the **actor-observer bias** (Jellison & Green, 1981). Actor-observer bias occurs because we tend to judge others only by the behavior we witness, and people's behavior may not always be a true reflection of their personalities.

Suppose you observe a stranger acting in a rude manner. If this is your only encounter with the person, you are likely to assume that the stranger has a rude disposition—that is, that he or she is a rude person. In most other situations, however, the same person might behave in a very polite fashion. Observing the stranger in most other situations, then, would lead to the assumption that he or she has a polite, respectful disposition. This may in fact be the case. The person might have acted rudely only because of the circumstances. For example, perhaps the person was provoked.

Fundamental Attribution Error The tendency to overestimate the effect of dispositional causes for another person's behavior, and to underestimate the effect of situational causes, is referred to as the **fundamental attribution error**. It is a common mistake that affects many of our interactions with other people. To further understand this concept, look at the photographs on page 471. If you observed this teenager in only one situation you might assume that she was either an extremely helpful person or a very rude person. That is, you might commit a fundamental attribution error and overlook or misinterpret the true causes of her behavior.

Self-Serving Bias People are more likely to attribute their own successes to dispositional, or personality, factors. They are also more likely to attribute their failures to situational factors (Campbell & Sedihides, 1999; Duval & Silvia, 2002). This is called a **self-serving bias**. The self-serving bias allows individuals to place the blame for their failures on circumstances outside their control. At the same time, however, it enables them to take full credit for their successes.

If Hannah's scholarship interview is a success, for example, she may attribute it to the fact that she is talented

A DAY IN THE LIFE

Taking a Stand

Have students consider whether a self-serving bias is primarily a healthy/positive perspective or a harmful/negative perspective. Encourage them to think of specific scenarios that support their point of view and to share these scenarios with the class. Then have volunteers for each point of view debate the question. Following the debate, have students discuss why individuals tend to attribute their own failures to situational factors and to attribute other people's failures to dispositional factors.

Role-Playing

Organize the class into small groups. Tell the members of each group that they are to write and perform a short skit in which the nonverbal communication being expressed in an interaction differs greatly from the verbal communication being expressed. Students may wish to focus on an interaction between parents and their child, between strangers in a social situation, or among a group of friends. After each group has presented its skit, have the class explain the disparity between the two forms of communication.

and motivated. If, on the other hand, the interview goes badly, she may attribute it to circumstances beyond her control—perhaps she had a headache that day, or the interviewer was in a bad mood.

Nonverbal Communication

It is not only what people say and do but how they say and do it that influences our perceptions of them. Forms of nonverbal, or unspoken, communication include facial expressions, gestures, posture, and the distance we keep from others. These and other forms of "body language" affect our perceptions of people, largely because they often indicate feelings. Feelings of sympathy or anger, for example, may be inferred from a concerned look or frown.

Some nonverbal forms of communication are learned early. Even young children can "read" a tone of voice, a facial expression, or other forms of non-verbal communication. Thus, before they understand all the words their parents are speaking, they can tell from nonverbal communication how their parents are feeling (Saarni, 1990).

Without necessarily being aware of it, people use nonverbal communication to send messages to other people (Patterson, 1991). They may even use nonverbal communication to mask their true feelings (DePaulo, 1992). For example, a parent who wishes to hide his fear or worry from his child might use nonverbal forms of communication, such as smiles and a relaxed bearing, to convince the child that all is well.

Physical Contact Touching is one way in which people communicate nonverbally. However, not all people use physical contact to communicate with others. For example, American women are more likely than American men to touch the people with whom they are interacting (Stier & Hall, 1984). There is also considerable cultural variation in the use of touch to communicate with others.

Touching can be an effective means of communication. In one experiment, college students who had filled out several personality questionnaires were asked by the experimenter to stay and help in another study. Students who were touched during the request were more likely to help in the subsequent study (Powell et al., 1994). In another study, waitresses received larger tips when they touched customers on the hand or shoulder while making change (Crusco & Wetzel, 1984).

A study in a nursing home found that the ways in which people respond to touch depend on many factors. In the study, whether touching was responded to favorably or unfavorably depended on the status of the staff member doing the touching, the type of touch, and the part of the body that was touched. Touching was not appreciated when it was inappropriate or forceful (Hollinger & Buschmann, 1993).

Eye Contact People can learn a great deal about the feelings of others from eye contact. When someone who is talking looks directly into the eyes of the

How do you think first impressions of this teen might vary from one situation to another?

471

Closing Section 4

Applying Ideas

Have students work in small groups to write short stories or plays that dramatize the topics covered in this section. Then have the groups annotate their creations with explanations of what phenomenon (e.g., eye contact, primacy effect) they are illustrating.

Reviewing Section

Have students complete the Section Review questions on page 472.

Extension

Have students observe nonverbal communication in a variety of situations. Some might observe the behavior of friends and family members, while others might conduct observations of strangers in public places. Students should produce written records and detailed evaluations of what they have observed. Have volunteers report their findings to the class for discussion.

Panel 1: DAGWOOD'S REALLY BEEN UNDER A LOT OF PRESSURE AT HIS OFFICE LATELY

Panel 2: AND WE HAVE SOME MAJOR REPAIR BILLS DUE ON THE HOUSE

Panel 3: IT'S NO WONDER THE POOR DEAR LOOKS SO WORRIED

Panel 4: BOY, I CAN'T DECIDE WHETHER TO MAKE A HAM AND CHEESE ON RYE OR EAT THE LEFTOVERS

Source: BLONDIE reprinted with special permission of King Features Syndicate.

listener, for example, the talker is usually telling the truth. Avoidance of eye contact, on the other hand, may indicate that the talker is lying. This is why a message is more believable and persuasive when the messenger makes eye contact with the audience.

One type of eye contact is gazing, or looking at someone with a steady, intent look that conveys eagerness or attention. Gazing usually is interpreted as a sign of liking or friendliness, and it may greatly influence relationships (Kleinke, 1986).

Another type of eye contact is staring, or looking fixedly with wide-open eyes. Staring is usually interpreted as a sign of anger. Being the object of staring makes most people uncomfortable, and they may try to avoid the stare. For example, one study found that drivers who were stared at by other drivers at an intersection crossed the intersection faster when the light changed (Ellsworth et al., 1972).

Whether or not they are aware of it, most people send unspoken messages that can greatly influence how other people see them. Thus, becoming more aware of nonverbal communication can increase our understanding of others.

SECTION 4 REVIEW

go. hrw .com **Homework Practice Online** Keyword: SY3 HP20

1. List several factors that influence perceptions of other people.

2. Define *fundamental attribution error.*

3. **Critical Thinking** *Analyzing Information* Think about a recent interaction you had with another person. What forms of nonverbal communication did you, or the other person, use to convey thoughts or feelings?

SECTION 5
Interpersonal Attraction

Attraction is a kind of attitude—an attitude of liking. Attraction to another person often leads to friendship or love. Factors that attract us to particular people as potential friends or partners include physical appearance, similarity to ourselves, and evidence that our attraction is returned.

Physical Appearance

Physical appearance tends to influence our choice of friends and partners. What qualities make someone physically attractive? There is no single answer. Some people find blond hair most attractive; others may prefer black hair. Some people may find a slim body build most attractive, while others may prefer a more muscular build. Clearly, people's ideas of attractiveness differ.

Universals of Beauty Although there is variation among people in the types of traits they consider attractive, some aspects of attractiveness appear to be widely shared or even universal. For example, a smiling person is generally perceived to be more attractive than a person who is frowning (Reis et al., 1990).

Studies have also found that certain types of facial features are attractive to most people. In one study, both British and Japanese people were asked to identify the types of features they found most attractive in women. People from both cultures identified large eyes, high cheekbones, and narrow jaws as the most attractive types of facial features (Perrett et al., 1994).

▶ Describe the role of attraction in friendships and love relationships.

This objective is assessed in the Section Review on page 475 and in the Chapter 20 Review.

Opening Section 5

Motivator

Work with students to brainstorm a list of sayings about interpersonal attraction. Examples include "Opposites attract" and "Absence makes the heart grow fonder." Write the sayings on the chalkboard. Explain that while there is always some mystery about why certain people are attracted to each other, psychologists have discovered certain generalizations about the factors that underlie interpersonal attraction. These factors are the focus of Section 5.

Another study investigated the kinds of faces that infants find most attractive (Langlois, 1994). This was judged by the amount of time the infants spent looking at the faces of strangers—the longer the gaze, the greater the presumed attraction. As early as the age of two months, infants in the study seemed to prefer faces that were also rated by adults as most attractive. This evidence suggests that we do not "learn" what is attractive by being socialized in a particular culture. Other research, however, indicates that people do learn what features are considered attractive.

Differences in Body Shape Preference
Although preferences for certain facial features may be universal, preferences for body shape vary greatly (Etcoff, 1994). There is, in fact, a great deal of variation in people's standard for attractiveness of body shape—both in the shape we prefer in others and the shape we perceive ourselves as having.

This was demonstrated in a study of college men and women (Fallon & Rozin, 1985). The men in the study tended to believe their own body shape closely approached the "ideal" shape that women find attractive. However, the women tended to believe that they were heavier than the "ideal" shape men find attractive.

The results of this study are important. They suggest that females are more likely than males to incorrectly think they are too heavy to be attractive. Not surprisingly, women are more likely than men to go on weight-loss diets, and they have far higher rates of eating disorders. (See Chapter 11.)

Evidence suggests that in the United States, many men prefer their partners to be shorter than themselves, whereas many women prefer their partners to be taller (Goode, 2000; Hensley, 1994). On the job as well as in relationships, tallness tends to be perceived as an asset for men, whereas height in women tends to have less impact on their jobs (Pierce, 1996; Wade et al., 2000).

This is not to say, however, that physical appearance will determine an individual's ability to succeed on the job or in relationships. The initial attraction one feels for another person may be based on the person's physical appearance. However, other traits usually become more important as people get to know one another better. Traits such as honesty, loyalty, warmth, and sensitivity tend to be more important than physical appearance in forming and maintaining long-term relationships.

Similarity and Reciprocity

You may be familiar with the saying "Birds of a feather flock together." This saying suggests that we are usually attracted to people who are like us. On the other hand, another popular saying asserts "Opposites attract." Which of these two contradictory statements is true? Generally speaking, the answer is that we are more attracted to people who are like us.

Similarity in Physical Attractiveness According to the **matching hypothesis**, people tend to choose as friends and partners those who are similar to themselves in attractiveness (Feingold, 1988b). One reason for this may be the fear of rejection—the belief that someone more attractive will not be interested in them (Bernstein et al., 1983).

Using Visuals

Have students rate the attractiveness of the people in the four photographs on this page. Then have them analyze the reasons for their ratings. Are there specific features they find especially attractive or unattractive? Do any of the people remind them of someone they know and like or dislike? Do the students tend to rate as most attractive the person who most closely resembles themselves?

Class Discussion

Help students link past and present learning by asking them to relate balance theory, which they learned about in Chapter 13, to the concept of reciprocity. How does the notion of reciprocity support the theory?

Although conceptions of beauty vary from culture to culture, studies have shown that certain aspects of attractiveness appear to be widely shared or even universal.

Teaching Section 5

Cooperative Learning

To help students understand the concept of reciprocity, have pairs of students try the following experiment. Suggest that they go to a variety of public places—libraries, stores, malls—and ask for assistance or service. Tell them to act friendly in some situations and cold and demanding in others. As they record their experiences, have them describe their own behavior in each situation and also note how friendly or responsive each potential "helper" was. Have volunteers describe evidence of reciprocity to the class.

Predicting Outcomes

Before students read about love on pages 474 and 475, have them reflect on the nature of "being in love" and speculate about the components of love that psychologist Robert Sternberg has identified in his triangular model. Then have students read the section on love and examine Figure 20.2 and compare Sternberg's model with their own. Which types of love depicted in Sternberg's model are likely to characterize long-term marriages? Why?

Journal Activity

Have students write about the characteristics they find most attractive in a friend and those they find most attractive in a potential mate. When they finish writing, ask students to discuss whether their two sets of characteristics are fairly similar or whether they look for different qualities in a romantic relationship than in a friendship.

Essay and Research Themes for A. P. Students

Theme 17

Cross-Curricular Link: Music

Have students examine the seven types of love relationships depicted in Figure 20.2. Then have students choose one of these relationships and write a song that illustrates the components of the relationship. Ask volunteers to perform their songs for the class, and have students determine which type of relationship is depicted in each song.

474

People are more likely to form relationships with people who are similar to themselves than with those who differ in terms of level of attractiveness, age, and level of education.

Similarity in Other Characteristics   People's friends and partners also tend to be similar to them in race, ethnicity, age, level of education, and religion (Michael et al., 1994). One reason we choose friends and partners with backgrounds that are similar to our own is that we tend to live among people who are similar to ourselves. Thus, these are the people we are most likely to meet, to know, to date, and possibly to marry (Michael et al., 1994).

Another reason people tend to choose friends and partners with similar backgrounds is that such people often have similar attitudes as well—and people tend to be attracted to others with attitudes similar to their own. In fact, similarity of attitudes is a key contributor to attraction in both friendships and romantic relationships (Cappella & Palmer, 1990; Laumann et al., 1994). Attitudes toward religion and children tend to be the most important factors in people's attraction to potential partners (Singh & Ho, 2000; Watson et al., 2000).

TRUTH OR fiction
■ REVISITED ■

It is not true that when it comes to choosing a partner or friend, "opposites attract." People are more likely to choose as partners—and also as friends—people who are similar to themselves in many ways.

Reciprocity   When we have feelings of attraction or affection for another person, we want that person to return those feelings. **Reciprocity** is the mutual exchange of feelings or attitudes. It applies to situations in which the person we like likes us back. In other words, our feelings are returned, or reciprocated. Like similarity, reciprocity is a powerful contributor to feelings of attraction (Sprecher, 1998).

Reciprocity of feelings is a major factor in forming romantic relationships, but it may also apply to casual encounters. Research shows that people are more open, warm, and helpful when they are talking with strangers who seem to like them (Clark et al., 1989; Curtis & Miller, 1986).

Friendship

Friends are people for whom one has affection, respect, and trust. Most people value friends because of the rewards that friendship offers. For example, friends are concerned about one another and help and support one another when they can. As friendships develop, people may evaluate, consciously or unconsciously, how well the relationship is providing the rewards they seek in the friendship.

The people we choose as friends tend to be people with whom we have frequent contact—a next-door neighbor or a student who sits beside us in class. The people we find attractive and the people who approve of us are the people we are likely to choose as friends. In addition, they are likely to be similar to us in important ways, such as in attitudes, in values, and often in their selection of other friends (Gonzales et al., 1983).

Love

The word *love* is used in everyday life in numerous ways. Love refers to the feelings of attachment that exist between children and their parents. Love also refers to feelings of patriotism for one's country or to feelings of passion about strongly held values such as freedom. Most commonly, however, love refers to the feelings of mutual attraction, affection, and attachment shared by people who are "in love."

To better understand the relationships of people in love, psychologist Robert Sternberg (1988) developed the **triangular model of love**, shown in Figure 20.2. As defined in the figure, Sternberg identifies seven types of love relationships, each of which is characterized by at least one of three components: intimacy, passion, or commitment.

Intimacy refers to closeness and caring. It is reflected by mutual concern and by the sharing of

Closing Section 5

For Further Research

Have interested students conduct further research into the subject of interpersonal attraction. Some students may wish to focus on the analyses of the subject found in traditional approaches to psychology, such as the Freudian approach. Others may wish to look into the latest research on the biological basis of attraction, such as the influence of human pheromones. Students should summarize their findings and present them orally in class.

Evaluating Ideas

Have students write a few paragraphs about whether or not their experiences with friendships and love relationships support the information provided in this section. Ask volunteers to read their paragraphs aloud.

Reviewing Section 5

Have students complete the Section Review questions on page 475.

The Triangular Model of Love

Liking
Intimacy Alone
(true friendships without passion
or long-term commitment)

Intimacy

Romantic Love
Intimacy + Passion
(lovers physically and emotionally attracted to each other but
without commitment, as in a
summer romance)

Companionate Love
Intimacy + Commitment
(long-term committed friendship such as a marriage in
which the passion has faded)

Consummate Love
Intimacy + Passion + Commitment
(a complete love consisting of all three
components—an ideal difficult to attain)

Passion

Commitment

Infatuation
Passion Alone
(passionate, obsessive
love at first sight without
intimacy or commitment)

Fatuous Love
Passion + Commitment
(commitment based on passion
but without time for intimacy to
develop; shallow relationship
such as a whirlwind courtship)

Empty Love
Commitment Alone
(decision to love each
other without intimacy
or passion)

FIGURE 20.2 *Robert Sternberg believes that love rela-
tionships are characterized by at least one of three components: intimacy, passion, or commitment. Consummate love combines all three components.*

feelings and resources. **Passion** refers to feelings of romantic and sexual attraction. In addition to verbal expressions of love, passion is reflected by many types of nonverbal communication, such as gazing, hugging, and kissing. **Commitment** refers to a couple's recognition that they are "in love" and want to be together, "for better or for worse." According to Sternberg (1988), consummate (or complete) love is an ideal that is difficult to attain and that is characterized by all three components.

Most couples start out with feelings of physical attraction that may develop into passion. If they are compatible, their intimacy and passion may grow. Eventually, they may decide to make a commitment to each other. Thus, from dating, to a steady relationship, to marriage, love changes as our

relationships endure, deepen, and become a more important part of our lives.

SECTION 5 REVIEW

go.
hrw
.com
**Homework
Practice
Online**
Keyword: SY3 HP20

1. How does physical attractiveness influence one's choice of friends and partners?
2. Why are most people attracted to people who are similar to themselves?
3. **Critical Thinking** *Evaluating* If you were to create a triangular model of friendship similar to the triangular model of love shown in Figure 20.2, what components of friendship would you think should make up the three corners of the triangle?

Chapter 20 REVIEW AND ASSESSMENT RESOURCES

Technology
► Chapter 20 Test Generator (on the One-Stop Planner)
► HRW Go site

Reinforcement, Review, and Assessment
► Chapter 20 Review, pp. 476–477
► Chapter Review and Activities with Answer Key
► Alternative Assessment Handbook
► Portfolio Assessment Handbook
► Chapter 20 Test (Form A or B)

PSYCHOLOGY PROJECTS

Linking to Community Invite someone who works in advertising, public relations, or human resources to the classroom to discuss how psychological insights into social cognition affect his or her daily work. Encourage students to prepare a list of questions that apply what they have learned

---

7. tendency of people to form opinions of others on the basis of first impressions

8. theory stating that people tend to explain the behavior of others in terms of dispositional factors or in terms of situational factors

9. the tendency to overestimate the effect of dispositional causes for another's behavior

10. a couple's recognition that they are in love and want to be together "for better or for worse"

Understanding Main Ideas

1. They are persistent beliefs that shape the ways that people see the world and interpret events.

2. Cognitive anchors are a person's earliest attitudes, which remain persistent throughout life.

3. Two-sided arguments tend to be more persuasive because they give one the opportunity to discredit an opponent's views; also, they seem more honest.

4. Prejudice, or a generalized attitude toward a specific group of people, often is based on stereotypes, or unchanging, oversimplified, and distorted beliefs.

5. An example might be attributing the trait of rudeness to someone who is generally polite but acts uncharacteristically rude the one time he or she is observed.

6. Reciprocity is the return of attraction and affection.

Thinking Critically

1. Students should give reasons why the slogans are effective, such as logical presentation, the use of an

476

Chapter 20 REVIEW

Writing a Summary

Using standard grammar, spelling, sentence structure, and punctuation, summarize the information in this chapter. Consider:
• how attitudes develop, and how persuasion affects attitudes and behavior
• the causes of prejudice, and factors that influence perceptions of people
• the role of attraction in friendships and romantic relationships

Identifying People and Ideas

Identify the following terms or people and use them in appropriate sentences.

1. attitude
2. cognitive evaluation
3. central route
4. sales resistance
5. scapegoat
6. social perception
7. primacy effect
8. attribution theory
9. fundamental attribution error
10. commitment

Understanding Main Ideas

SECTION 1 (pp. 460–462)
1. Summarize the relationship between attitudes and behavior.
2. What are cognitive anchors?

SECTION 2 (pp. 462–465)
3. Why are two-sided arguments generally more persuasive than one-sided arguments?

SECTION 3 (pp. 465–468)
4. What is the relationship between prejudice and stereotyping?

SECTION 4 (pp. 468–472)
5. What is an example of actor-observer bias?

SECTION 5 (pp. 472–475)
6. What is reciprocity?

Thinking Critically

1. **Making Generalizations and Predictions** What are several ways that advertising slogans might be effective in reinforcing or changing people's attitudes about a product or service?

2. **Analyzing Information** Using a central route and then a peripheral route, give examples of how you might persuade a friend to join you in a walk-a-thon for a good cause.

3. **Drawing Inferences and Conclusions** Why might interpreting events with a self-serving bias boost a person's self-esteem?

4. **Supporting a Point of View** Do you think that the saying "Beauty is in the eye of the beholder" is true? Explain your answer.

Writing About Psychology

1. **Summarizing** Go to the library to learn more about how a cultural group's perspectives can be affected by the group's traditional physical environment. Then create a visual that outlines what you have learned. Be sure to include captions for your visual.

2. **Evaluating** Over the next few days, collect examples of nonverbal communication you observe in other people. For each example, write a brief description of the feelings that were expressed. Also note whether the feelings were consistent with the people's words and whether it was the spoken or the unspoken message that seemed to make a greater impact on the recipient of the message. Share what you have learned from your observations in a brief report. Use the graphic organizer below to help you write your report.

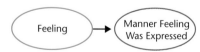

Feeling → Manner Feeling Was Expressed

in this chapter to the speaker's specialty. For example, if the guest works in the field of human resources, students might ask how a job applicant might go about creating a good first impression.

Cooperative Learning

Organize students into small groups. Have them design projects that examine the influence of social cognition on teen behavior. Areas of focus might be race relations in high school or parent-teen communication. Possible methods of research might include surveying their friends and discussing their own experiences. Have students set specific goals for their learning experiences, and ask that they create a product—such as a videotaped discussion or an oral report—through which to present their research findings.

Building Social Studies Skills

Interpreting Graphs

Study the bar graph below. Then use the information in the graph to help you answer the questions that follow.

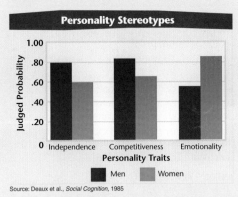

Personality Stereotypes

Judged Probability

Independence   Competitiveness   Emotionality

Personality Traits

■ Men   ■ Women

Source: Deaux et al., *Social Cognition*, 1985

1. Which of the following best reflects the information in the graph?
   a. People tend to believe that men are more emotional than women.
   b. People tend to believe that men are more likely to be competitive than women.
   c. People tend to believe that women are more likely to be independent than men.
   d. People tend to believe that women are more likely to be competitive than men.
2. How might a psychologist use this information when studying how people perceive other people?

Analyzing Primary Sources

Read the following excerpt, which discusses how children's interaction with other people affects how often the children smile. Then answer the questions that follow.

"Experience will do more than direct the smile; it will also determine its frequency. Experiments have shown that infants who receive no social stimulation after smiling, such as an adult's approving gaze, will begin smiling less often, somewhat in the manner of rats that stop their bar-pressing after the rewards cease. And infants raised in environments with inadequate social stimulation, such as foundling homes, will smile much less at 8 months or a year than will infants raised in middle-class homes. Nonetheless, the appearance of a reliable social smile by about 3 months of age is affected very little by learning. Maturation initiates, after which experience can differentiate."

3. What does the author mean by "maturation initiates, after which experience can differentiate"?
   a. A child's experiences have little effect on whether he or she smiles often.
   b. Whether a child smiles often is dictated by heredity.
   c. Most children learn a social smile as infants, but how often they smile later in life is affected by their experiences.
   d. Little is known about why some children smile more often than others.
4. What does the quote suggest about how experience might affect the way a person interacts with others?

"authority" to deliver the message, or frequent repetition.

2. Students may point out the importance of raising money for this cause (central route) and how much fun it will be to walk with their friends (peripheral route).

3. Interpreting events with a self-serving bias might lead to higher self-esteem because it means people are blaming circumstances rather than themselves for their failures.

4. Students may say that they agree because people's opinions vary in regard to the traits that they find attractive; for example, after you get to know someone better, he or she may become more beautiful in your eyes.

Writing About Psychology

1. Students' visuals should reflect an understanding of how a cultural group's perspectives can be affected by the group's traditional physical environment.

2. Students' reports should demonstrate an awareness of the various forms of nonverbal communication (touch, gesture, facial expression, and so on) and should analyze the congruence or disparity between the nonverbal and verbal cues they observed.

Building Social Studies Skills

1. b
2. This information should help psychologists be aware that people tend to have certain biases.
3. c
4. The study suggests that a child who receives another person's approval might be more inclined to interact with others.

PSYCHOLOGY PROJECTS

Cooperative Learning

Research in Psychology With a partner, watch several television commercials for a variety of products. Discuss the ways in which the advertisers try to sell their products. Do they take a central or a peripheral route? Whom do they use for a messenger? What, if anything, makes the messenger persuasive? With your partner, decide which two ads you think are likely to be the most effective for their intended audience. Describe the ads to the rest of the class and explain why you think they are effective.

⊟ internet connect

Internet Activity: go.hrw.com
KEYWORD: SY3 PS20

Choose an activity on social cognition to:
- create an annotated display on attitudes and behavior.
- design an advertisement employing methods of persuasion.
- create a theoretical profile analyzing prejudice and bias.

go hrw com

Social Interaction

CHAPTER RESOURCE MANAGER

	Objectives	Pacing Guide	Reproducible and Review Resources
SECTION 1: Group Behavior (pp. 480–484)	Identify how membership in a group can influence individual behavior.	**Regular** 1 day **Block Scheduling** .5 day *Block Scheduling Handbook with Team Teaching Strategies, Chapter 21*	**PS** Readings and Case Studies, Chapter 21 **REV** Section 1 Review, p. 484
SECTION 2: Conformity (pp. 484–486)	List the factors that lead people to conform to social norms.	**Regular** 1 day **Block Scheduling** .5 day *Block Scheduling Handbook with Team Teaching Strategies, Chapter 21*	**E** Research Projects and Activities for Teaching Psychology **REV** Section 2 Review, p. 486
SECTION 3: Obedience (pp. 487–489)	Explain why most people tend to obey authority figures.	**Regular** 1 day **Block Scheduling** .5 day *Block Scheduling Handbook with Team Teaching Strategies, Chapter 21*	**SM** Mastering Critical Thinking Skills 21 **REV** Section 3 Review, p. 489
SECTION 4: Aggression (pp. 490–492)	Summarize the various views on the causes of aggressive behavior.	**Regular** 1 day **Block Scheduling** .5 day *Block Scheduling Handbook with Team Teaching Strategies, Chapter 21*	**RS** Essay and Research Themes for Advanced Placement Students, Theme 18 **REV** Section 4 Review, p. 492
SECTION 5: Altruism (pp. 494–495)	Define altruism, and identify the factors that promote and the factors that inhibit altruistic behavior.	**Regular** 1 day **Block Scheduling** .5 day *Block Scheduling Handbook with Team Teaching Strategies, Chapter 21*	**REV** Section 5 Review, p. 495

Chapter Resource Key

PS	Primary Sources	**A**	Assessment		Video
RS	Reading Support	**REV**	Review		Internet
E	Enrichment		Transparencies		Holt Presentation Maker Using Microsoft® PowerPoint®
SM	Skills Mastery		CD-ROM		

One-Stop Planner CD–ROM

See the *One-Stop Planner* for a complete list of additional resources for students and teachers.

One-Stop Planner CD–ROM

It's easy to plan lessons, select resources, and print out materials for your students when you use the **One-Stop Planner CD-ROM with Test Generator.**

Technology Resources

 One-Stop Planner, Lesson 21.1
 Homework Practice Online
 Teaching Transparencies 41: Group Polarization
 HRW Go Site

 One-Stop Planner, Lesson 21.2
 Homework Practice Online
 HRW Go Site

 One-Stop Planner, Lesson 21.3
 Homework Practice Online

 One-Stop Planner, Lesson 21.4
 Homework Practice Online
 Teaching Transparencies 42: Television Viewing and Aggression
 CNN. Presents Psychology: Anger and Aggression

 One-Stop Planner, Lesson 21.5
 Homework Practice Online

Chapter Review and Assessment

 HRW Go site

REV Chapter 21 Review, pp. 496–497

REV Chapter Review Activities with Answer Key

A Alternative Assessment Handbook

A Chapter 21 Test (Form A or B)

A Portfolio Assessment Handbook

Chapter 21 Test Generator (on the One–Stop Planner)

Global Skill Builder CD-ROM

---

internet connect

HRW ONLINE RESOURCES

GO TO: go.hrw.com
Then type in a keyword.

TEACHER HOME PAGE
KEYWORD: SY3 Teacher

CHAPTER INTERNET ACTIVITIES
KEYWORD: SY3 PS21
Choose an activity on social interaction to:
- create a skit illustrating characteristics of group behavior.
- create a pamphlet explaining conformity.
- profile a theory of aggression.

CHAPTER ENRICHMENT LINKS
KEYWORD: SY3 CH21

ONLINE ASSESSMENT
Homework Practice
KEYWORD: SY3 HP21

Standardized Test Prep
KEYWORD: SY3 STP21

Rubrics
KEYWORD: SS Rubrics

CONTENT UPDATES
KEYWORD: SS Content Updates

HOLT PRESENTATION MAKER
KEYWORD: SY3 PPT21

ONLINE READING SUPPORT
KEYWORD: SS Strategies

CURRENT EVENTS
KEYWORD: S3 Current Events

Additional Resources

PRINT RESOURCES FOR TEACHERS

Baron, R., & Richardson, D. (1994). *Human aggression* (2nd ed.). New York: Plenum Press.

Milgram, S. (1975). *Obedience to authority.* New York: Harper & Row.

Miller, A. (1986). *The obedience experiments: A case study of controversy in social science.* New York: Praeger.

Sternberg, R. (1995). *Defying the crowd: Cultivating creativity in a culture of conformity.* New York: Free Press.

PRINT RESOURCES FOR STUDENTS

Eggert, L. (1994). *Anger management for youth: Stemming aggression and violence.* Bloomington, IN: National Educational Service.

Gardner, J. (1990). *On leadership.* New York: Free Press.

MULTIMEDIA RESOURCES

Conformity, obedience, and dissent (VHS). RMI Media Productions, Inc., 1365 North Winchester, Olathe, KS 66061.

Diffusing aggressive behavior (VHS). AIMS Media, 9710 De Soto Avenue, Chatsworth, CA 91311.

Generations of violence (VHS). Filmmakers Library, 124 East 40th Street, Number 901, New York, NY 10016.

SOCIAL INTERACTION

Introducing Chapter 21

Have students answer the following questions on a sheet of paper and then put aside their answers: Do you think there is too much emphasis on tests and grades in school? Why or why not? After students have finished writing, ask the class to discuss the question. Urge students to consider all the ideas raised by various members of the class. After several minutes of discussion, ask the students how many of them would modify their original answer in any way. What influenced them to change their minds? Tell the class that, as they saw in this exercise, other people often influence how we think, feel, talk, and act. Indeed, as students will learn in this chapter, other people influence virtually every aspect of our lives.

Sections

1 **Group Behavior**

2 **Conformity**

3 **Obedience**

4 **Aggression**

5 **Altruism**

Each of the five questions identified on page 478 corresponds to one of these sections.

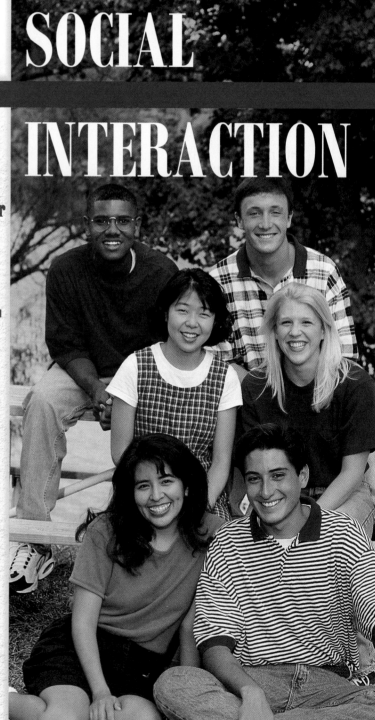

21 Chapter

SOCIAL INTERACTION

Read to Discover

1 How can membership in a group influence individual behavior?

2 What factors lead people to conform to social norms?

3 Why do most people tend to obey authority figures?

4 What are the various views on the causes of aggressive behavior?

5 What is altruism, and what are the factors that promote and the factors that inhibit altruistic behavior?

Each chapter begins with a vignette, called "A Day in the Life," that relates the information discussed in the chapter to the everyday events in the lives of a group of fictional high school students. The text of the chapter occasionally refers back to the vignette to demonstrate the application of the concept being discussed. An icon marked "A Day in the Life" is placed next to these references.

Copy the following graphic organizer onto the chalkboard, omitting the italicized text. Fill in the boxes as you discuss group behavior.

Group Behavior		
Social Facilitation	*Social Loafing*	*Risky Shift*

A DAY IN THE LIFE

June 15

"I can't believe we are graduating in four days," Janet said excitedly.

Janet and Linda were still setting up the picnic table when Marc, Hannah, Todd, and Dan arrived. They had decided to meet for a picnic lunch, and all they were able to talk about was memories of high school and the fact that it was almost over.

"Todd, remember when we first met?" Linda asked. "We were in introductory biology together. You really helped me a lot in that class—not to mention the fact that you always kept me laughing."

"I remember," Todd said. "I had just moved here, and you introduced me to your friends."

"I'd forgotten all about that," Dan replied. "Marc and I were at Janet's track meet that day."

"Hey, I made it to district finals that day," Janet reminded them.

"Of course you did," Hannah chimed in. "The track meet was at home, and all your friends were cheering you on."

They all sat quietly for a while, eating their lunches and thinking about their futures, their pasts, and their friends. Suddenly, Todd started laughing. "Do you remember the time we went to the amusement park, and we all decided to take the shortcut back to the gate? We ended up missing our bus home."

"Wait a minute, Todd!" Hannah exclaimed. "If I remember correctly, you were the one who insisted on that 'shortcut.' We just went along with you."

"Hey, it seemed like a good idea. Besides, it's not my fault that you all listened to me," Todd joked.

"Listening to you isn't always a bad idea," Dan said. "If it weren't for you, I would have fought that guy at the basketball game. Remember that? He bumped into me by accident, but I thought he shoved me on purpose. You were the only person who could calm me down."

"Who knows what any of us would be doing if we didn't have each other," Hannah added. "I'm excited about college, but I'm going to miss seeing all of you every day."

- - -

Key Terms

- social facilitation
- evaluation apprehension
- social loafing
- diffusion of responsibility
- risky shift
- social decision schemes
- majority-wins scheme
- truth-wins scheme
- two-thirds-majority scheme
- first-shift scheme
- group polarization
- authoritarian leaders
- democratic leaders
- laissez-faire leaders
- conform
- social norms
- explicit norms
- implicit norms
- foot-in-the-door effect
- catharsis
- altruism
- bystander effect

Todd often influenced his friends—to take a shortcut and to avoid a fight, for example—because they respected his opinions. Having an audience helped Janet run faster and play better. These are just two examples of social influence, or the way other people affect what we say and do. Other people can also influence us by giving us orders or pressuring us to adapt to their standards of behavior.

People behave differently when they are around other people than they do when they are by themselves. How people behave toward others depends on many factors. Sometimes people behave aggressively toward others; sometimes they help others. In this chapter, you will learn more about all of these aspects of social interaction.

Using Key Terms

Assign several of the key terms to each student. Then have students look up the meaning of their assigned terms in the chapter or in the Glossary and rewrite the definitions in their own words. Ask volunteers to read their definitions aloud to the class. Do the other students agree with the rewritten definitions? If not, how would they change them? Correct any misunderstandings.

Journal Activity

After students have read the "A Day in the Life" vignette, ask them to consider the ways in which they are influenced by their friends. Have them write in their journals about a time when encouragement from a friend or friends spurred them on to achieve a goal or improved their performance on a particular task.

WHY PSYCHOLOGY MATTERS

Psychologists study the ways people interact. Use CNNfyi.com or other current events sources to learn more about how psychologists study social interaction.

CNNfyi.com

479

1

Section Objective

▶ Identify how membership in a group can influence individual behavior.

This objective is assessed in the Section Review on page 484 and in the Chapter 21 Review.

Opening Section 1

Motivator

Ask students to name all the different leaders they can think of, such as political, civic, or religious leaders. Record their responses on the chalkboard. Then have students consider the ways in which the leaders they named differ from one another. Answers may include how the leaders are chosen, how much power they have, and how many people they influence. Tell students that in Section 1 they will learn more about different types of group leaders as well as about several other aspects of group behavior.

480

TRUTH **OR** **fiction** **?** Read the following statements about psychology. Do you think they are true or false? You will learn whether each statement is true or false as you read the chapter.

- People tend to take greater risks as part of a group than they would if they were acting alone.
- When there is no right or wrong choice, people often go along with the majority.
- Most people try to act as individuals and not simply "go along with the crowd."
- People seldom obey orders to do things that conflict with their own attitudes.
- It is human nature to be aggressive.
- People are more likely to help someone in trouble when no one else is present to help.

SECTION 1

Group Behavior

How people behave as part of a group often differs from how they behave as individuals. People may try harder, take greater risks, or make different decisions when they are with others than they would if they were alone. The ways in which groups affect individual behavior are discussed in this section.

Social Facilitation

Social facilitation refers to the concept that people often perform better when other people are watching than they do when they are alone. In other words, the presence of other people seems to facilitate and encourage one's performance. Hannah, for example, was not at all surprised that Janet had done so well at the track meet. She had witnessed before that Janet competed harder when her friends cheered her on.

Social facilitation is not limited to people. Psychologist Robert Zajonc (1980) found that dogs and cats—and even cockroaches—do things faster when they are in a group than when they are alone. These suggest that social facilitation may be a basic animal response. Zajonc believes that animals, including humans, respond in this way because the presence of others increases their level of excitement.

Competing on their home court with fans cheering them on usually motivates players to play harder. What concept of social psychology does this illustrate?

Evaluation apprehension, or the concern about the opinion of others, is another reason that the presence of other people may improve an individual's performance (Mullen et al., 1997; Sanna & Shotland, 1990). Evaluation apprehension may motivate people to try harder so that others will think more highly of them.

Social Loafing

Being a member of a group does not always improve one's performance. When people are working together toward a common goal rather than working on individual tasks, they may "slack off" and not try as hard. This behavior is referred to as **social loafing**. Social loafing is especially likely to occur when people see that other members of the group are not pulling their share of the load.

Social loafing may occur because of **diffusion of responsibility**—the tendency for people to feel less responsible for accomplishing a task when the effort is shared among members of a group. As part of a group, individuals are likely to feel less accountable for their actions. Therefore, they are less likely to worry about what others think of them because they have less evaluation apprehension. They may

Guided Practice

Create on the chalkboard a four-column chart titled "Group Decision Making." Ask students to provide the names of the four social decision schemes used in group decision making, and write these names in the chart. Then have students complete the chart by providing a description of each scheme and an explanation of how each scheme is used. Finally, lead the class in a discussion of the ways that being part of a group may affect the decision-making process.

Independent Practice

Organize the class into several small groups, and ask each group to consider the same choice—for example, which of two computers to buy—but assign each group a different decision-making scheme to use. After the groups have made their decisions, have representatives from each group explain how their group arrived at a decision. Urge the class as a whole to decide which decision-making scheme worked best for the type of decision that was made.

even feel that their contribution to the group's effort is not very important (Shepperd, 1993). When Todd said, "it's not my fault that you all listened to me [about the shortcut]," he was diffusing, or spreading out, his own responsibility for an unwise decision to the other members of the group.

Risky Shift

A related social phenomenon is the **risky shift**—the tendency for people to take greater risks when they are part of a group than they would as individuals acting on their own. People may feel more powerful (or less vulnerable) as part of a group. This is because the responsibilty for a particular situation or action is shared with the other group members (Kamalanabhan et al., 2000; Myers, 1996; Smith and Mackie, 1995). The risky shift may help explain such events as prison riots and mob attacks.

It is true that people tend to take greater risks as part of a group than they would if they were acting alone. This is because individuals can share responsibility for a decision.

Group Decision Making

Many important decisions are made by groups rather than by individuals. Committees, for example, are often appointed to study and make decisions about specific issues. Juries decide on the guilt or innocence of people accused of crimes. Similarly, a group of friends may make a joint decision about which movie to see. These are examples of group decision making.

Because many decisions are made by groups, psychologists have studied how being part of a group affects the decision-making process. They have identified a number of **social decision schemes**, or rules that govern group decision making (Gigone & Hastie, 1997; Stasser, 1999). These include the majority-wins scheme, the truth-wins scheme, the two-thirds-majority scheme, and the first-shift scheme.

Majority-Wins Scheme
In the **majority-wins scheme**, the group agrees to a decision that was initially supported by a majority of group members. For example, a group of five friends might be trying to decide what to do on the weekend—say, whether to go to a movie or to a video arcade. At first, three of the five friends might opt for the movie and the other two friends for the arcade. However, after discussing the two choices, all five friends might agree to go to the movie, the option that was initially supported by the majority.

The majority-wins scheme applies most often to situations in which there are no right or wrong choices. In the example just given, both the movie and the arcade were acceptable options—neither one was right or wrong. Rather, the preference of the majority guided the decisions of the others.

It is true that when there is no right or wrong choice, people often go along with the majority. This is called the majority-wins scheme of group decision making.

Truth-Wins Scheme
Often, the members of a group come to realize that one option is better than others after they learn more about the different choices available. This is referred to as the **truth-wins scheme**. Suppose that in the example just given, the five friends learn that the movie they hoped to see has been canceled and that another movie is being shown, one that interests them less. After gathering and sharing the information, the group might decide to go to the arcade instead, a decision that is based on a clearly better choice between their two options.

Two-Thirds–Majority Scheme
Some groups concur with a decision after two thirds of their members come to an agreement about the correct choice. This is called the **two-thirds-majority scheme**. It often applies to decisions made by juries. When two thirds of a jury initially vote for conviction, the remaining third may go along with the decision of the others.

First-Shift Scheme
The **first-shift scheme** applies to groups that are deadlocked, or split fifty-fifty, about a decision. If just one person changes his or her mind, or shifts from one side to the other, others may follow and shift to the opposite side as well. For example, a jury might be deadlocked, with

Cross-Curricular Link: Law

When a jury is deadlocked, or unable to agree on a verdict after a reasonable period of deliberation, the jury is referred to as a "hung jury." To help the jury reach a verdict, the trial judge may issue a "dynamite instruction." This instruction typically urges the jurors to consider the opinions of their fellow jurors and to yield their own views whenever possible.

☑ internet connect

TOPIC: Group Behavior
GO TO: go.hrw.com
KEYWORD: SY3 PS21
Have students access the Internet through the HRW Go site to research characteristics of group behavior. Then have students create a skit that illustrates characteristics of group behavior mentioned in the textbook. Students should also present a summary of how the group behaviors are illustrated in the skit.

Readings and Case Studies

481

Predicting Outcomes

Point out that polarization occurs in groups of people who share similar attitudes. Ask students to predict what might happen in a group of people who do not initially share similar attitudes. Would group members become more similar in their attitudes, or would they become more sharply divided? What factors might influence the outcome? *(Factors may include how persuasive particular members are and how strongly other members hold their attitudes.)* Then have students discuss why polarization may have both positive and negative outcomes.

Cooperative Learning

Tell the class that some people think there are natural leaders—that is, people who are born with leadership qualities. Other people think leadership depends on certain skills that, like other skills, can be learned. Have students consider both sides of the issue and determine which argument most closely matches their own beliefs about leadership. Organize students into two groups, based on their positions on this issue, for a group discussion. Then have volunteers from both sides of the issue debate their positions in front of the class.

Teaching Transparencies with Teacher's Notes

TRANSPARENCY 41:
Group Polarization

half believing the defendant is guilty and half believing the defendant is innocent. Those jurors who initially thought the defendant was guilty might follow the lead of the first juror who changes his or her vote from guilty to not guilty, even in the absence of additional information about the case.

Polarization

Members of a group usually share similar attitudes. Indeed, shared attitudes are often what attracts people to particular groups in the first place. For example, teens who are concerned about cruelty to animals might join an organization that has the goal of ending laboratory experimentation on animal subjects. Teens who are not as concerned about animal rights, on the other hand, are unlikely to join such a group.

The shared attitudes that group members hold are likely to grow stronger over time. This strengthening of a group's shared attitudes is called **group polarization**. It occurs as group members discuss and act upon the attitudes they share.

Polarization can be positive or negative. If group members are prejudiced against people of other races or religions, for example, then polarization is likely to increase their prejudice. If, on the other hand, group members are tolerant of people who are different, then polarization may make them even more so (Myers & Bishop, 1970; Zuber et al., 1992). Such polarization in group attitudes is illustrated in Figure 21.1.

Group Leadership

All groups, regardless of their nature, have leaders who serve several important functions in their groups. Leaders help group members identify the group's goals and establish and implement plans for reaching them. Leaders may also offer emotional support to group members.

Some leaders are appointed by outsiders; others are chosen by a vote of group members. The president of an organization might be elected by a vote of group members, for example. The president, in turn, might appoint a member of the group to head a committee to study a particular issue or complete a particular task.

Organizations such as businesses, schools, and the military usually have clear chains of command, or leadership. Group members know to whom they report and whose directions to follow.

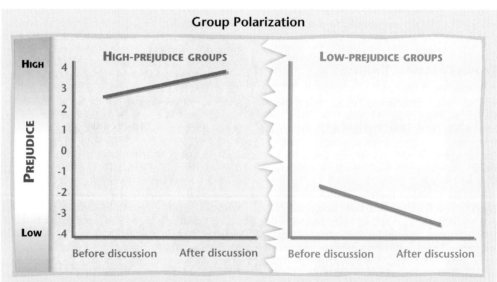

FIGURE 21.1 *A group's shared attitudes tend to grow stronger with discussion. In one study involving high school students, a discussion of racial issues increased prejudice in the high-prejudice group and decreased it in the low-prejudice group.*

Source: "Discussion Effects on Racial Attitudes" (1970) by D. G. Myers and G. D. Bishop, *Science, 169,* 778–779.

CASE STUDIES
AND OTHER TRUE STORIES

Discuss with students why people sometimes believe there is nothing they as individuals can do to change something they believe is wrong. Ask students to provide examples of individuals who have worked to end injustice and in so doing have changed the course of history. Then have students analyze how the progress of the civil rights movement of the 1950s and 1960s might have been different had it not been for Martin Luther King's unwavering commitment to nonviolent action.

For Further Research

Have interested students conduct library research to learn about Mohandas (Mahatma) Gandhi, his role in India's fight for independence from Great Britain, and his influence on Martin Luther King Jr. Have the students share what they learn with the rest of the class.

CASE STUDIES
AND OTHER TRUE STORIES
Dr. Martin Luther King Jr. and Nonviolent Action

People are usually influenced by the views of the majority. In some cases, however, the opinion of a single individual has influenced the behavior of the majority, and that minority influence has changed the course of history.

Researchers have investigated factors that enable a minority to influence the majority. They have found that the most influential individuals are those who hold steadfastly to

Dr. Martin Luther King Jr. (left)

their views and never waver, in words or actions, from what they believe. One of the best examples of such unyielding commitment is provided by Reverend Martin Luther King Jr. His belief in nonviolent action shaped the course of the civil rights movement throughout the 1960s and beyond.

King believed that the only way African Americans could achieve racial equality in the United States was through nonviolent action. Even as a boy, King reacted to racial insults and violence with nonviolence. When a school bully attacked him, he did not fight back. When a white woman in a store slapped him, he said nothing (Osborne, 1968).

King's extraordinary leadership qualities and his strong belief in nonviolent action changed the course of the civil rights movement. In 1955, inspired by Rosa Parks, King led a boycott of Montgomery, Alabama, city buses that eventually resulted in an integrated bus system there and in nearly every other city in the South as well.

King continued to lead nonviolent protests against racial inequality in the United States. He led lunch-counter sit-ins to desegregate eating facilities and organized prayer vigils to focus the nation's attention on the need to desegregate public parks and rest rooms. But he is probably best known for the 1963 March on Washington.

During this historic event, more than 200,000 people gathered at the Lincoln Memorial in Washington, D.C., to hear King deliver his famous speech, "I Have a Dream."

At these and other events King remained steadfast in his belief in nonviolence. Despite repeated arrests and physical violence against himself and his family, King never wavered in his belief that nonviolence was the best way to solve the problem of racial inequality.

King was feared and attacked by some white people because his methods were so effective. He was also criticized by African Americans who saw nonviolence as a sign of weakness. When one civil rights activist was shot soon after the start of a freedom march, some members of the movement questioned the wisdom of King's nonviolent approach. King, however, patiently urged his followers to remain true to the nonviolent movement. He was persuasive, and the march continued peacefully.

King's influence on the civil rights movement was profound. Nonviolence continually proved to be the most effective means of bringing about change. In 1964 Martin Luther King Jr. received the Nobel Peace Prize for his struggle to achieve racial equality through peaceful means. By 1965, because of his influence, civil rights organizations across the country had adopted nonviolent action as their primary method of addressing racial inequality.

For Your Information

Martin Luther King Jr. not only won the Nobel Peace Prize but in 1977 was posthumously awarded the Presidential Medal of Freedom for his battle against racial prejudice and discrimination. Moreover, in 1983, the U.S. Congress designated the third Monday in January a national holiday to commemorate King's birthday.

Closing Section 1

Applying Information

Ask students to choose one of the leadership styles discussed in the section and to draw a comic strip illustrating that style. Have volunteers show their comic strips to the class, and have the class try to determine which style of leadership is being portrayed.

Reviewing Section 1

Have students complete the Section Review questions on page 484.

► List the factors that lead people to conform to social norms.

This objective is assessed in the Section Review on page 486 and in the Chapter 21 Review.

Section 1 Review: Answers

1. Social facilitation is the tendency of people to perform better when other people are watching them than when they are alone. Social loafing is the tendency of people to "slack off" when they are working with others.

2. Four social decision schemes are the majority-wins scheme, the truth-wins scheme, the two-thirds-majority scheme, and the first-shift scheme.

3. Examples will vary. One type of group that might benefit from a laissez-faire style of leadership is a self-help group because a laissez-faire leader encourages group members to express and explore their own ideas.

A DAY IN THE LIFE Informal groups, such as groups of friends, may not have official leaders. However, some members are likely to have more influence over the group than others. This was true of Todd and his circle of friends. Todd tended to be the leader of the group and to influence the others because of his intelligence and leadership abilities. He influenced his friends to take a shortcut at the amusement park, for example, and he persuaded Dan not to fight.

Like Todd, group leaders often have certain personality traits and social skills that enable them to influence the decisions and behavior of others. For example, leaders tend to be more self-confident, outgoing, and intelligent than other group members (Smith & Mackie, 1995). Despite these similarities, leaders may differ in how they operate. In other words, they may have different styles of leadership. Leaders may be authoritarian, democratic, or laissez-faire.

Authoritarian Leaders   Authoritarian leaders exert absolute control over all decisions for the group. They tell other group members what to do and demand that group members obey their orders. Military leaders, for example, are usually authoritarian. They give orders to those of lesser rank and expect their orders to be carried out immediately and without question.

Democratic Leaders   Although military leaders tend to be authoritarian toward those below them in the chain of command, they are more democratic when they are planning strategies with other officers. **Democratic leaders** encourage group members to express and discuss their ideas and to make their own decisions. Such leaders may try to build a consensus—that is, to encourage unanimous agreement on a decision. Alternatively, they may request that group members take a vote and follow the decision of the majority.

Laissez-Faire Leaders   The term *laissez-faire* is French for "to let (people) do (as they choose)." Like democratic leaders, **laissez-faire leaders** encourage group members to express and explore their own ideas. However, laissez-faire leaders tend to take a less active role in the decision-making process. They tend to stand back from the group and allow group members to move in whatever direction they wish, even if the group seems to be making false starts or poor choices.

Comparing Leadership Styles   No one style of leadership is best for every group or situation. In times of crisis, authoritarian leaders may be more effective because they can make decisions quickly and know that those decisions will be carried out promptly. This is one reason nations often prefer authoritarian leaders when they are having serious problems.

In other situations, democratic or laissez-faire leaders may be more effective. Their styles of leadership allow group members to express themselves and grow as individuals. Such leadership may be important when the group is searching for new ways to solve a problem or when trying to help group members meet challenges in their lives.

SECTION 1 REVIEW

Homework Practice Online
Keyword: SY3 HP21

1. Explain the difference between social facilitation and social loafing.

2. List four social decision schemes.

3. **Critical Thinking**   *Drawing Inferences and Conclusions* Give an example of a group or situation that might benefit from a laissez-faire style of leadership. Explain your choice.

SECTION **2**
Conformity

The least direct social influence on behavior is the pressure to **conform**, or to modify one's attitudes and behavior to make them consistent with those of other people. People who conform bring their behavior in line with that of a group. The group may be a formal organization, such as a school club, or a loose collection of people, such as several friends who always hang out together. Linda, Marc, Todd, and the others in their circle of friends are an example of such a group.

Importance of Groups

Being accepted by a group can be important because groups help people satisfy many needs. Groups can fulfill an individual's needs for belonging, affection, and attention. Meeting such needs is one reason why many teens join clubs at school, sports teams, academic clubs, and other social organizations.

Motivator

Tell students to imagine that they have just arrived at an important social function dressed in a tuxedo or evening gown. As soon as they walk through the door, they realize that they have dressed inappropriately for the occasion. Everyone else is wearing school clothes. How do they feel, and why? *(Most would feel self-conscious and embarrassed because they failed to conform to social norms of appropriate dress.)* Tell students that in Section 2 they will learn more about social norms and why they exert such a powerful influence on people.

Demonstration

Ask seven volunteers to participate in a demonstration of Asch's study of conformity. In private, tell six of the volunteers to give the same wrong answer when you ask them which of three lines is the same length as a fourth. After all the volunteers have responded, explain to the class the rationale behind the study and ask the volunteer who did not receive the instruction to describe how it felt to agree (or disagree) with the others when they were wrong. Have students discuss what they learned about conformity from the demonstration.

Social norms vary from one group to another. People of different ages and occupations tend to have different standards of dress, for example. How might this be an example of both explicit and implicit norms?

⬛ internet connect

TOPIC: Conformity, the Individual, and Society
GO TO: go.hrw.com
KEYWORD: SY3 PS21

Have students access the Internet through the HRW Go site to research social norms and conformity. Then ask students to create pamphlet on the reasons people conform, how social norms are involved, and the importance of groups for the individual and society.

Groups are also important because they offer support to individuals when they are facing difficult problems. People who are grieving the loss of a loved one, for example, may benefit by joining a support group. (See Chapter 19.) Groups may also help people accomplish things they could not accomplish on their own. For instance, workers may join together to form a labor union in order to fight for better working conditions or higher wages.

Social Norms

Belonging to a group usually means following, or conforming to, the group's social norms. **Social norms** are the standards of behavior that people share. They serve as guidelines for what people should and should not do or say in a given situation. For example, social norms tell people what to eat, what to wear, and when and where to make a joke.

Social norms can be explicit or implicit. **Explicit norms** are spoken or written rules. Examples include traffic rules and school dress codes. **Implicit norms** are unspoken, unwritten rules. Examples include modes of dress or ways of greeting that are unique to a particular group. Although implicit norms are unstated, they nonetheless guide people's words and actions.

Social norms can be useful or harmful. They are useful if they help promote the safety and well-being of individuals or groups. Bathing regularly and not talking in a theater during a movie are examples of useful social norms. Social norms are harmful when they promote risky behavior. Smoking cigarettes—a norm in some groups—is an example of harmful social norms.

Asch's Studies of Conformity

To what extent will people conform to social norms? Psychologist Solomon Asch (1955) addressed this question in a series of well-known experiments. Asch wanted to determine whether people would go along with group opinion even when the group opinion differed from their own.

Procedure Asch asked participants in the study to look at three lines of varying length and to compare them with a standard line, as shown in Figure 21.2 on page 486. The participants were asked to indicate which of the three lines was the same length as the standard line. Each participant was tested in a group of several other people. However, the other group members were really Asch's associates, who were simply posing as study participants.

For the first few comparisons, all of Asch's associates gave the correct answer. However, for many of the remaining comparisons, all of the associates gave the same *wrong* answer. For example, they might have said that line 1 was the same length as the standard line.

Results When Asch's associates gave an answer that was obviously wrong, many study participants conformed to the group opinion and gave the same

Closing Section 2

Evaluating Ideas

Review with students the factors that lead people to conform to social norms. Then have students evaluate how important conformity is to societal cohesion. How might society be different if people were not pressured to conform to social norms? Would society even be possible?

Reviewing Section 2

Have students complete the Section Review questions on page 486.

Class Discussion

Many people believe that teens are in the age group most likely to succumb to peer pressure and conform to group norms. Have students discuss whether they think this is true and, if so, why.

Section 2 Review: Answers

1. Explicit norms are spoken or written; implicit norms are unspoken and unwritten.

2. Factors that influence people to conform include the presence of a collectivistic culture, the need to be liked and accepted by others, and unanimity of opinion in a group of up to eight members.

3. In Asch's studies, participants were asked, in a group of other people, to state their opinion about a readily observable fact. The experiment was "rigged" in that other group members gave the same wrong answer part of the time. A significant proportion of participants went along with the group's opinion even when they knew it was wrong.

wrong answer. About three fourths of study participants went along with group opinion at least once, one third went along with the group at least half the time, and one fourth went along with the group virtually all the time. Study participants who conformed to group opinion later admitted that they knew the answers they gave were incorrect, but they went along with the group so as not to appear different from the others.

TRUTH OR fiction
■ REVISITED ■

It is not true that most people try to act as individuals and not just "go along with the crowd." Asch's studies of conformity revealed that most people conform to those around them so as not to appear different.

Why Do People Conform?

"Going along with the crowd" is probably at least as common in everyday life as it was in Asch's experiments. Most people avoid talking, acting, or dressing differently from other members of the groups to which they belong. Why is conformity so common? Several factors may contribute to the tendency to

Asch's Conformity Experiment

| | 1 | 2 | 3 |
| **Standard line** | **Comparison lines** | | |

FIGURE 21.2 *In this example from Asch's studies, line 2 is clearly the same length as the standard line.*

conform to social norms (Bond & Smith, 1996; Myers, 1996; Smith & Mackie, 1995).

Cultural Influences Some cultures are collectivistic, which means that they place greater emphasis on the group than on its individual members. In many Asian cultures, for example, the person is seen primarily as part of the family and society rather than as an individual. (See Chapter 14.) In such cultures, individuals show a greater tendency to conform to the group, and they may feel extremely uncomfortable if they are singled out as different from the others in the group.

Need for Acceptance Some people conform to social norms in order to be liked and accepted by others. This need to conform stems from the belief that people who dress, talk, or act differently from other people stand out from the crowd and thus draw negative attention to themselves. In actuality, however, this is not always true.

People who depend the most on the acceptance and approval of others tend to be those with low self-esteem and high social anxiety (Singh & Sharma, 1989). They may value being liked more than they value being right. They may also be very self-conscious about standing out from others, fearing that others will ridicule or reject them if they appear different.

Other Factors Several other factors contribute to the tendency to conform to social norms. For example, the chances of conforming to a group's norms increase as the group grows in size—at least up to about eight members. Further increases in size (past eight members) seem to have little effect on the tendency to conform.

Individuals are more likely to conform to the group when all other members of the group are unanimous in their words and actions. However, if even one person disagrees with the rest of the group, others in the group also are less likely to conform.

SECTION 2 REVIEW

go. hrw .com **Homework Practice Online**

Keyword: SY3 HP21

1. What is the difference between explicit norms and implicit norms?

2. What factors influence people to conform to social norms?

3. **Critical Thinking** *Summarizing* How did Asch show that people tend to conform to the opinions of others?

Section Objective

▶ Explain why most people tend to obey authority figures.

This objective is assessed in the Section Review on page 489 and in the Chapter 21 Review.

Opening Section 3

Motivator

Point out to the class that people tend to conform to social norms in order to avoid feelings of embarrassment or isolation. In contrast, people tend to obey orders, rules, and laws in order to avoid discipline or punishment, such as being grounded, fined, court-martialed, or imprisoned. Ask students to give specific examples of consequences of failing to obey authority. Then tell the class that in Section 3 they will learn more about obedience and why most people tend to obey authority figures.

SECTION 3

Obedience

One of the most obvious and direct social influences on people's attitudes and behavior is the power of people in positions of authority. Parents often order their children to clean their own rooms or do their homework. Judges often order lawbreakers to pay fines or perform community service. Most children obey their parents, teachers, and other adults. Most adults obey police officers, judges, and other authority figures. Such obedience is necessary to protect the safety and well-being of the community and its people.

Throughout history, however, many people have also obeyed orders to commit immoral acts, such as killing innocent people. In the 1900s alone, Turks killed Armenians, Nazis killed Jews in Europe, and Serbs killed Muslims in Bosnia. In each case, those who did the killing justified their acts by saying they were "just following orders."

Milgram's Studies of Obedience

Are people who commit immoral acts unusual or abnormal? Or would most people be obedient in a similar situation? Yale University psychologist Stanley Milgram, whose own parents were killed by the Nazis during World War II, investigated this question in a series of studies conducted in the 1960s and 1970s. The purpose of Milgram's research was to determine whether the average person would obey the commands of authority figures.

Procedure In the first phase of his research, Milgram (1963) placed advertisements in local newspapers, seeking male volunteers to participate in a study of learning. In response, 40 men, ranging in age from 20 to 50, volunteered for the study. The volunteers represented a wide range of educational levels—from people who had not completed elementary school to others who had earned graduate degrees. Study participants also represented a variety of occupations, including teachers, engineers, laborers, and salespeople.

Instead of revealing the true nature of the study, Milgram told participants that its purpose was to investigate the effects that punishment has on memory. Some participants, Milgram explained, would be "teachers," and others would be "learners." In reality, all the volunteers who answered the advertisement

Scenes such as this one may come to mind when we hear the phrase "obedience to authority," but obedience characterizes many of our interactions in daily life. *Can you think of other examples of obedience?*

were assigned to the teacher group, whereas those in the learner group were Milgram's associates.

Study participants were told that learners were expected to learn word pairs that would be read to them from a list. After the learners had heard the entire list, the teachers read the words one at a time. Each learner was then asked to provide the word that was paired with the word read by the teacher. If a learner made the correct choice, nothing happened, and teacher and learner went on to the next test item. However, if a learner made an incorrect choice, the teacher was to deliver an electric shock. With each mistake a learner made, the teacher was to increase the amount of voltage.

As shown in the middle photograph in the series on page 488, learners were strapped into chairs and electrodes were attached to their wrists. The teachers sat at a console in an adjacent room. On the console were levers labeled with the voltage they controlled (from 15 to 450 volts) and the seriousness of the shocks they delivered (from slight to severe). Although the teachers were led to believe that the learners received shocks for each incorrect answer, the equipment did not really deliver shocks, and the learners were never hurt or put at risk in any way.

Teachers were first given a sample shock of 45 volts so that they would have some idea of what learners supposedly would be experiencing. A shock of 45 volts is not harmful, but it was unpleasant enough to convince teachers that high-voltage shocks would be painful, even dangerous. Teachers

Guided Practice

Lead the class in a discussion of why Milgram undertook additional studies of obedience with different types of study participants and in a variety of research settings. What did he expect to learn that would further his understanding of obedience? *(Using women and college students as study participants might reveal whether the tendency to obey differs by gender or age; using different research settings might reveal which situational factors influence the tendency to obey.)*

Independent Practice

Have students read more about Milgram's studies to find out how different types of study participants and research settings influenced the outcome of his research. Ask students to summarize what they read in a table that compares Milgram's results for different types of participants and research settings. Have students share their tables with the rest of the class.

Journal Activity

Ask students to keep a record of all the rules they follow in a one-day period. These may include rules for classroom behavior, rules for riding on the bus, and rules for doing homework. For each rule that students note, have them answer the following questions: Who made this rule? Why do you follow this rule?

Class Discussion

Ask students to discuss why the participants in Milgram's experiments tended to see the researcher as an authority figure. *(Possible reasons include the researcher's age, gender, professional position, and affiliation with a prestigious university.)* Also have students discuss the ethical considerations of Milgram's studies. Do the benefits derived from our increased knowledge of obedience outweigh the possible negative effects on the participants? Could (and should) such studies be conducted today?

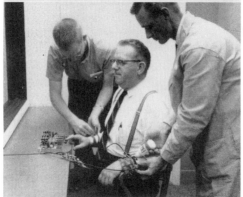

The machine and the procedure used in Stanley Milgram's classic study on obedience are pictured here. The bottom photograph in the series shows one of the few participants who refused to continue with the experiment.

Source: © 1965 by Stanley Milgram. From the film *Obedience.* Distributed by New York University Film Division and the Pennsylvania State University, PCR.

were told that they could quit at any time. However, if they hesitated to deliver a shock or to go on with the experiment, they were urged by repeated commands from the researcher to continue. The researcher also offered reassurances that the shocks, although painful, would cause no permanent damage.

Results As learners made errors, teachers delivered greater and greater voltage in each shock. At 300 volts, learners pounded on the other side of the wall, even screamed in make-believe pain. Yet 35 of the 40 participants continued with the experiment. Nine participants refused to continue somewhere between the 300-volt and the 450-volt level. However, the rest, almost two thirds of the participants, obeyed instructions to give shocks throughout the entire range of voltage, up to 450 volts, even though these participants later said that they had been afraid of harming the people receiving the shocks (Milgram, 1971).

Were the people who volunteered for Milgram's study abnormally insensitive, even cruel? Apparently not. They showed signs of great distress as the shocks they delivered increased in voltage. They sweated, bit their lips, trembled, stuttered, groaned, and dug their fingernails into their palms. Some even had fits of nervous laughter. Many also told the researcher that they wanted to stop. Nonetheless, most continued to deliver shocks of increasing voltage to the learners in the study.

Milgram repeated the experiment with other participants, including women and college students, and in other settings, including a storefront on a city street. In each phase of the research, at least half the participants obeyed the researcher and administered the entire series of electric shocks.

TRUTH
OR
fiction
■ REVISITED ■

It is not true that people seldom obey orders to do things that conflict with their own attitudes. Milgram's studies of obedience showed that the majority of people will obey such orders, even though doing so may cause them great emotional distress.

Why Do People Obey?

Why did the participants in Milgram's studies obey the researcher? What causes people, in general, to obey? Several causes have been identified.

Closing Section 3

Drawing Conclusions

Organize the class into several groups, and assign each group one of the reasons people tend to be obedient. Ask each group to write and present a brief skit that illustrates its assigned reason. Have the rest of the class try to identify which reason is illustrated by each skit.

Reviewing Section 3

Have students complete the Section Review questions on page 489.

Extension

Have students conduct library research to learn how the foot-in-the-door effect is used by advertisers and salespeople to sway other people to their point of view about particular products. Ask students to present their findings in a short oral presentation. Then have the class discuss why it is important for consumers to be aware of such psychological phenomena as the foot-in-the-door effect.

Socialization One reason people tend to be obedient is that they have been socialized from childhood to obey authority figures, such as parents, teachers, and police officers. Study participants saw the researchers in Milgram's studies as authority figures, so they obeyed orders to give shocks to the learners. To do otherwise would have conflicted with deeply held attitudes about correct behavior (Blass, 1991).

Foot-in-the-Door Effect Another reason people tend to be obedient to authority figures is the **foot-in-the-door effect**. This behavior is the tendency for people to give in to major demands once they have given in to minor ones (Burger, 1999). The foot-in-the-door effect is an example of how people may gradually change their attitudes to justify their behavior. (See Chapter 20.)

After participants in Milgram's studies had delivered small shocks to learners, it was easier for them to deliver increasingly larger shocks. In a similar way, soldiers become accustomed to obeying commands concerning relatively unimportant matters, such as how to dress, when and where to eat, and how to perform routine drills. Later on, they are more likely to obey commands relating to much more important matters that may involve risking their lives or taking the lives of other people.

Confusion About Attitudes People who are aware of their attitudes are more likely to behave in accordance with those attitudes (Fazio, 1990; Krosnick, 1989). As people become disturbed by what is happening around them—by the learners' screams and wall pounding in Milgram's studies, for example—they are likely to become less aware of, or at least more confused about, their own beliefs. Thus, they may be more likely to behave in ways that are in conflict with their attitudes.

Buffers When people are buffered, or protected, from observing the consequences of their actions, they are more likely to follow orders, even immoral ones. In the first phase of Milgram's research, for example, teachers and learners were placed in sep-

Obedience—even to immoral commands, as in Milgram's studies—may be an offshoot of the socially desirable respect for authority figures that most people learn in childhood.

arate rooms. Thus, the teachers could not see how their actions were affecting others. In later phases of the research, teachers and learners were placed in the same room so that the teachers could see the pain they were inflicting on the learners. Without the buffer of a wall to separate them from the people they thought they were hurting, compliance with the researcher's demands dropped from 65 percent to about 40 percent (Miller, 1986).

Today many soldiers are similarly buffered from their enemies. Their only contact with opposing forces may be a blip on a radar screen. Attacking their enemies may involve little more than pressing a button that launches a missile. The results of Milgram's studies suggest that obeying orders to kill enemies in this way may be easier than obeying orders to kill other human beings at close range.

SECTION 3 REVIEW

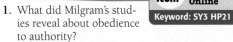

Homework Practice Online
Keyword: SY3 HP21

1. What did Milgram's studies reveal about obedience to authority?

2. Identify some of the reasons that explain why people tend to obey the orders of those in authority.

3. **Critical Thinking** *Analyzing Information* Give examples of situations in which obedience to authority is considered socially acceptable.

Class Discussion

Have students discuss how it is that some people are able to defy authority when the orders given by the authority figures are immoral. What personality traits might enable a person to refuse to comply in the face of disapproval and punishment? How are some people able to resist when others around them are following immoral orders?

Section 3 Review: Answers

1. Milgram's studies revealed that a majority of people will obey orders from authority figures, even when the orders conflict with their own attitudes.

2. Reasons people tend to obey the orders of those in authority include socialization, the foot-in-the-door effect, confusion about attitudes, and buffers.

3. Examples of obedience to authority that would be socially acceptable include obeying traffic laws and school regulations.

4
Section Objective

▶ Summarize the various views on the causes of aggressive behavior.

This objective is assessed in the Section Review on page 492 and in the Chapter 21 Review.

What's New in Psychology?

Evidence suggests that a genetic mutation may cause some males to be unusually aggressive. The gene in question normally produces an enzyme that breaks down the neurotransmitter serotonin. In males with the mutated gene, serotonin reaches abnormally high levels in the brain. Experts believe that the high levels of serotonin lead to aggression. The mutation is probably rare, so it cannot be the only cause of aggressive behavior. Indeed, the researchers caution that aggression is a complex behavior that cannot be explained with simplistic answers such as an aggression gene.

Goldberg, I. (1996). The bad seed: Amid controversy, scientists hunt for the 'aggression' gene. *Omni, 17* (5), 16.

Essay and Research Themes for A.P. Students

Theme 18

Technology Resources

CNN. Presents Psychology: Anger and Aggression

Opening Section 4

Motivator

Ask students how they express their feelings when they are angry. Possible responses may include hitting a pillow, holding the anger inside, or taking a brisk walk. Point out that some people express their anger through aggression, which refers to words or actions meant to hurt other people. Ask students to speculate on whether aggression is an inborn trait or a learned trait. Then tell the class that there are a number of views on the origin of aggression. These views are the focus of Section 4.

SECTION 4

Aggression

Aggression refers to words or actions that are meant to hurt other people. It is a serious and widespread social problem. For example, murder is the second-leading cause of death in the United States among young people between the ages of 15 and 24 (Centers for Disease Control, 2000), and more than a million children each year are victims of abuse. Children not only suffer from the results of aggression; they seem to be fascinated by it. For example, children are drawn to video games in which they can manipulate figures to kill or torture others.

Why are people aggressive? Several reasons have been suggested. They include biological, psychoanalytic, cognitive, learning, and sociocultural views.

Biological View

The brain and hormones appear to be involved in aggression. In response to certain stimuli, many lower animals react with instinctive aggression. For example, the male robin responds aggressively to the red breast of another robin. A brain structure (the hypothalamus) appears to be involved in

Children's games often involve make-believe aggression.

this instinctive reaction: Electrical stimulation of part of the hypothalamus triggers aggressive behavior in many kinds of animals. However, humans have more complex brains, and other parts of the brain apparently dampen possible aggressive instincts.

The male sex hormone testosterone is also involved in aggression. Testosterone appears to be connected with the tendencies to try to dominate and control other people. Men have higher testosterone levels than women do and are also usually more aggressive than women, particularly in contacts with male strangers (Pope et al., 2000). Studies show, for example, that aggressive 9- to 11-year-old boys are likely to have higher testosterone levels than less aggressive age-mates (Chance et al., 2000). Also, members of "wild" college fraternities have higher testosterone levels, on average, than members of "well-behaved" fraternities (Dabbs et al., 1996). Testosterone levels also vary with the occasion: men's testosterone levels tend to be higher when they are winning—whether at football or chess (Bernhardt et al., 1998).

Throughout the animal kingdom, more aggressive individuals are more likely to survive and transmit their genes to future generations. Aggression may be "natural" in people as in other species, but intelligence is also a key to survival in the case of humans. The capacity to outwit other species may be more important to human survival than aggressiveness. Now that people have organized themselves into societies in which many acts of aggression is outlawed or confined to sports, intelligence and organizational skills may be more important than aggressiveness to human survival.

TRUTH OR fiction
■ REVISITED ■

It is not true that it is human nature to be aggressive. While aggression may be a part of the biological makeup of our species, it is unlikely that all aggressive behavior is caused by genetic or biological factors.

Psychoanalytic View

Sigmund Freud believed that aggressive urges are unavoidable reactions to the frustrations of daily life. According to this view, it is normal for people to have urges to hurt other people who do not meet their wishes or demands. Such urges tend to be

490

Meeting Individual Needs: Learners with Limited English Proficiency

To help learners with limited English proficiency understand the concept of catharsis, illustrate the idea with a coiled spring or a whistling teakettle. Explain how the release of tension in the spring or the blowing off of steam by the teakettle is similar to what some psychologists believe happens when people watch aggressive sports or cheer for their team. Then have students debate whether the venting of feelings in this way actually decreases or increases aggressive behavior.

Applying Ideas

Make a statement that might be construed as either positive or negative, such as "You certainly have an eye for bargains." Tell students that one person might consider this a compliment, thinking the speaker meant that he or she is a smart shopper. Another person might be insulted, thinking the speaker meant he or she is cheap. Ask students to provide other examples of statements that could be interpreted positively or negatively. Then have them explain how cognitive psychologists view the relationship between interpretation and aggression.

---

repressed, however, because people fear hurting others (especially their parents) and, in turn, being rejected by them.

Freud also believed that repressed aggressive urges are likely to find other outlets. The urges might be expressed indirectly—for example, by the aggressive individual destroying other people's possessions or disobeying their orders. Alternatively, the urges might be expressed directly but toward strangers later in life.

Freud believed that the best way to reduce the tension caused by repressed aggressive urges and to prevent harmful aggression toward other people is to allow, or even encourage, less harmful expressions of aggression. For example, verbal aggression in the form of sarcasm or the expression of angry feelings might vent some of the aggressive feelings in the unconscious without causing bodily harm to other people. So might cheering on one's team or watching aggressive sports such as boxing or wrestling. Psychologists refer to such venting of aggressive impulses as **catharsis**.

Does catharsis really act as a safety valve, reducing feelings of tension and lowering the chances of harmful aggression toward others? Some studies have found that catharsis does seem to play this role (Doob & Wood, 1972). Other studies, however, have found that "letting off steam," either verbally or by watching aggressive sports, seems to encourage people to be more, not less, aggressive (Bushman et al., 1999). Thus, it is unclear whether catharsis increases or decreases aggressive behavior.

Cognitive View

Cognitive psychologists believe that people's behavior, including aggressive behavior, is not influenced by inherited tendencies or repressed urges. Instead, they maintain that aggressive behavior is influenced by people's values, the ways in which they perceive events, and the choices they make. According to this view, people choose to act aggressively because they believe that aggression is justified and necessary—either in general or in particular situations (Feshbach, 1994).

Some cognitive psychologists have suggested that frustration and suffering trigger feelings of anger and that these feelings in turn cause people to act aggressively (Rule et al., 1987). However, they also argue that people do not act aggressively automatically and without thought. Rather, people decide whether they will act aggressively on the basis of such factors as their previous experiences

These sports fans are obviously excited by the soccer match they are watching. **Is watching the aggressive play of a sports team a harmless way to vent aggressive urges, or does it encourage aggression?**

with aggression and their interpretation of other people's behavior (Berkowitz, 1994).

How people interpret the behavior of others may be especially important in this regard. Some people tend to interpret other people's behavior as intentionally insulting or cruel, even when it is not (Akhtar & Bradley, 1991; Crick & Dodge, 1994; Dodge et al., 1990). This interpretation may stir up feelings of anger that in turn lead to aggression (Lochman, 1992; Lochman & Dodge, 1994). That is what happened to Dan. When someone accidentally bumped into him at a basketball game, he thought he had been shoved on purpose. It made him so angry that he almost started a fight.

Learning Views

Learning theorists believe that people learn to repeat behaviors that are reinforced. Thus, when aggressive behavior is reinforced, people learn to behave aggressively.

One reason that aggression may be reinforced is that it helps people to get their own way. For example, teens who bully other people may be able to control others with force or threats of force. Although other people may stay out of their way, bullies are also likely to be rejected as friends by most of their peers. Thus, it is questionable whether such behavior is really reinforced.

A DAY IN THE LIFE

Closing Section 4

Demonstration

Demonstrate the high incidence of aggression on television by showing a videotape of a children's television program. Ask students to call out whenever they observe an act of aggression—including verbal aggression. Point out any acts of aggression that students miss. Ask a volunteer to keep a tally of aggressive acts as they are reported and to give the total number at the end of the demonstration. Then have students debate whether viewing aggression on television encourages children to act aggressively.

Taking a Stand

Ask students to explain how a bully's aggressive behavior might be viewed by each of the following: a biological psychologist, a psychoanalyst, a cognitive psychologist, and a learning theorist. Then have students state which of the views best explains the aggressive behavior and why.

Reviewing Section 4

Have students complete the Section 4 Review questions on page 492.

However, there is little question that other types of aggressive behavior are reinforced. In many sports, aggression helps players win games. Winning, in turn, gains them the admiration of fans and often, at least in professional sports, large paychecks.

Learning theorists also believe that people learn many behaviors by observing others. People observe aggressive behavior on television, in the movies, and in video games (Anderson & Dill, 2000; Huesmann & Miller, 1994; Yohota & Thompson, 2000). Many people also observe aggressive behavior in their own homes and neighborhoods. Thus, most people have ample opportunity to observe aggression and learn from their observations.

The role that television violence plays in teaching children aggressive behavior has received a considerable amount of attention. This is because most children spend a great deal of time watching television—more time, in fact, than they spend in school. Evidence suggests that by the time the average child reaches middle school, he or she has viewed more than 8,000 murders and 100,000 other acts of violence on television (Huston et al., 1992).

Most experts agree that watching violence on television leads people to act more aggressively (Holland, 2000). Figure 21.3 shows some of the data that support this conclusion. It shows how the seriousness of criminal acts committed by age 30 corresponds to the amount of television watched before age 8.

Watching violence on television may influence people to become more aggressive because television may reinforce an individual's ideas about violence and thus lessen his or her inhibitions against aggression. Children may also learn to imitate the acts of violence they see on television.

Sociocultural View

Sociocultural theorists argue that some cultures encourage independence and competitiveness and that this, in turn, promotes aggression. The United

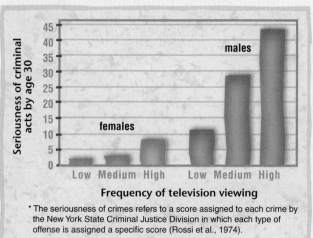

Television Viewing and Aggression

* The seriousness of crimes refers to a score assigned to each crime by the New York State Criminal Justice Division in which each type of offense is assigned a specific score (Rossi et al., 1974).

FIGURE 21.3 *This graph illustrates the results of a study that measured the seriousness of criminal acts by age 30 as a function of the frequency of television viewing at age 8.*

Huesmann, L. R., Eron, L. D., Dubow, E. F., & Seebauer, E. (1988). Television Viewing Habits in Childhood and Adult Aggression. *Child Development.*

States is a good example. Most Americans place a high value on individual rights and freedoms. They also emphasize competition. When so much importance is attached to the individual, getting along with others becomes less important. When one person is strongly encouraged to win over others, hostility and aggression may result.

Other cultures place greater value on the welfare of the group and encourage people to cooperate. This may reduce levels of aggression. Children in cultures such as Thailand and Jamaica, for example, where courtesy, respect, and cooperation are encouraged, tend to be less aggressive than children in the United States (Tharp, 1991).

SECTION 4 REVIEW

go.hrw.com **Homework Practice Online** Keyword: SY3 HP21

1. What is the biological view of aggressive behavior?

2. According to learning theorists, how do children learn aggressive behavior?

3. **Critical Thinking** *Evaluating* Why is it important to understand the causes of aggression?

Drawing Conclusions

Ask students to describe situations in which teens might be especially likely to conform to peer group norms because a situation requires almost total reliance on the peer group for support and social contact. *(Possibilities include a group of students visiting a foreign country or a school team visiting another school.)* Then have students analyze what personal traits might enable teens to remain true to their own beliefs in the face of peer pressure to engage in risky or potentially harmful behavior.

Have students explain how social factors rather than the threat of actual punishment worked to encourage the vast majority of the "ordinary men" in Reserve Police Battalion 101 to kill innocent people. *(Refusing to kill would have made the men appear weak. It would also have led them to be rejected by and isolated from their only social contacts. The end result might have been lowered self-esteem, depression, and similar emotional problems. The desire to be part of the group was stronger than the desire for personal honor.)*

READINGS IN

PSYCHOLOGY

CONFORMITY AND INDIVIDUAL CHOICE

How far will an individual deviate from his or her own beliefs to conform to the beliefs and actions of the majority? Could the power of social conformity influence an average man to commit murder? In the most extreme cases, the answer seems to be yes.

The following excerpts are from American historian Christopher R. Browning's book *Ordinary Men: Reserve Police Battalion 101 and the Final Solution in Poland* (1992). The book is a reconstruction of the events and motives that led 500 middle-aged, middle-class German men of Reserve Police Battalion 101 to launch a reign of terror against Jews in Poland in July 1942. By November 1943, these ordinary civilians had brutally killed at least 85,000 Jewish people.

It is important to note that the commanding officer, Major Trapp, explicitly offered to excuse any man who did not want to participate in the impending mass murder. Trapp's offer thrust responsibility onto each man individually. Unlike regular soldiers, these policemen bore the burden of choice. They were not "just following orders." The pressure to conform to their peers' expectations, however, was paramount.

Only the very exceptional remained indifferent to taunts of 'weakling' from their comrades and could live with the fact that they were considered to be 'no man.'. . . Killing was seen as a collective obligation, so not killing was asocial vis-à-vis one's comrades. Those who did not shoot risked isolation [and] rejection . . . —a very uncomfortable prospect within the framework of a tight-knit unit stationed abroad among a hostile population, so that the individual had virtually nowhere else to turn for support and social contact. (pp.184–185)

Browning notes that no member of Reserve Police Battalion 101 was physically harmed or officially punished for refusing to shoot. Instead, outright refusal—total nonconformity—brought other, more subtle, consequences.

There is the threat of isolation. . . . Stepping out could have been seen as a moral reproach of one's comrades: the nonshooter was potentially indicating that he was 'too good' to do such things. . . . Most nonshooters intuitively tried to diffuse the criticism of their comrades. . . . They pleaded not that they were 'too good' but rather that they were 'too weak' to kill. (p.185)

. . . most of those who did not shoot only reaffirmed the 'macho' values of the majority—according to which it was a positive quality to be 'tough' enough to kill unarmed, noncombatant men, women, and children—and tried not to rupture the bonds of comradeship that constituted their social world.

What, then, is one to conclude? . . . The reserve policemen faced choices, and most of them committed terrible deeds. But those who killed cannot be absolved by the notion that anyone in the same situation would have done as they did. For even among them, some refused to kill and others stopped killing. (p.188)

Yet 80 to 90 percent of the men proceeded to kill, though all of them—at least initially—were horrified and disgusted by what they were doing. To break ranks and step out, to adopt overtly nonconformist behavior, was simply beyond most of the men. It was easier for them to shoot. (p.184)

. . . Within virtually every social collective, the peer group exerts tremendous pressures on behavior and sets moral norms. If the men of Reserve Police Battalion 101 could become killers under such circumstances, what group of men cannot? (p.189)

Think About It

Analyzing Information What factors might have led more men to refuse to conform to the murderous actions of the rest of the group?

Primary Source Note

Description of Change: excerpted, bracketed

Rationale: excerpted to focus on main idea; bracketed to clarify meaning

Class Discussion

Remind the class that cognitive psychologists believe aggressive behavior reflects people's values and the choices they make. Have students discuss the values and choices of the men in the feature that led them to act so aggressively toward others.

Think About It: Answer

Two factors may have led more men to refuse to conform. First, most group members shared the attitude that those who refuse to kill are weak and unmanly. If group members instead had shared the attitude that those who refuse to kill are humane, then more of them might have refused to conform. The men also were in a situation in which they depended solely on other group members for social contact and support. If they could have turned instead to people outside the group for contact and support, more of them might have refused to conform to the group's actions.

493

Section Objective

▶ Define altruism, and identify the factors that promote and the factors that inhibit altruistic behavior.

This objective is assessed in the Section Review on page 495 and in the Chapter 21 Review.

Opening Section 5

Motivator

Privately ask a student to come to class a few minutes late and to drop the contents of his or her book bag when entering the room. Observe whether other students help the "latecomer" pick up the contents of the book bag. If they do not, help the person yourself. Then point out to the class that they have just observed an act of altruism. Explain what altruism is, and tell the class that in Section 5 they will learn what factors influence whether people are likely to act in an altruistic manner.

494

Altruism

Altruism is an unselfish concern for the welfare of other people. Altruistic people sacrifice their own well-being to help others in need. For example, an altruistic person might jump into the water to save someone who is drowning, even though doing so could put the would-be rescuer's own life in danger.

Explaining Altruism

Evolutionary psychologists believe that altruism, like aggression, is linked to genetics (Guisinger & Blatt, 1994; Rushton, 1989). Although altruistic behavior benefits other people, evolutionary psychologists believe it can also help people pass on their genes to future generations. At least it can do so if the altruistic behavior is directed toward relatives—that is, toward people who have many of the same genes as the altruist.

By helping their relatives survive and reproduce, evolutionary psychologists argue, early humans indirectly passed on their own genes to the next generation. In this way, genes for altruism have come to be part of the human gene pool. Thus, according to the evolutionary view, humans are altruistic by nature (Simon, 1990).

The evolutionary explanation of altruism has been criticized for many of the same reasons that the evolutionary explanation of aggression has been criticized: no clear-cut genetic basis for altruistic behavior has been found, and the tendency to act altruistically varies too widely to be under genetic control. The evolutionary view of altruism has also been criticized for failing to explain why people act altruistically toward those who are not related to themselves.

Factors Promoting Altruism

Research has shown that several factors influence whether a person will help others in particular situations. One factor is the person's state of mind. Many studies have found that people are more likely to help others when they are in a good mood (Berkowitz, 1987; Manucia et al., 1984). Being in a good mood seems to make people feel more generous and eager to help others (Carlson et al., 1988). It also may make people feel more powerful and thus better able to provide aid to those in need (Cunningham et al., 1990).

Altruism is just part of the job for the firefighter pictured here. **Can you think of other professions that require altruistic behavior?**

People who have problems themselves may also be more likely to act altruistically, perhaps because their own problems make them sensitive to the troubles of others (Thompson et al., 1980). People who are empathic—that is, able to put themselves in another's place—may be more likely to be altruistic for the same reason (Darley, 1993).

Being competent to help others seems to increase the chances that people will act altruistically. For example, registered nurses are more likely than people with no medical training to come to the aid of accident victims (Cramer et al., 1988). Similarly, police officers, who are trained to intervene in violent and dangerous situations, are more likely than the average person to help people in trouble. Being a good student himself, Todd felt competent to help others with their schoolwork and did so for Linda when they first met in biology class.

People with a strong need for approval also may be more likely to act altruistically. By doing so, they hope to gain the approval of others. In addition, a

A DAY IN THE LIFE

Teaching Section 5

Role-Playing

Ask several students to role-play a situation that demonstrates the bystander effect. Then generate a discussion of why people are less likely to help someone in need when other people are also present to help. Have students discuss the relationship between the bystander effect and the concept of diffusion of responsibility. What can be done to encourage people in groups to act altruistically?

Closing Section 5

Interpreting Ideas

Have students compare the factors that promote altruism with the factors that inhibit it. Then ask students to discuss how a cognitive psychologist or a behavior theorist might explain altruistic behavior.

Reviewing Section 5

Have students complete the Section Review questions on page 495.

---

sense of personal responsibility may increase the chances of altruistic behavior (Maruyama et al., 1982). Teachers and camp counselors, for example, are responsible for those in their care, and they are more likely to act altruistically toward them than others are.

Factors Inhibiting Altruism

There are also several factors that seem to make people reluctant to help others in distress. In some cases, people may not be aware that another person is in trouble. In fact, the less sure they are that another person needs help, the less likely they are to offer assistance (Shotland & Heinold, 1985).

Some people may fail to act altruistically because they think there is nothing they can do to help. Others may be afraid of making a social blunder and being ridiculed (Pantin & Carver, 1982). For example, someone who sees an individual with a disability struggling with a door may fear offending the person by offering help. Finally, people may fail to act altruistically, particularly in dangerous situations, because they fear injuring themselves in the attempt.

Bystander Effect

The chances of people helping someone in need also depend on how many other people are present to help. Research has shown that people are less likely to give aid when other bystanders are present. This is called the **bystander effect**.

A classic experiment by psychologists John Darley and Bibb Latané (1968) is one of many studies that have documented the bystander effect. In one phase of the study, participants were placed in separate cubicles and asked to talk with one another over an intercom. One of the participants was actually an associate of the researchers. When his turn came to talk, he called for help and then made sounds that suggested he was having an epileptic seizure.

Some study participants had been led to believe that they alone could hear the person having the seizure. Others had been led to believe that from one to four other participants could hear him as well. About 85 percent of participants who thought that no one else could hear the person came to his aid. However, when participants thought that others could also hear the individual in trouble, fewer of them tried to help. In fact, the more people who were presumed to be able to hear him, the less likely participants were to become involved. Only 31 percent of participants made an effort to help when they thought that four other people could hear the person in need.

TRUTH OR fiction ■ REVISITED ■

It is true that people are more likely to help someone in trouble when no one else is present to help. People are less likely to help a person in need when others are around. This is called the bystander effect.

It seems that diffusion of responsibility limits altruistic behavior. When people are members of a group, they are likely to stand back and wait for others to help the person in need. However, when others are not around, they are more likely to act altruistically.

SECTION 5 REVIEW

go.hrw.com **Homework Practice Online** Keyword: SY3 HP21

1. Define *altruism*.

2. What factors promote altruistic behavior? What factors inhibit it?

3. **Critical Thinking** *Categorizing* Describe two situations, one in which bystanders are likely to help a person in trouble and one in which bystanders are less likely to help. Explain your answer.

Whether we act altruistically to help others in need depends on many factors, including the presence of other bystanders who could also offer assistance.

2. Factors that promote altruistic behavior include being in a good mood, being sensitive to the problems of others, being empathic, being competent to help, needing the approval of others, and having a sense of personal responsibility for others. Factors that inhibit altruistic behavior include being unsure that another person needs help, believing that there is nothing one can do to help, being afraid of making a social blunder, and being afraid of getting hurt.

3. Answers will vary, but students should demonstrate an understanding of the bystander effect and the other factors that influence the likelihood of people acting altruistically.

Chapter 21 Review: Answers

Writing a Summary

See the section subtitles for the main topics in the chapter.

Identifying People and Ideas

1. the concept that people often perform better when other people are watching

2. concern about the opinion of others

3. the tendency to slack off when part of a group

4. the tendency for people to take greater risks as part of a group

21 Chapter REVIEW AND ASSESSMENT RESOURCES

Technology
▶ Chapter 21 Test Generator (on the One-Stop Planner)
▶ HRW Go site

Reinforcement, Review, and Assessment
▶ Chapter 21 Review, pp. 494–495
▶ Chapter Review and Activities with Answer Key
▶ Alternative Assessment Handbook
▶ Portfolio Assessment Handbook
▶ Chapter 21 Test (Form A or B)

PSYCHOLOGY PROJECTS

Linking to Community Invite a local judge, a police officer, a social worker, and a psychologist to hold a panel discussion on the nature of aggression. Ask the panel members to address the following questions:

■ How serious is the problem of aggression? Is aggression becoming more common?

---

5. group decision-making process in which the group makes decision in accordance with what the majority wants

6. the strengthening of a group member's attitudes

7. the standards people share

8. unspoken, unwritten rules

9. venting of aggressive impulses

10. an unselfish concern for the welfare of other people

Understanding Main Ideas

1. Diffusion of responsibility leads individuals in a group to take greater risks than they would if they were acting on their own.

2. Explicit norms are written or spoken. Implicit norms are unwritten and unspoken.

3. Obedience is behaving as someone else orders; conformity is matching one's behavior to that of other group members.

4. It allows people to vent aggressive feelings in ways that do not harm others.

5. It is the tendency for people to be less likely to help someone in need when other people are present.

Thinking Critically

1. An evolutionary psychologist would explain it as a way of increasing one's chances of surviving; a learning theorist would explain it in terms of reinforcement and observation.

2. Members would learn how much money the various options would raise and which would be feasible. Once they knew the facts

496

Chapter 21 REVIEW

Writing a Summary

Using standard grammar, spelling, sentence structure, and punctuation, summarize the information in this chapter. Consider:
• social norms, obedience to authority figures, and the ways group membership can influence individual behavior
• aggressive and altruistic behavior

Identifying People and Ideas

Identify the following terms or people and use them in appropriate sentences.

1. social facilitation
2. evaluation apprehension
3. social loafing
4. risky shift
5. majority-wins schemes
6. group polarization
7. social norms
8. implicit norms
9. catharsis
10. altruism

Understanding Main Ideas

SECTION 1 (pp. 480–84)
1. What is the relationship between diffusion of responsibility and the risky shift?

SECTION 2 (pp. 484–86)
2. How do explicit and implicit social norms differ?

SECTION 3 (pp. 487–89)
3. What is the difference between obedience and conformity?

SECTION 4 (pp. 490–92)
4. Why do some psychologists believe that catharsis can help prevent aggression?

SECTION 5 (pp. 494–95)
5. What is the bystander effect?

Thinking Critically

1. Analyzing Information How would an evolutionary psychologist and a learning theorist explain the tendency for people to obey authority figures?

2. Evaluating In what ways might a group of teens trying to raise money for a high school club come to a decision using the truth-wins social decision scheme?

3. Comparing and Contrasting How are the explanations of aggression provided by evolutionary psychologists and psychoanalysts similar and different?

4. Drawing Inferences and Conclusions How is the bystander effect related to evaluation apprehension?

Writing About Psychology

1. Summarizing Request permission to attend a meeting of a school or community organization. During the meeting, take notes on how the group's leader conducts the meeting. Afterward, review your notes and decide what style of leadership was used. How might the meeting have been conducted if another style of leadership had been used instead? Write a brief summary of what you have learned.

2. Analyzing Information Read more about the evolutionary explanation for human aggression or altruism. What types of evidence and arguments are used to back the claims that the behavior helps individuals survive, reproduce, and contribute their genes to the next generation? What evidence and arguments have been presented to refute the claims? Describe the evidence that supports and refutes the claims in a short written report. Conclude the report with a statement of your own position on the subject. Use the graphic organizer below to help you write your report.

Supports	Refutes

- Who are the chief victims of aggression?
- What are the major causes of aggression?
- How can teens help solve the problems of aggression?

Following the discussion, urge students to ask the panel members questions they have prepared in advance. When preparing their questions, students should consider how aggression adversely affects their own lives.

Cooperative Learning

Organize the class into groups of five or more. Instruct each group to write and perform a skit that illustrates one of the social decision schemes and one of the styles of group leadership discussed in the chapter. The members of each group should identify the type of group they will represent, who will lead them, and a specific decision the group must make. After the groups have performed their skits for the class, generate a discussion of how well the decision-making scheme and leadership style used matched the problem.

Building Social Studies Skills

Interpreting Graphs

Study the graph below. Then use the information in the graph to help you answer the questions that follow.

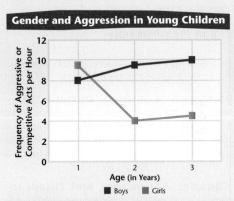

Gender and Aggression in Young Children

Frequency of Aggressive or Competitive Acts per Hour

Age (in Years)

■ Boys ■ Girls

Source: Maccoby, *The Two Sexes*, 1998

1. Which of the following statements best reflects the information presented in the graph?
   a. Aggression is an inherited trait.
   b. Aggression is a learned trait.
   c. As they grow older, girls remain as aggressive as boys.
   d. As they grow older, boys become more aggressive than girls.
2. What information would you request from the psychologist to learn more about this study and its usefulness?

Analyzing Primary Sources

Read the following excerpt, in which Thomas J. Socha and Diana M. Socha consider problems that arise during group communication among young children. Then answer the questions that follow.

"There are a number of interactional problems that prevent dialogue from occurring, which teachers and group facilitators need to consider. First, one child may dominate a group discussion with his or her voice, ideas, or behavior. . . . Second, the uncooperative child, the child who does not want to do his or her part, may be ignored by a group. . . . Third, turn taking was problematic in the discussions until a "no interrupting" rule was put in place. . . . Finally . . . it will be difficult for a teacher or group facilitator to resist participating. . . . Our analysis shows that children rely immediately on an adult for a solution and use that adult's authority to "fix" the problem, instead of learning communication strategies to manage it themselves."

3. Which of the following statements best reflects the arguments presented in the excerpt?
   a. Children are as capable of managing group communications as adults are.
   b. Children cannot function in groups.
   c. Adults will always lead children's groups, whether they intend to or not.
   d. Children's groups work best when some adult assistance is available.
4. What responsibilities and difficulties do adults face when they work with groups of children?

about the various options, they could reach a unanimous decision.

3. Both view human aggression as unavoidable but controllable. Evolutionary psychologists believe that a person's biological makeup strongly influences how aggressive that person is. Psychoanalysts, on the other hand, assert that aggression results from repressed anger and frustration.

4. People may be less likely to help another person when bystanders are present because they feel less responsible when the effort is shared by members of a group.

Writing About Psychology

1. Reports should include concrete examples that identify the leadership style observed; students should be able to apply other leadership styles to the group.

2. Students may take either side in the debate but should present the evidence for both sides in an objective manner.

Building Social Studies Skills

1. d
2. Students' answers will vary, but some students would request the researchers' definition of "aggressive and competitive acts."
3. d
4. Adults must ensure that all children in a group have the opportunity to share their ideas while at the same time not taking charge of the group or influencing the children with their own ideas.

PSYCHOLOGY PROJECTS

Linking to Community

Applying Psychology With several other classmates, work together to create a skit that shows how teens in the community are pressured to conform to their peers. As you work on the skit, help develop a supportive climate within the group. After presenting the skit, ask the class to identify the ways in which characters in the skit conformed to group norms. Help your group lead the class in a discussion of what might have happened if the individuals had decided not to conform.

☑ internet connect

Internet Activity: go.hrw.com
KEYWORD: SY3 PS21

Choose an activity on social interaction to:
- create a skit illustrating characteristics of group behavior.
- create a pamphlet that describes and explains conformity.
- profile one of the theories that attempts to explain aggression.

go.hrw.com

UNIT 7 REVIEW

▶ **TEACH**

Organize students into pairs and have them review the textbook's discussion of stereotypes and discrimination (pages 465–66). Then have each pair prepare a flyer that explains what these concepts are and how they can be combated.

▶ **PSYCHOLOGY IN ACTION**

Have students work in small groups to brainstorm different methods of convincing a group of people to take a certain action. Have each group make a list of at least five suggestions. Finally, have students discuss the issue as a class.

Have each pair present their flyers to the class.

▶ **EXTEND**

Have students review the problem in the Psychology in Action Simulation. Then point out that some people are likely to acquire prejudicial attitudes from their peers. Have each group use the problem-solving skills outlined in the simulation to develop a plan of action for dealing with prejudice

that stems from peer influence. Each group should create a report detailing their plan. Ask the groups to present their reports to the class.

UNIT 7

PSYCHOLOGY IN ACTION

YOU SOLVE THE PROBLEM . . .

How can students reduce prejudice in the community?

Complete the following activity in small groups. Imagine that your group is preparing a presentation about ways to reduce prejudice. Prepare a poster outlining the best way to accomplish this task.

1. Gather Information. Use your textbook and other resources to find information that might influence your plan of action. Remember that your poster must include adequate information to convince your classmates that your proposed method will be effective in dealing with prejudice. This information might include charts, graphs, or other

visuals. You may want to divide up different parts of the research among group members.

2. List and Consider Options. After reviewing the information you have gathered, list and consider the options you might use. Your final solution to the problem may be easier to reach if you consider all options. Be sure to record your possible options for the preparation of your poster.

3. Consider Advantages and Disadvantages. Now consider the advantages and disadvantages of taking each option. Your group should ask itself questions such as,

- Which course of action will have the best chance of being seen or heard by members of our community?
- What segments of the community are being targeted by this project?

Once you have considered the advantages and disadvantages, record them as notes for use in preparing your poster.

4. Choose and Implement a Solution. After considering the advantages and disadvantages, you should choose a solution. Then plan and create your poster for that solution. Be sure to make your poster very clear.

5. Evaluate the Effectiveness of the Solution. Once you have prepared your poster, write a paragraph evaluating the effectiveness of your group's recommendation. When you are ready, decide which group members will present the poster. Then take your report to the rest of the class. Good luck!

HOLT
PSYCHOLOGY:
PRINCIPLES IN PRACTICE

REFERENCE SECTION

R1

CAREERS IN PSYCHOLOGY

Overview

A career in psychology is bound to be fascinating, for the fundamental subject matter is, after all, us. That so many people decide to study human behavior, in all its diversity, should come as no surprise. The range of specializations and kinds of jobs available within the broad area of psychology are so varied that there may well be a career in psychology to suit almost everyone's interests.

But how can you start narrowing the field for yourself? What educational training and personality characteristics are required for each psychology-related career? How do you decide on a specialization and actually become a psychologist?

Career opportunities in the field abound on every educational level. If you are most interested in relating to people directly, and helping them deal with serious mental or emotional problems in therapy, perhaps you will consider becoming a clinical psychologist. This is the area that most people think of when they hear the word *psychologist.* Many clinical psychologists specialize in treating one or more specific problems, such as substance abuse, eating disorders, or phobias. Others specialize in group treatment settings, working as family therapists or couples therapists, for instance. But clinical psychology is just one of numerous possibilities.

Other careers in psychology do not necessarily involve working directly with people or doing therapy at all. If you enjoy working in a laboratory and conducting basic scientific research, you may be attracted to the exacting field of experimental psychology. Some fields offer a combination of research- and people-oriented work. As an industrial or organizational psychologist, for example, you might apply psychological techniques to work-oriented issues in a business environment.

The first step to pursuing a career in psychology is usually a four-year university degree, consisting of specific core courses. In addition, today's student is well-advised to take a course in computer science, which is mandatory for conducting research.

Not all careers related to psychology require graduate study. Options in psychological careers with a four-year bachelor's degree (B.A. or B.S.) alone do exist, although they tend to be somewhat limited in scope. Examples include working as an aide or a social worker in a mental hospital, hospice, nursing home, residential treatment center for disturbed youth, or

government agency. These same settings, among others, offer psychology-related careers in administration, human resources, and customer service.

Most careers in psychology, however, now require at least a master of arts or master of science degree (M.A. or M.S.), and often a doctoral degree (Ph.D. or Ed.Psy.). It takes about two years of study in a graduate program to earn a master's degree, and about four to six years above that to earn a doctoral degree.

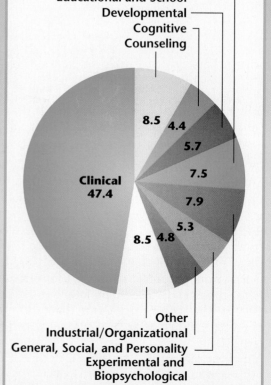

Doctoral Degrees Awarded in Psychology

Educational and School —
Developmental —
Cognitive —
Counseling —

8.5 4.4
5.7
7.5
Clinical 47.4 7.9
5.3
8.5 4.8

Other
Industrial/Organizational
General, Social, and Personality
Experimental and
Biopsychological

Career opportunities in the field of psychology are both numerous and diverse. Preparation for these careers generally begins with a doctoral degree. This graph illustrates the percentage of doctoral degrees awarded in the various areas of psychological specialization.

Source: Kyle, T. M. & Williams, S. (2000 May); 1998–1999 APA Survey of Graduate Departments of Psychology, Tables 13A & 13B.

Clinical psychologists are trained to diagnose and treat individuals with various psychological disorders such as this woman suffering from depression—as well as other social and adjustment problems.

For careers in educational, social, experimental, clinical, or counseling psychology, a doctoral degree is highly recommended. However, many people take some time off after receiving their undergraduate degree to gain valuable experience in laboratory or clinical work instead of plunging into years and years of schooling. In fact, if you intend to become a school or educational psychologist, your state may require that you first gain a few years of teaching experience.

Whatever career you ultimately select, it should be rewarding for you, personally. Rewarding opportunities in psychology exist on all levels.

Clinical Psychologist

About half of all graduate degrees in psychology are awarded in the demanding field of clinical psychology. In this sense, clinical psychology is the most popular branch of psychology. Some clinical psychologists work with individuals who suffer from severe psychological disorders, while others prefer to limit their practices to treating people with less

severe behavioral or adjustment problems. In the course of their work, clinical psychologists may deal with such diverse problems as severe depression and other psychological disorders, juvenile delinquency, drug abuse, marital problems, or eating disorders.

People often confuse clinical psychologists with psychiatrists. The distinction is a significant one, however. In treating their patients, clinical psychologists conduct interviews, practice methods of psychotherapy, and administer and interpret psychological tests. They are not, however, able to prescribe medication or administer other kinds of biological therapy. Psychiatrists, on the other hand, are medical doctors who specialize in the treatment of psychological disorders. By law, only psychiatrists have the right and responsibility to prescribe medication to their clients.

Many clinical psychologists with doctoral degrees maintain a private practice, where they see clients who voluntarily come to them for treatment. Others, however, work in veteran's hospitals, mental health clinics, schools for the mentally retarded, or correctional institutions, where they are generally assigned to a specific number of patients.

Many clinical psychologists teach—primarily in colleges, universities, or medical schools—where they pass on their experience and knowledge to others, rather than apply their skills directly. Still others conduct workshops on specific topics, and engage in the training of business professionals or other psychologists. Those with literary talents often write scholarly or popular books and articles.

Clinical psychologists may be self-employed, or hired by government, business, schools, universities, hospitals, prisons, or nonprofit organizations, as consultants or full-time employees. The field is extremely flexible, thus it is also becoming more competitive, as is admission to strong graduate programs. Clinical psychologists also must be licensed by the state in which they live and work.

Counseling Psychologist

Like clinical psychologists, counseling psychologists work with people experiencing distress. Counseling psychologists, however, tend to treat people who are confronted with stressful or highly emotional situations, rather than people who have more severe mental disorders. For example, a couple having marital difficulties might go to a counseling psychologist in the hopes of avoiding a divorce. The suicide of a family member may prompt a person to seek out a counseling psychologist's support and perspective for a few months.

People with a chronic physical disease or a catastrophic illness often look to counselors for help in coping with difficulties of various magnitudes that feel overwhelming. It may be that a high school student feels anxious because she believes that her parents expect too much of her, for instance, or that a formerly happy young man experiences depression after a job loss.

Differences between clinical and counseling psychologists are growing fainter. Both the work itself and the educational requirements in most graduate schools, are nearly identical. Also, the same types of employers that hire clinical psychologists are likely to hire counseling psychologists of the same educational level for the same positions. The final choice to become a clinical or a counseling psychologist ultimately may be determined by the specific graduate program that you find most appealing.

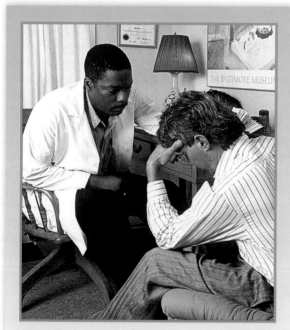

Counseling psychologists tend to work with patients who are faced with stressful or emotional situations. They help people to confront and overcome their fears or other disturbing emotions.

Both clinical and counseling psychologists use the techniques and theories with which they personally agree. They must be careful, however, not to impose their views on their clients. Both types of psychologists may use psychological assessments or tests to evaluate their clients. Graduate programs in counseling psychology, however, tend not to emphasize research as much as programs that train clinical psychologists.

Subspecialties in Counseling Psychology

Career counselors (also known as vocational counselors) administer interest-inventory and other psychological tests to help people make appropriate and gratifying career choices. They may work with university students, with adult career-changers, or in private businesses or corporations. Career counselors may lead workshops on job-searching skills, facilitate discussion and support groups, and sometimes work with motivated clients on a one-on-one basis. Some career counselors also function as intermediaries between industry and colleges, helping to place new graduates in jobs, or directing them to other resources. This career attracts outgoing people who love helping others and who thrive in a relatively fast-paced, upbeat environment that addresses a rather limited range of problems in a practical manner.

Rehabilitation counselors work with physically challenged individuals, helping them adapt to their disabilities and become self-sufficient and self-supporting. They work with people of all ages, whether handicapped after an accident, an illness, or from birth. Their primary job is a tough one: helping people face the hard reality of having physical limitations while remaining realistic, yet hopeful, about the client's potential.

Rehabilitation (or occupational) counselors help prepare clients for jobs that they are capable of doing. In some cases, they also arrange for additional training. Part of their job may entail soliciting potential employers for their clients while also acting as morale boosters in an individual's physical and emotional rehabilitative process.

A master's degree in rehabilitative counseling (often offered within university departments of education or health/kinesthesiology) is recommended, but a bachelor's degree in psychology, especially when combined with volunteer experience, may be an acceptable substitute. This can be an extremely rewarding career, though also a frustrating one, as in the case of any career that requires frequent contact with bureaucratic agencies. Rehabilitation counselors must demonstrate persistence, dedication, patience, and stamina.

Teachers of special education face similar tasks and issues as rehabilitation counselors (or therapists, as they are sometimes known). The objective of both special education teachers and rehabilitation counselors is the same: helping people with disabilities achieve their full potential.

School counselors (or school psychologists) work with students, teachers, and administrators to make the school the best possible environment for learning. One of their primary tasks is to help students who are having problems that interfere with learning. These problems may involve peers, families, teachers, coursework, or a combination of these and other factors. Such counselors must be observant and knowledgeable enough to identify and diagnose a student's problems, devise possible solutions, and make recommendations regarding a student's placement in special education or gifted classes.

Like other counseling psychologists, school counselors make use of a range of intelligence, interest, and psychological tests. A routine part of the job is administering and scoring standardized tests. More importantly, the school psychologist interprets these test results. This interpretation is then used to identify and address the special needs of individual students.

In some cases, school psychologists are also called in to resolve conflicts, either between students and teachers, students and parents, or students and other students. The psychologist will generally listen to both sides of the dispute and try to resolve the conflict with an amicable compromise.

Some states require school counselors to obtain teaching credentials and gain practical experience in the classroom. Training for school counselors usually takes place through a college's department of education, not necessarily within the psychology department. If you are tactful yet assertive, and flourish in the challenging school environment, this rewarding career may be high on your list of considerations.

Educational Psychologist

Should classrooms consist of only students of the same age, or should students be grouped according to skill levels, regardless of age? Should a school district revise its curriculum and teaching methods to meet the changing needs of students? How can computers facilitate learning in the classroom?

Educational psychologists study how people learn. They perform research—both in and out of the classroom—geared to facilitating the learning process and improving education as a whole. Although educational psychologists typically work for school districts, they are frequently employed by universities, where they engage in research and assist in training teachers and school counselors.

Unlike school psychologists, educational psychologists are more involved with theoretical issues that affect learning rather than with individual students. Their research often involves measuring a group's abilities and achievements by administering, and sometimes creating, standardized tests. Educational psychologists then use the results of these tests to help place students in specific programs and to develop curricula in schools.

Educational psychologists may focus on several other issues. They may, for example, study the psychological factors that affect a student's test-taking

The primary tasks of a school counselor are to administer, score, and interpret the results of standardized tests.

Educational psychologists do not generally work with individual students. They do, however, develop curriculum standards and teaching methods. Thus, indirectly, they have a profound effect on the individual student's education.

ability or school performance in general. They may research the effects that cultural and gender differences have on learning.

Educational psychologists also analyze the range of instructional methods available to teachers in the classroom. Then they use their research discoveries to expand or refine these instructional options.

Work for educational psychologists is not necessarily limited to the academic environment, however. Large corporations and government agencies often hire educational psychologists to devise staff training programs.

A bachelor's degree in psychology is the first step in the long, complex process of becoming an educational psychologist. Candidates are urged to gain teaching experience on the elementary, middle school, or high school levels before pursuing a doctoral program within a university's education or psychology department. Since the work of educational psychologists involves evaluating and interpreting research data, the training requires proficiency in mathematics, statistics, and computer science.

Depending on the graduate program, the final degree earned will be a Doctor of Education (Ed.D.) or a Doctor of Philosophy (Ph.D.). Although educational psychology is a difficult profession to break into, it is an attractive career for those who wish to influence the course of the educational system itself.

Developmental Psychologist

At what age do children develop the ability to think abstractly? Does isolation reduce short-term memory in elderly people? Why do infants need more sleep than older children? If questions related to stages of life intrigue you, perhaps you would want to become a developmental psychologist.

Developmental psychologists study the behavioral changes that occur at various stages in a person's life. In the past, developmental psychology was limited to the study of changes in the developmental stages of children. For this reason, it was called *child psychology.* Recently, however, researchers have become aware that people experience complex and interconnected physical, psychological, intellectual, and social changes throughout the entire life span.

Among the contemporary issues developmental psychologists are concerned with is the question of how our ability to perform certain tasks changes throughout our lifetime. Developmental psychologists also investigate language acquisition, changes in perception, creativity, sensory acuity, intellectual abilities, and emotions at different stages of life.

Most developmental psychologists focus on a certain period in the life span, such as infancy, childhood, adolescence, middle age, or old age. This last category, called *gerontology,* promises to be particularly important in the future, as the country's population ages and life spans increase.

Another topic of interest to developmental psychologists includes the changing roles of men and women in society. They study the impact of gender stereotyping and the implications of that stereotyping on a child's development.

Developmental psychologists usually work for universities, teaching and conducting research. Many combine academic careers with a secondary career in writing, as a natural outgrowth of their interests. Some developmental psychologists also work in clinical settings such as hospitals, prisons, nursing homes, schools, group homes, nursery schools, or hospices.

Developmental psychologists no longer limit their research to children. The field has expanded to address the behavioral changes that occur throughout the life span.

Social psychologists are often confused with social workers. Both focus on social behavior. Social workers, however, are more involved with individuals. Their work is more practical and less research oriented than the work of the social psychologist.

There is also a distinct overlap with the field of anthropology. Anthropologists also study social behavior, but they are more concerned with the social customs, rituals, and interactions of various groups of people.

Finally, social psychology is also closely related to sociology. There is, however, a distinct difference between the two. Social psychologists focus on the effects of group membership on the behavior of an individual person. Sociologists, on the other hand, are more concerned with the group as a whole—its structure and characteristics.

Some issues that social psychologists explore may involve gender studies, conformity, or peer

As our society changes, new and exciting issues will be raised. Developmental psychologists are likely to lead the way in answering these questions. The more we learn, the more we will understand about human development and behavior.

Social Psychologist

How do individuals behave in social and group situations? Do boys and girls play differently, and if so, why? Do people's styles of interacting change in the workplace?

Social psychologists study the effects of group membership on individual behavior. Their primary focus is, generally, how behavior in social situations affects individuals. However, social psychologists tend to focus on external influences and environments. They focus on such issues as attitudes, influence, and social cognition and interaction.

Social psychologists study the effects of group membership on individual behavior. They may be interested to study how this aggressive crowd as a whole affects the thoughts and behavior of any single individual in the crowd.

pressure. They may study more specific issues as well—such as the effects of prejudice and discrimination on self-esteem.

Many social psychologists prefer to conduct their research in a naturalistic environment rather than in a laboratory. In a naturalistic observation they have less control of the variables in the study, but the results are based on real-life factors.

Preparation for this multi-dimensional career is by no means uniform. Social psychologists usually first obtain a bachelor's degree in psychology, anthropology, or sociology. A doctoral degree in social psychology or anthropology offers the most flexibility and career advancement in research.

Many social psychologists are employed in research facilities or in universities. They may work in industry, where they can study consumer spending habits. They may work for the newspaper where they write articles on the causes and possible prevention of riots. The options in this field are vast and rewarding. People who enjoy observing others, gathering and synthesizing information, and being associated with academic settings are most likely to be happy in this stimulating field.

Experimental Psychologist

Why do people need sleep? What biological processes contribute to the feelings of happiness and sadness? Where in the brain does the ability to recognize faces reside?

Generally considered the most scientific of psychological disciplines, experimental psychologists conduct research into the basic biological processes related to behavior, thoughts, and emotions. They follow a set of strictly controlled scientific procedures to learn about the relationship between two or more variables. Their research usually emphasizes physiological studies of the nervous system, the brain itself, and the basic processes of thinking, feeling, remembering, and perceiving external stimuli.

Experimental psychologists lay the groundwork for more practical kinds of psychological research and counseling. This basic research, which may seem to have no practical value at the time it is conducted, has led other researchers to develop useful techniques for reducing stress, increasing motivation, enhancing memory, and encouraging longer attention spans, for example.

Experimental psychologists often work with animals. They try, however, to ensure that the animals are handled in a humane manner.

Experimental psychologists do not necessarily try to apply the knowledge they acquire. That is, they do not try to use their research to solve practical problems. They generally leave the actual application of research findings to psychologists from other fields.

In conducting their research, experimental psychologists often work with animals. They may compare the behavior of one species with that of another. In many cases, experimental psychologists use primates because their behavior is so similar to that of humans. The use of animals in research procedures is a matter of continual ethical debate. The benefits from using them, however, generally outweigh the potential harms. Also, experimental psychologists are careful to ensure that the animals receive humane treatment.

Temperament may be one of the most important factors when considering a career in experimental psychology because it takes a certain type of person to think in these process-oriented terms. Like those in other basic research fields, experimental psychologists tend to be highly detail-oriented, patient individuals who easily become absorbed in their work, and do not require regular, close contact with other people. They tend to be independent, abstract thinkers who prefer working in laboratory settings. A doctoral degree is mandatory for the most engrossing work in experimental psychology. Candidates must have strong preparation in the hard sciences, with a concentration on courses in neuroanatomy, physiology, biology and molecular biology, and genetics. Undergraduates often major in psychology, but a degree in any biological science, accompanied with appropriate courses in psychology, is usually an acceptable start.

Most graduate programs prefer candidates who have already demonstrated some competency in research and laboratory skills before entering the doctoral program. If a career in experimental psychology appeals to you, it would be wise to gain some exposure to research science as an undergraduate, or even while still in high school.

Industrial/Organizational Psychologist

What color package most attracts the eyes of shoppers? How can a company arrange cubicles to maximize space without isolating employees from each other? How would a department lay-off affect the company's morale, as a whole?

Psychology enters the workplace with industrial, or organizational, psychologists. Organizational psychologists are usually employed by business or government to figure out ways of increasing productivity, improving working conditions, and saving money in the process. Organizational psychologists generally consult with various divisions of one or more companies.

Organizational psychologists are often consulted by the marketing divisions of companies. Here, they conduct surveys and focus groups to help marketing divisions determine their advertising campaigns based on the psychological profile of their intended audience. They may also be called upon by the human resource department to create a new series of questions for interviewers, or to suggest ways to improve employee morale. They may also be called upon by the administrative department to assess the company's time-management program.

The more the workplace changes, the more need there will be for organizational/industrial psychologists to smooth things out. And so far, there is no sign that the workplace will cease changing.

Like counselors, organizational/industrial psychologists assume the titles indicated by the specific work they perform. If working for an oil company or a conservation organization, they may be called

environmental psychologists. If they work for an advertising firm, perhaps they will be called *consumer psychologists.* Working for a hospital, a health-care organization, or a government health agency on issues of preventive health and health promotion awareness, they may be called *health psychologists.*

As is the case throughout the psychological profession, a master's degree is usually the basic educational requirement for more challenging positions, with doctorates becoming more prevalent. Although industrial/organizational psychology is one of the less visible careers in psychology, it is one of the most far-reaching in terms of the work's impact on the public. The career choices available to those individuals qualified for industrial/organizational psychology are quite extensive. There are no fewer choices than there are types of industries. Industrial/Organizational psychology, thus, offers some of the most varied of career opportunities. The field is most appealing to people who have a knack for spotting trends, are relatively outgoing, and who get along well with a variety of individuals and groups.

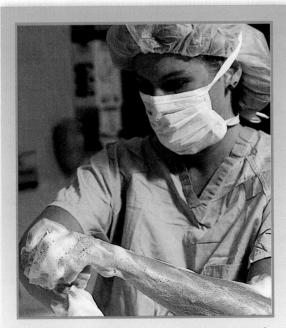

An organizational/industrial psychologist may be interested in studying how stressful work environments—such as that experienced by surgeons—affect a person's psychological health.

ETHICAL PRINCIPLES

OF PSYCHOLOGISTS

PREAMBLE

Psychologists work to develop a valid and reliable body of scientific knowledge based on research. They may apply that knowledge to human behavior in a variety of contexts. In doing so, they perform many roles, such as researcher, educator, diagnostician, therapist, supervisor, consultant, administrator, social interventionist, and expert witness. Their goal is to broaden knowledge of behavior and, where appropriate, to apply it pragmatically to improve the condition of both the individual and society. Psychologists respect the central importance of freedom of inquiry and expression in research, teaching, and publication. They also strive to help the public in developing informed judgments and choices concerning human behavior. This Ethics Code provides a common set of values upon which psychologists build their professional and scientific work.

This Code is intended to provide both the general principles and the decision rules to cover most situations encountered by psychologists. It has as its primary goal the welfare and protection of the individuals and groups with whom psychologists work. It is the individual responsibility of each psychologist to aspire to the highest possible standards of conduct. Psychologists respect and protect human and civil rights, and do not knowingly participate in or condone unfair discriminatory practices.

The development of a dynamic set of ethical standards for a psychologist's work-related conduct requires a personal commitment to a lifelong effort to act ethically; to encourage ethical behavior by students, supervisees, employees, and colleagues, as appropriate; and to consult with others, as needed, concerning ethical problems. Each psychologist supplements, but does not violate, the Ethics Code's values and rules on the basis of guidance drawn from personal values, culture, and experience.

GENERAL PRINCIPLES

PRINCIPLE A: COMPETENCE

Psychologists strive to maintain high standards of competence in their work. They recognize the boundaries of their particular competencies and the limitations of their expertise. They provide only those services and use only those techniques for which they are qualified by education, training, or experience. Psychologists are cognizant of the fact that the competencies required in serving, teaching, and/or studying groups of people vary with the distinctive characteristics of those groups. In those areas in which recognized professional standards do not yet exist, psychologists exercise careful judgment and take appropriate precautions to protect the welfare of those with whom they work. They maintain knowledge of relevant scientific and professional information related to the services they render, and they recognize the need for ongoing education. Psychologists make appropriate use of scientific, professional, technical, and administrative resources.

PRINCIPLE B: INTEGRITY

Psychologists seek to promote integrity in the science, teaching, and practice of psychology. In these activities psychologists are honest, fair, and respectful of others. In describing or reporting their qualifications, services, products, fees, research, or teaching, they do not make statements that are false, misleading, or deceptive. Psychologists strive to be aware of their own belief systems, values, needs, and limitations and the effect of these on their work. To the extent feasible, they attempt to clarify for relevant parties the roles they are performing and to function appropriately in accordance with those roles. Psychologists avoid improper and potentially harmful dual relationships.

PRINCIPLE C: PROFESSIONAL AND SCIENTIFIC RESPONSIBILITY

Psychologists uphold professional standards of conduct, clarify their professional roles and obligations, accept appropriate responsibility for their behavior, and adapt their methods to the needs of different populations. Psychologists consult with, refer to, or cooperate with other professionals and institutions to the extent needed to serve the best interests of their patients, clients, or other recipients of their services. Psychologists' moral standards and conduct are personal matters to the same degree as is true for any other person, except as psychologists' conduct may compromise their professional responsibilities or reduce the public's trust in psychology and psychologists. Psychologists are concerned about the ethical compliance of their colleagues' scientific and professional conduct. When appropriate, they consult with colleagues in order to prevent or avoid unethical conduct.

PRINCIPLE D: RESPECT FOR PEOPLE'S RIGHTS AND DIGNITY

Psychologists accord appropriate respect to the fundamental rights, dignity, and worth of all people. They respect the rights of individuals to privacy, confidentiality, self-determination, and autonomy, mindful that legal and other obligations may lead to inconsistency and conflict with the exercise of these rights. Psychologists are aware of cultural, individual, and role differences, including those due to age, gender, race, ethnicity, national origin, religion, sexual orientation, disability, language, and socioeconomic status. Psychologists try to eliminate the effect on their work of biases based on those factors, and they do not knowingly participate in or condone unfair discriminatory practices.

PRINCIPLE E: CONCERN FOR OTHERS' WELFARE

Psychologists seek to contribute to the welfare of those with whom they interact professionally. In their professional actions, psychologists weigh the welfare and rights of their patients or clients, students, supervisees, human research participants, and other affected persons, and the welfare of animal subjects of research. When conflicts occur among psychologists' obligations or concerns, they attempt to resolve these conflicts and to perform their roles in a responsible fashion that avoids or minimizes harm. Psychologists are sensitive to real and ascribed differences in power between themselves and others, and they do not exploit or mislead other people during or after professional relationships.

PRINCIPLE F: SOCIAL RESPONSIBILITY

Psychologists are aware of their professional and scientific responsibilities to the community and the society in which they work and live. They apply and make public their knowledge of psychology in order to contribute to human welfare. Psychologists are concerned about and work to mitigate the causes of human suffering. When undertaking research, they strive to advance human welfare and the science of psychology. Psychologists try to avoid misuse of their work. Psychologists comply with the law and encourage the development of law and social policy that serve the interests of their patients and clients and the public. They are encouraged to contribute a portion of their professional time for little or no personal advantage.

1. GENERAL STANDARDS

These General Standards are potentially applicable to the professional and scientific activities of all psychologists.

1.01 Applicability of the Ethics Code.

The activity of a psychologist subject to the Ethics Code may be reviewed under these Ethical Standards only if the activity is part of his or her work-related functions or the activity is psychological in nature. Personal activities having no connection to or effect on psychological roles are not subject to the Ethics Code.

1.02 Relationship of Ethics and Law.

If psychologists' ethical responsibilities conflict with law, psychologists make known their commitment to the Ethics Code and take steps to resolve the conflict in a responsible manner.

1.03 Professional and Scientific Relationship.

Psychologists provide diagnostic, therapeutic, teaching, research, supervisory, consultative, or other psychological services only in the context of a defined professional or scientific relationship or role. (See also Standards 2.01, Evaluation, Diagnosis, and Interventions in Professional Context, and 7.02, Forensic Assessments.)

1.04 Boundaries of Competence.

(a) Psychologists provide services, teach, and conduct research only within the boundaries of their competence, based on their education, training, supervised experience, or appropriate professional experience.

(b) Psychologists provide services, teach, or conduct research in new areas or involving new techniques only after first undertaking appropriate study, training, supervision, and/or consultation from persons who are competent in those areas or techniques.

(c) In those emerging areas in which generally recognized standards for preparatory training do not yet exist, psychologists nevertheless take reasonable steps to ensure the competence of their work and to protect patients, clients, students, research participants, and others from harm.

1.05 Maintaining Expertise.

Psychologists who engage in assessment, therapy, teaching, research, organizational consulting, or other professional activities maintain a reasonable level of awareness of current scientific and professional information in their fields of activity, and undertake ongoing efforts to maintain competence in the skills they use.

1.06 Basis for Scientific and Professional Judgments.

Psychologists rely on scientifically and professionally derived knowledge when making scientific or professional judgments or when engaging in scholarly or professional endeavors.

1.07 Describing the Nature and Results of Psychological Services.

(a) When psychologists provide assessment, evaluation, treatment, counseling, supervision, teaching, consultation, research, or other psychological services to an individual, a group, or an organization, they provide, using language that is reasonably understandable to the recipient of those services, appropriate information beforehand about the nature of such services and appropriate information later about results and conclusions. (See also Standard 2.09, Explaining Assessment Results.)

(b) If psychologists will be precluded by law or by organizational roles from providing such information to particular individuals or groups, they so inform those individuals or groups at the outset of the service.

1.08 Human Differences.

Where differences of age, gender, race, ethnicity, national origin, religion, sexual orientation, disability, language, or socioeconomic status significantly affect psychologists' work concerning particular individuals or groups, psychologists obtain the training, experience, consultation, or supervision necessary to ensure the competence of their services, or they make appropriate referrals.

1.09 Respecting Others.

In their work-related activities, psychologists respect the rights of others to hold values, attitudes, and opinions that differ from their own.

1.10 Nondiscrimination.

In their work-related activities, psychologists do not engage in unfair discrimination based on age, gender, race, ethnicity, national origin, religion, sexual orientation, disability, socioeconomic status, or any basis proscribed by law.

1.11 Sexual Harassment.

(a) Psychologists do not engage in sexual harassment. Sexual harassment is sexual solicitation, physical advances, or verbal or nonverbal conduct that is sexual in nature, that occurs in connection with the psychologist's activities or roles as a psychologist, and that either:(1) is unwelcome, is offensive, or creates a hostile workplace environment, and the psychologist knows or is told this; or (2) is sufficiently severe or intense to be abusive to a reasonable person in the context. Sexual harassment can consist of a single intense or severe act or of multiple persistent or pervasive acts.

(b) Psychologists accord sexual-harassment complainants and respondents dignity and respect. Psychologists do not participate in denying a person academic admittance or advancement, employment, tenure, or promotion, based solely upon their having made, or their being the subject of, sexual harassment charges. This does not preclude taking action based upon the outcome of such proceedings or consideration of other appropriate information.

1.12 Other Harassment.

Psychologists do not knowingly engage in behavior that is harassing or demeaning to persons with whom they interact in their work based on factors such as those persons' age, gender, race, ethnicity, national origin, religion, sexual orientation, disability, language, or socioeconomic status.

1.13 Personal Problems and Conflicts.

(a) Psychologists recognize that their personal problems and conflicts may interfere with their effectiveness. Accordingly, they refrain from undertaking an activity when they know or should know that their personal problems are likely to lead to harm to a patient, client, colleague, student, research participant, or other person to whom they may owe a professional or scientific obligation.

(b) In addition, psychologists have an obligation to be alert to signs of, and to obtain assistance for, their personal problems at an early stage, in order to prevent significantly impaired performance.

(c) When psychologists become aware of personal problems that may interfere with their performing work-related duties adequately, they take appropriate measures, such as obtaining professional consultation or assistance, and determine whether they should limit, suspend, or terminate their work-related duties.

1.14 Avoiding Harm.

Psychologists take reasonable steps to avoid harming their patients or clients, research participants, students, and others with whom they work, and to minimize harm where it is foreseeable and unavoidable.

1.15 Misuse of Psychologists' Influence.

Because psychologists' scientific and professional judgments and actions may affect the lives of others, they are alert to and guard against personal, financial, social, organizational, or political factors that might lead to misuse of their influence.

1.16 Misuse of Psychologists' Work.

(a)   Psychologists do not participate in activities in which it appears likely that their skills or data will be misused by others, unless corrective mechanisms are available. (See also Standard 7.04, Truthfulness and Candor.)

(b)   If psychologists learn of misuse or misrepresentation of their work, they take reasonable steps to correct or minimize the misuse or misrepresentation.

1.17 Multiple Relationships.

(a)   In many communities and situations, it may not be feasible or reasonable for psychologists to avoid social or other nonprofessional contacts with persons such as patients, clients, students, supervisees, or research participants. Psychologists must always be sensitive to the potential harmful effects of other contacts on their work and on those persons with whom they deal. A psychologist refrains from entering into or promising another personal, scientific, professional, financial, or other relationship with such persons if it appears likely that such a relationship reasonably might impair the psychologist's objectivity or otherwise interfere with the psychologist's effectively performing his or her functions as a psychologist, or might harm or exploit the other party.

(b)   Likewise, whenever feasible, a psychologist refrains from taking on professional or scientific obligations when pre-existing relationships would create a risk of such harm.

(c)   If a psychologist finds that, due to unforeseen factors, a potentially harmful multiple relationship has arisen, the psychologist attempts to resolve it with due regard for the best interests of the affected person and maximal compliance with the Ethics Code.

1.18 Barter (With Patients or Clients).

Psychologists ordinarily refrain from accepting goods, services, or other nonmonetary remuneration from patients or clients in return for psychological services because such arrangements create inherent potential for conflicts, exploitation, and distortion of the professional relationship. A psychologist may participate in bartering only if (1) it is not clinically contraindicated, and (2) the relationship is not exploitative. (See also Standards 1.17, Multiple Relationships, and 1.25, Fees and Financial Arrangements.)

1.19 Exploitative Relationships.

(a)   Psychologists do not exploit persons over whom they have supervisory, evaluative, or other authority such as students, supervisees, employees, research participants, and clients or patients. (See also Standards 4.05 - 4.07 regarding sexual involvement with clients or patients.)

(b)   Psychologists do not engage in sexual relationships with students or supervisees in training over whom the psychologist has evaluative or direct authority, because such relationships are so likely to impair judgment or be exploitative.

1.20 Consultations and Referrals.

(a)   Psychologists arrange for appropriate consultations and referrals based principally on the best interests of their patients or clients, with appropriate consent, and subject to other relevant considerations, including applicable law and contractual obligations. (See also Standards 5.01, Discussing the Limits of Confidentiality, and 5.06, Consultations.)

(b)   When indicated and professionally appropriate, psychologists cooperate with other professionals in order to serve their patients or clients effectively and appropriately.

(c)   Psychologists' referral practices are consistent with law.

1.21 Third-Party Requests for Services.

(a)   When a psychologist agrees to provide services to a person or entity at the request of a third party, the psychologist clarifies to the extent feasible, at the outset of the service, the nature of the relationship with each party. This clarification includes the role of the psychologist (such as therapist, organizational consultant, diagnostician, or expert witness), the probable uses of the services provided or the information obtained, and the fact that there may be limits to confidentiality.

(b)   If there is a foreseeable risk of the psychologist's being called upon to perform conflicting roles because of the involvement of a third party, the psychologist clarifies the nature and direction of his or her responsibilities, keeps all parties appropriately informed as matters develop, and resolves the situation in accordance with this Ethics Code.

1.22 Delegation to and Supervision of Subordinates.

(a)   Psychologists delegate to their employees, supervisees, and research assistants only those responsibilities that such persons can reasonably be expected to perform competently, on the basis of their education, training, or experience, either independently or with the level of supervision being provided.

(b)   Psychologists provide proper training and supervision to their employees or supervisees and take reasonable steps to see that such persons perform services responsibly, competently, and ethically.

(c)   If institutional policies, procedures, or practices prevent fulfillment of this obligation, psychologists attempt to modify their role or to correct the situation to the extent feasible.

1.23 Documentation of Professional and Scientific Work.

(a)   Psychologists appropriately document their professional and scientific work in order to facilitate provision of services later by them or by other professionals, to ensure accountability, and to meet other requirements of institutions or the law.

(b)   When psychologists have reason to believe that records of their professional services will be used in legal proceedings involving recipients of or participants in their work, they have a responsibility to create and maintain documentation in the kind of detail and quality that would be consistent with reasonable scrutiny in an adjudicative forum. (See also Standard 7.01, Professionalism, under Forensic Activities.)

1.24 Records and Data.

Psychologists create, maintain, disseminate, store, retain, and dispose of records and data relating to their research, practice, and other work in accordance with law and in a manner that permits compliance with the requirements of this Ethics Code. (See also Standard 5.04, Maintenance of Records.)

1.25 Fees and Financial Arrangements.

(a)   As early as is feasible in a professional or scientific relationship, the psychologist and the patient, client, or other appropriate recipient of psychological services reach an agreement specifying the compensation and the billing arrangements.

(b)   Psychologists do not exploit recipients of services or payors with respect to fees.

(c)   Psychologists' fee practices are consistent with law.

(d)   Psychologists do not misrepresent their fees.

(e)   If limitations to services can be anticipated because of limitations in financing, this is discussed with the patient, client, or other appropriate recipient of services as early as is feasible. (See also Standard 4.08, Interruption of Services.)

ETHICS

(f) If the patient, client, or other recipient of services does not pay for services as agreed, and if the psychologist wishes to use collection agencies or legal measures to collect the fees, the psychologist first informs the person that such measures will be taken and provides that person an opportunity to make prompt payment. (See also Standard 5.11, Withholding Records for Nonpayment.)

1.26 Accuracy in Reports to Payors and Funding Sources.

In their reports to payors for services or sources of research funding, psychologists accurately state the nature of the research or service provided, the fees or charges, and where applicable, the identity of the provider, the findings, and the diagnosis. (See also Standard 5.05, Disclosures.)

1.27 Referrals and Fees.

When a psychologist pays, receives payment from, or divides fees with another professional other than in an employer - employee relationship, the payment to each is based on the services (clinical, consultative, administrative, or other) provided and is not based on the referral itself.

2. EVALUATION, ASSESSMENT, OR INTERVENTION

2.01 Evaluation, Diagnosis, and Interventions in Professional Context.

(a) Psychologists perform evaluations, diagnostic services, or interventions only within the context of a defined professional relationship. (See also Standards 1.03, Professional and Scientific Relationship.)

(b) Psychologists' assessments, recommendations, reports, and psychological diagnostic or evaluative statements are based on information and techniques (including personal interviews of the individual when appropriate) sufficient to provide appropriate substantiation for their findings. (See also Standard 7.02, Forensic Assessments.)

2.02 Competence and Appropriate Use of Assessments and Interventions.

(a) Psychologists who develop, administer, score, interpret, or use psychological assessment techniques, interviews, tests, or instruments do so in a manner and for purposes that are appropriate in light of the research on or evidence of the usefulness and proper application of the techniques.

(b) Psychologists refrain from misuse of assessment techniques, interventions, results, and interpretations and take reasonable steps to prevent others from misusing the information these techniques provide. This includes refraining from releasing raw test results or raw data to persons, other than to patients or clients as appropriate, who are not qualified to use such information. (See also Standards 1.02, Relationship of Ethics and Law, and 1.04, Boundaries of Competence.)

2.03 Test Construction.

Psychologists who develop and conduct research with tests and other assessment techniques use scientific procedures and current professional knowledge for test design, standardization, validation, reduction or elimination of bias, and recommendations for use.

2.04 Use of Assessment in General and With Special Populations.

(a) Psychologists who perform interventions or administer, score, interpret, or use assessment techniques are familiar with the reliability, validation, and related standardization or outcome studies of, and proper applications and uses of, the techniques they use.

(b) Psychologists recognize limits to the certainty with which diagnoses, judgments, or predictions can be made about individuals.

(c) Psychologists attempt to identify situations in which particular interventions or assessment techniques or norms may not be applicable or may require adjustment in administration or interpretation because of factors such as individuals' gender, age, race, ethnicity, national origin, religion, sexual orientation, disability, language, or socioeconomic status.

2.05 Interpreting Assessment Results.

When interpreting assessment results, including automated interpretations, psychologists take into account the various test factors and characteristics of the person being assessed that might affect psychologists' judgments or reduce the accuracy of their interpretations. They indicate any significant reservations they have about the accuracy or limitations of their interpretations.

2.06 Unqualified Persons.

Psychologists do not promote the use of psychological assessment techniques by unqualified persons. (See also Standard 1.22, Delegation to and Supervision of Subordinates.)

2.07 Obsolete Tests and Outdated Test Results.

(a) Psychologists do not base their assessment or intervention decisions or recommendations on data or test results that are outdated for the current purpose.

(b) Similarly, psychologists do not base such decisions or recommendations on tests and measures that are obsolete and not useful for the current purpose.

2.08 Test Scoring and Interpretation Services.

(a) Psychologists who offer assessment or scoring procedures to other professionals accurately describe the purpose, norms, validity, reliability, and applications of the procedures and any special qualifications applicable to their use.

(b) Psychologists select scoring and interpretation services (including automated services) on the basis of evidence of the validity of the program and procedures as well as on other appropriate considerations.

(c) Psychologists retain appropriate responsibility for the appropriate application, interpretation, and use of assessment instruments, whether they score and interpret such tests themselves or use automated or other services.

2.09 Explaining Assessment Results.

Unless the nature of the relationship is clearly explained to the person being assessed in advance and precludes provision of an explanation of results (such as in some organizational consulting, pre-employment or security screenings, and forensic evaluations), psychologists ensure that an explanation of the results is provided using language that is reasonably understandable to the person assessed or to another legally authorized person on behalf of the client. Regardless of whether the scoring and interpretation are done by the psychologist, by assistants, or by automated or other outside services, psychologists take reasonable steps to ensure that appropriate explanations of results are given.

2.10 Maintaining Test Security.

Psychologists make reasonable efforts to maintain the integrity and security of tests and other assessment techniques consistent with law, contractual obligations, and in a manner that permits compliance with the requirements of this Ethics Code. (See also Standard 1.02, Relationship of Ethics and Law.)

3. ADVERTISING AND OTHER PUBLIC STATEMENTS

3.01 Definition of Public Statements.

Psychologists comply with this Ethics Code in public statements relating to their professional services, products, or publications or to the field of psychology. Public statements include but are not limited to paid or unpaid advertising, brochures, printed matter, directory listings, personal resumes or curriculum vitae, interviews or comments for use in media, statements in legal proceedings, lectures and public oral presentations, and published materials.

3.02 Statements by Others.

(a)   Psychologists who engage others to create or place public statements that promote their professional practice, products, or activities retain professional responsibility for such statements.

(b)   In addition, psychologists make reasonable efforts to prevent others whom they do not control (such as employers, publishers, sponsors, organizational clients, and representatives of the print or broadcast media) from making deceptive statements concerning psychologists' practice or professional or scientific activities.

(c)   If psychologists learn of deceptive statements about their work made by others, psychologists make reasonable efforts to correct such statements.

(d)   Psychologists do not compensate employees of press, radio, television, or other communication media in return for publicity in a news item.

(e)   A paid advertisement relating to the psychologist's activities must be identified as such, unless it is already apparent from the context.

3.03 Avoidance of False or Deceptive Statements.

(a)   Psychologists do not make public statements that are false, deceptive, misleading, or fraudulent, either because of what they state, convey, or suggest or because of what they omit, concerning their research, practice, or other work activities or those of persons or organizations with which they are affiliated. As examples (and not in limitation) of this standard, psychologists do not make false or deceptive statements concerning (1) their training, experience, or competence; (2) their academic degrees; (3) their credentials; (4) their institutional or association affiliations; (5) their services; (6) the scientific or clinical basis for, or results or degree of success of, their services; (7) their fees; or (8) their publications or research findings. (See also Standards 6.15, Deception in Research, and 6.18, Providing Participants With Information About the Study.)

(b)   Psychologists claim as credentials for their psychological work, only degrees that (1) were earned from a regionally accredited educational institution or (2) were the basis for psychology licensure by the state in which they practice.

3.04 Media Presentations.

When psychologists provide advice or comment by means of public lectures, demonstrations, radio or television programs, prerecorded tapes, printed articles, mailed material, or other media, they take reasonable precautions to ensure that (1) the statements are based on appropriate psychological literature and practice, (2) the statements are otherwise consistent with this Ethics Code, and (3) the recipients of the information are not encouraged to infer that a relationship has been established with them personally.

3.05 Testimonials.

Psychologists do not solicit testimonials from current psychotherapy clients or patients or other persons who because of their particular circumstances are vulnerable to undue influence.

3.06 In-Person Solicitation.

Psychologists do not engage, directly or through agents, in uninvited in-person solicitation of business from actual or potential psychotherapy patients or clients or other persons who because of their particular circumstances are vulnerable to undue influence. However, this does not preclude attempting to implement appropriate collateral contacts with significant others for the purpose of benefiting an already engaged therapy patient.

4. THERAPY

4.01 Structuring the Relationship.

(a)   Psychologists discuss with clients or patients as early as is feasible in the therapeutic relationship appropriate issues, such as the nature and anticipated course of therapy, fees, and confidentiality. (See also Standards 1.25, Fees and Financial Arrangements, and 5.01, Discussing the Limits of Confidentiality.)

(b)   When the psychologist's work with clients or patients will be supervised, the above discussion includes that fact, and the name of the supervisor, when the supervisor has legal responsibility for the case.

(c)   When the therapist is a student intern, the client or patient is informed of that fact.

(d)   Psychologists make reasonable efforts to answer patients' questions and to avoid apparent misunderstandings about therapy. Whenever possible, psychologists provide oral and/or written information, using language that is reasonably understandable to the patient or client.

4.02 Informed Consent to Therapy.

(a)   Psychologists obtain appropriate informed consent to therapy or related procedures, using language that is reasonably understandable to participants. The content of informed consent will vary depending on many circumstances; however, informed consent generally implies that the person (1) has the capacity to consent, (2) has been informed of significant information concerning the procedure, (3) has freely and without undue influence expressed consent, and (4) consent has been appropriately documented.

(b)   When persons are legally incapable of giving informed consent, psychologists obtain informed permission from a legally authorized person, if such substitute consent is permitted by law.

(c)   In addition, psychologists (1) inform those persons who are legally incapable of giving informed consent about the proposed interventions in a manner commensurate with the persons' psychological capacities, (2) seek their assent to those interventions, and (3) consider such persons' preferences and best interests.

4.03 Couple and Family Relationships.

(a)   When a psychologist agrees to provide services to several persons who have a relationship (such as husband and wife or parents and children), the psychologist attempts to clarify at the outset (1) which of the individuals are patients or clients and (2) the relationship the psychologist will have with each person. This clarification includes the role of the psychologist and the probable uses of the services provided or the information obtained. (See also Standard 5.01, Discussing the Limits of Confidentiality.)

(b)   As soon as it becomes apparent that the psychologist may be called on to perform potentially conflicting roles (such as marital counselor to husband and wife, and then witness for one party in a divorce proceeding), the psychologist attempts to clarify and adjust, or withdraw from, roles appropriately. (See also Standard 7.03, Clarification of Role, under Forensic Activities.)

4.04 Providing Mental Health Services to Those Served by Others.

In deciding whether to offer or provide services to those already receiving mental health services elsewhere, psychologists carefully consider the treatment issues and the potential patient's or client's welfare. The psychologist discusses these issues with the patient or client, or another legally authorized person on behalf of the client, in order to minimize the risk of confusion and conflict, consults with the other service providers when appropriate, and proceeds with caution and sensitivity to the therapeutic issues.

4.05 Sexual Intimacies With Current Patients or Clients.

Psychologists do not engage in sexual intimacies with current patients or clients.

4.06 Therapy With Former Sexual Partners.

Psychologists do not accept as therapy patients or clients persons with whom they have engaged in sexual intimacies.

4.07 Sexual Intimacies With Former Therapy Patients.

(a) Psychologists do not engage in sexual intimacies with a former therapy patient or client for at least two years after cessation or termination of professional services.

(b) Because sexual intimacies with a former therapy patient or client are so frequently harmful to the patient or client, and because such intimacies undermine public confidence in the psychology profession and thereby deter the public's use of needed services, psychologists do not engage in sexual intimacies with former therapy patients and clients even after a two-year interval except in the most unusual circumstances. The psychologist who engages in such activity after the two years following cessation or termination of treatment bears the burden of demonstrating that there has been no exploitation, in light of all relevant factors, including (1) the amount of time that has passed since therapy terminated, (2) the nature and duration of the therapy, (3) the circumstances of termination, (4) the patient's or client's personal history, (5) the patient's or client's current mental status, (6) the likelihood of adverse impact on the patient or client and others, and (7) any statements or actions made by the therapist during the course of therapy suggesting or inviting the possibility of a post-termination sexual or romantic relationship with the patient or client. (See also Standard 1.17, Multiple Relationships.)

4.08 Interruption of Services.

(a) Psychologists make reasonable efforts to plan for facilitating care in the event that psychological services are interrupted by factors such as the psychologist's illness, death, unavailability, or relocation or by the client's relocation or financial limitations. (See also Standard 5.09, Preserving Records and Data.)

(b) When entering into employment or contractual relationships, psychologists provide for orderly and appropriate resolution of responsibility for patient or client care in the event that the employment or contractual relationship ends, with paramount consideration given to the welfare of the patient or client.

4.09 Terminating the Professional Relationship.

(a) Psychologists do not abandon patients or clients. (See also Standard 1.25e, under Fees and Financial Arrangements.)

(b) Psychologists terminate a professional relationship when it becomes reasonably clear that the patient or client no longer needs the service, is not benefiting, or is being harmed by continued service.

(c) Prior to termination for whatever reason, except where precluded by the patient's or client's conduct, the psychologist discusses the patient's or client's views and needs, provides appropriate pretermination counseling, suggests alternative service providers as appropriate, and takes other reasonable steps to facilitate transfer of responsibility to another provider if the patient or client needs one immediately.

5. PRIVACY AND CONFIDENTIALITY

These Standards are potentially applicable to the professional and scientific activities of all psychologists.

5.01 Discussing the Limits of Confidentiality.

(a) Psychologists discuss with persons and organizations with whom they establish a scientific or professional relationship (including, to the extent feasible, minors and their legal representatives) (1) the relevant limitations on confidentiality, including limitations where applicable in group, marital, and family therapy or in organizational consulting, and (2) the foreseeable uses of the information generated through their services.

(b) Unless it is not feasible or is contraindicated, the discussion of confidentiality occurs at the outset of the relationship and thereafter as new circumstances may warrant.

(c) Permission for electronic recording of interviews is secured from clients and patients.

5.02 Maintaining Confidentiality.

Psychologists have a primary obligation and take reasonable precautions to respect the confidentiality rights of those with whom they work or consult, recognizing that confidentiality may be established by law, institutional rules, or professional or scientific relationships. (See also Standard 6.26, Professional Reviewers.)

5.03 Minimizing Intrusions on Privacy.

(a) In order to minimize intrusions on privacy, psychologists include in written and oral reports, consultations, and the like, only information germane to the purpose for which the communication is made.

(b) Psychologists discuss confidential information obtained in clinical or consulting relationships, or evaluative data concerning patients, individual or organizational clients, students, research participants, supervisees, and employees, only for appropriate scientific or professional purposes and only with persons clearly concerned with such matters.

5.04 Maintenance of Records.

Psychologists maintain appropriate confidentiality in creating, storing, accessing, transferring, and disposing of records under their control, whether these are written, automated, or in any other medium. Psychologists maintain and dispose of records in accordance with law and in a manner that permits compliance with the requirements of this Ethics Code.

5.05 Disclosures.

(a) Psychologists disclose confidential information without the consent of the individual only as mandated by law, or where permitted by law for a valid purpose, such as (1) to provide needed professional services to the patient or the individual or organizational client, (2) to obtain appropriate professional consultations, (3) to protect the patient or client or others from harm, or (4) to obtain payment for services, in which instance disclosure is limited to the minimum that is necessary to achieve the purpose.

(b)   Psychologists also may disclose confidential information with the appropriate consent of the patient or the individual or organizational client (or of another legally authorized person on behalf of the patient or client), unless prohibited by law.

5.06 Consultations.

When consulting with colleagues,

(1) psychologists do not share confidential information that reasonably could lead to the identification of a patient, client, research participant, or other person or organization with whom they have a confidential relationship unless they have obtained the prior consent of the person or organization or the disclosure cannot be avoided, and

(2) they share information only to the extent necessary to achieve the purposes of the consultation. (See also Standard 5.02, Maintaining Confidentiality.)

5.07 Confidential Information in Databases.

(a)   If confidential information concerning recipients of psychological services is to be entered into databases or systems of records available to persons whose access has not been consented to by the recipient, then psychologists use coding or other techniques to avoid the inclusion of personal identifiers.

(b)   If a research protocol approved by an institutional review board or similar body requires the inclusion of personal identifiers, such identifiers are deleted before the information is made accessible to persons other than those of whom the subject was advised.

(c)   If such deletion is not feasible, then before psychologists transfer such data to others or review such data collected by others, they take reasonable steps to determine that appropriate consent of personally identifiable individuals has been obtained.

5.08 Use of Confidential Information for Didactic or Other Purposes.

(a)   Psychologists do not disclose in their writings, lectures, or other public media, confidential, personally identifiable information concerning their patients, individual or organizational clients, students, research participants, or other recipients of their services that they obtained during the course of their work, unless the person or organization has consented in writing or unless there is other ethical or legal authorization for doing so.

(b)   Ordinarily, in such scientific and professional presentations, psychologists disguise confidential information concerning such persons or organizations so that they are not individually identifiable to others and so that discussions do not cause harm to subjects who might identify themselves.

5.09 Preserving Records and Data.

A psychologist makes plans in advance so that confidentiality of records and data is protected in the event of the psychologist's death, incapacity, or withdrawal from the position or practice.

5.10 Ownership of Records and Data.

Recognizing that ownership of records and data is governed by legal principles, psychologists take reasonable and lawful steps so that records and data remain available to the extent needed to serve the best interests of patients, individual or organizational clients, research participants, or appropriate others.

5.11 Withholding Records for Nonpayment.

Psychologists may not withhold records under their control that are requested and imminently needed for a patient's or client's treatment solely because payment has not been received, except as otherwise provided by law.

6. TEACHING, TRAINING SUPERVISION, RESEARCH, AND PUBLISHING

6.01 Design of Education and Training Programs.

Psychologists who are responsible for education and training programs seek to ensure that the programs are competently designed, provide the proper experiences, and meet the requirements for licensure, certification, or other goals for which claims are made by the program.

6.02 Descriptions of Education and Training Programs.

(a)   Psychologists responsible for education and training programs seek to ensure that there is a current and accurate description of the program content, training goals and objectives, and requirements that must be met for satisfactory completion of the program. This information must be made readily available to all interested parties.

(b)   Psychologists seek to ensure that statements concerning their course outlines are accurate and not misleading, particularly regarding the subject matter to be covered, bases for evaluating progress, and the nature of course experiences. (See also Standard 3.03, Avoidance of False or Deceptive Statements.)

(c)   To the degree to which they exercise control, psychologists responsible for announcements, catalogs, brochures, or advertisements describing workshops, seminars, or other non-degree- granting educational programs ensure that they accurately describe the audience for which the program is intended, the educational objectives, the presenters, and the fees involved.

6.03 Accuracy and Objectivity in Teaching.

(a)   When engaged in teaching or training, psychologists present psychological information accurately and with a reasonable degree of objectivity.

(b)   When engaged in teaching or training, psychologists recognize the power they hold over students or supervisees and therefore make reasonable efforts to avoid engaging in conduct that is personally demeaning to students or supervisees. (See also Standards 1.09, Respecting Others, and 1.12, Other Harassment.)

6.04 Limitation on Teaching.

Psychologists do not teach the use of techniques or procedures that require specialized training, licensure, or expertise, including but not limited to hypnosis, biofeedback, and projective techniques, to individuals who lack the prerequisite training, legal scope of practice, or expertise.

6.05 Assessing Student and Supervisee Performance.

(a)   In academic and supervisory relationships, psychologists establish an appropriate process for providing feedback to students and supervisees.

(b)   Psychologists evaluate students and supervisees on the basis of their actual performance on relevant and established program requirements.

6.06 Planning Research.

(a)   Psychologists design, conduct, and report research in accordance with recognized standards of scientific competence and ethical research.

(b)   Psychologists plan their research so as to minimize the possibility that results will be misleading.

(c)   In planning research, psychologists consider its ethical acceptability under the Ethics Code. If an ethical issue is unclear, psychologists seek to resolve the issue through consultation with institutional review boards, animal care and use committees, peer consultations, or other proper mechanisms.

(d) Psychologists take reasonable steps to implement appropriate protections for the rights and welfare of human participants, other persons affected by the research, and the welfare of animal subjects.

6.07 Responsibility.

(a) Psychologists conduct research competently and with due concern for the dignity and welfare of the participants.

(b) Psychologists are responsible for the ethical conduct of research conducted by them or by others under their supervision or control.

(c) Researchers and assistants are permitted to perform only those tasks for which they are appropriately trained and prepared.

(d) As part of the process of development and implementation of research projects, psychologists consult those with expertise concerning any special population under investigation or most likely to be affected.

6.08 Compliance With Law and Standards.

Psychologists plan and conduct research in a manner consistent with federal and state law and regulations, as well as professional standards governing the conduct of research, and particularly those standards governing research with human participants and animal subjects.

6.09 Institutional Approval.

Psychologists obtain from host institutions or organizations appropriate approval prior to conducting research, and they provide accurate information about their research proposals. They conduct the research in accordance with the approved research protocol.

6.10 Research Responsibilities.

Prior to conducting research (except research involving only anonymous surveys, naturalistic observations, or similar research), psychologists enter into an agreement with participants that clarifies the nature of the research and the responsibilities of each party.

6.11 Informed Consent to Research.

(a) Psychologists use language that is reasonably understandable to research participants in obtaining their appropriate informed consent (except as provided in Standard 6.12, Dispensing with Informed Consent). Such informed consent is appropriately documented.

(b) Using language that is reasonably understandable to participants, psychologists inform participants of the nature of the research; they inform participants that they are free to participate or to decline to participate or to withdraw from the research; they explain the foreseeable consequences of declining or withdrawing; they inform participants of significant factors that may be expected to influence their willingness to participate (such as risks, discomfort, adverse effects, or limitations on confidentiality, except as provided in Standard 6.15, Deception in Research); and they explain other aspects about which the prospective participants inquire.

(c) When psychologists conduct research with individuals such as students or subordinates, psychologists take special care to protect the prospective participants from adverse consequences of declining or withdrawing from participation.

(d) When research participation is a course requirement or opportunity for extra credit, the prospective participant is given the choice of equitable alternative activities.

(e) For persons who are legally incapable of giving informed consent, psychologists nevertheless (1) provide an appropriate explanation, (2) obtain the participant's assent, and (3) obtain appropriate permission from a legally authorized person, if such substitute consent is permitted by law.

6.12 Dispensing With Informed Consent.

Before determining that planned research (such as research involving only anonymous questionnaires, naturalistic observations, or certain kinds of archival research) does not require the informed consent of research participants, psychologists consider applicable regulations and institutional review board requirements, and they consult with colleagues as appropriate.

6.13 Informed Consent in Research Filming or Recording.

Psychologists obtain informed consent from research participants prior to filming or recording them in any form, unless the research involves simply naturalistic observations in public places and it is not anticipated that the recording will be used in a manner that could cause personal identification or harm.

6.14 Offering Inducements for Research Participants.

(a) In offering professional services as an inducement to obtain research participants, psychologists make clear the nature of the services, as well as the risks, obligations, and limitations. (See also Standard 1.18, Barter [With Patients or Clients].)

(b) Psychologists do not offer excessive or inappropriate financial or other inducements to obtain research participants, particularly when it might tend to coerce participation.

6.15 Deception in Research.

(a) Psychologists do not conduct a study involving deception unless they have determined that the use of deceptive techniques is justified by the study's prospective scientific, educational, or applied value and that equally effective alternative procedures that do not use deception are not feasible.

(b) Psychologists never deceive research participants about significant aspects that would affect their willingness to participate, such as physical risks, discomfort, or unpleasant emotional experiences.

(c) Any other deception that is an integral feature of the design and conduct of an experiment must be explained to participants as early as is feasible, preferably at the conclusion of their participation, but no later than at the conclusion of the research. (See also Standard 6.18, Providing Participants With Information About the Study.)

6.16 Sharing and Utilizing Data.

Psychologists inform research participants of their anticipated sharing or further use of personally identifiable research data and of the possibility of unanticipated future uses.

6.17 Minimizing Invasiveness.

In conducting research, psychologists interfere with the participants or milieu from which data are collected only in a manner that is warranted by an appropriate research design and that is consistent with psychologists' roles as scientific investigators.

6.18 Providing Participants With Information About the Study.

(a) Psychologists provide a prompt opportunity for participants to obtain appropriate information about the nature, results, and conclusions of the research, and psychologists attempt to correct any misconceptions that participants may have.

(b)   If scientific or humane values justify delaying or withholding this information, psychologists take reasonable measures to reduce the risk of harm.

6.19 Honoring Commitments.

Psychologists take reasonable measures to honor all commitments they have made to research participants.

6.20 Care and Use of Animals Research.

(a)   Psychologists who conduct research involving animals treat them humanely.

(b)   Psychologists acquire, care for, use, and dispose of animals in compliance with current federal, state, and local laws and regulations, and with professional standards.

(c)   Psychologists trained in research methods and experienced in the care of laboratory animals supervise all procedures involving animals and are responsible for ensuring appropriate consideration of their comfort, health, and humane treatment.

(d)   Psychologists ensure that all individuals using animals under their supervision have received instruction in research methods and in the care, maintenance, and handling of the species being used, to the extent appropriate to their role.

(e)   Responsibilities and activities of individuals assisting in a research project are consistent with their respective competencies.

(f)   Psychologists make reasonable efforts to minimize the discomfort, infection, illness, and pain of animal subjects.

(g)   A procedure subjecting animals to pain, stress, or privation is used only when an alternative procedure is unavailable and the goal is justified by its prospective scientific, educational, or applied value.

(h)   Surgical procedures are performed under appropriate anesthesia; techniques to avoid infection and minimize pain are followed during and after surgery.

(i)   When it is appropriate that the animal's life be terminated, it is done rapidly, with an effort to minimize pain, and in accordance with accepted procedures.

6.21 Reporting of Results.

(a)   Psychologists do not fabricate data or falsify results in their publications.

(b)   If psychologists discover significant errors in their published data, they take reasonable steps to correct such errors in a correction, retraction, erratum, or other appropriate publication means.

6.22 Plagiarism.

Psychologists do not present substantial portions or elements of another's work or data as their own, even if the other work or data source is cited occasionally.

6.23 Publication Credit.

(a)   Psychologists take responsibility and credit, including authorship credit, only for work they have actually performed or to which they have contributed.

(b)   Principal authorship and other publication credits accurately reflect the relative scientific or professional contributions of the individuals involved, regardless of their relative status. Mere possession of an institutional position, such as Department Chair, does not justify authorship credit. Minor contributions to the research or to the writing for publications are appropriately acknowledged, such as in footnotes or in an introductory statement.

(c)   A student is usually listed as principal author on any multiple-authored article that is substantially based on the student's dissertation or thesis.

6.24 Duplicate Publication of Data.

Psychologists do not publish, as original data, data that have been previously published. This does not preclude republishing data when they are accompanied by proper acknowledgment.

6.25 Sharing Data.

After research results are published, psychologists do not withhold the data on which their conclusions are based from other competent professionals who seek to verify the substantive claims through reanalysis and who intend to use such data only for that purpose, provided that the confidentiality of the participants can be protected and unless legal rights concerning proprietary data preclude their release.

6.26 Professional Reviewers.

Psychologists who review material submitted for publication, grant, or other research proposal review respect the confidentiality of and the proprietary rights in such information of those who submitted it.

7. FORENSIC ACTIVITIES

7.01 Professionalism.

Psychologists who perform forensic functions, such as assessments, interviews, consultations, reports, or expert testimony, must comply with all other provisions of this Ethics Code to the extent that they apply to such activities. In addition, psychologists base their forensic work on appropriate knowledge of and competence in the areas underlying such work, including specialized knowledge concerning special populations. (See also Standards 1.06, Basis for Scientific and Professional Judgments; 1.08, Human Differences; 1.15, Misuse of Psychologists' Influence; and 1.23, Documentation of Professional and Scientific Work.)

7.02 Forensic Assessments.

(a)   Psychologists' forensic assessments, recommendations, and reports are based on information and techniques (including personal interviews of the individual, when appropriate) sufficient to provide appropriate substantiation for their findings. (See also Standards 1.03, Professional and Scientific Relationship; 1.23, Documentation of Professional and Scientific Work; 2.01, Evaluation, Diagnosis, and Interventions in Professional Context; and 2.05, Interpreting Assessment Results.)

(b)   Except as noted in ©, below, psychologists provide written or oral forensic reports or testimony of the psychological characteristics of an individual only after they have conducted an examination of the individual adequate to support their statements or conclusions.

(c)   When, despite reasonable efforts, such an examination is not feasible, psychologists clarify the impact of their limited information on the reliability and validity of their reports and testimony, and they appropriately limit the nature and extent of their conclusions or recommendations.

7.03 Clarification of Role.

In most circumstances, psychologists avoid performing multiple and potentially conflicting roles in forensic matters. When psychologists may be called on to serve in more than one role in a legal proceeding - for example, as consultant or expert for one party or for the court and as a fact witness - they clarify role expectations and the extent of confidentiality in advance to the extent feasible, and thereafter as changes occur, in order to avoid compromising their professional judgment and objectivity and in order to avoid misleading others regarding their role.

7.04 Truthfulness and Candor.

(a) In forensic testimony and reports, psychologists testify truthfully, honestly, and candidly and, consistent with applicable legal procedures, describe fairly the bases for their testimony and conclusions. (b) Whenever necessary to avoid misleading, psychologists acknowledge the limits of their data or conclusions.

7.05 Prior Relationships.

A prior professional relationship with a party does not preclude psychologists from testifying as fact witnesses or from testifying to their services to the extent permitted by applicable law. Psychologists appropriately take into account ways in which the prior relationship might affect their professional objectivity or opinions and disclose the potential conflict to the relevant parties.

7.06 Compliance With Law and Rules.

In performing forensic roles, psychologists are reasonably familiar with the rules governing their roles. Psychologists are aware of the occasionally competing demands placed upon them by these principles and the requirements of the court system, and attempt to resolve these conflicts by making known their commitment to this Ethics Code and taking steps to resolve the conflict in a responsible manner. (See also Standard 1.02, Relationship of Ethics and Law.)

8. RESOLVING ETHICAL ISSUES

8.01 Familiarity With Ethics Code.

Psychologists have an obligation to be familiar with this Ethics Code, other applicable ethics codes, and their application to psychologists' work. Lack of awareness or misunderstanding of an ethical standard is not itself a defense to a charge of unethical conduct.

8.02 Confronting Ethical Issues.

When a psychologist is uncertain whether a particular situation or course of action would violate this Ethics Code, the psychologist ordinarily consults with other psychologists knowledgeable about ethical issues, with state or national psychology ethics committees, or with other appropriate authorities in order to choose a proper response.

8.03 Conflicts Between Ethics and Organizational Demands.

If the demands of an organization with which psychologists are affiliated conflict with this Ethics Code, psychologists clarify the nature of the conflict, make known their commitment to the Ethics Code, and to the extent feasible, seek to resolve the conflict in a way that permits the fullest adherence to the Ethics Code.

8.04 Informal Resolution of Ethical Violations.

When psychologists believe that there may have been an ethical violation by another psychologist, they attempt to resolve the issue by bringing it to the attention of that individual if an informal resolution appears appropriate and the intervention does not violate any confidentiality rights that may be involved.

8.05 Reporting Ethical Violations.

If an apparent ethical violation is not appropriate for informal resolution under Standard 8.04 or is not resolved properly in that fashion, psychologists take further action appropriate to the situation, unless such action conflicts with confidentiality rights in ways that cannot be resolved. Such action might include referral to state or national committees on professional ethics or to state licensing boards.

8.06 Cooperating With Ethics Committees.

Psychologists cooperate in ethics investigations, proceedings, and resulting requirements of the APA or any affiliated state psychological association to which they belong. In doing so, they make reasonable efforts to resolve any issues as to confidentiality. Failure to cooperate is itself an ethics violation.

8.07 Improper Complaints.

Psychologists do not file or encourage the filing of ethics complaints that are frivolous and are intended to harm the respondent rather than to protect the public.

ETHICS

GLOSSARY

Glossary

This glossary contains terms you need to understand as you study psychology. After each term there is a brief definition or explanation of the term as it is used in *Holt Psychology: Principles in Practice.* The page number refers to the page on which the term is introduced in the textbook.

Phonetic Respelling and Pronunciation Guide

Many of the key terms in this textbook have been respelled to help you pronounce them. The letter combinations used in the respellings throughout the narrative are explained in the following phonetic respelling and pronunciation guide. The guide is adapted from *Merriam-Webster's Tenth New Collegiate Dictionary, Merriam-Webster's New Geographical Dictionary,* and *Merriam-Webster's New Biographical Dictionary.*

MARK	AS IN	RESPELLING	EXAMPLE
a	alphabet	a	*AL-fuh-bet
ā	Asia	ay	AY-zhuh
ä	cart, top	ah	KAHRT, TAHP
e	let, ten	e	LET, TEN
ē	even, leaf	ee	EE-vuhn, LEEF
i	it, tip, British	i	IT, TIP, BRIT-ish
ī	site, buy, Ohio	y	SYT, BY, oh-HY-oh
	iris	eye	EYE-ris
k	card	k	KAHRD
ō	over, rainbow	oh	oh-vuhr, RAYN-boh
u̇	book, wood	ooh	BOOHK, WOOHD
ȯ	all, orchid	aw	AWL, AWR-kid
ȯi	foil, coin	oy	FOYL, KOYN
au̇	out	ow	OWT
ə	cup, butter	uh	KUHP, BUHT-uhr
ü	rule, food	oo	ROOL, FOOD
yü	few	yoo	FYOO
zh	vision	zh	VIZH-uhn

A syllable printed in small capital letters receives heavier emphasis than the other syllable(s) in a word.

A

absolute threshold   the smallest amount of a particular stimulus that can be detected, 78

accommodation   the process of adjusting existing ways of thinking to encompass new information, ideas, or objects, 241

acculturation   the process of adapting to a new or different culture, 339

achievement   knowledge and skills gained from experience and education, 206

achievement motivation   the desire to persevere with work and to avoid distraction in order to reach personal goals, 308

achievement test   test that measures the amount of knowledge one has in specific academic areas, 347

active coping   a response to a stressor that reduces stress by changing the situation to eliminate or lessen the negative effects of the stressor, 403

active listening   empathic listening in which the listener acknowledges, restates, and clarifies the speaker's thoughts and concerns, 444

actor-observer bias   the tendency to attribute one's own behavior to situational factors but to attribute the behavior of others to dispositional factors, 470

addiction   a compulsive need for and use of a habit-forming substance, 116

adolescent growth spurt a sudden, brief burst of physical growth during which adolescents typically make great gains in height and weight, 252

affiliation the desire to join with others and to be a part of something larger than oneself, 310

afterimage the visual sensation that occurs after the original stimulus has been removed, 84

agoraphobia a fear of crowded, public places, 416

algorithm a problem-solving strategy that eventually leads to a solution; usually involves trying random solutions to a problem in a systematic way, 179

altered state of consciousness a type of consciousness other than normal waking consciousness, 106

altruism unselfish regard for the welfare of others, 494

Alzheimer's disease an irreversible, progressive brain disorder characterized by the deterioration of memory, language, and eventually, physical functioning, 287

amphetamine a type of stimulant often used to stay awake or to reduce appetite, 118

anchoring heuristic the process of making decisions based on certain ideas or standards held by the decision maker, 193

anorexia nervosa an eating disorder characterized by extreme weight loss due to self-starvation, 265

anterograde amnesia the inability to form new memories because of brain trauma, 170

antianxiety drug a type of medication that relieves anxiety disorders and panic disorders by depressing the activity of the central nervous system, 451

antidepressant drug a type of medication used to treat major depression by increasing the amount of one or both of the neurotransmitters noradrenaline and serotonin, 452

antipsychotic drug a type of medication used to reduce agitation, delusions, and hallucinations by blocking the activity of dopamine in the brain; also called a major tranquilizer, 452

anxiety a psychological state characterized by tension and apprehension, foreboding, and dread, 415

approach-approach conflict a type of conflict involving a choice between two positive but mutually exclusive options, 388

approach-avoidance conflict a type of conflict involving a single goal that has both positive and negative aspects, 390

aptitude test a test that is designed to predict a person's future performance or capacity to learn, 348

archetypes original models from which later forms develop; in Jung's personality theory, archetypes are primitive images or concepts that reside in the collective unconscious, 330

assimilation the process by which new information is placed into pre-existing categories, 241

association areas areas of the cerebral cortex that are involved in such mental operations as thinking, memory, learning, and problem solving, 63

associationism a learned connection between two ideas or events, 12

attachment an active and intense emotional relationship between two people that endures over time, 234

attitude an enduring belief about people, places, or objects that evokes certain feelings and influences behavior, 460

attraction in social psychology, an attitude of liking (positive attraction) or disliking (negative attraction), 472

attribution theory the suggestion that there is a tendency to explain a person's behavior in terms of the situation or the person's personality, 468

auditory nerve the cranial nerve that carries sound from the cochlea of the inner ear to the brain, 86

authoritarian a leadership or parenting style that stresses unquestioning obedience, 237

authoritarian leader a leader who makes decisions for the group and tells other group members what to do, 484

authoritative a leadership or parenting style based on recognized authority or knowledge and characterized by mutual respect, 237

autonomic nervous system the subdivision of the peripheral nervous system that regulates body functions, such as respiration and digestion, 58

availability heuristic the tendency to make decisions on the basis of information that is available in one's immediate consciousness, 193

aversive conditioning a type of counterconditioning that links an unpleasant state with an unwanted behavior in an attempt to eliminate the behavior, 449

avoidance-avoidance conflict a type of conflict involving a choice between two negative or undesirable options, 390

axon a long tubelike structure attached to a neuron that transmits impulses away from the neuron cell body, 55

axon terminals small fibers branching out from an axon, 55

𝓑

balance theory the view that people have a need to organize their perceptions, opinions, and beliefs in a manner that is in harmony with those of the people around them, 309

basic research research that is conducted for its own sake, that is, without seeking a solution to a specific problem, 10

behavior observable and measurable actions of people and animals, 4

behaviorism the school of psychology, founded by John Watson, that defines psychology as the scientific study of observable behavior, **14**

behavior-rating scales systematic means of recording the frequency with which certain behaviors occur, **344**

bereaved suffering from the death of a loved one, **293**

binocular cues visual cues for depth that require the use of both eyes, **96**

biofeedback a system for monitoring and feeding back information about certain biological processes, such as blood pressure, **112**

biological perspective the psychological perspective that emphasizes the influence of biology on behavior, **18**

bipolar disorder a disorder in which a person's mood inappropriately alternates between extremes of elation and depression, **423**

blind spot the part of the retina that contains no photoreceptors, **83**

bulimia nervosa an eating disorder in which enormous quantities of food are consumed and then purged by means of laxatives or self-induced vomiting, **265**

bystander effect the tendency for a person to be less likely to give aid if other bystanders are present, **495**

C

case study an in-depth study of a single person or group to reveal some universal principle, **35**

catatonic stupor an immobile, expressionless, coma-like state associated with schizophrenia, **426**

catharsis in psychology, the release of aggressive energy through action or fantasy, **491**

cell body the part of a neuron that produces the energy needed for the activity of the cell, **55**

cellular damage theories the view that aging occurs because body cells lose the capacity to reproduce and maintain themselves as a result of damage, **285**

central nervous system the part of the nervous system that consists of the brain and spinal cord, **54**

central route a method of persuasion that uses evidence and logical arguments to influence people, **463**

cerebellum the area of the brain that is responsible for voluntary movement and balance, **60**

cerebral cortex the bumpy, convoluted surface of the brain; the body's control and information-processing center, **61**

cerebrum the large mass of the forebrain, consisting of two hemispheres, **61**

childhood the stage of life that follows infancy and spans the period from the second birthday to the beginning of adolescence, **231**

chromosome a microscopic threadlike structure in the nucleus of every living cell; it contains genes, the basic units of heredity, **70**

chunking a mental process for organizing information into meaningful units, or "chunks," **162**

circadian rhythm a regular sequence of biological processes, such as temperature and sleep, that occurs every 24 hours, **106**

classical conditioning a type of learning in which a neutral stimulus comes to elicit an unconditioned response when that neutral stimulus is repeatedly paired with a stimulus that normally causes an unconditioned response, **128**

clique a small, exclusive group of people within a larger group, **258**

closure the tendency to perceive a complete or whole figure even when there are gaps in sensory information, **93**

cochlea the fluid-filled structure of the inner ear that transmits sound impulses to the auditory nerve, **86**

cognitive activities private, unobservable mental processes such as sensation, perception, thought, and problem solving, **4**

cognitive anchors early attitudes and persistent beliefs that shape the ways in which people see and interpret the world, **461**

cognitive consistency the state in which a person's thoughts and behaviors match his or her beliefs and the expectations of others, **309**

cognitive-dissonance theory the theory that suggests that people make attitudinal changes to reduce the tension that occurs when their thoughts and attitudes are inconsistent with their actions, **310**

cognitive perspective the viewpoint that emphasizes the role of thought processes in determining behavior, **18**

cognitive restructuring a method of coping in which one changes the thoughts one has in a particular situation, **359**

collective unconscious Jung's concept of a shared, inherited body of memory that all humans have, **330**

commitment a pledge or promise, **475**

common fate the tendency to perceive objects that are moving together as belonging together, **94**

complementary the colors across from each other on the color circle, **84**

compulsion an apparently irresistible urge to repeat an act or engage in ritualistic behavior, such as hand washing, **416**

concept a mental structure used to categorize objects, people, or events that share similar characteristics, **178**

concrete-operational stage according to Piaget, the stage of cognitive development during which children acquire the ability to think logically, **243**

conditional positive regard an expression of esteem given only when an individual has exhibited suitable behavior, 240

conditioned response a learned response to a previously neutral stimulus, 130

conditioned stimulus a previously neutral stimulus that, because of pairing with an unconditioned stimulus, now causes a conditioned response, 130

conditioning a type of learning that involves stimulus-response connections, in which the response is conditional on the stimulus, 128

conductive deafness hearing loss caused by damage to the middle ear, thus interfering with the transmission of sound waves to the cochlea, 87

confirmation bias the tendency to look for information that confirms one's preconceived notions, 190

conform to change one's attitudes or behavior in accordance with generally accepted standards, 484

congruence agreement; in psychology, consistency between one's self-concept and one's experience, 335

consciousness awareness of oneself and one's environment, 103

conservation according to Piaget, the principle that the properties of substances remain the same despite changes in their shape or arrangement, 242

contact comfort the satisfaction obtained from pleasant, soft stimulation, 234

context-dependent memories information that is more easily retrieved in the context in which it was encoded and stored, 159

continuity the perceptual tendency to group stimuli into continuous patterns, 94

continuous reinforcement the reinforcement of a desired response every time it occurs, 139

control group in an experiment, the group that does not receive the treatment, 41

controlled experiment an experiment that uses both a control group and an experimental group to determine whether the independent variable influences behavior and, if so, how it does so, 41

conventional moral reasoning the level of moral development at which a person makes judgments based on conventional standards of right and wrong, 246

convergent thinking thinking that is limited to available facts, 187

corpus callosum the nerve fibers that connect the left and right hemispheres of the cerebral cortex, 61

correlation the relationship between variables, 39

counterconditioning a therapy procedure based on classical conditioning that replaces a negative response to a stimulus with a positive response, 135

creativity the ability to invent new solutions to problems or to create original or ingenious materials, 216

critical period a stage or point in development during which a person or animal is best suited to learn a particular skill or behavior, 229

cross-linking a possible cause of aging in which proteins within a cell bind together, toughening body tissues and eventually leading to the breakdown of various bodily processes, 286

cross-sectional method a method of research that looks at different age groups at the same time in order to understand changes that occur during the life span, 36

crowd large groups of people who share attitudes and a group identity, 258

culture-bound syndrome clusters of symptoms that define or describe an illness in a particular culture, 411

𝒟

decay disintegration; in psychology, the fading away of memory, 169

deductive reasoning a form of thinking in which conclusions are inferred from premises; the conclusions are true if the premises are true, 189

defense mechanisms psychological distortions used to remain psychologically stable or in balance, 326

defensive coping a response to a stressor that temporarily reduces stress but may be harmful in the long run because it neither changes the situation nor removes the stressor, 403

delusion an erroneous belief, as of persecution or grandeur, that may accompany certain psychotic disorders, 120

dementia a serious loss of cognitive function, 286

democratic leader a leader who encourages group members to express and discuss their ideas and to make their own decisions, 484

dendrites the branchlike extensions of a neuron that receive impulses and conduct them toward the cell body, 55

denial a defense mechanism in which the individual refuses to admit that a problem exists, 327

dependent variable in an experiment, the factor that is being measured and that may change in response to manipulations of the independent variable, 41

depersonalization a dissociative disorder characterized by persistent or recurrent feelings that one is unreal or is detached from one's own experiences or body, 421

depressant a drug that reduces neural activity and slows body functions, 117

depression a psychological disorder characterized by extreme sadness, an inability to concentrate, and feelings of helplessness and dejection, 423

detoxification the removal of a poisonous or otherwise harmful substance, such as alcohol or other drugs, from the body, **121**

developmental psychology the branch of psychology that studies the physical, cognitive, and social changes that occur throughout the life cycle, **228**

difference reduction a problem-solving method that involves reducing the difference between the present situation and the desired one, **182**

difference threshold the minimum difference that an individual can detect between two stimuli, **78**

diffusion of responsibility the sharing of responsibility for a decision or behavior among the members of a group, **480**

discrimination (1) in classical conditioning, the ability to distinguish the conditioned stimulus from other stimuli that are similar, **133**; (2) unfair treatment of a person or group based on prejudice, **465**

displacement the defense mechanism that shifts negative impulses toward a more acceptable object or person, **326**

dissociation a split in consciousness, **420**

distress stress that is damaging or negative, **386**

divergent thinking a thought process that attempts to generate multiple solutions to a problem, **187**

double-blind study an experiment in which neither the participant nor the researcher knows whether the participant has received the treatment or the placebo, **43**

dream analysis a technique used by psychoanalysts to interpret the content of patients' dreams, **441**

drives conditions of arousal or tension within an organism that motivate the organism; usually associated with a need, **300**

ℰ

echoic memory the sensory register in which traces of sounds are held and may be retrieved within several seconds, **161**

ego in psychoanalytic theory, the personality component that is conscious and that controls behavior, **325**

egocentrism in Piaget's theory, the inability of the preoperational child to understand another's point of view, **243**

ego integrity according to Erikson, a strong sense of identity during late adulthood that is characterized by the wisdom to accept the fact that life is limited, **288**

eidetic imagery the maintenance of a very detailed visual memory over several months, **161**

elaborative rehearsal a memory device that creates a meaningful link between new information and the information already known, **157**

electroconvulsive therapy a radical treatment for psychological disorders that involves passing an electric current through the brain of an anesthetized patient, **452**

emotions states of feeling that involve physical arousal, expressive behaviors, and conscious experience, **311**

emotional appeal a type of persuasive communication that influences behavior on the basis of feelings rather than on an analysis of the issues, **464**

empty-nest syndrome a sense of depression and a loss of purpose that some parents experience when the youngest child leaves home, **282**

encoding the translation of information into a form that can be stored in memory, **156**

encounter group a structured group that aims to foster self-awareness by focusing on how group members relate to one another in a setting that encourages frank expression of feelings, **440**

endocrine system the glands that secrete hormones into the bloodstream, **67**

episodic memory a memory of a specific experienced event, **154**

ethics rules and standards for proper and responsible behavior, **44**

ethnic group a group united by cultural heritage, race, language, or common history, **21**

eustress stress that is positive or motivating, **386**

euthanasia the act of killing or enabling the death of a hopelessly sick or injured individual in a relatively painless way; also called mercy killing, **292**

evaluation apprehension concern that others are judging one's performance, **480**

evolutionary perspective the theory focusing on the evolution of behavior and mental processes, **18**

experiment a controlled scientific procedure to determine whether certain variables manipulated by the researcher have an effect on other variables, **40**

experimental group in a study, the participants who receive the treatment, **41**

explicit memory a memory of specific information, **155**

explicit norms spoken or written rules of social behavior, such as traffic rules, **485**

extinction in classical conditioning, the disappearance of a conditioned response when an unconditioned stimulus no longer follows a conditioned stimulus, **131**

extrinsic rewards something external given in response to the attainment of a goal, such as good grades, **309**

extrovert   a person who tends to be active and self-expressive and to gain energy from interaction with others, **322**

F

first-shift scheme   situation in which one person changes his or her mind to break a deadlock, **481**

flashbulb memories   clear memories of emotionally significant moments or events, **154**

flooding   based on the principles of classical conditioning, a fear-reduction technique that involves exposing the individual to a harmless stimulus until fear responses to that stimulus are extinguished, **133**

foot-in-the-door effect   the tendency for people to comply with a large request after they have agreed to smaller requests, **489**

forced-choice format   a method of presenting test questions that requires a respondent to select one of several possible answers, **349**

formal-operational stage   according to Piaget, the stage of cognitive development during which people begin to think logically about abstract concepts, **244**

framing effect   the influence of wording, or the way in which information is presented, on decision making, **194**

free association   in psychoanalysis, the uncensored uttering of all thoughts that come to mind, **441**

free radical   an unstable molecule present in the human body that is thought by some scientists to be a cause of aging, **285**

functional fixedness   a barrier to problem solving that involves the tendency to think of objects only in terms of their common uses, **187**

functionalism   the school of psychology, founded by William James, that emphasizes the purposes of behavior and mental processes, **13**

fundamental attribution error   a bias in social perception characterized by the tendency to assume that others generally act on the basis of their dispositions, even when there is evidence suggesting the importance of their situations, **470**

G

gate theory   the suggestion that only a certain amount of information can be processed by the nervous system at a given time, **91**

gender   classifications of sex, based on mostly nonbiological traits such as physical structure and appearance, **364**

gender roles   the differing sets of behaviors that a culture considers appropriate for males or females, **364**

gender schema   the set of traits and behaviors by which a child learns to classify male and female gender roles and by which the child models and measures his or her own relation to those roles, **376**

gender stereotypes   oversimplified generalizations about the characteristics of males and females, **365**

gender typing   the process by which people learn to conform to gender roles, **372**

genes   the basic building blocks of heredity, **70**

general adaptation syndrome (GAS)   the three-stage sequence of behavior in response to stress, consisting of an alarm reaction, a resistance stage, and an exhaustion stage, **395**

generalization   the tendency to respond in the same way to stimuli that have similar characteristics, **132**

generativity   according to Erikson, the ability to create, originate, and produce throughout adulthood, **280**

Gestalt psychology   the school of psychology that emphasizes the tendency to organize perceptions into meaningful wholes, **16**

gifted   a term used to describe children with IQ scores above 130 or children with outstanding talent for performing at much higher levels than others of the same age and background, **216**

group polarization   the strengthening of a group's shared attitudes over time, **482**

H

hallucination   a false sensory perception that occurs in the absence of any actual stimulus, **120**

hallucinogen   a psychedelic drug, such as LSD, that distorts perceptions and evokes sensory images in the absence of actual sensory input, **120**

heredity   the genetic transmission of traits from one generation to the next, **69**

heritability   the proportion of variation among individuals that can be attributed to genes, **219**

heuristic   a strategy for making judgments and solving problems, **181**

homeostasis   an internal balance or equilibrium that is achieved through adjustments of the nervous system, **301**

hormones   chemicals produced by the endocrine glands that regulate specific body functions, **67**

hospice   a type of care for terminally ill patients; an organization that provides such care, **292**

humanistic perspective   the psychological view that assumes the existence of the self and emphasizes the importance of self-awareness and the freedom to make choices, **19**

humanistic therapy   a treatment method based on the assumption that most people are basically good and have a natural tendency to strive for self-actualization, **444**

hypnosis a condition in which people appear to be highly suggestible and to behave as if they are in a trance, **113**

hypothalamus the neural structure located below the thalamus that controls temperature, hunger, thirst, and various aspects of emotion, **61**

hypothesis a prediction or assumption about behavior that is tested through scientific research, **26**

ℐ

iconic memory the sensory register that briefly holds mental images of visual stimuli, **161**

id in psychoanalytic theory, the reservoir of unconscious psychic energy that strives to satisfy basic sexual and aggressive drives, **325**

identification in psychoanalytic theory, the process by which children adopt the values of their parents, **328**

identity achievement a stage in identity development in which a person has committed to an occupational direction and made decisions about important life questions, **262**

identity crisis a period of inner conflict during which one examines one's values and makes decisions about one's life direction, **260**

identity diffusion the constant search for meaning and identity without committing oneself to a set of personal beliefs or an occupational path, **262**

identity foreclosure the act of making a commitment based on other's values in order to avoid an identity crisis, **262**

identity moratorium a period of time in the development of identity in which a person delays making a decision about important issues but actively explores various alternatives, **262**

identity status according to Marcia, one of four reaction patterns or processes in the development of identity during adolescence, **262**

imbalance a state in which people who have strong feelings about each other disagree on a major issue, **310**

implicit memory a memory that consists of the skills and procedures one has learned, **155**

implicit norms unspoken, unwritten standards of behavior for a group of people, **485**

imprinting the process by which animals form strong attachments during a critical period very early in life, **235**

incubation effect the tendency to arrive at a solution after a period of time away from the problem, **185**

independent variable the factor that is manipulated by the researcher to determine its effect on another variable, **41**

inductive reasoning a form of thinking that involves using individual cases or particular facts to reach a general conclusion, **190**

infancy in humans, the stage of life from birth to age two, **231**

infantile amnesia the inability to remember events that occurred during one's early years (before age three), **169**

inferiority complex according to Adler, feelings of inadequacy and insecurity that serve as a central source of motivation, **330**

informed consent an agreement by an individual to participate in research after receiving information about the purpose of the study and the nature of the treatment, **46**

insomnia a sleep disorder characterized by recurring problems in falling asleep or staying asleep, **110**

instincts complex, unlearned behaviors that are present throughout a species, **300**

intelligence the capacity to learn from experience, solve problems, and adapt to a changing environment, **206**

intelligence quotient the ratio of mental age to chronological age multiplied by 100; the average performance for a given age is assigned a score of 100, **212**

interference the process that occurs when new information appears in short-term memory and replaces what was already there, **163**

intimacy feelings of closeness and concern for another person, **474**

intoxication a state of drunkenness characterized by impaired coordination and judgment, **117**

intrinsic rewards internal rewards, such as self-satisfaction, that are given in response to the attainment of a goal, **309**

introspection an examination of one's own thoughts and feelings, **12**

introvert a person who tends to be more interested in his or her own thoughts and feelings than in what is going on around him or her, **322**

ℐ

juvenile delinquency a violation of the law committed by a child or adolescent, **268**

ℋ

kinesthesis the sense that provides information about the position and movement of individual body parts, **92**

ℒ

laboratory observation the study of behavior in a controlled situation, **37**

laissez-faire leader a leader who stands back from decision making and allows group members to explore and express their own ideas, **484**

language the communication of ideas through sounds and symbols that are arranged according to the rules of grammar, **195**

language acquisition device according to Chomsky, the inborn ability of humans to acquire language, **199**

latent content according to Freud, the hidden meaning of a dream, **441**

latent learning learning that occurs but remains hidden until there is a need to use it, **145**

lateralization the development, prior to birth, of the tendencies of the brain's left and right hemispheres to specialize in certain functions, **372**

learning goals achievements that are motivated by the desire to enhance one's knowledge and skills, **309**

learning perspective the psychological point of view that emphasizes the effects of experience on behavior, **20**

lens the transparent structure of the eye that focuses light on the retina, **81**

limbic system a group of neural structures at the base of the cerebral hemispheres that is associated with emotion and motivation, **61**

lithium a chemical used to treat the mood swings of bipolar disorder, **452**

living wills legal documents in which the signer requests to be allowed to die rather than be kept alive by artificial means if disabled beyond a reasonable expectation of recovery, **293**

longitudinal method a type of research in which the same people are studied over a long time period, **36**

long-term memory the type or stage of memory capable of large and relatively permanent storage, **163**

M

maintenance rehearsal the repetition of new information in an attempt to keep from forgetting it, **157**

majority-wins scheme in group decision making, an agreement initially supported by a majority of the group members and then agreed to by all, **481**

mania a mood characterized by extreme elation and hyperactivity, **424**

manifest content according to Freud, the apparent and remembered content of a dream, **441**

matching hypothesis the view that people tend to choose other people similar to themselves in attractiveness and attitudes in the formation of interpersonal relationships, **473**

maturation developmental changes that occur as a result of automatic, genetically determined signals, **229**

means-end analysis a heuristic device in which a solution to a problem is found by evaluating the difference between the current situation and the goal, **183**

meditation a systematic narrowing of attention that slows the metabolism and helps produce feelings of relaxation, **112**

medulla a structure at the base of the brain stem that controls vital functions such as heartbeat and breathing, **59**

memory the processes by which information is encoded, stored, and retrieved, **154**

menarche a female's first menstrual period, **254**

menopause the cessation of menstruation; also, the biological changes that a woman experiences during the years of her declining ability to reproduce, **283**

mental age the level of intellectual functioning, which is compared to chronological age to give an IQ, **211**

mental retardation intellectual functioning that is below average, as indicated by an intelligence score at or below 70, **215**

mental set the tendency to approach a new problem in a way that has been successful in the past, **186**

midlife crisis a turning point experienced by many people between ages 45 to 65, when they realize that life may be half over and they feel trapped in meaningless life roles, **281**

midlife transition a period in middle adulthood when a person's perspective on his or her life may change significantly, **280**

migraine headache a headache characterized by sudden onset and severe throbbing pain on one side of the head, **399**

modeling the process of learning behavior through the observation and imitation of others, **374**

monocular cues cues for distance that may be available to either eye alone, **95**

morpheme the smallest meaningful unit of language, such as a prefix or suffix, **195**

motive a need or desire that energizes and directs behavior, **300**

multiple approach-avoidance conflict a conflict involving a choice between two or more options, each of which has both positive and negative aspects, **390**

myelin a white, fatty substance that insulates axons and enables rapid transmission of neural impulses, **55**

N

narcolepsy an uncommon sleep disorder characterized by brief attacks of REM sleep, often at inopportune moments, **112**

narcotic a type of drug that dulls the senses, relieves pain, and induces sleep; the term is usually reserved for those drugs derived from the opium poppy plant, **117**

naturalistic observation   the study of behavior in naturally occurring situations without manipulation or control on the part of the observer, **36**

need   the biological or psychological requirements for the well-being of an organism, **300**

negative correlation   an unpleasant stimulus between two variables in which one variable increases as the other variable decreases, **39**

negative reinforcer   an unpleasant stimulus that increases the frequency of behavior when it is removed, **137**

neuron   a nerve cell; the basic building block of the nervous system, **54**

neurotransmitter   a chemical messenger that carries impulses across the synaptic gaps between neurons, **56**

night terror   a sleep disorder characterized by high arousal and apparent terror; unlike nightmares, night terrors are seldom remembered, **111**

nonbalance   in balance theory, a condition in which people who dislike each other or have no feeling for each other feel indifferent if they disagree, **310**

nonconscious   descriptive of bodily processes, such as the growing of hair, of which we are not aware, **105**

nondirective therapy   a type of therapy in which the client rather than the therapist is encouraged to take the lead, **444**

norm   an established standard of performance or behavior, **347**

norm group   a group of test takers whose scores establish the norm for a particular test, **347**

nurturance   loving care and attention, **368**

O

obese   a condition characterized by excessive body fat, **304**

objective test   a test that has a group of standardized test items and specific answers that are considered to be correct, **350**

object permanence   the awareness that people and objects continue to exist even when they cannot be perceived, **242**

observational learning   learning by observing and imitating the behavior of others, **146**

obsession   a recurring thought or image that seems to be beyond control, **416**

olfactory nerve   the nerve that transmits information about odors from olfactory receptors to the brain, **89**

operant conditioning   learning that is strengthened when behavior is followed by positive reinforcement, **135**

opponent-process theory   according to Solomon, the idea that an intense emotion often is followed by its opposite, **314**

overregularization   the formation of plurals and the past tense of irregular nouns and verbs according to rules of grammar that apply to regular nouns and verbs; characteristic of the speech of young children, **199**

P

panic attack   an episode of intense dread in which a person experiences terror and other frightening sensations, such as chest pain, rapid heartbeat, or choking, **416**

partial reinforcement   a type of conditioned learning in which only some of the responses are reinforced, **140**

passion   an aroused state of intense desire for another person, **475**

patriarchy   a social organization marked by the supremacy of males in the clan or family, **276**

perception   the process of organizing and interpreting sensory information, **78**

performance goals   achievements motivated by a concrete, external reward, **308**

peripheral nervous system   the neurons that connect the central nervous system to the rest of the body, including the muscles and glands, **54**

peripheral route   a method of persuasion characterized by an emphasis on factors other than the message itself, **463**

personality   the pattern of feelings, thoughts, and behavior that sets people apart from one another, **321**

person-centered therapy   a humanistic therapy, developed by Carl Rogers, in which the therapist creates an accepting, empathic environment to facilitate the client's growth, **444**

persuasion   the attempt to influence people's attitudes and choices through argument, entreaty, or explanation, **462**

phobia   an excessive, irrational fear out of proportion to the actual danger, **415**

phoneme   the basic sound unit in a spoken language, **195**

photoreceptors   neurons that respond to light, **83**

placebo   an inert substance used in controlled experiments to test the effectiveness of another substance, **42**

pons   a brain structure located at the top of the brain stem that is involved in respiration, movement, and sleep, **59**

positive correlation   a relationship between variables in which one variable increases as the other variable also increases, **39**

positive reinforcers   encouraging stimuli that increase the frequency of a behavior when they are presented, **137**

postconventional moral reasoning   according to Kohlberg, a level of moral development during which moral judgments are derived from a person's own moral standards, **246**

posthypnotic suggestion   instructions given to a person under hypnosis that are supposed to be carried out after the hypnosis session has ended, **116**

post-traumatic stress disorder   a disorder that follows a distressing event outside the range of normal human experience and is characterized by intense fear, avoidance of stimuli associated with the event, and reliving of the event, **417**

preconscious   descriptive of information that is not conscious but is retrievable into conscious awareness, **105**

preconventional moral reasoning   according to Kohlberg, a level of moral development in which moral judgments are based on fear of punishment or desire for pleasure, **246**

prefrontal lobotomy   a radical form of psychosurgery in which a section of the frontal lobe of the brain is severed or destroyed, **453**

prejudice   an unjustifiable, and usually negative, attitude toward a person or group, **465**

premise   a statement or assertion that serves as the basis for an argument, **189**

preoperational stage   in Piaget's theory, the stage during which a child learns to use language but does not yet think logically, **242**

primacy effect   (1) the tendency to recall the initial item or items in a series, **162**; (2) the tendency to form opinions of others based on first impressions, **468**

primary reinforcers   stimuli, such as food or warmth, that have reinforcement value without learning, **137**

primary sex characteristics   the organs that make sexual reproduction possible, such as the ovaries and testes, **253**

principle   a rule or law, **6**

programmed theories   the view that aging is the result of genetics, **285**

projection   in psychoanalytic theory, the defense mechanism by which people attribute their own unacceptable impulses to others, **327**

projective test   a psychological test that presents ambiguous stimuli designed to elicit a response that reflects the test taker's feelings, interests, and biases, **352**

prototype   an original model on which others in the same category are patterned, **179**

proximity   the perceptual tendency to group together visual and auditory events that are near each other, **93**

psychoanalysis   the school of psychology, founded by Sigmund Freud, that emphasizes the importance of unconscious motives and conflicts as determinants of human behavior, **17**

psychoanalytic perspective   the perspective that stresses the influences of unconscious forces on human behavior, **19**

psychodynamic thinking   the theory that most of what fills an individual's mind is unconscious and consists of conflicting impulses, urges, and wishes, **17**

psychological constructs   theoretical entities, or concepts, that enable one to discuss something that cannot be seen, touched, or measured directly, **4**

psychological disorder   a pattern of behavior or a mental process that causes serious personal suffering or interferes with a person's ability to cope with everyday life, **410**

psychology   the scientific study of behavior and mental processes, **4**

psychosurgery   biological treatments in which specific areas or structures of the brain are removed or destroyed to change behavior, **453**

psychotherapy   the application of psychological principles and techniques to influence a person's thoughts, feelings, or behaviors in an attempt to help that person overcome psychological disorders or adjust to problems in living, **436**

puberty   the period of sexual maturation; the onset of one's ability to reproduce, **253**

pupil   the opening in the center of the eye that adjusts to allow light to enter, **81**

R

random sample   a survey population, selected by chance, which fairly represents the general population, **31**

rapid-eye-movement sleep   a stage of sleep characterized by rapid eye movements and linked to dreaming; also called REM sleep, **108**

rational-emotive therapy   a confrontational cognitive therapy, developed by Albert Ellis, that encourages people to challenge illogical, self-defeating thoughts and attitudes, **447**

rationalization   in psychoanalytic theory, the defense mechanism by which an individual finds justifications for unacceptable thoughts, impulses, or behaviors, **326**

reaction formation   in psychoanalytic theory, a defense mechanism by which the ego unconsciously switches unacceptable impulses into their opposites, **327**

reasoning   the process of drawing logical conclusions from facts and arguments, **189**

recall   retrieval of learned information, **168**

recency effect   (1) the tendency to recall the last item in a series, **162**; (2) the tendency for people to change their opinions of others based on recent interactions, **468**

reciprocity in interpersonal relationships, the tendency to return feelings and attitudes that are expressed about us, **474**

recognition a memory process in which one identifies objects or events that have previously been encountered, **167**

reflex an automatic, unlearned response to a sensory stimulus, **230**

regression in psychoanalytic theory, a defense mechanism by which an individual retreats to an earlier stage of development when faced with anxiety, **327**

reinforcement a stimulus or event that follows a response and increases the frequency of that response, **136**

relearning learning material a second time, usually in less time than it was originally learned, **169**

reliability the extent to which a test yields consistent results, **214**

replicate to repeat a research study, usually with different participants and in different situations, to confirm the results of the original study, **28**

representativeness heuristic the process of making decisions about a sample according to the population that the sample appears to represent, **192**

repression in psychoanalytic theory, the defense mechanism that removes anxiety-arousing thoughts, feelings, and memories from one's consciousness, **326**

resistance in psychoanalysis, a blocking from consciousness of issues that might cause anxiety, **441**

response an observable reaction to a stimulus, **128**

reticular activating system the part of the brain that is involved in attention, sleep, and arousal, **60**

retina the light-sensitive inner surface of the eye that contains the rods, cones, and neurons that process visual stimuli, **81**

retinal disparity a binocular cue for perceiving depth based on the difference between the two images of an object that the retina receives as the object moves closer or farther away, **96**

retrieval the process of recalling information from memory storage, **158**

retrograde amnesia the failure to remember events that occurred prior to physical trauma because of the effects of the trauma, **170**

risky shift the tendency to make riskier decisions as a member of a group than as an individual acting alone, **481**

sales resistance the ability to refuse a request or sales pitch, **464**

sample a representative segment of a target population, **31**

scapegoat a person or group unfairly blamed for the problems of others; to blame a person or group unfairly, **466**

schedule of reinforcement a timetable for when and how often reinforcement for a particular behavior occurs, **139**

schema an idea or mental framework that helps one organize and interpret information, **164**

schizophrenia a group of severe psychotic disorders characterized by distortions in thinking, perception, emotion, and behavior, **426**

secondary reinforcers stimuli that increase the probability of a response because of their association with a primary reinforcer, **137**

secondary sex characteristics sexual characteristics that are not involved in reproduction, such as the growth of facial hair in males and the rounding of hips and breasts in females, **253**

selective attention the focusing of attention on a particular stimulus, **104**

self-actualization according to Maslow, the self-motivated striving to reach one's potential, **302**

self-concept one's view of oneself as an individual, **335**

self-efficacy expectation a person's beliefs that he or she can bring about desired changes or goals through his or her own efforts, **393**

self-esteem the value or worth that people attach to themselves, **240**

self-help group a type of therapy group in which members share a common problem, such as alcoholism, **440**

self-report an interview or questionnaire in which a person reports his or her attitudes, feelings, and behaviors, **344**

self-serving bias the tendency to view one's successes as stemming from internal factors and one's failures as stemming from external factors, **470**

semantic memory a memory of general knowledge and information that can be recalled, **154**

semantics the study of meaning in language; the relationship between language and the objects depicted by the language, **196**

senile dementia a decrease in mental ability that sometimes occurs after the age of 65, **286**

sensation the stimulation of sensory receptors and the transmission of sensory information to the brain, **78**

sensorimotor stage according to Piaget, the stage during which infants know the world mostly in terms of their sensory impressions and motor activities, **242**

sensorineural deafness deafness that results from damage to the auditory nerve, **87**

sensory adaptation the process by which an organism becomes more sensitive to stimuli that are low in magnitude and less sensitive to stimuli that are constant, **80**

sensory deprivation a state in which there is little or no sensory stimulation, **307**

sensory memory the immediate, initial recording of sensory information in the memory system, **160**

separation anxiety distress that is sometimes experienced by infants when they are separated from their primary caregivers, **234**

shaping in operant conditioning, a procedure in which reinforcement guides behavior toward closer approximations of the desired goal, **142**

short-term memory memory that holds information briefly before it is stored or forgotten, **161**

signal-detection theory the idea that distinguishing sensory stimuli takes into account not only the strength of the stimuli but also such elements as setting and one's physical state, mood, and attitudes, **79**

similarity the perceptual tendency to group together elements that seem alike, **94**

simple phobia an anxiety disorder characterized by a persistent, irrational fear of a specific object or situation, **415**

single-blind study a study in which the participants are unaware of whether they are in the control group or the experimental group, **43**

sleep apnea a sleep disorder in which breathing is interrupted, **111**

social decision scheme rules for predicting the final outcome of group decision making, **481**

social facilitation improved performance of tasks because of the presence of others, **480**

socialization the guidance of people, especially children, into socially desirable behavior by means of verbal messages, the systematic use of rewards and punishments, and other teaching methods, **333**

social-learning theory the theory that suggests that people have the ability to change their environments or to create new ones, **20**

social loafing the tendency for people to exert less effort toward completing a task when they are part of a group than when they are performing the task alone, **480**

social norm explicit and implicit rules that reflect social expectations and influence the ways in which people behave in social situations, **485**

social perception the ways in which people form and modify their impressions of others, **468**

social phobia an irrational fear of social situations in which one might be exposed to the close scrutiny of others, **416**

sociocultural perspective in psychology, the perspective that focuses on the roles of ethnicity, gender, culture, and socioeconomic status in personality formation, behavior, and mental processes, **21**

somatic nervous system the division of the peripheral nervous system that connects the central nervous system with sensory receptors, muscles, and the skin, **57**

somatization the expression of psychological distress through physical symptoms, **421**

spinal cord a column of nerves within the spine that transmit messages to and from the brain, **57**

spontaneous recovery the reappearance of an extinguished conditioned response after some time has passed, **132**

standard deviation a measure of the distance of every score to the mean, **44**

standardized tests tests for which norms are based on the performance of a range of individuals, **344**

state-dependent memories memories in which information is more easily retrieved when one is in the same physiological or emotional state as when the memory was originally encoded or learned, **160**

status offenses actions that are illegal when committed by a minor, such as consuming alcohol, **269**

stimulant a drug that increases neural activity and speeds up body functions, **118**

stimulus a feature in the environment that is detected by an organism or that leads to a change in behavior, **128**

stimulus motives desires for increased stimulation, **306**

storage the maintenance of encoded information over time, **157**

stranger anxiety the fear of strangers that infants commonly display, **234**

stratified sample a sample drawn in such a way that known subgroups within a population are represented in proportion to their numbers in the general population, **31**

stress the physical and mental strain a person experiences in association with demands to adapt to a challenging situation, **386**

stressor an event or circumstance that produces stress, **386**

stroboscopic motion a visual illusion in which the perception of motion is generated by the presentation of a series of stationary images in rapid succession, **95**

structuralism the school of psychology, founded by Wilhelm Wundt, that maintains that conscious experience breaks down into objective sensations and subjective feelings, **13**

sublimation in psychoanalytic theory, the defense mechanism by which people channel their socially unacceptable impulses into more acceptable activities, **327**

successive approximations in operant conditioning, a series of behaviors that gradually become more similar to a desired behavior, **450**

superego according to Freud, the part of personality that represents the individual's internalized ideals and provides standards for judgment, **326**

survey a research technique for acquiring data about the attitudes or behaviors of a group of people, usually by asking questions of a representative, random sample, **29**

symbol an object or an act that stands for something else, **178**

synapse the junction between the axon terminals of the sending neuron and the dendrites of the receiving neuron, **55**

syntax the ways in which words and phrases are arranged into grammatical sentences, **195**

systematic desensitization a type of counterconditioning, used to treat phobias, in which a pleasant, relaxed state is associated with gradually increasing anxiety-triggering stimuli, **133**

𝒯

target population the total group to be studied or described and from whom samples may be drawn, **31**

taste aversion a type of classical conditioning in which a previously desirable or neutral food comes to be perceived as repugnant because it is associated with negative stimulation, **130**

test-retest reliability a method for determining the reliability of a test by comparing a test taker's scores on the same test taken on separate occasions, **214**

thalamus the structure of the brain that relays messages from the sense organs to the cerebral cortex, **61**

theory a set of assumptions about why something is the way it is and happens the way it does, **6**

thinking mental activity that involves understanding, manipulating, and communicating information, **178**

tip-of-the-tongue phenomenon the belief that a piece of information is stored in our memory although we cannot retrieve it easily, **160**

token economy a controlled environment in which people's desired behaviors are reinforced with tokens that may be exchanged for privileges or other rewards, **450**

trait an aspect of personality that is considered to be reasonably consistent, **322**

transference in psychoanalysis, the patient's transfer of emotions associated with other relationships to the therapist, **442**

transformed score a score that has been changed from a raw score in a systematic way, **212**

triangular model of love according to Sternberg, the components of love, which include passion, intimacy, and commitment, **474**

truth-wins scheme in group decision making, an agreement reached when members realize that one option is clearly better than the others, **481**

two-sided argument a method of discrediting an opponent by presenting his or her argument and then refuting it, **463**

two-thirds–majority scheme in group decision making, an agreement that is supported by two thirds of the members, **481**

𝒰

unconditional positive regard a consistent expression of esteem for the basic value of a person, **240**

unconditioned response in classical conditioning, an unlearned response, **130**

unconditioned stimulus in classical conditioning, a stimulus that elicits an unlearned, naturally occurring response, **130**

unconscious according to Freud, a reservoir of mostly unacceptable thoughts, wishes, feelings, and memories of which we are unaware but which influences our behavior, **105**

𝒱

validity the extent to which a test measures what it is suppose to measure, **214**

validity scale a group of test items that suggest whether or not the test taker is answering honestly, **345**

variables factors that are measured or controlled in a scientific study, **41**

vestibular sense the sense that provides information about the position of the body, **92**

visual acuity keenness or sharpness of vision, **83**

vocational interest inventories tests that are used to help people make decisions about career options, **348**

volunteer bias the concept that people who volunteer to participate in research studies often differ from those who do not volunteer, **33**

INDEX

R35

D

dark adaptation, 83
data
  ethical issues in using, 47
  using computers for collecting, 30
dating, 259, 268
deafness, 87–88
death and dying, 291–293
  and bereavement, 293
  and euthanasia, 292
  funerals, role of, 293
  stages of, 291–292
decay, 169
deception, 46
decibels, 85, 86*(illus.)*
decision making, 191–195
  and conflict, 388, 390
  and framing effect, 194
  and judgment, 191–195
  group, 481–482
  and overconfidence, 194–195
  shortcuts in, 191–194
deductive reasoning, 189, 189*(illus.)*
defense mechanisms, 326–327
  denial, 327
  displacement, 326–327
  effects of, 327
  projection, 327
  rationalization, 326
  reaction formation, 327
  regression, 327
  repression, 326
  sublimation, 327
defensive coping, 403
delta waves, 108
delusion, 120
dementia, 286–287
democratic leaders, 484
dendrites, 54*(illus.)*, 55*(illus.)*
denial, 327
deoxyribonucleic acid (DNA), 70, 70*(illus.)*
dependent variable, 41
depersonalization, 421
depersonalization disorder, 421
depressant, 117–118
  alcohol, 117
  narcotics, 117–118
depression
  cognitive therapy for treatment of, 448
  major, 423–424
  severe, 424
depth perception, 95–97, 96*(illus.)*, 97*(illus.)*

  and binocular cues, 96–97
  and monocular cues, 95–96
detoxification, 121
development, 228–247
  cognitive, 241–247
  critical periods in, 229
  father's role in, 238
  maturation, 229
  and nature-nurture debate, 228–229
  physical, 230–233, 23*(illus.)*
  psychosocial stages of, 327, 329
  social, 233–237, 239–241
  stages vs. continuity in, 229–230
  study of, 228–230
developmental psychologists, 9–10, 228
developmental psychology, 18, 228
***Diagnostic and Statistical Manual of Mental Disorders*, 4/e (DSM-IV)**, 413, 414*(illus.)*
diet, and health, 400
difference reduction, 182–183
difference threshold, 78–79
diffusion of responsibility, 480–481
discipline, classroom, 144
discrimination
  in adapting to environment, 132–133
  and identity formation, 264
  and prejudice, 466
disorders. *See* psychological disorders.
disorganized schizophrenia, 427
displacement, 326–327
dissociation, 420
dissociative amnesia, 420
dissociative disorders, 420–421
dissociative fugue, 420
dissociative identity disorder, 420–421
distress, 386, 391
divergent thinking, 187
diversity
  in psychology, 15
  in research, 32
divorce, 278–280
DNA (deoxyribonucleic acid), 70, 70*(illus.)*
dopamine, 56, 429
double-blind studies, 43–44
Down syndrome, 70, 70*(illus.)*
dream analysis, 325, 441
dreams and dreaming, 109–110
drill and practice, 170, 172
drive-reduction theory of motivation, 301
drives, 300
drug prevention programs, 267–268

limbic system, 61
links, constructing, 173
lithium, 452
Little Albert experiment, 134
Little Hans, case of, 328
living will, 293
lobes (of cerebral cortex), 61, 62(illus.)
lobotomy, prefrontal, 453
Locke, John, 13
longitudinal method, 36
long-term memory, 163(illus.), 163–164, 166
   capacity of, 164
   reconstructive aspects of, 164
   and schemas, 164, 166
Lorenz, Konrad, 235, 235(illus.)
loudness, 85, 86(illus.)
love, 474–475
   romantic, 276
   triangular model of, 474, 475(illus.)
LSD, 121

M

magazine surveys, 33–34
Magic Eye picture, 97, 97(illus.)
magnetic resonance imaging (MRI), 66, 66(illus.)
maintenance programs, 121
maintenance rehearsal, 157
major depression, 423–424
majority-wins scheme, 481
maladaptivity, 411
mal de ojo, 413(illus.)
male menopause, 284
malingering, 421
mandala, 329(illus.)
mania, 424
manic depression, 424
manifest content (of dreams), 441
manipulation, 307–308
mantra, 112
Marcia, James, 260, 262–263, 263(illus.)
marijuana, 120–121
marriage, 275–278
   and choice of spouse, 276, 278
   and divorce, 278–280
   history of, 276
Marshall, Thurgood, 289
Maslow, Abraham, 301–302, 302(illus.), 334
matching hypothesis, 473
mate selection, and gender differences, 370–371
mathematical abilities, and gender, 366–367

maturation, 229, 254
McDougall, William, 301
Mead, Margaret, 379
means-end analysis, 183, 183(illus.)
media violence, 146–147
Medical College Admissions Test (MCAT), 344, 348
meditation, 112, 112(illus.), 119
medulla, 59, 60(illus.)
memory, 153–173
   associations and, 173
   basic tasks of, 167–169
   capacity of, 164
   and cognitive perspective, 18
   context-dependent, 159
   echoic, 161
   and encoding, 155–156
   episodic, 154, 155(illus.)
   of eyewitnesses, 165
   hypnosis and, 115
   improving, 170, 172–173
   and limbic system, 61
   links and, 173
   long-term, 163–164, 166
   mnenomic devices and, 173
   procedural, 155
   as reconstructive, 164, 166(illus.)
   rehearsal and, 172
   repetition and, 170–172
   and retrieval, 158–160
   schemas, 164–166
   sensory, 160–161, 163(illus.)
   short-term, 161–163
   stages of, 163(illus.)
   state-dependent, 159–160
   and storage, 157–158
   See also forgetting.
menarche, 254
menopause, 283–284
   myths and realities about, 283(illus.)
menstruation, 254
mental age, 211–212
mental health professionals, 437–439
mental processes, 4
mental retardation, 215–216
   causes of, 216
   in Down syndrome, 70
   mild retardation, 215
   moderate retardation, 215–216
   profound retardation, 216
   severe retardation, 216
mental set, 186–187, 186(illus.)
Mesmer, Franz, 113
messenger, persuasive, 464

ACKNOWLEDGMENTS

For permission to reprint copyrighted material, grateful acknowledgment is made to the following sources:

American Psychiatric Association: "Some Culture-Bound Syndromes," "Categories of Psychological Disorders in the *DSM-IV*," "Two Examples of Somatoform Disorders," "Types of Mood Disorders and Their Characteristics," "Characteristics of Schizophrenia and Other Psychotic Disorders," and "Personality Disorders and Their Characteristics," adapted from the *Diagnostic and Statistical Manual of Mental Disorders, Fourth Edition, Text Revision.* Copyright © 2000 by the American Psychiatric Association.

American Psychological Association: "Ethical Principles of Psychologists and Code of Conduct" from *American Psychologist,* vol. 47, pp. 1597–1611, 1992. Copyright © 1992 by the American Psychological Association. Revised Fall 2002. For current standards, see http://www.apa.org/ethics.

Mathilda B. Canter and the American Psychological Association: From "Ethical Principles" from *Ethics for Psychologists: A Commentary on the APA Ethics Code* by Mathilda B. Canter, Bruce E. Bennett, Stanley E. Jones, and Thomas F. Nagy. Copyright © 1994 by the American Psychological Association.

R.N. Emde and the American Psychological Association: "Cardiac and behavioral inter-relationships in the reactions of infants to strangers" by J. J. Campos, R. N. Emde, T. Gaensbauer, and C. Henderson from *Developmental Psychology II,* 1975, p. 594. Copyright © 1975 by the American Psychological Association.

Jason Aronson Inc.: From *Cognitive Hypnotherapy* by E. Thomas Dowd, Ph.D., ABPP. Copyright © 2000 by Jason Aronson Inc.

Thomas J. Bouchard, Jr. and American Association for the Advancement of Science: From "Sources of Human Psychological Differences: The Minnesota Study of Twins Reared Apart" by Thomas J. Bouchard, Jr., David T. Lykken, Matthew McGue, Nancy L. Segal, and Auke Tellegen from *Science,* vol. 250, October 1990. Copyright © 1990 by American Association for the Advancement of Science.

Brooks/Cole, an imprint of the Wadsworth Group, a division of Thomas Learning, Fax 800 730-2215: "Figure 2.1 (behavior of young baboons and adults)" from *Human Behavior: A Systems Approach,* 1st Edition by V. Ellingstad and N. Heimstra. Copyright © 1974 by Brooks/Cole.

Butterworth-Heinemann Ltd.: From "From Crisis to Coping: Theories and Helping Practices" by J. Gibson-Cline, M. Dikaiou, and M. Haritos-Fatouras with B. Shafrir and G. Ondis from *Adolescence: From Crisis to Coping: A Thirteen Nation Study,* edited by Janice Gibson-Cline. Copyright © 1996 by Butterworth-Heineman Ltd.

Cambridge University Press: Figure 2.1 from *Language, Memory, and Aging,* edited by Leah L. Light and Deborah M. Burke. Copyright © 1988 by Cambridge University Press. From "Love Stories" by Robert J. Sternberg from *Personal Relationships,* vol. 3, 1996. Copyright © 1996 by Cambridge University Press.

Doubleday, a division of Random House, Inc.: From "The Psychotherapists" from *The Story of Psychology* by Morton Hunt. Copyright © 1993 by Morton Hunt.

Lawrence Erlbaum Associates, Inc.: From "Children's Task-Group Communication: Did We Learn It All in Kindergarten?" by Thomas J. Socha and Diana M. Socha from *Group Communication in Context: Studies of Natural Groups,* edited by Lawrence R. Frey. Copyright © 1994 by Lawrence Erlbaum Associates, Inc.

The Free Press, a division of Simon & Schuster, Inc.: From "Adolescence and Stress" by Anne C. Petersen and Ralph Spiga, and "Figure 8-3: Summary relationship between test anxiety and problem-solving performance" from *Handbook of Stress: Theoretical and Clinical Aspects,* edited by Leo Goldberger and Shlomo Breznitz. Copyright © 1982 by The Free Press.

Harvard University Press: poem 632 "The Brain is wider than the sky" from *The Poems of Emily Dickinson,* edited by Thomas H. Johnson. Copyright © 1951, 1955, 1979 by the President and Fellows of Harvard College. Published by The Belknap Press of Harvard University Press, Cambridge, Mass. From "Divergence in Childhood" from *The Two Sexes: Growing Up Apart, Coming Together* by Eleanor E. Maccoby. Copyright © 1998 by The President and Fellows of Harvard College.

Alfred A. Knopf, a division of Random House, Inc.: From *Beyond Freedom and Dignity* by B. F. Skinner. Copyright © 1971 by B. F. Skinner.

Pearson Education, Inc.: From "Self-Actualizing People: A Study of Psychological Health" from *Motivation and Personality* by Abraham H. Maslow. Copyright © 1954 by Harper & Row Publishers, Inc.; copyright © 1970 by Abraham H. Maslow.

Princeton University Press: From "Understanding 'Intelligence'" from *Inequality by Design: Cracking the Bell Curve Myth* by Claude S. Fischer et al. Copyright © 1996 by Princeton University Press.

Psychology Today: From "The Enigmatic Smile" by M. Konner from *Psychology Today,* pp. 42-44, 46, March 1987, as reprinted in *Psychology 88/89: Annual Editions.* Copyright © 1987 by Sussex Publishers, Inc.

Routledge: From Introduction: "Through the Looking Glass" from *Worlds of Sense: Exploring the Senses in History and Across Cultures* by Constance Classen. Copyright © 1993 by Constance Classen.

B. F. Skinner Foundation: From *Walden Two* by B. F. Skinner. Copyright © 1948, 1976 by B. F. Skinner.

Simon & Schuster, Inc.: From "Third Stage: Bargaining" from *On Death and Dying* by Elisabeth Kübler-Ross, M.D. Copyright © 1969 by Elisabeth Kübler-Ross.

University of Nebraska Press: From "The Actualizing Tendency in Relation to 'Motives' and to Consciousness" by Carl R. Rogers. Reprinted from 1963 *Nebraska Symposium on Motivation.* Copyright © 1963 and renewed © 1993 by the University of Nebraska Press.

Sources Cited:

Figure 4 from "Autobiographical Memory" by Martin A. Conway from *Memory,* edited by Elizabeth Ligon Bjork and Robert A. Bjork. Published by Academic Press, Inc., San Diego, CA, 1996.

"Figure 2.1 Physical Duration" from *The Unity of the Senses: Interrelations Among the Modalities* by Lawrence E. Marks. Published by Academic Press, Inc., San Diego, CA, 1978.

From "Plasticity of sensorimotor development in the human infant" from *The Causes of Behavior II,* edited by J. F. Rosenblith and W. Allinsmith. Published by Allyn and Bacon, Inc., Boston, MA, 1966.

From "Pathways to Change and Development: The Life of a School Psychologist" by Stephen Poland from *Career Paths in Psychology: Where Your Degree Can Take You,* edited by Robert J. Sternberg. Published by the American Psychological Association, Washington, D.C., 1997.

From "Problem Solving" by Alan Lesgold from *The Psychology of Human Thought,* edited by Robert J. Sternberg and Edward E. Smith. Published by Cambridge University Press, New York, 1988.

From "Individual Psychology" by Alfred Adler from *Psychologies of 1930,* edited by Carl Murchison. Published by Clark University Press, Worcester, MA, 1930.

From *Psychological Testing in Cultural Contexts* by Theodora M. Abel. Published by College & University Press Services, Inc., New Haven, CT, 1973.

Bar graph (Identical and fraternal twins as best friends) from *Entwined Lives: Twins and What They Tell Us About Human Behavior* by Nancy L. Segal, Ph.D. Published by Dutton, New York, 1999.

From *Lectures on Conditioned Reflexes* by Ivan Pavlov. Published by International Publishers, New York, 1928.

From "Historical Antecedents" from *Disorders of Personality: DSM-IV™ and Beyond* by Theodore Millon with Roger Davis. Published by John Wiley & Sons, Inc., New York, 1996.

ILLUSTRATIONS

All art, unless otherwise noted, by Holt, Rinehart and Winston, Inc.

Abbreviated as follows: (t) top; (b) bottom; (l) left; (r) right; (c) center.

Unit 1: Chapter 1: Page 8 (b), Doug Walston; 17 (t), Doug Walston; **Chapter 2:** Page 31 (b), Doug Walston; **Unit 2: Chapter 3:** Page 57 (r), Jean E. Calder; 68 (l), Jean E.Calder; **Chapter 4:** Page 86 (b), Digital Art; 89 (b), Jean E. Calder; 93 (b), Doug Walston; **Chapter 5:** Page 106 (t), Stephen Durke / Washington-Artists' Represents, Inc.; 113 (t), Stephen Durke / Washington-Artists' Represents, Inc.; **Unit 3: Chapter 6:** Page 129 (t), Blake Thornton / Rita Marie and Friends; 130 (b), Blake Thornton / Rita Marie and Friends; **Chapter 8:** Page 180, Blake Thornton / Rita Marie and Friends; 184 (l), Stephen Durke / Washington-Artists' Represents, Inc.; 187 (r), Blake Thornton / Rita Marie and Friends; **Unit 4: Chapter 10:** Page 231 (r), Blake Thornton / Rita Marie and Friends; 237 (t), Digital Art; **Unit 5: Chapter 14:** Page 338 (t), Blake Thornton / Rita Marie and Friends; **Chapter 17:** Page 396 (t), Blake Thornton / Rita Marie and Friends.

PHOTOGRAPHY

All photos, unless otherwise noted, by Sam Dudgeon or Victoria Smith/Holt Rinehart Winston.

Abbreviated as follows: (t) top; (b) bottom; (l) left; (r) right; (c) center, (bckgd) background, (bdr) border.

Table of Contents: Page iv (bl), Cleo/PhotoEdit/PictureQuest; iv (cl), Archive Photos/Getty Images; v (bl), Mehmet Biber/Photo Researchers, Inc.; v (cl), Diane Schuimo/Photographs; vi (bl), H.S. Terrace/Animals Animals/Earth Scenes; vi (cl), Ian Shaw / Tony Stone Images; vi (tl), Mitch Kezar/Tony Stone Images; vii (bl), Richard Hutching/PhotoEdit; vii (c), SuperStock; vii (tl), L. Kesterson/Sygma; viii (bl), SuperStock; viii (cr), John Henley/The Stock Market; viii (tl), Zigy Kalunzy / Tony Stone Images; ix (bl), Elizabeth Zuckerman/ PhotoEdit; ix (cl), Bob Daemmrich/Bob Daemmrich Photography; ix (tl), Giraudon/Art Resource; x (bl), Bruce Ayres/Tony Stone Images; x (cl), Derek Bayes/Tony Stone Images; x (tl), Michael Newman/ PhotoEdit; xi (bl), Frank Siteman/Tony Stone Images; xi (cl), Hulton Archive/Getty Images; xi (tl), Michael Newman/PhotoEdit; xx (all), Courtesy CNNfyi.com; xxi (tr), John Langford/HRW Photo; xxxix (tr), ©Art Montes DeOcal/Getty Images/FPG International.

Skills Handbook: Page S4 (tl), Warren Anatomical Museum, Harvard Medical School; S17 (br), Tom McCarthy/PhotoEdit; S17 (c), David Phillips/HRW.

Unit One: Page 1(c), Cleo/PhotoEdit/PictureQuest.

Chapter One: Page 5(t), Bob Daemmrich/Bob Daemmrich Photography; 6(b), Yoav Levy/PhotoTake; 7 (c), Ghislain & Marie David de Lossy/Getty Images/The Image Bank; 9(t), Paul Meredeth/Tony Stone Images; 11(t), Bob Daemmrich/Bob Daemmrich Photography; 12(b), Archive Photos; 13(t), Corbis- The Bettmann Archive; 13(b), Corbis—The Bettmann Archive; 14(c), Archive Photos; 15(c), AP/Wide World Photos; 16(t), Corbis-The Bettmann Archive; 16(b), L.L.T. Rhodes/Animals Animals/Earth Scenes; 17(b), NY Public Library Prints Division; 19(t), Yoav Levy/PhotoTake; 21(t), Bob Daemmrich/Bob Daemmrich Photography; **Chapter Two:** Page 28(t), SuperStock; 30(b), Jeff Greeenberg/Photo Edit; 32(c), Mark Scott/FPG International; 35(t), Jim Pickerell/Tony Stone Images; 37(t), David Macdonald/Animals Animals/Earth Scenes; 39(bckgd),Russell Dian/ HRW; 42(b), Michael Newman/PhotoEdit; 47(t), Michael Schwarz/The Image Works;

Unit Two: Page 51(bl), Chris Cheadle/Tony Stone Images;

Chapter Three: Page 56(t), Brad Mangin/Duomo; 56(b), SuperStock; 58(t), Richard Hutchings/PhotoEdit; 64(tl), Roon Chapple/FPG International; 64(tr), SuperStock; 65(c), Warren Anatomical Museum, Harvard Medical School; 66(bl), Jim Pickerell/Tony Stone Images; 66(br), Charles Thatcher/Tony Stone Images; 67(t), Jan Halaska/Tony Stone Images; 69(t), Charles Thatcher/Tony Stone Images; 70(b), Mugshots/The Stock Market; 72(t), Cosmo Condina/Tony Stone Images; **Chapter Four:** Page 80(t), Peter A. Simon/PhotoTake; 82 (all), Reuters NewsMedia Inc./CORBIS; 85(t), Diane Schuimo/Fundamental Photographs; 87(b), Kurt Viavant/Sipa Press; 88(t), Bob Daemmrich/Bob Daemmrich Photography; 92(t), William R. Sallaz/Duomo; 95(t), Kim Taylor/Bruce Coleman, Inc.; **Chapter Five:** Page 105(t), Bob Daemmrich/The Image Works; 107(t), Richard Haynes/ HRW109(t), © 1996 Michael Parkes/Steltman Galleries New York. Desert Dream oil painting on wood, 110 x 90cm.; 111(t), Jane Meddaugh/David Frazier Photolibrary; 112(b), Bill Wassman/The Stock Market; 115(t), The Bettmann Archive; 117(t), Culver Pictures, Inc.; 119(c), Mehmet Biber/Photo Researchers, Inc.; 120 (tl), courtesy of National Clearinghouse for Alcohol and Drug Information; 121(t), M. Siluk/The Image Works;

Unit Three: Page 125(br), Robert A. Propper/Leo de Wys, Inc.;

Chapter Six: Page 128(b), ©1992 Molkenthin/The Stock Marke; 131(b), Ed Degginger/Animals Animals/Earth Scenes; 133(t), James Hackett/Leo de Wys, Inc.; 134(c), Tom McCarthy/The Stock Market; 139 (br), Will Hart/PhotoEdit; 141(t), SuperStock; 143 (c), Michael L. Abramson/TimePix; 144(t), Mitch Kezar/Tony Stone Images, Inc.; 145(b), Will & Deni McIntyre/Photo Researchers, Inc.; 146(b), Dion Ogust/The Image Works; 149(t), Jose L. Pelaez/The Stock Market; 149(t), Jose L. Pelaez/The Stock Market; **Chapter Seven:** Page 155 (tr), Thomas E. Franklin/The Record (Bergen County, NJ)/ CORBIS/ SABA; 156(t), Ian Shaw/Tony Stone Images; 158(t), H. Kaiser/Leo de Wys, Inc.; 161(b), Micahel Krasowitz/FPG International; 165(c), John Neubauer/PhotoEdit; **Chapter Eight:** Page 178(t), Copyright © 1996 by the American Psychological Association. Reprinted with permission.; 179(t), Charles Gupton/Tony Stone Images; 182(b), Amy Etra/PhotoEdit; 183(t), Bob Daemmrich/The Image Works; 185(tl), SuperStock; 185(tc), SuperStock; 185(tr), SuperStock; 188(b), Bruce

Ayres/Tony Stone Images; 192(b), SuperStock; 193 (tr), Chris Trotman/Duomo/CORBIS; 194(b), Jon Riley/Tony Stone Images; 196(b), Joe Carini/The Image Works; 197(b), Universal Press; 198(b), Chip Henderson/Tony Stone Images; 199(b), Craig Newbauer/Peter Arnold; 200(c), H.S. Terrace/Animals Animals/Earth Scenes; 201 (bl), Michael Newman/PhotoEdit; 207(t), Bob Daemmrich/Bob Daemmrich Photography; 207(b), AP/Wide World Photos; 209(c), L. Kesterson/Sygma; 210(t), David Frazier/David R. Frazier Photolibrary; 212(t), Laura Dwight/ PhotoEdit; 216(t), Bob Daemmrich/Bob Daemmrich Photography; 216(b), Dick Luria/FPG International; 217(c), Corbis-The Bettmann Archive; 218(t), Scala/Art Resource, NY; 219(b), David Young Wolff/Tony Stone Images; 220(b), N. Rowan/The Image Works; 221(t), Bob Daemmrich/Bob Daemmrich Photography;

Unit Four: Page 225(b), Dan Bosler/Tony Stone Images;

Chapter Ten: Page 228(b), SuperStock; 230(b), Laura Dwight/Peter Arnold, Inc.; 232(t), Super Stock; 233(t), Mark Richards/PhotoEdit; 234(b), Tim Brown/Tony Stone Images; 235(t), Martin Rogers/Tony Stone Images; 235(b), Nina Leen, Life Magazine © Time, Inc.; 238(c), Chuck Savage/The Stock Market; 240(t), Ariel Skelley/The Stock Market; 241(c), Archive PhotosLine: Archive Photos/A.F.P.; 242(t), Michael Newman/ PhotoEdit; **Chapter Eleven:** Page 254(t), Richard Hutchings/ PhotoEdit; 255(c), Mark Richards/PhotoEdit; 258(tl), Laura Dwight/PhotoEdit; 259(t), Bob Daemmrich/Bob Daemmrich Photography; 260(b), Bob Daemmrich/Tony Stone Images; 264(t), Robert Sorbo/AP/Wide World Photos; 266(t), Bob Daemmrich/Bob Daemmrich Photography; 267(t), Tom McCarthy/PhotoEdit; 268(t), Rhoda Sidney/PhotoEdit; 255(c), Mark Richards/PhotoEdit; 258(t), David Frazier/ David Frazier Photolibrary; 259(t), Bob aemmrich/Bob Daemmrich Photography; 260(b), Bob Daemmrich/Tony Stone Images; 264(t), Robert Sorbo/AP/Wide World Photos; 266(t), Bob Daemmrich/Bob Daemmrich Photography; 267(t), Tom McCarthy/ PhotoEdit; 268(t), Rhoda Sidney/PhotoEdit; **Chapter Twelve:** Page 275(t), SuperStock; 276(t), Paul Rees/Tony Stone Images; 278(t), M. Greenlar/The Image Works; 279(b), Michael Newman/PhotoEdit; 281(t), SuperStock; 282(t), United Media; 282(b), Michael Newman/PhotoEdit; 284(bckgd), HRW; 284 (bl), © Walter Hodges/Getty Images/Stone; 285(t), Zigy Kaluzny/ Tony Stone Images; 286 (tl), Walter Hodges/CORBIS; 288(t), SuperStock; 290(t), Tom McCarthy/Photo Edit; 292(t), SuperStock; 293(t), Leslye Borden/PhotoEdit;

Unit Five: Page 297(b), Super Stock;

Chapter Thirteen: Page 298(r) HRW/Michelle Bridwell; 301(t), SuperStock; 303(t), Eric R. Berndt/Unicorn Stock Photos; 304(t), Picture taken by J.A.F. Stevenson, a collaborator on the original study, but first published by Neal E. Miller in an article summarizing a number of studies from his laboratory.; 306(t), Bob Daemmrich/The Image Works; 307(b), Super Stock; 308(tl), Harlow Primate Laboratory, University of Wisconsin (Madison); 308(tr), James McLoughlin/FPG; 309(b), John Henley/The Stock Market; 311(b), Bob Daemmrich/Bob Daemmrich Photography; 314(t), SuperStock; 315(bl), M. Eastcott/The Image Works; 315(br), Michael Goldman/FPG; 315(bcl), David Frazier/David Frazier Photolibrary; 315(bcr), Comstock; **Chapter Fourteen:** Page 25(t),Reuters/Corbis-Bettmann; 327(b), Lawrence Migdale/Tony Stone Images; 329(t), Giraudon/Art Resource, NY; 330(tl), John Neubauer/PhotoEdit; 330(tr), Ben Simmons/The Stock Market; 334(t), SuperStock; 335(b), Rhoda Sidney/The Image Works; 337(b), Charles Gupton/ The Stock Market; **Chapter Fifteen:** Page 345(t), Bonnie Kamin/

PhotoEdit; 346(c), Super Stock; 347(t), Martha M Bride/Unicorn Stock Photos; 348(t), Laura Elliott/Comstock; 349(cl), SuperStock; 349(cr), Thomas Ives/The Stock Market; 349(bl), Bob Daemmrich/ Bob Daemmrich Photography; 349(br), Ted Horowitz/The Stock Market; 350(t), SuperStock; 352(b), Bob Daemmrich/Bob Daemmrich Photography; 355(t), Robert Brenner/PhotoEdit; 357(t), Comstock; 358(b), Bob Daemmrich/Bob Daemmrich Photography; 359(t), SuperStock; **Chapter Sixteen:** Page 365(tl), SuperStock; 365(tc), SuperStock; 365(tr), Tony Freeman/PhotoEdit; 366(b), Tony Freeman/PhotoEdit; 368(t), Tony Freeman/PhotoEdit; 370(tl), John Giffin/Image Works; 370(tcl), Fujifotos/The Image Works; 370/371(tcr), Super Stock; 371(tr), SuperStock; 374(t), Tony Freeman/Photo Edit; 376(b), Elizabeth Zuckerman/PhotoEdit; 378(t), SuperStock; 378(b), D. Young-Wolff/Photo Edit; 379(t), Margret Mead Papers, Manuscript Divison, Library of Congress;

Unit Six: Page 383(br), Super Stock;

Chapter Seventeen: Page 387(b), Joes Pelaez/The Stock Market; 388(t), Michael Newman/PhotoEdit; 392(t), Jose L. Pelaez/The Stock Market; 392(b), The Stock Market; 393(t), Bob Daemmrich; 394(t), David Young-Wolff/PhotoEdit; 395(t), SuperStock; 397(t), Tony Freeman/PhotoEdit; 398(b), SuperStock; 400(c), Christian Michaels/ FPG; 403(bl), Michael Newman/PhotoEdit/PhotoEdit; 405(t), Michael Newman/PhotoEdit; **Chapter Eighteen:** Page 410(t), Art Montes DeOcal/FPG; 412(c), UPI/Corbis-Bettmann; 416(t), Luis Rosendo/FPG; 417(b), Bob Dammrich/Image Works; 418 (tc), AP/ Wide World Photos; 426(b), Derek Bayes/Tony Stone; 427 (tr), Benelux Press/Getty Images/FPG International; 428(t), Monkmeyer/ Grunnitus; 431(t), Ron Chapple/FPG; **Chapter Nineteen:** Page 436(t), Zigy Kaluzny/Tony Stone; 439(t), David Harry Stewart/Tony Stone; 440(t), F. Pedrick/The Image Works; 442(t), Bruce Ayres/Tony Stone; 445(c) HRW/Michelle Bridwell; 448(t), Peter Steiner/The Stock Market; 449(t), Michael Newman/Photo Edit; 449(c), Michael Newman/Photo Edit; 449(b), Michael New man/Photo Edit; 453(t), Will & Deni McIntyre/Tony Stone;

Unit Seven: Page 457(br), composite, David Young-Wolff/ Photo Edit, © 1996 Daivd Eisenberg/Development Center for Appropriate Technology/Habitat for Humanity; **Chapter Twenty:** Page 460(b), Myrleen Ferguson/Photo Edit; 461(t), Michael Newman/Photo Edit; 462(b), Paul Conklin/Photo Edit; 463(b), Stock Market; 463 (bl), Phil Sandlin/AP/Wide World Photos; 464(t), Courtesy of Save The Children; 465(t), Reuters/ Bettmann; 466(b), Michael Newman/Photo Edit; 467(c), Archive Photos; 473(bl), Art Wolfe/Tony Stone; 473(br), Bob Daemmrich/ HRW; 473(bcl), Bill Wassman/The Stock Market; 473(bcr), Zviki-Eshet/The Stock Market; 474(t), Tony Freeman/Photo Edit; **Chapter Twenty-One:** Page 480(t),Chuck Savage/The Stock Market; 483(c), Archive Photos; 485(tl), Eastcott/The Image Bank; 485(tc), Stock Market ©1994 Latin Stock/Carlos Goldin/Stock Market; 485(tr), David Young Wolff/Tony Stone Images; 487(t), Anthony Edgeworth/Stock Market; 488(t)(c)(b), From the film OBEDIENCE, © 1965 by Stanley Milgram, and distributed by PennState Media Sales. Permission granted by Alexandra Milgram; 489(b), R Hutchings/Photo Edit; 490(b), Leanna Rathkelly/Tony Stone Images; 491(t), Glyn Kirk/Tony Stone; 494(t), Frank Siteman/Tony Stone; 495(b), Michael Newman/Photo Edit;

Careers: Page 508(t), SuperStock; 509(b), Michael Newman/Photo Edit; 510(b), Martha M. Bride/Unicorn Stock Photos; 511(t), Comstock; 512(t), Ariel Skelley/The Stock Market; 512(t), Glyn Kirk/ Tony Stone; 513(t), Michael Schwarz/The Image Works; 514(b), SuperStock;